Risk Management and Insurance

SEVENTH EDITION

Risk Management and Insurance

SEVENTH EDITION

S. Travis Pritchett
The University of South Carolina

Joan T. Schmit
University of Wisconsin—Madison

Helen I. Doerpinghaus
The University of South Carolina

James L. Athearn
The University of North Carolina

WEST PUBLISHING COMPANY

Minneapolis/St. Paul   New York   San Francisco   Los Angeles

Production Credits

Copy Editor: Bonnie Goldsmith
Interior Design: Roslyn M. Stendahl
Composition: Parkwood Composition

Index: Schroeder Indexing Services
Cover Image: The Dead River; DownEast Whitewater Rafting, Inc.

Photo Credits

2, 19 Stephen Simpson/FPG International Corp.; 24, 42 Arnulf Husmo/Tony Stone Worldwide; 50, 73 Mark Richards/PhotoEdit; 76, 94 Peter Gridley/FPG International Corp.; 120, 137 David Woodfall/Tony Stone Images; 140, 164 Tony Freeman/PhotoEdit; 170, 199
continued following index

West's Commitment to the Environment

In 1906, West Publishing Company began recycling materials left over from the production of books. This began a tradition of efficient and responsible use of resources. Today, 100% of our legal bound volumes are printed on acid-free, recycled paper consisting of 50% new paper pulp and 50% paper that has undergone a de-inking process. We also use vegetable-based inks to print all of our books. West recycles nearly 27,700,000 pounds of scrap paper annually—the equivalent of 229,300 trees. Since the 1960s, West has devised ways to capture and recycle waste inks, solvents, oils, and vapors created in the printing process. We also recycle plastics of all kinds, wood, glass, corrugated cardboard, and batteries, and have eliminated the use of polystyrene book packaging. We at West are proud of the longevity and the scope of our commitment to the environment.

West pocket parts and advance sheets are printed on recyclable paper and can be collected and recycled with newspapers. Staples do not have to be removed. Bound volumes can be recycled after removing the cover.

Production, Prepress, Printing and Binding by West Publishing Company.

 PRINTED ON 10% POST CONSUMER RECYCLED PAPER  Printed with **Printwise** Environmentally Advanced Water Washable Ink

British Library Cataloguing-in-Publication Data. A catalogue record for this book is available from the British Library.

COPYRIGHT © 1962, 1969   By Meredith Corporation
COPYRIGHT © 1977, 1981,
1984, 1989   By WEST PUBLISHING COMPANY
COPYRIGHT © 1996   By WEST PUBLISHING COMPANY
610 Opperman Drive
P.O. Box 64526
St. Paul, MN 55164-0526

Printed in the United States of America

03 02 01 00 99 98 97 96   8 7 6 5 4 3 2 1 0

Library of Congress Cataloging-in-Publication Data

Risk management and insurance / S. Travis Pritchett . . . [et al.].—7th ed.
    p. cm.
   Rev. ed. of: Risk and insurance/James L. Athearn, S. Travis
Pritchett, Joan T. Schmit. 6th ed. c1989.
   Includes bibliographical references and index.
   ISBN 0-314-06427-3 (hard: alk. paper)
   1. Insurance. 2. Risk (Insurance) I. Pritchett, S. Travis.
II. Athearn, James L. Risk and insurance.
HG8051.A82 1996
368'.01—dc20
95-45304
CIP

....

To Bertha, John and Meri
S.T.P

To Elizabeth, Cathy, Tom and Mary
J.T.S

To Wayne
H.I.D.

....

Contents

CHAPTER 3

CHAPTER

CHAPTER

CHAPTER 21

Individual Health Insurance Contracts 500

Preface

News reports of various events, such as the earthquake that devastated Kobe, Japan; Hurricane Andrew that ripped through the Caribbean and Florida; the bombed-out municipal building in Oklahoma City; and a simple fender bender on Main Street, highlight the extent and variety of risky situations to which people and organizations are exposed. Such events involve both personal and financial loss, each best managed through planning and preparation. This book primarily addresses planning and preparation for financial security, which we refer to as *risk management*. The steps taken to manage financial risks, however, will often assist also in managing personal risks.

The book is operational. It is concerned with what you need to know and what you need to do. As you proceed chapter by chapter, you learn how to manage risk and make the best use of insurance and other risk-handling techniques. Both insurance and situations involving risk are complex; therefore, we discuss fundamental principles first and then apply them to real-world situations. To keep the book a reasonable length for an introductory course, only topics that meet one or both of the following tests are included:

1. Is this essential for the reader's understanding?
2. Will this help the reader as a risk manager and consumer of insurance products?

Because the field of risk management and insurance is broad and dynamic, you will not know all there is to know about it when you finish this book. You will, however, have a great deal of knowledge and skill that will help you as a business or personal consumer and provide a foundation for further study.

This edition continues to reflect our belief that knowledge and skill are most readily acquired when complex matters—such as risk and insurance—are presented in an uncomplicated format. We have endeavored to keep up with what is most important for the beginning student in a constantly changing field, provide as much material as can be dealt with effectively in one course, add depth, and discuss each topic in terms that are relevant for the reader.

Consumer Applications at the end of each chapter demonstrate how to use what you have learned, and represent our continued focus on the needs of the manager of risks (as opposed to the seller of risk management techniques, primarily insurers). This seventh edition includes applications about how to analyse homeowners insurance (chapter 8), automobile insurance (chapter 9), life insurance (chapters 13–15), and HMOs (chapters 18, 20).

New to This Edition

Ethical Dilemmas are found throughout the text. Their intent is to raise a question related to chapter material that involves conflict between at least two competing interests, leading to an ethical dilemma. For instance, if safety requirements outside of the United States are lower than within the United States, what is a corporation's duties when conducting business outside of the United States? Similarly, what is an insurer's responsibility regarding the use of health information for identifying potential policyholders? Is it ethical, for example, to deny coverage to someone who has a genetic predisposition to some disease? These dilemmas do not have exact answers and are intended to offer opportunities for discussion of complex problems in risk management and insurance. We provide questions to generate discussion and also offer an outline in chapter 1 of how to approach evaluation of ethical dilemmas.

Organization of the material has been revised, with discussion of property and liability risk management near the front of the text. We made this modification in the belief that property and liability insurance best demonstrates the legal fundamentals and organization of insurance contracts, paving the way for later, more complex contractual issues.

Increased coverage of business risk management and insurance is part of this new organization. Two chapters (10 and 11) now address business property and business liability risks. A chapter on the liability risk generally (7) has also been added. Combined with **expanded coverage of employee benefits,** professional risk management issues are more extensively addressed in this edition. The employee benefits material, previously found in one chapter, now is examined in three fundamental issues, as well as life and disability risks (chapter 17); medical care (chapter 18); and retirement plans (chapter 19).

New chapters on interest-sensitive and variable life insurance (chapter 14), individual health insurance contracts (chapter 20), and individual financial management of retirement (chapter 22) expand our discussion of personal risks. **Electronic spreadsheets** are used in several places to illustrate material. These new chapters, along with the expanded employee benefits chapters, add material on subjects such as Medical Savings Accounts, insurance taxation, disability income plans, Medigap policies, and national health insurance.

Updates and Expansions

Global Perspectives are now found in nearly all chapters. For example, chapter 18 includes discussion of medical care systems worldwide. Chapter 6 includes information on political risks that tend to be relevant on a global basis. Chapter 10 incorporates discussion of insurance issues that develop for multinational organizations.

Key Terms at the end of each chapter list important vocabulary. A review of these terms can help you evaluate your understanding of the chapter.

Discussion Questions and Cases for each chapter provide the basis for class discussion. The cases, in particular, offer an opportunity to apply what you have learned.

Appendices include sample insurance policies, a standard mortality table, and a listing of insurance regulators throughout the United States, including addresses and telephone numbers.

Supplements

Several supplements are available with the text. These include:

Instructor's Manual with Test Bank by Pritchett, Schmit, and Doerpinghaus. This manual provides outlines of each chapter and answers to the end-of-chapter discussion questions and cases. Multiple choice and true/false test questions are also provided.

WESTEST 3.1 Computerized Testing is available to those instructors who want a computerized version of test questions offered in the instructor's manual.

Transparency Masters of key illustrations in the text are also available.

Acknowledgments

This book lists four authors, but it is the product of countless suggestions and a great deal of help from many people. Our publisher, West Publishing Company, has provided us with talented and energetic editing, marketing, and production work. Many people at West offered their expertise and enthusiasm to enhance the quality of this text. Among them are Esther Craig, Sharon Adams-Poore, Michelle McAnelly, and Stephanie Buss.

Important suggestions were made by a number of readers who were willing to offer detailed comments on the book as it was being revised. These reviewers include:

Saul W. Adelman
Miami University

Mary Ann Boose
Indiana State University

Stephen P. D'Arcy
University of Illinois at Urbana

William R. Feldhaus
Georgia State University

Albert A. Freeman
Asheville-Buncombe Technical Comm. Coll.

George L. Granger
East Tennessee State University

J. Smith Harrison
South Carolina Wind and Hail Association (Columbia, SC)

Douglas G. Heeter
Ferris State University

Robert E. Hoyt
University of Georgia

J. David Lofton
University of Southwestern Louisiana

Michael J. McNamara
Memphis State University

Craig Merrill
Brigham Young University

John S. Moore
Western Washington University

Phyllis S. Myers
Virginia Commonwealth University

Robert Puelz
Southern Methodist University

J. Allen Seward
Baylor University

Jack A. Taylor
Birmingham-Southern College

K. S. Maurice Tse
Indiana University

Geungu Yu
Jackson State University

Gale K. Zumpano
University of Alabama

Some of the chapter cases contributed to the fourth edition by Professors John H. Thornton of North Texas State University and Terrence E. Williams of the University of South Dakota appear in this edition, perhaps in modified form. Frederick W. Schroath contributed a chapter on international insurance to the fifth edition, some of which is incorporated into the current edition. Deanie Harris, Harriet Bradham, Ellen Rouche, and Betty McLees of the University of South Carolina, and Lisa Helsing Bastion, Brenda Brugger, and Polly Sponsler of the University of Wisconsin-Madison were our safety nets in their assistance on manuscript typing, index revision, chapter material collection, and various administrative tasks.

STP
JTS
HID
JLA

About the Authors

S. TRAVIS PRITCHETT holds the W. Frank Hipp Chair of Insurance at the University of South Carolina. Having taught since 1969, he has been given the Motar Board and Alfred G. Smith Teaching Excellence Awards at South Carolina. In 1989, he was the first professor in the U.S. chosen for the Insurance Educator of the Year Award presented by the Professional Insurance Agents Insurance Foundation. He is Past President of the American Risk and Insurance Association, the Risk Theory Society, the Academy of Financial Services, and the Southern Risk and Insurance Association. Between 1987 and 1991, Professor Pritchett served as Editor for the Journal of Risk and Insurance. He serves on the editorial boards of Benefits Quarterly and the Journal of the American Society of CLU and ChFC. His research primarily examines financial issues concerning the life-health segment of the insurance industry, employee benefits, and personal financial planning.

JOAN T. SCHMIT is the American Family Insurance Professor of Risk Management and Insurance at the University of Wisconsin-Madison, where she has been a faculty member since 1988. Prior to joining the faculty of Wisconsin, Professor Schmit taught at the University of South Carolina. She has received numerous teaching awards at both schools, including the Alfred G. Smith Teaching Excellence Award, the Mable W. Chipman Award for Teaching Excellence, and the William H. Kiekhofer Award for Teaching Excellence, this last a university-wide honor at the University of Wisconsin. Professor Schmit is Past President of the American Risk and Insurance Association and of the Risk Theory Society. She is also on the editorial boards of the CPCU Journal, and the Journal of Insurance Regulation. Her research interests are in the property and liability risk management fields, focusing on the interaction between law and economics. This interest has led to the analysis of the effects of tort reforms on insurance availability, defendant and plaintiff behavior, and overall system costs.

HELEN DOERPINGHAUS, Associate Professor of Insurance, has been on the faculty of the University of South Carolina since 1987. She received her doctoral from the Wharton School at the University of Pennsylvania in insurance and health care finance. She teaches undergraduate and graduate courses primarily in the areas of risk management and employee benefits. Dr. Doerpinghaus has received the University's Michael J. Mungo Teaching Award, the Mortar Board Teaching Award, and the College of Business Administration's Alfred G. Smith Teaching Award. She has published articles on insurance and employee benefits in various scholarly journals. She serves on the board of directors of the American Risk and Insurance Association, and is Vice President of the Southern Risk and Insurance Association.

JAMES L. ATHEARN is Distinguished Professor Emeritus at the University of South Carolina. Following several years of teaching economics at Ohio State University, he received the first postdoctoral fellowship awarded by the S. S. Huebner Foundation at the University of Pennsylvania. Subsequently, he taught at the University of Florida; the University of Montana, where he was Dean, and the University of South Carolina, where he held the W. Frank Hipp Chair of Insurance before retiring in 1982. A Past President of the American Risk and Insurance Association, he is the author of several books and numerous articles on insurance topics. He and his wife, Helen, now enjoy their view in Glacier National Park, Montana, and spend the winter in Carefree, Arizona.

PART I

Fundamentals of Risk Management and Insurance

Risk

Introduction

As we write this material, a violent hurricane is heading for the United States mainland. Winds may reach category 5, the strongest designation. At the same time, fires burn out of control in various parts of the world, including France, England, and the western U.S. Wars are raging, volcanoes are erupting, traffic deaths are mounting, the number of cancer cases is increasing, and a myriad of other losses are occurring. Some of these losses are common and somewhat predictable. Many others are shocking, unexpected events. Each involves **risk,** which we define as variability in future outcomes.

Risk and how we manage it are critical aspects of our lives. This text is devoted to the topics of risk and risk management, with emphasis on the use of insurance to manage risk. In the first chapter, our objective is to offer a theoretical understanding of risk, including discussion of methods to measure it. While the theory is overshadowed in later chapters by practical issues of risk management and insurance, a good foundation in risk concepts will provide a much easier journey through the remainder of the text.

Chapter one, therefore, includes the following topics:

1. The concept of risk, especially those areas particular to risk management.
2. Why risk matters in our lives.
3. How risk can be measured and evaluated.
4. Important elements of risk that affect our management of it.
5. Methods to manage risk, including insurance.

As stated previously, risk is variability in future outcomes. Risk exists when we are in a state of the world in which outcomes may differ from expectations. The possibility of lower than expected outcomes is critical to the definition of risk, because so-called "losses" produce the negative quality associated with not knowing the future, and managing the future is the essence of risk management. In this text, lower than expected values are termed "losses," and higher than expected outcomes are termed "gains." While some situations involve the possibility of gain as well as loss (termed **speculative risks**), we are concerned almost exclusively with situations in which no gain is possible. The latter are termed **pure risks.** We recognize, however, that pure and speculative risks often are closely linked. In evaluating the expected financial returns for a new product (speculative risk), for example, issues concerning product liability, workplace accidents, and other potential losses, which would be categorized as pure risks, must be considered.

Risk has no meaning without **loss** being the outcome of concern, and most of the discussion in this book will be about situations that involve potential for *economic loss*. This term implies that loss must be capable of being expressed in an easily measurable economic unit, such as dollars. Many losses, however, cannot be fully measured or described in economic terms.[1] For example, the death of a family pet may be felt as a great loss, but is not measurable totally in economic terms. One may know the cost of buying another pet of the same kind, but this is not the only diminution in value. Although we concentrate on economic loss, you might find some of the risk management techniques introduced in this chapter (and developed in chapter 2) equally useful in managing risk of noneconomic losses.

Remember that for risk to exist, it must be *possible* for loss to occur. Loss may or may not occur under risk, but no risk exists when the probability of loss is either zero or 100 percent, because under these conditions the outcome is not variable. When we know what is going to happen as a result of an activity during a particular time, such as a day or year, no risk exists, and thus the activity is outside the purview of this text. Instead, our concern is with unfavorable, unpredictable deviations from expectations.

Variability derives from deviations from expectations. The greater the size of deviations, the greater the variability, and the more difficult becomes the task of planning. Much of a risk manager's job involves estimating future outcomes (losses) and the variability of those future outcomes. The risk manager prefers to quantify this variability. Some basic techniques for measuring variability will be described later in this chapter. A **risk manager,** whether holding the title or not, is the person whose job involves minimizing the negative aspects of not knowing the future.

While variability in future outcomes is our definition of risk, other authors choose other characterizations. Table 1–1 offers a sampling of some of these definitions. Recognize that "risk," although a commonly used word, does not possess a universal definition.

---

1. Risk theorists are also interested in the effect of risk on our utility. Utility involves both economic factors and emotional reaction to risk and can be considered the "value" we assign to something.

TABLE 1–1

Definitions of Risk

DORFMAN *Introduction to Risk Management & Insurance,* **4th Edition**	Risk is variation in possible outcomes of an event based on chance.
GREENE & TRIESCHMANN *Risk & Insurance,* **7th Edition**	Risk is uncertainty as to loss.
MEHR & CAMMACK *Principles of Insurance,* **3rd Edition**	Risk equals uncertainty. Risk has principally to do with the uncertainty of a loss.
MEHR & HEDGES *Risk Management Concepts & Applications*	Risk may be defined as the possibility that losses will be greater than is normal, expected, or usual.
REJDA *Principles of Risk Management & Insurance,* **4th Edition**	Risk is uncertainty concerning the occurrence of a loss.
RIEGAL *Insurance Principles & Practices,* **4th Edition**	Risk is the possibility of an unfortunate occurrence.
SNIDER (ED.) *Risk Management,* **2nd Edition Published for S. S. Huebner Foundation for Insurance Education**	There is common agreement that risk involves chance events and that the element of uncertainty is inherent in the outcome of any risk situation.
VAUGHAN *Fundamentals of Risk & Insurance,* **5th Edition**	Risk is a condition in which there is a possibility of an adverse deviation from a desired outcome that is expected or hoped for.
WILLIAMS, HEAD, HORN, & GLENDENNING *Principles of Risk Management & Insurance,* **2nd Edition**	"Risk" is used in Risk Management & Insurance literature & practice to mean 1) the possibility of loss, 2) the probability of loss, 3) a peril, 4) a hazard, 5) the property or person exposed to damage or loss, 6) potential losses, 7) variation in potential losses, and 8) uncertainty concerning loss.
WILLIAMS & HEINS *Risk Management & Insurance,* **6th Edition**	Risk is defined as the variation in possible future outcomes.

Attitudes Toward Risk

Although we have defined risk and discussed the important elements of risk, we have not talked about why risk matters. Why do we care about variability in future outcomes? The answer is that most of us are **risk averse.**

To be risk averse implies that a person is willing to pay in excess of the expected return in exchange for some certainty about the future. To pay an insurance premium, for example, is to forgo wealth in exchange for the insurer's promise that covered losses will be paid. Some people refer to this as an exchange of a certain loss (the premium) for an uncertain loss. An important aspect of the exchange is that the premium is larger than the average or expected loss because insurer expenses and profit are in-

ETHICAL *Dilemma*

How Much Caution is Enough?

The existence of risk implies that some type of loss is possible. Risk management involves preparations for loss, including efforts to prevent, reduce, and finance loss. A personal dilemma each of us faces is, "How much caution is enough?" The question arises in making decisions about our own safety, as well as decisions that affect others.

Governments often add another dimension to this problem. Safety regulations may prohibit freedom. For example, some motorcyclists vehemently oppose helmet requirements, believing they deserve the freedom to choose their own destiny. The same applies to the use of seat belts, regulations banning fireworks, and limitations on the availability of certain products, such as saccharine.

The motorcyclist who opposes helmet laws likely thinks that she or he hurts no one else if injured in an accident. However, many motorcyclists lack medical and/ or disability insurance. The public then bears the cost of medical care and may have to support the person for some time, even for life. Furthermore, and more importantly, society loses the value of that person's abilities, whether temporarily or permanently. Economic and emotional costs to others are significant.

Still, independence is highly valued in the United States. People ask: Should the government be allowed to take away freedoms in order to save us from our own "foolishness"? How far should government go in this process? What are our own responsibilities, and how can they be enforced? How much risk should government manage for us?

Applying Ethical Theories to Decision Making

Instructions: Answer Questions 1 through 6 to obtain the information necessary for performing an ethical analysis. Based on this information, develop a policy option that has the strongest ethical basis.

1. Who are all the people affected by the action (stakeholder analysis)?
2. Is the action beneficial to me (egoism)?
3. Is the action supported by the social group (social group relativism)?
4. Is the action supported by national laws (cultural relativism)?
5. Is the action for the greatest good of the greatest number of people affected by it (utilitarianism)?
6. Are the motives behind the action based on truthfulness and respect/integrity toward each stakeholder (deontology)?

- *If answers to Questions 2–6 are all yes,* do it.
- *If answers to Questions 2–6 are all no,* do not do it.
- *If answers to Questions 2–6 are mixed,* amend your decision.
- *If answers to Questions 5 and 6 are yes,* this is the *most* ethical action. You may need to amend your decision in consideration of any "no" answer to Questions 2–4.
- *If answers to Questions 5 and 6 are no,* this is the *least* ethical action. Amend your decision in consideration of these objections.
- *If answers to Questions 5 and 6 are mixed,* this is *moderately* ethical. Amend your decision in consideration of the shortcomings revealed by Questions 5 or 6. You may need to further amend your decision in consideration of any "no" answers to Questions 2–4.

cluded. A person willing only to pay the average loss as a premium would be considered **risk neutral.** Someone who accepts risk at less than the average loss, perhaps even paying to add risk such as through gambling, is a **risk seeker.**

Risk aversion is important, because such an attitude may result in lost opportunities. Many examples are possible. A vaccine manufacturer worried about potential liability lawsuits may choose not to introduce a promising new treatment. A land developer concerned about erosion might decide not to build a new convention center. The list could be quite long and even could become absurd—fear of being in an auto accident might keep us indoors indefinitely, for example. The point is that our negative reaction toward uncertain possible future losses (risk aversion) leads us to want to manage the future, and thus to manage risk. By managing risk, we develop opportunities that might otherwise not be feasible.

Measurement of Risk

SPECIFIC MEASUREMENT TECHNIQUES

To manage the future, we need to have some idea about possible outcomes and how likely each outcome is to occur. Estimates of the future typically are based primarily on historical and/or theoretical data. These data, then, are used to develop probabilities, or likelihoods, of the future occurrence of each event. Representations of all possible outcomes along with their associated probabilities are called **probability distributions,** which are discussed in some detail in chapter 2. An example is shown in table 1–2. The most important probabilities for risk managers are those associated with frequency and severity of losses. **Frequency** is a measure of how often incidents occur (for example, the number of injuries that occur in a plant during a specified period of time). Typically, the risk manager will relate the number of incidents to a base (for instance, to develop an average frequency, the number of injuries in the plant may be related to the average number of employees). **Severity** is a measure of the amount of damage caused by each incident.

Average Value

Probability distributions allow us to measure expectations of the future as well as variability of those expectations. Our best guess of the future typ-

TABLE 1–2

Loss Probabilities

OBSERVATION	LOSS VALUE	LOSS CATEGORY	# OBSERVATIONS	PROBABILITY
1	$ 100	$ 100	3	3/8 = .375
2	100	500	2	2/8 = .250
3	100	1,000	3	3/8 = .375
4	500		8	8/8 = 1.000
5	500			
6	1,000			
7	1,000			
8	1,000			
	$4,300			

ically is measured as the **mean** or **average.** The sample mean is the sum of all observed outcomes divided by the number of observations. The mean in some situations can be defined as the sum of the products of each possible outcome multiplied by its probability. In equation form, the mean is:

(1)
$$\text{sample mean} = \sum_{i=1}^{n} X_i/n$$

where X_i = value of observation i
n = number of observations,

or

(2)
$$\text{mean} = \sum_{j=1}^{m} X_j * P(X_j)$$

where X_j = value of category j of possible events
m = number of categories
$P(X_j)$ = probability (relative frequency) of category j

We can use table 1–2 to illustrate these equations. The mean can be calculated using either equation 1 or 2.

$$\$4,300/8 = \$537.50$$

or

$$(\$100 \cdot .375) + (500 \cdot .25) + (1000 \cdot .375) = \$537.50$$

Variability

The variability of outcomes, or "risk," can be measured in a number of ways. One measure is the **range.** The range equals the difference between the largest value and the smallest value of possible outcomes. In table 1–2, the range equals $\$1,000 - 100$, or $\$900$. Note that in most cases, zero will also be a possible outcome, although it is omitted in our example.

A more common measure of variability is the **variance.** The variance of a probability distribution is equal to the average squared difference of each outcome from the mean. In equation form, the sample variance is represented as:

(3)
$$\text{Variance} = \sum_{i=1}^{n} (X_i - \overline{X})^2/n$$

where X_i = value of observation i
$\overline{X}$ = mean of the distribution
n = number of observations

(4)
$$\text{Variance} = \sum_{j=1}^{m} (X_j - \overline{X})^2 P(X_j)$$

where X_j = value of category j of possible events

m = number of categories

$P(X_j)$ = probability (relative frequency) of category j

The variance measures the appropriateness of the mean as an estimate of likely outcomes. If each observation is quite a distance, on average, from the mean, then our estimate is not very reliable as a predictor of the future. Variance uses squared differences because positive and negative values would otherwise offset each other, giving us a poor idea of how much variability exists. The variance in our example equals 152,343.74. This is a large value, but what does it mean?

To provide some meaningful measure of risk, statisticians often use the square root of the variance. The square root of variance provides a value comparable with the original expected outcomes. Remember that variance uses *squared* differences; therefore, taking the square root returns the measure to its initial unit of measurement. The square root of the variance is termed the **standard deviation.** In our example, the standard deviation equals 390.31. On average, each observation is approximately 390 units (dollars) away from the mean of $537.50.

If we compare this standard deviation with another distribution of equal mean and larger standard deviation, we could say that the second distribution is riskier than the first. It is riskier because the observations are, on average, further away from the mean than in the first distribution. Larger standard deviations, therefore, represent greater risk, everything else being the same. Of course, distributions seldom have the same mean.

What if we are comparing two distributions with different means? In this case, we would need to consider the **coefficient of variation,** which equals the standard deviation of a distribution divided by its mean. The coefficient of variation gives us a *relative* value of risk. In our example, the coefficient of variation equals .73. The smaller this value, the lower the relative riskiness of the distribution.

Data Sources

Armed with these tools to measure variability, a risk manager is better able to make informed decisions. An important issue, however, is the general lack of data on which to develop probability distributions. Often the events under consideration are new or rare, making data collection difficult. A small organization, for example, may experience a specific type of loss no more than once every five years, on average. Unfortunately, three losses could occur in a single year, with none the next fifteen years. Even the most sophisticated data analysis techniques have trouble with these situations.

LAW OF LARGE NUMBERS

Availability of only small data sources (or sometimes none at all) is troublesome because most estimation techniques rely on numerous observations for accuracy. The benefit of many observations is well stated by the **law of large numbers,** an important statistical doctrine for the successful management of risk.

The law of large numbers holds that as a sample of observations is increased in size, the relative variation about the mean declines. An example, given in table 1–3, may help explain. The important point is that with larger samples we feel more confident in our estimates.

A risk manager (or insurance executive) uses the law of large numbers to estimate future outcomes for planning purposes. The larger the sample

TABLE 1–3

Law of Large Numbers

Assume that the riskiness of two groups is under consideration by an insurer. One group is comprised of 1,000 units and the other of 4,000 units. Each group anticipates incurring 10 percent losses within a specified period, such as a year. The first group, therefore, is expected to have 100 losses; the second group expects 400 losses. This example demonstrates a binomial distribution, one where only two possible outcomes exist, either loss or no loss. The average of a binomial equals the sample size times the probability of "success." Here we will call success a loss (not implying that a loss has any of the usual desirable connotations of the word "success") and use the following symbols:

$$n = \text{sample size}$$
$$p = \text{probability of "success"}$$
$$q = \text{probability of "failure"} = 1 - p$$
$$n \cdot p = \text{mean}$$

For group 1 of our example, then, the mean is 100

$$(1000) \cdot (.10) = 100$$

For group 2 the mean is 400

$$(4000) \cdot (.10) = 400$$

The standard deviation of a distribution is a measure of risk or dispersion. For a binomial distribution, the standard deviation is

$$\sqrt{n \cdot p \cdot q}$$

In our example, the standard deviations of group 1 and group 2 respectively are 9.5 and 19.

$$\text{Group 1} \quad \sqrt{(1000)(.1)(.9)} = 9.5$$
$$\text{Group 2} \quad \sqrt{(4000)(.1)(.9)} = 19$$

Thus, while the mean, or expected number of losses, quadrupled with the quadrupling of the sample size, the standard deviation only doubled. Through this illustration you can see that the *proportional* deviation of actual from expected outcomes decreases with increased sample size. The relative dispersion has been reduced. The coefficient of variation (the standard deviation divided by the mean) is often used as a relative measure of risk. In the above example, group 1 has a coefficient of variation of 9.5/100 or .095. Group 2 has a coefficient of variation of 19/400 = .0475, indicating the reduced risk. (Insurance premiums reflect risk, so group 1 members can expect to pay a higher risk charge per member than can group 2 members.)

Taking the extreme, consider an individual (n = 1) who attempts to retain the risk of loss. That person either will or will not incur a loss, and even though the probability of loss is only 10 percent, how does that person know whether or not he or she will be the unlucky one out of ten? Using the binomial distribution, that individual's standard deviation (risk) is $\sqrt{(1)(.1)(.9)} = .3$, a much higher measure of risk than that of the insurer. The individual's coefficient of variation is .3/.1 = 3, demonstrating this higher risk. More specifically, the risk is 63 times (3/.0475) that of the insurer, with 4,000 units exposed to loss.

size, the lower the relative risk, everything else being equal. The ability to pool experience, therefore, is quite desirable and is discussed further in chapter 3 where insurance operations are presented.

Elements of Pure Risk

An important criterion for the law of large numbers to operate effectively is that the observations all generate from essentially the same type of conditions (i.e., all observations are similar or "homogeneous"). Someone managing risk, therefore, needs to know the particular characteristics of the underlying potential losses. These can be described in terms of exposures, perils, and hazards.

EXPOSURES

Although most insurance professionals describe risk as some form of variability, many continue to use the word "risk" to denote the property or person exposed to losses. Most insurance industry education and training materials, in contrast, use the term **exposure** to describe the property or person facing a condition in which loss or losses are possible. We also will use the term exposure this way.

The categorization of insurance "risks" often begins by putting them into broad types of exposures. The pure risks that confront individuals, families, firms, and other organizations may, for example, cause personal, property, or liability exposures.[2] Each of these categories receives extensive attention in future chapters and is introduced briefly below.

Personal Loss Exposures

Because all losses are ultimately borne by people, it could be said that all exposures are personal. Some, however, have a more direct impact on people. Exposure to premature death, sickness, disability, unemployment, and dependent old age are examples of **personal loss exposures.** An organization may also experience loss from these events when such events affect employees.

Property Loss Exposures

Property owners face the possibility of both direct and consequential (indirect) losses. If your car is damaged in a collision, the direct loss is the cost of repairs. The **consequential losses** are the time and effort required to arrange for repairs, the loss of use of your car while repairs are being made, and the additional cost of renting another car while repairs are being made. **Property loss exposures** are associated with both "real" property such as buildings, and "personal" property such as automobiles and the contents of a building.

Liability Loss Exposures

Under our legal system, you can be held responsible for causing damage to others. Thus, you are exposed to the possibility of **liability loss exposures** by having to defend yourself against a lawsuit. In addition, you may become legally obligated to pay for injury to persons or damage to property.

PERILS

Perils are the immediate causes of loss. People are surrounded by potential loss because the environment is filled with perils such as floods, theft, death, sickness, accidents, fires, tornadoes, and lightning. Table 1–4 is a list of some perils.

Although various efforts have been made to categorize perils, doing so is difficult. We could talk about **natural** and **human perils.** Natural perils

---

2. More refined categorization will be made by an insurer or risk manager before using the law of large numbers. For example, property exposures involve real and personal property, mobile and immobile property, owned and non-owned property, etc.

TABLE 1–4

Types of Perils

NATURAL PERILS	
Generally Insurable	**Generally Difficult to Insure**
Windstorm	Flood
Lightning	Earthquake
Natural combustion	Epidemic
Heart attacks	Volcanic eruption
	Frost

HUMAN PERILS	
Generally Insurable	**Generally Difficult to Insure**
Theft	War
Vandalism	Radioactive contamination
Hunting accident	Civil unrest
Negligence	
Fire and smoke	

are those over which people have little control, such as hurricanes, volcanoes, and lightning. Human perils, then, would be the causes of loss within the control of individuals, including suicide, war, and theft. Sometimes losses caused by recessions will be considered caused by human perils, but they may be separated into a third category labeled **economic perils.** Employee strikes, arson for profit, and similar situations also are generally considered economic perils.

Another method of peril categorization is division into insurable and noninsurable perils. Typically, the noninsurable perils are those that might be considered catastrophic to an insurer or would encourage policyholders to cause loss. In both instances, the problem for the insurer is the security of its financial standing.

HAZARDS

Hazards are the conditions that lie behind the occurrence of losses, increasing the probability of losses, their severity, or both. Certain conditions are referred to as being "hazardous." For example, when summer humidity declines and temperature and wind velocity rise in heavily forested areas, the likelihood of fire increases. Conditions are such that a forest fire could start very easily and be difficult to contain. In this example, both the probability of loss and its severity are increased by low humidity. The more hazardous the conditions, the greater the probability and/or severity of loss. Two kinds of hazards—physical and intangible—affect the probability and severity of losses.

Physical Hazards

Physical hazards are the tangible conditions of the environment that affect the frequency and/or severity of loss. Examples include slippery roads that increase the chance of an automobile accident, poorly lit stairwells that add to the likelihood of slips and falls, and old wiring that may increase the likelihood of a fire. The following example describes these hazards.

Location, construction, and use represent physical hazards that affect property. The location of a building affects its susceptibility to loss by fire, flood, earthquake, and other perils. If the building is located near the fire department and a good water supply, there is less chance that it will suffer a serious loss by fire than if it is in an isolated area with neither water nor firefighting service.

Construction affects the probability and severity of loss. While no building is fireproof, some types of construction are less susceptible to loss from fire than others. What is susceptible to one peril, however, is not necessarily susceptible to all. For example, a frame building is more apt to burn than a brick building, but it may suffer less damage from an earthquake.

Use or occupancy may also create physical hazards. A building will have a greater probability of loss by fire if it is used for a fireworks factory or a dry-cleaning establishment than if it is used as an office building. An automobile used for business purposes may be exposed to greater chance of loss than the typical family car if the business car is used more extensively and in more dangerous settings. Similarly, people have physical characteristics that affect loss. Some of us have brittle bones, weak immune systems, or vitamin deficiencies. Any of these characteristics could increase the probability or severity of health expenses.

Intangible Hazards

Intangible hazards, attitudes and culture (nonphysical conditions), also affect the probability and severity of loss. Traditionally, authors of insurance texts present these conditions as moral and morale hazards, which are important concepts but do not define the full range of nonphysical hazards.[3] Even the distinction between moral and morale hazards is fuzzy, and generally their existence may lead to physical hazards.

Moral hazards involve dishonesty on the part of insureds. In the context of insurance, moral hazards are conditions that encourage insureds to cause losses intentionally. Generally, moral hazards exist when a person can gain from the occurrence of a loss. For example, an insured who will be reimbursed for the cost of a new stereo system due to the loss of an old one has an incentive to cause loss. Such an incentive increases the probability of loss.

Morale hazards, in contrast, do not involve dishonesty. Rather, morale hazards are attitudes of carelessness and lack of concern that increase the chance a loss will occur or increase the size of losses that do occur. Poor housekeeping (for example, allowing trash to accumulate in the attic or basement) and careless cigarette smoking are examples of morale hazards that increase the probability of loss by fire. Often such lack of concern occurs because an insurer is available to pay for losses.

Many people unnecessarily and often unconsciously create morale hazards that can affect their health and life expectancy. These hazards include excessive use of tobacco, drugs, radiation, and other harmful substances; poor eating, sleeping, and exercise habits; unnecessary exposure to falls,

....
3. The authors thank Leroy L. Phaup for suggesting the intangible hazard.

poisoning, electrocution, venomous stings and bites, and air pollution; and other dangers to life and limb.

In addition to moral and morale hazards, legal and cultural conditions exist that increase loss frequency and/or severity. These **societal hazards** likely change over time, and yet can be quite significant. Many people today believe, for example, that business activities are more prone to litigation in the United States than anywhere else because of a greater "litigious attitude" in the United States. Doing business in the U.S., therefore, is considered hazardous. In contrast, outside of the U.S., a number of other societal hazards exist. The former eastern bloc countries, for instance, are currently experiencing a high incidence of political turmoil, which has resulted in losses. Terrorism, war, and rebellion may be more likely in some countries and regions than in others.

Hazards are critical characteristics to analyze because our ability to reduce their effects will reduce both overall costs and variability. Hazard management, therefore, can be a highly effective risk management tool.

Methods of Handling Pure Risk

The optimal method(s) to manage pure risk depends upon a number of characteristics, including the nature of the exposure situation and the circumstances of the person or organization exposed to loss. Nearly always, more than one method is appropriate. For example, losses that are reduced but not eliminated must still be financed. Thus, both reduction and financing techniques are appropriate.

Available risk management techniques can be categorized as follows[4]:

1. Avoidance
2. Loss control
3. Loss financing

AVOIDANCE

Avoidance occurs when there is no possibility of the occurrence of some event (that is, the probability equals zero). General property, liability, and personal loss potentials cannot be avoided, but specific aspects of these potentials can.

You can avoid loss from a bungee cord accident by not participating in bungee cord activities. You cannot, however, avoid all accidents during recreational activities without eliminating all recreation. Thus, even when avoidance is possible, it may not be feasible. For instance, you can avoid the possibility of drowning by staying away from water. Such practical behavior would preclude all water transportation and water sports. To avoid the potential completely, however, requires prohibiting airplane trips over waterways, use of bridges, use of walkways over water, even baths. Clearly, some attempts to avoid drowning are not feasible. What is feasible is avoidance of the more narrowly defined potential to drown while participating in water sports or using water transportation.

---

4. Other categorizations are also possible.

This example illustrates that opportunities to avoid loss potentials are feasible only when the event avoided is rather narrowly defined.[5] We must also consider the consequences of avoidance prior to choosing it. Avoidance of one loss potential may create another. Some people choose to travel by car instead of plane, for example, because of their fear of flying. While they have successfully avoided the possibility of being a passenger in an airplane accident, they have increased their probability of an automobile accident. Automobile deaths per mile traveled are far more frequent than are aircraft fatalities. By choosing cars over planes, these people actually raise their probability of injury.

LOSS CONTROL

Loss control represents those efforts designed to minimize the overall frequency and size of outcomes. These efforts generally are categorized as either prevention or reduction techniques.

Loss prevention efforts are aimed at reducing the probability of a loss occurring. The objective of **loss reduction** efforts, on the other hand, is to lessen the severity of loss. If you want to ski in spite of the hazards involved, you may take instruction to improve your skills and reduce the likelihood of your falling down a hill or crashing into a tree. At the same time, you may engage in a physical fitness program to toughen your body to withstand spills without serious injury. Using both loss prevention and reduction techniques, you attempt to abate both the probability and severity of loss.

The magnitude of losses suffered by a firm during a year is a function of the frequency and severity of accidents, fire, and other loss-causing incidents. Loss prevention and reduction efforts are directed toward decreasing both frequency and severity. For example, attempts are made to prevent fires. Because some buildings will have fires in spite of such efforts, however, it is necessary to use automatic sprinkler systems to reduce their severity.

You make similar efforts in your own household. For example, you prevent the accumulation of oily rags, sawdust, and trash in your workshop because such refuse is susceptible to fires. In this way, you minimize the hazards associated with the peril of fire. You may also decide to install smoke and heat alarms in your workshop and elsewhere in your home; they do not prevent fires, but they can help reduce the severity of losses.

The goal of loss prevention and reduction is to reduce losses to the minimum compatible with a reasonable level of human activity and expense. At any given time, economic constraints place limits on what may be done, although what is considered too costly at one time may be readily accepted at a later date. Such reconsideration is influenced as much by our sense of values as it is by our wealth, although these two factors may be interrelated. Thus, during one era, little effort may have been made to prevent injury to employees, because employees were regarded as expendable. The general notion today, however, is that such injuries are prevented because they have become too expensive, due to changing concepts of the value of human life and the social responsibility of business.

....

5. A business, for instance, could avoid certain product liabilities by choosing never to manufacture or sell a given product, but to avoid *all* product liability would require never manufacturing or selling *any* product.

LOSS FINANCING

Losses do occur, and when they occur, some mechanism for financing them must be employed. **Loss financing** can be accomplished through retention or transfer.

Retention

When losses are paid from an individual's or organization's own funds, these losses have been financed by **retention.** Retention may be chosen, or may derive from a lack of awareness that a potential for loss exists. An example of the latter might be the people affected by the flood damage in Chicago during the spring of 1992, despite the area not being in an identified flood zone.

Some potential losses are retained because their significance is underestimated. Many people retain certain liability risks (for example, those associated with large automobile liabilities) not because they are unaware, but because they think they are unlikely to suffer such a loss. Their decision is based on ignorance. They in effect say, "It won't happen to me." What they fail to consider is that it *can* happen to them with a probability large enough for a prudent person to worry; and if it does happen, it may very well prove a financial disaster. A similar attitude causes some families to retain the risk of disability or death of the person who is the sole or main source of family income. Many young people are foolishly guided by the low frequency of such losses among persons of their age group, rather than by the severity of such losses when the decision to retain the risk is made.

Other potential losses are prudently retained because the dollar amount is relatively unimportant. If such losses do occur, they may be somewhat inconvenient but not burdensome. For example, there is a possibility that you may lose a textbook today or that your ballpoint pen may be damaged, but you retain these losses because the severity of loss is insignificant.

There are also cases in which part or all of an important risk is retained after careful analysis of the risk and the alternative methods of handling it. The arrangement made for handling the burden of losses may be merely to charge them off as an operating expense. Alternatively, some estimate of long-term average losses may provide the basis for creating a fund from which to pay for losses sustained. Such a fund may be in the form of cash or near-cash, or it may merely be a bookkeeping entry that represents an unidentified portion of a firm's assets.

The extent to which risk retention is feasible depends upon the accuracy of loss predictions and the arrangements made for loss payment. Because organizations are more likely to use the law of large numbers than is the typical individual, retention is especially attractive to large organizations. When an organization uses a highly formalized method of retention on an insurable risk, it is sometimes said the organization has "self-insured" the risk. Full discussion of this concept will be presented after the nature of insurance has been analyzed.

Transfer

As noted earlier, avoidance of risk means staying out of the game, so to speak. People avoid a risk by avoiding the activity or situation that creates it. When they **transfer** a risk, on the other hand, they stay in the game but shift the financial aspects of risk to someone else. Transfer can be accomplished only when the risk and the activity or situation involving it are separable. For example, industrial accidents involve the risk of employee injury that may cause pain, loss of income, and medical expense. The dollar cost of lost income and medical expense can be separated from the activity and shifted by having someone else, such as an insurer or self-insured employer, bear the loss. But the pain cannot be borne by someone else. That risk cannot be separated from the activity. Moreover, transfer of risk is not always complete or dependable. Transfer to a financially weak insurer, for instance, may be undependable.

Some risks may be transferred through the formation of a corporation with limited liability for its stockholders. Others may be transferred by contractual arrangements, including insurance.

Corporations   The owner or owners of a firm face a serious potential loss in the responsibility for the payment of debts and other financial obligations when such liabilities exceed the firm's assets. If the firm is organized as a *sole proprietorship,* the proprietor faces this risk. His or her personal assets are not separable from those of the firm, because the firm is not a separate legal entity. The proprietor has unlimited liability for the firm's obligations. General partners in a *partnership* occupy a similar situation, each partner being liable without limit for the debts of the firm.

Because a corporation is a separate legal entity, investors who wish to limit possible losses connected with a particular venture may create a corporation and transfer such risks to it. This does not prevent losses from occurring, but the burden is transferred to the corporation. The owners suffer indirectly, of course, but their loss is limited to their investment in the corporation. A huge liability claim for damages may take all the assets of the corporation, but the stockholders' personal assets beyond their stock in this particular corporation are not exposed to loss. Such a method of risk transfer sometimes is used to compartmentalize the risks of a large venture by incorporating separate firms to handle various segments of the total operation. In this way, a large firm may transfer parts of its risks to separate smaller firms, thus placing limits on possible losses to the owners. Courts, however, may not approve of this method of transferring the liability associated with dangerous business activities. For example, a large firm may be held legally liable for damages caused by a small subsidiary formed to manufacture a substance that proves dangerous to employees and/or the environment.

Contractual Arrangements   Some risks are transferred by a *guarantee* included in the contract of sale. A noteworthy example is the warranty provided the purchaser of an automobile. When automobiles were first manufactured, the purchaser bore the burden of all defects that developed during use. Somewhat later, automobile manufacturers agreed to replace defective parts at no cost, but the buyer was required to pay for any labor involved. Currently, manufacturers typically not only replace defective parts but also pay for labor, within constraints placed on time and mileage. The owner has, in effect, transferred a large part of the risk of purchasing a new automobile back to the manufacturer. The buyer, of course, is still subject to the inconvenience of having repairs made, but he or she does not have to pay for them.

Similar warranty contracts are now available to transfer the risk of repair losses from the buyers of many household appliances to the manufacturers. As the nature of durable goods becomes more complicated and the cost of repairs rises, such a transfer of risk becomes an important consideration in making a choice among competing brands, particularly when the warranty is included in the price of the product.

Bailments provide another method of transferring risk through contractual arrangements. A bailment exists when personal property is placed in the hands of another for safekeeping, servicing, processing, and so on. The arrangement usually provides that the bailee—the person or firm holding the property—is responsible to the owner only for damage to the property that results from the bailee's negligence.[6] The bailment, however, may provide an opportunity for the owner to transfer specified risks to the bailee by contract. This is quite common in fur storage, for example. The owner of a fur is encouraged to store it by the storage company's promise to be responsible for any loss to the fur during storage, irrespective of negligence. The bailee, in turn, may transfer the risk to an insurance company.

Leases and *rental agreements* often transfer risk from one party to another. A typical rental agreement, for instance, provides that the property rented shall be returned to the owner in good condition, except for ordinary wear and tear. When you sign a lease for an apartment, such a provision places the burden of possible loss or damage to the property on you. Many people underestimate the risk they assume by signing such an agreement. Some leases contain a **hold-harmless clause** designed to shift certain risks from owner to tenant. This clause specifies that the tenant agrees to hold the owner harmless from liability arising out of the ownership or use of the premises during the term of the lease. Many tenants who sign leases do not realize that they have agreed to pay for losses normally paid by the owner. On the other hand, if the tenant cannot pay because she or he has no financial assets, the burden will be borne by the owner despite the hold-harmless clause.

Contracts of suretyship are another risk transfer device. In such a contract, a third party (known as the surety) guarantees that it will perform as specified in the contract if the person who is obligated fails to do so. The endorser of a note is a surety who says to the creditor, "If the person who signed this note and to whom you loaned this money does not repay it in accordance with the terms of the note, I will." This transfers the risk of default from the creditor to the surety. When you endorse a check for deposit in your bank account, you are acting as a surety. If the check bounces, you are responsible for reimbursing the bank.

Clearly, it is neither possible nor feasible to list, much less discuss, all the methods of transferring risk. They are limited only by the imagination. Those mentioned merely illustrate some of the possibilities. Perhaps the most important arrangement for the transfer of risk is **insurance.**

Insurance is a common form of planned risk transfer as a financing technique for individuals and most organizations. The insurance industry has grown tremendously in industrialized countries, developing sophisticated products, employing millions of people, and investing billions of dollars. Because of its core importance in risk management, insurance is the centerpiece of this text. In chapter 2 you will read about the risk management process, including the use of insurance. Chapters 3, 4, and 5 follow with specific analysis of the insurance product. Later chapters are devoted to the various exposures to pure risk and to the means of managing those risks, especially through insurance.

....

6. This type of loss ("negligence" of bailees) is discussed in chapter 7.

The Risk of Driving an Automobile

Chapter 1 has introduced basic concepts about risk, but you may not yet understand the relevance to you of risk management. Let's consider an example that applies to most of us, and explore the general concepts of risk management.

THE RISK

Almost everyone drives (and many own) an automobile. That simple act, generally taken for granted, involves extensive risk. Say you drive the car to school. You expect to reach school without incident. Unfortunately, automobile accidents are somewhat frequent. You may, therefore, be involved in a fender bender, or a more severe accident.

The variability of those outcomes, from no loss to large potential liabilities (what if you hit a school bus, for example?), is the risk involved in driving. Substantial uncertainty in outcomes exists.

All three types of exposures discussed in chapter 1 are involved: property damage to the vehicle, liability for bodily injury and property damage to others, and personal losses if you also are injured. The peril is the auto accident, and possible hazards include poor weather conditions, heavy traffic, and poor vehicle maintenance. Can you think of others?

MANAGING RISK

We all take various steps to manage risks associated with driving an automobile, sometimes consciously, sometimes unconsciously. What are they?

Avoidance

Many large cities have mass transit opportunities that allow residents and visitors to function without automobiles. Subways and buses are used by millions of commuters. In some locations, jobs and stores are close enough to residences that walking or biking is possible. Where these options exist, people can successfully avoid the risk of loss from driving an automobile (that is, reduce the probability of loss to zero).

Note that the individual is *not* avoiding loss caused by an automobile. This broader situation would involve no potential loss as a pedestrian or from accidents between buses

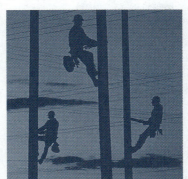

(or bicycles) and automobiles. Avoidance of these is almost impossible without strict curtailment of activities.

Note also that avoidance of loss from using an automobile involves loss of certain benefits. The most significant benefit lost may be flexibility. Reliance on mass transit implies a willingness to arrange your schedule according to the subway or bus system. It may also involve inconvenience in getting to the mass transit pick-up. The comfort of mass transit is generally less than that of a car. Avoidance, therefore, eliminates risk only at a cost.

Loss Prevention and Reduction

Most of us are unwilling to avoid the potential losses associated with driving an automobile. We do, however, have available various opportunities to reduce loss frequency and/or severity.

Efforts to reduce loss frequency are termed "loss prevention." A number of such measures can be applied to driving, including driver training; driving during off-peak hours; following traffic rules; choosing not to drive when tired, drunk, on medication, or otherwise mentally impaired; maintaining vehicles; and driving defensively rather than aggressively.

Efforts to minimize loss severity are termed "loss reduction." We can list many driving-related loss reduction possibilities, including driving cars with seat belts and air bags; choosing sturdy vehicles not easily damaged (although these have the possibility of causing greater damage to others); knowing CPR; and being prepared for an emergency.

Both loss prevention and loss reduction reduce risk by reducing variability in outcomes. They also involve costs. Some are direct monetary costs (adding the expense of air bags, for example). Others are costs of time and convenience, such as driving in off-peak hours. You will be willing to incur these costs only if the apparent benefit of doing so exceeds the expense. This is always true in implementing risk management decisions. We do not choose to eliminate all risk because that would be too costly. Instead, we accept some level of risk and try to manage it efficiently.

Loss Financing

When losses occur despite our efforts to prevent, reduce, or avoid them, we must finance them. We may plan for the financing (generally the best procedure), or we may find ourselves with an unplanned loss.

As individuals, our primary method of loss financing is insurance. We do well to transfer our automobile risks to an insurance company that can combine our risk with those of thousands of other drivers, thereby reducing variability in total outcomes. This is how the law of large numbers operates.

Our needs for insurance come in various forms. The greatest risk may involve potential liabilities for injuring other people and damaging their property. These liabilities could be in amounts too large for most of us to pay out of pocket.

We also need to protect against our own injuries and damage to the car. Because medical expenses and lost income could be substantial values, transfer of these risks to insurers generally is desirable. Damage to the automobile, however, may be retained, depending on the value of the car. Insurance is best used to protect against high-value, low-frequency risks. A "junker car," therefore, may not be worth insuring. All these options of insuring, retaining, preventing, and reducing are discussed in the following chapters.

Key Terms

risk	liability loss exposure
speculative risk	peril
pure risk	natural peril
loss	human peril
risk manager	economic peril
risk averse	hazard
probability distribution	physical hazard
frequency	intangible hazard
severity	moral hazard
mean	morale hazard
average	societal hazard
range	avoidance
variance	loss control
standard deviation	loss prevention
coefficient of variation	loss reduction
law of large numbers	loss financing
exposure	retention
personal loss exposure	transfer
consequential loss	hold-harmless clause
property loss exposure	insurance

Discussion Questions

1. Explain why use of the *squared* differences from the mean is necessary in calculating the variance. Try a numerical example.

2. In a particular situation it may be difficult to distinguish between moral hazard and morale hazard. Why? Define both terms.

3. Give examples of perils, exposures, and hazards for a university or college. Define each term.

4. Does the transfer of risk eliminate losses? Why, or why not?

5. A number of methods to deal with pure risk were presented in the text. Identify and define each, and discuss circumstances under which each is appropriate.

6. What is the law of large numbers? Why is it important?

7. Inflation causes both pure and speculative risks in our society. Can you give some examples of each? How do you handle such risks?

8. Some people with complete health insurance coverage tend to visit doctors more often than required. Is this tendency a moral hazard, a morale hazard, or simple common sense? Explain.

9. Proprietors have unlimited liability for the obligations of their proprietorship, and general partners are in the same position with regard to partnerships. Liability of those who own a corporation, on the other hand, is limited to their investment. Explain what relevance this has for risk management.

10. Transferring risk to someone whose ability to bear loss is less than yours is hardly an effective way to handle risk. Nevertheless, many landlords who are better off financially than their tenants include a hold-harmless clause in leases or rental agreements. Why? Is this method of handling risk free of cost to the landlord?

Cases

1.1 One medical practice that has been widely discussed in recent years involves "defensive medicine," in which a doctor orders more medical tests and x-rays than she or he might have in the past—not because of the complexity of the case, but because the doctor fears being sued by the patient for medical malpractice. The extra tests may establish that the doctor did everything reasonable and prudent to diagnose and treat the patient.

1. What does this tell you about the burden of risk?
2. What impact does this burden place on you and your family in your everyday life?
3. Is the doctor wrong to do this, or is it a necessary precaution?
4. Is there some way to change this situation?

1.2 Thompson's department store has a fleet of delivery trucks. The store also has a restaurant, a soda fountain, a babysitting service for parents shopping there, and an in-home appliance service program.

1. Name three perils associated with each of these operations.
2. For the pure-risk situations you noted in part 1 of this case, name three hazards that could be controlled by the employees of the department store.
3. If you were manager of the store, would you want all these operations? Which—if any—would you eliminate? Explain.

1.3 Omer Laskwood, the major income earner for a family of four, was overheard saying to his friend Vince, "I don't carry any life insurance because I'm young, and I know from statistics few people die at my age."

1. What are your feelings about this statement?
2. How does Omer perceive risk relative to his situation?
3. What characteristic in this situation is more important than the probability of loss?
4. Are there other risks Omer should consider?

1.4 The council members of Flatburg are very proud of the new proposed airport they are discussing at a council meeting. When it is completed, Flatburg will finally have regular commercial air service. Some type of fire protection is needed at the new airport, but a group of citizens is protesting that Flatburg cannot afford to purchase another new fire engine. They could use the downtown facilities, or they could move the downtown facilities five miles out to the airport. Someone suggested a compromise—move them halfway. As the council members left their meeting that evening, they had questions regarding this problem.

1. What questions would you raise?
2. How would you handle this problem using the information discussed in this chapter?

CHAPTER

2

Risk Management

Introduction   In August of 1992, Hurricane Andrew destroyed homes and businesses in Florida, flooded parts of Louisiana, and took the lives of residents in both areas. The dollar value of loss far exceeded any other recorded natural catastrophe. Andrew followed by only three years the second most costly hurricane, Hugo, which struck the East Coast a bit further north, hitting the Carolinas with great force. Yet miraculously, Hugo's "human losses," those associated with injuries and death, were minimal. Was this outcome miraculous, or was it the result of excellent planning and preparation? Persons familiar with Hurricane Hugo know that substantial planning and preparation was done by government officials and others. Citizens, with few exceptions, evacuated endangered coastal areas and followed other directions from the governor of South Carolina.

The planning and preparation for a hurricane, or for any loss potential, is the process of risk management. In this chapter we will define risk management and outline a step-by-step approach to help reduce the costs of risks. This approach could allow both individuals in their personal lives and executives in organizations to participate in daily activities without constant worry over what will happen in the future. The intent is to help meet personal and professional objectives with minimal negative interference. In this chapter, you will explore:

1. Risk management.
2. How risk management is performed.
3. The objectives of risk management.
4. How risk management fits within your daily activities.

Risk management can be described as the decision-making process by which an organization or individual reduces the negative consequences of risk. Recall that risk has been defined as variability in future outcomes and that in this text we are concerned with situations involving losses, not gains. Management is involved because the process includes leading, controlling, directing, and organizing for some stated purpose, which in the case of risk management is to reduce the "costs" associated with risk. Such costs are defined in the following paragraphs.

When we are uncertain about what will happen in the future, we need to make contingency plans. To do so involves costs. For example, a hospital must have back-up generators on hand so that if its regular supply of electricity is lost, essential life-supporting machinery will not be without power. The back-up generator is used only when the regular electricity is out; hence, it is a duplication of assets and an added cost. Such techniques to reduce loss costs are termed **loss control** and represent one of four costs of risk.

A second cost of risk is the **lost opportunity** when some activity is curtailed due to uncertainty regarding its consequence. The potential for product liability litigation, for example, has been cited as a reason for reduced research and development efforts in the United States. As a result, firms lose the opportunity to earn a profit, and consumers lose the opportunity to buy a product. Trampolines are one product made temporarily unavailable because of liability concerns and breast implants may become another. The opportunities lost because of concern over risk are sometimes called the "social costs of risk."

Risk also involves **psychological costs.** Uncertainty over future losses may cause worry and anxiety. As stated above, worry and anxiety may result in lost opportunities. The negative emotions themselves are additional costs of risk.

A fourth cost of risk is the **financing of losses** that do occur. Often, losses are financed through the purchase of insurance. The price of insurance includes insurer expenses and profits beyond the payment of losses. Without insurance, the buyer would not have the costs of insurer expenses and profits, but would have to deal with uncertainty in paying for losses as well as the expenses of administering the payment of loss and possibly the cost of borrowing funds when loss occurs.

The actual losses that occur represent a cost of risk management rather than a true cost of risk. Their importance, however, deserves explicit mention. If we do our risk management jobs well, losses will be manageable; yet even manageable losses represent an expense or cost to individuals and organizations.

The risk management function, then, has the objective of reducing the costs of (1) loss/risk control; (2) lost opportunities; (3) psychological costs; (4) loss/risk financing; and (5) actual losses. Of these costs, the easiest to measure are the costs of financing and the actual loss costs. Attempts to quantify psychological and opportunity costs likely would result in such nebulous numbers as to be of little meaning; and loss control costs often are so tied into general business expenses (such as employee training) that clear identification of them is troublesome. As a result, specific efforts aimed at measuring the "cost of risk" tend to use the dollars spent on insurance premiums, uninsured losses, and risk management departmental expenses. A recent study using these measures found the average cost risk per surveyed firm was $9,591,421, which represented .52 percent of revenues or .21 percent of assets.[1]

The person(s) performing the function of reducing costs of risk may be called a risk manager, but typically only rather large organizations employ people under such a title. In many situations, risk management is performed by several people, and often it is done without a formal background in the field. In fact, all of us are managers of our own risks, whether we have studied risk management or not. Every time you lock your house or car, check the wiring system for problems, or pay an insurance premium, you are performing the functions of a risk manager. So, while we will refer to a risk manager in this text, keep in mind that many other people also manage risks.

The Risk Manager as a Decision Maker

In a small firm, the owner usually performs the risk management function, establishing policy and making decisions. In larger organizations, the risk manager holds a staff position, and his or her authority depends upon the policy adopted by top management. The dimensions of this authority are outlined in a policy statement. The risk manager may be authorized to make decisions in routine matters, but restricted to making recommendations in others. For example, the risk manager may recommend that the costs of employee injuries be retained rather than insured, but a final retention decision of such magnitude would be made by top management. Avoidance decisions may also be made at higher levels, because they frequently require sacrificing an opportunity to make profits. For example, a new product may have potential for both great profits and huge liability losses. The liability risk can be avoided only by keeping the product off the market, but if that is done the profits it could generate are not realized. In such a situation, the risk manager is an adviser to top management rather than a decision maker.

The risk manager's status has grown with the complexity of the environment in which organizations operate. For example, risk managers were almost unheard of in hospitals in 1970. But following the liability insurance crisis that arose in the mid-1970s for medical care providers, hospital chief executives quickly recognized the benefits of risk management. Now all major hospitals have risk managers. The liability insurance crisis of the mid-1980s again focused attention on the role of the risk manager, this time in virtually all lines of business. Typically, the hospital risk manager reports directly to the chief executive officer. In most other large organizations, it is typical for a risk manager to report to the chief financial officer.

This reporting relationship probably began as the risk manager position evolved from that of insurance buyer to insurance manager to risk manager; the insurance buying function was a subset of other finance and

1. James D. Blinn, Sandra R. Duncan, Barbara Goodwin, "1990 Cost of Risk Survey: A Yardstick for Managers," *Risk Management,* February 1991.

controller activities. In an organization today, the risk manager should be at a sufficiently high staff level to allow effective work relationships with all departments. The position requires formal recognition on the organizational chart and respect within the informal organizational structure.

The Risk Management Process

We have stated that risk management is a decision-making process. This is important, because the risk management framework shares many characteristics with other functions that require decisions. As a result, the following pages will be familiar to those of you who have studied other decision-making processes, and all readers can observe the links across functions requiring decisions. Table 2–1 presents the risk management process in a concept summary form.

RISK MANAGEMENT DECISIONS FOR ORGANIZATIONS

Set Objectives

Any successful decision-making procedure requires that the intended outcomes, or objectives, be known up front. How could we choose, for example, between the purchase of a Plymouth Caravan and a Jaguar without knowing

TABLE 2–1

Concept Summary: The Risk Management Process

ACTION	
1. Set Objectives	1. Coincide with general organizational/individual goals.
	2. Focus primarily on risk-return trade-off.
	3. Consider attitude toward safety and willingness to accept risk.
2. Identify Problems	1. Problems are combination of perils, exposures, hazards.
	2. Need to use multiple methods of identification.
	3. Identification is essential to effective management.
3. Evaluate Problems	1. Measure loss frequency and severity.
	2. Relate to organizational characteristics and goals.
	3. Utilize probability analysis.
	4. Consider maximum probable and maximum possible loss.
4. Identify & Evaluate Alternatives	1. Basic choice of avoidance, loss control, loss financing.
	2. Loss control involves loss prevention and reduction.
	3. Loss financing involves transfer and retention.
	4. Generally use more than one method.
	5. Evaluation based on cost, effect on loss frequency and severity, and risk characteristics.
5. Choose Alternatives	1. Decision making rules available to choose among the alternatives.
	2. Choice should be based on objectives set in first step.
6. Implement Alternatives	1. Requires negotiating skills.
	2. Success includes a "big picture" perspective or organizational activities.
7. Monitor System	1. Loop back to step one and re-evaluate each element of the process.
	2. Choice is made in a dynamic environment, requiring continual evaluation.

ETHICAL *Dilemma*

Conflicting Organizational Objectives

Organizations and individuals are faced with many objectives, some of which conflict with one another. Such conflicts can lead to ethical dilemmas. Let's consider the organization that sets high profitability goals. What does this organization do when product testing of one of its most successful products reveals a significant potential to injure the public, but not for another twenty years? More difficult, what if testing reveals a low potential (probability) for harm, but a very serious harm? The cost to eliminate the potential for harm may be enormous, yet human life is precious and valuable. What is the proper action to take?

We all willingly accept some potential for loss in our lives, in part because elimination of that potential is impossible. We could not function in a world without risk. Such a world would require never using electricity or fire or sharp objects, never even eating because of the potential for spoilage. The question, thus, becomes one of how much risk we are willing to accept and at what cost. Does a surgeon have the duty to warn patients of every imaginable problem that might arise during or after treatment? Which problems must be discussed verbally, rather than by providing patients with a written list of risks and their likelihood of occurring? Must the homeowner reveal the real potential for water damage in the basement when attempting to sell a house? Ought a product manufacturer recall all its products following a terrorist threat that could harm users?

the intended use of and preferences for various automobile characteristics? The risk management process, therefore, begins with objectives.

Individuals likely will have objectives regarding careers, family relationships, and community involvement. Organizations may list objectives involving profits, employee safety, civic responsibility, innovation, and others. The individual's risk management process is discussed later in the chapter. Here we will focus on organizations.

Regarding risk management, the primary objectives will focus on the tradeoff between risk and return. The less risk we are willing to accept, the more expensive the process. Whatever objectives are chosen, success in meeting them depends somewhat on the ability to communicate them effectively.

Risk management objectives can be communicated in a number of ways. First are the stated organization's goals (or mission) that likely include broad concepts of customer satisfaction, growth, profits, or, for nonprofit organizations, other measures of success, such as the number of individuals served and social responsibility.

Second is a **risk management policy statement,** which is a specific means of communicating risk management objectives. Risk management policy statements have had a place for many years in discussions of the risk management process. This emphasis began in the 1970s, first in a book by Mehr and Hedges,[2] and later in an article by Close and O'Connell.[3]

Mehr and Hedges detail various requirements of a risk management policy statement. These include: a statement of goals in a form that makes it possible to determine whether or not these goals are being met or have been reached; a set of measurable standards against which a risk manager's performance may be evaluated; and clear-cut guides to determine which risk management techniques should be used to meet organizational goals. An example of a risk management policy statement is shown in table 2–2.

Objectives may also be communicated through two additional documents: the risk manager's job description and/or a **risk management manual.** A manual provides specific guidelines for detailed risk management problems, such as how to handle the kidnapping of an organization executive. These two documents are more precise and detailed than the organization's mission statement or risk management policy statement. Advertisements, employee training programs, and other public activities offer further insight into an organization's philosophies and objectives. To be effective, risk management objectives must coincide with those of the organization generally, and both must be communicated consistently.

Identify Problems

Having set and communicated objectives, the next step in the process is to identify the many problems that could cause an organization to fail in meeting its objectives. The characteristics of such "problems" can be placed in three categories, as discussed in chapter 1: (1) perils; (2) exposures; and (3) hazards. Identification is critical, because a problem that is unknown can be managed well only by accident.

Risk managers use the following approaches to identify perils, exposures, and hazards:

1. Advice from insurance agents, brokers, and risk management consultants.
2. Insurance policy checklists.
3. Financial statement analysis.
4. Flow chart analysis.
5. Communication with other departments.
6. Inspections of the organization's facilities and operations.
7. Review and analysis of historical data on losses.

Advice from Insurance Agents, Brokers, and Consultants Some agents and brokers are so "insurance oriented" that they sometimes ignore uninsurable risks, but professionals in the field have become aware of risk management. They can render valuable service in both identifying and evaluating risks.

2. Robert I. Mehr and Bob A. Hedges, *Risk Management: Concepts and Applications* (Homewood, Ill.: Richard D. Irwin, Inc., 1974), chapter 2.
3. Darwin B. Close and John O'Connell, "A Guide to Formulation of Risk Management Policy Statements," *CPCU Annals,* vol. 29, no. 3 (1976): 195–200.

Title
RISK MANAGEMENT POLICY STATEMENT
Company/Location/Department/Section
SUBSIDIARIES—ALL LOCATIONS

1. Purpose
    1.1 To establish company policy in respect of Risk Management and Insurance.

2. Scope
    2.1 This policy will extent to the Company's locations worldwide.

3. Policy
    3.1 It is the basic corporate policy and a corporate goal to control exposures to risk of loss (except speculative risk) which arises from external causes. To achieve this goal and minimize the adverse effects of accidental losses, a Risk Management Program has been established.
    3.2 Risk Management is the planning, organizing, directing, and controlling of resources to minimize adverse effects of accidental losses at the least possible cost. It is a rational decision-making process consisting of separate risk management steps as follows:
        3.2.1 Identify and analyze exposures which may lead to accidental losses.
        3.2.2 Formulate feasible risk management alternatives for dealing with these exposures, i.e.,
            • Risk avoidance
            • Loss prevention
            • Risk retention
            • Risk transfer
        3.2.3 Select the best alternative technique.
        3.2.4 Implement the chosen technique.
        3.2.5 Monitor the results.
    3.3 The purchase of insurance is one part of the broader Risk Management Program. While the actual operation of the Corporate Risk Management and Insurance Department embraces more than just the purchase of appropriate insurance coverages, this function continues to be one of the department's major responsibilities. The highly technical nature of the insurance business plus the inherent advantages of centralized purchases combine to place this responsibility solely within the jurisdiction of the Corporate Risk Management and Insurance Department. Insurance coverages may be purchased at a local level only after the department has been fully appraised of the need for such purchase and, of course, has approved such purchase.

4. General Responsibilities
    4.1 The Corporate Risk Management and Insurance Department is responsible for planning and managing the corporate risk program and purchasing all required coverages by:
        4.1.1 Determining the amount of insurance or policy limits required in conjunction with permissible retentions and/or deductibles, if any.
        4.1.2 Determining where best the risk may be placed.
        4.1.3 Placing the risk.
        4.1.4 Making periodic evaluations so as to update values or policy limits.
        4.1.5 Reviewing leases, contracts, and other documents whose operation may adversely affect present or proposed forms of coverage.
        4.1.6 Establishing the appropriate allocation of premium between two or more entities receiving benefits under one policy form.
    4.2 The Corporate Risk Management and Insurance Department is also responsible for planning the corporate risk program so as to embrace the functions of safety, security, and property conservation by:
        4.2.1 Coordinating and reviewing inspection reports rendered by inspectors from carriers and other sources.
        4.2.2 Analyzing loss experience so that all pertinent levels of management are aware of specific problems, if any.
        4.2.3 Formulating and disseminating general policies dealing with risk management, along with other items of interest.

TABLE 2–2—*continued*

Risk Management Policy Statement

Title
RISK MANAGEMENT POLICY STATEMENT
Company/Location/Department/Section
SUBSIDIARIES—ALL LOCATIONS

4.3 Local management is responsible for applying the risk management program to all facets of its own operations. Local management is held directly responsible for implementing the corporate risk program in respect of exposure, or risk, by:

4.3.1 Reducing or eliminating exposures whenever practical.

4.3.2 Reporting any material changes in the exposures presently covered.

4.3.3 Complying with the conditions and warranties on policies of insurance presently in force.

4.3.4 Maintaining corporate properties so that the risk of damage or destruction is minimized.

4.3.5 Promptly reporting all accidents or incidents to the respective carrier and the Corporate Risk Management and Insurance Department.

4.3.6 Assisting carriers or their legal representatives in actions brought against the Company.

4.3.7 Promptly evaluating all recommendations made by authorized inspectors and effecting immediate correction of those deemed to be desirable. It should be recognized and understood that in those cases when insurance companies classify their recommendations as "mandatory," this means that a decision not to comply may result in cancellation of insurance protection or increased rates.

5. Other

5.1 Effective loss and accident prevention activities and the maintenance of appropriate insurance protection will provide the highest degree of protection against loss of assets and assure continuity of operations.

5.2 Technical counsel and other services relative to loss and accident prevention activities are available to each operating unit and upon request will be provided by the Corporate Risk Management and Insurance Department and/or appropriate outside insurance representatives.

APPROVED

Organizations may also employ risk management consultants, many of whom are well prepared through education and experience to work with all phases of the risk management process. Consultants work for a fee, either on an hourly or per job basis, and do not receive commissions from insurers. Agents and brokers typically are compensated by commissions that are a percentage of the insurance premiums paid by their clients. Some people believe commissions create a conflict of interest that causes some agents and brokers to overemphasize insurance as a solution to risk management problems. Objectivity is important in an era when large organizations are placing greater emphasis on retention and are using insurance primarily for catastrophic levels of risk.

Insurance Policy Checklists   These checklists itemize the policies or types of insurance needed by various kinds of organizations. They are concerned only with insurable loss exposures, but can be useful. Insurable exposures confronting the firm are not the only exposures, but they are a large part of the total. Some risk managers develop their own checklists by modifying insurance policy checklists and published exposure checklists.

Financial Statement Analysis   The analysis of financial statements involves an examination of the balance sheet and income statement, as well as financial forecasts and budgets. Current balance sheets provide clues to the present property exposures of the firm, while forecasts and budgets reveal exposures that will arise in the future. Budgets, for example, show planned expenditures for future operations and purchases of property. Risk managers who know about such plans can identify the exposures and make timely recommendations. Advice concerning fire prevention and control is more helpful while a new structure is in the planning stage than after it is constructed. For example, if a building needs a fire suppression sprinkler system, it is much less expensive to have it installed while the building is under construction than after the building has been completed.

Flow Chart Analysis Flow charts graphically depict the operations of the organization, starting with economic inputs at one end and progressing through various processes and locations to product or service output at the other end. Used in conjunction with a checklist, they are helpful in identifying possible losses to property and operations. A risk manager can readily identify bottlenecks that can create a situation in which a small loss in actual property damage leads to a large loss in profits due to a temporary shutdown for repairs.

Communication with Other Departments Communication has the dual purpose of making everyone risk conscious and helping the risk manager find out what is happening. No one can possibly know about everything that goes on in the organization, so help is essential. In addition, employees who are risk conscious can help by identifying exposures and keeping the risk manager informed of changes in activities, processes, property, products, and services. This information will alert him or her to new possibilities for loss. A new activity, for example, may require inspection to assure compliance with all OSHA regulations. New processes, products, or services may create a liability exposure. Newly acquired property may or may not be covered by present insurance.

Inspections of Facilities and Operations A risk manager or outside expert can visualize potential losses by a physical inspection of the organization's facilities and observation of its operations. This method of identifying loss exposures is enhanced when the risk manager is familiar with the industry in which the organization operates. It is helpful to know the kinds of losses that other organizations in the same industry have experienced. It is also helpful to know that many insurance companies employ inspectors who will help the risk manager make inspections, demonstrate methods to identify exposures, and offer assistance in deciding how to manage those exposures identified.

Review and Analysis of Historical Data The sophisticated risk manager accumulates loss data over time (both the organization's own loss experience and industry experience) and uses various quantitative techniques to analyze the data. While data analysis is primarily used in the evaluation step of the risk management process, data on types of losses can help in the identification stage. Some common exposures are shown in table 2–3.

Evaluate Problems

Identification of risk management problems is difficult because there is so much to observe. Once done, however, problems ought to be evaluated

TABLE 2–3
···

Common Loss Exposures for
Organizations

	EXPOSURE	PERIL	POSSIBLE LOSS
Personal	Employee	Disability	Income, services, extra expenses
	Employee	Death	Income, services, extra expenses
	Employee	Old age	Income, services, extra expenses
Property	Buildings, equipment	Damage or destruction	Asset, income, extra expense
	Trade secrets	Theft	Income
	Inventory	Damage or destruction	Asset, income
Liability	Activities	Lawsuit	Asset, extra expense
	Property	Lawsuit	Asset, extra expense

with the intent of choosing appropriate mechanisms to reduce their adverse consequences.

As discussed in the introductory chapter, two important characteristics of potential losses must be measured for evaluation purposes. These are **loss frequency** and **loss severity.** Together, these characteristics help us understand the magnitude and riskiness of the problem under consideration. From estimates of loss frequency and severity, exposures can be classified as **unbearable, difficult to bear,** and **relatively unimportant.** The categories are "fuzzy," in that no strict rule can be applied to designate which one is appropriate in a given situation. Nonetheless, the categories provide some structure for the problem.

Unbearable risks are those so large that an organization's finances would be disrupted enough to cause bankruptcy. Difficult to bear risks would seriously impair the organization's ability to operate, but not lead to bankruptcy. Relatively unimportant exposures to loss would not materially affect the organization's activities. For example, a number of asbestos manufacturers were forced to file for bankruptcy during the 1980s in response to the barrage of lawsuits filed by people injured from exposure to asbestos products. This exposure was unbearable for those firms in the long run. For other firms, the litigation involving asbestos caused them to change their corporate structure but not to file for bankruptcy. The exposure was difficult to bear. Virtually no firm involved in the asbestos industry would today consider the exposure relatively unimportant. An example of relatively unimportant exposures might come from the potential loss associated with pilferage of office supplies that inevitably occurs at every business organization. Most firms account for this loss as part of their normal operating expenses.

If the significance of a risk is overestimated, resources may be wasted in dealing with it. On the other hand, if it is underestimated, the organization may inadvertently be left exposed to the possibility of serious loss. Accurate evaluation helps the risk manager formulate a priority list that shows the relative importance of each risk to the firm. The nature of each risk can then be analyzed to determine the best alternative for dealing with it. The organization's choice is influenced by the relative significance of the risk and the feasibility of each alternative from the mechanical, engineering, legal, and economic points of view.

TABLE 2–4

Probability Distribution of Total Dollar
Losses

TOTAL DOLLAR LOSSES PER YEAR	PROBABILITY
$ 0	.200
1,000	.230
5,000	.200
25,000	.130
100,000	.100
300,000	.070
500,000	.040
1,000,000	.020
5,000,000	.008
10,000,000	.002

The relative significance of pure risk can be based on information obtained from the probability distribution for losses associated with all types of loss exposures. A **probability distribution** is a table in which possible outcomes are listed with the appropriate probability (or relative frequency) of occurrence of each outcome. All possible, mutually exclusive outcomes ought to be represented so that the sum of probabilities equals one. The nature of a probability distribution is depicted in table 2–4. This table shows a hypothetical distribution of total losses for a year. For simplicity, specific dollar values are given. Assume, for illustration purposes, that these dollar amounts represent the only possible outcomes; that is, losses cannot fall in between these values. Using this assumption, we know that 23 percent of all "events" are expected to yield a loss of $1,000. That is, out of 100 events, 23 will result in a $1,000 loss. This example demonstrates that probability is a measure of frequency.

Two elements are relevant in the risk manager's use of probability analysis: (1) probability reflects the *long-run* frequency; and (2) the environment is assumed to be *stable*. The first point refers to the law of large numbers. In essence, probability analysis requires a large volume of data, which is often unavailable to the risk manager. Reliance on industry or government information and generation of data through computer simulation may alleviate the problems posed by small data sets.

The second point is important because of the dynamic nature of our society; that is, the world is not stable. Use of data on automobile accidents during the 1940s is of little value in estimating automobile accidents in the 1990s. The environment has not been stable in such areas as road conditions, vehicle performance, safety controls, and driver training. Risk managers respond to the changing environment by limiting use of old data, and updating what data are included in estimates for factors expected to impact future outcomes.

Taking those potential shortcomings into account, the risk manager can use information provided by probability distributions in many ways. He or she can determine several helpful measurements. For instance, the probability of no loss is .20. Because the probabilities sum to 1.0, we also know that the probability of some loss is 1.0 − .20 = .80. Thus, we prepare for losses. The expected total dollar losses are calculated in two steps. First, each possible loss outcome is multiplied by its probability of occurrence.

The resulting values are then summed together. An example is shown in table 2–5. This expected loss indicates the average annual loss the organization with a large number of independent exposures can anticipate during a year.[4] The expected value can also be viewed as the cost of losses in a full insurance program. Of course, the total insurance premium would have to cover the insurer's operating expenses, taxes, risk, profit, and other elements, as will be explained later.

A distribution also gives information about how likely it is that losses will be difficult to handle or even unbearable. For example, if we decide that losses of $100,000 or more would be difficult to handle, the probability of having *a difficult loss* (or losses) is .100 + .070 + .040 + .020 + .008 + .002, or .24.

Assume further that losses are considered unbearable at or above $1,000,000. The probability of such a loss would be .020 + .008 + .002, or .030. On the average, unbearable losses would occur three times during a 100-year period, because we have presented the data so that one year represents one "event." This average would result only if conditions remain unchanged.

Often, the risk manager will use these probability concepts in a **management information system.** Data are the lifeblood of risk managers, permitting them to make informed decisions. A major task of the risk manager, therefore, is to quantify the organization's loss history, including types of losses, amounts, circumstances surrounding them, dates, and other relevant facts. Such a quantification may be called a risk management information system, or RMIS. An RMIS provides the risk manager with trends, such as a preponderance of workplace injuries in a particular plant, and increases or decreases in number and size of losses. The history may also permit establishment of probability distributions, as discussed, which help the risk manager decide how best to manage risks. Those decisions must include consideration of financial concepts such as the time value of money. A number of computer programs (and models) have been developed to assist the risk manager in this task.

TABLE 2–5

Expected Loss

OUTCOME	×	PROBABILITY	=	EXPECTED OUTCOME
0		.200		0
1,000		.230		230
5,000		.200		1,000
25,000		.130		3,250
100,000		.100		10,000
300,000		.070		21,000
500,000		.040		20,000
1,000,000		.020		20,000
5,000,000		.008		40,000
10,000,000		.002		20,000
				$135,480

4. The calculations are sufficiently complex to require a Monte Carlo simulation or some other computer program. "Independent" in this statistical context means that a loss of one exposure, such as a building in St. Louis, does not change the probability of loss for another of the many buildings belonging to the same organization.

Identify and Evaluate Alternatives

This whole process of setting objectives and identifying and evaluating problems is undertaken with the intent of implementing a program to meet the organizational and risk management objectives. Alternative methods to manage risk, therefore, must be identified and evaluated. These alternatives include avoidance, loss prevention and reduction, retention, and transfer. Each was discussed in chapter 1 and is given attention throughout the text. The insurance transfer mechanism is given particular emphasis.

Choose Alternatives

Having reviewed the organizational risk management problems and alternative management techniques, choices (selections) can be made. Often, more than one option will be implemented. For example, unless avoidance is used, some financing technique is required, whether it be retention or transfer, and may be accompanied by a loss control technique.

The selection process likely involves many facets. Not only must expected frequency and severity of loss be considered, but also the risk attitude of the organization's decision-maker(s). The more risk averse the decision-making individual or group is, the less variability will be acceptable. In addition, monetary concerns do not constitute the only criteria for decisions. Other important factors include objectives of social responsibilty, reputation, and tradition. Proctor and Gamble, for example, has instituted in some of their plants a target of "zero accidents," which may reduce profits but also meet employee safety needs.

A number of decision-making rules are available to risk managers. It is possible, although generally not advisable, to make decisions based on intuition. More often, decisions are based on data.

One relatively simple decision process is illustrated in figure 2–1. This illustration may be called a **risk management matrix.** On one axis, cat-

FIGURE 2–1

Risk Management Matrix

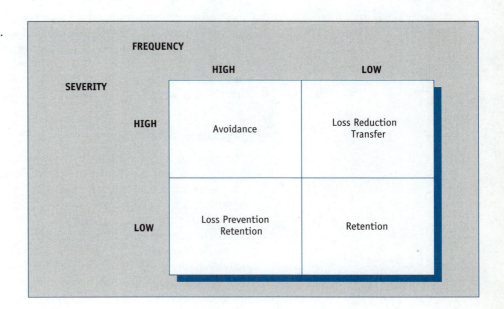

egories of relative frequency are listed; on the other are categories of relative severity. The simplest of these matrices is one with just four cells (as shown).

Starting with the upper lefthand corner of high frequency and high severity, we find "avoidance." This suggests that a situation falling in this category is best avoided. An example might be a firm that is considering construction of a building on the banks of the Mississippi. Flooding would be a common occurrence and likely cause significant damage each time.

Moving down to the corner characterized by high frequency and low severity, we find "loss prevention" and "retention." Where frequency is significant, efforts to prevent losses may be useful. In addition, if losses are of low value, they may be easily paid out of the organization's or individual's own funds (an exception occurs if frequency makes the total value unbearable). Highly frequent losses are predictable and are generally more cost-effectively financed through retention. An example might be losses due to wear and tear on equipment. Such losses are predictable and of low annual value. A second example might be employee pilferage of supplies.

The upper righthand corner represents situations involving low frequency and high severity. Here we find "loss reduction" and "transfer." For large-valued potential losses, reduction is an effective way to minimize risk. Furthermore, a low-probability but high-valued event involves significant risk, which is more effectively managed when transferred, usually through the purchase of insurance. An example might be loss due to liability through the manufacture of a defective product, or loss caused by an interruption of business due to damage to a factory.

The fourth corner, representing both low frequency and low severity, shows "retention." Because loss control techniques tend to be less effective with loss situations that rarely happen and are low value when they do, no control is recommended. Furthermore, little risk exists in such a scenario, making retention a generally appropriate financing tool. Examples might include someone driving through the parking gate and damaging it, and loss of the pet gerbil to a visiting python.

Another common decision process is to accept a project that provides a positive return to the organization of sufficient value to meet the organization's goals. Such a process may be referred to as **cash flow analysis,** in which the actual flow of funds over the life of the project is estimated and valued. An example of cash flow analysis is given in the appendix to this chapter.

Implement Alternatives

The risk manager's job is nearly completed at this point. Objectives are determined and communicated. Problems are identified and evaluated, as are alternative tools to manage those problems. Selection has been made of which tools to employ, and how those tools are to be implemented. Throughout the text, we will discuss methods of implementation. Keep in mind that implementation requires knowledge and skill. If insurance is the chosen option, for example, care is needed to be certain that the policy provides the intended coverage, that the insurer is solvent, that the premium is appropriate, and sometimes that the premium is properly allocated among organizational divisions. Likewise, the institution of a loss control program requires upper management's endorsement, employee training, and generally a well-prepared plan. We will touch on some of these topics later in the text; others can be learned only through experience, since they differ according to situations.

Monitor System

Even after all this analysis and planning, the job still is not done. The process of risk management is continuous, requiring constant monitoring of the program to be certain that (1) the options implemented were correct and have been implemented appropriately; and (2) the underlying problems have not changed so much as to require revised plans of managing them. When either of these conditions exist, the process returns to the first step and the cycle repeats. In this way, risk management can be considered a systems process, one in never-ending motion.

GLOBAL RISK MANAGEMENT

All business disciplines must respond to the reality of interdependence of national economies. A major cause of this interdependence is the growth of multinational organizations. Ford Motor Corporation, for example, is no longer a U.S. company, but rather an organization based in the United States with divisions dispersed around the globe. Our interdependence became clear in 1987 when the stock market crash on Wall Street was followed by massive drops in value at stock markets in Japan, the United Kingdom, and elsewhere.

We would be remiss in this global economic framework to omit discussion of risk management outside of the United States. And yet discussion of global risk management is limited by the realization that the fundamentals of risk management cross national borders.

The major distinctions between risk management within U.S. (and Canadian) borders and outside those borders lie either in variations in attitudes toward risk and risk management or in hazards that affect the size and probability of loss. Don't be fooled, however, by this simple categorization of differences into thinking that global risk management is easy. An effective global risk management program requires extensive knowledge of local laws and customs, as well as a keen ability to organize diverse systems.

Variations in Attitudes

The United States is famous for its orientation toward safety. Even in the early days of property insurance, the U.S. first developed firefighting units and then contemplated the need for fire insurance. The rest of the world went straight for the insurance. The U.S. remains a leader in safety planning around the globe. Innovations in the development of fire-resistant materials, earthquake-proof construction, ergonomically sound workstations, and safe highways generally occur in the U.S.

A preference for safety over financing might signify a risk-averse attitude. Yet in developing financial schemes, firms in the U.S. tend to utilize retention programs more often than do their counterparts overseas. Thus, the use of large deductible, captives, and other means of retention are more common in the U.S. than elsewhere.[5]

The greater use of insurance outside the U.S. appears due in part to the importance of long-term, close relationships between insureds and insurers. Unlike the U.S., where one-year policies are the norm, some firms overseas enter into twenty- or thirty-year agreements.

A second reason for heavier reliance on insurance overseas is that insurers offer lower credits for deductibles than they do in the U.S. Use of deductibles, therefore, is not cost-effective. Deductibles are discussed in chapter 6.

Variation in Hazards

Some potential losses are more severe or frequent across national boundaries. Liability losses, for example, are believed to be both more frequent and larger inside the U.S. than anywhere else in the world. In contrast, losses associated with political instability, such as government seizure of assets, may be more common and of larger value outside the U.S. than within it. The risk associated with political instability is termed **political risk** and is discussed in chapter 6. Liability risks are presented in chapter 7.

RISK MANAGEMENT DECISIONS FOR FAMILIES

Early in this chapter, we indicated that risk management is performed informally by many people, including ourselves for our own potential loss situations. The risk management process just described for an organization applies equally well for an individual or family. In fact, much of the remainder of this text is devoted to the management of risks faced by individuals and families.

The main distinction between familial and organizational risk management is that managing risks tends to be quite a bit more complex for organizations. Otherwise, our analysis applies equally well in either setting.

Risk management is more complicated for an organization than it is for a family for a number of reasons. First, the average organization has far more property exposed to risk than does the average family. Second, organizations engage in a greater variety of activities that expose them to unpredictable losses. Third, the responsibility of the organization for the actions of others is far broader than in the case of the family. No family has 5,000 members, but many organizations have that many employees, any one of whom may get into trouble while acting as an agent of the employer. Fourth, organizations have certain responsibilities imposed by law, such as workers' compensation, which expose them to loss. Fifth, most organizations either voluntarily or involuntarily (through union pressure) assume part of the life and health risks to which their employees are ex-

---

5. See Norman A. Baglini, *Global Risk Management: How U.S. Corporations Manage Foreign Risk* (New York: Risk Management Society Publishing, Inc., 1983), and Joan T. Schmit, Kendall Roth, and Rick G. Winch, "Managing Domestic Versus Foreign Risks," in *Insurance, Risk Management, and Public Policy,* edited by Sandra G. Gustavson and Scott E. Harrington (Boston, Kluwer Academic Publishers, 1994).

posed. Finally, as mentioned earlier, large organizations have more alternatives in handling risk than the family does.

We must also mention that while risk management for an organization may be more complex than it is for a family, the family's needs may be relatively more significant. The disability of a family's main income-earner, for example, is devastating not only emotionally but also financially. A corporation, in contrast, has limited liability, so that its owners may not be devastated by a corporate "disability" (although the employees could well be devastated).

The Risk Management Process

How can you apply the risk management process? Let's look at property risks associated with home ownership.

THE HOME RISK

Setting Objectives

Consider your property exposure as a homeowner (now or in the future). Your first step in risk management ought to be setting objectives. Begin with broad, philosophical considerations. For example, you might set an objective of managing all your liability, personal, and property (including home) risks as best as possible, spending no more than 5 percent of annual family income on insurance and on loss prevention and reduction programs. A limit on expenditures is required, because you cannot prevent or insure against all potential losses. Your objectives for managing home risks, therefore, must be coordinated with objectives for all other risks. Set your objectives to coincide with your attitude toward uncertainty, ability to pay for losses, and potential for loss. You might consider protection (loss prevention and reduction) more important than insurance on some types of property, for example, because of sentimental value.

In addition to such broad, philosophical objectives, you ought to set objectives about specifics, including the amount of loss you can and are willing to bear. That is, you need to decide on an insurance policy deductible level, the types of property and perils to be covered (or not covered), the relation of the insurance amount to the value of the property (do you want to insure for the full value, only the amount required by your lender, or some other amount?), and whether or not you want insurance to cover the re-placement value or depreciated value of the lost property. Determine also what kind of service you require from your insurance agent and insurance company. Do you want your insurer to be of the highest financial standing? You can obtain financial data from *Best's Reports,* published annually by the A.M. Best Company and likely found in your local library. Do you want an agent in town, or are you willing to buy insurance through the mail? How important is service from your insurance company? Call the Department of Insurance in your state for available information regarding consumer complaints against insurance companies doing business in your state, and the ratio of number of complaints to number of policies sold by those companies. The point is, decide what your goals are before developing your program. Then build your program with constant reference to your goals. Also, because some of your objectives are likely to conflict with others, set priorities that will help you balance them.

Identify Problems

After setting objectives, you as the family risk manager must identify perils, exposures, and hazards. Homeowners' policy options include variations in covered perils. As discussed in chapter 8, you can buy a policy that covers all perils not excluded, or one that lists the covered perils. One such list is shown in table 2–6. Your agent can help you determine the importance of perils covered in some but not all policies to decide which policy best meets your needs. Your agent can also help you identify your exposures. Checklists have been developed to aid family risk managers

TABLE 2–6

Perils Covered in Homeowner's Form 2

Fire or lightning	Falling objects
Windstorm or hail	Weight of ice, snow, or sleet
Explosion	Collapse
Riot or civil commotion	Accidental discharge or overflow of water or steam
Aircraft	Rupture of heating or A-C system
Vehicles	Freezing plumbing and heating or A-C
Smoke	Artificially generated electricity
Vandalism or malicious mischief	Volcanic eruption
Theft	Glass breakage

FIGURE 2-2

Checklist for Your Home
Loss Exposures-Contents

Identifying Property and Personal Loss Exposures

Section B-Contents*

Living Room	Quantity	Date of Purchase	Price Paid	Dining Room	Quantity	Date of Purchase	Price Paid
Couch				Table			
Chairs				Chairs			
				Rug(s)			
Rugs							
				Silverware			
Tables							
				China			
Lamps				Linen			
				Glassware			
TV							
Radio				Drapes			
Artwork							
				Artwork			
Other							

in this task. An example of such a checklist is shown in figure 2-2. Typically, the insurance commissioner of your state and insurance agents' organizations will have similar checklists available. Use one as a guideline in recognizing your property exposures. You may find various types of exposures not included in the checklist, so remember that the checklist is merely a guideline to get you started.

Evaluate Exposures

Having completed the identification process, your next step is to evaluate exposures to determine how best to meet your objectives. A family ought to focus on the value of having the property available—including inconvenience, cost of replacement, and sentimental attachment—as well as the likelihood of loss. In addition, the family's financial ability to bear the loss without insurance ought to be considered. For example, loss to your house may result in extreme inconvenience and unbearably high financial burden, whereas loss to other property, such as your car, may be less burdensome because of available public transportation, rental vehicles, and carpools. Likely your car also represents a smaller financial loss. Thus, efforts to protect the house become more important than efforts to protect the car.

FIGURE 2–2—*continued*

Checklist for your Home
Loss Exposure-Contents

Other			

Kitchen	Quantity	Date of Purchase	Price Paid
Table/Chair			
Stove			
Refrigerator			
Major Appliances			
Small Appliances			
Utensils			
Curtains			
Rugs			

Artwork			
Cookware			
Other			

Den/Family Room	Quantity	Date of Purchase	Price Paid
Couch			
Chairs			
Tables			
Rugs			
TV & Radio			
Stereo			
Curtains			
Artwork			
Other			

This is an excerpt from an eleven-page checklist.
Reprinted with permission by the National Association of Professional Insurance Agents.

Selecting Methods

The purpose of evaluating exposures is to determine how best to manage the risk of losing them. Few (if any) of us have a choice other than to purchase insurance on our houses, because of the large percent of our wealth associated with a house. Yet, choice does exist on the size of the deductible, the amount of coverage above what is required by your lender, the specifics of the policy (such as perils, conditions, etc.), the agent and company from whom to buy the policy, and loss prevention and loss reduction techniques to implement. The actions you choose ought to be based on the objectives you set at the beginning. If the objective is to minimize the frequency and severity of losses, then smoke detectors, deadbolt locks, fire extinguishers, and burglar alarms are appropriate. If your family has extensive assets, a relatively large deductible is appropriate. The less you are able to withstand uncertainty, the lower the deductible, the higher the value of coverage, and the broader the perils you want covered. Insurance availability and cost will also affect your decision. When insurance is readily available and/or inexpensive, you will choose it more willingly than retention, and vice versa.

Implementing and Monitoring the Program

Choosing the proper means of managing risks is not the end of your task. The plan decided upon must be put into place. Insurance must be purchased, and loss control techniques installed. Techniques for choosing agents and policies are discussed in later chapters, and they too must be imple- mented. Finally, your risk management program requires continual monitoring or review. As the family and environ- ment change, so too might objectives and exposures change, as well as alternatives to handling risk. Annual re- view of your risk management program (from start to finish) is desirable.

Key Terms

risk management
loss control
psychological costs
risk management policy statement
risk management manual
loss frequency
loss severity
unbearable risks
difficult to bear risks

relatively unimportant risks
probability distribution
management information system
risk management matrix
cash flow analysis
political risk
present value
net cash flow

Discussion Questions

1. What are the adverse consequences of risk? Give examples of each.

2. What is a probability distribution? How can a risk manager use one?

3. Provide examples of loss prevention and loss reduction that you can implement in your personal risk management program. Define both terms. How will you decide whether or not to implement them?

4. Architects design buildings to be functional and attractive. What con- tribution can a risk manager make during the planning stage?

5. Describe the seven steps of the risk management function. Provide a recent example of how a firm or individual demonstrated their efforts to manage risk.

6. What difficulties might a risk manager encounter in convincing man- agement to implement loss control? How can a risk manager deal with these difficulties?

7. Suggest a good approach to identifying your personal risks, including sources of information and what can be gleaned from those sources.

8. Some firms provide annual medical screening tests, weight control programs, exercise facilities, and other health-related programs for em- ployees. Do you think this is just another form of compensation, or may there be other reasons for such programs?

9. Name the divisions suggested by Mehr and Hedges for an organiza- tion's risk management policy statement. Why is it necessary to specify a particular organization's overall objectives rather than immediately dis- cussing risk management objectives?

10. It has been said that, "the most important thing in the world is to know what is most important now." What do you think is the most important risk for you now? What do you think will be the most important risk you will face twenty-five years from now?

2.1 Brooks Trucking has never had a risk management program. It provides trucking services over a twelve-state area from its home base in Cincinnati, Ohio. Shawana Lee, Brooks Trucking's Financial Vice-President, has a philosophy that "lightning can't strike twice in the same place." Because of this, she does not believe in trying to practice loss prevention or loss reduction.

1. If you were appointed its risk manager, how would you identify the pure-risk exposures facing Brooks?
2. Do you agree or disagree with Shawana? Why?

2.2 Devin Davis is an independent oil driller in Oklahoma. He feels that the most important risk he has is small property damages to his drilling rig, because he constantly has small, minor damage to the rig while it is being operated or taken to new locations.

1. Do you agree or disagree with Devin?
2. Which is more important, frequency of loss or severity of loss? Explain.

2.3 Yu-Luen Pa does not believe that risk management can properly be used by a family. "After all," she argues, "my family is such a small group of people that I cannot predict when losses will happen. I can't manage risk—it's too uncertain." Explain why you agree or disagree with Yu-Luen.

2.4 As an agent for an independent insurance agency, you have been pondering a presentation you have to make to the Wompu's Sports Car Club. Your task is to explain how a family moves through various growth stages, such as newly married, young children at home, children in high school and college, and finally the "empty nest" retirement years. The methods by which a family handles risk associated with these changes vary through the years. You want to give examples of how the risk varies and how it can be successfully dealt with by the family during its lifetime.

1. Set up examples to explain these family changes and the changing risks associated with them.
2. Note the obstacles that could surface within a family through the years that would make it difficult for them to transfer various forms of risk.

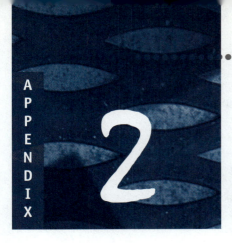

Cash Flow Analysis

Cash flow analysis is a decision rule by which the present value of cash inflows is compared with the present value of cash outflows for a given project. If the inflows exceed the outflows on this basis, the project meets the organization's profitability goals and may be implemented if other goals are also met (those goals may involve stability, liquidity, and social responsibility objectives).

Present value calculations allow decision makers to compare two or more cash streams that have unequal timing. That is, present value allows us to consider the investment opportunities of holding cash now (in the present) rather than later. Think about your preference for receiving a scholarship of $500 either now or one year from now. Generally, we prefer the cash now, because we are able to use it for productive purposes. Thus, we would even be willing to take something less than $500 in order to receive the funds now. How much less depends on other opportunities to use the money.

Generally, we calculate the present value as follows:

$$PV = (\$ \text{ Funds Available in Future}) * 1/(1+r)^t$$

where r equals the opportunity cost of money (i.e., return available from other uses) and t equals the number of periods until the funds are available. If our opportunity cost for the scholarship is 5 percent, then the present value equals

$$(500)(1/(1+.05)^1) = \$476$$

In other words, we would be willing to receive $476 or more today, versus $500 in one year.

A risk manager uses this concept of present value to make decisions about risk management options. Typically, these options will involve a stream of cash flows, which may be considered annuities. The calculation for the present value of an annuity is

$$PV \text{ annuity} = (\$ \text{ annual stream of funds})*[\{1 - 1/(1 + r)^t\} \div r]$$

The present value of four annual scholarships of $500 with an opportunity cost of 5 percent, then, equals

$$\$500 * 3.54 = \$1,770$$

Receiving $1,770 now is of equal value under these assumptions to four annual payments of $500 starting in one year.

For illustration, let's consider the decision of whether or not to add a sprinkler system to an existing building. Assume that the sprinkler would cost $20,000 to build. Further, assume that the expected loss distributions with and without the sprinkler are as shown in table 2–7, that the expected life of the system is ten years, that the effective tax rate is .30, and that an annual inspection costs $100. The cash flow analysis is shown in table 2–8.

Note that the **net cash flow** is negative. The net cash flow is the comparison of the present value of cash inflows with the present value of cash outflows. If the net cash flow is negative, we know that the expected return of the project does not cover the expected costs. If the expected return were the only consideration, this project would be rejected. Reasons to accept would include objectives of safety, and concern that estimated values are not precise. Estimating risk, however, can be incorporated into the analysis by employing a more conservative interest assumption.

One remaining observation on this analysis is that *cash flow* is the centerpiece. Thus, in calculating taxes, we consider the effect of depreciation (we used straight-line depreciation on the $20,000 sprinkler). In calculating flows, however, depreciation is otherwise irrelevant.

TABLE 2–7

Loss Distributions With and Without a Sprinkler

NO-SPRINKLER	PROBABILITY	LOSS	E(VALUE)
	.80	0	0
	.10	1,000	100
	.06	40,000	2,400
	.03	75,000	2,250
	.01	150,000	1,500
			6,160

WITH SPRINKLER	PROBABILITY	LOSS	E(VALUE)
	.80	0	0
	.10	200	20
	.06	25,000	1,500
	.03	37,000	1,110
	.01	62,000	620
			3,250

TABLE 2–8

Cash Flow Analysis of Sprinkler System

Change in Expected Losses	2,910
Change in Expected Costs (Inspection)	(100)
Before Tax Change in Cash Inflow	2,810
Tax	
Change in Cash Flow	2,810
Change in Depreciation	(2,000)
Taxable Income	810
Change in Tax Requirements	
810 * .30	(243)
After Tax Cash Flow	$2,567

$$PV_{sprinkler} = 2{,}567 * \{[1 - 1/(1.05)^{10}] \div 05\}$$
$$= 2{,}567 * 7.72 = 19{,}817.24$$
$$\text{Net Cash Flow} = PV_{cash\ inflow} - PV_{cash\ outflow}$$
$$= 19{,}817.24 - 20{,}000 = (\$182.76)$$

3

Insurance

Introduction   Imagine yourself at work, or perhaps at the library studying, when you receive a message that your house or apartment is in flames. By the time you get home, everything is destroyed. Your personal documents, treasured CD collection, family photos, clothes, furniture—all of them gone forever. What will you do? Where will you live? How can you afford to buy even the most essential items?

If you have planned for such an event, you likely will have insurance to pay for part if not all of the economic losses. Your emotional loss is more difficult to manage, and may require time to heal. If you have not purchased insurance, even the economic loss may

be unmanageable. How is it that most individuals cannot conveniently pay for such losses, but insurers can? Are insurers able to accept the risk of any possible loss? Do situations exist when we might be better off not buying insurance? In this chapter, you will consider:

1. What insurance is and how it works.
2. What types of loss potential are insurable and why.
3. How insurers protect against catastrophic loss through reinsurance.
4. What is meant by the term "self insurance," and when it is an appropriate risk management tool.

Nature of Insurance

Everybody knows what insurance is—or do they? Sometimes a person will say, "I'm not going to buy insurance on my camera. I will insure it myself." As you shall see, such a person is not insuring his or her camera but is, instead, simply retaining any loss that may occur. Distinctions between insurance and retention are highlighted in this chapter.

DEFINITION OF INSURANCE

A brief survey of insurance literature reveals differences of opinion among authors concerning how the term should be defined. Regardless of definition, however, the literature indicates that all authors are referring to the same thing when they say "insurance." The following is our definition:

> **Insurance** is a *social device,* in which a *group* of individuals (called "insureds") *transfer risk* to another party (called an "insurer") in order to combine loss experience, which permits *statistical prediction* of losses and provides for payment of losses from *funds contributed* (premiums) by all members who transferred risk.

Insurance (1) is a *social device,* in that people and organizations help themselves and each other by exchanging relatively small premiums for economic security against potentially large losses; (2) involves a large *group* of people or organizations who are exposed to similar risks; (3) allows each person or organization who becomes an insured to *transfer* risk to the whole group, as evidenced by an insurance contract issued by an insurer; (4) involves the systematic *accumulation of funds* through the *statistical prediction* of losses and calculation of premiums; and (5) pays for losses in accordance with the terms of the insurance contract. An insurance contract is a legal document setting forth the agreement between the insured and the insurer.

An alternative, although similar, definition is offered by the Internal Revenue Service. Recent tax rulings have held that a contract must possess three characteristics for it to be considered insurance: risk shifting, risk distribution, and "insurance risk."[1] For now, what is important to know regarding the IRS definition is that insurance serves the purpose of reducing variability for the insured by placing the variability of outcomes on the insurer (risk shifting), while requiring that all members in the group pay for losses through premium charges (risk distribution). In addition, the covered event cannot be speculative; it involves only the opportunity for loss or no change, an "insurance risk." These characteristics are relevant in determining if a contract is insurance, and therefore if premiums are tax deductible for the insured.

Consideration of these three characteristics of insurance is important. If the contract is not considered to be insurance by the IRS, then premiums paid by business insureds are not tax deductible as an ordinary business expense for organizations. Risk financing mechanisms that do not meet the IRS definition of insurance may be called "self insurance," which is a form of retention. Retention programs are discussed later in this chapter. In addition, insurance is a heavily regulated industry. The nature of the

---

1. Humana, Inc. v. Commissioner, 88-1403, U.S. State Tax Court (1989).

contract as insurance or noninsurance will affect the type and degree of regulation involved in the transaction. A discussion of the regulation of the insurance industry is presented in chapter 26

BENEFITS OF INSURANCE

Two fundamental services are provided by insurance. First, by reimbursing insureds for the economic aspects of losses, insurance helps individuals and organizations prevent financial harm (for example, bankruptcy) when insured perils occur. Second is the reduction of uncertainty and worry about our inability to predict individual future outcomes. These services are provided by spreading the economic burden of losses among members of the group, while also improving predictability of average results through pooling of experience.

Insurance is understood by most people to be critical to a well-functioning economy. For example, we are able to finance homes because lenders, through insurance, are able to protect their loan interests in the homes. Likewise, businesses are able to export goods because their financial interests in those goods are protected by insurance against loss in transit. Municipalities are able to offer services to the public because they are protected by insurance against liability losses.

Insurance also has been essential in responding to challenges of individual and societal catastrophes. Through disability insurance, families are protected against the financial havoc (loss of income) that accompanies injury or illness of a key income earner. Health insurance further protects the family from the exorbitant costs of high-technology health care. Society is similarly protected when natural (and artificial) events lead to widespread losses. The United States experienced massive property damage in 1989, first from Hurricane Hugo and later in the San Francisco earthquake. In 1992, the Los Angeles riot and Hurricane Andrew caused similarly large losses. Without insurance, affected communities likely would still be in shambles. Instead, hundreds of insurance personnel were sent immediately to the damaged areas. Those personnel made on-the-spot cash payments to policyholders for their essential needs. Claims adjusters worked overtime to submit claim reports as quickly as possible, responding to the need for a rapid cleanup process. Even so, many homes and businesses destroyed by Hurricane Andrew have not yet been rebuilt.

Mayers and Smith list economies of scale and efficiencies of specialization in claims management as primary benefits of insurance to corporate policyholders. They also note that when conflicting objectives may affect the level of safety in an organization, the parties who desire long-term safety may be able to use insurance requirements as a mechanism to override the conflict.[2]

Of course, in many cases, loss prevention is better than loss financing to most of us, because a loss prevented saves anguish, expense, and time. The insurance industry responds to prevention needs by conducting and supporting research on, for example, new fire-resistant materials, fire-fighter training, engineering techniques to thwart the effects of earth-

2. David Mayers and Clifford W. Smith, Jr., "On the Corporate Demand for Insurance," *Journal of Business (1982).*

quakes, wind, and other perils, and a host of other safety programs. Insurers are in the business of safety, as well as finance.

The insurance industry in the United States directly employs over 1.5 million people. Furthermore, every one of us is affected by insurance in some facet of our lives. For example, we buy automobile insurance, are protected by workers' compensation insurance, use products covered by liability insurance, and receive better health care because we have health insurance. Clearly, insurance has become an integral part of our lives.

INSURANCE VERSUS GAMBLING

You may occasionally hear a remark such as, "The insurance company is betting that my house won't burn down, and I'm betting that it will." It is true that in both gambling and insurance, money changes hands on the basis of chance events. You pay a premium to insure against loss to your house caused by fire and other perils. If no insured loss occurs, the insurance company keeps the premium and you receive no money.[3] On the other hand, if an insured peril occurs, the insurance company pays for the loss. Similarly, if you bet Jon Smith $100 that East will win its ball game with West, money will change hands on the basis of what is to you and Smith a matter of chance.

In spite of the similarity of these insurance and gambling transactions, however, there is a fundamental difference between them. In gambling, the risk of loss is created by the transaction itself, while in insurance the risk exists without the transaction. You are not exposed to risk in connection with the East-West ball game until you make a wager with Smith. You are, however, exposed to the possibility that various perils will cause damage to your home, whether or not you insure it. Thus, *gambling* is an activity that *creates risk* for the participants, whereas *insurance* is a device that *transfers existing risk* from one party to another, such as an insurer.[4]

In addition, in gambling you can win. For example, you can bet $100 and win $1,000. The net result is a $900 gain, at least on this one bet. Insurance, however, only *restores* what you already owned. For example, you may pay a $100 premium for automobile collision insurance, create $1,000 damage to your car in a wreck, and have the insurer pay the garage that repairs your car. The net result is that you have a car of the same value (ignoring the mismatched old and new paint) as before the insured event occurred.[5]

....

How Insurance Works

A definition of insurance and discussion of how it differs from other financial transactions involving risk provide an indication of what it is. A full understanding, however, requires an analysis of how insurance works.

....

3. It would be incorrect to say that you receive nothing at all for the premium payment. Remember that one of the benefits of insurance is the peace of mind you get from being relieved of the uncertainty and worry associated with the possibility of financial loss. You are paying for a product, albeit an intangible one.
4. State laws generally will not allow you to buy insurance unless you are actually exposed to the possiblity of loss. If you could, the transaction would be gambling, since there was no way for you to lose before accepting the wager.
5. This "indemnity" concept will be discussed in chapter 4.

In this section, therefore, we will discuss the basic principles of risk transfer, loss sharing, and discrimination in pricing. Some familiarity with these principles is essential to an understanding of insurance.

RISK TRANSFER (ASSUMPTION)

Insurance is created by an insurer that, as a professional risk-bearer, *assumes* the financial aspect of risks *transferred* to it by insureds. The insurer assumes risk in that it promises to pay whatever loss may occur as long as it fits the description given in the policy and is not larger than the amount of insurance sold. The loss may be zero, or it may be many thousands of dollars. In return for accepting this variability in outcomes (our definition of risk), the insurer receives a premium. Through the premium, the policyholder has paid a certain expense in order to transfer the risk of a possible large loss. The insurance contract stipulates what types of losses will be paid by the insurer.

Most insurance contracts are expressed in terms of money, although some compensate insureds by providing a service. A life insurance contract, for example, obligates the insurer to pay a specified sum of money upon the death of the person whose life is insured. A liability insurance policy not only requires the insurer to pay money on behalf of the insured, but also to provide legal and investigative services needed when the event insured against occurs. The terms of some health insurance policies are fulfilled by providing medical and hospital services (for example, a semi-private room and board, plus other hospital services) for the insured when he or she is ill or injured.

Whether the insurer fulfills its obligations with money or with services, the burden it assumes is financial. The insurer does not guarantee that the event insured against will not happen. Moreover, it cannot replace sentimental value or bear the psychological cost of a loss. A home may be worth only $80,000 for insurance purposes, but have many times that value to the owner in terms of sentiment. The death of a loved one can cause almost unbearable mental suffering that is in no way relieved by receiving a sum of money from the insurer. Neither of these aspects of loss can be measured in terms of money; therefore, such risks cannot be transferred to an insurer. Because these noneconomic risks create uncertainty, it is apparent that insurance cannot completely eliminate uncertainty. Yet, insurance performs a great service by reducing the financial uncertainty created by risk.

LOSS SHARING (RISK DISTRIBUTION)

In general, the bulk of the premium required by the insurer to assume risk is used to compensate those who incur covered losses. Loss sharing is accomplished through premiums; therefore, group losses are shared by the group members.

Although premiums pay for losses incurred by members of the group, they are intended to reflect each insured's expected losses. For this purpose actuaries, charged with determining appropriate rates (prices) for coverage, estimate the likelihood (probability) of loss and the corresponding size (severity) of loss. These estimates are made for a series of categories of insureds, with each category intended to group insureds who are similar with regard to their likelihood and size of loss. An underwriter then has the job of determining which category is appropriate for each insured. Actuaries combine the likelihood and size information to arrive at an average, or expected loss. Estimates generally are based on empirical data or theoretical relationships, making them objective estimates. When the actuary must rely on judgment rather than facts, the estimates are termed subjective. In most cases, both objective and subjective estimates are used in setting rates. For example, the actuary may begin with industry-determined rates based on past experience and adjust them to reflect the actuary's "feelings" about the insurer's own expected experience.

A life insurer may estimate that 250 of the 100,000 forty-year-old insureds it covers will die in the next year. If each insured carries a $1,000 policy, the insurer will pay out $250,000 in claims (250 × $1,000). To cover these claims, the insurer requires a premium of $2.50 from each insured ($250,000/100,000), which is the average or expected cost per policyholder. (An additional charge to cover expenses, profit, and the risk of actual losses exceeding expected losses would be included in the actual premium. A reduction of the premium would result from the insurer sharing its investment earnings with insureds.)

Predictions

The life insurer that estimates its claim payments at $250,000 is unlikely to be right on target. Actual claims may exceed or be less than expected; therefore, the insurer requires a buffer to protect itself against excessive losses. The relative size of this buffer reflects the insurer's ability to make reliable estimates for the pooled group.

The insurer is not required to predict which of the insureds will experience loss. Rather, the insurer needs only to know *how many* in the group will experience loss (assuming each carries a similar amount of coverage.) The large pool of exposures for which the insurer has assumed risk provides the insurer with a base upon which to make predictions. The larger that base, the more accurate the prediction and the smaller the needed reserve. Thus, insurance not only provides certainty to insureds, it also reduces overall risk for society, permitting productive use of funds in medium and long-term investments rather than setting them aside in less productive liquid assets.

This statistical phenomenon through which the pooling of experience reduces risk is termed the **law of large numbers** (discussed in chapter 1). The law of large numbers holds that the larger the number of trials, the more nearly experience will approximate the underlying (true) probability. Thus, in tossing a coin, if the probability of heads is 50 percent, results should more and more closely approach 50 percent heads as the number of trials increases. Those who perform the experiment find that this is correct, but are surprised at how large a number of trials is involved. One experiment involving more than 70,000 tosses of the coin resulted in a distribution of heads and tails that was not quite 50–50.

Pooling

The unique contribution of pooling to the insurer as a risk-bearer should now be apparent—it is a function of the law of large numbers. Insurer operations are affected by this law in two ways. First, if accurate estimates of the probability distribution are to be made prior to actually providing insurance, a large number of cases must be considered. If the empirical method is used to determine, for example, the probability of death during age twenty-five, a large number of cases must be observed in order to define a reliable estimate.

Second, after an estimate of probability has been made, the law of large numbers can be used by an insurer as the basis for predicting future experience only when dealing with sufficiently large numbers. If, for example, an insurance company provides one person with $100,000 of life insurance for one year in exchange for a $150 premium, its underwriting income (ignoring operating expenses) will be either $150 or a loss of $99,850. That is, the person whose life is insured will either die or not die during that year. There is some probability that a person at a given age will die during the year, but even if the insurance company knows exactly what that probability is, such information will not allow it to predict the outcome for one individual.

As discussed previously, as far as an individual is concerned, knowing the probability of death during the coming year is of almost no help in predicting the future. Therefore, with respect to one individual's life, the insurer is in no better position to make predictions than is the individual. Given a large number of similar lives, however, the insurer can make rather accurate predictions of what will happen within the group.

Some scientists believe the law of large numbers applies to every natural occurrence in the universe. We are aware of how this law applies to human mortality, fires, auto accidents, and the like, because their probability is revealed in a relatively short time. For other events, such as earthquakes, tidal waves, and typhoons, it may take centuries for the law of large numbers to reveal a pattern.

DISCRIMINATION

In order for the law of large numbers to work, the pooled exposures[6] must have approximately the same probability of loss (follow the same probability distribution). In other words, the exposures need to be homogeneous (similar). Insurers, therefore, need to **discriminate** (classify) exposures according to expected loss. For this reason, twenty-year-old insureds with relatively low rates of mortality are charged lower rates for life insurance than are sixty-year-old insureds, holding factors other than age constant. The rates reflect each insured's expected loss.

If the two groups were charged the same rate, problems would arise. As previously stated, rates reflect average loss costs. Thus, a company charging the same rate to both twenty-year-old insureds and sixty-year-old insureds would charge the average of their expected losses. Because the probability of death increases exponentially with age, the average would exceed the twenty-year-old insured's expected loss and be less than the sixty-year-old insured's expected loss. Having a choice between a policy from this company and one from a company that charged different rates

---

6. Remember from chapter 1 that an exposure is the property or person facing a condition in which loss is possible.

ETHICAL *Dilemma*

When is "Discrimination" in Insurance Appropriate?

The AIDS epidemic is a concern of major proportions. The cost in lives is almost too great to fathom. The cost in dollars is also tremendous. As of this writing, premature death is a certainty to those who contract the virus. Further, medical care received by the typical AIDS patient runs into the tens of thousands of dollars. As a result, both life and health insurers want to identify high-risk insurance applicants so that homogeneity of exposure units and individual rate equity[7] are maintained.

Strong debate has been voiced over whether or not life and health insurers should be able to test for AIDS or HIV exposure, and further, whether or not they should be allowed to deny coverage to those who test positive. The test itself is considered an invasion of privacy, because the results could be used by others to deny people jobs, housing, and the like.

Even without concern over the improper use of test results by individuals not associated with insurers, questions arise as to the ethical nature of denying health insurance to someone in such extreme need of health care. This situation presents a classic example of the struggle between an insurer's need to be able to select its insureds and society's need to avoid undue hardship on certain segments of the population.

A good discussion could develop from considering some of the following questions. How are other policyholders affected when insurers are limited in their ability to select? When is it appropriate to allow insurers freedom of selection? What alternatives exist to provide protection to those people who would be selected out of coverage? Is it fair to accomplish social objectives through private firms such as insurers? Does AIDS present a role for expansion of social insurance (e.g., coverage of persons with AIDS under Medicare immediately upon diagnosis)?

based on age, the sixty-year-old insureds would choose this lower-cost, single-rate company while the young insureds would not. As a result, sixty-year-old policyholders would be overrepresented in the group of insureds, making the average rate insufficient. This phenomenon on the part of those age sixty is called adverse selection.

Adverse selection occurs when insurance is purchased more often by people/organizations with higher than average expected losses than by people/organizations with average or lower than average expected losses. That is, insurance is of greater use to insureds whose losses are expected to be high (insureds "select" in a way that is "adverse" to the insurer). On this basis alone no problem would exist, because insurers could simply

7. Individual rate equity exists when policyholders are charged rates that reflect their expected costs (both losses and expenses) to insurers.

charge higher premiums to insureds with higher expected losses. Information asymmetries, however, typically prevent insurers from being able to distinguish completely among insureds. Furthermore, the insurer wants to aggregate in order to use the law of large numbers. Thus, some tension exists between limiting adverse selection and employing the law of large numbers.

Adverse selection, then, can result in greater losses and/or greater expenses or lower investment returns than are expected for the group. Insurers try to prevent this by learning enough about applicants for insurance to identify such people so they can either be rejected or put in a rating class whose members have a loss probability similar to theirs. Many insurers, for example, require medical examinations for older applicants for life insurance, or for anyone who applies for a large amount of insurance.

Some insurance policy provisions are designed to reduce adverse selection. The suicide clause in life insurance contracts, for example, excludes coverage to most applicants who purchase life insurance in contemplation of taking their own lives.[8] The preexisting conditions provision in health insurance policies is designed to avoid paying benefits to people who buy insurance because they are aware, or should be aware, of an ailment that will require medical attention or disable them in the near future.[9]

Ideal Requisites for Insurability

Are all pure risks insurable by private (nongovernmental) insurers? No. The private insurance device is not suitable for all risks. Many risks are uninsurable. So that you may understand why some risks cannot be insured, this section is devoted to a discussion of the requirements that must generally be met if a risk is to be insurable in the private market. As a practical matter, many risks that are insured privately meet these requirements only partially or, with reference to a particular requirement, not at all. Thus, in a sense, the *requirements* listed describe those which would be met by the *ideal* risk. Nevertheless, the bulk of the risks insured fulfill—at least approximately—most of the requirements. No private insurer can safely disregard them completely.[10]

A risk that was perfectly suited for insurance would meet the following requirements:

1. The number of similar exposure units would be large.
2. Losses that occurred would be fortuitous.

----

8. Very few who contemplate suicide will wait the required one or two years (the length of time varies with state law) until the contract's suicide limitation expires. Of the few who wait this long, some will change their minds. Because the insurer would have difficulty determining an insured's intent at the time of purchase, the Suicide Clause excludes all deaths (regardless of intent) that are caused by suicide during the specified period.

9. Recent health care reforms have limited the ability of insurers to reduce adverse selection through the use of preexisting conditions limitations (see chapter 19).

10. Government-insuring organizations make greater deviations from the ideal requisites for insurability. They are able to accept greater risks because they often make their insurance compulsory and have it subsidized from tax revenues, while private insurers will operate only when a profit potential exists. The nature of government insurance programs will be outlined later in this chapter.

3. A catastrophe could not occur.
4. Losses would be definite.
5. The probability distribution of losses would be determinable.
6. The potential severity of loss would be significant, but the probability would not be high (economic feasibility).

The sixth requirement influences the consumer *demand* for insurance and looks at what is economically feasible from the perspective of potential insureds. The other requirements influence the willingness of insurers to *supply* insurance and are concerns held by insurers.

MANY SIMILAR EXPOSURE UNITS

For an insurance organization to insure a possible loss exposure, a preference exists for the exposure to have a large number of similar units. The concepts of **mass** and **similarity** are thus considered before an insurer accepts a loss exposure. Some insurance is sold on exposures that do not possess the requirements of mass and similarity, but such coverage is the exception, not the rule.

Mass

A major requirement for insurability is mass; that is, there must be large numbers of exposure units involved. For automobile insurance, there must be a large number of automobiles to insure. For life insurance, there must be a large number of persons. An automobile insurance company cannot insure a dozen automobiles, and a life insurance company cannot insure the lives of a dozen persons. You will recall that arriving at accurate probability distributions requires observation of a large number of events. After the probabilities and severities of loss have been estimated, they can be relied upon for prediction of actual losses only with reference to a large group. The insurance company is in no better position to predict losses for you than you are for yourself.

How large is a "large group"? For insurance purposes, the number of exposure units needed in a group depends upon the extent to which the insurer is willing to bear the risk of deviation from its expectations. Suppose the probability of damage to houses is 1/1,000. An insurer might assume this risk for 1,000 houses with the expectation that one claim would be made during the year. If no houses were damaged, there would be a 100 percent deviation from expectations, but such a deviation would create no burden for the insurer. On the other hand, if two houses were damaged, the claims to be paid would be twice the expected number. This could be a severe burden for the insurer, assuming average or higher loss severities. By increasing the number of similar houses insured to 10,000, the expected number of losses increases to ten but the stability of experience is increased. That is, there is a *proportionately* smaller deviation from expected losses than with a group of 1,000 houses. Similarly, if the group is increased to 100,000 houses, the variation between actual and expected losses would be likely to increase in absolute terms, but decline proportionately.

Figure 3–1 is a representation of this discussion. Note that as the number of houses (n) increases, the number of expected losses also increases, but the relative deviation from this number declines. The number of

Assume the probability of loss is .001.[*]

	n = 1,000	n = 10,000	n = 100,000
Expected number of loss (n * .001)	1	10	100
Standard deviation ($\sqrt{n}$ * .001 * .999)	1	3.16	9.99
Relative standard deviation (standard deviation ÷ expected number of losses)	1	.316	.0999

[*]Assuming a binomial distribution.

houses required to assure that actual experience will be the same as that expected on the basis of the true underlying probability distribution is infinitely large. The number required for practical purposes is a function of the amount of risk the insurer is able and willing to bear and the underlying probability distribution. Remember that the insurer's risk decreases when it is able to use the law of large numbers.

Similarity

The loss exposures to be insured and those observed for empirical probability distributions must be similar. The exposures assumed by insurers are not identical, no matter how carefully they may be selected. No two houses are identical, even though physically they may appear to be. They cannot have an identical location, and perhaps more importantly they are occupied by different families. Nevertheless, the units in a group must be *reasonably similar* in characteristics if predictions concerning them are to be accurate.

Moreover, probability distributions calculated on the basis of observed experience must also involve units similar to each other. Observing the occupational injuries and illnesses of a group of people whose age, health, and occupations were all different, for example, would not provide a basis for calculating workers' compensation insurance rates for a group of clerical workers whose age, health, and other characteristics were similar. In particular, clerical work typically involves much lower probabilities of work-related loss than do occupations such as logging timber or climbing utility poles. Estimates based on experience require that the exposure units observed be similar to each other. Moreover, such estimates are useful only in predicting losses for exposures similar to those whose experience was observed.

FORTUITOUS LOSSES

The risks assumed by an insurer must involve only the *possibility,* not the certainty, of loss to the insured. Losses must be **fortuitous,** that is, they must be a matter of chance (accidental). Ideally, the insured should have no control or influence over the event to be insured. In fact, this situation prevails only with respect to limited situations. As mentioned in chapter 1, intangible and physical hazards influence the probability of loss. Prediction of potential losses is based on a probability distribution that has been estimated by observing past experience. Presumably, the events observed were, for the most part, fortuitous occurrences. The use of such estimates for predicting future losses is based on the assumption that future losses will also be a matter of chance. If this is not the case, predictions cannot be accurate.

SMALL POSSIBILITY OF CATASTROPHE

The possibility of catastrophic loss may make a loss exposure uninsurable. A catastrophic potential to an insurer is one that could imperil the insurer's solvency. When an insurer assumes a group of risks, it expects the group as a whole to experience some losses but only a small percentage of the group members to suffer loss at any one time. Given this assumption, a relatively small contribution by each member of the group will be sufficient to pay for all losses. If it is possible for a large percentage of all insureds to suffer a loss simultaneously, however, the "relatively small contributions" would not provide sufficient funds. Similarly, a single very large loss would also require large contributions. Thus, a requisite for insurability is that there must be no excessive possibility of **catastrophe** for the group as a whole. There must be limits that insurers can be reasonably sure their losses will not exceed. Insurers build up surpluses (net worth) and contingency reserves to take care of deviations of experience from the average, but such deviations must have practical limits. If losses cannot be predicted with reasonable accuracy and confidence, it is impossible to determine either insurance premium rates or the size of surpluses required.

Catastrophic losses may occur in two circumstances. In the first, all or many units of the group are exposed to the same loss-causing event, such as war, flood, or unemployment. For example, if one insurer had assumed the risk of damage by wind (hurricane) for all houses in the Miami, Florida, area, it would have suffered a catastrophic loss in 1992 when many structures were damaged simultaneously (and in fact several insurers were unable to withstand the degree of dependency they experienced in this event). This is an example of **dependent** exposure units. Exposure units are dependent if loss to one affects the probability of loss to another. Thus, fire at one location in your neighborhood increases the probability of fire at other homes in the area. Their experience is dependent. In the early days of insurance in the United States, many fire insurance companies concentrated their business in small areas near their headquarters. This worked in New York, for example, until a major fire devastated large sections of the city in 1835. Because of their concentrated exposures, several insurers suffered losses to a large percentage of their business. The insurers were unable to pay all claims and several went bankrupt.

A second type of catastrophe exposure arises when a single large value may be exposed to loss. The possibility of Barbra Streisand's death or incapacity due to other causes while on tour in 1994, for example, would have created extraordinarily large loss of income. Likewise, an oil rig that could be destroyed by an explosion, hurricane, or other peril represents a catastrophic potential. A few large insurers could handle such a significant exposure, but most would do so through reinsurance, which is discussed later in this chapter.

The existence of the catastrophe potential explains why insurance companies limit the amount to which they will commit themselves on any one exposure, and why property insurers limit their total commitments in any one city or area. Moreover, certain perils such as nuclear energy are difficult to insure, partly because of the catastrophe exposure and partly because there is limited experience upon which to base predictions.

DEFINITE LOSSES

Losses must be *definite in time, place, and amount,* because in many cases, insurers promise to pay in dollar amounts for losses if they occur during a particular time and in a particular geographical area. For example, the contract may cover loss by fire at a specified location. For this contract to be effective, it must be possible to determine *when, where, and how much* loss occurred. If this cannot be established, it is impossible to determine whether the loss is covered under the terms of the contract. The fact that "pain and suffering" is hard to measure in dollar terms increases the insurer's risk when calculating rates for liability insurance.

In many cases, it is also difficult to determine objectively whether a person is disabled; thus, the peril of disability is difficult to insure. On the other hand, death usually meets the requirement of definiteness because it is ordinarily easy to establish. Only when the insured mysteriously disappears or there are questions about whether "brain death" constitutes legal death do problems arise. One other reason the requirement of definiteness is essential is that it is necessary to accumulate data for future predictions. Unless such data can be accurate, they cannot provide the basis for useful predictions.

DETERMINABLE PROBABILITY DISTRIBUTION

For an exposure to loss to be insurable, the expected loss must be calculable. Ideally, this means that there is a **determinable probability distribution** for losses within a reasonable degree of accuracy. Insurance premium rates are based on predictions of the future which are expressed quantitatively as expected losses. Calculation of expected losses requires the use of estimated probability distributions. Some probability distributions can be derived from theoretical relationships, such as the outcomes expected when a die is rolled. Other distributions, however, must be calculated from experience.

Probability distributions based on experience are useful for prediction, however, only when it is safe to assume that factors shaping events in the future will be similar to those of the past. For this reason, mortality (death) rates during times of peace are inappropriate for estimating the number of insured deaths during times of war. Similarly, the introduction of new technologies such as foam blanketing makes past experience of fire damage a poor indicator of future experience. Yet, because the technology is new and no theory exists as to what ought to be the losses, the actuary has little information on which to base lower rates. The actuary must use subjective estimates as well as engineering information to develop proper rates.

When the probability distribution of losses for the exposure to be insured against cannot be calculated with reasonable accuracy, the risk is uninsurable. An example of purported uninsurability due to inability to predict losses is the nuclear power industry. Insurance experts convinced government officials in 1957 that the risk of loss caused by an incident at a nuclear power site was too uncertain (because of lack of experience and unknown maximum severity) for commercial insurers to accept without some government intervention. As a result, the government limited the liability of owners of nuclear power plants for losses that would arise from such incidents.

ECONOMIC FEASIBILITY

For insurance to be **economically feasible** for an insured, the size of the possible loss must be significant to the insured and the cost of insurance must be small compared with the potential loss. Otherwise, the purchase of insurance is not practical. If the possible loss is not significant to those exposed, insurance is inappropriate. Retention (bearing the financial loss yourself) of many risks is almost automatic because the loss would not be a burden. You may expect to lose your ballpoint pen, but do not consider insuring yourself against the possibility because such a loss is not important—it would be inconvenient, perhaps, but not burdensome. If all the people who own automobiles were wealthy, it is doubtful that much automobile collision insurance would be written, because such losses would not be significant to the wealthy owners. Insurance is feasible only when the possible loss is large enough to be of concern to the person who may bear the burden.

The possible loss must also be relatively large compared with the size of the premium. If the losses the insurer pays plus the cost of insurer operations are such that the premium must be very large in relation to the potential loss, insurance is not economically feasible. When the expected loss is high relative to the maximum possible loss, budgeting is preferable to insurance. The use of deductibles (a form of retention) to eliminate insurance reimbursement for frequent small losses helps make automobile collision premiums economically feasible.

The deductible eliminates claims for small losses. Small automobile collision losses have such high probability and the cost of settling them is so great that the premium for covering them would be very large compared with the size of actual losses. For example, if a policy with a $200 deductible costs $85 more than one with a $500 deductible, you may consider $85 too large a premium for $300 of insurance. Insurance is best suited for risks involving large potential losses with low probabilities. Large losses are important because insureds cannot bear them, and low probabilities for large losses make premiums relatively small compared with the possible losses. In other situations, insurance may not be economically feasible for the person or business facing risk.

Types of Insurance

Many types of insurance policies are available to families and organizations who do not wish to retain their own risks. The following questions may be raised about an insurance policy:

1. Is it personal or commercial?
2. Is it life-health or property-liability?
3. Is it issued by a private insurer or a government agency?
4. Is it purchased voluntarily or involuntarily?

As you read through this section, you may refer to figure 3–2 to follow the pattern of questions. To simplify the presentation, the terms "personal" and "commercial" have not been used in the figure. These terms are used primarily by the insurance industry; however, understanding them will make you a wiser insurance consumer.

PERSONAL OR COMMERCIAL

Personal insurance, used by individuals and families, includes life, health, property, and liability insurance. **Commercial insurance** is the term used by businesses and other organizations to describe property-liability insurance.[11] The distinction between personal and commercial forms of insurance is of significance primarily to insurers. An insurance company is likely to have two divisions, for example, within its underwriting department: a personal lines group and a commercial group. Personnel in the first group are trained to look for risk factors (e.g., driving records and types of home construction) that influence the frequency and severity of claims among individuals and families; the commercial group has underwriting experts on risks faced by organizations. Personnel in other functional areas such as claims adjustment also may specialize in either personal or commercial lines.

LIFE-HEALTH OR PROPERTY-LIABILITY

Life-health insurance covers exposures to the perils of premature death,[12] medical expenses, disability, unemployment, and dependent old age. Private life insurance companies provide insurance for these perils, and the public voluntarily decides whether or not to buy their products. Health insurance is provided primarily by life-health insurers but is also sold by some property-liability insurers.

The Social Security program provides substantial amounts of life-health insurance on an involuntary basis. Unemployment insurance, another involuntary program, covers the peril of lost income caused by having a job terminated and being unable to find new employment. These governmental programs will be discussed in chapters 16 and 12, respectively.

Property-liability insurance covers property exposures such as direct and indirect losses of property caused by perils such as fire, windstorm, and theft. It also includes insurance to cover the possibility of being held legally liable to pay damages to another person. Workers' compensation insurance is required by law and carried by employers to respond primar-

---

11. Life-health insurers will use the term "employee benefits" to describe its business with organizations. Commercial insurance is a term used by property-liability insurers for the same purpose.

12. A death is considered premature when it occurs well before a person reaches normal life expectancy, which is approximately 79 years for females and 72 years for males in the United States.

FIGURE 3–2

Types of Insurance

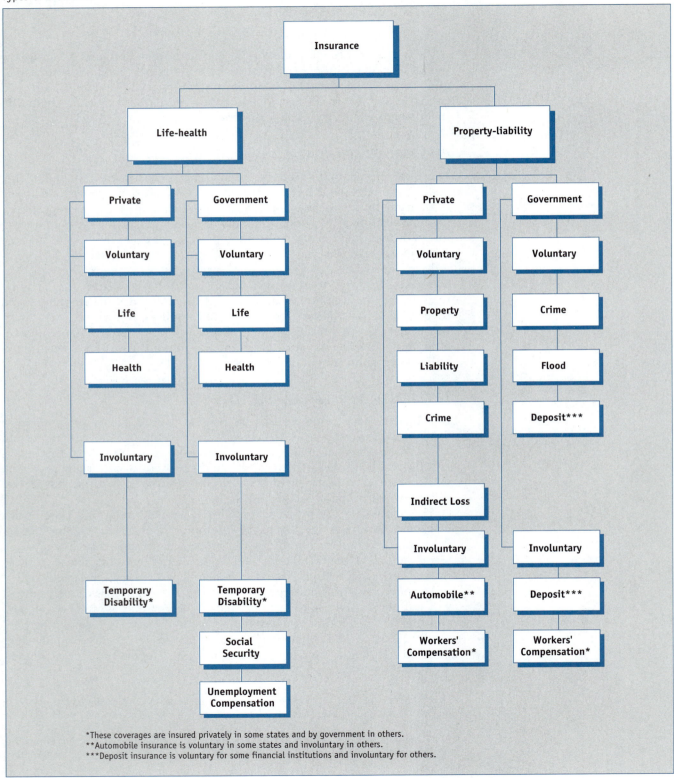

*These coverages are insured privately in some states and by government in others.
**Automobile insurance is voluntary in some states and involuntary in others.
***Deposit insurance is voluntary for some financial institutions and involuntary for others.

ily to cases of strict liability for work-related employee injuries and illnesses. Before the passage of multiple-line underwriting laws in the late 1940s and early 1950s, property and liability insurance had to be written by different insurers. Now they frequently are written in the same contract (for example, homeowner's and commercial package policies, which will be discussed in later chapters).

A private insurer can be classified as either a life-health or a property-liability insurer. Health insurance may be sold by either. Some insurers specialize in a particular type of insurance, such as property insurance. Others are affiliated insurers, in which several insurers (and sometimes noninsurance businesses) are controlled by a holding company; all or almost all types of insurance are offered by some company in the group. In the 1980s, some insurers followed the movement toward full financial services, whereby insurers are affiliated with investment bankers, mutual funds, money market funds, and other types of financial institutions. The full financial services movement allowed consumers the alternative of getting all types of personal financial services from one agent/broker or from an affiliated group of financial advisers at the same place. The trend in the 1990s, however, seems to be back toward specialization.

PRIVATE OR GOVERNMENT

Insurance is provided by both privately owned organizations and state and federal agencies. Measured by premium income, the bulk of property-liability insurance is provided by private insurers. Largely because of the magnitude of the Social Security program, however, government provides about one-third more personal insurance than the private sector. Our society has elected to provide certain levels of death, health, retirement, and unemployment insurance on an involuntary basis through governmental (federal and state) agencies. If we desire to supplement the benefit levels of social insurance or to buy property-liability insurance, some of which is required, private insurers provide the protection.

Overlaps exist between government and private insurers. This primarily involves the coverage of catastrophic losses such as floods and property damage in high crime areas where only a few private insurers elect to provide insurance.

VOLUNTARY OR INVOLUNTARY

Most private insurance is purchased voluntarily, although some types, such as on mortgages and car loans, are required by law or contracts. In many states, the purchase of automobile liability insurance is mandatory, and if the car is financed the lender will require property damage coverage. Government insurance is involuntary under certain conditions for certain people. Most people are required by law to participate in the Social Security program, which provides life-health coverage. Unemployment insurance is also a form of involuntary social insurance provided by the government. Some government insurance, however, is available to those who want it, but no one is required to buy it. Crop insurance, for example, is available to farmers through a federal government agency, but purchase is voluntary. The medical expense (non-hospital) part of Medicare is also optional to eligible people.

Nature of Reinsurance

Reinsurance is a system that reduces risk for an insurer. In effect, it is a method whereby an insurer transfers risk (buys insurance) rather than assumes risk (sells insurance). The use of reinsurance expands risk sharing and makes the insurance transaction safer for the original consumer as well as the original insurer.

DEFINITION OF REINSURANCE

Reinsurance is an arrangement by which an insurance company transfers all or a portion of its risk under a contract (or contracts) of insurance to another company. The company transferring risk is called the **ceding insurer,** and the company assuming risk is the **reinsurer.** In effect, the insurance company that has issued policies of insurance purchases insurance protection from another insurer. Typically, the reinsurer assumes responsibility for part of the losses under an insurance contract; however, in some instances the reinsurer assumes full responsibility for the original insurance contract. As with insurance, reinsurance involves risk transfer, risk distribution, and coverage against "insurance risk."

HOW REINSURANCE WORKS

Reinsurance may be divided into three types: (1) treaty, (2) facultative, and (3) a combination of these two. Any one type may be further classified as proportional or nonproportional. The original insurer (the ceding company) may have a **treaty** with a reinsurer. Under a treaty arrangement, the original insurer is obligated *automatically* to reinsure any new underlying insurance contract that meets the terms of the prearranged treaty, and the reinsurer is obligated to accept certain responsibilities for the specified insurance. On the other hand, with a **facultative** arrangement both the original insurer and the reinsurer retain full decision-making powers with respect to each insurance contract. As each insurance contract is issued, the original insurer decides whether or not to seek reinsurance and the reinsurer retains the flexibility to accept or reject each application for reinsurance on a case-by-case basis. The *combination* approach may require the original insurer to offer to reinsure specified contracts (like the treaty approach) while leaving the reinsurer free to decide whether to accept or reject reinsurance on each contract (like the facultative approach). Alternatively, the combination approach can give the option to the original insurer and automatically require acceptance by the reinsurer on all contracts offered for reinsurance. In any event, a contract between the ceding company and the reinsurer spells out the agreement between the two parties.

When the reinsurance agreement calls for **proportional** (or pro rata) **reinsurance,** the reinsurer assumes a prespecified percentage (for example, 70 percent) of both premiums and losses. Expenses are also shared in accord with this prespecified percentage. Because the ceding company has incurred operating expenses associated with the marketing, evaluation, and delivery of coverage, the reinsurer often pays a **ceding commission** to the original insurer. Such a commission may make reinsurance profitable to the ceding company, in addition to offering protection against catastrophe and improved predictability.

Nonproportional reinsurance obligates the reinsurer to pay losses when they exceed a designated threshold. **Excess-loss reinsurance,** for instance, requires the reinsurer to accept amounts of insurance that exceed the ceding insurer's retention limit. As an example, a small insurer might reinsure all property insurance above $25,000 per contract. The excess policy could be written per contract or per occurrence. Both proportional and nonproportional reinsurance may be either treaty or facultative.

In addition to specifying the situations under which a reinsurer has financial responsibility, the reinsurance agreement places a limit on the amount of reinsurance the reinsurer must accept. For example, the SSS Reinsurance Company may limit its liability per contract to four times the ceding insurer's retention limit, which in this case would yield total coverage of $125,000 ($25,000 retention plus $100,000 in reinsurance on any one property). When the ceding company issues a policy for an amount that exceeds the sum of its retention limit and SSS's reinsurance limit, it would need still another reinsurer, perhaps TTT Reinsurance Company, to accept a second layer of reinsurance. The excess-loss arrangement is depicted in figure 3–3. A proportional agreement is shown in figure 3–4.[13]

BENEFITS OF REINSURANCE

A ceding company uses reinsurance mainly to protect itself against losses in individual cases beyond a specified sum (i.e., its retention limit), but competition and the demands of its sales force may require issuance of policies of greater amounts. A company that issued policies no larger than its retention would severely limit its opportunities in the market. Many insureds do not want to place their insurance with several companies, preferring to have one policy with one company for each loss exposure. Furthermore, agents find it inconvenient to place multiple policies every time they insure a large risk.

In addition to its concern with individual cases, a company must protect itself from catastrophic losses of a particular type (such as a windstorm), in a particular area (such as a city or a block in a city), or during a specified period of operations (such as a calendar year). An **aggregate reinsurance** policy can be purchased for these potential situations. Sometimes they are considered excess policies, as described above, when the excess retention

FIGURE 3–3

An Example of Excess-Loss Reinsurance

Original policy limit of $200,000 layered as multiples of primary retention	
$ 75,000	Second reinsurer's coverage (equal to the remainder of the $200,000 contract)
$100,000	First reinsurer's limit (four times the retention)
$ 25,000	Original insurer's retention

13. This discussion has not covered all types of reinsurance. For example, life insurers use the yearly renewable term reinsurance plan and the coinsurance reinsurance plan, which are not explained in this textbook.

Assume 30-70 split, premiums of $10,000, expense of $2,000, and a loss of $150,000. Ignore any ceding commission.

	TOTAL EXPOSURE	PREMIUM	EXPENSES	NET PREMIUM*	LOSS
Reinsurer	70%	7,000	1,400	5,600	105,000
Ceding Insurer	30%	3,000	600	2,400	45,000
Total	100%	10,000	2,000	8,000	150,000

*Net Premium = Premium - Expenses

is per occurrence. An example of how an excess per occurrence policy works can be seen from the damage caused by Hurricane Andrew in 1992. Insurers who sell property insurance in hurricane—prone areas probably choose to reinsure their exposures, not just on a property-by-property basis, but also above some chosen level for any specific event. Andrew was considered one event and caused billions of dollars of damage in Florida alone. A Florida insurer may have set limits, perhaps $100 million, for its own exposure to a given hurricane. For its insurance in force above $100 million, the insurer can purchase excess or aggregate reinsurance.

Other benefits of reinsurance can be derived when a company offering a particular line of insurance for the first time wants to protect itself from excessive losses and also take advantage of the reinsurer's knowledge concerning the proper rates to be charged and underwriting practices to be followed. In other cases, a rapidly expanding company may have to shift some of its liabilities to a reinsurer to avoid impairing its capital.[14] Reinsurance often also increases the amount of insurance the underlying insurer can sell. This is referred to as "increasing capacity."

Reinsurance is significant to the buyer of insurance for a number of reasons. First, reinsurance increases the financial stability of insurers by spreading risk. This increases the likelihood that the original insurer will be able to pay its claims. Second, reinsurance facilitates placing large or unusual exposures with one company, thus reducing the time spent seeking insurance and eliminating the need for numerous policies to cover one exposure. This reduces transaction costs for both buyer and seller. Third, reinsurance helps small insurance companies stay in business, thus increasing competition in the industry. Without reinsurance, small companies would find it much more difficult to compete with larger ones.

Individual policyholders, however, rarely know about any reinsurance that may apply to their coverage. Even for those who are aware of the

....
14. The immediate balance sheet effect of issuing a policy of insurance is to add more to liabilities than to assets. Most expenses in connection with issuing the policy are incurred immediately, but no allowance is made for this fact in the requirements for establishing the liability account, called "reserves." Thus, a short-run drainage of surplus (net worth) occurs that can be relieved through reinsurance.

reinsurance, whether it be on a business or individual contract, most insurance policies prohibit direct access from the original insured to the reinsurer. The prohibition exists because the reinsurance agreement is a separate contract from the primary (original) insurance contract, and thus the original insured is not a party to the reinsurance agreement.

Nature of Self-Insurance

Financing that is neither insurance nor reinsurance generally involves retention. Within this category is **self-insurance.** True self-insurance differs significantly from mere failure to buy insurance. A self-insurer establishes a scheme for handling risk that is fundamentally the same as insurance.

A risk perfectly suited for self-insurance would have the same characteristics as one ideally qualified for insurance. That is, the potential losses would be significant, but the accompanying probabilities would not be high (relatively speaking); the probability distribution would be calculable; the number of similar exposure units would be large; losses would be accidental and definite; and a catastrophe could not occur. Losses would be predicted by an actuary, and funds (reserves) could be accumulated in special accounts to cover self-insurance losses, except for relatively small routine losses that could be paid from the organization's working capital (the equivalent of a deductible in an insurance contract, see chapter 6).

However, self-insurance differs from insurance in that risk transfer is not necessary under self-insurance. The person or organization exposed to loss has a sufficiently large exposure based upon which to make predictions, as well as a sufficiently large financial base from which losses would be paid. A firm employing 100,000 workers, for instance, likely has a sufficiently large exposure base to predict employee accidents and their financial consequences quite accurately. If too many worked in a single location, however, a potential for catastrophe exists.

In most parts of this book, the term "self funding" is used in lieu of self-insurance. Self funding indicates that the retention scheme does not include special loss reserve funds as a true self-insurance program would, nor does it adequately meet the ideal requisites of insurance. If a husband and wife of ordinary means decide not to buy property and liability insurance on their home, they are practicing retention of the self-funding type. This decision does not meet enough of the ideal requisites of insurance to call it self-insurance. Furthermore, the term self-insurance is considered a misnomer by some, because the definition of insurance includes the element of transfer, which is absent in self-insurance.

A **captive insurance company** is one form of self-insurance. Broadly defined, a captive insurer is one that provides insurance coverage to its parent company and other affiliated organizations. The captive is controlled by its policyholder-parent. Some captives sell coverage to nonaffiliated organizations. Others are comprised of members of industry associations, resulting in captives that closely resemble the early mutual insurers. Earlier in the chapter we discussed IRS-specified characteristics that are necessary for a contract to be considered insurance. The definition is important for the determination of deductibility of premiums and was expressed in a legal ruling involving Humana, Inc., which owns a large number of hospitals, and its captive insurance company, Health Care Indemnity. Health Care Indemnity is an insurance corporation. Its stock is owned exclusively by Humana, Inc., and its primary business is to provide medical malpractice insurance to Humana, Inc. and the other corporations owned by Humana. If it chose to, Health Care Indemnity might also sell insurance to organizations not affiliated with Humana. Alternatively, Humana could have joined forces with other hospital corporations and formed an association captive.

Forming a captive insurer is an expensive undertaking. Capital must be contributed in order to develop a net worth sufficient to meet regulatory (and financial stability) requirements. Start-up costs for licensing, chartering, and managing the captive are also incurred. And of course, the captive needs constant managing, requiring that effort be expended by the firm's risk management department and/or that a management company be hired.

To justify these costs, the parent company considers various factors. One is the availability of insurance in the commercial insurance market. During the liability insurance crisis of the 1980s, for example, pollution liability coverage became virtually nonexistent. Chemical and other firms formed captives to fill the void. Another factor considered in deciding upon a captive is the opportunity cost of money. If the parent can use funds more productively (i.e., can earn a higher after-tax return on investment) than can the insurer, the formation of a captive may be wise. The risk manager must assess the importance of the insurer's claims adjusting and other services (including underwriting), the deductibility of premiums, regulatory constraints against use of non-admitted (non-licensed) insurers, and access to the reinsurance market. One currently popular use of captives is to coordinate the insurance programs of a firm's foreign operations. An added advantage of captives in this setting is the ability to manage exchange rate risks as well as the pure risks more common to risk managers. Perhaps of primary significance is that captives give their parents access to the reinsurance market, which offers relatively cheap insurance.

A new development for risk managers regarding self-insurance options is the availability of risk retention groups. President Reagan signed into law the **Liability Risk Retention Act** in October 1986 (an amendment to the Product Liability Risk Retention Act of 1981). The Act permits formation of retention groups (a special form of captive) with fewer restrictions than existed before. The retention groups are similar to association captives. The Act permits formation of such groups in the U.S. under more favorable conditions than have existed generally for association captives. The Act may be particularly helpful to small businesses that could not feasibly self-insure on their own, but can do so within a designated group. How extensive will be the use of risk retention groups is yet to be seen.

Captives, including risk retention groups, are examples of the variety of loss financing options available to organizations but not to families. Organizations can also take advantage of hybrid retention and insurance products. Innovations in this area continue.

How to Make Insurance Function Well

PREVENTING MISREPRESENTATIONS

Your insurance company relies on the information you provide. By law, therefore, if you provide information that is misleading, the insurance company may be able to deny coverage for a claim you make. Clearly you want to avoid this occurrence; otherwise, you would not have purchased the policy in the first place. Your obligation to the insurance company is not only to provide correct information, but to provide complete information.

What do you need to tell the insurance agent when you go to purchase automobile insurance? The agent knows most of what is needed. He or she will ask for the make and model of the automobile, the year of manufacture, and whether or not there are any outstanding loans on the vehicle. The agent will also ask if you have had any accidents or traffic violations in the past three to five years, where you keep ("garage") the automobile, and how you use it (for work or for pleasure only).

You might be tempted to tell the agent that you keep the automobile at your parents' home, because rates there are cheaper. If you are using it primarily at school, however, to tell the agent otherwise may be considered a misrepresentation that would permit the insurer to deny coverage on a claim. Be certain to tell the agent that the automobile is being used at school. The agent may still give you the rate applicable to your parents' locale, and you have avoided the possibility that the insurer will argue that you have been untruthful, which could make the policy voidable.

You may also be tempted to tell the agent that you have not had any traffic violations, when actually you have had three in the past year. Certainly your insurance premium will be lower if the agent thinks you have a clean record than if the agent knows the truth, but that premium savings will mean very little to you when the insurer notifies you of denial of coverage because of dishonesty. Coverage may also be denied if you simply fail to notify the insurer of certain facts that clearly affect the insurer's view of whether or not to accept you as a policyholder.

A recent example illustrates the point. An out-of-state student at the University of South Carolina decided not to renew his auto insurance policy because he could not afford the premium. In South Carolina (as in many states) it is

illegal to drive without minimum amounts of automobile liability insurance. The student had an accident and convinced the reporting officer to allow him to obtain insurance on the spot rather than be put in jail. He called an insurer in his home state. The insurer provided coverage, but *the student failed to tell the insurer of the accident* that had just occurred. If the student makes a claim under this policy and the insurer finds out about the accident, the insurer has good cause for denying coverage.

On the other hand, you have various options to make yourself a more desirable policyholder, thus reducing premiums. These are actions you can take without having to tell untruths or hide important facts.

FITTING THE REQUISITES OF AN IDEALLY INSURABLE RISK

You can save many dollars in lower insurance premiums if you are reasonably close to an ideally insurable risk. What can you do?

Safe driving is a key to maintaining reasonable auto insurance premiums. Avoiding traffic violations and accidents helps reduce the probability of loss to a level that promotes economic feasibility of premiums. Likewise, you ought to include as large a deductible as you can bear on the physical damage portion of the policy (the part that pays for damage to your car). Use of a deductible eliminates coverage for the small, frequent losses—those losses that are so highly predictable that retaining them is cheaper than transferring them.

You can help yourself further by purchasing a car that places you in a group of similar (homogeneous) insureds. A flashy sports car with jacked-up rear wheels will *not* put you in a large, homogeneous group of insureds. Furthermore, a car that is easily damaged and/or expensive to repair will force up your physical damage premiums. People who own specialty cars, such as Bradleys, find insurance quite expensive and difficult to obtain because of the uniqueness of the exposure.

Where you garage (keep) the car and use the car will also affect your premiums. Living outside the city limits ought to reduce insurance costs. Those costs can be reduced further if you use the car for pleasure only, instead of driving to and from work. Riding the bus or in a friend's car will lower the probability of an accident, making you a more desirable policyholder. Living outside the city limits has a similar effect.

Finally, you can lower auto insurance premiums through variations in personal habits. If you do not drink or smoke, you may be eligible for premium discounts. Discounts are also often available for drivers who have passed driving courses. As a student, you can reduce premiums by maintaining a B average. Ask your agent about such discounts.

Key Terms

insurance
law of large numbers
discriminate
adverse selection
mass
similarity
fortuitous
catastrophe
dependent
determinable probability
   distribution
economically feasible
personal insurance
commercial insurance
life-health insurance

property-liability insurance
reinsurance
ceding insurer
reinsurer
treaty
facultative
proportional reinsurance
ceding commission
nonproportional reinsurance
excess-loss reinsurance
aggregate reinsurance
self-insurance
captive insurance company
Liability Risk Retention Act

Discussion Questions

1. When you buy a service contract on your new refrigerator, are you buying insurance? Explain.

2. Mr. and Mrs. Kaiser each own retail businesses. Mr. Kaiser has ten locations, each valued at $50,000, while Mrs. Kaiser has one location valued at $500,000. Can either of these businesses self-insure against property losses from fire, theft, windstorm, and other causes? What additional information would be helpful to you in answering this question?

3. Occasionally, Insurer X will reinsure part of Insurer Y's risks, and Insurer Y will reinsure part of Insurer X's risks. Doesn't this seem like merely trading dollars? Explain.

4. Some large insurance companies cede part of their risks to a smaller company. Since a large company is usually financially stronger than a small company, does this seem reasonable? Explain.

5. Professor Kulp said, "Insurance works well for some exposures, to some extent for many, and not at all for others." Do you agree? Why, or why not?

6. Insurance requires a transfer of risk. Risk is uncertain variability of future outcomes. Does life insurance meet the ideal requisites of insurance when the insurance company is aware that death is a *certainty?*

7. Distinguish between the different types of reinsurance and give an example of each. What are the advantages of reinsuring?

8. Define insurance using the three elements described in the chapter as required by the IRS. Explain how auto liability insurance fits the definition of insurance.

9. What is meant by the term self insurance? Is it insurance according to the IRS's definition?

10. What are the benefits of insurance to individuals and to society?

Cases

3.1 Hatch's furniture store has many perils that threaten its operation each day. Explain why each of the following perils may or may not be insurable. In each case, discuss possible exceptions to the general answer you have given.

1. The loss of merchandise because of theft when the thief is not caught and Hatch's cannot establish exactly when the loss occurred.

2. Injury to a customer when the store's delivery person backs the delivery truck into that customer while delivering a chair.

3. Injury to a customer when a sofa catches fire from internal combustion and burns the customer's living room. Discuss the fire damage to the customer's home, as well as the customer's bodily injury.

4. Injury to a customer's child who runs down an aisle in the store and falls.

5. Mental suffering to a customer whose merchandise is not delivered on the schedule to which Hatch's had agreed.

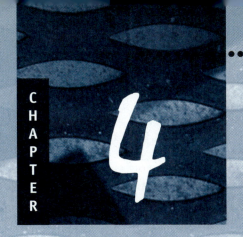

Fundamental Doctrines Affecting Insurance Contracts

Introduction   Have you purchased insurance? Filed an insurance claim? Participated in an insurance sales presentation? If you answered yes to any of these questions, the complexity of the insurance transaction with its multiple provision, legalistic wording, and technical nature is known to you. Others will quickly see that complexity; and yet, each of us can learn to manage the insurance transaction effectively and efficiently.

In chapter 3 we discussed the nature of insurance, which helps us understand the function of insurance organizations. The focus of chapter 4 is the insurance contract itself. You will explore

1. Agency law, especially applied to insurance.
2. Basic contractual requirements.
3. Important distinguishing characteristics of insurance contracts.

AGENT

Insurance is sold primarily by agents. The underlying contract, therefore, is affected significantly by the legal authority of the agent, which in turn is determined by well-established general legal rules regarding agency.

The **law of agency,** as stated by Hynes, "deals basically with the legal consequences of people acting on behalf of other people or organizations."[1]

Agency involves three parties: the principal, the agent, and a third party. The **principal** (insurer) creates an agency relationship with a second party (the agent) by authorizing him or her to make contracts with third parties (policyholders) on the principal's behalf. The source of the agent's authority is the principal. Such authority may be either expressed or implied. When an **agent** is appointed, the principal expressly indicates the extent of his or her authority. The agent also has, by implication, whatever authority is needed to fulfill the purposes of the agency. By entering into the relationship, the principal implies that the agent has the authority to fulfill the principal's responsibilities.

From the public point of view, the agent's authority is whatever it appears to be. This is sometimes referred to as **apparent authority.** If the principal treats a second party as if the person were an agent, then an agency is created. Agency law and the doctrines of waiver and estoppel have serious implications in the insurance business.

BINDING AUTHORITY

The law of agency is significant to insurance in large part because the only direct interaction most buyers of insurance have with the insurance company is through an agent. Laws regarding the authority and responsibility of an agent, therefore, affect the contractual relationship.

One of the most important of these agency characteristics is called the "binding authority." In many situations an agent is able to secure ("bind") coverage for an insured without any additional input from the insurer. The agreement that exists before a contract is issued is called a **binder.** This arrangement, described in the offer and acceptance section presented later, is common in the property and liability insurance areas.

In life and health insurance, however, an agent's ability to secure coverage is generally more limited. Rather than issuing a general **binder** of coverage some life insurance agents may be permitted to issue only a **conditional binder.** A conditional binder implies that coverage exists only if the underwriter ultimately accepts (or would have accepted) the application for insurance. Thus, if the applicant dies prior to the final policy issuance, payment is made only if (i.e., is conditioned on whether) the applicant would have been acceptable to the insurer as an insured. The general binder, in contrast, provides coverage immediately, even if the applicant is later found to be an unacceptable policyholder and coverage is cancelled at that point.

1. J. Dennis Hynes, *Agency and Partnership: Cases, Materials and Problems,* 2nd ed. (Charlottesville, Va.: The Michie Company, 1983), p. 4.

WAIVER AND ESTOPPEL

The agent's relationship between insured and insurer is greatly affected by doctrines of waiver and estoppel.

Waiver is the intentional relinquishment of a known right. In order to waive a right, a person must know he or she has the right, and must give it up intentionally. If a risk is undesirable at the time the agent assumes it on behalf of the company, and he or she knows it, the principal (the insurer) will have waived the right to refuse coverage at a later date. This situation arises when an agent insures a risk the company has specifically prohibited. Suppose, for example, that the agent knew an applicant's seventeen-year-old son was allowed to drive the covered automobile and also knew the company did not accept such risks. If the agent issues the policy, the company's right to refuse coverage on this basis later in the policy period has been waived.

In some policies, the insurer attempts to limit an agent's power to waive its provisions. The business property policy, for example, provides that

> The terms of this insurance shall not be waived, changed, or modified except by endorsement issued to form a part of this policy.

Unfortunately for the insurer, however, this will not prevent a waiver by its agent. For example, the business property policy provides that coverage on a building ceases after it has been vacant for over sixty days. What if the insured mentions to the agent that one of the buildings covered by the policy has been vacant sixty days, but says the situation is only temporary. If the agent says, "Don't worry, you're covered," the right of the insurer to deny coverage in the event of a loss while the building is vacant is waived. The policy may provide that it cannot be orally waived, but that generally will not affect the validity of the agent's waiver. From the insured's point of view, the agent is the company and the insurer is responsible for the agent's actions. Knowledge of the agent typically is knowledge of the insurer. Ultimately, the insurer may hold the agent liable for such actions, but with respect to the insured, the insurer cannot deny its responsibilities.

Estoppel occurs when the insurer or its agent has led the insured into believing that coverage exists. The insurer cannot later claim that no coverage existed. For example, when an insured specifically requests a certain kind of coverage when applying for insurance, that coverage likely exists even if the policy wording would imply otherwise. This is because the agent implied such coverage at the time of sale, and the insurer is estopped from denying it.

AGENCY BY ESTOPPEL

An agency relationship may be created when the conduct of the principal implies that an agency exists—an agency by estoppel. In such a case, the principal will be estopped from denying the existence of the agency (recall the binding authority of some agents). This situation may arise when the company suspends an agent, but the agent retains possession of blank policies. People who are not agents of a company do not have blank policies in their possession. By leaving them with the former agent, the company is acting as if he or she is a current agent. If such policies are issued by the former agent, the company is estopped from denying the existence of an agency relationship and will be bound by the policy.

If an agent who has been suspended sends business to the company which the company accepts, the agency relationship will be ratified by such action and the company will be estopped from denying the contract's existence. The company has the right to refuse such business when it is presented, but it waives the right when the business is accepted.

Requirements of a Contract

When an agent sells an insurance policy, he or she is selling a contract. A contract is an agreement enforceable by law. For any such agreement to be legally enforceable, it must meet the following minimum requirements:

1. There must be an offer and an acceptance.
2. There must be consideration.
3. The parties to the contract must be competent.
4. Its purpose must be legal.
5. The contract must be in legal form.

OFFER AND ACCEPTANCE

Offer and **acceptance** are essential elements to the creation of a contract. An agreement is reached when one party makes an offer and the other party accepts it. If the party to whom the offer was made requests a change in terms, a counteroffer is made which releases the first offerer from the terms of the original offer. In the making of insurance contracts, usually the buyer offers to buy and the insurer accepts or rejects the offer. When you call an insurance agent for insurance on your new automobile and the agent says, "You are covered," you have made an offer to buy and the agent has accepted on behalf of his or her company. As stated previously, this acceptance is called a binder. Your offer may be verbal, as in this case, or it may be in the form of a written application. Remember that this process differs for life and health insurance.

CONSIDERATION

A contract also requires the exchange of **consideration.** Consideration is the price each party demands for agreeing to carry out his or her part of the contract. The value of the consideration is usually unimportant, but lack of consideration will cause the contract to be considered a gift and therefore unenforceable. In many cases, insurance contracts stipulate that the consideration inducing the insurer to make promises to the insured is both the premium *and* certain conditions specified in the policy. Such conditions may include maintenance of a certain level of risk, timely notice of loss, and periodic reports to insurers of exposure values. Conditions will be explained in detail later in the text. The insurer's consideration is its promise to pay losses. Consideration, therefore, does not necessarily imply dollars.

COMPETENT PARTIES

Another essential element for a contract is that the parties to the contract must be **competent parties.** Most people are competent to contract, but there are exceptions. Insane or intoxicated persons are not competent. Minors may enter into contracts, but such contracts may be voided (or terminated). Upon reaching majority (age eighteen in some states, age twenty-one in others), the young person may ratify or reject the contract. If ratified, the contract would then have the same status as one originally entered into by competent parties.

A minor who enters into an insurance contract, therefore, may void it during infancy or when he or she reaches majority. Ratification of a policy at the age of majority can be accomplished (by oral or written communication) either explicitly or implicitly (by continuing the policy). Some states have laws giving minors the power to enter into binding life insurance contracts on their own lives as young as age fourteen.

LEGAL PURPOSE

A contract must have a **legal purpose.** If it does not, to enforce the contract would be contrary to public policy. A contract by a government employee to sell secret information to an agent of an enemy country, for example, would not have a legal purpose and would be unenforceable. For the same reason, a contract of insurance to cover losses caused by the insured's own arson would be illegal, contrary to public policy, and thus unenforceable.

LEGAL FORM

Contracts may be either oral or written; they must, however, follow a specific **legal form,** which may vary from state to state. As noted, some insurance contracts are—at least initially—oral. Most states do not have laws directly prohibiting oral contracts of insurance. They do, however, require that contract "forms" (the written version of standardized insurance policy provisions and attachments) be approved before being offered for sale. Moreover, the nature and general content of some policies are specified by law. Most states require that certain provisions be included in life and health insurance contracts. Thus, although some contracts may be oral, insurance contracts must—for the most part—be in writing, and must conform to the requirements of the states in which they are sold.

Distinguishing Characteristics of Insurance Contracts

In addition to the elements just discussed, insurance contracts have several characteristics that differentiate them from most other contracts. Risk managers must be familiar with these characteristics in order to understand the creation, execution, and interpretation of insurance policies. Insurance contracts are:

1. Based on utmost good faith.
2. Contracts of adhesion.
3. Contracts of indemnity.
4. Personal.

BASED ON UTMOST GOOD FAITH

When an insurer considers accepting a risk, it must have accurate and complete information to make a reasonable decision. Should it assume the risk and, if so, under what terms and conditions? The person who makes these decisions is an **underwriter,** and the process is known as **underwriting.** Because insurance involves a contract of **uberrimae fidei,** or **utmost good faith,** potential insureds are held to the highest standards of truthfulness and honesty in providing information for the underwriter. In the case of contracts other than for insurance, it is generally assumed that each party has equal knowledge and access to the facts, and thus each is subject to requirements of "good faith," not "utmost good faith." In contrast, eighteenth-century ocean marine insurance contracts were negotiated under circumstances that forced underwriters to rely on information provided by the insured, because they could not get it firsthand. A ship being insured, for example, might be unavailable for inspection because it was on the other side of the world. Was the ship seaworthy? The underwriter could not inspect it, so he (they were all men in those days) required the insured to warrant that it was. If the warranty was not strictly true, the contract was voidable. The penalty for departing from utmost good faith was having no coverage when a loss occurred. Today the concept of utmost good faith is implemented by the doctrines of (1) representation, (2) concealment, and (3) warranties.[2]

Representations

When you are negotiating with an insurer for coverage, you make statements concerning the exposure. These statements are called **representations.** They are made for the purpose of inducing the insurer to enter into the contract, i.e., provide you with insurance. If you misrepresent a **material fact,** the insurer can void the contract and you will have no coverage, even though you may possess the insurance policy. In essence, the contract never existed.

Note that "material fact" has been specified. If the insurer wants to void a contract it has issued to you in reliance upon the information you provided, it must prove that what you misrepresented was material. That is, the insurer must prove that the information was so important that if the truth had been known, the underwriter would not have made the contract or would have done so only on different terms.

If, for example, you stated in an application for life insurance that you were born on March 2 when, in fact, you were born on March 12, such a misrepresentation would not be material. A correct statement would not alter the underwriter's decision made on the incorrect information. The

---

2. Warranties are stringent requirements that insureds must follow for coverage to exist. They were considered necessary in the early days of marine insurance because insurers were forced to rely on the truthfulness of policyholders in assessing risk (often the vessel was already at sea when coverage was procured, and thus inspection was not possible). Under modern conditions, however, insurers generally do not find themselves at such a disadvantage. As a result, courts rarely enforce insurance warranties, treating them instead as representations. Our discussion here, therefore, will omit presentation of warranties. [See Kenneth S. Abraham, *Insurance Law and Regulation: Cases and Materials* (Westbury, NY: The Foundation Press, 1990) for a discussion.]

ETHICAL *Dilemma*

Automobile Insurance

Automobile insurance represents a major expense for most of us. Furthermore, the cost generally seems out of proportion with what we think the insurer is likely to pay out on our behalf, and premiums seem determined more by factors generally out of our control (location, gender and age, for example) than by our driving record.

Given this setting, we might be tempted not to inform our insurer that we've brought the car to school. Where a vehicle is garaged is a significant pricing element for most insurers in most states. A university town often is congested; vandalism near student housing may be higher than elsewhere; and we may allow more people to use the car than we would in our hometowns, all of which might lead to higher insurance premiums (of course, the opposite conditions may also exist). Let's assume rates are higher in our college location. Given that the insurer has never needed to pay a claim for us up to this point, despite collecting large premiums, we might feel that it is only fair to maintain the low rate associated with using our cars in our hometowns. If we consider the large home offices of major insurance companies, we might further believe that they make plenty of money. Many people think insurers are too wealthy.

However, as you know from chapter 4, if you get caught misrepresenting the use of your car, your insurer can deny coverage. You have talked with your parents, though, and they agree to tell anyone who asks that you generally keep the car at home, only occasionally driving back and forth to school.

Even if you never have an accident, does this seem right? Should you be able to recover the large premiums you have paid to insurers for so long? Are insurers failing to treat you justly by giving too little attention to your driving record? Knowing that other insureds are similarly misrepresenting the truth, do you consider this action acceptable?

The issues related to acceptable rating factors in all lines of insurance are significant and hotly debated. Later chapters in this book will take up the question again. Our intent here is to consider the need to be honest with insurance companies. Do we, for instance, have the right to decide when to tell an insurer the truth, or is it morally appropriate to take up the issue with insurance regulators instead, so that all of society plays by the same rules?

policy is not voidable under these circumstances. On the other hand, suppose you apply for life insurance and state that you are in good health, even though you've just been diagnosed with a severe heart ailment. This fact likely would cause the insurer to charge a higher premium, or not to sell the coverage at all. The significance of this fact is that the insurer may contend that the policy never existed (it was void), and so loss by any cause (whether related to the misrepresentation or not) is not covered.

Several exceptions to this rule apply, as presented in chapters discussing specific policies.

It is not uncommon for students to misrepresent to their auto insurers where their cars are garaged, particularly if premium rates at home are lower than they are where students attend college. Because location is a factor in determining premium rates, where a car is garaged is a material fact. Students who misrepresent this or other material facts take the chance of having no coverage at the time of a loss. The insurer may elect to void the contract. Thus, for students to think they have insurance under such circumstances may prove a delusion.

Concealment

Telling the truth in response to explicit application questions may seem to be enough, but it is not. You must also reveal those material facts about the exposure that only you know and that you should realize are relevant. Suppose, for example, that you have no insurance on your home because you "don't believe in insurance." Upon your arrival home one afternoon, you discover that the neighbor's house—only thirty feet from yours—is on fire. You promptly telephone the agency where you buy your auto insurance and apply for a homeowners policy, asking that it be put into effect immediately. You answer all the questions the agent asks, but fail to mention the fire next door. You have intentionally concealed a material fact you obviously realize is relevant. You are guilty of **concealment,** and the insurer has the right to void the contract.

When the underwriter relies on you to give all material facts, you must do so. You cannot hold the insurer to the contract if you conceal material information. You are not, however, expected to be an insurance expert. If the insurance company requires the completion of a long, detailed application, an insured who fails to provide information the insurer neglected to ask about cannot be proven guilty of concealment unless it is obvious that certain information should have been volunteered. Clearly, no insurance agent is going to ask you when you apply for insurance if the neighbor's house is on fire. You should understand the relevance of this condition (if you know it), and must tell the agent. The fact that the agent does not ask does not relieve you of the responsibility.

In both life and health insurance, most state insurance laws limit the period (usually one or two years) during which the insurer may void coverage for a concealment or misrepresentation. Other types of insurance contracts do not involve such time limits.

CONTRACTS OF ADHESION

Insurance policies are contracts of **adhesion.** Unlike contracts formulated by a process of bargaining, most insurance contracts are prepared by the insurer and then accepted or rejected by the buyer. You do not specify the terms of coverage, but rather accept the terms as stipulated. Thus, you "adhere" to the insurer's contract. Some contracts are written by risk managers or brokers[3] who then seek underwriters to accept them, but not many. Most people go to an agent to request coverage.

....

3. Brokers represent the buyer, rather than the insurer. See the discussion in chapter 25.

The fact that buyers usually have no influence over the content or form of the insurance policies they buy has had a significant impact on the way courts interpret policies when there is a dispute.[4] When the terms of a policy are ambiguous, the courts favor the insured because it is assumed that the insurer that writes the contract should know what it wants to say and how to state it clearly. When the terms are not ambiguous, however, the courts have been reluctant to change the contract in favor of the insured. Further, the policy language generally is interpreted according to the insured's own level of expertise and situation, not that of an underwriter who is knowledgeable about insurance.

A violation of this general rule occurs, however, when the courts believe that reasonable insureds would expect coverage of a certain type. Under these conditions, regardless of the ambiguity of policy language (or lack thereof), the court may rule in favor of the insured. Courts are guided by the **expectations principle** (or reasonable expectations principle), which may be stated as follows:

> The objectively reasonable expectations of applicants and intended beneficiaries regarding the terms of insurance contracts will be honored even though painstaking study of the policy provisions would have negated those expectations.[5]

Thus, the current approach to the interpretation of contracts of adhesion is threefold: First, to favor the insured when terms of the contract drafted by the insurer are ambiguous; second, to read the contract as an insured would; third, to determine the coverage on the basis of reasonable expectations of the insured.

INDEMNITY CONCEPT

Many insurance contracts are contracts of **indemnity.** This means the insurer agrees to pay no more (and no less) than the actual loss suffered by the insured. For example, suppose your house is insured for $100,000 at the time it is totally destroyed by fire. If its value at that time is only $80,000, that is the amount the insurance company will pay.[6] You cannot collect $100,000, because to do so would exceed the actual loss suffered. You would be better off after the loss than you were before. The purpose of the insurance contract is—or should be—to restore you to the same economic position you had before the loss, not to improve your situation. Of course, the principle of indemnity usually leads the insurer to pay no more than an actual loss. Often, however, less will be paid.

The indemnity principle has practical significance both for the insurer and for society. If insureds could gain by having an insured loss, some

---

4. Some policies are designed through mutual effort of insurer and insured. These "manuscript policies" might not place the same burden on the insurer regarding ambiguities.
5. See Robert E. Keeton, *Basic Text on Insurance Law* (St. Paul, Minn.: West Publishing Company, 1971), p. 351. While this reference is now about 25 years old, it remains perhaps the most popular insurance text available.
6. In some states, a valued policy law requires payment of the face amount of property insurance in the event of total loss, regardless of the value of the dwelling. Other policy provisions, such as deductibles and coinsurnace, may also affect the insurer's effort to "indemnify" you.

would deliberately cause losses. This would result in a decrease of resources for society, an economic burden for the insurance industry, and, ultimately, higher insurance premiums for all insureds. Moreover, if losses were caused intentionally rather than as a result of chance occurrence, the insurer likely would be unable to predict costs satisfactorily. An insurance contract that makes it possible for the insured to profit by an event insured against violates the principle of indemnity and may prove poor business for the insurer.

The doctrine of indemnity is implemented and supported by several legal principles and policy provisions, including the following:

1. Insurable interest.
2. Subrogation.
3. Actual cash value provision.
4. Other insurance provisions.

Insurable Interest

If a contingency, such as a fire or auto collision, will cause loss to a person or firm, that person or firm has an **insurable interest.** A person not subject to loss does not have an insurable interest. Stated another way, someone who would be harmed by change has an insurable interest. Most often this "change" is viewed in economic terms. The law concerning insurable interest is important to the buyer of insurance, because it determines whether the benefits from an insurance policy will be collectible. Thus, all insureds should be familiar with what constitutes an insurable interest, when it must exist, and the extent to which it may limit payment under an insurance policy.

Basis for Insurable Interest Many situations constitute an insurable interest. The most common is ownership of property. As the owner of a building, you will suffer financial loss if it is damaged or destroyed by fire or other peril. Thus, you have an insurable interest in the building.

If you finance your purchase (i.e., take out a loan) and provide a mortgage on the building for security, the lender also has an insurable interest in the building. For the lender, loss to the security, such as the building being damaged or destroyed by fire, may reduce the value of the loan. On the other hand, an unsecured creditor generally does not have an insurable interest in the general assets of the debtor, because loss to such assets does not directly affect the value of the creditor's claim against the debtor.

If part or all of a building is leased to a tenant who makes improvements in the leased space, such improvements become the property of the building owner on termination of the lease. Nevertheless, the tenant has an insurable interest in the improvements, because he or she will suffer a loss if they are damaged or destroyed during the term of the lease. This commonly occurs when building space is rented on a "bare walls" basis. To make such space usable, the tenant must make improvements.

If a tenant has a long-term lease with terms more favorable than would be available in the current market, but which may be cancelled in the event that the building is damaged, the tenant has an insurable interest in the lease. This is called a **leasehold interest.** A bailee who is responsible for the safekeeping of property belonging to others, and who must return it in good condition or pay for it, has an insurable interest. When you take your clothes to the local dry-cleaning establishment, for example, it acts as a bailee, responsible to return your clothes in good condition.

You have an insurable interest in your own life and may have such an interest in the life of another.[7] An insurable interest in the life of another person may be based on a close relationship by blood or marriage, such as a wife's insurable interest in her husband. It may also be based on love and affection, such as that of a parent for a child, or on financial considerations. A creditor, for example, may have an insurable interest in the life of a debtor, and an employer may have an insurable interest in the life of a key employee.

When Insurable Interest Must Exist The time at which insurable interest must exist depends upon the type of insurance. In property insurance, the interest must exist at the time of the loss. As the owner of a house, you have an insurable interest in it. If you insure yourself against loss to the house caused by fire or other peril, you can collect on such insurance only if you still have an insurable interest in the house at the time the damage occurs. Thus, if you transfer unencumbered title to another person before the house is damaged, you cannot collect from the insurer, even though your policy may still be in force. You no longer have an insurable interest. On the other hand, if you have a mortgage on the house you sold, you will continue to have an insurable interest in the amount of the outstanding mortgage until the loan is paid. You are a secured creditor.

As a result of the historical development of insurance practices, life insurance requires an insurable interest only at the inception of the contract. When the question of insurable interest in life insurance was being adjudicated in England, such policies provided no cash surrender values; payment was made by the insurer only if the person who was the subject[8] of insurance died while the policy was in force. An insured who was also the policyowner and unable to continue making premium payments simply sacrificed all interest in the policy.

This led to the practice of some policyowners/insureds selling their policies to speculators who, as the new owners, named themselves the beneficiaries and continued premium payments until the death of the insured. If such purchasers could not collect policy proceeds when the insured died because they lacked an insurable interest at the time of the insured's death, they would be unwilling to buy the policy. Marketability was assured by requiring an insurable interest only at the inception of the policy. Any subsequent policyowner did not need to be concerned about the matter of insurable interest. With the advent of cash surrender values in life insurance

....

7. Although a person who dies suffers a loss, he or she cannot be indemnified. Because the purpose of the principle of insurable interest is to implement the doctrine of indemnity, it has no application in the case of a person insuring his or her own life. Such a contract cannot be one of indemnity.

8. The person whose death requires the insurer to pay the proceeds of a life insurance policy is usually listed in the policy as the **insured.** He or she is also known as the **cestui que vie** or the **subject.** The **beneficiary** is the person (or other entity) entitled to the proceeds of the policy upon the death of the subject. The **owner** of the policy is the person (or other entity) who has the authority to exercise all the prematurity rights of the policy, such as designating the beneficiary, taking a policy loan, and so on. Often the insured is also the owner.

policies, the practice of selling policies to avoid forfeiture was generally discontinued because the owner of the policy usually could obtain as much by surrendering it to the insurance company for cash as by selling it.[9]

Because the legal concept of requiring an insurable interest only at the inception of the life insurance contract has continued, it is possible to collect on a policy in which such interest has ceased. For example, if the life of a key person in a firm is insured, in whose life the firm has an insurable interest because his or her death would cause a loss to the firm, the policy may be continued in force by the firm even after the person leaves its employ, and the proceeds may be collected when he or she dies. This seldom occurs, however, because usually there is an agreement between the employer and employee that allows the employee to acquire ownership of the policy in the event employment is terminated.

Extent Insurable Interest Limits Payment   In the case of property insurance, not only must an insurable interest exist at the time of the loss, but the amount the insured is able to collect is limited by the extent of such interest. For example, if you have a one-half interest in a building that is worth $100,000 at the time it is destroyed by fire, you cannot collect more than $50,000 from the insurance company no matter how much insurance you purchased. If you could collect more than the amount of your insurable interest, you would make a profit on the fire. This would violate the principle of indemnity. An exception exists in some states, where valued policy laws are in effect. These laws require insurers to pay the full amount of insurance sold if property is totally destroyed. The intent of the law is to discourage insurers from selling too much coverage.

In contrast to property insurance, life insurance payments are usually not limited by insurable interest. Most life—and some health—insurance contracts are considered to be **valued policies.**[10] That is, they are contracts to pay a stated sum upon the occurrence of the event insured against, rather than to indemnify for loss sustained. For example, a life insurance contract provides that the insurer will pay a specified sum to the beneficiary upon receipt of proof of death of the person whose life is the subject of the insurance. The beneficiary does not have to prove that any loss has been suffered, because he or she is not required to have an insurable interest.

Some health insurance policies provide that the insurance company will pay a specified number of dollars per day while the insured is hospitalized. Such policies are not contracts of indemnity; they simply promise to make cash payments under specified circumstances.

Although an insurable interest must exist at the inception of a life insurance contract to make it enforceable, the amount of payment is usually not limited by the extent of such insurable interest. The amount of life insurance collectible at the death of an insured is limited only by the amount insurers are willing to issue and by the insured's premium-paying

9. With the introduction of HIV into our ecosystem, however, new markets for life insurance have emerged, and moral questions about selling life insurance policies have resurfaced.
10. Some property insurance policies are written on a valued basis, but precautions are taken to assure that values agreed upon are realistic, thus adhering to the principle of indemnity.

ability.[11] However, the amount of the proceeds of a life insurance policy that may be collected by a creditor-beneficiary is generally limited to the amount of the debt and the premiums paid by the creditor, plus interest.[12]

Subrogation

The principle of indemnity is also supported by the right of **subrogation.** This right gives the insurer whatever claim against third parties the insured may have as a result of the loss for which the insurer paid. If your house is damaged because a neighbor burned leaves and negligently permitted the fire to get out of control, you have a right to collect damages from the neighbor, because a negligent wrongdoer is responsible to others for the damage or injury he or she causes.[13] If your house is insured against loss by fire, however, you cannot collect from both the insurance company and the negligent party who caused the damage. Your insurance company will pay for the damage and is then subrogated to (i.e., given) your right to collect damages. The insurer may then sue the negligent party and collect from him or her. This prevents you from making a profit by collecting twice for the same loss.

The right of subrogation is a common-law right the insurer has without a contractual agreement. It is specifically stated in the policy, however, so you will be aware of it and refrain from releasing the party responsible for the loss. The personal auto policy, for example, provides that

> If we make a payment under this policy and the person to or for whom payment was made has a right to recover damages from another, that person shall subrogate that right to us. That person shall do whatever is necessary to enable us to exercise our rights and shall do nothing after loss to prejudice them.
>
> If we make a payment under this policy and the person to or for whom payment is made recovers damages from another, that person shall hold in trust for us the proceeds of the recovery and shall reimburse us to the extent of our payment.

---

11. Life and health insurance companies have learned, however, that overinsurance may lead to poor underwriting experience. Because the loss caused by death or illness cannot be measured precisely, defining overinsurance is difficult. It may be said to exist when the amount of insurance is clearly in excess of the economic loss that may be suffered. Extreme cases, such as the individual whose earned income is $300 per week but who may receive $500 per week in disability insurance benefits from an insurance company while he or she is ill, are easy to identify. Life and health insurers engage in financial underwriting to detect overinsurance. The requested amount of insurance is related to the proposed insured's (beneficiary's) financial need for insurance and premium-paying ability.

12. This is an area in which it is difficult to generalize; the statement made above is approximately correct. The point is that the creditor-debtor relationship is an exception to the statement that an insurable interest need not exist at the time of the death of the insured and that the amount of payment is not limited to the insurable interest that existed at the inception of the contract. For further discussion, see Kenneth Black, Jr. and Harold Skipper, Jr., *Life Insurance,* 12th ed. (Englewood Cliffs, N.J.: Prentice-Hall, 1994) pp. 187–88.

13. See chapter 7 for a discussion of the concept of negligence liability.

Actual Cash Value

This clause is included in many property insurance policies. An insured generally does not receive an amount greater than the actual loss suffered, because the policy limits payment to **actual cash value.** A typical property insurance policy says, for example, that the company insures "to the extent of actual cash value . . . but not exceeding the amount which it would cost to repair or replace . . . and not in any event for more than the interest of the insured."

Actual cash value is not defined in the policy, but a generally accepted notion of it is the replacement cost at the time of the loss, less physical depreciation including obsolescence. If the roof on your house has an expected life of twenty years, roughly half its value is gone at the end of ten years. If it is damaged by an insured peril at that time, the insurer will pay the cost of replacing the damaged portion, less depreciation. You must bear the burden of the balance. For example, if the replacement cost of the damaged portion is $2,000 at the time of a loss, but the depreciation is $800, the insurer will pay $1,200 and you will bear an $800 expense. Note that book values are irrelevant in determining actual cash value. Thus, original cost and accounting depreciation are ignored for insurance valuation purposes.

Another definition of actual cash value is **fair market value,** which is the amount a willing buyer would pay a willing seller. For auto insurance, where thousands of units of virtually the same property exist, fair market value may be readily available. The NADA retail value, for instance, may be used as a guide. For other types of property, however, the definition may be deceptively simple. How do you determine what a willing buyer would be willing to pay a willing seller? The usual approach is to compare sales prices of similar property and adjust for differences. For example, if three houses similar to yours in your neighborhood have recently sold for $90,000, then that is probably the fair market value of your home. You may, of course, believe your house is worth far more because you think it has been better maintained than the other houses. Such a process for determining fair market value may be time-consuming and unsatisfactory, so it is seldom used for determining actual cash value. Such a process may, however, be used when replacement cost minus depreciation is far greater than market value, because of obsolescence and/or the deterioration of the area in which a dwelling is located.

Property insurance is often written on a **replacement cost** basis, which means that there is no deduction for depreciation. With such coverage, the insurer would pay $2,000 for the roof loss mentioned above earlier and you would not pay anything. This coverage may or may not conflict with the principle of indemnity, depending upon whether you are better off after payment than you were before the loss.

If $2,000 provided your house with an entirely new roof, you have gained. You now have a roof that will last twenty years, rather than ten years. On the other hand, if the damaged portion that was repaired accounted for only 10 percent of the roof area, having it repaired would not increase the expected life of the entire roof. You are not really any better off after the loss and its repair than you were before the loss. Actually, you may be worse off if the repaired part of the roof does not blend in well with the old, undamaged part. It may, in fact, stand out like a black eye. If you have ever had a fender on your car repainted, you are aware of this problem.

When an insured may gain, such as by having a loss paid for on a replacement cost basis, there is a potential moral or morale hazard. The insured may be motivated to be either dishonest or careless. If your kitchen has not been redecorated for a very long time and looks shabby, for example, you may not worry about leaving a kettle of grease unattended on the stove. The resulting grease fire will require extensive redecoration as well as cleaning of furniture and, perhaps, replacement of some clothing (assuming that the fire is extinguished before it gets entirely out of control).

Or, you may simply let your old house burn down. Insurers try to cope with these problems by providing in the policy that, when the cost to repair or replace damage to a building is more than some specified amount, the insurer will pay not more than the actual cash value of the damage until actual repair or replacement is completed. The insurer in this way discourages you from destroying the house in order to receive a monetary reward. Arson generally occurs with the intent of financial gain. Some insurers will insure personal property only on an actual cash value basis, because the opportunity to replace old with new may be too tempting to some insureds. Fraudulent claims on loss to personal property are easier to make than are fraudulent claims on loss to buildings. Even so, insurers find most insureds to be honest, permitting the availability of replacement cost coverage on most forms of property.

Other Insurance Provisions

The purpose of **other insurance provisions** in insurance contracts is to prevent insureds from making a profit by collecting from more than one insurance policy for the same loss. If you have more than one policy protecting you against a particular loss, there is a possibility that by collecting on all policies you may profit from the loss. This would, of course, violate the principle of indemnity.

Most policies (other than life insurance) have some provision to prevent insureds from making a profit from a loss through ownership of more than one policy. The homeowners policy, for example, provides in the other insurance, or pro rata liability, clause that:

> If a loss covered by this policy is also covered by other insurance, we will pay only the proportion of the loss that the limit of liability that applies under this policy bears to the total amount of insurance covering the loss.[14]

Suppose you have a $150,000 homeowners policy in Company A with $75,000 personal property coverage on your home in Montana, and a $100,000 homeowners policy in Company B with $50,000 personal property coverage on your home in Arizona. Both policies provide coverage of personal property anywhere in the world. If $5,000 worth of your personal

----

14. See Appendix A, Section I—Conditions.

property is stolen while you are traveling in Europe, because of the "other insurance" clause you cannot collect $5,000 from each insurer. Instead, each company will pay its pro rata share of the loss. Company A will pay $3,000 and Company B will pay $2,000. You will not make a profit on this deal, but you will be indemnified for the loss you suffered. The proportions are determined as follows:

Amount of insurance, Company A	$ 75,000
Amount of insurance, Company B	50,000
Total amount of insurance	125,000
Company A pays $\frac{75,000}{125,000} \times 5,000 =$	3,000
Company B pays $\frac{50,000}{125,000} \times 5,000 =$	2,000
Total paid	$ 5,000

PERSONAL

Insurance contracts are **personal.** They insure against loss to a person, not to the person's property. For example, you may say, "My car is insured." Actually, you are insured against financial loss caused by something happening to your car. If you sell the car, insurance does not automatically pass to the new owner. It may be assigned,[15] but only with the consent of the insurer. The personal auto policy, for example, provides that

> Your rights and duties under this policy may not be assigned without our written consent.

Because people affect the probability of loss, underwriters are as concerned about the insured person as they are about the nature of the property involved, if not more so. If you have an excellent driving record and are a desirable insured, the underwriter is willing to accept your application for insurance. If you sell your car to an eighteen-year-old male who has already wrecked two cars this year, however, the probability of loss increases markedly. Clearly, the insurer does not want to assume that kind of risk without proper compensation, so it protects itself by requiring written consent for assignment.

Unlike property insurance, life insurance policies are freely assignable. This is a result of the way life insurance practice developed before policies accumulated cash values. Whether or not change of ownership affects the probability of the insured's death is a matter for conjecture. In life insurance, the policyowner is not necessarily the recipient of the policy proceeds. As with an auto policy, the subject of the insurance (the life insured) is the same regardless of who owns the policy. Suppose you assign your life insurance policy (including the right to name a beneficiary) to your spouse while you are on good terms. Such an assignment may not affect the probability of your death. On the other hand, two years and two

---

15. A complete assignment is the transfer of ownership or benefits of a policy; that is, to give someone else all rights of ownershp in the policy.

spouses later, the one to whom you assigned the policy *may* become impatient about the long prospective wait for death benefits. Changing life insurance policyowners may not change the risk as much as, say, changing auto owners, but it could (murder is quite different from stealing). Nevertheless, life insurance policies can be assigned without the insurer's consent.

Suppose you assign the rights to your life insurance policy to another person and then surrender it for the cash value before the insurance company knows of the assignment. Will the person to whom you assigned the policy rights also be able to collect the cash value? To avoid litigation and to eliminate the possibility of having to make double payment, life insurance policies provide that the company is not bound by an assignment until it has received written notice. The answer to this question, therefore, is generally no. The notice requirements, however, may be rather low. A prudent insurer may hesitate to pay off life insurance proceeds when even a slight indication of an assignment (or change in beneficiary) exists.

Identifying Your Firm's Insurance Problems

As a part-time bookkeeper for High Country, Inc., a small manufacturing firm, you mention to Ms. Langdon, your boss and the owner of the firm, that you are taking this course. A day or two later, she says to you, "Drop the bookkeeping for a week and look over our insurance. I think we're paying too much premium, and I'm not sure we need all the insurance we have."

The thought that you have become a risk manager after reading four chapters of this book is gratifying. The thought that you may bomb on this assignment, however, makes you feel acutely uncomfortable. You may be able to respond with "I don't know" when your professor asks you a question about the material in this week's assignment, but your boss is accustomed to a great deal more than that. She is a hard-headed businessperson who makes lots of money, hates to pay taxes, and believes that insurance is a necessary evil. She thinks you are a bright young person who could go a long way in this business, and you would like to preserve that illusion. What can you do?

First, you can recognize that, as bookkeeper, you know more about the business than you might think. Second, you can adopt a goal. Let's say you decide to write a report entitled, "Some Aspects of Our Insurance Program You Ought to Know About." Third, you can go back through this chapter and look for some signals that may lead to the discovery of problems. You can put together some prospective signals as follows:

1. Insurable interest.
2. Actual cash value.
3. Other insurance.

INSURABLE INTEREST

In examining the various property insurance policies the firm has, you find that the insured's name and address on all the buildings is High Country, Inc. This seems reasonable until you recall that the company pays rent every month for some premises. By investigating, you find that one check goes to Ms. Langdon's son and one to her daughter, both of whom are away at college.

This puzzles you, so you talk to Mr. Davidson, who has been Ms. Langdon's secretary since the day she started the

business twenty-seven years ago. Davidson says, "Ms. Langdon gave Building #3 to Jack, Jr. and Building #5 to Denise a long time ago so she could pay them rent instead of an allowance. That way, the money sent to them is a deductible expense for income tax purposes, and Ms. Langdon does not have to put them through school with money on which she has paid taxes."

Armed with this bit of intelligence, you go back through the insurance policies and find that you were right the first time. The named insured for all buildings, including #3 and #5, is High Country, Inc.

Query: Does High Country, Inc. have an insurable interest in buildings owned by Jack Langdon, Jr. and Denise Langdon? If not, can it collect on the insurance if there is a loss? Can Jack or Denise? You now have one item for your report.

ACTUAL CASH VALUE

In examining the property insurance on High Country's buildings, you find that the amount of insurance has been increased every year to keep it equal to the actual cash value. As the bookkeeper, you are aware that this means replacement cost minus depreciation. Some of the buildings are quite old but in good repair. Building #2, for example, is twenty-five years old but still suitable for its use as a warehouse. The amount of insurance on it is $200,000. How much would it cost to replace it? When you ask Ms. Bronson, the plant superintendent responsible for construction and maintenance, she estimates at least $400,000. If the building is totally destroyed by fire, High Country will be paid $200,000 by the insurance company, but replacement costs will be $400,000.

Query: Does High Country have $200,000 readily available or could Ms. Langdon borrow that much? Should they try to get the insurance policies changed to a replacement cost basis? You have another item for your report.

OTHER INSURANCE

When you checked the insurance on Building #2, you found two policies, each in the amount of $100,000. One was issued by Pacific Fire Insurance Company and the other by Square Deal Insurance, a company owned partly by Ms.

Langdon's husband's first cousin. When you ask Mr. Davison about this, he tells you, "The company has a low financial rating, but Ms. Langdon wanted to help her husband's cousin get started."

Query: What happens when there is a loss? The other insurance provision of both policies says that each company will pay its share. If Square Deal is defunct when High Country has a loss, Pacific Fire will pay its share but who will pay Square Deal's share? If your state has an insolvency association, the association may pay. But how quickly? Under the best of circumstances, settling a loss with more than one company can be more time consuming than settling with only one company. If one company is unable to pay its share, you have a real problem. Perhaps High Country should have insurance with only one (strong) company. Another item for your report.

REPRESENTATIONS

An attachment to the policies specifies that High Country, Inc. employs guards to be present when the plant is not operating. The company receives a premium discount for including this provision. In your bookkeeping duties, you do not recall handling any salary checks or expense reports for night guards.

Query: If a loss occurs when a guard should have been on duty but was not, what responsibility does the insurer have to pay the loss? Does High Country employ guards? If so, how are they paid? If not, do they wish to hire guards or to change the policy provision requiring them? This too is an item for your report.

YOUR REPORT

Because I don't know enough about insurance to analyze costs, interpret all contract provisions, and so forth, I cannot make a complete insurance analysis. I have, however, discovered some problems that should be brought to your attention. They are:

1. High Country does not have an insurable interest in Buildings #3 and #5 because they are owned by your children, not the firm. Our insurance agent should issue policies to them.

2. The insurance on Building #2 is enough to pay for its actual cash value but only half enough to replace it. We should ask our agent about replacement cost insurance on it and our other buildings.

3. There are two insurers on Building #2, and one of them is pretty weak financially. We would be far better off to have all our property insurance with one strong company. Under the present arrangement, each company is required to pay only half of each loss. If the weak company becomes insolvent, we would be paid for only half of a loss, and it could be inconvenient collecting from the state insolvency fund. Even under the best of circumstances, it is easier to settle claims with one company than with two.

4. According to our policies, there must be a guard on duty whenever the plant is not operating. If there is not, our coverage is suspended. If we had a fire at such a time, the insurer(s) would pay us nothing. We need some system to assure that guards will be on duty when they are required.

5. Perhaps the major problem with our insurance is that it is not part of a total program for handling the risks to which High Country is exposed. We should buy insurance the same way we buy a prescription for medicine—that is, after our problem(s) has been diagnosed. We may have too much insurance or not enough. I suggest that we ask our insurance agent to identify all the risks to which High Country is exposed, help us evaluate them, and show us how they should be handled. We need a risk management program, not just an insurance program.

Key Terms

law of agency
principal
agent
apparent authority
binder
conditional binder
waiver
estoppel
offer
acceptance
consideration

competent parties
legal purpose
legal form
underwriter
underwriting
uberrimae fidei
utmost good faith
representations
material fact
concealment
adhesion

expectations principle
indemnity
insurable interest
leasehold interest
valued policies
subrogation

actual cash value
fair market value
replacement cost
other insurance provisions
personal

Discussion Questions

1. What are the requirements of a contract? Provide an example.

2. Assuming you are a key employee, your employer can buy an insurance policy on your life and collect the proceeds even if you are no longer with the firm at the time of your death. Clearly, if you leave the firm, your employer no longer has an insurable interest in your life and would gain by your death. Would this situation make you uncomfortable? What if you learned that your former employer was in financial difficulty? Do you think the law should permit a situation of this kind? How is this potential problem typically solved? Explain.

3. Michelle Rawson recently moved to Chicago from a small rural town. She does not tell her new auto insurance agent about the two speeding tickets she got in the past year. What problem might Michelle encounter? Explain.

4. You cannot assign your auto policy to a purchaser without the insurer's consent, but you can assign your life insurance policy without the insurer's approval. Is this difference really necessary? Why, or why not?

5. What "rules" am I violating if I sell my car but continue my insurance policy on the car?

6. May the fact that an insurance policy is a contract of adhesion make it difficult for insurers to write it in simple, easy-to-understand terms? Explain.

7. Explain the concepts of waiver and estoppel and provide an example of each.

8. If your house is destroyed by fire because of your neighbor's negligence, your insurer may recover from your neighbor what it previously paid you under its right of subrogation. This prevents you from collecting twice for the same loss. But the insurer collects premiums to pay losses and then recovers from negligent persons who cause them. Isn't that double recovery? Explain.

9. If you have a $100,000 insurance policy on your house but it is worth only $80,000 at the time it is destroyed by fire, your insurer will pay you only $80,000. You paid for $100,000 of insurance but you get only $80,000. Aren't you being cheated? Explain.

10. Who makes the offer in insurance transactions? Why is the answer to this question important?

4.1 Henrietta Hefner lives in northern Minnesota. She uses a woodburning stove to heat her home. Although Henrietta has taken several steps to ensure the safety of her stove, she does not tell her insurance agent about it because she knows that most woodburning stoves represent uninsurable hazards.

1. Explain to Henrietta why she ought to tell her insurance agent about the stove.

2. What coverage would the insurer be required to provide if a windstorm (a covered peril) damaged Henrietta's home? (Assume the insurer discovers the woodburning stove while investigating the windstorm damage.)

4.2 Walter Brown owns a warehouse in Chicago. The building would cost $400,000 to replace at today's prices, and Walter wants to be sure he's properly insured. He feels he'll be better off to have two $250,000 replacement cost property insurance policies on the warehouse, because "then I'll know if one of the insurers is giving me the run-around. Anyhow, you have to get a few extra dollars to cover expenses if there's a fire—and I can't get that from one company."

1. If the building is totally destroyed by fire, how much may Walter collect without violating the concept of indemnity?

2. What is Walter's insurable interest? Does it exceed the value of the building?

4.3 Recent litigation over insurance coverage in commercial liability policies has focused on the meaning of the term "occurrence." For example, problems have developed in determining coverage for loss due to cancers caused by inhalation of asbestos fibers. Did loss "occur" when asbestos was inhaled, when cancers developed, or at some other time?

1. What characteristic of insurance would you expect courts and insureds to use in making these decisions?

2. How is the insured business firm benefited and/or impaired by this characteristic?

4.4 During the application process for life insurance, Bill Boggs indicated that he had never had pneumonia, when the truth is that he did have the disease as a baby. He fully recovered, however, and with no permanent ill effects. Bill was unaware of having had pneumonia as a baby until, a few weeks after he completed the application, his mother told him about it. Bill was aware, however, that he regularly smoked three or four cigarettes a day when he answered a question on the application about smoking. He checked a block indicating that he was not a smoker, realizing that nonsmokers qualified for lower rates per $1,000 of life insurance. The insurer could have detected his smoking habit through blood and urine tests. Such tests were not conducted because Bill's application was for a relatively small amount of insurance compared to the insurer's average size policy. Instead, the insurer relied on Bill's answers being truthful.

Twenty months after the issuance of the policy on Bill's life, he died in an automobile accident. The applicable state insurance law makes life insurance policies contestable for two years. The insurer has a practice of investigating all claims that occur during the contestable period. In the investigation of the death claim on Bill Boggs, the facts about Bill's episode of pneumonia and his smoking are uncovered.

1. Will Bill's statements on the application be considered misrepresentations? Discuss what you know about misrepresentations as they could apply in this case.

2. Since the cause of Bill's death was unrelated to his smoking habit, his beneficiary will not accept the insurer's offer to return Bill's premiums plus interest. The beneficiary is insisting on pursuing this matter in court. What advise do you have for the beneficiary?

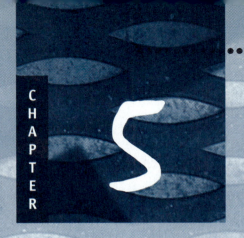

CHAPTER 5

Structure and Analysis of Insurance Contracts

Introduction   As discussed in chapter 4, an insurance policy is a contractual agreement subject to rules governing contracts. Understanding those rules is necessary to comprehend an insurance policy. It is not, however, enough. We will be spending quite a bit of time in the following chapters discussing the specific provisions of various insurance contracts. These provisions add substance to the general rules of contracts already presented and should give you the skills needed to comprehend any policy.

In chapter 5 we offer a general framework of insurance contracts. Because most policies are somewhat standardized, it is possible to present a framework applicable to almost all insurance contracts. Our intent, therefore, is that you will be able to:

1. Identify the five major parts of an insurance policy.
2. Discuss the purpose and effect of each part.
3. Understand why insurance contracts do not cover all possible losses.

Entering Into the Contract

You may recall from chapter 4 that every contract requires an offer and an acceptance. This is also true for insurance. The offer and acceptance occur through the application process.

APPLICATIONS

Although much insurance is sold rather than bought, the insured is still required to make an **application,** which is an offer to buy. The function of the agent is to induce you to make an offer. As a practical matter, the agent also fills out the application for you and then asks you to read and sign it. The application identifies you in more or less detail, depending upon the type of insurance. It also provides information about the exposure involved.

For example, in the application for an automobile policy you would identify yourself, describe the automobile to be insured, indicate the use of the automobile, where it will be garaged, who will drive it, and other facts that help the insurer assess the degree of risk you would represent as a policyholder. Some applications for automobile insurance also require considerable information about your driving and claim experience, as well as information about others who may use the car. In many cases, such as life insurance, the written application becomes a part of the policy. An example is included in appendix E. Occasionally, before an oral or written property/liability application is processed into a policy, a temporary contract, or binder, may be issued.

BINDERS

As discussed in chapter 4, property-liability insurance coverage may be provided while the application is being processed. This is done through the use of a **binder,** which is a temporary contract to provide coverage until the policy is issued by the agent or the company.

In property-liability insurance, an agent who has binding authority can create a contract between the insurance company and the insured. Two factors influence the granting of such authority. First, some companies prefer to have underwriting decisions made by specialists in the underwriting department, so do not grant binding authority to the agent. Second, some policies are cancellable; others are not. The underwriting errors of an agent with binding authority may be corrected by cancellation if the policy is cancellable. Even with cancellable policies, the insurer is responsible under a binder for losses that occur prior to cancellation. If it is not cancellable, the insurer is obligated for the term of the contract.

The binder may be written or oral. When you telephone an agent and ask to have your house insured, the agent will ask for the necessary information, give a brief statement about the contract—the coverage and the premium cost—and then probably say, "You are covered." At this point, you have made an oral application and the agent has accepted your offer by creating an oral binder. The agent may send you a written binder to serve as evidence of the contract until the policy is received. The written binder shows who is insured, for what perils, the amount of the insurance, and the company in which coverage is placed.

In most states an oral binder is as legal as a written one, but in case of a dispute it may be difficult to prove its terms. Suppose your house burns after the oral binder has been made but before the policy has been issued, and the agent denies the existence of the contract. How can you prove there was a contract? Or, suppose the agent orally binds the coverage, a fire occurs, and the agent dies before the policy is issued. Unless there is evidence in writing, how can you prove the existence of a contract? Suppose the agent does not die and does not deny the existence of the contract, but has no evidence in writing. If the agent represents only one company, he or she may assert that the company was bound and the insured can collect for the loss. But what if the agent represents more than one company? Which one is bound? Typically, the courts will seek a method to allocate liability according to the agent's common method of distributing business. Or, if that is not determinable, relevant losses might be apportioned among the companies equally. Most agents, however, keep records of their communication with insureds, including who is to provide coverage.

CONDITIONAL AND BINDING RECEIPTS

Conditional and binding receipts in life insurance are somewhat similar to the binders in property-liability insurance but contain important differences. If you pay the first premium for a life insurance policy at the time you sign the application, the agent will give you either a conditional receipt or a binding receipt. The **conditional receipt** does not bind the coverage at the time it is issued, but it does put the coverage into effect retroactive to the time of application if you meet all the requirements for insurability as of the date of the application. A claim for benefits because of death prior to issuance of the policy generally will be honored, but only if you were insurable when you applied. Some conditional receipts, however, require the insured to be in good health when the policy is delivered.

In contrast, with a **binding receipt,** even if you are found not to be insurable but you die while your application is being processed, a claim for the death benefit will be paid. Thus, the binding receipt provides interim coverage while your application is being processed, whether or not you are insurable.[1] This circumstance parallels the protection provided by a binder in property-liability insurance.

The Contract

Having completed the offer and the acceptance and met the other requirements for a contract, a contract now exists. What does it look like? Insurance policies are composed of five major parts: the declarations, insuring agreement, exclusions, conditions, and endorsements and riders.[2] These parts typically are identified in the policy by headings. Sometimes, however, they are not so prominently displayed, and it is much more common to have explicit section designations in property-liability contracts

---

1. In a few states, the conditional receipt is construed to be the same as the binding receipt. See William F. Meyer, *Life and Health Insurance Law: A Summary,* 2nd ed. (Cincinnati: International Claim Association, 1990), pp. 196–217.
2. A section titled "definition" is also becoming common.

than it is in life-health contracts. Their general intent and nature, however, has the same effect.

DECLARATIONS

Generally, the declarations section is the first part of the insurance policy. Some policies, however, have a cover (or "jacket") ahead of the declarations. The cover identifies the insurer and the type of policy.

Declarations are statements that identify the person(s) or organization(s) covered by the contract, give information about the loss exposure, and provide the basis upon which the contract is issued and the premium determined. This information may be obtained orally or in a written application. The declarations section may also include the period of coverage and limitations of liability. (The latter may also appear in other parts of the contract.)

Period of Coverage

All insurance policies specify the **period of coverage** during which they apply. Life and health policies may cover for the entire life, a specified period of years, or to a specified age. Health policies and term life policies often cover for a year at a time. Most property insurance policies are for one year or less (although longer policies are available). Perpetual policies remain in force until cancelled by you or the insurer. Liability policies may be for a three-month or six-month period, but most are for a year. Some forms of automobile insurance may be written on a continuous basis, with premiums payable at specified intervals, such as every six months. Such policies remain in force as long as premiums are paid or until they are cancelled. Whatever the term during which any policy is to be in force, it will be carefully spelled out in the contract.

Limitations of Liability

All insurance policies have clauses that place **limitations of liability** (maximum amount payable) on the insurer. Life policies promise to pay the face amount of the policy. Health policies typically limit payment to a specified amount for total medical expenses during one's lifetime and have internal limits on the payment of specific services, such as surgery. Property insurance policies specify as limits actual cash value or replacement value, insurable interest, cost to repair or replace, and the face amount of insurance. Limits exist in liability policies for the amount payable per claim, sometimes per injured claimant, and sometimes per year. Defense services, provided in most liability policies, are limited only to the extent that litigation falls within coverage terms and the policy proceeds have not been exhausted in paying judgments or settlements. Because of the high cost of providing defense in recent years, however, attempts to limit insurer responsibility to some dollar amount have been made.

Retained Losses

In many situations, it is appropriate not to transfer all of an insured's financial interest in a potential loss. In chapter 2, for example, we discussed the benefit of retention for the insured when losses are predictable and manageable. For the insurer, some losses are better left with the insured because of moral hazard concerns. Thus, an insured might retain a portion of covered losses through a variety of policy provisions. Some such provisions are deductibles, coinsurance in property insurance, copayments in health insurance, and waiting periods in disability insurance. Each is discussed at some length later in the book. For now, realize that the existence of such provisions typically are noted in the declarations section of the policy.

INSURING CLAUSES

The second major element of an insurance contract, the **insuring clause** or agreement, is a general statement of the promises the insurer makes to the insured. Insuring clauses may vary greatly from policy to policy. Most, however, specify the perils and exposures covered, or at least some indication of what they might be.

Variation in Insuring Clauses

Some policies have relatively simple insuring clauses, such as a life insurance policy, which could simply say, "The company agrees, subject to the terms and conditions of this policy, to pay the amount shown on page 2 to the beneficiary upon receipt at its Home Office of proof of the death of the insured." Package policies are likely to have several insuring clauses, one for each major type of coverage and each accompanied by definitions, exclusions, and conditions. An example of this type is the personal automobile policy, described in chapter 9.

Some insuring clauses are designated as the "insuring agreement," while others are hidden among policy provisions. Somewhere in the policy, however, it states that the "insurer promises to pay . . ." This general description of the insurer's promises is the essence of an insuring clause.

Open-Perils versus Named-Perils

The insuring agreement provides a general description of the circumstances under which the policy becomes applicable. The "circumstances" include the covered loss-causing events, called **perils.** They may be specified in one of two ways.

A **named-perils** policy covers only losses caused by the perils listed. If a peril is not listed, loss resulting from it is not covered. For example, one form of the homeowner's policy HO-2, insures for direct loss to the dwelling, other structures, and personal property caused by eighteen different perils. Only losses caused by these perils are covered. Riot or civil commotion is listed, so a loss caused by either is covered. On the other hand, earthquake is not listed, so a loss caused by earthquake is not covered.

An **open-perils** (formerly called "all risk") policy covers losses caused by all perils except those excluded. The exclusions in an open-perils policy are more definitive of coverage than in a named-perils policy. Generally, an open-perils policy provides broader coverage than a named-perils policy, although it's conceivable, if unlikely, that an open-perils policy would have such a long list of exclusions that the coverage would be narrower.

Moreover, policies written on a named-perils basis cannot cover all possible causes of loss because of the "unknown peril." There is always the possibility of loss caused by a peril that was not known to exist and so was not listed in the policy. For this reason, open-perils policies cover many perils not covered by named-perils policies. This broader coverage usually requires a higher premium than a named-perils policy but is often preferable because it is less likely to leave gaps in coverage.

A recent situation may illustrate an unknown peril. Several emergency room workers were overcome by toxic fumes emanating from the body of a patient in cardiac arrest. An autopsy of the patient did not reveal the cause of the fumes, and no reports of prior similar circumstances have come forth. Before this incident, the peril was unknown and would not have been in a named-perils policy for the health care workers. Consequently, the loss would be covered under an open-perils policy but not under a named-perils policy.[3]

Very few, if any, policies are "all risk" in the sense of covering every conceivable peril. Probably the closest approach to such a policy in the property insurance field is the comprehensive glass policy, which insures against all glass breakage except that caused by fire, war, or nuclear peril. Most life insurance policies cover all perils except for suicide during the first year or the first two years. Health insurance policies often are written on an open-perils basis, covering medical expenses from any cause not intentional. Some policies, however, are designed to cover specific perils such as cancer. Limited peril policies are popular, because many people fear the consequences of certain illnesses. Of course, the insured is well advised to be concerned with (protect against) the loss, regardless of the cause.

Exposures to Loss

Generally, the exposures to be covered are also defined (broadly speaking) in the insuring agreement. For example, the liability policy states that the insurer will pay "those sums the insured is legally obligated to pay for damages . . ." In addition, "The Company shall have the right and duty to defend . . ." The exposures in this situation are legal defense costs and liability judgments or settlements against the insured.

In defining the exposures, important information such as the basis of valuation and types of losses covered is needed. Various valuation methods have already been discussed. Actual cash value and replacement cost are the most common means of valuing property loss. Payments required of defendants, either through mutually acceptable settlements or court judgments, define the value of liability losses. The face value (amount of coverage) of a life insurance policy represents the value paid upon the insured's death. Health insurance policies employ a number of valuation methods, including an amount per day in the hospital or per service provided, or, more likely, the lesser of the actual cost of the service or the customary and prevailing fee for this service. Health maintenance organ-

---

3. Most health insurance policies are open-peril; therefore, the expenses incurred by the workers because of their exposure to the fumes were likely covered. The point is that this situation was completely unexpected.

izations promise the provision of services *per se* rather than a reimbursement of their cost.

The types of covered losses are also generally stated in the insuring agreement. Many property insurance policies, for example, cover only **direct loss.** Direct losses to property are the values physically destroyed or damaged, not the losses caused by inability to use the property. Other policies cover only the loss of use, called **consequential loss.**

Liability policies, on the other hand, may cover liability for **property damage, bodily injury, personal injury,** and/or **punitive damages.** Property damage liability includes responsibility both for the physical damage to property and the loss of use of property. Bodily injury is the physical injury to a person, including the pain and suffering that may result. Personal injury is the nonphysical injury to a person, including damage caused by libel, slander, false imprisonment, and the like. Punitive damages are assessed against defendants for "gross negligence," supposedly for the purpose of punishment and to deter others from acting in a similar fashion.

EXCLUSIONS AND EXCEPTIONS

Whether the policy is open-perils or named-perils, the coverage it provides cannot be ascertained without considering the **exclusions,** which represent the third major part of an insurance policy. You do not know what the policy covers until you find out what it does not cover. Unfortunately, this is not always an easy task. In many policies, exclusions appear not only under the heading "exclusions" in one or more places, but also throughout the policy and in various forms. The homeowners policy section I (which provides property coverage) has two lists of exclusions identified as such, plus others scattered throughout the policy. The last sentence in the description of loss of use coverage, for example, says, "We do not cover loss or expense due to cancellation of a lease or agreement." In other words, such loss is excluded. In "Perils Insured Against," the policy at one point says, "We insure for risks of physical loss to the property . . . . Except," followed by a list of losses or loss causes. Under the heading "Additional Coverages," several coverages are listed and then the following sentence appears: "We do not cover loss arising out of business pursuits . . ." Thus, such loss is excluded.

A policy may exclude specified locations, perils, property, or losses. Perhaps a discussion of the exclusions in some policies and the reasons for them will help you find them in your policies.

Reasons for Exclusions

Four broad reasons, with some overlap, exist for placing exclusions in insurance policies. Each relates to some element(s) of the requisites of an ideally insurable risk, as discussed in chapter 3.

One reason exclusions exist is to *avoid financial catastrophe* for the insurer, which may result if many dependent exposures are insured and/or a single, large-value exposure is insured. Because war would affect many exposures simultaneously, losses caused by war are excluded in most policies in order to avoid catastrophe.

Exclusions also exist to limit coverage of *nonfortuitous* events. Losses that are not accidental make prediction difficult, cause coverage to be expensive, and represent circumstances in which coverage would be contrary to public policy. As a result, losses caused intentionally (by the insured) are excluded. So too are naturally occurring losses, which are expected. Wear and tear, for instance, is excluded from coverage. Adverse selection and moral hazard are limited by these exclusions.

Adverse selection is limited further by use of specialized policies and endorsements that *standardize the risk*. That is, limitations (exclusions) are placed in standard policies for exposures that are nonstandard. Those insureds who need coverage for such nonstandard exposures purchase it specifically. For example, homeowners policies limit theft coverage on jewelry and furs to a maximum amount ($2,500). Exposures in excess of the maximum are atypical, representing a higher probability (and severity) of loss than exists for the average homeowner. Insureds who own jewelry and furs with values in excess of the maximum must buy special coverage (if desired).

Similarly, some exclusions exist to *avoid duplication* of coverage with policies specifically intended to insure the exposure. For example, neighbors Smith and Jones may have very similar exposures to loss from liabilities arising out of their home activities. Smith, however, received three speeding tickets within the past year, while Jones had none. Generally, an insurer may believe that Smith's automobile liability exposure ought not be lumped in with that of Jones, even if their "home" risks are similar. The homeowners liability coverages exclude automobile liability, workers' compensation liability, and other such exposures that are nonstandard to home and personal activities. Other policies specifically designed to cover such exposures are available and commonly used. To duplicate coverage would diminish insurers' ability to discriminate among insureds and could result in moral hazard if insureds were paid twice for the same loss. A policy clause, termed an **other insurance clause,** addresses the potential problem of duplicating coverage when two or more similar policies cover the same exposure. Through this type of provision, the insurer's financial responsibility is apportioned in such a way that payment in excess of the insured's loss is avoided.

These four reasons for exclusions are manifested in limitations on:

- locations
- perils
- property
- losses

Following is a discussion of the purpose(s) of limiting locations, perils, property, and losses.

Excluded Locations

Some coverages are location specific, such as to buildings. Other policies define the location of coverage. Automobile policies, for example, cover the United States and Canada. Mexico is not covered because of the very high auto risk there. In addition, some governmental entities in Mexico will not accept foreign insurance. Some property policies were written to cover movable property anywhere in the world *except* the eastern bloc countries, likely due to difficulty in adjusting claims. With the breakup of the communist bloc, these limitations are also being abandoned. Yet coverage may still be excluded where adjusting is difficult and/or the government of the location has rules against such foreign insurance.

Excluded Perils

Some perils are excluded because they can be covered by other policies or because they are unusual and require separate rating. The earthquake peril requires separate rating and is excluded, for example, from homeowners policies. It can be insured under a separate policy or added by endorsement for extra premium. Many insureds do not want earthquake coverage, either because they live in an area not prone to earthquakes and/or they think their property is not exposed to the risk of loss caused by an earthquake and do not want to pay the premium required. Given the choice of a homeowners policy, for example, that excluded the earthquake peril at a saving of $50 per year and one that included earthquake coverage but cost $50 more per year, they would choose the former. Many arguments have been made about why insureds make this choice. They include: an expectation that federal disaster relief will cover losses, so purchase of insurance is unnecessary; the high deductible (often 10 percent of the value) that makes insurance undesirable; and a belief that "loss won't happen to me." Thus, to keep the price of their homeowners policies competitive, insurers exclude the earthquake peril. It is also excluded because it is an extraordinary peril that cannot easily be included with all the other perils covered by the policy. It must be rated separately.

Some perils, such as those associated with war, are excluded because commercial insurers consider them uninsurable. Nuclear energy perils, such as radiation, are excluded from most policies because of the catastrophe exposure. Losses to homeowners caused by the Three Mile Island incident in 1979, for example, were not covered by their homeowners' insurance.[4]

Transportation policies usually exclude marring and scratching of the insured property because the loss is partially or wholly within the control of the insured or a bailee, who may be careless if such losses are covered. Losses due to wear and tear are excluded because they are inevitable rather than accidental and thus not insurable. Similarly, inherent vice, which refers to losses caused by characteristics of the insured property, is excluded. For example, certain products, such as tires and various kinds of raw materials, deteriorate with time. Such losses are not accidental and are, therefore, uninsurable.

Excluded Property

Some property is excluded because it is insurable under other policies. Homeowners policies, as previously stated, exclude automobiles because they are better insured under automobile policies. Other property is excluded because the coverage is not needed by the average insured, who

4. In 1979 a nuclear meltdown occurred at the Three Mile Island utility plant. Homeowners were forced to evacuate, and property in the area was damaged.

would, therefore, not want to pay for it. For example, most "floater" policies exclude property on exhibition because of the extra hazard, but such coverage is available for an additional premium.[5]

Liability policies usually exclude damage to or loss of others' property in the care, custody, or control of the insured, because property insurance can provide protection for the owner and/or the bailee against losses caused by fire or other perils. Other possible losses, such as damage to clothing being dry-cleaned, are viewed as a business risk involving the skill of the dry cleaner. Insurers do not want to assume the risk of losses caused by poor workmanship or poor management.

Excluded Losses

Losses resulting from ordinance or law—such as those regulating construction or repair—are excluded from most property insurance contracts. Policies that only cover direct physical damage exclude loss of use or income resulting from such damage. Likewise, policies only covering loss of use exclude direct losses. Health insurance policies often exclude losses (expenses) considered by the insurer to be unnecessary, such as the added cost of a private room or the cost of elective surgery.

CONDITIONS

The fourth major part of an insurance contract is the conditions section. **Conditions** enumerate the duties of the parties to the contract and, in some cases, define the terms used. Some policies list them under the heading "Conditions," while others do not identify them as such. Wherever the conditions are stated, you must be aware of them. You cannot expect the insurer to fulfill its part of the contract unless you fulfill the conditions. Remember that acceptance of these conditions is part of the consideration given by the insured at the inception of an insurance contract. Failure to accept conditions may release the insurer from its obligations. Many conditions found in insurance contracts are common to all. Others are characteristic of only certain types of contracts. Some examples follow.

Notice and Proof of Loss

All policies require that the insurer be notified when the event, accident, or loss insured against occurs. The time within which notice must be filed and the manner of making it vary. The homeowners policy, for example, lists as one of the insured's duties after loss to "give immediate notice to us or our agent" and to file proof of loss within sixty days. A typical life insurance policy says that payment will be made "upon receipt . . . of proof of death of the insured." A health policy requires that "written proof of loss must be furnished to the Company within 12 months of the date the expense was incurred." The personal auto policy says, "We must be notified promptly of how, when, and where the accident or loss happened."

In some cases, if notice is not made within a reasonable time after the loss or accident, the insurer is relieved of all liability under the contract. A beneficiary who filed for benefits under an accidental death policy more

....
5. Floater policies cover property wherever it may be, rather than at only specified locations.

ETHICAL *Dilemma*

The Agent's Responsibility

Insurance policies are complex contracts. Most people require the assistance of insurance agents in interpreting their policies. Yet the agent is an employee or representative of an insurance company and may actually have a greater interest in the profitability of the insurer than in the policyholder's ability to have claims paid.

Think about the following example: an insured suffers windstorm damage to her home. In filing the insurance claim, the insured overstates the value of certain property, or so the agent believes. The agent, however, does not know how to prove that the values are inflated. Simultaneously, the agent realizes that the insured failed to claim coverage for debris removal, which is a covered expense. Even though the debris removal expense is less than the inflated values, the agent feels that the trade-off is sufficient not to pursue the issue further. What do you think? Is the agent obligated to inform the insured of all possible coverages? What is the agent's responsibility to the insurer and to all other policyholders whose premiums will rise from the filing of fraudulent claims? Is the agent responsible for payment of the claim, or merely for passing the completed claim form to the insurer, whose claims adjuster will investigate? In this instance, should the agent notify the adjuster of either or both issues? What would you do?

than two years after the insured's death was held in one case to have violated the notice requirement of the policy.[6] The insurer is entitled to such timely notice so it can investigate the facts of the case. Insureds who fail to fulfill this condition may find themselves without protection when they need it most—after a loss.

Suspension of Coverage

Because there are some risks or hazardous situations insurers want to avoid, many policies specify acts, conditions, or circumstances that will cause the **suspension of coverage** or, in other words, that will release the insurer from liability. The effect is the same as if the policy were cancelled or voided, but when a policy is suspended, the effect is only temporary. When a **voidance of coverage** is incurred in an insurance contract, coverage is terminated. Protection resumes only by agreement of the insured and insurer. Suspension, in contrast, negates coverage while some condition exists. Once the condition is eliminated, protection immediately reverts without the need for a new agreement between the parties.

Some life and health policies have special clauses that suspend coverage for those in military service during wartime. When the war is over or the insured is no longer in military service, the suspension is terminated and coverage is restored. The personal auto policy has an exclusion that is

....
6. *Thomas v. Transamerica Occidental Life Ins. Co.*, 761 F. Supp. 709 (1991).

essentially a suspension of coverage for damage to your auto. It provides that the insurer will not pay for loss to your covered auto "while it is used to carry persons or property for a fee," except for use in a share-the-expense car pool. The homeowners policy (form 3) suspends coverage for vandalism and malicious mischief losses if the house has been vacant for more than thirty consecutive days. A property insurance policy may suspend coverage while there is "a substantial increase in hazard."

You can easily overlook or misunderstand suspensions of coverage or releases from liability when you try to determine coverage provided by a policy. They may appear as either conditions or exclusions. Because their effect is much broader and less apparent than the exclusion of specified locations, perils, property, or losses, it is easy to underestimate their significance.

Cooperation of the Insured

All policies require your cooperation, in the sense that you must fulfill certain conditions before the insurer will pay for losses. Because the investigation of an accident and defense of a suit against the insured are very difficult unless he or she will cooperate, liability policies have a specific provision requiring cooperation after a loss. The businessowners policy, for example, says that, "The insured shall cooperate with the Company, and upon the Company's request, assist in . . . making of settlements; conducting of suits . . . ."

It is not unusual for the insured to be somewhat sympathetic toward the claimant in a liability case, especially if the claimant is a friend. There have been situations in which the insured was so anxious for the claimant to get a large settlement from the insurer that the duty to cooperate was forgotten. If you do not meet this condition and the insurer can prove it, you may end up paying for the loss yourself.

This is illustrated by the case of a mother who was a passenger in her son's automobile when it was involved in an accident in which she was injured. He encouraged and aided her in bringing suit against him. The insurer was released from its obligations under the liability policy, on the grounds that the cooperation clause was breached.[7] The purpose of the cooperation clause is to force insureds to perform the way they would if they did not have insurance.

Protection of Property After Loss

Most property insurance policies contain provisions requiring the insured to protect the property after a loss in order to reduce the loss as much as possible. An insured who wrecks his or her automobile, for example, has the responsibility for having it towed to a garage for safekeeping. In the case of a fire loss, the insured is expected to protect undamaged property from the weather and other perils in order to reduce the loss. You cannot be careless and irresponsible just because you have insurance. Yet, the requirement is only that the insured be reasonable. You are not required to put yourself in danger or to take extraordinary steps. Of course, views of what is "extraordinary" may differ.

....
7. *Beauregard v. Beauregard,* 56 Ohio App. 158, 10 N.E.2d 227 (1937).

Examination

A provision peculiar to some disability income policies gives the insurer the right to have its physician examine the insured periodically during the time he or she receives benefits under the policy. This right cannot be used to harass the claimant, but the insurer is entitled to check occasionally to see if he or she should continue to receive benefits. Property insurance policies have a provision that requires the claimant to submit to examination under oath,[8] as well as make records and property available for examination by representatives of the insurance company.

ENDORSEMENTS AND RIDERS

Sometimes (maybe often), but not always, an insurance policy will include a fifth major part: the attachment of endorsements or riders. Riders and endorsements are two terms with the same meaning. **Riders** are used with life-health policies, whereas **endorsements** are used with property-liability policies. A rider or endorsement makes a change in the contract to which it is attached. It may increase or decrease the coverage, change the premium, correct a statement, or make any number of other changes.

The home replacement cost guarantee endorsement, for example, provides replacement cost coverage for a dwelling insured by a homeowners policy, regardless of the limit of liability shown in the declarations. This keeps the amount of insurance on the dwelling up-to-date during the term of the policy. A waiver of premium rider increases the benefits of a life insurance policy by providing for continued coverage without continued payment of premiums if the insured becomes totally disabled. The sound receiving and transmitting equipment endorsement limits coverage of CB radio equipment to that which is permanently installed "in the opening of the dash or console of the automobile normally used by the motor vehicle manufacturer for the installation of a radio."

Endorsements and riders are no easier to read than the policies to which they are attached. Actually, the way some of them are glued or stapled to the policy may discourage you from looking at them. Nevertheless, they are an integral part of the contract you have with the insurer and cannot be ignored. When their wording conflicts with that in exclusions or other parts of the contract, the rider or endorsement takes precedent, negating the conflict.

----

8. Why under oath? Because an oath is "a solemn calling upon God to witness to the truth of what one says," some people will tell the truth under oath when they would not do so otherwise. They may not be sure what "being under oath" means, but they feel that it is a rather serious state of affairs.

Examining the Insurance Transaction

Let's look at the chronology of an insurance experience to see how you can apply what we have discussed in this chapter. The sequence of events is usually as follows:

1. You call the agent or the agent calls you about insurance.
2. You apply for a policy.
3. The insurer decides the terms under which it will insure you.
4. You receive the policy.
5. You pay premiums.
6. You have, or do not have, a loss.

THE APPLICATION

If the transaction is made by telephone, the agent fills out the application and, if your signature is required, asks you to stop by the office and sign it. If you get together in person, the agent asks you questions, fills out the application, and asks you to sign it. The application includes a description of what you want and the information the insurer needs. Similar to the process of ordering a car, before you get around to the written application (order), you have discussed what you want and the terms of the purchase. The application reduces to writing what you have discussed. Remember, in this whole process you are negotiating a contract. The application should indicate what you want and what it will cost. If it does not have all this information, get what you need in writing separately.

Read the application carefully before you sign it. This sounds obvious, but many people have a tendency to skip the reading because they assume that what they have said is what the agent put in the application. But the agent could have misunderstood, edited or ignored what you said. That is improbable, but it has happened. Some agents are not ethical. Because an insurance contract is one of utmost good faith, you must be sure you don't conceal or misrepresent anything. Otherwise, your insurer may deny your request for payment following a loss.

GET A BINDER

If you apply for property or liability insurance, get a written binder from the agent. It is proof of what you ordered and provides coverage immediately. Oral binders are as binding as written ones, but it can be difficult to establish their existence and terms. A binder is a temporary contract and, for your own protection, you should insist on its being written.

GET A BINDING RECEIPT OR CONDITIONAL BINDER

Most life insurance agents will ask you to pay the first premium when you sign the application. By getting the first premium immediately, they avoid having to collect it from you when they deliver the policy. This is usually to your advantage as well. Recognize the benefit for you if the policy is purchased using a conditional binder or, ideally, a binding receipt. Remember that under a conditional binder the application will be processed and, if you qualify, a policy will be issued regardless of what happens to you in the meantime. By getting a binding receipt instead, you are assuring immediate life insurance protection even if you are not insurable. The difference could be significant; however, binding receipts are rarely available.

If the agent cannot issue a binding receipt, get a conditional receipt. At least you will have interim coverage if you are insurable.

RECEIPT OF POLICY

When you take delivery on your new car, what do you do? You probably examine the car carefully to be sure that everything you ordered has been delivered. Is it the color you ordered? Does it have the options you ordered? You may overlook something, but you surely make an effort to see that you are getting what you ordered, because you know you will have to pay for it anyway.

When your insurance policy is delivered, what do you do? Stick it in a drawer? If your agent delivers the policy, you should go over it with him or her carefully to assure that you've gotten what you ordered and you understand what you are getting, including limitations due to exclusions. Refer to the policy checklist shown in figure 5–1 so you won't overlook anything. Remember that the policy you receive is the entire contract between you and the insurance company. Regardless of what you may have been promised, in the process of filling out the application and during other discussions, if it isn't in the policy you don't get it.

FIGURE 5–1

Insurance Policy Checklist

1. Who is insured?
2. Is the information in the declarations correct?
3. What property or types of liabilities are covered? Or, whose life or health is covered?
4. What perils are covered?
5. What losses are covered?
6. What perils, losses, or property are excluded?
7. Does it provide the amount of insurance you requested?
8. Does it have all the endorsements you requested?
9. Does it have the deductible(s) you requested?
10. Does it have the coinsurance clause you requested?
11. How are coverages limited?
12. Under what circumstances can the insurer increase the premium?
13. When is the policy in effect?
14. Where does protection apply?
15. What conditions suspend coverage?
16. What claim settlement alternatives are there?
17. Is the premium payment method suitable?
18. What are your rights and obligations?

PREMIUM PAYMENTS AND CONDITIONS

You must pay premiums to keep an insurance policy in force, but that isn't all you have to do. Beware of the conditions! This is not to imply that they are unfair, but to remind you that you have a conditional contract. If you don't fulfill the conditions, the insurer does not have to keep its promises. An insurance policy is a contract that creates a continuing relationship between you and the insurance company. If it is to be successful, you must do your part. You must know not only your rights but also your obligations.

WHEN YOU HAVE A LOSS

Many people learn most of what they know about their insurance after they have a loss. Such is the case too with many consumer products; we find out how they operate only after purchase. The difference between buying a personal computer and buying insurance, however, is that the computer can be tested in the store before purchase. If it does not quite fit your needs, it can be traded in for a new one, with only the loss of its value in trade-in. Insurance, in contrast, cannot be tested for feel and function before it is used. The policyholder learns about its mechanics only upon the occurrence of a loss, and trade-in is not possible (at least regarding the current loss). Settlement of losses, therefore, is a critical activity for insureds.

Loss settlement procedures and suggestions for problem solving are discussed in chapter 24.

Key Terms

application	consequential loss
binder	property damage
conditional receipt	bodily injury
binding receipt	personal injury
declarations	punitive damages
period of coverage	exclusions
limitations of liability	other insurance clause
insuring clause	conditions
perils	suspension of coverage
named-perils	voidance of coverage
open-perils	riders
direct loss	endorsements

Discussion Questions

1. Dave was just at his insurance agent's office applying for health insurance. On his way home from the agent's office, Dave had a serious accident that kept him hospitalized for two weeks. Would the health insurance policy Dave just applied for provide coverage for this hospital expense?

2. Lightning struck a tree in the Gibsons' yard, causing it to fall over and smash the bay window in their living room. The Gibsons were so distraught by the damage that they decided to go out for dinner to calm themselves. After dinner, the Gibsons decided to take in a movie. When they returned home, they discovered that someone had walked through their broken bay window and stolen many of their valuable possessions. The Gibsons have a homeowners policy that covers both physical damage and theft. As the Gibsons' insurer, do you cover all their incurred losses? Why, or why not?

3. In the chapter on automobile insurance, you will find that portable stereos and tape decks are excluded from coverage. What do you think the insurance company's rationale is for such an exclusion? What are other reasons for insurance policy exclusions? Give examples of each.

4. Joe Phelps is a chemistry aficionado. For his twenty-ninth birthday last month, Joe's wife bought him an elaborate chemistry set to use in their attached garage. The set includes dangerous (flammable) substances, yet Joe does not notify his homeowners insurer. What problem might Joe encounter?

5. Joe Phelps (prior question) has another insurance problem. He had an automobile accident last month in which he negligently hit another motorist while turning right on red. The damage was minor, so Joe just paid the other motorist for the repairs. Fearing the increase in his auto insurance premiums, Joe did not notify his insurer of the accident. Now the other motorist is suing for whiplash. What is Joe's problem, and why?

6. What are the shortcomings of limited peril health insurance policies, such as coverage for loss caused solely by cancer, from a personal risk management point of view?

7. When you apply for a life insurance policy, agent Dawn Gale says, "If you will give me your check for the first month's premium now, the policy will cover you now if you are insurable." Is this a correct statement, or is Dawn just in a hurry to get her commission for selling you the policy? Explain.

8. In deciding between a named-perils and open-perils policy, what factors would you consider? Define both terms and explain your answer.

9. List the four reasons for exclusions and give examples of each (other than those discussed in the chapter).

10. Your careless driving results in serious injury to Linda Helsing, a close personal friend. Because she knows you have liability insurance and the insurer will pay for damages on your behalf, she files suit against you. Wouldn't it be unreasonable for your insurer to expect you not to help Linda pursue maximum recovery in every conceivable way? Explain.

5.1 Kevin Kaiser just replaced his old car with a new one and is ready to drive the new car off the lot. He did not have collision insurance on the old car, but he wants some on the new one.

He calls his friend Dana Goldman, who is an insurance agent. "Give me the works, Dana. I want the best collision coverage you have." Soon after he drives the car away, he is struck by an eighteen-wheeler and the new car is totaled.

Kevin then discovers that he has collision insurance with a $500 deductible which he must pay. He is upset, because to him "the works" meant full insurance for all losses he might have due to collision. Dana had thought that he wanted a more cost-efficient coverage, and had used the deductible to lower the premium. The applicable state law and insurer underwriting practices allow deductibles as low as $250, although they can be much higher.

1. Kevin wants to take Dana to court to collect the full value of the auto. What would you advise him?

2. What does this tell you about oral contracts?

5.2 A. J. Jackson was very pleased to hear the agent say that she was covered the moment she finished completing the application and paid the agent the first month's premium. A. J. had had some health problems previously and really didn't expect to be "covered" until after she had taken her physical and received notice from the company. The agent said that the conditional binder was critical for immediate coverage. "Of course," said the agent, "this coverage may be limited until the company either accepts or rejects your application." The agent congratulated A. J. again for her decision. A. J. began to wonder the next morning exactly what kind of coverage, if any, she had.

1. What kind of coverage did A. J. have?

2. Did her submission to the agent of the first month's premium have any impact on her coverage? Why?

3. If you were the agent, how would you have explained this coverage to A. J.?

5.3 LeRoy Leetch had a heck of a year. He suffered all the following losses. Based on what you know about insurance, which would you expect to be insurable, and why?

1. LeRoy's beloved puppy, Winchester, was killed when struck by a school bus. He has losses of burial expenses, the price of another puppy, and his grief due to Winchester's death.

2. Part of Skylab (NASA's space expedition) enters the earth's orbit and plummets onto LeRoy's greenhouse. The structure, worth $3,000, is completely destroyed.

3. LeRoy has an expensive collection of rare clocks. Most are kept in his spare bedroom and were damaged when a fire ignited due to faulty wiring. The loss is valued at $15,000.

4. Heavy snowfall and a rapid thaw caused flooding in the LeRoy's town. Damage to his basement was valued at $2,200.

5. Weather was hard on the exterior of LeRoy's house as well. Dry rot caused major damage to the first story hardwood floors. Replacement will cost $6,500.

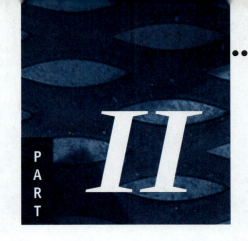

Property and Liability Risks

The Property Exposure

Introduction   Imagine yourself at the library, studying diligently. The sky turns dark and you hear what sounds like the faint rumble of a train. In an instant, you realize that a tornado is coming, and you head for cover. You later learn that the storm hit nearby, demolishing your apartment, leaving the downtown area in a shambles, and damaging parts of the campus. How can the town and university function in the days ahead? How will you manage without clothes, shelter, or any of your personal belongings?

Proper planning beforehand will help lessen the trauma of the rebuilding process. Such planning requires knowledge of the property exposures that might be affected by a storm and an understanding of available property risk management techniques, including property insurance.

This chapter considers the following questions:

1. What is the difference between a direct and consequential loss?
2. What are some loss control methods especially well suited to property exposures?
3. How did property insurance evolve?
4. What types of property and events typically are covered by insurance? What types are excluded?
5. When a loss occurs, what factors affect the insurance coverage amount, and how?

Nature of the Property Exposure

Property can be classified in a number of ways, including its mobility, use value, and ownership. Sometimes these varying characteristics will affect potential losses and, in turn, affect decisions about which risk management options work best. A discussion of these classifying characteristics, including consideration of global property exposures, follows.

PHYSICAL PROPERTY

Physical property generally is categorized as either real or personal. **Real property** represents permanent structures (realty) that if removed would alter the functioning of the property. Any building, therefore, is real property. In addition, built-in appliances, fences, and other such items typically are considered real property.

Physical property that is mobile (i.e., not permanently attached to something else) is considered **personal property.** Included in this category are motorized vehicles, furniture, business inventory, clothing, and similar items. Thus, your house is real property, while your stereo and car are personal property. Some property, such as carpeting, is not easily categorized. The risk manager needs to consider the various factors discussed below in determining how best to manage such property.

Why is this distinction between real and personal property relevant? One reason is that dissimilar properties are exposed to perils with dissimilar likelihoods. When flood threatens your house, the opportunities to protect it are limited. Yet threatened flood damage to something mobile may be thwarted by movement of the item away from floodwaters. You may be able, for example, to drive your car out of the exposed area and to move your clothes to higher ground.

A second reason to distinguish between real and personal property is that appropriate valuation mechanisms may differ between the two. We will discuss later in this chapter the concepts of "actual cash value" and "replacement cost new." Because of moral hazard issues, an insurer may prefer to value personal property at actual cash value (a depreciated amount). The size of depreciation on real property, however, may outweigh concerns about moral hazard. Because of the distinction, valuation often varies between personal and real property.

LOSS OF USE

When property is physically damaged or lost, a cost beyond the physical loss is possible, which is the cost associated with being unable to use that property. Often this is called a **consequential property loss.**[1] Let's first discuss the loss of use of business property, which may result in lost profits due to reduced revenues or increased expense, and then discuss the loss of use of family property.

---

1. Sometimes such losses are referred to as "indirect losses." We will save that term, as is the custom in the insurance industry, to refer instead to situations in which undamaged property loses value due to loss or damage to other property. An expensive chess set values each piece at higher amounts, for example, when the set is complete than when some pieces are missing.

Business Property

Business interruption losses occur when an organization is unable to sell its goods or services, and/or unable to produce goods for sale. Generally, these losses will be due to some property damage. Such lost revenues typically translate into lost profits. The 1992 Chicago flood, for example, required that Marshall Fields' downtown store close its doors for several days while crews worked to clean up damage caused by the floodwaters.[2] When the loss is caused by property damage not owned by the business, it is considered a **contingent business interruption.** If Marshall Fields reduced its orders to suppliers of its goods, for instance, those suppliers may experience contingent business interruption loss caused by the water damage, even though their own property was not damaged.

Alternatively, some organizations choose to continue operating following property damage, but are able to do so only by incurring additional costs. These costs, which also reduce profits, are termed **extra expense** losses. Continuing with the 1992 Chicago flood example, consider the various accounting firms who could not use their offices the second week in April. With the upcoming tax deadline, these firms chose to rent additional space in other locations so they could meet their clients' needs. The additional rental expense (and other costs) resulted in reduced profits to the accounting firms. Yet a variety of service organizations, including accountants, insurance agents, and bankers, prefer to incur such expenses in order to maintain their reputation of reliability upon which long-term success and profits are dependent. Closing down, even temporarily, could badly hurt the organization.

Family Property

Individuals and families too may experience costs associated with loss of use. If your home is damaged, you may need to locate (and pay for) temporary housing. You may also incur abnormal expenses associated with the general privileges of home use, such as meals, entertainment, telephones, and similar conveniences. Likewise, if your car is unavailable following an accident, you must rent a car or spend time and money using other forms of transportation. Thus, while a family's loss of use tends to focus on extra expenses, its effect may be as severe as that of an organization.

GLOBAL PROPERTY EXPOSURES

As mentioned in chapter 2, the fundamental principles of risk management do not differ for exposures within and outside the United States. Various risk attitudes and hazards, however, do differ across borders. One area typically given greater attention for non-U.S. exposures is political risk.

---

2. In April 1992, part of Chicago's underground tunnel system was flooded when the river pushed back a wall far enough to cause a rapid flow of water into the tunnels. Water levels rose high enough to damage stored property, force electrical supplies to be shut off, and cause concern about the stability of structures built above the tunnels.

Political risk can be defined as unanticipated political events that disrupt the earning or profit-making ability of an enterprise. Nationalization of an industry or expropriation of an enterprise are extreme examples of political risk. The imposition of exchange controls that would restrict or prohibit the transfer of profits back to the home country is another form of political risk.

Despite periodic public discontent in the United States, notably the L.A. riots in 1992, the Chicago riots in 1968, various labor activities, prison lockouts, and other events, the U.S. governmental authority has remained generally stable since the end of the Civil War. Such stability, however, is rare in many parts of the world. Governmental instability leads to both speculative and pure risks. Organizations that operate in some fashion outside of the United States must consider these risks.[3]

To provide coverage for such risks, the United States government in 1948 established an insurance program administered through the Overseas Private Investment Corporation (OPIC). Coverages available include expropriation, confiscation, war risks, civil strife, unfair calling of guarantees, contract repudiation, and currency inconvertibility. These coverages are defined in table 6–1. OPIC insurance is available only in limited amounts, and only in certain developing countries that have signed bilateral trade agreements with the United States for projects intended to aid development. Some private insurers, however, also provide political risk insurance. Private insurers do not have the same restrictions as OPIC, but country limits do exist to avoid catastrophe (dependent exposure units). Additional coverages such as kidnap, ransom, and export license cancel-

TABLE 6–1

Political Risk Insurance Definitions*

EXPROPRIATION: acts by governments which prevent the owners of business operations from being able to continue those operations and exercise their rights regarding the operations. In effect, expropriation involves the involuntary takeover of business by governments.

CONFISCATION: acts by governments which prevent an owner's use of property.

WAR, REVOLUTION, AND INSURRECTION: attempts by organized groups to overthrow the governmental authority or oust it from a particular geographic region. Compensable damages result from military actions (including sabotage) by the revolutionary forces or the government defenders.

CIVIL STRIFE: politically motivated attacks on U.S. property, such as those connected with terrorist activities.

UNFAIR CALLING OF GUARANTEES: refusal to honor reexport licenses, preventing contractors from taking equipment out of the country upon contract completion.

CONTRACT REPUDIATION: arbitrary contract termination or material default, without fair compensation, by a foreign government (or private entity when induced by the direct/indirect interference of the foreign government).

CURRENCY INCONVERTIBILITY: to prevent/restrict conversion of local currency to U.S. dollars or other hard currency for use in external payment of imported goods or services through the direct operation of a law, decree, or regulation of the host country, or failure of exchange authorities to act on a proper application for converting local currency.

*These definitions represent paraphrasing from those used by the Overseas Private Investment Corporation (OPIC) and the American International Group (AIG) political risk policies.

3. Political risks exist within the U.S. as well, but at generally low probabilities. The U.S. boycotts of Olympic games is an example of a U.S. political risk.

lation are also provided by private insurers. Recent poor experience in this line of insurance has made coverage more difficult and costly to obtain.

METHODS FOR MANAGING POTENTIAL PROPERTY LOSSES

This text focuses on the use of insurance for managing risks, yet all available tools are important for consideration. Regarding property exposures, the desired tools may differ between physical losses and loss of use. Global property exposures may also call for special treatment.

Loss control is an essential aspect of managing any risk. For physical property exposures, consideration ought to be given to controls such as sprinklers, alarms, inspections (for wiring problems, boiler maintenance, and the like), security systems, and educational programs. Controlling effects from loss of use might include pre-loss contractual arrangements for use of space or machinery if needed, diversification of suppliers and buyers to limit dependence on any single one, and preparation of a detailed plan of action in the event of a major work shutdown.

The use of loss control and loss financing outside of the U.S. tends to differ from practices within the United States. Such variations may reflect cultural differences, insurance markets that do not offer price reductions for improved (lower) loss experience, unavailability of safe materials, or some combination of factors. Most people do believe, however, that safety has been given greater attention in the U.S. than elsewhere. A U.S.-based firm, therefore, needs to decide whether or not to implement general safety programs globally or just locally. With regard to political risks, a global organization can reduce losses by maintaining positive local relationships, employing local workers whenever possible, and responding to local attitudes.

Unless avoidance is used, some form of loss financing is always required. Most families and organizations purchase insurance for physical property damage. Large organizations with geographically dispersed properties very likely use extensive retention programs, because property losses are quite predictable. Coverage against and/or preparation for loss of use, however, tends to receive less attention than does the possibility of direct property damage. This is unfortunate, because loss of use can greatly exceed direct property damage and often leads to bankruptcy of affected firms. The proper tools to protect against property risks will depend on characteristics of the individual or organization exposed to loss, as well as of the potential loss itself. A discussion of some of these issues was presented in chapter 2. Property insurance is discussed generally below, and more specifically in following chapters.

General Property Coverage

While property insurance as a distinct contractual agreement did not become known (at least as far as the authors are aware) until the seventeenth century, the practices of risk transfer and loss distribution have been used for ages. Religious communities, for example, shared the burdens of member losses by contributing to a general fund and/or offering "in kind" compensation when disaster hit. Often, when a member lost a house to fire, the others would bring supplies and help rebuild it. Risk shifted, in essence, to the group, with each member contributing a small portion of the cost.

As population density has increased, opportunities for catastrophic fires have grown. With minimal firefighting ability and the construction of buildings too close to one another to stop the spread of fire, a single spark could result in acres of destruction. It is believed that such conditions, which contributed to the tremendous losses in the London fire of 1666, also led to the first property insurance contract. This story is presented in most discussions of early property insurance. Its validity is uncertain, but the general theme is believable. Nicholas Barbón is said to have become a construction contractor following the London fire. He is believed to have offered an unusual promise: that he would rebuild any of his structures for free were it again destroyed by fire. This promise of Barbón's was so popular that eventually it became available at a fee separate from the construction of a building. Thus began property insurance as an industry.

The value of such a promise was limited, however, because opportunities for catastrophic fire losses remained. Limitations on communication and transportation (no phones, no cars) made dispersion of covered properties difficult for insurers. Thus, when fire damaged large geographic areas, insurers often had too many simultaneous claims to be able to pay all their obligations. Some insureds, therefore, had no coverage. In later years, regulators and industry leaders encouraged efforts to overcome communication and transportation limitations in hopes of yielding a wider geographical distribution of exposures covered by each insurer. If this were accomplished, a single fire would be unlikely to bankrupt any given insurer, because only a small portion of the insurer's policyholders would be affected.

Geographical dispersion, however, caused its own problems. By removing the local ties between insurer and policyholder, the two parties were unlikely to know each other directly. Without a personal relationship, the two had little or no basis of trust. In response, insurers needed to develop extensive policy provisions to account for the various situations in which the insured might find itself, and which previously were managed through the direct relationship of the parties. These provisions were drafted separately by each insurer, leading to lack of uniformity in coverage. The provisions also became quite lengthy and complex. Consumers found themselves unable to compare products, or even understand their provisions.

The growth of the industry in this somewhat haphazard manner served ultimately to cause insureds confusion and frustration about coverage. This confusion led to extensive use of our judicial system for interpretation of policy language, which in turn yielded extensive costs in time, effort, and legal counsel. The only logical solution appeared to be standardization (or uniformity) of policy language.

The first **standard fire policy** (SFP) came into effect during the late 1800s. Two revisions of the SFP were made, in 1918 and 1943. Most recently, the SFP has been largely removed from circulation, replaced instead by homeowners policies for residential property owners and the **commercial package policy** (CPP), or some close variant, for commercial property owners. The SFP was simple (compared with prior contracts) and relatively clear. Most of its original provisions are still found in current policies, updated for the needs of today's insured. A copy of an SFP is shown on the following page to provide an example of property insurance

STANDARD FIRE INSURANCE POLICY for Alabama, Alaska, Arizona, Arkansas, Colorado, Connecticut, Delaware District of Columbia, Florida, Georgia, Hawaii, Idaho, Illinois, Indiana, Iowa, Kansas, Kentucky, Louisiana, Maine, Maryland, Michigan, Mississippi, Missouri, Montana, Nebraska, Nevada, New Hampshire, New Jersey, New Mexico, New York, North Carolina, North Dakota, Ohio, Oklahoma, Oregon, Pennsylvania, Rhode Island, South Carolina, South Dakota, Tennessee, Utah, Vermont, Virginia, Washington, West Virginia, Wisconsin and Wyoming.

No.　　　　　　　　　　　　　　　　　　　　　　　　　　　　　　　　　　　　NONASSESSABLE

STANDARD FIRE POLICY

Insured's Name and Mailing Address

Policy Term:　INCEPTION (Mo. Day Year)　　EXPIRATION (Mo. Day Year)　　YEARS

$_____
Div. on Exp Pol.　　　Renewal of _____

It is important that the written portions of all policies covering the same property read exactly alike. If they do not, they should be made uniform at once.

INSURANCE IS PROVIDED AGAINST ONLY THOSE PERILS AND FOR ONLY THOSE COVERAGES INDICATED BELOW BY A PREMIUM CHARGE AND AGAINST OTHER PERILS AND FOR OTHER COVERAGES ONLY WHEN ENDORSED HEREON OR ADDED HERETO

Item No.	DESCRIPTION AND LOCATION OF PROPERTY COVERED Show address (No., Street, City, County, State, Zip Code), construction, type of roof and occupancy of building(s) covered or containing property covered. If occupied as a dwelling state if building is a seasonal or farm dwelling. If commercial state exact nature of product (and whether manufacturer, wholesaler or retailer) or the service or activity involved.	Protection Class	Dwelling Business Only			
			No. of Families	Feet From Hydrant	Miles From Fire Dept.	Zone
1.						

Item No.	PERIL(S) INSURED AGAINST AND COVERAGE(S) PROVIDED (INSERT NAME OF EACH)	Per Cent of Co-Insurance Applicable	Deductible Amount	Amount of Insurance	Rate	Prepaid or Installment Premium Due At Inception	Installment Premium Due At Each Anniversary
1.	FIRE AND LIGHTNING EXTENDED COVERAGE			$ x x x x x x x		$	$

Special provision applicable only in State of Mississippi—**Total Insurance**—See form attached—
Item 1, $　　　　　; Item 2, $　　　　　; Item 3, $

Special provision applicable only in State of So. Carolina—**Valuation Clause**—See form attached—
Item , $　　　　; Item , $　　　　; Item , $

TOTAL(S)	$		$
TOTAL PREMIUM FOR POLICY TERM PAID IN INSTALLMENTS	$		

Subject to Form No(s).　　　　　　　　　　　　　　　　　　　　　　　　　　**attached hereto.**

INSERT FORM NUMBER(S) AND EDITION DATE(S)

Mortgage Clause: Subject to the provisions of the mortgage clause attached hereto, loss, if any, on building items, shall be payable to:

INSERT NAME(S) OR MORTGAGEE(S) AND MAILING ADDRESS(ES)

COUNTERSIGNATURE DATE	AGENCY AT	AGENT

IN CONSIDERATION OF THE PROVISIONS AND STIPULATIONS HEREIN OR ADDED HERETO

AND OF the premium above specified, this Company, for the term of years specified above from inception date shown above At Noon (Standard Time) to expiration date shown above At Noon (Standard Time) at location of property involved, to an amount not exceeding the amount(s) above specified, does insure the insured named above and legal representatives, to the extent of the actual cash value of the property at the time of loss, but not exceeding the amount which it would cost to repair or replace the property with material of like kind and quality within a reasonable time after such loss, without allowance for any increased cost of repair or reconstruction by reason of any ordinance or law regulating construction or repair, and without compensation for loss resulting from interruption of business or manufacture, nor in any event for more than the interest of the insured, against all **DIRECT LOSS BY FIRE, LIGHTNING AND BY REMOVAL FROM PREMISES ENDANGERED BY THE PERILS INSURED AGAINST IN THIS POLICY, EXCEPT AS HEREINAFTER PROVIDED,** to the property described herein while located or contained as described in this policy, or pro rata for five days at each proper place to which any of the property shall necessarily be removed for preservation from the perils insured against in this policy, but not elsewhere.

Assignment of this policy shall not be valid except with the written consent of this Company.

This policy is made and accepted subject to the foregoing provisions and stipulations and those hereinafter stated, which are hereby made a part of this policy, together with such other provisions, stipulations and agreements as may be added hereto, as provided in this policy.

TA8-3

1 **Concealment,** This entire policy shall be void if, whether
2 **fraud.** before or after a loss, the insured has wil-
3 fully concealed or misrepresented any ma-
4 terial fact or circumstance concerning this insurance or the
5 subject thereof, or the interest of the insured therein, or in case
6 of any fraud or false swearing by the insured relating thereto.
7 **Uninsurable** This policy shall not cover accounts, bills,
8 **and** currency, deeds, evidences of debt, money or
9 **excepted property.** securities; nor, unless specifically named
10 hereon in writing, bullion or manuscripts.
11 **Perils not** This Company shall not be liable for loss by
12 **included.** fire or other perils insured against in this
13 policy caused, directly or indirectly, by: (a)
14 enemy attack by armed forces, including action taken by mili-
15 tary, naval or air forces in resisting an actual or an immediately
16 impending enemy attack; (b) invasion; (c) insurrection; (d)
17 rebellion; (e) revolution; (f) civil war; (g) usurped power; (h)
18 order of any civil authority except acts of destruction at the time
19 of and for the purpose of preventing the spread of fire, provided
20 that such fire did not originate from any of the perils excluded
21 by this policy; (i) neglect of the insured to use all reasonable
22 means to save and preserve the property at and after a loss, or
23 when the property is endangered by fire in neighboring prem-
24 ises; (j) nor shall this Company be liable for loss by theft.
25 **Other Insurance.** Other insurance may be prohibited or the
26 amount of insurance may be limited by en-
27 dorsement attached hereto.
28 **Conditions suspending or restricting insurance. Unless other-**
29 **wise provided in writing added hereto this Company shall not**
30 **be liable for loss occurring**
31 (a) while the hazard is increased by any means within the con-
32 trol or knowledge of the insured; or
33 (b) while a described building, whether intended for occupancy
34 by owner or tenant, is vacant or unoccupied beyond a period of
35 sixty consecutive days; or
36 (c) as a result of explosion or riot, unless fire ensue, and in
37 that event for loss by fire only.
38 **Other perils** Any other peril to be insured against or sub-
39 **or subjects.** ject of insurance to be covered in this policy
40 shall be by endorsement in writing hereon or
41 added hereto.
42 **Added provisions.** The extent of the application of insurance
43 under this policy and of the contribution to
44 be made by this Company in case of loss, and any other pro-
45 vision or agreement not inconsistent with the provisions of this
46 policy, may be provided for in writing added hereto, but no pro-
47 vision may be waived except such as by the terms of this policy
48 is subject to change.
49 **Waiver** No permission affecting this insurance shall
50 **provisions.** exist, or waiver of any provision be valid,
51 unless granted herein or expressed in writing
52 added hereto. No provision, stipulation or forfeiture shall be
53 held to be waived by any requirement or proceeding on the part
54 of this Company relating to appraisal or to any examination
55 provided for herein.
56 **Cancellation** This policy shall be cancelled at any time
57 **of policy.** at the request of the insured, in which case
58 this Company shall, upon demand and sur-
59 render of this policy, refund the excess of paid premium above
60 the customary short rates for the expired time. This pol-
61 icy may be cancelled at any time by this Company by giving
62 to the insured a five days' written notice of cancellation with
63 or without tender of the excess of paid premium above the pro
64 rata premium for the expired time, which excess, if not ten-
65 dered, shall be refunded on demand. Notice of cancellation shall
66 state that said excess premium (if not tendered) will be re-
67 funded on demand.
68 **Mortgagee** If loss hereunder is made payable, in whole
69 **interests and** or in part, to a designated mortgagee not
70 **obligations.** named herein as the insured, such interest in
71 this policy may be cancelled by giving to such
72 mortgagee a ten days' written notice of can-
73 cellation.
74 If the insured fails to render proof of loss such mortgagee, upon
75 notice, shall render proof of loss in the form herein specified
76 within sixty (60) days thereafter and shall be subject to the pro-
77 visions hereof relating to appraisal and time of payment and of
78 bringing suit. If this Company shall claim that no liability ex-
79 isted as to the mortgagor or owner, it shall, to the extent of pay-
80 ment of loss to the mortgagee, be subrogated to all the mort-
81 gagee's rights of recovery, but without impairing mortgagee's
82 right to sue; or it may pay off the mortgage debt and require
83 an assignment thereof and of the mortgage. Other provisions

84 relating to the interests and obligations of such mortgagee may
85 be added hereto by agreement in writing.
86 **Pro rata liability.** This Company shall not be liable for a greater
87 proportion of any loss than the amount
88 hereby insured shall bear to the whole insurance covering the
89 property against the peril involved, whether collectible or not.
90 **Requirements in** The insured shall give immediate written
91 **case loss occurs.** notice to the Company of any loss, protect
92 the property from further damage, forthwith
93 separate the damaged and undamaged personal property, put
94 it in the best possible order, furnish a complete inventory of
95 the destroyed, damaged and undamaged property, showing in
96 detail quantities, costs, actual cash value and amount of loss
97 claimed; **and within sixty days after the loss, unless such time**
98 **is extended in writing by this Company, the insured shall render**
99 **to this Company a proof of loss,** signed and sworn to by the
100 insured, stating the knowledge and belief of the insured as to
101 the following: the time and origin of the loss, the interest of the
102 insured and of all others in the property, the actual cash value of
103 each item thereof and the amount of loss thereto, all encum-
104 brances thereon, all other contracts of insurance, whether valid
105 or not, covering any of said property, any changes in the title,
106 use, occupation, location, possession or exposures of said prop-
107 erty since the issuing of this policy, by whom and for what
108 purpose any building herein described and the several parts
109 thereof were occupied at the time of loss and whether or not it
110 then stood on leased ground, and shall furnish a copy of all the
111 descriptions and schedules in all policies and, if required, verified
112 plans and specifications of any building, fixtures or machinery
113 destroyed or damaged. The insured, as often as may be reason-
114 ably required, shall exhibit to any person designated by this
115 Company all that remains of any property herein described, and
116 submit to examinations under oath by any person named by this
117 Company, and subscribe the same; and, as often as may be
118 reasonably required, shall produce for examination all books of
119 account, bills, invoices and other vouchers, or certified copies
120 thereof if originals be lost, at such reasonable time and place as
121 may be designated by this Company or its representative, and
122 shall permit extracts and copies thereof to be made.
123 **Appraisal.** In case the insured and this Company shall
124 fail to agree as to the actual cash value or
125 the amount of loss, then, on the written demand of either, each
126 shall select a competent and disinterested appraiser and notify
127 the other of the appraiser selected within twenty days of such
128 demand. The appraisers shall first select a competent and dis-
129 interested umpire; and failing for fifteen days to agree upon
130 such umpire, then, on request of the insured or this Company,
131 such umpire shall be selected by a judge of a court of record in
132 the state in which the property covered is located. The ap-
133 praisers shall then appraise the loss, stating separately actual
134 cash value and loss to each item; and, failing to agree, shall
135 submit their differences, only, to the umpire. An award in writ-
136 ing, so itemized, of any two when filed with this Company shall
137 determine the amount of actual cash value and loss. Each
138 appraiser shall be paid by the party selecting him and the ex-
139 penses of appraisal and umpire shall be paid by the parties
140 equally.
141 **Company's** It shall be optional with this Company to
142 **options.** take all, or any part, of the property at the
143 agreed or appraised value, and also to re-
144 pair, rebuild or replace the property destroyed or damaged with
145 other of like kind and quality within a reasonable time, on giv-
146 ing notice of its intention so to do within thirty days after the
147 receipt of the proof of loss herein required.
148 **Abandonment.** There can be no abandonment to this Com-
149 pany of any property.
150 **When loss** The amount of loss for which this Company
151 **payable.** may be liable shall be payable sixty days
152 after proof of loss, as herein provided, is
153 received by this Company and ascertainment of the loss is made
154 either by agreement between the insured and this Company ex-
155 pressed in writing or by the filing with this Company of an
156 award as herein provided.
157 **Suit.** No suit or action on this policy for the recov-
158 ery of any claim shall be sustainable in any
159 court of law or equity unless all the requirements of this policy
160 shall have been complied with, and unless commenced within
161 twelve months next after inception of the loss.
162 **Subrogation.** This Company may require from the insured
163 an assignment of all right of recovery against
164 any party for loss to the extent that payment therefor is made
165 by this Company.

STATE EXCEP-TIONS
FLORIDA AND WISCONSIN: The words "five days'" in line 62 are changed to "ten days'."
IDAHO: The words "five days" in line 58 are changed to "twenty days."
KANSAS: The words "demand and" in line 58 and "on demand" in lines 65 and 67 are deleted. The words "twelve months" in line 161 are changed to "sixty months."
MAINE: The words "five days" in line 62 are changed to "ten days'." The words "twelve months" in line 161 are changed to "two years."
NEW YORK: The words "twelve months" in line 161 are changed to "two years."
NORTH CAROLINA: The words "twelve months" in line 161 are changed to "three years."
NORTH DAKOTA: The words "twelve months" in line 161 are changed to "thirty-six months."
OREGON: The word "Noon" in the In Consideration provision is changed to "12:01 A.M."
WYOMING: The words "sixty days" in line 151 are changed to "forty-five days." The words "twelve months" in line 161 are changed to "four years."

language. You might find it interesting to refer to the SFP when reading about standard property insurance provisions.

General Property Coverage Provisions

Both the homeowners and CPP policy forms will be presented in detail in later chapters. In this section, however, we will offer some general guidelines to understanding property insurance. Four topics will be discussed: covered property, covered losses, covered perils, and determination of payment.

COVERED PROPERTY

Most property insurance policies utilize the distinction between real and personal property to designate what is covered, when, and for how much. In the homeowners policy, for example, separate sections are devoted to dwelling and other structures (i.e., real property) and personal property. Similarly, coverage "a" of the buildings and personal property form of the commercial package policy relates to buildings, while coverage "b" relates to business personal property. The insured must read the insuring agreement(s) of the relevant insurance policy to determine specifics about types of covered property.

COVERED LOSSES

Previously we discussed the distinction between physical damage, or loss of property, and the loss caused by being unable to use that property. The physical damage or loss of property is termed **direct loss.** The loss of use, defined earlier, is considered a consequential loss. This differentiation can be significant, because the impact of a consequential loss may be several multiples of that related to the direct loss. An insured would be more apt to recognize the need for the direct loss coverage, because it is more obvious. In turn, a significant uninsured consequential loss exposure may occur.

Both the homeowners and commercial property policies provide consequential loss coverage. Included in the protection are such added expenses as renting extra space for living or for conducting business while the covered property is being repaired, and the loss of profits or rental income that would accrue from the unavailability of the premises for use. Note also that although we are focusing on the homeowners and commercial property policies, many other policies also provide property coverage. The most obvious example to you may be your auto policy, which covers certain losses to your vehicles. We are using the homeowners and commercial property policies for illustration here because they provide sufficiently broad coverage to include most of the general provisions discussed in this chapter. The auto policy is more narrow, not providing coverage for real property, for example.

COVERED PERILS

Coverage of perils on either a named or open basis has been discussed previously. In many property policies, perils are covered in one of three ways: a basic list, a broad list, or everything covered unless excluded (open perils). In addition, a number of specialized coverages have developed over time. As a result, specific policies exist to cover particular causes of loss. These include crime, transportation (ocean and inland marine), flood, earthquake, and explosion of major power equipment (boiler and machinery).

The development of property insurance in this way is a historical artifact. With fire insurance as the catalyst, policies were devised to cover just one or several perils. As insurers became more familiar with rating and underwriting a variety of perils, extensions of coverage beyond fire became the norm. Today, the inclusion of most perils in a single policy (or package) seems to be most prevelent. Examples of basic, broad, and open perils coverages are found in chapter 8 (homeowner's policies) and chapter 10 (commercial package policies). We should also note that ocean marine coverage, which protects against losses associated with water transportation, mostly for shipment of cargo, developed quite differently. Ocean marine provided broad, open-perils-type coverage from the start.

DETERMINATION OF PAYMENT

Once it is determined that a covered peril has caused a covered loss to covered property, several other policy provisions are invoked to calculate the covered amount of compensation. Important provisions in this calculation are the valuation clause, deductibles, coinsurance and other insurance clause.

Valuation Clause

The intent of insurance is to indemnify an insured. Payment on an **actual cash value** basis is most consistent with the indemnity principle, as discussed in chapter 4. Yet, the deduction of depreciation can be both severe and misunderstood. In response, property insurers often offer coverage on a **replacement cost new** (RCN) basis, which does not deduct depreciation in valuing the loss. Rather, RCN is the value of the same property that has been lost or destroyed if it were bought new or rebuilt on the day of the loss.

You might recall the example we used in chapter 4. We considered the possibility that your ten-year-old roof (with an expected life of twenty years) was destroyed by a covered peril. The cost to repair the roof may be $4,000, but depreciation is equal to $2,000. Under RCN, the full $4,000 loss is covered, and you have a new roof. As mentioned in chapter 4, such valuation may, or may not, promote moral/morale hazards.

Deductibles

The cost of insurance to cover frequent losses (as experienced by many property exposures) is high, eventually approaching the amount of insurance protection afforded by the insurer. To alleviate the financial strain of frequent small losses, many insurance policies include a deductible.

A deductible requires you to bear some portion of a loss before the insurer is obligated to make any payment. The purpose of deductibles is to reduce costs for the insurer, thus making lower premiums possible. The insurer saves in three ways. First, the insurer is not responsible for the amount you bear. Second, because most losses are small, the number of

ETHICAL *Dilemma*

Should You Make a Claim?

Not too long ago, a medium-sized city in the United States experienced a significant hailstorm. Most of the damage was to automobiles out in the open, but other property was also affected, especially roofs. Suppose that your roof was nearing the age when replacement is appropriate, and hail damage added relatively little to the poor status of the roof. Separating the hail damage from the normal wear and tear, however, was quite difficult. If you have replacement cost coverage, repair of the hail-damaged roof would give you a new roof, free! Free, of course, except for any premium paid, deductible, increase in premium, or guilt. What is appropriate? You paid for replacement cost coverage. The storm caused some, even if only minor, damage. Is it your fault that the roof was near replacement time anyway? Would it have made a difference to your insurer had you just put in a new roof last year? Think about the positive and negative arguments to making an insurance claim for your roof. Also consider the insurer's appropriate response to such a claim on insurance coverage.

claims for loss payment is reduced, thereby reducing the claims processing costs. Third, the moral and morale hazards are lessened, because you are more interested in preventing loss when you have to bear part of the burden.[4]

The small, frequent losses associated with property exposures are good candidates for deductibles, because their frequency minimizes risk (the occurrence of a small loss is nearly certain) and their small magnitude makes retention affordable. The most common forms of deductibles in property insurance are:

1. Straight deductible
2. Franchise deductible
3. Disappearing deductible

A **straight deductible** requires you to pay for all losses less than a specified dollar amount, and that specified amount of all other losses. If, for example, you have a $200 deductible on the collision coverage part of your auto policy, you pay the total amount of any loss that does not exceed $200. In addition, you pay $200 of every loss in excess of that amount. If you have a loss of $800, therefore, you pay $200 and the insurer pays $600.

A **franchise deductible** is similar to a straight deductible, except that once the amount of loss equals the deductible, the entire loss is paid in full.

---

4. For example, residents of a housing development had full coverage for windstorm losses (that is, no deductible). Their storm doors did not latch properly, so wind damage to such doors was common. The insurer paid an average of $100 for each loss. After doing so for about six months, it added a $50 deductible to the policies as they were renewed. Storm door losses declined markedly when insureds were required to pay for the first $50 of each loss.

This type of deductible is common in ocean marine cargo insurance, although it is stated as a percentage of the value insured rather than a dollar amount. The franchise deductible is also used in crop hail insurance, which provides that losses less than, for example, 5 percent of the crop are not paid, but when a loss exceeds that percentage, the entire loss is paid.

The major disadvantage with the franchise deductible from the insurer's point of view is that the insured is encouraged to inflate a claim that falls just short of the amount of the deductible. If the claims adjuster says your crop loss is 4 percent, you may argue long and hard to get the estimate up to 5 percent. Because it invites moral hazard, a franchise deductible is appropriate only when the insured is unable to influence or control the amount of loss, such as in ocean marine cargo insurance.

The **disappearing deductible** is a modification of the franchise deductible. Instead of having one cut-off point beyond which losses are paid in full, a disappearing deductible decreases as the amount of the loss increases. If, for example, the deductible is $500 and the relevant proportion 111 percent, then 111 percent of the loss above the deductible is paid up to the point at which the deductible disappears, and losses are paid in full. This concept is illustrated in table 6–2.

At one time, homeowners policies had a disappearing deductible. Unfortunately, it took only a few years for insureds to learn enough about its operation to recognize the benefit of inflating claims. As a result, it was replaced by the straight deductible.

The small, frequent nature of most direct property losses makes deductibles particularly important. Deductibles help maintain reasonable premiums because they eliminate administrative expenses of the low-value, common losses. In addition, the nature of property losses causes the cost of property insurance per dollar of coverage to decline with the increasing percentage of coverage on the property. That is, the first 10 percent value of the property insurance is more expensive than the second (and so on) percent value. The cost of property insurance follows this pattern because most property losses are small, and so the expected loss does not increase in the same proportion as the increased percent of the property value insured.

Coinsurance

Besides making *first-dollar coverage* (coverage without a deductible) expensive, the nature of property losses provides disincentives for insureds to buy adequate amounts of insurance. To illustrate, consider an insured who

TABLE 6–2

How the Disappearing Deductible Disappears

AMOUNT OF LOSS	LOSS PAYMENT	DEDUCTIBLE
$ 500.00	$ 0.00	$500.00
1,000.00	555.00	445.00
2,000.00	1,665.00	335.00
4,000.00	3,885.00	115.00
5,000.00	4,955.00	5.00
5,045.50	5,045.00	0.00
6,000.00	6,000.00	0.00

knows that most property losses are small.[5] To save money, the insured buys coverage of only 50 percent of the value of the property (premiums are determined in part by the amount of insurance purchased). To charge this insured the same *rate* (price per unit of insurance) as an insured who purchases full coverage would be inequitable, because the cost incurred by the insurer as claims per unit of insurance (for example, per $100 of property) is greater at low values of a given piece of property than at high values. A **coinsurance** provision may be used to avoid such an inequity (and to encourage purchase of insurance closer to the value of the property). Table 6–3 illustrates how rate inequities can develop.

A coinsurance provision first requires that you carry an amount of insurance equal to a specified percentage of the value of the property. The provision (clause) further stipulates a penalty to be applied for failure to carry sufficient insurance. Thus, through the penalty, the insured may be a "coinsurer" if insurance is purchased at less than the required value. The price per unit of insurance declines with the insured's acceptance of a higher coinsurance percentage.

Rates can be reduced for insureds who buy more insurance to value, because charging the same rate regardless of the ratio of insurance to value is not justified by the underlying probability distribution. As the ratio of loss to value goes up, the number of losses in each category of severity declines. For example, there are many losses in which the loss-to-value ratio is less than 10 percent, fewer losses in which it is between 10 and 20 percent, and so on. The number of losses in which the loss-to-value ratio exceeds 80 or

TABLE 6–3

Illustration of Potential for Rate Inequities (Need for Coinsurance Provisions)

Assume 50,000 policyholders, each of whom owns a building valued at $1,000,000 (for a total value of $50,000,000,000). For these 50,000 policyholders, the insurer expects the following losses next year:

5 total losses	$ 5,000,000
95 partial losses (average $150,000 per loss)	14,250,000
TOTAL	$19,250,000

The pure premium rate equals expected losses per exposure unit. One exposure unit for property insurance is $100 of value.

If all the 50,000 insureds buy full coverage, then

$$\text{Pure Premium Rate} = \frac{19,250,000}{500,000,000^*} = .0385 \text{ or approximately 4 cents per \$100 of insurance}$$

If instead, the 50,000 insureds buy coverage of 50 percent of value, then

$$\text{Pure Premium Rate} = \frac{16,750,000^{**}}{250,000,000} = 0.67 \text{ or approximately 7 cents per \$100 of insurance}$$

*$50,000,000,000 value divided by $100 (one exposure unit)
**The full $14,250,000 of partial losses are assumed to fall below 50% of the value. This is added to the 5 total losses at the 50% coverage ($2,500,000) for a total of $16,750,000.

5. Vaughan has said that "statistics gathered by fire-rating bureaus indicate that about 85% of all fire losses are for less than 20% of the value of the property, while only about 5% result in damage in excess of 50% of the property's value." Emmett J. Vaughan, *Fundamentals of Risk and Insurance*, 5th ed., New York: (John Wiley & Sons, 1989).

90 percent is very small compared with the number in the lower percentages. The marginal cost for providing additional increments of insurance declines as the percentage of insurance to the value of the property increases. Therefore, the larger the amount of insurance purchased on any given structure, the lower the unit price can be. Conversely, the smaller the ratio of insurance to value, the higher the unit price must be.

What happens when you fail to have the amount of insurance you agreed to purchase? Nothing happens until you have a partial loss. At that time, you are subject to a penalty. Suppose in January you bought an $80,000 policy for a building with an actual cash value of $100,000, and the policy has an 80 percent coinsurance clause. By the time the building suffers a $10,000 loss in November, its actual cash value has increased to $120,000. The coinsurance limit is calculated as follows:

$$\frac{\text{Amount of insurance carried}}{\text{Amount you agreed to carry}} \times \text{Loss}$$

$$= \frac{\$80,000}{\$96,000 \ (80\% \ \text{of} \ \$120,000)} \times \$10,000 = \$8,333.33$$

Who pays the other $1,666.67? You do. Your penalty for failing to carry the agreed amount of insurance is to bear a part of the loss.

What if you have a total loss at the time the building is worth $120,000, and you have only $80,000 coverage? According to the coinsurance formula, the insurer would pay:

$$\frac{\$80,000}{\$96,000} \times \$120,000 = \$99,999.99$$

You would not receive $99,999.99, however, because the total amount of insurance is $80,000, which is the maximum amount the insurer is obligated to pay. When a loss equals or exceeds the amount of insurance required by the applicable percentage of coinsurance, the coinsurance penalty has no effect. The insurer is not obligated to pay more than the face amount of insurance in any event, because a typical policy specifies this amount as its maximum coverage responsibility.

You save money buying a policy with a coinsurance clause because the insurer charges a reduced premium rate, but you assume a significant obligation. The requirement is applicable to values only at the time of loss, and the insurer is not responsible for keeping you informed of value changes. That is your responsibility.

Values can change imperceptibly. They may increase because the cost of construction has risen. They may also increase as improvements are made to the property. A large additional investment in a plant building creates obvious changes in value, but the cumulative effect of a series of small improvements may easily escape your attention. You may be so busy with the improvements that you forget about your insurance. This situation illustrates why risk managers must review their program continuously to keep it up to date. An option available, and discussed in chapter 10, is to negate the coinsurance clause and simply agree to buy insurance equal to 100 percent of the value of the property at the time the insurance is purchased. Technically, "coinsurance" applies only on an actual cash value basis, but similar provisions may be effective for properties covered on a replacement cost basis. Care should be taken in the purchase of sufficient limits either way.

Other Insurance Clause

It is possible to have more than one policy covering the same property exposure. In that event, arrangements are required to prevent multiple payment on a loss. As noted in chapter 4 in connection with the indemnity principle, an *other insurance* provision is included in most policies to prevent an insured from making a profit on multiple loss payments.

Four types of other insurance provisions are commonly used, and each is described below with respect to property insurance. Keep in mind, however, that an other insurance provision typically becomes relevant for property losses typically only with poor risk management. While coverage may apply for two or more policies in other situations even when proper risk management is followed (for example, when a negligent driver is using a friend's car; in this situation, both the driver's and car owner's policies may be applicable), this condition is rare for property losses. It is unwise to purchase multiple policies on the same property, the most likely situation to result in the application of the other insurance provision for property losses.

One type of other insurance provision is the **pro rata liability clause.** An example of this clause is given in chapter 4. Pro rata liability apportions losses among two or more insurers in the proportion that each policy limit bears to the total amount of coverage on the property.

A second type of other insurance provision creates **primary and excess insurance.** The primary insurer pays first, and the excess insurer pays only after the limits of the primary policy are exhausted.

The commercial property policy stipulates in the second section of its other insurance provision that:

> . . . we will pay only for the amount of covered loss or damage in excess of the amount due from that other insurance, whether collectible or not.

If a business purchases a commercial property policy (discussed in chapter 10) with a limit of $50,000 on personal property, and also owns a special policy on certain unusual equipment with a limit of $10,000, the other insurance clause would come into play for any loss in excess of $10,000 on that property. A $15,000 covered loss, for example, would result in payment of $10,000 from the special policy and $5,000 from the commercial property policy (minus any applicable deductibles or coinsurance penalties). Another example of excess property insurance is the difference in conditions coverage discussed in the international section of chapter 10.

A third other insurance provision is termed **joint loss.** Under this arrangement, each policy contributes proportionally, similarly to the pro rata liability apportionment. Under joint loss, however, the basis of apportionment is the amount each policy would have contributed had no other policy applied. In the example above, where a $50,000 and a $10,000 policy applied toward a $15,000 loss, the first policy would have paid $15,000 and the second $10,000 (if the other policy were not in effect), yielding an apportionment basis of $25,000. Contributions under this arrangement would have been

$$\$9,000 = \left(\frac{15,000}{25,000} \times 15,000\right) \text{ and }$$

$$\$6,000 = \left(\frac{10,000}{25,000} \times 15,000\right) \text{ respectively.}$$

A fourth method to apportion losses among several policies is that of **contribution by equal shares.** Under this method, the loss is distributed evenly across the policies until the lowest face value is reached. At this point, the policy with the lowest face value has no additional coverage to provide on the loss. The remaining policies provide for payment of the remaining loss until the next lowest limit is reached, and so on.

The four forms of other insurance provisions are illustrated in table 6–4.

Generally, purchase of more than one policy to cover the same property exposure is unwise. Two policies issued on the same interest that do not agree in their terms are said to be **nonconcurrent.**[6] If you acquire nonconcurrent policies, you may incur an uninsured loss. Nonconcurrency could result in a pro rata liability distribution of loss based on the relative amount of insurance afforded under each policy, even if one is inapplicable. The outcome is payment less than full. Nonconcurrency does not apply in liability coverage, nor does it apply when two different exposures (such as direct and consequential losses) are involved.

TABLE 6–4
....

Other Insurance Provisions

Loss:	$200,000			
Face Amount:	Policy 1: $ 50,000			
	Policy 2: $100,000			
	Policy 3: $250,000			

	RECOVERY			
	Pro Rata Liability	**Primary/Excess***	**Joint Loss**	**Equal Shares**
Policy 1	$ 25,000	$ 50,000	$ 28,570	$50,000
Policy 2	$ 50,000	$100,000	$ 57,140	$75,000
Policy 3	$125,000	$ 50,000	$114,290	$75,000

*Policy 1 is primary, 2 excess of $50,000, and 3 excess of $150,000.

....
6. S. S. Huebner, Kenneth Black, Jr., and Robert S. Cline, *Property and Liability Insurance*, 3rd ed., Englewood Cliffs, NJ (Prentice-Hall, Inc.: 1982) p. 81.

Managing Global Property Exposures

The world sometimes seems to be shrinking, as travel across national borders becomes more commonplace, economic unions of several countries are developed, the United Nations takes a stronger role in world politics, and business enterprises spread among many nations. All of these conditions, and especially the last, have implications for risk management. Let's consider some of them with respect to property exposures.

NATURE OF EXPOSURES

As discussed at the start of this chapter, categorization of property into real and personal exposures, as well as direct and consequential exposures, is valuable. Some particular issues might arise for global exposures. For example, a common practice is to ship goods into a country for specialized processing and then ship them out again, either as finished or semi-finished goods.

The value of this personal property, therefore, changes as it flows between nations. Insurance coverage needs to provide protection in both nations (all three if shipped to a third country), which could pose problems if either or both nations impose restrictions on the purchase of insurance. Further, the insurance amount must be flexible to reflect increases in value. Coverage is also needed while goods are in transit, not just while those goods are at specified locations.

In addition to insurance needs, a plan to move goods in and out of various countries relies on government willingness to permit it. Sometimes governments unexpectedly close borders, or impose severe import/export restrictions. Alternate plans and diversification of operations will help reduce the impact of such actions. Close and positive relationships with local governments and leaders may also prove helpful.

A slightly different problem may arise regarding real property. Permanent structures are more likely subject to government takeover (expropriation) and local vandalism. Real property cannot be removed from danger, as can personal property. Businesses, therefore, might choose to rent space rather than own realty. They are then subject to landlord whims, but minimize the potential for loss of valuable property.

Consequential losses may also involve some peculiarities on a global basis. Currency inconvertibility (or even just major adjustments in exchange rates) may greatly affect a firm's profits. Furthermore, global organizations may be dependent on various nations for supply and purchase of its goods. Political instability, to distinguish global exposures from domestic exposures, may cut off that supply/purchasing source. For example, many firms are hesitant to become heavily involved in trade with mainland China because of uncertainty over governmental actions. Labor is inexpensive in mainland China, which would encourage development of manufacturing plants; however, such actions involve risk.

GENERAL PROPERTY INSURANCE

In chapter 10 we discuss some specifics of global insurance policies. Here we wish to discuss only those associated with political risk.

Decisions about whether or not to purchase political risk insurance should be made after considering several factors. Cost, of course is one. Cost must be weighed against the likelihood of loss, as well as the potential severity. Political risk analysts sell their information to organizations with the intent of helping to evaluate size and frequency of potential losses. Such information is used both to assess the value of operating in a particular locality, as well as to provide guidance in proper risk management. Sometimes it is preferable to implement loss control rather than to purchase insurance.

If insurance seems appropriate, then the type of coverage to purchase must be chosen. Coverage from the Overseas Private Investment Corporation (OPIC) tends to be less expensive and broader than commercial insurance, but its availability is limited. Commercial insurance is also limited. A risk manager might succeed in obtaining it from Lloyd's of London along with other purchases. The American International Group (AIG) might have a broader selection and/or lower cost. Sometimes other sources also exist.

IMPLEMENTING LOSS CONTROL

As mentioned in the text, most commentators on the subject believe that safety is given a higher priority in the United States than elsewhere. If this is true, or possibly even if it is not, then risk managers of global organizations must evaluate the appropriateness of implementing either worldwide safety programs or more localized loss control.

To decide which is preferable, the risk manager should consider corporate philosophy regarding centralization versus decentralization; the relative benefit of implementing safety in reduced insurance costs; corporate attitude toward safety; local attitude toward safety (and imposition of rules by headquarters); and overall risk management objectives. This process is not too dissimilar from considering multiple domestic locations; perhaps the issues are simply highlighted in a global context.

Key Terms

real property
personal property
business interruption
contingent business interruption
extra expense
political risk
standard fire policy
commercial package policy
direct loss
consequential loss
actual cash value

replacement cost new
straight deductible
franchise deductible
disappearing deductible
coinsurance
pro rata liability clause
primary and excess insurance
joint loss
contribution by equal shares
nonconcurrent

Discussion Questions

1. Distinguish between direct and consequential losses.

2. What is a deductible? Provide illustrative examples of straight, franchise, and disappearing deductibles.

3. What is the purpose of coinsurance? How does the policyholder become a "coinsurer"? Under what circumstances does this occur?

4. Describe the need for other insurance provisions. Give an example of one such provision.

5. What is a standard policy? Why is a standard policy desirable (or undesirable)?

6. Explain the importance of geographical spread in property insurance.

7. What is different about international property exposures as compared with U.S. property exposures?

8. Provide an example of a business interruption loss and of an extra expense loss.

9. Why should a policyholder avoid the purchase of two policies of the same type on the same property?

10. How can knowledge of the history of property insurance help today's students of risk management and insurance?

6.1 Linda Winchester carries three insurance policies on her $400,000 warehouse. The limits are as follows:

Policy 1	$75,000
Policy 2	$100,000
Policy 3	$145,000

A recent fire caused $93,000 of a covered loss to the warehouse. Illustrate the various ways by which the loss might be apportioned among the policies. Assume none of the policies has an applicable coinsurance provision.

6.2 Hurricane Iniki in 1992 caused extensive damage to one of the Hawaiian Islands. A significant loss in tourist activity resulted. Assume the Koehn Hotel experienced $500,000 in damage to its property. Furthermore, assume Koehn typically brought in $100,000 of revenue per month, on which it incurred $80,000 of fixed and variable expenses. For two months following Iniki, the Koehn Hotel was shut down, but still incurred expenses of $50,000. The hotel further spent $15,000 of extra money on advertising before reopening. Based on this information, what would be the insurable consequential losses of the Koehn Hotel from Hurricane Iniki? What could be done to reduce those losses?

6.3 Assume you live on the Texas gulf, where hurricane damage can be extensive. Further assume that you own a two-story frame home valued at $120,000. The house is nicely (although not expensively) furnished. One room is used for your office, where you have placed a computer, printer, fax machine, and your personal library. Almost all your income is generated from work done at home. You also own a 1993 Honda Civic, which you need to get into town, about twenty miles away. Your closest neighbor lives a mile to the south of you, and your property is home to many trees.

1. Identify important property exposures and hazards associated with this scenario.

2. Describe some recommended loss control techniques to manage the described risks.

3. What would be some general mechanisms you could employ to estimate potential losses?

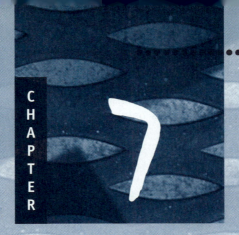

The Liability Risk

Introduction   The headlines are eye-catching: "Manufacturer to Pay Millions for Injury to Customer," "Hospital Sued for Wrongful Birth," "Parent Liable to Children for Automobile Accident." All relate to stories about one party paying another party for some harm associated with their interaction. Fear exists in corporate boardrooms, hospitals, and our own homes that one of us might be the party who must pay. In this chapter we will discuss the various situations that could lead to liability, defenses against liability, and current policy issues regarding the legal system in the United States.

You will consider how to:
1. Define liability and have an appreciation for its intended purpose and operation.
2. Identify various modifications to and defenses against liability, which could be helpful if you are ever involved in a liability lawsuit.
3. Discuss most of the situations that could result in liability and the characteristics of those situations that are likely to affect liability.

Nature of the Liability Exposure

Legal liability is the responsibility, based in law, to remedy some wrong done to another person or organization. Several aspects of this definition deserve further discussion. One involves the "remedy" of liability. A person who has been "wronged" or harmed in some way may ask the court to remedy or compensate for the harm. Usually this will involve monetary compensation, but it could also involve some behavior on the part of the person who committed the wrong, the **tortfeasor.** For example, someone whose water supply has been contaminated by a polluting business may request an injunction against the business to force the cessation of pollution. A realtor who is constructing a building in violation of code may be required to halt construction, based on a liability lawsuit.

When monetary compensation is sought, it can take one of several forms. **Special damages** compensate for those harms generally easily quantifiable into dollar measures. These include medical expenses, lost income, and repair costs of damaged property. Sometimes special damages are termed **economic damages.** Those harms that are just as real, but which are not specifically quantifiable, are called **general damages.** Examples of general damages include pain and suffering, mental anguish, and loss of consortium (companionship). The third type of monetary liability award is **punitive damages.** As will be discussed later in the chapter, controversy surrounds the use of punitive damages. At this point, let's refer to them as awards intended to punish a tortfeasor for exceptionally undesirable behavior. Punitive damages are not intended to compensate for actual harm incurred.

A second important aspect of the definition of liability is that it is "based in law." In this way, liability differs from other exposures because it is purely a creation of societal rules (laws), which reflect social norms. As a result, liability exposures will differ across societies (nations) and over time. In the United States, liability is determined by the courts and by laws enacted by legislatures.

The risk of liability is twofold. Not only may you become liable and suffer loss, but some person or organization may become liable to you. You need to know about both sides of the coin, so to speak. Your financial well-being or that of your organization can be adversely affected by your responsibility to others or by your failure to understand their responsibility to you. If you are the party harmed, you would be the **plaintiff** in litigation. The party being sued is the **defendant.** In some circumstances the parties will be both plaintiffs and defendants.

BASIS OF LIABILITY

The liability exposure may arise out of either statutory or common law, as shown in figure 7–1. **Statutory law** is the body of written law created by legislatures. **Common law,** on the other hand, is based on custom and court decisions. In evolving common law, the courts are guided by the doctrine of **stare decisis.** Under this doctrine, once a court decision is made in a case with a given set of facts, the courts tend to adhere to the principle thus established and apply it to future cases involving similar facts. This practice provides enough continuity of decision making so that many disputes can be settled out of court by referring to previous deci-

FIGURE 7–1

Basis of Liability Risk

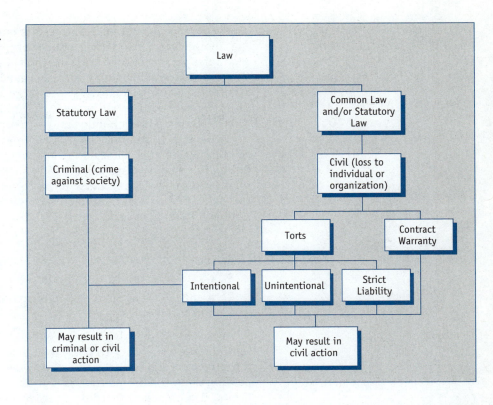

sions. Some people believe that in recent years, as new forms of liability have emerged, continuity has not been as prevalent as in the past.

As illustrated in figure 7–1, the field of law includes criminal law and civil law. **Criminal law** is concerned with acts that are contrary to public policy (crimes), such as murder or burglary. **Civil law,** in contrast, deals with acts that are not against society as a whole, but rather cause injury or loss to an individual or organization, such as carelessly running a car into the side of a building. A civil wrong may also be a crime. Murder, for instance, attacks both society and individuals. Civil law has two branches, one concerned with the law of contracts and the other with the law of torts. Civil liability may stem from either contracts or torts.

Contractual liability occurs in many settings. When you sign a rental agreement for tools, for example, the agreement may provide that the tools will be returned to the owner in good condition, ordinary wear and tear excepted. If they are stolen or damaged, you are liable for the loss. As another example, if you offer your car for sale and assure the buyer that it is in perfect condition, you have made a **warranty.** A warranty is simply a form of contract. If the car is not in perfect condition, you may be liable for damages because of a breach of warranty. This is why some sellers offer goods for sale on an "as is" basis; they want to be sure there is no warranty.

A **tort** is "a private or civil wrong or injury, other than breach of contract, for which the court will provide a remedy in the form of an action for damages."[1] That is, all civil wrongs, except breach of contract, are torts.

1. H. J. Black, *Black's Law Dictionary,* 5th ed. (St. Paul, Minn.: West Publishing Company, 1983), p. 774.

A tort may be intentional, in that it is committed for the purpose of injuring another person or the person's property, or it may be unintentional. Examples of intentional torts include libel, slander, assault, and battery. While a risk manager may have occasion to be concerned about liability arising from intentional torts, the more frequent source of liability is the unintentional tort. By definition, unintentional torts involve **negligence.**

If someone suffers bodily injury or property damage as a result of your negligence, you may be liable for damages. Negligence refers to conduct or behavior. It may be a matter of doing something you should not do, or failing to do something you should. Negligence can be defined as a failure to act reasonably that causes harm to others. It is determined by proving the existence of four elements (sometimes people use three, combining the last two into one). These are:

1. A duty to act (or not to act) in some way.
2. Breach of that duty.
3. Damage or injury to the one owed the duty.
4. A causal connection, called a **proximate cause,** between the breach and the injury.

An example may be helpful. When a person operates an automobile, that person has a duty to obey traffic rules and to drive appropriately for the given conditions. A person who drives while drunk, passes in a no-passing zone, or drives too fast on an icy road (even if within set speed limits) has breached the duty to drive safely. If that person completes the journey without an incident, no negligence exists because no harm occurred. If, however, the driver causes an accident in which property damage and/or bodily injury results, all elements of negligence exist, and legal liability for the resulting harm likely will be placed on the driver.

A difficult aspect of proving negligence is showing that a breach of duty has occurred. Proof requires showing that a reasonable and prudent person would have acted otherwise. Courts use a variety of methods to assess "reasonableness." One is a cost-benefit approach, which holds behavior to be unreasonable if the discounted value[2] of the harm is less than the cost to avoid the harm.[3] In this way, courts use an efficiency argument to determine the appropriateness of behavior.

A second difficult aspect of proving negligence is to show a proximate cause between the breach of duty and resulting harm. Proximate cause has been referred to as an unbroken chain of events between the behavior and harm. The intent is to find the relevant cause, one that could be deterred through assessing liability. The law is written to encourage behavior that is done with consideration of its consequences.

Liability will not be found in all the circumstances just described. The defendant has available a number of defenses, and the burden of proof may be modified under certain fact situations.

----

2. The discounted value of the harm is the size of the potential loss times the probability that the loss would occur.
3. This was first stated explicitly by Judge Learned Hand in *U.S. v. Carroll Towing Co.,* 159 F. 2d 169 (1947).

TABLE 7–1

Defenses Against Liability

Assumption of Risk
Contributory Negligence
Comparative Negligence
Last Clear Chance
Sovereign, Familial, and Charitable Immunity

DEFENSES

A number of defenses against negligence exist, with varying degrees of acceptance. A list of defenses is shown in table 7–1. One is **assumption of risk.** The doctrine of assumption of risk holds that if the plaintiff knew of the dangers involved in the act that resulted in harm, but chose to act in that fashion nonetheless, the defendant will not be held liable. An example would be a bungie cord jumper who is injured from the jump. One could argue that a reasonable person would know that such a jump is very dangerous. If applicable, the assumption of risk defense bars the plaintiff from a successful negligence suit. The doctrine was particularly important in the nineteenth century for lawsuits involving workplace injuries, where employers would defend against liability by claiming that workers knew of job dangers. With workers' compensation statutes in place today, the use of assumption of risk in this way is of little importance. Further, many states have abolished the assumption of risk doctrine in automobile liability cases, disallowing the defense that a passenger assumed the risk of loss if the driver was known to be dangerous or the car unsafe.

A second defense found in just a few states is the doctrine of **contributory negligence,** which disallows any recovery by the plaintiff if the plaintiff is shown to be negligent to any degree in not avoiding the relevant harm. Thus, the motorist who was only slightly at fault in causing an accident may recover nothing from the motorist who was primarily at fault. In practice, a judge or jury is unlikely to find a plaintiff slightly at fault where contributory negligence applies. Theoretically, however, the outcome just described is possible.

The trend today is away from use of contributory negligence. Instead, most states follow the doctrine of **comparative negligence.** As the name implies, the court compares the relative negligence of the parties and apportions recovery on that basis. At least two applications of the comparative negligence rule may be administered by the courts. Assume that in the automobile example both motorists experienced damages of $100,000, and that one motorist was 1 percent at fault, the other 99 percent at fault. Under the **partial comparative negligence** rule, only the motorist less than 50 percent at fault receives compensation. The compensation equals the damages multiplied by the percent not at fault, or $99,000 (100,000 × .99) in our example. Under the **complete comparative negligence** rule, the damages would be shared by both parties. The motorist who was 1 percent at fault still receives $99,000, but must pay the other motorist $1000 (100,000 × .01), resulting in a net compensation of $98,000. Because few instances exist when a party is completely free of negligence and our society appears to prefer that injured parties be compensated, comparative negligence has won favor over contributory negligence. An important question, though, is how the relative degrees of fault are determined. Gen-

Assume that two drivers are involved in an automobile accident. Their respective losses and degrees of fault are as follows:

	LOSSES	DEGREE of FAULT
Dan	$18,000	.60
Kim	$22,000	.40

Their compensation would be determined as follows:

	CONTRIBUTORY	PARTIAL[1] COMPARATIVE	COMPLETE[2] COMPARATIVE
Dan	0	0	7,200
Kim	0	13,200	13,200

[1]Only when party is less at fault than the other is compensation available. Here Dan's fault exceeds Kim's. Dan receives no compensation.

[2]Complete comparative negligence forces an offset of payment. Kim would receive $6,000 from Dan ($13,200–7,200).

erally, a jury is asked to make such an estimate, based on the testimony of various experts. Examples of the application of contributory and comparative negligence are shown in table 7–2.

Last clear chance is a further defense to liability. Under the last clear chance doctrine, a plaintiff who assumed the risk or contributed to an accident through negligence is not barred from recovery if the defendant had the opportunity to avoid the accident but failed to do so. For instance, the motorist who could have avoided hitting a jaywalker, but did not, had the last clear chance to prevent the accident. The driver in this circumstance could not limit liability by claiming negligence on the part of the plaintiff. Today the doctrine has only minor application. It may, however, be used when the defendant employs the defense of contributory negligence against the plaintiff.

Last in this listing of defenses is **immunity.** Where immunity applies, the defendant has a complete defense against liability, merely because of its status as a protected entity, professional, or other party. For example, governmental entities in the United States were long protected under the doctrine of **sovereign immunity.** Sovereign immunity held that governments could do no wrong, and therefore could not be held liable. That doctrine has lost strength in most states, but still exists to some degree in certain circumstances. Other immunities extend to charitable organizations and family members. Like sovereign immunity, these too have lost most of their shield against liability.

MODIFICATIONS

Doctrines of defense are used to prevent a successful negligence (and sometimes strict liability) lawsuit. Other legal doctrines modify the law to assist the plaintiff in a lawsuit. Some of these are discussed here and listed in table 7–3.

Rules of negligence hold that an injured person has the burden of proof; that is, he or she must prove the defendant's negligence in order to receive compensation. Courts adhere to these rules unless reasons exist to modify them. In some situations, for example, the plaintiff cannot possibly prove negligence. The court may then apply the doctrine of **res ipsa loquitur,** which shifts the burden of proof to the defendant. The defendant must prove innocence. The translation of res ipsa loquitur is "the thing speaks for itself." The doctrine may be used upon proof that the situation causing

Res Ipsa Loquitur
Strict Liability
Vicarious Liability
Joint and Several Liability

injury was in the defendant's exclusive control, and that the accident was one that ordinarily would not happen in the absence of negligence. Thus, the event "speaks for itself."

Illustrations of appropriate uses of *res ipsa loquitur* may be taken from medical or dental treatment. Consider the plaintiff who visited a dentist for extraction of wisdom teeth and was given a general anesthetic for the operation. Any negligence that may have occurred during the extraction could not be proved by the plaintiff, who could not possibly have observed the negligent act. If, upon waking, the plaintiff has a broken jaw, *res ipsa loquitur* might be employed.

Doctrines with similar purposes to *res ipsa loquitur* may be available when a particular defendant cannot be identified. Someone may be able to prove by a preponderance of evidence, for example, that a certain drug caused an adverse reaction, but be unable to prove which company manufactured the particular bottle consumed. Courts may shift the burden of proof to the defendants in such a circumstance.[4]

Liability may also be "strict" (or, less often, absolute), rather than based on negligence. That is, if you have property or engage in an activity that is ultra-dangerous to others, you may become liable on the basis of **strict liability,** without regard to fault. In some states, for example, the law holds owners or operators of aircraft liable with respect to damage caused to persons or property on the ground, regardless of the reasonableness of the owner's or operator's actions. Similarly, if you dam a creek on your property to build a lake, you will be liable in most situations for injury or damage caused if the dam collapses and floods the area below. In products liability, discussed later in this chapter, a manufacturer may be liable for harm caused by use of its product, even if the manufacturer was reasonable in producing it. The manufacturer, thus, is strictly liable.

In some jurisdictions, the owner of a dangerous animal is liable by statute for any harm or damage caused by the animal. Such liability is a matter of law. If you own a pet lion, you may become liable for damages regardless of how careful you are. Similarly, the responsibility your employer has in the event you are injured or contract an occupational disease is based on the principle of liability without "fault."[5] Both situations involve strict liability.

In addition, liability may be vicarious. That is, the liability of one person may be based upon the tort of another. An employer, for example, may be liable for damages caused by the negligence of an employee who is on

....

4. Two such theories are called Enterprise Liability and Market Share Liability. Both rely on the plaintiff's inability to prove which of several possible companies manufactured the particular product causing injury when each company makes the same type of product. Under either theory, the plaintiff may successfully sue a "substantial" share of the market, without proving that any one of the defendants manufactured the actual product that caused the harm for which compensation is sought.
5. Workers' compensation is discussed in chapter 12.

ETHICAL *Dilemma*

International Safety Standards

Product liability is one of today's most prominent forms of business liability. Laws regarding such liability, however, vary extensively across national boundaries (and sometimes even across state boundaries). A question then arises for firms that sell products on a multinational basis: whose law should govern the safety of those products?

A number of recent cases have made this question particularly relevant. For example, ought Gerber Baby Foods be forced to meet U.S. Food and Drug Administration standards when selling its goods in South America, Africa, or elsewhere outside the United States?

Although beyond the realm of product liability, a similar question involves workplace safety. When Union Carbide's plant emitted toxic chemicals into the air in Bhopal, India, we learned that operating safety in Bhopal did not meet the same kinds of standards as enforced in the U.S. Many people wonder if multinational firms ought not to apply their highest requirements for safety around the globe.

Of course, safety is expensive. One reason to locate operations abroad is to take advantage of such cost differentials. If we were to apply similar safety standards universally, many developing countries would lose jobs and economic development. Are we willing to sacrifice food, clothing, and shelter for a safe work environment? How safe is safe enough? Who decides the appropriate level of safety? A suitable answer to all these questions requires the development of an ethical foundation.

---

duty. Such an agency relationship may result in **vicarious liability** for the principal (employer) if the agent (employee) commits a tort while acting as an agent. The principal need not be negligent to be liable under vicarious liability. The employee who negligently fails to warn the public of slippery floors while waxing them, for instance, may cause his or her employer to be liable to anyone injured by falling. Vicarious liability will not, however, shield the wrongdoer from liability. It merely adds a second potentially liable party. The employer and employee in this case may both be liable.

A controversial modification to negligence is use of the joint and several liability doctrine. **Joint and several liability** exists when the plaintiff is permitted to sue any of several defendants individually for the full harm incurred. Alternatively, the plaintiff may sue all or a portion of the group together. Under this application, a defendant may be only slightly at fault for the occurrence of the harm, but totally responsible to pay for it. The classic example comes from a case in which a Disney World patron was injured on a bumper car ride.[6] The plaintiff was found 14 percent contri-

---

6. *Walt Disney World Co. v. Wood,* 489 So. 2d 61 (Fla. 4th Dist. Ct. Appl. 1986), upheld by the Florida Supreme Court (515 So. 2d 198, 1987).

butorily at fault; another park patron was found 85 percent at fault; and Disney was found 1 percent at fault. Because of the use of the joint and several liability doctrine, Disney was required to pay 86 percent of the damages (the percent the plaintiff was not at fault). Note that we consider this case an exceptional use of joint and several liability, not the common use of the doctrine.

SIGNIFICANCE OF THE LIABILITY RISK

The liability risk is significant for several reasons. Among these are (1) the financial responsibility may be large; (2) claim frequency has increased; (3) the cost of defense may be substantial; and (4) uncertainty about the claim outcome exists.

Possible Size of Judgment or Settlement

In the mid– to late–1980s, liability became a "crisis" to Americans through increased insurance premiums, canceled coverage, and extensive media attention. Insurers, business executives, and even former President Bush claimed that the tort system had grown out of control, awarding damages in absurd circumstances and for amounts far beyond reason. They cited evidence such as that provided by Jury Verdict Research, Inc. (JVR). JVR reported that from 1974 through 1984 the average yearly increase in award size of four common injury categories was 14.26 percent. In addition, JVR recorded 588 million-dollar civil liability verdicts in 1989, quite a jump since 1962 when the first such award was recorded. The 588 cases represent 13 percent of all personal injury verdicts. In 1988, 488 cases involved verdicts of at least one million dollars, representing 10 percent of all personal injury verdicts.[7]

In rebuttal, trial lawyers contended that the JVR statistics were distorted by a few very large awards. If the median verdict, rather than the mean verdict, were considered, the change in size would parallel changes in inflation. Furthermore, lawyers argued that informative numbers should include effects of defendant victories, out-of-court settlements, and appellate court reductions in awards. The JVR reports are said to exclude these factors. Whichever side is right, liability insurance with premiums of more than $115 billion in 1995 is a costly element of American society.

Frequency of Lawsuits

The liability "crisis" was purportedly a reflection of an increase in claim frequency as well as claim severity. The Insurance Information Institute reports that civil cases filed in United States federal district courts increased sixfold between 1940 and 1982, to 206,000, while the U.S. population increased by less than a twofold amount.[8] Even former Chief Justice Warren E. Burger complained that "the public has an almost ir-

---

7. The four categories are cervical strain, knee injuries, vertebrae fractures, and wrongful deaths of adult males. *Insurance Facts: Property/Casualty Fact Book, 1985–86* (New York: Insurance Information Institute), p. 51, citing Jury Verdict Research, Inc. (no listed publication).
8. *Insurance Facts*, p. 55. Some of these data are old because the crisis subsided and interest in collecting such information diminished.

rational focus—virtually a mania—on litigation as the way to solve all problems."[9]

Trial lawyers counter these claims with arguments that lawsuits merely have kept pace with population growth and inflation. The National Center for State Courts, for example, conducted a study that "shows that litigation has declined in most states in recent years. The states that do show increases primarily are the ones that have seen large population growth."[10]

Those who do believe that litigiousness is on the rise in the United States offer several reasons for the rise. One, law schools have oversupplied us with lawyers. These lawyers need to earn a living. Two, the public is more aware of the availability of large awards because of publicity on unusual cases. Three, juries view the availability of insurance proceeds and corporate assets as reasons to provide victims with compensation. By compensating in this manner, a sense of wealth sharing develops. Jury members do not feel bad when an insurer or corporation is assessed damages, because individuals are not directly involved. This is commonly referred to as the "deep pocket syndrome." Yet, if these circumstances exist, a number of the requisites of insurability are violated, reducing the availability of such coverage.

For one, rapid legal changes make the past a poor predictor of the future. As a result, estimation of loss is hampered. Dramatic changes could nearly destroy predictability, because there is no basis upon which to estimate the future. Furthermore, premiums may become infeasible with increased frequency of loss. Because the potential size of liability losses is unlimited, increased frequency makes insurance (transfer) a high-cost tool and a less desirable management technique. Remember that frequent, severe loss potentials may be appropriately handled through avoidance because they are too costly to finance.

Cost of Defense

Verdicts illustrate the loss potential of the liability exposure, but a verdict is only part of the story. If someone sues you or threatens to sue you for damages, a great deal of time, effort, and worry are involved in settling the claim. Whether the claim is groundless or not, you must defend yourself in order to prevent having to pay large sums of money. If you ignore the problem, the plaintiff may win the case by default. You must hire an attorney if you want to prevent such a loss. The attorney may, in turn, find it necessary to hire an investigator to determine all the facts of the case. If the attorney thinks that the plaintiff may get a judgment against you, the attorney may recommend that you attempt to compromise with the plaintiff. This will involve an out-of-court settlement.

One issue for which the amount of resources expended in defense costs has become an acute problem in litigation over liability is asbestos-related injuries. A 1983 study (the most recent reported research) conducted by the Rand Corporation concluded that approximately $800 million had been spent on legal expenses in asbestos litigation between 1970 and 1982.[11]

9. David Lauter, "Report Says Litigation Explosion is a 'Myth,'" *National Law Journal* (April 28, 1986), p. 46.

10. Lauter, p. 46. *Insurance Facts: Property/Casualty Fact Book, 1995* (New York: Insurance Information Institute), p. 59.

11. Kakalik, et al., *Costs of Asbestos Litigation* (Santa Monica, CA.: The Institute for Civil Justice, Rand Corp. 1983).

That represented 80 percent of the total paid expenses *and compensation.* It should be remembered, however, that $345 million in expenses represents activities for claims not yet settled. Still, the Rand study showed asbestos litigation defense expenses to be substantially higher in relation to compensation paid than exists in other products liability and medical malpractice cases. The concern is that experience in asbestos litigation may be indicative of future trends. A 1992 Rand study came to similar conclusions with hazardous waste (pollution) litigation. Of the approximately $470 million spent by insurers in 1989 on claims involving inactive hazardous waste sites, $410 million went to transactions costs.[12]

Uncertainty of Outcome

While many cases result in verdicts that favor the defendant, the possibility of loss is cause for considerable worry. Even if an adverse decision can be appealed to reduce the size of the judgment, such action is expensive and the results are uncertain. Thus, the defendant in a suit for damages involving negligence may be faced with a choice between paying more in a compromise settlement than appears warranted, or devoting considerable funds to attorney's fees without any assurance of success. A large verdict may spell financial ruin, and further appeals may drain the defendant of resources. Furthermore, regardless of how such negotiations and appeals are finally concluded, they may involve negative publicity.

Many people feel, however, that the greatest level of uncertainty regarding liability is that the same set of facts often result (or are believed to result) in vastly differing outcomes. That is, defendants (and plaintiffs too) have considerable uncertainty about jury behavior. Some of the differences come from variations in the juries themselves; others from the laws of the different states and territories.

Major Sources of Liability

Individuals, families, firms, and other organizations are exposed to countless sources of liability. These may be related to the property they own or control, or to their activities (including using an automobile, providing professional services, or manufacturing products).

PROPERTY

You not only have a duty to the public with regard to your activities, but also in connection with real and personal property you own or for which you are responsible. The duty—the degree of care—varies with the circumstances. The owner or tenant of premises, for example, does not owe the same duty to all those who enter the property. The highest degree of care is owed to invitees, whereas the standard of care is less for licensees and lowest for trespassers.

A **trespasser** is a person who enters the premises of another without either express or implied permission from a person with the right to give

12. Jan Paul Acton and Lloyd S. Dixon, *Superfund and Transactions Costs* (Santa Monica, CA: The Institute for Civil Justice, Rand Corp., 1992).

such permission. Generally, the only duty owed to a trespasser is to refrain from taking steps to harm him or her. There are several exceptions to this, the most important concerning trespassing children. This exception is discussed in connection with the doctrine of "attractive nuisance."

A **licensee** is a person who enters premises with permission but (1) not for the benefit of the person in possession, or (2) without a reasonable expectation that the premises have been made safe. If your automobile breaks down and you ask the owners of the nearest house to use their telephone, the permission you receive to enter the house makes you a licensee. Because a licensee is the party who receives the benefit of entering the property, he or she is entitled to a minimum degree of care by the owner or tenant. An owner or tenant must avoid harm to licensees and must warn licensees of any dangerous activity or condition of the property. They need not, however, make the place safer than it is normally.

An **invitee** is a person who enters the premises with permission and for the benefit of the person in possession. The invitee is entitled to a higher degree of care than a licensee. Thus, a customer in a store is an invitee, whether or not he or she makes a purchase. The property owner is expected to maintain safe premises for invitees and to warn of dangers that cannot be corrected.

For the most part, it is a person's reasonable expectations that determine his or her status. If you may reasonably expect that the premises have been made safe for you, you are an invitee. For example, if I invite you to a party at my home, you are an invitee. If you should reasonably expect to accept the premises as is without special effort on the part of the possessor, then you are a licensee. The distinction between a licensee and an invitee is not always clear, because it depends on reasonable expectations. Further, the courts have tended in recent years to place little weight on these distinctions. The question becomes, "What is reasonable of the property owner?" Generally, the owner has the responsibility to provide a reasonably safe environment.

In one case, a guest who fell on a slippery floor was awarded damages against the homeowner. In another case, a visitor fell down steps that were not properly lighted because a worker had failed to turn on a light. Although it was the worker who was negligent, the homeowner had to pay because the worker was his representative. Thus, the property owner's liability was vicarious; he was not negligent, but his employee was. In another case, a homeowner repaired a canopy and then hired a painter. When the painter crawled onto the canopy, the canopy collapsed. The homeowner was held liable for the injuries sustained.

Tenant's Liability to Public

If you are a tenant, you cannot assume that the owner alone will be liable for defects in the premises. In many cases, the injured party will sue both owner and tenant. Furthermore, the owner may shift responsibility to you by means of a **hold-harmless clause** in the lease. A hold harmless agreement, described earlier in chapter 1, is a contractual provision that transfers financial responsibility for liability from one party to another. This is particularly important to understand, because many tenants who sign a lease do not realize they are assuming such liability by contract. A typical clause is as follows:

> . . . That the lessor shall not be liable for any damage, either to person or property, sustained by the lessee or by any other person, due to the building or any part thereof, or any appurtenances thereof, becoming out of repair, or due to the happening of any accident in or about said building, or due to any act or neglect of any tenant or occupant of said building, or of any other person.

The gist of this clause is to transfer the financial aspects of the landlord's potential liability to the tenant.

Tenant's Liability to Owner

If your negligence results in damage to premises you lease, you may be liable to the owner. The fact that the owner has insurance to cover the damage does not mean you will not be required to pay for the loss. After the insurer pays the owner, the insurer receives subrogation of the owner's right to recover damages, meaning that the insurer is given legal recourse against you for any liability you may have to the owner.

Animals

Ownership of pets and other animals may also result in liability. Anyone owning an animal generally is responsible for damage or injury the animal may cause. In many jurisdictions, if the owner acted reasonably in controlling the animal, no liability will result. For example, in many places a pet dog that has been friendly and tame need not be leashed. Once that dog has bitten someone, however, more control is required. If the dog bites a second person, the owner is likely to be held liable for the harm. In this case, the owner had forewarning.

Likewise, anyone owning dangerous animals, such as poisonous snakes or lions, is held to a higher standard of care. In this case, *strict* liability may be applied. Knowledge of the potential danger already exists; thus, the owner must be given strong incentives to prevent harm. Pit bulls may be the most recent addition to this list of dangerous animals. We all know or should have heard of attacks made by these dogs, and therefore we have knowledge of their ferocity.

Attractive Nuisance

In some cases, small children are attracted by dangerous objects or property. In such circumstances, the owner has a special duty toward the children, especially if they are too young to be entirely responsible. This is called the doctrine of **attractive nuisance.** An attractive nuisance is anything that is (1) artificial, (2) attractive to small children, and (3) potentially harmful. People who own power lawn mowers, for example, must be especially watchful for small children who may be injured through their own curiosity. If you leave your mower running while you go in the house to answer the telephone and there are small children in the neighborhood who may be attracted to the mower, you may be held financially responsible for any harm they experience. The most common attractive nuisance is the swimming pool. Although some courts have held that those who own swimming pools are not necessarily baby-sitters for the community, it appears that pool owners do have the duty of keeping children out. There have been many cases in which children entered a neighbor's pool without permission and drowned. The result is a suit for damages and in many cases a verdict for the plaintiff.

Hazardous Waste

An increasingly important area of potential liability involving property derives from the possibility that land may be polluted, requiring cleanup and/or compensation to parties injured by the pollution. Because of significant legislation passed in the 1970s and 1980s, the cleanup issue may be of greater concern today than previously.

In 1980 the U.S. Congress passed the Comprehensive Environmental Response, Compensation, and Liability Act (known as either CERCLA or Superfund). This act places extensive responsibilities on organizations involved in the generation, transportation, storage, and disposal of hazardous waste. Responsibility generally involves cleaning or paying to clean polluted sites that are dangerous to the public. Estimates of total program costs run from $100 billion to $1 trillion, giving an indication of the potential severity of liability judgments. Any purchaser of realty (or creditor for that purchase) must be aware of these laws and take steps to minimize involvement in CERCLA actions.

ACTIVITIES

People also may be liable for damages caused by their own actions or those of someone else. In negligence suits, you will be judged on how a "reasonable" person in the same or similar circumstances with your training and ability would have acted. You will be judged according to different criteria for non-negligence suits.

Automobile Liability

Ownership and operation of an automobile is probably the most common source of liability any individual will encounter. With about 195 million automobiles in the U.S. and millions of people driving them, automobile accidents cause an amazing amount of death and destruction.

There are over 33 million automobile accidents every year, and the total cost involved is more than $96 billion. A motor vehicle death occurs in the U.S. on average once every eleven minutes and an injury once every nineteen seconds.[13] Property damage caused by an automobile can easily reach $25,000 or more. In the case of bodily injuries, claims of $100,000 are common. Although stories about large damage suits appear in the newspapers almost daily, smaller claims have become so commonplace that they are no longer considered newsworthy. The automobile policy

---

13. *Insurance Facts,* p. 75.

will be discussed in chapter 9. At this point we will outline the problem as it affects you and your family.

As the driver of an automobile, you are responsible for its careful and safe operation. If you do not operate it in a reasonable and prudent fashion and someone is injured as a result of such lack of care, you may be held liable for damages. If, for example, you carelessly drive through a stop sign and run into another car, you may be liable for the damage done.

Through either direct or vicarious liability, the owner of an automobile may be responsible for the damage it causes when driven by another person. In some states, the **family purpose doctrine** makes the owner of the family car responsible for whatever damage it does, regardless of which member of the family may be operating the car at the time of the accident. The theory is that the vehicle is being used for a family purpose, and the owner as head of the family is therefore responsible.

Many parents assume responsibility for their children's automobile accidents without realizing they are doing so. In some states, minors between the ages of sixteen and eighteen are issued driver's licenses only if their application is signed by a parent or guardian. What many parents do not realize is that by signing the application they may assume responsibility for damage arising from the child's driving any automobile. Ordinarily, a child is responsible for his or her own torts, but the parent may become liable by contract.

Vicarious liability is possible in other settings as well. If you lend your car to a friend, Sid Smith, so he can go buy a case of liquor for a party you are having, he will be your agent during the trip and you may be held responsible if he is involved in an accident. Your liability in this case is vicarious; you are responsible for Smith's negligence. On the other hand, if Smith is not a competent driver, you may be held directly liable for putting a dangerous instrument in his hands. In such a case, it is your own negligence for which you are responsible.

A special problem for employers is the risk known as **nonownership liability.** If an employee offers to drop the mail at the post office as he or she drives home from work, the firm may be held liable if the employee is involved in an accident in the process. This possibility is easily overlooked, because the employer may not be aware that employees are using their cars for company business.

Professional Liability

Most people have a great deal of respect for professionals. Members of a profession claim to have met high standards of education and training, as well as of character and ethical conduct. They are expected to keep up with developments in their field and maintain the standards established for the profession. As a result, the duty a professional owes to the public is considerably greater than that owed by others. Along with this duty, of course, comes liability for damage caused by failure to fulfill it. People *expect* more from a professional, and when they don't get it, some sue for damages.

The risk to which physicians and surgeons are exposed illustrates the position of a professional. In taking cases, doctors represent that they possess—and the law imposes upon them the duty of possessing—the degree of learning and skill ordinarily possessed by others in their profession.

Doctors must use reasonable care and diligence and their best judgment in exercising their skill and applying their knowledge. If they fail to do so, they are guilty of malpractice. Medical malpractice is discussed in more detail later in this chapter.

Two cases illustrate the risk to which medical doctors are exposed. A plastic surgeon who made his patient look worse instead of better had to pay $115,000 for the damage. A court awarded $4.5 million to a girl suffering acute kidney failure as a result of malpractice.

The number of medical malpractice lawsuits has increased enormously during the past three decades, and the size of verdicts has multiplied several-fold. At the same time, suits against other professionals have become common. Attorneys, accountants, architects, druggists, engineers, real estate brokers, and insurance agents are exposed to this risk. Hospitals and clinics also may be liable for damages.

Operations

Many firms are exposed to liability from their operations. Contractors are particularly susceptible to **operations liability** because they perform most of their work away from their premises. Their greatest liability exposure, therefore, is on the job, rather than arising from their own premises. Bystanders may be injured by equipment, excavations may damage the foundation of adjacent buildings, blasting operations may damage nearby property or injure someone. If harm is caused while performing the job, as opposed to a negligently completed job, the liability may be an operations one.

Product Manufacture

Products liability is one of the most widely debated sources of risk for a firm. The basis for such liability may be negligence, warranty, or strict liability in tort.

Products liability is a somewhat unusual aspect of common law, because its development has occurred primarily within the twentieth century. One explanation for this late development is the doctrine of **privity.** The privity doctrine required a direct contractual relationship between a plaintiff and defendant in a products suit. Thus, a consumer injured by a product had a cause of action only against the party from whom the product was purchased. The seller, however, likely had no control over the manufacture and design of the product, limiting potential liability. Consumers' only recourse was to claim a **breach of warranty** by the seller; this cause of action is still available.[14]

Once the privity doctrine was removed, **negligence** actions against manufacturers surfaced. Demonstrating a manufacturer's negligence, however, is troublesome, due to the manufacturer's total control of the production process. You may recall that the doctrine of *res ipsa loquitur* becomes relevant in such a circumstance, placing the burden of proof on the manufacturer.

....
14. See Dix W. Noel and Jerry J. Phillips, *Products Liability in a Nutshell* (St. Paul, Minn.: West Publishing Co., 1981).

By 1963, members of the judiciary for the United States seemed to have concluded that consumers deserved protection beyond *res ipsa loquitur*. Thus developed strict liability in products, as stated by Justice Traynor:

> A manufacturer is strictly liable in tort when an article he places on the market, knowing that it is to be used without inspection for defects, proves to have a defect that causes injury to a human being.[15]

These three doctrines of breach of warranty, negligence, and strict liability are available today as causes of action by a consumer in a products liability case. Each is briefly described below.

Breach of Warranty

Many products are warranted suitable for a particular use, either expressly or by implication. The statement on a container of first-aid spray, "This product is safe when used as directed . . .," is an *express* warranty. If you use the product as directed and suffer injury as a result, the warranty has been breached and the manufacturer may be held liable for damages. On the other hand, if you use the product other than as directed and injury results, the warranty has not been breached. Directions on a container may create an implied warranty. A statement such as "apply sparingly to entire facial surface," for example, implies that the product is not harmful for such use, thus creating an *implied* warranty. If the product is harmful even when the directions are followed, the warranty has been breached.

Negligence

When a firm manufactures a product, sells a commodity, or acts in one of the other points in the marketing chain, it has a duty to act reasonably in protecting users of the commodity from harm. Failure to fulfill this duty constitutes negligence and may provide the basis of liability if harm results. According to Noel and Phillips, "negligence in products cases is most likely to involve a failure to warn or to warn adequately of foreseeable dangers, a failure to inspect fully or test, a failure in either design or production to comply with standards imposed by law or to live up to the customary standards of the industry."[16] For example, failure to warn that the paint you sell may burn skin unless removed immediately may result in injury to the buyer and a liability for the seller. The products liability exposure can extend over the life of a product, which may be a very long time in the case of durable goods. A number of proposals have been made both nationally and at the state level to limit the time period during which such responsibility exists.

Strict Liability

A firm may be held liable for damage caused by a product even though neither negligence nor breach of warranty is established. This is called strict liability. The doctrine of *strict liability* is illustrated by the following statement made in a case opinion:

15. *Greeman v. Yuba Power Products, Inc.*, 377 P.2d 897 (Cal 1963).
16. Noel and Phillips, p. 30.

The plaintiffs must prove that their injury or damage resulted from a *condition* of the product, the *condition* was an unreasonably dangerous one and that the *condition* existed at the time it left the manufacturer's control.[17]

The doctrine of strict liability has been applied primarily based on the description provided in 1965 by the American Law Institute in section 402 of the Second Restatement of Torts. It reads as follows:

1. One who sells any product in a defective condition unreasonably dangerous to the user or consumer or to his property is subject to liability for physical harm thereby caused to the ultimate user or consumer, or to his property, if

   a. the seller is engaged in the business of selling such a product, and

   b. it is expected to and does reach the user or consumer without substantial change in the condition in which it is sold.

2. The rule stated in Subsection (1) applies although

   a. the seller has exercised all possible care in the preparation and sale of his product, and

   b. the user or consumer has not bought the product from or entered into any contractual relation with the seller.

The important aspects of this description are that the product was sold in a *defective* condition, which makes it *unreasonably dangerous,* thereby causing *physical harm* to the *ultimate user.* Thus, the manufacturer and/or seller of the product may be held liable even if "all possible care in the preparation and sale" of the product was undertaken, and even if the injured party was not the buyer. Because of the extent of this liability, it is not surprising that manufacturers hope to eliminate or at least limit the use of strict liability.

Completed Operations

Closely related to products liability is liability stemming from activities of the firm in installing equipment or doing other jobs for hire off its own premises, called **completed operations.** Defective workmanship may cause serious injury or property damage for which the firm may be held liable. For example, a roofing company employee was injured in a fall from a fire escape when a cable broke. The court held the fire escape company negligent for using a cable of insufficient size. Here the liability arises from the unsatisfactory outcome of the work, not from the actual performance of the work, as with operations liability.

Contingent Liability

Generally, a firm that hires an independent contractor is not liable for damage or injury caused by the contractor. There are, however, a number of exceptions to this general rule, resulting in **contingent liability.** In some situations, the firm may be liable for an independent contractor's negligence if the firm did not use reasonable care in selecting someone

17. *Suvada v. White Motor Company,* 32 Ill.2d 614, 210 N.E. 2d 182 (1965).

competent. If the activity to be performed by an independent contractor is inherently dangerous, the firm is strictly liable for damages and cannot shift its liability to the contractor. The fact that the contractor agrees to hold the firm harmless will not relieve it from liability. A firm that hires an independent contractor to do a job and then interferes in details of the work may also find itself liable for the contractor's negligence.

Liquor Liability

Many states have liquor laws—or **dramshop laws**—which impose special liability on anyone engaged in any way in the liquor business. Some apply not only to those who sell liquor but also to the owner of the premises on which it is sold. The laws are concerned with injury, loss of support, and damage to property suffered by third parties who have no direct connection with the store or tavern. If, for example, liquor is served to an intoxicated person or a minor and the person served causes injury or damage to a third party, the person or firm serving the liquor may be held liable. In some cases, liability has been extended to employers providing alcohol at employee parties.

Liability Issues

The basic concept of liability—that the wrongdoer should pay for damage he or she causes—has had broad support for many years. Indeed, as we shall discuss in chapter 9, there is a general belief that not only should automobile drivers pay for damage they cause, but they should also be required to prove their financial ability to do so.

During the past two decades, however, there has been growing concern that use of the liability concept has been carried too far. The circumstances under which liability is found and the size of awards for damages have expanded so much that the cost of the system may, at least in some areas, be exceeding the benefit to society. These developments have been particularly apparent in medical malpractice liability and product liability.

MEDICAL MALPRACTICE LIABILITY

As noted earlier, the number of medical malpractice suits and the size of awards have grown markedly since 1970. Part of this growth reflects the abundance of medical malpractice and that plaintiffs' attorneys have found this field a lucrative one. With the growth of private health insurance and Medicare, far more people have access to health care and a greater proportion of a growing population is exposed to the possibility of malpractice.

Another factor contributing to the increase is a change in doctor-patient relationships. Unlike the days when a family had one doctor who took care of almost all health problems, the modern health care system is more specialized; many patients are dealing primarily with doctors they do not know. Faith and friendship with the family doctor have been displaced by impersonal, brief contact with a specialist who may be more efficient than friendly. Furthermore, publicity about fraud by some doctors under the Medicare and Medicaid programs and about the amount of unneeded medical procedures (often performed as a defense against lawsuits) has reduced the prestige of the medical profession. As a result, there has been a decrease in confidence and a rise in willingness to sue.

Some of the increase in lawsuits, however, has been caused by a combination of unrealistic expectations based on news about modern medical miracles and the belief by some that people are entitled to perfect care. When they do not get it, they feel entitled to compensation. After all, they reason, it must be someone else's fault.

One result of the surge in medical malpractice suits has been a scarcity of professional liability insurance in the private market and a dramatic increase in the cost of protection for both doctors and hospitals. These costs, of course, are passed along by most doctors to the consumer. They represent one factor contributing to rising health care costs.

Another result is the rise of *defensive medicine*. Doctors and hospitals are guided not only by what is good for the patient but also by their own interests in preventing liability losses. The latter, of course, leads to practices that may not be medically necessary and that increase the size of the patient's bill. The total effect of defensive medicine on the cost of health care is difficult to determine, but it is likely significant.

PRODUCT LIABILITY

As already discussed, product liability suits were rare prior to the 1960s, and awards were small by today's standards. Two legal changes altered the scope of the product liability system. First came the abolition of the privity rule. With the expansion of trade to include wholesalers and retailers, especially with respect to automobiles, the concept of privity seemed inappropriate. Then in 1963, strict liability was brought to the arena of products cases. With strict liability, an injured party could receive damages by showing that the product was inherently dangerous, and also defective. The result was a subtle shift from focus on the manufacturer's behavior to the product's characteristics.[18]

Since 1963, the United States has seen a rapid increase in product liability litigation. One of the most difficult and common forms of litigation today involves strict liability due to defective warnings. Another source of consternation is the "mass tort" area, in which thousands of people are injured by the same product or set of circumstances, such as the Dalkon Shield and asbestos products. The Dalkon Shield was an intrauterine device used by women as a contraceptive. Some of these women experienced severe medical problems allegedly due to the defective nature of the product. Asbestos is an insulation material made of tiny fibers that when inhaled may cause respiratory ailments. Thousands of workers using asbestos in the 1930s and 1940s have been diagnosed with various forms of cancer.

The increase in product liability litigation and awards is believed to have been a major cause of the liability insurance "crisis" of the mid-1980s. The cost of insurance increased so much that some firms have gone out of business, while others have discontinued production of the items that seem to be causing the trouble.

In some circumstances, the discontinuance of a product line may not be very newsworthy. In others, however, the results could be quite detri-

18. Many people consider strict product liability to be anything but a subtle shift from negligence. For a discussion of the difference, however, see *Barrett v. Superior Court (Paul Hubbs)*, 272 Cal. Rptr. 304 (1990).

mental. The threat of lawsuits, for instance, appears to have been the impetus for several vaccine manufacturers to leave the business. Merck & Co. is now the sole producer of the combined measles, mumps, and rubella (MMR) vaccine. Similarly, only two companies, Lederle Laboratories of American Cyanamid and Connaught Laboratories, sell the diphtheria, pertussis, and tetanus (DPT) vaccine. The cost of the DPT vaccine increased from $2.80 a dose to $11.40 a dose in one year, purportedly due in part to increased legal and insurance costs.[19] Legal and insurance costs have risen in response to litigation brought against vaccine manufacturers to compensate for the adverse reactions some children have to the medication. If litigation continues, all manufacturers may be forced to quit operating, leaving the responsibility to the government.

In other circumstances, companies have not only terminated the manufacture of products, but have filed for bankruptcy. Johns Manville Corporation, an asbestos manufacturer, and A. H. Robbins, a producer of intrauterine devices (the Dalkon Shield), are two examples of companies who filed for Chapter 11 bankruptcy in order to get out from under the weight of liability suits. In November 1991, over 100,000 asbestos bodily injury claimants were litigating with asbestos producers.[20] Estimates of the number of deaths alone in the next twenty years caused by exposure to asbestos range from 74,000 to 450,000. Keene Corporation extimates that it continues to pay defense attorneys $60 million per year to defend against asbestos liability.[21]

While these examples suggest a harsh, and perhaps inappropriate, system, whether or not this perception is accurate has generated considerable debate. Some information suggests that the perception is far worse than the reality; yet, if perceptions are leading to dramatic business decisions, some change seems warranted. The nature of that change is uncertain.

SUGGESTED SOLUTIONS

A number of suggestions have been made to alleviate the problems of product liability and malpractice (professional) liability. A few have been enacted into law in some states. Some would limit the right to use or improve the defendant's defenses; others would reduce the incentive to sue or provide an alternative to legal action.

In both areas, proposals are included that would limit the compensation available to plaintiffs' attorneys. Most plaintiffs compensate their attorneys with a percentage (typically one-third) of their award, called a **contingency fee.** The advantage of a contingency fee system is that low-income plaintiffs are not barred from litigation because of inability to pay legal fees. A disadvantage is that lawyers have incentives to seek very large awards, even in situations that may appear only marginally appropriate for litigation. Reduced contingency fee percentages and/or caps on lawyer compensation have been recommended as partial solutions to increases in the size of liability awards and the frequency of litigation itself. Similarly,

19. Michael Brody, "When Products Turn into Liabilities," *Fortune* (March 3, 1986), p. 22.
20. Stacy Adler Gordon, "Asbestos Compensation Program Proposed," *Business Insurance* (November 11, 1991), p. 1.
21. Wade Lambert, "Keene's Asbestos Fight Spreads Beyond Courts, Onto Ad Pages," *Wall Street Journal* (June 29, 1992), p. 38.

shorter **statutes of limitation,** which determine the time frame within which a claim must be filed, have also been proposed as a means to reduce the number of liability suits.

Placing caps on the amount of damages available and eliminating the **collateral source rule** are recommendations that focus on the size of liability payments. Caps on damages typically take one of two forms. They limit recovery either for general damages or for punitive damages. Often, when actually awarded, general and punitive damages far exceed the special damages; thus, they dramatically increase the size of the award and can add significant uncertainty to the system.

The collateral source rule is a legal doctrine that prevents including in the litigation information about a plaintiff's financial status and/or compensation of losses from other sources. In a setting in which a plaintiff has available payments from workers' compensation or health insurance, for example, the jury is not made aware of these other payments when determining an appropriate liability award. The plaintiff may, therefore, receive double recovery.

Another prominent recommendation is to abolish or limit the use of joint and several liability. As previously described, joint and several liability has the potential to hold a slightly-at-fault party primarily responsible for a given loss. The extent of use of the doctrine, however, is disputed.

Given these conflicting ideas and data, in October 1985, the attorney general of the United States established a tort policy working group. The group consisted of representatives from ten governmental agencies as well as the White House. The purpose was to examine the claims of a crisis in liability insurance availability and affordability, and to report on the extent, causes, and policy implications of whatever crisis existed. Eight reforms of tort law were recommended in the group's report:

1. Retain fault-based standard for liability, as opposed to strict liability.

2. Base causation findings on credible scientific and medical evidence and opinions.

3. Eliminate joint and several liability in cases where defendants have not acted in concert.

4. Limit noneconomic damages to a fair and reasonable amount (the working group suggests a $100,000 limit).

5. Provide for periodic, instead of lump-sum, payments of damages for future economic damages.

6. Reduce awards in cases where a plaintiff can be compensated by collateral sources,[22] to prevent double recovery.

---

22. You may recall that insurance is based on the doctrine of indemnity. Most policies, therefore, contain other insurance provisions and exclusions of certain losses compensable by other means. Liability, however, is said to exist in part to deter undesirable actions; therefore, to permit deductions of other available compensation from a tortfeasor's obligation is to limit the deterrence effect. Thus developed the collateral source rule, which prevents defendants from benefiting from the plaintiff's receipt of money from other sources, such as health insurance. This provision of the group's recommendations would void the collateral source rule. The group's rationale is that compensation, not deterrence, has become the focus of liability.

7. Limit attorneys' contingency fees to reasonable amounts on a "sliding scale"; specifically, the working group suggests 25 percent for the first $100,000, 20 percent for the second $100,000, and 10 percent for the remainder.

8. Develop arbitration and other alternative dispute resolution methods to resolve cases out of court.

Many of these suggestions have been encompassed in federal and state bills. Some have been enacted, although most remain in committee or under consideration. During the 1992 presidential campaign, then Vice President Dan Quayle fought hard for many of these reforms, claiming they were needed to aid U.S. business competitiveness. In 1995, Congress' Contract with America includes tort reform among its ten promised actions.

In the interim, state insurance commissioners have taken action in response to rapidly rising insurance premiums and declining amounts of available coverage. Some have denied insurers the right to cancel policies across the board for a certain class of insureds. Others have mandated more restrictive cancellation privileges than previously existed. In the chapter on business property and liability insurance, we will discuss a new insurance policy and regulators' reactions to it.

Becoming Liability Risk Conscious

Like strange diseases with unpronounceable names, the liability risk seems rather remote. Does it affect you? If so, what can you do about it? Let's examine these questions.

DOES LIABILITY RISK AFFECT YOU?

Not infrequently, students reading about the liability risk for the first time believe they really don't need to be concerned about it. "I don't have any assets," or "You can't get blood out of a turnip," they may say. Well, you may or may not be judgment proof. And maybe you can't get blood out of a turnip, but not everyone knows that and they may try.

What is a *judgment?* Webster's says it is "an obligation (as a debt) created by the decree of a court." If the court grants a plaintiff a judgment against you, that person is your creditor and you are his or her debtor. You may not be able to pay the debt, but you are wrong if you think that your inability to pay means you won't be injured. The judgment may, in effect, be a mortgage against your future.

In most states, the party who gets the judgment against you can attach your property, both real and personal. Many states limit a creditor's rights with regard to certain kinds of property, but if you are at all successful in your career, such laws offer little protection. Although judgments expire periodically in some states, they are usually renewable. This gives the creditor a continuing right to take property you may acquire in the future. This ongoing threat may not bother you, but many people find it a real psychological burden.

And that isn't all. Many states allow *garnishment* of part of your wages by your creditor. This is a legal process by which your employer is required to make deductions from your salary to pay your creditor. Having a judgment against you will not enhance your reputation, particularly with your employer. Unhappily, you may not be able to keep it a secret.

WHAT CAN YOU DO?

If it is possible for you to become liable for damages, and if it is unlikely that you are judgment proof, what can you do? The most important thing is to train yourself to be conscious of the liability risk. Remember that every piece of property you have and every activity you engage in in-

volves a possible liability exposure. Look at every situation from this point of view. Unless you identify risks, you can't do anything about them. A liability checklist may be helpful.

Liability Checklist

It is probably impossible to create a checklist of liability risks that will include every exposure for every individual or family. Table 7–4 may, however, serve as a starting point. As we discuss some of the items it contains, you may think of others.

Almost any activity may inadvertently lead to liability because of a momentary lapse in judgment that results in injury or damage. Your hobbies can involve liability exposure. Are you a model airplane enthusiast? Could careless operation of your model airplane cause it to hit someone? Have you signed any contracts lately? Did they have hold-harmless clauses? When you rent tools or equipment, it is not unusual for the contract you sign to provide that you are responsible for any injury caused to anyone, even if the real cause was faulty maintenance by the equipment rental shop. You may assume this risk without realizing it.

Your children may damage a neighbor's property. Kids have been known to build under the neighbor's porch. You may cause a forest fire if you are careless with your campfire. You may cause your neighbor's home to burn if your trash fire gets out of control through your carelessness.

When your neighbor borrows your chainsaw, what responsibility do you have to him or her? Are you responsible for defects in the saw that may cause injury? Suppose you don't check to see that your neighbor knows how to handle the saw and, as a result, he or she is injured. Could you be held liable? Suppose you are target shooting and the neighbor's eight-year-old son comes along and asks to "take just one shot." If he accidentally shoots someone, you may be responsible for putting a dangerous instrument into the hands of an incompetent.

Your home is your major asset and also a major source of liability exposure. Your swimming pool may be considered an attractive nuisance, so it's your responsibility to protect the neighbors' children. Every power tool you have involves a similar exposure. Your lawn mower, power saw, electric hedge trimmer, and other tools can cause injury to a curious

TABLE 7–4

Possible Sources of Personal Liability

ACTIVITIES	PROPERTY

Home or Work
  occupation
  contracts
  home maintenance
Recreational
  golf
  camping
  archery
  hunting
Social
  club member
  home entertaining
	Home
	  swimming pool
	  lawn mower
	  other power tools
	  poorly maintained walkways,
	    steps
	  pets
	Vehicles
	  automobile
	  motorcycle
	  snowmobile
	  boat
	  airplane
	  off-road recreational vehicle

child. You may become liable to a person who trips over your child's tricycle or inadvertently steps on an abandoned skateboard. Even your dog can cause liability by hurting someone or by damaging a neighbor's property.

What about social activities? You know you have responsibilities for guests in your home and are aware of the potential for liability. But what about social organizations to which you belong? Are you a member of an association? If so, you may have liability in connection with its activities. This means you may become liable, along with other members of the association, for the actions of a member. That's a real shocker, isn't it? If you belong to a fraternity, soror-

ity, or similar organization, is it an association and what are the possible liability risks for you? When you realize that you may become legally liable for the actions of other people, the possible scope of such liability should get your attention.

How to Cope

After you have become liability risk conscious and are able to identify potential sources of loss, how can you cope with them? First, you can avoid some. For example, when you sign an equipment rental agreement, read it. Look for hold-harmless clauses. Tell the rental people you don't mind being responsible for the equipment itself, but you have a policy against assuming someone else's liability exposure. Most of the time, they won't know what you're talking about, because they use what they call a "standard form" and don't read it themselves. If you persist, however, they may agree to strike out hold-harmless clauses.

Second, be careful. Most of us believe we're always careful, but if we think about each situation from the perspective of potential loss, we are inclined to be more careful. One reason people who work on high-voltage power lines are so deliberate in each move they make is because one wrong move may be their last. You don't have to look at every move you make exactly that way, but you can be more careful than you have been. For example, is your campfire out? Maybe? Or absolutely?

Third, you can transfer your risks. Does your liability insurance cover you for *this* exposure? Does your employer's liability insurance cover you? Does the association to which you belong have liability insurance to protect itself and its members?

Key Terms

legal liability	*stare decisis*
tortfeasor	criminal law
special damages	civil law
economic damages	contractual liability
general damages	warranty
punitive damages	tort
plaintiff	negligence
defendant	proximate cause
statutory law	assumption of risk
common law	contributory negligence

comparative negligence
partial comparative negligence
complete comparative negligence
last clear chance
immunity
sovereign immunity
res ipsa loquitur
strict liability
vicarious liability
joint and several liability
trespasser
licensee
invitee
hold-harmless clause

attractive nuisance
family purpose doctrine
nonownership liability
operations liability
products liability
privity
breach of warranty
negligence
completed operations
contingent liability
dramshop laws
contingency fee
statutes of limitation
collateral source rule

Discussion Questions

1. Distinguish between criminal and civil law, and between strict liability and negligence-based liability.

2. Betsy Boomer does not own a car and she must rely on friends for transportation. Last month, Betsy asked Freda Farnsworth to drive her to the store. Freda is known to be a reckless driver, but Betsy is not in a position to be choosy. On the way to the store, Freda is distracted by Betsy and hits the median strip, forcing the car into a telephone pole. The car, of course, is damaged, and Betsy is injured. Describe Freda's possible liability and the various defenses to or modifications of liability that her lawyer may try to employ in her defense.

3. What is the impact of *res ipsa loquitur* on general doctrines of liability? What seems to be the rationale for permitting use of this modification?

4. Ceci Willis sells books door-to-door. What responsibilities do you owe her when she visits your home? How would the circumstances change if you were the book seller and Ceci came to your home as a potential buyer? What if you owned several pet panthers?

5. What was the "liability crisis"? How might elimination of the "collateral source rule" and a shortened statute of limitations affect the availability and affordability of liability insurance?

6. Your neighbor's small children run wild all day, every day, totally ignored by their parents. You have forcibly ejected them from your swimming pool several times but they return the next day. Your complaints to their parents have had no effect. Do you think it is fair to hold you responsible for the safety of these children simply because your swimming pool is an attractive nuisance? Aren't their parents being negligent? Can you use their negligence in your defense in the event one of the children drowns in your pool and they sue you for damages?

7. Describe when strict liability applies in products. What is the practical effect of this doctrine?

8. How does the contingency fee system work? How might it affect the frequency and severity of liability exposures?

9. Considering the factors involved in establishing responsibility for damages based on negligence, what do you think is your best defense against such a suit?

10. A physician or surgeon may become liable for damages on the basis of contract or negligence. Why is the latter more common than the former? Does your answer to this question tell you something about managing your liability risks? What?

Cases

7.1 Your neighbor's English bulldog, Cedric, is very friendly, but you wouldn't know it by looking at him. Last Monday, a rather strange set of circumstances happened at the neighbor's home. The substitute mail carrier met Cedric as he was approaching the mailbox. Because the mail carrier is afraid of even small dogs, he collapsed from fright at the sight of Cedric approaching, fell to the ground, and broke his left arm. A motorist, who observed this situation while driving by, rammed the neighbor's parked car. The parked car then proceeded down the street through two fences, finally stopping in Mrs. Smith's living room.

1. Is there a case for litigation involving your neighbor?
2. Where does the motorist's liability fit into this picture?

7.2 In an interesting case in Arizona, Vanguard Insurance Company vs. Cantrell vs. Allstate Insurance Company, 1973 C.C.H. (automobile) 7684, an insurer was held liable for personal injuries inflicted on a storeowner when its insured robbed the store and fired a warning shot to scare the owner. The robber's aim was bad, and he hit the owner. Because he had not intended to harm the owner, the insured convinced the court that the exclusion under a homeowners policy of intentional injury should not apply.

1. What reasoning might the court have applied to reach this decision?
2. Do you agree with this decision? Why, or why not?

7.3 Most states have a vicarious liability law regarding the use of an automobile. For instance, California and New York hold the owner liable for injuries caused by the driver's negligence, whereas Pennsylvania and Utah make the person furnishing an automobile to a minor liable for that minor's negligence. Ohio, Indiana, Texas, Hawaii, and Rhode Island make the parent, guardian, or signer of the minor's application for a license liable for the minor's negligence.

1. Why do these states do this?
2. Do you agree with this approach? Why, or why not?
3. If you are a resident of a state that has no such vicarious liability statute, does this mean you are unaffected by these laws? Why or why not?

7.4 In Steyer vs. Westvaco Corporation, 1979 C.C.H. (fire & casualty) 1229, and in Grand River Lime Company vs. Ohio Casualty Insurance Company 1973 C.C.H. (fire & casualty) 383, industrial operators were held liable for damages caused by their discharge of pollutants over a period of years, even though they were not aware of the damage they were causing when discharging the pollutants.

1. How might this decision affect the public at large?
2. What impact will it have on liability insurance?
3. Since the discharge of pollutants was intentional, should it be insurable at all?

Managing Home Risks

Introduction

A home is a special place where friends and family gather, where we spend most of our nonworking hours, and where many memories are founded. It is also a place filled with potential loss.

Have you watched news reports of devastating fires and wondered how you would cope as an owner or resident whose worldly possessions were destroyed? Where would you stay and how would you pay for it? Could you remember what you lost? What is its value?

If a friend is hurt while visiting your home, who will pay her medical bills? As your invitee, she might be forced, through her health insurer, to sue you.

These and many other pure risks associated with your home are very real. A partial listing of home risks is shown in table 8–1. They need to be managed carefully. One of the most important risk management tools to finance such losses is the homeowners policy. We will discuss this coverage in detail here, including both property and liability insurance.

TABLE 8–1

Risks of Your Home

1. Liability
2. Damage to, or destruction of, the home
3. Loss of use of the home
4. Loss of, or damage to, personal property
5. Defective title

The chapter includes discussion of information that will help you:

1. Communicate intelligently with your agent about the property and liability insurance needs for your house.
2. Determine whether or not coverage applies for various loss situations.
3. Appreciate the different types of homeowners policies, and when each is appropriate.

Packaging Coverages

Homeowners policies are similar to automobile policies in that they combine several coverages into one policy. They are a combination of property and liability insurance, along with a little health insurance for guests and residence employees. The persons insured vary from coverage to coverage and place to place.

If the insurer promised *only* you that it would pay for damage *only* to your desk caused *only* by fire and *only* when the desk was at a specified location, the contract would be simple and easy to understand. But when protection is extended to the property at other places, and to other property, other causes of loss, and other people under some, but not all, circumstances, the contract becomes complicated. When the insurer adds liability insurance for you and for some, but not all, other people, plus medical expense coverage for others but not you, things go from bad to worse as far as complexity is concerned. To say that homeowners policies are multidimensional is, indeed, an understatement. But they are also well organized, and the provisions are stated in relatively simple terms so you can determine who is covered, what is covered, the amount of coverage, and the conditions and exclusions.

Homeowners policies are sometimes referred to as **package policies,** because they combine coverages that were previously provided by several policies and a number of endorsements. Before the availability of homeowners policies, someone trying to replicate coverage would have needed to buy a standard fire policy with a dwelling, building, and contents broad form, a personal property floater, and a comprehensive personal liability policy. In today's homeowners policies, packaging reduces cost and premiums by reducing administrative and marketing costs. It also provides broader protection and eliminates many gaps in coverage.

The packaging of home coverages began in 1958. Since then, a number of modifications and revisions have been implemented. The most significant revisions came in 1976 when the standard fire policy was omitted (the relevant provisions meshed with other parts of the homeowners policy), a more readable format and style were introduced, and verbiage was reduced. An example of an attempt at readability is the use of "you" and "we" to denote "insured" and "insurer," respectively.

Because of the extensiveness of the 1976 policy modifications, you might expect a period during which insurers made adjustments to policy provisions in response to court interpretations of them. Such adjustments were made in 1982, 1984, and 1991 to respond to policy interpretation for broader coverage than was intended. Each adjustment, however, has been relatively minor when compared with the 1976 modifications. A major modification anticipated in the future is the implementation of the "rainbow homeowners" policy. As discussed by Dye,[1] the rainbow homeowners concept is to color code the homeowners policy and to restructure it by placing all coverages in one section, all exclusions in another, and so on. The restructure would be an attempt to reduce the confusion that arises when coverage is provided through an exception to an exclusion, as discussed later in this chapter. We can look forward to this more readable

1. William M. Dye, "The Rainbow Homeowners: Dropping the Other Shoe," *CPCU Journal,* vol. 40, no. 2 (1987): pp. 72–74.

format in the near future. The 1991 form will be considered subsequently. A sample policy is found in Appendix A.

Homeowners Policy Forms

First we will look at the different kinds of homeowners policies shown in table 8–2. Then we will examine the homeowners special form in some detail.

As shown in figure 8–1, each policy consists of three parts: a **declarations page,** a homeowners policy jacket, and a policy form attached to the jacket. The declarations page looks like the first page of Appendix A. It identifies the specifics that are unique to the insured, such as the covered location, and also lists policy limits, period of coverage, the name of the insurer, and similar information. The policy jacket includes general, universal provisions, such as the title of the coverage, and acts to bind together the remaining policy parts. The policy form is the substance of the contract, spelling out the specific coverage provisions. Several types of forms are available from which the insured can choose.

Following the declarations page, the balance of each form is divided into two sections. Section I pertains to direct and indirect property losses related to the dwelling, other structures, personal property, and loss of use. A stated deductible ($250 in most states), which can be increased, applies to section I coverages. Section II includes personal liability coverages for you and medical payments to others. Each section lists the coverages provided, the perils insured against, and the exclusions and conditions applicable to that section. Finally, conditions applicable to both sections are listed. Table 8–3 outlines the coverages in section I, amounts of insurance for each coverage, and the perils included for the various forms. Note that the limit for coverages B, C, and D is a specified percentage of the amount of insurance on the dwelling (coverage A) in forms 1, 2, and 3. Thus, when you decide upon the amount of insurance to have on your house, you have automatically selected the amount for other coverages. If additional amounts of coverage are needed, they are available with payment of additional premium. Forms 4 (for tenants) and 6 (for condominium unitowners) do not cover a dwelling or other structures; the amount for coverage D is based on that selected for coverage C (personal property). The basic amount for section II (coverages E and F) is the same for all forms but can be increased for additional premium. The insuring agreements, exclusions, and conditions for section II are the same for all forms.

The basic differences among the forms are in the property coverages provided in section I. Forms 4 and 6 do not include insurance on the dwelling and other structures, because 4 is for tenants and 6 is for condominium owners. The latter have an interest in the building in which they live as well as related structures, but such property is insured on behalf of the owner and all occupants in a common separate policy. Lim-

TABLE 8–2

Homeowners Policy Forms*

HO-1. Basic form	HO-4. Contents broad form
HO-2. Broad form	HO-6. Condominium unit owners form
HO-3. Special form	HO-8. Modified coverage

*The numbering and content vary in some states.

FIGURE 8–1

Homeowners Policy Structure

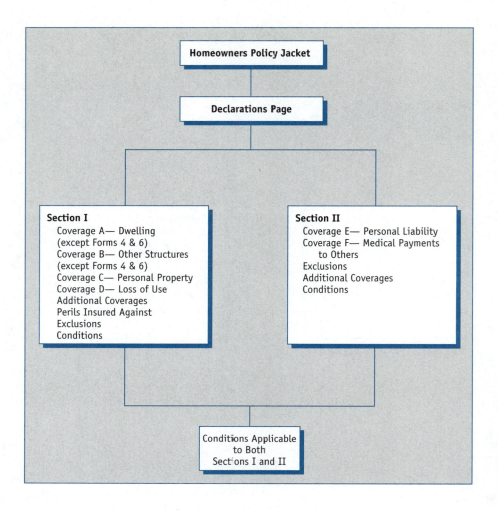

ited coverage for permanent appliances is provided in Part A. Form 8 is for older homes that may involve special hazards. The valuation provision used in form 8 on the building is actual cash value, not replacement cost new. The perils covered represent another basic difference among the forms. Some are named perils while others are open perils. Note that form 8 has a much shorter list of covered perils than the others.

The Special Form (HO-3)

We will examine form HO-3 in some detail, because it is representative of the various forms and is the most popular homeowners policy. We will, in effect, take a guided tour through the policy, referring to the part in Appendix A we are discussing so you can refer to it for more detail as we go along. Our purpose is to familiarize you with its structure and content so you will know what to look for and how to find it in any homeowners policy. Your own policy may differ slightly from the one provided in the appendix due to state and company peculiarities. The basic coverage, however, is the same.

TABLE 8–3

Section 1
Homeowners Coverages

COVERAGE	FORM HO-2	FORM HO-3	FORM HO-4	FORM HO-6	FORM HO-8
A	15,000 minimum	15,000 minimum	Not included	$1,000 minimum	Varies by company
B	10% of A	10% of A	Not included	Not included	10% of A
C	50% of A	50% of A	$6,000 minimum	$6,000 minimum	50% of A
D	20% of A	20% of A	20% of C	40% of C	10% of A
PERILS COVERED UNDER SECTION 1					
	Fire or lightning	Open perils A,B,&D	Contents same as	Contents same as	Fire or lightning
	Windstorm or hail	Contents same as	HO-2 (except	HO-2	Windstorm or hail
	Explosion	HO-2	glass	Also covers	Explosion
	Riot or civil		breakage)	improvements	Riot or civil
	commotion			(e.g., carpet,	commotion
	Aircraft			wallpaper)	Aircraft
	Vehicles			up to $1,000	Vehicles
	Smoke				Smoke
	Vandalism or				Vandalism or
	malicious				malicious mischief
	mischief				Theft (limited)
	Theft				Volcanic eruption
	Glass breakage				
	Falling objects				
	Weight of ice,				
	snow, or sleet				
	Collapse				
	Accidental				
	discharge				
	or overflow				
	of water				
	or steam				
	Rupture of				
	heating or				
	A-C system				
	Freezing				
	plumbing				
	and heating				
	or A-C				
	Artificially				
	generated				
	electricity				
	Volcanic eruption				

Note: Form HO-5 provided contents and real property coverage on an open perils basis. That coverage is now available through endorsement HO-15 to the HO-3 form, eliminating the need for HO-5. HO-1 provided a list of perils similar to that of HO-8 (i.e., shorter than the others), and is no longer in use in most states.

INSURING AGREEMENT AND DEFINITIONS

These two parts of the policy follow the declarations page. They are the same in all homeowners forms. The insuring agreement says:

> We will provide the insurance described in this policy in return for the premium and compliance with all applicable provisions of this policy.

Two aspects of this agreement should be noted. First, the portion following the words "in return for" is the consideration that is vital to the contract. Unless you comply with the provisions of the policy, the consideration is incomplete. The insurer is saying, "If you comply with the provisions, we will provide the insurance described in the policy." Second, you must look further in the policy to find out what insurance is described.

Before you can determine this, you must know the meaning of the terms used in the policy. Words or phrases printed in bold letters are defined in detail under the heading "definitions." Because definitions are crucial to an understanding of the scope of coverage, these terms are listed separately in table 8–4. Several other terms are defined in the body of the policy.

Armed with this terminology, you are prepared to examine the following parts of section I:

1. Coverages.
2. Perils insured against.
3. Exclusions.
4. Conditions.

SECTION I—COVERAGES

Coverage A—Dwelling

The dwelling on the **residence premises** (i.e., your house), plus structures attached to the dwelling, such as an attached garage, are insured in coverage A. Also covered are materials and supplies on or adjacent to the residence premises for use in the construction, alteration, or repair of the dwelling or other structures. Land is not included.

Coverage B—Other Structures

The exposures insured in coverage B are structures on the residence premises that are separated from the dwelling, such as a detached garage. Coverage B does not apply to any structure used for business purposes or rented to any person not a tenant of the dwelling, unless used solely as a private garage. The location of this exclusion and the way it is stated illustrate two important points generally made in chapter 5. First, exclusions are not always called exclusions. They may appear as "we do not cover," or following the word "except." Second, they may appear anyplace in the policy, not just under the heading "Exclusions."

Coverage C—Personal Property

This part of the policy says:

> We cover personal property owned or used by any insured while it is anywhere in the world.

1. Bodily injury	5. Occurrence
2. Business	6. Property damage
3. Insured	7. Residence employee
4. Insured location	8. Residence premises

Note that this definition includes property you own as well as that belonging to others while you are using it. If you borrow your neighbor's lawnmower, it is protected by your insurance as if it were yours.

If the insured requests, coverage C will apply to personal property owned by others while it is "on the part of the residence premises occupied by an insured," and to property of guests and residence employees while at any residence occupied by an insured. For example, if you store property of a friend at your residence premises, even though you are not using the property, you can cover the property under your policy. Or, if a guest at your cottage (not the residence premises) has property damaged while visiting you there, that property too can be covered.

Property usually situated at an insured's residence other than the residence premises (such as the cottage described above) is subject to a limit of 10 percent of coverage C or $1,000, whichever is greater. Coverage C, remember, is 50 percent of coverage A unless specifically amended to provide some other amount. Protection of $100,000 for coverage A, then, results in a $50,000 limit for coverage C. Ten percent of coverage C in this case is $5,000, which is greater than $1,000, and therefore is the limit on personal property usually kept at a residence other than the residence premises. If you, as a member of your parents' household, rent a room at school, the personal property normally kept in your school room is subject to this limit. Property brought there for a special occasion, perhaps when your sister drives up for a visit, is not subject to this limit.

Two provisions in coverage C merit careful attention. One is **special limits of liability** and the other is **property not covered.** Under the first, dollar limits are placed on some property for loss caused by any peril, and on other property for loss caused by theft. These special limits should call your attention to any gaps in coverage if you have the kind of property listed. You may want to cover the gaps with a scheduled personal property endorsement added to your policy. This endorsement is explained later in the chapter.

Most of the exclusions and limitations have the purpose of standardizing the risk, with coverage available by endorsement or in other policies. For example, much of the property not covered is related to conduct of a business and, therefore, not suited for homeowners coverage. A business-related policy or endorsement should be used to cover those items.

Some exclusions are of greater interest to a typical full-time college student than others. An example is the exclusion from coverage of tape players, their tapes, citizen band radios, and their accessories, all used in a motor vehicle. These items would be included in the automobile policy, sometimes under a special endorsement.

Coverage D—Loss of Use

This coverage protects you from losses sustained because the premises cannot be lived in as a result of a direct loss to either the premises or neighboring premises. **Additional living expense** is provided if a loss covered under section I makes the residence uninhabitable. If a similar loss makes the part of the residence rented to others uninhabitable, the policy pays for its **fair rental value.** If a civil authority prohibits you from using the premises as a result of direct damage to neighboring premises by a peril insured against in this policy, both additional living expense and fair rental value loss will be paid for a period not exceeding two weeks. The two-week limit does not apply except for **loss of use** due to actions by a civil authority.

An important characteristic of coverage D is that it covers only *additional* expenses. A family forced out of its home for a week due to fire damage, therefore, will not receive payment for all expenses incurred during that week. Suppose that the family normally spent $250 a week on groceries, but had to pay $400 while away from the damaged premises. Only the difference, $150, plus other added expenses would be compensable.

Additional Coverages

At this juncture, you might think that every conceivable source of loss in connection with your home and personal property has either been covered, modified, or excluded. Such is not the case.

Ten additional items of coverage are provided under the **additional coverages** section of the policy. First is *debris removal,* which provides payment for the cost of removing (1) debris of covered property damaged by a covered peril; (2) ash, dust, or particles from a volcanic eruption that has caused direct property loss; and (3) fallen trees that damage covered property. This additional protection is needed because other coverages provide only for the cost of repair or replacement of damaged property, not for the cost of hauling away the debris.

Several provisions in the *additional coverages* section of the policy are intended to encourage the insured to take steps that reduce the size of a loss after it has occurred. One is *reasonable repairs,* which provides payment for repairs made solely to protect property from further damage. For example, a temporary patch in the roof, following a covered loss, would be paid in order to prevent more extensive damages inside while awaiting permanent repairs. The conditions section further stipulates that if the insured fails to protect property in this way, some further damage might not be covered.

Similarly, *property removed* from premises endangered by a covered peril is covered while removed "against loss from any cause" for no more than thirty days. If this provision were not included, you might be better off to leave personal property in your house while it burned to the ground rather than remove it and risk having it damaged or destroyed by a peril other than those included in the policy.

The insurer also promises to pay *fire department service charges* incurred to save or protect covered property from a covered peril. Up to $500 per loss, without application of a deductible, is available.

Trees, shrubs, and other plants are also addressed in additional coverages. Loss to these items on the residence premises is covered if caused by one of several named perils. You should note that windstorm, ice, insects, and disease are not among the covered perils. No more than $500 per tree, shrub, or plant is available, with a total limit of 5 percent of coverage A.

Many of us have as many credit cards as we do trees, shrubs, or plants. In most cases, we are responsible for up to $50 per card if the card is used by a thief. The homeowners policy will pay up to $500 (or more in some policies) for such loss under the *credit card, fund transfer card, forgery and counterfeit money* coverage. The $500 limit is for loss caused by any single person, regardless of the number of cards or other instruments involved. No deductible applies to this coverage.

Many of us may also belong to an association of property owners (e.g., condominium projects). As members, we may be assessed charges for damage to association property. The *loss assessment* provision in the additional coverages section of the homeowners policy provides up to $1,000 to cover such charges. This provision has its greatest applicability in the condominium unit owners form (HO-6), but is included in all of the homeowners forms.

The additional coverages section also provides for direct physical loss to covered property due to two situations previously considered perils: *collapse* of a building, and loss caused to or by glass or safety glazing material. The definition and covered causes of collapse are outlined in this provision. Coverage is more narrowly defined for loss caused by collapse than had been the case when it was included under the open perils protection to real property. The glass coverage actually is slightly broader than that found in previous versions of the policy.

The tenth additional coverage found in the HO-3 is for *landlord's furnishings.* Up to $2,500 coverage is available to cover a landlord's appliances and other property located in an apartment on the residence premises that is usually available for rental. The same perils that are available for coverage C apply to this protection, except that theft is excluded.

SECTION I—PERILS INSURED AGAINST

Coverages A and B—Dwelling and Other Structures

Under this heading, the policy says:

> We insure against risk of direct loss to property described in Coverages A and B only if that loss is a physical loss to property; however, we do not insure loss . . .

The most important aspect of the agreement is that coverage is *open perils* (sometimes also referred to as "all risk"), but a close second is the delimiting phrase *"we do not insure loss."* Three exceptions to coverage follow this phrase. Through these exceptions, the coverage, while open perils, does not protect for all losses under all circumstances. The first exception is for collapse other than as provided in additional coverages. The second exception lists six circumstances in which protection is not afforded under the policy. In general, these circumstances relate to especially hazardous situations or nonfortuitous events, such as theft to or in a dwelling under construction or loss due to wear and tear. The third exception is for loss excluded under the section I-exclusions portion of the policy.

Coverage C—Personal Property

Unlike the open perils protection for the dwelling and other structures, personal property is covered against direct loss on a named perils basis, including the following:

1. Fire or lightning.

2. Windstorm or hail.

3. Explosion.

4. Riot or civil commotion.

5. Aircraft.

6. Vehicles.

7. Smoke.

8. Vandalism or malicious mischief.

9. Theft.

10. Falling objects.

11. Weight of ice, snow, or sleet.

12. Accidental discharge or overflow of water or steam.

13. Rupture of a steam or hot water heating system, air conditioning or automatic fire protective sprinkler system, or hot water heater.

14. Freezing of a plumbing, heating, air conditioning or automatic fire protective sprinkler system or household appliance.

15. Sudden and accidental damage from artificially generated electrical current.

16. Volcanic eruption.

Most of these perils are listed along with some explanation of what they involve, as well as specific exclusions. For example, damage by windstorm or hail to personal property in a building is not covered unless the opening is caused by wind or hail. Therefore, if hail broke a window and damaged property inside, the loss would be covered. If the window was left open, however, damage to property would not be covered. Similarly, furnishings, equipment, and other personal property is covered only if such property is inside a fully enclosed building. So, if your curtains are damaged by a windstorm while the window is left open, coverage C of HO-3 will not pay for the loss.

Smoke damage is covered if it is sudden and accidental, but not if it is caused by smoke from agricultural smudging or industrial operations. If, for example, your oil furnace malfunctions and spreads smoke throughout the house, the insurer will pay for redecorating and having smoky furniture and clothing cleaned. On the other hand, if you hang your clothing outside on the clothesline and it needs cleaning because of exposure to emissions from a coal-burning power plant, you will have to pay for any resulting loss.

Theft includes damages caused by attempted theft as well as loss of property from a known location when it is likely that the property has been stolen. If someone damages your bicycle in an attempt to steal it, such damage is covered. The second part of the theft definition is sometimes referred to as **mysterious disappearance.** Suppose, for example, you leave your camera at your table in McDonald's, go to the counter for another cup of coffee, return to your table, and find the camera gone. Was it stolen, or did it leave under its own power? It was probably stolen, so the loss is covered. Mysterious disappearance coverage requires that there be loss of property from a known place in such a fashion that theft is the likely cause.

Several exceptions to the theft coverage are enumerated in the policy. First, the HO-3 does not include loss caused by theft committed by any insured. This sounds absurd until you consider how many people are included in the definition of insured, which includes any resident relative and anyone under age 21 in the care of one of these resident relations.

Second, theft in or from a dwelling under construction or of materials and supplies for use in the construction is excluded because the risk is too great. Theft from any part of a residence rented by an insured to other than an insured is also excluded. If you rent a room to an outsider, for example, and he or she steals something from that room, the loss is not covered.

The third exception is one particularly important to typical college-age students. Unless an insured is residing there, theft from a residence owned by, rented by, rented to, or occupied by an insured, other than the *residence premises,* is excepted. Property of students kept at school, however, is covered as long as the student has been there within forty-five days. If you go home for winter break and your dorm room (or apartment) is broken into, your property is covered if you were not gone more than forty-five days at the time of the theft, subject of course to other policy exclusions and limitations.

Falling objects is the next listed peril. If a tree falls on your canoe, the damage is covered because the tree is a falling object. This peril does not, however, include loss to property contained in a building, unless the roof or an exterior wall of the building is first damaged by a falling object. If you drop a hammer on a piece of china, the loss is not covered. If the roof is damaged by a falling tree which, in turn, damages the china, the loss is covered. Similarly, damage to personal property caused by the weight of ice, snow, or sleet or the collapse of part or all of a building is covered.

Loss caused by accidental discharge or overflow of water or steam from a plumbing, heating, air conditioning, or automatic fire protective sprinkler system, or from a household appliance, is covered. Water could leak from a washing machine, for example, and cause damage to a painting hung on the wall of a room below. Sudden and accidental tearing asunder, cracking, burning, or bulging of a steam or hot water heating system, an air conditioning or automatic fire protective sprinkler system, or a hot water heater could damage not only the premises but personal property. Such loss is covered.

Loss caused by freezing of a plumbing, heating, air conditioning, or automatic fire protective sprinkler system, or of a household appliance, is covered. This does not include loss on the residence premises while the dwelling is unoccupied, unless you arrange to maintain heat in the building or shut off the water supply and drain the system. If you leave your home during the winter for several weeks or months, losses caused by cold weather will not be covered unless you take the same precautions as would a prudent person who did not have insurance.

Damage to some property caused by a short circuit in your electrical system is covered. Excluded is loss to a tube, transistor, or similar electronic component. Thus, damage to your television or personal computer is not covered.

SECTION I—EXCLUSIONS

We have already noted so many exceptions and limitations that you would think an exclusion's section is hardly worthwhile. Yet, eleven additional items are listed as general exclusions from section I coverages. These are listed in table 8–5.

Some of these exclusions deserve comment. The law in your city, for example, may provide that a building that does not comply with the building code is permitted to stand, but if it is damaged by fire or other peril to the extent of 50 percent of its value, it must be demolished. The first exclusion listed in table 8–5 says, in effect, "We will pay for the loss caused directly by an insured peril, but not one caused by an ordinance." If your garage does not meet building code requirements and is damaged by fire to such an extent that it must be razed, the insurer will pay only for the first damage. You will bear the rest of the loss.

If earth movement damages your house, the loss will not be paid. If, however, the damage is not total, and fire, explosion, or breakage of glass follows the earth movement, the *additional* loss caused by the following perils is covered. Of course, determining the property value following earth movement is not an easy task. Homeowners who want earthquake protection can purchase an endorsement for additional premium. This endorsement is discussed later in the chapter.

The water damage exclusion is not identical with the earth movement exclusion, but works in the same way. That is, it excludes loss caused by specified water damage and then says, "direct loss by fire, explosion, or theft resulting from water damage is covered." Specified exclusions are for flood, backup of sewers or drains, water seepage below the ground, and overflow of a sump.

Under the fourth exclusion listed in table 8–5, loss caused by power failure off the residence premises is not covered. If the power failure results in the occurrence of a covered peril, however, loss caused by the covered peril is covered. Thus, if lightning strikes a power station, cutting off electricity that heats your greenhouse, loss caused by frost to your plants is not covered. The freezing and bursting of your pipes, a covered peril, on the other hand, is covered.

The neglect exclusion can be confusing, especially because "neglect" is not defined in the policy. People often negligently cause damage to their homes, such as smokers who fall asleep with lit cigarettes in their hands. But negligence is not neglect, and these incidents are not excluded. Rather, the exclusion has the purpose of encouraging insureds to act at the time of loss to minimize the severity. You are not expected to run into a burning building to recover property. You are, however, expected to make temporary repairs to holes in the roof caused by wind damage in order to prevent further damage by rain before permanent repairs can be made.

TABLE 8–5

Listed Exclusions

1. Ordinance or law	6. War
2. Earth movement	7. Nuclear hazard
3. Water damage	8. Intentional loss
4. Power failure	9. Weather conditions
5. Neglect	10. Act or decision of governmental body
	11. Third-party negligence

The war and nuclear hazard exclusions require little explanation. Their purpose in the homeowners policy, of course, is to avoid the catastrophe potential.

Insurers have added four more exclusions (numbered 8 through 11 in table 8–5) in recent years, because of several court decisions providing broader coverage than insurers intend. The intentional loss exclusion is directed toward court decisions that permitted insureds not guilty of any misrepresentation or concealment to collect for arson damage caused by another insured. The purpose is to discourage arson, or at least to avoid paying for it.

Remaining are three exclusions, use of which is motivated by the doctrine of "concurrent causation." According to this doctrine, when a loss is caused simultaneously (concurrently) by two or more perils, at least one of which is not excluded, the loss is covered. The doctrine has been used most frequently in cases where earth movement, aggravated by negligent construction, engineering, or architecture of the building or weather conditions was the cause of loss. Courts considered the negligence of third parties a concurrent peril, not excluded, resulting in coverage.[2] By excluding weather conditions, act or decision of governmental body, and third-party negligence, insurers are responding to the concurrent causation doctrine.

SECTION I—CONDITIONS

As you have seen, there are several ways to place bounds around coverages provided by the policy, including:

1. Special limits of liability, as in coverage C.
2. Listing property not covered, as in coverage C.
3. Listing losses not covered, as in additional coverages and perils insured against.

Another place where coverages may be limited is the conditions section. Conditions outline your duties, the company's duties and options, what happens in the event of a dispute between you and the company about the amount of a loss, and the position of mortgagees and bailees.[3] Table 8–6 lists the conditions in section I of the policy.

Because the contract is conditional (i.e., your rights are dependent on fulfillment of certain duties), you must be familiar with the conditions. Your failure to fulfill one may result in a loss not being paid. This point is emphasized by condition 8, which provides that you cannot bring legal action against the insurer unless you have complied with the policy provisions and the action is started within one year after the occurrence causing loss or damage.[4] Two other duties warrant further discussion: "your duties after loss" and "loss settlement."

....

2. *Safeco Insurance Co. of America v. Guyton*, 692 F.2d 551 (1982), and *Premier Insurance Co. v. Welch*, 140 Cal.App.3d 420 (1983).

3. A mortgagee is the lending agency; when you borrow money to buy a home, you sign a note and a mortgage. You are the mortgagor who executes a mortgage in favor of the mortgagee. A bailee is a person who holds another person's property; the bailor is the person who leaves his or her property with the bailee.

4. If the one-year time limit conflicts with state law, the law prevails. In South Carolina, for example, it is six years.

TABLE 8–6

Section I—Conditions

1. Insurable interest and limit of liability	9. Our option
2. Your duties after loss	10. Loss payment
3. Loss settlement	11. Abandonment of property
4. Loss to a pair or set	12. Mortgage clause
5. Glass replacement	13. No benefit to bailee
6. Appraisal	14. Nuclear hazard clause
7. Other insurance	15. Recovered property
8. Suit against us	16. Volcanic eruption period

Your Duties After Loss

When a loss occurs, you must do the following:

1. Give immediate notice to the company or its agent and, in case of theft, also to the police. In case of loss or theft of credit cards, you must notify the credit card company.

2. Protect the property from further damage, make reasonable and necessary repairs to protect it, and keep an accurate record of repair expenditures. If, for example, a falling tree makes a hole in the roof of your house, you should have temporary repairs made immediately to prevent water damage to the house and its contents in case of rain. The insurer will pay for such repairs, as noted in the additional coverages.

3. Prepare an inventory of damaged personal property showing the quantity, description, actual cash value, and amount of loss.

4. Exhibit the damaged property as often as required and submit to examination *under oath*. The practical reason for the latter requirement is simply that many people are far more reluctant to lie under oath than they are otherwise. They may not understand what being "under oath" means, but they feel that it is a rather serious situation.[5]

5. Submit to the company, within sixty days of its request, a signed, sworn statement of loss that shows the time and cause of loss; your interest and that of all others in the property; all encumbrances on the property; other insurance that may cover the loss; and various other information spelled out in the policy.

Preparing an inventory (duty 3) after a loss is, for most people, a very difficult task. Generally, the loss adjuster for the insurance company will help you, but that does not assure a complete inventory. The only way to deal with this problem is *before* a loss. You should have an inventory not only before a loss but at the time you buy insurance so you will know how much insurance you need. Often insureds will use photographs and/or videotapes of their homes and belongings to supplement an inventory. An up-to-date inventory of your household furnishings and personal belongings can help you do the following:

1. Determine the value of your belongings and your personal insurance needs.

....

5. One definition of oath is, "a solemn, usually formal, calling upon God to witness to the truth of what one says."

2. Establish the purchase dates and cost of major items in case of loss.

3. Identify exactly what was lost (most people cannot recall items accumulated gradually).

4. Settle your insurance claim quickly and efficiently.

5. Verify uninsured losses for income tax deductions.[6]

Loss Settlement

Personal property losses are paid on the basis of actual cash value at the time of loss, not exceeding the cost to repair or replace. Carpeting, domestic appliances, awnings, outdoor antennas, and outdoor equipment, whether or not attached to buildings, are paid on the same basis. Typically, anything permanently attached to a building is considered to be part of the building. You would expect such losses to be settled the same as buildings. But the phrase "whether or not attached to buildings," makes them coverage C (personal property) losses rather than coverage A or B (real property).

The provision for settling losses to buildings is, to say the least, confusing. Here is how it works: If the total amount of coverage equals at least 80 percent of the current replacement cost of your home (at least $80,000 on a $100,000 structure, for example), you are paid the full cost of replacing or repairing the damage up to the policy limits. There is no deduction for depreciation.

On the other hand, if the amount of coverage is less than 80 percent of the replacement cost, the insurer will pay the larger of (1) the actual cash value, which is replacement cost minus depreciation, or (2) that proportion of the cost to repair or replace, without deduction for depreciation, which the total amount of insurance on the building bears to 80 percent of its replacement cost. An example may help clarify what the policy says.

Suppose that at the time of a $20,000 loss your home has a replacement value of $100,000. And suppose you have $70,000 worth of insurance on it. The loss could be settled as follows:

$$\frac{\text{Amount of insurance carried}}{80\% \text{ of replacement cost}} \times \text{loss} = \text{payment}$$

$$\frac{\$70,000}{\$80,000} \times \$20,000 = \$17,500$$

If, however, the actual cash value of the loss was greater than $17,500, you would be paid the larger amount. This example demonstrates that unless there is no depreciation, you would have to bear part of the loss. On the other hand, if construction of the house was completed the day before the loss occurred, depreciation would be zero, actual cash value would equal replacement cost, and the loss would be paid in full. In most

6. "Taking Inventory" (New York: Insurance Information Institute, 1992): p. 2. Copies of this booklet are available from the Consumer Affairs Department, Insurance Information Institute, 110 William Street, New York, N.Y. 10038. The Property Loss Research Bureau, 20 North Wacker Drive, Chicago, Ill. 60606 publishes a "Personal Property Inventory Booklet" you may also find helpful.

cases, of course, depreciation is greater than zero, so actual cash value is less than replacement cost.

Clearly, you are well advised to carry an amount of insurance equal to at least 80 percent of the replacement value of your house. But even if you do, what happens in the event of a total loss? If you have $80,000 insurance on your $100,000 house and it burns to the ground, you will lose $20,000. Remember that insurance works best against high value, low probability losses. It may be valuable to know also that replacement cost estimates do not include the value of foundations or land, which are not insured.

Furthermore, if you have $80,000 insurance at the beginning of this year, will that be 80 percent of the value of your house later in the year? If the price trend shown in table 8–7 continues, you should (1) consider adding an **inflation guard endorsement** to your policy to increase the amount of insurance automatically every year, or (2) increase the amount of insurance to between 90 and 100 percent of replacement value and keep the amount up to date every time you pay the premium. That will assure being paid in full for partial losses and provide more complete protection against a total loss. Some insurers also offer a replacement cost guarantee endorsement whereby replacement cost is covered, even if it exceeds the limit of liability.

The extent of *underinsurance* is well illustrated by a study of the Syca-more Canyon fire in Santa Barbara, California, in 1977.[7] The fire destroyed 195 homes. Less than 4 percent of the dwellings were fully insured on a replacement cost basis, and only 6 percent of the homeowners had fully covered contents. The average payment received from insurance companies was $61.51 for each $100 of replacement value of the buildings, and the average payment on contents was $39.53 per $100 of depreciated value.

DETERMINING COVERAGES

If you are like most people, the previous discussion has provided you with some new information. Yet, the homeowners policy still remains a puzzle with pieces that do not seem to fit. How do you determine what coverage you have? Different people will find alternative methods of breaking a puzzle's code. We offer one method here that may help get you started. Figure 8–2 is a visual representation of the verbal path that follows.

TABLE 8–7
....

Private Residential Construction Costs Index

YEAR	INDEX	YEAR	INDEX	YEAR	INDEX
1975	48.0	1981	77.0	1987	100.0
1976	52.0	1982	83.5	1988	102.2
1977	56.6	1983	88.5	1989	106.3
1978	61.7	1984	93.5	1990	109.7
1979	67.4	1985	96.2	1991	113.0
1980	73.0	1986	98.0		

1987 as base year

Source: U.S. Dept. of Commerce, Economics & Statistics Administration Bureau of Economic Analysis.

....
7. *The Lesson of the Sycamore Fire, Santa Barbara, California* (Santa Barbara, Cal.: Independent Insurance Agents of Santa Barbara, 1982): pp. 48–49.

FIGURE 8–2

Determining Coverages

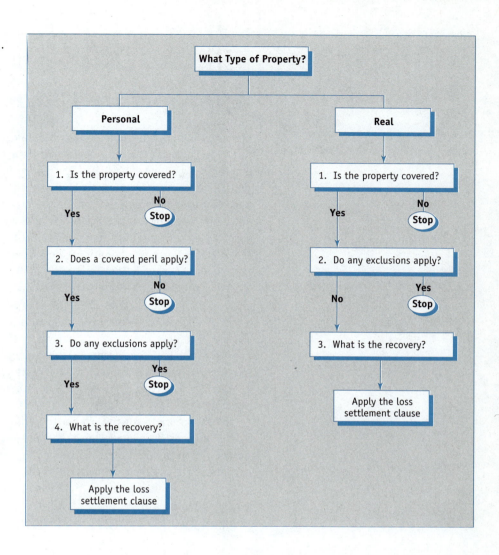

To determine coverage once loss has occurred, ask yourself which type of property (real or personal) is involved in the loss. If both, consider each type separately.

If real property is involved, be certain it is covered by the policy (i.e., consult the declarations page to see if a premium was paid for coverage A. Next, check the exclusions listed under section I-perils insured against for coverages A and B, as well as those listed under section I-exclusions. If no exclusion applies, refer to the provisions of the loss settlement clause to determine how much of the loss will be compensated.

When the loss involves personal property, the process is slightly more complicated. First, make certain that the property is covered by referring to the *special limits of liability and property not covered* provisions of coverage C under section I-property coverages. You hope the property is not listed here. Next, look to section I—perils insured against for coverage C for a listing of covered loss-causing events. If the loss was caused by a peril that is not listed, no coverage exists. If loss was caused by a covered peril, refer to section I—exclusions for limitations on protection. Last, apply the

Appropriate Claims Behavior

Claims brought under homeowners insurance coverage often involve several different valuations of losses. For example, when a fire damages one's home, coverage may be sought under part A of the policy for damage to the house itself, under part B for any damage caused to personal belongings, and also under part C for expenses of living elsewhere while the home is being repaired. Each of these three coverages will involve distinct provisions, evaluations, limits, and so on. In some ways, three claims rather than one are being made for the loss. Many insureds will not understand their obligations for proving such losses, including the valuation of loss and the special provisions for additional coverages.

Under these conditions questions might arise as to whether it is appropriate to try to pay a fair amount for the whole claim, or to be concerned with the individual parts. It might be, for example, that an insurer has difficulty measuring the exact value of the personal property that was lost. The insurer further may believe that the claim for part B exceeds its true value. Yet, the insurer may also know that the insured can claim amounts for debris removal that the insured has not requested; and between the two errors, the insurer may consider the claim to be approximately fair.

Is it appropriate for the insurer to withhold information from its insured, even if the result is an overall claim that appears appropriate? Does the insurer have an obligation to negotiate each part of a claim, or is it sufficient to seek an overall settlement? Would your impression of the insurer's responsibility differ if only one error existed, yielding a claim that was too low? Too high? If it would, why would your impression differ?

provisions of the loss settlement clause to determine how much you will be paid for the loss.

SECTION II—LIABILITY COVERAGES

As discussed in chapter 7, many of our daily activities may result in our involvement in litigation. The liability exposures that are standard to homeowners are covered in the homeowners policy, including defense costs. This liability protection is found in coverage E. Medical expenses incurred by others in circumstances that might result in litigation, but not necessarily, are provided in coverage F.

Coverage E—Personal Liability

The insuring agreement for coverage E includes two promises by the insurer: to pay damages for which the insured is legally liable; and to "provide a defense at our expense by counsel of our choice, even if the suit is groundless, false, or fraudulent." Both promises are of significant value, given the frequency of lawsuits, the size of awards, and the cost of defense. Note that the coverage is on an open perils basis; therefore, all events not excluded from coverage are included. One limitation is that damages must be either bodily injury or property damage, not personal injury. Personal injuries include bodily injuries, and also encompass injuries to an individual that are not physical harms to the body. Libel, for example, is a personal injury but not bodily injury. Coverage for personal injuries is discussed later in the chapter. In addition, defense is provided only until the amount paid by the insurer for damages (court judgments or negotiated settlements) equals the limit of liability. Thereafter, the insured is responsible for defense. Deciding upon a sufficient amount for coverage E, therefore, is best done by considering both the exposure to liability and to extended litigation.

Coverage F—Medical Payments

You may at times be wise to pay for medical expenses of other people without requiring that they prove your fault. You may, for instance, feel morally obligated, or you may merely hope to avoid litigation by remaining on friendly terms with the injured person.

Coverage F of the homeowners policy provides funds for such events. Specifically, medical expenses will be paid if incurred within three years of an accident and arising out of one of five possible situations. This coverage differs from that found in your auto policy. In the auto policy, coverage is for you and your passengers. Here (in a homeowners policy), the coverage is for losses incurred by others. The five covered situations are:

1. To a person on the insured location with the permission of an insured.
2. Arising out of a condition on the insured location.
3. Caused by the activities of an insured.
4. Caused by a residence employee in the course of employment.
5. Caused by an animal owned by or in the care of an insured.

Expenses incurred by regular residents of the residence premises, except for residence employees, are not covered. The insured, children, and spouses of the insured living at the residence and others living there are excluded so that this policy does not become a first-party health insurance policy for them.

SECTION II—EXCLUSIONS

The exclusions to section II coverage in the homeowners policy are found in three subsections. The first is a list of exclusions to both coverage E and coverage F. The second is a list of exclusions applicable only to coverage E. The third is a list of exclusions applicable only to coverage F.

All the exclusions fit the general purposes of exclusions discussed in chapter 5. Among the group of exclusions shared by coverages E and F, for instance, is for nonfortuitous losses which are expected or intended by the insured. Also excluded are nonstandard exposures and exposures/risks generally covered under other policies, such as business and professional loss potentials and motor vehicle, aircraft, and watercraft exposures. War, as a catastrophic exposure, is excluded. Premises that are owned by, rented to, or rented by an insured, but are not insured locations, are also excluded.

Exclusions applying solely to coverage E similarly follow the purposes discussed in chapter 5. Exclusion 2. a. omits coverage for most contractually assumed liabilities; these are nonfortuitous risks. Exclusions 2. b. and c. avoid duplicate coverage by negating protection for the insured's own property or property in the care of the insured, both of which may be covered in section 1. Similarly, duplicate coverage is avoided through 2. d. where payments for bodily injury are available from various work-related laws. The catastrophic nuclear exposure is excluded in 2. e. Finally, exclusion 2. f. omits coverage for bodily injury to the named insured or any resident relative of the named insured. The purpose of this last exclusion is to avoid liability when one family member sues another. Historically, immunity from liability due to negligence existed between family members. Increasing numbers of jurisdictions are negating that immunity. Thus, the resident relative exclusion may create a gap in coverage needed by the insured.

Four exclusions apply to coverage F. The first is for medical payments to resident employees while away from the residence premises and arising out of events not related to employment duties. The second is where other available compensation exists. Third is the nuclear exclusion. The fourth exclusion clarifies the intention of omitting protection for the named insured and resident relatives, who are assumed to be covered by health insurance.

SECTION II—ADDITIONAL COVERAGES

Section II of the homeowners policy provides four additional coverages. These are:

1. Claim expenses.
2. First aid expenses.
3. Damage to property of others.
4. Loss assessment.

The claim expenses and first aid expenses coverages stipulate what the insurer will pay of those costs. Claim expenses refer generally to costs associated with litigation, such as premiums on bonds and prejudgment interest assessed against the insured, other than the actual cost of defense. First aid expenses are those associated with bodily injury liability as covered under the policy, and therefore are not limited to the conditions required for medical payments to apply, but do require the possibility of an insured's liability. The coverage for damage to property of others is an added (small) benefit to cover others' property losses when you are not liable. You may at times feel a moral obligation to pay for someone's property damage even though you are not legally liable for such damage. This is similar to times when you feel a moral obligation to pay for someone's medical expenses (coverage F). When you are using someone else's property, coverage may exist in section I, but what about the friend's coat that is damaged by your dog? You are not using the coat, and you'd rather not be sued for it. **Damage to property of others** provides up to $500 for such purposes. Of interest is that coverage applies even when loss is caused intentionally by an insured who is under 13 years old, such as when a child throws a rock through a window. These types of intentional activity might be excluded under the liability coverage if the courts consider the child able to "intend" harm. The loss assessment provision is the same as that found in section I, except that it covers liability assessments instead of property assessments.

SECTION II—CONDITIONS

Just as section I contains a set of limiting conditions, section II contains a set of conditions that limit and clarify coverage. Section II conditions are listed in table 8–8.

The *limit of liability* condition clarifies that the maximum coverage available is the amount shown in the declarations. The *severability of insurance* condition provides coverage separately to each insured, although the total available for any one occurrence is the limit shown in the declarations. *Duties after loss* and *duties of an injured person* are similar to the duties stipulated in the section I conditions, as is the *suit against us* condition. *Payment of claim,* in regard to coverage F, merely emphasizes that payment is made without regard to fault. The *bankruptcy of an insured* condition requires the insurer be responsible for payment even if the insured would be relieved of his or her obligation due to bankruptcy. Finally, the *other insurance* clause makes coverage E excess of other collectible liability insurance, unless another policy with a similar other insurance clause or excess other insurance clause is involved as collectible. Other insurance clauses are discussed generally in chapter 6.

SECTIONS I AND II—CONDITIONS

Nine conditions apply to the entire contract. Three are discussed below. Refer to the sample policy in Appendix A for the remaining six conditions.

Cancellation

For various reasons, either the insured or the insurer may want to terminate the policy prior to the end of the policy period. You may cancel the policy at any time by giving the insurer written notice. State insurance regulations, however, have increasingly limited the cancellation privileges of insurers. As stated in the 1991 edition of the HO-3, four situations exist under which the insurer may cancel the policy.

First, nonpayment of premium is a justified reason for cancellation. Second, a new policy in effect less than sixty days may be cancelled for any reason. Third, a material misrepresentation or substantial change (in-

TABLE 8–8

Homeowners Section II Conditions

1. Limit of liability	5. Payment of claim—coverage F—medical payments to others
2. Severability of insurance	
3. Duties after loss	6. Suit against us
4. Duties of an injured person—coverage F. Medical payments to others	7. Bankruptcy of an insured
	8. Other insurance—coverage E—personal liability

crease) in risk will permit cancellation. For example, an insured who began to store large amounts of flammables on the premises after purchasing the policy may cause the insurer to cancel when such use becomes known to the insurer. The policy may also be cancelled at renewal date for any reason. The first two reasons require ten-day written notice; the last two reasons require thirty-day written notice. Premium refunds are available. While this is the standard homeowners cancellation provision, some states may place restrictions on insurers that require different wording.

Assignment

Because of the personal nature of insurance, policy rights of ownership are not transferable (assignable) without the written permission of the insurer. As a result, when you sell your house, you cannot automatically transfer the insurance on it to the new owner.

Subrogation

Various provisions that limit over-indemnification were discussed in chapter 4. One of these was subrogation, whereby the insured is required to transfer to the insurer any rights to recovery available from a third party. The transfer is made only to the extent of payment made by the insurer. For example, if part of an airplane detaches and falls on your house, the resulting damage is covered within the limits of your policy because it is a "falling object." Payment is limited by the loss settlement clause and deductible. If you did not have insurance, you likely would attempt to collect from the airline. The insurer, upon payment of your loss, has your right to sue the airline. Generally, the insured will be reimbursed for any out-of-pocket expenses not covered by insurance (such as deductibles and coinsurance) from any amount the insurer collects from the third party. If such collection exceeds the amount paid by the insurer to the insured, that too is the property of the insured. An additional point worth emphasizing is that the insured is precluded from interfering with the insurer's subrogation rights by, for example, settling with a negligent party without the insurer's consent.

Endorsements

In addition to the inflation guard endorsement mentioned earlier, there are several other homeowners policy endorsements you should consider, including the following:

1. Earthquake.
2. Personal property replacement cost.
3. Scheduled personal property.
4. Business pursuits.
5. Personal injury.

EARTHQUAKE ENDORSEMENT

This endorsement can be added to your policy to cover losses such as those suffered by residents of the San Francisco Bay area when a 1994 earthquake caused damage of $20–30 billion. Unfortunately, only approximately 10 percent of the damage was covered by insurance, despite the frequency of earthquakes in California. The low reimbursement rate is due to several factors, including the failure of the majority of homeowners to purchase the endorsement and the effect of a deductible of 2 percent[8] of the insurance applicable separately to dwellings and other structures. A minimum deductible of $250 applies to any one loss. The endorsement covers damage caused by earthquakes, landslides, volcanic eruptions, and earth movement.

PERSONAL PROPERTY REPLACEMENT COST ENDORSEMENT

Coverage C of HO-3 pays for loss on an actual cash-value basis, which means replacement cost minus depreciation. Except for something you bought very recently, you are underinsured from the replacement cost point of view. For example, your four-year-old TV might cost $700 to replace today. If it has depreciated 10 percent per year, the insurer will pay you $420 in the event it is stolen or destroyed this year. You will have to find another $280 if you want to replace it. You can protect yourself from this unfavorable development by adding a personal property replacement cost endorsement to your homeowners policy. In the event of a loss, it will pay you the lower of the following:

1. The full cost of replacement (if replacement cost exceeds $500, actual replacement must occur).
2. The cost incurred to repair or restore the item.
3. The limit of coverage C.
4. Any special limit stipulated in the policy.
5. Any limit separately endorsed to the policy.

SCHEDULED PERSONAL PROPERTY ENDORSEMENT

Some of the special limits that apply to personal property may be too low for you. Your jewelry or furs, for example, may be worth far more than the $1,000 limit. Such property can be listed and specifically insured to provide adequate coverage against all risks by adding the scheduled personal property endorsement. Another alternative is to pay extra premium to have the main policy's limit for a particular category of personal property, such as jewelry, watches, and furs, increased. Note, however, that this leaves your coverage on a named-perils basis rather than changing it to open perils. The insurer may require an appraisal at your expense before agreeing to a specified value.

BUSINESS PURSUITS ENDORSEMENT

Personal liability coverage and medical payments to others coverage do not apply to bodily injury or property damage arising out of business pursuits of any insured, or out of rendering or failing to render professional services. The business pursuits exclusion, however, does not apply to ac-

---

8. Ten percent in some states.

tivities that are ordinarily incident to nonbusiness pursuits. For example, your liability exposure in connection with an occasional garage sale would be covered. If you conduct garage sales regularly, however, such activity is a business pursuit and liability coverage does not apply. Liability stemming from rental operations, except for occasional rental of your residence or rental to no more than two people, is also excluded. Normal part-time employment, such as an after-school job, is not considered a business pursuit. But what about regular, full-time summer employment as a lifeguard? Such employment could be considered a business pursuit.

The business pursuits endorsement eliminates these exclusions, but it does not cover an insured while operating a business owned or financially controlled by the insured, or a partnership or joint venture of which he or she is a member. It is designed for a person who is an employee of a business firm but may not be covered by the firm's liability insurance. If you are a teacher or salesperson, or have other employment, you may need the coverage provided by the business pursuits endorsement.

PERSONAL INJURY ENDORSEMENT

The liability coverage of your homeowners policy provides protection against losses caused by bodily injury or property damage for which you may be responsible. **Bodily injury** is defined as "bodily harm, sickness, or disease . . ." It does not include the following, which are considered to be **personal injury** and are added by the personal injury endorsement:

1. False arrest, detention or imprisonment, or malicious prosecution.
2. Libel, slander, defamation of character, or violation of the right of privacy.
3. Invasion of right of private occupation, wrongful eviction, or wrongful entry.

Could you become liable for personal injury? Suppose you write a letter to the editor of the local paper in which you make a defamatory statement about a person. You could be sued for libel. Or, suppose you make an oral defamatory statement about someone. You could be sued for slander.

Other Risks

Two major risks that are too significant to be retained and cannot be avoided are not covered by the insurance discussed thus far in this chapter. These are the possibility of losses by flood or title defect.

THE FLOOD RISK[9]

Homeowners policies exclude loss caused by flood because of the problem of adverse selection. In some situations, this major gap in coverage can be filled by purchasing a flood insurance policy. Flood insurance is available through the National Flood Insurance Program, a federal program that provides flood insurance to individuals in flood-prone communities. Com-

9. We are grateful to Julia Aasberg for her assistance in preparing this section of the text.

munities must apply to the program in order for citizens to become eligible to buy flood insurance policies. In addition, the communities must undertake certain required loss control activities under a program administered by the Federal Insurance Administration.

Property owners, renters and business people in flood hazard areas of communities that have qualified for the National Flood Insurance Program may purchase flood insurance. The policy covers losses that result directly from river and stream, coastal and lakeshore flooding. Structures that are covered by flood insurance include most types of walled and roofed buildings that are principally above ground and affixed to a permanent site. The contents of a fully enclosed building are also eligible for coverage, however flood insurance policies do not automatically provide this coverage. It must be specifically requested. Commercial structures, multiple family dwellings and single family residences are also eligible for coverage.

Flood insurance provides coverage for structures and (if covered) personal property or contents on an actual cash value basis. Flood policies do not offer replacement coverage for contents. If a single family residence is insured for 80% of its replacement cost, damage to the structure will be reimbursed on a replacement cost basis. Flood policies have a $500 deductible that applies separately to both the structure and contents coverage. Higher deductibles, with commensurate premium credits, are available. There is a $50 minimum per year premium.

Two layers of coverage are available. The first is emergency coverage, available to residents of flood-prone communities as soon as the community enters the program. The rates are partially subsidized by the federal government.

Once a flood rate map is completed, a "second layer" or "regular" layer of coverage is available at actual rather than subsidized rates. Insurance under the regular program is only available to communities that have passed required ordinances and have undergone studies by the Army Corps of Engineers.

In September 1994, Congress enacted the National Flood Insurance Reform Act. One of the major provisions of the act was to provide for a substantial increase in the amount of flood insurance coverage available. The new coverage limits available under the regular program are shown in table 8–9.

The Reform Act also increased the waiting period from five to 30 days before a flood insurance policy is effective. This 30-day waiting period begins the day after the data of application for flood insurance. This is a

TABLE 8–9

Available Limits National Flood Insurance Program, as of September 1994

COVERAGES	TOTAL INSURANCE AVAILABLE
Building	
Single Family	$250,000
2–4 Family	$250,000
Other Residential	$250,000
Non-Residential (including small business)	$500,000
Contents	
Residential	$100,000
Non-Residential (including small business)	$500,000

measure to reduce potential adverse selection from individuals who may be "downriver" from rising flood waters. The waiting period does not apply to the initial purchase of flood insurance coverage when the purchase is in connection with the making, increasing, extension or renewal of a loan.

The Reform Act added an optional extension for mitigation insurance to help policyholders rebuild their substantially repetitively damaged homes and businesses according to the floodplain management code, including their community's flood proofing and mitigation regulations. This was previously unavailable under the flood insurance policy, however substantially damaged structures were still required to be rebuilt according to floodplain management code.

Flood insurance may be required by law, such as under FHA, VA and federally-insured bank or savings and loan association mortgage agreements. Under a provision in the Reform Act of 1994, if a lender discovers at any time during the term of a loan that a building is located in a special flood hazard area, the lender must notify the borrower that flood insurance is required. If the borrower fails to respond, the lender must purchase coverage on behalf of the borrower.

Flood insurance can be purchased through any licensed property or casualty insurance agent or from some direct writing insurers. Some insurers actually issue the flood insurance policies, in partnership with the federal government, as a service and convenience for their policyholders. In those instances, the insurer handles the premium billing and collection, policy issuance and loss adjustment on behalf of the federal government. These insurers are called Write Your Own (WYO) insurers. About 88% of all flood insurance policies in force are WYO policies. The remaining 12% of flood insurance policies are ordered by agents not involved with WYO program directly from the federal government.

Another important result of the National Flood Insurance Reform Act of 1994 involves the availability of Federal Disaster Relief funds following a flood disaster. Individuals who live in communities located in special flood hazard areas which participate in the National Flood Insurance Program and who do not buy flood insurance will no longer be eligible for automatic federal disaster aid for property losses suffered as a result of a flood.

THE TITLE RISK

A **title defect** is a claim against property that has not been satisfied. One example of such a claim is a lien filed by an unpaid worker or materials supplier. Another sample is a spouse whose signature does not appear on the deed signed by the other spouse when the property was sold. Her or his claim is based on the community property interest she or he has in their real property regardless of who originally paid for it.

If there is a defect in the title to your property, an informed buyer will insist that it be removed (cleared) before the title is acceptable, even though it may have originated many years ago. The clearing process can be time-consuming and expensive. You may have to pay off a lien-holder, a person who has a dower interest in the property, or the heirs of such persons.

There are two approaches to the risk of your suffering an unbearable loss when a previously undetected defect in the title to your property is discovered. One is loss prevention, having a competent attorney search the records at the county courthouse to ascertain if a claim against the property exists. In many areas, certain firms compile records, called abstracts, for property in the area they serve. In such cases, the abstract, rather than the county records, is examined by an attorney, who then renders an opinion as to the soundness of the title possessed by the seller. The shortcomings of this method of handling the risk are that the records may be incomplete or inaccurate, or that the attorney who examines them may overlook something. The attorney does not provide a guarantee that the title is clear of defects; he or she merely renders an opinion.

The other approach to handling the title risk is to buy title insurance. A title insurance policy protects you against loss caused by a defect in the title that existed at the time the policy was issued. It does not cover defects that come into existence after the policy is issued. The insurer says,

> If anything was wrong with the title to this property at the time this policy was issued, we will defend you and pay for the loss caused when it is discovered, within policy limits.

Before making this promise, the insurer attempts to determine if defects exist. If any are found, they are described in the policy and excluded from coverage, or a policy is not issued until they have been removed. A single premium is paid for the policy, and it remains in force indefinitely. As a general rule, it cannot be assigned. When title to the property is transferred, the purchaser must buy his or her own title insurance policy if protection is desired.

Personal Umbrella Liability Policies

Umbrella liability policies protect against catastrophic losses by providing high limits over underlying coverage or a deductible if there is no basic coverage. They are an "umbrella" to cover you against liability losses unusual in their nature and/or size. There are no standard umbrella policies, as there are in auto and home insurance. All do, however, have the following characteristics in common:

1. They are excess.
2. They are broader than most liability policies.
3. They require specified amounts and kinds of underlying coverage.
4. They have exclusions.

EXCESS AND BROAD

Unlike other liability policies, umbrella policies do not provide first-dollar coverage. They pay only after the limits of underlying coverage, such as your auto or homeowners policies, have been exhausted. Furthermore, they cover some exposures not covered by underlying coverage. A typical umbrella policy covers personal injury liability, for example, whereas auto and homeowners policies do not. When there is no underlying coverage for a covered exposure, however, a deductible is applied. Some personal umbrella liability policies have deductibles (also called the "retained limit") as small as $250, but deductibles of $5,000 or $10,000 are not uncommon.

MINIMUM UNDERLYING COVERAGE

Buyers of umbrella coverage are required to have specified minimum amounts of underlying coverage. If you buy a personal umbrella policy, for example, you may be required to have at least $100,000/$300,000/$50,000[10] (or a single limit of $300,000) auto liability coverage and $300,000 personal liability coverage (section II in your homeowners policy). If you have other specified exposures, such as aircraft or boats excluded by your homeowners policy, the insurer will require underlying coverage of specified minimum limits. Clearly, an umbrella liability policy is not a substitute for adequate basic coverage with reasonable limits.

EXCLUSIONS

Umbrella policies are broad, but they are not without limitations. Typically, they exclude the following:

1. Obligations under workers' compensation, unemployment compensation, disability benefits, or similar laws.
2. Owned or rented aircraft, watercraft excluded by the homeowners policy, business pursuits and professional services, unless there is underlying coverage.
3. Property damage to any property in the care, custody, or control of the insured, or owned by the insured.
4. Any act committed by or at the direction of the insured with intent to cause personal injury or property damage.
5. Personal injury or property damage for which the insured is covered under a nuclear energy liability policy.

---

10. In chapter 9, automobile limits are explained. These values represent $100,000 coverage per person for bodily injury liability and $300,000 total for all bodily injury liability per accident. Property damage liability coverage is $50,000 per accident.

Consumer Applications

Shopping for Home Insurance and Reducing Costs

You can buy insurance for your home from many different sources, and premiums can vary greatly. Table 8–10 shows the range of annual premiums for a homeowners form 3 policy to cover a single-family frame dwelling. The startling difference between high and low prices clearly demonstrates that it pays to shop for home insurance.

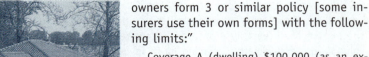

As with any kind of insurance, price isn't the only consideration, but the possibility of saving 40 or 50 percent a year on your home insurance is worth some effort. The range of prices may not be as great where you live, but a good guess is that there is enough variation to justify shopping. Who knows—you may find more variation in prices rather than less.

HOW TO SHOP

First, contact your state insurance department for information on buying home insurance. Names, addresses, and telephone numbers of insurance departments are provided in Appendix G. They may be able to give you information about premiums charged by companies licensed in your state. This will help you avoid the high-priced companies.

Second, organize information the insurer will need. Figure 8–3 can be used as a guide. Your house is one of the following types of construction:

1. Frame.
2. Brick, stone, or masonry veneer.
3. Brick, stone, or masonry.
4. Frame with aluminum or plastic siding.

Third, decide what insurance you want. You will say to the insurer or agent: "Please give me a quote on a home-

owners form 3 or similar policy [some insurers use their own forms] with the following limits:"

Coverage A (dwelling) $100,000 (as an example)

Coverage E (liability) $25,000 (as an example)

Coverage F (medical payments), $500 per person (as Coverage F an example)

"I would like a quote for the policy with various section I deductibles, including $100, $250, and $500. I would also like to know what the annual premium would be for higher limits on coverages E and F, such as $100,000 or $300,000 on coverage E."

Fourth, contact several independent agents, several exclusive agency companies, and one or more insurance-by-mail insurers for quotes.

Fifth, be sure you give everyone you talk to the same information and ask for the same quotes. You won't get exactly comparable quotations from everyone you talk to, but they will be closer to what you want if you are specific.

Sixth, make a form similar to figure 8–4 and enter the quotes. You will have to make one form for the limits you requested and other forms for increased limits on coverages E and F. Then you can compare annual premiums for the basic limits and also for increased limits. Make a note of any differences in coverage. Not all insurers will have the same choice of deductibles, for example. With this information, you can decide which company will provide you with what you want at the best price.

HOW TO REDUCE HOME INSURANCE COSTS

First, when you buy or build a home, consider insurance costs. It costs more to insure a frame home than one made

TABLE 8–10

Annual Premiums for $75,000 Policy with $100 Deductible

	PITTSBURGH	PHILADELPHIA	YORK COUNTY
Low	$172	$289	$125
Medium	$216	$371	$162
High	$281	$441	$208

SOURCE: Pennsylvania Insurance Department, "Pennsylvania Consumers' Guide to Homeowners Insurance," April 1986.

of brick, stone, or masonry, because average losses are higher. You will also find that, in many areas, frame houses cost more to maintain.

Second, choose the largest deductible you can bear. Consider, however, that you want enough premium reduction to offset the extra burden you will have in the event of a loss. Also, keep in mind that the premium reduction for various deductibles is not the same for all insurers.

Third, price other forms. An HO-2 provides less coverage than an HO-3 but costs less. Remember that you have to bear the burden of potentially uninsured losses. You may sacrifice valuable protection without saving much in premiums.

Fourth, community factors that affect insurance premium rates may seem beyond your control, but you can help influence them. You can encourage better fire department service, improvements in the water system and building code, and a better police department. These improvements not only lead to reduced insurance premiums, but also save property and lives.

Fifth, before deciding on an insurer, go to the library and read the report on it in *Best's Insurance Reports*. Also inquire about financial ratings made by Standard and Poors, Moodys, Duff and Phelps, and Weiss. On quotes from independent agents, you may need to ask who is the insurer.

Also, consider policyholder service and claims service. Information may be available from friends and family members who have interacted with insurers. In addition, the state insurance regulator may have a record of complaints against the insurer.

FIGURE 8–3

INVENTORY
of the contents of your home

Name_____

Address_____

_____

Date of Inventory _____

Revised_____ Date _____

Revised_____ Date _____

Revised_____ Date _____

Revised_____ Date _____

Revised_____ Date _____

We recommend that you complete this inventory promptly. Make sure you are adequately insured and return this folder to your agent to keep in your file.

You may want to attach a few photographs.

Your Agent:

KITCHEN, LAUNDRY ROOM

No. of Items	Item	Year Purch'd	Cost
	Books		
	Bric-a-brac*		
	Cabinets, and contents*		
	Closet contents*		
	Cookers		
	Crockery		
	Crystal		
	Cutlery		
	Dishes		
	Dryer		
	Elec. appliances (Record on Page 3)		
	Freezer		
	Glassware		
	Ironing board		
	Kitchen utensils		
	Linens		
	Portable dishwasher		
	Pots and pans		
	Refrigerator		
	Silverware		
	Stove		
	Tables		
	Washing machine		

*Where applicable, itemize contents in extra space provided.

TOTAL $ _____
(Record on page 20)

MASTER BEDROOM

No. of Items	Item	Year Purch'd	Cost
	Air cond. window units		
	Bedding		
	Beds		
	Books		
	Bric-a-brac*		
	Bureaus, and contents*		
	Chairs		
	Chests, and contents*		
	Closet contents*		
	Curtains/Shades		
	Desk		
	Dresser, and contents*		
	Dressing table		
	Lamps		
	Mattresses		
	Rugs		
	Sewing machine		
	Springs		
	Tables		
	Wall shelves		

*Where applicable, itemize contents in extra space provided.

TOTAL $ _____
(Record on page 20)

FIGURE 8–4
....

HOMEOWNERS INSURANCE
QUOTATION WORKSHEET

Applicant: _____

Address of property to be insured: _____

Number of losses in last 3 years if covered by insurance: _____

Dwelling:

Number of apartments or households in building: _____

Construction:
(frame, brick, etc.)   _____   Age of dwelling   _____
Number of stories   _____   Age of roof   _____
Number of rooms   _____   Age/type of furnace _____
Total square feet   _____

Major Options
Central air   _____
Cen. vacuum   _____
Cen. bur. al.   _____
Smoke dec.   _____
Other   _____

Owner occupant   [ ] Yes   [ ] No

Inside city limits [ ] Yes   [ ] No

Outside city limits [ ] Yes   [ ] No

Current Dwelling Replacement Cost	Current Market Value of Dwelling & Land	Purchase Price of Dwelling
Name of Fire Department	Distance from Hydrant/Station	

Cost of Your Insurance _____   Annual Premium _____

Property Coverage & Amount (% of replacement cost)		Company Name _____	Company Name _____
A.	Dwelling _____	$	$
B.	Appurtenant structures _____	$	$
C.	Unscheduled personal property _____	$	$
D.	Additional living expense _____	$	$
Liability Coverage & Amount			
E.	Personal liability (bodily injury and property damage) _____	$	$
F.	Medical payments _____	$	$
Deductible amount		$	$
Scheduled personal property		$	$
Other coverage(s)		$	$
Total Annual Premium		$	$
Installment charges		$	$
Total Annual Cost of Homeowner's Insurance		$	$

package policies

additional coverages

declarations page

mysterious disappearance

residence premises

inflation guard endorsement

special limits of liability

damage to property of others

property not covered

bodily injury

additional living expense

personal injury

fair rental value

title defect

loss of use

Discussion Questions

1. Name three exclusions in section I of the homeowners policy, and describe why each exclusion is appropriate.

2. Provide an example of a loss covered under section II of the homeowners policy.

3. Mrs. Gotcheaux's home in San Francisco was damaged by an earthquake. Subsequent to the earthquake a gas line exploded and a fire broke out, completely destroying the house. Mrs. Gotcheaux's homeowners policy explicitly excludes coverage for any damage caused by earth movement. Nevertheless, she files a claim with her insurer under her HO-3 policy. As Mrs. Gotcheaux's insurer, how would you handle her claim?

4. Why might auto policies exclude tapes and CB equipment?

5. The Rupnick's home was damaged in a fire, forcing them to stay at a nearby hotel for two weeks while repairs were being done. Due to the circumstances, the Rupnicks ate out every day, doubling the amount they would normally spend on food at home during a two-week period to $400. When the Rupnicks filed a claim for damages under their HO-3, they included the $400 cost of eating out as an expense resulting from the fire. How will the insurer respond to this claim for food? Explain.

6. Will the inflation guard endorsement alone assure that you have enough insurance on your home? Why, or why not? Discuss the application of the endorsement.

7. What is the justification for the provision that damage to your home (coverages A and B) will be paid on a replacement basis up to the limits of your coverage if you have coverage equal to 80 percent of replacement cost, but on a less favorable basis if you have a smaller amount of insurance? Do you think this provision is reasonable?

8. What protection is provided by title insurance, and who receives that protection?

9. Under what conditions ought a homeowner to consider the purchase of a personal umbrella policy?

10. Homeowners' coverage of damage to property of others is limited to $250 per occurrence. Does purchase of such coverage violate the buying principles discussed in chapter 25? Why do you suppose this is in the policy?

8.1

Bill has a homeowners policy with the special form (HO-3). His home has a replacement value of $80,000, and the contents are worth $45,000 at replacement cost or $35,000 at actual cash value. He has a detached greenhouse with heat and humidity control that houses his prized collection of exotic flowers. The flowers are valued at $11,000, and the greenhouse would cost $7,500 to replace at today's prices.
His policy has the following coverages:

Dwellings	$60,000
Unscheduled personal property	$30,000
Personal liability, per occurrence	$25,000

A property coverage deductible of $250 per occurrence applies. Analyze each of the following situations in light of the above information. Determine all applicable coverage(s) and limit(s) and explain all factors that might affect the coverage provided by the policy. Use the specimen policy in Appendix C to make your analysis.

1. A windstorm causes $20,000 in repair-cost damages to the house, and subsequent wind-blown rain causes damage to the contents of the house—$18,000 in replacement cost, or $11,000 at actual cash value. The greenhouse is a total loss, as are the exotic plants. Debris removal of the greenhouse to satisfy the city's health laws costs $350, and further debris removal to clear the way for repairs costs another $280. Two maple trees valued at $600 each are blown down, and their removal costs another $400. Bill must move his family to a nearby rental home for two months during repairs to the house. Rental costs are $600 per month, utilities at the rental house are $150 more per month, and his mortgage payments of $550 per month continue payable. It costs Bill another $80 per month to commute to work and to drive his children to their school. The telephone company charges him $50 to change his telephone to the rental unit and back to his home again.

2. After Bill and his family return to their home, faulty wiring (done during repair) causes a short and a small fire. All the family clothing has to be washed because of smoke damage, at a cost of $1200. Repair to the walls requires an additional $4,700. What might be the effect of subrogation in this case?

8.2

Brenda Joy is an accountant in a small Kansas town. She works out of her home, which has a replacement value of $125,000 and an actual cash value of $105,000. Brenda purchased an HO-3 with the following limits:

Coverage A:	$110,000, $250 deductible
Coverage E:	$300,000
Coverage F:	$ 5,000

Discuss the application of Brenda's HO-3 to the following losses.

1. One of Brenda's clients sues her for negligent accounting advice. The suit alleges damages of $75,000.

2. A friend of Brenda's visits at Brenda's home and slips over a stack of books Brenda laid on the floor temporarily. Brenda takes the friend to the hospital, where treatment is received costing $645.

3. Brenda is the star pitcher for the local softball team. Unfortunately, Brenda's game was off last month and she beaned an opponent. The opponent's attorney filed a notice of claim against Brenda, asserting damages of $500,000.

4. Neighborhood children often run through Brenda's yard. Recently a group did just that, with one child falling over a rock hidden in the grass. The child needed stitches and an overnight stay in the hospital. It is not clear if the child's parents will sue.

8.3 As a newly graduated lawyer, Quinn Krueger was able to find a well-paying job and as a result a large enough mortgage to buy a nice house. The mortgage company required that Quinn also purchase a homeowners policy, and so Quinn obtained an HO-3 with $95,000 on coverage A (the replacement cost value), $60,000 for coverage C, $100,000 of coverage E, and $2,000 on coverage F. How would Quinn's insurer react to the following losses? Explain.

1. Coming home late one night, Quinn accidentally hits the attached garage with her vehicle. Damage to the garage involves repairs of $2,300. The car needs repairs costing $3,200.

2. Quinn owns an electric guitar and likes to play it loudly. Neighbors sue Quinn for nuisance, claiming damages of $25,000 (the reduction in the value of their house).

3. Heavy snowfall, followed by rapid melting, results in high water levels. Quinn finds herself dealing with an overflow in her basement. It causes $2,700 in damage to personal property and requires repairs of $1,700 to the basement.

4. Thieves are not common in Quinn's neighborhood, but a group (police believe) of crafty criminals break into her house. The break-in damages the doorway, requiring $685 in repairs. The thieves take a Persian rug valued at $8,300, a television worth $500, jewelry assessed at $3,000, a CD player costing $450, and silverware worth $1,200.

CHAPTER 9

Managing Automobile Risks

Introduction The automobile is an incredibly important element of U.S. society. We own approximately 120 million cars, vans, and trucks. We are involved in over 30 million automobile accidents annually, and more than 40,000 Americans are killed on the roads each year. Motor vehicle fatalities, in fact, far outnumber those that occur at work. Perhaps it is our desire for individual freedom that allows us to accept such high probabilities of injury.

When an automobile accident occurs, the costs can be tremendous. People may be badly injured, requiring extensive medical care, rehabilitation, and income replacement. They may also be disfigured or experience other emotional trauma. Vehicles likely are damaged or destroyed, as may be other property, such as a building into which the vehicle collided.

For most individuals, the best way to plan for high value, relatively low probability events is to purchase insurance. In this chapter, we will focus on the type of automobile policy most of us buy. We will also discuss financial responsibility laws, which require drivers (and/or auto owners) to buy insurance or have similar financial resources in case an accident occurs.

Some states go one step further. Because some legislators believe that the liability system involves undue transaction costs, is slow, and may be unfair, various state laws have been passed to eliminate or modify automobile liability under certain circumstances. These laws generally are called no-fault laws, and they are the first topic discussed in this chapter.

This chapter provides answers to the following questions:

1. Should fault be abandoned with respect to use of a motor vehicle?
2. How can we assure adequate compensation to "victims" of automobile accidents, including availability of insurance?
3. What coverages are provided under a typical auto policy?
4. What factors are appropriate in determining auto insurance prices?

·····························

NO-FAULT

An issue debated extensively over the past several decades is whether or not to maintain a fault-based compensation mechanism for automobile accidents. In response to the debate, over half the states in the U.S. have passed *mandatory first-party benefits* (also known as **no-fault**) laws. Subject to various limitations, such laws require that insurers compensate insureds for the insureds' medical expenses, lost wages, replacement service costs, and funeral expenses incurred as a result of an automobile accident. These benefits are provided without regard to who caused the accident and are usually termed **personal injury protection** (PIP) or **basic economic loss** (BEL).

Under the no-fault concept, first-party benefits such as PIP or BEL are provided without regard to fault, so as to negate legal battles. If you were involved in a multi-car accident where tort law applied, a suit between the parties likely would result. The suit would be an attempt to place "blame" for the accident, thereby also placing financial responsibility for the losses incurred. Under the no-fault concept, each injured party would receive compensation from his or her own insurance company. No need would exist to expend resources in determining "fault." Furthermore, the worry of being hit by someone who does not have automobile liability insurance would be eliminated. You already have a form of limited no-fault insurance in the coverages that compensate for damage to your car (discussed later in the chapter). The no-fault PIP or BEL benefits extend first-party coverage to expenses associated with bodily injury.

No-fault automobile laws are not uniform, yet they typically fall into three categories. **Pure no-fault** exists only theoretically. Such a plan would abolish completely the opportunity to litigate over automobile accidents. Only specific damages (economic losses, such as medical expenses and lost wages) would be available under pure no-fault, but these would be unlimited. Michigan's no-fault law is more like pure no-fault than are the laws of other no-fault states.

Michigan's plan, however, is an example of a **modified no-fault** law. Under a modified plan, rights to litigate are limited but not eliminated. Generally, suit can be brought against an automobile driver only when "serious" injury has resulted from the accident or special damages exceed a given dollar amount, called a "threshold." For nonserious injuries and those resulting in losses below the threshold, only no-fault benefits are available. Serious injuries, or those resulting in losses in excess of the dollar-value threshold, permit the injured party to take legal action, including claims for general damages (such as pain and suffering).

Some states do not limit rights to litigate but do require that insurers offer first-party coverage similar to what is available in no-fault states. An injured party can be compensated from his or her own insurer. The insurer in turn can sue the negligent driver. Because rights to litigate are not affected, these programs are called **add-on plans** or *expanded first-party coverage*. The intent, apparently, is to reduce delays in payment for loss caused by litigation while continuing the deterrent effect of liability.

A more recent approach is **choice no-fault.** According to its authors,[1] a choice plan would allow motorists either to purchase PIP coverages at

························

1. Jeffrey O'Connell, Stephen Carroll, Michael Horowitz, and Allan Abramse, "Consumer Choice in the Auto Insurance Market," *Maryland Law Review* 52 (1993): pp. 1016–1062.

financial responsibility levels or remain in the tort system. Those who choose PIP are then precluded from seeking pain-and-suffering damages and are also immune from claims for such damages. They would receive PIP payments up to the limit and would be eligible to initiate a tort claim solely for economic damages above the PIP limit. Payments would be made on a periodic basis rather than in a lump sum (to reflect the timing of one's loss of income) and would be in excess of all other collateral sources. One exception to the tort limitation is when injury is caused by a tortfeasor's abuse of drugs or alcohol; then no limit on one's right to sue would apply.

For those who choose to remain in the tort system, actions for compensation would be made against a motorist's own insurer for both economic and noneconomic damages when caused by a PIP motorist. This system, called "tort maintenance coverage," would operate similarly to the current use of uninsured motorists' coverage (discussed later in the chapter). If economic damages exceed a motorist's own tort maintenance coverage, an action can be made against the PIP insured to recover that excess (but only for economic losses). Accidents between two tort liability motorists would be handled as they are today. Further, no change would occur in any claim for property damage.

The intent of the choice plan is to allow the auto insurance market to determine the best mechanism for compensating parties injured in motor vehicle accidents. The authors of this plan believe that savings in litigation expenses will be so great as to weigh in favor of choosing no fault.

No-Fault Appraised

Interest in no-fault grew from the belief that the tort system is slow, erratic in its results, and expensive considering the portion of the premium dollar used to compensate persons injured in automobile crashes.[2] If the tort system could be bypassed, all the expenses of the process—including costs of defense and plaintiff's counsel—could be eliminated. This would make more dollars available for compensation at no additional cost to insureds and, perhaps, even reduce the cost of insurance. Proponents of no-fault assert that enough money is spent on automobile insurance to compensate all crash victims but that the tort system wastes funds on the question of fault. Therefore, the concept of fault should be abandoned and the funds used more effectively. Furthermore, proponents argue that evidence is weak (if it exists at all) that insurance premiums actually reflect loss potentials and therefore work to deter unsafe driving.

Opponents of no-fault argue that it is simply compulsory health insurance with restrictions on tort action. They observe that workers' compensation was designed to reduce litigation by abandoning employers' liability, but that in recent times litigation in that field has been increasing. Opponents of no-fault assert that many people who favor no-fault do so primarily because they expect it will be cheaper than the present system when, in fact, it may cost more, for the reasons presented in the next paragraph. They also point out that those who wish to cover their own life

---

2. See Jeffrey O'Connell, "No-Fault Auto Insurance: Back by Popular (Market) Demand," *San Diego Law Review* 26 (1989). Most studies regarding these aspects of fault-based laws are now old. Emphasis has turned recently to premium levels, as discussed.

and health risks associated with the automobile on a voluntary basis may do so without giving up their right to sue the party at fault; such insurance is readily available and has been for a long time.

The most recent comprehensive study of automobile no-fault laws was conducted by the Rand's Institute for Civil Justice.[3] A number of results can be pulled from the study. The most important result likely is the realization that a successful state no-fault plan must consider the particular characteristics of the state. Thus, no general plan design can be offered as the "best." In addition, the authors note that while transaction costs can be lowered through no-fault, compensation tends to increase, and therefore overall system costs either stay approximately equal under no-fault as under fault, or rise under no-fault. The speed of payment definitely improves under a no-fault plan. No other general conclusions were available from the study.

How Can We Assure Adequate Compensation?

FINANCIAL RESPONSIBILITY LAWS

Every state has some kind of **financial responsibility law** to induce motorists to buy auto liability insurance so victims of their negligence will receive compensation. A typical law requires evidence of financial responsibility when a driver is involved in an accident or convicted of a specified offense, such as driving while intoxicated. The simplest way to prove such responsibility is to have an auto liability insurance policy with specified limits that meet or exceed the minimum limits set by various state legislatures. For example, the financial responsibility law in Arizona requires insurance of $15,000/$30,000/$10,000.[4]

Several states also have **unsatisfied judgment funds** that respond in situations when an injured motorist obtains a judgment against the party at fault but cannot collect because the party has neither insurance nor resources. The maximum amount the injured party may claim from the fund is usually the same as that established by the state's financial responsibility law. When the fund pays the judgment, the party at fault becomes indebted to the fund and his or her driving privilege is suspended until the fund is reimbursed.

Financial responsibility laws increased the percentage of drivers with auto liability insurance, but many drivers remained uninsured. Therefore, about half the states require evidence of insurance prior to licensing the driver or the vehicle. Unfortunately, in many such states only about 80 or 90 percent of the drivers maintain their insurance after licensing. Even a **compulsory auto liability insurance law** does not guarantee that you will not be injured by a financially irresponsible driver. A compulsory auto liability insurance law requires automobile registrants to have specified liability insurance in effect at all times; however, numerous drivers find ways to operate motor vehicles without insurance.

3. Stephen J. Carroll, James S. Kakalik, Nicholas M. Pace, John L. Adams, *No-Fault Approaches to Compensating People Injured in Automobile Accidents,* The Institute for Civil Justice, RAND, R-4019-1CJ, 1991.
4. $15,000 per person and $30,000 per accident bodily injury liability coverage, and $10,000 per accident property damage liability. Generally, the financial responsibility limits are lower than we would advise most insureds to buy.

Assuring Auto Insurance Availability

The assumption underlying laws requiring motorists to buy automobile liability insurance is that it is available. Unfortunately, some drivers cannot buy insurance through usual channels because, as a group, their losses are excessive. As a result, people injured by such drivers might not be able to collect anything for their losses. Presumably this problem could be solved by charging higher premium rates for such drivers. Yet auto insurance rates are closely regulated in many states, and insurers cannot adjust them easily. Adverse selection is also a problem. Where rates are permitted flexibility, there is a so-called **"substandard" market** in which some companies offer limited auto coverage to high-risk drivers at high premium rates.

The methods of creating a market for people who cannot buy auto insurance through the usual channels are listed in figure 9–1. Known as the **residual market,** they are created by state law.

AUTO INSURANCE PLANS

Auto insurance plans were formerly called **assigned risk plans** because they operate on an assignment basis. Drivers who cannot buy auto liability insurance through the usual channels can apply to such a plan. They are assigned to an insurer who must sell them coverage that meets the requirements of the financial responsibility law. Every company writing auto insurance in the state is a member of the plan and each must take its share of such business. If a company writes 10 percent of the auto insurance business in the state, it has to accept 10 percent of the qualified applicants. In most states, an insurer can reduce its quota by voluntarily insuring youthful drivers. Persons who have criminal records or frequent accidents or violations are excluded in some plans. Most motorists insured through the plan pay a surcharge in addition to the regular premium, although in some states those with good records pay the regular premium.

In spite of generally higher rates than the voluntary market, auto insurance plans have caused significant losses to the auto insurance industry. Many insureds dislike the plans because of high rates and the stigma connected with being assigned. Moreover, many insureds in such plans are not bad drivers on the basis of their driving records but have the misfortune to be in an undesirable classification (such as young, unmarried males) that prevents them from obtaining insurance through regular channels.

REINSURANCE FACILITIES

Where there is a **reinsurance facility**—Massachusetts, North Carolina, New Hampshire, and South Carolina—every auto insurer is required to issue auto insurance to any licensed driver who applies and can pay the premium. The insurer can transfer the burden of bad risks to the facility, a pool to which all auto insurers belong. As members of the pool, insurers share in both premiums and losses. The insured generally knows nothing about this arrangement; like all other insureds, he or she receives a policy

FIGURE 9–1

Auto Insurance Residual Market

Auto insurance plans	Joint underwriting associations
Reinsurance facilities	Maryland state fund

issued by the company to which he or she applied. In some states, however, a specific insurer is designated to service the policy or pay for losses of a given insured; then the insured likely knows his or her status in the facility.

JOINT UNDERWRITING ASSOCIATIONS

Where there is a **joint underwriting association**—Florida, Hawaii, and Missouri—all automobile insurers in the state are members and the association is, in effect, an insurance industry company. Several insurers are appointed as servicing carriers to act as agents for the association. An applicant for insurance who cannot meet underwriting requirements in the regular market is issued a policy by the servicing carrier on behalf of the association; so far as the policyholder is concerned, the association is his or her insurer. Premiums and losses are shared by all the auto insurers in the state, similar to the auto insurance plan. The JUA differs from an auto insurance plan in that only designated servicing carriers are able to issue coverage to participants.

MARYLAND STATE FUND

This government-operated residual market company provides coverage to drivers who cannot obtain insurance through the regular market. In spite of high premiums, however, it has suffered heavy losses. Originally, it was to bear such losses itself (through taxation), but the law now requires that the private insurance industry subsidize the fund.

RESIDUAL MARKET EVALUATED

Three groups are affected by attempts to make automobile insurance available to everybody—the insurance companies, high-risk drivers, and other insureds. The insurance companies are responsible for establishing and managing the plans, as well as bearing the losses they generate. Even though high-risk drivers pay high prices for their insurance, others have to pay higher premium rates than they would if there were no involuntary market, because most plans have suffered losses in excess of premiums (and investment income) paid by high-risk drivers. The excess losses are spread among all insured drivers in the state. Thus, good drivers as a group are paying part of the cost of providing auto liability insurance for bad drivers.

Personal Auto Policy

The **personal auto policy** (PAP) is the automobile insurance contract purchased by most individuals, whether to meet financial responsibility laws or just to protect against the costs associated with auto accidents. It begins with a declarations page, general insuring agreement, and list of important definitions. These are followed by the policy's six major parts:

1. Part A—Liability coverage
2. Part B—Medical payments coverage

3. Part C—Uninsured motorists coverage
4. Part D—Coverage for damage to your auto
5. Part E—Duties after an accident or loss
6. Part F—General provisions

Each of the first four parts has its own insuring agreement, exclusions, and other insurance provisions, but most conditions are in parts E and F. In a sense, each of the first four parts is (almost) a separate policy and the PAP is a package that brings them all together. Each part is made effective by indicating in the declarations that the premium has been paid for that specific part and the coverage applies. When you receive your policy, check the declarations to be sure they show a premium for all the coverages you requested, and see that the information relating to your policy is correct.

Parts E and F apply to the entire policy. As we discuss each part, you will find reference to the specimen policy in Appendix B helpful.

DECLARATIONS

The *declarations* identify you by name and address and show the term of the policy, the premiums charged, the coverages provided, and the limits of liability of the coverages. You—and your spouse, if you are married— are the *named insured(s)*. A description of the automobile(s) covered—by year, name, model, identification or serial number, and date of purchase— is included. The loss payee for physical damage to the automobile is listed to protect the lender who has financed the automobile's purchase, and the garaging address is shown. The latter is an important underwriting factor. Loss frequency and severity vary from one area (called *territory* by rate-makers) to another. For example, losses are generally greater in urban than in rural areas. Although many people drive all over the country, most driving is done within a rather short distance of the place the car is typically garaged. Thus, the place where it is garaged affects the premium.

Where is your car garaged if your home is in a rural area but you are attending a university in a large city or different state? It would be wise to talk to your agent about this question. He or she will—or should—know what the insurer's interpretation is about identifying the proper "garaging" location. You, of course, want to avoid misrepresenting a material fact, which could void the policy.

DEFINITIONS

Definitions are crucial elements of insurance policies, because the meaning of a term may determine in a particular instance whether or not you have coverage. Any term found in quotations in the policy is defined. Some are defined in the definitions section, others within the separate coverage sections.

Those found in the definitions section include the following. "You" and "your" refer to the "named insured" shown in the declarations, and the spouse if a resident of the same household. "We," "us," and "our" refer to the insurance company. A private passenger auto is deemed to be owned by a person if leased under a written agreement to that person for a continuous period of at least six months. "Bodily injury" occurs when there is bodily harm, sickness, or disease, including resulting death. "Property damage" involves physical damage to, destruction of, or loss of use of tangible property. A "business" includes trade, profession, or occupation.

"Family member" means a resident of your household related to you by blood, marriage, or adoption. This includes a ward or foster child. "Occupying" means in, upon, getting in, on, out, or off. It may seem ridiculous to define a common word such as "occupying," but a reading of the exclusions for medical payments coverage shows how crucial the definition may be. A recent example provides helpful illustration. A woman walked to her car, and while unlocking the door was struck by another vehicle. The insurer included this scenario under the category of "occupying."

"Trailer" means a vehicle designed to be pulled by a private passenger auto or pickup, panel truck, or van. It also means a farm wagon or farm implement being towed by one of the vehicles listed.

"Your covered auto" includes four categories:

1. Any vehicle shown in the declarations.
2. Any of the following types of vehicles you acquire during the policy period, provided you request the insurer to insure it within thirty days after you become the owner:
   a. a private passenger auto
   b. a pickup, panel truck, or van under specified conditions
3. Any trailer you own.
4. Any auto or trailer you do not own while used as a temporary substitute for any other vehicle described in this definition that is out of normal use because of its breakdown, repair, servicing, loss, or destruction.

The reason you must notify the insurer if you want a replacement vehicle covered for physical damage is that probably the replacement vehicle will be more valuable than the one it replaced. If you replace a five-year-old Cadillac with a new one, the insurer will be assuming a larger exposure and will want additional premium. The liability risk, in contrast, ought not to change significantly with a new vehicle.

LIABILITY COVERAGE—PART A

As mentioned in chapter 7, liability coverage is sometimes referred to as *third-party coverage* because it is payable to someone other than the insured. That is, payment goes to a third party other than the insured and the insurer, the two parties to the contract. On the other hand, coverages that provide for payment to the insured—such as for damage to your auto—are called *first-party coverage* because the insured is the party of the first part in the contract. The insurer is the party of the second part. Part A of the PAP is third-party coverage.

In the PAP, the liability insuring agreement can be paraphrased as:

> We will pay damages for bodily injury or property damage for which any insured becomes legally responsible because of an auto accident. We will settle or defend, as we consider appropriate, any claim or suit asking for these damages. Our duty to settle or defend ends when our limit of liability for this coverage has been exhausted.

In the liability part of the PAP, the policy defines insured as:

1. You or any family member, for the ownership, maintenance, or use of any auto or trailer.

2. Any person using your covered auto.

3. For your covered auto, any person or organization, but only with respect to legal responsibility for acts or omissions of a person for whom coverage is afforded under this part.

4. For any auto or trailer other than your covered auto, any person or organization, but only with respect to legal responsibility for acts or omissions of you or any family member for whom coverage is afforded under this part. This provision applies only if the person or organization does not own or hire the auto or trailer.

The first two definitions are understandable, but the third and fourth are nearly incomprehensible. An example may help. If I lend you my covered auto to take children to the church picnic, you become a covered person, according to number 2. The policy will cover your liability in connection with an accident on the way to the picnic. It will also, according to number 3, cover any liability the church may have in connection with the accident. If, on the other hand, I borrow your car to take the children to the church picnic, I am a covered person according to number 1, and the church's liability for any accident I might have is covered by number 4. In both situations, coverage for the organization stems from the fact that the driver is a covered person.

Defense

If claims are brought against you or other covered persons, the liability coverage provides *legal defense,* the cost not being considered part of the insurer's limit of liability. Defense costs often run into thousands of dollars, making this a significant benefit of liability insurance. In some types of liability insurance (such as pollution), the defense coverage may exceed the indemnity coverage. If you are found liable, the insurer pays on your behalf to the plaintiff(s), up to the limit(s) of liability under the policy. The insurer's responsibility to defend ends when that limit is reached (i.e., is paid in award or settlement to third-party claimants).

The insurer retains the right to settle claims without your approval if it finds this expedient. Such action keeps many cases out of court and reduces insurance claims expenses. It can, however, cause a rude surprise for you in at least two ways. One, if you want to contest the claim because it seems improper, but the insurer finds it simpler and cheaper to settle, the insurer may settle despite your protests. Two, you have no say in who will defend you.

Supplementary Payments

In addition to the limit for liability, the insurer will pay up to $250 for the cost of bail bonds required because of an accident, if the accident results in bodily injury or property damage covered by the policy. Note that this would not cover the cost of a bond for a traffic ticket you receive when there is no accident. Premiums on appeal bonds and bonds to release attachments are paid in any suit the insurer defends. Interest accruing after a judgment is entered and reasonable expenses incurred at the insurer's request are paid. Up to $50 a day for loss of earnings because of attendance at hearings or trials is also available.

Single or Split Limits

Although liability coverage under the PAP usually is subject to a single, aggregate limit (called a combined single limit, or CSL), it can be divided by use of an endorsement into two major subparts: bodily injury liability and property damage liability. Bodily injury liability applies when the use of your car results in the injury or death of pedestrians, passengers of other vehicles, or passengers of your automobile. Property damage liability coverage applies when your car damages property belonging to others. Although the first thing you probably think about under this coverage is the other person's car, and you are right, this coverage could also cover street signs, fences, bicycles, telephone poles, houses, and other types of property. Remember, however, that it does not apply to your house or to other property you own, because you cannot be legally liable to yourself.

If you choose a **single limit** of liability to cover all liability, including both property damage and bodily injury, then the insurer will pay on your behalf for all losses up to this limit for any single accident, whether they are property-related or injury-related. The only limit you are concerned with in this case is the single, or aggregate limit. Once all losses equal this limit, you will have to bear the burden of any further liability.

If you choose a **split limit** of liability, a set of two limits will be specifically applied to bodily injury, and a single, aggregate limit applied to property damage. For the bodily injury limits, one limit applies per person, per accident, and a second limit is the aggregate the insurer will pay for your liability to all persons injured in an accident. The limit for property damage is shown separately. Thus, your limits are shown as, for example:

Bodily injury	$150,000 each person
	$300,000 each accident
Property damage	$ 50,000 each accident

In insurance jargon, these limits would be described as 150/300/50. Alternatively, a single limit, say $300,000, could be purchased to cover all liabilities from any one accident.

Whether you have single or split limits, the need for adequate limits is imperative. As table 9–1 illustrates, premiums increase less than proportionately as limits are raised. Note that increasing the single limit from $25,000 to $3,000,000 only slightly more than doubles the premium, although coverage increases more than onehundred-fold. Also note the clarifying language in "limit of liability," which states that the amount shown is the maximum payable, regardless of the number of covered persons, claims made, vehicles or premiums shown in the declarations, or vehicles involved in the auto accident. If two vehicles shown in the declarations are involved in the same accident, therefore, twice the limit of liability will not be available. At least, this is the intent of the insurer. Various state courts have interpreted the policy differently, permitting what is called "stacking." **Stacking** may occur when a single policy covers two vehicles

TABLE 9-1

Factors for Increased Auto Liability Limits

$BI Limits*	FACTOR**	PD LIMITS	FACTOR	SINGLE LIMITS	FACTOR
$ 50/100	1.00	$ 5,000	1.00	$ 25,000	.906
100/200	1.26	10,000	1.05	50,000	1.00
100/300	1.31	15,000	1.06	100,000	1.08
300/300	1.39	20,000	1.07	200,000	1.24
250/500	1.43	25,000	1.08	300,000	1.31
500/1,000	1.56	50,000	1.13	500,000	1.39
1,000/1,000	1.68	100,000	1.18	1,000,000	1.53
1,000/2,000	1.76	150,000	1.23	2,000,000	1.71
1,500/3,000	1.91	500,000	1.33	3,000,000	1.81
2,500/5,000	2.13	1,000,000	1.43	4,000,000	1.91
5,000/10,000	2.36	5,000,000	1.64	5,000,000	1.97
10,000/10,000	2.60	10,000,000	1.69	10,000,000	2.17

*Thousands.
**Factor is applied to base rate, e.g., the rate for $100/200 is 1.26 times the rate for 50/100. These factors are for vehicles eligible for personal injury protection.

SOURCE: Insurance Services Office, *Personal Auto Manual*. Copyright Insurance Services Office, 1981, 1983.

and the court interprets this situation to yield a limit of liability equal to double the amount shown in the declarations.

Exclusions

The wording of the insuring agreement of part A provides for open perils liability coverage. All events resulting in automobile liability, therefore, are covered unless specifically excluded. Twelve exclusions apply to part A, nine of which identify unprotected persons and three that specify non-covered vehicles. The exclusions, listed in table 9–2, can be discussed in terms of the purposes of exclusions presented in chapter 5.

Perhaps the easiest exclusion to understand is that of intentionally caused (*nonfortuitous*) harm. Aside from the insurer's moral hazard problem, public policy calls for this omission of coverage. For much the same reason, several exclusions exist to prevent *duplicate coverage,* which would result in over-indemnification. Property damage to owned or used property, for instance, ought to be covered under other property insurance contracts such as a homeowner's policy and is, therefore, excluded in the PAP.

Another exclusion to avoid duplicate coverage is that of bodily injury to an employee of the covered person who is eligible for workers' compensation benefits. If the employee is a domestic employee, workers' compensation benefits may not be available; hence, the exclusion applies only if such benefits are required or available.

Various activities require separate insurance coverage in order to *standardize the risk* of the general policy. Anyone using a motor vehicle as a taxi, for example, represents greater risk than one who does not. Thus, persons using a vehicle as a "public livery or conveyance" are excluded from coverage. Because persons employed in the automobile business[5] rep-

5. The "automobile business" is the business of selling, repairing, servicing, storing, or parking vehicles designed for use mainly on public highways.

The Insurer will not cover

A. The liabilities of any person

  1. who intentionally causes loss

  2. who damages property he or she owns or is transporting

  3. who damages property he or she is renting, using, or has in his or her care (with some exceptions)

  4. who causes bodily injury to his or her employees, except to domestic employees if workers' compensation is not available

  5. whose liability arises out of the use of a vehicle as a public livery or conveyance, except for car-pooling

  6. who is engaged in the automobile business, except for "your" (and family members') use of the covered auto

  7. who is using the automobile for business, except for the use of a private passenger auto; pickup panel truck or van "you" own; or trailer used with either of the preceding two vehicles

  8. who is using a vehicle without a reasonable belief of permission to do so

  9. who is insured under a nuclear energy policy, or would be except that policy limits have been exhausted

B. Liabilities arising out of maintenance or use of

  1. a vehicle with less than four wheels

  2. a vehicle other than "your covered auto" which is owned by "you" or available for "your" regular use

  3. a vehicle other than "your covered auto "which is owned by or available for the regular use of any family member (except "you" use)

NOTE: Some of the exclusions are paraphrased. See part A of appendix B for the actual wording, which may be interpreted by courts differently than we have done here.

resent a significant risk while in their employment status, they too are excluded. You can understand that the insurer prefers not to provide coverage to the mechanic while he or she is test driving your car. The automobile business is expected to have its own automobile policy, with rates that reflect its unique hazards.

Certain other occupations require the use of vehicles that are hazardous regardless of who operates them. Large garbage trucks, for example, are difficult to control. Insurers do not provide liability protection while you operate such a vehicle. Insurers, however, do not exclude all business uses of motor vehicles. Specifically excepted from the exclusion are private passenger autos (for example, those of traveling salespeople); owned pickups, or vans; trailers used with any of these vehicles; and any vehicle used in a farming or ranching business.

Insurers also standardize the risk through exclusion of coverage while "using a vehicle without a reasonable belief that that person is entitled to do so." The insurance company rates the policy according to the insured's characteristics, which include who the insured allows to use the covered auto. A thief, or someone without belief of permission to use the covered auto does not reflect these characteristics. Questions sometimes arise when an insured's child allows a friend to use the covered car, despite parents' admonitions to the contrary. Court rulings are mixed on the application of the exclusion in such a setting. Generally, such persons represent greater risks. The use of a motor vehicle with less than four wheels also represents a greater risk than one with at least four wheels. It too is excluded.

To prevent *catastrophic exposure,* the PAP excludes persons covered under nuclear energy liability policies. This exclusion is a standard provision in all liability policies.

The final two exclusions are confusing. Their purpose is to prevent insureds from obtaining more coverage than was purchased. Thus, no coverage applies for accidents arising out of ownership, maintenance, or use of a motor vehicle "you" own or have available for regular use if it is not a declared auto in the declarations section of the policy. If such protection were available, you would need only to purchase coverage on one vehicle instead of on all your owned vehicles. The second exclusion is the same, except it applies to motor vehicles owned by or available for the regular use of "family members." This last exclusion does not apply to "you." Remember that "you" is the named insured and the named insured's spouse. Thus, if the named insured uses a noncovered vehicle owned by a family member (perhaps a son or daughter living at home), liability coverage exists. On the other hand, the family member who owns the noncovered vehicle is not protected while driving the undeclared auto.

Other Provisions

Part A also has provisions for *out-of-state* coverage and other insurance. The out-of-state provision takes care of a situation in which your liability limits comply with the financial responsibility or compulsory insurance law in your state but are inadequate in another state. It provides that, under such circumstances, your policy will provide at least the minimum amounts and types of coverage required by the state in which you are driving. Suppose you have limits of 15/25/15 ($15,000/$25,000/$15,000), the limits required in the state where your car is garaged. If you are driving in a state that requires 25/50/20 ($25,000/$50,000/$20,000) and are involved in an accident, your insurer will interpret your policy as if it had the higher limits. Thus, even though the limits you have meet only the requirements where you live, your policy will provide the limits you need in any state or province in which you may be driving.

Other Insurance

The liability coverage of the PAP is excess with regard to a nonowned vehicle. In the event of a loss while you are driving a friend's car, your insurer will pay only the amount by which a claim (or judgment) exceeds the limits of your friend's auto insurance. In such a situation, your friend's insurance is *primary coverage* (it pays first) and your insurance is *excess coverage.* By this means, coverage on the vehicle is always primary. If, however, two excess policies apply, then the "other insurance" provision calls for a pro rata distribution of liability. For example, if you were driving a friend's car whose insurance had expired and you were an insured under two policies (as, perhaps, a resident relative of two insureds who bought separate policies on their vehicles), these two policies would share in any liability attributable to you on a pro rata basis. This example, however, is quite unusual.

MEDICAL PAYMENTS COVERAGE—PART B

Medical payments coverage, which is optional in some states and from some insurers, overlaps with family health insurance coverage. You may consider it unnecessary if you have excellent health insurance. Your own family health insurance does not cover nonfamily members riding in your vehicle, so it is narrower than is medical payments coverage. Yet, if you are liable, part A will provide coverage. If not, your passengers may have their own health insurance.

Insuring Agreement

Under part B, the insurer agrees to pay reasonable expenses incurred within three years from the date of an accident for necessary medical and funeral services because of bodily injury caused by an accident and sustained by a covered person. A covered person means you or any family member, while occupying, or as a pedestrian when struck by, a motor vehicle designed for use mainly on public roads, or a trailer of any type. It also includes any other person occupying your covered auto.

Note that you or a family member would be covered by your PAP medical payments protection while occupying a nonowned car, but not other passengers in the vehicle. No benefits are paid if you are struck by a machine not designed for use on the highway, such as a farm tractor.

Exclusions

Medical payments coverage is similar to liability coverage in that it is provided on an open perils basis within the category of automobile use. Seven of the exclusions to part A (liability) are nearly identical to exclusions found in part B (medical payments). These are:

1. While occupying a motor vehicle with less than four wheels.
2. While occupying your covered auto when it is being used as a public livery or conveyance.
3. During the course of employment if workers' compensation is available.
4. Involving a vehicle you own or have available for your regular use other than your covered auto.
5. Occupancy by someone other than "you" of a nondeclared vehicle owned by or available for the regular use of a family member.
6. While occupying a vehicle when it is being used in the business or occupation of a covered person, unless the vehicle is a private passenger auto, pickup, or van owned by the insured, or trailer used with one of these means of transportation.
7. While occupying a vehicle without reasonable belief of permission.

Three additional exclusions apply to the medical payments coverage. The first denies coverage "while occupying a vehicle located for use as a residence or premises." Thus, while "trailers" are covered autos, a house trailer represents a nonstandard risk under part B and is excluded.

The other two exclusions are intended to avoid catastrophic exposure. The first of these omits coverage for losses caused by discharge of a nuclear weapon; war; civil war; insurrection; or rebellion or revolution. The second denies coverage for loss as a consequence of nuclear reaction; radiation; or radioactive contamination.

Other Conditions

The limit of liability for medical payments is on a per person basis, such as $5,000 per person. This is the maximum limit of liability for each person injured in any one accident. If you have two autos insured with a medical payments limit for each shown on the declarations page, you cannot add all (i.e., stack) the limits together. It may appear that you have $10,000 in medical payments coverage because you have $5,000 on each vehicle, but such is not intended by the insurer.

When there is other applicable auto medical payments insurance, your policy will pay on a pro rata basis. With respect to nonowned automobiles, however, the PAP is excess. That is, it pays only after the limits of all other applicable insurance have been exhausted.

Any amounts payable by this coverage are reduced by any amounts payable for the same expenses under part A (liability) or part C (uninsured motorists). Thus, a passenger in your car who is injured cannot recover under both liability and medical payments coverages for the same losses. Nor can you recover under both medical payments and the uninsured motorists coverages. Injured parties are entitled to indemnity, but not double payment.

UNINSURED MOTORISTS COVERAGE—PART C

Uninsured motorists coverage pays for bodily injuries (and property damage in some states) caused by an accident with another vehicle whose driver is negligent and either (1) has no liability insurance or less than that required by law, (2) was a hit-and-run driver, or (3) was a driver whose insurance company is insolvent. Covered persons include you or any family member, any other person occupying your covered auto, and any other person entitled to recovery because of bodily injury to a person in the first two categories. An example of "any other person entitled to recovery" is one who has suffered loss of companionship as a result of a spouse (who was in one of the first two categories) being injured in an accident.

Minimum coverage is the amount required to comply with your state's financial responsibility or compulsory insurance law. You can, however, purchase additional coverage up to the limit you purchased under part A. In addition, if you purchase increased amounts of uninsured motorists coverage, you are eligible to buy *underinsured motorists coverage,* which is discussed later in this chapter.

Uninsured Motor Vehicle

Because you can recover under part C of the PAP only if you are involved in an accident with a negligent driver of an uninsured motor vehicle, the definition of such a vehicle is crucial. The policy defines it as a land motor vehicle or trailer of any type, with the following specifications:

1. One to which no bodily injury *liability bond* or policy applies at the time of the accident.[6]

2. One to which there is a bodily injury liability bond or policy in force, but the limit of liability is less than that specified by the financial responsibility law in the state where your covered auto is garaged.

3. A hit-and-run vehicle whose operator/owner cannot be identified and that hits you or any family member, a vehicle you or any family member are occupying, or your covered auto.

4. One to which a bodily injury liability bond or policy applies at the time of the accident, but the company denies coverage or is insolvent.

However, an uninsured motor vehicle *does not include* any vehicle or equipment:

1. Owned by, furnished, or available for the regular use of you or any family member.

2. Owned or operated by a self-insurer under any applicable motor vehicle law, except a self-insurer which is or becomes insolvent.

3. Owned by any governmental unit or agency.

4. Operated on rails or crawler treads.

5. Designed mainly for use off public roads while not on public roads.

6. While located for use as a residence or premises.

Exclusions

Perhaps because the definition of an uninsured motor vehicle is so limited, only six exclusions apply to part C. Like the prior two parts, uninsured motorist coverage excludes loss:

1. Involving an undeclared motor vehicle owned by you or any family member.

2. While occupying your covered auto when it is being used as a public livery or conveyance.

3. While using a vehicle without reasonable belief of permission.

In addition, exclusion A2 denies payment to a covered person "if that person or the legal representative settles the bodily injury claim without our consent." Just because a negligent driver is an uninsured motorist, he or she is not free from liability. The insurer, therefore, does not want its subrogation rights to be adversely affected by agreements between the insured and negligent driver, which could include collusive and fraudulent situations.

....

6. Some states that require auto liability insurance permit self insurance but require the attainment of an availability bond issued by an approved bonding or insurance company. The bond assures that, if the self-insured becomes liable for damages but cannot pay, the issuer of the bond will. The injured party is paid, and the self-insured becomes indebted to the bonding or insurance company.

On the other hand, the auto insurer does not want to make uninsured motorists payments available through subrogation to a workers' compensation or disability benefits insurer. If the accident occurred during the course of employment, resulting in workers' compensation benefits, the compensation insurer might seek such subrogation. Exclusion B prevents this type of activity.

Last, the coverage is not intended to pay for punitive damages. These are excluded. Additionally, the insuring agreement is specific in promising to pay *compensatory* damages only. Punitive damages are not compensatory.

Other Provisions

The limit of liability provision for uninsured motorists coverage is virtually the same as for medical payments (although the actual limit is usually quite different). The other insurance provision is the same as that for parts A and B; namely, pro rata for your covered auto and excess for a nonowned auto. In the event of a dispute concerning the right to recover damages or their amount, either party—you or the insurer—can demand binding arbitration. Local rules as to procedure and evidence apply.

Underinsured motorists coverage fills in the coverage gap that arises when the negligent party meets the financial responsibility law of the state, but the auto accident victim has losses in excess of the negligent driver's liability limit. In such circumstances, when the negligent driver meets the legal insurance requirements but is legally responsible for additional amounts, the driver is not an uninsured motorist. The negligent driver may not have available other noninsurance resources to pay for the loss, leaving the injured party to bear the financial strain. Underinsured motorists coverage permits the insured to purchase coverage for this situation.

You may purchase underinsured motorists coverage in amounts up to the amount of liability (part A) protection you purchased. The same amount of uninsured motorists coverage must also be purchased. The underinsured motorists coverage will pay the difference between the at-fault driver's liability and the at-fault driver's limit of liability insurance, up to the amount of underinsured motorists coverage purchased. For example, assume you were hit by another motorist, incurring damages of $60,000. Further assume that the other driver is found liable for the full amount of your loss, but carries insurance of only $30,000, which meets the financial responsibility law requirement. An underinsured motorists coverage equal to your limit of liability coverage, say $100,000, would cover the remaining $30,000 of loss above the at-fault driver's insurance. Your total payment, however, could not exceed the underinsured motorists coverage limit of liability. If your loss were $115,000, therefore, you would receive $30,000 from the at-fault driver's insurer and $70,000 from your own insurer. The remaining $15,000 loss remains the responsibility of the at-fault driver, but you may have difficulty collecting it.

COVERAGE FOR DAMAGE TO YOUR AUTO—PART D

Part D of the PAP is first-party property insurance. The insurer agrees to pay for direct and accidental loss to your covered auto and to any other nonowned auto used by you or a family member, subject to policy limitations and exclusions. Automobile equipment, generally meaning those items normally used in the auto and attached to or contained in it, are also covered. All of this is subject to a deductible.

You have the option of buying coverage for your automobile on an open perils basis by purchasing both **collision** and **other than collision**[7] coverage. You may instead opt to buy just collision (although it may be difficult to find a company to provide just collision coverage) or just other than collision, or neither. A premium for the coverage must be stated in the declarations for coverage to apply. The distinction between the two coverages may be important, because collision protection generally carries a higher deductible than other than collision coverage.

Collision means the upset (turning over) of the covered auto or "nonowned auto," or collision with another object. Every other type of loss-causing event is considered "other than collision." To help you identify certain ambiguous perils as either collision or other than collision, a list is provided in the policy. You might mistakenly take this list as one of exclusions. Rather, the perils shown in table 9–3 are other than collision perils and are therefore covered along with other nonexcluded perils if other than collision coverage applies. For example, loss caused by an exploded bomb is neither collision nor among the events listed as examples of other than collision. Because breakage of glass may occur in a collision or by other means, the insurer will allow you to consider the glass breakage as part of the collision loss, negating dual deductibles.

In addition to the above, the insurer will pay up to $15 per day (to a maximum of $450) for *transportation expenses* in the event your covered auto is stolen. Transportation expenses would include car rental or the added cost of public transportation, taxis, and the like. You are entitled to expenses beginning forty-eight hours after the theft and ending when your covered auto is returned to you or its loss is paid. You must notify the police promptly if your covered auto is stolen.

Some insurers offer *towing and labor coverage* for additional premium. If your car breaks down, this coverage pays the cost of repairing it at the place where it became disabled or towing it to a garage. The limit of liability is $25 and a typical premium is $4 or $5. Considering the fact that you can get towing service and many other services for about the same cost from automobile associations, adding towing and labor to your policy may not be a bargain. Furthermore, if your car is disabled by collision or other than collision loss, the cost of towing it to the garage will be paid under those coverages.

Exclusions

Two of the exclusions found in part D (the first and third) have already been discussed. The remaining exclusions are dominated by limitations on

TABLE 9–3

Other Than Collision Losses

1. Missiles and falling objects	6. Hail, water, or flood
2. Fire	7. Malicious mischief or vandalism
3. Theft or larceny	8. Riot or civil commotion
4. Explosion or earthquake	9. Contact with bird or animal
5. Windstorm	10. Breakage of glass

7. In some policies this is called **comprehensive coverage.**

the coverage for automobile equipment. Part D exclusions are listed in table 9–4. One important exclusion reflects the high frequency of theft losses to certain equipment. Exclusion 4 omits coverage for sound equipment unless permanently installed in the automobile. It also eliminates coverage on tapes, records, and other equipment designed for the reproduction of sound. Loss to citizens band radios, two-way mobile radios, telephones, and scanning monitor receivers, unless the item is permanently installed in the opening of the dash or console of the auto, is also denied. Radar detecting equipment is excluded in number 9.

Other excluded items are custom furnishings in pickups and vans (exclusion 10) and loss to awnings or cabanas and equipment designed to create additional living facilities (exclusion 8). Such equipment represents nonstandard exposures for which insurance can be bought through endorsement.

Recall that trailers you own, whether declared or not, are defined as covered autos. To obtain property insurance on those trailers, they must be declared (permitting the insurer to charge a premium). Exclusion 6 provides this requirement by omitting coverage on camper bodies and trailers not shown in the declarations, unless newly acquired and you request coverage within thirty days of acquisition.

Nonfortuitous losses are also excluded. Certain losses are expected or preventable, such as damage due to wear and tear, freezing, mechanical or electrical breakdown, and road damage to tires. These are omitted in exclusion 2.

TABLE 9–4

....

Personal Auto Policy
Part D Exclusions

The Insurer will not pay for loss

1. occurring while the covered auto or any nonowned auto is being used as a public livery or conveyance

2. due to wear and tear; freezing; mechanical or electrical breakdown or failure; or road damage to tires

3. due to radioactive contamination; discharge or any nuclear weapon (even if accidental); war; civil war; insurrection; rebellion or revolution

4. to equipment designed for the reproduction of sound, unless the equipment is permanently installed; or to other electronic equipment unless necessary for operation of the auto

5. to the covered auto or any nonowned auto due to governmental destruction or confiscation because you or any family member engaged in illegal activities or violated EPA/DOT standards

6. to a camper body or trailer not shown in the declarations unless it is new (30 days old) or you notify the insurer of its acquisition

7. to a nonowned auto if used by you or any family member without a reasonable belief of permission to do so

8. to awnings or cabanas; or to equipment designed to create additional living facilities

9. to equipment designed or used for the detection or location or radar

10. to custom furnishings or equipment in or upon any pickup or van

11. to a nonowned auto damaged while being maintained or used by any person who is engaged in the automobile business (servicing, etc.)

12. to a nonowned auto damaged while the driver is engaged in any business, unless the nonowned auto is a private passenger auto or trailer used by "you" or any "family member"

NOTE: Some of the exclusions are paraphrased. See part D of appendix B for the actual wording, which may be interpreted by courts differently than we have done here.

An exclusion new in the 1989 PAP is number 5, which denies coverage for loss or destruction because the government seized the vehicle. This exclusion follows the development of new laws associated with illegal drug trafficking and the handling of hazardous waste.

Prior to revisions in 1986, the PAP covered damage to nonowned autos (including temporary substitutes) for liability only. If you were driving a friend's car or a rental vehicle, the old policy would cover damage to that vehicle only if you were legally liable. The 1986 form provides property damage coverage for nonowned autos in part D, negating the requirement that you be liable. The 1989 form goes one step further by including temporary substitutes (cars used because the declared vehicle is out of commission) in part D rather than part A.

The amount of coverage available for nonowned autos, however, is limited to the maximum available (actual cash value) on any declared auto. In addition, a deductible likely applies, and three exclusions relevant to nonowned autos have been added. First, a nonowned auto used without reasonable belief or permission to do so is not covered. Second, a nonowned vehicle damaged while being driven by someone performing operations associated with the automobile business (servicing, repairing, etc.) is not covered. Last, if the nonowned auto is driven by anyone in any business operation (other than a private passenger auto or trailer driven by "you" or any "family member"), the auto is not covered.

Other Provisions

The *limit of liability* is the lesser of the actual cash value of the stolen or damaged property or the amount necessary to repair or replace it. The insurer reserves the right to pay for the loss in money or repair or replace the damaged property. If the car is stolen and recovered, the insurer will pay for the damage resulting from the theft. If the cost to repair or replace your damaged vehicle exceeds its actual cash value, the insurer can pay you for a total loss. If your car is worth $5,000 but it would cost $6,000 to repair it, the insurer will pay you $5,000, less the deductible.

The *no benefit to bailee* provision says, "This insurance shall not directly or indirectly benefit any carrier or other bailee for hire." If your car is damaged or stolen while in the custody of a parking lot or transportation company, your insurer will pay you and then have the right of subrogation against a negligent bailee. If other insurance covers a loss, your insurer will pay its share on a pro rata basis. If there is a dispute concerning the amount of loss, either you or the insurer may demand an appraisal, which is binding on both parties. As a practical matter, appraisal is seldom used by an insured, because the cost is shared with the insurer.

The other insurance provision is pro rata except for nonowned autos, which is excess. In prior coverages, nonowned autos were included in the liability part, not part D.

DUTIES AFTER AN ACCIDENT OR LOSS—PART E

When an accident or loss occurs, you must notify the company promptly, indicating how, when, and where it happened. Notice should include the names and addresses of any injured persons and any witnesses. You can

ETHICAL *Dilemma*

Claims Inflation

Does your car have any dings or scratches on its exterior? Any car older than a few months (weeks?) probably has a few. Small scratches aren't worth getting fixed on their own, but what if you had a minor auto accident involving only property damage? Couldn't you just ask the auto body shop to include those costs in repair estimates? The insurer is a big company; it won't even feel the effects of another couple of hundred dollars on your claim.

Many people feel justified in adding a few hundred dollars to their auto insurance claims. After all, they've been paying premiums for something! They might even make a deal with the body shop to charge the insurer more than the cost of the repairs and split the difference between the car owner and body shop.

Does this seem ethical? Who pays for those losses? Would it make a difference if "everybody else was doing it"? Also important is to consider the insurer's obligation in preventing overpayment of claims. How far should the insurer go in its investigations of claims? What should be the insurer's response when it finds out about overcharging?

Insurance fraud is considered a major cost to the insurance industry (and consumers). Answers to the questions posed above are not as clear as might appear at first blush, and represent issues currently being debated among regulators and legislators.

notify your agent or call the company. You must also comply with the following conditions:

1. Cooperate with the insurer in the investigation, settlement, or defense of any claim or suit.
2. Promptly send the company copies of any notices or legal papers received in connection with the accident or loss.
3. Submit, as often as reasonably required and at the insurer's expense, to physical exams by physicians it selects as well as examinations under oath.
4. Authorize the company to obtain medical reports and other pertinent records.
5. Submit a proof of loss when required by the insurer.

A person seeking uninsured motorists coverage must also notify the police promptly if a hit-and-run driver is involved, and send copies of the legal papers if a suit is brought. The requirement that you notify the police concerning a hit-and-run driver is to discourage you from making such an allegation when, in fact, something else caused your accident. If, for example, you do not have coverage for damage to your auto but you do have uninsured motorists coverage, you may be tempted to use the latter after you fail to negotiate a sharp curve in the road. Having to report a hit-and-run driver to the police may deter you from making such an assertion.

If an accident causes damage to your car, or if it is stolen, you must also fulfill the following duties:

1. Take reasonable steps after loss to protect the auto and its equipment from further loss. The company will pay for reasonable cost involved in complying with this requirement.

2. Notify the police promptly if your car is stolen.

3. Permit the company to inspect and appraise the damaged property before its repair or disposal.

The first duty listed means that you cannot just walk off and abandon your automobile after an accident. If you do, it may very well be stripped as an abandoned car. The second duty, prompt notification of the police in the event of theft, increases the probability that stolen property will be recovered. This requirement also reduces the moral hazard involved; people have been known to sell a car and then report it stolen. The third duty, permitting company appraisal, allows the insurer to inspect and appraise the loss before repairs are made in order to keep down costs. If you could simply take your damaged car to a repair shop, have the work done, and then send the bill to the insurance company, costs would increase immensely. The most common question you hear upon entering many (if not most) repair shops is, "Do you have insurance?"

GENERAL PROVISIONS—PART F

Several *general provisions* apply to the whole contract. Following is a brief summary of each.

1. Bankruptcy or insolvency of a covered person shall not relieve the insurer of any obligations under the policy. The fact that you are bankrupt does not relieve the insurance company of its obligation to pay a third-party claimant or you.

2. Changes in the policy can be made only in writing, and may affect the premium charged. If the form is revised to provide more coverage without a premium increase, the policy you have will automatically provide it.

3. You cannot start legal proceedings against the insurer until there has been full compliance with all the terms of the policy.

4. If a person who receives payment from the insurer has the right to recover damages from another, the insurer has the right to subrogation. Such a person must help the insurer to exercise its rights and do nothing after a loss to prejudice them. This would apply, for example, to a passenger in your car who is injured, receives payment under the medical payments coverage, and has the right to recover damages from a liable third party or a first-party health insurer. The company's subrogation right, however, does not apply under damage to your auto coverage against any person using your covered auto with a reasonable belief that he or she has the right to do so. If it were not for this provision, a person who borrowed your car with

your permission and had a wreck would wind up paying for the damage if he or she was at fault.

5. The policy's territorial limits are the United States, its territories and possessions, Puerto Rico, and Canada. Note that this does not include Mexico. If you are going to drive your car in Mexico, it is imperative that you buy Mexican insurance. You will have ample opportunity to do so virtually any place you cross the border.

6. The policy cannot be assigned without permission of the insurer.

7. You can cancel the policy by returning it to the insurer or providing advance written notice of the date *cancellation* is to take effect.

8. The insurer can cancel the policy at any time for nonpayment of premium. During the first sixty days the policy is in effect, the insurer can cancel upon ten days' notice for any reason, unless the policy is a renewal or continuation policy. After the first sixty days or if the policy is a renewal or continuation policy, the insurer can cancel only for nonpayment of premium or if your driver's license or that of any driver who lives with you or customarily uses your covered auto is suspended or revoked. In such instances, twenty days' notice must be given. If your state requires a longer notice period or special requirements concerning notice, or modifies any of the stated reasons for termination, the insurer will comply with them.

9. If you have another policy issued by this company and both apply to the same accident, the maximum limit under all the policies will not exceed the highest applicable limit of liability under any one policy. In other words, you cannot stack them. If this policy has a single limit for liability of $300,000 and another policy you have with this company has a single limit of $200,000, your total coverage if both apply to the same accident is $300,000.

INSURING OTHER VEHICLES

A *miscellaneous type vehicle endorsement* can be added to the PAP to insure motorcycles, mopeds, motorscooters, golf carts, motor homes, and other vehicles. The endorsement does not cover snowmobiles; they require a separate endorsement. The miscellaneous type vehicle endorsement can be used to provide all the coverages of the PAP, including liability, medical payments, uninsured motorists, and physical damage coverage. With a few exceptions, the PAP provisions and conditions applicable to these coverages are the same for the endorsement.

NO-FAULT COVERAGES

The liability coverage in the PAP protects you against loss if you are responsible to someone else for bodily injury or property damage because of an accident that was your fault. All the other coverages pay benefits without regard to fault. Thus, they could be referred to as *no-fault coverages*. This term, however, generally refers to legally required coverage added to the auto policy to compensate you and members of your family who are injured in an auto accident. This coverage, as discussed earlier, is called *personal injury protection* (PIP) or *basic economic loss* (BEL).

In some states, the PIP provides only medical payments, whereas in other states it will also replace part of your income if you are disabled in an auto accident. It may also include payments to replace uncompensated personal services, such as those of the parent who maintains the home. If you operate your vehicle in a no-fault state, your coverage will conform with the state law. Usually, there is an aggregate limit per person per accident for all benefits provided by the PIP.

Auto Insurance Premium Rates

Pricing insurance is different from pricing most other goods and services for two reasons. First, cost depends on the future. The insurer must estimate under conditions of uncertainty how many losses there will be, how much they will cost, and when they will occur. Second, cost is influenced by the purchaser. The cost to manufacture a bottle of beer is the same whether you buy it or I buy it. On the other hand, if I drive 50,000 miles per year and you drive 10,000 miles per year, other things being equal, I am more likely to be involved in an auto accident than you are.

Laws regulating insurance require that insurance premium rates be adequate to assure the ability of the insurer to fulfill the promises it sells. They also require that rates be equitable—that is, that they be fair. This does not mean that everyone should pay the same price for a particular policy, but that the price each person pays should reflect accurately the amount of expected losses, expenses, and risk he or she brings to the group of insureds.

Auto insurance is (1) virtually a necessity for most of us, (2) expensive for many people, and (3) sold at a wide range of prices greatly influenced by purchaser characteristics. As a result, there is considerable controversy about insurance pricing fairness. Some claim that the factors used to classify purchasers for pricing purposes are either entirely unsound or are given the wrong weight. Those factors objected to most frequently are (1) age, (2) gender, (3) marital status, and (4) place of residence.

Young, unmarried male drivers object to paying higher premiums than female drivers, married males, and older drivers. People who live in urban areas object to paying more for auto insurance than those who live in rural areas. A common complaint from young drivers is, "I have a perfect driving record, yet I pay more for auto insurance than some older people who have had an accident. My driving record proves that I'm a good risk, but I'm being ripped off." Parents whose sons reach their teens and begin to drive the family car are equally vehement when their auto insurance premiums leap upward. How can all these situations that appear inequitable to the purchasers of auto insurance be justified? This question has been addressed in various ways.

Currently, several states prohibit the use of gender as a rate classification basis. In 1980, the Florida insurance department dealt with the problem by prohibiting use of gender and marital status for auto insurance ratemaking, but the prohibition was temporarily stopped by court order. Testimony before the court established that there is actuarial justification for sex and marital status factors. The Louisiana insurance department issued a similar order, but it too was set aside by the court. In 1977, Los Angeles County sued the California insurance commissioner and two insurance companies, contending that geographical rating territories discriminated against urban residents. This led to a massive study of California's fourteen million drivers. While the study is now old, it remains the most comprehensive of its type, and continues to be used in the debate over permissible rating factors.

The conclusion of the study was that no single factor, such as an individual's accident record, provides an adequate measure of insurance loss potential. The most accurate predictions are those based on a combination of factors, including driving record, age, gender, annual mileage, and place of residence. As figure 9–2 illustrates, the study revealed that young male drivers have twice as many accidents as older males, and males of all ages have more accidents than females of the same age. As table 9–5 shows, however, the major factor causing higher accident frequencies for male drivers seems to be the number of miles driven, although this is not true

FIGURE 9–2

Age, Gender, and Number of Accidents per 100 Drivers

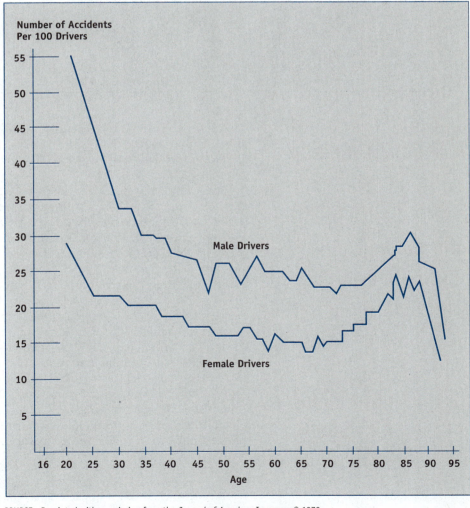

SOURCE: Reprinted with permission from the *Journal of American Insurance* © 1979.

TABLE 9–5

Sex of Drivers Involved in Accidents, 1975–1991

| | DRIVERS IN ALL ACCIDENTS | | | | DRIVERS IN ALL ACCIDENTS | | | |
| | MALE | | FEMALE | | MALE | | FEMALE | |
Year	Number	Rate*	Number	Rate*	Number	Rate**	Number	Rate**
1975	19,100,000	212	8,400,000	195	46,500	52	9,600	22
1976	19,600,000	206	8,800,000	191	48,100	51	10,900	24
1977	20,600,000	209	9,300,000	193	51,900	53	11,800	25
1978	21,700,000	209	9,800,000	192	51,500	50	15,500	30
1979	20,600,000	202	9,100,000	180	52,700	52	12,500	25
1980	20,100,000	200	9,700,000	192	56,100	56	12,200	24
1981	20,500,000	200	9,500,000	183	53,200	52	11,800	23
1982	20,600,000	198	9,900,000	186	48,800	47	11,500	22
1983	20,400,000	187	10,300,000	184	46,300	43	11,700	21
1984	21,800,000	192	11,200,000	190	47,600	42	13,300	23
1985	21,400,000	185	11,600,000	191	46,800	40	12,700	21
1986	22,100,000	196	12,900,000	177	46,400	41	13,100	18
1987	20,700,000	192	12,300,000	148	45,500	42	13,500	16
1988	22,500,000	204	13,700,000	155	49,200	45	14,800	17
1989	14,100,000	95	8,700,000	143	47,000	32	14,800	24
1990	12,170,000	80	7,630,000	121	46,800	31	15,400	24
1991	12,070,000	86	7,430,000	97	43,600	31	14,200	19

*Number of drivers in all accidents per 10,000,000 miles driven.
**Number of drivers in fatal accidents per 1,000,000,000 miles driven.

SOURCE: *Insurance Facts: Property/Casualty Fact Book, 1985–86, 1993,* Insurance Information Institute.

for fatal accidents. Many people argue, therefore, that mileage ought to play a much more significant role in automobile rating, especially because it is a controllable characteristic.[8] This question is discussed further in chapter 25, on regulation.

The California study also showed that varying rates by geographical territory appears valid, with higher rates charged in urban than in rural areas. In addition, it was found that drivers who have had prior accidents are more apt to have accidents in a subsequent period, but the vast majority of accidents in any given time period involve drivers who have had no previous accidents. Therefore, it appears that driving records help in estimating future loss potential of drivers who have had accidents, but they are not the only factor to be considered. A clean record does not necessarily imply a low risk. For insurance rating purposes, the study concludes, "factors other than the individual's past driving record must be assessed in order to properly predict the total cost of losses."

Despite these results, general public perception is that auto insurance rating is unfair. California drivers decided to take matters into their own hands and in 1988 passed Proposition 103, legislation that set strict guidelines for insurance pricing activities. Proposition 103 also called for an elected insurance commissioner and provided that commissioner with expanded powers. A major selling point of this legislation to voters was the

8. Patrick M. Butler, Twiss Butler, Laurie L. Williams, "Sex-Divided Mileage, Accident, and Insurance Cost Data Show that Auto Insurers Overcharge Most Women," *Journal of Insurance Regulation* (March 1988): pp. 243–284.

imposition of limitations on insurer use of geography as a rating factor. Specifically, Proposition 103 requires insurers to set prices primarily based on driving record, years of driving experience, and annual miles driven. Insurers are further restricted in their ability to incorporate age, gender, and zip code in their rating process.

Types of Automobile Policies

There are two general types of auto insurance policies: commercial use and personal use. The Insurance Services Office, a ratemaking advisory organization, has developed standard forms for each category. In the personal use category is a *personal auto policy*. In the commercial category is a *business auto policy*.

Some insurers issue the standard policies; others issue policies that are similar but not identical. Variations result from competition that motivates insurers to try to differentiate their products. The PAP is the newest of the policies for personal use automobiles, having virtually displaced other personal use forms. You will probably buy a PAP or a policy similar to it, and so we have discussed it in detail.

Bear in mind, however, that your policy may differ in some significant ways from the PAP. The major differences are in the perils covered, persons insured, exclusions and definitions, and the presence of *personal injury protection* (PIP) coverage or no-fault provisions that are required in some states. To understand your own coverage, therefore, be sure to read the specifics of your policy.

Shopping for Auto Insurance

Spread over a lifetime, auto insurance is one of our more significant purchases. Yet it's a product whose quality cannot be fully known by the buyer until it is too late to return it. That is, we cannot take insurance out for a test run, see it, feel it, or smell it. How can we choose the appropriate product?

HOW TO SHOP FOR AUTO INSURANCE

First, contact your state insurance department for information on buying insurance. Some departments have detailed information about premiums charged by companies licensed in their state. If you have that information, you can decide which insurers to avoid.

In your quest for low insurance costs, you might consider purchasing a make and model of automobile that has good collision loss experience. Your state insurance department might also have information on this. If you are worried about insurance costs, don't buy a "muscle car," sports car, or high-performance car. They boost the price of insurance.

Next, prepare information (often referred to as "specifications") an insurer will need to give you a price quote. The "Quotation Worksheet" of figure 9–3 can be used as a guide.

As part of these specifications you need to decide what coverage and limits you want. The "Insurance Quotes—Semiannual Premiums" section of figure 9–3 can be used for this process. To consider price-quantity variations, you likely should inquire about several different limits and also several deductible levels. A relatively small increase in the deductible often results in a substantial premium savings. A substantial increase in liability limits often is available at relatively little additional premium. Thus, while we recommend purchase of the limits/deductibles that meet your needs, we realize that cost variations will affect your choices.

After preparing this information, contact an independent agent and ask her or him for quotes from several companies. You may also wish to contact several exclusive-agency companies and insurance-by-mail companies (whose names may be available from your state insurance department) and repeat the process. The degree to which your state insurance regulator has price information will affect the amount of shopping required to find the right coverage at a good price. Be certain to talk with friends and relatives about their experiences with particular agents and insurers. You are buying a service and ought not to consider price as the only factor in your choice. Insurer financial strength and service are also significant factors. Also be certain that you are asking for quotes on the same basic policy, limits, and deductibles; otherwise, your comparisons will be invalid.

Organize the information collected so that you can identify the best price for each combination of limits and deductibles. You must then determine which combination best serves your needs. Remember that insurance works best for the low probability, high value losses.

Next, look for the following discounts:

1. Good student.
2. Nondrinkers.
3. Nonsmokers.
4. Second car.
5. Driver training.
6. Safety devices.

Furthermore, if you have more than one car, don't use both of them to drive to work. "Pleasure use only" is cheaper than "to and from work."

Last, don't duplicate insurance. If you have adequate health insurance to protect you against medical expense, why buy medical payments with your auto insurance? Some insurers add accidental death insurance to an auto policy for extra premium. If you need life insurance, buy a policy that provides benefits for death by any cause.

HOW TO REDUCE INSURANCE COSTS

Table 9–6 illustrates the divergence in premiums that can be found across insurers. These quotes are based on the same information: coverage for a 21-year-old single male with no dependents who commutes twenty-four miles to work round-trip. He had no accidents or violations in the past three years and travels approximately 20,000 miles annually in his three-year-old GMC Jimmy S15, 4-wheel drive.

FIGURE 9–3

Automobile Insurance Quotation Worksheet

Rating Information

	Age	Sex	Marital Status	% Use of Car	Annual Mileage: _____
Principal Operator	_____	_____	_____	_____ %	Number of days per week or weeks out of 5 weeks if driving in a car pool: _____
Other Driver(s)	_____	_____	_____	_____ %	Number of miles one way if driving to and from work every day: _____

Number of accidents or moving violations in the last 3 years: _____
List on separate sheet. Use date of conviction for violations.

Type of Auto(s)	Make	Model & Year
Auto 1	_____	_____
Auto 2	_____	_____

INSURANCE QUOTES—SEMIANNUAL PREMIUMS

Liability Limits		Company 1	Company 2	Company 3
Bodily Injury:	_____ per person			
Bodily Injury:	_____ per accident			
Property Damage:	_____ per accident			
Uninsured Motorist				
Bodily Injury:	_____ per person			
Bodily Injury:	_____ per accident			
Property Damage:	_____ per accident			
Physical Damage to Insured Vehicle				
Comprehensive:	_____ deductible			
Collision:	_____ deductible			
Other Coverages:				
TOTAL SEMIANNUAL PREMIUM:				
Membership Fees: (if applicable)				
Finance Charges:				
TOTAL SEMIANNUAL COST:				

Office of the Commissioner of Insurance (Wisconson), *Consumer's Guide to Auto Insurance,* 1992.

TABLE 9–6

Annual Premium for Identical Auto Insurance for Same Car

	Low	High
Milwaukee	$692	$1,384
Madison	$478	$1,040
Green Bay	$545	$1,085

Office of the Commissioner of Insurance *Consumer's Guide to Auto Insurance,* (Wisconsin), 1992.

The insurance limits are 25/50/10 for part A, $1,000 for part B, 25/50 for part C, and a $100 deductible on the collision.[9] As this illustration demonstrates, shopping around for automobile insurance can be worthwhile.

In addition to shopping around, you can reduce costs in other ways. One way is to choose the largest deductible you can afford. The higher the deductible, the lower the premium. A second way to save is to drop coverage for damage to your vehicle on an old (low value) vehicle. Insurers will not pay more than the actual cash value of a car, regardless of the cost to repair it. Bear these costs yourself, just as you do with the deductible.

Key Terms

no-fault
personal injury protection
basic economic loss
pure no-fault
modified no-fault
add-on plans
choice no-fault
financial responsibility law
unsatisfied judgment funds
compulsory auto liability
  insurance law
substandard market
residual market
auto insurance plans

assigned risk plans
reinsurance facilities
joint underwriting association
personal auto policy
single limit
split limit
stacking
medical payments coverage
uninsured motorists coverage
underinsured motorists coverage
collision coverage
other than collision coverage
comprehensive coverage

Discussion Questions

1. Some auto insurance policies are written with a single limit for liability, whereas others have split limits. The PAP can be written either way. Which do you prefer? Why?

2. Do you think it is socially desirable to do away with age, gender, and marital status as classification factors for auto insurance premium rates? Why, or why not?

3. Chris Malmud says, "Buying uninsured motorist coverage is an awkward substitute for life and health insurance. Besides that, it protects you only in certain situations. I'd rather spend my money on more and better life and health insurance." Do you agree? Why, or why not?

4. Automobile financial responsibility laws require you to have some minimum amount of auto liability insurance. If liability insurance is to protect you from loss caused by your negligence, why should the law force you to buy it? Don't you think this is a decision for you to make? Explain.

5. Morton C. Salt currently has a PAP with only both bodily injury and property damage liability coverages. While hurrying home one evening, Mr. Salt smashed through his garage door. There was damage to his car

9. We do not recommend such low limits or a deductible of only $100 for persons with significant assets or earning power. Consideration of one's ability to compensate injured parties due to negligence would also suggest higher limits.

and extensive damage to the garage and its contents. Will Morton be able to collect for these damages under his PAP? Explain.

6. The insuring agreement for part D of the PAP shown in Appendix B lists ten perils that are covered under other than collision coverage. Explain the meaning of this list and what protection is afforded under the policy for loss caused by one of the perils. Explain further the coverage for loss caused by a peril neither listed in the insuring agreement nor considered collision (such as lightning damage).

7. The deductible for other than collision is usually smaller than for collision coverage. Does this make sense to you? How do you account for it?

8. Discuss three general forms of automobile no-fault laws presented in the text. What are their advantages and disadvantages?

9. Explain how "choice no-fault" would operate in your state.

10. If you permit a friend to drive your car, does he or she have protection under your policy? How will losses be shared if your friend has a PAP on his or her own auto and negligently causes an accident while driving your car?

Cases

9.1 The Helsings (who have a PAP) are involved in an automobile accident (which was not their fault) on their way home from a dinner party. Although they are unharmed, their car is disabled. The police recommend that they leave the car by the side of the road and take a taxi home. When the Helsings return to the scene of the accident, they find that their car has been stripped down to the chassis. The Helsings submit a claim to their insurance agent for the entire loss. Are the Helsings covered under the PAP? Explain. What if the Helsings had not contacted the police?

9.2 Barney has a PAP with liability limits of 25/50/15 and collision coverage with a $200 deductible. While pulling his boat and trailer—which are not listed in the policy's declarations—to the lake, he passes a car, loses control, sideswipes the car he is passing with his trailer, then rams a tree with his car. The losses are as follows:

Barney (medical expenses)		$ 1,300
Barney's girlfriend (medical expenses)		2,450
Driver of other car		
lost income	10,000	
medical expenses	13,500	
mental anguish	20,000	43,500
Passenger of other car		
lost income	5,500	
medical expenses	3,400	8,900
Barney's car		4,000
Barney's boat		800

Barney's trailer	500
Farmer's tree	300
Other driver's Mercedes	29,800

Using the PAP in Appendix B, explain what will and will not be paid by Barney's insurance contract, and why.

9.3 While attending classes at her college, Lisa parks her Corvette on the street and locks it. When she returns, it is gone. She reports its loss to her insurer and notifies the police immediately. Because she must commute to school and to work, she rents a car for $140 per week, or $22 per day for any part of a week. Twenty-three days after her car disappeared, it is recovered. It has been driven over 12,000 miles, its right side has been destroyed in an accident, and the interior has been vandalized. The low estimate for repair of the exterior and interior damage is $23,000. The actual cash value of her car is $16,000. Lisa has a PAP with other than collision coverage and a $200 deductible. Explain her coverage to her, noting what she can expect to recover from her insurer, and why.

CHAPTER 10

Business Property Insurance

Introduction In the preceding four chapters, you have read about property and liability exposures generally, and how families insure home and auto exposures specifically. In some ways, risk management may seem like common sense—spend money on loss control as long as the return for doing so is at least as great as the cost, for instance. The application of risk management decisions, however, including decisions regarding insurance, is a highly complex process. More than common sense is required to make consistently good risk management decisions.

Businesses, which typically confront a greater diversity of risk management concerns, must make even more challenging decisions than do families. In chapters six and seven we highlighted the general property and liability exposures for families. In this chapter you will read about several insurance programs available to businesses to transfer risk connected with property exposures.

We will consider:

1. The philosophy behind the commercial package policy.
2. The coverages provided in the building and personal property (BPP) and business income coverage (BIC).
3. Special property coverages also found in the commercial package policy program.
4. Special insurance needs associated with international exposures.

In chapter six you read about the commercial package policy (CPP) program begun by the insurance services office (ISO) in 1986. This program permits businesses (i.e., commercial insureds) to select among a variety of insurance options, something like a cafeteria where we can choose the items we want and reject those we don't. The broad option categories can be thought of as "modules."

The program is considered a "package" because it combines both property and liability options in the same policy. Further, within each of the property and liability coverages are various options available to tailor protection to the needs particular to the insured. We will examine the basic property and liability coverages, and the general CPP program. We will also consider special international programs.

The CPP works as illustrated in figure 10–1. As you can see, every policy includes three standard elements: the cover page, common policy conditions, and common declarations. The rest of the policy (which may be a "package" if several coverages are chosen) is comprised of choices among the modules that follow. Here and in chapter 11, we will focus on the first two modules, which involve a series of choices among policy types, often referred to as "forms."

The common conditions and declarations of the CPP are general statements about who the insured is and what the requirements of the insured/insurer are, regardless of which forms are chosen. Each individual module incorporates its own declarations and conditions for more specific provisions.

Commercial Property Coverages

Most commercial organizations have similar property exposures, in the general sense of having buildings and contents exposed either as owners or renters. These exposures, along with business income exposures, can be insured through the property module of the CPP. A sample policy is included in Appendix C.

The property module of the CPP begins with property declarations and conditions. These provisions identify the covered location, property values (and limits), premiums, deductibles, and other specific aspects of the coverage. These pages make the insurance unique for a given policyholder by identifying that policyholder's specific exposures. The information in the declarations must be accurate for the desired protection to exist.

The remainder of the property coverage consists of:

- the building and personal property coverage form (BPP)
- one of three causes of loss forms for the BPP
- the business income coverage form (BIC)
- one of three causes of loss forms for the BIC
- endorsements

DIRECT PROPERTY COVERAGE: THE BUILDING AND PERSONAL PROPERTY FORM

The BPP provides coverage for direct physical loss to buildings and/or contents as described in the policy. Separate sections with distinct limits

FIGURE 10–1

Contents of the ISO Commercial Package Policy (CPP)

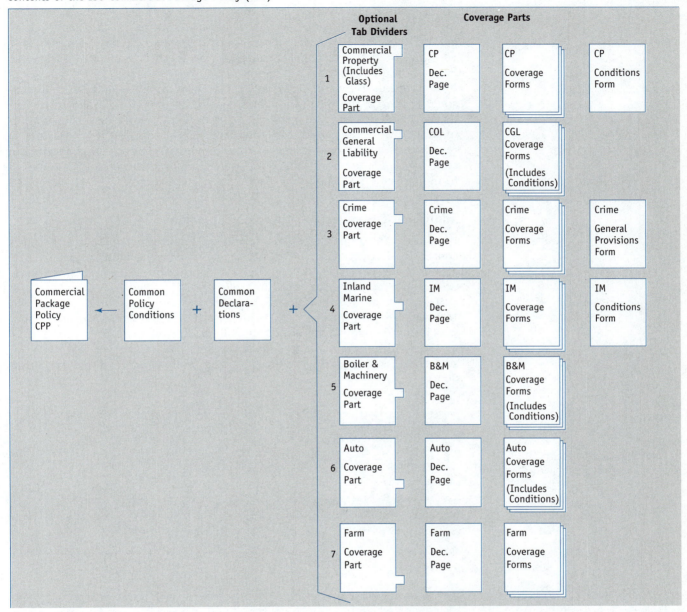

Taken from Rodda, William; Trieschmann, James; Wiening, Eric; Hedges, Bob; *Commercial Property Risk Management and Insurance,* (Malvern, Penn.: The American Institute for Property and Casualty Underwriters, 1988).

of insurance are available for both buildings and contents to account for differing needs of insureds. Some insureds will be tenants, who do not need building coverage. Others will be landlords, who have limited or no need for contents coverage. Many insureds, of course, will need both in varying degrees.

Covered Property

What constitutes a "building" and "business personal property" may appear obvious. The insurer, however, must be very precise in defining its intent because, as you know, insurance is a contract of adhesion. Ambiguities, therefore, are generally construed in favor of the insured. Table 10–1 lists the items defined as "buildings" in the BPP; table 10–2 lists those items defined as "business personal property."

In addition to limiting coverage by defining building and business personal property, the BPP lists specific property that is excluded from protection. These items are listed in table 10–3. Reasons for exclusions in insurance were discussed in chapter five. You might find it worthwhile to match the various reasons for exclusions with the excluded properties in table 10–3. The exercise will help you understand the policy, as opposed to memorizing provisions.

Additional Coverages and Coverage Extensions

In addition to paying for repair or replacement of the listed property when caused by a covered peril, the BPP pays for other related costs. The BPP also extends coverage under specified conditions. These coverage additions and extensions are listed in table 10–4.

The value of these additional and extended coverages can be significant. **Debris removal,** for example, is a cost often overlooked by insureds, but which could involve thousands of dollars. Recent tornadoes in the midwestern United States caused heavy property damage; yet for many insureds, the most significant costs involved removal of tree limbs and other debris.

TABLE 10–1

Building
As Defined in [paraphrased] ISO
Building and Personal Property Coverage
Form, 1989

> The building or structure described in the declarations, including
> - completed additions
> - permanently installed fixtures; machinery; and equipment
> - outdoor fixtures
> - personal property used to maintain or service the building, structure, or premises
> - additions under construction, alterations, and repairs to the building or structure; and related materials, equipment, supplies, and temporary structures, on or within 100 feet of the described premises (if not covered by other insurance)

TABLE 10–2

Business Personal Property
As Defined in [paraphrased] ISO
Building and Personal Property Coverage
Form, 1989

> Business personal property owned by the insured and located in or on the building described in the declarations or in the open (or in a vehicle) within 100 feet of the premises, consisting of
> - furniture and fixtures
> - machinery and equipment
> - stock [defined in the policy]
> - all other personal property owned by the insured and used in the insured's business
> - labor, materials, or services furnished or arranged by the insured on personal property of others
> - the insured's interest in tenants' improvements and betterments
> - leased personal property for which the insured has a contractual responsibility to insure

TABLE 10–3

....

Listed Property Not Covered
As Defined in [paraphrased] ISO
Building and Personal Property Coverage
Form, 1989

- accounts, bills, currency, deeds, evidences of debt, money, notes, or securities
- most animals
- automobiles held for sale
- bridges, roadways, walks, patios, or other paved surfaces
- contraband
- cost of excavations, grading, backfilling, or filling
- foundations of buildings, structures, machinery, or boilers
- land, water, growing crops, or lawns
- personal property while airborne or waterborne
- pilings, piers, wharves, or docks
- property specifically covered under another form
- retaining walls not part of described building
- underground pipes, flues, or drains
- cost to research, replace, or restore the info on valuable papers and records
- most vehicles or self-propelled machines
- while outside of buildings: grain, hay, straw, or other crops; and fences, radio or television antennas, trees, shrubs, or plants

TABLE 10–4

....

Additional Coverages and Coverage
Extensions
As Defined in [paraphrased] ISO
Building and Personal Property Coverage
Form, 1989

Additional Coverages

....

- debris removal
- preservation of property
- fire department service charges
- pollutant cleanup and removal

Coverage Extensions

- newly acquired or constructed property
- personal effects and property of others
- valuable papers and records—cost of research
- property off premises
- outdoor property

An interesting additional coverage is **pollutant cleanup and removal.** This provision specifies the conditions under which and the extent to which protection for clean-up costs are paid by the insurer. Because of large potential liabilities, coverage is narrowly defined to those situations caused by a covered loss, and only for losses at the described premises. The amount of available protection is also limited.

The extended coverages primarily offer protection on properties not included in the definition of covered buildings and personal property. The intent is to provide specific and limited insurance for these properties, which is why they are separated from the general provision. Newly acquired property and property of others, for instance, involve exposures distinct from the general exposures, requiring special attention in the coverage extensions. Some of the coverage extensions offer protection against loss caused by a short list of causes to property otherwise excluded. Outdoor equipment is an example.

Valuation

As has been discussed in prior chapters, property insurance payments may be made on either a replacement cost new (RCN) basis or an actual cash value (ACV) basis. If the insured chooses actual cash value, then the **provision 7 valuation** of **section E, loss conditions** applies. Referring to the sample policy in Appendix C, you will note that the valuation provision involves a number of parts. Parts (b) through (f) explain the insurer's intent for valuation in situations on RCN when ACV may be difficult to measure or inappropriate. Part (o), for instance, permits payment at RCN for relatively small losses, those valued at $2,500 or less.

If the insured chooses, the valuation provision just discussed is overridden by the **optional coverages** section 3, **replacement cost new.** Choice of this optional coverage must be designated in the declarations. Further, the insured ought to recognize the need for higher limits than if ACV is used. Typically, the insurer does not charge a higher rate for RCN coverage; however, more coverage is needed, which translates into a higher premium. For RCN to be paid, the insured must actually repair or replace the covered property. Otherwise, the insurer will pay on an ACV basis.

Limits of Insurance

As just discussed, we need to take care in selecting an amount of insurance that will cover our potential losses. The insurer will not pay more than the limit of insurance, except for the coverage extensions and two coverage additions (fire department charges and pollution cleanup). In addition to concern over having a sufficient amount of insurance to cover the value of any loss, some insureds will need to worry about violation of the **coinsurance** provision, which is found under section E, **additional conditions.**

Coinsurance, discussed in chapter 6, is used to limit pricing inequities among policyholders. As noted, coinsurance violation may cause undesired and unexpected retention of losses.

The BPP continues to include a coinsurance provision as a major condition of coverage. The sample policy found in Appendix C includes several examples of how the coinsurance provision works. Most insureds, however, choose to override the coinsurance clause with an **agreed value option,** found in section G, **optional coverages.** The agreed value option requires the policyholder to buy insurance equal to 100 percent of the value of the property, as determined at the start of the policy. If the insured does so, then the coinsurance provision does not apply and all losses are paid in full, up to the limit of insurance.

The agreed value option, however, does not assure that the policyholder will have sufficient limits of insurance to cover a total loss, especially in times of high inflation. To ward off unwanted retention of loss values above the limit of insurance, the insured can purchase the **inflation guard option** found in section G, optional coverages. The inflation guard provides for automatic periodic increases in limits, with the intent of keeping pace with inflation. The amount of the annual increase is shown on a percentage basis in the declarations.

Causes of Loss

We have just described the major elements of the BPP form. A full understanding of the coverage requires a thorough reading and consideration of the impact of each provision. As for which perils are covered, the property section of the CPP offers three options: the **basic causes of loss** form; the **broad causes of loss** form; and the **special causes of loss** form.

Causes of Loss–Basic Form

The basic causes of loss form is a named–perils option that covers eleven named perils, listed in table 10–5. In referring to the sample policy in Appendix C, you will note that some perils are defined and others are not. When no definition exists, then the common use of the term, supplemented by court opinions, will provide its meaning.

Fire, for example, is not defined, because it has a generally accepted legal meaning. Insurance policies only cover certain fires. While excessive heat may be sufficient for the fire protection to apply, oxidation that results in a flame or glow is typically required. Further, the flame must be "hostile," not within some intended container. For instance, if I throw something into a fireplace, intentionally or not, that fire is not hostile and the loss likely is not covered.

A review of the policy and reference to chapter 8, where many of these same perils were discussed as they apply to homeowners coverage, may clarify which loss situations are payable on the basic causes of loss form. Review of the exclusions is just as important.

Exclusions found in the basic causes of loss form can be categorized as follows:

- ordinance of law
- earth movement
- governmental action
- nuclear hazards
- power failure
- war and military action
- water damage
- "other," involving primarily water, steam, and electrical appliances

Most of these exclusions involve events with catastrophic potential. We suggest that you read this section and determine which reasons for exclusion apply.

Causes of Loss–Broad Form

The broad causes of loss form is also a named-perils coverage. It differs from the basic form in adding four perils, as listed in table 10–5. Geography may dictate to some extent preference for the broad form, because of the ice and snow coverage. Further, note that the water damage peril is for the "sudden and accidental leakage of water or steam that results from the breaking or cracking of part of an appliance or system containing water or steam [not a sprinkler system]." It does *not* cover floods or other similar types of catastrophic water damage. In fact, all the exclusions listed for the basic form, except the last "other" category and some aspects of the water damage limitations, are also found in the broad and special forms.

In addition to adding these four perils, the broad form includes a provision to cover "collapse" caused by the named perils or by hidden decay;

Basic Form	Broad Form
• fire	• basic form perils, plus
• lightning	• weight of snow, ice, or sleet
• explosion	• water damage
• windstorm or hail	• falling objects
• smoke	• breakage of glass
• aircraft or vehicles	
• riot or civil commotion	
• vandalism	
• sprinkler leakage	
• sinkhole collapse	
• volcanic action	

hidden insect or vermin damage; weight of people or personal property; weight of rain that collects on a roof; or use of defective materials in construction, remodeling, or renovation. While this "collapse" additional coverage does not increase the amount of coverage available (as do the other additional coverages), it does expand the list of covered loss situations.

Causes of Loss–Special Form

The special form causes of loss is an "open perils" or "all risk" coverage form. That is, instead of listing those perils that are covered, the special form provides protection for all causes of loss not specifically excluded. In this form, then, the exclusions define the coverage. Remember that all those exclusions listed for the basic form, except for the "other" category and some aspects of the water damage exclusion, apply to the special form.

Most of the additional exclusions found in the special form relate either to catastrophic potentials or nonfortuitous events. Among the catastrophe exclusions are boiler or machinery explosions. Nonfortuitous exclusions relate to such things as wear and tear, smoke from agricultural smudging, and damage to a building interior caused by weather conditions, unless the building exterior is damaged first. For a full listing of the exclusions, refer to the sample policy in Appendix C.

Some experts believe that the greatest benefit of the special form over the broad form is coverage against theft. You may recall that theft is not a listed peril in the broad (nor basic) form.

Coverage of theft from any cause, however, is too costly for most policyholders. The special form, therefore, includes some limitations on this protection. For instance, employee dishonesty and loss of property that appears to have been stolen but for which there is no physical evidence of theft ("mysterious disappearance") are not covered. In addition, certain types of property such as patterns, dyes, furs, jewelry, and tickets are covered against theft for specified amounts only.

In addition to extending coverage for theft, the special form also provides coverage for property in transit. While the rest of the policy requires that damage occur at the described premises or within 100 feet, this provision offers up to $1,000 of coverage for the insured's personal property while in a motor vehicle more than 100 feet from the premises. Coverage, however, is for a limited set of named perils.

Other Policy Provisions

We have described the covered property, valuation, ar[...]
The policy also incorporates a number of other prov[...]
tioned. Provisions exist, for example, that specify the [...]
and insurer when a loss occurs, the existence of a ded[...]
apportion loss when other insurance exists.

These kinds of provisions were discussed general[...]
specifically, with regard to homeowners and auto coverage, in chap[...]
and 9. Every policyholder must be aware of these clauses in order to grasp
the full extent of coverage. Examine the policy shown in Appendix C to
challenge yourself in interpreting these particular policy elements.

CONSEQUENTIAL PROPERTY COVERAGE: BUSINESS INCOME COVERAGE (BIC)

In addition to the cost of repairing and/or replacing damaged or lost property, a business is likely to experience some negative consequences of
being unable to use the damaged or lost property. Those negative consequences typically involve reduced revenues (sales) or increased expenses,
both of which reduce net income (profit). The commercial property policy
provides coverage for net income losses through the business income coverage (BIC) form. The BIC protects against both **business interruption**
and **extra expense** losses.

Business Interruption

When operations shut down (are interrupted) because of loss to physical
property, a business likely loses income. The BIC covers the loss of "(a)
Net Income (Net Profit or Loss before income taxes); and (b) Continuing
normal operating expenses incurred, including payroll." Normal operating
expenses are those costs associated with the activity of the business, not
the materials that may be consumed by the business. Included among
operating expenses are payroll, heat and lighting, advertising, and interest
expenses.

The intent of the BIC is to maintain the insured's same financial position
with or without a loss. Payment, therefore, does not cover all lost revenues,
because those revenues generally cover expenses, some of which will not
continue. Yet because some expenses continue, coverage of net income alone
is insufficient. An example of a BIC loss is given in the box on page 250.

Extra Expense

In addition to losing sales, a business may need to incur various expenses
following property damage in order to minimize further loss of sales. These
extra expenses are also covered by the BIC. A bank, for example, could
not simply shut down operations if a fire destroyed its building, because
the bank's customers rely on having ready access to financial services. As
a result, the bank is likely to set up operations at a temporary location
(thus reducing the extent of lost revenues) while the damaged property is
being repaired. The rent at the temporary location plus any increase in
other expenses would be considered covered extra expenses.

Causes of Loss

The same three perils options available for the BPP are also available for the BIC. Because the BIC requires that the covered income loss result from direct physical loss or damage to property described in the declarations, most insureds choose the same causes of loss form for both the BPP and the BIC.

Business Income Coverage (BIC) Hypothetical Loss

In the spring of 1992, Chicago experienced an unusual "flood," apparently caused by damage to an underground tunnel system. Many firms were required to shut down offices in the damaged area. Among them were large accounting organizations, just two weeks before the tax deadline of April 15. Assume the following hypothetical conditions for one of those firms.

Pre-loss Financial Information	
Average monthly revenues	$500,000
Average April revenues	
(stated in 1992 dollars)	700,000
Average monthly payroll	300,000
Average April payroll	550,000
Monthly heat, electricity, water	25,000
Monthly rent for leased office	45,000
Monthly interest expense	10,000
Monthly marketing expense	15,000
Monthly other expenses	10,000
Net Income in April	$ 45,000

Post-loss Financial Information for April 1992	
Revenues	$600,000
Payroll	540,000
Utilities	30,000
Rent on downtown space	0
Rent for temporary space	50,000
Interest expense	10,000
Marketing expense	22,000
Other expenses	20,000
Net Loss	($ 72,000)

This firm experienced both a reduction in revenue and an increase in expenses. The resulting profit (net income) loss is the covered loss in the BIC. For this example, the loss equals $117,000, the sum of the income not received ($45,000) that would have been expected without a loss, plus the actual lost income ($72,000) incurred. Such a substantial loss for a two-week period is not unusual.

Coinsurance

The coinsurance provision of the BIC is one of the more confusing parts of any insurance policy. Its purpose is the same as that discussed in chapter 6 generally and mentioned previously in this chapter regarding the BPP, which is to maintain equity in pricing. Its application is also similar. The difficulty comes in defining the underlying value of the full exposure, which is needed to apply any coinsurance provision.

Remember that a BIC loss equals net income plus *continuing* operating expenses. Coinsurance, however, applies to net income plus *all* operating expenses, a larger value. The amount of insurance required to meet the coinsurance provision is some percentage of this value, with the percentage determined by what the insured expects to be the maximum period of interruption. If a maximum interruption of six months is expected, for example, the proper coinsurance percentage is 50 percent (6/12). If it is nine months, a coinsurance percentage of 75 percent (9/12) is appropriate.

Because of the complexity of the coinsurance provision, however, many insureds choose an agreed value option. This option works under the same principles as those discussed with regard to the BPP. Using the example illustrated in the box on page 250, we can demonstrate the application of the coinsurance provision. Coinsurance requirements apply to net income plus operating expenses ($95,000 + $405,000 per month on average, or $6,000,000 for the year). If a 50 percent coinsurance provision is used because the expected maximum period of interruption is six months, then the amount of insurance required is $3,000,000 (.50 × $6,000,000). If the April example is representative, a six-month interruption would result in a much lower loss. Our estimates, however, are often low, and additional coverages raise the amount of insurance appropriate for such losses; hence, insurers require coverage at the higher value.

Other Options

The BIC includes a number of options designed to modify coverage for the insured's specific needs. Three options that affect the coinsurance provision are the **monthly limit of indemnity; maximum period of indemnity; and payroll endorsements.**

The monthly limit of indemnity, as defined in the sample policy in Appendix C, negates the coinsurance provision. Instead, a total limit is listed, as is the percentage of that limit available each month. The policy uses the example of a $120,000 limit and 1/4 monthly amount. For this example, only $30,000 (1/4 × 120,000) is available each month. An organization with stable earnings and expectations of a short period of restoration would likely find this option of interest.

The maximum period of indemnity option also negates the coinsurance provision of the BIC. Instead of limiting the amount payable per month, however, this option limits the duration of coverage to 120 days (or until the limit is reached, whichever comes first). Both the maximum period of indemnity and monthly limit of indemnity address the fact that the standard policy cannot be used with a coinsurance provision of less than 50 percent (6 months).

Instead of negating the coinsurance provision, as do the two options just discussed, the payroll endorsements allow the insured to deduct some or all of its payroll from the value of operating expenses before calculating the coinsurance requirement. Doing so will allow the insured to purchase less insurance (pay lower premiums, usually) and still meet the coinsurance provision. It also excludes payroll from covered expenses, however, and so the insured must feel confident that payroll would not be maintained during a shutdown. A common payroll endorsement includes ninety days of payroll expense in the coinsurance calculation (and BIC coverage), assuming that a short shutdown might allow the insured to continue to pay employees. For a longer shutdown, termination of employment might be more cost effective.

The commercial package policy is designed to accommodate separate and sometimes special property needs of insureds that are not covered in the BPP and BIC of the commercial property program. These include crime, inland marine, boiler and machinery, and policies designed for small businesses.

COMMERCIAL CRIME COVERAGE

Historically, crime losses have been insured separately from other property losses. Perhaps the separation has been intended to standardize the risk; exposure to crime loss may involve quite different loss control needs, and thus frequency and severity estimates, from exposure to fire, weather damage, or other BPP–type losses. Furthermore, within the crime coverage, employee dishonesty typically has been insured separately from other property crimes, likely also in an effort to recognize variations in risk and loss control needs between the two. Furthermore, employee dishonesty protection began as a bond (called a **fidelity bond**), which was a guarantee provided to employers by each employee promising loyalty and faithfulness, and stipulating a mechanism for financial recovery should the promise be broken. As a result, bonding companies developed to protect against employee crimes, while insurers expanded their coverage separately to protect against other property—related crimes.

Today, however, an insured is able to purchase the commercial crime coverage part of the commercial package policy and cover all types of crimes. Table 10–6 lists the options for crime coverage. An insured would choose those options relevant to its needs, attach declarations and conditions appropriate to the crime policy, and then attach all of it to the common declarations and conditions of the commercial package policy. Most likely the insured has also chosen a BPP and BIC as well, and may include several other coverage parts.

INLAND MARINE

You may recall that the BPP covers personal property while it is located at the described premises. Many businesses, however, move property from one location to another and/or have specialized personal property that require insurance coverage not intended by the BPP. These needs are often met by inland marine (IM) insurance. Examples of property needing IM coverage are shown in table 10–7.

Inland marine insurance is an outgrowth of **ocean marine** insurance, which is coverage for property while being transported by water (including coverage for the vessels doing the transporting). IM tends to be broad coverage, often on an open-perils basis, and generally for replacement cost. Exclusions tend to involve nonfortuitous events, such as wear and tear and intentionally caused loss. The protection IM provides is for inland transportation and specialized equipment.

TABLE 10–6

....

Commercial Crime Coverage—Coverage Options

Form A—Employee Dishonesty (Blanket)
Form A—Employee Dishonesty (Scheduled)
Form B—Forgery or Alteration
Form C—Theft, Disappearance and Destruction
Form D—Robbery and Safe Burglary
Form E—Premises Burglary
Form F—Computer Fraud
Form G—Extortion
Form H—Premises Theft and Robbery Outside the Premises
Form I—Lessees of Safe Deposit Boxes
Form J—Securities Deposited with Others
Form K—Liability for Guests' Property—Safe Deposit Box
Form L—Liability for Guests' Property—Premises
Form M—Safe Depository Liability
Form N—Safe Depository Direct Loss

TABLE 10–7

....

Examples of Property Appropriate for Inland Marine Coverage

Dentistry Equipment
Theatrical Sets
Mobile Inventory

BOILER AND MACHINERY COVERAGE

When a boiler or similar piece of machinery explodes, the cost tends to be enormous. Typically, the entire building is destroyed, as are surrounding properties. Anyone in or near the building may be killed or badly injured. Furthermore, the overwhelming majority of such explosions can be prevented through periodic inspection and excellent maintenance. As a result, a boiler inspection industry developed, and ultimately became an inspection and insurance industry.

Boiler and machinery (B&M) coverage protects against loss that results from property damage to the insured's own property, and to nonowned property, (bodily injury liability coverage can be added by endorsement), all caused by explosions or other sudden breakdowns of boilers and machinery. The bulk of the premium, however, goes toward costs of inspection and loss control. Any business that uses a boiler or similar type of machinery needs to consider purchase of this coverage, because the potential loss is large while the probability of loss is low if proper care is maintained.

BUSINESSOWNERS POLICY

In 1976, the insurance services office (ISO) developed its first businessowners policy (BOP), which was designed for small businesses in the office, mercantile, and processing categories, and also for apartment houses and condominium associations. The intent was to provide a comprehensive policy that would omit the need for small businesses to make numerous decisions, while also incorporating coverage on exposures often overlooked. The original BOP was one policy covering both property and liability exposures. The current program incorporates the BOP into the

ETHICAL *Dilemma*

How to Show Trust in Employees

Embezzlement is a major concern for many businesses. A difficulty in controlling it arises, however, in the conflict between demonstrating trust in one's employees and implementing detection techniques that may be perceived as distrustful. A further wrinkle develops in realizing that the crime policy requires employers to notify their fidelity insurers when they learn of *any* unlawful behavior by their employees, regardless of the circumstance of that behavior. If such notification is not provided, coverage may be suspended.

We can think of several scenarios that would pose ethical dilemmas. Consider, for example, a person who is working two jobs to help support her aging mother. At the end of her rope one evening, she fights with her husband, who calls the police. She is charged with domestic violence, even though everyone recognizes that the stress caused her to throw the vase. Should her employer tell the crime insurer about this legal infraction? Or should the employer try to protect the employee's reputation?

As a second example, consider a teenage worker at a bakery who steals a few loaves of bread because he does not have enough to eat at home (his father was paralyzed in an auto accident, and his mother cannot support the whole family on her secretary's salary). Should the employer press charges against the teenager? Are other workers taking even worse advantage of the employer but not getting caught? Does it matter that the teenager is such a good worker that he makes more profit for the company than the value of the stolen goods (while other workers take extended lunch breaks and work slowly on the line)?

Consider a third scenario. Two employees share a job. At some point, an embezzlement by one or the other becomes known, but both deny it. No proof can be found to identify the culprit. Should both be fired? Kept working at the firm? Given new jobs? What can be done to protect the reputation of the innocent employee?

Development of firm policies regarding employee misdeeds, before the occurrence of a loss, may help give direction in this and other situations. Communication of such policies to workers is essential. Demonstrating both trust and vigilance takes energy and thought, but it can be accomplished.

commercial package policy through separate property and liability policies designed for small businesses. When these coverages are combined, they provide protection nearly identical to the old BOP policy.

The property portion of the businessowners program covers both direct and consequential losses, combining the types of coverage found in the BPP and BIC. An inflation guard is standard, as is a seasonal fluctuation for personal property. The inflation guard increases the building's coverage limit by some stated percentage automatically each year. The **seasonal fluctuation** permits recovery of lost personal property up to 125 percent of the declared limit, as long as the average value of the personal property over the prior twelve months is not greater than the limit. For organizations with fluctuating stock values, this provision is helpful. Coverage is on a replacement cost new basis without a coinsurance provision.

The policy also provides business income loss for one year of interruption without a stated dollar limit or coinsurance requirement. Many small businesses are prone to ignore this exposure, which is why the coverage is included automatically.

Coverage can be purchased either on a named-perils basis or open risk. The named-perils form covers the causes of loss listed in table 10–5, which are the same perils available in other coverage forms. One additional peril, "transportation," is also covered in the BOP. The transportation peril affords some inland marine protection.

Global Property Exposures[1]

Many firms today spread their operations beyond a single country's border, which forces management to think globally instead of domestically. Although many risk management problems are the same no matter where they are encountered, some unique problems arise when companies cross national borders. Even basic tasks of identification and measurement of risks faced by an organization can be complicated by different legal and monetary systems, lack of data, and language and cultural barriers. The nature of such problems is explained in this section, followed by discussions of property-liability coverages in other countries, and coverages, such as political risk insurance, specific to foreign investment.

LAWS AND REGULATIONS IN FOREIGN COUNTRIES

The risk manager must learn about the legal environment in which the foreign facility is located. Often the decision to undertake operations in a particular country is made apart from any risk management considerations. Although the legal environment may have been carefully reviewed from the standpoint of firm operations, little information may have been obtained about insurance requirements and regulations. For example, in many countries social insurance is much broader than in the United States and there are few, if any, alternatives available to the risk manager. Workers' compensation, retirement benefits, automobile insurance, and property insurance, in some cases, must be purchased from state monopolies. Even when private alternatives are available, tax considerations and the difficulty of enforcing contracts with nonauthorized carriers may render these options undesirable.

In addition, the risk manager may be forced by regulations to purchase local coverage that is inadequate in covered perils or limits of liability. Particularly in less developed countries, there simply may not be adequate insurance capacity to provide desirable amounts and types of coverage.

1. Much of this discussion was written by Frederick W. Schroath for the fifth edition of the text (1984).

The risk manager then must decide whether or not to ignore the regulations and use nonadmitted coverage.

Nonadmitted coverage involves contracts issued by a company not authorized to write insurance in the country where the exposure is located. **Admitted insurance** is written by companies so authorized. Nonadmitted contracts have advantages to some U.S. policyholders: they are written in English; use United States dollars for premiums and claims, thus avoiding exchange rate risk; utilize terms and conditions familiar to United States risk managers; and provide flexibility in underwriting. However, such contracts may be illegal in some countries, and the local subsidiary is subject to penalties if their existence becomes known. Further, premium payment may not be tax deductible, even in countries where nonadmitted coverages are permitted. If nonadmitted insurance is purchased where it is prohibited, claim payments must be made to the parent corporation, which then has to find a way to transfer the funds to the local subsidiary.

Coverage is also affected by the codification of the legal system under which the country operates. The *Napoleonic code,* for example, is used in France, Belgium, Egypt, Greece, Italy, Spain, and several other countries. Under this legal system, liability for negligence is treated differently than under the United States system of common law: any negligence not specifically mentioned in the code is dismissed. The common law system is based on legal precedence, and the judges play a much more significant role.

DATA COLLECTION AND ANALYSIS

Another problem facing the international risk manager is the collection of adequate statistical information. Economic and statistical data commonly available in the United States may simply be nonexistent in other parts of the world. For example, census data that provide an accurate reflection of mortality rates may not be available because of the irregularity and method by which they are collected. Even in industrialized countries statistics may need careful scrutiny, because the method used to produce them may be vastly different from that typical to the risk manager. This is particularly true of rate-making data. Data may also be grossly distorted for political reasons. Officially stated inflation rates, for instance, are notoriously suspect in many countries.

Faced with this lack of reliable information, the risk manager has little choice but to proceed with caution until experience and internal data collection can supplement or confirm other data sources. Contacts with other firms in the same industry and with other foreign subsidiaries can provide invaluable sources of information.

Data collection and analysis are not only a problem in this broad sense. They are also troublesome in that communication between the corporate headquarters and foreign operations becomes difficult due to language barriers, cultural differences, and often a sense of antagonism that a noncitizen has authority over decisions. Particularly difficult under these circumstances are the identification and evaluation of exposures, and the implementation of risk management tools. Loss control, for instance, is much more advanced and accepted in the United States than in most other countries. Encouraging foreign operations to install sprinklers, implement safety programs, and undertake other loss control steps generally is quite difficult. Further, risk managers of United States-based multinational firms may have difficulty persuading foreign operations to accept retention levels as high as those used in the United States. Retention simply is not well accepted elsewhere.

EXCHANGE RATE RISK

Any multinational transaction, where payments are transferred from one currency to another, is subject to **exchange rate risk.** Under the current system of floating exchange rates, the rate of currency exchange between any two countries is not fixed and may vary substantially over time. To illustrate the effect of exchange rate risk on an insurance transaction, let us assume a French subsidiary purchased a three-year property contract from a nonadmitted United States insurer in 1980. In mid-1980, one United States dollar was worth approximately four French francs; by the summer of 1983, the dollar was worth eight francs. When this contract was renewed in 1983, then, its premium for the same coverage was twice that of 1980.[2]

INTERNATIONAL PROPERTY-LIABILITY COVERAGES

Due to the regulation, local demand, custom, legal restrictions, and insurance capacity, contract provisions abroad may vary considerably from standard United States forms. In some cases, coverage may be broader than United States forms, but most American firms feel there are substantial gaps in the coverage provided in many overseas markets. Examples of these gaps include:

1. Coverage for limited perils abroad, relative to that available in the U.S.
2. Coverage on an ACV basis only in property insurance policies.
3. Unavailability of coinsurance below a 100 percent rate in property insurance policies.
4. No automobile liability coverage if the driver is under the influence of alcohol or other drugs.
5. Stricter disclosure provisions regarding changes in risk and filing a proof of loss, relative to U.S. practices.
6. Varying policy periods from country to country and by type of coverage. In some cases, the contract period may be for as long as ten years. Cancellation provisions also vary widely.
7. Insufficient liability insurance. Some liability insurance may contain substantial percentage deductibles, or may not cover as many types of liability as in the U.S.

Several means of developing a global insurance program (in which international operations have the same or similar insurance coverages as do domestic operations) exist. One is to purchase local (admitted) coverage through affiliates of an international insurer (CIGNA, AIG, and Lloyd's are the three main sources of international insurance) with the broadest coverage available, and to fill in remaining gaps with a **difference in conditions** policy (DIC). A DIC is a promise to cover differences between the

....

2. By 1994, the dollar was worth 5.79 French Francs, showing the volatility of exchange rates.

global program (generally the same coverage and amounts as purchased for domestic operations) and the local coverage. For example, some local property policies do not cover windstorm. The DIC would fill this gap.

Another option is to buy as much local coverage as possible and reinsure the exposure with a captive. A captive is a subsidiary that insures affiliate companies (and sometimes other firms as well) of the parent and the parent itself. The captive approach aids the firm in managing exchange rate risk as well as insurable risks by controlling the flow of funds across borders through the insurance transaction. Captives are discussed in chapter 3.

Cutting the Cost of Business Insurance

Your firm can reduce its insurance costs by controlling losses, because the "product" being purchased from an insurer is not as expensive to provide. Your firm can also reduce its insurance costs through use of a successful purchasing strategy. For this consumer application, let's postpone our discussion of loss reduction, and focus on how your firm can affect the cost of insurance through its buying practices, assuming it is a desirable risk.

BUYING INSURANCE FOR THE FIRM

Buying insurance for the firm is like buying it for a family or individual, but you may need more help from agents or brokers in determining what you need and shopping for it. What should you do the first time you buy? Before you start shopping, you have to decide exactly what you're looking for. Suppose you decide you want a commercial property policy with a BPP and BIC, but you do not know which causes of loss form or coinsurance provision to choose. Get prices on several options so you can compare them.

Ask About Services

Price alone isn't enough. You need service. The most important services for your firm include:

1. Help in determining insurance needs.
2. Help in shopping for coverage.
3. Help with loss prevention.
4. Help with claim settlement.

If you tell an agent, broker, or company representative that you are concerned about adequate coverage, price, and service, he or she will recognize that you are a reasonable, rational buyer. Although you cannot be sure ahead of time what quantity and quality of service you will receive, you can request a written statement of what to expect. This does not mean a brochure extolling the virtues of the selling organization, but a specific statement tailored to your needs. Such a statement has two functions:

1. It tells you what to expect.
2. It gives you something to refer to at renewal time.

What to Do at Renewal Time

When a policy anniversary or renewal time rolls around, a quality agent, broker, or company representative will suggest a review of your needs and coverages. In addition to that, you should review the service you have received and check on insurance costs. If your firm is a desirable risk, you have a good bargaining position. Use it—but don't abuse it.

Question the premium at renewal time. Ask the agent, broker, or company representative to check on it. How does it compare with alternatives? *Caveat:* Although you should ask about cost at renewal time and check with other sources occasionally to see what is available in the insurance market, it is foolish to hop from agent to agent or company for a few dollars. People who never question price frequently pay too much, but start with the assumption that your agent, broker, or company representative will treat you appropriately. If you are too lethargic, you may not get the best deal. If you are fickle and unreasonably demanding, however, no one wants your business.

REDUCE COST BY REDUCING LOSSES

Loss prevention and reduction pay off in two ways. First, they save the firm money it would lose on uninsured losses. Second, they lead to reductions in premium rates. Let's look at a few examples of how losses can be controlled.

Employee Dishonesty

Employee dishonesty losses exceed those caused by burglary, robbery, and theft committed by persons not employed by their victims. They are probably equal to or greater than annual fire losses. Your firm can prevent embezzlement by taking the following steps:

1. **Carefully select employees.** Check their background so you won't hire someone with past criminal behavior related to the duties for which she or he would be hired. *Caveat:* Be careful you don't violate federal law in this process. There are limits to what you can ask a prospective employee, and an improperly conducted investigation can violate privacy rights and result in a lawsuit against the employer.

2. **Be aware of an employee's spending pattern.** Many embezzlers have been discovered through their spending habits. Example: Young man, salary $2,000 per month, owns one automobile, one pickup; just bought a new Corvette for himself and a three-carat diamond for his wife. Did he win big at the dog races or is he stealing from you?

3. **Maintain adequate internal control.** The duties of one employee should serve as a check on the duties of another. Don't have one person in charge of ordering, billing, and receiving. Every employee should be required to take a regular annual vacation. Have his or her duties performed by another employee during such an absence; don't just let the work stack up until the employee's return.

4. **Report embezzlement to the insurer immediately upon discovery,** but beware of a false accusation that could lead to a personal injury suit. If dishonest employees go scot-free, others may be tempted, and condoning dishonesty can negate coverage for a subsequent incident.

5. **Have outside accountants make frequent and complete audits,** and follow their advice with regard to the improvement of internal controls.

6. **Be cognizant of troubled employees.** Effective broad-based assistance programs can help thwart an embezzlement loss.

Property Damage

If you are going to build or remodel a building, ask your insurer for advice while you are in the planning stage. For firms with a risk management function, encourage the insurer to work with the risk manager, safety engineers, and architects to build a safe structure. By following such advice, you can reduce property insurance premium rates markedly. The most important factors are construction, layout (arrangement of space), and protection. From the fire loss point of view, the best construction is fire resistive, the worst is wood frame. A wood frame, however, may withstand an earthquake more successfully. Incorporation of fire walls and fire partitions at the time of construction can reduce the probability of a fire spreading, thereby reducing losses. Protection features such as sprinkler systems and detection and alarm systems also reduce losses.

Use of good lighting systems and guard patrols reduce vandalism and burglary losses. Proper roof construction should limit the occurrence of collapse. Boiler explosions can be avoided by quality maintenance and frequent inspections. Purchase of nonbreakable windows will protect against glass breakage.

Some of these insurance premium rate-reducing features can be built in only at the time of building or remodeling. Others, such as a sprinkler system, can be added later, but only at considerably greater cost. Because the cost of the insurance (or losses) is, like death and taxes, always with us, you may save considerable money over the long term by considering fire prevention during the planning stage.

Key Terms

agreed value option
optional coverages
inflation guard option
basic causes of loss
broad causes of loss
special causes of loss
business interruption
extra expenses
monthly limit of indemnity

maximum period of indemnity
payroll endorsements
fidelity bond
ocean marine coverage
seasonal fluctuation
nonadmitted coverage
admitted insurance
exchange rate risk
difference in conditions policy

Discussion Questions

1. What types of property are covered in the BPP? What are some examples of excluded property, and why are they excluded?

2. How can an insured get around the coinsurance provision in the BPP? Why might an insured prefer to do this?

3. What are the primary differences among the three causes of loss forms available in the commercial property policy? Why not always choose the special form?

4. What kinds of losses are covered in the BIC? Provide examples.

5. How does the insured choose a limit of insurance for the BIC?

6. When would the monthly limit of indemnity, maximum period of indemnity, or payroll endorsement be appropriate?

7. What is a fidelity bond?

8. What is inland marine insurance?

9. What are the advantages of using a businessowners policy?

10. What special problems arise for global property exposures?

Cases

10.1 Assume that the Seinfeld Shoe Station owns the $1 million building in which it operates, maintains inventory and other business properties in the building worth $700,000, and sometimes has possession of other businesses' property up to a value of $50,000 while it is being repaired. For each of the following losses, what if anything will Seinfeld's BPP insurer pay? Limits are $1 million on coverage A and $800,000 on coverage B. The broad causes-of-loss form is used. Explain your answers.

1. Wind damage rips off tiles from the roof, costing $20,000 to replace. The actual cash value is $17,000.

2. An angry arsonist starts a fire. The building requires repairs of $15,000, $17,000 of inventory is destroyed, and $2,000 of other people's property is burned.

3. A water pipe bursts, destroying $22,000 of inventory and requiring $10,000 to repair the pipe.

10.2 Seinfeld also bought a BIC with a limit of $250,000 and a 50 percent coinsurance clause. No other endorsements are used. A limited income statement for last year is shown below.

Revenues		2,000,000
Cost of Goods Sold	800,000	
Utilities	200,000	
Payroll	400,000	
Other Expenses	300,000	1,700,000
Profit		$ 300,000

1. How much in expenses does Seinfeld expect to be noncontinuing in the event of a shutdown? Explain.

2. What is the longest shutdown period Seinfeld would expect following a loss?

3. If a three-month closing occurred following the roof collapsing due to the weight of snow, what do you think would be the loss? Explain.

10.3 Maben's Masters is an international golfing goods manufacturer, specializing in high-quality, high-priced golfing equipment. Maben's Masters has locations in the United States (its headquarters), Great Britain, Australia, Germany, and Brazil, each producing various goods. Total revenues last year were $1,000,000,000, with 40 percent in the U.S. and the rest somewhat evenly spread in the other four locations. Property located in the U.S. is worth $35 million, approximately $15 million each in the other locales.

1. How would you advise Maben's Masters regarding their international property exposure?
2. Discuss some risk management concerns peculiar to global enterprises.
3. What additional types of information would be helpful in your effort to advise Maben's Masters?

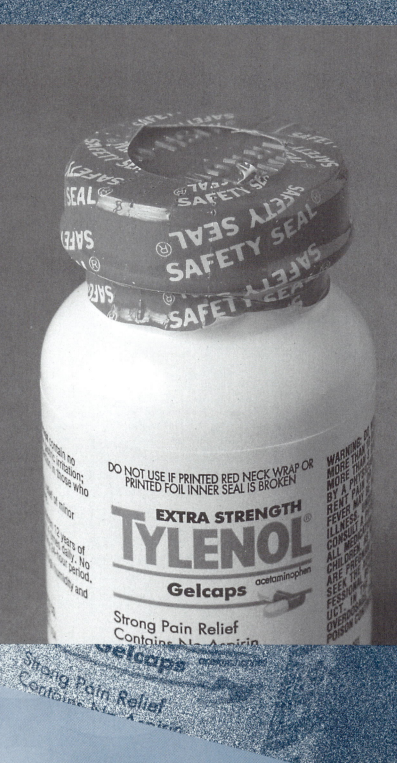

Business Liability Insurance

Introduction   As a current or future business executive, you will be making decisions for your organization that affect its success and survival, including marketing strategies, expansion opportunities, and selection of personnel. Within all these decisions are risk management issues that require attention. Failure to consider risk management could cause the business to fail, or at least be less successful.

An example helps illustrate. In June 1993, various reports were made of consumers finding syringes in soft drink cans, primarily Pepsi products. The incidents caused large expenses for Pepsi and other beverage manufacturers. The degree to which Pepsi prepared for product tampering and sabotage lessened these losses. Otherwise, Pepsi might have been unable to recreate its market in a highly competitive industry.

In chapter 10 we discussed business risk management for property exposures. In this chapter, we will use the foundation built in our discussion of the commercial package policy (CPP) to investigate business liability risk management. A coverage part available in the CPP is the commercial general liability (CGL) policy that most businesses purchase.

Business liability exposures receive substantial media attention and play a large role in a business executive's list of concerns. Some of the prominent areas of concern were presented in chapter 7; you might want to review those now. You may also find that reading the newspaper brings many of these ideas to life, as examples are found daily. Why not bring examples to class for discussion?

This chapter will:

1. Review business liability exposures.
2. Present a discussion of liability insurance offered through the CPP in the form of the comprehensive general liability policy.
3. Consider how an umbrella liability policy might contribute to the success of an organization's risk management program.
4. Briefly introduce techniques available to manage other business liability exposures.

Business Liability Risks

As discussed in chapter 7, businesses have a wide variety of liability exposures. Many of these are insurable through the CGL. Table 11–1 lists some of the common business liability exposures covered in traditional insurance policies.

Remember that for each of these exposures, liability may result from several sources. The organization might be negligent; strict liability might apply; or the organization could be vicariously liable. The point is that a business must be aware of the ethical and legal rules governing its operations and respond appropriately. Knowledge that a product may harm users results in a high level of responsibility for the producer and retailer of that product. Even without actual knowledge, responsibility often exists if the decision makers within the organization *should have known* of the danger.

Keep in mind, therefore, that even though we will focus in this chapter on the insurance coverages available to finance business liability losses, safety cannot be ignored. The costs of insurance and of lost reputation can be greatly diminished through conscientious, safe behavior. And some liabilities might not be covered by insurance.

Commercial General Liability Policy[1]

In chapter 10 we discussed at length the property module of the commercial package policy (CPP). In chapters 8 and 9, we discussed the packaging of family exposures in the homeowners and auto policies. Each of these policies covers both property and liability exposures. A business organization that wishes to coordinate its property and liability exposures in a similar way can do so through purchasing both the property and liability modules of the CPP.

The liability module of the CPP is the **commercial general liability** (CGL) **policy.** It replaces the liability coverage previously available through the comprehensive general liability policy. In 1986, the CGL was made part of the new modular approach introduced by the insurance services office in the form of the CPP. A sample CGL is given in Appendix D.

CGL POLICY FORMAT

The format of the CGL is very similar to that of the BPP and BIC (chapter 10). The complete contract includes:

- common policy declarations page
- common policy conditions

TABLE 11–1

Business Liability Risks

1. Premises	5. Contingent liability
2. Operations	6. Contractual liability
3. Products	7. Liquor laws
4. Completed operations	8. Automobiles, aircraft, boats

---

1. Much of this discussion paraphrases the CGL. A full understanding of the policy requires a direct analysis of it.

- CGL declarations
- CGL coverage form
- any appropriate endorsements

The common declarations and policy conditions are the same as those used with the property module. The rest is specific to the CGL. The CGL itself is comprised of five sections:

1. Coverages
2. Who is an insured
3. Limits of insurance
4. CGL conditions
5. Definitions

Coverage is available either on an occurrence or on a claims-made basis. If the claims–made option is chosen, a sixth section is incorporated into the policy, the extended reporting periods provision.

COVERAGES

The CGL provides three coverages:

1. Bodily injury and property damage liability
2. Personal and advertising injury liability
3. Medical payments

Each coverage involves its own insuring agreement and set of exclusions. Each also provides a distinct limit of insurance, although an aggregate limit may apply to the sum of all costs under each coverage for the policy period. Other aggregates also apply, as discussed in the policy limits section below.

Coverage A—Bodily Injury and Property Damage Liability

The CGL provides open-perils coverage for the insured's liabilities due to "bodily injury" or "property damage" experienced by others. The bodily injury or property damage must arise out of an "occurrence," which is "an accident, including continuous or repeated exposure to substantially the same general harmful conditions." If the policy is a **claims-made policy,** the event must take place after a designated **retroactive date,** and a claim for damages must be made during the policy period. Under the claims-made policy, an insured's liability is covered (assuming no other applicable exclusions) if the event causing liability occurs after some specified retroactive date and the claim for payment by the plaintiff is made within the policy period. This differs from an occurrence policy, which covers liability for events that take place within the policy period, regardless of when the plaintiff makes a claim. The claims-made policy may lessen the insurer's uncertainty about likely future payments, because the time lag between premium payments and loss payments generally is smaller with claims made than with occurrence.[2]

....

2. By requiring insurers to include an option for an extended reporting period (see paragraph to follow), some, if not all, of this benefit is lost.

TABLE 11–2

Claims-Made Coverage Example

Assume a policy purchased on January 1, 1990, that provides $1,000,000 per occurrence of claims-made coverage with a retroactive date of January 1, 1988, and a one-year policy period. Further assume that the policy is cancelled on December 31, 1990, and that the insured purchased a one-year extended reporting period.

The following losses occur:

AMOUNT	DATE OF INJURY	DATE OF CLAIM	INSURER RESPONSIBILITY
$100,000	3/15/88	3/15/89	−0[1]
100,000	3/15/88	3/15/90	100,000[2]
100,000	3/15/90	3/15/91	100,000[3]
100,000	3/15/90	3/15/92	−0[4]
100,000	3/15/91	3/15/91	−0[5]

[1] The claim precedes the coverage period. No coverage exists under this policy.
[2] The event follows the retroactive date and the claim is brought during the policy period.
[3] The event follows the retroactive date and the claim is brought in the extended reporting period.
[4] The claim follows the end of the reporting period (assuming our date of claim is date of notice to the insurer). No coverage exists under this policy.
[5] Even though the claim is brought within the extended reporting period, the event occurs after policy cancellation. No coverage exists under this policy.

If the claims-made policy is purchased, a retroactive date must be defined. In addition, an **extended reporting period** must be included for the policy to be legal. The extended reporting period applies if a claims-made policy is cancelled. It provides coverage for claims brought after the policy period has expired for events that occurred between the retroactive date and the end of the policy period. An example is shown in table 11–2. The standard extended reporting form is very limited, and so insureds may purchase additional extensions.

The claims-made policy was introduced (first in medical malpractice insurance, later in other policies) in response to increased uncertainty about future liabilities. An occurrence policy could be sold today, and liability associated with it determined thirty or more years later. With changing legal and social norms, the inability of insurers to feel confident with their estimates of ultimate liabilities (for pricing purposes) led them to develop the claims-made coverage.

"Bodily injury" (BI) is defined as bodily injury, sickness, or disease sustained by a person, including death resulting from any of these at any time. **"Property damage"** (PD) is defined as (a) physical injury to tangible property, including all resulting loss of use of that property; or (b) loss of use of tangible property that is not physically injured.

In addition to covering an insured's liability due to bodily injury or property damage, the insurer promises to defend against suits claiming such injuries. The **cost of defense** is provided in addition to the limits of insurance available for payment of settlements or judgments, as is payment of interest that accrues after entry of the judgment against the insured. The insurer, however, has the general right to settle any suit as it deems appropriate. Further, the insurer's obligation to defend against liability ends when it has paid out its limits for any of the coverages in settlements or judgments.[3]

....

3. Some limitations exist in various states. See Kenneth S. Abraham, *Insurance Law and Regulation* (Westbury, N.Y., The Foundation Press, Inc., 1990): pp. 549–550.

So far this coverage sounds extremely broad, and it is. A long list of exclusions, however, defines the coverage more specifically. Table 11–3 lists these exclusions.

We can discuss the exclusions as they relate to the four general reasons for exclusions, as presented in chapter 5. Several relate to situations that may be *nonfortuitous*. Exclusion (a), which denies coverage for intentionally caused harm, clearly limits nonfortuitous events. Exclusion (b), an exclusion of contractually assumed liability, also could be considered a nonfortuitous event because the insured chose to enter into the relevant contract. Pollution liability (exclusion f), likewise, may arise from activities that were known to be dangerous. Damage to the insured's own products or completed operations (exclusions k, l, and m) indicates that the insurer is not willing to provide a product warranty to cover the insured's poor workmanship, a controllable situation.

A number of exclusions are intended to *standardize the risk and/or limit duplicate coverage* when other coverage does or should exist. Liquor liability, for instance, is not standard across insureds. Entities with a liquor exposure must purchase separate coverage to protect against it. Likewise, we know that workers' compensation, disability benefits, and unemployment compensation (exclusions d and e) all are covered by specialized contracts or governmental programs. Separate policies also exist for autos, aircraft, watercraft, and mobile equipment (exclusions g and h), because these "risks" will not be standard for organizations with similar general liability exposures. Last in this category is property owned by or in the care, custody, and control of the insured. These are exposures best handled in a property insurance policy, in part because the insured cannot be liable to itself for damage, and in part because the damage should be covered whether or not caused by the insured's carelessness.

Some exclusions apply because of the *catastrophic potential* of certain situations. In addition to the possible nonfortuity of pollution losses, the potential damages are catastrophic. Cost estimates to clean hazardous

TABLE 11–3

CGL Section A Exclusions (paraphrased)

a. BI or PD that is expected or intended by the insured.
b. Contractually assumed BI or PD, except for a list of specific contracts or for situations where the insured would have been liable even without the contract.
c. Liquor liability.
d. Obligations of the insured under workers' compensation, disability benefits, or unemployment compensation law or similar law.
e. Employment-related injuries to the insured's employees.
f. Harm caused by pollution.
g. Liabilities arising out of the ownership or use of autos, aircraft, or watercraft.
h. BI or PD arising out of the use or transportation of mobile equipment.
i. War-related injuries.
j. PD to owned and used property (property in the insured's care, custody, and control).
k. Damage to the insured's own product.
l. Damage to the insured's own completed (operations) work.
m. Impairment of property without physical damage, due to some defect in an insured's product or failure of the insured to perform as contractually promised.
n. Costs associated with a product recall.

waste sites in the U.S. run into the hundreds of billions of dollars. Similarly, war-related injuries (exclusion i) are likely to affect thousands, possibly hundreds of thousands of people simultaneously. The war risk practically defines catastrophe, because it affects so many people from a single situation, not too unlike a product recall (exclusion n). Most manufacturers produce tens of thousands of products in each batch. If a recall is necessary, the whole batch generally is affected. This situation also has some element of nonfortuity, in that the insured has some control over deciding upon a recall, although limited separate coverage is available for this exposure. A memorable example occurred when Johnson & Johnson recalled all of its Tylenol products following the lethal tampering of several boxes. Even though Johnson & Johnson undertook the recall to prevent future injury (and possible liability), its insurer denied coverage for the recall costs.

Coverage B—Personal and Advertising Injury Liability

Coverage A provides protection against physical injury or damage due to the insured's activities. Despite the many exclusions, it provides broad coverage for premises, products, completed operations, and other liabilities. It does not, however, provide protection against the liabilities arising out of nonphysical injuries.

"Personal injury" involves harms to a person that are not bodily. It is defined in the policy to include the situations listed in table 11–4. **"Advertising injury"** may also be personal injury, but it is specific to oral or written publications, advertising activities, or infringement of copyright, title, or slogan. Table 11–5 lists what is considered advertising injury.

This manner of providing coverage can be considered a named-perils approach. Protection is afforded for all situations actually named. Not covered are liabilities deriving from such activities as defamation of character, humiliation, or discrimination. Insurers are, however, willing to add these coverages to the policy for a fee under some conditions.

TABLE 11–4

CGL Personal Injury

1. False arrest, detention, or imprisonment.
2. Malicious prosecution.
3. Wrongful entry into or eviction of a person from premises the person occupies.
4. Oral or written publication of material that slanders or libels a person or organization, or disparages a person's or organization's goods, products, or services.
5. Oral or written publication of material that violates a person's right of privacy.

TABLE 11–5

CGL Advertising Injury

1. Oral or written publication of material that slanders or libels a person or organization, or disparages a person's or organization's goods, products, or services.
2. Oral or written publication of material that violates a person's right of privacy.
3. Misappropriation of advertising ideas or style of doing business.
4. Infringement of copyright, title, or slogan.

Only two exclusions apply to coverage B. The first denies coverage for any known violation of a law, for knowingly publishing false material, or for damage caused by communication first published prior to the start of the policy period. The second exclusion applies to advertising injury and denies coverage for four situations: (1) breach of contract; (2) failure of goods, products, or services to perform as advertised; (3) improperly described prices of goods, products, or services; and (4) actions committed by an insured who is in the business of advertising, broadcasting, publishing, or telecasting.

The effect of coverage B, therefore, is to extend protection beyond physical bodily injury and property damage. It broadens the types of harms covered.

Coverage C—Medical Payments

We have discussed medical payments coverage in both the homeowners and auto policy. The CGL medical payments coverage is similar to what is found in the homeowners policy. It provides payment for first aid, necessary medical and dental treatment, ambulance, hospital, professional nursing, and funeral services to persons other than the "insured." The intent is to pay these amounts to people injured on the insured's premises or due to the insured's operations, regardless of fault. That is, medical payments coverage is not a liability protection.

The medical payments coverage is not intended to provide health insurance to the insured nor to any employees of the insured (or anyone eligible for workers' compensation). Nor will it duplicate coverage provided in other sections of the CGL or fill in where coverage A excludes protection. War is also excluded.

WHO IS AN INSURED

The CGL is very specific and detailed in defining whose liability is covered. Some of these are obvious, others are not. Some of the more obvious insureds are: the named insured and his/her spouse if an individual; members (partners) and their spouses, as well as the organization, if the named insured is a partnership or joint venture; and if the named insured is a business other than a partnership or joint venture, then the organization, executive officers, directors, and stockholders. In each instance, insured status exists only when performing the function that leads to being an insured.

A number of other situations also lead to insured status. These include: (1) employees for most employment-related activities (health care is a notable exception); (2) the organization's real estate manager; (3) legal representatives if the insured dies; (4) drivers of mobile equipment owned by the named insured and for which no other insurance exists; and (5) additional affiliated organizations, but coverage is only temporary with the intent that the insurer be notified of these additions.

LIMITS OF INSURANCE

The limits of insurance, as you know by now, define the maximum responsibility of the insurer under specified situations. In prior forms, the

TABLE 11–6

CGL Limits of insurance

1. General aggregate limit.
2. Products—Completed operations aggregate limit.
3. Personal and advertising injury limit.
4. Per occurrence limits for A and C.
5. Fire damage limit.
6. Medical expense limit.

CGL listed limits only per occurrence, which seemed fine until "mass tort" litigation became somewhat common. Recall that mass tort litigation involves situations where thousands of potential plaintiffs have been injured or harmed by generally similar conditions. Exposure to asbestos and use of medicines are two examples. With mass tort litigation, insurers experienced much heavier losses than anticipated.

In response, the current CGL has been written with six different applicable limits, as listed in table 11–6. Several of the limits apply on an annualized basis, others on a per person or per occurrence basis. For example, the fourth limit lists the per occurrence limit for coverages A and C. Coverage B involves a per person maximum, as stated in limit three. A per person maximum is also relevant for coverage C, as specified in limit six. A per event (fire) limit is applicable for fire legal liability related to property the insured rents, as discussed in the fifth limit.

The other two limits are annual aggregates. The general aggregate limit is the most the insurer will pay in the policy year for all three coverages, excluding products and completed operations, which has a separate annual aggregate. The products-completed operations aggregate is the most the insurer will pay within a policy year for all related judgments and settlements under coverage A for products and completed operations liabilities.

A paragraph at the beginning of this policy provision states that the limits are not intended to be "stacked," regardless of the number of insureds, claims made, or persons or organizations making claims. This statement is in response to court interpretation of insurance policies that permit multiple limits (i.e., stack one on top of another) based on the number of insureds or similar qualities.

CGL CONDITIONS

Like all other policies, the CGL includes an extensive conditions section, primarily outlining the duties of the insured and insurer. Subrogation, other insurance, proper action in the event of loss, and similar provisions are spelled out in the conditions section.

DEFINITIONS

Words used in insurance policies might not have the same interpretation as when used in other documents or conversations. To specify its intent, insurers define significant terms (remember that insurance is a contract of adhesion, so ambiguities are read in the manner most favorable to the insured). Some defined terms in the CGL have already been discussed, including "bodily injury," "property damage," "personal injury," "advertising injury," and "occurrence." In total, fifteen terms are defined in the CGL. Like the rest of the policy, a full interpretation of coverage requires reading and analyzing these definitions.

Umbrella Liability Policy

Today, $1,000,000 of liability coverage, the standard limit for a CGL, is insufficient for many businesses. Furthermore, liabilities other than those covered by the CGL may be of significant importance to a business. To obtain additional amounts and a broader scope of coverage, a business can purchase an **umbrella liability policy.**

As figure 11–1 shows, the umbrella liability policy provides excess coverage over underlying insurance. Except for excluded risks, it also provides excess over a specified amount, such as $25,000, for which there is no underlying coverage. Typically, you are required to have specified amounts of underlying coverage, such as the CGL with a $1,000,000 limit and automobile insurance with the same limit. When a loss occurs, the basic contracts pay within their limits and then the umbrella policy pays until its limits are exhausted. If there is no underlying coverage for a loss covered by the umbrella, you pay the first $25,000 (or whatever is the specified retention) and the umbrella insurer pays the excess.

The umbrella policy covers bodily injury, property damage, personal injury, and advertising injury liability, similar to what is provided in the CGL. Medical expense coverage is not included. The limits of coverage, however, are intended to be quite high, and the exclusions are not as extensive as those found in the CGL. Most businesses find umbrella liability coverage an essential part of their risk management operations.

The Businessowners Policy

As discussed in chapter 10, insurers have for several decades made available specialized insurance policies for small businesses through the businessowners policy (BOP). In 1987, the BOP was split into modules of property and liability, instead of being offered solely as a single contract (the property portion is described in chapter 10). Still, the coverages directed toward small businesses are available through the commercial pack-

FIGURE 11–1

Umbrella Liability Policy

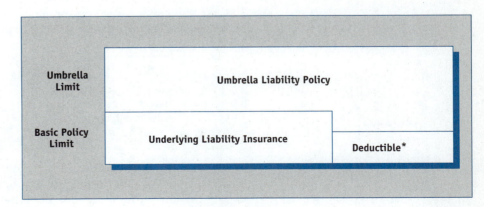

*Deductible applied when there is no underlying insurance coverage.

age policy. The coverage is nearly identical to that of the CGL just described, although it is only available on an occurrence basis and usually at limits lower than that purchased by other insureds.

Other Liability Risks

What about the business liability exposures not covered by the CGL? Space limitations prohibit discussing all of them, but several merit some attention: automobile, professional liability, and workers' compensation. Workers' compensation is discussed later in the text.

AUTOMOBILE LIABILITY

If the business is a proprietorship and the only vehicles used are private passenger automobiles, the personal auto policy or a similar policy is available to cover the automobile exposure. If the business is a partnership or corporation or uses other types of vehicles, other forms of automobile insurance must be purchased if the exposure is to be insured. The coverages are similar to the automobile insurance discussed in chapter 9.

PROFESSIONAL LIABILITY

The nature and significance of the professional liability risk were discussed in chapter 7. Most professionals insure this exposure separately with either **malpractice insurance** or **errors and omissions insurance.** The former is professional liability insurance for physicians, surgeons, and dentists whose practice involves exposure to bodily injury liability. The latter is for attorneys, insurance agents, accountants, and similar professionals whose services are provided with an expectation of certain abilities, and which could result in nonbodily injury if performed inappropriately (below the accepted standard for the profession).

Malpractice Insurance

There are no standard malpractice policies for all the professions exposed to the bodily injury risk; even in the medical field, many companies use their own contracts. A discussion of medical malpractice insurance, however, will illustrate some of the common characteristics of such coverage.

First, the coverage is very broad. In one medical malpractice policy, for example, the insurer promises to pay on behalf of the insured

> all sums which the insured shall become legally obligated to pay as damages because of injury . . . caused by a medical incident which occurs . . . in the practice of the insured's profession . . . including service . . . as a member of a formal accreditation, standards review, or similar professional board or committee.

A medical incident is defined as "any act or omission in the furnishing of professional . . . services . . . by the insured, an employee of the insured, or any person acting under the personal direction, control, or supervision of the insured." Thus, protection is provided for the professional's own acts as well as those of persons for whom he or she may be responsible. Note, however, that protection is for the insured; it is not for persons other than the insured, who need their own professional liability insurance. If a doctor's liability stems from the act of a nurse, the doctor's liability is covered but the nurse's is not.

The breadth of coverage provided is revealed by the scope of the term "medical incident" and the fact that the term "injury" is not defined. Injury, therefore, includes bodily injury, property damage, and personal injury. Note also that coverage is not restricted to accidental or unintentional acts. A surgeon who becomes liable because he or she used the wrong procedure is covered, even though there was no accident and the act (but not the outcome) was intentional.

Second, unlike professional liability policies in the past, which required the insured's consent to settle a lawsuit, some contracts give the insurer the power to settle "any claim or suit as it deems expedient." Thus, the insured's permission to settle a claim is not required. Some insureds prefer the previous arrangement, because they believe that settling a claim is, in effect, admission of an error on their part. As the market for malpractice insurance tightened during the 1970s, however, they had to accept whatever coverage was available. The insurers, in turn, wanted to avoid the expense of battling with claimants in court whenever possible.

Third, like the new CGL, many malpractice contracts are of the claims-made type. As discussed earlier, an occurrence policy covers loss causes that occurred during the policy period, with no time limit on the discovery of the injury. An error made by a surgeon in 1970 and discovered ten years later would be covered by the contract in effect in 1970. This obligation led to what insurers call the "long tail" of claims, which made pricing the coverage extremely difficult. As costs escalated beyond insurer expectation, claims made in the 1980s for errors made ten to fifteen years earlier greatly exceeded the premiums received during the policy period. A claims-made policy avoids the problem of predicting claims far into the future by specifying that the policy in effect at the time a claim is made covers the loss, regardless of when the insured made the error that is the basis for the claim. Issues related to the U.S. liability system are discussed in chapter 7. One issue involves possible tort doctrine changes that are believed by many to have increased liability awards dramatically in recent years, thus expanding insured losses beyond insurers' expectations.

Errors and Omissions Insurance

This insurance is sometime referred to as "E and O coverage." It provides protection against liability for damage caused by an error or omission by the insured. It would, for example, cover the liability of an insurance agent whose client suffered damage (typically a financial loss) because the agent failed to provide the insurance the client ordered.

Although E and O insurance does not cover liability for bodily injury, it is similar to malpractice insurance in some respects. Many policies are written on a claims-made rather than an occurrence basis. As with most liability policies, consent of the insured is not needed for out-of-court settlement of claims against the insured.

Some E and O insurance has a single aggregate limit for the policy period, rather than a limit for each incident leading to claims. Usually, a

ETHICAL *Dilemma*

What Type of Tort System Works Best?

Lawmakers around the country continue to debate the value of reforming the tort system. In today's environment, legislative reformation of the tort system implies a stiffening of the rules in favor of defendants. These include placing limitations on when punitive damages are available, curtailing imposition of joint and several liability, repealing collateral source rules, and capping amounts available for non-economic damages. As voters, we all have the opportunity to sway the direction of these legislative initiatives, and so we have an obligation to analyze them.

Let's consider the proposal to place caps on noneconomic damages. Various states have already passed such legislation, others are debating the idea. As a voter, you need to know the implications of these initiatives. Those people in support of caps believe that caps will aid the American economy by reducing the uncertainty that accompanies large potential liabilities. A stronger economy means jobs and income security. Because noneconomic damages are difficult to quantify, there may be no strong pattern in their size from one jury to another. Predicting them, therefore, is difficult. In addition, they tend to be large.

In contrast, opponents to caps consider them inequitable. Plaintiffs with small noneconomic damages are paid in full, while those with larger losses are paid increasingly smaller percentages of their damages as those damages grow. Furthermore, the caps imply that noneconomic damages are less legitimate than economic harms, even though their existence may be obvious (consider the concert pianist who loses a hand due to a defective product.)

Ethically, we have a number of issues to consider. Among them are the following questions: What is society's responsibility in protecting individuals? Is an increase in consumer safety worth the loss of jobs from business liability uncertainty? How much safety is enough? Too much? Do pain and suffering have value? Do businesses place sufficient value on human suffering? How much standardization do we want across tort cases? The tort reform movement in the 1980s and 1990s is complex and laden with ethical questions. We can benefit from considering them specifically.

---

deductible is applied to each claim. Deductibles range from $250 to $100,000 or more.

Global Liability Exposures

Global business insurance needs were mentioned in chapter 10. Liability issues do not differ significantly from the property issues discussed there. One distinction is that liability may occur globally from a single manufacturing or operating decision. For example, a U.S. manufacturer that sells its products globally could be sued by consumers worldwide if the product leads to widespread injuries. The value of centralizing risk management activities, therefore, may be greater for liability exposures than for property exposures. Increasingly, U.S. laws are being applied around the globe, especially with respect to activities of U.S.-based organizations. Still, development of a deep understanding of the legal system wherever the organization operates is an essential part of a successful risk management program.

Global Risk Management

We are finding ourselves increasingly in a global economy, and as such, development of global risk management expertise is necessary for successful business practices. Throughout the text we have discussed various global risk management issues. Here, we pull together a number of those discussions.

GETTING STARTED

We have used the risk management process as a framework for the management of risk because we believe that it works. We suggest, therefore, that the process be applied to global exposures.

SET OBJECTIVES

Our first task in the risk management process is to set objectives. Remember that risk management objectives should be consistent with the organization's overall objectives. Set up a meeting with top management to discuss the organization's global risk management objectives. Prepare beforehand with a set of guidelines that can be discussed in the meeting. Be precise in setting your objectives, and discuss with management methods to measure success. When the process is completed, the list you have agreed upon with top management should be written, voted on, and then distributed to stockholders, decision-makers, and employees of the organization. You cannot achieve most objectives on your own. Knowledge and acceptance of them by all involved parties is essential.

GATHER DATA (Identification and Measurement)

Objectives in hand, the process of understanding organizational global risk management problems can begin in earnest. In chapter 2 we discussed *identification* tools including checklists, surveys, and inspections. For global exposures, unique problems of communication, culture, and distance may pose special needs. You may find the use of a risk management expert for your international operations may be more valuable than for U.S. operations. Oddly enough, you may also find that despite the distance and language differences, personal inspection by the risk manager is more important outside than inside the U.S. Acceptance of the home office's authority may be weaker outside the U.S. if a sense exists of being a cultural outsider and/or being ignored. Personal attention may alleviate these feelings.

A major element of gathering data involves development of an understanding of local laws and cultural norms. In many places, strict limitations exist on the use of insurance; these must be followed. Likewise, laws regarding acceptable business operations that prevent liability differ from nation to nation. You might do well to learn about and meet the most stringent requirements among those countries, thereby stabilizing operations and surpassing by some margin the required behavior of any given country. General safety practices also vary across borders. The risk manager would be wise to become familiar with the general norm and the rationale for it, and then work toward acceptance of a global safety standard. The DuPont Corporation is known for its ability to heighten safety awareness throughout the world in this fashion.

Having identified an organization's global risk management issues (exposures, perils, and hazards), you can measure their importance and characteristics. Measurement typically involves estimating loss distributions (frequencies and severities), maximum probable loss, maximum possible loss, and the like (see chapter 2 for a discussion). Information gathered on cultural norms will assist in evaluating the stability of these estimates; that is, evaluating their accuracy or riskiness. The intent is to use the data gathered to predict future losses, as well as the impact of possible actions on those losses.

MAKING DECISIONS

Having set objectives and gathered data, the risk manager is in a position to make decisions. Part of the data-gathering stage was to identify available options for managing risk. These include financing losses through locally purchased insurance, globally purchased insurance, retention, or a combination.

Here is where the thorny issue of centralization versus decentralization emerges. Economies of scale may make centralization (such as purchase of a global insurance policy) appropriate. Sensitivity to local needs, however, may call for decentralization. Referral to your risk management objectives and communication with local management as well as corporate management will help determine the appropriate path.

IMPLEMENTATION AND MONITORING

The decision-making part of the process is so difficult that often we forget to give attention to the implementation part. Successful implementation requires excellent management skills for coordination of effort, and loyalty to the decisions made. Safety will not be achieved without employee acceptance of it, for example. Implementation, therefore, means that you will need to communicate with all members of the organization and solicit their involvement in the process.

Implementation also implies constant monitoring to keep the system up-to-date. As laws and conditions change, so too must the risk management program change. Being open to change is an enormous asset in successful risk management. Monitoring of the system requires reevaluation of the decisions made. Are those decisions still appropriate? Have loss estimates proved reasonably accurate? Are new risk management options available that may be superior to the options in place? Have the choices implemented accomplished what was intended? In essence, monitoring is the process of cycling through the risk management endeavor (beginning with objectives, identification, etc.) on an endless path.

Key Terms

commercial general liability policy
occurrence-based policy
claims-made policy
retroactive date
extended reporting period
bodily injury
property damage

cost of defense
personal injury
advertising injury
umbrella liability policy
malpractice insurance
errors and omission insurance

Discussion Questions

1. Provide an example of expenses that would be covered under each of the three CGL coverages.

2. Compare occurrence and claims-made policies.

3. What responsibility does a CGL insurer have with regard to litigation expenses for a lawsuit that, if successfully pursued by the plaintiff, would result in payment of damages under the terms of the policy?

4. Provide a detailed rationale for excluding pollution, auto accidents, and liquor liability in the CGL.

5. How does "personal injury" differ from "bodily injury"?

6. Why do insurers incorporate both per occurrence and annual aggregate limits?

7. Who needs an umbrella liability policy? Why?

8. How does malpractice differ from errors and omissions?

9. Provide an example of a global liability exposure.

10. What are the advantages and disadvantages of a centralized risk management program?

. . . .

11.1 Assume the Koehn Kitchen Corporation, a manufacturer of kitchen gadgets, experiences the following losses:

1. A consumer chops off his finger while using Koehn's Cutlery Gizmo. The consumer sues Koehn for medical expenses, lost income, pain and suffering, and punitive damages.

2. An employee of Koehn is injured while delivering goods to a wholesaler. The employee sues for medical expenses and punitive damages.

3. Koehn uses toxic substances in its manufacturing process. Neighbors of its plant bring suit against Koehn, claiming that a higher rate of stillbirths are occurring in the area because of Koehn's use of toxics. (Consider the variation that an explosion emitted toxics, rather than normal operations).

4. Koehn's Mighty Mate Slicing Machine must be recalled because of a product defect. The recall causes massive losses.

Based on information in this chapter, which parts of any of these losses are covered by Koehn's CGL? Explain your answer.

11.2 Assume that the Baker-Leetch Pet Store has a CGL with a $1,000,000 aggregate limit. Under both occurrence and claims-made scenarios, would the following losses be covered? The policy commences July 1, 1995, and ends June 30, 1996. If claims-made, the retroactive date is July 1, 1994, and a one-year extended reporting period applies.

1. The pet shop sold a diseased gerbil in August 1994. The gerbil ultimately infected the owner's twenty cats and dogs (they breed the animals), who all died. A lawsuit was filed against Baker-Leetch in September 1995. What if the lawsuit were filed in September 1996? September 1997?

2. The pet shop provided dog training in July 1995, and guaranteed the results of the training. In December 1996, one of the trained dogs attacked a mail carrier, causing severe injuries. The mail carrier immediately sued Baker-Leetch.

3. The pet store sold an inoculated rare and expensive cat in October 1995 (so it claimed). The cat contracted a disease in October 1996, that would not have occurred if the animal truly had been properly inoculated. The owners sued in December 1996.

11.3 The Goldman Cat House is a pet store catering to the needs of felines. The store is a sole proprietorship, taking in revenues of approximately $1,700,000 annually. Products available include kittens, cat food, cat toys, cages, collars, cat litter and litter boxes, and manuals on the care of cats. One manual was written by the store owner, who also makes up his own concoction for cat litter. All other goods are purchased from national wholesalers. Two part-time and two full-time employees work for Goldman. Sometimes the employees deliver goods to Goldman customers.

1. Identify some of Goldman Cat House's liability exposures.

2. Would Goldman be best advised to purchase an occurrence-based or claims-made liability policy?

3. What liability loss control techniques would you recommend for Goldman?

Workers' and Unemployment Compensation

Introduction Between 1984 and 1994, workers' compensation costs grew an average of 12 percent a year. During the same period, average weekly wages increased 5 percent per year and the overall Consumer Price Index rose at a 4 percent rate. What caused this alarming growth in claims? Potential causes include the effect of attorney involvement, medical care costs, fraud, the assigned risk plan in each state, the broadening of the scope of covered injuries, and other issues. The early 1990s saw reforms in workers' compensation legislation in many states and some return to normal loss ratios for this line of business by the mid-1990s. Yet challenges of controlling costs remain. Similarly, unemployment is always of concern to the public, politicians, employers, and employees. While losses cannot be predicted accurately, costs fall directly on employers. The average cost as a percentage of payroll is similar to that for workers' compensation.

After reading this chapter, you will be acquainted with:

1. Workers' compensation laws and benefits.
2. Workers' compensation insurance.
3. Self-insurance of workers' compensation costs.
4. State funds and second-injury funds.
5. Workers' compensation issues.
6. Unemployment compensation.

Workers' Compensation Laws and Benefits

Each year, approximately 2,000,000 workers miss one or more days of work due to a work-related injury or illness, approximately 14,000 are killed, and many experience permanent partial impairments. Each state, and certain other jurisdictions such as the District of Columbia and territories, have a workers' compensation system to enforce a series of state laws designed to pay workers for their work-related injuries and illnesses.

HISTORY AND PURPOSE

In the nineteenth century, before implementation of workers' compensation laws in the United States, employees were seldom paid for work-related injuries. A major barrier to payment was that a worker had to prove an injury was the fault of his or her employer in order to recover damages. The typical employee was reluctant to sue his or her employer out of fear of losing the job. For the same reason, fellow workers typically refused to testify on behalf of an injured about the circumstances surrounding an accident. If the injured employee could not prove fault, the employer had no responsibility. The injured employee's ability to recover damages was hindered further by the fact that even a negligent employer could use three **common law defenses:** the fellow-servant rule, the doctrine of assumption of risk, and the doctrine of contributory negligence.

Under the **fellow-servant rule,** an employee who was injured as a result of the conduct of a fellow worker could not recover damages from the employer. The **assumption of risk doctrine** provided that an employee who knew, or should have known, of unsafe conditions of employment assumed the risk by remaining on the job. Further, it was argued that the employee's compensation recognized the risk of the job. Therefore, he or she could not recover damages from the employer when injured because of such conditions. If an employee was injured through negligence of the employer but was partly at fault, the employee was guilty of **contributory negligence.** Any contributory negligence, regardless how slight, relieved the employer of responsibility for the injury.

These defenses made recovery of damages by injured employees virtually impossible, placing the cost of work-related injuries on the employee. As a result, during the latter part of the nineteenth century, various **employer liability laws** were adopted to modify existing laws and improve the legal position of injured workers. The system of negligence liability was retained, however, and injured employees still had to prove that their employer was at fault to recover damages.

Even with modifications, the negligence system proved costly to administer and inefficient in protecting employees from the financial burdens of workplace injuries.[1] The need for more extensive reform was recognized. In Germany, Bismarck's social insurance programs of the latter half of the 1800s had been providing compensation for industrial accidents; other European countries had adopted this strict liability prototype. Beginning with

---

1. A counterargument is postulated in "Challenges to Workers' Compensation: A Historical Analysis," by Edward D. and Monroe Berkowitz, in *Workers' Compensation Adequacy, Equity & Efficiency,* eds. John D. Worral and David Appel (Ithaca N.Y.: ILR Press, 1985). The authors contend that workers were becoming successful in suing employers. Thus, workers' compensation developed as an aid to employers in limiting their responsibilities to employees.

Wisconsin in 1911, United States jurisdictions developed the concept of workers' compensation that compensated workers without the requirement that employers' negligence must be proved (i.e., strict employer liability). Costs were born directly by employers (e.g., in the form of workers' compensation insurance premiums), and indirectly by employees who traded off wages for benefits. To the extent, if any, that total labor costs were increased, consumers (who benefit from industrialization) shared in the burden of industrial accidents through higher prices for goods and services. Employees demanded higher total compensation (wages plus benefits) to engage in high-risk occupations, resulting in incentives for employers to adopt safety programs. By 1948, each jurisdiction had similar laws.

In compromising between the interests of employees and employers, the originators of workers' compensation systems limited the benefits available to employees to some amount less than the full loss. They also made those benefits the sole recourse of the employee against the employer for work-related injuries. This give-and-take of rights and duties between employers and employees is termed a **quid pro quo,** literally meaning "this for that." The intent was for the give-and-take to have an equal value, on the average. You will see in our discussion of current workers' compensation issues that some doubt exists as to whether or not equity has been maintained. An exception to the sole recourse concept exists in some states for the few employees who elect, prior to injury, not to be covered by workers' compensation. Such employees, upon injury, can sue their employer; however, the employer in these instances retains the three defenses described earlier.

In addition to every state and territory having a workers' compensation law, there are federal laws applicable to longshore workers and harbor workers, to nongovernment workers in the District of Columbia, and to civilian employees of the federal government. Workers' compensation laws differ from jurisdiction to jurisdiction, but they all have the purpose of assuring that injured workers and their dependents will receive benefits without question of fault.

In the early 1970s, a nonpartisan group called "The National Commission on State Workmen's Compensation Laws" reached consensus on five broad objectives for an ideal workers' compensation program:

1. Broad scope of covered employees, injuries, and diseases.
2. Substantial protection against loss of income.
3. Prompt and comprehensive medical and rehabilitation care.
4. Encouragement of safety.
5. An effective delivery system.

The commission suggested federal intervention for failure to comply with these recommendations. Fear of being superseded by the federal government caused state legislators to improve their workers' compensation programs substantially during the 1970s. Subsequent rapid growth in claims led to many states tightening their laws in various ways during the 1990s. We will look at how states have responded to the other commission objectives as we consider:

1. Coverage.
2. Benefits.

3. How benefits are provided.

4. Employer's risk.

No state is in full compliance with the commission's recommendations. Over fifty jurisdictions, including Washington, D.C., and U.S. territories such as Puerto Rico, develop and administer their own workers' compensation laws. Consequently, questions about the law in specific jurisdictions should be directed to the particular workers' compensation commission, the exact title of which varies by jurisdiction.

COVERAGE

Coverage under workers' compensation is either inclusive or exclusive. Further, it is compulsory or elective, depending upon state law. A major feature is that only injuries and illnesses that "arise out of and in the course of employment" are covered.

Inclusive or Exclusive

Inclusive laws list all the employments that are covered; **exclusive laws** cover all employments except those that are excluded. Typically, domestic service and casual labor are excluded. Agricultural workers are excluded in nineteen jurisdictions, whereas their coverage is compulsory in twenty-seven jurisdictions. Coverage of farm workers is entirely voluntary in four jurisdictions. Some states limit coverage to occupations classified as hazardous. The laws of thirty-nine states apply to all employers in the employments covered; others apply only to employers with more than a specified number of employees, such as three or more. Any employer can comply voluntarily.

Compulsory or Elective

In all but three states, the laws regarding workers' compensation are compulsory. In these three states (New Jersey, South Carolina, and Texas) with **elective laws,** either the employer or the employee can elect not to be covered under the law. An employer who opts out (i.e., elects not to come under the law) loses the common law defenses discussed earlier. If the employer does not opt out but an employee does, the employer retains those defenses as far as that employee is concerned. If both opt out, the employer loses the defenses. It is unusual for employees to opt out, since those who do must prove negligence in order to collect and must overcome the employer's defenses.

An employer who does not opt out must pay benefits to injured employees in accordance with the requirements of the law, but that is the employer's sole responsibility. Thus, an employee who is covered by the law cannot sue his or her employer for damages. The law is the employee's **sole remedy.**[2] By coming under the law, the employer avoids the cost of litigation and the risk of having to pay a large judgment in the event an injured employee's suit for damages is successful. During the mid-1990s,

---

2. Also called "exclusive remedy." Later in this chapter, we will discuss some of the current methods used by employees to negate the exclusive remedy rule. Workers' compensation is losing its status as the employee's sole remedy against the employer.

approximately 50 percent of Texas employers—primarily small ones—had opted out of the system; a less-pronounced trend toward opting out was developing in South Carolina. Virtually all employers that opt out reduce their likelihood of being sued by providing an alternative employee benefit plan which includes medical and disability income benefits as well as accidental death and dismemberment benefits for work-related injuries and illnesses.[3] In addition, the employer purchases employers' liability insurance to cover the possibility of being sued by injured employees who are not satisfied with the alternative benefits.

Proponents of an opt-out provision argue that competition from alternative coverage provides market discipline to lower workers' compensation insurance prices. Furthermore, greater exposure to common law liability suits may encourage workplace safety. Opponents see several drawbacks of opt-out provisions:

- Some employers may fail to provide medical benefits or provide only modest ones, resulting in cost-shifting to other segments of society.
- The right of the employee to sue may be illusory because some employers may have few assets and no liability insurance.
- Employees may be reluctant to sue the employer, especially when the opportunity to return to work exists and/or family members may be affected.
- Safety incentives may not be enhanced for employers with few assets at risk.[4]

Covered Injuries

In order to limit benefits to situations in which a definite relationship exists between an employee's work and the injury, most laws provide coverage only for injuries "arising out of and in the course of employment." This phrase describes two limitations. First, the injury must **"arise out of employment,"** meaning that the job environment was the cause. For example, the family of someone who has a relatively nonstressful job but dies of cardiac arrest at work would have trouble proving the work connection, and therefore would not be eligible for workers' compensation benefits. A police officer or firefighter, on the other hand, who suffers a heart attack (even while not on duty) is presumed in many states to have suffered from work-related stress.

The second limitation on coverage is that the injury must occur **"while in the course of employment."** That is, the loss-causing event must take place while the employee is on the job. An employee injured while engaged in horseplay, therefore, might not be eligible for workers' compensation because the injury did not occur while the employee was "in the course of employment." Likewise, coverage does not apply while traveling the normal commute between home and work. Along these same lines of

3. Employee benefits are discussed in chapters 18–20. Alternative coverage never exactly duplicates a state's workers' compensation benefits.
4. Various concepts and statistics in this chapter are based on research described in S. Travis Pritchett, Scott E. Harrington, Helen I. Doerpinghaus, and Greg Niehaus, *An Economic Analysis of Workers' Compensation in South Carolina* (Columbia, S.C.: Division of Research, College of Business Administration, University of South Carolina, 1994).

reasoning, certain injuries generally are explicitly excluded, such as (1) those caused by willful misconduct (i.e., willful failure to follow safety rules), (2) those resulting from intoxication, and (3) those that are self-inflicted.

Subject to these limitations, all work-related injuries are covered, even if due to employee negligence. In addition, every state provides benefits for **occupational disease,** which is defined in terms such as "an injury arising out of employment and due to causes and conditions characteristic of, and peculiar to, the particular trade, occupation, process or employment, and excluding all ordinary diseases to which the general public is exposed."[5] Some states list particular diseases covered, whereas others simply follow general guidelines such as those given in the preceding sentence.

BENEFITS

Four types of benefits are provided for by workers' compensation laws: (1) medical, (2) income replacement, (3) survivors', and (4) rehabilitation.

Medical

All laws provide unlimited **medical care benefits** for accidental injuries. Many cases do not involve large expenses, but it is not unusual for medical bills to run into many thousands of dollars. Medical expenses resulting from occupational illnesses may be covered in full for a specified period of time and then terminated. While the medical component of the Consumer Price Index grew 115 percent between 1980 and 1990, workers' compensation medical costs rose approximately 275 percent.[6] Unlike nonoccupational health insurance, workers' compensation does not impose deductibles and coinsurance to create incentives for individuals to control their demand for medical services. Forty-five percent of the total workers' compensation claim costs is for medical expenses. This percentage has grown from approximately 33 percent in the early 1980s.

Income Replacement

All workers' compensation laws provide an injured employee with a weekly income while disabled as the result of a covered injury or disease. Income replacement benefits are commonly referred to by industry personnel as **indemnity benefits.** The size and duration of indemnity payments depend upon the following factors:

1. Whether the disability is total or partial, and temporary or permanent.

2. An employee's amount of benefit.

---

5. J. D. Long and D. W. Gregg, eds., *Property and Liability Insurance Handbook* (Homewood, Ill.: Richard D. Irwin, Inc., 1965), p. 521. At times we shorten our description of covered perils to "injuries" rather than "injuries and illnesses" because state laws often define occupational illnesses to be injuries.

6. Some, but far from all, of the higher growth rate for workers' compensation medical costs can be explained by the growth in the labor force.

3. Maximum duration of benefits.

4. Waiting period.

5. Cost-of-living adjustments.

Degree and Length of Disability   **Total disability** refers to the condition of an employee who misses work because he or she is unable to perform all the important duties of the occupation. **Partial disability,** on the other hand, means the employee can perform some, but not all, of the duties of his or her occupation. In either case, disability may be permanent or temporary. **Permanent total disability** means the person is not expected to be able to work again. **Temporary total disability** means the employee is expected to be able to return to work at some future time.[7]

Partial disability may be either temporary or permanent. **Temporary partial** payments are most likely to be made following a period of temporary total disability. For example, a person can perform some but not all work duties and thereby qualifies for temporary partial benefits. Such benefits are based on the difference between wages earned before and after an injury. They account for a minor portion of total claim payments.

Most laws specify that the loss of certain body parts constitutes **permanent partial disability.** These cases are called **scheduled injuries.** Benefits expressed in terms of number of weeks of total disability payments are usually provided in such cases. For example, the loss of an arm might entitle the injured worker to 200 weeks of total disability benefits; the loss of a finger might entitle him or her to thirty-five weeks of benefits. No actual loss of time from work or income is required, under the assumption that loss of a body part causes a loss of future income.

Table 12–1 shows the average weeks of compensation for selected scheduled injuries. Permanent partial claims account for over 50 percent of all income replacement benefits.

TABLE 12–1

Average Weeks of Compensation for Selected Scheduled Injuries, 1992

LOSS OR LOSS OF USE	AVERAGE FOR 46 STATES & DC
Arm	248
Hand	197
Thumb	66
First Finger	40
Second Finger	32
Third Finger	23
Little Finger	17
Leg	224
Foot	155
Great Toe	33
Other Toe	10
Eye	149
Hearing (one ear)	59
Hearing (both ears)	178

SOURCE: *Survey of Workers' Compensation Laws* (Chicago: Alliance of American Insurers, 1992).

Note: Various refinements apply in some states. Alaska, Florida, Kentucky, and Washington are not represented in these data.

7. The amount of weekly income benefits is the same for both permanent and temporary total disability.

Amount of Benefit Weekly benefits for death, disability, and, often, disfigurement are determined primarily by (1) the employee's **average weekly wage** (i.e., average earned income per week during some specified period prior to disability) and (2) a **replacement ratio** expressed as a percentage of the average weekly wage. Jurisdictions also set **minimum weekly benefits** (subject to not exceeding the actual average wage of a low-income worker) as well as **maximum weekly benefits** that limit payments to high-income earners. Forty-one jurisdictions use 100 percent of the average weekly wage for all of its workers as the maximum wage base. The maximum weekly benefit, then, is the product of its maximum wage base and its replacement percentage. Table 12–2 shows a distribution of maximum weekly disability benefits.

The replacement percentage for disability benefits ranges from 60 in one jurisdiction to 70 in two others, but in most jurisdictions it is 66-2/3. The percentage reflects the intent to replace income after taxes and other work-related expenses, since workers' compensation benefits are not subject to income taxation.[8]

Twenty jurisdictions lower their permanent partial maximum payment per week below their maximum for total disability. For these jurisdictions, the average permanent partial maximum is 60.7 percent of their total disability maximum. With respect to death benefits, thirty-one jurisdictions use 66-2/3 percentage in determining survivor benefits for a spouse only; five of these use a higher percentage for a spouse plus children. The range of survivor benefits for a spouse plus children is 60 percent in Idaho to 75 percent in Texas.

Duration of Benefits In thirty-nine jurisdictions, no limit is put on the duration of temporary total disability. Nine jurisdictions, however, allow benefits for less than 500 weeks; two specify a 500-week maximum. The limits are seldom reached in practice because the typical injured worker's

TABLE 12–2

Maximum Weekly Disability Benefits for Total Disability in 51 Jurisdictions, 1992

MAXIMUM WEEKLY BENEFIT	NUMBER OF JURISDICTIONS
$225–300	8
301–400	17
401–500	16
501–600	3
601–700	5
701–750	2
Average = $411	

SOURCE: *Survey of Workers' Compensation Laws* (Chicago: Alliance of American Insurers, 1992).

8. In Ohio, a replacement rate of 72 percent applies in the first twelve weeks, followed by sixty-six and two-thirds for the remainder of the disability. In Washington, the percentage depends on your "conjugal status"—an unmarried person receives 60 percent, married without children calls for 65 percent, married with four children results in a 73 percent benefit. An alternative approach used in three states is the replacement of 80 percent of **spendable income,** which is earnings after all tax deductions. Disability income payments from Social Security are coordinated with workers' compensation to limit total payments to no more than 80 percent of the claimant's average monthly wage.

condition reaches "maximum medical improvement" that terminates temporary total benefits earlier. Maximum medical improvement is reached when additional medical treatment is not expected to result in improvement of the person's condition.

In forty-three jurisdictions, permanent total benefits are paid for the duration of disability/lifetime. These jurisdictions generally do not impose a maximum dollar limit on the aggregate amount that can be paid. The remaining jurisdictions[9] specify a maximum number of weeks between 400 and 550. Various limits apply to permanent partial disability claims, with an average weekly limit around 500 weeks.

Waiting Periods Every jurisdiction has a **waiting period** before indemnity payments (but not medical benefits) for temporary disability begin; the range is from three to seven days. The waiting period feature has the advantage of (1) giving a financial incentive to work, (2) reducing administrative costs, and (3) reducing the cost of benefits. If disability continues for a specified period (typically, two to four weeks), benefits are retroactive to the date disability began. This provision is similar to a franchise deductible. Moral hazard is created among employees who reach maximum medical improvement just before the time of the retroactive trigger. Some employees will malinger long enough to waive the waiting period. Hawaii does not allow retroactive benefits.

Cost-of-Living Adjustment Fifteen jurisdictions have an automatic cost-of-living adjustment (COLA) for weekly benefits. In some cases, the COLA is effective only after disability has continued for one or two years. Because benefit rates are usually set by law, those rates in jurisdictions that lack automatic increases for permanent benefits become out-of-date rapidly during periods of inflation.

Survivor Benefits

In the event of a work-related death, all jurisdictions provide **survivor income benefits** for the surviving spouse and dependent children, as well as a burial allowance. The survivor income benefit for a spouse plus children is typically (in thirty jurisdictions) sixty-six and two-thirds percent of the worker's average weekly wage. In some jurisdictions this percentage is the same for a spouse only, but in others a spouse alone receives only 35 or 50 percent. Several jurisdictions provide additional income for one child only. Thirty-three jurisdictions provide death benefits "through widowhood and for children to age 18" (modified to ages 22–25 for full-time students in several jurisdictions).[10] The remaining jurisdictions specify survivor benefit limits between 400 and 500 weeks. Burial allowances range from $700 to $6,000, with a 1992 average of $3,060.

Rehabilitation

Most people who are disabled by injury or disease make a complete recovery with ordinary medical care and return to work able to resume their

9. Indiana, Mississippi, South Carolina, Tennessee, Texas, Virginia, and Wyoming.
10. "Widowhood" is usually defined as lasting until either the remarriage or death of the spouse, whichever is earlier.

former duties. Many workers, however, suffer disability of such a nature that something more than income payments and ordinary medical services is required to restore them, to the greatest extent possible, to their former economic and social situation. **Rehabilitation** is the process of accomplishing this objective.

Rehabilitation involves the following:

1. Physical-medical attention in an effort to restore workers as nearly as possible to their state of health prior to the injury.

2. Vocational training to enable them to perform a new occupational function.

3. Psychological aid to help them adjust to their new situation and be able to perform a useful function for society.

About one-fourth of the workers' compensation laws place this responsibility on the employer (or the insurer, if applicable). Most of the laws require special maintenance benefits to encourage disabled workers to cooperate in a rehabilitation program. Nearly all states reduce or stop income payments entirely to workers who refuse to participate.

HOW BENEFITS ARE PROVIDED

Workers' compensation laws hold the employer responsible for providing benefits to injured employees. Employees do not contribute directly to this cost. In most states, employers may insure with a private insurance company or qualify as self-insurers.

Various **residual market** mechanisms, such as assigned risk pools and reinsurance facilities, allow employers considered uninsurable access to workers' compensation insurance. Insurers are required to participate, and insureds are assigned to an insurer in various ways. Even though rates for this residual market segment are substantially higher than those for the regular market, the approximately 25 percent of total workers' compensation premiums in this market produces large losses (in excess of income) that must be absorbed solely by private insurers. In the early 1990s, residual market losses were running around $2 billion annually; by the mid-1990s, losses had decreased somewhat. Partly to avoid sharing residual market losses, many employers, especially large ones, self-insure the workers' compensation risk.

Eighteen jurisdictions have **state operated workers' compensation funds.** In six of these, the state fund is exclusive; that is, employers are not permitted to buy compensation insurance from a private insurance company but must insure with the state fund or self-insure.[11] Where the state fund is *competitive* (that is, optional), employers may choose to self-insure or to insure through either the state fund or a private insurer.

EMPLOYER'S RISK

Industrial accidents create two possible losses for employers. First, employers are responsible to employees covered by the workers' compensa-

---

11. Three of the six permit self-insurance. Exclusive funds are called **monopolistic state funds.**

tion law for the benefits required by law. Second, they may become liable for injuries to employees not covered by the law.[12] The risks associated with these exposures cannot be avoided without suspending operations—hardly a viable alternative.

Where permitted, self-insurance of this exposure is common. Self-insurance is desirable in part because of the predictability afforded by legislated benefits. In addition, employers can buy coverage (called excess loss insurance) for very large losses similar to the umbrella liability policy discussed in chapter 11.

Workers' Compensation Insurance

Both risks just mentioned can be transferred to an insurer by purchasing a workers' compensation and employers' liability policy.

COVERAGE

The workers' compensation and employers' liability policy has three parts Under part I—**Workers' Compensation**—the insurer agrees:

> to pay promptly when due all compensation and other benefits required of the insured by the workers' compensation law.

The policy defines "workers' compensation law" as the law of any state designated in the declarations, and specifically includes any occupational disease law of that state. The workers' compensation portion of the policy is directly for the benefit of employees covered by the law. The insurer assumes the obligations of the insured (i.e., the employer) under the law and is bound by the terms of the law as well as the actions of the workers' compensation commission or other governmental body having jurisdiction. Any changes in the workers' compensation law are automatically covered by the policy.

Four limitations or "exclusions" apply to part 1. These limitations include any payments in excess of the benefits regularly required by workers' compensation statutes due to (1) serious and willful misconduct by the insured; (2) the knowing employment of a person in violation of the law; (3) failure to comply with health or safety laws or regulations; or (4) the discharge, coercion, or other discrimination against employees in violation of the workers' compensation law. In addition, the policy refers

12. For example, many workers' compensation laws exclude workers hired for temporary jobs—such employees are called casual workers. Injured employees who are classified as casual workers are not entitled to benefits under the law but may recover damages from the employer if they can prove that their injuries were caused by the employer's negligence. The employer's liability risk with regard to excluded employees is the same as it would be if there were no workers' compensation law. Similarly, certain emerging theories such as dual capacity and third-party actions over (discussed in the issues section of this chapter) are potential sources of employer liability outside the workers' compensation system.

only to state laws and that of the District of Columbia; thus, coverage under any of the federal programs requires special provisions.

Part 2, **Employers' Liability,** protects against potential liabilities not within the scope of the workers' compensation law, yet arising out of employee injuries. The insurer agrees to pay damages for which the employer becomes legally obligated because of:

> bodily injury by accident or disease, including death at any time resulting therefrom . . . by any employee of the insured arising out of and in the course of his employment by the insured either in operations in a state designated in . . . the declarations or in operations necessary or incidental thereto.

Examples of liabilities covered under part 2 are those to employees excluded from the law, such as domestic and farm laborers. Part 2 might also be applicable if the injury is not considered work-related, even if it occurs on-the-job.

Part 3 of the workers' compensation policy provides **Other States Insurance.** Previously, this protection was available by endorsement. Part 1 applies only if the state imposing responsibility is listed in the declarations. An employee injured while working out of state may be covered by that state's compensation law. To account for this potential gap, part 3 allows the insured to list states (perhaps all) of incidental exposure. Coverage is extended to these named locales.

COST

Based on Payroll   The premium for workers' compensation insurance typically is based on the payroll paid by the employer. A charge is made for each $100 of payroll for each classification of employee. This rate varies with the degree of hazard of the occupation.[13] For example, the highest rate from a private insurer in one state, which has average rates, is $77.10 per $100 of weekly payroll. This is for classification number 5701, wrecking buildings.[14] On the other hand, clerical classifications in the same state are rated at 28 cents per $100 of payroll. Large employers can elect to have their own claims experience have a major impact on costs through a process called experience rating (see the Consumer Applications near the end of this chapter).

Factors Affecting Rate   The rate for workers' compensation insurance is influenced not only by the degree of hazard of the occupational classification but also by the nature of the law and its administration. If the benefits of the law are high, rates will tend to be high. If they are low, rates will tend to be low. Moreover, given any law—whether benefits stipulated

---

13. Rates are made for each state and depend upon the experience under the law in that state. Thus, the rate for the same occupational classification may differ from state to state.
14. No, this is not an error. The rate is $77.10 per $100 of payroll. By way of comparison, the second highest rate is $28.40 for classification number 5040, iron erection. Apparently, wrecking buildings is almost three times as hazardous as erecting iron for bridges, highrise buildings, and other structures.

by the law are high, low, or otherwise—its administration will affect premium rates. If those who administer the law are conservative in their evaluation of borderline cases, premium rates will be lower than in instances where administrators are less circumspect in parceling out employers' and insurers' money. Most laws provide that either the claimant or the insurer may appeal a decision of the administrative board in court on questions of law, but if both the board and the courts are inclined toward generosity, the effect is to increase workers' compensation costs.

Workers' compensation may be a significant expense for the employer. Given any particular law and its administration, costs for the firm are influenced by the frequency and severity of injuries suffered by workers covered. The more injuries there are, the more workers will be receiving benefits. The more severe such injuries, the longer such benefits must be paid. It is not unusual to find firms in hazardous industries having workers' compensation costs running from 10 to 30 percent of payroll. This can be a significant component of labor costs. Moreover, there are many other non-wage costs for employers, such as Social Security, unemployment compensation taxes, and voluntary employee benefits (group life and health insurance or group pensions).

Self-Insurance

Most state workers' compensation laws permit an employer to retain the workers' compensation risk if it can be proved that the employer is financially able to pay claims. Some states permit the risk to be retained only by employers who furnish a bond guaranteeing payment of benefits.

The major question for the self-insurance of the workers' compensation risk is whether the firm has a large enough number of exposure units (employees) so that its losses are reasonably stable and can be predicted with some accuracy. Clearly, an employer with ten employees cannot make an accurate prediction of workers' compensation benefit costs for next year. Such costs may be zero one year and several thousand dollars another year. On the other hand, as the number of the firm's employees increases, workers' compensation losses become more stable and predictable. Just how stable losses must be in order for self-insurance to be feasible depends upon the employer's ability and willingness to pay for losses that exceed expectations. The employer's ability to pay for loss is a second important factor considered by regulators in determining whether or not to permit self-insurance.[15]

State Funds

A third method of assuring benefit payments to injured workers is the state fund. State funds are similar to private insurers except that (1) they are operated by an agency of the state government, and (2) most are concerned only with benefit payments under the workers' compensation law

15. We address the incentives to self-insure in the Consumer Applications section of this chapter.

and do not assume the employers' liability risk.[16] This usually must be insured privately. The employer pays a premium (or tax) to the state fund and the fund, in turn, provides the benefits to which injured employees are entitled. Some state funds decrease rates for certain employers or classes of employers if their experience warrants it.

Cost comparisons between commercial insurers and state funds are difficult because the state fund may be subsidized. Moreover, in some states, the fund may exist primarily to provide insurance to employers in high-risk industries—for example, coal mining—that are not acceptable to commercial insurers. In any case, employers who have access to a state fund should consider it part of the market and compare its rates with those of private insurers.

Second-Injury Funds

NATURE AND PURPOSE

If two employees with the same income each lost one eye in an industrial accident, the cost in workers' compensation benefits for each would be equal. If one of these employees had previously lost an eye, however, the cost of benefits for him or her would be much greater than for the other worker (probably more than double the cost). Obviously, the loss of both eyes is a much greater handicap than the loss of one. To encourage employment in these situations, **second-injury funds** are part of most workers' compensation laws. When a subsequent injury occurs, the employee is compensated for the disability resulting from the combined injuries. The insurer (or employer) who pays the benefit is then reimbursed by the second-injury fund for the amount by which the combined disability benefits exceed the benefit which would have been paid only for the last injury. The need for second-injury funds has been diminished, by passage in 1990 of the federal Americans With Disabilities Act.

FINANCING

Second-injury funds are financed in a variety of ways. Some receive appropriations from the state. Others receive money from a charge made against an employer or an insurer when a worker who has been killed on the job does not leave any dependents. Some states finance the fund by annual assessments on insurers and self-insurers. These assessments can be burdensome. For example, between 1982 and 1992, assessments against insurers and self-insurers in South Carolina fluctuated between 9 and 18 percent of regular costs.

Workers' Compensation Issues

EXCLUSIVITY

Perhaps due in part to innovative plaintiff's attorneys paid by the contingency fee system, malleable judges, and states' unwillingness or inability to meet (or surpass) the National Commission's 1972 recommendations,

---

16. Some, such as the Utah State Fund, provide both workers' compensation and employer's liability coverages.

the exclusivity of workers' compensation has been under attack for some time. Employers, of course, benefit from having their liabilities limited to what is stipulated in workers' compensation laws. When the benefits received by workers are a close approximation of what would be received under common law, employees too receive a clear advantage from the law. Today, however, there is a perception that workers' compensation provides inadequate compensation for many injuries. With high awards for punitive and general damages (neither available in workers' compensation) in tort claims, workers often perceive the exclusivity of compensation laws as inequitable.

As a result, workers attempt to circumvent the exclusivity rule. One method is to claim the employer acts in a **dual capacity,** permitting the employee an action against the employer in the second relationship as well as a workers' compensation claim. For example, an employee injured while using a product manufactured by another division of the company might seek a products liability claim against the employer. Dual capacity has received limited acceptance.

A second means of circumventing the exclusivity of workers' compensation is to claim the employer intentionally caused the injury. Most states exempt intentional injury from workers' compensation because such incidents are not accidental. Frequently, this claim is made with respect to exposure to toxic substances. Employees claim that employers knew of the danger, but encouraged employees to work in the hazardous environment anyway. This argument too has received limited acceptance, yet litigation of these cases is costly. Further, their mere existence likely indicates at least a perception of faults in the workers' compensation system.

A third circumvention of the exclusivity of workers' compensation is the third-party action over. It begins with an employee's claim against a third party (not the employer). For example, the employee may sue a machine manufacturer for products liability if the employee is injured while using the manufacturer's machine. In turn, the third party (the manufacturer in our example) brings an action against the employer for contribution or indemnification. The action against the employer might be based on the theory that the employer contributed to the loss by failing to supervise its employees properly. The end result is an erosion of the exclusive remedy rule—as if the employee had sued the employer directly.

SCOPE OF COVERAGE

Another current issue in workers' compensation is the broadening of the scope of covered claims. The original intent of workers' compensation laws was to cover only work-related physical injuries. Later, coverage was extended to occupational illnesses that often are not clearly work-related, as is for example, a broken bone. Claims for stress, heart attacks, and cumulative trauma have been increasing at a rapid pace in some states. The National Council on Compensation Insurance estimates that 5 percent of claims nationwide involve stress. Repetitive motion injuries account for about half of all work-related injuries reported to the U.S. Department of Labor via the workers' compensation system. While losses are usually real and significant, the ideal requisites of insurance may be violated. Questions arise on some claims about whether a work-related loss actually occurred, when it occurred, where it occurred, and the extent of disability.

One approach to controlling claims for stress and heart attacks is for the law to spell out clearly when these conditions are or are not compensable. With respect to stress, for example, a law could specify that:

1. Only disabilities caused by real workplace events that are *extraordinary* when compared to the normal work environment are compensable.

2. The extraordinary work environment mentioned above must be the *predominate* cause of the stress illness.

3. Diagnosis and assessment must be determined only by a licensed psychiatrist.

4. Claims are excluded that arise
   a. shortly after employment
   b. resulting from personnel decisions
   c. caused by verbal disagreements with the employer
   d. from problems with a fellow employee without the employer's knowledge
   e. primarily from alcoholism or other drug abuse.[17]

Control of cumulative trauma (e.g., carpal tunnel injuries) claims is perhaps best achieved by a combination of loss prevention/reduction programs (e.g., proper posture, equipment positioning, and regular hand-stretching exercises for workers such as personal computer operators), medical cost containment, and rehabilitation of injured workers.

PERMANENT PARTIAL CLAIMS

Permanent partial disability claims account for approximately half of all money spent on work-related disability claims. Under some state statutes, a lack of objective guidelines creates problems in measuring the degree of disability and its permanency. Subjectivity invites attorney involvement. A "Policy Statement on Permanent Partial Disability" written in 1992 by The National Conference of State Legislatures Blue Ribbon Panel on Workers' Compensation says:

> Based on one study of experience in 13 states over a recent five-year period, about 3 percent of temporary total disability claims involved attorneys, whereas over 31 percent of the partial disability claims involved lawyers.

In some states, attorneys represent over 75 percent of claimants with large permanent partial claims. The concern is that the strict liability nature of the workers' compensation system is designed to be less litigious than a tort system and to provide benefits administratively without resorting to the use of attorneys.

Attorney involvement varies substantially among the states. It is encouraged by factors such as:

1. The complexity of the law.
2. Weak early communication to injured workers.

....
17. Pritchett, Harrington, Doerpinghaus, and Niehaus.

ETHICAL *Dilemma*

Workers' Compensation and Fraud

Fraud is a potential problem with respect to all parties associated with workers' compensation. Employees may exaggerate the length of a period of disability (a process called malingering). They also may fabricate otherwise noncompensable claims. The base for workers' compensation insurance premiums is the insured employer's payroll, with different rates applying to the payroll for various job classifications based on degree of risk. Employers may understate payroll or misclassify employees. Some employers terminate certain employees who are immediately hired by an employee-leasing company that then leases employees back to their original employer. One of the ways employee-leasing companies claim to reduce personnel cost is by administering payroll and benefits. Since a leasing company works with several employers, it is hard for a workers' compensation insurer to monitor its activity. The company may underreport its total number of employees and misclassify some of the work it performs for clients. Still another potential type of fraud occurs when insurance claim adjusters take kickbacks from claimants to cover up fraud that should be reported to the insurer. Attorneys, medical doctors, and other health care providers can initiate or be an accessory to fraud.

There are documented cases of laid-off California employees being enticed by unethical attorneys, assisted by unethical mental health specialists, to fabricate work-related stress claims rather than apply for lower unemployment benefits. Attorneys actually solicited potential claimants from the waiting lines at unemployment offices. Such cases were a factor leading California to tighten its workers' compensation law in 1993.

When a small employer considers its workers' compensation premiums to be excessive for its recent level of claims and perceived risk, is it unethical to underreport payroll or misclassify employees to reduce its premiums? (Assume that in the last three years its workers' compensation premiums have been twice as large as its claims.)

Suppose a friend of yours, with a history of occasional outpatient psychiatric treatment for anxiety and depression, loses her job when an employer of five years downsizes its work force by 20 percent. Would it be ethical for this friend to contact an attorney for assistance in filing a workers' compensation claim for temporary disability benefits based on job stress?

3. Advertisements by attorneys.

4. Failure to begin claim payments soon after the start of disability.

5. Employee distrust of some employers and insurers.

6. Employee concern that some employers will not rehire injured workers.

7. The subjective nature of benefit determination (e.g., encouraging both parties to produce conflicting medical evidence concerning the degree of impairment).

The solution may be a system that settles claims equitably and efficiently through promoting agreement and timely return to work. The Wisconsin system may be the best example of this type of system, characterized by prompt delivery of benefits, low transaction costs, and clear communication between employers and employees.

MEDICAL EXPENSES

All medical care costs have, for decades, grown much faster than the overall Consumer Price Index. Workers' compensation medical care costs are of special concern. The high reimbursement rate (100 percent of allowable charges) by workers' compensation relative to lower rates (e.g., 80 to 90 percent) in nonoccupational medical plans creates a preference for workers' compensation among employees and medical care providers who influence some decisions about whether or not a claim is work-related. Another problem has been the somewhat limited use of medical cost containment techniques by workers' compensation insurers and self-insurers.[18] Options available to better manage the medical care component of workers' compensation include:

1. Allowing the employer to select the treating physician.
2. Allowing the use of health maintenance organizations and other forms of managed care.[19]
3. Setting fee schedules and per diem amounts to limit payments to physicians, hospitals, and other medical care providers.
4. Integrating occupational and nonoccupational medical benefit systems on a twenty-four-hour basis.

Workers' compensation is a quasi social-private insurance scheme of significant concern to its many stakeholders. Unemployment compensation, in contrast, is a purely social insurance program because of the high risk associated with projecting future rates of unemployment and associated claims. Private insurers are not willing to provide this type of insurance.

Unemployment Compensation

Unemployment compensation programs pay weekly cash benefits to workers who are involuntarily unemployed. The following sections cover state laws, coverage, how benefits are financed, and administration of unemployment compensation.

18. The medical insurance techniques mentioned here are explained fully with respect to employee benefit plans in chapter 19.
19. These terms are explained in chapter 19.

STATE LAWS

State unemployment compensation programs were established as a result of federal legislation. However, each state creates, finances, and administers its own law. Like workers' compensation, the law transfers to the employer at least part of the financial element of a risk faced by the employee. Unlike most workers' compensation programs, however, the firm's risk manager has no choice with regard to how the risk is handled. Neither private insurance nor self-insurance is permitted. Management can, however, reduce the cost by (1) stabilizing the firm's employment and (2) preventing payment of unjustified benefits.

Federal Tax Offset

Prior to the adoption of the Social Security Act of 1935, there was considerable opposition to the idea of state laws dealing with the problem of unemployment compensation. This opposition stemmed at least partly from the fear that a state adopting such a program would place business and industry within its borders at a competitive disadvantage unless all states had similar legislation. The unemployment provisions of the Social Security Act solved this problem by placing a 3.4 percent tax on payrolls and permitting employers who pay the tax a 2.7 percent offset. In order to receive this offset, employers must prove that an equivalent amount has been paid into a state system of unemployment compensation which meets the standards set forth by the federal law.[20]

Employers Subject to Tax

The federal tax applies to firms that have one or more employees in each of twenty weeks during the year, or firms that pay $1,500 or more in wages during any calendar quarter. As of January 1987, coverage has been extended to agricultural employers that have ten or more employees in each of twenty weeks during the year or that pay $20,000 or more in wages during any calendar quarter. New provisions to include domestic and municipal employees, as well as employees of nonprofit organizations, have also been added. Under the federal law, only the first $7,000 of annual wages of each employee is subject to the tax, but most states have a higher wage base; Alaska tops the list at $21,600. Sixteen states have a wage base in excess of $10,000.

COVERAGE

The federal law established minimum standards for coverage and benefits. Unless a state law meets the standards, no tax offset is permitted. Every state meets the standards, and in many cases they are exceeded. Today, all states cover state and local government employees, several cover farm workers, and a few cover domestic workers. About 97 percent of the civilian labor force is covered.

----

20. Employers whose state tax is less than 3 percent as a result of experience rating are permitted to offset 90 percent of what they would have paid without experience rating. Without this provision, experience rating could not be used to reduce the employer's tax burden.

Unemployment compensation is designed to relieve workers in certain industries and occupations of part of the economic burden of temporary unemployment. Three aspects of benefit payments are important: (1) amount and duration, (2) qualifications for benefits, and (3) disqualifications.

Amount and Duration

The amount of the weekly benefit payment a worker may receive while unemployed varies according to the benefit formula in the law of each state. Usually the amount is about one-half to two-thirds of the worker's full-time weekly pay within specified limits. The maximum ranges from $95 to $250 a week for a worker without dependents. Minimum benefits range from $5 to $60 a week. Some states provide an additional allowance for certain dependents of the unemployed worker. With the passage of the 1986 Tax Reform Act, all unemployment benefits are fully taxable to the recipient for federal income tax purposes.

Most state laws have a waiting period—typically one week—between the time an unemployed worker files a claim for benefits and the time benefit payments begin. This is designed to place the burden of short-term temporary unemployment on the worker as well as to decrease the cost of the plan, thereby making possible greater coverage of more significant unemployment losses.

The number of weeks for which benefits are paid is a function of the work history of the worker. Those whose earnings record is the highest and longest are entitled to the largest benefits for the maximum length of time. In most states, the maximum number of weeks benefits can be paid is twenty-six. A federal-state program of extended benefits may continue payments for another thirteen weeks during periods of high unemployment, such as occurred in the early 1990s. In an "economic emergency," federal funding may continue payments for another twenty-six weeks.

Qualifications for Benefits

In order to qualify for benefits, unemployed workers must fulfill certain conditions. They must register for work at a public employment office and file a claim for benefits. They must have been employed in a job covered by the state unemployment compensation law.[21] They must have earned a specified amount of pay or worked for a specified length of time, or both. They must be able to work, be available for work, and be willing to take a suitable job if it is offered to them. In most states, an unemployed worker who is sick and, therefore, unable to work is not entitled to unemployment compensation benefits. Some states, however, permit payments to disabled workers who are otherwise qualified.[22]

....

21. An unemployed federal civilian or ex-serviceperson may be entitled to benefits under the conditions of a state law for determining benefit eligibility. The amount he or she may receive will be the same as if federal pay had been covered under the state law. Costs of the benefits are paid by the federal government.

22. Several states have compulsory temporary disability insurance laws to provide income (and, in one state, medical) benefits for disabled workers who are not receiving unemployment benefits. Some of these plans pay partial benefits to workers receiving workers' compensation benefits. Others exclude these workers.

Disqualifications

Unemployed workers may be disqualified from benefits even if they meet the qualifications described above. Most state laws disqualify those who quit voluntarily without good cause or who were discharged for just cause. Those who refuse to apply for or accept suitable work, or are unemployed because of a work stoppage caused by a labor dispute may be disqualified. Other causes for disqualification are receiving pay from a former employer, receiving workers' compensation benefits, receiving Social Security benefits, or being deemed an independent contractor and, therefore, not an employee.

The effect of disqualification varies from state to state. In some cases, it means that the unemployed worker receives no benefits until he or she has again qualified by being employed for a specified length of time in covered work. In other cases, disqualification results in an increase in the waiting period. Some state laws not only increase the waiting period but also decrease the benefits.

HOW BENEFITS ARE FINANCED

Noncontributory

Most unemployment compensation insurance is *noncontributory:* employers pay all the cost in most states.[23] The **Federal Unemployment Tax Act** places a tax on employers at the rate of 6.2 percent of workers' pay in covered jobs, excluding anything over $7,000 paid to a worker in a year. Up to 5.4 percent can be offset by employers who pay a state tax or have been excused through experience rating. Thus, the maximum state tax that can be offset is 5.4 percent. Revenue from this tax is deposited in the Federal Unemployment Trust Fund and credited to the state for the payment of benefits under its plan. The remaining part of the federal tax goes into general federal revenues. Congress appropriates money for grants to the states for their administration of the program. If appropriations for this purpose are less than the federal share of the payroll tax, the remainder of such revenue is put into a reserve fund for aid to the states in payment of benefits when state reserves are low.

Experience Rating

All states have **experience rating;** that is, they reduce the contribution of employers whose workers have little unemployment. The theory of this rating system is that it encourages employers to reduce unemployment and stabilize employment to the extent that they can. One other effect, however, is to make employers interested in disqualifying workers who apply for benefits, because it is benefits paid out of their account that reflect their experience under the plan.[24] This has led to considerable discussion of disqualification standards and administration.

23. Employees contribute in Alabama, Alaska, and New Jersey.
24. This does not necessarily mean that employers try to cheat employees out of benefits. There are many borderline cases in which there is room for argument about whether or not the unemployed worker is really *involuntarily* unemployed. Experience rating emphasizes the fact that employers pay the cost of benefits and motivates them to be interested in disqualifications. As in other human relations situations, one can find examples of bad behavior by both employers and employees.

ADMINISTRATION

The federal portion of the unemployment compensation insurance program is administered by the Employment and Training Administration in the Department of Labor. Every state has its own employment security agency: some are independent; others are in the State Department of Labor or some other state agency. Typically, the agency is also responsible for the administration of state employment search offices. There are more than 2,500 such offices in the United States where claims for benefits may be filed. Claimants apply for benefits and register for employment at the same time. The function of the office is to find employment for claimants or provide benefits.

In recent years, unemployment compensation has attracted less attention than workers' compensation. Worker's compensation has attracted more attention because its costs seemed to be out of control during the 1980s and early 1990s. By the mid-1990s, they were under control again, primarily as a result of changes in state laws. These changes tended to tighten the conditions under which benefits are payable and added stricter claim controls through improved administrative procedures.

Reducing Workers' Compensation Costs

As noted earlier, workers' compensation costs can be a significant burden for a firm. Whatever their size, however, these costs are only part of the total cost of occupational injury and disease. If your firm insures this risk, the premium you pay is the direct cost. You may not be aware that indirect costs of industrial accidents, such as lost time, spoiled materials, and impairment of worker morale, can be just as significant. How can you reduce these costs? First, you may reduce costs by loss prevention and reduction; second, you may self-insure the risk.

LOSS PREVENTION AND REDUCTION

Most industrial accidents are caused by a combination of physical hazard and faulty behavior. Once an accident begins to occur, the ultimate severity is largely a matter of chance. Total loss costs are a function of accident frequency and severity. Frequency is a better indicator of safety performance than severity, because chance plays a greater part in determining the seriousness of an injury than it does in determining frequency.

Accident Prevention Program

The first consideration is to reduce frequency by preventing accidents. Safety must be part of your thinking, along with planning, and supervising. Any safety program should be designed to do two things: (1) reduce hazards to a minimum and (2) develop safe behavior in every employee. A safety engineer from your workers' compensation insurer (or a consultant if you are self-insured) can give you expert advice and help with your program. He or she can identify hazards so they can be corrected. This involves plant inspection, job safety analysis, and accident investigation.

The safety engineer can inspect your plant to observe housekeeping, machinery guarding, maintenance, and safety equipment. He or she can help you organize and implement a safety training program to develop employee awareness and safe practices. He or she can analyze job safety to determine safe work methods, and can set job standards that promote safety. Your insurer will provide you with accident report forms and instructions on accident investigation. This is essential because every accident demonstrates a hazardous condition or an unsafe practice, or both. The causes of accidents must be known if you are going to prevent them. Inspections, job safety analysis, and accident investigations that lead consistently to corrective action are the foundations of accident prevention.

Loss Reduction

Accident frequency cannot be reduced to zero because not all losses can be prevented. After an employee has suffered an injury, however, action may reduce the loss. First, if you provide immediate medical attention, you may save a life. Moreover, recovery will be expedited. This is why many large plants have their own medical staff. It is also why you should provide first-aid instruction for your employees. Second, you or your insurer should manage the care of the injured worker, including referrals to low-cost, high-quality medical providers. Third, arrange for an injured worker to take advantage of rehabilitation. Rehabilitation is not always successful but experience has shown that remarkable progress is possible, especially if it is started soon enough after an injury. The effort is worthwhile from both the economic and humanitarian points of view. All of society benefits.

INSURANCE OR SELF-INSURANCE?

Is your firm large enough to self-insure and, if so, can you save money by doing so? Unless you have at least several hundred employees and your workers' compensation losses have a low covariance with other types of retained exposures, self-insurance is not feasible. Unless self-insurance will save money, it is not worthwhile. What are the possible sources for saving money? Ask yourself the following questions about your present arrangement:

1. Does your insurer pay benefits too liberally?
2. Does it bear the risk of excessive losses?
3. Does it bear the risk of employers' liability?
4. Does it administer the program?
5. How large is the premium tax paid by the insurer?
6. How large is the insurer's profit on your business?
7. What is your share of losses in the assigned risk plan?

As a self-insured firm you will still provide the benefits specified by the workers' compensation law(s) in the state(s) where you operate. Therefore, self-insuring reduces benefits only if you or your outside self-insurance administrator will settle claims more efficiently than your insurer.

Unless your firm is very large you probably would decide to buy stop-loss insurance for excessive losses; and you would buy insurance for your employer's liability (i.e., part B of a workers' compensation insurance policy). Would you administer the self-insured program? Yes, unless you hire an outside administrator. In either event, your administrative expenses might be similar to those of your insurer. As a self-insurer you would save the typical premium tax of between 2 and 3 percent your insurer is required to pay to the state(s) where you do business. Profits are difficult to calculate because the insurer's investment income must be factored in along with premiums, benefit payments, expenses, and your own opportunity cost of funds. While the workers' compensation line of business produces losses in some years and profits in others, over a period of several years (the "long run") you would expect the insurer to make a profit on your business. You could retain this profit by self-insuring.

Firms that do not qualify for insurance based on normal underwriting guidelines and premiums can buy insurance through an assigned risk plan, i.e., the residual market. Because of inadequate rates and other problems, large operating losses are often realized in the residual market. These losses become an additional cost to be borne by insurers and passed on to insureds in the form of higher premiums. Assigned risk pool losses are allocated to insurers on the basis of their share of the voluntary (nonassigned risk) market by state and year. These losses can be 15 to 30 percent or more of premiums for employers insured in the voluntary market. This "burden" can be avoided by self-insuring. Many firms have self-insured for this reason, resulting in a smaller base over which to spread the residual market burden.

If your firm is large enough to self-insure, your workers' compensation premium is experience rated. What you pay this year is influenced by your loss experience during the past three years. The extent to which your rate goes up or down to reflect bad or good experience depends upon the credibility assigned by the insurer. This statistical credibility is primarily determined by the size of your firm. The larger your firm, the more your experience influences the rate you pay during succeeding years.

If you want this year's experience to influence what you pay this year, you can insure on a retrospective plan. It involves payment of a premium between a minimum and a maximum, depending on your loss experience. Regardless of how favorable your experience is, you must pay at least the minimum premium. On the other hand, regardless of how bad your experience is, you pay no more than the maximum. Between the minimum and the maximum, your actual cost for the year depends on your experience that year.

Several plans with various minimum and maximum premium stipulations are available. If you are conservative with respect to risk, you will prefer a low minimum and a low maximum, but that is the most expensive. Low minimum and high maximum is cheaper, but this puts most of the burden of your experience on you. If you have an effective loss prevention and reduction program, you may choose the high maximum and save money on your workers' compensation insurance.

In choosing between insurance and self-insurance, you should consider the experience rating plans provided by insurers, as well as the advantages and disadvantages of self-insurance. The process of making this comparison will, undoubtedly, be worthwhile.

Key Terms

common law defenses
fellow-servant rule
assumption of risk doctrine
contributory negligence
employer liability laws
quid pro quo
inclusive laws
exclusive laws
elective laws
sole remedy
arise out of employment
while in the course of
    employment

occupational disease
medical care benefit
indemnity benefit
total disability
partial disability
permanent total disability
temporary total disability
temporary partial
permanent partial disability
scheduled injuries
average weekly wage
replacement ratio
minimum weekly benefits

maximum weekly benefits

spendable income

waiting period

survivor income benefits

rehabilitation

residual market

state operated workers'
    compensation funds

monopolistic state funds

workers' compensation

employers' liability

other states insurance

second-injury funds

dual capacity

unemployment compensation

benefit formula

federal unemployment tax act

experience rating

Discussion Questions

1. Many workers' compensation laws exclude casual workers from coverage. Why? Who is a "casual employee?"

2. A worker is entitled to workers' compensation benefits when disability "arises out of and in the course of employment." A pregnant employee applies for medical and income benefits, alleging that her condition arose out of and in the course of the company's annual Christmas party. Is she entitled to benefits? Why, or why not?

3. Is the rationale for workers' compensation laws the same as that for no-fault auto insurance plans?

4. How do you account for the range in maximum weekly disability income benefits for workers' compensation reflected in table 12–2?

5. What is the quid pro quo in workers' compensation? How is the exclusivity element of the quid pro quo being eroded? Why is such erosion important?

6. What are the arguments for and against allowing employers to opt out of the workers' compensation systems in South Carolina, Texas, and New Jersey? Given the rapid increases in workers' compensation costs, would you argue that other states should return to offering an opt-out provision? (Note: In the early days of workers' compensation laws in the United States, opt-out provisions were common because of concern about whether making workers' compensation mandatory was constitutional—now, a nonissue.)

7. The frequency of workers' compensation claims due to stress has increased. How can the law provide for legitimate stress claims while reducing illegitimate ones?

8. Ann and Dick both have excellent jobs in Boston. She is transferred to Los Angeles. Dick quits his job so he can go with her. Should he receive unemployment compensation benefits? Why, or why not?

9. Do unemployment compensation benefits help stabilize our economy? Please explain.

10. Do you think experience rating of unemployment compensation contributions helps stabilize employment? Why, or why not?

12.1

Franco Chen, a production foreman for Acme Machine Company, was discussing an unusual situation with Bill Johnson, a line supervisor. "Bill, I've got a bit of a problem. That new applicant for the number 7 drill press job seems to be just the person we need. He has the skill and experience to handle the job. The fact that he has sight in only one eye doesn't affect his ability to perform adequately. Yet I am worried about two things. First, he said he lost his sight in the bad eye because of a steel shaving from a drill press ten years ago. That bothers me about this job, and a possible reoccurrence. Second, I know that management would be upset if he lost his only good eye, because he would be totally blind and the workers' compensation settlement would be much higher for him than for a less experienced worker with two good eyes. It's a hard decision for me to make."

Bill replied, "I don't know much about the technical aspects of that problem, but I think I would hire the experienced fellow. In fact, the Americans with Disabilities Act requires that we not discriminate against him."

1. What obligation (if any) does the company have toward the new worker, if he is hired, to make his workplace "extra" safe?

2. How much added workers' compensation risk will the company be assuming by hiring the one-eyed worker rather than a worker with normal vision?

12.2

As risk manager for Titanic Corp., you want to embark on a stringent work safety program that would cost the business at least $500,000 per year for the next three years, and $300,000 per year thereafter. Workers' compensation losses average about $600,000 per year, and you estimate that you can reduce them by one-third. Your plan is opposed by the financial vice president as a "bleeding heart" program that is not even close to being cost efficient.

1. In light of your knowledge of workers' compensation costs, employers' liability exposures, and trends in court decisions, what arguments can you make in favor of the safety program?

2. Give some examples of activities you might include in this safety program.

12.3

Professor Applegate had just finished her lecture to the class on the theory of unemployment compensation. In the hall, Jack Armbuster told his friend that his father's company, Armbuster Construction, paid rather extensive unemployment premiums due to the seasonal nature of their work. Jack said that Professor Applegate's comment that unemployment payments tended to keep skilled labor in a market through short periods of unemployment made sense. Jack said he could now see some possible benefit in paying higher unemployment premiums and having your crew ready to go back to work on a day's notice, rather than having them move hundreds of miles away in search of new construction projects in an acceptable climate. Jack's friend shared his view.

1. Does Professor Applegate's idea make sense to you? Why or why not?

2. What argument can you make against it?

12.4 Jeanne quits her job because her boss continually makes advances to her. She applies for unemployment compensation benefits while she looks for another job, but her former employer challenges her benefits on the grounds that her unemployment was voluntary because she quit her job with his firm.

1. What do you think her chances of collecting benefits are?
2. Do you think she should be able to collect?
3. Could an employer make a workplace so hostile as to force resignations in order to escape unemployment compensation costs?

P A R T III

Life, Health and Retirement Risks

Daughter of
W.B. & S.M.Munger

CHAPTER 13

Life Insurance

Introduction   As you go through stages in the typical life cycle, your needs for life insurance are likely to change. First, you may die young, long before the end of your income-earning years, while other family members are still dependent on your earnings. Persons who are not wealthy and have dependent children (i.e., most young parents) usually need large amounts of death protection to provide continuation of income in the event of an income earner's premature death. Life insurance can be thought of as a contract providing a hedge against an untimely death. When you purchase life insurance, you buy a contract for the future delivery of dollars. Second, your death, whenever it occurs, will create final expenses such as funeral costs and the payment of debts. If you are wealthy, perhaps later in your life cycle, estate taxes and settlement expenses may require more liquidity than you want to maintain in your investment portfolio. Life insurance provides the necessary liquidity because its payment is triggered by your death.

Since the timing of death is uncertain, it is not feasible for the average person to self-fund death benefits. Although you may retain part of these life risks, a major portion must be transferred or your family may suffer catastrophic losses. Smart decisions about life insurance require understanding both the nature of life insurance and the different types available.

This chapter examines:

1. Basic concepts underlying how life insurance works.
2. Traditional types of life insurance contracts: term, whole life, and endowment policies.

Life insurance, like other forms of insurance, is based on three concepts: pooling many exposures into a group, accumulating a fund by contributions (premiums) from the members of the group, and paying from this fund for the losses of those who die each year. That is, life insurance involves the group sharing of individual losses. To set premium rates, the insurer must be able to calculate the probability of death at various ages among its insureds, based on pooling.

POOLING

The simplest illustration of pooling is one-year term life insurance. If an insurer promises to pay $100,000 at the death of each insured who dies during the year, it must collect enough money to pay the claims. If past experience indicates that 0.1 percent of a group of young people will die during the year, one death may be expected for every 1,000 persons in the group. If a group of 300,000 is insured, 300 claims (300,000 × .001) are expected. Because each contract is for $100,000, the total expected amount of death claims is $30 million (300 claims × $100,000). To collect enough premiums to cover *mortality costs* (the cost of claims), the insurer must collect $100 per policyowner ($30 million in claims/300,000 policyowners).

Other Premium Elements

In addition to covering mortality costs, a life insurance premium must reflect several adjustments. First, the premium is reduced to recognize that the insurer expects to earn *investment income* on premiums paid in advance. In this manner, most of an insurer's investment income benefits consumers. Second, the premium is increased to cover the insurer's marketing and administrative *expenses*. Taxes levied on the insurer also must be recovered. In calculating premiums, an actuary usually increases the premium to cover the insurer's *risk* and *expected profits*. Risk charges cover any deviations above the predicted level of losses and expenses. The major **premium elements** for term life insurance are shown in figure 13–1. The actual prediction of deaths and the estimation of other premium elements are complicated actuarial processes.[1]

PROBABILITY OF DEATH

The prediction of deaths is based on past observations. If the prediction is to be accurate, the group insured must be similar to the one observed. From the law of large numbers, you know it is necessary to insure a large number of people with similar exposures to loss so that actual experience will approximate the underlying probabilities. The smaller the number insured, the greater may be the relative variations from the average, necessitating a larger risk charge to cover any unfavorable deviations from expectations.

....

1. For more information on premium computations see Kenneth Black and Harold Skipper, *Life Insurance,* 12th ed. (Englewood Cliffs, N.J.: Prentice-Hall, Inc., 1994). Contracts that accumulate cash values provide an additional and more significant source of investment income sharing, demonstrated in chapter 14.

FIGURE 13–1

Term Premium Elements

```
Mortality cost
–  Investment income
+  Expense charge
+  Taxes
+  Risk charge
+  Profit
_____
=  Gross premium charge
```

Characteristics of the Mortality Rate

In the previous example of pooling, an assumption was made about the number of people expected to die during the year. This figure is known as the *"mortality rate"* and may be expressed in four ways: (1) in terms of the number of deaths per 1,000; (2) as a fraction, in which the numerator is the number of expected deaths and the denominator is the number in the group; (3) as a decimal; or (4) as a percentage. Thus, the mortality rate for a specific sex and age, which is also referred to as the "death rate," may be expressed as 10 per 1,000, 1/100, 0.01, or 1 percent. The mortality rate is a measure of the probability of death during a given year. Different rates are developed for males and females because females on average outlive males by several years. Group insurance purchased by employers uses the same rate for males and females, called **unisex rates.**

The mortality rate has two important characteristics that greatly influence insurer practices and the nature of life insurance contracts. First, yearly probabilities of death rise with age. Second, for practical reasons, actuaries set at 1.0 the probability of death at an advanced age, such as 99. That is, death during that year is considered a certainty, even though some people survive. An understanding and appreciation of these characteristics will provide the basis for much of our later discussion. They can be illustrated with the mortality curve.

Mortality Curve

If we plot the probability of death for males by age, as in figure 13–2, we have a **mortality curve** that illustrates the relationship between age and the probability of death. This curve shows that the mortality rate for males is relatively high at birth but declines until age 10. It then rises to age 21 and declines between age 22 through 29. This decline apparently reflects many accidental deaths among males in their teens and early 20s, followed by a subsequent decrease. The rise is continuous for females above age 10 and for males after age 29. The rise is rather slow until middle age, at which point it begins to accelerate. At the more advanced ages, it rises very rapidly.

The mortality curve shows why life insurance for a term of one year costs relatively little for young people. The probability that a death benefit payment will be made during that year is very low. Death rates for both females and males, based on the Commissioner's 1980 Mortality Table (the table discussed above), are shown in Appendix F. The rates in this table are higher than current ones because life expectancies for females and males have increased since the 1980 table was constructed. They also include safety margins that make them somewhat higher than the rates experienced now by most life insurers, even in the current AIDS

FIGURE 13–2

Male Mortality Curve Based on 1980 CSO Table

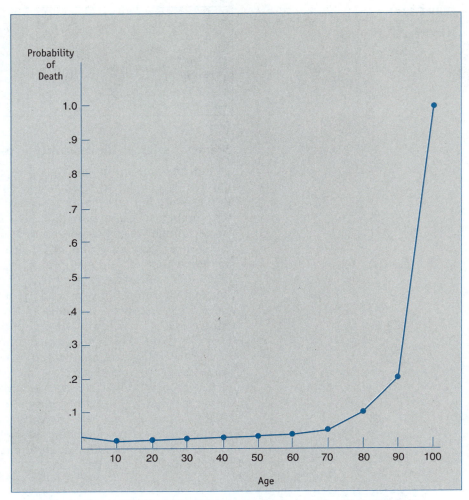

See Appendix F for the 1980 CSO Table. Additional data on mortality rates can be found in the Statistical Abstract of the United States, an annual government publication.

environment. Even with safety factors, the 1980 probability of death for the typical age 25 female is only 0.116 percent, or 1.16 per 1,000.

The mortality curve also indicates why the cost of **yearly renewable term** life insurance, purchased on a year-by-year basis, becomes prohibitive for most people's budgets beyond the middle years. The theory of insurance is that the losses of the few can be paid for by relatively small contributions from the many. If, however, a large percentage of those in the group suffer losses (e.g., because all members of the group are old), the burden on one's budget becomes too great, substantial adverse selection is experienced, and the insurance mechanism fails.

LEVEL-PREMIUM PLAN

The mortality curve shows that yearly renewable term life insurance, where premiums increase each year as mortality increases, becomes prohibitively expensive at advanced ages. For example, the mortality table in Appendix F shows a mortality rate of .06419 for a male age 75. Thus, just

ETHICAL *Dilemma*

Should Life Rates be Based on Gender?

A few states no longer allow automobile insurers to charge different rates to males and females. Yet, while the gap is closing, young male drivers, as a group, still cause more losses than young female drivers as a group. Over a decade ago, the Supreme Court ruled that employers using annuities to fund retirement benefits were discriminating against women by collecting higher contributions from women than from men during their working years and then making equal annuity payments during retirement. Because women as a group at a typical retirement age such as 65 are expected to live several years longer than men of the same age, sex-distinct annuities per dollar of investment pay less per month to women than to men. The same amount of available money at retirement must be spread over more benefit years for women as a group. Employers continuing to pay retirement benefits through annuities were forced by the Supreme Court to use unisex annuities. That is, the mortality rates of men and women were merged to produce an average life expectancy greater than that for men alone and less than that for women alone. Retirement benefits went up for the women and down for the men involved.[2]

As shown by the mortality table in Appendix F, death rates differ for males and females. These differences are used to justify different individual-policy life insurance rates. For example, one insurer charges men age 25 $160.00 and women age 25 $141.00 for $100,000 of yearly renewable term life insurance. For a $100,000 straight life insurance policy purchased at age 25, the same insurer charges men $958.00 and women $819.00. Yet when we compare a particular man to a particular woman of the same age and seemingly the same state of insurability (health, moral behavior, occupation, financial condition, and so forth), the man may outlive the woman. Still, insurers use the observed difference in average experience for large groups of males and females to justify different life rates based on gender, arguing that doing so creates actuarial equity. That is, premiums should differ because expected outcomes (death benefits x probabilities) are different for groups of males and females.[3]

Are sex-distinct life insurance rates ethical, for individual products in the United States as it approaches the 21st century? Does this practice represent unreasonable discrimination (sometimes called "social inequity") against males based on a factor over which they have no control? Is sufficient equity created by charging you a rate that reflects the average mortality of others of your own sex (normally called "actuarial equity" and viewed by insurers as nondiscriminatory)?

2. Mortality experience for large groups varies also by race. However, life insurers voluntarily stopped differentiating rates by race decades ago.
3. Recall that unisex rates are used for life insurance sold to groups (e.g., to an employer as part of an employee benefits plan) as opposed to individuals.

the mortality element of the annual premium for a $100,000 yearly renewable term life insurance policy would be $6,419 (.06419 × 100,000). At age 90, ignoring other premium elements and adverse selection, the mortality cost would be $22,177 (.22177 × 100,000). This high cost, from a budget perspective, coupled with adverse selection, can leave the insurer with a group of insureds whose mortality is even higher than would be anticipated in the absence of adverse selection. Healthy people tend to drop the insurance, while unhealthy people try to pay premiums because they think they may soon have a claim. This behavior is built into renewal rates on term insurance, resulting in renewal rates that rise substantially above rates for new term insurance for healthy people of the same age. A system of spreading the cost for life insurance protection, over a long period or for the entire life span, without a rise in premiums, is essential for most individuals. This is the function of level-premium life insurance.

A **level premium** remains constant throughout the premium-paying period, instead of rising from year to year.[4] Mathematically, the level premium is the amount of the constant *periodic payment* over a specified period (ending before the specified date in the event of death), equivalent to a hypothetical *single premium* that could be paid at the beginning of the contract, discounting for interest and mortality. The hypothetical single premium at the beginning can be thought of as similar to a mortgage that is paid for by periodic level premiums.

As figure 13–3 shows, the level premium for an **ordinary (whole) life** policy (which provides lifetime protection, issued at age 25 in the illustration) is greater during the early years than premiums for a yearly renewable term policy for the same period. The excess (see the shaded area between age 25 and a little beyond age 50 in figure 13–3) and its investment earnings are available to help pay claims as they occur. It is this accumulation of funds, combined with a decreasing amount of true insurance protection (i.e., the net amount at risk to the insurance mechanism), that makes possible a premium that remains level even though the probability of death rises as the insured grows older. In later years, the true cost of insurance protection (i.e., the probability of death at a particular age times the decreased amount of protection) is paid for by the level premium plus a portion of the investment earnings produced by the policy's cash value. In summary, the level premium is higher than necessary to pay claims and other expenses during the early years of the contract, but less than the cost of protection equal to the total death benefit during the later years. The concept of a level premium is basic to an understanding of financing death benefits at advanced ages.

The accumulation of funds is a mathematical side effect of leveling the premium to accommodate consumers' budgets. Beginning in the 1950s, however, insurers began to refer to the accumulated funds as *living benefits* that could meet various savings needs. Today, the payment of premiums greater than the amount required to pay for a yearly renewable term policy often is motivated, at least in the minds of consumers, by the objective of creating savings or investment funds.

....

4. While this discussion is about using a level premium to finance death benefits for one's entire life, the principle may be applied to any duration, including a short-duration term policy such as one with a ten-year term. In addition, instead of leveling over one's whole life, the premium may be leveled over a shorter period, such as to age 65.

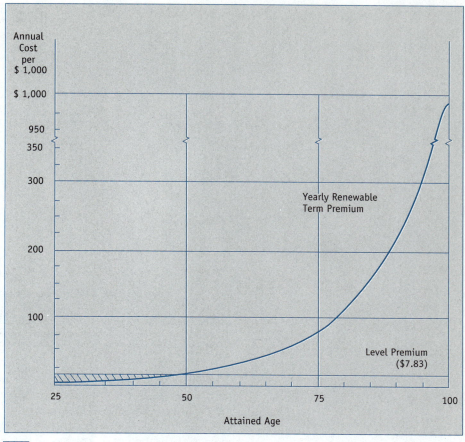

▨ : Premiums that exceed the cost of yearly renewable term life insurance.
Based on nonsmoker rates for a $50,000 policy with a selected company.

Effects of the Level-Premium Plan

From an economic standpoint, the level-premium plan does two things.
First, the insurer offers an installment payment plan with equal payments
over time. Second, the level-premium plan makes possible life insurance
policies made up of two elements: protection and investment.[5]

As discussed, although the periodic premium payments exceed death
benefits and other expenses for an insured group during the early years
of the policy, they fall short during later years (see figure 13–3). The insurer accumulates a **reserve** to offset this deficiency. The insurer's reserve
is similar in amount, but not identical, to the sum of cash values for the
insured group. The reserve is a liability on the insurer's balance sheet,
representing the insurer's debt to you and reflecting the extent to which
your future premiums and the insurer's assumed investment income will
not be sufficient to cover the present value of future claims on your policy.
At any point, the present value of the reserve fund, future investment
earnings, and future premiums are sufficient to pay the present value of

....
5. Aspects of implementing the decision to purchase life insurance are discussed in chapter 22.

FIGURE 13–4

Proportion of Protection and Cash Value in Ordinary Life Contract (Issued to a Male Age 25)

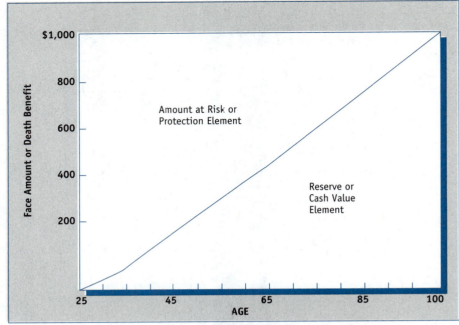

This table shows the cash value (investment) figures for a selected ordinary life policy. The insurer's reserve would be slightly higher than the cash value in the early contract years.

all future death claims for a group of insureds. When an insured dies, the insurer is obligated to pay the beneficiary the face amount (death benefit) of the policy. Part of this payment is an amount equal to the reserve.

The difference between the reserve at any point in time and the face amount of the policy is known as the **net amount at risk** for the insurer, and the **protection element** for the insured. As figure 13–4 illustrates, this element declines each year because the reserve (investment or **cash value,** from your perspective) increases. The protection/net-amount-at-risk element is analogous to decreasing term insurance. All whole life and endowment policies have a combination of cash value and protection. You may prefer to think of life insurance merely as a contract to deliver dollars in the event of a contingency.

The amount at risk for the insurer (that is, your protection element) decreases as the cash value element increases with age; thus, less true insurance (protection) is purchased each year. This decreasing amount of insurance is one of the reasons why the annual cost of pure insurance (that is, your protection element) to your insurer is less than the sum of the level premium plus investment earnings, even at advanced ages when mortality rates significantly exceed the premium per $1,000 of death benefit. Over time, the growing amount of investment earnings (due to your increasing cash value) more than offsets the inadequacy of the level premium. The periodic addition of part of these investment earnings to your cash value explains why the cash value in your policy continues to grow throughout the life of your contract (see figure 13–4).

From an insurer's perspective, the reserve is a liability that will have to be paid when you either die or surrender your policy. A similar amount is an asset from your perspective and is called the cash value. The separation of a whole life policy into protection and investment elements is an economic or personal finance concept, rather than an actuarial one. Actuaries deal with large groups of insureds rather than individual policies and look at an individual policy as an indivisible contract.

The cash value is appropriately classified as an asset on your personal balance sheet because you have three options that make it valuable to you:

1. You may surrender (discontinue) your policy and receive the cash value as a refund.

2. You may take a loan from your insurer for an amount that does not exceed your cash value, without any collateral except your cash value and without any questions qualifying you for the loan.

3. You may leave the cash value in the contract and eventually let it mature as part of your death claim.

If you exercise either option 1 or 2, you convert your paper asset into cash, the ultimate among liquid assets. The third option has value because it avoids reducing the amount of your death benefit by the outstanding balance on your policy loan (the exercise of option 2). Remember that your death benefit consists of the protection plus the cash value element in your policy.

Life insurers may offer many different policies, but each can be classified as one or some combination of the following six basic plans:

1. Term life.
2. Whole life.
3. Endowment life.[6]
4. Universal life.
5. Current assumption whole life.
6. Variable life.
7. Variable universal life.

The first three are discussed in this chapter, the others in chapter 14. Although universal life, variable life, and variable universal life are considered separate types of life insurance, their components fit the first three basic types.

Traditional Life Insurance Contracts

The primary function of term insurance is to create a principal sum for a beneficiary in the event of the insured's death during a specific period (that is, during the term). It is pure protection. Other types of life insurance provide varying combinations of protection and cash values.

Changes in new sales of life insurance sold directly to individuals is shown in table 13–1. Between 1983 and 1993, variable universal life grew at the expense of more traditional policies. Whole life and term policies, however, still accounted for 66 percent of new individual life insurance, as of 1993. The 20 percent volume of universal and variable products in

6. Although endowments may still be considered a basic type of insurance, their sales volume has dropped below 0.5 percent of life insurance sales as consumers have shown a disinterest in relatively short-term insured savings plans that usually have heavy front-end expense loads.

TABLE 13–1

Individual Life Insurance Product Mix
(in Percentage of Face Amount)

POLICY TYPE	1983	1993
1. Whole Life		
Straight Life	17%	18%
Limited Payment Life	2	2
Modified Life	3	1
2. Term	50	45
3. Family Plan Policies	7	7
4. Enhancements	1	2
5. Universal Life	14	10
6. Variable Life	2	2
7. Variable Universal	—	8
8. Other Combined Coverage	4	1
Total	100	100

Note: Figures exclude credit life insurance and single premium policies. Credit life insurance accounts for 1.9 percent of all life insurance in force; single premiums, including dividends used to purchase paid-up insurance, excess premiums that exceed planned periodic premiums, and single premiums applied to riders accounted for 14.1 percent of all 1993 ordinary life insurance premiums.

SOURCE: *Life Insurance Fact Book Update, 1994* (Washington, DC: American Council of Life Insurance), p. 12.

1993 was down from highs of 32 percent in 1984 and 1987, influenced strongly by lower interest rates after 1987 that depressed the sale of universal life policies. The average size policy purchased in 1993 was $81,140. The average amount of insurance per household was $111,600, 2.3 times the disposable personal income per household.[7] In 1983, this ratio had been 1.8. In 1993, 58 percent of households owned individual life insurance. Households with annual incomes below $25,000 are less likely (37 percent ownership) to own individual policies than are higher-income households (e.g., 75 percent ownership with household income of $75,000 or more).

Purchases by individuals, as opposed to employers and others, accounted for 66 percent of all new life insurance in 1993,[8] compared to 70.1 percent in 1983. While term insurance accounted for only 22 percent of the number of individual policies sold in 1993, 45 percent of the amount of individual insurance was term.[9] Term insurance provides a higher death benefit per dollar of premium than do policies with cash values. The percentage of term was down from 50 percent in 1983, as new variable universal policies attracted some consumers who in earlier years would have bought term. Term life insurance is sold in most parts of the world.

TERM INSURANCE

Term life insurance provides *protection* for a specified period called the policy's *term* or duration. When a company issues a one-year term life policy on your life, it promises to pay the face amount of the policy if you die during the one-year term.

In this respect, a term life insurance contract is similar to property insurance. In a property insurance contract, the insurer promises to pay

7. *Life Insurance Fact Book, 1994* (Washington, D.C.: American Council of Life Insurance), p. 15.
8. *Life Insurance Fact Book, 1994*, p. 8.
9. *Life Insurance Fact Book, 1994*, p. 11.

if the insured property is damaged or destroyed by insured perils during the term of the policy. If the property is not damaged or destroyed during that time, there is no payment. No survival benefits exist. Obviously, the term (or duration) for which protection is provided is an important feature of a term policy.

Duration

The length of term policies varies from one month to those that are effective to age 100.[10] The usual terms, however, are one-, five-, ten-, fifteen-, and twenty-year. Ten-year term is currently the most popular form of term contract. Term policies are often not renewable beyond age 65 or 70 because of adverse selection that increases with age. Yet increasingly, yearly-renewable term (YRT) policies are renewable to age 95 or 100, although it would be unusual for a policy to stay in effect at advanced ages because of the amount of premium. YRT policies are subject to high lapse rates (that is, failure to be renewed) and low profitability for the insurer.

Short-term life policies involve no investment element. Long-term contracts (for example, term to age 65) *when accompanied by a level premium* can accumulate a small cash value element in the early years, but this is depleted during the latter part of the term because then the cost of mortality exceeds the sum of the level premium and the investment earnings. The result is that no survivor benefits are available at the end of the renewability period. Two options are typically available with term insurance sold directly to individuals: renewability and convertibility.

Renewability

If you buy a term policy you may want to continue protection for more than one term. Unless the policy contains an option giving you the right to do so, you must, at the end of each term, make a new application to the insurer and provide new evidence of insurability. If your health has deteriorated or you are for any other reason considered a poor risk, you may be unable to obtain insurance or be subjected to higher-than-standard premiums. Magic Johnson learned he was HIV positive when he applied for a life insurance policy before the birth of a child.

This risk may be handled by purchasing *renewable term insurance*. The **renewability option** gives you the right to renew the policy for a specified number of additional periods of protection, at a predetermined schedule of premium rates, without evidence of insurability. Renewability protects your insurability for the period specified. After that period has elapsed, you must again submit a new application and prove insurability.

Each time the policy is renewed, the premium rises because you are older, and older age groups experience higher mortality.[11] Because each premium increase leads to adverse selection, whereby the less healthy tend to renew and the most healthy tend to discontinue, the renewable feature increases the cost of protection. A strong renewable feature, how-

---

10. Term insurance for periods of one to eleven months is called "preliminary" or "initial" term.

11. With non-level premium structures such as those of YRT life, your premium will increase yearly rather than at the end of the ten-year period or so of level premiums.

ever, is valuable if you buy term life insurance. You may in the future become unhealthy and even uninsurable.

Convertibility

You can also buy a term policy with a **convertibility option.** This option provides the right to convert the term policy to a whole life or another type of insurance, before a specified time, without proving insurability. If, for example, you at age 28 buy a term policy renewable to age 65 and convertible for twenty years, you may renew each year for several years and then, perhaps at age 36, decide you prefer cash-value life insurance. Your motivation may be that the premium, though higher than that of the term policy at the age of conversion, will remain the same year after year; the policy can be kept in force indefinitely; or you may want to include cash values among your investments.

The right to convert to whole life insurance or another policy such as universal life makes it possible to obtain such insurance regardless of the condition of your health, your occupation, or other factors that influence your insurability. Because many people at some point in their lives become uninsurable or insurable only at higher-than-standard (called substandard) rates—some at surprisingly low ages—this is an important right. The option protects you against the possibility that your life insurance may expire before your need for it does. Many term contracts are both renewable and convertible. Some companies issue term policies that are automatically converted to another plan of insurance at a specified date.

Most conversions are made at **attained age** premium rates. That is, the premium for the new policy is based on your age at the time of the conversion. You pay the same rate as anyone else who could qualify for standard rates based on good health and other insurability factors. The option results in no questions about your insurability. The **original age** method gives you the premium rate that would have applied had you originally taken out the cash-value policy instead of the term policy. This method is usually not attractive because at the time you convert you have to reimburse the insurer for the difference in what premiums would have been for the different policies, plus interest on this difference (essentially, an amount equal to the reserve on the new policy).

Death Benefit Pattern

The death benefit in a term policy, as explained in the contract, will either remain level, decrease, or increase over time. Each pattern of protection fits specific needs. For example, a decreasing term policy may be used as collateral for a loan on which the principal is being reduced by periodic payments. An increasing amount of protection helps maintain your purchasing power during inflation. The increasing benefit is likely to be sold as a rider to a level benefit policy.

When you purchase a home, you are likely to be offered **mortgage protection** insurance. If you buy this contract, you own *decreasing term insurance* in which the only unique feature is a rate of face value decrease that corresponds to the unpaid principal of your loan. Otherwise, mortgage protection is like other decreasing term policies.[12] **Credit life** insurance is similar to mortgage protection. Its death benefit changes, up or down, as the balance changes on an installment loan or other type of consumer loan. For example, Mastercard and Visa balances are often covered by credit life insurance. In most states, credit life premiums are higher than those for other forms of term insurance available to young, healthy persons.

Premium Patterns

An insurer's nonsmoker's rates may be 40 percent or so lower than those for smokers. The YRT contract usually has a table of premiums that increase each year as you age and as time elapses since you established insurability. Because of adverse selection, as you grow older the guaranteed premiums may become higher than the current cost of a new policy at your attained age.

Reentry term allows you to redemonstrate your insurability periodically, perhaps every five years, and qualify for a new (lower) *select table* of rates that are not initially loaded for adverse selection. If you cannot qualify for the new rates, usually because of worsening health, you can either pay the higher rates of the initial premium table (called *ultimate rates*) or lapse the policy. Because your insurability problem is likely to produce higher rates at competing insurers, you are likely to continue paying higher rates with your first company.

Front-end-loaded term has been highly promoted by a few companies. The major purpose of the high first-year premium has been to create funds to pay substantial commissions to agents. The term policy is often sold as part of a term and annuity (or term and mutual fund) package. Sales emphasis is put on the performance of the investment part of the package. Often, the marketing ploy is to get access to a large initial sum of money by convincing you to surrender an existing cash-value life insurance policy and roll the cash over into the proposed annuity or mutual fund. The front-end load is a negative from your perspective because its major function is to enable the insurer to pay high commissions to your agent.

WHOLE LIFE INSURANCE

Whole life insurance, as its name suggests, provides for payment of the face value upon your death regardless of *when* it may occur. As long as the premiums are paid, the policy stays in force. Thus, whole life insurance is referred to as *permanent insurance*. This ability to maintain the policy throughout one's life is the key characteristic of whole life insurance.

....

12. Before buying a mortgage protection policy, you will want to consider the pros and cons of paying off your mortgage at the time of death. Will your spouse's income be sufficient to meet the mortgage payments? Is the interest rate likely to be attractive in the future? Will the after-tax interest rate be less than the rate of growth in the value of the house, resulting in favorable leverage?

Some forms of mortgage protection insurance insure both you and your spouse. The death benefit is paid when the first of you dies, assuming either of you dies before the end of the policy's duration. Mortgage protection policies often include a conversion feature.

There are three traditional types of whole life insurance: (1) ordinary or straight life, (2) limited-payment life, and (3) single-premium life. The difference between them is in the arrangements for premium payment. (See Appendix E for a sample straight life policy.)

In recent years, the flexibility of whole life insurance policies has been enhanced by the development of various premium payment patterns. The newer forms include *graded premium whole life,* where (by the use of a combination of decreasing term insurance and increasing amounts of whole life insurance) premiums begin relatively low and increase over ten years or so before becoming level for the remainder of life; *vanishing premium plans* in which accumulated dividends (i.e., refunds from the insurer) or the cash values of dividend additions and future projected dividends are sufficient to substitute for future premiums; *indeterminate premium plans* that after a few years adjust, subject to a maximum premium, future premiums to reflect the insurer's future expected operating experience with respect to mortality, investment returns, and expenses; and *current assumption whole life,* that will be discussed in some detail later in this chapter.[13]

Straight Life

The premium rate for a **straight life** policy is based on the assumption that premiums in equal periodic amounts will be paid as long as you live up to an advanced age, such as 90 or 100. In effect, you are buying the policy on an installment basis and the installments are spread over the balance of your lifetime, as explained earlier in our discussion of the level premium concept. This provides the lowest possible level outlay for permanent protection.

As shown in figure 13–4, the level-premium policy consists of a protection element and a cash value element. The cash value builds to equal the face value of the policy by an advanced age such as 90 or 100. If you are still alive at this advanced age, the insurer will pay your death benefit as if you were dead. By this time, the cash value equals the face amount and no real insurance element exists. The options available with regard to this value are discussed in chapter 15. It may be noted here, however, that because of the cash value you do not promise to pay premiums all your life but have several alternatives available. You can, for example, convert the policy to one which requires no further premium payments, but has a lower face amount for the remainder of your life.

A basic straight life policy typically has a face amount (death benefit) that remains level over your lifetime. The pattern can change, however, by using dividends to buy additional amounts of insurance or by purchasing a cost of living adjustment rider. In 1993, straight life policies made up 36 percent of the new policies sold and 18 percent of new death benefits.

---

13. The nature of dividends and paid-up additions mentioned in describing vanishing premium plans will be described in more detail later.

Limited-Payment Life

Like straight life, limited-payment life, offers lifetime protection but limits premium payments to a specified period of years or to a specified age. After premiums have been paid during the specified period, the policy remains in force for the balance of your life without further premium payment. The policy is called *paid up*. A *20-pay life* policy becomes paid up after premiums have been paid for 20 years, a *life-paid-up-at-65* becomes paid up at age 65, and so on. The shorter premium payment period appeals to some buyers. For example, you may see a life-paid-up-at-65 policy as ending premiums around the time you expect to begin living on retirement pay. If you die before the end of the premium-paying period, premium payments stop and the face amount is paid. As illustrated in table 13–2, for a given amount of insurance issued at a given age, annual premium payments (and cash values) are larger for limited-payment life insurance than for straight life. In 1993, limited-payment policies accounted for 10 percent of the new policies sold, but only 2 percent of the amount of new insurance, suggesting that most limited-payment policies have low face amounts. These policies are mainly sold on the lives of children (called juvenile insurance) or as business insurance where there is a need to fully pay for a policy by a certain date, such as the time you expect an employee to retire.

Single-Premium Life

Whole life insurance may be bought for a **single premium**—the ultimate in limited payment. Single premiums are large (for example, $150 per $1,000 of insurance for a male nonsmoker at age 35) because no further payment is required. Mathematically, the single premium is the present value of future benefits, with discounts both for investment earnings and mortality. Cash and loan values are high compared with policies bought on the installment plan (see figure 13–5). In 1991, a little over half of all new single-premium life insurance was whole life, one-third was in variable life policies, and the remainder was primarily in universal contracts. Single-premium life insurance is bought almost exclusively because of its investment features; protection is viewed as a secondary benefit of the transaction. In the Depression of the 1930s, substantial sums of money

TABLE 13–2

Annual Premium Per $1,000 of Death Benefit and Guaranteed Cash Values Issued to Nonsmoking Males Age 25*

	YEARLY RENEWABLE TERM	STRAIGHT LIFE	LIFE PAID UP @ 65	20-PAY LIFE
Annual Premiums	$1.45	$ 7.18	$ 8.74	$ 10.82
5th Year Cash Value	0.00	10.00	12.00	24.00
10th Year Cash Value	0.00	45.00	50.00	80.00
15th Year Cash Value	0.00	88.00	97.00	153.00
20th Year Cash Value	0.00	140.00	154.00	243.00
Cash Value at Age 65	0.00	430.00	499.00	499.00

*Current life insurance premium rates may be found in *Best's Flitcraft Compend,* A. M. Best Company, Olwick, NJ 08858. The rates in this table are for $100,000 non-participating policies. Larger policies have slightly lower rates. Policies for females also have lower rates. The yearly renewable term rate increases each year; by age 45 it is $2.42.

FIGURE 13–5

Protection and Cash Value Elements for Single Premium and Installment Forms of Cash Value Life Insurance

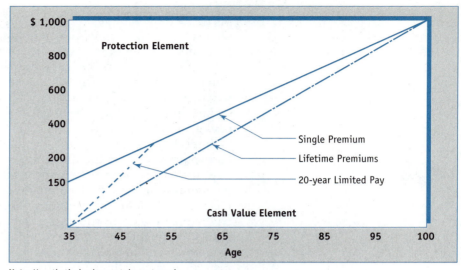

Note Hypothetical values not drawn to scale.

flowed into single-premium life insurance because the life insurance industry was having far fewer bankruptcies than the banking industry. Following the stabilization of banks in the late 1930s with the passage of legislation to create bank account insurance mechanisms (that is, the Federal Deposit Insurance Corporation and the Federal Savings and Loan Insurance Corporation), single-premium life insurance became an insignificant product until the 1980s. In the 1980s and 1990s it was being viewed as an attractive investment largely because tax law changes had eliminated a number of tax-sheltered investments but had left favorable treatment of *inside interest buildup* (that is, investment returns on cash values).[14]

Tax Aspects

In the U.S., you typically pay individual life insurance premiums out of funds on which you previously had paid income taxes. That is, premiums are paid from after-tax income. They are deductible in many countries around the world. Exceptions to this general rule in the U.S. include:

- Life insurance payable to a charity.
- Life insurance required by an alimony agreement.
- Life insurance bought through an Internal Revenue Code (IRC) Section 457 deferred compensation plan for state employees.
- Group term life insurance premiums paid by an employer for the benefit of employees. These are deductible as an ordinary business expense and, do not impute taxable income, on the first $50,000 of coverage, to employees.

14. Tax law changes in 1988 made single-premium surrenders and policy loans undesirable because any gain over net premiums becomes taxable immediately. Furthermore, gains are subject to an additional 10 percent tax penalty if the policyowner is less than age fifty-nine and one-half. Thus, the tendancy of single-premium buyers is to let the policy mature as a death claim. At that time there are no adverse income tax effects.

In general, when premiums are paid from after-tax income, death benefits are *not* part of the beneficiary's or anyone else's gross income.[15] Therefore, whether you die soon or long after purchasing a $100,000 life insurance policy on your life, your named beneficiary, irrespective of relationship to you, would not incur any federal income taxes on the proceeds, including gains within the cash value portion of the policy. Nontaxable proceeds also include nonbasic benefits such as term riders, accidental death benefits, and paid-up additions. *Exceptions* include:

- Benefits received as alimony.
- Benefits from an IRC Section 457 plan for state employees.
- Benefits in whole or part resulting from a policy transferred to another person for a valuable consideration (the so-called *transfer* for value rule).[16]
- Benefits from a policy that fails to meet the IRC Section 7702 definition of life insurance.[17]

The cash value of a life insurance policy, whether straight life, limited premium, single premium, or another type, earns investment returns. Under most current forms of life insurance, all or almost all of the investment return (inside interest build-up) is used either to increase your cash value or provide dividends; none or only a small part of each increase goes to the insurer to cover its expenses and profit. The inside interest build-up is subject to federal income tax *only* if you surrender (cancel) the policy for its cash value and receive more than your net premiums paid (that is, premiums minus dividends).[18] For example, you may surrender a policy with the following tax effect:

Cash Value		$25,000
Minus Net Premiums Paid:		
Gross Premiums	$30,000	
− Dividends	7,000	23,000
Taxable Gain		$ 2,000

The entire taxable gain is subject to income taxation at your marginal rate in the year you surrender the policy for its cash value. An interesting aspect of this tax law is that your cost basis (net premiums paid) includes the cost of your insurance protection that is generally a nondeductible personal expense, along with your contributions to the cash value element of the contract. Therefore, the cost of insurance protection becomes a deduction from your investment earnings before taxes are assessed on the remainder.

---

15. IRC Section 101(a)(1). Unlike federal income taxation, federal estate taxes on the right to transfer assets at death apply to death proceeds from life insurance where the insured owned the policy. Estate taxes are explained in chapter 22.

16. This rule does not apply when the transfer is from one spouse to another, when the transfer is a bona fide gift, in connection with certain transfers involving a business, and when the policy is acquired by the insured.

17. In general, the definition of life insurance sets forth two tests to see that a policy includes a significant protection element, rather than being predominantly an investment vehicle. When a policy fails both tests, only its protection element would receive favorble Section 101(a)(1) treatment of death benefits.

18. The exception is for loans from single-premium policies. See footnote 14.

Some life insurance policies include dividends, and these policyholder dividends are excluded from federal income taxation. The federal government reasons that dividends constitute the return of an original overcharge of premiums. Thus, it is assumed that funds (premiums) on which you previously have paid taxes are being returned as policyowner dividends. More will be said about dividends later in this chapter.

Except for single-premium life insurance, the purchase of most life insurance is motivated primarily by a need for death protection. The availability of private life insurance reduces pressures on government to provide welfare to families that experience premature deaths of wage earners. Furthermore, life insurance is owned by a broad cross section of U.S. society. This, along with effective lobbying by life insurers, may help explain the tax treatment of life insurance.

Investment Aspects

The typical buyer of life insurance, however, does not expect to pay income taxes on proceeds from his or her policy. Instead, the expectation is for the policy to mature eventually as a death claim. At that point, all proceeds (protection plus cash value) of life insurance death claims are exempt from income taxes under Section 101(a)(1). In practice, most policies terminate by being lapsed or surrendered prior to death as needs for life insurance change.

Life insurers offer participation in portfolios of moderate-yield investments (such as high-grade industrial bonds, mortgages, real estate, and common stock) in which cash values are invested, with potentially no income tax on the realized investment returns. Part of each premium, for all types of cash-value life insurance, is used to make payments on the protection element of the contract, but the protection element also has an expected return. This return is equal to your probability of death multiplied by the amount of protection. Thus, the need to pay for protection in order to gain access to the cash value element of a single-premium or other investment-oriented plan should not be viewed as a consumer disadvantage if you need additional life insurance protection. The participation (dividend) feature of a policy has a major effect on its cost and worth.

Participation Feature

Mutual life insurers have always sold their term and cash-value life products on a participation basis. Stock life companies have also made limited use of participating policies.[19] Participating contracts pay **dividends** for the purpose of retrospectively refunding higher-than-necessary premium margins *and* sharing company profits with policyowners. Thus, as investment returns escalate above previous expectations or as mortality rates decline, as in the 1970s and 1980s, dividends provide a mechanism for life

---

19. Mutual insureres have no stockholders. Thus, they share profits with policyholders who effectively own such companies. Stock insurers, however, are owned by outside stockholders, a third party that shares in the profits or losses of these companies. The distinction is explained more fully in chapter 24.

TABLE 13–3

Net Rate of Investment Income for U.S.
Life Insurers: 1915–1994*

Year	Rate	Year	Rate	Year	Rate
1915	4.77%	1970	5.34%	1985	9.87%
1920	4.83	1971	5.52	1986	9.64
1925	5.11	1972	5.69	1987	9.39
1930	5.05	1973	6.00	1988	9.41
1935	3.70	1974	6.31	1989	9.47
1940	3.45	1975	6.44	1990	9.31
1945	3.11	1976	6.68	1991	9.09
1950	3.13	1977	7.00	1992	8.58
1955	3.51	1978	7.39	1993	8.04
1960	4.11	1979	7.78	1994	7.63
1965	4.61	1980	8.06		
1966	4.73	1981	8.53		
1967	4.83	1982	8.87		
1968	4.97	1983	9.08		
1969	5.15	1984	9.65		

*The returns are for general investment portfolios supporting traditional life insurance products, such as straight life, that have guaranteed cash values and face amounts. It does not include investments that support variable insurance products where the investments are primarily in equities.

The calculations use industry aggregates. The reported net rate of investment income is determined by dividing net investment income by mean insurer assets (beginning-of-year plus end-of-year) less half the net investment income.

Federal income taxes were deducted from these returns before 1940. Since 1940, the rates are before federal income taxes.

SOURCE: *Life Insurance Fact Book, 1995,* p. 36.

insurers to share these windfalls with consumers, including policyholders who purchased insurance many years ago.[20]

The gradual increase in investment returns over about forty years between 1945 and 1985 (see table 13–3) was a major factor in actual dividends over this period being greater than those illustrated to consumers at the time of purchase. Falling interest rates along with retention of higher-than-normal percentages of net income moderated increases in policyowner dividends in the late 1980s and into the 1990s. Several large mutuals reduced dividend scales in 1992, 1993, and 1994, reflecting lower investment earnings as well as attempts to strengthen their net worth. Net worth to assets is one of the main measures of an insurer's financial strength. Consumer interest in the financial strength of life insurers increased in 1991 following the financial failures of several large life insurers.

Dividends allow the *sharing* of current investment, mortality, expense, and lapse experience with the policyholder. Investment returns usually have more influence on the size of dividends than do the other factors. The fact that insurer investment portfolios tend to have many medium- and long-term bonds and mortgages that do not turn over quickly creates a substantial lag, however, between the insurer's realization of higher yields on new investments and the effect of those higher yields on average **portfolio re-**

20. Most insurers choose to share substantially with persons who have held policies with their company for years; others primarily make their new policies look attractive to prospective customers. The latter practice represents an ethical breach by these insurers.

turns that affect dividends. Thus, in a period of rising interest rates such as the late 1970s and early 1980s, dividends do not increase as sharply as yields on new bonds and money market instruments. The lag between higher current yields and average portfolio returns results in dividends not responding quickly to the inflation that often underlies increased yields. The use of average portfolio returns in dividend calculations can cause current rates of return on participating whole life policies, for example, to be lower than the current return being realized on other insurance products that use **new money** methods. With new money portfolio methods, the insurer credits you with returns realized on new investments made at the time your premiums are paid, rather than the average returns on all of the investments in its portfolio. This partly explains the drop in popularity during the early and mid-1980s of straight life insurance funded primarily by investment portfolios with medium-to-long maturity instruments bought when returns were relatively low. On the other hand, in periods such as the early 1990s when interest rates on new investments were low, lags resulted only in gradual drops in average returns for participating whole life products and make whole life policies look attractive compared to the performance of products funded by short-term investment portfolios that are affected very quickly by the new lower rates.[21]

Participating whole life insurance continues to be a major product line for mutual insurers. Sales illustrations are used by agents in presenting the product to the consumer. For products with the participation feature, dividends projected for long periods into the future are a significant part of the sales illustration. Generally, the illustrations are based on the *current* experience of the insurer with respect to its investment returns, mortality experience, expenses, and lapse rates. Table 13–4 shows a sales illustration that might be used for a 20-year-old male nonsmoker who is interested in buying a participating straight life policy. We shall briefly explain the illustration and the importance of the projected dividends.

Column 1 indicates that the illustrated annual values are shown for the first twenty years (through age 40), and at the selected ages of 60, 65, and 74. Column 2 shows that the annual premium for the policy is a level amount of $919 due, incidentally, at the beginning of each year rather than at the end, as indicated by the title for column 1. Column 3 illustrates the dividends the insurer would expect to pay if its future operating experience remained exactly like its current experience. You can be sure that the insurer's future investment, mortality, and expense experience will *not* be the same. Notice the asterisk beside "dividend" and the wording of the insurer's footnote cautioning the consumer that the dividends ". . . are not estimates or guarantees of future results, which may be larger or smaller." Are dividends simply a refund of initial overcharges in premium, as is assumed by federal tax policy? A "no" answer seems obvious by observing that after the thirteenth policy year, the illustrated dividends exceed the premium every year. By age 74, the illustrated dividend is over 46 times greater than the annual premium. Another interpretation is to recognize that had the insurer projected current experience on investments, mortal-

---

21. Universal life (see chapter 14) often is funded by rather short-term investments. Consequently, universal life tends to be more popular in periods of high current interest rates (for example, 1986) than in times when current rates are relatively low (for example, 1994).

TABLE 13–4

Sales Illustration of a $100,000 Participating Straight Life Policy for a Male Nonsmoker, Age 20. (Dividends to be used to purchase paid-up additions.)

(1) End of Year	(2) Cash Outlay	(3) Dividend*	(4) Total Payments	(5) Cash Value Increase*	(6) Cash Value Total*	(7) Cash Value Guaranteed	(8) Death Benefit*
1	919	50	919	49	49	0	100,397
2	919	90	1,838	614	664	522	101,086
3	919	138	2,757	699	1,363	1,077	102,099
4	919	186	3,676	787	2,151	1,666	103,408
5	919	238	4,595	886	3,037	2,292	105,015
6	919	293	5,514	994	4,032	2,960	106,906
7	919	353	6,433	1,110	5,142	3,669	109,081
8	919	419	7,352	1,238	6,380	4,420	111,552
9	919	491	8,271	1,377	7,758	5,215	114,317
10	919	569	9,190	1,528	9,286	5,054	117,382
11	919	655	10,109	1,694	10,981	6,940	120,750
12	919	745	11,028	1,866	12,848	7,870	124,402
13	919	841	11,947	2,057	14,905	8,849	128,338
14	919	927	12,866	2,244	17,150	9,876	132,481
15	919	1,023	13,785	2,449	19,599	10,953	136,842
16	919	1,128	14,704	2,672	22,272	12,082	141,431
17	919	1,243	15,623	2,914	25,186	13,264	146,255
18	919	1,369	16,542	3,176	28,362	14,499	151,325
19	919	1,508	17,461	3,463	31,826	15,790	156,654
20	919	1,660	18,380	3,773	35,600	17,137	162,251
Ages							
@60	919	13,300	36,760	19,469	237,123	45,099	459,839
@65	919	20,539	41,355	28,815	361,127	53,289	610,503
@74	919	42,543	49,625	55,451	743,564	67,806	1,031,259

*Dividends assume no loans; loans will reduce dividends. Illustrated dividends (1995 scale) reflect claims, expense, and investment experience and are not estimates or guarantees of future results, which may be larger or smaller. This illustration does not reflect that money is paid and received at different times. Interest of 8 percent applies to policy loans.

ity, expenses, and lapses in calculating the premium, the $919 annual premium would have been much smaller and no dividends would be illustrated. Insurers use more conservative premium factors and thereby shift substantial risk about future performance to the consumer.

Column 4 shows a simple accumulation of the premiums in column 2. Columns 5, 6, and 8 are influenced strongly by the amount of dividends illustrated and their use to purchase dividend additions. When you select the dividend additions option, at the end of each year, your dividend (for example, $50 in the first year) is used to purchase a single premium life insurance policy. In the first year, this addition to the illustrated basic $100,000 policy has a cash value of $49 (see column 5) and a face amount of $397 (see the value in column 8, year 1 and subtract the policy's original $100,000 face value). Compare the total cash values in column 6 with the guaranteed cash values in column 7. The differences are the cash values in the dividend additions (single premium policies) purchased with the illustrated dividends. By the twentieth year, total cash values are a little over twice those actually guaranteed, and by age 65 are almost seven times greater than the minimum guaranteed.[22]

Dividend additions increase the amount of death benefit as well as cash values. If dividends had been taken in cash, the death benefit in column 8 would have remained level at $100,000 over time. Instead, based on the sales illustration, dividend additions increase this amount to over $1,000,000 at age 74. Dividends and their use have a powerful impact on life insurance sales illustrations. They are highly unlikely to remain at the level illustrated. Many illustrations made in the early 1980s were not being realized by the mid-1990s. Their use represents a controversial market conduct issue. Consumers need to monitor whether or not their insurers are being overly optimistic in printing sales illustrations.

ENDOWMENT LIFE INSURANCE

Endowments provide for payment of the face amount of the policy in the event of your death during a specified period, or the face amount at the end of such period if you are still living. Thus, the insurer makes two promises: (1) to pay for death during the endowment period and (2) to pay for survival to a specified date (maturity value). Payment of the entire face amount is a certainty, assuming you continue to pay the relatively high premiums.

Endowment insurance, like whole life insurance, is a combination of increasing investment and decreasing term insurance. At the inception of the contract, the term insurance part equals the face amount of the policy. In a relatively short period of time (for example, ten or twenty years or at age 65), the investment element equals the face amount, and the contract matures even if you are still living. In essence, this is an insured savings plan. Cash values are available if you want to borrow them or if you surrender the contract before the end of the endowment period. Whole life insurance can be considered an endowment at an advanced age such as 90 or 100 when the cash value equals the face value. The term "endowment," however, is usually reserved for contracts that have the unique characteristic of a short duration.

Except when the endowment policy is used to fund a qualified retirement plan,[23] the maturity value of the contract is subject to the same federal income tax treatment as applies to the surrender of a whole life contract. That is, the excess of the maturity value over the net premiums paid (gross premiums minus dividends received) is taxable income at the end of the endowment period.

---

22. These large numbers, if they are never realized, do not necessarily reflect a high rate of return on the cash value element of the contract. This subject is addressed in chapter 16.
23. Qualfied retirement plans are discussed in chapter 20.

Choosing a Type of Life Insurance

When should you buy term insurance? When should you buy a whole life policy? Should you buy endowment insurance? Let's see how you can make the best choice.

USES OF TERM INSURANCE

Term life insurance is best when your need for protection is temporary or when you need a great deal of protection but cannot afford a large premium. As you will see when we discuss the programming of life insurance needs in chapter 22, many young families need a surprisingly large amount of life insurance to provide income continuation in the event of the death of a major wage earner. Most married persons with children cannot afford to fill all their needs with cash value life insurance. For this group, it may be more important to satisfy protection rather than savings needs.

At younger ages, term life insurance premium rates are relatively low, so a sizable amount can be bought for a modest sum. For example, a male age 25 can buy a $100,000 yearly renewable term policy for about $12 per month. If you plan to keep the term policy for more than ten years, you will want a reentry feature. Term rates will rise rapidly at older ages. Reentry term will moderate the increase as long as you remain insurable at standard rates. A convertible feature is highly desirable unless you are convinced (for example, by the results of dynamic life insurance programming) that you will not need the protection represented by the term policy in advanced years.

You may also prefer term insurance if you need death protection but believe you have investment alternatives superior to the investment choices available through cash-value life insurance policies. Most people can find an investment strategy consistent with their risk/return preferences[24] among the basic types of life insurance. This chapter described the new money and portfolio approaches, and in the next chapter we will examine life products with

equity investment alternatives and the ability to transfer funds among a family of portfolios. We also will look at ones that offer flexible premiums. The different tax treatment of alternative investments may lead you to a combination of term life insurance and an investment that defers income taxation on your periodic investment contributions. For example, persons eligible for individual retirement accounts, 401(k) plans, or other tax-deferred retirement programs may want to buy term insurance for their death protection needs but direct long-term investment dollars to annuities, mutual funds, or other investments through the tax-deferred program. The life insurance products we have discussed shelter (or defer, if you surrender the policy) income taxes on investment earnings (inside interest buildup), but premiums generally are paid with after-tax income.[25] Persons who opt for the term plus other tax-deferred investments should have other sources of savings for emergency needs because programs that defer income taxes on contributions have 10 percent penalties on withdrawals before age 59½.

Perhaps the major flaw in the buy-term-and-invest-the-difference strategy, however, is that the majority of Americans lack the discipline required for regular contributions to the "other investment." Pressures to consume often overcome the desire to invest. Cash value life insurance is sometimes considered as "forced savings." This classification assumes that you are more likely to pay life insurance premiums when they are due than you are to contribute regularly to a savings or investment program. This reasoning overlooks the fact that life insurance **lapse rates** are not close to zero. A lapse rate is the ratio of the number of policies lapsed or surrendered to the average number of policies in force. In 1993, 17.4 percent of policies were lapsed during their first two years. After two years, the annual

---

24. Investment theory and empirical studies show a positive correlation between risk and expected returns for investments. The traditional cash-value life insurance policies we are discussing are supported by portfolios of medium-risk investments. Consequently, the size of their expected returns on investment would also fall in the medium range.

25. A small percentage of the population (that is, those working for state governments) is eligible for cash-value life insurance under Internal Revenue Code section 457 plans that exempt premiums from current taxes. However, the death benefits under such plans are subjected to federal income taxes if you die before retirement. Most employed individuals do not pay income taxes on premiums paid by their employers for group term life insurance.

lapse rate was 5.8 percent.[26] The reasoning also ignores the availability of "forced savings" plans available through payroll deductions where you work and through periodic deductions from bank accounts.

CREDIT LIFE INSURANCE

Many people buy term life insurance without realizing it. When you make an installment loan at the bank or other lender to buy furniture or an automobile, for example, credit life insurance may be part of the deal. Decreasing term insurance pays the balance of your debt to the bank in the event of your death. Where credit life insurance premium rates are not prudently regulated, the cost of such protection is usually excessive. In a few states a bank may, for example, charge 1 percent of the original amount of an installment loan per year, which is a premium rate of $10 per thousand dollars of protection. This is more than five times as much per thousand as the rate shown in table 13–2 for one-year renewable term insurance at age 25.

If you borrow frequently or are often in debt, continuously, you can save money by purchasing an individual term policy in an amount equal to your maximum indebtedness, instead of buying the credit life insurance offered by a bank or other lending agency. (An exception exists for older persons and persons in poor health. Credit life rates are averages that reflect mortality experience for a wide range of ages and insurability status.) Lenders may be able to require an assignment of life insurance to assure that the debt will be paid in the event of your death, but they cannot require you to buy it from them.

MORTGAGE LIFE INSURANCE

Also called mortgage redemption insurance, this is simply a longer-lived form of credit life insurance. It is decreasing term, the amount of which declines as your monthly payments reduce the balance due on the mortgage. Typically, it is offered to you by the lending agency at the time you make arrangements to finance the purchase of your home. At that time, you should find out what the costs are so that you can compare this insurance with protection from some other source. You can easily get quotes by calling several life insurance agents. Mortgage life rates with some insurers are highly competitive.

USES OF WHOLE LIFE INSURANCE

Unless you plan to keep a life insurance policy in force for an extended period, such as fifteen years or more, you

should buy term rather than whole life. Term is cheaper in the short run, and you can buy a larger amount per dollar of premium. On the other hand, traditional whole life has the advantage of a level premium for persons who keep it in force for a long period. The term life premium is lower than the whole life premium initially, but eventually becomes larger (see figure 13–3) and ultimately rises to levels that are prohibitive for most budgets, particularly in retirement years.

Which is better, straight life or limited-payment? If you want the same amount of life insurance both before and after retirement, straight life requires lifetime premium payments. Limited-payment, such as life-paid-up-at-65, does not have this drawback. You can change straight life to paid up permanent insurance at any time, but the death benefit will be reduced. We believe the only reason to buy a cash value life insurance policy with a premium larger than that for straight life would be when you have all the death protection you need but still want more funds flowing into the investment element of cash value life insurance. Then you might opt for a medium- or high-premium current assumption policy (or a universal or variable policy) with the flexibility to increase premiums above the target level. These newer policies have essentially made limited-payment and endowment policies obsolete.

An interesting issue is whether an existing whole life insurance policy should be replaced by a newer whole life, universal, variable, or buy-term-and-invest-the-difference plan. For a replacement to be justified, the new policy must have a lower cost of protection or a higher return on the investment element than is expected for the older policy. As a generalization, replacement of participating policies and current assumption whole life policies is usually not in your best interest because they have mechanisms to share current and future company operating experience with you. To justify replacing these policies, you would need to be with a poorly performing company and/or one that does not equitably share its good fortunes with consumers. Of course, such companies exist. But many fine-performing, consumer-oriented insurers also have many of their policies indiscriminately replaced. Some buy-term-and-invest-the-difference schemes (usually a high-priced term policy with investments made in mutual funds or annuities) have replaced millions of whole life insurance policies with total disregard of whether the consumer's welfare is enhanced. Be wary of the replacement artist!

USES OF ENDOWMENT INSURANCE

Federal tax law changes in the 1970s and 1980s resulted in reducing the appeal of endowment policies as savings vehicles. An exception is the use of individual endowment policies to fund qualified retirement plans offered by small

26. *Life Insurance Fact Book, 1994,* p. 67. The lapse rates shown are for all types of policies combined.

employers. Some plans perform well in the retirement market. Endowments are used sparingly in the juvenile insurance market as college savings mechanisms. Those with normal commission scales for agents and short maturities, such as ten or fifteen years, seldom have attractive after-tax rates of return on the savings element because their expense loads, primarily to pay commissions to agents, are higher than those for competing investments.

Endowment life insurance is widely used in many Asian and European countries. Short duration policies (three to ten years) are common in Asian countries; single-premium endowments are popular in some European countries. Korea and certain other countries make significant use of endowments for education purposes. In the U.S., uses other than in small corporate retirement plans are limited.

Key Terms

premium elements	attained age
mortality rate	original age
unisex rates	mortgage protection
mortality curve	credit life
yearly renewable term	reentry term
level premium	front-end-loaded term
ordinary (whole) life	whole life
reserve	straight life
net amount at risk	single premium
protection element	dividends
cash value	portfolio returns
term life	new money
renewability option	endowments
convertibility option	lapse rates

Discussion Questions

1. An early assessment society provided death benefits by requiring a contribution from all members whenever one member died. What problems would you expect with such an arrangement?

2. List and describe the elements that make up a life insurance premium.

3. Would you expect one-year term insurance that is renewable and convertible to require a higher premium than one-year term insurance without these features? Explain.

4. Explain why an investment (cash value) segment becomes a part of a level-premium life insurance contract.

5. In what way is the reentry feature of term insurance desirable to policyholders? Is it a valuable policy feature after you become unhealthy?

6. What is the purpose of a front-end expense load in a term insurance policy? Are there any consumer benefits in this design?

7. How may the participating whole life policy share higher-than-expected investment earnings?

8. What is attractive from a policyowner's viewpoint about the way returns (inside interest build-up) on cash-value life insurance policies other than single-premium policies are taxed?

9. Explain the nature of the reserve an insurer accumulates in connection with its level-premium life insurance policies.

10. What justification do you have for including your cash values on life insurance you own among assets on your personal balance sheet?

Cases

13.1 George and Mary Kays are very excited over the news that they are to be parents. Since their graduation from college three years ago, they have purchased a new house and a new car. They owe $130,000 on the house and $8,000 on the car. They did not purchase life insurance with either of these debts. In fact, their only life insurance consists of $75,000 of term coverage on George and $50,000 on Mary. This coverage is provided by their employers as an employee benefit. Their personal balance sheet shows a net worth (assets minus liabilities) of $80,000. George is rapidly moving up within his company as special projects engineer. His current annual salary is $60,000. In anticipation of the new arrival, George is considering the purchase of additional life insurance. He feels that he needs at least $500,000 in coverage, but his budget for life insurance is somewhat limited. The couple has decided that Mary will stay at home with the new baby and put her career on hold for ten years or so while this baby and perhaps a later sibling or two are young.

1. As George's agent, advise him as to the type(s) of life insurance that seem(s) most appropriate for his situation.
2. George indicates to you that his financial situation will change in five years when he receives a one-time payment of approximately $100,000 from his uncle's estate. In what way would this affect the type of life insurance you recommend to George?

13.2 Your wealthy Aunt Mabel, age 64, recently talked to you, her life insurance agent, regarding her desire to see that her great-niece has the funds to attend college. Aunt Mabel is in very good health and expects to live for many years to come. She does not know if she should put aside money in certificates of deposit at the bank, buy more insurance on herself, or choose some other plan of action. She simply knows that her great-niece will need at least $80,000 to pay for her college education in ten years. What type of investment and/or insurance program would you recommend for her? Why?

13.3 Phil Pratt has decided that the lowest-premium form of life insurance is definitely the best buy. Consequently, he has purchased a $250,000 yearly renewable term life insurance policy as his only life insurance.

1. Explain why you agree or disagree with Phil's philosophy.
2. Will his decision have any possible adverse effects in later years?

3. Are there any realistic alternatives available to him without making premiums too high at a young age?

13.4 Betty Bick, age 40, is considering the purchase of a limited-payment participating life insurance policy which would be paid up at age 60. She plans to work until then and does not wish to pay any premiums after she retires, but she definitely wants whole life insurance protection. Betty earns $45,000 per year as a branch manager for a commercial bank. As a single mother she has been unable to accumulate much wealth. At this time, Betty has dependent children ages 10 and 14.

1. Explain to her any alternatives that would meet the criteria she has established.

2. Why do you think her choice is a good (or bad) one? What additional information would you like to have before feeling confident about your answer?

13.5 Assume you as an agent are counseling Scott Browne, age 20, on the sales illustration for a straight life policy, as depicted in table 13–4 of this chapter. While you want to sell Scott a policy, satisfy his insurance needs, and receive about $500 in commissions, you also want to provide your client with ethical advice.

1. Explain to Scott the nature of policyholder dividends as paid by mutual life insurers.

2. Educate Scott on the extent to which the illustrated values depend on the illustrated dividends being paid in the future. Remember that Scott may not know they are not guaranteed.

3. What should you and Scott know about the insurer that furnished this sales illustration?

Interest-Sensitive and Variable Life Insurance

Introduction Cash values in the traditional life insurance policies we examined in chapter 13 are by-products of leveling the premium payment. Future cash value amounts are specified at the time of purchase, based on long-run assumptions about factors such as mortality, investment returns, and expenses. Universal life, current assumption whole life, variable life, and universal variable life differ from traditional life insurance by periodically having cash values determined directly by the amount of premium paid, the amount of investment earnings credited, mortality charges, and expense charges. Many consumers prefer this method of having cash values flow directly

from the structure of the policy and the insurer's future performance.

Choosing either interest-sensitive or some type of variable life policy creates flexibility with respect to: (1) deciding on the amount of premium payments over time, (2) changing the amount of death protection provided, and (3) changing the investment risks you assume in the cash value element.

In this chapter we discuss:
1. Universal life insurance.
2. Current assumption whole life insurance.
3. Variable life insurance.
4. Variable universal life insurance.

Universal life insurance contracts were introduced to the market in 1979 to bolster stock insurer profits. Universal policies were advertised as offering competitive investment features and the flexibility to meet changing consumer needs. When expense charges are set at reasonable levels, the investment part of the contract can be competitive on an after-tax basis with money market mutual funds, certificates of deposit, and other short-term instruments offered by investment companies, banks, and other financial institutions. Most insurers invest funds from their universal life contracts primarily in short-term investments so they will have the liquidity to meet policyholder demands for cash values. Some other insurers use investment portfolios that are competitive with medium and long-term investment returns.

A key feature of the product is its flexibility. As a policyowner, you can:

1. Change the amount of premium periodically.

2. Discontinue premiums and resume them at a later date.

3. Change the amount of death protection (subject to restrictions).

Universal life was introduced during a period of historically high double-digit interest rates. Sales illustrations often projected high investment returns for many years into the future, resulting in illustrated cash values that surpassed those of traditional cash value policies. Traditional policy illustrations projected dividends and cash values using average investment returns for a portfolio of securities and mortgages purchased during periods of low, medium, and high interest rates. Consumers were attracted to the high new money rates of the early 1980s, which resulted in universal life going from a zero market share of death benefits before 1979 to 14 percent in 1983 and to 38 percent by 1985. Subsequently, new money rates fell and universal life sales followed, with a 10 percent market share of life insurance sold directly to individuals in 1993.[1]

SEPARATION OF ELEMENTS

Traditional cash-value life insurance products do not clearly show the separate effect of their mortality, investment, and expense components. The distinguishing characteristic of universal life contracts is a clear separation of these three elements. This is called unbundling. The separation is reported to you, at least annually, by a disclosure statement. The disclosure statement shows:

1. The *gross* rate of investment return credited to your account.[2]

2. The charge for death protection.

3. Expense charges.

4. The resulting changes in accumulation value and in cash value.

---

1. *Life Insurance Fact Book, 1994.* (Washington, D.C.: American Council of Life Insurance), pp. 10–12.

2. The advertised rate of return credited to your account is likely to be higher than the true rate of return being earned on the cash value element of your contract. This subject is discussed in chapter 16.

This **transparency** allows you to see how your policy operates internally, after the fact.

The insurer maintains separate accounting for each policyowner. The account has three income items:

1. New premiums paid.
2. Guaranteed interest.
3. Excess interest.

The cash outgo items, from a consumer perspective, consist of:

1. A mortality charge for death protection.
2. Administrative and marketing expenses.
3. Withdrawals or loans.

The difference between income and outgo becomes a new contribution to (or deduction from) the **accumulation-value** account. Visualize this as the level of liquid in an open container where the three income items flow in at the top and the outgo items are extracted through a spigot at the bottom. Accounting usually occurs on a monthly basis, followed by annual disclosure of the monthly cash flows. The steps in the periodic **flow of funds** for a universal life policy are shown in figure 14–1. The first premium is at least a minimum amount specified by the insurer; subsequent premiums are flexible in amount, even zero if the cash value is large enough to cover the current cost of death protection and any applicable expense charges.

Administrative and marketing expense charges are subtracted each period. Some policies do not make explicit deductions. Instead, they recover

FIGURE 14–1

Flow of Funds for Universal Life

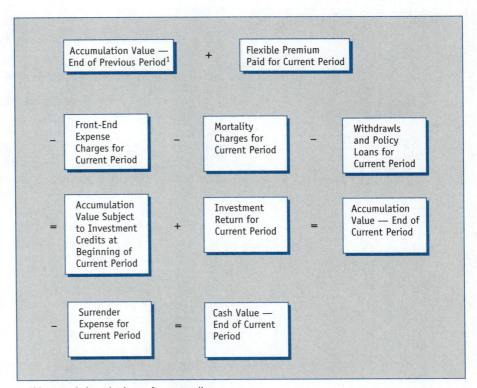

1. This accumulation value is zero for a new policy.

their expenses by lowering investment credits or increasing mortality charges (limited by guaranteed maximums). Another periodic deduction is for mortality. The policyowner decides whether withdrawals (that is, partial surrenders of cash values) or policy loans are made. They cannot exceed the current cash value. If you withdraw the entire cash value, your contract terminates. Withdrawals and loans reduce your death benefit as well as your cash value, preventing adverse selection against the insurer.

After deductions at the beginning of each accounting period for expenses, mortality, and withdrawals, your accumulation value is increased periodically by the percentage that reflects the insurer's current investment experience (subject to a guaranteed minimum rate) for the portfolio underlying universal life policies.

The difference between your accumulation value and what you can withdraw in cash (i.e., the cash value) at any point in time is determined by surrender expenses. "Surrender expenses" and other terms will become clearer as aspects of universal life are discussed in more detail in the next few pages.

DEATH BENEFIT OPTIONS

Figure 14–2 shows two **death benefit options** that are typically available. Type A keeps a level death benefit by making dollar-for-dollar changes in the amount of protection as the investment (cash value account) increases or decreases. This option is expected to produce a pattern of cash values and protection like that of a traditional, ordinary life contract (see figure 13–3). When a traditional, straight life contract is issued, the policy stipulates exactly what the pattern of cash values will be and guarantees them. In universal life contracts, you are provided an illustration of cash values for thirty years or so, assuming:

1. A specified level of premium payments.
2. A guaranteed minimum investment return.
3. Guaranteed maximum mortality rates.

Another column of the illustration will show values based on current investment and mortality experience. Company illustration practices also usually provide a column of accumulation and cash values based on an intermediate investment return (i.e., a return between the guaranteed and current rates).

The type B option is intended to produce an increasing death benefit. The exact amount of increase will depend on future non-guaranteed changes in cash value, as described in the discussion of type A policies. The type B alternative is analogous to buying a yearly, renewable *level* term insurance contract and creating a separate investment account.

With either type you, as the policyowner, may use the contract's flexibility to change the amount of protection as your needs for insurance change. Like traditional life insurance contracts, additional amounts of protection require evidence of insurability, including good health, to protect the insurer against adverse selection. Decreases in protection are made without evidence of insurability. The insurer simply acknowledges your request for a different death benefit by sending notification of the change. Your contract will specify a minimum amount of protection to comply with

FIGURE 14–2

Two Universal Life Death Benefit
Options

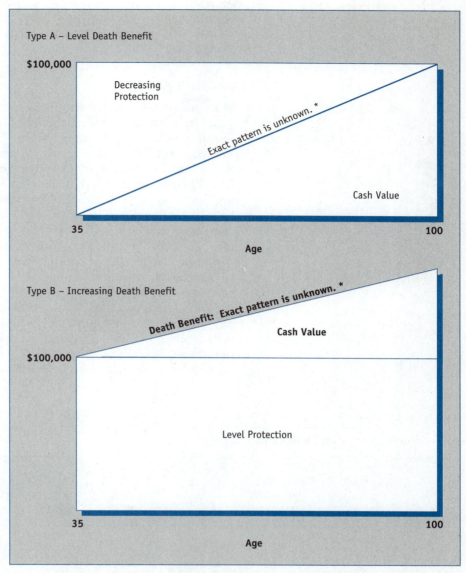

Type A – Level Death Benefit

$100,000

Decreasing Protection

Exact pattern is unknown. *

Cash Value

35   100

Age

Type B – Increasing Death Benefit

Death Benefit: Exact pattern is unknown. *

Cash Value

$100,000

Level Protection

35   100

Age

*Cash values may decrease and even go to zero, for example, due to low investment returns or inadequate premium payments.

federal tax guidelines. These guidelines must be met to shelter the contract's investment earnings (commonly called inside interest build-up) from income taxes.

Cost of living adjustment (COLA) riders and options to purchase additional insurance are available from most insurers. **COLA riders** increase the death benefit annually, consistent with the previous year's increase in the Consumer Price Index. Thus, if inflation is 3 percent, a $100,000 type A policy reflects a $103,000 death benefit in the second year. Of course, future mortality charges will reflect the higher amount at risk to the insurer, resulting in higher costs of death protection and lower cash values, unless premiums or investment returns increase concomitantly. Options to purchase additional insurance give you the contractual right to purchase stipulated amounts of insurance at specified future ages (generally limited to age 40) and events (e.g., birth of a child) without evidence of insurability.[3]

PREMIUM PAYMENTS

Most universal policies require a minimum premium in the first policy year. In subsequent years, the amount you pay is your decision, subject to minimums and maximums set by insurers and influenced by IRS rules. For example, tables 14–1 and 14–2 illustrate guaranteed and projected values, respectively for a hypothetical policy. The premium payments illustrated in column B of both tables start with a high initial premium of $1,000 and decrease to $500 and $250 for years two and three, respectively. This hypothetical policyowner totally discontinues premium payments after the third year, but decides to leave the policy in force. As a result, death benefits cease in the tenth year using guaranteed mortality and interest assumptions, while they continue until the fifteenth year using projections of current assumptions. Before the coverage terminates, the insurer would send a reminder that coverage will terminate on a certain date unless additional premiums are paid. At this time, the policyowner could elect to pay a premium anywhere between the minimum and maximum. The illustrations show how universal policies can be used primarily for protection. Most insurers would prefer that you continue to pay premiums and accumulate large cash values. This gives the insurer more

TABLE 14–1

Guaranteed Values for a Type B Universal Life Policy*

A AGE	B ANNUAL PREMIUM PAYMENT	C MAXIMUM MORTALITY CHARGE[1]	D EXPENSES[2]	E 4.5% INTEREST[3]	F GUARANTEED ACCUMULATION (END OF YEAR)	G SURRENDER VALUE[4] (END OF YEAR)	H GUARANTEED DEATH BENEFIT (END OF YEAR)
25	$1,000	$177	$56	$35	$ 802	$302	$100,802
26	500	173	46	49	1,132	682	101,132
27	250	171	41	53	1,223	823	101,223
28	0	170	36	46	1,063	713	101,063
29	0	171	36	39	895	595	100,895
30	0	173	36	31	717	467	100,717
31	0	178	36	23	526	326	100,526
32	0	183	36	14	321	171	100,321
33	0	191	36	4	98	0	100,098
34	0	200	18	2	0**	0	0**

*All values are rounded to the nearest dollar.

Notes:
1. Annual maximum mortality rate times $100,000 of protection.
2. A monthly charge of $3.00 plus a 2% premium tax.
3. A guaranteed rate.
4. The surrender charge is $500 in the first year, decreases $50 per year, and disappears after 10 years.

**These two values go to zero in the sixth month of the tenth year.

---

3. See chapter 15 for further discussion.

TABLE 14-2

Projected Values for a Type B Universal Life Policy*

A AGE	B ANNUAL PREMIUM PAYMENT	C CURRENT MORTALITY CHARGE[1]	D EXPENSES[2]	E 8.0% INTEREST	F PROJECTED ACCUMULATION (END OF YEAR)	G PROJECTED SURRENDER VALUE (END OF YEAR)[3]	H PROJECTED DEATH BENEFIT (END OF YEAR)
25	$1,000	$133	$56	$ 65	$ 876	$ 376	$100,876
26	500	130	46	96	1,296	846	101,296
27	250	128	41	110	1,487	1,087	101,487
28	0	128	36	106	1,429	1,079	101,429
29	0	128	36	101	1,366	1,066	101,366
30	0	130	36	96	1,296	1,246	101,296
31	0	134	36	90	1,216	1,016	101,216
32	0	137	36	83	1,126	976	101,126
33	0	143	36	76	1,023	923	101,023
34	0	150	36	67	904	854	100,904
35	0	158	36	57	767	767	100,767
36	0	168	36	45	608	608	100,608
37	0	180	36	31	423	423	100,423
38	0	194	36	15	208	208	100,208
39	0	209	33	14	0**	0**	0**

*All values are rounded to the nearest dollar.

Notes:
1. 75% of 1980 CSO rates times $100,000 of protection.
2. A monthly charge of $3.00 plus a 2% premium tax.
3. The surrender charge is $500 in the first year, decreases $50 per year, and disappears after 10 years.

**These three values go to zero in the twelfth month of the fifteenth year.

funds on which it can earn an investment spread (profit) and reduces the likelihood that you will let the policy lapse.

Insurers encourage regular premium payments in at least three ways. First, they usually set a target premium, for example, $750 annually.[4] Under a reasonable set of mortality and interest assumptions, payment of target premiums should produce large cash values and keep the policy in force for your lifetime. However, there is no guarantee that the target premium is set sufficiently high to avoid the accumulation value going to zero, resulting in policy termination. Second, the insurer sends reminders of the target premium. For example, reminders will be sent monthly if you express a preference for monthly premiums. Third, as for other types of insurance, many insurers encourage you to sign a preauthorized bank draft that gives the insurer the right to collect the periodic target premium from your checking account.

MORTALITY CHARGES

Almost all universal life insurance policies specify that mortality charges are levied monthly. The charge for a particular month is determined by

4. If the illustration in table 14-2 had included premium payments of $750 for ages 26 through 39 and all other assumptions remained the same, the projected surrender value at the end of age 39 would be $17,079 and the projected death benefit would be $117,079, rather than the zeros in the table.

multiplying the **current mortality rate** by the current amount of protection (net amount at risk to the insurer). The current mortality charge can be any amount determined periodically by the insurer as long as the charge does not exceed the guaranteed **maximum mortality rate** specified in your contract. Maximum mortality rates typically are those in the conservative 1980 CSO Mortality Table (see Appendix F).[5] Table 14–1, column C, reflects 1980 CSO rates. For simplicity, annual (rather than monthly) mortality rates are shown. Since table 14–2 illustrates a policy with a level amount of protection equal to $100,000, the mortality charge for a particular year is the current mortality rate for the insured's age multiplied by the net amount at risk of $100,000. For example, the charge for age 30 is .0013 × $100,000 = $130.00. The net amount at risk for a type A policy will be the difference between the level face amount/death benefit (for example, $100,000) and your cash value. Thus, in type A policies you effectively pay for a decreasing amount of term insurance.

The current practice among most insurers is to set current mortality rates below the specified maximums. For example, table 14–2 illustrates charges based on rates that are 75 percent of the maximums shown in table 14–1. An insurer's board of directors periodically revises these charges, considering the advice of its actuaries and what other insurers are charging for similar policies. The difference between the actual charge and the current death claim experience of the insurer is an element of profit or loss for the insurer. The mortality charges in tables 14–1 and 14–2, for simplicity, are shown as annual deductions from the beginning-of-the-year accumulation value (previous end-of-year accumulation value plus current year's premium payment). This demonstrates that the deduction for death protection is independent of your current premium payments. Notice that the contract terminates when the accumulation account (including the latest premium) is insufficient to cover the cost of protection.

Mortality charges vary widely among insurers and may change after a policy is issued. Consumers should not, however, choose an insurer solely by a low mortality charge. Expense charges and investment returns also factor into any determination of a policy's price. It is also unwise to choose a policy solely on the basis of low expenses or high advertised gross investment returns.[6]

EXPENSE CHARGES

Insurers levy expense charges to help cover their costs of marketing and administering policies. The charges can be grouped into **front-end expenses** and **surrender expenses** (back-end expenses). Front-end expenses are applied at the beginning of each month or year. They consist of some combination of: (1) a percentage of new premiums paid (for example, 5 percent, with 2 percent covering premium taxes paid by the insurer to the state), (2) a small flat dollar amount per month or year (for example, $1.50

---

5. Other maximums would be specified for persons in poor health, dangerous jobs, or other situations that call for special treatment at the time of contract issuance. Different rates are charged for smokers and nonsmokers. In most states, rates differ by gender for contracts issued to individuals rather than groups.

6. Methods that integrate all three factors are described in chapter 16.

per month), and (3) a larger flat dollar amount in the first policy year (for example, $50). Universal life policies began with high front-end expenses, but the trend has been toward much lower or no front-end expenses due to competition among companies. Those that levy front-end expenses tend to use only a percentage of premium load in both first and renewal policy years. Policies with large front-end loads seldom levy surrender expenses.

As most early issuers of universal policies lowered their front-end charges, they added surrender charges. Whereas front-end expenses reduce values for all insureds, surrender expenses transfer their negative impact to policyowners who terminate their policies. Tables 14–1 and 14–2 implicitly illustrate ten-year surrender charges by showing column G surrender values lower than column F accumulation values until the eleventh year. The actual surrender charges are the dollar differences between columns F and G, beginning at $500 in the first year and decreasing $50 per year until they disappear after ten years. The implicit illustration of surrender expenses is consistent with industry practice. Often the charges continue for fifteen or twenty years, usually decreasing yearly to eventually reach zero. They are expressed either as flat dollar amounts (our example), flat dollar assessments per $1,000 of face amount (for example, $10 per $1,000), or as decreasing percentages of the first year's premium.

Surrender charges help your insurer recover its heavy front-end underwriting expenses and sales commissions. Questions exist about whether or not they create equity between short-term and persisting policyholders. A few insurers issue universal policies with neither front-end nor surrender charges. These insurers, of course, still incur operating expenses. Some lower operating expenses by distributing their products directly to consumers or through financial planners who charge separate fees to clients. These "no-load" products still incur marketing expenses for the insurers that must promote (advertise) their products through direct mail, television, and other channels. They plan to recover expenses and make a profit by margins on actual mortality charges (current charges greater than company death claim experience) and margins on investment returns (crediting current interest rates below what the company is earning on its investment portfolio). Thus, even "no-load" contracts have hidden expense loads. Expense charges of all types, like current mortality rates, vary widely among insurers. Advertised investment returns are likely to vary in a narrower range.

INVESTMENT RETURNS

Different investment credits are shown in tables 14–1 and 14–2. Table 14–1, column E, shows a **guaranteed investment return** of 4.5 percent of the accumulation account. A guaranteed rate (for example, 4, 4.5, or 5 percent) is paid even if insurers earn less than this amount on the investment of policyowner funds.[7]

Table 14–2, relative to table 14–1, reflects an increase in the assumed investment return from 4.5 percent to a **current investment return** of 8.0 percent (see column E). In this illustration, the current return consists

---

7. This happened to many life insurers in the 1940s, when their actual investment returns were less than the guaranteed increases on traditional cash-value life insurance and annuities.

of two parts: the guaranteed rate plus an **excess rate** of 3.5 percent. The excess component allows the insurer's management team to offer a total return that considers both the insurer's investment earnings and competition from other insurers. At times, an insurer may credit policies with a higher return than it is earning currently because of competitive pressure.

Insurers reserve the right to change the current rate periodically. Some guarantee a new rate for a year; others only commit to the new rate for a month or a quarter.

The **indexed investment strategy** used by some insurers ties your rate of return on cash values to a published index, such as rates on 90-day U.S. Treasury bills or Moody's Bond Index, rather than leaving it to the insurer's discretion and its actual investment portfolio returns. This approach also provides a guarantee between 4 and 5 percent.

Some insurers use a **new money rate** for universal contracts. As explained in chapter 13, this approach credits your account with the return an insurer earns on its latest new investments. The practice dictates investment of universal life funds in assets with relatively short maturities in order to match assets with liabilities. When short-term rates are relatively high, such as in the early 1980s, the new money approach produces attractive returns. When short-term returns drop, as they did after the mid-1980s, the approach is not attractive. This undoubtedly was responsible for universal life's drop in market share from 38 percent in 1985 to 10 percent in 1993.

Other insurers use a **portfolio rate** that reflects the average return on a portfolio of short, medium, and long maturity debt instruments. Common stocks, real estate, and other equities also may be included in this portfolio. Some insurers segregate funds coming from universal sales and create a unique portfolio rate for this business. Others commingle funds from universal and other products. Portfolio rates reflect the average return over time and look best to consumers in times of relatively low current interest returns.

Current Assumption Whole Life Insurance

In most respects, **current assumption whole life** policies work like universal life. The major difference is that, similar to traditional whole life contracts, the policyowner is expected to pay premiums regularly at the levels set by the insurer. These policies do not have the flexible premium arrangements characteristic of universal life. Some current assumption designs emphasize low premiums (for example $6.00 per year per $1,000 at age 25) and expect the premiums, with periodic adjustments, to be paid during your entire lifetime. Low-premium policies emphasize protection and appeal primarily to families or businesses with modest incomes. Medium and high-premium alternatives for the same initial face amount might have premiums of $10.00 and $15.00 respectively. They emphasize cash values in the protection/investment mix and reduce the chances of the insurer having to request higher premiums to avoid the contract lapsing in later years.

After a current assumption contract is issued, the outlook for prospective (future) mortality and expenses can result in periodic increases or decreases in premiums. Some insurers adjust premiums annually; others make changes at three- or five-year interals.

The higher-premium versions of current assumption policies usually include a contract provision allowing the policyowner to stop premium payments and essentially have a non-guaranteed, paid-up contract for the initial face amount. This **vanishing premiums provision** is triggered when your cash-value account has a balance equal to a net single premium for this amount of death benefit at your attained age.[8] The net single premium is determined with current (at the time of vanish) investment and mortality assumptions. If future experience with the insurer's investments and mortality turns out to be less favorble, the single premium may prove to be insufficient. You could either resume premium payments or let the policy lapse. Thus, the policyowner retains some financial risk even for higher-premium current assumption policies where premiums have vanished.

As is characteristic of universal life policies, minimum guaranteed interest rates are typically 4.0, 4.5, or 5.0 percent. Current assumption whole life is technically a non-participating policy, as is most universal life. Yet, like universal life, it shares the insurer's investment and mortality expectations with you (e.g., through excess interest credits). It is sometimes referred to as **interest-sensitive whole life** because of its participatory investment feature. The accumulation value and cash value are determined in the same manner as was described earlier for universal life policies.

The death benefit is usually a fixed, level amount, analogous to a type A universal life contract. Some insurers, however, offer an alternative death benefit equal to the original stated face amount plus the accumulation fund balance, analogous to a type B universal life design.

An annual disclosure statement shows the current investment credit, mortality charge, any applicable expenses, and surrender charges. Although the premium is not flexible, the current assumption product provides far more flexibility and transparency for consumers than is available in traditional whole life policies.[9]

Variable Life Insurance

Variable life insurance was designed to overcome the fears created by the impact of inflation on life insurance values. Policies with level or decreasing death benefits are most susceptible to inflation.

OBJECTIVE: STABLE DEATH BENEFITS

If life insurance is to perform the income replacement function meaningfully, in many situations purchasing power must be maintained. Over

8. Participating traditional whole life policies of the type discussed in chapter 13 also offer a vanishing premium provision. It is implemented by adding dividend values and normal cash values when they equal a net single premium.

9. Traditional policies, on the other hand, specify their guaranteed cash values on a year-by-year basis, but do not specify the rates of investment credits, mortality, and expenses that underlie the cash value schedules. While adjustments are made through dividends, some insurers have not disclosed the investment credits and other factors underlying the dividend calculations. Insurers are under pressure to share more information with agents and consumers, using a form titled Information Questionnaire that was constructed by the American Society of CLU and ChFC.

ETHICAL *Dilemma*

The Credibility of Sales Illustrations

A recent survey of life insurance agents named sales illustration usage as their most important ethical issue. The concern is about the projection of dividends for traditional whole life policies and the projection of cash values for interest-sensitive policies such as current assumption whole life and universal life. For decades, the use of illustrations had produced little concern among consumers, agents, and regulatory agencies. The trend in interest rates and mortality rates had been favorable for about forty years, until the mid 1980s when interest rates began to decline.[10] Mortality continues to show modest improvements. Concern also exists about the practice of projecting additional mortality improvements into the future.

During the early 1990s, many insurers needed to strengthen net worth by retaining a larger share of earnings, federal income taxes on life insurers increased, market values of real estate fell, and other factors affecting earnings were adverse. As a result, numerous insurers cut dividends on participating policies. Investment credits on interest-sensitive policies were cut also, from double-digit rates in the early 1980s to around 6.0 percent in the mid-1990s. Just looking at the effect of compound interest on an annual investment of $1,000 over a forty-year period shows the significance of basing illustrations on interest rates that are unlikely to be realized over the life of a policy. Assuming annual compounding with interest payable at the end of each period for forty years, a $1,000 per year investment will accumulate to $165,048 at 6 percent interest, $280,781 at 8 percent, and $487,852 at 10 percent. The financially naive person who relies on an illustration at 10 percent is likely to be disappointed with policy performance in a period of

time, the policy must provide a death benefit that remains about the same in terms of the ability to purchase goods and services.

Your primary objective when buying variable life insurance should not be higher cash values for the purpose of surrendering the policy or making policy loans. These are desirable secondary benefits of a policy with the primary purpose of providing larger death benefits.

THEORY OF VARIABLE INSURANCE PRODUCTS

The theory of variable life insurance (and variable annuities) is that the prices of the stock and other equities purchased by the insurer for this product will rise as fast, over the long run, as increases in the level of

---

10. The long-term trend in average net rates of investment income for U.S. life insurers is shown in table 13–3.

declining interest rates, even if they remember the insurer's caveat that the illustrated values are not guaranteed.

What you as a life insurance consumer need to understand is that policy values will depend on the insurer's future performance regarding investment returns, mortality experience, and other non-guaranteed factors.

The illustration of vanishing premiums has been part of the problem. In the high interest rate environment of the early 1980s, sales illustrations often showed premiums vanishing between five and ten years. Vanish points were not guaranteed; however, in some instances, they were relied on. After premiums vanish, the insurer reserves the right to require resumption of premiums. This occurs when the insurer's actual operating experience does not live up to its expectations at the point at which premiums vanished. These caveats may be omitted or not highlighted on sales illustrations. By the mid 1990s, many policyowners were being told that their vanish points would be extended several more years into the future because the insurer's actual investment returns had been well below those being realized (and illustrated) at the time of the sale. This failure to live up to illustrations on several types of cash value life policies has been a source of widespread consumer discontent, and embarrassment to insurers.

Are agents who deliver unrealistic illustrations (e.g., those projecting unrealistically high interest rates) as responsible as the insurers making such illustrations? What is the training and monitoring responsibility of insurers? Is it ethical to illustrate values dependent upon the long-run continuation of interest rates that appear historically high for the investment risk being taken, even with the written caveat that they are not guaranteed? Should regulators allow only illustrations reflecting guaranteed values? Would development of self-regulatory organizations (like the National Association of Securities Dealers for investment brokers) be preferable to strict regulation? Do consumers have a responsibility to be skeptical of illustrations? Or is consideration of actuarial pricing factors beyond reasonably expected comprehension for the typical consumer?

prices for consumer goods. It is assumed that the forces in the economy affecting the one will affect the other in a similar fashion. Furthermore, it is assumed that equities will share in the growth of the economy, so that you will benefit not only by storing purchasing power but by accumulating it more rapidly than is possible with traditional methods of saving.[11] Thus, it is hypothesized that investments supporting variable products will tend to keep pace with changes in the standard of living as well as the cost of living. Investments supporting variable life insurance are held in one or more separate account(s). This distinguishes them from investments underlying other life and health insurance contracts.

The developers of variable products recognized that common stock prices sometimes fail to advance as rapidly as inflation for periods of sev-

---

11. Over long periods of time, high-grade common stocks have outperformed fixed-dollar bond investments by about 5 percent per year.

eral years. Stock prices and consumer prices sometimes even move in opposite directions. When variable annuities were first introduced in the United States in 1952, one had only to look back to the 1940s for a decade of poor common stock performance relative to inflation.[12] Common stock prices were below their 1940 level in eight of the next ten years. Thus, from the beginning of variable products in the United States, insurers were aware that long periods could produce disappointing results. Large drops in common stock prices later occurred in 1970, 1974, and 1987, while inflation continued. Even recognizing these weaknesses in the underlying theory and having observed several of them with respect to variable annuities, variable life insurance was introduced to the United States market in 1976. It had been successful in Europe and Canada for several years before. In recent years, insurers have moved away from a concentration on common stock separate accounts. Now, more balanced portfolio approaches are allowed by giving each variable life consumer a choice of investing in a combination of between five and twenty different separate accounts with varying investment objectives and strategies. For example, you might add more short-term stability by placing part of your money in a short-term bond fund, while maintaining a significant equity element in one or more common stock funds.

Each separate account makes investments in publicly traded securities that have readily determinable market values. Market values are needed to determine the current values of cash/accumulation values and death benefits. Cash values will vary daily, and death benefits will vary daily, monthly, or annually.

Variable life transfers all investment risks to the policy owner. Unlike universal life, for example, which guarantees the fixed-dollar value of your accumulation fund and a minimum return (e.g., 4.5 percent), variable insurance products make no guarantee of either principal or returns. All the investment risk (upside or downside) is yours. Cash values (but not death benefits) can go to zero as a result of adverse investment experience.

HOW IT WORKS

The Model Variable Life Insurance Regulation produced by the National Association of Insurance Commissioners sets guidelines that help establish the form of the product. Certain basic characteristics can be identified.

Variable life is, in essence, a whole life product that provides variable amounts of benefit for your entire life. It requires a *level* premium; therefore, your out-of-pocket contributions will not change with changes in the cost of living. This limits the extent to which death benefits can increase over time, since no new amounts of insurance can be financed by defining the premium in constant dollars. All increases in death benefits must come from favorable investment performance.

Contracts specify a minimum death benefit, called the face amount. In one design, this minimum stays level during the life of the contract. Another design uses increasing term insurance to provide automatic increases of 3 percent per year for fourteen years, at which point the minimum face amount becomes level at 150 percent of its original face

------

12. Variable annuities are discussed in chapter 23.

value. Assuming continuation of premium payments, the face amount can never go below the guaranteed minimum. It can increase, however.

Each separate account is in essence a different mutual fund. For example, one contract offers five investment accounts: (1) guaranteed interest, (2) money market, (3) a balance of bonds and stocks, (4) conservative common stock, and (5) aggressive common stock. You could allocate all net premiums (new premiums minus expense and mortality charges) to one account or divide them among any two or more accounts. Currently, approximately 75 percent of separate account assets are in common stocks. Some policies limit the number of changes among the available accounts. For example, some contracts set a limit of four changes per year. Administrative charges may accompany switches among accounts, especially when one exceeds the limit. Since the changes are made inside a life insurance product where investment gains are not subject to income taxes (unless the contract is surrendered), gains at the time of transfer among accounts are not taxable.

It is assumed that investments in the underlying separate accounts will earn a modest compound return, such as 4 percent. This **assumed rate of return** is generally a rate necessary to maintain the level of cash values found in a traditional fixed-dollar straight life contract. Then, if *actual investment returns* exceed the assumed rate: (1) cash values increase more than assumed, and (2) these increases are used partly to purchase additional death benefits.

The additional death benefits are usually in the form of term insurance. The amount of term insurance can change (upward or downward) daily, monthly, or yearly, depending on the provisions of your contract. The total *death benefit,* at a point in time, becomes the amount of traditional straight life insurance that would be supported by a reserve equal to the policy's current cash value.

If *separate account values fall below the assumed rate,* (1) your cash value falls, and (2) one-year term elements of death protection are automatically surrendered. The net result is a new death benefit that corresponds to the amount of straight life that could be supported by your new cash value, subject to the minimum death benefit. These variable aspects are what give the contract its name. The nature of variable life insurance, with one-year term additions, is depicted in figure 14–3.

Policy loans or contract surrenders can be handled by transferring funds out of the separate account. Loans are typically limited to 90 percent of your cash value at the time of the latest loan. Surrenders equal the entire cash value minus any applicable surrender charge.

Some variable contracts are issued on a participating basis. Since investment experience is reflected directly in cash values, dividends reflect only unanticipated experience with respect to mortality and operating expenses.

Variable life insurance is technically a security as well as insurance. Therefore, it is regulated by the Securities and Exchange Commission (SEC) that enforces the Investment Company Act of 1940, the Securities Act of 1933, and the Securities Exchange Act of 1934, as well as by state insurance departments. The SEC requires that you be given a **prospectus** before being asked to sign an application for variable life. The prospectus explains the risks you bear and usually illustrates how the death benefit and cash values would perform if future investment experience results in

FIGURE 14–3

Hypothetical Values for a Variable Life
Insurance Contract

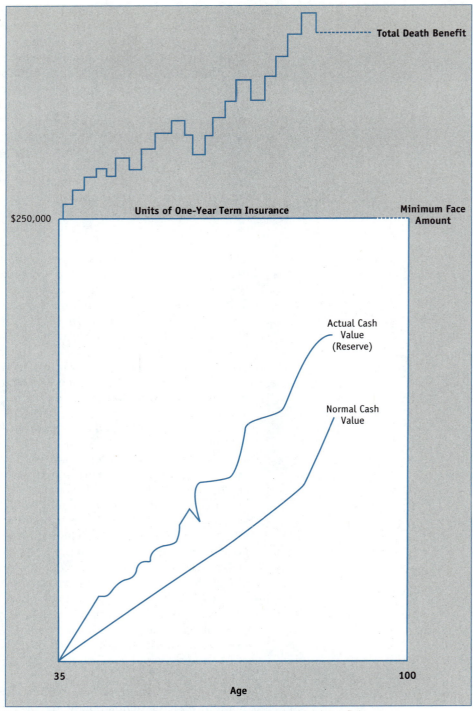

Note: The relationship depicted between the Actual Cash Value and the Total Death Benefit is
approximate. It has not been drawn precisely to scale.

returns of 0, 4, 6, 8, 10, and 12 percent. Returns also can be illustrated based on historical experience of the Standard and Poor's 500 Stock Price Index. Because the product is a security, it can be sold only by agents who register with and pass an investments examination given by the National Association of Security Dealers.

A mid-range assumption (for example, 4 percent) produces a contract that performs exactly like traditional straight life insurance. The zero percent return would produce the minimum face amount; the cash value would be below normal for a period and go to zero at an advanced age. Because cash values cannot be negative, your policy would continue from the time the cash values reach zero until your death without cash values. At your death, the minimum face amount would be paid. The 8 and 12 percent returns would produce cash values that grow much faster than those normal for an ordinary life policy; the total death benefit would continue to grow above the minimum face amount. These illustrations all assume continuous payment of the fixed annual premium.

SUMMARY OF VARIABLE LIFE

Your cash value in a variable life policy fluctuates with the market value of one or more separate accounts. Death benefits, subject to a minimum face amount, vary up or down as the cash value changes. Success in achieving the objective of maintaining a death benefit that keeps pace with inflation depends on the validity of the theory that certain investments are good inflation hedges.

You should recognize that all investment risks are borne by you, rather than by the insurer. The issuer of a variable life policy assumes only mortality and expense risks. Variable life is decreasing in popularity, probably because its fixed premium at a guaranteed level is higher initially than premiums on competing products. In 1993, variable life accounted for 2 percent of new life insurance purchases (measured by amount of face value), whereas a newer version called variable universal life represented 10 percent of new purchases.[13] Thus, let us turn our attention to variable universal life.

Variable Universal Life Insurance

In 1985, **variable universal life** was marketed for the first time. It combines the premium and death benefit flexibility of a universal policy design with the investment choices of variable life. This policy is also called *flexible premium variable life insurance.* Some insurers allow all premiums to vary after the first year of the contract. Others specify minimum premiums that would, if paid, continue death protection at least through age 65. Premiums can exceed these minimums. Single-premium policies are also available.

Like the universal life policyowner, you decide periodically whether to decrease death protection (subject to the contract's minimum face amount) or increase death benefits (subject to evidence of insurability). One design

13. See table 13.1.

specifies a fixed face amount, like universal life's type A design (see figure 14–2), and allows investment experience to affect only cash values. Another design, like variable life, allows the total amount of protection to increase when cash values exceed their normal level for a straight life contract.

As with variable life, the assets backing variable universal policies are invested in separate accounts. Your choices are like those for variable life policies, and you continue to assume all investment risks. The flow of funds due to expenses, mortality charges, and policy loans for both variable and variable universal work like those in universal policies. The outlook for the sale of variable universal policies is bright because the contract combines:

1. The premium flexibility of universal life.
2. The death benefit flexibility of universal life.
3. Greater investment flexibility than universal life.
4. The disclosure of universal and variable life.
5. The ability to withdraw cash values as policy loans without any tax penalties. (This is an advantage in comparison to annuities, rather than other types of life insurance.[14])
6. Separate accounts are not general assets of an insurer. Therefore, they are protected in the event of the insurer's insolvency.

The major drawback of variable universal life, as with variable life, is the transfer of all investment risk to you.[15]

Taxation

Universal life, current assumption whole life, variable life, and variable universal life are taxed exactly like the traditional life insurance contracts discussed in chapter 13. Thus, premiums are typically paid with after-tax dollars; cash value and accumulation funds grow without income taxation (except when a contract is surrendered); loans against the cash value can be made without tax effects unless they cause the contract to terminate; funds can be transferred among separate accounts without taxation; and death benefits are received without being subject to income taxation. When a contract is discontinued by surrender for its cash value, or interest is not paid on maximum-loaned policies, any gain is subject to income taxation.[16] Death benefits may be included in your gross estate and subjected to estate taxes.[17]

---

14. Annuities are discussed in chapter 23.
15. A hybrid variable life policy combines some elements of variable life (for example, a regular premium but one that begins low and increases until leveling a few years later) with certain elements common to variable universal life, such as flexible death benefits.
16. See chapter 13.
17. See chapter 22.

Consumer Applications

Adjusting Life Insurance for Inflation

You buy life insurance so your dependents will have income when you die. The death benefit is stated in terms of dollars, but what your family needs are goods and services. The ideal solution is to increase savings and investments to the extent that the increase at least equals the increase in death needs. After all, insurance is merely a substitute for other assets. If the growth in other estate assets is not sufficient to offset the impact of inflation, you may need a larger amount of life insurance to ensure an adequate amount of assets upon death. What are your choices?[18]

RELY ON A PARTICIPATING OR INTEREST-SENSITIVE POLICY

Participating policies, current assumption whole life policies, and universal life policies recognize inflation in a limited manner. Participating contracts can respond to inflation through dividends. Dividends can be used each year to purchase additional amounts of paid-up life insurance, but these small amounts of additional protection seldom keep pace with inflation.

Interest sensitive contracts partly recognize inflation by crediting investment earnings directly to cash values. We say "partly recognize" because cash values in these policies are primarily invested in short-term debt instruments like government securities and in short-term corporate bonds, and the interest rates for these have an expected inflation component at the time they are issued. The expected inflation component is there because, in addition to a basic return on the money being loaned and an increase to reflect financial risks of failure, investors in debt instruments require an incremental return to cover their projections of future inflation rates. Thus, contracts with direct crediting of insurer investment returns to cash values give some recognition to inflation. The recognition is weak, however, for two reasons. First, the protection element of these contracts does not respond quickly, or at all for type A contracts, to inflation.[19] The protection element is expressed in fixed dollars and, as a storehouse of value and purchasing power, the dollar certainly is not ideal. Second, in a portfolio of primarily debt instruments, all except newly purchased parts reflect inflation expectations formed in the past. These expectations can grossly underestimate current and future rates of inflation.

BUY MORE LIFE INSURANCE

As long as you are insurable, you can buy more life insurance as your needs increase. What if you become uninsurable? You can protect yourself against that possibility by buying a policy with a guaranteed insurability option; however, this has four drawbacks. First, the option is limited to a specified age, such as 40, and you may need more insurance after that age. Second, you must buy the same kind of insurance as the policy you have. Third, the premium will be higher due to your age. For example, one company offering straight life for $8.13 per thousand at age 25 charges $15.56 per thousand at age 40. This could present a budget problem if your real (inflation-adjusted) income has not increased. Fourth, the opportunities to buy additional insurance are not related to the rate of inflation. On the other hand, unlike other arrangements discussed below, you don't lose the next option if you fail to exercise one.

BUY A COST-OF-LIVING RIDER OR POLICY

Another alternative is the **inflation rider** or **cost-of-living rider,** which automatically increases the amount of insurance as the Consumer Price Index rises. It provides term insurance as an addition to the face amount of your permanent or term policy up to a point such as age 55. If, for example, you have a $100,000 whole life policy and the CPI goes up 5 percent this year, $5,000 of one-year term insurance is automatically written for next year at the pre-

---

18. When you buy life insurance for business purposes or estate settlement expenses, the needs also are likely to increase with inflation.

19. Small recognition in total death benefits exists in type B universal policies because any increases in cash values as a result of higher interest rates are added to a level amount of protection. Dividends may be used to buy additional amounts of insurance, but the relationship to inflation is weak. Dividend options are discussed in chapter 15.

TABLE 14–3

Inflation Rider Option (at 5 percent annual inflation)

YEAR	CONSUMER PRICE INDEX	BASIC INSURANCE AMOUNT	OPTION AMOUNT	TOTAL DEATH BENEFIT
1995	1.00000	$100,000		$100,000
1996	1.05000	100,000	$ 5,000	105,000
1997	1.10250	100,000	10,250	110,250
1998	1.15763	100,000	15,763	115,763
1995	1.21551	100,000	21,551	121,551
1996	1.27628	100,000	27,628	127,628
1997	1.34010	100,000	34,010	134,010
1998	1.40710	100,000	40,710	140,710
1999	1.47746	100,000	47,746	147,746
2000	1.55133	100,000	55,133	155,133
2001	1.62889	100,000	62,889	162,889
2002	1.71034	100,000	71,034	171,034
2003	1.79586	100,000	79,586	179,586
2004	1.88565	100,000	88,565	188,565
2005	1.97993	100,000	97,993	197,993
2006	2.07893	100,000	107,893	207,893
2007	2.18287	100,000	118,287	218,287
2008	2.29202	100,000	129,202	229,202
2009	2.40662	100,000	140,662	240,662
2010	2.52659	100,000	152,659	252,659
2011	2.65330	100,000	165,330	265,330

mium rate for your age. You are billed for it along with the premium notice for your basic policy.

Since your premium increases with each increase in coverage, you may conclude that you bear the risk of keeping your coverage up with inflation. Keep in mind that no evidence of insurability is required. You do not have to accept (and pay for) the additional insurance if you don't want it. If you refuse to exercise the option, however, it is no longer available. In other words, you can't say, "I'm short of funds this year, but I will exercise the option next year." Table 14–3 illustrates how the inflation rider option would affect your total amount of insurance if you had bought a $100,000 whole life policy in 1995 and the inflation rate was 5 percent every year.

BUY A VARIABLE OR VARIABLE UNIVERSAL LIFE POLICY

The face amount of variable life and variable universal life (except for the level face amount type) policies fluctuates with the performance of one or more separate accounts. You have the option of directing most of your premiums into common stock accounts where long-run returns are expected to offset CPI increases.

If you buy a variable life policy, you assume the risk that the equity markets may be going down at the same time that the CPI is going up. Should you buy a variable life policy? The answer depends on you. How much investment risk are you willing to take in coping with inflation?

Key Terms

universal life
unbundling
disclosure statement
transparency
accumulation value
flow of funds
death benefit options
COLA riders
target premium
current mortality rate
maximum mortality rate
front-end expenses
surrender expenses
guaranteed investment return

current investment return
excess rate
indexed investment strategy
new money rate
portfolio rate
current assumption whole life
vanishing premiums provision
interest-sensitive whole life
variable life
assumed rate of return
prospectus
variable universal life
inflation rider (cost of living rider)

Discussion Questions

1. Universal life insurance sales peaked at 38 percent of new purchases of life insurance by individuals in 1985; by 1993, universal life had only a

10 percent market share. Explain how "new money" rates of return on short-term investments may have influenced this change.

2. What elements of a universal life contract are separated or unbundled relative to their treatment in a traditional life insurance policy? How does a "disclosure statement" help implement the separation and create transparency?

3. When the issuer of a universal life policy does not levy explicit charges to cover its administrative expenses, how may it recover expenses (and, maybe, profits also)?

4. Explain the two death benefit options that are available to you when you purchase a universal life or current assumption policy.

5. Explain the difference between the "maximum mortality rate" and the "current mortality rate" for a universal life policy.

6. Why is the cash value of a high-premium current assumption whole life policy larger than that of a low-premium policy at the end of twenty years, assuming both policies have equal face amounts, are purchased by a healthy person age 25, and premiums are paid for all twenty years?

7. When the dollar value of your home increases because of inflation, the insurer normally automatically increases the amount of insurance on your dwelling and its contents. Why does your life insurer require evidence of insurability before allowing you to increase the face value of your universal life insurance policy? (Assume no cost of living rider or guaranteed insurability rider.) How do you explain this difference between insuring homes and human lives?

8. What is the major difference between a current assumption life policy and a universal life policy? Why might a life insurer prefer issuing current assumption policies?

9. What is the objective of variable life insurance? Can this objective be achieved through a variable universal life policy with a level face amount (i.e., one like a type A universal life contract)?

10. Who bears the investment risk in variable life and universal variable life policies? How does this differ from investment risks borne by the buyer of a universal life policy?

Cases

14.1 Lane Golden has just purchased a universal life insurance policy from Midwest Great Life. Initially, Lane pays a first-month premium of $100. Her policy has (1) a front-end load of $2.00 per month, (2) a surrender charge equal to 100 percent of the minimum first-year premiums of $1,200 ($100 per month), decreasing 20 percent of the original surrender charge per year until it disappears after five years, (3) a current monthly mortality rate of $0.15 per $1,000 of protection (amount at risk), and (4) a current monthly investment return of 0.667 percent. Her policy is a type B one, with a level $100,000 protection element.

1. Construct a flow of funds statement, like the one in figure 14–1, for the first month of Lane's policy.

2. Explain why her accumulation value and cash value will be equal if she continues her policy for more than five years.

14.2 Your neighbor, Walt Fanaya, recently approached you as you were on your way to work as an agent of Lotze Life Insurance Company. He said, "Say—you know what bothers me about life insurance? It's a bad deal. If I die tomorrow your company pays the face amount but you keep all the savings that belong to me now! I don't think that is fair!" Your response was, "Walt, there are other ways to look at that. Let's make an appointment for tomorrow, and I'll show you how to have your cake and eat it, too."

1. What did Walt mean by his complaint?

2. What solution(s) did you have in mind using your universal life death benefit options?

14.3 As a senior vice president with Old Reliable Life, you are chairing a committee that has been charged with recommending the current investment return and current mortality rate to be used with Old Reliable's universal life policies during the next quarter. Your investment portfolio for universal life is in short-term bonds; short-term interest rates have been declining during the last two years and are expected to decline more during the next few months. Old Reliable is currently crediting a 7.0 percent return to customers, while earning 7.5 percent. The industry average return for universal policies is 7.4 percent. You observe that some of your competitors are crediting current investment returns that probably slightly exceed the rate their portfolio is actually earning. You are concerned about providing a competitive return in order to attract new customers. For the next quarter, your investment vice president has forecasted an average new money return of 6.9 percent.

In recent quarters, your current mortality charges have been pegged at 65 percent of 1980 CSO rates, the maximum rates allowed in your contracts. Old Reliable's actual mortality experience for its population of insureds has remained steady for several years at approximately 60 percent of the 1980 CSO table rates for various ages. Your actuary does not expect any change in mortality rates during the foreseeable future.

1. Recognizing that typical customers are better able to judge the competitiveness of current investment returns than to judge current mortality rates, make recommendations for next quarter's current investment returns and current mortality rates. Your recommendations will be considered by Old Reliable's full board of directors.

2. Reflect on the ethical implications of your recommendations. In other words, is the tradeoff you have made between expected contributions to the insurer's expenses and profits, versus fairness to consumers, an ethical one?

Life Insurance Policy Provisions

Introduction A life insurance contract's provisions add value in the form of a renewal guarantee, a policy loan option, a set of alternative methods of payout, several ways of receiving dividends from a participating policy, and so forth. When you buy life insurance, you will want to compare policy provisions, prices, and the quality of the insurer.[1] The variation among contracts is significant.

This chapter examines:
1. The importance of contractual provisions.
2. The different types of dividend options.
3. The uses of nonforfeiture options.
4. How special provisions affect interest-sensitive contracts.
5. Why additional premiums are required when certain options are added.

---

1. Methods of comparing prices are discussed in chapter 16; chapter 24 provides information about how to compare insurers.

| **Major Provisions** | The major policy provisions are listed in figure 15–1 and included in the specimen whole life insurance policy in Appendix E.[2] Not listed is the insuring agreement explaining the benefits that will be paid subject to the terms and conditions of the policy, upon the death of the insured. |

THE CONTRACT

Entire Contract

The written policy and the attached application constitute the entire agreement between the insurer and policyowner. Because of this **entire contract provision,** agents cannot, verbally or in writing, change or waive any terms of the contract. A change is valid only after endorsement by an officer of the insurer. This may require submission of the policy to the insurer for endorsement.

Statements in the application are considered representations, rather than warranties. This means that only those material statements that would have caused the insurer to make a different decision about issuance of the policy, its terms, or premiums will be considered valid grounds to void the contract.

Incontestable Provision

A typical **incontestable provision** makes a contract incontestable after it has been in force for two years during the lifetime of the insured.[3] If you die before the end of the two years, the policy is contestable on the basis of material misrepresentations, concealment, and fraud in the application. When the insurer contests a policy, it challenges its validity from inception. If you live beyond the contestable period, the policy cannot be contested even for fraud. An exception is fraud of a gross nature, such as letting someone else take your medical exam. While the incontestable clause may force the insurer to do considerably more investigating (part

FIGURE 15–1

Major Life Insurance Policy Provisions by Group

The Contract
- Entire contract
- Incontestability
- Suicide
- Mistatement of age or sex

Ownership
- Policy ownership
- Assignment

Premium Payment
- Grace period
- Reinstatement
- Post-death refund

Dividends
- Six options

Nonforfeiture
- Cash value
- Extended term insurance
- Paid-up insurance

Policy Loans

Beneficiaries

Settlement Options

2. This specimen is referred to subsequently without repeating its location, Appendix E.
3. An increase in death benefits, such as in a universal life policy, remains contestable with respect to statements relevant to the addition, until the addition has been in force for two years.

ETHICAL *Dilemma*

Representations, Concealments, and Life Insurance Applications

Mary Z. Floyd, age 45, risk manager with the Price Concrete Company in her home town, is completing the application form for a universal life insurance policy. Mary, recently divorced, is the mother of Otis Ira Floyd, aged 10. Otis is mentally retarded to a degree that he will need financial assistance throughout his life. Mary has concluded that Otis's father cannot be depended on to provide for Otis. Consequently, Mary is applying for $500,000 of insurance on her life to help provide for her son in the event of her death. In response to a question concerning the beneficiary, she has listed "First National Bank of Santa Domino, Trustee for the estate of Mary Z. Floyd, under her will dated May 14, 1996." The separate trust agreement names Otis as the sole beneficiary. Broad powers are given to the trustee for the use of judgment in making decisions about Otis's welfare. The trust would not become effective until Mary's death. Life insurance proceeds could be the major source of funding for the trust.

Mary is pondering how to answer questions about her health on the application. She considers her health history to be perfect, except for having been diagnosed with rheumatic fever following a bout of strep throat while on a family trip to Spain at age 12. It is possible that she had some damage to her heart valves at the time. In her adult years, however, doctors have not detected any heart murmur. Her family physician's periodic examinations, as recent as one year ago, have continued to record "excellent health." About six months ago, however, Mary began experiencing episodes of shortness of breath and mild chest pain while engaging in rigorous exercise. Two weeks ago, she saw a cardiologist on a self-referral basis, her family physician having recently died. A stress test produced acceptable but borderline results. In addition, a slightly irregular heart rate was detected. The cardiologist believes Mary is developing aortic stenosis, a narrowing of the aortic valve, that could be caused by her childhood rheumatic fever. Mary is scheduled to have further tests next week, including an echocardiogram that would detect any leaking valves. She continues to be able to work long hours and engage in other normal activities of life. The cardiologist has not reported her initial diagnosis of "possible aortic stenosis" to anyone, except to list it on a health insurance claim form that went to an administrative organization that pays claims for the self-insured medical plan sponsored by the Price Concrete Company. Heart valve problems can lead to congestive heart failure if left untreated.

In response to a question about visits to physicians, Mary has listed the name of her family physician, her last "routine checkup," and his conclusion that she was in "excellent health." Another question asks about "other medical practitioners," still another asks specifically about any heart problems.

Should she give information about the visit to the cardiologist? She truly believes she continues to be in good health. If she lists the visit to the cardiologist, the insurer is likely to request a copy of her records and may conclude that Mary is not insurable at this time. The insurer to which she is applying is financially strong, with a management policy of reinsuring all life insurance policies above a retention limit of $150,000. If she does not report the results of her recent visit to the cardiologist, the insurer is likely to uncover this fact in its underwriting investigation. Given the large amount of life insurance being applied for, it undoubtedly will obtain (favorable) information from the records of her family physician. If she develops a serious heart problem, it can probably be corrected with surgery. Mary is confident that she will live well beyond the contestable period for life insurance. What advice do you have for Mary?[4]

of the "underwriting process") before contracts are issued than would otherwise be the case, and perhaps does result in some claims being paid that should not be, it is a great boon to the honest policyowner who wants to be confident that his or her insurance proceeds will be paid upon death.

Contracts other than life insurance are usually contestable throughout their existence. At one time, life insurance contracts also could be contested at any time, so no insured could ever be sure that a claim would be paid promptly, if at all. Since the insured would be unavailable for questioning, the beneficiary might be in a difficult situation. As early as 1864, therefore, insurance companies began to incorporate an incontestable clause in the contract on a voluntary basis; today, such a clause is required by state statute.

When grounds to void a contract within the contestable period exist, the insurer's obligation is limited to the return of premiums. Practice includes the refund of interest on the premiums. When an insurer exercises the contestable clause to void a contract (for example, because of material misrepresentation on the application), the process is called a **rescission.** The insurer claims that the contract was never legally in force, demands return of the contract, and presents the insured with a return of his or her premiums plus interest. The options of the policyowner (or those of the legal representative if the insured/policyowner is deceased, as is usually the case in a rescission) are (1) to accept the returned premiums, or (2) if he or she does not agree that the insurer has sufficient grounds for the rescission, to sue the insurer for payment in the event of a death claim (or continuance of the policy).

Suicide

The **suicide provision** provides that if the insured commits suicide within two years (one year with some states and companies) from the date the policy was issued, the sole obligation of the insurer is to return the premiums. When coverage is increased under a universal life or variable universal policy, the additional insurance is subject to a new suicide exclusion period. This provision is a compromise between two conflicting theories. One is that, since insurance operates on the basis of chance occurrences,

4. Most insurers require a physical examination for a person Mary's age who is applying for $500,000 of insurance.

it is unfair to expect the company to bear the burden of what may not be a matter of chance. Paying such claims is like paying a policyowner on a fire policy who burns his or her own house down. On the other hand, the purpose of life insurance is to provide for the beneficiary, who, in many cases, was dependent upon the insured. The loss to the beneficiary is just as great whether the death was from suicide, accident, or natural causes.

The time period during which payment for suicide is excluded will, presumably, protect the company to a large degree from adverse selection and moral hazard by those contemplating suicide when they purchase the insurance. At the same time, restricting the exclusion to this period offers protection to the beneficiary. It is felt that very few people would plan suicide for as much as one or two years ahead and actually carry out the suicide at that time.

If the company wishes to deny a claim on the grounds that death was caused by suicide during the period of exclusion, it must prove conclusively that the death was suicide. Because there is a strong presumption against suicide on the grounds that everyone has an instinct for self-preservation, proving suicide can be very difficult.

Misstatement of Age and Sex

When you apply for life insurance, your age and sex have a direct bearing on its cost. They are, therefore, material facts. Thus, the **misstatement of age or sex** would ordinarily provide grounds, within the contestable period, for rescinding the contract. Most state laws, however, require that all policies include a provision that if age and/or sex has been misstated, the amount of the insurance will be adjusted to that which the premium paid would have purchased at the correct age and/or sex (see section 1 of the specimen policy).[5]

For example, if a 26-year-old man purchases a straight life policy with a face amount of $100,000 and states that his age as of his nearest birthday[6] is 25, the premium in Company X would be quoted as $1,000. Upon learning the insured's correct age, the company can reduce the face amount to $97,561, which is the amount of death benefit that the $1,000 annual premium would buy at a rate of $1,025 per thousand at age 26 in Company X. On the other hand, if the insurer finds that the insured has overstated his age, an upward adjustment is made in the amount of insurance. Because the adjustment for misstatement of age is merely the operation of a policy provision, it is not affected by the incontestable clause. Age discrepancies are commonly found when death certificates show a different age from that reflected in the policy. Proof of the correct age is then sought. Adjustments are also made when the insured's sex is misstated. Most age and sex misstatements result from errors by the agent or underwriter.

....

5. Some insurers use one provision to correct misstatements of age or sex to cover the possible misstatement of either.

6. The majority of insurers use your age as of your nearest birthday rather than your actual age as the basis for premium determination.

OWNERSHIP

Policy Ownership

Ownership refers to rights. When you say, "I own this car," you mean you have the right to use the car, sell it, lend it, and so on. The owner of a life insurance policy also has rights, such as the ability to assign the policy to someone else, designate the beneficiary, make a policy loan, or surrender the policy for its cash value. When you as the insured fill out the application for a policy, one item of concern is the **ownership provision;** it may simply be labeled "rights." At that point, you indicate to whom the rights belong. Typically, you mark the square entitled "insured." The policyowner and the insured are the same person.

You can, however, designate a trust or another person, such as your spouse, as the owner of the policy. If you select yourself to be owner and later decide to transfer ownership to a trust or another person, you may do so either by making an absolute assignment or by executing an ownership form, which may be obtained from the insurance company.

Assignment

As mentioned, the owner of a life insurance policy can transfer part or all of the rights to someone else. The **assignment provision** provides, however, that the company will not be bound by any assignment until it has received notice, that any indebtedness to the company shall have priority over any assignment, and that the company is not responsible for the validity of any assignment. This provision helps the company avoid litigation about who is entitled to policy benefits, and it protects the insurer from paying twice.

PREMIUM PAYMENT

Premiums are payable on the due date on a monthly, quarterly, semiannual, or annual basis. The first premium must be paid in advance while you are in good health and otherwise insurable. Subsequent premiums are due in advance of the period to which they apply. Insurance companies send a notice to the policyowner indicating when the premium is due. The time horizon over which premiums are payable depends on the type of policy (e.g., through age 99 for a straight life policy), and will be stated on the declarations page.

Grace Period

The law requires that the contract must contain a provision entitling the policyowner to a **grace period** within which payment of a past-due premium (excluding the first premium) must be accepted by the insurer. The grace period is almost always thirty-one days. In spite of the fact that the premium is past due during this period, the policy remains in force. If the insured dies during this period, before the premium is paid, the face amount of the policy minus the amount of the premium past due will be paid to the beneficiary. If the premium is not paid during the grace period of a traditional policy, a nonforfeiture option (to be discussed later) becomes effective. The purpose of the grace period is to prevent unintentional lapses.[7] If it were not for this provision, an insured whose premium was paid one day late would have to prove his or her insurability in order to have the policy reinstated.

In variable, universal, and other flexible-premium policies, the grace period is usually sixty days. This only has meaning when your cash value is not large enough to cover expense and mortality deductions for the next period. Most insurers notify you of such a situation. The cash surrender value in the first few policy years may be zero due to surrender charges. In that event, most universal and variable policies also contain a grace period exception clause. This clause states that during a specified period of time (generally the first few policy years, even if the policy has a negative surrender value), as long as at least the stated minimum premium has been paid during the grace period, the policy will continue in force.

Reinstatement

Following your failure to pay a fixed premium within the grace period, you may want to reinstate your policy. The **reinstatement provision** provides that, unless the policy has been surrendered for cash, it may be reinstated at any time within five (in some cases, three, ten, or more) years after default. Payment of all overdue premiums on the policy and other indebtedness to the insurer, plus interest on these items, is required along with payment of the current premium. Usually, you must also provide satisfactory evidence of insurability.[8]

Evidence of insurability may be as strict in the case of reinstatement as it is for obtaining new life insurance. The company is concerned about your health, occupation, hobbies, and any other factors that may affect the probability of death. If the policy lapsed recently, however, most insurers only require a simple statement that you are in good health and consider yourself insurable.

Why would you apply for reinstatement instead of new insurance? There may be features in the old policy that are preferable to those currently available. For example, reinstatement avoids beginning another suicide exclusion period in a new policy. Sometimes reinstatement is preferable because a new policy involves new surrender charges or heavy front-end costs, all or part of which you have already paid on your old policy. However, a new policy may or may not cost more than reinstating the old one. The only way to find out is to make cost comparisons.[9]

Universal and variable policies typically provide reinstatement without requiring payment of back premiums. In this event, the cash value of the reinstated policy equals the amount provided by the premium paid, after deductions for the cost of insurance protection and expenses.

7. The automatic premium loan discussed later in this chapter is also designed to deal with this problem for traditional policies. The grace period is found in section 1 of the specimen policy.

8. The reinstatement provision of the specimen life policy (see section 3) does not require evidence of insurability when you apply for reinstatement within thirty-one days after the grace period expires.

9. Cost comparison methods are discussed in chapter 16.

Post-Death Premium Refund

After the death of the insured, insurers refund any premium paid but unearned. For example, if you paid an annual premium and died nine months after the due date, 25 percent (reflecting the remaining three months of the year) of the annual premium would be refunded. Most insurers explain their practice in a contract **premium refund provision.** A study shows that 18 percent of insurers calculate the refund from the end of the month in which death occurs; the remainder use the date of death.[10]

DIVIDEND OPTIONS

Participating policies share in the profits the insurer earns because of (1) lower than anticipated expenses, (2) lower than expected mortality, and (3) greater than expected investment earnings. The amounts returned to policyowners are called dividends. Dividends also involve the return of abnormally high (redundant) premiums. Dividends are payable annually on the policy anniversary. They are not guaranteed, but are a highly significant element in many policies.[11]

When you purchase a participating life insurance policy, you have one or more of the following **dividend options:**

1. Paid in cash.
2. Applied toward payment of the next premium.
3. Left with the insurer to accumulate at interest.
4. Used to buy paid-up additional insurance.
5. Used to buy one-year term insurance (provided by some companies).
6. Used to pay up the policy through a vanishing premium provision.

The majority of companies offer only the first four of these options.[12] Companies that offer the one-year term insurance option usually limit the amount of term insurance to the amount of your cash value.[13] The selection of the appropriate dividend option is an important decision.

NONFORFEITURE VALUES AND OPTIONS

In the early history of cash value life insurance, it was customary for the insurer to keep the reserve if payments were stopped, on the grounds that the policyowner forfeited the value. This was obviously unfair to policyowners. Eventually, some life insurers voluntarily adopted the policy of refunding the reserve (liability), minus a surrender charge, to the policyowner who surrendered (returned) the policy to the company. This practice is now required by all state insurance laws.[14]

---

10. John H. Thornton and Kennes C. Huntley, "A Survey of Life Insurance Policy Provisions," *Journal of the American Society of CLU & ChFC,* vol. XLIV, no. 3 (May 1990): p. 74.

11. See section 4 of the specimen life policy. In interest-sensitive policies, earnings are shared with you in the form of higher accumulation and cash value, as opposed to dividends.

12. See section 4 of the specimen life policy for additional explanation.

13. Thornton and Huntley, pp. 73–74.

14. Elizur Wright, the Massachusetts Insurance Commissioner during the mid-1800s, campaigned for the nationwide adoption of nonforfeiture laws. Massachusetts adopted the first law in 1861.

When you stop making premium payments in traditional cash value policies, several **nonforfeiture options** are available to you. The policy-owner can:

1. Take a check for the surrender (cash) value.
2. Continue the policy in force as extended term insurance.
3. Continue the policy in force with a smaller face amount that is paid-up.

The policy lists these amounts in a Table of Guaranteed Values.[15] Term life policies do not have policy loan or nonforfeiture values unless premiums are level for an extended number of years and cash values are provided.

Cash Value

As pointed out in chapter 13, the cash value life plan results in the accumulation of a reserve (or cash value element, from the insured's perspective) that usually increases as each year passes. If you decide to terminate your contract and the entire death benefit, you receive a refund. The amount subject to refund is called the **cash value.** The total cash value consists of (1) the amount in the Table of Guaranteed Values, (2) the cash value of any paid-up additions, and (3) any dividend accumulations.

Extended Term Insurance

If premiums remain unpaid at the end of the grace period, the usual automatic option is **extended term insurance.** The death benefit continues at its previous level for as long as the cash value will support this amount of term insurance. The cash value is applied as a net single premium[16] at the insured's attained age, and this determines the length of term insurance coverage.

Paid-up Insurance

As an insurance alternative to extended term, you can apply your cash value as a net single premium for **paid-up insurance.** The new policy will have a lower lifetime death benefit than existed prior to your discontinuance of premium payments.

With universal, current assumption, and variable policies, you may discontinue premium payments at any time without lapsing the policy, as long as the surrender value is sufficient to cover the next month's monthly deduction for cost of insurance and expenses. An extended term insurance option is not specifically mentioned because periodic deduction of mortality charges from your cash value is the equivalent of an automatic extended term insurance provision. Extended term is also the explicit automatic option in the specimen life policy (see section 5) and in almost all traditional cash value policies when the policy was issued on a standard or preferred basis (that is, without extra premium being charged because

---

15. See page 4 of the specimen life policy.
16. See chapter 13.

of adverse health, a dangerous occupation, or other abnormal risk). Requiring the paid-up option *with a lower face amount* limits adverse selection. The automatic option applies only when the policyowner fails to select an option following his or her nonpayment of a required premium.

POLICY LOAN

You have the right under the **policy loan provision** to borrow an amount up to the cash value from the insurer at a rate of interest specified in the policy. The majority of insurers use a fixed rate of interest; the most common rate is 8 percent. Other companies use a variable rate; a small number give the policyowner a choice between a fixed rate and a variable rate. If you choose a variable rate, the wording of your contract may call for the greater of either Moody's Composite Yield on corporate bonds for the month ending two months prior or the cash value rate plus one or more percent.[17] (Fixed rates of 5 or 6 percent are found in older policies.)

Interest is payable on the anniversary date of the policy, and sometimes interest for the first year is deducted in advance from your loan proceeds. When you die, however, the proceeds of the policy are reduced by any outstanding loans and interest due. For example, a policy with a face value of $250,000 and loans plus unpaid interest equal to $20,000 would pay $230,000 to the beneficiary. Although the loan right is a valuable one, it can at least partially defeat the major purpose of the insurance program.

The insurer reserves the right to defer policy loans for up to six months; however, this provision is not exercised unless an insurer is experiencing severe financial problems. Policy loans are private and convenient because they do not involve any credit check or justification. Repayments are made only if and when you want to make them.

A few insurers encourage the repayment of policy loans on participating policies by **direct recognition** of your average policy loans for the year when calculating your annual dividends. For example, on certain policies your insurer may allow 8 percent investment credit on cash values left with the insurer and 4.75 percent on borrowed cash values.

Many contracts have an **automatic premium loan provision** or make this an available option. It provides that if you fail to pay the premium, a loan in the amount of the premium due will automatically be made at the end of the grace period, if there is enough unencumbered cash value to cover the loan and the interest for one premium-paying period. A small minority of companies place restrictions on the use of the provision. Some limit the number of automatic loans by exercising the extended term nonforfeiture option after, for example, two years of automatic loans. Extended term keeps the death benefit in force longer than would a series of automatic premium loans. The automatic premium loan provision, however, is a valuable one to request when you buy traditional life insurance, since it is easy to overlook payment of a premium. The provision reduces the likelihood of needing to go through the reinstatement process.

The mechanics of a universal or variable life policy that provides for the deduction of mortality and other expenses from your cash value are

17. See Thornton and Huntley, p. 74. Moody's Composite Yield is the average interest rate for a portfolio of seasoned corporate bonds of various maturities.

the equivalent of an automatic premium loan with no interest credit or charge. The exception is a policy that pays a lesser interest rate when the accumulation value is below a specified amount.

BENEFICIARY PROVISION

The purpose of the **beneficiary provision** is to enable the owner of the policy to designate to whom the proceeds shall be paid when the insured dies. If no beneficiary is named, the proceeds will go to the owner's estate. There are no legal or contractual restrictions on the designation of a beneficiary. It is not necessary that the beneficiary have an insurable interest; only the policyowner needs this interest.

A **revocable beneficiary** can be changed at will only by the policyowner. Most people prefer the revocable provision. **Irrevocable beneficiary** designations, on the other hand, can be changed only with the consent of the beneficiary. For example, a divorced spouse, as part of a property settlement, may be given an irrevocable interest in life insurance on his or her former spouse. The former spouse, as the insured and policyowner, would be required to continue premium payments but could not make a policy loan or other changes that would diminish the rights of the irrevocable beneficiary.

A beneficiary must survive the insured in order to be entitled to the proceeds of the policy. It is customary, therefore, to name one or more beneficiaries who are entitled to the proceeds in the event that the primary (first-named) beneficiary does not survive the insured. These are known as **contingent,** secondary, or tertiary **beneficiaries.** Such beneficiaries are named and listed in the order of their priority.[18]

If the insured and the primary beneficiary die in the same accident and no evidence shows who died first, there is a question as to whether the proceeds shall be paid to the estate of the primary beneficiary or to a contingent beneficiary. In states where the Uniform Simultaneous Death Act has been enacted, the proceeds are distributed as if the insured had survived the beneficiary. Where this act is not in effect, the courts have usually reached the same conclusion. If no contingent beneficiary has been named, the proceeds go to the estate of the policyowner, thus subjecting them to estate taxes, probate costs, and the claims of creditors. Probate costs are levied by the court that certifies that an estate has been settled properly. Probate costs (but not estate taxes) are avoided when benefits go to a named beneficiary.

A similar problem arises when the primary beneficiary survives the insured by only a short period. In such a case, the proceeds may be depleted by going through the estate of the beneficiary or because an annuity-type settlement option had been selected. This problem can be solved by adding a **common disaster provision** (or survivorship clause), which provides that the beneficiary must survive the insured by a specified period of time (for example, seven to thirty days) or must be alive at the time of payment to be entitled to the proceeds. If neither of these conditions is fulfilled, the proceeds go to a contingent beneficiary or to the estate of the policyowner if a contingent beneficiary has not been named. A sur-

----

18. See section 8 of the specimen life policy for typical provisions concerning beneficiaries.

vey of life insurance policy provisions found only about one in four insurers that included a specific clause to handle questions of survivorship.[19]

Policyowners should designate the beneficiary clearly. No questions should exist about the identity of the beneficiary at the time of the insured's death. In designating children as beneficiaries, one must keep in mind that a minor is not competent to receive payment. In the event of the death of the insured prior to the maturity of a beneficiary child, a guardian may have to be appointed to receive the proceeds on behalf of the child. As a general rule, policyowners should avoid naming minors as beneficiaries. Where the objective is a substantial estate to benefit a child or children, the preferable approach would be to name a trust as beneficiary. The child or children could be the beneficiary(ies) of the trust.[20]

SETTLEMENT OPTIONS

Life insurance is designed to create a sum of money that can be used when the insured dies or the owner surrenders a cash-value policy. In the early days of life insurance, the only form in which the death proceeds or cash value of a policy were paid was in a lump sum. Because a lump-sum payment is not desirable in all circumstances, several additional **settlement options** (also called payment plans) have been developed and are now included in most policies.[21] Many companies have discontinued printing specific details of settlement options (such as the dollars payable) in the policy form, on the premise that only the conservative guaranteed options could be printed. Actual proceeds paid use current settlement options with nonguaranteed, current interest assumptions.

The owner may select an option in advance or leave the choice to the beneficiary. The owner may also change the option from time to time if the beneficiary designation is revocable. The settlement options for death proceeds usually are:

1. Cash or lump-sum payment.
2. Periodic payments of interest.
3. Equal installments of principle and interest over a *fixed period*, possibly with periodic payment of excess interest.
4. Equal payments under a *fixed-amount option*, with payments made until all principle and interest are exhausted.
5. Income guaranteed to continue as long as the beneficiary lives.[22]

Special Provisions for Interest-Sensitive Policies

Universal and other interest-sensitive policies include the provisions discussed in other parts of this chapter. In addition, they must have distinguishing features to provide flexibility and the separation of their protection, cash value, and expense elements.

19. Thornton and Huntley, pp. 72–84.
20. Trusts are discussed in chapter 22.
21. Payment plans for the specimen life policy are described in section 9. The interest option is automatic in the specimen policy until you select cash or another option.
22. Settlement options for life insurance policies are similar to options given to buyers of annuities. Descriptions of annuity payment options are in chapter 23.

MINIMUM, TARGET, AND ADDITIONAL PREMIUMS

A **minimum premium** is required for the first one- or two-year period for universal policies. The minimum is well below (for example, approximately half) the amount of premium required by a traditional straight life contract. The **target premium** is usually the equivalent of an annual level premium for a traditional straight life policy, based on liberal (high) investment and (low) mortality assumptions, but you are not required to pay this amount except for current assumption policies. Remember, current assumption policies do not offer premium flexibility. Additional premium deposits are allowed, periodically or in lump sums, subject to limitations. The usual limitation requires that the policy have at least the minimum amount of protection (often called the **minimum risk amount**) required by federal tax laws to allow favorable taxation of inside interest buildup. The policy must have a significant insurance element or it will be disqualified by the IRS for favorable tax treatment. Insurers often prevent adverse selection by requiring evidence of insurability if the payment of additional premium increases the amount of death benefit by more than the amount of additional premium in the case of a type B (cash value plus level protection) policy.

CHANGES IN COVERAGE

The **changes in existing coverage provision** specifies the conditions under which a policyowner can change the total face amount of the policy. Any requested decreases take place on a monthly anniversary date and reduce the most recent additions to coverage (if any) before affecting the initial face amount. A **minimum face amount** will be defined, and in some policies will equal the **initial face amount** at the time of purchase. Requests for increases in coverage must be made on a supplemental application and are subject to evidence of insurability. As described earlier, additions are also subject to a new suicide period and to the incontestable clause based on statements made to induce more coverage.

INTEREST RATE

Both the guaranteed and excess (if any) interest rates will be described in an **interest rate provision.** Monthly compounding applies. Excess returns are calculated in a manner solely determined by the insurer.[23] The provision usually explains that excess interest does not apply to policy loans. A higher interest rate may apply after the accumulation value exceeds a minimum amount, such as $800.

Life Insurance Riders

Through the use of **riders,** life insurance policies may be modified to provide special benefits. Under specified circumstances, these riders may waive the premium, provide disability income, provide accidental death benefits, guarantee issuance of additional life insurance, and pay accelerated death benefits (before death).

---

23. Guaranteed and excess interest are explained in chapter 14.

WAIVER OF PREMIUM

The **waiver of premium rider** is offered by all life insurance companies and is included in about half of the policies sold. Some companies automatically provide it without charging an explicit amount of additional premium. The rider provides that premiums due after commencement of the insured's total disability shall be waived for a period of time. A waiting period of six months must be satisfied first. In flexible premium contracts such as universal and variable life, the waiver of premium provision specifies that the target premium will be credited to the insured's account during disability.[24] If a premium was paid after disability began and before the expiration of a waiting period, the premium is refunded.

When disability begins before a certain age, usually age 60, premiums are waived as long as the insured remains totally disabled. A few insurers provide a paid-up policy at age 65. Many offer no benefit for disability that begins after age 60. For disability that begins between ages 60 and 65, some insurers provide benefits to age 65, and occasionally as long as to age 70. Term insurance contract riders stipulate that premiums are not waived beyond the maximum time the policy is renewable.

Waiver of premium has no effect on any other provision of the policy. Your rights and benefits continue just as they would if you continued making premium payments. The waiver of premium benefit does not increase family income, but it releases premium dollars for other uses and keeps insurance protection in force. Cash values continue to increase and dividends (if the policy is participating) continue to be paid. The rider is like having a disability income policy with the benefit equal to your premium. If you have enough long-term disability income insurance and other sources of income to pay premiums and all other normal living expenses, you probably do not need to pay for a waiver of premium provision.[25] Most people who become disabled for extended periods, however, have inadequate income, and definitions of disability—for example, in group long-term disability income plans—may be more strict than the one used in a waiver of premium provision.

Definition of Disability

To qualify for disability benefits, disability must be total and permanent, and must occur prior to a specified age. The waiver of premium rider in the specimen life policy uses age 65 but limits the duration of the waiver when disability begins after age 60. Disability may be caused by either accidental injury or sickness; no distinction is made. Typically, for the first two years of benefit payments, you are considered totally disabled whenever, because of injury or disease, you are unable to perform the duties of *your regular occupation.* Beyond two years, benefits usually continue only if you are unable to perform the duties of *any occupation* for which you are qualified by reason of education, training, and experience. A minority of insurers use this more restrictive definition from the inception of the

---

24. An alternative to the waiver of premium rider for flexible premium contracts waives only the amount required to cover mortality cost and expense deductions.
25. Separate policies providing disability income insurance are discussed in chapter 21.

period for which waiver of premium is claimed. Most insurers and courts interpret the definition liberally. Most riders define blindness or loss of both hands, both feet, or one hand and one foot as presumptive total disability. Typically, disability longer than six months is considered to be permanent. Circumstances may later contradict this assumption, as proof (e.g., a physician's statement) of continued disability is usually required once a year up to age 65.

DISABILITY INCOME

The **disability income rider** provides a typical income benefit of $10 per month per $1,000 of initial face amount of life insurance for as long as total disability continues and after the first six months of such disability, provided it commences before age 55 or 60. Payments are usually made for the balance of the insured's life as long as total disability continues; under some contracts, payments stop at age 65 and the policy matures as an endowment. This is less favorable than continuation of income benefits.

The definitions of disability for these riders are like those for waiver of premium provisions. Most disability income insurance is now sold either through a group plan (for example, an employer offers the coverage to employees) or as separate individual policies. Most life insurers do not offer this rider.

ACCIDENTAL DEATH BENEFIT

The **accidental death benefit rider** is sometimes called **double indemnity.** It usually provides that double the face amount of the policy will be paid if the insured's death is caused by accident, and, sometimes, triple the face amount if death occurs while the insured is riding as a paying passenger in a public conveyance.[26] Figure 15–2 illustrates the accidental death benefit rider. Because it does not add much cost to the premium and *appears* to double the protection of the policy, it is very popular.

The loss of income resulting from death, however, is likely unrelated to the cause of death. The loss can be just as great whether one dies of natural causes or by accident. Unreimbursed medical expenses may ac-

FIGURE 15–2

Accidental Death Benefit Rider

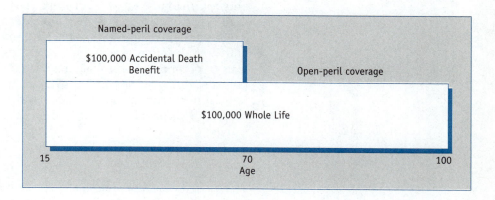

....

26. Policies with flexible face amounts usually issue the accidental death rider for a fixed amount equal to the basic policy's initial face amount.

company both accidents and illnesses. The drawback with this rider is that many insureds tend to think of protection in terms of the double indemnity benefit and forget that it is payable only in the event of death caused by accident. Do not accept the illusion that, with an accidental death rider, you have twice as much protection. Many people advocate the purchase of double indemnity because accidents claim more lives than all other causes of death combined for persons age 15 to 24. They forget that the possible size of a loss is more important than the probability of the loss occurring. It is worthwhile noting that 22 percent of deaths in the age group of 25 to 44 are caused by accidents. Approximately 4 percent of all deaths among the U.S. population are due to accidents. About half of these are in automobile accidents.

A typical definition of accidental death is, "Death resulting from bodily injury independently and exclusively of all other causes and within ninety days after such injury."[27] Certain causes of death are typically excluded: suicide, violations of the law, gas or poison, war, and certain aviation activities other than as a passenger on a scheduled airline. This rider is usually in effect to the insured's age 70.[28]

GUARANTEED INSURABILITY OPTION

Many insurers will add a **guaranteed insurability option** (GIO) to policies for an additional premium. This gives the policyowner the right to buy additional amounts of insurance, usually at three-year intervals up to a specified age, without proof of insurability. The usual age of the last option is 40; a small number of insurers allow exercise of the option up to age 65. The amount of each additional purchase is usually equal to or less than the face amount of the original policy. If a $50,000 straight or interest-sensitive life policy with the GIO rider is purchased at age 21, the policyowner can buy an additional $50,000 every three years thereafter to age 40, whether or not the insured has become uninsurable. By age 40, the total death benefit would equal $350,000. The new insurance is issued at standard rates on the basis of the insured's attained age when the option is exercised. The GIO rider ensures one's insurability. It becomes valuable if the insured becomes uninsurable or develops a condition that would prevent the purchase of new life insurance at standard rates. Some parents, particularly those with impaired health, buy life insurance on children just to get access to the GIO rider while the children are healthy.

The details of this rider and its name vary depending on the insurer, but they all follow the same general pattern. If the original policy has a waiver of premium provision and/or accidental death benefit, the new policies will have the same provisions if the policyowner wants them. Further, if the original policy has a waiver of premium provision and the insured is disabled, some insurers will issue new policies with premiums waived.

27. Instead of requiring death within ninety days, a minority of insurers specify a longer period such as 120 days, 180 days, one year, or even as long as the rider is in force (for example, to age 70). A few do not specify any time limit. See Thornton and Huntley, p. 75.
28. An accidental death rider is included on page 17 of the specimen life policy.

ACCELERATED DEATH BENEFITS

Some medical conditions regularly result in high medical expenses for the insured and his or her family or other caregivers. The need for funds may significantly exceed benefits provided by medical and disability insurance because of deductibles, coinsurance, caps on benefits, exclusions, and (perhaps primarily) from having purchased inadequate coverage. **Accelerated death benefits,** introduced into South Africa in 1983 and the U.S. in 1988, are triggered by either the occurrence of a catastrophic (dread) illness or diagnosis of a terminal illness, resulting in payment of a portion of a life insurance policy's face amount prior to death.

Catastrophic Illness Coverage

When a **catastrophic illness rider** is added to a life insurance policy (usually requiring additional premium), a portion (usually 25 to 50 percent) of the face amount is payable upon diagnosis of specified illnesses. The named illnesses differ among insurers but typically include organ transplantation.

Terminal Illness Coverage

Riders providing payment of part of a life policy's face amount upon diagnosis of a **terminal illness** have become common. Often, the coverage is provided without additional premium. The benefit (for example, 50 percent of the face amount) can usually be claimed when two doctors agree that the insured has six months or less to live. The small number of claims for terminal illness benefits suggests a reluctance among many insureds to accept the opinion that death is imminent.

As benefits are paid out under either a catastrophic or terminal illness rider, the face amount of the basic policy is reduced an equal amount and an interest charge applies in some policies. Cash values are reduced either in proportion to the death benefit reduction or on a dollar-for-dollar basis.

Decisions for the Life Insurance Policyowner

Among the important choices you make concerning a life insurance policy are:

1. Who should own the policy?
2. Which dividend option should you select?
3. Which settlement option should you choose?

Let's see how to make these decisions.

owner you can change the beneficiary, make policy loans, and surrender the policy.

You may or may not need the help of an attorney, life insurance professional, or financial planner to decide who should own the insurance on your life, but you should make the decision carefully. Without the help of a professional, your decision could still result in estate tax liability because of contingent ownership, either expressed or implied.

WHO SHOULD OWN THE POLICY?

When you buy a car or house, you give careful consideration to the matter of ownership. Should you own it? Should your spouse own it? Or should you own it jointly? In contrast, most people who buy life insurance automatically name themselves as policyowners. As you will see when we discuss estate planning in chapter 22, there may be situations in which consideration should be given to having someone other than yourself as owner of the policy on your life.

One such situation is when you want to reduce the size of the insured's taxable estate in order to reduce the burden of estate taxes. If you are both the owner of and the insured in life insurance in the amount of $300,000, for example, when you die the proceeds of the policy go to your beneficiary but are considered part of your taxable estate. On the other hand, if you have not been the owner during the three years preceding your death, the proceeds are not part of your estate for tax purposes. The difference this can make in your estate depends on its total size. If your taxable estate without the insurance is zero, the tax is zero. But if all the insurance proceeds are included at minimum federal estate tax rates, the tax is $111,000 on the policy proceeds, and would be $165,000 at rates for taxable estates exceeding $10 million. Some state estate taxes, in addition, might exceed the allowance allowed at the federal level.

Life insurance proceeds are included in the insured's estate when the "estate" is the beneficiary, even if someone else owns the policy. Thus, for estate tax purposes, it is wise to be neither the policyowner nor the beneficiary. When estate taxes are not a problem or when achieving other objectives is more important, which is true for most people, there are advantages to owning your policy: as

WHICH DIVIDEND OPTION SHOULD YOU SELECT?

If you have budget problems, you may be tempted to take policy dividends in cash. Before you make that choice, you should consider applying dividends toward the annual premium payment, especially if you are paying monthly premiums for a policy that is a few years old.

Why? Suppose the monthly premium is $19.13. Twelve payments equal $229.56. But if you paid annually, the premium would be $216.83, a savings of $12.73. Using monthly premiums results in an annual interest charge of 12.65 percent.[29] If your dividend is $121.38, the cash required to pay the annual premium is $95.45. If you can save an interest cost of 12.65 percent by paying out $94.45 annually, that's wise. Because dividends usually increase every year, your cash outlay is likely to go down every year.

Suppose you don't need the cash. Should you leave dividends to accumulate at interest? That depends on the interest rate the insurer pays on such deposits, and on your alternatives. If the insurer pays 5 percent on deposits and your savings bank pays 7 percent, don't leave money with the insurer. One advantage of leaving it with the insurer, of course, is the simple fact that if you don't see it, you won't spend it. You may, however, pay dearly in lost earnings by accepting this low-risk/low-return investment. You, of course, still have the option to withdraw your accumulations at will. Interest payments for both dividend accu-

....

29. The annual percentage rate cost of using monthly premiums was calculated using the direct ratio method. For the formula and explanation of this method, see Joseph M. Belth, "A Note on the Cost of Fractional Premiums," *Journal of Risk and Insurance,* vol. 45, no. 4 (1978): pp. 683–687.

mulations and bank savings are subject to income taxes annually.

Unless you have more life insurance than you need or have a serious budget problem, you are probably better off to use the dividends to buy paid-up additions (that is, small additional amounts of single-premium whole life insurance with premiums reflecting your attained age). Most participating policyowners choose this option. Use of paid-up additions will increase both your cash values and death benefit. The cash value in each addition initially equals the amount of the dividend (there are no front-end expense loads) and grows in the future. It is shielded from income taxes since the growth is part of your "inside interest buildup." These additional amounts of cash value will be a source of higher dividends if the insurer has investment earnings in excess of those assumed in establishing a cash-value schedule for the paid-up additions. You should recognize that single-premium life insurance has the highest premium per $1,000 of death benefit of all forms of life insurance. In buying paid-up additions, the mix of savings and protection favors savings. Dividend additions may be the only source of additional insurance to offset inflation when your health is impaired and you are unable to buy new insurance at a reasonable premium. Usually, no evidence of insurability is required to change to this option with respect to future dividends.

Your policy also may allow you to use one-year term insurance, with the additional death benefit equal to either the amount of cash value in your policy or all the term coverage that can be purchased with your current dividends. The better choice between this and paid-up additions depends on your situation. If you need a significant amount of new protection now, choose one-year term. If you expect to need death benefits over a long period of time, choose paid-up additions. If you die soon, your beneficiary will be better off financially if you selected term. If you live to a ripe old age, you will be pleased if you chose the paid-up additions.

Other dividend options are available in some policies. The **vanishing premium option** has become common and is another reason to use either the paid-up additions or the accumulation option in the early contract years. The vanishing premium option allows you to use the total of your cash value (including the part in paid-up additions) and dividend accumulations as a single premium at your attained age to "pay up" your original face amount of insurance. Even then, your premium is not guaranteed to remain vanished. The insurer can ask for a resumption of premium payments if its future operating experience deteriorates. Sales illustrations sometimes show when the cash values and accumulations are projected to equal the single premium. At current dividend levels, premiums can often van-

ish in ten or twelve years. You should remember that future dividends can be lower, as well as higher, than illustrated. Thus, the actual vanish period is likely to differ from the illustration. You may, of course decide at that point that you prefer to continue to pay premiums and choose another dividend option because you need the additional protection (provided by either paid-up additions or term bought by dividends), or because you like the cash value features of your policy.

WHICH SETTLEMENT OPTION SHOULD YOU CHOOSE?

As noted earlier, most companies will permit a beneficiary to place lump-sum death proceeds under a different settlement option. Considering the emotional circumstances in which cash life insurance proceeds may become available, it may be in the best interest of your beneficiary to select some other option and specify that it can be changed by the beneficiary. If you don't know what other choice to make, specify the interest option, along with the right to make withdrawals or change to another option. This avoids a situation in which a large sum of money is handed to someone unprepared to manage it.

Should the proceeds be left at interest for a long time? That depends partly upon the needs of the beneficiary, his or her ability to manage funds, the interest rate paid, and taxation. Your policy specifies the minimum rate to be paid, but the current rate may be considerably higher. Therefore, when you compare alternatives, find out what the insurer is currently paying. If the insurer pays 6 percent on deposits and a larger return is readily available at no more risk, it would be beneficial to move the money. Convert both returns to their after-tax equivalents. The insurer's rates, however, may be quite competitive.

Should the proceeds be used to provide monthly income? Here again, any settlement options listed in your policy show the minimum income provided. If you are trying to help a friend make the choice, ask the insurer what amount of income per $1,000 of death proceeds is currently offered. Also, find out if any excess earnings are available in the form of annual dividends or excess interest payments. Then compare the information with available alternatives that liquidate the principal sum over time. Also, determine how these returns compare with what can be obtained elsewhere, including through life annuities.[30]

When you look at alternatives, be sure they are truly comparable to the safety and service provided by the insurer. Remember that money left with the insurer is protected from creditors of the beneficiary. Moreover, the risk of losing the money is very low for financially sound insur-

---

30. Annuities, discussed in chapter 23, promise lifetime benefits.

ers. This does not mean that differences between what the insurer offers and what is available elsewhere should be disregarded. It does mean, however, that you should not risk a lot for a little, especially when a steady and certain income is at stake.

Trusts, as discussed in chapter 22, provide more flexibility in investments and management. You may want to discuss this alternative with a professional insurance agent or financial planner. Obtain information on the investment returns, after administration expenses, for the trust departments in your community and compare these data with the expected returns under life insurance settlement options. Remember that only settlement options, as annuities, can promise lifetime income, and that insurers cannot agree to exercise discretion with respect to the payment of benefits. Instead, they pay the same amounts each period to the designated beneficiaries.

Key Terms

entire contract provision
incontestable provision
rescission
suicide provision
misstatement of age or sex
ownership
ownership provision
assignment provison
grace period
reinstatement provision
premium refund provision
dividend options
nonforfeiture options
cash value
extended term insurance
paid-up insurance
policy loan provision
direct recognition
automatic premium loan
    provision
beneficiary provision
revocable beneficiary

irrevocable beneficiary
contingent beneficiaries
common disaster provision
settlement options
minimum premium
target premium
minimum risk amount
changes in existing coverage
    provision
minimum face amount
initial face amount
interest rate provision
riders
waiver of premium rider
disability income rider
accidental death benefit rider
double indemnity
guaranteed insurability option
accelerated death benefits
catastrophic illness rider
terminal illness
vanishing premium option

Discussion Questions

1. The premium on Bill Brown's traditional whole life policy was due September 1. On September 15, he mailed a check to the insurance company. On September 26, he died. When the insurance company presented the check to the bank for collection, it was returned because there were insufficient funds in Bill's account. Does the company have to pay the claim presented by Bill's beneficiary? Why, or why not? What provisions might result in payment?

2. Clancy knew he could not meet the physical requirements for insurability, so he had his twin brother, Clarence, take the physical examination in his place. A policy was issued, and three years later, Clancy died. The insurance company claims manager learned that Clancy's twin took the examination in his place and refused to pay the claim. Clancy's beneficiary sued the company for the proceeds, claiming that the two-year contestable period had expired. Did the company have to pay? Why, or why not?

3. If you intentionally burn your house down, the property insurance company will refuse to pay for it. If you commit suicide after your life insurance policy has been in force for two years, however, the insurer will pay the face amount to your beneficiary. Isn't this a departure from the concept that insurance is to pay for fortuitous losses? Please explain.

4. People buy life insurance because they don't know when they may die or what may cause their death. Although accidental death benefits are paid only when death is caused by accident, the accidental death benefit rider has great sales appeal. How do you account for this apparent inconsistency in the way people make decisions?

5. If you don't need life insurance now but realize you may need it sometime in the future, would you be interested in buying a guaranteed insurability option, if it were available, without buying a policy now? Please explain.

6. Why is it usually unwise to name a minor child as beneficiary of a life insurance policy? What complications exist when this is done?

7. When would a life insurer initiate the process of rescission? When faced with a rescission, what are the options of the policyowner (or those of the legal representative following the death of the policyowner/insured)?

8. What desirable features characterize the policy loan provision of a cash-value life insurance policy, relative, for example, to borrowing money from a bank? How do policy loans affect death benefits?

9. Explain how universal life policies transfer mortality risk (subject to a limit) to you. Does the provision that creates this risk have an "up side" that may allow you to participate in your insurer's good fortunes?

10. Describe the nature of what is purchased by the dividend on a life insurance policy when it is used to buy "paid-up additions."

Cases

15.1 Therese Thomas misstated her age on her application for life insurance, saying she was 25 when she really was 28; otherwise, she answered the questions correctly. After three years, she died of injuries from a fall while riding a horse. When her sister, the beneficiary, submitted proof of death to the insurer, the insurer sent a check for about 9 percent less than the face amount. The sister is considering bringing suit against the insurer, contending that the incontestable clause prevents the insurer from paying less than the face amount. Is the sister right? Explain what guidance is available in the language of the policy.

15.2 The following insureds have accidental death benefit riders on their life insurance policies. Discuss why you think this rider will or will not pay the beneficiary in each of the following situations.

1. The insured dies from a fall through a dormitory window on the tenth floor. The door to his room is locked from the inside, and the

window has no ledge. There is no suicide note. He had not appeared despondent.

2. The insured dies in a high-speed single-car automobile accident, on a clear day and with no apparent mechanical malfunction in the vehicle. He had been very depressed about his job and had undergone therapy with a counselor, during which he had discussed suicide; however, there is no note.

3. The insured contracts pneumonia after she is hospitalized due to injuries received from a fall from a ladder while rescuing a cat from a tree. She has a history of pneumonia and other serious respiratory problems. She dies of pneumonia thirty days after the fall.

15.3 Assume you are advising Mr. Nash Antonic about what to do with a $200,000 straight life insurance policy on which he has paid annual premiums for the past thirty years. The policy specifies that premiums are payable for life (through age 99). Nash plans to retire in three months at age 63. Continuing to pay the premiums during retirement will put some strain on Nash's budget. Yet he definitely does not want to surrender the policy for its cash value because his wife, Jelena, is 48 and has a modest income from her job as a secretary. He considers the current cash value of $95,000 to be insufficient to help with her retirement income. Given his current intentions about income from his private retirement plan, survivor benefits will not be paid to Jelena following Nash's death. Nash has some concern about his health, having had a mild heart attack five years ago and currently facing the possibility of a heart bypass operation.

1. Tell Nash about the nonforfeiture options in his policy besides the cash value option.

2. Assume that the extended term insurance option would provide continuation of the $200,000 death benefit for fifteen years. Further assume that acceptance of the reduced paid-up option would reduce the death benefit to $150,000. Do you think either option is appropriate for Nash?

Evaluating Life Insurance Costs

Introduction

Do not assume that life insurance costs pretty much the same regardless of where you buy it. Smart shoppers compare the costs (or rates of return) of different policies. A common misconception is that a low premium is the same as a low cost.[1] In addition to your policy's premium, your cost of insurance protection is strongly affected by cash values, dividends, and the amount of death benefit. As was said in chapter 14 in the discussion of cash flows for universal life insurance, universal cash values (and dividends in participating whole life) are influenced by the insurer's mortality charges, expense charges, and investment credits. These same factors affect current assumption whole life and variable life. Thus, in judging a policy's cost, consider more than the premium. A premium is not a cost or price; the premium covers a package of protection, cash values, and dividends in proportions that vary from policy to policy.[2]

Insurer characteristics such as financial strength, investment performance, lapse rates, credibility of historical dividend illustrations, and so forth further affect the value of different contracts. When you buy life insurance, you will want to compare the quality of the insurer as well as prices. Price variations among contracts are significant.[3]

In this chapter, you will become acquainted with the following methods of ranking policies by cost or value:

1. Interest-adjusted net cost methods.
2. Cash accumulation method.
3. Belth yearly rate of return.
4. Linton rate of return.

---

1. This relationship holds for nonparticipating term insurance but not for participating term and cash-value policies ranging from whole life to universal variable life.
2. Insurance specialists use the terms "cost" and "price" synonymously in describing the sacrifice a policyowner makes per $1,000 of life insurance protection.
3. Chapter 25 provides information about how to compare insurers.

Traditional Net Cost Method

As late as the 1970s, life insurance salespeople often demonstrated the cost of a policy over a period of years simply by adding up all the premiums paid and subtracting from this total: (1) the dividends received and (2) any cash value at the end of the selected period (usually ten or twenty years). The result, the total net cost, was divided by the number of years in the period and the face amount (in thousands) to show the annual average cost per thousand dollars of face amount (i.e., the net cost). Subtraction of the cash value implied that the policyowner surrendered the policy for its cash value at the end of the period. As the example in column 1 of table 16–1 shows, the annual net cost calculated by this **traditional net cost method** is startlingly low compared with the annual premium. In fact, the net cost is negative, implying that one can have life insurance protection for twenty years without costs.

This method of cost calculation ignores opportunity costs by the policyowner, thus giving the impression that life insurance can be costless or even profitable. It is like saying, "If you will give me a million dollars for a year, I will let you live in my house free for the year and then give the million dollars back to you. It will cost you nothing to live in the house." Clearly, use of the house is not free because giving up the use of a million dollars for a year involves sacrifice. If you could earn 5 percent interest per annum after taxes, the cost of living in the house would be $50,000 for the year. So it is with the premium dollars you give up to have a life insurance policy in force for twenty years. In addition, the traditional net cost method is subject to actuarial manipulation by insurers because cash

TABLE 16–1

20-Year Values and Cost Indexes per $1,000 for $100,000 Participating Straight Life Policy (issued to male, age 35, 5 percent interest)

	(1) TRADITIONAL NET COST, WITHOUT INTEREST	(2) SURRENDER COST INDEX, WITH INTEREST	(3) NET PAYMENT COST INDEX, WITH INTEREST
Annual premium per $1,000	$ 13.86	$ 13.86	$ 13.86
Accumulated premiums	277.20	481.21	481.21
Less projected dividends*	146.17	190.34	190.34
Less 20th-year cash value	285.09	285.09	**
Equals 20-year index	−154.06	5.78	290.87
Cost index per year	−7.70	0.17	8.38

YEAR	PROJECTED DIVIDEND	YEAR	PROJECTED DIVIDEND	YEAR	PROJECTED DIVIDEND
1	$ .10	8	$ 3.67	15	$ 11.55
2	.16	9	4.76	16	13.08
3	.38	10	6.01	17	14.67
4	.74	11	7.40	18	15.37
5	1.26	12	8.93	19	16.03
6	1.91	13	9.83	20	16.86
7	2.72	14	10.74	Total	$146.17

*The dividend deduction includes any *terminal dividends* due upon surrender of a policy. Terminal dividends are paid only to policyowners who surrender their policies. Theoretically, they represent a return of your share of the insurer's net worth.

**The cash value is not deducted in calculating the net payment cost index.

values and dividends do not increase at constant rates over the period of analysis, as is assumed by this method. Most cash-value policies start with very small increases in cash values (and dividends if the policy is a participating one). These values are then increased rapidly as the policy approaches its twentieth year, the point at which cost comparisons are usually made. Because the method often produces misleading results, its use to compare costs is now illegal in all states.

Interest-Adjusted Net Cost Methods

Most state insurance laws require that life insurers disclose the results of the surrender cost index and the net payments indexes for both the guaranteed values and illustrated values for any policy presented to a prospective customer. These techniques take into consideration the consumer's cost—the interest you could earn if you were to invest the money being illustrated as premium payments over selected periods (usually ten or twenty years).

SURRENDER COST INDEX

The **surrender cost index,** a refinement of the older traditional net cost method, is illustrated in column 2 of table 16–1. There you can see the effect of accumulating both premiums and dividends at interest. On the one hand, you are measuring the sacrifice (opportunity cost) involved in paying premiums; on the other hand, you are measuring the benefits of accumulating dividends at interest. The cash value is not adjusted for interest because it already has built-in interest credits. The net result is a total surrender cost of $5.78 (column 2) for the twenty-year period, as opposed to −$154.06 (column 1) when interest is ignored. The surrender cost of $5.78 may also seem low for insurance over twenty years. This figure would have been higher, however, had the opportunity cost of money been set above 5 percent.

In the traditional net cost method, the average cost per year was calculated simply by dividing the net cost figure by twenty (column 1). When interest at 5 percent is recognized, however, the cost for twenty years is annualized by dividing it by a **conversion factor** of 34.719 to arrive at the surrender cost index (column 2) per year.[4] The index is not simply an average for the twenty-year period but a measure of the annual cost, assuming an interest rate of 5 percent. It is the amount of money required annually to accumulate at 5 percent interest the total surrender cost for the period the policy was assumed to be in force. If you invested $0.17 (that is, 0.1748 before rounding) every year at a net return of 5 percent per annum, you would have $5.78 at the end of twenty years.

NET PAYMENT COST INDEX

Both the traditional net cost method and the surrender cost method are designed to measure the sacrifice you make when you surrender a policy

---

4. One dollar per annum accumulated at 5 percent per year for 20 years = $34.719. You may recognize this accumulation as the future value of an annuity of one dollar.

for cash after having paid premiums for a number of years. The assumption is that you will live for a specified number of years and then surrender the policy for its cash value. The methods measure cost from the "if I live" point of view.

The **net payment cost index,** on the other hand, measures the cost if you keep the policy in force until the day you die. This is the "if I die and the beneficiary gets the policy proceeds" point of view. Column 3 of table 16–1 shows how this index is calculated. The method is appropriate for all policies except type B universal and type B universal-variable policies, where the beneficiary receives both the cash value plus a level amount of protection.

For other types of policies with level death benefits, the net payment index is similar to the surrender cost index, except the net payment index ignores the deduction of cash values at the end of the period. A personal economics view of life insurance assumes the death benefit includes the cash value (plus a decreasing amount of protection).[5] If dividends were the same every year, one could compare the net payments index with that for another policy by simply subtracting the dividend from the annual premium. But dividends are not the same every year; they need to be accumulated at interest.[6]

The surrender cost index and the net payment cost index can both be used when shopping for life insurance. The surrender cost index looks at cost from the "if I live" point of view. The net payment cost index looks at cost from the "if I die" point of view. The consumer must ask: Which index is more important for me? Will I live twenty years (or some other period of time) and then surrender the policy? Or will I keep the policy for a specific period and then die? No one knows when he or she will die. But if you are *sure* you are not going to surrender the policy, then the net payment cost index is more significant to you than the surrender cost index. On the other hand, if you think you may surrender the policy sometime, the reverse is true.

Three critical assumptions underlie these indexes. First, it is assumed that 5 percent is what the consumer would be able to earn by periodically investing relatively small sums over twenty years in a noninsurance investment. Second, the assumption is that the insured will pay all premiums for twenty years and then surrender the policy to the insurer (or die, in the case of the net payments index). Because these assumptions are highly questionable, the result of the calculation is appropriately viewed as an *index,* rather than a precise dollar outlay for the policy's protection element. Index numbers are meaningful only when they are compared to index numbers for other *similar* policies calculated with the same assumptions. Having similar premiums is especially important.

The third critical assumption is whether or not the projected dividends that have been deducted in the calculations are credible. One can assume with reasonable confidence that the future stream of dividends will differ

---

5. See chapter 13 for an explanation.
6. An alternative is to accumulate the dividends and divide the total by the conversion factor (34.719 at 5 percent) to calculate the **equivalent level dividend,** which can be subtracted from the annual premium to arrive at the net payment cost index. In this case, accumulated dividends $190.34 divided by 34.719 = $5.48. In turn, $13.86 minus $5.48 = $8.38.

ETHICAL *Dilemma*

Marketing High-priced Life Insurance

Earl Gustafsen, age 55, has been a special agent with an all-lines (property-liability and life-health) insurer for 26 years. He plans to retire in eight years. As a special agent, he promotes his employer's insurance products to approximately 100 agents who, in turn, sell these products, along with those of other insurers, to consumers. Earl has a strong code of personal ethics, based largely on his religious convictions. He has been successful in his job partly because he has been enthusiastic about his employer's products being among the best in the industry.

Earl is disturbed upon reading an authoritative new book that compares the prices of the leading life insurance policies sold by the 50 largest life insurers in the United States. The comparisons include insurer names. The policies sold by Earl's insurer are among the highest-priced ones in every comparison where they appear, often having prices more than twice as high as similar products. In most instances, the lowest-cost products are issued by financially secure, highly reputable insurers, so Earl has no basis on which to justify the high prices of the products he has been promoting.

You are Earl's close friend. What advice do you have for him? He is considering seeking new employment, although terminating his current employment would impose a 25 percent penalty on the pension benefits he has earned. Should he seek new employment? Should he continue to promote his employer's property, liability, and health products that he still believes in, while not mentioning the life products? Suppose he follows the latter course: how should he respond when agents inquire about his employer's life products? Should he just repress his new-found knowledge and adopt a buyer-beware attitude?

from those shown in table 16–1. What is not known is the direction of the change. If the overall trend in investment returns (compared to current experience) is upward over the selected period, actual dividends can be expected to be larger than the projections. If the trend is downward, dividends are likely to be lower. Trends in mortality and operating expenses are likely to have less influence than investments. The difference between dividend projections and histories is also influenced by insurer management philosophy. In the past, a few insurers have realized good experience but failed to share much with existing policyowners. Consumers can obtain information on actual versus projected dividends for a large sample of insurers by looking at periodic studies published in *Best's Review* (Life-Health edition). If dividends were reduced to zero in all twenty years for the participating policy illustrated in table 16–1, its surrender index per year would be $5.65, rather than $0.17.

It is unwise to select a participating whole life policy on the basis of a low premium. The correlation between premiums and measures of costs, especially the surrender cost measure, is not strong. Premiums and the two measures of interest-adjusted net cost are shown in table 16–2. Ranks are shown in parentheses, with the six companies listed by their 20-year cost indices. Each of the insurers represented in table 16–2 had the highest financial rating given by the A.M. Best Company.

Cash Accumulation Method

The **cash accumulation method** is used to compare the costs of two or more policies. The method is also helpful in comparing a life insurance policy that generates cash values with the alternatives of term life insurance plus a separate investment.[7] Comparisons for the two or more alternative mixes of protection and investments are made by comparing illustrated cash values on the basis of guaranteed minimum values and one or more selected interest rates.

The steps in the technique are:

1. Set premiums (plus investment deposits, if applicable) equal for all alternative products.
2. Set death benefits equal in all years.[8]
3. Simulate cash values for the alternatives at the guaranteed interest rate, plus one or more interest rates.[9]
4. Compare cash values.

Other purchase factors held equal, one chooses the policy with larger cash values. Other primary purchase factors include contract provisions, quality of the insurer, agent service, credibility of illustrations, and whether interest is credited on a new money or a portfolio basis. The decision may still be complicated by different guaranteed interest rates on

TABLE 16–2

Interest-Adjusted Net Costs for Selected Straight Life Policies (issued to a nonsmoking female, age 35, 5 percent interest)

PREMIUM	20-YEAR SURRENDER COST (RANKS IN PARENTHESES)	20-YEAR NET PAYMENT COST (RANKS IN PARENTHESES)
$ 942 (2)	− 1.04 (1)	$5.70 (3)
1001 (4)	.06 (2)	6.71 (4)
1247 (6)	.25 (3)	7.69 (6)
1036 (5)	.63 (4)	5.44 (1)
872 (1)	1.26 (5)	5.58 (2)
947 (3)	1.98 (6)	7.14 (5)

SOURCE: *Best's Flitcraft Compend*, A. M. Best's Co., Inc., 1994.

7. Annual contributions to the separate investment would be determined by deducting the term insurance premium from the premium for the cash value policy. Assumed investment returns for the separate investment fund would be equal to that for the cash value policy, or to a projected after-tax rate that seems reasonable given the risk inherent in the separate investment.

8. It is easy to set death benefits equal in the first year. A computer is useful in maintaining equal death benefits in subsequent years.

9. This step requires annual cash flow calculations of the type discussed in chapter 14. Agents and insurers can provide the numbers to you in the form of sales illustrations using specified assumptions for premiums, death benefits, and interest rates.

contracts, preferences switching from one contract to another in different years, and so forth. The cash accumulation technique and its complications are illustrated in table 16–3.

Table 16–3 compares two universal life policies with type A (level) death benefits for a 45-year-old nonsmoking male. The comparisons have been simplified by showing values only for every fifth year after year five. First, compare the guaranteed values. Policy X has higher values through year ten; policy Y is preferred thereafter. Closer analysis reveals that maximum mortality charges for both policies are based on the same 1980 C.S.O. mortality table. Both also guarantee the same interest rate of 4 percent. The obvious explanation is different expense charges. Further analysis would reveal higher expense charges (especially surrender charges) for policy Y during the first ten years and much lower front-end expenses (relative to policy X) after year ten.

Next, compare the two policies on the basis of current assumptions, reflecting 6.75 percent interest for both policies, current mortality rates (lower for policy X, as revealed by analysis not shown here), and contractual expense charges. Between years two and five[10] the preference is for policy X. After year ten, the clear preference on a cash accumulation basis is for policy Y. Closer analysis of data (not presented here, for simplicity) shows much lower expense charges for policy Y, especially front-end expenses expressed as a percentage of premiums after year ten.

The cost analysis on both guaranteed and 6.75 percent interest assumptions leaves the consumer with the dilemma of preferring policy X in the early policy years and policy Y later. This suggests a need to consider how likely you are to surrender your policy (or request a maximum policy loan) in the first ten years or so. If your estimate of surrender is low, you are

TABLE 16–3

Two Universal Life Policies (issued to nonsmoking male, age 45)

POLICIES X and Y*			CASH SURRENDER VALUES			
			Guaranteed Basis		Current Assumptions	
Year	Planned Annual Premium	Death Benefit	Policy X (4.0%)	Policy Y (4.0%)	Policy X (6.75%)	Policy Y (6.75%)
1	$1,500	$100,000	$ 0	$ 0	$ 0	$ 132
2	1,500	100,000	773	342	889	617
3	1,500	100,000	1,976	820	2,246	1,326
4	1,500	100,000	3,195	1,934	3,678	2,739
5	1,500	100,000	4,432	3,069	5,186	4,251
10	1,500	100,000	10,788	10,100	14,389	14,907
15	1,500	100,000	16,928	17,803	27,065	30,616
20	1,500	100,000	22,027	23,520	44,867	49,789
25	1,500	100,000	23,662	26,694	69,491	76,568
30	1,500	100,000	17,833	23,513	105,091	116,062

*In the years not shown in this comparison, assumed annual premium payments continue at $1,500 and death benefits are $100,000.

10. Details for all years (not shown in table 16–3) show the shift to higher values for policy Y occurs in year eight.

likely to consider policy Y to be preferable on a cash accumulation basis, other factors held equal. If your likelihood of early surrender is high, you should purchase a term policy. Expense charges make most cash values unattractive in early contract years. Surrender charges do not affect accumulation values. The fact that cash values equal accumulation values after surrender charges disappear helps make universal life contracts attractive in the long run.

Yearly Rate of Return Method

With a cash-value life insurance policy, the premium covers two valuable elements: a protection element and a cash value element. The value of the two-part package can be judged in either of two ways. First, methods like the interest-adjusted surrender cost attach an assumed rate of return (for example, 5 percent) to the cash value element of the contract in order to determine a cost of the protection element.[11] Alternatively, you can attach, by assuming a price of annual renewable term insurance (ART), a value to the protection element of your policy in order to calculate a rate of return for the investment portion. The two methods rank policy values equally well. Essentially, examining the rate of return on the cash value element adds sophistication and insight to the cash accumulation method.

Perhaps the major advantage of a rate of return measure is that most people—by having some familiarity with rates of return on bank certificates of deposit, government bonds, and other savings and investment instruments—have an intuitive feel for whether a given rate of return figure is low, high, or somewhere in between. A refinement to keep in mind, of course, is that low-risk investments such as treasury bills are expected to produce much lower returns than higher-risk investment alternatives such as common stocks. The portfolios backing most types of cash value life insurance (with the exception of common stock and other equity funds available through variable life policies) are typically somewhere in the middle of the spectrum of investment risk (and expected returns). Thus, medium investment returns are the proper norm in judging rates of return on universal, straight, and other forms of whole life insurance.

Professor Joseph M. Belth of Indiana University developed a formula called the **yearly rate of return** (YROR) to determine the rate of return on a particular year's investment in a cash value life insurance policy.[12] The method is especially useful in answering the question: How did my insurer treat me last year? An insurer's annual premium notice probably includes the necessary data, except for an ART rate for your nearest age during the year of analysis. YRORs for a period of years also can help detect trends or changes. Examination of YRORs for future years, using illustrated data, will help you decide whether your insurer plans to treat you equitably through-

11. A technical weakness of the surrender cost method is its division by the face amount of a policy rather than the amount of protection (that is, the face amount minus the cash value) in determining the cost per $1,000.
12. Joseph M. Belth, *Life Insurance: A Consumer's Handbook,* 2nd ed. (Bloomington, Ind.: Indiana University Press, 1985): pp. 89–91.

out the expected life of your policy. To make this judgment you would want to calculate estimated YRORs for several future years, perhaps to age 75 or so. Request current data from your insurer, recognizing that dividends on participating policies and current interest rates on interest-sensitive policies will be illustrations rather than guarantees.

Let us look at the formula for calculating YROR figures.

$$YROR_t = \frac{CV_t + D_t + (YP_t)\,(F_t - CV_t)\,(0.001)}{P_t + CV_{t-1}} - 1$$

where:

$YROR_t$	=	yearly rate of return for policy year t
CV_t	=	cash value (actual or illustrated) at the end of policy year t
D_t	=	policyowner dividend (actual or illustrated) at the end of policy year t, (if not already deducted from the premium or used to buy paid-up additional amounts of insurance and thereby already reflected in total cash values)
YP_t	=	assumed yearly price of ART insurance per $1,000 of protection for policy year t
F_t	=	death benefit (actual or illustrated) at the end of policy year t
P_t	=	premium (actual or illustrated)[13] paid at the beginning of policy year t.

Benefits derived from your policy are expressed in the numerator of the formula. Your *investment* in the contract for the year is captured in the denominator. Your benefits consist of:

1. Cash value at the end of the year (CV_t).

2. The current year's dividend (D_t).

3. The value of insurance protection during the year [(YP_t) ($F_t - CV_t$) (.001)].

Recognize that the value of protection for the year is determined by multiplying a term insurance rate times an amount equal to the death benefit minus the cash value [$F_t - CV_t$], expressed in thousands of dollars of protection (hence the multiplication by .001). Your investment for the year is the sum of:

1. The premium you pay in advance for the current year (P_t).

2. Your cash value in the contract at the beginning of this year (CV_{t-1}).

In summary,

$$YROR = \frac{Benefits}{Investments} - 1$$

To illustrate, we will calculate YROR for the twenty-fifth year of an actual participating straight life policy issued to one of the authors in 1969. His latest premium notice includes the following:

---

13. "Actual or illustrated" has been included in the definition of terms for the YROR formula to recognize that the analysis can be made with actual (historical) data, illustrated (projected) policy values, or a combination of actual and illustrated values.

Face amount, including paid-up additions = 70,101

Annual premium = 558

Current year's annual dividend (used to purchase
paid-up additions) = 1,773

Current cash value = 32,121

Cash value increase during the past year = 2,747

The other data needed to calculate YROR is an ART premium rate for a male age 55. Assume we do not have access to ART rates. A reasonable proxy is to use a rate equal to 75 percent of the male age 55 death rate in the 1980 CSO mortality table reproduced in Appendix F.[14] The result is: $.75 \times 10.47 = 7.85$.

With these data,

$$YROR = \frac{32,121 + 0 + (7.85)(70,101 - 32,121)(.001)}{558 + (32,121 - 2,747)} - 1$$

$$= \frac{32,419.14}{29,932} - 1$$

$$= 1.0831 - 1 = 8.31\%$$

An 8.31 percent return for the twenty-fifth year relative to returns on investments with similar risks and tax characteristics in that year leads to the conclusion that this existing policyowner is being treated well by his insurer.

Linton Yield Method

The **Linton yield method** ascribes a value to the protection element of the policy for each year, based on current premium rates. This value shows how much of each year's premium should be allocated to protection. The balance of the premium is allocated to savings. By comparing the accumulated value of the hypothetical savings stream with the policy's cash value at the end of any period, the compound annual rate of return (ROR) can be calculated. Look for the annual rate of return that the hypothetical stream of savings would need to earn to equal the amount of cash value in the insurance policy at the end of the period (a computer helps in making this calculation). If the same assumption is made about the cost of protection per thousand dollars, then the one with the higher ROR is a better buy. This average ROR over a period of years is a desirable adjunct to YROR figures.

14. The 1980 CSO mortality table added safety factors to its underlying mortality rates. The result is conservative death rates that exceed competitive rates for annual renewable term insurance. Implicit in the use of a "competitive" rate for term insurance is the assumption that the insured meets "average" insurability standards.

Some people prefer the YROR and ROR methods to interest-adjusted indexes because they avoid the problem of selecting an interest rate for a long period of time.[15] Annual renewable term rates used in rate of return methods, on the other hand, are guaranteed for the life of the policy.[16] Note that the ART rate selected is crucial to the computation of rates of return. The lower the ART rate, the lower the rate of return and *vice versa*. Thus, instead of arguing about which interest rate to select, those who use YROR and/or ROR for policy cost comparison can debate which ART rates should be used. After ART rates are selected, the same rates need to be used for all contracts being compared.

One of the shortcomings of YROR and ROR methods for persons buying life insurance for protection is that they emphasize *return* rather than *cost*. The term "return" is typically used in connection with an investment. What return did you make this year on the stock you bought? *Life insurance, on the other hand, is bought by most people primarily for protection.* Rate of return calculations are desirable primarily for single-premium, high-premium current assumption, high-premium universal, and other life policies purchased with significant investment motives.

ROR ILLUSTRATIONS

A study by Professors Cherin and Hutchins of San Diego State University revealed a broad array of Linton rates of return for universal life insurance policies. A summary of their results is shown in table 16–4. The results

TABLE 16–4

20-Year Rates of Return for 60 Universal Life Policies (Males age 45; $100,000 increasing death benefit; $2,000 annual premium payments for 20 years)

	NUMBER OF INSURERS		
ROR	Current Advertised Interest Rate	ROR with Low Term Rates	ROR with Average Term Rates
13.00 – 13.99%	1		
12.00 – 12.99	22		2
11.00 – 11.99	22		5
10.00 – 10.99	8		12
9.00 – 9.99	2	4	23
8.00 – 8.99	4	4	9
7.00 – 7.99	1	15	4
6.00 – 6.99		19	4
5.00 – 5.99		9	1
4.00 – 4.99		1	
3.00 – 3.99		5	
2.00 – 2.99		2	
1.00 – 1.99		1	
Mean	11.19%	6.41%	9.36%

SOURCE: Cherin and Hutchins, pp. 700–701.

NOTE: "ROR" means rate of return.

15. In our net payment cost comparison we used 5 percent. This is the rate required by all insurance regulators. It may seem low at times by current standards but not compared with historic levels. The real concern, of course, is what interest rates will be in the future.
16. Reentry term rates should not be used in rate of return calculations.

were calculated using both low- and medium-level term insurance rates. The average current advertised rate at the time of purchase in 1983 was 11.19 percent. Crediting the advertised rate for each insurer and deducting its current mortality rates and contractual expense charges over a twenty-year period produced average RORs of 6.41 percent using the lowest term rates found for a sample of twenty insurers selling yearly renewable term insurance. When RORs were calculated using average term insurance rates for the twenty insurers, the average ROR increased to 9.36 percent. The results are shown in table 16–4. The differences in the three average returns show us that advertised current rates, relative to buying term insurance and investing the difference, are likely to be higher than true rates of return on the cash value element of universal life insurance (e.g., 11.19 percent advertised, versus 9.36 percent with average term rates). The results also show the sensitivity of the ROR to different term insurance rates used in calculations.[17]

---

17. Anthony C. Cherin and Robert E. Hutchins, "The Rate of Return on Universal Life Insurance," *Journal of Risk and Insurance*, Vol. LIV, No. 4 (1987): pp. 691–711.

Consumer Applications

Comparing Costs

COMPARISON OF TERM POLICY COSTS

It is easier to compare term policy costs than those of cash-value policies because you evaluate term purely from an "if I die" point of view. There are no cash values to consider. With guaranteed cost, level-premium term policies, all you compare is premium rates. If, for example, the annual premium rate for a ten-year level-premium term policy is $5 per $1,000 from Company C and $6 per $1,000 from Company D, it is clear that the policy from Company C is less expensive.

ART policies, however, have a different rate per $1,000 each year. Two guaranteed cost policies may have approximately equal premium rates for the first year—or several years—but be quite different thereafter. Cost comparison for participating policies is more complicated. Even if the premium rates for two policies are identical every year, it is unlikely that dividends will be. Thus, the time factor and the applicable interest rate cannot be ignored.

To take an extreme case, suppose two participating ART policies have identical premium rates for ten years, but Policy J pays a $1 per $1,000 dividend at the end of every year and Policy K pays a $10 per $1,000 dividend at the end of the tenth year. At 5 percent interest, the accumulated value of dividends paid by Policy J is $2.02 ($12.02 − $10.00) more than the dividend paid by Policy K. Because of the time value of money, dividends paid in early years reduce cost more than dividends paid later, just as large dividends reduce the cost more than small dividends.

Clearly, except for level-premium, guaranteed-cost policies, the cost of term insurance cannot be compared by looking at premium rates. Instead, interest-adjusted net payment cost indexes must be compared. Remember that lower index numbers mean better buys—holding quality of company, agent service, and other factors constant.

COMPARISONS OF CASH-VALUE POLICIES

Interest-adjusted surrender cost indexes, net payment indexes, the cash accumulation method, YROR, and ROR results all help you decide on the relative value of competing life insurance proposals. They can also help you decide how an insurer has treated you as a consumer historically, especially the YROR method.

Since most insurers issuing universal life and current assumption life policies express significant expense charges as rear-end surrender charges, it is important to recognize these expenses in the analysis. The conservative approach is to use surrender values as the cash values in all calculations. We, however, recommend that costs (or rates of return) be calculated on two bases: "if I surrender" and "if I continue." The former uses surrender values in the calculations; the latter uses accumulation values. The weight to attach to each approach will depend on how likely you are to surrender a universal (or current assumption whole life) policy. The weight that you attach to the "if I continue" index for a specific year would be one minus your surrender probability, since you will either surrender or continue the policy in a particular year. You may also consider the "if I surrender" figure as a maximum cost and the "if I continue" figure as a minimum cost.

All methods will show that cash value forms of life insurance are poor buys *if* you surrender the policy within a few years. Over long periods of time, their costs are almost always lower than the cost for alternative term insurance. After you have identified a few low-cost policies, select one from a financially strong insurer with an impressive investment track record. Also, pick one with an investment strategy consistent with your own investment objectives. For example, if you want to maximize long-run returns, go with an insurer that calculates returns on a portfolio basis. What you are looking for is a policy that, over time, has low mortality charges, low expense loads, and high investment credits to your cash value account.[18] This combination will produce both a low cost for protection and a relatively high ROR. Any study of interest-adjusted surrender costs and ROR, using the same sample of policies, will have a strong

---

18. Low expense loads are most likely to be found with "no-load" or "low-load" policies. All policies have implicit, if not explicit, expense charges. Consequently, there are no true "no-load" policies. These policies are primarily promoted by fee-only financial planners. When calculating price in this instance, deduct the financial planner's fee from the cash value, since this is a substitute for insurance company marketing expenses.

negative correlation, since they are different, but valid, approaches to determining value. The significance of this correlation is that if you have one of these measures you do not need the other, since they represent two ways of obtaining similar contract rankings. Just be sure you have one reliable measure of consumer value. ROR methods are more reliable than interest-adjusted methods. Both are suspect when non-guaranteed illustrated values are used, including historically high current interest rates.

Key Terms

traditional net cost method
surrender cost index
conversion factor
net payment cost index

equivalent level dividend
cash accumulation method
yearly rate of return
Linton yield method

Discussion Questions

1. Name the steps used in calculating an interest-adjusted surrender cost index. How do these steps differ from those for the traditional net cost method?

2. J. Edwin Logan says, "I am never going to surrender the straight life insurance policy I buy. Therefore, all I am going to use for cost comparison purposes is the net payment cost index." Do you share this view? Why, or why not?

3. Using the cash accumulation method to compare life insurance policies, you generally prefer the contract with the larger cash value. What factors might lead you to a different decision?

4. The yearly rate of return (YROR) method can be viewed as a way to relate your benefits for a particular year to your investments in the contract for that year. Describe, in words, the benefits and investments reflected in this method.

5. What are the basic similarities and differences between the interest-adjusted surrender cost index and the Linton yield method (ROR) for comparing life insurance costs?

6. In addition to a policy premium, what other factors must be considered when comparing life insurance costs?

7. Usually some assumptions must be made before the cost of an insurance policy can be calculated. What are these assumptions, and why are they important?

8. What is the major shortcoming of the YROR and ROR methods? Why might these methods not be appropriate measures of cost for the average life insurance consumer?

9. Explain why it is easier to compare costs for term policies as opposed to whole life or other cash value policies.

10. Your eccentric Uncle Bud has just made the following statement: "I'm not going to waste my time talking to five different insurance agents. I've known Jim Spitz all my life, and he represents a reputable company. I know he'll give me a good deal." How would you respond to your uncle?

16.1 Betty McLees, age 35, has just heard a sales presentation by an agent who told her that all cash value life insurance gives very poor returns on investment. The agent told her that she should buy term life insurance only, and invest the difference between the term insurance premiums and whole life premiums in a growth-oriented common stock mutual fund that the agent sells. Betty has owned a $50,000 participating whole life insurance policy since she was 23. She is considering cashing it in to pay the first premium for an equal amount of 20-year decreasing yearly renewable term life insurance, and investing the remaining cash value in the mutual fund. In the current year, the term insurance cost for Betty would be $1.75 per $1,000.

1. What factors should Betty consider before making this decision?

2. She has a current premium notice that includes the following information: annual premium of $530, face amount of $50,000, annual dividend (used to reduce the premium due) of $200, current cash value of $5,000, and cash value increase during the last year of $650. Can you calculate a rate of return that will let her know how her insurer is treating her? What is the rate of return for this latest year?

16.2 Carlos Fañaya is not happy with the life insurance surrender cost comparisons he has read about in a consumer magazine. "They just don't use realistic interest rates in making the cost calculations," he says. "There is no way that I would be happy with anything less than 12 percent on my investments. Therefore, the comparisons have no meaning to me."

1. What advice would you give Carlos?

2. How would you explain the interest rate assumptions?

16.3 Joseph Kannady is favorably impressed by the proposal he has for a participating whole life policy with the Pan Mexican Mutual Life Insurance Company. The sales illustration shows ten- and twenty-year interest-adjusted surrender and net payments costs on both a guaranteed cost basis and an illustrations basis. The difference is that the illustrations numbers deduct the value of projected dividends (see table 16.1, columns 2 and 3).

1. Joseph learns from the agent that Pan Mexican projects its dividends on the assumption that its current experience with respect to investment portfolio returns, mortality experience, and operating expenses will continue throughout the policy's life (possibly to Joseph's age 100). Current investment returns in general and Pan Mexican's average portfolio returns are at historic highs. What confidence exists that Pan Mexican will fulfill its dividend projections on Joseph's policy?

2. Joseph is interested in comparing Pan Mexican's actual dividend history with illustrations it made in the past. Why might he want this information? In what publication can periodic studies of actual versus projected dividends be found?

CHAPTER 17

Life and Health Insurance Provided by Social Security

Introduction We have identified and evaluated the major life risks to which a family is exposed and examined the voluntary methods available for handling the economic losses caused by death. To effectively plan how to deal with these risks, it is necessary to consider possible Social Security benefits that may be available as well. Social Security provides income continuation in the event of death, disability, or retirement. It also provides medical expense benefits for disabled or retired persons and specified dependents. In 1994, over 42 million beneficiaries were receiving some type of cash benefit under Social Security. About 71 percent of the beneficiaries were retired or dependents of retirees, about 12 percent were disabled workers or dependents, and about 17 percent were survivors of former workers.[1]

Social Security is the foundation of employee benefits for most U.S. workers, covering most full-time, part-time, and temporary employees. Employers and employees pay a significant payroll tax to fund the program.

After reading this chapter, you will have examined these questions:

1. What is Social Security?
2. Who is covered under Social Security?
3. When are you eligible for benefits?
4. What types of benefits are available?
5. What are the benefit amounts?
6. How are benefits financed?
7. How is Social Security administered?
8. How financially sound is the Social Security system today? How sound will it be in the future?
9. What are the global trends in social security systems worldwide?

---

1. These statistics are from the *Social Security Bulletin,* Summer 1994, Vol. 57, No. 2, pp. 90–132. The Social Security law specifies many requirements that must be met to qualify for certain benefits. When you have a potential claim, consult the nearest district office of the Social Security Administration. This chapter covers the major provisions of the program but may not mention a point that could affect your claim.

Definition of Social Security

There are many governmental programs designed to provide economic security for individuals and families. Both public assistance and **social insurance** programs are (1) organized and undertaken by the government and (2) have the broad social purpose of reducing want and destitution. However, social insurance is different from public assistance: social insurance is an *insurance* program that is compulsory for nearly all Americans, eligibility criteria and benefits are specified by law, and financing is wholly or partially covered by the employer. Unlike public assistance (or *welfare*), employers and employees pay into the social insurance system to earn their right to benefits. Some examples of social insurance programs include **Social Security,** workers' compensation, and unemployment compensation.[2]

Public assistance or welfare benefits are financed from federal and state funds that come from general revenues and are not based on any contributions that have been made by the recipients or on their behalf. Some examples of public assistance programs are Aid to Families with Dependent Children (AFDC) and Medicaid, both of which pay benefits solely based on need. While public assistance programs have a role in providing economic security, they are not insurance programs since the insurance principles of measuring the risk of the insured or spreading the cost of losses among those exposed do not apply. While it is appropriate and necessary to include possible social insurance benefits in individual financial planning—in the event of economic loss due to premature death, disability, or retirement—it is not appropriate to include public assistance; one of the purposes of financial planning is to avoid the need for public assistance.

When most people talk about Social Security, they are referring to a social insurance program that was created in 1935. Originally, this program was a compulsory pension plan known as "Old-Age Insurance" or OAI. Later, survivors' benefits were added and the program was referred to as "Old-Age and Survivors' Insurance" or OASI. When disability benefits were added, it became OASDI and, with the addition of hospital and medical benefits, it became the **OASDHI** program. The Social Security Administration now refers to the program as "Social Security" in its publications.[3]

Coverage Requirements

Today, nearly all employees in private industry, most self-employed persons, and members of the armed forces are covered by Social Security. Coverage is compulsory for well over 90 percent of all workers in the United States, which means that Social Security taxes must be paid on their wages. The major exceptions are railroad workers, who are covered by the Railroad Retirement Act, and federal government employees who, before 1984, were covered by other programs. Prior to 1984, state and local government bodies could elect not to cover certain employees under Social Security. With few exceptions, this option is no longer allowed. Municipal

---

2. Workers' compensation and unemployment compensation are social insurance programs discussed in chapter 12.
3. One of the most complete sources of information concerning the Social Security program is the *Social Security Handbook,* which is frequently revised by the Social Security Administration and is available from the U.S. Government Printing Office, Washington, D.C.

governments that elected out prior to 1984 do have the option to voluntarily join the Social Security program. Ministers are covered automatically unless they request a waiver on religious grounds. Members of religious sects whose beliefs prohibit acceptance of benefits are exempt.

Eligibility for Benefits

In order to be eligible to receive benefits, you must achieve insured status. With insured status you may be either fully insured, currently insured, or disability insured, depending upon your work history. If you are **fully insured,** most types of Social Security benefits are payable. If you do not have enough work experience to be fully insured, you may be **currently insured,** and you would be eligible for some survivor benefits. The amount of work required to become insured is measured in quarters of coverage. In 1995, an employee earned one quarter of credit for each $630 of earnings, up to a maximum of four quarters each year. You get four quarters of coverage for $2,520, even if you earned this much in only one day. The quarterly measure of earnings is adjusted every year to account for increases in average wages.

You are fully insured when you have forty quarters of coverage, or when you have a minimum of six quarters of coverage and, if greater, at least as many quarters of coverage as there are years elapsing after 1950 (or after you reach age 21, if later). For example, a person age 25 who has six quarters of coverage is fully insured, whereas a person age 40 needs nineteen quarters of coverage to be fully insured. You are currently insured if you have at least six quarters of coverage in the thirteen-quarter period ending with the quarter of death. **Disability insured** status is gained by having twenty quarters of coverage in the forty quarters ending when disability begins. Less rigorous disability requirements apply if you are under age 31 or blind.

Types of Benefits

The types of benefits available from Social Security are apparent from the acronym, OASDHI: (1) old age (or retirement), (2) survivors', (3) disability, and (4) health (or Medicare) benefits. The insured status of a worker determines who (i.e., the worker and/or his or her family) is entitled to collect these benefits.

OLD AGE OR RETIREMENT BENEFITS

A fully insured worker is eligible to receive most benefits, including retirement income benefits. A spouse or divorced spouse of a retired worker is entitled to a monthly benefit if he or she is (1) at least age 62 or (2) caring for at least one child of the retired worker (under age 16, or disabled if disability began before age 22). A dependent child, grandchild, or great-grandchild of a retired worker who is (1) under age 18, (2) a full-time student between 18 and 19, or (3) disabled, if disability began before age 22, is also entitled to a benefit. The beneficiaries of retirement benefits are shown in figure 17–1.

FIGURE 17–1
....

Who Gets Monthly Benefits If a
Fully Insured Worker Retires?

1. Retired worker (at age 62 or over).
2. Spouse or divorced spouse of retired worker (age 62 or over).
3. Spouse of retired worker (at any age, if caring for a child under 16 or disabled).
4. Dependent child of retired worker (under age 18, or 18 or 19 if in school).

Age 65 has become the traditional **normal retirement age** in our society. A fully insured worker can elect to receive full **retirement benefits** at age 65, or reduced benefits as early as age 62. However, in recognition of financial pressures on the Social Security system and the increased life expectancy for men and women today, the Social Security Amendments of 1983 redefined the age for full benefits eligibility. Beginning with persons who reach age 62 in the year 2000, the age of qualification for full benefits will increase in steps until it levels at age 67 in 2022. The new normal retirement ages are shown in figure 17–2.

SURVIVORS' BENEFITS

Survivors' benefits protect the surviving dependents of a fully or currently insured deceased worker. The surviving spouse is entitled to monthly income payments if caring for a child who is under age 16 or a child who is disabled by a disability that began before age 22. A child of a fully or currently insured deceased worker is entitled to benefits if he or she (1) is under age 18, is disabled by a disability that began before age 22, or is age 18 or 19 and a full-time student attending an elementary or secondary school, (2) was dependent on the deceased worker, and (3) is not married. Figures 17–3 and 17–4 summarize who gets monthly benefits if a fully insured or currently insured worker dies.

A widow or widower of a fully insured deceased worker is qualified for benefits at age 50 if disabled, and otherwise at age 60. A divorced spouse also qualifies, subject to having been married to the worker at least ten years and not being remarried. A parent of a fully insured deceased worker is entitled to benefits if he or she (1) is at least age 62, (2) was receiving at least half of his or her support from the child,[4] (3) has not remarried since the child's death, and (4) is not entitled to a retirement or disability benefit equal to or larger than this survivors' benefit.

YEAR OF BIRTH	NORMAL RETIREMENT AGE	YEAR OF BIRTH	NORMAL RETIREMENT AGE
Before 1938	65	1955	66 + 2 months
1938	65 + 2 months	1956	66 + 4 months
1939	65 + 4 months	1957	66 + 6 months
1940	65 + 6 months	1958	66 + 8 months
1941	65 + 8 months	1959	66 + 10 months
1942	65 + 10 months	1960	67
1943–1954	66		

....
4. At the time of the child's death, or at the beginning of a disability that lasted until the child's death, or when the child became eligible for retirement or disability benefits.

FIGURE 17–3

Who Gets Monthly Benefits If a
Fully Insured Worker Dies?

1. Spouse or divorced spouse of deceased worker (at least age 60, or at any age if caring for a child who is under age 16 or who is disabled).
2. Disabled spouse of deceased worker (at age 50 or over).
3. Dependent parent of deceased worker (at age 62 or over).
4. Dependent child or grandchild of deceased worker.
5. Dependent child age 18 or over if disabled since before age 22.

FIGURE 17–4

Who Gets Monthly Benefits If a
Currently Insured Worker Dies?

1. Dependent child or grandchild of deceased worker.
2. Widow or widower (not remarried) of deceased worker (any age if caring for a child).

In addition to these monthly benefits, a small lump-sum death payment of $255 is made upon the death of a worker who is fully or currently insured. It is paid to the spouse living with the worker at the time of death, or a spouse otherwise entitled, or children entitled as described above. In the absence of a spouse or children, the death benefit is not paid. It is the only benefit that has not increased since the Social Security legislation was passed in 1935.

DISABILITY BENEFITS

A fully insured worker who has a medically determinable physical or mental condition that prevents any *substantial gainful work*[5] is entitled to monthly **disability benefits** after a waiting period of five full months if he or she is under age 65 and has been disabled for twelve months or is expected to be disabled for at least twelve months, or if he or she has a disability that is expected to result in death. The definition of disability for a widow or widower of a deceased worker is even more restrictive.[6] A spouse or child of a disabled worker is entitled to a monthly benefit upon meeting the same qualifications as those previously listed in connection with retirement benefits. Figure 17–5 shows who gets monthly benefits if a fully insured worker is disabled. Note that to receive benefits the worker must be fully insured, meet the disability insured status, and meet the definition of disability. Disability benefits may be stopped if the disabled worker refuses to participate in rehabilitation. They may be reduced if disability benefits are received from workers' compensation or under a federal, state, or local law.[7]

HEALTH OR MEDICARE BENEFITS

Medicare consists of two parts: (A) the basic hospital insurance benefits plan and (B) the voluntary supplementary medical benefits plan. Eligibility requirements are shown in figure 17–6.

5. Earnings of $500 or more per month are considered substantial.
6. Rather than being unable to engage in "substantial gainful activity," a widow or widower must be unable to engage in "any gainful activity." In addition, disability is determined solely on the basis of the severity of the impairment. For workers, factors such as age, education, and work experience are considered.
7. Social Security disability benefits are reduced if benefits from all of these sources exceed 80 percent of the highest of several measures of your former earnings.

FIGURE 17–5

Who Gets Monthly Benefits If a Fully
Insured Worker is Disabled?

1. Disabled worker.
2. Dependent child or grandchild of disabled worker.
3. Spouse of disabled worker (if caring for child under 16 or disabled).
4. Spouse of disabled worker (at least age 62).

Note: A worker with disability that began at or after age 31 must have worked in covered employment half of the last ten years. A worker with a disability that began before age 31 must have worked in covered employment half of the quarters between age 21 and the onset of disability (but not less than six quarters).

FIGURE 17–6

Who Is Eligible for Medicare?

1. Almost all persons age 65 and older.
2. Persons under age 65 who have been entitled to disability benefits for at least 24 months (but not their dependents).
3. Insured workers and dependents of all ages needing kidney dialysis or a transplant.
4. Disabled widows or widowers under 65, disabled divorced spouses under 65, and disabled children 18 or older may be eligible.*

*For details, contact a Social Security office.

Medicare Part A: Hospital Benefits

Part A hospital insurance benefits are automatically effective upon application, without payment of premium, for persons who are eligible for Social Security or railroad retirement benefits at age 65. You do not have to retire to be covered for hospital benefits; however, Medicare is the secondary payer for persons who continue to work between ages 65 and 69 and have medical coverage through their employers. Individuals age 65 and over who are not eligible for Social Security or railroad retirement benefits may enroll in Medicare Part A by paying a premium ($261 per month in 1995) if they also enroll for Medicare Part B, the supplementary medical benefits plan. The Medicare Part A plan provides:

1. Inpatient hospital services for up to ninety days in each **spell of illness or benefit period,**[8] subject to a flat amount of deductible during the first sixty days and a daily coinsurance charge during the next thirty days. At 1995 benefit levels, you would pay the first $716 of hospital charges and Medicare would pay the rest for up to sixty days. For the next thirty days, you would pay $179 a day and Medicare would pay the rest.[9] A ninety-day hospital confinement, therefore, would cost you $6,086.[10]

2. Inpatient services during a sixty-day lifetime reserve, available with you paying a coinsurance rate of $358 per day in 1995.

3. Posthospital extended care in a skilled nursing facility for up to 100 days in each spell of illness. After the first twenty days, you would pay $89.50 per day (in 1995) and Medicare would pay the rest.

8. A **spell of illness** begins the day a patient is admitted to a hospital. It ends when the patient has been in neither a hospital nor a facility primarily furnishing skilled nursing or rehabilitative services for sixty days. There is no limit on the number of ninety-day benefit periods a person can have. A 190-day lifetime limit applies to inpatient psychiatric care.
9. The Medicare deductibles and participation amounts are increased annually.
10. The assumption here is that hospital charges will always exceed $179/day at all U.S. hospitals for days 60–90. This is a reasonable assumption.

4. Posthospital home health services for an unlimited time, if home-bound.

5. Hospice care, primarily in your home, when your life expectancy is six months or less. No payment is made in a hospital nursing facility or home for what is considered primarily custodial care.

Medicare Part B: Medical Benefits

Anyone eligible for the basic hospital benefits plan and anyone age 65 or over who is either a citizen or a lawfully admitted alien with at least five years residence in the United States is eligible for **Part B medical benefits,** which are supplementary. Those receiving Social Security or railroad retirement benefits are enrolled automatically unless they elect not to be covered. Each person who enrolls pays a monthly premium, which was $46.10 in 1995.

Part B requires you to pay an annual deductible (of $100 in 1995), as well as 20 percent of allowable charges for most covered expenses.[11] Services for which Part B pays 100 percent include home health services and clinical laboratory services (such as blood tests and urinalysis). Part B pays 50 percent of approved charges for most outpatient mental health services. Figure 17–7 shows the types of medical expenses covered by Medicare Part B.

Noncovered charges include routine physical examinations; routine care of the eyes, ears, and feet; drugs; most immunizations; and cosmetic surgery. Doctors must bill Medicare directly, rather than having patients file Medicare claims. Some physicians and surgeons accept Medicare's reasonable charge as full payment, but others charge patients an additional fee above the reasonable charge. However, beginning in 1991, doctors are limited in the additional amount they may charge patients.

Amount of Benefits

As we have discussed, Medicare benefits are stated in terms of services provided. Payments may be made directly to the provider of care or on a reimbursement basis to the insured. The amount paid is the same for all

FIGURE 17–7

Medical Expenses Covered by Medicare Part B

1. Doctors' services, including house calls, office visits, and services in the hospital and other institutions.
2. Hospital diagnostic studies and other services on an outpatient basis.
3. Services and supplies to outpatients.
4. Outpatient physical therapy and speech pathology furnished by specified agencies.
5. Dentists' bills for bone surgery.
6. Outpatient psychiatric treatment.
7. Home health services, up to 100 visits per year.
8. Diagnostic tests.
9. Radiation therapy.
10. Surgical dressings and similar items.
11. Ambulance service under certain circumstances.
12. Dialysis services and supplies.
13. Outpatient rehabilitation services.

11. Allowable charges are only *reasonable costs,* as determined by the Health Care Financing Administration of the Department of Health and Human Services, and these are payable only for amounts beyond the $100 deductible and 20 percent copayment requirement.

TABLE 17–1

Social Security Benefits

			BENEFITS FOR LIVING WORKERS AND THEIR DEPENDENTS			
			Benefits for Dependents			
			Spouse Not Caring for Child		**Child or Spouse Caring for Child**	**Maximum Family Benefit for Disability**
Average Indexed Monthly Earnings	**Age 65 Retirement Benefit or Disability Benefit**	**Age 62 Retirement Benefit**	**Age 65**	**Age 62**		
	100% of PIA	80%* of PIA	50% of PIA	37.5% of PIA	50% of PIA	**
500	407	326	203	153	203	425
1,000	567	454	283	213	283	850
1,500	727	582	363	273	363	1,090
2,000	887	710	443	333	443	1,330
2,500	1,047	838	523	393	523	1,570
3,000	1,133	906	566	425	566	1,699
3,500	1,208	966	604	453	604	1,812

*For those born in 1960 or later, the retirement benefit at age 62 will be 70% of PIA under current law.

**The maximum family benefit for disability benefits is subject to a constraint that limits the family benefit to the smaller of (a) 150 percent of PIA or (b) 85 percent of the disabled workers AIME (or 100 percent of PIA, if larger).

persons enrolled. In contrast, the amount of survivors', disability, and retirement benefits is not the same for everyone. Instead, these benefits are based on the insured's covered earnings since 1950 or after the year the insured reached age 21, if later.

PRIMARY INSURANCE AMOUNT

The **primary insurance amount** (PIA) is the basic unit used to determine the amount of monthly benefits. Before 1978, you could calculate your average monthly earnings by a fairly simple method and determine your PIA from a table that showed the PIA for various levels of average monthly earnings. Because this method penalized workers with a long work history that included the lower wages of fifteen or twenty years ago, the PIA is now based on a person's **average indexed monthly earnings** (AIME). In the calculation of the AIME, earnings for prior years, up to the maximum Social Security wage base, are adjusted to what they would have been if wage levels in earlier years had been the same as they are now.

Consequently, there is no easy way to make an estimate of your PIA. You cannot just calculate a simple average of your wages and consult a table. The Social Security Administration has computerized wage histories for all workers, and the PIA calculation is made by the computer when an application for benefits is processed. Unless you apply for benefits, the only way you can obtain an estimate of your PIA is to calculate it yourself. At your request, the Social Security Administration will furnish a record of your historical Social Security earnings.

After you have determined your AIME, your PIA in 1995 would be determined by the following formula:

TABLE 17–1 (continued)

Social Security Benefits

BENEFITS FOR SURVIVORS OF DECEASED WORKERS					
Spouse Not Caring for Child					
Age 65	Age 50 and Disabled or Age 60	One Child Alone	One Parent	Spouse and One Child or Two Children Alone or Two Parents	Maximum Family Benefit for Survivors and Retirement
100% of PIA	71.5% of PIA	75% of PIA	82.5% of PIA	150% of PIA	150–175% of PIA
407	291	305	336	610	610
567	405	425	467	850	879
727	520	545	600	1,090	1,314
887	634	665	732	1,330	1,608
1,047	749	785	864	1,570	1,832
1,133	810	850	935	1,699	1,982
1,208	864	906	997	1,812	2,114

AIME	PIA
up to $426	90% of AIME
$426–$2,567	$383.40 + 32% of the AIME above $426
over $2,567	$1,068.52 + 15% of the AIME above $2,567

The three AIME ranges, called *bend points,* increase as average wages in the economy increase. The percentages do not change unless Congress amends the law. The formula shows that benefit levels, expressed as **replacement ratios,** are weighted in favor of lower-income workers. Here a replacement ratio is defined as your Social Security benefit divided by your AIME. You may or may not think the disparate replacement ratios are equitable, but they meet the social objectives of the system. It is not unusual for social insurance programs to redistribute wealth to lower-income groups. 1995 benefit levels for various beneficiaries are shown in table 17–1.

OTHER FACTORS AFFECTING BENEFIT AMOUNTS

As described above, your AIME determines your PIA as a retired or disabled worker, and the benefit levels for other beneficiaries are a percentage of your PIA. If you qualify both as a worker and as the spouse of a worker, you will receive whichever PIA amount is greater, but not both. However, other factors also may affect your benefit amount. There is a maximum family benefit limitation, and if three or more survivors or dependents of a retired worker are eligible for benefits, usually the maximum is reached.[12] When the family maximum is reached, the worker's benefit is not reduced but the benefits of the survivors or dependents are reduced proportionately. There is also a minimum PIA for very low-wage workers who have been covered by Social Security for at least ten years. This attempts to address the broad social purpose of Social Security: reducing want and destitution by providing an adequate income to insured workers.

Benefit amounts are affected by early and late retirement. Early retirement benefits (prior to age 65) are permanently reduced in amount, since the length of the expected benefit pay-out period is longer than it would have been from normal retirement age.[13] Likewise, postponing retirement past age 65 results in a permanently increased benefit amount to compensate for the shortened length of the expected pay-out period and to encourage older workers to continue working full-time.[14] Full benefits begin at age 70 even if you continue to work full-time. Benefit amounts are also affected by automatic cost-of-living adjustments linked to increases in the Consumer Price Index.[15] In addition, workers receiving Social Security disability income may have Social Security benefits reduced to offset other disability benefits received from governmental programs such as workers' compensation to reduce the moral hazard of malingering.

The retirement benefit may be reduced for a retired worker under age 70 whose annual earned income exceeds a specified amount. This provision is called the **earnings test.** Its purpose is to limit monthly cash benefits to those who have earned income and to reduce the cost of the Social Security program. In 1995, a beneficiary under age 65 lost $1 of benefits for every $3 earned above $8,160. Those ages 65 to 69 may earn $11,280 before benefits decrease. The exempt amount increases annually as average wages increase.

Financing of Benefits

Social Security benefits are financed through payroll taxes paid by employers and employees and by a special tax on earnings paid by the self-employed. The tax rate for employers and employees is 6.2 percent for OASDI and 1.45 percent for HI (Medicare). Self-employed rates are 12.4 percent for OASDI and 2.9 percent for HI, which are equal to the combined employer and employee tax rates.[16] The tax rates are intended to remain

12. In 1995, the formula for calculating the family maximum was (150% of the first $544 of PIA) + (272% of the PIA greater than $544 and less than or equal to $785) + (134% of the PIA greater than $785 and less than or equal to $1,024) + (175% of the PIA greater than $1,024).

13. Based on a normal retirement age of 65, retirement before age 65 results in a permanently reduced benefit equal to 5/9 of 1 percent of the worker's PIA for every month that retirement precedes age 65. The fraction will be greater for persons born in 1938 and later years.

14. Those born from 1917 to 1924 receive an increased retirement benefit of 3 percent for each year of delayed retirement up to age 70. For those turning 65 after 1990, the delayed retirement credit will increase gradually until it reaches 8 percent per year by 2009.

15. In years where OASDI reserves fall below 20 percent of expected benefits, the cost-of-living adjustment is limited to the lesser of (1) the increase in the Consumer Price Index or (2) the average annual wage increase used to adjust the taxable wage base.

16. Federal income tax law helps equalize the Social Security tax treatment for the self-employed. Someone who is self-employed first reduces self-employment income by 7.65 percent before calculating the amount of Social Security tax due. Then "taxable income" is reduced by one-half of the Social Security tax.

constant, but the taxable wage base is adjusted annually to reflect increases in average wages. For example, the 1995 base was $61,200, so that employers, employees, and the self-employed paid OASDI taxes on an individual's wages up to $61,200. If wages increase 5 percent next year, then the tax rates would remain the same but the taxable wage base would increase by 5 percent, thus increasing total Social Security tax revenue (all else being equal). Wages beyond the threshold are not subject to the OASDI tax, but they are subject to the Medicare tax.

Social Security benefits are also financed through federal income taxes of up to 85 percent of the benefits paid to certain recipients. More specifically, taxes are payable on 50 percent of the Social Security benefit by single persons whose taxable incomes (including 50 percent of Social Security benefits and any interest on tax-exempt bonds) are between $25,000 and $34,000 (between $32,000 and $44,000 for married couples filing joint returns). If income exceeds $34,000 for single persons (or $44,000 for married couples filing jointly), up to 85 percent of the Social Security benefit is taxable.

Taxing Social Security benefits is a relatively recent phenomenon, designed to increase income and increase the financial soundness of the program. In 1984, legislation required that at most 50 percent of a family's Social Security benefits be subject to taxation. In 1993, the maximum increased to 85 percent. These laws affected mostly higher-income recipients. In fact, the 1993 increase affects only 11 percent of recipients, who now must include more of their benefits for taxation than they did under prior law. Eight percent of families pay the same under the 1993 law as they did under the prior law. More than 80 percent of beneficiaries do not have sufficient income to be required to include any Social Security benefits in taxable income under either new or old tax law.[17]

Tax receipts are allocated to three trust funds from which benefits are paid. These are the old-age and survivors' trust fund (for retirement and survivors' benefits), the disability insurance trust fund, and the hospital insurance trust fund. The supplementary medical benefits (i.e., Medicare Part B benefits) are financed by monthly premiums from persons enrolled in the program, along with amounts appropriated from the general revenue of the federal government. These funds are deposited in a fourth trust fund, the supplementary medical insurance trust fund.

The Social Security system is primarily a *pay-as-you-go system,* with limited use of funds already on deposit in the trust funds. For the most part, current tax revenues are used to pay the current benefits of Social Security recipients. This is quite different from financing with traditional, private insurance, where funds are set aside in advance to accumulate over time and benefits are paid to those who contributed to the fund.

Administration

The Social Security program is administered by the Social Security Administration, an agency of the United States Department of Health and Human Services. Local service is provided by offices located in the principal cities and towns of the fifty states and Puerto Rico. Applications for Social Se-

17. David Pattison, "Taxation of Social Security Benefits Under the New Income Tax Provisions: Distributional Estimates for 1994," *Social Security Bulletin,* Vol. 57, No. 2, Summer 1994.

curity numbers and the various benefits as well as the enrollment for the medical insurance plan are processed by the district office.

Disability determination—the decision as to whether or not an applicant for disability benefits is disabled as defined in the law—is made by a state agency (usually the vocational rehabilitation agency) under agreements between the state and the secretary of the Department of Health and Human Services. Qualification for hospital and medical benefits is determined by the district office, but claims for such benefits are processed through private insurer intermediaries under contract with the Social Security Administration.

The first decision concerning a person's qualification for benefits under the various parts of the program is made at the local level. Simple, effective procedures exist for appeal by any applicant for whom the decision is unsatisfactory. There is no charge for such appeals, and the agency strives to provide courteous assistance to the claimant.

Social Security Issues

The major Social Security issue is financing. Can (or will) our society pay for the system? Originally designed to operate with advance funding, it has for many years operated on an unfunded, pay-as-you-go basis. As a result, this generation of workers is paying for the benefits of current beneficiaries, such as disability income and survivors' benefits, and benefits for those who are retired. Social Security taxes have increased much faster than the general level of prices and even faster than the cost of health care during the past two decades. When the first payroll tax was collected in 1937, the maximum annual payment by a covered worker was $30 (benefits ranged from $10 to $85). By 1995, the maximum annual payment for OASDI taxes by a covered worker was $3,794.40, more than 125 times that much.[18] The taxable wage base has also increased dramatically during this period. Most people pay more in Social Security than in federal income tax.

The number of retired workers has increased faster than the number working. In 1945, there were forty-two workers per retiree. Currently, this has decreased to approximately three workers per retiree and is expected to decline to two by the year 2020. The Social Security funding burden is being borne by a shrinking sector of society as birth rates have declined and longevity has increased. This trend will continue as the "baby boomers" move out of the work force and into retirement. Retired workers are concerned about the certainty of their benefits and future required tax rates. The current generation of taxpayers has serious doubts about the ability of the Social Security system to deliver benefits at current inflation-adjusted levels.

Such doubts are understandable, considering recent problems of the OASI program, which is by far the largest part of the system. In fiscal 1982, the OASI trust fund paid out $15 billion more than it received. Its surplus was completely wiped out, and it was forced to borrow $600 million from the disability insurance trust fund. Although the latter fund was expected to run surpluses for the foreseeable future, the OASI program's needs were

18. The 1.45 percent Medicare tax on wages is unlimited, since it is paid up to and beyond the taxable wage base on all earnings.

so great that even if the two funds were pooled, they would have run out of money by 1984. In this section we discuss the history of Social Security problems and issues, as well as recent legislation and the outlook for the future.

PROBLEMS DEVELOPED GRADUALLY

Awareness of the problems of Social Security financing has come only recently; the program's troubles developed gradually over a long period and recognition was late in coming. As recently as 1971, the Social Security Advisory Council erred in telling Congress that the program was greatly overfinanced and would accumulate reserves approaching $1 trillion by 2025. As a result, in 1972 Congress increased benefits by 20 percent, cut future tax rates, pegged benefits to the Consumer Price Index, and tied the wage base (subject to payroll tax) to future increases in average earnings. Unfortunately, by the following year the economy was a victim of both recession and inflation. Because benefits were indexed to inflation, expenditures soared while unemployment reduced tax revenues and pushed more workers into retirement. By 1975, retirement benefits paid out exceeded revenues from payroll taxes. In 1976, the Social Security Administration projected that the disability insurance fund would be depleted by the end of 1979 and that the OAS fund would suffer a similar fate by 1983.

Congress reacted in 1977 by raising future tax rates and revising the formula for retirement benefits. These changes, however, proved to be inadequate as inflation continued and recessions occurred again in 1980, 1981, and 1982. In May 1982, the Reagan administration proposed major cost reductions in the retirement system, but withdrew its proposal when the Democratic leader in the House of Representatives charged that the Republicans were willing to "balance the budget on the backs of the elderly." This led to "an explosion of protest," and the attempt to deal with Social Security's financial problem was considered a serious political error.

The following year, President Reagan appointed the bipartisan national Commission on Social Security Reform to create a plan to rescue the Social Security system from financial collapse. Faced by the possibility that Social Security trust funds would be exhausted by July 1983, the commission produced a plan which called for about $169 billion of increased revenues and cost reductions by 1989. It would accelerate scheduled tax increases, tax some benefits, provide incentives for workers to retire later, and delay the annual cost-of-living adjustment.

1983 LEGISLATION

The commission report provided the basis for the Social Security Amendments of 1983. In essence, the 1983 legislation increased revenue and reduced benefits to make the Social Security system more financially sound. The amendments raised payroll tax rates and included use of some general revenues for Social Security purposes. They blanketed into the Social Security system all federal workers hired after 1983, as well as elected and appointed federal officials and all employees of nonprofit organizations, to increase the number of people paying into the system. Future withdrawal from Social Security by state and local governmental units was prohibited. As noted earlier, some retirement, survivors', and disability benefits for

ETHICAL *Dilemma*

The Social Security System

The OASDHI system is not a public assistance program where benefits are awarded based on financial need. Instead Social Security is an *insurance* program where employers and employees pay "premiums" (i.e., payroll taxes) in order to provide benefits for employees and their dependents in the event of retirement, death or disability. While all types of insurance use pooling to redistribute premium and investment income from the insured group to those who suffer different sized losses, the Social Security system involves intentional rather than random redistribution.

One way to see the redistribution of income from higher paid to lower paid workers is to look at the benefits formula. In order to calculate benefits, first the average indexed monthly earnings (AIME) of the worker is computed. This takes the worker's covered wages over the years and indexes them to reflect wage inflation over time. Next the AIME is used to calculate the primary insurance amount (PIA). In 1995 the PIA equaled

> 90% of the first $426 of AIME, plus
> 32% of AIME between $426 and $2,567, plus
> 15% of AIME in excess of $2,567

Note that the benefit formula more heavily weights the first dollars of the AIME. Consequently, a worker with twice the AIME of another worker would receive more benefits, all else being equal, but would receive *less than* twice the benefits of the worker with the lower AIME. Thus typically the lower paid worker receives a better benefits return on payroll taxes contributed to the system.

The Medicare portion of Social Security redistributes income as well. Unlike the OASDI taxes which are taken out only on wages up to the taxable wage base (which was $61,200 in 1995), the Medicare tax (HI) is paid on all wages without limit. However, benefits are set by law and are the same for all Medicare recipients.

Clearly the OASDHI tax system does more than fund OASDHI benefits. The system redistributes income from higher to lower wage earners. This may not be strictly fair or equitable, especially for those with higher earnings who subsidize the system. However, the system was designed to set a priority on lifting families out of need rather than strictly ensuring equity. In order to evaluate the system, you might consider several questions: Would you benefit or lose from the current program design? Would most people be better off with an alternative approach? Does everyone in the system receive some non-economic benefit by setting the priority on economic protection of lower paid workers?

beneficiaries with total taxable income above specified levels are now subject to federal income taxation, and these income taxes go to the Social Security trust funds.

The amendments curtailed benefits. The annual cost-of-living benefit adjustment was shifted from June to December. Instead of using the annual change in the Consumer Price Index, the increase is based on whichever is less: the average annual wage increase or the annual change in the CPI. Moreover, the increase will be reduced by a specified amount for any year in which the OASDI fund balance is less than 15 percent of annual benefit payments (20 percent after 1988). Retirement age for full benefits was scheduled to increase gradually over time, but the eligibility age (of 65) for Medicare was unchanged. The law provided for a gradual reduction in early retirement benefits over a period of ten years.

The only significant liberalization in the 1983 legislation affected the earnings test. The $1 reduction in benefits for each $2 earned above the exempt amount was decreased to $1 for $3, effective in 1990. This change in the law was designed to reduce the disincentives to the elderly for earning income while drawing Social Security benefits.

THE FUTURE

The legislative reforms of 1983 made a significant difference in the financial soundness of the OASI trust fund. By the time the current baby boomers are ready to retire, a very large fund will have accumulated if current projections are realized, and benefits should be adequately funded until near the end of the baby boomer retirement period. Projections are that the OASI trust fund will be able to pay benefits until about 2035 under current law.[19] However, long-range deficits are expected thereafter. Both the disability insurance (DI) trust fund and the hospital insurance (HI) trust fund are projected to be depleted by the turn of the century.[20] Clearly, there is need for review and reform to ensure the *long-term* solvency of the program.

Some experts are also concerned about the large OASI fund accumulation in the interim. First, since Social Security revenues and expenses are reported as a part of the federal budget, the size of the federal budget deficit is masked. Masking the true size of the deficit does little to encourage Congress to enact significant budget reform. Some fear that Congress will not be able to leave the large fund untouched for future benefit payment, leaving future retiree benefits unfunded. The fear that benefits may be expanded once funds accumulate is perhaps well-founded, given the history of the Social Security program.[21]

When the system was established in 1935, its purpose was to provide wage-related pensions through compulsory employer and employee contributions to a trust fund that would operate as an insurance scheme. It was not created to provide the bulk of retirement income to average wage earners. On the contrary, the concept was a "floor of protection" that would be supplemented by savings and private pensions.

By 1940, however, the benefit structure was modified to consider need. The change gave low-income workers greater benefits relative to earnings than high-income workers. In addition, the concept of advance funding was abandoned in favor of pay-as-you-go funding. From that time on, the

19. Projections are based on mid-range actuarial assumptions. If these assumptions are not realized, deviations from the projections will occur.
20. "Actuarial Status of the Social Security and Medicare Programs," *Social Security Bulletin*, Vol. 57, No. 1, Spring 1994.
21. See, for example, Robert J. Myers, "The Role of Social Security in the Smoke-and-Mirrors Budget Deficit," *Benefits Quarterly*, First Quarter 1994.

congressional urge to respond to needs was irresistible. In 1939, benefits for dependents and survivors were added. In 1956, disabled workers under age 65 became eligible for benefits. In 1961, early retirement at age 62 was added. In 1965, hospital insurance under Medicare was made part of the Social Security system. In 1972, benefits were indexed to the inflation rate.

During the same period, the concept that Social Security should provide only a "floor of protection" was discarded—at least in the public mind—in favor of the belief that benefits should be adequate to provide a "reasonable level of living." Clearly, the latter costs more than the former. In the late 1970s and 1980s, Congress finally reduced some benefits. For example, college students are no longer eligible for benefits, parents under age 60 receive benefits until the youngest child is age 16 rather than 18, and the method of paying hospitals has tightened considerably.

Whether the objective of the Social Security program is to provide a "floor of protection" or a "reasonable level of living" remains an open question. Reform, however, will require agreement by politicians and the public on not only what benefits citizens are entitled to but what benefits taxpayers are willing to fund.

Global Trends in Social Security Systems

In many countries, financing the government social security system has become increasingly difficult. There are several reasons for this. Benefit levels have increased in many nations through the political process to the point where the tax rates necessary to support benefits are at an all-time high. For example, free or very low-cost medical care may be available to everyone; disability benefits may require little proof of inability to work and generous disability payments result in the moral hazard of malingering. Demographic trends in other industrialized nations mirror those in the United States: the population is aging, fewer workers finance the pay-as-you-go system for retirees, and the declining birthrate suggests that this trend is unlikely to be reversed. In addition, other governments also face the problem of growing budget deficits. Governments in some developing countries may be perceived as unable to administer the social security system fairly and efficiently.

Experts anticipate a shift from public sector social insurance plans to private sector plans, especially for retirement benefits.[22] Private sector organizations, particularly insurance companies, have successfully managed retirement savings and income for decades and are in a position to improve management and funding practices. Several countries have already begun to privatize the social security system, namely, Chile, Peru, Mexico, Italy, and Japan. In Chile (beginning in 1981) and Peru (in 1993), for example, workers are required to contribute to their own retirement fund, and contributions are invested by a private pension fund manager selected by the worker. In both these countries, the pre-funded privatized system appears to be working well. Some countries also are moving toward privatized medical care systems.

The trend toward privatization is worldwide, including both industrialized and developing countries. The potential for market expansion for insurers and other financial institutions is tremendous.

22. This discussion draws on "A Global Trend: Privatization and Reform of Social Security Pension Plans," W. G. Poortvliet and T. P. Laire, *The Geneva Papers on Risk and Insurance,* July 1994.

Consumer Applications

Estimating Your Benefits and Covering Medicare Gaps

In order to estimate your Social Security benefits, you must know how to calculate your average indexed monthly earnings (AIME). Here is how to do it, using the worksheet in figure 17–8:

1. Begin with the later of 1951 or your age 22 and enter your actual yearly earnings in column 2. (You may include years before age 22 and after age 62 if they increase your average or are needed to qualify you for insured status.)

2. Enter the appropriate maximum Social Security wage or earnings base amounts in column 3. We have supplied amounts for 1984 through 1995. To extend the base for earlier or later years, consult an official Social Security publication such as the *Social Security*

Bulletin: Annual Statistical Supplement in your local library, or call the nearest Social Security district office in your state.[23]

3. Obtain the indexing factors for your year of eligibility and enter them in column 4. Your year of eligibility is the earlier of the year you reach age 62, die, or become disabled. You can obtain the indexing factors directly from your Social Security office, or you can calculate the indexes from the average wage figures that are included in publications such as the *Social Security Bulletin: Annual Statistical Supplement.*

23. Superintendent of Documents, U.S. Government Printing Office, Washington, D.C., annual.

FIGURE 17–8

Social Security Indexed Earnings Worksheet

		THE LESSER OF		
		COLUMN 2 COLUMN 3		
(1)	(2)	(3)	(4)	(5)
Year	Your Actual Earnings	Social Security Taxable Wage Base ×	Indexing Factor =	Indexed Earnings For Year
1984	_____	37,800	_____	_____
1985	_____	39,600	_____	_____
1986	_____	42,000	_____	_____
1987	_____	43,800	_____	_____
1988	_____	45,000	_____	_____
1989	_____	48,000	_____	_____
1990	_____	51,300	_____	_____
1991	_____	53,400*	_____	_____
1992	_____	55,500	_____	_____
1993	_____	57,600	_____	_____
1994	_____	60,600	_____	_____
1995	_____	61,200	_____	_____

Total for years _____ through _____
Divide by months
Equals AIME

*This is the taxable wage base for OASDI taxes. Medicare taxes are levied on a higher base from 1991 on.

The formula for calculating each year's index is:

$$\text{Index for Year} = \frac{\text{National Average Annual Earnings for Your Indexing Year}}{\text{National Average Annual Earnings for Year}}$$

Your **indexing year** is the second year before your year of eligibility. For example, if you become disabled in 1995, your indexing year is 1993. You can include earnings for the final two years on an unindexed basis. In cases of death or disability, earnings for the year of eligibility are included in the calculation only if this increases your AIME. If earnings for this latest year are lower than the indexed values for other years in your calculation, they will be dropped.

4. Multiply the lesser of column 2 or column 3 by the indexing factors. Enter the products in column 4.

5. Cross out as many years of low or no earnings as you are allowed to delete. The number of years you can delete depends on your age in the year of eligibility, as shown in figure 17–9.[24] Now decide, in the event of eligibility due to death or disability, whether it helps to delete earnings for your year of eligibility also. You must leave at least two years for disability or survivor benefits and at least five for retirement. Years in which you were considered disabled by Social Security may also be dropped out unless you worked part of a disability year, and these earnings would raise your AIME. Years of disability are called a **disability freeze** on your earnings record.

Consider earnings after age 62 only if they can increase your AIME by being higher than the indexed earning for earlier years. Although your regular computation base stops with the year you become 62, earnings between ages 63 and 70 can be substituted for years of lower earnings.

6. Total the indexed earnings that remain.

7. Divide that sum by the number of months' (years times twelve) earnings in the total. The result is your AIME.

You are now ready to find the primary insurance amount (PIA) that corresponds to your AIME. Look in a schedule like the one in table 17–1, use the PIA formula, or consult a current Social Security publication. Remember that the bend points in the PIA formula change annually.

If you started working at age 22 in 1988 and calculated your AIME in 1995, you would have what is shown in table 17–2. Benefits would be based on this calculation if you became disabled, according to the strict Social Security definition of disability, or died with eligible survivors in 1995. The calculation keeps your 1995 earnings, since this increases your AIME. Earnings for 1988 are crossed out because at age 29 you can drop one year and this is your lowest year of earnings. After dividing the total of $333,268 by 84 months, your AIME is $3,967.

An AIME of $3,967 would produce a monthly PIA of $1,279.[25] Any dependent or survivor benefits would be a percentage of your $1,279 benefit, subject to a family maximum of $2,237.[26]

FIGURE 17–9

Relationship Between Age and Years of Deleted Earnings

WORKER'S AGE	YEARS TO BE DELETED*
Less than 27	0
27–31	1
32–36	2
37–41	3
42–46	4
47 and Over	5

*If you had no earnings and cared for a child under age 3, you may qualify for up to three additional dropout years.

24. You may notice that a dropout year is earned for every five years of work, up to a maximum of five dropout years.

25. The PIA is: ($426).90 + ($2,567 − 426).32 + ($3,967 − 2,567).15 = $1,279.

26. The family maximum benefit is: ($544)1.50 + ($785 − 544)2.72 + ($1,024 − 785)1.34 + ($1,278.52 − 1,024)1.75 = $2,237.

(1) Year	(2) Your Actual Earnings	(3) Social Security Taxable Wage Base	(4) Indexing Factor	(5) Indexed Earnings for You
1988	$22,000	$45,000	1.196	
1989	29,000	48,000	1.151	$ 33,376
1990	34,000	51,300	1.100	37,403
1991	38,000	53,400	1.016	40,302
1992	45,000	55,500	1.009	45,387
1993	55,000	57,600	1.000	55,000
1994	65,000	60,600	1.000	60,600
1995	75,000	61,200	1.000	61,200
			Total 1988 through 1995	$333,268
			Average Indexed Monthly Earnings (AIME)	$ 3,967

Key Terms

social insurance	Medicare
Social Security	Part A hospital insurance benefits
OASDHI	spell of illness or benefit period
fully insured	Part B medical benefits
currently insured	primary insurance amount
disability insured	average indexed monthly earnings
normal retirement age	replacement ratio
retirement benefits	earnings test
survivors' benefits	indexing year
disability benefits	disability freeze

Discussion Questions

1. How does social insurance differ from public assistance?

2. How does a worker become fully insured under Social Security? What benefits are fully insured workers entitled to?

3. What is the difference between Medicare Part A and Medicare Part B? Does a retiree need both?

4. Why is it important to index earnings in calculating AIME? What does the PIA represent?

5. How does the earnings test affect Social Security benefits?

6. Social Security benefits are financed largely through payroll taxes. Up to the maximum earnings base, the more you earn, the more tax you pay. Income benefits, however, favor lower-income workers. You may earn twice as much as I do and pay twice as much tax, but you will not be entitled to twice as much income benefit. Do you think this is fair? If not, should it be changed? How?

7. Do you think Social Security coverage should be voluntary? Why, or why not?

8. In recent years, insurance regulatory authorities have exerted pressure on private insurers to issue insurance policies that can be easily understood by the average person so they will know what benefits are provided. The Social Security Administration does not have to do this. Do you think it should? Why, or why not?

9. From time to time, you may hear that Social Security is in financial trouble and that you may not receive the benefits you expect. Do you think this is true? If it is true, what should be done about it?

10. Would you favor U.S. privatization of the Social Security retirement program, as other countries have done? Please explain.

Cases

17.1 Mr. C. J. Abbott worked hard all his life and built up a successful business. His daily routine involves helping with management decisions in the business, even though the majority of it is now owned and managed by his sons. He continues to draw a salary from the company sufficient to cover his expenses each month. C. J. is fully insured under Social Security and applied for benefits at age 65. However, he does not presently receive, nor has he ever received, Social Security benefits. He celebrated his 66th birthday last May.

1. Why doesn't C. J. receive any Social Security benefits? Does this tell you anything about how much he is earning at the business?
2. Why do you think C. J. continues to work?
3. Will C. J.'s benefits be increased any for his work beyond age 65? (Assume he starts drawing benefits at age 70.)
4. What is the logic behind the provision in the Social Security law that leads to a fully insured individual like C. J. not receiving Social Security retirement benefits after age 65?

17.2 Mrs. Estelle Martin retires in 1994 at age 62 with an AIME of $1,800. Her 62-year-old husband of forty-eight years, Arthur, has no covered earnings under Social Security. They provide full support for a grandchild, Justin, age 4. Assume Mr. Martin retires that same year.

1. What would be the amount of Estelle's PIA in 1994?
2. Would Arthur be entitled to a benefit? If so, how much?
3. Would Justice be entitled to a benefit? If so, how much?

17.3 Your father-in-law was employed by a state agency for forty years before his retirement last year. He was not covered by Social Security on his state job. During the last five years of his career with the state government, however, you employed him on a part-time basis to do some surveying work on a housing development for which you had an engineering contract. You paid both the employer's and employee's Social

Security tax, deducting the latter from his wages during the time you employed him.

When he retired, he applied for Social Security retirement benefits. Several months later, he was notified that he was not entitled to benefits because the work he did for you was "in the family," and not bona fide employment. The implication in the notice he received was that the job you gave him was designed to qualify him for Social Security benefits rather than to provide him with "real" employment.

1. What should your father-in-law do?

2. How can you help him?

17.4 Medicare costs have turned out to be much greater than expected when the program was first enacted. The number of people eligible for Medicare and the benefit amounts have increased through the years. For example, Medicare covers not only medical expenses for eligible retirees, but also kidney dialysis and kidney transplants for persons of all ages (as of 1972).

1. Why does Medicare have deductibles, coinsurance, and limitations on benefits that create gaps in coverage for insureds?

2. Considering the fact that many older people worry about what is not covered by Medicare, do you think the gaps should be eliminated?

3. Should Medicare be expanded to cover everyone for a broad array of medical services without regard to age or work history? Do you favor expanding Medicare into a national health insurance plan?

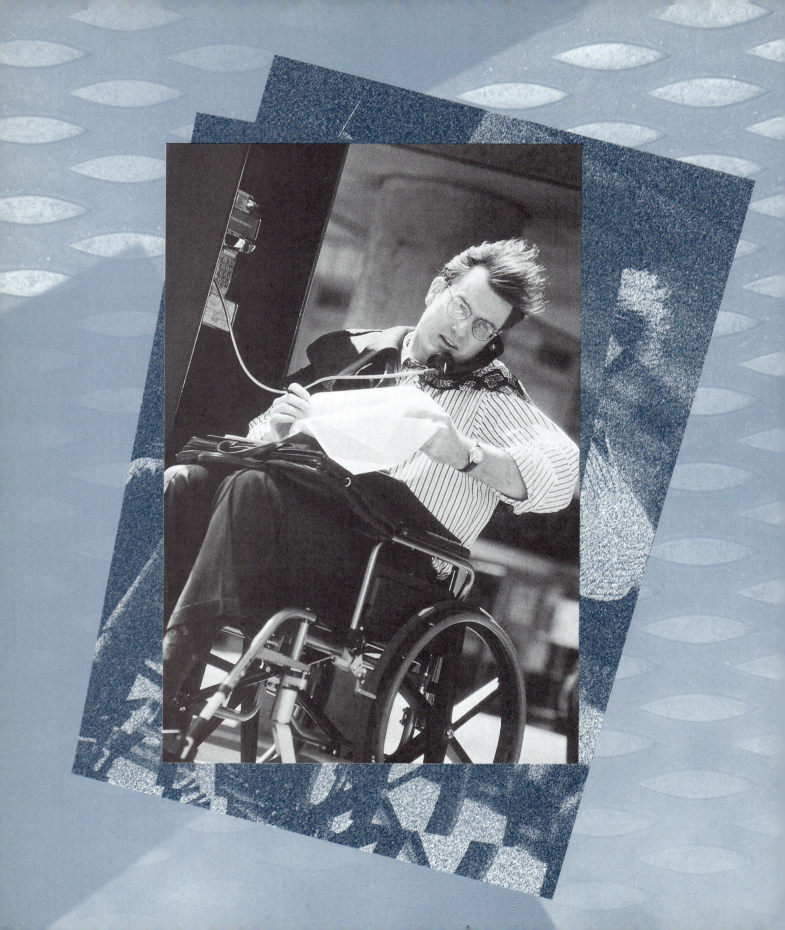

CHAPTER 18

Employee Benefits: Fundamentals, Life, and Disability Risks

Introduction Organizations are concerned with managing **human resource risk.** Employees or their dependents may experience a loss of income due to premature death, disability, or retirement, as well as economic losses due to medical expenses. These risks affect employers, since employee welfare suffers and work productivity can be affected. In addition, society has come to expect employers to provide some economic security for workers, and employees left without income protection may reflect poorly on the employer.

Most employers provide employer-sponsored benefit programs to mitigate the human resource risk and increase the economic security of employees. **Employee benefits** may be defined as any compensation, other than wages, that workers receive for time worked. Employee benefits include Social Security, group insurance, retirement plans, paid vacations, holiday and sick leave, child care benefits, employer discounts, educational benefits, moving expenses, and many other miscellaneous benefits. The United States Chamber of Commerce estimates that expenditures on employee benefits averaged about 40 percent of

employer payroll in the mid-1990s.[1] Clearly, employee benefits are a significant component of total employee compensation and are important in recruiting, retaining, and rewarding workers.

Employee benefits are examined in several chapters of this text. Social Security is discussed in chapter 17, and the importance of employee benefits and Social Security in the development of a total financial plan is demonstrated in chapter 22. Chapter 19 focuses on group medical expense insurance plans, and chapter 20 focuses on retirement plans.

This chapter describes the fundamentals of group insurance, as well as how group life and disability insurance plans protect workers. In discussing group employee benefits, and particularly life and disability insurance, special attention will be given to:

1. Employer objectives.
2. Nature of group insurance.
3. Group life insurance plans.
4. Group disability insurance plans.
5. The flexibility issue.
6. Compliance with nondiscrimination laws.
7. Multinational employee benefit plans.

1. *Employee Benefits: Survey Data from Benefit Year 1993*, U.S. Chamber of Commerce Research Center, 1994 Edition.

Employer Objectives

The first step in managing an effective employee benefit program, as with the other aspects of risk management discussed in chapter 2, is setting objectives. Objectives take into account both (1) the economic security needs of employees and (2) the financial constraints of the employer. Without objectives, a plan is likely to develop incrementally into a haphazard program.

Employers can use several methods to set objectives for benefit plans. They may investigate what other organizations in the region or within the industry are doing, and then design a competitive package of their own to recruit and retain qualified employees. Benefits may be designed to compete with plans offered for unionized workers. Employers may survey employees to find out what benefits are most desired and then design the benefits package with employees' responses in mind.

Employer objectives are developed by answering questions such as the following:

1. Who is eligible for each type of benefit?
2. Should seniority, position, salary, and other characteristics influence the amount of each employee's benefit?
3. How might a specific benefit affect employee turnover, absenteeism, and morale?
4. How should benefits be funded?
5. Should the benefits program be designed to adjust to differing needs among employees?
6. How do laws and regulations influence benefit plan design?
7. To what extent should tax preferences affect plan design?

In answering questions like these, management must keep in mind the effect of its benefits decisions on the organization's prime need to operate at an efficient level of total expenditure with a competitive product price. Efficiency requires management of total labor costs, wages *plus* benefits. Thus, if benefits are made more generous, this can have a dampening effect on wages, all else being equal. Financial constraints are a major factor in benefit plan design.

Nature of Group Insurance

Individuals receive economic security from individually purchased insurance and from group insurance. Both types of coverage may provide protection against economic loss caused by death, disability, or sickness. To the covered person, the differences between the two types of coverage may not be noticeable. However, there are some important differences, specifically in underwriting, administration, and pricing.

UNDERWRITING

Individually purchased life and health insurance involve individual underwriting. The purchaser files an application and, in some cases, takes a medical examination. On the basis of this and other information, the underwriter decides whether or not to issue insurance, and on what terms.

The merits of each application are decided individually. **Group underwriting** does not involve an application to the insurer by each participant, or a medical examination (except in some very small employer groups). The employer makes one application for the entire group, and, instead of selecting individual insureds, the insurer makes an underwriting decision based on group characteristics, such as the number of employees, employer location, employee demographics, and past claims experience. If the group characteristics are satisfactory to the underwriter, no consideration is given to the health or habits of individuals within the group, provided that employees sign up for insurance during their **eligibility period.**[2]

Generally, employees are first eligible for benefits either immediately upon hiring or following a three–to six–month **probationary period.** Many employers use the probationary period to save administrative costs, since short-term employees (e.g., those employed less than three or six months) are never brought into the group plan. Following hiring or the probationary period (whichever the employer requires), the employee's eligibility period usually extends for thirty-one days, during which employees may sign up for group insurance coverage. In order for coverage to become effective, most group plans require that the employee be **actively at work** on the day that coverage would normally become effective. Being at work provides some evidence of good health and helps reduce adverse selection.

Enrollment after the eligibility period usually means that the employee will have to provide evidence of insurability. The employee may have to complete a questionnaire or have a medical examination to show that he or she is in good health. This provision helps reduce adverse selection. Most employers allow only full-time employees to participate in the benefit plan. Generally, employees working more than thirty hours per week are considered full-time. Thus, to be insured, the employee must (1) satisfy the probationary period, (2) enroll, (3) be actively at work, and (4) be a full-time employee.

In most group health insurance plans, employees electing group insurance at the first opportunity are covered, except for expenses due to a medical condition existing prior to the beginning of employment. For example, someone who has arthritis prior to taking the job would be covered for all medical expenses except those related to treatment of arthritis. **Preexisting condition clauses** may prohibit payment for preexisting conditions for three to twelve months, depending on the employer's policy.[3] This provision also helps reduce adverse selection.

Some employers provide minimal benefits for part-time employees. For example, a half-time employee may have coverage worth approximately half of what a full-time employee's coverage is worth. Most employers, however, do not provide benefits for part-time workers. The trend toward increased use of part-time workers in service industries has resulted in

2. In recent years, however, small groups have been an exception. Consideration may be given to the health of individuals, even when employees sign up for insurance during the eligiblity period.
3. Additional discussion of preexisting condition clauses and continuation provisions through COBRA is presented in chapter 19.

many employees working at two or more part-time jobs and not qualifying for group benefits through any employer.

ADMINISTRATION

The administration of group insurance differs from individual insurance in that the contract is made with the employer rather than with each individual. The employer receives a **master contract** that describes all the terms and conditions of the group policy. The employer, in turn, provides each insured employee with a **certificate of insurance** as evidence of participation. **Participants** in the benefit plan may include employees, their dependents (including a spouse and children under a specified age, such as 21, when enrolled in school), retirees, and their dependents. Participants receive a booklet describing the plan, distributed by the employer at the time the plan goes into effect or when eligibility begins, whichever is later.

Administration of group insurance also differs from individual insurance in that the employer may be responsible for the record keeping ordinarily done by the insurer, especially if the group is large. Administration is simplified by the employer paying periodic premiums directly to the insurer. If employees are required to contribute toward the premium, the employer is responsible for collection or payroll deduction of employee contributions, as well as for payment to the insurer of the total group premium amount.

Most large employer plans are **self-insured,** and employers, rather than insurers, pay claims and bear the risk that actual claims will exceed expected claims. Some employers with self-insured plans also administer the benefits themselves. However, insurers and **third-party administrators** (or **TPAs**) administer many (even large) self-funded plans under an **administrative services only (ASO)** contract. The employer transfers record keeping and claim payment functions to the insurer or TPA, paying about 5 to 10 percent of the normal premium for administrative services.

In addition, the employer may purchase **stop loss insurance** from the same or another insurer or TPA for protection against unexpectedly high claims. Stop loss coverage is a form of reinsurance or excess insurance for self-insured plans. Purchase of an ASO contract and stop loss insurance gives the employer the potential cash flow and expense advantage of self-funding, while reducing the employer's administrative burden and potential for catastrophic risk.

Adverse Selection

There is potential for adverse selection in group insurance. Adverse selection occurs when employees more likely than the average employee to have a loss seek insurance. This results in poor claims experience for the group. Careful benefit design and administration can reduce adverse selection. Requiring evidence of insurability after the eligibility period has elapsed also helps (as discussed above). Employees are more likely to join the plan during the initial eligibility period rather than waiting until their health declines, because then they can no longer provide evidence of insurability.

State insurance *minimum participation requirements* also help reduce the effects of adverse selection on the average cost of insurance per employee.

Insurance laws may require that a minimum percentage of the group be enrolled in the benefit plan to ensure that there are enough healthy employees and dependents to help offset the high claims that can be expected from unhealthy employees or dependents. Every group, insured or self-insured, can anticipate enrollment by the unhealthy. The likelihood of achieving minimum participation (meaning at least 75 percent) is increased by **employer sharing of costs,** characteristic of all true group insurance plans. Most states and insurers require that 100 percent of employees be covered in a *noncontributory* plan, in which employees do not pay for the cost of their coverage. In *contributory* plans, where employees pay all or part of the premium amount, 75 percent of employees must participate.[4] This helps protect the plan from adverse selection that may occur from the absence of individual underwriting during the eligibility period.

Participation requirements are reduced significantly (for example, to 25 percent) for **supplemental plans.** Supplemental plans allow employees to choose additional group insurance coverage paid for entirely by themselves. For example, supplemental life coverage can allow an employee to increase the face amount of group life insurance coverage, and supplemental group disability coverage can allow for a cost-of-living benefit increase for periods of long-term disability. In recent years, the use of supplemental plans has grown, largely due to the flexibility they provide to employees at little or no cost to employers.

The potential for adverse selection may be greater with supplemental benefits than with nonsupplemental benefits. Since employees pay the premium for supplemental coverage, it is likely that those who anticipate a benefit are more willing to participate. Despite this, supplemental plans are popular because they allow employees to tailor benefits to meet their individual needs through a convenient payroll deduction plan.

Firms with a small number of employees may have difficulty purchasing or maintaining group insurance on their own, due to potential adverse selection problems. For example, in small groups, individual employees who develop health problems often are dropped at renewal under current small group marketing practices in states without small group reform bills. Other small group employers may have trouble finding an insurance carrier willing to service their group if one or more individuals are in ill health. Many of these firms, however, have access to group insurance by participating in a **multiple employer trust (MET)**. The MET makes available to small employers, often in the same industry group and with as few as one or two employees each, benefits similar to those available to large groups. METs often are organized for a trade association, union, or other sponsoring organization by an insurer or third-party administrator. When small employers come together through an MET to purchase insurance, they have access to group underwriting treatment, products, and services similar to those available to large employers.

Some METs in recent years have suffered from mismanagement and bankruptcy. In some instances, this occurred when managers attempted to enhance the marketability of the MET by lowering premiums to the

---

4. Contributory and noncontributory plans are discussed in more detail in this chapter in the section on pricing.

point that they were insufficient to cover claims. Other MET failures were attributable in part to dishonesty and fraud on the part of management. As a result, some METs were unable to pay employees their promised benefits. Consequently, state regulation of METs has increased in recent years to better protect workers covered by these plans.

Another benefit design feature that reduces adverse selection is *automatic determination of benefits,* in which the employee's benefit amount is set by a formula. Life insurance benefit formulas, for example, may vary according to earnings, job classification, length of service, or some combination of factors. Disability formulas vary by earnings or job classification. Medical benefits specify the same benefit amounts for single or family coverages. When benefits are automatically determined, higher-than-average-risk employees cannot take advantage of group insurance to obtain excessive amounts of coverage that would likely result in a higher overall group premium.

Both **flexible benefit programs** that allow employee input into the amount of each benefit, and supplemental plans that allow employees to purchase additional amounts of a specific benefit on a fully contributory basis undoubtedly involve adverse selection. This has to be reflected in higher rates for flexible and supplemental benefits. However, given the diversity in needs among single, married, divorced, younger, older, male, and female employees in the typical group, the advantages of tailoring benefits to employee-perceived needs by giving employees a voice in benefit decisions may well outweigh the cost of some adverse selection. Flexible benefit programs are discussed later in this chapter.

PRICING

Some employers require employees to pay part of the cost of the group insurance premium. These plans are **contributory plans.** The balance of the plan is paid by the employer. **Noncontributory plans,** on the other hand, are those in which the employer pays all the premium. Frequently, group life and disability insurance plans are noncontributory, but do require the employees to contribute if other family members are covered. Due to rising premiums, however, medical expense insurance coverage for employees only is not as frequently noncontributory as it used to be. Premiums, whether contributory or noncontributory, are paid by the employer to the insurer. Often, contributory premium amounts are transferred from the employee through payroll deduction.

Group insurance is usually less expensive than individual insurance for several reasons: (1) with group coverage, the insurer deals with one insured instead of many, streamlining marketing costs; (2) the employer takes care of much of the administrative detail; (3) commission scales on group business are lower than they are on individual policies; (4) medical examinations are not needed because underwriting is done on a group basis and provides the employment process a form a screening; (5) the employer pays part (or all) of the costs (which is more economically efficient than having employees pay with after-tax dollars); and (6) the employer often does some monitoring to eliminate false or unnecessary claims for health care benefits. In addition, group insurance theory maintains that the replacement by younger employees of employees who retire or quit keeps average mortality and morbidity rates from rising to prohibitive levels. That is, a *flow of persons through the group* tends to keep average costs down. This is often true when the number of employees in a group is growing, but is less true for an organization that is downsizing.

Group life and health insurance rates are usually quoted by insurers as one monthly rate (for example, $0.15 per $1,000 of coverage in the case of life insurance) for all employees. This rate is based on a weighted average, taking into account the age, sex, and accompanying mortality and morbidity rates for each employee in the group. Since mortality and morbidity rates increase with age, groups with a higher proportion of older people, for example, may have relatively higher premiums. Thus, an average rate for the group is high for younger employees and low for older employees, relative to the cost of individually purchased insurance. This usually does not create an adverse selection problem for the employer, however, because after the employer's contribution is deducted, the cost to the employees is a bargain for all, young and old. In group plans where employees contribute most of the premium, however, the plan may not have a low cost for younger employees relative to what they could pay for similar coverage in the individual market.

Most small organizations, for example, those with fewer than fifty employees, have their entire premium based on pooled claims experience for similar-sized firms. However, larger employers are likely to have **experience-rated premiums,** in which the group's own claims experience affects the cost of coverage. Experience rating allows employer groups to benefit directly from their own good claims experience, and provides a direct economic incentive for risk managers to control claims.

With experience rating, the weight or *credibility* given to a group's own experience increases with the number of participants. The experience of smaller groups (for example, those with fewer than 500 or 1,000 employees) is not considered sufficiently statistically credible or reliable to determine premiums completely. Insurers, therefore, use a weighted average of the group's loss experience and the pooled experience for groups of similar size in developing the claims charge. For example, the group's actual loss experience may be weighted at 70 percent of the claims charge and the pooled experience for groups of similar size may carry a weight of 30 percent. If the group had a loss experience of $80,000 and the pool experience was $100,000, then the claims charge for the experience-rated premium would be $86,000 per year.[5] A larger group would have more statistically reliable experience and might receive an 80 percent weighting for its own experience and a 20 percent weighting for the pooled experience, resulting in a claims charge of $84,000. Thus, the larger the group, the more credit the group receives for its own claims experience and the lower the experience-rated claims charge. The experience-rated claims charge makes up the bulk of the total premium due, but the final experience-rated premium also includes administrative charges and fees.

Premiums for larger organizations, however, can reflect *only* the group's own loss experience. With *prospective experience rating,* the group's claims experience for the previous few years, plus an inflation factor, partly or completely determine the premium for the current year. A *retrospective*

....

5. $(.70)(\$80,000) + (.30)(\$100,000) = \$86,000/\text{year}.$

experience rating plan uses loss experience to determine whether premium refunds (or dividends) should be paid at the end of each policy year.

Group insurance premiums paid by the employer are a deductible business expense and are not taxable income to employees except for amounts of term life insurance in excess of $50,000 per person and all group property-liability insurance. Employee premium contributions are not tax deductible, except when flexible spending accounts are used.[6] Proceeds paid from group life insurance at death are not taxable income to the beneficiary, but are included in the estate of the insured, if he or she is the owner, for federal estate tax purposes (see chapter 22).

Group disability insurance premiums paid by the employer are also a deductible business expense for the employer, and do not result in an immediate tax liability for the employee. Employee contributions for premiums are made from after-tax dollars. With respect to the taxation of disability benefits when they are received, the portion of benefits paid from coverage paid for by employer contributions is taxable to the employee when received. For example, if the employer pays one-third of the premium amount for disability coverage, then if the employee becomes disabled and receives benefits, one-third of the benefits are taxable income to the employee. Benefits attributable to coverage paid for by the employee with after-tax dollars are not taxable. Thus, in this example, two-thirds of the disability benefit amount would not be taxable income. Explaining taxation of disability income to employees can be a challenge to the benefits manager.

Group Life Insurance

Group life insurance is the oldest of the employer-sponsored group insurance benefits, dating from 1912. The most common type of group life insurance offered by employers is *yearly renewable term* coverage. Yearly renewable term coverage is the least expensive form of protection the employer can provide for employees during their working years. Due to a shorter average life expectancy, older employees and males have relatively higher premium rates. The premium for the entire group is the sum of the appropriate age-sex based premium for each member of the group. Obviously, the employee's particular premium will increase yearly with age. However, if younger employees continue to be hired, the lower premium for new hires can offset increases due to aging employees hired some years earlier. Also, if young employees replace older ones, premiums will tend to stabilize or decrease. This flow of covered lives helps maintain a fairly stable average total premium for the employer group.

Most group term life insurance provides death benefit amounts equal to twice the employee's salary. Some provide three or four times salary, but some states and many insurers set limits on maximum benefits. Insurers' underwriting limitations are usually related to the total volume of insurance on the group. Additional amounts of term life insurance may be available on a supplemental basis. Employers sponsor the supplemental plan, and employees usually pay all the premium through payroll deduc-

6. Flexible spending accounts are described later in this chapter.

tion. This allows employees to increase life insurance based on their individual needs.

Many group plans terminate all group life insurance when the employee retires. Those that allow employees to maintain coverage after retirement usually reduce substantially the amount of insurance available. If an employee is insurable at retirement, additional life insurance may be purchased on an individual basis. Alternatively, the employee can use the **conversion privilege** in most group plans (regardless of the reason that employment terminates) to buy an equal or lower amount of permanent life insurance with level premiums based on the employee's attained age. Because mortality rates increase rapidly after middle age, the costs of conversion are burdensome for all but those with high income during retirement.

Another way employers fund life insurance for retirees is through a **retired lives reserve.** With a retired lives reserve, employers not only purchase yearly renewable term insurance on an active employee, but they also make level contributions to a retired lives reserve with an insurer or a trust fund for that employee during the working years. At retirement, the employer uses the funds set aside in the retired lives reserve to purchase term insurance for the employee during retirement. The employer's contributions to the retired lives reserve are a tax-deductible business expense, and investment earnings held by a trust are sheltered from taxation. Generally, the Internal Revenue Service limits the amount of coverage per retiree to a face amount of $50,000.

A small percentage of group life insurance plans use permanent insurance to cover an employee, both as an active worker and as a retiree. Cash values are accumulated in the employee's younger years, and investment earnings on these cash values maintain reduced amounts of life insurance on the employee's life during retirement. For tax reasons, the savings element in group permanent plans is usually financed by employee contributions.

Group universal life insurance is available from many employers. This insurance is usually offered as a supplement to a separate program of group term benefits. Universal life premiums are paid by employees and are administered through payroll deduction. A substantial amount of coverage (for example, twice annual salary up to a maximum of $100,000 in face amount) is available without evidence of insurability. Low administrative expenses and low agents' commissions usually result in reasonably priced insurance.[7] Group universal life insurance plans have become increasingly popular with both employers and employees. Employers are able to sponsor a life insurance plan that covers workers during their active years and into retirement, at little or no cost to the employer. For example, the employer's expense may be limited to the costs of providing explanatory material to new employees, making payroll deductions of premiums, and sending a monthly check for total premiums to the insurer. Group universal life insurance is also popular with employees, largely because of the flexibility of the product.

Employers may provide other forms of group death benefits, such as the **survivor income benefit plan,** which pays monthly benefits related

7. See chapter 14 for a description of universal life insurance.

to the employee's salary and the number of dependents. For example, a plan may provide, in addition to Social Security survivor benefits, 25 percent of the employee's former earnings to a spouse for as long as the spouse lives and is unmarried. Benefits of 5 percent per dependent child under age 18 (or students under 22) may also be provided, up to a maximum of two or three children and an overall maximum of $2,500 per month. This type of coverage recognizes that needs are related to earnings, the number of dependents, and the life expectancy of a non-remarried spouse, and that the major need is for replacement of future income. Survivor income plans often are combined with a relatively small lump-sum death benefit that helps with funeral costs and other final expenses. The plans have been available for many years without gaining much popularity. The lack of popularity may be related to higher benefits going to, on average, younger employees with children, whereas employee benefit design decisions often are influenced heavily by older executives who fail to qualify for large benefits.

Group Disability Insurance Plans

Group disability income coverage provides economic security for employees who are unable to work due to illness or injury. Disability income coverage is important, since employee disability can mean not only reduced income but additional medical and rehabilitation expenses. An extended disability may result in greater economic hardship for the family than does the premature death of the employee. Employers, however, are less likely to provide group disability insurance than group life or medical expense insurance. In 1993, while 88 percent of U.S. employers provided life insurance and 97 percent provided medical insurance, only 37 percent provided short-term disability insurance and 57 percent provided long term disability coverage for employees.[8] This may be due in part to the tendency of employees and employers to underestimate the likelihood or the seriousness of a disability.

GROUP SHORT-TERM DISABILITY PLANS

Disability income may be provided on a short- or long-term basis.[9] The most common method of providing for short-term disability income is through sick leave plans (also called **salary continuation plans**).[10] With sick leave plans, employees accumulate leave, typically at a rate of one day per month of work up to a maximum of twenty-six weeks. In the event of illness or disability, the employee uses sick leave and receives 100 percent income replacement beginning on the first day of illness or disability.

For employees with adequate length of service, sick leave provides some protection in the event of disability, but for new employees who have not

8. *Employee Benefits: Survey Data from Benefit Year 1993,* U.S. Chamber of Commerce Research Center (1994): p. 26.
9. See chapter 21 for a discussion of individual short- and long-term disability insurance policies.
10. In 1993, 73 percent of employers provided sick leave. *Employee Benefits: Survey Data from Benefit Year 1993,* U.S. Chamber of Commerce Research Center, (1994): p. 26.

yet accrued sick leave, a salary continuation plan offers little economic security. Another drawback to sick leave plans results from plan designs that require no waiting period and pay full income replacement. This encourages the use of sick leave a day or two at a time by employees who feel they have earned the benefit and view it as a form of personal time off. Some employers try to reduce moral hazard by buying sick leave back, perhaps half of an employee's unused sick leave days above the maximum accumulation level. Employers also may require medical certification for extended periods of sick leave to further deter abuse of leave time.

Leave policy is changing significantly among employers today. More and more employers are eliminating specific leave definitions (such as sick leave, personal leave, and vacation leave) and consolidating leave into a total number of personal days off each year. This is especially common with sick leave and personal leave, when employees are allowed to take off for personal illness, the illness of other family members, or to attend to personal business. This flexibility allows employees to better meet personal needs, facilitates advance work scheduling and planning in some instances, and reduces the moral hazard potential of claiming sick leave for personal leave purposes.

Employees depending solely on salary continuation plans who have disabilities extending beyond the number of days of accrued leave are left with insufficient income protection. Some employers also provide **short-term disability income** replacement through insured plans. Generally, all full-time employees are eligible for coverage under a short-term disability insurance plan after meeting a three-month probationary period. Unlike sick leave, these plans do not pay benefits until after an **elimination period,** typically from one to seven days of absence from work due to disability. The employee may be required periodically to provide medical evidence of disability and to submit continuing evidence. These plans pay for the duration stipulated in the employer's policy, usually ranging from three months to two years (although the majority pay for one year at most). Group short-term disability insurance plans do not provide full income replacement, but pay 65 to 75 percent of salary. This provision reduces moral hazard and encourages employees to return to work.

The **definition of disability** determines when the employee is eligible for benefits. Short-term disability insurance policies generally define disability as the inability of the employee to perform *any and every* duty of the job. This liberal definition allows disabled workers to qualify for benefits relatively easily when compared with the definition of disability used by most group long-term disability insurance policies. Generally, group short-term disability policies pay only for nonoccupational disability, and workers' compensation benefits cover employees for short-term occupational income loss.

GROUP LONG-TERM DISABILITY PLANS

The eligibility criteria for group **long-term disability insurance** is often different than that for short-term insured plans. Unlike short-term insured plans, which generally cover all full-time workers, long-term disability plans usually cover only salaried workers after they meet a probationary period lasting from three months to one year. Long-term disability plans also have an elimination period prior to payment of benefits, ranging from three to six months. The elimination period is often equivalent to the pay-out duration for the short-term disability plan. If the elimination period is longer than the period covered by short-term income replacement, the employee may have a gap in coverage.

The definition of disability used for long-term plans is generally more restrictive than for short-term plans. Most contracts pay only if the employee is unable to engage in the *material duties* of the job. Thus, a worker unable to perform every duty of his or her occupation might be eligible for short-term disability benefits but would not be eligible for *long-term* disability benefits if he or she could perform the *material duties* of the job. Significantly fewer long-term disability policies have an even more restrictive definition, which pays only if an employee is unable to engage in any occupation for which she or he is reasonably qualified by education, experience, or training.

Some group long-term policies use a dual definition of disability. For example, benefits are payable while the own-occupation definition applies for a relatively short period of time, for example, two or three years. After that, long-term benefits are paid only if the employee is unable to engage in any reasonable occupation for which he or she is or can become qualified. Use of both definitions provides economic security to the employee and an economic incentive to find reasonable, gainful employment.

The benefit period for long-term policies can vary greatly. Employees may be covered only two, five, or ten years, or they may be covered until retirement age or for life. Typically, group long-term plans pay no more than 60 to 65 percent of salary to disabled employees. In addition, a maximum dollar benefit amount may apply. Group disability benefits are usually coordinated with other disability income, for example, from Social Security or workers' compensation. Employees may be able to obtain additional non-group disability insurance in the individual market to increase their total amount of protection, although seldom to the level of full income replacement. This ensures that the disabled person has an economic incentive to return to work.

Most group long-term disability contracts include a rehabilitation provision. This allows insureds to return to work on a trial basis for one or two years while partial long-term disability benefits continue. If disabled employees are unable to perform in the new job, long-term disability benefits are fully restored. By providing this safety net, insurers encourage disabled workers to attempt to return to work through rehabilitative employment. Insurers may also assist with training and rehabilitation costs, since these can be far less than continuing benefit payments for those who do not return to work.

Long-term disability benefit amounts may also be affected by supplemental benefits made available to employees through payroll deduction. Cost-of-living adjustments can be added to prevent the erosion of purchasing power of the disability income benefit. Survivors' benefits can protect employee dependents after the death of the disabled employee.

Group long-term disability contracts contain several important exclusions. Benefits are not paid unless the employee is under a physician's care. Benefits are not paid for self-inflicted injuries, and preexisting condition clauses may restrict coverage. Generally, benefits are not paid if the employee is gainfully employed elsewhere. Benefits payable due to mental illness and substance addiction are typically limited in amount.

In the past, long-term disability claims experience (both frequency and duration) for hourly workers has been especially unfavorable (relative to salaried employees). This may be because hourly workers are more likely to be in jobs that are monotonous and produce lower satisfaction, factors which do not help keep employees at work or encourage them to return quickly. Disability claim frequency among hourly workers has risen especially during periods of economic recession, when job security is threatened. Hourly employees may choose to make a disability claim rather than to be laid off with temporary and minimal unemployment benefits. Unfavorable claims experience is consistent with employer and insurer reluctance to provide hourly workers with long-term disability insurance.

In the last few years, however, there has been a shift in long-term disability claims experience for salaried workers. The frequency and duration of claims by salaried employees and highly paid professionals, particularly physicians, have increased significantly. Increased claims among physicians may be due in part to an increasingly litigious environment for practicing medicine and to health care financing reform initiatives that threaten the traditional practice of medicine, factors that can negatively affect physician job satisfaction. Among non-medical professionals, the increased incidence may be due to a more stressful business environment characterized by firm downsizing, especially among mid- and upper-management employees. Employers and insurers are paying attention to the increased incidence of claims among salaried employees, and in some cases are limiting the amount of benefits payable for long-term disability to reduce any potential moral hazard problems.

Group long-term disability insurance is an important benefit for employees, but it is much less often provided than are sick leave plans or short-term disability coverage. Many employees believe that the Social Security disability benefits will provide adequate protection. However, the weakness in Social Security disability protection rests in the stringent definition of disability. Many persons stop working for health reasons but cannot qualify for Social Security disability benefits. A substantial need exists for more group long-term disability income coverage to fill the gap.

The Flexibility Issue

Employers have been interested in flexible benefit plans since the early 1970s. These plans give the employee choices among an array of benefits or cash and benefits. Few flexible plans were adopted until tax issues were clarified in 1984. At that time, it became clear that employees could choose between taxable cash income and nontaxable benefits without adversely affecting the favorable tax status of a benefit plan. However, since then the rules regarding cafeteria plans and flexible spending accounts have continued to change, resulting in some employer hesitancy to adopt these plans.

Despite the uncertain legislative environment, flexible plans became very popular in the mid-1980s, particularly among large employers. Employers are attracted to flexible benefit plans because, relative to traditional designs, they:

1. Increase employee awareness of the cost and value of benefit plans.
2. Meet diverse employee economic security needs.

ETHICAL *Dilemma*

Living Benefits

Historically, the purpose of life insurance was to provide financial resources to beneficiaries following the death of the insured. Today, however, families experience economic loss, not only from the death of the income earner, but also if the insured has a prolonged illness or extensive medical treatment prior to death. This risk is increasingly important with advances in medical science which lead to increased treatment costs and longer life expectancies. The risk due to burdensome medical costs prior to death can devastate a family financially, and life insurance proceeds are not available to help until after the death of the insured.

Life insurance policies have changed to meet the changing needs of policyholders. Many life insurance policies today allow benefits to be paid early in the event that the insured has a terminal illness or catastrophic medical expenses. The insured must provide evidence that life expectancy is less than six months or one year, or proof that the insured has a catastrophic illness such as cancer, renal failure, or needs an organ transplant. The insured then can receive *living benefits* or *accelerated death benefits* rather than the traditional death benefit.

Living benefits are limited in amount, typically from 25 to 50 percent of the face amount of the life insurance policy. The balance of the benefit (minus insurer expenses) is paid to beneficiaries after the death of the insured. Generally, adding the living benefits rider does not increase total group costs, and employers and employees will not pay more for the option.

Benefit managers must consider whether living benefits are a good option to offer employees. The effect on various groups of employees should be examined. Employees with terminal illnesses or catastrophic medical expenses might prefer to have access to life insurance proceeds prior to death. This reduces financial stress to themselves and their families. However, final pay-out of the policy to beneficiaries following death of the insured is significantly reduced. Timing of the payout (i.e., pre- or post-death) affects those beneficiaries that are responsible for the medical expenses of the deceased far less than those beneficiaries who are not paying treatment costs. The benefits manager may consider whether the policy is provided primarily for the benefit of the insured (i.e., the employee) or the beneficiary, where there is a conflict of interests with respect to the timing of the payment of policy proceeds.

The benefits manger needs to recognize the importance of effectively communicating to employees how living benefits work. Effective communication reduces the possibility that beneficiaries are confused or disappointed with the final death settlement amount in the event that the insured selected living benefits. Given these considerations, if adding the rider improves the welfare of some or all employees without diminishing the welfare of others, at little or no cost to the group, then the benefits manager may want to consider making the change.

3. Help control total employer costs for the benefit plan.

4. Improve employee morale and job satisfaction.

How flexible benefit plans accomplish these goals will become clear through discussion of cafeteria plans and flexible spending accounts.

CAFETERIA PLANS

Flexible benefit plans frequently are called **cafeteria plans** because they allow selection of the types and amounts of desired benefits. A cafeteria plan usually involves three elements:

1. Flexible benefit credits.

2. Minimum levels of certain benefits.

3. Optional benefits.

In a cafeteria plan, the employer generally allows each employee to spend a specified number of flexible credits, usually expressed in dollar amounts. The number of credits assigned each year may vary with employee salary, length of service, and age. Some employers allow the employee to spend the flexible credits on a combination of benefits and cash, whereas others require that all credits be applied to benefits.

The employer may restrict employee benefit choice to some degree, since the employer has a vested interest in making sure that some minimal level of economic security is provided to employees. For example, the organization might be embarrassed if the employee did not elect medical expense benefits and was subsequently unable to pay a large hospital bill. Most flexible benefit plans specify a minimum level of certain benefits judged to be essential. For example, a core of medical, death, and disability benefits may be specified for all employees. The employee can elect out of a core benefit by supplying written evidence that similar benefits are available from another source, such as the spouse's employer or the military retirement system.

Each benefit will have a per unit price. For example, group term life insurance, above a core level equal to one year's pay, may be available in units of $10,000 up to a maximum of five times the employee's annual pay. The price of a unit may vary with the employee's age and sex. Evidence of insurability may be required at some level, such as three times annual pay. If the employee chooses additional units of an optional benefit, the employee spends credits equal to the price of each selected unit. After the credits are exhausted, the employee may be allowed to select additional benefits on a payroll deduction basis. Through the selection process, employees become aware of the cost and value of their benefits.

Cafeteria plans also help control employer benefit costs. Employers set a dollar amount on benefit expenditures per employee and employees choose within that framework. This maximizes employee appreciation, since employees choose what they want, and minimizes employer cost, since employers do not have to increase coverage for all employees in order to satisfy the needs of certain workers.

Cafeteria plans have been especially effective in controlling group medical expense insurance costs. Employees often are offered several alternative medical plans, including an HMO and a PPO, plans designed to control costs.[11] In addition, employees may be charged lower prices for traditional plans with more cost containment features. For example, a comprehensive medical insurance plan may have an option with a $100 deductible, 90 percent coinsurance, a $1,000 out-of-pocket or stop loss provision, and a $1 million maximum benefit. A lower-priced comprehensive plan may offer the same maximum benefit with a $2,000 deductible, 80 percent coinsurance, and a $4,000 stop loss provision. The employee uses fewer benefit credits to get the lower option plan, and the cost sharing requirements likely reduce claim costs, too. Likewise, long-term disability insurance choices will attach lower prices per $100 of monthly benefit with an option that insures 50 percent of income rather than 60 or 70 percent. Here again, lower prices attract employees to options with more cost sharing, and the cost sharing helps contain claims.

Cafeteria plans are well suited to meet the needs of a demographically diverse work force. The number of women, single heads of households, and dual career couples in the work force has increased dramatically in the past decade, and benefit needs vary across employees more than ever before. A single employee with no dependents may prefer fewer benefits and more cash income. Someone covered by medical benefits through a spouse's employer may prefer to use benefit dollars on more generous disability coverage. An older worker may prefer more generous medical benefits and fewer life insurance benefits, once the children are grown. Clearly, economic security needs vary, and job satisfaction and morale may improve by giving employees some voice in how benefits, a significant percentage of total compensation, are spent.

However, both higher administrative costs and adverse selection discourage employers from implementing cafeteria plans. Record keeping increases significantly when benefit packages vary for each employee. Computers help, but do not eliminate the administrative cost factor. Communication with employees is both more important and more complicated, since employees are selecting their own benefits and all choices must be thoroughly explained. Employers are careful to explain but not to advise about benefit choices, because then the employer would be liable for any adverse effect of benefit selection on the employee.

Cafeteria plans may have some adverse selection effects, since an employee selects benefits that he or she is more likely to need. Those with eye problems, for example, are more likely to choose vision care benefits, while other employees may skip vision care and select dental care to cover orthodontia. The result is higher claims per employee selecting each benefit. Adverse selection can be reduced by plan design and pricing. The employer may require, for example, that those selecting vision care must also choose dental care, thus bringing more healthy people into both plans. Pricing helps by setting each benefit's unit price high enough to cover the true average claim cost per employee or dependent, while trying to avoid excessive pricing that would discourage the enrollment of healthy employees.

....

11. Chapter 19 provides further discussion of HMOs and PPOs.

FLEXIBLE SPENDING ACCOUNTS

Flexible spending accounts (FSAs) allow employees to pay for specified benefits (which are defined by law) with before-tax dollars. In the absence of a flexible spending account, the employee would have purchased the same services with after-tax dollars. An FSA can either add flexibility to a cafeteria plan or can accompany traditional benefit plans with little other employee choice. The employer may fund the FSA exclusively, the employee may fund the account through a salary reduction agreement, or both may contribute to the FSA.

The employee decides at the beginning of each year how much to personally contribute to the FSA, and then signs a salary reduction agreement for this amount. The legal document establishing the employer's program of flexible spending accounts will specify how funds can be spent, subject to the constraints of Section 125 in the Internal Revenue Code. For example, the simplest kind of FSA is funded solely by an employee salary reduction agreement and only covers employee contributions to a group medical insurance plan. The salary reduction agreement transforms the employee contribution from after-tax dollars to before-tax dollars, often a significant savings. A more comprehensive FSA, for example, may allow the employee to cover medical premium contributions, uninsured medical expenses, child care, and legal expenses. The catch with an FSA plan is that the employee forfeits to the employer any balance in the account at year's end. This results in flexible spending accounts primarily being used to prefund highly predictable expenses on a before-tax basis.

Compliance with Nondiscrimination Laws

Administration and design of group employee benefit plans have been affected by federal regulation through the Age Discrimination in Employment Act, the Civil Rights Act, and the Americans with Disabilities Act. The Employee Retirement Income Security Act (ERISA) also pertains to employee benefit plans, but since it primarily concerns retirement plans, ERISA is discussed in chapter 20. The Social Security Act was discussed in chapter 17; the Health Maintenance Organization Act is discussed in chapter 19 with medical care delivery systems. Federal legislation is concerned with nondiscrimination in coverage and benefit amounts for plan participants.

AGE DISCRIMINATION IN EMPLOYMENT ACT

The Age Discrimination in Employment Act (ADEA) was first passed in 1967 and is known primarily for eliminating mandatory retirement on the basis of age. That is, employees cannot be forced to retire at any age, with the exception of some executives who may be subject to compulsory retirement. Employee benefits are also affected by the ADEA, since the law was amended to require that benefits must be continued for older, active (not retired) workers. Most benefits can be reduced to the point where the cost of providing benefits for older workers is no greater than for younger workers. The Act makes this an *option*; employers are not required to reduce benefits for older workers. Employers choosing to reduce some benefits for older workers generally do not reduce benefits except for active workers over age 65, even though reductions prior to age 65 may be legally allowed based on cost.

The employer may reduce benefits on a benefit-by-benefit basis based on the cost of coverage, or may reduce benefits across the board based on the overall cost of the benefit package. For example, with the benefit-by-benefit approach, the amount of life insurance in force might be reduced at older ages to compensate for the extra cost of term coverage at advanced ages. Alternatively, several different benefits for an older worker might be reduced to make the total cost of the older worker's package commensurate with the cost of younger workers' packages.

Life and disability insurance may be reduced for older workers. Acceptable amounts of life insurance reductions are specified by law. For example, employees age 65 to 69 may be eligible for life insurance benefit amounts equal to 65 percent of the amounts available to eligible employees under age 65; employees age 70 to 74 may receive only 45 percent. Disability benefits provided through sick leave plans may not be reduced on the basis of age. Reductions in benefit amounts for short-term disability insured plans are allowed, but are relatively uncommon in actual practice. Long-term disability benefits may be reduced for older workers through two methods. Benefit amounts may be reduced and duration remain the same, or benefit duration may be curtailed and amounts remain the same. This is justified on the basis of cost, since the probability of disability and the average length of disbaility increase at older ages.

Medical benefits may not be reduced for older, active employees. Employers must offer older workers private group medical benefits that are equal to those offered to younger participants, even if active workers over age 65 are eligible for Medicare. Medicare is the secondary payer for active employees over age 65, covering only those expenses not covered by the primary payer, the employee's group medical insurance.[12]

THE CIVIL RIGHTS ACT

Traditionally, employee benefit plans have not been required to provide benefits for pregnancy and other related conditions. Including disability and medical benefits for pregnancy can significantly increase costs. However, in 1978 the Civil Rights Act was amended to require employers to provide the same benefits for pregnancy and related medical conditions as are provided for other medical conditions. If an employer provides sick leave, disability, or medical insurance, then the employer must provide these benefits in the event of employee pregnancy. Spouses of male and female employees must also be treated equally with respect to pregnancy-related conditions. This federal regulation applies only to plans with more than fifteen employees, but some states impose similar requirements on smaller employers.

AMERICANS WITH DISABILITIES ACT

The 1990 Americans with Disabilities Act (ADA) forbids employers with more than fifteen employees from discriminating against disabled persons

---

12. See chapter 17 for a more detailed discussion of Medicare.

in employment. Disabled persons are those with physical or mental impairments limiting major life activities such as walking, seeing, or hearing. The ADA requires that employee benefits, as a privilege of employment, be provided in a nondiscriminatory manner as well. Employees with disabilities must be given equal access to medical expense insurance coverage and disability coverage. If the medical plan does not cover certain treatment needed by persons with disabilities, such as vision care, the employer does not have to add vision care treatment. However, if vision care is provided by the plan, then vision care must also be offered to employees with disabilities. In addition, specific disabilities, such as vision impairment, or disability in general cannot be excluded from coverage.

OTHER NONDISCRIMINATION LAWS

Federal **nondiscrimination rules** discourage employers from providing benefits only to selected groups of employees, specifically those who are highly paid or hold key positions within the organization. Coverage of a broad class of employees is beneficial not only for lower-paid workers but for society as a whole, since private sector provision for economic security reduces the likelihood that the public sector will need to provide for employees and their families in the event of illness, disability, or premature death. Federal nondiscrimination rules are not uniform across benefits. In 1986, the Tax Reform Act attempted to remedy this through *Section 89* regulations, but these were repealed in 1989 due to the complexity and administrative burden they imposed on employers and on government. The nondiscrimination rules in place prior to 1986 were reinstated to encourage employers to cover a broad class of employees in their benefit plans.

Multinational Employee Benefit Plans

Multinational corporations manage the human resource risk across national boundaries. The most common concern of multinational employers is the benefit needs of **expatriates,** United States citizens working outside the United States. However, the employer is also concerned with managing benefits for employees who are not United States citizens, but who are working in the U.S. In addition, benefits must be considered for employees who are not U.S. citizens and who work outside the U.S. and outside the employee's home country.

The corporation designs multinational benefit policy to achieve several objectives. First, the plans need to be sufficient to attract, retain, and reward workers in locations around the world where a corporate presence is required. The plan needs to be fair for all employees, within the corporation itself, within the industry, and within the country where employees are located. In addition, the multinational benefit policy needs to facilitate the transfer of workers across national boundaries whenever necessary, with a minimum of overall transaction costs.

Typically, the multinational employer tries to protect the expatriate from losing benefits when the employee transfers outside the U.S. A premium may be paid at the time of the move to compensate the employee for international relocation. The corporation often provides the expatriate with the same life, long-term disability, medical, and pension benefits as those provided to their U.S. employees. However, in some cases the employee may receive medical care or short-term disability benefits like those of the host country. When employers provide benefits in several international locations, they may use an **international benefit network** to cover employees across countries under one master insurance contract. This can simplify international benefit administration. The employer also must take into consideration the social insurance systems of the host country, and coordinate coverage as necessary with the employee's home country's system.

Cultural and regulatory factors differ among countries and affect benefit design, financing, and communication. This makes international employee benefits management a dynamic and challenging field. With the continued globalization of business in the 1990s, career opportunities in international benefits management are likely to grow.

Getting the Most from Employee Benefits

If your salary is $750 a week, how big is your check? Do you look? Of course you do, and you're probably disappointed to see that it is about $500 after taxes and other deductions. Your salary, however, may be only three-fourths (or less) of your total compensation. The other part is employee benefits. Look at it this way: if your salary is $750 per week, your employee benefits may be worth an additional $250 per week and you don't have to pay income tax on and take other deductions from the $250.

If your employer failed to provide these benefits, you would have to take over half of your $750 paycheck to purchase similar coverages in the individual market. On an after-tax basis, benefits probably account for more than a third of your total compensation. How can you use them to the best advantage?

First, know your coverage. Know what the benefits are. Study your employee benefits booklet as carefully as you would inspect a new car. If there is anything you don't understand, ask your supervisor or benefits administrator. If they don't know, keep asking until you find out. Second, use your knowledge. Don't buy any other insurance until you know what your employer provides. Now, let's look at your life and disability benefits and make a few specific suggestions.

LIFE INSURANCE

View your group term life insurance as you would any other yearly renewable (and probably convertible) life insurance. Coordinate it with Social Security survivor benefits in determining your needs for individual life insurance. It will be in force only as long as you are with your present employer. After most job terminations, employees immediately move to another employer that offers a similar amount of group life insurance. You can convert almost all plans to a permanent form if you quit your job, but you will pay the premium and it will be substantial if you are advancing in years. This is true of all term and cash-value insurance purchased at advanced ages.

Who owns your group life insurance? Because the matter of ownership is usually not mentioned when you sign up for employee benefits, you are probably the owner. Is that the way you want it? If not, you will have to take the initiative to change ownership. If the clerk who handles employee benefits tells you it can't be done, keep pushing the matter.

It doesn't cost your employer anything and it may be important to you if you have a large estate. If you are the owner at the time of your death, the proceeds will become part of your estate for tax purposes.

Disability Income

It is important to check the definition of disability used in your short-term and long-term disability plans. Is it an own-occupation definition, a reasonable occupation definition, or any occupation definition? For a long-term disability policy, there may be a dual definition that changes after a short time, for example, the first two years of receiving benefits. Also check to see what the elimination period is for your long-term disability income insurance. There may be a gap in coverage between when your short-term insurance ends and your long-term insurance begins.

Certain limitations of group long-term disability coverage may affect your benefits dramatically. For example, benefits may replace a percentage of income up to a specified maximum amount. Is this maximum amount too low for higher-income earners to maintain their standard of living? What about cost-of-living adjustments? Does your plan provide for these? If not, the purchasing power of your benefit could erode during a long period of disability. Group long-term disability insurance policies may not include a conversion option. If coverage terminates, the disabled employee may not continue to receive benefits. Check with the benefits manager to find out how these provisions affect your benefits.

Beware of provisions that reduce your long-term disability income benefit. Some plans use a coordination of benefits provision to offset Social Security disability income benefits, workers' compensation benefits, veterans and other governmental programs, and group-sponsored plans such as retirement plans with disability benefits. Some plans have so many offsets that they really don't provide much income to most disabled persons. This is not to say that there should not be offsets, but to warn you that simply adding up all the disability income benefits you might receive may be misleading. Some of the benefits you add may, instead, be offset. Looked at from that point of view, your total disability income may be inadequate. Know your coverage!

human resource risk
employee benefits
group underwriting
eligibility period
probationary period
actively at work
preexisting condition clauses
master contract
certificate of insurance
participants
self-insured
third-party administrator (TPA)
administrative services only (ASO)
stop loss insurance
employer sharing of costs
supplemental plans
multiple employer trust (MET)
flexible benefit programs

contributory plans
noncontributory plans
experience-rated premiums
conversion privilege
retired lives reserve
group universal life insurance
survivor income benefit plan
salary continuation plan
short-term disability income
elimination period
definition of disability
long-term disability insurance
cafeteria plans
flexible spending accounts (FSA)
nondiscrimination rules
expatriates
international benefit network

Discussion Questions

1. What is meant by the organization's "human resource risk"? How do employee benefit plans mitigate this risk?

2. What methods do employers use to set objectives for a benefits plan?

3. What is the difference between the "probationary period" and the "eligibility period" in group insurance? What is an "elimination period" in group disability insurance?

4. How do employers protect themselves from the risk of catastrophic financial loss when they self-insure a benefits program?

5. Describe three group insurance provisions that reduce the potential for adverse selection.

6. Discuss two ways that an employer may set up a life insurance plan for retirees. What are the strengths and weaknesses of each approach?

7. Why do most group disability insurance plans limit income replacement to no more than 60 percent of salary, even if employees are willing to pay more to get 100 percent coverage? Does this seem fair to you? Why, or why not?

8. Cafeteria plans have become increasingly popular in the 1990s. What factors contributed to the increased use of these plans?

9. How might a flexible benefit plan achieve desirable goals for your employer as well as for you?

10. Why might the benefits manager of a multinational corporation use an international benefits network?

18.1

Rosa Sanchez, single and 25, received two job offers after college graduation. Both were with organizations that she respected, and the nature of the work at each place sounded very interesting to her. One job was with a larger, well-established firm and offered $22,000 per year in salary plus noncontributory benefits worth $7,000 per year. The other job was with a small business and offered a salary of $30,000 per year without benefits. Rosa's mother suggested that she make the choice between the two jobs based on which offered better total compensation.

1. What factors should Rosa consider in determining the better package? Which package do you think maximizes her total compensation?

2. Which employer is economically better off (all else being equal), the one offering salary plus benefits or the one offering salary only? Explain your answer.

18.2

Henry Zantow, the comptroller for Xanex Industries, was discussing the supposed advantages of a true cafeteria plan versus a "traditional" plan with Lloyd Olsen. Lloyd agreed with Henry that a cafeteria plan certainly seemed the better of the two plans. Both Henry and Lloyd looked at each other and in the same breath said, "I wonder why anyone would choose a traditional plan?"

1. What is your answer to this question?

2. If the corporation decides to use a cafeteria plan, why might it want a minimum level of core benefits?

18.3

Jan Czyrmer, the employee benefits manager at Ludlow Enterprises, wants to restructure the leave policy for the company. He is concerned that employees abuse sick leave policy, taking sick leave time for personal reasons not related to illness. He wants to abolish particular types of leave (such as sick leave, vacation leave, personal leave) and give employees a certain number of general leave days per year to use as they choose.

1. If upper management objects to Jan's idea of a major restructuring of leave, what can he do to prevent abuse of current sick leave policy? Are there steps that can be taken to reduce moral hazard within the traditional leave system?

2. What advantages might Jan cite to convince upper management that consolidating leave may be helpful for Ludlow Enterprises?

18.4

Yolanda Freeman is evaluating whether federal nondiscrimination laws have helped or hurt employees.

1. Which federal laws particularly affect employee benefits? Which workers are particularly affected by each law?

2. Who pays the cost of requiring that benefits be paid on a nondiscriminatory basis? Do additional benefit costs have any effect on employee wage levels?

3. If federal laws did not require coverage for certain employees and their dependents, who would pay for benefits for these individuals? Do you think that social welfare is maximized by mandating coverage for certain workers and their dependents through these nondiscrimination laws?

Employee Benefits: Medical Care

Introduction   The costs of health care and the insurance that helps finance this care are of major social concern in the United States. The United States historically has spent more on health care per capita than any other country.[1] From 1962 to 1992, national health care expenditures as a percentage of gross domestic product rose from 5.5 percent to 13.8 percent.[2] Health care costs, particularly the hospital component, have grown much faster than the average cost of other consumer goods and services. With the rising cost of care, medical insurance becomes increasingly important, since it provides economic security for individuals against the risks of medical expenses that may be difficult to budget.

Most private (nongovernmental) medical expense insurance is provided through employer groups. Among all employee benefits sponsored by employers, medical insurance is both the most commonly offered and the most expensive to the employer. In 1993, 97 percent of medium- to large-sized employers offered some type of group medical insurance, and the average amount spent by employers on medical coverage was approximately 11 percent of payroll.[3] In group plans, generally, the employee is covered and the spouse and unmarried children (up to age 18, or 22 or 25 for full-time students) may or may not be, depending on whether the employer or employee pays the extra premium for dependent coverage and whether the dependents are covered under other policies.

After reading this chapter, you will have examined the following aspects of group medical expense insurance:
1. Traditional fee-for-service group medical expense coverage.
2. Medical insurance policy provisions.
3. Cost containment initiatives for traditional fee-for-service policies.
4. Health maintenance organizations.
5. Preferred provider organizations.
6. Managed care plans.
7. Other medical care plans.
8. Medical care systems worldwide.

1. However, the 1990 per capita health care costs increased more rapidly in Canada, France, and the United Kingdom and are projected to continue to do so in the future. See the *Source Book of Health Insurance Data 1993* (Washington, D.C.: Health Insurance Association of America), p. 78.
2. These statistics are published annually by the U.S. Department of Health and Human Services, Health Care Financing Administration.
3. *Employee Benefits: Survey Data from Benefit Year 1993*, U.S. Chamber of Commerce Research Center (1994): pp. 9, 26.

Traditional Fee-for-Service Medical Expense Coverage

The traditional method for providing group medical expense benefits has been by paying **health care providers** a fee for services rendered. Health care providers include health *professionals,* such as physicians and surgeons, as well as health *facilities,* such as hospitals and outpatient surgery centers. Medical expense benefits may be provided on an indemnity, service, or valued basis.

Indemnity benefits apply the principle of indemnity by providing payment for loss, such as hospital expense, within specified limits and for specified causes. The insured (the covered employee or dependent) would receive, for example, the actual costs incurred up to but not exceeding $300 per day for up to 90 days while confined in a hospital. If the cost were $280 per day, the insurer would pay $280. If it were $350 per day, the insurer would pay only $300. Other dollar limits would be placed on benefits for other types of charges, such as those for ancillary charges (such as x-ray, laboratory, and drugs) made by the hospital.

With a policy providing **service benefits,** the insurer pays for specified services from health care providers participating in the group insurance plan, rather than paying a specific number of dollars for services rendered. For example, the insurer might pay the cost of a semiprivate room for up to 90 days of hospital confinement. This concept of service benefits originated with Blue Cross plans, but now they are offered by most commercial insurers as well. Most health care providers participate in group plans that provide service benefits. However, if the insured uses a nonparticipating provider, say, in the event of emergency treatment, generally the insured is reimbursed on an indemnity basis. Consequently, the insured is usually better off economically using a participating provider whenever possible.

In a **valued policy,** the insurer agrees to pay the insured a specified amount of money upon the occurrence of a particular event, such as $100 per day for a hospital confinement. It is not specified as to whether the insured uses the money to pay the hospital, replace lost income, or for some other purpose. Valued policies are primarily used as supplements to other health care coverages.

There are five major classifications of traditional fee-for-service medical expense insurance: (1) hospital expense, (2) surgical expense, (3) medical expense, (4) major medical, and (5) comprehensive medical insurance. The first three types are called "basic" coverage and provide a limited set of services or reimburse a limited dollar amount. As the names suggest, major medical and comprehensive medical insurance provide coverage for large losses.

BASIC HEALTH CARE BENEFITS

Basic health care benefits cover hospital, surgical, and medical expenses. These coverages are limited in terms of the types of services (or expenditure reimbursements) they provide, as well as the dollar limits of protection. As figure 19–1 shows, basic medical coverage generally provides first-dollar coverage instead of protection against large losses.

The **basic hospital policy** covers *room and board* (for a specified number of days) and *hospital ancillary charges,* such as those for x-ray imaging and laboratory tests. The basic hospital policy primarily provides benefits

FIGURE 19–1

Basic Medical Coverage

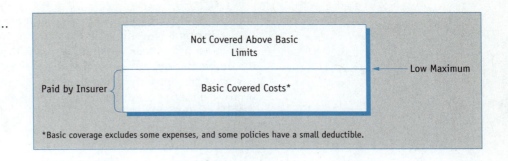

*Basic coverage excludes some expenses, and some policies have a small deductible.

during a hospital confinement. In addition, it covers outpatient surgery and limited emergency care in case of an accident. Many policies today have a small deductible, such as $75 or $125 per hospital confinement, in order to reduce claims and premiums.

Ancillary charges may be covered on a *schedule* basis, such as $40 for a chest x-ray, or more commonly on a *blanket* basis for all x-rays, laboratory, work, and other ancillary charges, with a maximum limit such as $5,000 for all such charges. Maternity coverage is included in group medical expense insurance policies, since the Civil Rights Act forbids employer-sponsored health insurance plans from treating pregnancy differently from any other medical condition.[4] Common limits on basic hospital insurance include nonduplication of coverage provided by workers' compensation and limits on expenditures for treatment of mental disorders.

The **basic surgical policy** usually pays providers according to a schedule of procedures, regardless of whether the surgery is performed in a hospital or elsewhere. The policy lists the maximum benefit for each type of operation. For example, up to $800 may be paid for an appendectomy. A second approach sometimes used by insurers is to pay benefits up to the "usual and customary" surgical charges in the geographical region where the operation is performed.[5] Usual and customary charges are defined as those below the 90th percentile of charges by all surgeons in a geographical region for the same procedure, and typically are higher than most fee schedule amounts.

A **basic medical expense policy** covers all or part of doctors' fees for hospital, office, or home visits due to nonsurgical care. Often a plan provides benefits only when the insured is confined to a hospital. Most policies have an overall limit of a daily rate (such as $50) multiplied by the number of days (for example, a 120-day maximum) in the hospital, whereas others simply have a daily limit or a limit per visit. Common exclusions are routine examinations, eye examinations, x-rays, and prescription drugs.

4. The effect of the Civil Rights Act on *group* pregnancy benefits is discussed in chapter 18. See chapter 21 for a discussion of *individual* policies. Maternity coverage is excluded under many individual policies, unless care is needed for abnormal complications not resulting from routine pregnancy. An individual may purchase optional maternity coverage in the individual market, but the premium is quite high at younger ages because of the frequency of claims and the significant expense of even a routine or normal delivery.

5. Insurers use different terms to describe what we have called "usual and customary" charges. Some add "prevailing"; others add "reasonable." In all cases, the purpose is to cap reimbursement for any specific procedure.

Basic health care coverage has been criticized for encouraging treatment in the hospital, the most expensive site for medical care delivery. For example, both the basic hospital and medical policies cover services primarily delivered on an inpatient basis. Newer basic policies provide better coverage for outpatient services. For example, some provide x-ray and laboratory benefits on an outpatient basis (up to a small maximum benefit) and cover the cost of preadmission tests, done on an outpatient basis prior to hospital admission.

MAJOR MEDICAL AND COMPREHENSIVE INSURANCE

The hospital, surgical, and medical expense insurance policies previously discussed are basic contracts in the sense that they provide for many of the expenses caused by poor health but on a somewhat selective basis and with rather low limits. They are weak in the breadth of their coverage as well as their maximum benefit limits. Two insurance policies have been developed to correct for these weaknesses: (1) major medical insurance and (2) comprehensive medical insurance.

Major Medical Insurance

Major medical insurance covers the expense of almost all medical services prescribed by a doctor. It provides coverage for virtually all charges for hospitals, doctors, medicines, blood, wheelchairs, and other medically necessary items. Typically, employers provide group major medical coverage in conjunction with group basic health care coverage, and both policies may be sold to the employer by the same or different insurance carriers. Major medical policies have four fundamental features: (1) high maximum limits, (2) a large deductible, (3) coverage of a broad range of different medical services, and (4) coinsurance provisions.

Maximum limits on benefits vary upward from $10,000 per person, with a typical maximum benefit of $250,000 or more. Some policies offer unlimited maximum benefits. The limit applies to the total amount the insurer will pay. It may apply to each injury or illness separately, but typically applies to all injuries and illnesses irrespective of whether they are related, over the insured's lifetime. A small percentage of policies have lower internal limits that apply to a calendar year, a policy year, or a benefit year.[6] Large limits reduce the likelihood that the insured will bear the cost of potentially catastrophic expenses associated with some illnesses and accidents.

Internal policy limits often apply to specified services. Hospital room and board charges are usually limited to the hospital's most prevalent semi-private rate. Private duty nursing care, as with outpatient psychiatric services, may be covered at a low coinsurance rate, such as 50 percent, when care is provided outside of a hospital. All charges are subject to a usual and customary test. Benefits for surgeons' and physicians' fees can be less than the entire amount that is billed because actual charges exceed the insurer's schedule of what is usual and customary.

....

6. A policy year is from one anniversary date of the policy to the next. A benefit year begins at the inception of a disability and runs for the succeeding twelve months.

FIGURE 19–2

Major Medical Insurance

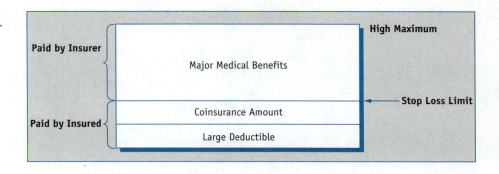

As figure 19–2 shows, the deductible in policies is large, ranging from $300 to $2,000. Its purpose is to eliminate small claims and restrict benefits to the more financially burdensome expenses, thus making possible high limits and broad coverage at a reasonable premium rate. A new deductible must be satisfied each **benefit period.** In group insurance, the benefit period is usually a calendar year. Group major medical contracts often have a "corridor deductible," under which basic contract benefits are not counted toward the major medical deductible requirement. The insured has to pay the deductible after the basic contract benefits are exhausted, before the major medical begins to pay.[7]

As with maximum limits, the deductible can consist of charges for all illnesses and injuries, or be restricted to only one illness and its medically related conditions. The deductible also applies to each individual; however, many policies require only that two or three family members meet the deductible each year. This reduces the possibility of deductibles causing financial hardship when several family members have serious illnesses or injuries during the same year.

The **coinsurance provision** gives the percentage of expenses the insurer will pay in excess of the deductible. It may vary from 70 to 90 percent; 80 percent is common. The insured bears the remainder (for example, 20 percent) of the burden, up to a **stop loss limit,** for example, $1,000, after which 100 percent of covered charges are reimbursed. Some group contracts include the deductible in the stop loss limit and others do not (figure 19–2 shows the deductible included in the stop loss limit.)

Deductibles and coinsurance requirements are **cost sharing** provisions that increase the personal cost to the insured of using medical services. When insureds pay part of the cost, they tend to use fewer unnecessary or discretionary medical services. That is, deductibles and coinsurance provisions reduce moral hazard and help keep group insurance premiums affordable.[8] The stop loss limit protects the insured from *excessive* cost sharing, which could be financially devastating.

Assume that an employer provides no basic health insurance, but instead provides a major medical policy with a $500 deductible, an 80 percent coinsurance clause, a $1,000 stop loss limit provision that ignores

7. Individual major medical policies may count amounts paid by basic policies toward the major medical deductible. See chapter 21 for a discussion of individual policies.
8. With traditional fee-for-service plans, there is still an economic incentive for medical providers to recommend and provide unnecessary services.

EXPENSES	COVERED CHARGES	NOT COVERED
Hospital room and board (20 days private room @ $225)	$4,000	$500 for private room
Hospital ancillary charges, $3,500	3,500	
Surgeon's fee, $1,500	1,350	$150 above the usual and customary fee
Physician's fees for office visits, $400	400	
Drugs and wheelchair rental, $600	600	
	$9,850	$ 650
− Deductible	500	500
Balance	$9,350	
First $5,000 paid @ 80% = $4,000		1,000
Remainder paid @ 100% = 4,350		$2,150 Amount You Pay
Insurer pays: $8,350		

the deductible, a $1 million maximum benefit, an internal limit of the most prevalent semiprivate room-and-board rate, and a usual and customary charges provision. Using these assumptions, figure 19–3 shows the calculation of what the insured would collect on a hypothetical claim under this policy.

Comprehensive Medical Insurance

With major medical policies, the insurer pays most of the cost for medical services. However, major medical policy cost sharing still may be sizeable, putting a heavy financial burden on the insured. This was illustrated in figure 19–3. **Comprehensive medical insurance** deals with this problem by providing smaller deductibles, typically $100 to $300 per individual per calendar year (see figure 19–4). Any eligible expenses incurred during the calendar year usually can be used to satisfy the deductible. Comprehensive plans are not sold with basic hospital, surgical, and medical expense insurance. Comprehensive medical insurance is designed as a stand-alone policy that provides broad coverage for a range of inpatient and outpatient services. Except for the smaller deductible, the provisions of a comprehensive plan are usually the same as those in a major medical plan. The comprehensive policy is sold mainly on a group basis.

LIMITED CONTRACTS

The medical expense insurance policies discussed so far are generally rather broad, in the sense that eligible expenses are paid regardless of the cause of injury or illness (with some exceptions). Thus, all eligible expenses from illness or injuries not excluded by the policy are covered and, for the most part, the exclusions are not numerous. However, many employers offer the option of additional coverage through **limited contracts,** policies that pay only for eligible expenses of a specified illness or injury.[9] These limited contracts are an important part of **voluntary benefits,** op-

....
9. Limited contracts for disability income are discussed in chapter 21.

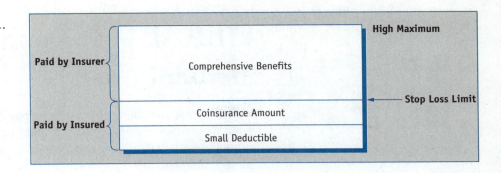

tional benefits for which the employer makes no premium contribution and which the employee elects at will and funds through payroll deduction. Limited contract benefits are usually paid on a reimbursement basis.

There are many different types of limited contracts. A common one is the "dread disease policy." The dread disease policy, which originated as the polio policy prior to the development of an effective vaccine for polio, provides for reimbursement of a broad range of medical expenses up to a high limit of coverage if the insured contracts one of the diseases listed. The diseases included are low in frequency, but high in severity. Currently, cancer policies constitute the bulk of dread disease policies. The policy pays only in the event that the insured contracts cancer.

Some employees do not recognize that the need of an individual or family for medical expense reimbursement is the same, regardless of the disease contracted. Limited contracts are not a substitute for more expensive but broader protection, such as that provided by major medical or comprehensive plans. Limited contracts may lead to a false sense of security if the employee does not appreciate their limitations.

Medical Insurance Policy Provisions

Some medical insurance policy provisions (for example, deductibles, coinsurance, and stop loss limits) have already been discussed in this chapter, and other general plan provisions, such as who pays the premium and preexisting condition provisions, are covered in chapter 18. Here we discuss three additional policy provisions that are especially important with group medical insurance, namely, coordination of benefits, continuation provisions, and retiree eligibility for benefits. Cost containment provisions are discussed in the next section of this chapter.

COORDINATION OF BENEFITS

Today, many employees and their dependents are eligible for group medical expense coverage under more than one plan. For example, the husband and wife of a dual-career couple may be eligible either as an employee or as the spouse of an employee. Children may be eligible under both the father's and the mother's plan. Workers with more than one permanent part-time job may be eligible for coverage with more than one employer. Coordination is needed to prevent duplicate payment of medical expenses when employees or their dependents are covered under more than one group policy.

ETHICAL *Dilemma*

Medical Care

Medical care is something that everyone needs at some point in life. Most people agree that a health care system providing universal care (or medical services to all) would be desirable. Some people believe that medical care is not only desirable, but is a right to which everyone is entitled. The ethical dilemma rests in the fact that, although universal access is desirable, medical care is costly. Who will pay for the cost of universal coverage? Should those who can afford to pay cover the cost of those who cannot?

The current health care system in the United States covers most people through private, employment-based plans or through public plans targeted to specific groups, such as the elderly and the poor. However, about 15 percent of the population is uninsured, and lack of insurance limits access to medical care services. The uninsured generally are able to get care from some hospital emergency rooms and clinics, but the choice and quality of care are restricted.

In the current health care system, costshifting occurs; those who pay for care absorb some of the cost of those who do not pay. For example, employer-provided plans often pay hospital rates that are increased to cover costs of those in the hospital who do not pay. Even though costshifting is a burden, many employers fear that moving to a health care system that provides true universal coverage would be far more expensive than the current system.

Consider for a moment who is entitled to medical care and who should pay. Several factors may affect your beliefs: your own employment status, whether your employer is large enough and financially able to provide a medical expense insurance plan, whether you or a family member has a chronic illness. The ethical dilemma is difficult to resolve, but merits consideration.

The **coordination of benefits provision** establishes a system of primary and secondary insurers. The primary insurer pays the normal benefit amount, as if no other insurance were in force. Then the secondary insurer pays the balance of the covered health care expenses. The total payments by the primary and secondary insurers are limited to 100 percent of the covered charges for the applicable policies. Estimates are that coordination of benefits reduces the total cost of health insurance by over 10 percent by reducing duplicate payment.

An employee's group plan is always considered primary for expenses incurred by the employee. For example, in a dual-career couple, the husband's primary coverage is with his employer, the wife's with her employer, and each has secondary coverage through the spouse's plan. When a child is insured under both parents' plans, the policy of the parent whose birthday falls first in the year is the primary policy. However, in the case of separation or divorce, the primary coverage for the child is through the custodial parent. Secondary coverage is through stepparents, and coverage through the noncustodial parent pays last. In some cases, these rules may not establish a priority of payment, and then the policy in effect for the longest period of time is primary. Any group plan that does not include a coordination of benefits provision is considered the primary insurer by all insurers that have such provisions. This encourages almost universal use of the coordination of benefits provision.

Allowing insureds to be covered under more than one policy means that these insureds may not have to pay deductible or coinsurance requirements. However, group policies sometimes stipulate that the secondary payer cannot reimburse the deductible amounts required by the primary policy. This is designed to preserve the effect of the cost sharing requirement, namely, to control the use of unnecessary or excess services by the insured and to reduce moral hazard.

CONTINUATION PROVISIONS

The Consolidated Omnibus Budget Reconciliation Act (**COBRA**) of 1985 requires that employers of more than twenty employees who maintain a group medical plan must allow certain minimum **continuation provisions.** COBRA's continuation provisions require that former employees, their spouses, divorced spouses, and dependent children be allowed to continue coverage at the individual's own expense upon the occurrence of a *qualifying event* (which otherwise would have resulted in the loss of medical insurance). The qualifying events are shown in figure 19–5. Most terminations of employment, except for gross misconduct, activate a 31-day right to convert the health insurance that the employee or dependent had before the qualifying event (vision and dental benefits need not be offered). If the employer does not meet the COBRA continuation provisions, it cannot deduct its contributions toward the cost of the plan in figuring its federal income taxes. The employer can charge for the cost of conversion coverage, but the charge cannot exceed 102 percent of the cost of coverage for employees generally. Some events require coverage continuation for eighteen months, and others require thirty-six months of coverage.

The employee has a valuable right with COBRA, because continuation of insurance is possible without evidence of insurability. In addition, the group rate may be lower than individual rates in the marketplace. However, COBRA subjects employers to adverse selection costs and administrative costs beyond the additional 2 percent of premium collected. Many terminated healthy employees and dependents will immediately have ac-

FIGURE 19–5

COBRA Qualifying Events Leading to Continuation of Health Insurance Opportunities

1. Voluntary (and in some cases involuntary) termination of employee's employment.
2. Employee death.
3. Reduction of hours worked resulting in coverage termination.
4. Divorce or legal separation from an employee.
5. Entitlement by an employee for Medicare.
6. Dependent child ceases to meet dependent child definition.
7. Employer filing for Chapter 11 bankruptcy.

NOTE: For each event, it is assumed that the person was covered for group medical benefits immediately prior to the qualifying event.

SOURCE: COBRA

cess to satisfactory insurance with another employer, but many newly hired unhealthy employees may not. This is due to the preexisting condition clauses that many group insurance plans have.[10] Preexisting condition clauses may prohibit payment for preexisting conditions for three to twelve months, depending on the employer's policy. Thus, unhealthy employees terminating one job and going to another job may pay the cost of COBRA at the former job until the preexisting condition period elapses at the new job, in order to ensure that expenses due to the preexisting condition are insured.

RETIREE ELIGIBILITY FOR GROUP MEDICAL BENEFITS

As discussed in chapter 18, most group medical plans allow active, permanent, full-time employees to be eligible for group coverage. By law, employers that offer group medical insurance are required to offer it to active workers over age 65, and for these employees Medicare becomes a secondary payer. Some employers choose to offer continuation of group medical benefits to employees who have retired. This coverage is like medigap insurance, where Medicare is the primary payer and the group plan is secondary.[11] Typically, the retiree plan is less generous than the plan for active workers, since it is designed to simply "fill the gaps" left by Medicare.

Historically, employers have paid medical premiums or benefits for retirees out of current revenues, recognizing the expense in the period that it was paid out. However, in 1993 the Financial Accounting Standards Board (FASB) began phasing in a requirement that employers recognize the present value of future retiree medical expense benefits on the balance sheet during the employees' active working years. The negative effect of these new rules on corporate earnings is significant. Consequently, many employers are cutting back on medigap benefits promised to retirees (through increased cost sharing provisions, for example), and in some cases are eliminating employer-sponsored medigap coverage altogether.

Cost Containment Initiatives for Traditional Fee-for-Service Policies

Medical costs have been rising at a rapid rate, and such costs create both a strong demand for health insurance and a strong desire to develop effective methods to control costs. These methods are called **cost containment techniques.**

Cost containment techniques have been developed for traditional fee-for-service plans, as will be discussed next. In addition, health maintenance organizations and preferred provider organizations were developed to control costs, and managed care techniques emerged most recently to serve this same purpose. These other important cost containment mechanisms are discussed in subsequent sections of this chapter.

10. See chapter 18 for more discussion of preexisting condition clauses.
11. See chapter 17 for a discussion of Medicare, and chapter 21 for a discussion of medigap insurance.

Cost containment techniques for traditional fee-for-service plans can be categorized as follows:

1. Plan design techniques.
2. Administration and funding techniques.
3. Utilization monitoring techniques.

PLAN DESIGN TECHNIQUES

Early health insurance design incorporated the traditional insurance cost control techniques of (1) deductibles, (2) coinsurance, (3) limits on coverage, and (4) exclusions. Deductibles and coinsurance shift costs to the insured, with the expectation that demand for health care services will be less than it would be without these features.

A study conducted by the Rand Corporation for the United States Department of Health and Human Services confirms that the use of deductibles and coinsurance provisions reduces overall health care expenditures.[12] Some fifteen years since the release of the study results, these findings remain important in understanding the relationship between insurance policy design, the demand for medical services, and cost control. During that period, many employers have increased employee cost sharing by raising deductibles and having coinsurance percentages (usually 80 percent) apply to inpatient as well as outpatient charges.

Limits on coverage or policy limits consist of (1) maximum allowances per unit of health service (for example, a $40 limit per visit to a physician's office); (2) internal limits, such as 50 percent coinsurance or treatment of mental illness, in a major medical or comprehensive plan that provides 80 percent coinsurance for all other covered charges; (3) maximum limits per year or lifetime, such as $100,000 per year and a $1 million lifetime limit on major medical benefits; and (4) the coordination of benefits when they are available under more than one plan.

Exclusion of routine eye examinations, eyeglasses, hearing examinations, and most dental expenses under otherwise broad insurance plans undoubtedly reduced expenditures on these types of services, at least until separate policies started covering these items. Dental insurance has become prevalent, and vision care is increasingly common.

ADMINISTRATIVE AND FUNDING TECHNIQUES

Retention consists of an insurer's operating expenses and profit, and is a portion of the premium not expected to be returned to insureds as benefits. Retention comprises between 5 and 10 percent of total premiums for large employers.[13] Employers have reduced retention in two ways. First, they negotiated with insurers for lower retention elements. Second, more than half of large employers shifted from insured to primarily self-insured plans.

---

12. Willard G. Manning, Joseph P. Newhouse, Naihua Duan, Emmett B. Keeler, Arlene Leibowitz, and M. Susan Marquis, "Health Insurance and the Demand for Medical Care: Evidence from a Randomized Experiment," *American Economic Review*, vol. 77, no. 3 (1987): pp. 251–77.
13. Large employers are defined here as those with more than fifty employees.

Insurers continue to have a role in many self-insured group plans, but it is mainly administrative. They (1) pay claims, (2) provide other administrative services, and (3) reinsure catastrophic claims. Through self-insurance, employers may be able to avoid state premium taxes (usually 1 or 2 percent of premiums) levied on insurance, eliminate most of the insurers' potential profits, and, in some cases, earn higher investment returns on reserves for health claims than those normally earned by group insurers. In addition, self-insured plans do not have to comply with state laws mandating coverage of medical care benefits (for example, alcoholism and infertility benefits). A small percentage of employers totally administer their plans, eliminating any insurer involvement. The overall effect of these changes on the cost of health care can be characterized as significant in absolute dollar savings, yet minor as a percentage of total costs.

UTILIZATION MONITORING TECHNIQUES

We have discussed some important information from the Rand study about the effect of cost sharing on the demand for medical services. The Rand study found that more generous insurance coverage is likely to mean more demand for medical services. The study found that while cost sharing affects demand for services, only about 10 percent of the tremendous post-World War II increase in health care costs is attributable to the availability of insurance.[14] The study attributes most of the cost increase to technological advances in medicine, inflation, and increases in real income. Consistent with this finding, efforts to control costs have not been limited to variables in contract design. Utilization techniques developed by insurers and employers in the last fifteen years are designed to reduce the use of the most costly forms of health care—hospitalization and surgery. Some of these techniques are listed in figure 19–6. Most group plans use some or all of these methods to control costs. The first ten are discussed briefly in this section, and the others are described later in more detail.

Second surgical opinion contract provisions provide for the payment of 100 percent of usual and customary surgical costs when the insured seeks a second opinion before undergoing elective or nonemergency surgery, and a lower percentage, usually from 50 to 80 percent, if the insured proceeds with surgery after only one opinion. Second surgical opinions do not require that two surgeons agree that surgery needs to be done before the insurer will pay for the procedure. A second surgical opinion provision only requires that the insured get a second opinion to increase the infor-

FIGURE 19–6

Health Care Cost Containment Methods

1. Second surgical opinions.	9. Statistical analysis of claims.
2. Ambulatory surgical centers.	10. Prospective payment.
3. Preadmission testing.	11. Business coalitions.
4. Preadmission certification.	12. Wellness programs.
5. Extended care facilities.	13. Health maintenance organizations.
6. Hospice care.	14. Preferred provider organizations.
7. Home health care.	15. Managed care plans.
8. Utilization review organizations.	

14. Manning et al., p. 269.

mation available before making a decision about whether to have the surgery. Most people, however, do not want to have surgery, and often opt for an alternative treatment if one is available.

The same dual reimbursement rates apply for minor surgical procedures, where surgery is performed in an **ambulatory surgical center** or as an outpatient at the hospital or surgeon's office. The policy pays a greater percent of the cost when the surgery is performed on an outpatient basis. The objective is to avoid paying for hospital room and board, if hospitalization is not needed for recovery. Dual reimbursement rates also encourage **preadmission testing,** where patients have diagnostic tests done on an outpatient basis prior to surgery to reduce the total time spent in the hospital.

Most group fee-for-service plans require **preadmission certification** for hospitalization for any nonemergency condition. The insured or the physician of the insured contacts the plan administrator for approval for hospital admission for a specified number of days. The administrative review is usually made by a nurse or other health professional. The plan administrator may approve the requested length of stay, approve a shorter stay, or require the procedure to be done on an outpatient basis. The recommendation is based on practice patterns of physicians in the region, and an appeals process is available for patients with conditions that require admissions and lengths of stay outside of the norm.

Extended care facilities or nursing facilities, **hospice care** for the dying, or **home health care** following hospital discharge may be recommended to reduce the length of hospitalization. Extended care facilities provide basic medical care needed during some recoveries, rather than the intensive and more expensive medical service of a hospital. With hospice care, volunteers and family members help to care for a dying person in the hospital, at home, or in a dedicated hospice facility. Home health care is an organized system of care at home that substitutes for a hospital admission or allows early discharge from the hospital. The insurer covers the cost of physicians' visits, nurses' visits, respiratory therapy, prescription drugs, physical and speech therapy, home health aids, and other essentials. Cancer, diabetes, fractures, acquired immune deficiency syndrome (AIDS), heart ailments, and many other illnesses can be treated as effectively and less expensively with home health, hospice, and extended care.

Employers or their insurers often contract for reviews by an outside **utilization review organization,** sometimes called a Professional Review Organization (PRO). Utilization review organizations, run by physicians, surgeons, and nurses, offer peer judgments on (1) whether a hospital admission is necessary, (2) whether the length of the hospital stay is appropriate for the medical condition, and (3) whether the quality of care is commensurate with the patient's needs. When problems are identified, the utilization review organization may contact the hospital administrator, the chief of the medical staff, or the personal physician. When treatment deviates substantially from the norm, the physician may be asked to discuss the case before a peer review panel. The medical insurance policy may refuse to pay for care considered unnecessary by the reviewing organization.

Utilization review organizations, third-party administrators, and many large employers collect and analyze data on health care claims. This **statistical analysis of claims** has the purpose of identifying any overutilization or excessive charges by providers of medical care. These studies usually establish standard costs for a variety of **diagnostic related groups (DRGs)**. Each DRG is a medical or surgical condition that recognizes age, sex, and other determinants of treatment costs. By looking at each provider's charges on a DRG basis, the analyses can identify high- and low-cost providers.

Another cost containment technique using DRGs is **prospective payment.** In 1983, the federal government adopted the practice of paying a flat fee for each Medicare patient based on the patient's DRG. Prospective payment provided an economic incentive to providers, specifically hospitals, to minimize length of stay and other cost parameters. Use of prospective payment proved effective, and other insurers and employers now use similar methods. Assignment of incorrect or multiple DRGs to obtain higher fees can be problematic, and monitoring is necessary to keep costs as low as possible.

Business coalitions engage in statistical analysis and other efforts to control health care costs. Through coalitions, businesses in a city or region combine their medical care purchasing power to identify low-cost providers and negotiate discounts with them. In return for the discounts, coalition members increase employee awareness of the need to control costs by distributing lists of low-cost physicians and hospitals to influence employee use patterns. These efforts have resulted in formal arrangements called preferred provider organizations, described later in this chapter. Coalitions also get involved in regional health care planning, often to oppose construction of new hospitals or the expansion of old ones. These coalition activities are motivated by the hypothesis that the supply of health care providers creates its own demand. Some coalitions also create their own utilization review organizations.

Another cost containment initiative by employers has been to sponsor **wellness programs** designed to promote healthy lifestyles and reduce the incidence and severity of employee medical expenses. The programs vary greatly in scope. Some are limited to educational sessions on good health habits and screening for high blood pressure, cholesterol, diabetes, cancer symptoms, and other treatable conditions. More extensive programs provide physical fitness gymnasiums for aerobic exercise such as biking, running, and walking. Counseling is available, usually on a confidential basis, as an aid in the management of stress, nutrition, alcoholism, or smoking.

One criticism of wellness programs is that they primarily attract persons who already have healthy lifestyles. Top management endorsement may enable wellness programs to attract wider participation. More recently, some employers have moved toward programs that target the needs of particular employees in poor health, in an effort to better control medical claim costs. Employers with successful wellness programs believe not only that the programs help control medical costs, but that wellness efforts improve employee morale and productivity.

The cost containment methods listed in figure 19–6 show that businesses are taking an active role in managing health care costs. These methods are no longer experimental, and most are here to stay. New techniques for containing costs will continue to emerge as long as rising medical care costs remain a top concern of employers.

Health Maintenance Organizations

Health maintenance organizations (HMOs) have been around for over fifty years. In the 1970s, they gained national attention for their potential to reduce health care costs. Today, about 36 percent of people with private medical insurance are covered through an HMO.[15]

HISTORY

The HMO concept is generally traced back to the Ross-Loos group, which was a temporary medical unit that provided medical services to Los Angeles construction workers building an aqueduct in a California desert in 1933. Henry J. Kaiser offered the same service to construction workers for the Grand Coulee Dam in Washington state. During World War II, what is now called the Kaiser Permanente plan was used for employees in Kaiser shipyards.[16] In the 1960s, the United Auto Workers union enrolled approximately 60,000 members in a group practice[17] HMO. The major turning point in popularity for HMOs occurred with the passage of the Health Maintenance Organization Act of 1973.

This act requires an employer to subscribe exclusively to an HMO or to make this form of health care financing and delivery available at the option of employees, provided an HMO that qualifies under the act is located nearby and requests consideration.[18] This mandate is called *dual choice* because the HMO generally becomes an alternative choice for employees to the traditional fee-for-service group plan. With passage of the HMO Act and increased public acceptance of this nontraditional health care system, enrollment in HMOs grew from 3.5 million subscribers in 1972 to 41.4 million in 1992.[19] Sponsors include insurance companies, government units, Blue Cross Blue Shield, hospitals, medical schools, consumer groups, unions, and other organizations.

In recent years, most HMOs have preferred to market their services without forcing themselves on employers by invoking the HMO Act. This is important because an HMO that gains access to a group by asking the sponsor to comply with the dual choice provisions of the HMO Act must charge the same premium to all participants.[20] The HMO that markets its services without demanding dual choice, however, can recognize age, sex, and other underwriting factors in setting both individual and group rates. Recognition of these factors produces rates more competitive with an employer's insurance and self-insurance alternatives.

NATURE OF HMOS

HMOs provide a comprehensive range of medical services, including physicians, surgeons, hospitals, and other providers, emphasizing preventive

---

15. *Source Book of Health Insurance Data,* (1993): p. 35.
16. Today, Kaiser Permanente is one of the largest HMOs in the United States, with operations scattered across the country.
17. A group practice HMO is defined later in the chapter.
18. Employers engaged in interstate commerce with more than twenty-five employees must comply.
19. *Source Book of Health Insurance Data,* (1993): p. 41.
20. This system is called community rating.

care. The HMO either employs providers directly or sets up contracts with outside providers to care for subscribers. Thus, the HMO both finances care (like an insurer) and provides care (unlike an insurer). The HMO estimates the cost of care for a subscriber during the next year and sets a **capitated fee** that is the equivalent of a premium. In return for a capitated fee, the HMO has a contractual obligation to provide all necessary health care services to the subscriber. In order to remain profitable, the HMO must provide total care to subscribers at a cost that does not exceed capitated fee income.

With traditional fee-for-service insurance, providers are legally and physically separated from the third-party insurance companies that provide the funding (insurance) for patient care. In other words, the employer pays the premiums to one organization and the employee receives care from independent providers. The independent providers are paid fees for each service they deliver, and economic incentives are for providers to deliver more services.

The scope of HMO coverage is broader than that of most fee-for-service plans. For example, HMOs cover routine checkups even when the employee is not ill. Deductibles and coinsurance apply only to minor cost items, such as physician office visits and prescription drugs (for example, a $3.00 copayment may be required for each of these services). The employee has lower cost sharing requirements than with traditional fee-for-service plans as long as the employee is treated within the HMO.

Two basic types of HMOs are available. Some of the oldest and largest plans are not-for-profit **group practice associations.** In this arrangement, HMO physicians and other providers work for salaries. In **individual practice associations,** which can be either for-profit or not-for-profit organizations, contractual arrangements are made with physicians and other providers in a community who practice out of their own offices and treat both HMO and non-HMO members. Often, a physician, selected as an HMO member's primary physician is paid a fixed fee per HMO member. When physicians are paid by salary or per patient, the primary physician acts as a gatekeeper between the patient, specialists, hospitals, and other providers. Both types of HMOs pay for and refer subscribers to specialists when they consider this necessary. However, if the HMO subscriber sees a specialist without a referral from the HMO, then the subscriber is responsible for paying the specialist for the full cost of care (i.e., no other insurance applies). HMOs either own their own hospitals or contract with outside hospitals to serve subscribers.

COST-SAVING MOTIVATION

Because the HMO receives an essentially preset, fixed annual income (the capitation fee plus investment income on reserves) and has promised to provide all the care the subscriber needs (with a few exclusions), it is financially at risk. If the HMO overtreats subscribers, it will lose money. Consequently, no economic incentive exists to have subscribers return for unnecessary visits, to enter the hospital if treatment can be done in an ambulatory setting, or to undergo surgery that is unlikely to improve quality of life. This is the key aspect of an HMO that is supposed to increase efficiency relative to traditional fee-for-service plans. Evidence suggests that HMOs use less hospitalization and surgery compared to traditional insured plans.

A major criticism of HMOs is the limited choice of providers for subscribers. The number of physicians, hospitals, and other providers in the HMO may be quite small with both group and individual practice associations. Some individual practice plans overcome the criticism by enrolling almost every physician and hospital in a geographic region, and then paying providers on a fee-for-service basis. By paying on a fee-for-service basis, however, these arrangements may destroy the main mechanism that helps HMOs control costs. Another concern expressed by critics is that HMOs do not have proper incentives to provide high-quality care. There is, however, little evidence that conclusive differences in the quality of care exist between traditional fee-for-service plans and HMOs.[21]

Preferred Provider Organizations

Preferred provider organizations (PPOs) were first formed in the 1980s as another approach to containing costs in group health insurance programs. PPOs are groups of hospitals, physicians, and other health care providers that contract with insurers, third-party administrators, or directly with employers to provide medical care to members of the contracting group(s) at discounted prices per unit of service. They provide a mechanism for organizing, marketing, and managing fee-for-service medical care. While PPOs vary in design, a typical one would include the features shown in figure 19–7. In 1992 there were more than 680 PPOs covering almost 50 million employees across the country.[22]

Unlike most HMOs, PPOs give employees and their dependents a broad choice of providers. The insured can go to any provider on an extensive list supplied by the employer or insurer. The insured can also go to a provider not on the list. If the insured goes to a preferred provider, most PPOs waive most or all of the deductibles and coinsurance features of the health plan. When nonpreferred providers are seen, the insured pays the deductibles and copayments. Providers such as doctors and hospitals are in abundant supply in most urban areas. The majority operate on a fee-

FIGURE 19–7

PPO Features

1. A large group of preferred physicians.
2. One or more preferred hospitals.
3. Other preferred health care providers, such as pharmacies and home health care serivces.
4. Access to all other providers.
5. Waiver of deductibles and coinsurance provisions when insureds use preferred providers.
6. Negotiated discounts on a fee-for-service pricing basis.
7. Insurer, other third-party administrator, or employer promises of prompt payments to providers.
8. Utilization review.

---

21. See, for example, Sloss, E. M., Keeler, E. B., Brook, R. H., et al., "Effect of a Health Maintenance Organization on Physiologic Health: Results from a Randomized Trial," *Annals of Internal Medicine,* May 1987: pp. 1–9.
22. *Source Book of Health Insurance Data,* 1993, p. 45.

for-service basis and are concerned about competition from HMOs. In order to maintain their market share of patients, providers are willing to cooperate with PPOs. The income they give up in price discounts, they expect to gain through an increase of patients. Employers and insurers like PPOs because they are not expensive to organize and they direct employees to low-cost providers. The primary incentive for employees to use preferred providers is the avoidance of deductibles and coinsurance provisions.

In most PPOs, the risk of expenses exceeding an expected level remains with the insurer and employer. Some PPOs shift some risk to providers by holding a percentage of the provider reimbursement for services (for example, 20 percent) until the end of the year, at which time it is paid only to providers judged cost effective.

Cost effectiveness would not be achieved, even with discounts, if providers got insureds to accept more service(s) than necessary for the proper treatment of injury or illness. Therefore, many PPOs monitor their use of services. In 1992, approximately 83 percent of employees covered under PPOs were subject to utilization review, 88 percent to inpatient preadmission authorization, 44 percent to incentives to encourage use of ambulatory surgery, and 51 percent to penalties for non-urgent use of the emergency room. During that same period, the percentages of employees in traditional fee-for-service plans who were subject to these same restrictions was at least 10 percent less than those in PPOs. For example, only 72 percent of employees in traditional plans were subject to utilization review and only 31 percent were subject to ambulatory surgery provisions.[23] PPOs continuously monitor utilization of services to identify the least expensive, effective mode of care. Periodically, new DRG statistical studies are made. The result may be deletion from the list of those providers who do not meet cost or quality standards and the addition of others.[24] The providers added to the list may be dropped at a future date if they do not meet the stated standards.

Many states have passed laws to regulate PPO activities. No specific federal laws have been passed for PPOs, but sponsors must avoid violation of federal antitrust laws because they involve businesses (physicians, hospitals, insurers, and others) cooperating on a mutually beneficial venture.

Managed Care Plans

The most recent concept in the area of health care cost containment is **managed care.** When the term first came into use in the late 1980s, it referred to cooperation between the insurer and provider to select treatment for insureds on a case-by-case basis that was both effective and minimized costs. Today, the term *managed care* can refer to a wide array of different cost control arrangements. For example, traditional fee-for-service insurance policies may implement a limited degree of managed care through second surgical opinion and preadmission certification provisions. HMOs and PPOs reflect a much greater degree of managed care

23. *Source Book of Health Insurance Data,* 1993, p. 46.
24. Some PPOs have been set up without statistical analysis to identify low-cost providers. These are likely to be marketing schemes organized by a hospital and its medical staff.

because the behavior of insureds is controlled to a larger extent. Insurers and providers may merge to provide managed care to employers. For example, an insurer and a hospital chain may combine their skills in marketing, actuarial pricing, data management, finance, and medical service delivery in order to provide high quality, cost-efficient care to employer groups.

As the concept of managed care has grown in the 1990s, several characteristics are common across health care plans. Managed care plans typically control access to providers. Managed care fee-for-service plans control access through provisions such as preadmission certification; PPOs control access by providing insureds with economic incentives to choose efficient providers; and HMOs control access by covering services provided only by HMO providers. Managed care plans typically engage in utilization review, monitoring service usage and costs on a case-by-case basis. In addition, managed care plans usually have economic incentives for providers and for insureds to minimize costs. For example, providers may be compensated on a capitated basis or through bonuses for providing quality care at minimal cost. Insureds can be rewarded through lower cost sharing requirements when efficient providers are chosen.

Most employers today use some form of managed care in their medical benefit plans because managed care has been shown to control costs. Given rising medical costs, efforts among providers and insurers to discover new managed care methods are not likely to diminish in the near future.

Other Medical Care Plans

Another way in which employers may provide for coverage of employee medical expenses is through use of individual employee **medical savings accounts (MSAs).** MSAs are similar to individual retirement accounts (IRAs) in that deposits are made to an account for the employee, who uses the fund to cover medical expenses (rather than retirement expenses). MSAs provide an economic incentive to employees to be cost conscious and use only necessary care, since employees retain the balance of their own accounts.

A catastrophic medical expense insurance policy is usually purchased in conjunction with an MSA. For example, the catastrophic policy may have a deductible of $3,000, so that all medical expenses less than $3,000 are paid from the MSA, but in the event of medical costs exceeding $3,000, the catastrophic policy offers full protection. A catastrophic policy is less expensive than traditional policies or HMOs and PPOs. The premium saved by purchasing only catastrophic coverage can be used to fund the MSA.

Employer and employee contributions to the MSA are limited in amount. MSA contributions are not exempt from federal tax, but are from state taxes in a few states. Proposals for federal tax exemption have been made. However, until federal tax law is changed, MSAs are not likely to be widely adopted by employers.

Other proposals for health care reform that would affect employers include those for **national health insurance.** These proposals vary in design, but all seek to provide universal health care coverage, i.e., medical services for everyone. Here we describe three leading national health insurance reform proposals: managed competition plans, play-or-pay plans, and single payer plans.

Managed competition plans typically would require all employers to provide insurance to all employees. Employers would be allowed to form large purchasing groups in order to negotiate rates and control costs through competition. Individuals not covered through employment would receive subsidized coverage through the purchasing groups. Government standard-setting boards would oversee operation of the entire system. Managed competition is a reform proposal that is consistent to a degree with the traditional, private, employment-based system.

A second national health insurance plan is the *play-or-pay plan.* Here again, employers would be required to provide coverage, or "play." If they did not, then they would "pay" a payroll tax to a public program that would cover individuals not covered at work. Here again, subsidies would make coverage affordable to individuals in the public program. This proposal is also a type of private, employment-based system.

A *single payer plan,* however, would replace existing private and public insurance plans with one national governmental plan providing universal coverage. The Canadian system is an example of a single payer plan. Most proposals would require no cost-sharing by individuals (i.e., no deductibles or coinsurance), and physician fee schedules and hospital budgets would be used to control costs. This system would be funded by taxes, and unlike the other proposals is not a private, employment-based system.

Employers are involved in the ongoing debate on health care insurance and reform initiatives at the local, state, and federal level. Preferences for the different proposals vary based on employer characteristics, such as the size, location, and industry type of the organization. All employers, however, are concerned with reform initiatives because any major change in the health care system will affect the cost and delivery of employee medical benefits.

Medical Care Systems Worldwide

The level of health care services within a country varies with the level of economic development. Countries that are more developed or industrialized have modern health services available to most of the population, whereas in poorer countries, health care systems are very limited. Among the countries with more extensive health care systems, financing methods vary greatly. Some nations have a public, nationalized health service, others have social insurance programs, and others finance health services through private, voluntary insurance plans.

With a purely public, nationalized health service model, the state owns and operates the health care system. For example, hospitals are owned by the state and doctors are employees of the state. The state provides universal coverage (or care to everyone), funded through general tax revenues. The system in the United Kingdom most closely follows this model.

The social insurance model integrates the public and private sectors to finance health care. Employers and employees pay a payroll tax to private insurers, who in turn contract with physician groups to provide care. Hospitals may be publicly or privately owned. Those people not covered by employment (such as the unemployed or elderly) are insured by the state. Germany uses a social insurance program to provide most health care services.

The private, voluntary system does not require employers, employees, or individuals to participate in a health insurance plan. Typically, larger employers provide health insurance for employees. Individuals not covered at work may buy health insurance themselves. A portion of the population, however, may be uninsured, which limits their access to medical services. Insurers, physicians, and hospitals operate in the private sector to provide services. The United States is the principle example of a private, voluntary system.

Most countries finance health care primarily through one of these systems. However, most countries also have sub-systems in place. For example, in the United Kingdom, the national health service covers everyone, but about 10 percent of the population also has private, supplemental health insurance. Private policies cover services that may not be readily accessible otherwise. Likewise, the social insurance system is often supplemented by private insurance that covers deductibles or coinsurance costs. Germany and France have social insurance systems augmented by voluntary, private insurance. In the United States, although private insurance predominates, more than 40 percent of medical care is provided by governmental programs (for example, for the poor and elderly). Combination systems allow adjustment of a country's health care system to provide service for those not well served by the predominant system.

Although there are many different approaches to health care financing, the objectives across systems are similar: to provide high-quality care to many people at an affordable price. Achieving these objectives is of great concern, not only in the United States, but worldwide. As we learn more about other health care systems, we have an excellent opportunity to consider the effects of different systems on the availability, quality, and price of health care.

Consumer Applications

Choosing Between Traditional Fee-for-Service Health Insurance and an HMO Option

As an employee, you are likely to be asked to choose periodically between some combination of a traditional health insurance plan, one or more HMOs, and a PPO. Or, you may have these same options of individual protection. It is impossible to choose intelligently without knowing the exact provisions of each plan and understanding your personal situation. Assume your choice is between the traditional, comprehensive medical insurance and the HMO plan out-

lined in figure 19–8. Also assume the same employee contributions for each option. Let's discuss some of the pros and cons of each plan.

COMPREHENSIVE PLAN FEATURES

Some advantages of the traditional, comprehensive medical insurance plan are shown in figure 19–9; disadvantages appear in figure 19–10. Although the list of disadvantages is longer than the list of advan-

FIGURE 19–8

Hypothetical Comparison of a Comprehensive and HMO Plan

FEATURE	COMPREHENSIVE PLAN	HMO
General Description	Comprehensive plan covering all services prescribed by a licensed physician or surgeon, subject to the usual exclusions described in the chapter.	Formed in 1987, an individual practice HMO with fifteen "gatekeeper" physicians paid by an annual capitation per patient. Referrals to specialists when "gatekeeper" recommends this. Providence Hospital used except for out-of-the-area emergencies.
Maximum Benefits	$1 million lifetime limit.	No maximum.
Deductibles and Copayments	$200 comprehensive deductible per calendar year, limited to three per family; 80 percent coinsurance.	Copayments of $20 for emergency room, $5 per office visit, and $4 per prescription.
Stop Limit Provision	$750/year per family member after payment of $200 deductible.	None.
Hospital Services	Semiprivate care subject to plan deductible and coinsurance; intensive care when medically necessary; and a 30-day limit on substance abuse and mental health care.	Same as comprehensive.
Surgical Care and Medical Care in the Hospital	Paid in full subject to a usual and customary fee schedule.	Full coverage.
Outpatient Psychiatric Services	Limited to 50 percent coinsurance, a $50 per visit covered charge, and 50 visits per year.	Full payment for twenty visits per year.
Routine Preventive Care	None, except an initial pediatric newborn exam at the usual and customary fee.	Full coverage for routine physicals, immunizations, physical therapy, and well baby care.
Second Opinion Surgery	Full coverage.	Full coverage.
Prescription Drugs	Covered (except contraceptives), subject to deductibles and coinsurance.	Covered (including contraceptives), subject to a $4 per prescription copayment.
Routine Eye and Hearing Care	None.	One eye exam and one hearing exam per year. Glasses and hearing aids not covered.
Chiropractors	Covered.	Covered only if recommended by the gatekeeper.

FIGURE 19–9
....

Traditional Insurance Advantages

1. Complete employee choice of providers.
   —Medical doctors, chiropractors, osteopaths, podiatrists, psychologists.
   —Hospitals and other providers.
   —No geographical constraints.
2. Maintain established provider relationships.

tages, their importance may not outweigh the advantage of access to a wide variety of providers. You may be primarily concerned about the financial disincentives. Deductibles and copayments may discourage needed care if you are low on cash. The communication and administrative procedures can be problematic for people who do not understand when they have a valid claim. Understanding and filing claim forms may be difficult for many. Your employer or insurer may offer employees only limited advice.

HMO FEATURES

Some of the attractive features of the HMO option are shown in figure 19–11. The HMO requires copayments, but they are small relative to the $200 deductible and 80 percent coinsurance feature in the comprehensive medical insurance plan. Coverage of routine care is broader. The absence of a maximum on benefits is a minor point, since you are highly unlikely to have lifetime medical expenses that exceed the $1 million limit on the comprehensive plan. You may think of the reduction of unnecessary hospitalization and surgery that characterizes most HMOs as features that primarily appeal to the cost-saving instincts of premium payers. But this is not their only attraction. It is dangerous to be in a hospital or undergo surgery. Many hospitals are full of infections, and most staffs make more mistakes than they care to admit. You may be safer at home, unless your condition

FIGURE 19–10
....

Traditional Insurance Disadvantages

1. Financial disincentives.
   —Deductibles.
   —Coinsurance (subject to stop limit maximum).
   —Usual and customary fee schedules.
   —Limits on mental health, alcoholism, and drug treatment.
2. No coverage of routine physicals, immunizations, or contraceptives.
3. Communication/administrative disincentives.
   —Need to understand benefits.
   —Claim forms must be filed.
   —Sufficient benefit counseling unavailable in some instances.

FIGURE 19–11
....

HMO Advantages

1. Little financial disincentives for members to seek care.
2. No claim forms.
3. Broad coverage.
   —Preventive care/routine physicals.
   —Immunizations.
   —Optometry (limited).
   —Family planning.
   —Hearing exams.
4. Reduction of unnecessary hospitalization and surgery.
5. No maximum on catastrophic illness.

is serious. We tend to trust our physician and follow his or her advice. The HMO places the physician at risk for unnecessary care in the sense that his or her time commitment to you is greater when you are hospitalized and/or undergo surgery. Yet his or her income remains the same (with the exception of the individual practice HMO forms that use fee-for-service).

Features of this HMO that you may view negatively are shown in figure 19–12. The limited choice of providers may concern you. Will the gatekeeper recommend a specialist when you need to see one, even though symptoms seem minor? Your HMO is rather new. Will it develop a reputation for high-quality care? Is it possible that you might want care at a Harvard University-affiliated hospital, Johns Hopkins, University of California-San Francisco, the Mayo Clinic, or another highly respected medical institution? Under what (nonemergency) conditions will your HMO assume the costs of care in any facility other than their affiliate, Providence Hospital? What are the chances that this relatively new HMO will go bankrupt and leave you looking for new health care protection, perhaps at a time when your health has deteriorated and you are not viewed as a desirable underwriting risk? These questions may or may not be important to you. The answer partly depends on the quality of your HMO, its normal network of providers, and whether you have (or may develop) a unique health problem.

SITUATIONAL FACTORS

You may prefer the comprehensive plan if you have an established doctor-patient relationship and do not want to switch family doctors. You may also want to maintain the opportunity to choose freely among providers if the need for nonroutine care arises. If you have a serious disease or travel frequently, you may want unencumbered access to providers outside your immediate geographic area.

Compare the premiums for each plan. If the employee pays part of the premium, which option is more expensive

FIGURE 19–12
....

HMO Disadvantages

1. Limited choice of providers.
2. Control by gatekeepers.
3. Inconvenient location of providers for some.
4. Concerns (maybe unfounded) about the quality of care.
5. No or limited chiropractic care.
6. Emergency ambulatory centers excluded.
7. Lack of a long track record for quality care.

for you? Consider not only the premium, but also the cost-sharing requirements. Given your health status, which do you think will result in greater total costs (i.e., premium plus deductibles and coinsurance)? The availability of cash for deductibles and coinsurance may make the comprehensive plan financially burdensome. This may override all other factors and lead you to the HMO.

You may have small children who need frequent, routine preventive care that is only insured under the HMO option. You may be new to your locality and not want to seek out a family practitioner with little or no guidance. You can assume (rightly or wrongly) that the HMO has screened its panel of physicians to some extent. In any event, ask about your doctor's medical class standing, board certifications, and the quality of his or her residency program. The choice between traditional insurance and HMO systems is not a simple one. Application of the factors discussed to your situation will help you make a decision with some confidence.

Key Terms

health care providers
indemnity benefits
service benefits
valued policy
basic health care benefits
basic hospital policy
basic surgical policy
basic medical expense policy
major medical insurance
maximum limits
internal policy limits
benefit period
coinsurance provision
stop loss limit
cost sharing
comprehensive medical insurance
limited contracts
voluntary benefits
coordination of benefits provision
COBRA
continuation provisions
cost containment techniques
retention

second surgical opinion
ambulatory surgical center
preadmission testing
preadmission certification
extended care facilities
hospice care
home health care
utilization review organization
statistical analysis of claims
diagnostic related group (DRG)
prospective payment
business coalitions
wellness programs
health maintenance organization
    (HMO)
capitated fee
group practice associations
individual practice associations
preferred provider organization
    (PPO)
managed care
medical savings account (MSA)
national health insurance

Discussion Questions

1. How do indemnity benefits differ from service benefits? Which would you prefer to have?

2. What is the purpose of including deductible and coinsurance provisions in group medical expense insurance policies?

3. How does a basic medical expense insurance policy differ from a major medical insurance policy? If you could only have one, which would you prefer? Why?

4. How important are limited contracts in providing employees with adequate medical expense insurance? Please explain.

5. The intent behind passage of COBRA was to reduce the number of uninsured persons. How does COBRA work to achieve this objective?

6. Explain how second surgical opinion provisions work to control health care costs.

7. What services are provided by a home health service? How do home health services reduce overall health care expenses?

8. What is the purpose of statistically analyzing health care claims? What role did claims analysis play in the formation of preferred provider organizations?

9. How do PPOs differ from group practice HMOs? Is there much difference between a PPO and an individual practice HMO that pays its providers on a fee-for-service basis?

10. Managed care is used in a variety of plans ranging from traditional fee-for-service to PPOs and HMOs. Describe the characteristics of managed care that are common across all these plans.

Cases

19.1 Raymond Chang has a basic and a major medical policy through his employer. The basic policy has no deductible or coinsurance requirement and pays for covered charges up to a policy limit of $30,000. His major medical plan requires him to pay a $300 deductible each year and 20 percent of covered charges up to a stop loss limit of $1,500 (which does not include the major medical deductible amount). The policy maximum is $500,000 per lifetime. Raymond has a skiing accident and ends up in the hospital for several weeks. He receives a bill for $45,000 in covered charges (charges covered under both the basic and major medical plan).

1. How much will the basic policy cover?
2. How much will the major medical plan pay?
3. How much will Raymond himself pay out-of-pocket?

19.2 Riley Fleming has severe arthritis. When she changed jobs she was concerned about the preexisting condition clause in the new employer's medical expense policy. The clause dictated that the new plan would not cover treatment for her arthritis until after she had been enrolled for coverage for twelve months.

1. Is there any insurance available to Riley to cover arthritis treatment during the first year at her new job? Will she need to have two policies (one with the new employer and one to cover the arthritis treatment) while the preexisting condition clause is in effect?
2. If coverage is available, who pays for the insurance?
3. Does the new employer's policy cover Riley's medical expenses in the first year other than those associated with the arthritis?

19.3 Anna Claire's Costumes, Inc. has experienced medical benefit cost increases of 16 and 19 percent over the last two years. The benefits manager believes that high hospitalization rates and unnecessarily long hospital stays may explain this. The company wants to control costs by reducing hospitalization costs.

1. What cost control methods could be implemented to achieve this objective?

2. Would employees still have adequate protection with these new techniques in place?

3. How do employees gain in the long run if the company contains medical benefit costs?

19.4 Marguerite Thomas, a Canadian, and Margaret Phythian, a Minnesotan, meet every summer in Vermont at their cabins on the lake. One evening they were discussing health care. Each woman tried to convince the other that the health care system in her country was superior. In Canada, Marguerite enjoys nationalized health care, where everyone is covered. She does not worry that she may need care she can't afford. She is willing to pay the taxes necessary to support the system. She doesn't mind waiting several weeks to get certain elective procedures done because she knows that everyone is getting the care they need and she is willing to wait her turn. Margaret, however, likes the high-quality, high-tech care available to her in the Twin Cities through her employer-provided HMO. She gets high quality care and never needs to wait for treatment. She also likes the lower tax rate she pays, partly because the U.S. government isn't funding a nationalized health system.

1. If Marguerite and Margaret were unemployed or had low income, which system might they prefer? Would this change if they were in high income tax brackets? Please explain.

2. Which system would you prefer? What trade-offs are you willing to make to have this type of health care system?

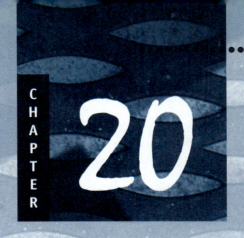

Employee Benefits: Retirement Plans

Introduction Individuals rely on several sources for income during retirement: Social Security, employer-sponsored retirement plans, and individual savings. In chapter 17 we discussed how Social Security, a public retirement program, provides economic security for retired workers and their families. However, for many, Social Security benefits fail to provide enough income for them to maintain their preretirement standard of living.

Employees may receive additional retirement income from employer-sponsored retirement plans. In 1993, more than 80 percent of medium-and large-sized employers contributed to retirement plans for employees, with contributions averaging 6.5 percent of payroll.[1] Clearly, private retirement benefits are an important component of employee compensation. In this chapter we discuss the objectives of group retirement plans, how plans are structured, and current issues important to employers and employees.

The chapter presents:
1. The purpose of retirement plans.
2. The nature of qualified pension plans.
3. Elements of pension plan design.
4. Pension plan funding techniques.
5. Other qualified defined contribution plans.
6. Nonqualified tax-favored retirement plans.
7. Retirement trends worldwide.

1. *Employee Benefits* 1994, U.S. Chamber of Commerce, p. 22.

The Purpose of Retirement Plans

Maintaining personal savings for retirement can be difficult. Some employees may not have the discipline to save or the financial expertise to structure a savings plan effectively. The primary purpose of an employer-sponsored retirement plan is to assist employees in saving for retirement.

However, *employers,* benefit also from having an adequate retirement program. A good retirement plan helps attract and retain qualified employees. Morale can be enhanced if employees view a retirement plan as evidence of employer concern for their economic well-being. Employers also benefit because a good retirement plan encourages older employees to retire, making room for new hires or promotions. In addition, providing a retirement plan makes a favorable public relations statement, since the community observes the employer taking care of employees.

The Nature of Qualified Pension Plans

SIGNIFICANCE

A retirement plan may be qualified or nonqualified. The distinction is important to both employer and employee because qualification produces a plan with a favorable tax status. With a **qualified plan,** employer contributions to an employee's pension during the employee's working years are deductible as a business expense but are not taxable income to the employee until they are received as benefits. Moreover, investment earnings on funds held by the trustee for the plan are not subject to income taxes as they are earned. Because funds required to provide benefits accumulate faster when tax sheltered, pension costs are reduced. This also makes higher benefits possible. At retirement, the portion of the benefits financed by *employer* contributions is considered taxable income. Any contributions made by the employee from after-tax dollars are not subject to federal income taxes when they are returned as retirement benefits, but the investment earnings are taxable income when received.

Most nonqualified plans do not allow employer funding contributions to be deducted as a business expense unless they are classified as compensation to the employee, in which case they become taxable income for the employee.[2] Investment earnings on these nonqualified accumulated pension funds are also subject to taxation at the employer level. Retirement benefits from a nonqualified plan are a deductible business expense when they are paid to the employee, if not previously classified as compensation.

REQUIREMENTS

In order to be qualified, a plan must fulfill the requirements shown in figure 20–1. These requirements prevent those in control of the organization from using the plan primarily for their own benefit. The requirements are enforced by the United States Internal Revenue Service, the

---

2. Special nonqualified plans with tax-favored arrangements are discussed at the end of the chapter.

1. The plan must be legally binding, in writing, and must be communicated clearly to all employees.
2. The plan must be for the exclusive benefit of the employees or their beneficiaries.
3. The principal or income of the pension plan cannot be diverted to any other purpose, unless the assets exceed those required to cover accrued pension benefits.
4. The plan must benefit a broad class of employees and not discriminate in favor of highly compensated employees.
5. The plan must be designed to be permanent and have continuing contributions.
6. The plan must comply with the Employee Retirement Income Security Act and subsequent federal laws.

United States Department of Labor, and the Pension Benefit Guaranty Corporation (PBGC).[3]

Elements of Pension Plan Design

The Employee Retirement Income Security Act of 1974 (**ERISA**) is a federal law that regulates the design, funding, and communication aspects of private, qualified retirement plans. Aspects of ERISA have been amended by subsequent tax acts. The purpose of ERISA is two-fold: to protect the benefits of plan participants and to prevent discrimination in favor of highly compensated employees (i.e., those who control the organization).[4]

Within the guidelines and standards established by ERISA and other federal laws, the employer must make some choices regarding the design of a qualified retirement plan. Design elements include:

1. Eligibility and coverage requirements.
2. Retirement age limits.
3. Vesting provisions.
4. Type of plan.

ELIGIBILITY AND COVERAGE REQUIREMENTS

A pension plan must establish **eligibility criteria** for determining who is covered. Most plans exclude certain classes of employees. For example, part-time or seasonal employees may not be covered. Separate plans may be set up for those paid on an hourly basis. Excluding certain classes of employees is allowed, provided the plan does not discriminate in favor of highly compensated employees.

Individual employees are included in the plan only after they attain a specified age, usually 21, and after a specified number of years of service, usually one year.[5] This is partly to reduce costs of enrolling employees who leave employment shortly after being hired, and partly because most younger employees attach a low value to benefits they will receive many

....

3. The Pension Benefit Guaranty Corporation will be described later in this chapter.
4. ERISA defines highly compensated and non-highly compensated employees based on factors such as employee salary, ownership share of the firm, and whether the employee is an officer in the organization.
5. The service requirement may be extended to two years in the small minority of plans that have immediate vesting. Vesting is defined later in the chapter.

years in the future. The Age Discrimination in Employment Act eliminates all maximum age limits for eligibility. Even when an employee is hired at an advanced age, such as 71, the employee must be eligible for the pension plan within the first year of service if the plan is offered to other, younger hires in the same job.

In addition to eligibility rules, ERISA has **coverage requirements,** designed to improve participation by non-highly compensated employees. All employees of businesses with related ownership (called a **controlled group**) are treated for coverage requirements as if they were employees of one plan. The employer's plan must meet one of the coverage requirements outlined in figure 20–2. In addition to these requirements each plan within a controlled group will have to cover either fifty employees or 40 percent of all employees, whichever is less.

Although the objective of coverage rules is to improve participation by non-highly compensated employees, the expense and administrative burden of compliance discourages small employers from having a qualified retirement plan. In fact, the majority of small businesses do not offer qualified plans. It is not mandatory that the employer establish a qualified plan; rather, it is only mandatory that those with qualified plans comply with ERISA regulations. The end result is that regulations designed to protect non-highly compensated employees may also end up hurting these employees.

RETIREMENT AGE LIMITS

In order to reasonably estimate the cost of some retirement plans, it is necessary to establish a retirement age for plan participants.[6] For other types of plans, setting a retirement age clarifies the age at which no additional employer contributions will be made to the employee's plan.[7] The **normal retirement age** is the age at which full retirement benefits become available to retirees. Most private retirement plans specify age 65 as the normal retirement age.[8] Allowing private benefits to begin at about the

FIGURE 20–2

Retirement Plan Coverage Requirements

1. Ratio Percentage Test: The percentage of covered non-highly compensated employees must be at least 70 percent of the percentage of covered highly compensated employees (for example, if 90 percent of highly compensated employees are covered, at least 63 percent of the eligible non-highly compensated employees must be included).
2. Average Benefit Test: The average benefit (expressed as a percentage of pay) for non-highly compensated employees must be at least 70 percent of the average benefit for the highly compensated group.

Note: If an employer also offers a 401(k) plan (discussed later in this chapter), salary deferrals under the 401(k) are considered in applying one of the coverage requirements.

6. Establishing a retirement age is necessary in estimating the cost of a defined benefit plan. This type of plan will be described later in the chapter.

7. Establishing a retirement age to limit employer contributions may be important to a defined contribution plan. This type of plan will be described later in the chapter.

8. For employees hired within five years of the plan's normal retirement age (for example, age 62, in a plan with age 65 as the normal retirement age), normal retirement can be defined as five years from the date of participation in the plan.

same time as full Social Security benefits facilitates the selection of a retirement date by the many employees that need both benefits. This also facilitates *integration* of social and private benefits.[9]

Early retirement may be allowed, but that option must be specified in the pension plan description. Usually, early retirement permanently reduces the benefit amount. For example, an early retirement provision may allow the participant to retire as early as age 55 if he or she also has at least thirty years of service with the employer. The pension benefit amount, however, would be reduced to take into account the shorter time available for fund accumulation, as well as the likelihood that the benefit will be paid for more years in total.

Mandatory retirement is considered age discrimination, except for executives in high policy-making positions. Thus, a plan must allow for *late retirement*. Deferral of retirement beyond the normal retirement age does not interfere with the accumulation of benefits. That is, working beyond normal retirement age may produce a pension benefit greater than would have been received at normal retirement age. However, a plan can set some limits on total benefits (for example $50,000 per year) or on total years of plan participation (for example, 35 years). These limits help control employer costs.

VESTING PROVISIONS

A pension plan may be contributory or noncontributory. A **contributory plan** requires the employee to pay all or part of the pension fund contribution. A noncontributory plan is funded only by employer contributions; that is, the employee does not contribute at all to the plan. ERISA requires that if an employee contributes to a pension plan, the employee must be able to recover these contributions, with or without interest, if she or he leaves the firm. However, this does not apply to employer contributions.

Employer contributions may be recovered by an employee leaving the organization if the employee is vested. **Vesting,** or the employee's right to benefits for which the *employer* has made contributions, depends on the plan provisions. ERISA established minimum standards to assure full vesting within a reasonable period of time. The employer usually chooses one of two vesting schedules, shown in figure 20–3: a cliff vesting schedule or a graded vesting schedule. ERISA, however, does allow the employer to choose a schedule for more rapid vesting than these two stipulated schedules.

Vesting is important for several reasons. Prior to passage of ERISA in 1974, a plan could provide for no vesting prior to normal retirement age. This meant that employees who left the organization before retirement would receive no benefit from the employer's contributions. Vesting provisions allow employees to change jobs without losing certain pension benefits, which is important today since the trend is to change jobs more frequently than in the past.

When a vested employee leaves an organization, the employee typically has the right to the retirement benefit upon reaching normal retirement age. In some plans, the benefit available at retirement age is frozen in

----

9. Integration of pension benefits is described later in the chapter.

FIGURE 20–3

Vesting Alternatives

1. Cliff Vesting: Full vesting of employer contributions after five years.
2. Graded Vesting: 20 percent vesting after three years and 20 percent per year thereafter, until 100 percent vesting occurs after seven years.

Note: Top-heavy plans, or plans that according to ERISA rules discriminate in favor of highly compensated employees, have to meet more stringent vesting schedules.

amount at the point of job termination, and if a long period elapses before retirement, inflation may take a heavy toll on the purchasing power of the benefit.[10] This controls the employer's cost of vesting, but reduces the value of the vested benefit to employees.

Some plans provide a cash settlement at termination of employment. This distribution is taxable income in the year it is made, unless the employee carefully follows federal tax rules for moving the funds directly into a rollover individual retirement account (IRA). Employees not rolling the funds over must pay penalties in addition to income taxes in the year pension funds are received. Despite the tax consequences, employees often like to spend their vested cash settlement prior to retirement. However, if they do, they may be without adequate income when they retire. This problem can be exacerbated by frequent job changes and multiple cash settlements during an employee's working years.

Pension plans that disproportionately favor highly compensated employees are called *top-heavy plans*. Such a plan may be identified by applying ERISA rules (for example, the coverage rules). A top-heavy plan must meet a more stringent (faster) vesting schedule. The minimum schedule for a top-heavy plan requires 100 percent cliff vesting after two years of service or graded vesting beginning after two years of service (at 20 percent), with 100 percent vesting after six years of service.

TYPE OF PLAN

The employer chooses a pension plan from two types, a defined benefit or a defined contribution plan. Both are qualified plans, providing tax-favored arrangements for retirement savings and subject to ERISA regulation.

Defined Benefit Plans

A **defined benefit plan** has the distinguishing characteristic of clearly defining, by its benefit formula, the amount of benefit that will be available at retirement. That is, the benefit amount is specified in the written plan document, although the amount that must be contributed to fund the plan is not specified. A defined benefit plan that allows early retirement specifies how the early retirement benefit amount is calculated relative to the benefit available at normal retirement age. Similarly, a deferred retirement benefit is also specified.

In a defined benefit plan, several benefit formulas may be used:

1. A flat dollar amount.
2. A flat percentage of pay.

---

10. This applies to defined benefit plans, described later in the chapter.

3. A flat amount unit benefit.
4. A percentage unit benefit.
5. A cash balance plan.

Each type has advantages and disadvantages, and the employer selects the formula that best meets both the needs of employees for economic security and the budget constraints of the employer.

The defined benefit formula may specify a *flat dollar amount,* such as $500 per month. It may provide a formula by which the amount can be calculated, yielding a *flat percentage* of current annual salary (or the average salary of the past five or so years). For example, a plan may specify that each employee with at least twenty years of participation in the plan receives 50 percent of his or her average annual earnings during the three consecutive years of employment with the highest earnings. A *flat amount unit benefit* formula assigns a flat amount (for example, $25) with each unit of service, usually with each year. Thus, an employee with thirty units of service at retirement would receive a benefit equal to thirty times the unit amount (for example, 30 × $25 = $750 per month). This formula is used mainly in union-negotiated plans.

The advantage to flat amount formulas is that they are easy to explain to plan participants and simple to administer. However, flat dollar amount and flat amount unit formulas do not accommodate well differences in salary, and flat percentage formulas do not accommodate well differences in length of service.

The most popular defined benefit formula is the *percentage unit benefit* plan. It recognizes both the employee's years of service and level of compensation. For example, the benefit may be defined as 1.5 percent of the compensation base per year of service. Thus, the amount of annual benefit, assuming compensation of $30,000 and thirty years of service, would be .015 × 30 × $30,000 = $13,500.

When the compensation base is described as compensation for a recent number of years (for example, the last three or highest consecutive five years), the formula is referred to as a **final average formula.** Relative to a **career average formula,** which bases benefits on average compensation for all years of service in the plan, a final average plan tends to keep the initial retirement benefit in line with inflation. How well this performs depends on the extent to which an employee's compensation keeps up with inflation.

Two types of service are involved in the benefit formula: past service and future service. *Past service* refers to service prior to the installation of the plan. *Future service* refers to service subsequent to the installation of the plan. If credit is given for past service, the plan starts with an initial past service liability at the date of installation. To reduce the size of this liability, the percentage of credit for past service may be less than that for future service, or a limit may be put on the number of years of past service credit. Initial past service liability may be a serious financial problem for the employer starting or installing a pension plan.

The newest type of defined benefit plan is the *cash balance* plan. Unlike the other formulas, the cash balance plan does not guarantee the amount of benefit that will be available for the employee at retirement. Instead, the cash balance plan sets up an individual account for each employee, and credits each participant annually with a plan contribution (usually a percentage of compensation). The employer also guarantees a minimum interest credit on the account balance. For example, an employer might contribute 5 percent of an employee's salary to the employee's plan each year, and guarantee a minimum rate of return of 4 percent on the fund. If investment returns turn out to be higher than 4 percent, the employer may credit the employee account with the higher rate. The amount available to the employee at retirement varies, based on wage rates and investment rates of return. Although the cash balance plan is technically a defined benefit plan, it has many of the same characteristics as defined contribution plans, discussed later in the chapter. These characteristics include individual employee accounts, a fixed employer contribution rate, and an indeterminate final benefit amount, since employee compensation changes over time and interest rates may turn out to be well above the minimum guaranteed rate.

Defined benefit plans may provide for adjustments to account for inflation during the retirement years. A plan that includes a **cost-of-living adjustment (COLA)** clause has the ideal design feature: benefits increase automatically with changes in a cost-of-living or wage index. To limit the potential cost of a COLA, a maximum increase of 4 or 5 percent per year is typical. COLAs are common in governmental plans but are seldom found in private plans. The problem created by final average benefit formulas and COLAs is that future cost levels for an employer increase and become difficult to predict accurately.

Many plans integrate the retirement benefit with Social Security benefits. An **integrated plan** coordinates Social Security benefits (or contributions) with the private plan's benefit (or contribution) formula. Integration reduces private retirement benefits based on the amount received through Social Security, thus reducing the cost to employers of the private plan. Integration also allows employers to favor highly compensated employees to some degree, although ERISA limits the tax shelter available for these employees even with integration. Using integration formulas to favor higher-income earners is justified on the basis that lower-income earners are favored through Social Security benefit formulas (since the wage replacement rate is higher in Social Security for lower-income earners).

There are two basic methods to integrate pension plans. The simplest way is the *offset method,* which reduces the private plan benefit by a set fraction. This approach is only applicable to defined benefit plans. The second integration method is the *integration-level method.* Here, a threshold of compensation, such as $10,000, is specified, and the rate of benefits or contributions provided below this compensation threshold is lower than the rate above it. The integration-level method may be used for defined benefit or defined contribution pension plans.

Distributions are benefits paid out to participants or their beneficiaries, usually at retirement. Tax penalties are imposed on plan participants who receive distributions (except for disability benefits) prior to age 59 1/2. However, ERISA requires that benefits begin by age 70 1/2, whether retirement occurs or not. Depending on the provisions of the particular plan, distributions may be made (1) as a lump sum, (2) as one of several life annuity options, or (3) over the participant's life expectancy.

The longest time period over which benefits may extend is the participant's life expectancy.[11] ERISA requires that pension plan design make spousal benefits available. Once the participant becomes vested, the spouse automatically is eligible for a qualified **preretirement survivor annuity.** This provision gives lifetime benefits to the spouse if the participant dies before the earliest retirement age allowed by the plan. Once the participant reaches the earliest retirement age allowed by the plan, the spouse becomes eligible for benefits under a **joint and survivor annuity** option. This qualifies the spouse for a lifetime benefit in the event of the participant's death. Upon the employee's retirement, the spouse remains eligible for this benefit. These benefits may be waived only if the spouse signs a notarized waiver.

The maximum annual benefit from a defined benefit plan was initially limited to $90,000 (indexed for inflation) at age 65.[12] The maximum is reduced for early or late retirement relative to the Social Security retirement age (which is scheduled to increase from 65 to 67 by the year 2027). These benefit restrictions are not appealing to some highly compensated employees, but do serve to achieve ERISA's purpose of preventing excessive discrimination in their favor.

Defined benefits, up to specified levels, are guaranteed by the **Pension Benefit Guaranty Corporation (PBGC),** a federal insurance program somewhat like the Federal Deposit Insurance Corporation (FDIC) for commercial bank accounts. All defined benefit plans contribute an annual fee (or premium) per pension plan participant to finance benefits for members of insolvent terminated plans. The premium amount takes into account, to a degree, the financial soundness of the particular plan, measured by the plan's unfunded vested benefit. Thus, plans with a greater unfunded vested benefit pay a greater PBGC premium (up to a maximum amount), providing an incentive to employers to adequately fund their pension plans. Despite this incentive, there is national concern about the number of seriously underfunded pension plans insured by the PBGC. If these plans were unable to pay promised retirement benefits, the PBGC would be liable, and PBGC funds may be insufficient to cover the claims. Taxpayers could end up bailing out the PBGC. Careful monitoring of PBGC fund adequacy continues, and funding rules may be tightened to keep the PBGC financially sound.

Defined Benefit Cost Factors

Annual pension contributions and plan liabilities for a defined benefit plan must be estimated by an actuary. The defined amount of benefits becomes the employer's obligation, and contributions must equal whatever amount is necessary to fund the obligation. The estimate of cost depends on factors such as salary levels; normal retirement age; current employee ages; and assumptions about mortality, turnover, investment earnings, administra-

---

11. Life expectancy can be recalculated annually to recognize that it increases with age (or survival).

12. The defined benefit maximum annual benefit in 1995 reached $120,000.

tive expenses, and salary adjustment factors (for inflation and productivity). These factors determine estimates of how many employees will receive retirement benefits, how much they will receive, when benefits will begin, and how long benefits will be paid.

Normal costs reflect the annual amount needed to fund the pension benefit during the employee's working years. **Supplemental costs** are the amounts necessary to amortize any past service liability over a period that may vary from ten to thirty years. Total cost for a year is the sum of normal and supplemental costs. Under some methods of calculation, normal and supplemental costs are estimated as one item. Costs may be estimated for each employee and then summed to yield total cost, or a calculation may be made for all participants on an aggregate basis.

Defined benefit plan administration is expensive compared to defined contribution plans, because of actuarial expense and complicated ERISA regulations. This explains in part why about 75 percent of the plans established since the passage of ERISA have been defined contribution plans.

Defined Contribution Plans

A **defined contribution plan** is a qualified pension plan in which the contribution amount is defined but the benefit amount available at retirement varies. This is in direct contrast to a defined benefit plan, in which the benefit is defined and the contribution amount varies. As with the defined benefit plan, when the defined contribution plan is initially designed, the employer makes decisions about eligibility, retirement age, integration, vesting schedules, and funding methods.

The most common type of defined contribution plan is the *money purchase* plan. This plan establishes an annual rate of employer contribution, usually expressed as a percentage of current compensation; for example, a plan may specify that the employer will contribute 10 percent of an employee's salary. Separate accounts are maintained to track the current balance attributable to each employee, but contributions may be commingled for investment purposes. In order to prevent discrimination in favor of the highly compensated, ERISA limited allowable contributions to the lesser of (1) $30,000 or (2) 25 percent of employee compensation.[13]

The benefit available at retirement varies with the contribution amount, the length of covered service, investment earnings, and retirement age. Some plans allow employees to direct the investment of their own pension funds, offering several investment options. Generally, retirement age has no effect on a distribution received as a lump sum, fixed amount, or fixed period annuity. Retirement age only affects the amount of income received under a life annuity option.

From the perspective of an employer or employee concerned with the adequacy of retirement income, the contributions that typically have the longest time to accumulate with compound investment returns are the smaller ones. They are smaller because the compensation base (to which the contribution percentage is applied) is lowest in an employee's younger

---

13. The $30,000 limit was not increased until the inflation-adjusted defined benefit limit of $90,000 reached $120,000 (in 1995), after which the defined contribution limit is set equal to one-fourth of the defined benefit limit.

years. This is perhaps the major disadvantage of defined contribution plans. It is also difficult to project the amount of retirement benefit until retirement is near, which complicates planning. In addition, the speculative risk of investment performance (positive or negative returns) is borne directly by employees.

From an employer's perspective, however, such plans have the distinct advantage of a reasonably predictable level of pension cost, because they are expressed as a percentage of current payroll. Since the employer only promises to specify a rate of contribution and prudently manage the plan, actuarial estimates of annual contributions and liabilities are unnecessary. The employer also does not contribute to the Pension Benefit Guaranty Corporation, which applies only to defined benefit plans. Most new plans today are defined contribution plans, not surprising given their simplicity, lower administrative cost, and limited employer liability for funding.

Pension Plan Funding Techniques

ERISA requires advance funding of qualified pension plans. An advance funded plan accumulates funds during the period in which employees are actively working for the organization. Pension expense is charged against earned income while pension obligations are accumulating, instead of being deferred until employees have retired. Pension plans are funded either through (1) noninsured trust plans, or (2) insured plans.

NONINSURED TRUST PLANS

With a **noninsured trust plan,** the employer creates a trust to accumulate funds and disburse benefits. The trustee may be an individual, a bank, a trust company, an insurer, or some combination of co-trustees. The duties of the trustee are to invest the funds contributed by the employer to the trust (and by the employees, if contributory), accumulate the earnings, and pay benefits to eligible employees. The trustee makes no guarantee with regard to earnings or investments.

Under a defined benefit trust plan, a consulting actuary is employed to make estimates of the sums that should be put into the trust. The employer is in effect a self-insurer. The consulting actuary does not guarantee that the estimates will be accurate.[14] There is also no guarantee as to the expense of operating the plan. Thus, the employer that chooses a noninsured trust to fund a defined benefit plan should be large enough and financially strong enough to absorb differences between actual experience and past estimates of mortality, investment returns, and other cost factors.

INSURED PLANS

Several insurer options are available for funding pension plans, as shown in figure 20–4.

---

14. There is no implication here that such estimates will *not* be reasonably accurate; the point is that they are not guaranteed for the employer. Adjustments will need to be made in funding levels from time to time to reflect corrections for differences between assumptions and actual realized investment returns, mortality results, etc.

FIGURE 20–4

Insured Plan Options

1. Group deferred annuity contracts.
2. Group deposit administration contracts.
3. Immediate participation guarantee contracts.
4. Separate accounts.
5. Guaranteed investment contracts.

Group Deferred Annuity Contracts

The **group deferred annuity** is a contract between insurer and employer to provide for the purchase of specified amounts of deferred annuity for employees each year. For example, an annuity that would pay retirees $50 per month beginning at age 65 might be purchased by the employer from the insurer each year for each employee. The employer receives a master deferred annuity contract, and certificates of participation are given to individuals covered by the plan. Group plans usually require some minimum number of participants, to lower administrative expenses per employee.

Under this plan, all actuarial work is done by the insurer, which also provides administrative and investment services. Neither the employees nor the employer are subject to risk of investment return fluctuations. The only risk is the possible failure of the insurer. The employer's sole responsibility is to report essential information to the insurer and pay the premiums.

Group Deposit Administration Contracts

The **deposit administration** arrangement requires the employer to make regular payments to the insurance company on behalf of employees, and these contributions accumulate at interest. An actuary estimates the amount of annual employer deposits necessary to accumulate sufficient funds to purchase annuities when employees retire. The insurer guarantees the principal of funds deposited, as well as a specified minimum rate of interest. However, the insurer has no direct responsibility to employees until they retire, at which time an annuity is purchased for them. Before retirement, the employee's position is similar to that under an uninsured trust plan. After retirement, the employee's position is the same as with a group deferred annuity contract.

Immediate Participation Guarantee Contracts

The **immediate participation guarantee contract (IPG)** plan is a form of deposit administration; the employer makes regular deposits to a fund managed by the insurance company. The insurer receives deposits and makes investments. An IPG may be structured like a trust plan in that the insurer makes no guarantee concerning the safety of investments or their rate of return. However, some IPGs may guarantee the fund principal and a minimum rate of return.

The IPG is distinctive from other deposit administration contracts and attractive to employers, in that it gives employers more flexibility after an employee retires. The employer has the option to pay retirement benefits directly from the IPG fund, rather than locking into an annuity purchased from the insurer. This gives the employer control over the funds longer. The employer can also purchase an annuity for the retired employee.

Separate Accounts

Separate account plans are another modification of deposit administration contracts and are designed to give the insurer greater investment flexibility. They are not commingled with the insurer's other assets, and therefore are not subject to the same investment limitations. At least part of the employer's contributions are placed in separate accounts for investment in common stocks. Other separate accounts pool money for investment in bonds, mortgages, real estate, and other assets. Usually the funds of many employers are pooled for investment purposes, although a large firm may arrange for a special, separate account exclusively for its own funds. Separate accounts may be used to fund either fixed-dollar or variable annuity benefits.

Guaranteed Investment Contracts

Guaranteed investment contracts (GICs) are arrangements used by insurers to guarantee competitive rates of return on large, lump-sum transfers (usually $100,000 or more) of pension funds, usually from another type of funding instrument. For example, an employer may terminate a trust plan and transfer all the funds in the trust to an insurer who promises to pay an investment return of 7 percent for each of the next ten years. At the end of the specified period, the GIC arrangement ends and the fund balance is paid to the original investor, who may decide to reinvest in another GIC.

Other Qualified Defined Contribution Plans

Employers may offer a variety of defined contribution plans, other than money purchase plans, to assist employees in saving for retirement. These may be the only retirement plan offered by the organization, or they may be offered in addition to a defined benefit plan or a defined contribution money purchase plan. Many are designed to provide economic incentives to employees to encourage productivity and profitability for the organization. These plans are presented in figure 20–5.

GROUP DEFERRED PROFIT-SHARING PLANS

Profit-sharing plans provide economic incentives for employees, since firm profits are distributed directly to employees. In a **deferred profit-sharing plan,** a firm puts part of its profits in trust for the benefit of employees.

FIGURE 20–5

Other Qualified Defined Contribution Plans

1. Group deferred profit-sharing plans.
2. Savings plans.
3. 401(k) plans.
4. Employee stock ownership plans (ESOPs).

Typically, the share of profit allocated is related to salary; that is, the share each year is the percentage determined by the employee's salary divided by total salaries for all participants in the plan. The maximum amount of contribution cannot exceed 15 percent of the employee's salary. Some employers also consider years of service in making profit-sharing allocations.

Suppose, for example, that a plan provides for allocating an amount equal to 5 percent of annual basic salary for each person employed by the firm for ten years or less, and 10 percent for people employed for over ten years. Deposits would be recorded in the trust at the end of the year as follows:

EMPLOYEE	BASIC SALARY	YEARS SERVICE	PERCENT DEPOSIT	AMOUNT DEPOSIT
Adams, J.	$16,000	8	5%	$ 800
Brown, M.	20,000	11	10	2,000
Cramer, T.	30,000	7	5	1,500

Consideration of years of service can result in discrimination in favor of highly compensated employees. Discrimination would disqualify the plan for favorable tax treatment. Because of this possibility, most deferred profit-sharing plans consider salaries only and not length of employment. When the plan meets the qualifications established by the Internal Revenue Code, contributions to the trust are deductible from income by the firm, but are not taxable income to employees until benefits are received.

Deferred profit-sharing plans are similar to money purchase plans, except for the nature of the contributions. As qualified plans they must meet eligibility and vesting standards. However, many deferred profit-sharing plans have more relaxed eligibility and vesting standards than the minimum provisions required by ERISA. This may be attributable to the fact that employers also benefit from employee ownership of the plan, due to the incentive nature of the profit-sharing arrangement.

SAVINGS PLANS

A **savings plan** is a defined contribution plan that allows employees to contribute after-tax dollars to an individual account during employment in order to save for retirement. The investment returns on the account are not taxable until they are received as benefits. A profit-sharing savings plan allows employees and employers to contribute to the account, usually through a matching program in which employee contributions are matched by employer profit-sharing contributions. For example, employees may be allowed to contribute up to 6 percent of salary, and employers match one-half a percent for each percent saved by the employee. Thus, an employee saving 6 percent of salary would receive an employer contribution of 3 percent. Contributions to a savings plan are limited to prevent discrimination in favor of highly compensated employees more able to take advantage of the plan.

401(K) PLANS

Another qualified defined contribution plan is the **401(k) plan,** which allows employees to defer wage compensation for retirement.[15] For example, if an employee with a gross salary of $30,000 chooses to defer $2,000 for retirement in a 401(k) plan, then the employee will have a taxable salary that year of $28,000 (all else being equal). The primary difference between a savings plan and a 401(k) plan is that the 401(k) plan allows employees to save on a pre-tax basis. A 401(k) plan may stand alone or may be part of a profit-sharing plan, allowing employer contributions to augment employee savings.

Contributions to a 401(k) plan are limited. In 1987, the salary deferral was limited to $7,000 of income (indexed annually).[16] In addition, an employee's contribution cannot exceed 25 percent of the reduced salary amount, so that lower-income earners are well below the $7,000 limit. The total contribution amount to a 401(k) plan, by both employees and employers, cannot exceed 15 percent of the organization's payroll of reduced salaries.

Strict requirements are put on withdrawals, such as only allowing them for hardships (that is, heavy and immediate financial needs), disability, death, retirement, termination of employment, or reaching age 59 1/2. As in all other qualified retirement plans, a 10 percent penalty tax applies to withdrawals before age 59 1/2. The penalty undoubtedly discourages contributions from employees who want easier access to their savings.

Strict discrimination rules apply to 401(k) plans to guard against a plan favoring highly compensated employees. In addition, the plans must meet the general qualifications of a pension or profit-sharing plan. Investment accumulations and previously deferred salary are taxable when paid out as benefits. The majority of large employers offer 40l(k) plans in addition to either a defined benefit or money purchase pension plan. Under these circumstances, *combined* contributions cannot exceed the lesser of 25 percent of employee pay or $30,000 per year, unless a defined benefit plan requires a contribution above these limits. In the latter case, no contributions are allowed to the 40l(k) or other defined contribution plan.

EMPLOYEE STOCK OWNERSHIP PLANS

An **employee stock ownership plan (ESOP)** is a special form of profit sharing. The unique feature of an ESOP is that all investments are in the employer's common stock. Proponents of ESOPs claim that this ownership participation increases employee morale and productivity.

An ESOP represents the ultimate in investment concentration, since all contributions are invested in one security. This is distinctly different from the investment diversification found in the typical pension or profit-sharing plan. To alleviate the ESOP investment risk for older employees, employers are required to allow at least three diversified investment portfolios for persons over age 55 who also have at least 10 years of partici-

---

15. According to the Internal Revenue Code, tax-exempt and governmental agencies are not allowed to establish 401(k) plans, but instead may adopt 403(b) plans, which are similar.
16. In 1995, the 401(k) limit reached $9,240.

pation in the plan. Each diversified portfolio would contain several issues of nonemployer securities, such as common stocks or bonds. One option might even be a very low-risk investment, such as bank certificates of deposit. This allows use of an incentive-type qualified retirement plan without unnecessarily jeopardizing the retiree's benefit.

Nonqualified, Tax-Favored Retirement Plans

In addition to the qualified pension and profit-sharing plans previously discussed, other tax-favored retirement income plans are available. While these other plans technically are not qualified, they allow employers to deduct contributions, accumulations to the fund accrue tax-free, and employees are taxed on employer contributions and investment accumulations only when benefits are received.

SIMPLIFIED EMPLOYEE PENSION PLANS

A **simplified employee pension (SEP)** is similar to an employer-sponsored individual retirement account (IRA). With a SEP, the employer makes a deductible contribution to the IRA, but the contribution limit is much higher than the $2,000 annual deduction limit of the typical IRA. The SEP contribution is limited to the lesser of $30,000 or 15 percent of the employee's compensation. Coverage requirements ensure that a broad cross-section of employees is included in the SEP. Employers are not locked into an annual contribution amount, but when contributions are made, they must be allocated in a way that does not discriminate in favor of highly compensated employees. The main advantage of the SEP is low administrative cost compared with most qualified retirement plans, and for this reason small businesses find SEPs particularly attractive.

KEOGH PLANS

Keogh plans (HR-10 plans) are for people who earn self-employment income. Contributions can be made based on either full- or part-time employment. Even if the employee is a retirement plan participant with an organization that has one or more qualified defined benefit or defined contribution plans, the employee can establish a Keogh plan based on self-employment earned income. For example, the employee may work full-time for wages or salary but part-time as a consultant or accountant in the evenings and on weekends. Saving part of net income from self-employment is what Keogh is all about. Proprietors, partners, and employees can be covered in the same plan. Contribution limits are the same as those for regular defined benefit or money purchase plans. The Keogh plan may be designed as either type of plan.

Retirement Trends Worldwide

Many industrialized countries worldwide, including the United States, Japan, and European nations, have aging populations. In the United States, we talk about the aging of the "baby boomers," the large group of people born between 1946 and 1964, and the lower birth rates of post-boomer

ETHICAL *Dilemma*

Ethics of Employee-Directed Investment

Many employers allow employees to choose the investment vehicle for their individual defined contribution account. The pension plan is required to offer a range of investment choices and permit opportunities to switch investments during the year. Some employees appreciate the opportunity to direct their investment and control this aspect of retirement savings. In addition, properly managed employee-directed investment reduces employer liability for investment return.

A disadvantage to employee-directed investment, however, is that plan participants often lack investment experience. Unlike professional pension fund managers, employees tend to be cautious investors, choosing lower-risk vehicles with commensurately lower rates of return. Over the long term, retirement benefit amounts generated through employee-directed investment may be significantly less than those achieved with professional fund investors.

Both employees and employers can pay a high price for poor investment performance. Those eligible to retire, but who have insufficient private pension funds to do so, may remain in the work force longer than is desirable to employers. Large numbers of individuals in this situation could also put pressure on the government to increase Social Security benefits, placing a burden on the next generation of workers.

Educating employees about investment can make a difference in retirement benefit adequacy. The employer can explain the positive relationship between investment risk and rate of return, as well as the various funds available to employees. Participants may be given printed information on investing, as well as computer software that allows them to explore the effect of different investment vehicles on their own retirement fund. Meetings where choices are explained and questions addressed are also helpful. Employers are careful to advise employees on the options available, but not on how funds should be invested. For example, the employee benefits manager does not answer an employee's question about how the manager's own funds are invested, since that may be construed as an authoritative recommendation. Employee education on investment not only helps employees, but also assists employers who gain from the ability to recruit, retain, and retire satisfied workers.

populations. As the baby boomers matured, they first put a strain on many social institutions (such as school systems) and then caused rapid growth in the labor force. With their retirement, they will also have a significant impact on public and private retirement systems. Retirement systems in Europe and Japan are likely to undergo similar strain during this period, not only because of the large numbers of people retiring but also due to trends toward early retirement and longer life expectancies, trends also seen in the United States.

In chapter 17, we discussed how the U.S. Social Security system was modified by the 1983 amendments to better prepare for funding the anticipated baby boomer retirement. Throughout the world, modifications to social insurance systems are being made to address the challenges of aging societies, usually through increases in funding, limits to benefits, or privatization. Private retirement plans will also be affected by this boom in retirement.

There is global concern about how government-sponsored and private retirement plans may be affected in the future. In order to pay retiree benefits, pension funds, which are net buyers of assets at the present time, may become net sellers of assets. The sale of large quantities of assets to fund the increased number of retirements may negatively affect the price of the assets, perhaps jeopardizing retirees' security.[17] The fact that many countries worldwide will be experiencing similar boom retirement periods makes it unlikely that pension assets will remain at previous price levels (all else being equal). Pension assets may be discounted until enough demand for them is generated by the less numerous, younger workers to sufficiently clear the markets.

Preparing for retirement is an uncertain business in most industrialized countries. There are disincentives to save, since saving more may yield less than it does today if asset values fall. However, for that same reason (i.e., potentially decreased asset values), increased savings for retirement is important. Prudent plan funding and disciplined saving may be the safest strategy for individuals, employers, and governments.

....

17. See Sylvester J. Schieber and John B. Shoven, "The Consequences of Population Aging on Private Pension Fund Saving and Asset Markets," *National Bureau of Economic Research Working Paper, no. 4665* (Cambridge, Massachusetts: National Bureau of Economic Research, March 1994).

Getting the Most From Your Private Group Retirement Plan

More than 80 percent of medium- to large-sized employers offer some type of private group retirement plan, at a cost of more than 6 percent of payroll. Increases in contributions to pension plans have gone up faster than payroll costs.[18] The value of the plan to you can be substantial. It makes sense to be informed about your group retirement plan and to make the most of this important financial resource.

First, get a copy of the plan document describing the type of coverage you have. Do you have a defined contribution plan or a defined benefit plan? Perhaps you have both. Many employers offer a profit-sharing, savings, or 401(k) plan in addition to a defined benefit or defined contribution money purchase plan. 40l(k) plans have become popular "second plans," and of course these offer employees an excellent opportunity to defer income for retirement.

Check to see who contributes to the plan. Defined contribution plans are more likely to allow employee contributions than are defined benefit plans. If employees are allowed to contribute, you may want to make regular contributions so that your retirement income is adequate to maintain your preretirement standard of living. Vesting will protect employer contributions if you leave the plan before retirement, so find out what vesting schedule applies to your group and how leaving the plan affects the benefits.

If you have a defined benefit pension plan, what is the benefit formula? Are salary level and years of service rec-ognized? Check to see if the formula is integrated. A defined contribution plan also may allow integration, so check to see if you are affected. The larger the integration amount, the smaller your retirement benefit will be.

Perhaps your employer offers a plan that allows you to direct pension fund investments. This gives you a choice of the risk and return tradeoff you prefer. Generally, investment in common stocks is riskier than in bonds, but the return is greater. In fact, past experience suggests that over time (such as during your working career), common stocks tend to outperform all other investments. Remember that performance needs to be sufficient to at least keep up with inflation. Inflation is an important consideration when you are saving for any length of time, especially over a twenty- or thirty-year period. Educate yourself about the investment choices available to you, and choose wisely. Monitor investment performance, but don't react to every shift in the market. Keep a long-term perspective and only make changes as needed.

Remember that retirement planning is not a one-time event but a process that requires your continuing education and ongoing evaluation. Check with the Social Security Administration every three years to make sure they have an accurate record of your wage history. Stay in touch with your employee benefits manager to find out about any changes being made to your private pension plan. Monitor investment performance, both for your group pension plan and for any individual savings programs you may establish. The ultimate benefit to you and your family will more than compensate you (literally) for your investment of time and attention in retirement planning.

18. *Employee Benefits Report 1994*, U.S. Chamber of Commerce, pp. 22, 25.

Key Terms

qualified plan	normal retirement age
ERISA	contributory plan
eligibility criteria	vesting
coverage requirements	defined benefit plan
controlled group	final average formula

career average formula
cost-of-living adjustment (COLA)
integrated plan
preretirement survivor annuity
joint and survivor annuity
Pension Benefit Guaranty
    Corporation (PBGC)
normal costs
supplemental costs
defined contribution plan
noninsured trust plan
group deferred annuity
deposit administration

immediate participation guarantee
    contract (IPG)
separate account plans
guaranteed investment contracts
    (GIC)
deferred profit-sharing plan
savings plan
401(k) plan
employee stock ownership plan
    (ESOP)
simplified employee pension (SEP)
Keogh plan

Discussion Questions

1. There has been a proposal that all private pension plans be required to provide full vesting at the end of one year of participation. If you were the owner of a firm employing fifty people and had a qualified pension plan, how would you react to this proposal? Please explain.

2. As an employee with a defined benefit pension plan, which would you prefer: a flat amount benefit formula that specifies $1,000 per month, or a percentage unit benefit formula that says your benefit will be 1.5 percent per year times your average annual salary for your highest three consecutive years of employment? Please explain.

3. As an employer, would you prefer a defined contribution pension plan or a defined benefit plan? Please explain.

4. Which is preferable from an employee's point of view: a defined contribution or a defined benefit pension plan? Please explain.

5. As an employee, would you prefer a deferred or an immediate (cash at the end of the year) profit-sharing plan? If your income doubled, would your choice change? Please explain.

6. Some employers have deferred profit-sharing plans instead of defined benefit or defined contribution money purchase plans. Why?

7. As an employee benefits manager, you must recommend to the firm's CEO a defined contribution plan to add to the existing defined benefit retirement plan. First describe the hypothetical firm, giving firm size, profitability, and stability of the work force. Then explain your choice of a deferred profit-sharing plan, a savings plan, a 401(k), an ESOP, or some combination of these (such as a profit-sharing savings plan).

8. Cash balance plans have become increasingly popular in recent years. Why do employers like cash balance plans relative to other types of defined benefit plans?

9. Social Security retirement benefits are adjusted annually to offset the effect of inflation, but few private pension plans follow this practice. Why not?

10. Explain the difference between a group deferred annuity contract and a deposit administration contract. Which offers more protection to employers against the risk of inadequate funding of a promised defined benefit?

Cases

20.1 Lloyd Olsen, personnel manager of Sturdy Biscuit Company, is pondering a question of funding the company's pension plan. Sturdy Biscuit Company employs 300 people and has a history of sound financial management. Knowing that he has to present a proposal to the board of directors next week, Lloyd is considering presenting the advantages and disadvantages of both a bank administered trust plan and an insurer separate account plan. He feels that once the board clearly understands the alternatives, they can make the best decision.

1. Help Lloyd construct a comparison of the two approaches.
2. Outline the advantages and disadvantages. How might the board decide?

20.2 Jackson Appliances has twelve employees. The owner, Zena Jackson, is considering some system to reward them for their loyalty and to provide some funds to help them with their living expenses after they retire. Explain why a SEP might be a good choice for the company and explain how it works. Are there other alternatives Zena should consider?

20.3 Charles Dillard's company pension plan allowed him to begin participating at age 21. He worked for the company for twenty years, leaving at age 41. He was promised $20 per month in retirement benefits, to begin at age 65, for each year he was covered by the plan, but he finds when he leaves that he will not be allowed to take the current value of these benefits out of the plan. Instead, he must wait until he is 65 and take the benefits at that time.

1. Why would the law allow this arrangement?
2. Why not let Charles take the present value of his benefits with him to his new employer, and add this to his plan there?
3. Why not simply let him take the money out now and use it as he sees fit?

20.4 Henry Wooster meets with the employee benefits manager to discuss enrolling in the company's 401(k) plan. He finds that if he enrolls, he must choose the amount of salary to defer and also direct fund investment. Having no college education and no business experience, Henry lacks confidence about making these decisions.

1. Should Henry enroll in the 401(k)? Do the advantages outweigh the difficulties he may have in managing the plan?
2. What would you recommend that Henry do to educate himself about fund management? How can the benefits manager help?
3. Is it appropriate for the employer to establish a plan that requires employees to take this much responsibility for retirement planning? Please explain.

Individual Health Insurance Contracts

Introduction Individuals are concerned about managing their personal health risks, specifically the risk of being without sufficient income or means of paying for care in the event of an illness, injury, or disability. In chapter 17, we discussed the health insurance coverage provided through Social Security and explained that coverage for retirement medical expenses and serious disabilities is available for individuals with sufficient work history. In chapters 18 and 19, we described private group medical and disability insurance offered by employers choosing to sponsor voluntary employee benefit plans. In this chapter, we will discuss individual health insurance contracts that are voluntarily purchased, with no link to employment or work history.

Individual contracts are an important source of insurance for unemployed people or those without employer-sponsored health benefits. Some of the policy characteristics of individual contracts are similar to those of group contracts; however, there are important differences which will be explored here. We also investigate two additional health insurance contracts, long-term care insurance and policies that supplement Medicare, both of which are increasingly important with the aging of the population, longer life expectancies, and the trend toward earlier retirement.

This chapter examines:
1. Individual medical expense insurance contracts.
2. Dental insurance.
3. Individual disability income insurance contracts.
4. Long-term care insurance contracts.
5. Medicare supplements.
6. Health insurance policy provisions.
7. Global perspectives on individual health insurance.

Individual Medical Expense Insurance Contracts

Various medical expense insurance contracts are available in the private, non-group market. The policies providing the broadest coverage are similar to those group medical policies discussed in chapter 19, namely, basic medical expense insurance, major medical insurance, and comprehensive medical insurance.[1] Other types of policies reimburse only for specific illnesses (such as cancer), pay only a per diem amount for medical expenses, or are otherwise very limited in coverage. The consumer needs to read individual policies carefully.

For an individual or family managing the risk of illness or injury without the assistance of employer-sponsored benefits, a broad-based, individually purchased policy should provide the foundation of the medical insurance program. The first type of coverage in the non-group market is basic health insurance, which is similar to that in the group market: a **basic hospital policy,** a **basic surgical policy,** and a **basic medical expense policy.** These may be sold individually or together. As in group insurance, there is little or no cost sharing through deductibles or coinsurance provisions, and there are low dollar limits of coverage. Covered services are limited (compared to the services covered by major medical or comprehensive policies).

The basic hospital policy covers *room and board* (usually for a specified number of days) and *hospital ancillary services* (such as x-ray imaging and laboratory tests). The benefit for room and board is limited to a specified maximum per day and a specified number of days. Generally, the higher the room and board benefit, the higher the premium. Ancillary services are also limited, either on a *scheduled basis* (such as $35 for a certain laboratory test) or on a *blanket basis* (with a maximum limit, for example, of $4,000).

A major difference between individual and group basic hospital policies concerns maternity benefits. As discussed in chapter 19, the Civil Rights Act requires that group policies treat pregnancy the same as any other medical condition. However, individuals may purchase policies that cover *complications* due to pregnancy but not routine maternity care. Routine maternity care may be added through an insurance rider, which can be expensive because of adverse selection. That is, those more likely to need maternity benefits tend to purchase the rider.

As in group insurance, the individual basic surgical policy pays surgeons for services, whether the surgery is performed in the hospital or elsewhere. The policy either lists the maximum benefit amount for each procedure or pays up to the "usual and customary" charges, based on physician practice patterns in the region. If the surgeon charges more than the maximum amount covered by the policy, the individual pays the difference out-of-pocket.

The third basic policy, basic medical expense insurance, covers doctors' fees for nonsurgical services provided in the hospital, office, or home. Policy limits may restrict coverage to doctors' visits in the hospital only, and a daily maximum benefit amount can be imposed. Other typical exclusions are routine physical examinations, eye examinations, and prescription

---

1. Some individuals also join HMOs. For a more detailed discussion of basic, major medical, and comprehensive medical policies, as well as HMOs, see chapter 19.

drugs. Basic surgical and basic medical policies are fairly similar in the individual and group market.

Major medical and comprehensive insurance policies in the individual market are also similar to those sold in the group market. As in the group market, major medical policies are often sold in conjunction with basic policies. **Major medical policies** require insureds to *cost share* through deductible and coinsurance provisions. Cost sharing provides an economic incentive to insureds to price shop and use only needed care. Major medical policies cover a broad range of services and offer high limits of coverage. However, individual policies may exclude maternity coverage except for complications related to pregnancy. **Comprehensive policies** are similar to major medical insurance in that they cover a broad range of services, require cost sharing, and have high limits of coverage. The notable difference is that comprehensive contracts stand alone and are not sold in conjunction with basic policies.

Anyone purchasing non-group medical expense insurance should read the policy carefully, since provisions and exclusions across contracts vary greatly (even more so than in the group market). Covered services, cost-sharing requirements, and coverage limits should be noted. A coordination of benefits provision typically is included to designate the primary insurer in the event that other insurance (such as workers' compensation or Social Security) is available.[2]

Dental Insurance

Most medical insurance policies do not cover dental expenses. The notable exception is the major medical or comprehensive policy which covers selected dental surgery, injuries to natural teeth, or fractures and dislocations of the jaw. **Dental insurance policies,** available in both the individual and group market, typically pay for normal diagnostic, preventive, restorative, and orthodontic services, as well as services required because of accidents. Diagnostic and preventive services include checkups and x-rays. Restorative services include procedures such as fillings, crowns, and bridges, and orthodontia includes braces and realignment of teeth.

Dental insurance policies encourage better dental health by not applying a deductible or coinsurance to charges for checkups and cleaning. By having first-dollar coverage, insureds are more likely to seek routine diagnostic care, which enables early detection of problems and may reduce total expenditures. Dental policies not only cover routine care but also protect insureds against more expensive procedures such as restorative services. For restorative and orthodontic services, insureds usually pay a deductible or coinsurance amount. A fee schedule limits the amount paid per procedure, so the insured may also pay out-of-pocket for the cost of services above the scheduled amount. Policy maximums are specified on an annual and lifetime basis, such as $2,000 per year and $50,000 during a lifetime.

Many dentists consult with the insured in advance of the procedure to determine what will be paid by insurance. The dentist lists what needs to

---

2. See chapter 19 for a discussion of coordination of benefits.

be done and then the dentist or the insured checks with the insurer to determine coverage. Most policies exclude coverage for purely cosmetic purposes, losses caused by war, and occupational injuries or sickness.

Individual Disability Income Insurance Contracts

Most people recovering from an acute illness or accident miss a few days or weeks of work. What may not be obvious is that more than 14 percent of the United States population is limited in the ability to perform some major activity, and more than 4 percent are unable to do a major job assignment due to chronic disease or disability.[3] Table 21–1 provides data, with partial and total disability combined, on the incidence of disability related to gender, income, and age. Generally, the probability of disability is greater for women, for those with lower income, and for older people.

Disability income insurance replaces lost income when the insured is unable to work. Income replacement is especially critical with disability because the individual faces not only the risk of reduced earnings but also the risk of additional expenses resulting from medical or therapeutic services. In chapter 17 we discussed the Social Security disability program, which covers most employees in the United States. However, qualifying under the Social Security definition for disability is difficult, and fewer than 13 percent of the people with activity limitation due to disability receive benefits through Social Security.[4] Workers' compensation is another source of disability insurance, but only for disability arising from employment-related injury or illness (see chapter 12). Some employers provide private group disability insurance, as discussed in chapter 18, but this employee benefit is much less commonly offered than are life, medical, or retirement

TABLE 21–1

Number of Days per Year of Limited Ability to Perform Employment or Housework (1991)

GENDER	
Male	6.4
Female	8.2
FAMILY INCOME (PER YEAR)	
Under $10,000	10.7
$10,000–19,999	8.2
$20,000–34,999	7.3
$35,000 and over	6.4
AGE	
18–44	7.0
45–64	6.4
65 and over	8.8

SOURCE: U.S. Department of Health and Human Services, National Center for Health Statistics, as adapted from a table in the *Source Book of Health Insurance Data 1993*, p. 134.

3. *Source Book of Health Insurance Data 1993*, p. 129.
4. Ibid., pp. 129, 140.

benefits.[5] Individuals may want to purchase disability coverage on their own, in case they are not eligible for Social Security, workers' compensation, or private employer-sponsored plans, or simply because they want additional protection.

DEFINITION AND CAUSE OF DISABILITY

Definitions of disability vary more among individual policies than among group policies. **Total disability** may be defined as the complete inability to perform *any and every duty* of the individual's own job. Alternatively, it may be defined as the inability to engage in any *reasonable and gainful occupation* for which the individual is (or could become) qualified by education, training, or experience. Some policies combine these two definitions, with the more liberal (from the insured's point of view) "own occupation" definition satisfying the requirement for total disability during an initial short-term period (for example, two years), and the more stringent definition being used thereafter. **Partial disability** is even more difficult to define than total disability. It is usually measured in terms of the inability to perform some of the important duties of the job. Some policies pay partial disability only if partial disability follows total disability or only if a loss of income results.

Some contracts provide income benefits for disability caused by *accident only,* others for both *accident and sickness.* It is necessary to distinguish between losses caused by accident and those caused by sickness, because the benefits can differ. Some policies provide that income losses resulting from injuries due to accident must start within ninety days after the injury. Losses resulting from injuries which begin after the ninety-day period are deemed to have resulted from sickness. Moreover, a loss is not considered caused by accident unless it results "directly and independently of all other causes." This provision is designed to eliminate from the definition of accidental bodily injury income losses actually caused by illness. For example, a person who suffers a heart attack and is injured when falling to the ground would not qualify for accident benefits but would qualify for sickness benefits.

Preexisting conditions are excluded from individual policies[6] by the statement that insurance is provided for "loss resulting from sickness contracted and first treated by a physician while this policy is in force." A more liberal provision (from the insured's point of view) would exclude benefits only for preexisting conditions that cause disability during the first two policy years. A preexisting condition excludes benefits only when it is not disclosed on the application or a specific rider excludes this cause of disability. The purpose of the clause is to avoid adverse selection from persons who have a serious illness before buying the insurance.

BENEFITS

As with group insurance, both short-term disability and long-term disability policies are available for individuals. **Short-term disability policies**

5. See chapter 18 for a detailed discussion of short-term and long-term disability insurance plans. Here we discuss disability policies briefly, highlighting how individual policies differ from those available in the group market.
6. Preexisting conditions are not excluded from group disability policies.

(STD) are those with benefits payable up to two years. Short-term plans may restrict benefits to periods as short as thirteen or twenty-six weeks. Individual STD plans may limit benefit duration to six months for the *same cause* of disability, sometimes requiring the insured to return to work for up to ninety days before establishing a new maximum benefit period for disability from the same cause.

Long-term disability policies (LTD) are those that pay benefits for longer periods, such as five years, ten years, until a set retirement age, or for life. Long-term disability policies often assume that the insured will become eligible for retirement benefits from Social Security or private retirement plans at age 65. To coordinate benefits, the disability policy defines the maximum duration as age 65. LTD benefits for any shorter period would expose the insured to a potentially devastating income loss, since neither disability nor retirement income would be provided for this period.

Long-term benefits do not cost proportionately more than short-term coverage. From the consumer's point of view, the longer term policy is a better buy. It protects against an *unbearable* risk: the *long-term* loss of income. This is a good example of the "large loss principle," where insurance purchase should be governed by the potential severity of loss, rather than the frequency of loss. The large loss principle should govern disability income insurance purchases even though most disabilities are of relatively short duration.

Policies pay benefits after an elimination or waiting period. The **elimination period,** like a deductible in medical insurance, reduces moral hazard. For STD policies the elimination period typically extends from a few days to two weeks; for LTD policies the period extends from one month to one year. Here, as in group coverage, the insured may be covered during the LTD waiting period by benefits from the STD policy or a salary continuation plan (i.e., sick leave).

Individual contracts generally state the amount of the benefit in terms of dollars per week or month, unlike group policies that state benefits as a percentage of the insured's basic earnings. In either case, the insurer is wary of having the benefit equal to anything approaching full earnings. Typically, the amount is limited to about two-thirds of earned income because benefits are typically not taxable. The purpose of this limitation is to reduce moral hazard by providing an economic incentive for employees to return to work.

Benefits may differ for disabilities resulting from accident rather than sickness. Benefits for sickness are not as generous as those for accidents. For example, a policy may provide benefit payments for five years if disability is caused by accident, but only two years if caused by sickness. Some long-term policies pay to age 65 for sickness, but for life when the cause of disability is accidental. Benefits for partial disability, which are more likely to be provided by individual contracts rather than group contracts, often are only for disability caused by accident. Some policies pay no benefits if the sickness or accident is work-connected and the employee receives workers' compensation benefits. Such policies are called *nonoccupational.* Others supplement workers' compensation benefits up to the point at which the insured gets the same payment for occupational and nonoccupational disabilities. Some individual policies specify a maximum combined benefit for Social Security and the private policy. The insured can purchase a plan with a **social insurance substitute,** which replaces

Social Security benefits if the individual does not qualify under their strict definition of disability.

Often, individual policies are not coordinated with other disability income benefits. The relatively few individual policies that coordinate disability benefits use the **average earnings provision.** This provision addresses the problem of overinsurance, which may occur when a person has more than one policy.[7] For example, a person whose salary is $2,000 per month may have two disability income policies, each of which provides $1,200 per month income benefits. In the event of total disability, assuming no coordination provision, the insured loses $2,000 per month salary and receives $2,400 in benefits. This reduces the incentive to return to work and may lead to benefit payment for a longer time than anticipated when the premium rate was established.

The average earnings clause provides for a reduction in benefit payments if the total amount of income payments under all insurance policies covering the loss exceeds earnings at the time disability commences, or exceeds the average earnings for two years preceding disability, whichever is greater. The amount of the reduction is the proportion by which all benefits would have to be reduced in order to prevent total benefits from exceeding average earned income. In the preceding illustration, for example, total insurance exceeded income by one-fifth, in which case the benefits of each policy containing an average earnings clause would be reduced so that disability benefits do not exceed predisability earnings. A reduction of the payment provided by each policy from $1,200 to $1,000 per month eliminates the excess.

The insured may have policies in place that do not have an average earnings clause, and could receive benefits in excess of predisability earnings. This provides an income advantage during a period of disability. A further advantage to the insured is the absence of federal income taxes on disability benefits from individual policies (as well as employee-paid group policies). In addition, the disabled insured has few, if any, work expenses, such as clothing and transportation costs. Insurance underwriters recognize these advantages, as well as the potential for moral hazard, and may be unwilling to issue a large policy when benefits are otherwise available.

Long Term Care Insurance Contracts

A significant risk that individuals face later in life is the risk of insufficient resources to pay for nursing home services. Generally, wealthy individuals are able to pay these expenses from their private income or savings. Those with few resources who qualify for Medicaid are covered through public assistance or welfare. Others who are neither wealthy nor poor often find it difficult to afford such care, which can cost upwards of $30,000 per year. Some people mistakenly think that long-term nursing care is covered by Medicare; Medicare only covers a limited number of days of skilled nursing care after a period of hospitalization.[8]

7. In group insurance, coordination of benefits provisions address the problem of overinsurance.
8. See chapter 17 for a discussion of Medicare.

Long-term care insurance (LTC) can be purchased by individuals to cover the costs of nursing homes, home health care, or other related services for the elderly.[9] Generally, benefits are expressed as a maximum daily benefit, such as $50 or $100 per day, with an overall policy limit, such as five years of benefits or a $100,000 lifetime maximum. Waiting or elimination periods are not uncommon; for example, a policy may not pay the first ninety days of nursing home expenses.

Eligibility for benefits depends not only on whether the insured has bought an LTC policy, but on whether the policy covers the type of care needed. LTC policies specify three types of care: *skilled nursing care, intermediate nursing care,* and/or *custodial care.* Not all policies cover all types of care. Most cover skilled nursing care, which requires medical professionals, such as nurses, to treat the patient on a 24-hour basis under the direction of a physician. Patients typically need this type of attention for a relatively short period of time, immediately after hospitalization or following an acute illness. However, some individuals may require skilled nursing care for longer periods. Skilled nursing care is the most expensive kind of long-term care. Intermediate nursing care is for those not requiring around-the-clock assistance by medical professionals. This type of care typically extends for longer periods than does skilled nursing care.

Custodial care provides individuals with assistance in activities of daily living, such as bathing, dressing, and eating. Medical staff are not required. Although it is the least intensive kind of care, custodial care is often needed for the longest period of time and thus can be the most costly care overall. Coverage of custodial care varies across policies. Some contracts cover custodial care only if a doctor states that it is medically necessary. Others cover only if the insured is unable to perform a certain number of activities of daily living.

LTC insurance policies typically cover skilled, intermediate, and/or custodial nursing care in a nursing home facility. Some policies also cover **home health care,** in which all or a portion of these services are provided in the insured's own home. Coverage of home health care is becoming increasingly common, since insureds generally prefer to be at home and total costs may be lower than if care is provided in a medical facility.

Generally, long-term contracts are sold to individuals over 50 years of age. Policies become very expensive with advanced age (for example, over 70). Once the policy is purchased, the premium does not increase with the insured's age, unless the premium is increased across the entire class of insureds due to greater-than-expected claims. Premium increases or changes in the insured's situation may cause some individuals to stop making payments on the LTC policy. In those cases, a *nonforfeiture option* can be important, since it allows people who have been paying premiums for a number of years to receive a reduced benefit if they stop making payments. Another important LTC policy is inflation protection. Many LTC policies offer the option of indexed benefits or nonindexed adjustments of three to five percent a year. Given the trend of rising health care costs, inflation protection is important.

Health status and preexisting conditions affect whether LTC policies are issued and what their benefits are. Policies generally exclude coverage for

---

9. *Group* long-term care insurance is being offered by an increasing number of employers, but it is still only a small part of the long-term care insurance market.

mental and nervous disorders, other than Alzheimer's disease. However, if the individual *already* has Alzheimer's disease before purchasing the policy, Alzheimer's may be excluded from coverage. Individuals who *already* have other severely disabling conditions before applying for LTC coverage may be denied by the underwriter. Less severe medical conditions usually do not affect issue of the policy, but coverage of a nursing home stay resulting from a preexisting medical condition is generally not covered for the first six months to a year that the policy is in force. Most LTC contracts state that as long as the insured continues to make premium payments, the insurer cannot cancel the policy. This protects insureds who may experience a change in health status after purchasing a LTC policy.

Long-term care insurance can provide an important component of economic protection for elderly people. Given the aging population and the rising cost of medical care, the significance of LTC insurance is not likely to diminish soon. However, consumers should remember that LTC insurance is a relatively new product that continues to evolve. Consequently, individual LTC policy provisions vary greatly, and the consumer should read the contract carefully before making any purchase.

Medicare Supplementary Insurance

Medicare health insurance is provided through the Social Security system for covered persons over age 65, as well as those under 65 with kidney disease (see chapter 17). Medicare, however, does not completely cover the cost of all medical services needed by elderly people. Private individual health contracts, known as **"Medigap" insurance,** supplement the coverage provided by Medicare.[10]

Various Medigap policies have been available, representing a range of benefits and premiums. In the past, the wide variety of products, as well as unethical sales practices by agents, made it difficult for consumers to understand policy provisions or compare contracts. Lengthy preexisting condition requirements limited the protection offered by many policies. Many people purchased duplicate coverage, not realizing that the additional policies provided no extra protection. Many of the policies were not good buys, returning less than 60 cents in benefits for each dollar of premium.

In 1990, legislation required standardization of Medigap policies to make it easier for consumers to understand and compare various policy provisions. Ten standardized policies (developed by the National Association of Insurance Commissioners) are now approved for sale in the individual Medigap market. Preexisting condition clauses cannot exceed six months. In addition, loss ratios, the ratio of benefits paid to premiums received, are required to be at least 60 percent. Legislation outlawed the sale of duplicate policies, and agents can be fined for deceptive sales practices.

The ten standard Medigap plans range from Plan A to Plan J. Plan A, the least expensive contract, is the basic policy and covers a *core of benefits*. Plans B through J cover the core of benefits as well as additional benefits

10. The statutory definition of a Medigap policy excludes employer-sponsored group medical plans. However, retirees may have employer-sponsored supplemental policies that pay expenses not covered by Medicare (see chapter 19). The Medigap definition does include Medicare supplemental products sold by HMOs to individuals.

that increase as one moves toward Plan J, which provides the most coverage and has the greatest premium. Comparing the ten standardized policies on the basis of benefits and price is straightforward, and the insured simply decides what to purchase based on need for coverage and willingness or ability to pay. However, not all insurers selling Medigap coverage sell all of the plans.

Like long-term care insurance, Medigap insurance can provide an important element of economic security for elderly people. Given the current funding shortfalls of Medicare and the national concern with the federal budget deficit, additional public funding of medical care for the elderly is unlikely. Thus, the importance of Medigap insurance is not likely to diminish anytime soon.

Health Insurance Policy Provisions

Among the various individual health insurance policies are several common contract provisions. Some have been discussed, such as preexisting condition and average earnings clauses. Others are similar to those in life insurance policies, such as the grace period, the incontestable clause (also referred to as the "time limit on certain defenses"), reinstatement, waiver of premium (in disability contracts), assignment clauses, and the cost-of-living rider, all discussed in chapter 13. Several provisions not yet discussed are continuance provisions, change of occupation clause, and the option to purchase additional disability insurance. To protect the consumer, state laws require health policies to include these provisions. Most consumers, however, do not know what provisions are necessary to provide adequate protection.

CONTINUANCE PROVISIONS

Because health insurance is a unilateral contract, an insured does not have to pay the next premium, but the policy will not continue in force unless it is paid. To stop the insurance, all an insured has to do is ignore the premium notice. But suppose an insured is satisfied with the policy and is willing to pay the premium. What guarantee does he or she have that it can be kept in force? The answer depends on the **continuance provision.**

Individual health insurance policies (including medical and disability contracts) handle continuance in several different ways:

1. No provision.
2. Cancellable by the insurer at any time.
3. Cancellable only on an anniversary date, or date the premium is due.
4. Conditionally renewable.
5. Guaranteed renewable.
6. Noncancellable and guaranteed renewable.

No Provision

The policy simply terminates upon expiration of its term. This is similar to a five-year term life insurance policy; after five years, it expires. If the insured wants more coverage, she or he has to be insurable and buy another policy.

Cancellable by the Insurer at Any Time

With this provision, the policy does not have a term. It simply remains in force as long as the premium is paid and the insurer is willing to accept it. Coverage may terminate at any time.

Cancellable Only on an Anniversary Date or Date the Premium is Due

If the anniversary date is January 1 and premiums are paid annually, the insured is guaranteed coverage for one year. If premiums are paid monthly, however, coverage is provided for only one month at a time. If they are paid weekly, coverage is certain for only a week at a time.

Conditionally Renewable

The insurer can terminate the policy only on an anniversary date and only under circumstances specified in the policy. The policy may provide, for example, that the insurer can terminate coverage when the insured retires, or it can refuse to renew all policies of its kind in the state. This means the company cannot cancel only one contract, but can cancel all the policies in the same group. If an insured has many claims, the only way the insurer can cancel the policy is to terminate all insureds with the same type of policy in the state. Thus, the policy is "class cancellable." On the other hand, if no claim has been filed but overall loss experience with the group is bad, the company may terminate all contracts in the group. If an insured is elderly or in poor health, finding other coverage may be difficult or impossible.

Guaranteed Renewable

The insurer agrees that the insured has the right to continue the policy in force for a substantial period of time—to age 65, for example. The insurer has no right to make any changes *except* the premium rate for a class of insureds. The insurer can change the premium rate for all insureds of a certain age, in a certain territory, or with a particular policy form. It cannot change the premium on an individual contract without changing the premiums of all insureds in the classification. It cannot, in other words, single out individuals.

Noncancellable and Guaranteed Renewable

Under this type of renewal guarantee, the insured has the right to continue the policy in force for a substantial period of time—to age 65, for example—by paying premiums when due. The insurer has no right to make any changes. The premium may be level or it may increase according to a schedule provided in the policy. Thus, the premium pattern may be like level-premium term life insurance to age 65, or it may be like annual renewable term life insurance to age 65. This is the best continuance provision and the most expensive. The purpose of insurance is to reduce un-

ETHICAL *Dilemma*

The Individual Health Insurance Market

Doctors have been among disability insurers' favorite customers.[11] This can be explained, in part, because when physicians are disabled, they tend to return to work quickly. Recently, however, the trend has changed.

One of the largest U.S. disability insurers, UNUM, had physician claims increase 60 percent in the first six months of 1994 from one year earlier.[12] Doctors are making more claims and, in a surprising number of cases, are not returning to work. Many claims are for mental and nervous conditions. Other insurers have experienced similar trends. As a result, insurers are increasing premiums, tightening policy provisions (for example, not writing "own occupation" coverage), and underwriting more stringently. Benefits for stress-related disorders, such as mental and nervous conditions as well as for treatment of substance abuse, are being reduced. Some insurance companies are increasing marketing efforts to individuals in lower-income brackets, since disability income replacement benefit payments are lower for this group than for physicians.

The increase in physician claims, which seems to be associated with reduced job satisfaction, can be linked with health care reform. Reform efforts toward managed care have resulted in cost control initiatives, monitoring of doctors, and a reduction, in some cases, of physician income.[13] In addition, claims have increased because many individual disability policies written in the late 1980s for professionals were quite generous, and doctors could receive more on disability than they could by returning to work in a managed care environment.

Whether the increase in doctors' disability claims represents compromised ethics or outdated policy provisions and marketing efforts can be debated. However, insurers argue that for doctors to have continued access to individual disability coverage, insurers must adopt policy provisions, premiums, and benefit levels appropriate to a new medical service business environment, one likely to continue to change and evolve throughout the 1990s.

certainty, and this provision eliminates any uncertainty about an insured's power to keep the coverage in force and the amount of premium to be charged.

CHANGE OF OCCUPATION

The **change of occupation provision** is commonly included in contracts designed for sale to individuals whose occupations generally are not haz-

11. Self-employed people, like doctors and lawyers, are usually not covered by group disability plans, but purchase their own insurance in the individual market.
12. "More Physicians Heal Themselves on Disability Income," *The Wall Street Journal*, November 7, 1994, p. B6.
13. See chapter 19 for a discussion of managed care.

ardous. It provides that if the individual changes to a more hazardous occupation than the one at the time of application for insurance, benefits are reduced to what the current premium would provide. The clause is similar in effect to the operation of the misstatement of age clause in a life insurance policy. If an insured changes to a less hazardous occupation, however, benefits remain unchanged but the premium is reduced.

OPTIONS TO PURCHASE ADDITIONAL DISABILITY INSURANCE

A major problem with long-term disability income insurance is the impact of inflation on a fixed dollar benefit amount. Before disability begins, a solution is to get periodic updates in coverage by buying additional policies, provided you remain insurable. A better solution is an **option to purchase rider** that allows you to purchase additional amounts of disability income benefits. This option allows the insured to increase the amount of coverage, regardless of insurability (recognizing health, occupation, and financial condition), on certain policy anniversaries such as those nearest one's 25th, 30th, 35th, 40th, 45th, and 50th birthdays. The insurer guards itself against overinsurance by reserving the right to apply its financial underwriting standards. These standards specify a relationship between current earnings and the sum of disability income benefits with all insurers. The new policy will not cover any preexisting disability when issued.

A **cost-of-living rider** adjusts benefits for inflation, similar to the rider found in life insurance. The benefit amount is adjusted for inflation with limits per year (for example, a maximum of 8 or 10 percent). Liberal policies continue to make increases available as long as the insured meets financial underwriting standards for more coverage. If a policy has an option to purchase additional insurance, insureds may want the cost-of-living increases to begin only during periods of disability. In the absence of an option to purchase rider, a cost-of-living rider can be used to provide adjustments before and after an actual disability. A cost-of-living rider without a cap on total benefits before an advanced age (such as 65) exposes the insurer to potentially larger benefits than an option to purchase additional benefits, and thus tends to be significantly more expensive.

Global Perspective on Individual Health Insurance

Individual disability insurance contracts are sold throughout the world. The market in each country depends, in part, on whether disability coverage is offered through other channels, such as the social insurance system or through employment. The market is also dependent on the adequacy of those benefits. Another factor affecting demand is per capita income. Where income is higher (all else being equal), individuals are more able to afford coverage and may want to replace a higher portion of income than that replaced through social insurance.

In Japan, employers traditionally have provided disability protection to workers and their families. However, global competition has forced companies to become more cost conscious, making employee benefits less generous than in the past. In addition, the government is concerned about containing social insurance costs, and is therefore unwilling to add more benefits to current programs.

As a result, there is tremendous growth potential in the market for individual disability income contracts in Japan.[14] Per capita income in Japan is high relative to the rest of the world, and social insurance replaces less than 40 percent of predisability earnings. The need for coverage exists, as well as the personal resources to pay for the product.

U.S. disability insurers have been licensed to sell long-term disability coverage in Japan. In order for a U.S. insurer to be successful, careful study of Japanese culture, administrative practices, and claim management practices is required. To the degree possible, hiring local people who understand the culture also helps ensure success. The goal is to find and implement the *best practices* in marketing, underwriting, and claims management to produce a viable insurance product throughout the world.

....

14. "The World's Largest Undeveloped LTD Market," *National Underwriter: Life & Health/Financial Services,* January 23, 1995, p. 33.

Buying Health Care Insurance

The health insurance consumer is confronted with hundreds of health policies on the market. If you are just graduating from college, you may prefer to continue a student health policy or a COBRA extension of your parents' policy until you get a job. (COBRA was explained in chapter 19.) Once employed, if you don't have an employer-sponsored plan, you may want to buy a health policy on your own. How do you as a consumer make a choice? To help you understand the differences among policies, we outline some features and drawbacks of basic and major medical plans, and then present buying principles that should help when you're in the market for health insurance.

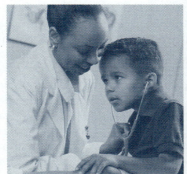

BUYING BASIC HOSPITAL, SURGICAL, AND MEDICAL INSURANCE

Buying basic health insurance can be confusing because it is difficult to compare benefits and costs of dissimilar policies. Although no checklist can cover every conceivable aspect of an insurance contract, even a simple one can help you identify important features so you can look at those first. After you evaluate them, you can look at other provisions.

Figure 21–1 provides a set of guidelines to follow in evaluating proposals for a basic policy. The daily hospital benefit usually refers to the maximum payable for a semiprivate room. A guide to determining the amount you need can be obtained easily by calling a local hospital or the state hospital association for rates in your area. If a policy does not indicate a semiprivate room rate, ask the agent to specify in writing what type of room is being quoted. The maximum benefit period can be as short as thirty days or as long as two years. The longer the maximum stay, the higher the premium, but the increase is not proportional for more coverage. Ancillary hospital expenses (such as x-rays and lab tests) are usually a specified sum multiplied by the number of days you stay in the hospital. Consider any amount less than twenty times your room and board benefits to be weak coverage. "In full" coverage is the ultimate benefit for ancillary charges.

Surgical expense benefits will be subject to a maximum limit listed in a schedule of surgical procedures or will cover an unspecified amount, not exceeding usual and customary charges. In the former case, if the limit you select is too low to cover usual and customary charges, you will have to pay the difference. In any event, you pay the difference, if any, between your surgeon's total charge and the insurance benefit. Even with usual and customary coverage, you may incur charges that exceed your insurance benefits, unless the expense is reduced by the surgeon.

Amounts listed for inpatient and outpatient medical expenses provide benefits equal to the charges for service, not exceeding usual and customary charges. The number of days for which inpatient medical expense is paid may be less than the maximum number of days the hospital benefit is provided.

You may want supplemental benefits added to the basic policy, depending upon what is excluded. For example, the policy may exclude pregnancy benefits, private nursing benefits, or other desired benefits. The addition of x-ray and laboratory benefits for outpatient tests is an excellent way to broaden basic coverage. Find out how much this will cost.

Three other items are of crucial importance. First, how much is the deductible? Does it apply to different benefits

FIGURE 21–1

Basic Hospital-Surgical-Medical
Insurance Checklist

Coverage Questions
1. Daily hospital benefit. . .Maximum per day $_____
   (Maximum benefit period _____ days)   _____
2. Ancillary hospital expense. . .Maximum   _____
3. Surgical expense. . .Schedule or usual and customary   _____
4. Inpatient medial expense. . .Per day   _____
5. Outpatient medical expense. . .Maximum   _____
6. Deductible   _____
7. Supplemental benefits/premium
   _____ Normal pregnancy   _____
   _____ Private nursing   _____
   _____ X-ray and lab   _____
   _____ Other   _____
8. List the covered persons _____ , _____ , _____
9. Continuation provision? (yes or no)   _____

Cost Questions
1. Annual premium   _____
2. Quarterly premium, if needed for budgeting   _____

separately or as a group? Second, who is covered? If you have dependents, you may want benefits for them. Third, what is the continuance provision? Is the policy guaranteed renewable with premium rates subject to change? Or is it noncancellable? If the latter, is the annual premium level or will it increase according to a schedule?

A checklist helps you evaluate the merits of any policy. However, unless the various policies provide similar kinds and amounts of coverages, it is very difficult to compare cost. For this reason, you are better off to create a simple specification list based on the checklist, and then shop for policies that meet those specifications. Figure 21–2 shows a sample specification.

If you go to an agent, broker, or company officer and say, "This is what I want," you may be shown policies that provide more coverage than you asked for in your specifications. Others, however, will respond to your request the best they can. The result will be several similar policies so you can compare costs. Cost isn't everything, but if you want to compare several policies that have most of the features you want, it's a good place to start. After you identify the policies that fit your needs and your budget, you can compare details. This procedure will bring you closer to what you need than if you try to shop without a checklist.

BUYING MAJOR MEDICAL INSURANCE

A major medical policy has the following features:

1. High maximum limits
2. Large deductible
3. Coinsurance
4. Broad coverage

When you read this list, you probably think a major medical policy covers virtually any medical expense. Some policies, however, reduce coverage with internal limits and

exclusions (sometimes called exceptions). A classic example of internal limits is a surgical schedule like the one in a basic policy. It places dollar limits on surgical procedures and further limits payment by requiring that charges be "usual and customary." Another method to limit coverage is to list all "eligible medical expenses." This restricts payment to items listed, which is the opposite of what you might think of as broad coverage. Most major medical policies are open perils contracts and only list exclusions. So when purchasing a major medical policy, beware of limitations on the coverage.

When you find a policy that provides truly broad coverage, it is worthwhile to determine the price of the policy with various maximum benefit amounts and various deductible/coinsurance/stop limit combinations. Select the combination that offers you adequate maximum benefits, broad coverage, and a reasonable tradeoff between cost and risk-retention. The format shown in figure 21–3 may help you compare policies. A copy of the form is used for each policy and for each maximum benefit amount.

BUYING PRINCIPLES FOR HEALTH CARE INSURANCE

The buying principles discussed in chapter 25 are applicable to the purchase of health insurance. These guidelines are:

1. Use the large loss principle.
2. Avoid first-dollar coverage.

FIGURE 21–3

Format for Comparing Major Medical Insurance Policies

| Company name _____ |
| Maximum benefit per person/family _____ |
| Per year ( )   Lifetime ( )   Per Occurrence ( ) |

(1) If your coinsurance/stop limit is. . . _____ And, (2) if your deductible is. . .	___%/$___	___%/$___	___%/$___
$ _____ per (occurrence, year)	$ _____ premium	$ _____ premium	$ _____ premium
$ _____ per (occurrence, year)	$ _____ premium	$ _____ premium	$ _____ premium
$ _____ per (occurrence, year)	$ _____ premium	$ _____ premium	$ _____ premium
The, (3) your premium is. . . (fill in the boxes) (4) List exclusions and internal limits: _____ _____ _____ _____			

FIGURE 21–2

Sample Specification

Daily hospital benefit (semiprivate)	$ 300
Maximum benefit period	365 days
Miscellaneous hospital expense	$12,000
Maximum surgical expense	$ 4,000
Inpatient medical expense per day	$ 100
Outpatient medical expense per day	$ 80
Deductible	$ 250
Pregnancy	$ 3,500
X-ray and lab annual maximum	$ 500
Persons covered	You and spouse
Continuance provision	Noncancellable and guaranteed renewable.

3. Carefully read contract provisions.

4. Buy from a reputable insurer.

5. Compare costs.

Use the Large Loss Principle

Severity is the best measure of the importance of a risk. You want to be prepared for health care costs that would be financially burdensome to you. Health care expenses can be catastrophic for all but the most wealthy. Thus, if there is any feasible way to afford the premium, buy major medical or comprehensive medical insurance with a large maximum benefit. Consider a maximum of at least $250,000 and see if you can afford a lifetime maximum of $1 million or more. The extra protection is worth the additional premium.

Avoid First-Dollar Coverage

Because of the high frequency of small health care expenses, you pay a high price for first-dollar coverage. Retain, through deductibles, as much loss as your budget will permit. The appropriate amount of deductible is very much a function of your own financial situation (income, liquidity, financial commitments, and so on). With this caveat, let us suggest that your major medical deductible should be at least $250, and preferably $500 or more. The reduction in premiums may free up enough premium dollars to allow you to follow the large loss principle with respect to other aspects of your policy.

Consider Contract Provisions

Health insurance contract provisions vary widely. The objective should be to insure broadly where breadth is an option. All contracts exclude war and a few other potential losses. But avoid as many exclusions and internal limits as you can and read the definitions of covered charges, causes of disability, definitions of disability, and other clauses that define what is and is not covered. If there are definitions or provisions that you do not understand, ask the company to explain them in writing.

Include a stop limit provision at the level of $1,500 plus your deductible. Otherwise, the coinsurance provision could prevent even a policy with a large maximum benefit from meeting your insurance needs. Your share of a $50,000 loss could be $10,000 (20 percent participation through 80 percent coinsurance), plus the deductible and any expenses not covered by the usual and customary limitation, internal limits, and exclusions of your policy. You don't need this when sickness strikes.

Buy from a Reputable Insurer

The largest health insurers aren't always the best. Some sell policies with very restrictive contract provisions and then compound this problem by lowering the amount paid on eligible claims. Compare each insurer's policy provisions and ask your state insurance commissioner's complaint section about each company's claims practices. Also, check on the cancellation provision. Look for noncancellable and guaranteed renewable coverage. Also, remember to check their financial and policyholder ratings. Insist on an A+ rating in the latest issue of Best's.

Beware of health insurance marketed by direct mail. Advertisements may be deceptive. Some reputable insurers market health insurance in this way; so do many fly-by-night operators. Be sure the company is licensed in your state.

Compare Costs

Cost is important. But first, use specifications to be sure you are comparing costs for similar coverage. Basic coverage should be less expensive than major medical or comprehensive medical insurance because basic plans only provide a little coverage when you are confined to a hospital or have surgery. Major medical and comprehensive medical contracts provide broader coverage. Even here, use specifications of coverage to increase the comparability of the contracts.

MEDIGAP INSURANCE

Older people must handle their savings with care because it's too late in life to replace anything they lose. They appreciate their Social Security check and Medicare but worry about what isn't covered—the gaps. As a result, they are susceptible to a smooth sales pitch and scarce tactics. Many have ended up burdened with several health insurance policies but inadequate coverage. What would you advise an older person who is worried about the gaps in Medicare? Tell him or her the following:

1. You have some protection now when you buy a "Medigap" policy to cover gaps in Medicare. Congress has regulated the market to limit the types of policies sold and to require that the policies be relatively sound. This was done to protect elderly people from bad products, unethical sales techniques, and hard-to-understand policies. So when an agent calls on you, ask for a written proposal that shows what Medicare covers, what you would have to pay if you did not have Medigap policy, and what part of that gap the policy you are looking at will pay. Tell the agent that you want to send the proposal to a friend of yours who is a sharp young insurance student before you buy anything.

2. Don't buy a cancer policy or a "dread disease" policy. They promise to give large benefits for what appears to be a small premium, but the coverage is very lim-

ited. What if you have a disabling stroke instead of cancer?

3. Prices and benefits vary across policies. Read what benefits are offered, compare prices, and decide what is best for you.

4. Ask the agent what the company's historical and anticipated loss ratio is for this policy. The loss ratio is the percentage of the premium paid to, or on behalf of, the policyholder. The higher the loss ratio, the better the product (all else being equal).

5. Buy only one policy. That's all you need to cover the gaps left by Medicare. Read the policy as soon as you get it. You should be able to return it in ten days and get your money back if you don't want it.

6. If there is anything in the policy that you don't understand, ask the agent to explain it. Then tell him or her that you want the explanation in writing so you can keep it with the policy for future reference. Tell the agent that what he or she says is easier to understand than the policy.

Key Terms

basic hospital policy
basic surgical policy
basic medical expense policy
major medical policies
comprehensive policies
dental insurance policies
disability income insurance
total disability
partial disability
preexisting conditions
short-term disability policies (STD)

long-term disability policies (LTD)
elimination period
social insurance substitute
average earnings provision
long-term care insurance (LTC)
home health care
medigap insurance
continuance provision
change of occupation provision
option to purchase rider
cost-of-living rider

Discussion Questions

1. How do individual and group medical insurance policies differ regarding
a. maternity benefits?
b. general policy provisions and exclusions?

2. What types of services are covered by dental insurance contracts? Why are individuals given first-dollar coverage for some services but not for others?

3. Would someone with Social Security, workers' compensation, and an employer-provided group disability plan have any reason to purchase disability insurance in the individual market? Please explain.

4. What is meant by the statement: "The benfits of a disability income policy are no better than the definition of disability"?

5. How do disability benefits differ when total disability results from sickness rather than accident? Can you image why insurers might have written contracts this way?

6. Explain how the average earnings provision of a disability contract works. What is the purpose of the provision?

7. If custodial care is the least expensive type of service covered by long-term care insurance, why is it important to make sure your contract covers this type of care?

8. Why is inflation protection important for disability and long-term care contracts? How is inflation protection handled?

9. Which continuance provisions are most expensive in terms of premium (all else being equal)? Why is this the case?

10. What purpose does the change of occupation provision serve? Does this protect the insured or the insurer?

21.1 Diana Antonoplos, your friend from high school, is trying to decide what is the best health insurance policy to buy. She has offers for a cancer policy with a low premium, a major medical policy with a higher premium, and a hospital policy with a premium that falls midway between the other two. All policies are noncancellable until age 65.

1. Discuss the major features that will affect Diana's decision. Explain what you would look for, and why.

2. If you were to buy only one policy and had a limited—but adequate—budget, which product would you choose?

21.2 Talitha Byrd has a long-term disability income insurance contract and is disabled. After the sixty-day waiting period, she begins receiving the $1,200 per month in benefits. Although this is less than her predisability income of $2,000 per month, she is able to get along quite nicely. Even though she is not eligible for Social Security disability benfits, after two years the insurer tells her that it is stopping payment under the contract.

1. Why might the insurer stop payment after two years?

2. What might Talitha do to receive payments again?

3. How could she have prevented this problem when she was selecting a disability income policy?

21.3 Darnell Walker's mother is surprised when he tells her she may want to look into buying an individual long-term care contract. She is 71 years old and already has Medicare coverage.

1. Does Medicare pay for long-term care?

2. What types of services should she make sure are covered by the policy? What policy provisions may be important for her?

3. Darnell is 50 years old. The long-term care premium at his age is low. Do you think he should buy it now while it is inexpensive?

21.4 Profitability of U.S. disability insurers has declined in recent years. As a result, insurers wonder whether they can continue to write noncancellable "own occupation" policies. Why would these types of policies threaten insurer profitability? Are there ways the insurer could achieve the same end without withdrawing these policies from the market?

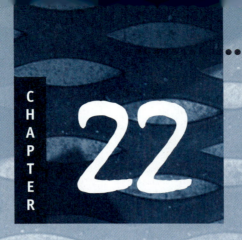

Individual Financial Management of Life and Health Risks

Introduction Parents produce income and services for the benefit of each other and their children. Either death or disability will stop this production. Death will also subject families to estate settlement costs that reduce assets. If the need for cash while the estate is being settled forces asset liquidation under unfavorable circumstances, resources may also be decreased. In addition, the death of a parent will leave the family without the financial management skills, love, emotional support, and counseling that person provided.

Disability may stop income production and increase expenses, such as those for medical care. Disability or death of non-income producers may also increase expenses. For example, high medical expenses may pose a problem for the family budget, and child care services may be needed.

Family status has a strong influence on the need for life insurance. If you remain single throughout life, your needs for non-business-related life insurance are likely to be relatively small because the major need comes from your financial obligations to persons who survive you. You, for example, may feel some responsibility to help support your parents in their old age. If you marry, you may desire to supplement your spouse's income in the event of your premature (i.e., before attaining normal life expectancy) death. Your obligation is likely to be increased greatly by the presence of children in your household. You may also want individual life insurance in connection with your small business and/or to provide liquidity for a large estate. In any event, the need to remain self-sufficient heightens your awareness of the need for disability income insurance.

This chapter focuses on how you can determine the amounts of life and health insurance that are appropriate for your situation. We will use the risk management part of the financial planning process to determine these needs. After studying this chapter you will have examined:

1. How to use the risk management/financial planning process to identify and evaluate life-health risks.
2. How to calculate income continuation needs for a hypothetical family.
3. The essence of estate planning.
4. How to identify business life-health risks.

Financial Planning Process

Financial planning is a process of establishing financial objectives and creating a plan to implement those objectives. The process integrates knowledge about taxes, insurance, investments, and related fields such as estate planning. The purpose is to meet goals (including wealth accumulation during your lifetime), protect assets, and, eventually, distribute your estate in a manner consistent with your stated objectives. The six steps in the process require:

1. Organizing and analyzing your financial data.
2. Establishing your objectives.
3. Developing alternative ways to achieve your objectives.
4. Deciding which risk management and investment plan is most likely to achieve your objectives.
5. Implementing the plan.
6. Evaluating performance periodically and revising the plan.

These steps are similar to those for risk management (see chapter 2). The major difference is more consideration of investment management. Tax information is also a major consideration in financial planning because both insurance and investment decisions are often influenced by tax laws. Financial planning includes estate planning, requiring decisions about asset conservation and distribution.

A major part of individual financial planning is the evaluation of all types of pure risks facing the family. With respect to these risks, the financial planner becomes a risk manager and concentrates on measuring the need for protection. More specifically, the financial planner determines what will happen to cash flow and assets if any of the following perils occur:

1. Death of income producer.
2. Disability of income producer.
3. Disability or death of non-income producer.
4. Unusual medical expenses.
5. Long-term care.[1]

HANDLING POTENTIAL LOSSES

How can these exposures be handled? There are several alternatives. First, some losses are so regular that they can be budgeted. A few years of experience will show how many visits to the doctor and dentist, for example, can be expected under normal circumstances. Second, an emergency fund can bear the burden of unexpected small losses that cannot be handled through the regular family budget and other sources of liquidity such as your ability to borrow from credit cards, life insurance cash values, and banks. Of course, you should not rely on borrowing more than you can conveniently repay following an emergency. Your sources of liquidity should be large enough to cover first-dollar losses such as small medical

---

1. Retirement planning for individuals is the subject of chapter 23.

and hospital expenses. It is also important to provide funds to take the place of income that may be lost because of short-term disability. The appropriate level of retention can be combined with insurance by the use of deductibles and elimination periods.

But what about the possibility of large expenses or loss of income because of death or long-term disability? Clearly, these exposures cannot be satisfactorily borne by the typical family, even if it does have an emergency fund and other sources of liquidity—possible losses are simply too large and unpredictable. Unless such losses are adequately covered by Social Security or group life and health insurance, they must be insured on an individual basis if the remaining exposure is to be transferred.

Income Continuation for the Dowd Family

In this section, the income continuation needs for a single-parent family, the Dowds, will be evaluated to see how much life and health insurance they may need. The risk management component of the financial planning process will be used to look at the family's present resources, income needs, and insurance needs in the event of the wage earner's death, disability, high medical expenses, or retirement. First, we will describe the family and its finances.

DATA COLLECTION

The Dowd family has three members:

1. Lori, age 35.
2. Liz, age 6.
3. Bob, age 4.

Liz and Bob see a pediatrician at least once a year. Lori had a routine check-up about six months ago. Apparently, all three are healthy.

Financial Situation

Lori is a branch bank manager whose gross yearly income is $50,000. Her former husband lives in another state and refuses to pay alimony or child support. Lori has given up on trying to get him to help support the family. He shows no interest in the children.

A balance sheet and cash flow statement are important in evaluating Lori's current ability to meet her needs and in establishing post-loss objectives. Lori has constructed tables 22–1 and 22–2.

On the balance sheet, you may wonder why the value of furniture and other personal property is only $10,000. The sums listed are liquidation values; these items probably have a replacement value between $30,000 and $40,000. But our concern, in the event of Lori's death, is how much the items would sell for if they had to be liquidated to meet family income needs. Unlike houses and automobiles, limited demand exists for used furniture and clothing.

TABLE 22–1

Balance Sheet
(End-of-Year Market Value)

Assets	
Checking account	$ 500
Certificates of deposit	3,000
Life insurance cash values	4,500
401(k) retirement plan (vested value)	15,000
Automobile	10,000
House	85,000
Furniture and other personal property	10,000
Total	$128,000
Liabilities	
Credit card balances	$ 1,000
Other household account balances	500
Automobile loan balance	8,000
Life insurance loan against cash values	4,000
Home mortgage balance	75,000
Total	$ 88,500
Net Worth	$ 39,500

The family has four types of basic resources in addition to the assets shown in table 22–1. These resources are provided by:

1. Social Security.
2. Lori's employer.
3. Individual insurance.
4. Personal savings and investments.

TABLE 22–2

Annual Cash Flow Statement

Income	
Lori's salary	$50,000
Investment income	*
Total cash flow	$50,000
Taxes	
Social security	$ 3,825
Federal income	4,300
State income	1,700
Total SS and income taxes	$ 9,825
Disposable personal income	$40,175
Expenses	
State sales taxes	$ 1,300
Personal property taxes (home and auto)	1,175
401(k) retirement savings contribution	2,000
Dependent medical & dental insurance	1,500
House payments, including homeowners insurance	8,900
Utilities	2,700
Food	3,200
Automobile payments and expenses	3,600
Child care	4,500
Clothes	1,800
Miscellaneous expenses	9,000
Total expenses	$39,675
Savings	$ 500

*Investment earnings of approximately $1,500 are being reinvested in the certificates of deposit and 401(k) plan.

Based on Lori's earnings history, we estimate that the following Social Security benefits would be available to her and/or the children in the event of her death or disability:[2]

1. Lori's death: $255 burial allowance plus $600 per month survivor benefits to each child until each is age 18 (or age 19 if still a full-time high school student).

2. Lori's disability: $1,200 per month until her younger child reaches age 18; then $800 per month for the remainder of Lori's total and permanent disability. Survivor benefits and disability income benefits are expected (based on the current Social Security law) to keep pace with inflation.

3. Medicare benefits following two years of Lori's total and permanent disability.

Lori's employee benefit plan at the bank provides her and the children with the benefits outlined in table 22–3.

Individual Coverage

Lori has a $15,000 whole life policy that her parents purchased when she was young and turned over to Lori when she finished college. Lori recently borrowed most of the policy's $4,500 cash value to help make the down payment on the family home. She purchased credit life insurance to cover the balance of her automobile loan. She has not purchased life or disability insurance associated with her home mortgage.

Personal Savings and Investments

At the present time, Lori's personal savings and investments are small, consisting of $3,000 in certificates of deposit at her bank and a $15,000 vested value in her 401(k) plan. Her yearly savings of $500 are 1 percent of her gross income. In addition, she is contributing 4 percent of gross income to her 401(k) plan and her employer matches 50 percent of this amount. If these savings rates can be continued over time and earn reasonable returns, her total savings and investments will grow quickly.

OBJECTIVES

In Case of Death

In the event of her premature death, Lori would like her children to live with her sister, Kay, and Kay's husband, Robert, who have expressed willingness to assume these responsibilities. Lori has not, however, formally created a legal document expressing this wish. Kay and Robert have three small children of their own, and Lori would not want her children to be any financial burden to them. Taking care of her children's nonfinancial needs is all that Lori expects from Kay and Robert.

----

2. For definitions of insurance terms with which you are not familiar, consult the glossary or chapter 13 for life insurance, chapter 17 for Social Security, and chapters 19 and 21 for health insurance.

Group Life Insurance
—Term insurance equal to two times annual salary for active employees.
—$5,000 term insurance for retirees.

Short-Term Disability
—Paid sick leave equal to income for ninety days.

Long-Term Disability
—Long-term disability (LTD) income to age 70 equal to two-thirds of annual salary in last year of employment, minus total Social Security and employer-provided pension benefits; 90-day waiting period; no adjustment for inflation.

Group Comprehensive Preferred Provider Medical Care
—$200 annual deductible per family member.
—90 percent coinsurance for preferred providers; 75 percent coinsurance for non-network providers.
—$1 million aggregate lifetime limit.
—Stop-loss provision after $1,000 out-of-pocket coinsurance expenses per person per year.
—Benefits terminate upon job termination or retirement.

Dental Coverage
—$50 per person annual deductible; no deductible on preventive care.
—80 percent coinsurance.
—$1,000 per person per year limit.
—$1,000 per person lifetime limit on orthodontic work.
—$50,000 aggregate family lifetime limit on other care.
—Benefits terminate upon job termination or retirement.

401(k) Plan
—Employer matches 50 percent of employee contributions up to a maximum employee contribution of 6 percent of basic pay, subject to the annual maximum limit on 401(k) contributions.

Defined-Benefit Pension Plan
—Pension at age 65 equal to 40 percent of average final three years salary, minus half of primary Social Security retirement benefit, with no provision for benefits to increase after retirement. Early retirement is allowed between ages 60 and 65, subject to a reduction in benefits. Reductions equal 4 percent for each year the retiree is below age 65.

Lori's values influence her *objectives*. Her parents paid almost all her expenses, including upkeep of a car, while she earned a bachelor's degree. Lori recognizes that her children are currently benefiting from her well-above-average income. When they reach college, she wants them to concentrate on their studies and enjoy extracurricular activities without having to work during the academic year. They would be expected to work during the summers to earn part of their spending money for school. Lori decides that, if she dies prematurely, she wants to provide $12,000 per year before taxes for each child through age 17 when they will graduate from high school, both having been born in August. During their four years of college, Lori wants $18,000 per year available for each child. She realizes that inflation can devastate a given level of income in only a few years. Thus, she wants her expressed objectives to be fulfilled in real (uninflated) dollars. We will present a simple planning solution to this problem.[3]

....
3. If you were a financial planner advising Lori, your own values and financial situation might lead you to believe that Lori's objectives are either extravagant or too frugal. You would want to help Lori quantify the future cost of food, clothing, education, and other items that she wants to finance for her children, but you must be careful not to project your values on your client. It is the client's wishes you want to help clarify, not what you would do in the client's shoes.

In Case of Disability

In the event of Lori's total disability, she recognizes that expenses associated with her working would cease but that extra money might be needed for her care and medical expenses not covered by insurance due to the deductible, coinsurance feature and exclusions. In a financial sense, disability can be worse than death. Lori would like to continue living in her home, which has a substantial mortgage payment. After looking at her current cash flow statement (see table 22–2) and factoring in the likely changes in the event of her disability, she concludes that $36,000 per year (before taxes) would be desirable if she were disabled. Again, the need is for purchasing power in real dollars over time.

Medical and Dental Care

Lori's main objective with respect to necessary medical care is access for her and the children to dentists, physicians, hospitals, pharmacists, and other health care providers without severe impacts on her budget. She defines a "severe impact" as uninsured medical expenses that exceed the balance of her checking account plus $2,000.

ALTERNATIVE SOLUTIONS/EXPOSURE EVALUATION

The next step in the financial planning process requires determining:

1. The amount of money required to meet Lori's objectives.
2. Any gaps that exist between what is desired and Lori's current financial resources.
3. Alternatives available to fill the gaps.

Money Required for Death

Determination of the amount of money required to meet Lori's objectives for her children in the event of her premature death is complicated by the following:

1. We do not know when Lori will die.
2. The family's income needs extend into the future possibly eighteen years (assuming Lori dies now and income is provided until her younger child is age 22).
3. Social Security will make its payments *monthly* over fourteen of the eighteen years.
4. Lori's two life insurance policies (and any new policies) would, most likely, make *lump-sum payments* at the time of her death, although her objective calls for the provision of support over many years.
5. Lump sums of money can be invested, and these investment earnings can provide part of the family's future income needs.
6. Lump sums may be liquidated over the period of income need, but we need to be sure the money does not run out before the period ends.
7. The effects of inflation must be recognized.

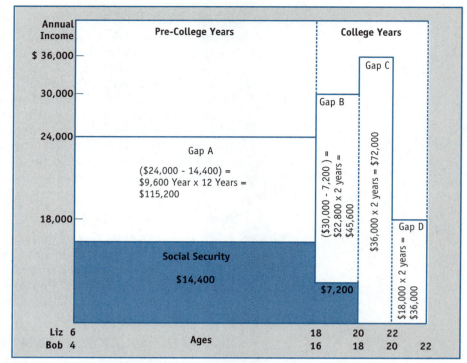

Both the required amounts of income and Social Security benefits are shown in real (uninflated) dollars.

Static Life Insurance Planning

With some simplifying assumptions, these problems can be solved by a technique that we will call **static life insurance planning.** The technique is static in the sense that it only considers the worst possible scenario ("maximum possible loss," as defined in chapter 2): Lori dies this year. Also, the technique does not recognize various changes (for example, re-marriage and a third child) that Lori may be expecting to occur at some point during the planning period.

Figure 22–1 reflects the assumption that Lori dies today by showing Liz's and Bob's current ages at the left, on the horizontal axis. The figure continues until Lori's objectives are met when Bob is assumed to complete college at age 22.

The vertical axis of figure 22–1 shows Lori's real income objective of $12,000 per year per child prior to age 18. Recognize that Lori plans for much of this money to be spent by her sister and brother-in-law for her children's food, utilities, transportation, child care, school expenses, and other basic needs. She does not plan for her children to have excessive amounts of spending money. During college, each child has $18,000 per year, which will provide financial access to modestly priced private colleges and out-of-state universities. The maximum annual need of $36,000 per year, depicted in figure 22–1, occurs during the last two years of Liz's planned college period, when it is assumed that Bob also will have begun college. Social Security benefits begin at $14,400 and remain at this level (in real terms) until Liz's benefit terminates at age 18. Bob's benefit of $7,200 continues until he is 18.

Looking at the differences (gaps) between Lori's objectives and the income expected from Social Security (see figure 22–1, gaps A through D), we see an increase in the size of the gaps as Social Security payments decline and then stop as Bob's college years begin. The simplest way to summarize the amount of the gaps is to add the following:

A. ($24,000 − 14,400) × (12 years) = $115,200
B. ($30,000 − 7,200) × (2 years) = 45,600
C. ($36,000) × (2 years) = 72,000
D. ($18,000) × (2 years) = 36,000
　　　　　　Total　　　　　　　　= $268,800

This period while children remain dependent is called the **family dependency period.** A subsequent period during which support might be provided to a spouse is not depicted since Lori is not married. Such a period may be called a **spousal dependency period.**

What are the problems with saying $268,800 is needed to fulfill Lori's objectives, assuming she dies now? Reviewing our list of seven complications, we can recognize two major problems. First, inflation is likely to increase her nominal (inflated dollar) needs. Current Social Security legislation provides for annual benefit increases to reflect the lesser of inflation or wage increases over time. Thus, we can assume that real-dollar Social Security benefits will increase approximately at the rate of inflation. Our concern becomes the effect of inflation on the gap between total income needs and Social Security. In the first year, we know this gap is $9,600. If there is 4 percent inflation, the gap in nominal dollars would be $13,664 by the beginning of the tenth year and $64,834 by the beginning of the sixteenth year, the second year when both Liz and Bob are expected to be in college. Our $268,800 total understates the nominal dollar need substantially.

Second, we have ignored the opportunity to invest the lump-sum insurance benefits (existing and yet-to-be-purchased) and net worth. With such an opportunity, investment earnings would provide part of the future cash flow needs. Unlike the possibility of inflation, the failure to recognize this time value of money overstates the size of the gaps.

You may use the $268,800 figure depicted in figure 22–1 if you are willing to assume that the net return on investments will be just sufficient to cover the rate of expected inflation. This is not an unrealistic assumption for the conservative investor who would make "low-to-medium risk/low-to-medium expected return" investments. Before you disagree, look at long-run historical returns for corporate and government bonds, for example, and recognize that a small percentage of the returns will be absorbed by federal and state income taxes.[4] Relatively conservative investments may be suitable where the purpose is safety of principal in the interest of supporting two children, following the death of their sole financial support (other than Social Security). The static life insurance planning technique produces approximate rather than exact estimates of death needs.

．．．．．．．．．．．．．．．．．．．．．．．．
4. Lori's sister and brother-in-law also may incur sales charges in managing the money, or a trust (to be discussed later in this chapter) will levy periodic management fees.

At this point, we have only estimated Lori's gross death needs for the family dependency period.

Total Needs

Total death needs for most situations can be grouped into four categories:

1. Final expenses.
2. Family dependency period.
3. Spousal dependency period.
4. Special needs.

We have only looked at the family dependency period. To complete Lori's financial planning for death, assume that her **final expenses** consist of funeral costs of $4,500, $1,500 to pay her current bills, and $3,000 for an executor to settle her estate. Nothing is required to fund a spousal dependency period in Lori's case. The **special needs** category could include college expenses that we have placed in the family dependency period, care of a dependent parent, or other expenses that do not fit neatly in the other three categories.

Lori's total needs above Social Security are:

Final Expenses	$ 9,000
Family Dependency Period	268,800
Total Needs	$277,800

Net Needs

Life insurance is a substitute for other assets that for one reason or another, at the current time, have not been accumulated. Thus, the need for new life insurance as a result of the life insurance planning process consists of:

$$\text{Net Needs} = \text{Gross Death Needs} - \text{Resources}$$

Consideration of Existing Resources

Are Lori's current net worth and life insurance adequate to meet her objectives if she dies now? From the balance sheet provided earlier (table 22–1), we know that she has a net worth of $39,500.[5] This is a liquidation value that is net of sales commissions, depreciation, and other value-reducing factors. Her current life insurance consists of a $100,000 term policy through her employer and a $15,000 individual policy. The proceeds from the individual policy will be $11,000 after the insurer deducts the $4,000 loan. Her automobile loan will be paid by credit life insurance. We show this loan repayment below as a life insurance resource. Lori's net needs after recognizing existing resources are:

....

5. It is feasible that all furniture, jewelry, and so on would not be liquidated. In a two-parent family, the surviving spouse might want to retain the house and all furnishings.

Total needs		$277,800
Resources (minus):		
Net worth	$ 39,500	
Group life insurance	100,000	
Individual life insurance	11,000	
Credit life insurance	8,000	158,500
Net Needs		$119,300

Solutions

Lori has three main ways of reacting to the finding that her current resources would be $119,300 short of meeting her financial objectives associated with death. First, she could reevaluate her objectives, decide to lower the amount of financial support for Liz and Bob, and calculate a lower total. Second, she could decide to tighten her budget and increase her savings/investment program. Third, she could buy an additional life insurance policy in the amount of, let's say, $125,000. Life insurance premiums would vary upward from approximately $175 for next year for an annual renewable term policy to higher amounts for other types of insurance.[6] We would recommend that Lori, assuming she maintains her current objectives, buy additional life insurance. Savings as an alternative to life insurance is not a viable solution because she could die before contributing much to her savings program. Nevertheless, she should continue to save.

Other Life Insurance Planning Issues

Lori's situation certainly does not cover all planning possibilities. For example, another person might want to extend the family dependency period far beyond age 22 to provide support to a disabled child. Another person might want to contribute to a spouse's support for the remainder of his or her life. In this case, we would recommend using the life insurance planning technique to quantify the need up to an advanced age, such as 65. Then get price quotations on a life annuity for the remainder of the person's lifetime.[7]

Dynamic Life Insurance Planning

In practice, life insurance agents and financial planners use computers to calculate life insurance needs. This allows easy modification of assumptions. What if a spouse works during the spousal dependency period? What if average after-tax investment income is expected to exceed average expected inflation by 2 percent (or 4 percent)? What if we assume that the needs of survivors are a percentage of a changing standard of living (i.e., income) over time? These and other assumptions can be handled easily by using electronic spreadsheets to conduct **dynamic life insurance planning.** Dynamic life insurance planning considers anticipated changes in income, number of children, investments, and other factors. Then it produces the amount of net need as it changes from year to year. The

6. For discussion, see chapters 13 and 14.
7. Annuities will be discussed in chapter 23.

dynamic approach emphasizes the need for an insurance plan that has sufficient flexibility to change as one's situation changes.[8] This approach can be applied to Lori Dowd, using the facts and assumptions shown in table 22–4.

The dynamic approach (see table 22–5) produces lower gross family dependency period needs than the static approach because of the positive difference between the after-tax investment return assumptions and the inflation assumption. Increasing degrees of investment risks are assumed. Also, estimated needs decrease as the discount rate (investment assumption) increases from 5 to 7 percent. This is an expected reward for investment risk taking. Furthermore, the growth in Lori's personal savings and investment program (also shown in table 22–5) would increasingly reduce her net needs as death is assumed later in the planning period. Simply subtracting each year's "personal savings and investment" figure from the corresponding "present value of income gap" produces a pattern of decreasing needs.

Recognize that the spreadsheet results shown in table 22–5 are merely inputs into a net death needs estimate. You would still need to add final expenses and subtract all other resources. Existing life insurance ($119,000 in 1995) and net worth beyond that categorized as "personal savings and investment" (for example, current home equity) would be included in "other resources." Recognizing the pattern in which net needs (reflecting deductions such as the growing "personal savings and investments" reflected on the last line of table 22–5 from the "present value of income gap") will decrease over time, Lori may want to consider purchasing decreasing term insurance as her form of additional insurance.[9]

Insurance on the Lives of Children

What about Liz and Bob? If either were to die between now and adulthood, the only category of needs would be final expenses. Considering the costs of funerals and Lori's current liquidity (see table 22–1), small policies could be justified on each child. Where a child might inherit a health problem,

TABLE 22–4

Facts and Assumptions in Applying Dynamic Life Insurance Planning to Lori Dowd

1. The 1995 after-tax income for Lori is taken from Table 22–2. Subsequently, her income is expected to increase at the inflation rate of 4 percent per year.
2. Lori dies at the beginning of 1996.
3. Alternatively, death is deferred until each subsequent year.
4. Social Security survivor benefits increase annually by 4 percent.
5. Income needs for Liz and Bob grow at 4 percent per year.
6. The income deficits are discounted at 5 percent, and alternatively at 7 percent, reflecting after-tax rates of return above the 4 percent inflation assumption.
7. Potential growth in other resources is recognized by allowing personal savings and investments to increase over time due to annual contributions (7 percent, including her employer's 401(k) contribution of each year's gross salary) and annual investment returns of 8 percent.

8. The term "dynamic life insurance programming" was coined by Joseph M. Belth. See Joseph M. Belth, "Dynamic Life Insurance Programming," *Journal of Risk and Insurance,* vol. 31, no. 4 (1964): pp. 539–56. We have substituted "planning" for "programming."
9. If Lori had a husband who contributed significantly to the family, we would go through the same life insurance planning process for him.

TABLE 22-5

Gross Family Dependency Needs for Lori Dowd, Assuming Death in 1996 or Later Years

	1995	1996	1997 ...	2000 ...	2003 ...	2006 ...	2009 ...	2012
Age of Children								
Liz	6	7	8	11	14	17	20	23
Bob	4	5	6	9	12	15	18	21
Income Sources								
Lori's After-Tax Income	40,175							
Social Security—Liz*		7,488	7,788	8,760	9,854	11,084	0	0
Social Security—Bob*		7,488	7,788	8,760	9,854	11,084	0	0
Total Sources	40,175	14,976	15,575	17,520	19,707	22,168	0	0
Income Needs								
Family	40,175							
Liz**		12,480	12,979	14,600	16,423	18,473	31,170	0
Bob**		12,480	12,979	14,600	16,423	18,473	31,170	35,062
Total Needs	40,175	24,960	25,958	29,200	32,846	36,947	62,340	35,062
Income Gap		9,984	10,383	11,680	13,138	14,779	62,340	35,062
Present Value of Income Gap								
At 5 percent (annuity due)		245,309	247,091	250,321	249,600	243,749	184,954	35,062
At 7 percent (annuity due)		204,961	208,625	218,475	225,908	229,804	181,001	35,062
Personal Savings & Investments*		23,115	28,823	50,096	79,067	117,907	169,118	236,201

*Social Security survivor benefits would have been $7,200 per child with death in 1995.

**In 1995 dollars, income needs are $12,000 per child until age 18 and $18,000 per child for the ages of 18 through 21.

***Personal savings and investments are assumed to increase during Lori's lifetime due to two sources: new annual contributions equal to 7 percent of Lori's 1995 and future gross income, and an 8 percent tax-deferred annual return on investment. It is further assumed that the annual contribution will increase during Lori's work life at 4 percent per year due to salary increases. Approximately 86 percent of the investments are in the 401(k) plan and will be reduced by income taxes after Lori's death. Assuming the children are named beneficiaries of the 401(k) plan, the proceeds can be liquidated evenly (or faster) over the life expectancies of Liz and Bob. Each year, the amount liquidated would be added to other sources of taxable income.

engage in a dangerous occupation, or take up a dangerous hobby such as hang gliding, some parents buy policies with guaranteed insurability options on the lives of children. In effect, the parent pays for an option that creates future access to life insurance at standard rates during adulthood. Grandparents sometimes buy cash value life insurance on young children as a means of access to the cash value element of the policy. As discussed in chapter 13, the cash value element has the advantage of income-tax-free inside interest buildup prior to any lifetime surrenders of the policy. The downside is the administrative expenses and commissions that reduce the true rate of return on the policy.[10]

Disability

In the event of a long-term period of total disability (possibly for the remainder of life), Lori set a disability income objective of $3,000 per month after federal and state income taxes. This is approximately 90 percent of her current income after the deduction of Social Security taxes, federal income taxes, and state income taxes (see table 22-2).

10. See the rate of return discussion in chapter 16.

FIGURE 22–2

After-Tax Family Income If Lori Is
Totally Disabled

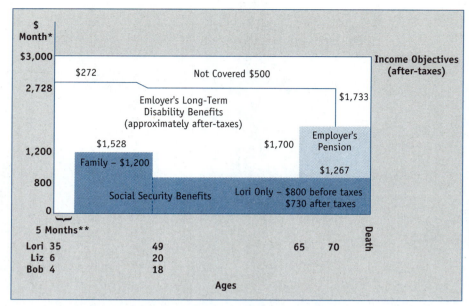

*This figure is drawn in real (uninflated) dollars.
**After 90 days sick leave and Social Security elimination periods have expired.

From our earlier data collection (see table 22–3), we know that sick leave would pay Lori's full salary for ninety days; after five months, Social Security would pay $1,200 per month until Bob is age 18 (including benefits available to minor children) and $800 per month for the remainder of her total disability; her employer's long-term disability plan would pay two-thirds of her salary ($2,778 per month) until age 70 minus Social Security and pension benefits. Her employer's defined benefit pension plan design, we assume, would provide for service credits during disability but would not pay benefits until age 65. At that time, her pension benefit would be $1,267 per month (that is, 40 percent of her last three years' salary minus 50 percent of her Social Security benefit).

Any disability income benefits coming from premiums previously paid by Lori's employer would be subject to federal and state income taxes. As we know from chapter 17, Lori's entire Social Security benefit would not be taxed while the family Social Security benefit is $1,200 (in uninflated terms) because Lori's adjusted gross income ($1,578 × 12 months = $18,936 from the LTD plan, plus one-half of her Social Security benefit, $400 × 12 months = $4,800) is less than the $25,000 threshold before partial taxation of a single person's Social Security benefit. Part of the Social Security benefit would be taxable when the before-tax LTD benefit increases to $1,978 per month when Bob's benefit stops at his attainment of age 18. LTD benefits are expressed as an amount per month. Consequently, the vertical axis in figure 22–2 shows Lori's objective and existing benefits on a monthly basis. The figures are after-tax estimates. Federal and state income taxes initially are estimated to be $50 per month. In later years, they are estimated to be approximately $278 per month, resulting in combined after-tax disability income of approximately $1,700 per month (that is, $2,778 before taxes minus $800 from Social Security minus $278 for taxes).

Figure 22–2 shows an unfilled after-tax gap of $272 per month in the years before the younger child reaches age 18, and approximately $500 per month between then and age 65. What alternative does Lori have to fill this gap? At the present time, her investments ($3,000 in certificates of deposit, $15,000 401(k) balance, and $500 in non-borrowed life insurance cash values), as reflected in table 22–1, would not produce enough annual income to close the gap. She may want to consider purchasing, on an individual basis, an LTD policy with a monthly benefit of $300. Most insurers, however, are unlikely to issue a policy to someone who has group LTD coverage like Lori's. (When an individual such as Lori personally pays the premiums on a disability income policy, benefits are not subject to income taxes. Therefore, the $300 benefit is in after-tax dollars.) The gap will widen quickly relative to the current dollar depiction in figure 22–2.

Our analysis revealed that Lori's employer's plan does not adjust future benefits for inflation during a period of disability. Increases in Social Security during the disability, however, would not be deducted from the employer-provided benefit. Consequently, it is important that any individual plan include a cost-of-living provision. In addition, an option to purchase additional amounts of individual LTD insurance would be needed to protect Lori as the gap widens in real-dollar terms.[11] Over time, assuming Lori can continue to work and contribute to her 401(k) plan, income from this plan should fill any gap between the employer's plan and Lori's disability income objectives.[12] At that point, any individual LTD could be discontinued. Cost-of-living provisions are becoming common in group LTD plans. Thus, when her employer's plan is revised next, this weakness may disappear.

Medical Care

As far as medical expenses are concerned, the Dowd family has excellent coverage. Their medical insurance program has no financially burdensome gaps. The maximum yearly deductibles for both medical and dental care are $750 (3 persons × $250). The stop-loss provision of the medical care plan limits Lori's part (coinsurance) of medical care expenses to $1,000 per family member per year. Additional coinsurance and some uncovered charges are expected for dental care, but these items should be budgetable. While the deductibles and medical coinsurance together could be $3,750 in one year, there exists only a very low probability of all three family members incurring heavy medical expenses in the same year. Maximum benefits of $1 million per person are more than adequate for all but a few, rarely occurring catastrophic illnesses.

A few potential expenses are excluded by the medical plan, but their chances of being financially burdensome are also too small for concern. Orthodontic care is usually an elective treatment, but Lori may need and want this for at least one of the children. If it is chosen, the cost is likely to be two or three times the $1,000 dental plan benefit. Lori can save for this or work it into her budget at the time.

....
11. Lori's $36,000 objective is 72 percent of her $50,000 salary.
12. The balance in a 401(k) plan can be used to provide income, without income tax penalties, in the event of retirement due to disability.

Long-Term Care

As Lori ages, her likelihood of needing care in a nursing home or through home health services will increase. At her current age of 35, the chance of needing long-term care is relatively insignificant. However, approximately 40 percent of persons over age 65 enter a nursing home before dying. Approximately 7 percent of persons between ages 75 and 84 are in nursing homes at any given time; for those 85 and older, over 20 percent are confined.[13] Some will be there for a short time; others will be confined for years. Even with good health habits and medical care, Lori should not ignore the likelihood of reaching this stage of life. More importantly, the severity of loss, as reflected in the cost of nursing home care, is high. Average costs are around $24,000 per year and can reach $40,000 or more.

Very few people near Lori's age of 35 make explicit financial plans to handle old-age dependency in the form of nursing or home health care. Yet it is during the early and middle stages of life that planning should begin because it is then that earnings have time to multiply with compound returns. Also, long-term care insurance premiums (usually on a level-premium basis) are budgetable. Lori needs to prepare for the contingency of long-term care. The funding alternatives are income from Social Security (disability or retirement), private retirement plan income, personal investments, and Medicaid. A reasonable objective is to avoid exhausting one's personal assets and having to rely on the public Medicaid system. Some people have an aversion to accepting public assistance. Further, the standard of care may be below what one may purchase with conscious planning.

Assuming Lori continues a career with her current employer (and the validity of this is questionable), her pension plan plus Social Security is expected to cover 40 percent of her preretirement salary. Remember, however, that her defined benefit pension is not designed to keep pace with inflation, and that is likely to seriously erode its purchasing power by the time she is 75. Continuation of her 401(k) contributions at their current levels, no major withdrawals, and investment primarily in inflation hedges during both pre- and post-retirement years should, along with Social Security and her private pension, provide adequate funding for her long-term care. If funding in these programs is not on track when her children's college expenses are fully funded, serious consideration should be given to purchasing a long-term care insurance policy as a supplement to her retirement income. A greater need for long-term care insurance exists in two situations:

1. When projected retirement income and personal investments provide income below the projected costs of nursing homes.

2. When a spouse is likely to continue to need funds to maintain a household (in addition to nursing home costs).

Prolonged Life Risk

A relatively new loss exposure created by advances in medical science is not dealt with in the planning process, although it has become a real

---

13. See Edward E. Graves and Burton T. Beam, Jr., *Meeting the Need for Long-Term Care* (Bryn Mawr, Pa.: American College, 1989).

ETHICAL *Dilemma*

Terminal Illness and Death

Your state agency allows living wills and may recommend forms that you can feel safe in signing without an attorney. Is such an arrangement morally wrong because it may let a life end naturally? For some people, it is. Others disagree. Only you and members of your family can decide. Many people make the decision by ignoring the possibility and doing nothing. Increasing numbers of people, however, have lawyers help them handle this risk by drawing up the necessary documents. What do you think? Is a living will justified in the case of some illnesses but not others? Do you personally want a living will?

The right to die is an even more pronounced issue. Dr. Jack Kevorkian, a retired pathologist, has sparked national debate by assisting with the suicides of several terminally ill people in Michigan. Michigan authorities have attempted (unsuccessfully, at this writing) to prosecute Dr. Kevorkian. Oregon passed a right-to-die act in 1994. Undoubtedly, the constitutionality of the law will be challenged.

Do you believe a person has a right to end his or her life by suicide? The Old Testament's King Saul took his own life by falling on his sword. He did this during a battle in which he was critically wounded and believed, based on past practices of the Philistines, that his enemies would soon mutilate him.[14] Does the existence of a terminal condition influence your view? Is reduction of medical expenses in this final stage of life a factor in your thinking? Does your view change when you think specifically about a member of your family?

---

concern for many people. The risk is so new it does not have a generally accepted name. We will call it the "prolonged life" risk.

The **prolonged life risk** is the possibility that at some time, perhaps late in your life, you may be kept alive through the use of support systems for a long period at great expense and suffering, although you may be terminally ill with no prospect for recovery. As medical science develops greater ability to prolong life, the probability that this will happen to you increases.

Once begun, your doctor may not stop life-support efforts because of ethical considerations, the risk of criminal charges, and the possibility of a malpractice suit. Your family may be able to obtain a court order authorizing their discontinuance, but that is a difficult process both legally and emotionally.

How can you handle this risk? You can, while you are still of sound mind, execute a **special power of attorney,** often called a **living will,** that gives a designated person(s) authority to have such life-sustaining efforts discontinued under specified circumstances. Examples are: when two physicians render the opinion that you have undergone an irreversible cessation of total spontaneous brain function; when you are unconscious

---

14. See 1 Samuel, Ch. 31:1–9.

for a period of thirty days; or when your condition is terminal and irreversible and there is no reasonable medical expectation of your recovery.

OTHER FINANCIAL PLANNING STEPS

We have just finished step three in the financial planning process. Three additional steps remain: (1) deciding on insurance and investment plans, (2) implementation, and (3) periodic review and revision. We recommended in step 3, "Developing alternative ways to achieve your objectives," that Lori purchase additional life and disability income insurance. We also concluded that her current medical and dental insurance plans meet her objectives. Chapters 13, 14, 15, 16, and 21 have examined how to decide between different life and disability insurance plans, and their options. Chapter 25 will provide more information on buying insurance. Investments are important in financial planning but are beyond the scope of this book.

Implementation, as we know from studying the risk management process, requires that Lori purchase insurance, execute a will, and take other steps to see that her objectives are realized. Her will, among other things, will formalize her desire that her sister and brother-in-law be appointed guardians of her children. The will should also specify who she wants to manage the assets that would be left for the beneficial use of her children in the event of her premature death.

We do not know the future, but we can confidently predict that Lori's financial objectives and abilities to achieve these objectives will change over time. Consequently, periodic review is important. Needs change as people get older; the solution is to revise the plan every few years. Factors such as a major promotion at work, unanticipated inflation, a child's performance in school, marriage, divorce, or a death will materially change one's situation.

Estate Planning

Estate Planning is the process of arranging for the conservation and transfer of property—your estate—to heirs upon your death. As part of the financial planning process, it involves determining your objectives regarding the disposition of your estate and selecting the tools to achieve them. The basic tools are wills, trusts, life insurance, and gifts.

The property you own is known as your **estate.** When you die, your estate is settled in accordance with the provisions of your will or, if there is no will, in accordance with your state's "laws of descent and distribution." The settlement process, called **probate,** is carried out by an **executor** or **administrator** under the supervision of a probate court judge.[15] The executor is named in your will, but if you have no will or the person named as executor cannot serve, the court appoints an administrator to assist with probate. The functions of an executor or administrator are to

15. In some states the person who settles your estate is called your "personal representative," irrespective of whether you had a will.

assemble your assets, pay all your debts and taxes, and make proper distribution of the remaining property. Your executor or administrator may hire an attorney to do the paperwork, provide guidance on complicated matters, obtain court approval of potentially questionable actions, and prepare final reports to the probate court and the United States Internal Revenue Service.

OBJECTIVES

In the estate planning process, you have several objectives. They are:

1. Conserve property values between the time of your death and transfer to heirs.
2. Transfer your property to certain persons or entities in accordance with your wishes.
3. Assure that heirs who are dependent on you receive the advice and help they may need in your absence.
4. Accomplish the transfer with minimum administration and legal fees.
5. Keep taxes at a minimum, consistent with the achievement of your other objectives.

The first three objectives should take precedence. It is more important that the persons and entities you love and respect benefit from your estate than it is to save transfer costs or taxes. Ideally, all objectives are achieved with proper planning.

WILLS

The major reason to have a **will** is to assure that your estate will be distributed in accordance with your wishes. A valid will must usually be in writing, signed by you while mentally competent, and signed by two or more witnesses. Requirements vary by state, resulting in the need to revise your will when you move from one state to another. If you die without a will it is said you died **intestate.** In such a case, your estate is distributed in accordance with the laws of the state in which you were a resident. If you were married with two or more children, many states would provide that one-third of your estate would go to your spouse and two-thirds would be distributed to the children. If you were married with no children, one half might go to your spouse and the remainder to your parents and siblings. Your state's division, in the condition of intestacy, might be quite different from your wishes. Further, dying intestate might reduce your marital deduction and thereby increase your estate taxes (explanation to follow).

A frequently overlooked complication to dying intestate is the problems that may arise in connection with minor beneficiaries. It may be difficult for the surviving spouse to manage property inherited by minor children. Unless he or she is the **guardian** of the child's estate, which does not occur automatically, a sale of such property may be impossible.

Suppose, for example, no will exists and ownership of the family home is divided among a wife and two children. Suppose also that the house is larger and more expensive to maintain than necessary, and the wife wants to trade the equity in it for a smaller home. She will not be able to do so unless she arranges for the appropriate court to authorize the sale and/or appoint her guardian of the children's estate. This can be complicated, expensive, and slow.

TRUSTS

What is a trust? Suppose you were given $100,000 and asked to invest it and give the income to the giver's daughter. As holder of the property, you are the **trustee.** As trustee you are obligated to administer the trust in accordance with the terms of the trust agreement. Often, the **trust agreement** (that is, the legal document) gives the trustee discretionary power to use both income and principal solely for the needs of the trust beneficiary or beneficiaries. The person giving the property is called the **grantor, donor, trustor, settlor,** or **creator** of the trust. The daughter, as recipient of the income earned under your management, is called the **beneficiary.** The property (money) is the **corpus** of the trust. The arrangement between the trustor and trustee is known as a **trust.**

Testamentary Trust

The most widely used trusts are **testamentary trusts.** They are part of a will and become effective after the death of the **testator** (the person for whom the will is written). For example, a testamentary trust can be created in a will to handle the problem previously mentioned in connection with minor beneficiaries. Suppose you want to leave half of your property to your children but want your spouse to manage it on their behalf. Instead of leaving the property to them directly in your will, you can create a testamentary trust and designate your spouse as trustee, or your spouse and a bank as co-trustees. The trustee or co-trustees would have whatever authority you granted in the provisions of the trust.

In the Dowd family case, Lori should consider creating a testamentary trust with her children as beneficiaries. A big decision for Lori would be whom to name as trustee. Logical options include: her sister Kay and brother-in-law Robert as co-trustees, Kay alone, Robert alone, Kay and/or Robert and a bank or trust company as co-trustees, and a bank as the sole trustee. If a bank is named, it appoints a bank employee, usually with the title of "trust officer," to see that the wishes of the trust creator are carried out. Lori obviously thinks Kay and Robert have good judgment or she would not have appointed them guardians of her children. If one or both is/are named trustees without the involvement of a bank, they must be capable of prudent investment decisions with respect to large sums of money. They may or may not have this financial knowledge. Banks or trust companies are often made trustee or co-trustee because of their expertise in the management of the trust corpus. When the major trust asset is life insurance proceeds (for example, in the Dowd case), the trust is called an insurance trust. The trust would be named as beneficiary of any policy proceeds that the grantor wants as part of the trust's corpus.

Living Trust

A **living trust**—also called an **inter vivos trust**—is established during the lifetime of the creator. A living trust can be either revocable or irrevocable, depending upon the wishes of the creator. The trust can be used to reduce the cost of probating the estate, since property in a trust does not go through the probate process. Trust property should be designed separate from your estate for probate purposes; therefore, putting property into a trust reduces the size of your estate. Both administrative and legal costs are reduced because the executor or administrator and attorney have less to do with a small estate than with a large one. Probate courts are inclined to approve administration fees based on the size of the estate. Moreover, in some states, lawyers are permitted to charge a specified percentage of the estate value, regardless of how little time and effort are required.

If you create a living trust, put all your property into it, and name yourself and your spouse trustees, what happens when you die? Nothing, because the trust has a life of its own. As trustee, your spouse can continue to manage trust property just as he or she did during your lifetime.[16]

Another advantage of a living trust to your family is that trust income and assets are just as readily available after your death as they were before. In contrast, income and assets of an estate may be temporarily unavailable while the probate process grinds along at what may be a snail's pace. If your spouse has to ask the court to approve a partial distribution or special living allowance during probate in order to have money to live on, that request adds to legal costs and, sometimes, causes a long delay.

LIFE INSURANCE

When you die, taxes, administrative costs, mortgages, and all your bills must be paid before the remainder of your estate is transferred to heirs. Sale of estate assets for this purpose reduces the amount available for heirs. Furthermore, it may be difficult to sell certain assets for their true worth, especially if business assets or real estate are involved. So, in addition to life insurance needed to continue income for your survivors, you may need life insurance to pay outstanding income taxes, administrative costs, estate taxes, and other indebtedness to assure that your survivors receive *all* of your estate rather than just part of it. Unless your situation qualifies as an exception, your estate taxes will be due nine months after your death.

If your estate is large enough to be subject to estate taxes, you should recognize that the proceeds of life insurance policies on your life will be included in your estate for tax purposes, regardless of how the beneficiary is named, if you owned the policies when you died. When taxes are a factor, you should consider having your policies owned by an irrevocable living trust or another person. Even if you are the owner, the administrative costs of probate, but not estate taxes, are avoided by having life insurance proceeds paid to a third-party beneficiary rather than to your estate. Thus, when your objectives can be achieved by naming third-party beneficiaries, heirs will be better off. At a minimum, however, be sure your executor has sufficient liquidity to pay debts, taxes, and other admin-

---

16. Unless you have full confidence in your spouse's management ability, it may be advisable to have a co-trustee appointed upon your death. At advanced ages you may want an outside trustee because neither spouse may be mentally or physically capable of managing a large sum of money.

istrative costs without selling assets at prices that may be depreciated during the relatively short period available for estate settlement.

In calculating federal estate taxes, the deceased is given an unlimited marital deduction. This means that any amount passing to a spouse escapes taxation. This may, however, simply defer the tax problem until the death of the spouse (assuming he or she has not remarried and has not consumed or given away assets). A couple may want to avoid the liquidation of a family business, real estate, or other illiquid assets on short notice by having life insurance provide the necessary estate settlement costs. Since insurance proceeds to cover estate taxes are needed only at the death of the second of the two spouses, the preferred policy may be **second-to-die life insurance** (see chapter 14).[17]

GIFTS

Persons with estates worth more than $600,000 may decide that they can achieve their objectives and reduce federal estate taxes by a program of gifts. There is no estate tax limit on the deduction of gifts, during one's lifetime or at death, to qualified charitable organizations. Religious, scientific, literary, educational, and a few other organizations are included. Money or other property given to charitable organizations is totally exempt from federal estate taxes. Gifts by one spouse to the other are also totally exempt.

Limits apply to nontaxable transfers to individuals. Still, a program of gifts can result in large sums passing untaxed to other individuals and reducing the size of the donor's taxable estate. The main **gift tax rule** excludes from federal estate taxation the first $10,000 given each year to each recipient. In addition, there is no limit on the number of recipients. For example, a person with two children and three grandchildren could give $50,000 every year without taxes by annually giving at least $10,000 to each child and grandchild. If less than $10,000 is given to one of the recipients, the exclusion is limited to the amount of the gift. So, if one gives $15,000 to a daughter and $5,000 to a granddaughter, the exclusion would be $15,000 ($10,000 for the daughter and $5,000 for the granddaughter).

Recipients do not have to be related to the donor. Gifts must be of a present interest in order to qualify. This means that the recipient must have full possession and enjoyment of the property at the time of the gift, rather than at some future date.

When the donor is married and his or her spouse consents to a gift, the annual exclusion increases to a maximum of $20,000 per recipient per year. Thus, in our example with five recipients, the annual deduction could increase to $100,000 if there is a consenting spouse. Lifetime gifts that exceed the limits described above are taxable. As we will see soon, no actual federal tax would be due, however, until the sum of taxable living gifts exceeds $600,000. The sum of all taxable gifts (i.e., those exceeding the annual limits described above) is added back to the estate at the time of death, with a credit for taxes paid on gifts over $600,000. In summary, a simple way to reduce federal estate taxes is to give away annually part

17. The use of a buy-sell agreement, often funded by life insurance, to avoid liquidation of a small business is discussed near the end of this chapter.

of your estate. It should be emphasized at this point that gifts need to be consistent with the objectives of the estate owner, such as seeing that grandchildren have funds for college, while concurrently allowing the grantor sufficient assets for his or her lifetime support.[18]

Fundamentals of Federal Estate and Gift Tax Calculations

Executors or administrators for decedents whose gross estates when added to the sum of previously granted taxable gifts are over $600,000 must file a federal unified estate and gift tax form. The tax is on the sum of transfers at death and taxable gifts made while living. Tax rates are graduated, starting at 18 percent on taxable estates under $10,000 and going to 60 percent on amounts above $10 million. Since you receive a credit equivalent to taxes on the first $600,000 of the estate tax computation base, the important rate is the 37 percent rate that applies by the time your estate exceeds $600,000. The major steps in this **estate tax calculation** are shown in figure 22–3.

The gross estate is essentially the fair market value, at the time of death or at the alternate valuation date six months after death, of all property interest of the decedent. Property used in farming or other closely held businesses is subject to special valuation rules. The definition of property interest is broad. It even includes life insurance proceeds from policies that you own or that are payable to your estate regardless of ownership.

Funeral expenses, expenses of administering the estate, mortgages, and other debts are **allowable deductions** from the gross estate. The result of their subtraction from the gross estate yields the **adjusted gross estate** (see step 1 in figure 22–3).

All **charitable gifts** are a further deduction. The major deduction for most families, however, is the **marital deduction.** All property left outright or as a qualified terminal interest[19] to a surviving spouse qualifies for this deduction. Since the deduction can go up to 100 percent of the adjusted gross estate, the **taxable estate** goes to zero when all net assets are left to a surviving spouse. The taxable estate at the time of death consists of the adjusted gross estate minus charitable gifts, and the amount qualifying for the marital deduction (see step 2 of figure 22–3).

FIGURE 22–3

Federal Estate Tax Calculation Steps

1. Gross Estate − Allowable Deductions = Adjusted Gross Estate
2. Adjusted Gross Estate − Charitable Gifts − Marital Deduction = Taxable Estate
3. Taxable Estate + Adjusted Taxable Gifts = Tax Computation Base
4. Tax Computation Base × Tax Rate = Tentative Federal Estate Tax
5. Tentative Federal Estate Tax − Unified Credit − State Estate Tax Credit − Previously Paid Estate and Gift Taxes − Foreign Death Taxes Paid = Federal Estate Tax Due

18. The reasons to consider giving away your ownership rights in life insurance are presented in the next section.
19. A qualified terminal interest gives a person the sole right to all income during his or her lifetime and the right to specify the ultimate disposition of the property.

Because estate taxes combine living transfers with transfers triggered by death, the sum of **adjusted taxable gifts** made after 1976 is added to the taxable estate. The result is called the **tax computation base** (see step 3). The amount of adjusted taxable gifts is the sum of gifts that have exceeded the annual gift tax exclusion allowance since 1976.

Step 4 requires the multiplication of the tax computation base by the appropriate tax rate. The schedule of rates is shown in table 22–6. The product of this multiplication is the **tentative federal estate tax.** The tax is labeled tentative because step 5 allows for the deduction of (1) a **unified credit,** (2) a **state estate tax credit** for a limited amount of taxes paid to the state of domicile, (3) **previously paid estate and gift taxes,** and (4) **foreign death taxes paid**. Only after adjustment for any of these applicable deductions can one determine the amount of **federal estate tax due.** Because the tax is due nine months after death, the estate plan should provide liquid assets to avoid having to sell illiquid assets at below normal market prices. Providing liquidity is often the purpose of life insurance for persons with large estates.

The adjustment that applies to all estates that are large enough, after estate planning, to produce a tentative tax is the unified credit. The credit is $192,800. It becomes a dollar-for-dollar offset against the tentative tax. As a result, no federal taxes are due unless the tax computation base exceeds $600,000. If Lori Dowd were to die now, no federal estate taxes would be due.

Business Life and Health Risks

If you own an interest in a business as a sole proprietor, partner in a partnership, or stockholder in a *close corporation,*[20] you are exposed to three death and disability risks. First, it may be difficult for you or your heirs to sell your interest in the firm for its full value in the event of your death or long-term total disability. Second, you are exposed to possible loss if a key employee dies or becomes totally and permanently disabled. Third, a lender may want you to assign life insurance as collateral for business debt.

SELLING THE FIRM

The possibility that your interest in the firm cannot be sold for its full value if you die or become totally disabled can be handled with a **buy-and-sell agreement** created between you and a prospective purchaser while you are alive and well. Prospective purchasers include the following:

1. Key employees in a sole proprietorship.
2. Your partners in a partnership.
3. Other stockholders in a close corporation.

Buy-and-Sell Agreement

In a buy-and-sell agreement, you agree to sell and the prospective purchaser agrees to buy your interest in the firm in the event of your death or long-

20. A close corporation is owned by very few stockholders. It is said to be "closely held," in contrast with one that is owned by hundreds or thousands of stockholders.

TAX COMPUTATION BASE		
More Than	**But Less Than**	**Tenatative Tax**
$ 0	$ 10,000	18%
10,000	20,000	$ 1,800 + 20% of excess over $ 10,000
20,000	40,000	3,800 + 22% of excess over 20,000
40,000	60,000	8,200 + 24% of excess over 40,000
60,000	80,000	13,000 + 26% of excess over 60,000
80,000	100,000	18,200 + 28% of excess over 80,000
100,000	150,000	23,800 + 30% of excess over 100,000
150,000	250,000	38,800 + 32% of excess over 150,000
250,000	500,000	70,800 + 34% of excess over 250,000
500,000	750,000	155,800 + 37% of excess over 500,000
750,000	1,000,000	248,300 + 39% of excess over 750,000
1,000,000	1,250,000	345,800 + 41% of excess over 1,000,000
1,250,000	1,500,000	448,300 + 43% of excess over 1,250,000
1,500,000	2,000,000	555,800 + 45% of excess over 1,500,000
2,000,000	2,500,000	780,800 + 49% of excess over 2,000,000
2,500,000	3,000,000	1,025,800 + 53% of excess over 2,500,000
3,000,000	10,000,000	1,290,800 + 55% of excess over 3,000,000
10,000,000	21,040,000	5,140,800 + 60% of excess over 10,000,000
21,040,000	No Limit	11,764,800 + 55% of excess over 21,040,000

term total disability. The agreement establishes the price for your interest or includes a formula by which the price can be determined at the time of sale. The price may be a lump sum upon your death, or income for life or a specified period in the event of your disability. This agreement, subject to adequate funding, assures a market for your business interest should you die or become disabled. In a partnership or close corporation buy-and-sell agreement, you make the same agreement with regard to your partners' or other stockholders' interests so they are protected just as you are.

Funding the Agreement

Where does the money come from to fulfill obligations undertaken in a buy-and-sell agreement? In some cases, funds dedicated to this purpose are set aside. This method is often used when one of the partners, for example, is uninsurable. Because the event that creates the need for funds (death or disability) may occur before funds have been accumulated, purchase of life insurance and disability income insurance is preferable. It is virtually the only way to be sure that lack of funding will not prevent the agreement from being fulfilled. In a sole proprietorship, your employee-purchasers buy insurance to pay for your interest in the event of your death or disability. In a partnership or close corporation, the partners or stockholders buy insurance on each other. If one of them dies or becomes disabled, you (and your other partners or stockholders) are able to buy out his or her interest and continue to control the business. On the other hand, the buy-and-sell agreement assures you, should you become disabled (or your heirs, in the event of your death), of a market for your business interest and assures business associates that they can buy the interest.

KEY EMPLOYEE RISK

A **key employee** is one whose contribution to the firm is crucial to its success. The death or disability of such an employee can cause significant losses to your firm and, perhaps, even impair its credit rating. Loss of your outstanding sales manager, for example, can cause a drastic drop in sales and profits. Replacing him or her may be difficult, time-consuming, and costly.

Most firms have one or more such employees. These key employees must be identified and an estimate made of the total loss that would result in case of death or disability. Then an adequate amount of life and disability income insurance can be bought on each key employee, with the firm named as the beneficiary.[21]

21. Business firms are exposed to other life and health risks through workers' compensation laws (see chapter 12) and employee benefit plans (see chapters 18–20).

Consumer Applications

Estate Tax Reduction Techniques

Estate planning can be complicated; therefore, persons with wealth should seek advice from an attorney, a certified public accountant who specializes in taxation, a trust officer, an investment specialist, and a life insurance agent. When you see your advisors, examine the following techniques that have potential to reduce your federal estate taxes:

1. Transfer ownership rights in life insurance.
2. Use charitable and marital deductions.
3. Consider using trusts.
4. Make gifts early and periodically.
5. Consider locating in a state with estate or inheritance taxes within the federal deductible allowance.

Remember that the definition of property interest is broad enough to include proceeds from life insurance in which you held incidents of ownership such as the right to change the beneficiary or make policy loans. If your objectives can be achieved without being the owner of some or all of the life insurance on your life, transfer ownership rights to others. For example, assume your large estate includes a $100,000 life insurance policy on your life. Your objectives include bequeathing at least this amount of money to your son, James. The entire proceeds can be removed from your gross estate by irrevocably transferring, at least three years prior to death, all policy ownership rights to James. If James is a minor or irresponsible, you will want to transfer the policy to a living trust called an insurance trust. The potential disadvantage to you is that in the future, James (or the trust) will have sole discretion about changing the beneficiary, borrowing from the cash value, surrendering the policy, and exercising other ownership rights.

If the policy has a cash value at the time of the ownership transfer, there may be gift tax implications. Rather than the face amount being a taxable living gift, the interpolated terminal reserve (essentially, the amount of cash you would receive if the policy were surrendered to your insurer at the time of transfer) plus any premiums paid in advance and accumulated dividends would be considered a taxable gift when the policy is transferred. The gift would be eligible for a $10,000 annual gift tax exclusion ($20,000

if you have a spouse and he or she consents).[22] A gift tax form will need to be filed for amounts exceeding these exclusion limits; however, no gift taxes will be payable until the taxes on the sum of your predeath gifts (up to $600,000) exceed the unified credit of $192,800. The main point is that $10,000 (or $20,000) plus the difference between the eventual death benefit and the taxable gift—a substantial portion of most policies before very advanced ages—will never enter the gross estate. You can still pay future premiums, if you choose, without incurring a taxable gift, provided the amount of premium and other gifts to James do not exceed the annual gift tax exclusion.

Because charitable gifts and property that qualify for the marital deduction are deducted in arriving at your taxable estate, you will want to think of ways to maximize these deductions to the extent you can do so and still achieve your primary objectives. Do these objectives include helping your alma mater, church, or other charitable organizations? Gifts can be made while you are living (with the advantage of a gift tax exclusion) or through your will, but make them clear. For example, do not just assume that your spouse will someday, after your death, make a gift to your alma mater; make this specific bequest in your will *and* create a charitable deduction for the eventual estate tax computation.

How much do you want to leave your spouse? A desirable tax reduction technique is to see that a will is written to pass more to a spouse with children, for example, than would be allowed by your state's intestacy law. Your attorney or accountant can help you calculate the optimum marital deduction from the standpoint of minimizing estate taxes and leaving you flexibility to transfer directly some property to parties other than your spouse.

The unlimited nature of the marital deduction does not mean it is always desirable to leave 100 percent of an adjusted gross estate to a surviving spouse. Whatever is left of this bequest (and its value may have grown) at the time of the receiving spouse's death will become part of his or her gross estate. Also, leaving everything to your spouse

---

22. Policies on which no future premiums are payable are valued on the basis of what the insurer would charge as a single premium for a comparable policy at the insured's current age.

nullifies the estate tax credit worth $192,800 on the first $600,000 of the estate at the time the first member of the couple dies.

The $192,800 credit at the time of the first death can be utilized and the size of the surviving spouse's estate can be reduced by using a **credit shelter trust.** The spouse typically loses little benefit relative to receiving the entire estate. Both spouses with wealth need to implement provisions in their will establishing a credit shelter trust when the first of them dies. The provision would place $600,000 of assets (minus taxable gifts made during life) in the trust, resulting in no tax through the tax credit on a tax computation base of this size.[23] The remainder of the estate, upon the first death, would escape taxation by operation of the marital deduction. If desirable, the trust instrument could provide that all income on the $600,000 go to the surviving spouse. The trust instrument would specify that, at the death of the second spouse, the trust's corpus go to children, other heirs, or a charity to avoid being part of the second spouse's estate.

23. An underlying assumption here is that each spouse would own enough property to have a tax computation base of at least $600,000.

You have at least two ways to reduce the amount of adjusted taxable gifts that become part of your estate tax computation base. First, you can use a program of periodic planned gifts for a particular recipient, rather than a smaller number of large gifts. For example, gifts of $15,000 per year over five years to one donee, assuming no spousal consent, will produce adjustable taxable gifts of $25,000 [that is, $75,000 − ($10,000 × 5 years)]. One $75,000 gift to the same recipient will produce an adjustable taxable gift of $65,000. Second, because the amount added back is the value at the time of a gift, the appreciation in the value of property between the time of gift(s) and your death escapes transfer taxes. This encourages early gifting of appreciating property, provided the gifts are consistent with your objectives.

Since federal law places limits on the amount of deductible state inheritance taxes (levied on persons who receive property) or state estate taxes (paid by the estate), it is sensible (other factors being equal) to live in a state whose rates do not exceed the allowable maximum. Some states begin taxing estates long before the $600,000 minimum allowed by federal law and produce total state taxes that exceed the allowable federal deduction for state estate and inheritance taxes. Wealthy people have a tendency to avoid settling in such states.

Key Terms

financial planning	testamentary trusts
static life insurance planning	testator
family dependency period	living trust/inter vivos trust
spousal dependency period	second-to-die life insurance
final expenses	gift tax rule
special needs	estate tax calculation
dynamic life insurance planning	allowable deductions
prolonged life risk	adjusted gross estate
special power of attorney	charitable gifts
living will	marital deduction
estate planning	taxable estate
estate	adjusted taxable gifts
probate	tax computation base
executor/administrator	tentative federal estate tax
will	unified credit
intestate	state estated tax credit
guardian	previously paid
trustee	estate and gift taxes
trust agreement	foreign death taxes paid
grantor/donor/trustor/settlor/ creator	federal estate tax due
beneficiary	buy-and-sell agreement
corpus	key employee
trust	credit shelter trust

1. Describe how family risk management is a part of personal financial planning. In what ways is financial planning a broader concept?

2. Describe how family cash flow is changed by the death or total, permanent disability of a major income producer. Why is an investment program not a viable solution to these potential cash flow problems?

3. Explain how life insurance, Social Security survivor benefits, and family net worth are complements and substitutes for each other.

4. With respect to static life insurance planning, discuss several factors that complicate the determination of the amount of life insurance needed by a family.

5. Describe briefly the major categories that can be used to group cash flow needs for most situations involving the death of a main family wage earner.

6. Why is it important for most adults to have a will? What does it mean to die intestate? Can this influence the size of one's marital deduction in the calculation of federal estate taxes?

7. Distinguish between living and testamentary trusts.

8. What role does life insurance often play in estate planning for wealthy people?

9. Would you prefer to have your best friend act as trustee for your estate, or have the trust department of your bank perform that function? Please explain.

10. At death, how are federal estate and gift taxes influenced by living gifts that exceeded annual gift tax exclusion limits?

Cases

22.1 After discussing the mechanics of determining life and health needs with Jim, your neighbor, you both begin to reflect on your individual situations. You determine that in the case of your death, your family would need $1,000 per month during the family dependency period, in addition to benefits from Social Security, your current life insurance, and a small net worth. Your solution is to purchase the necessary amount of life insurance, with the type to be determined by your budget limitations.

After some thought, Jim responds that after considering his situation and budget, his solution is rather simple. If he were to die prematurely, his wife and four-year-old child would be hard pressed for only the length of time it took his wife to find a new husband, preferably one with money. To Jim, these were the facts of life. After all, his wife is young and attractive, and she could not stay in mourning all her life.

1. Are there any problems with Jim's approach? What are they? How can they be solved?

2. Can Jim rely on Social Security survivor benefits to help pay for his child's college expenses?

22.2 When Lori Dowd looked at the results of her life insurance planning (see figure 22–1), she suddenly realized that Social Security provides significant survivor benefits. Lori had previously thought of Social Security as only useful in retirement years. She is curious about the extent to which she would need more life insurance if Social Security survivor benefits did not exist.

Recognize that Lori's children have benefits of $600 per month beginning in 1995. The benefits are currently designed to increase with inflation or wage changes, which we will assume to be 4 percent per year. Further assume that a lump sum of money for the children's welfare could earn 1/4 percent per month after taxes and inflation (i.e., approximately 7.23 percent per year). The older child, Liz, is expected to receive her benefit for 144 months; the younger child, Bob, is expected to receive his for 168 months.

(Note: You may want to use a financial calculator or a spreadsheet. Alternatively, you can solve the problem by hand by using a present value of an annuity of one factor of 120.8041 for Liz's 144 payments and a factor of 137.0435 for Bob's 168 payments. This problem assumes you have learned present value mathematics, perhaps in an accounting or finance class.)

22.3 Bill Masters, age 55, has accumulated a sizable estate. Included are a $250,000 home, with only $20,000 in unpaid mortgage balance; his personally owned business, which has assets of $4 million and liabilities of $2.5 million; a common stock portfolio with a market value of $1.5 million; and $250,000 of personally owned life insurance. He has a wife, Jane, age 53, and three children, all of whom are married college graduates.

1. Why should Bill plan his estate?

2. Is there any reason to consider additional life insurance in this plan?

22.4 Calculate the federal estate taxes that would be owed by the estate of Bill Masters, assuming the following facts in addition to those given in Case 22.3: the values shown are fair market values; funeral expenses are $5,000; estate administration fees are $25,000; a testamentary gift of $50,000 will go to Bill and Jane's alma mater; 50 percent of the adjusted gross estate will go outright to Jane, the remainder divided equally among the children; no living gifts exceeded the annual gift tax exclusion limits; and the $76,200 estate tax paid to Bill's state is equal to the maximum credit on his federal form.

22.5 Using a spreadsheet, prepare a life insurance plan for the Milne family; facts and data follow. Pattern your answer on table 22–5 page 533. Your conclusion should explain how much life insurance is needed to meet the needs.

Steven and Ramona Milne of Atlanta, Georgia, are both 32 years old. Their children, Jesse and Milo, are ages 4 and 2, respectively. All members of the household are in excellent health and have normal life expectancies. Steven is a pediatrician in his second year of independent practice. Ra-

STEVE AND RAMONA MILNE
BALANCE SHEET
(END-OF-YEAR MARKET VALUES)

Assets

Checking Account	$ 1,000
Government bond fund	3,000
Stock mutual funds	3,000
IRA (Ramona)	8,000
Keogh retirement plan (Steven)	15,000
Automobiles	16,000
House and lot	215,000
Personal property	10,000
Total	$271,000

Liabilities

Credit card balances	$ 1,000
Other household account balances	500
Automobile loan balance	14,500
Home mortgage balance	173,000
Total	$189,000

Net Worth	**$ 82,000**

ANNUAL CASH FLOW STATEMENT

Steven's income	$100,000
Investment income	Assume reinvestment
Total cash flow	$100,000

Taxes

Social Security	$ 10,637
Federal income	13,500
State income	4,000
Total income + SS taxes	$ 28,137
Remaining disposable income	71,863

Other Expenses

Property taxes (home and auto)	$ 2,500
Sales taxes	2,800
House payment, including insurance	19,200
Automobile expense, including insurance	8,500
Food and household items	5,000
Utilities	3,600
Contributions	6,000
Medical and dental insurance	3,000
Term life insurance	700
Vacations and entertainment	2,500
Preschool tuition	1,400
Clothes	1,500
Other expenses	7,163
Total expenses	$63,863

Savings and Investments

Keogh contributions	$ 6,000
Mutual fund contributions	2,000

Total Expenses, Savings, and Investments	**$71,863**

mona, a homemaker since the birth of Jesse, holds a current CPA designation. A former tax manager for a Big Six accounting firm, she would return to work in a less stressful position if Steven were·to die prematurely. In the event of Steven or Ramona's premature death, a nanny would be hired at a cost of $12,000 per year (1995 dollars).

Two years ago, they purchased a $215,000 home, making a $40,000 down payment from money saved while Ramona was working. The home mortgage is for 15 years at 7 percent interest. They have no educational loans. An automobile loan payment is reflected in the annual cost of transportation included in their balance sheet and cash flow statement following.

Steven expects his income to grow at 5 percent per year for five years, and thereafter at the expected rate of inflation, 4 percent. In the event of his premature death, Ramona would return to work with expected after-tax earnings of $35,000 per year (1995 dollars) and expected growth of 4 percent per year. Each child would be eligible for a Social Security survivor benefit of $11,000 per year (1995 dollars). Both Jesse and Milo are assumed to attend college (bachelors and masters degrees) for six years each at a cost of $9,000 per year (1995 dollars). In addition, the surviving spouse would expect expenses equal to 80 percent of those reflected on the current cash flow statement (after income and Social Security taxes), plus the cost of a nanny through 2005 ($63,090 in 1995 dollars). After 2009, the mortgage payment will drop out of the budget. For expense purposes, they would expect the family net worth to continue to be used to produce retirement security rather than income. When you calculate net needs, assume there is $200,000 of term life insurance on the lives of both Steven and Ramona.

The planning horizon ends when Milo is assumed to complete a masters degree at age 23. At this point, the mortgage will have been paid off for several years and various other household expenses are expected to have decreased. Ramona and Steven believe Ramona's income should be sufficient to support her desired lifestyle then, should Steven predecease her.

23

Individual Financial Management of Retirement

Introduction   The typical college-age person is three times as likely to live into retirement years as to die earlier. Consequently, it is important to begin preparing for retirement during your working years.

Retirement income comes primarily from three sources: (1) Social Security, (2) employer-sponsored retirement plans, and (3) personal resources.[1] **Personal resources** consist of (1) income from employment during retirement (perhaps part-time), (2) accumulations created by individual contributions to tax-deferred savings/investment vehicles, (3) other personal investments, and (4) inheritances, if any. One reason to plan wisely is to avoid having to work part-time during retirement. Several factors increase the need to plan effectively for sufficient personal resources:

- Inflation over your working years will multiply the dollars you will need to maintain purchasing power. Over a forty-year working career, 4 percent inflation, for example, will reduce the purchasing power of a dollar to 21 cents. Twenty years into retirement, the same rate of inflation will reduce this 21 cents to 10 cents.[2]

- More than a third of all employees are not offered employer-provided retirement benefits. The trend in coverage is not encouraging, particularly for those working for small employers. Job changes can significantly reduce the amount of employer-provided benefits, even if you work for employers that sponsor retirement plans. You may leave some jobs before becoming vested. Upon job termination at a young age, you may consume a lump sum distribution rather than reinvesting it. A vested benefit may be frozen in amount for many years with no inflation adjustments.

- Life expectancy has increased from around age 47 for males and 49 for females at the beginning of the twentieth century to age 80 for males and 84 for females. Advances in the treatment of cancer, cardiovascular disease, and other major causes of death are on the horizon. Combining longer life expectancy with a trend toward younger retirement means funds for the typical future retiree will be needed over a long period.

---

1. Social Security is discussed in chapter 17; employer-sponsored retirement plans are discussed in chapter 20. The three sources are often viewed as three legs of a stool supporting retirement.
2. If 4 percent inflation sounds too high, consider 3 percent. Over 40 years, 3 percent inflation reduces the purchasing power of a dollar to 31 cents, and to 17 cents in another twenty years.

- Social Security benefits are likely to be reduced, relative to today's benefit levels, as one way of managing an upcoming crisis in the financing of this retirement program.

These trends can be viewed as challenges. With proper planning, sufficient funds can be accrued for retirement years. This chapter presents an approach to estimating the amount you or the person you are advising needs to invest periodically to accumulate the necessary retirement income. This chapter examines:

1. The role of the risk management/financial planning process as it applies to retirement.
2. How to determine the periodic contributions required to accumulate the desired level of personal resources for retirement.
3. The nature and uses of annuities as the major retirement funding vehicle offered by life insurers to individual consumers.

Retirement Planning for Lori Dowd

In chapter 22 we used the Dowd family to illustrate the planning process for handling certain nonretirement personal loss exposures. In the current chapter, we apply the financial planning process to Lori Dowd's retirement income needs. The same steps are followed.

DATA COLLECTION

The process starts with collecting data on the individual's Social Security earnings, employer-sponsored retirement plans, and personal assets that may be used in retirement years. Remember that Lori is a single parent, age 35, earning $50,000 a year as a branch bank manager. Her Social Security earnings record began at age 22 when she was earning $15,000 per year as a new college graduate. Her current earnings are projected to reach $58,000 in real (uninflated) terms by age 50 and then remain at this level in real terms until she retires.

Two retirement plans were described in table 22–3, as follows:

- 401(k) Plan—Employer matches 50 percent of employee contributions up to a maximum employee contribution of 6 percent of basic pay, subject to the annual maximum limit on 401(k) contributions.
- Defined-Benefit Pension Plan—Pension at age 65 equal to 40 percent of average final three years salary, minus 1/2 of primary Social Security retirement benefit, with no provision for benefits to increase after retirement. Early retirement is allowed between ages 60 and 65, subject to a reduction in benefits. Reductions are equal to 4 percent for each year the retiree is below age 65.

From Lori's balance sheet (table 22–1), we know she has $15,000 vested in her 401(k) account. Her house, valued at $85,000 with a $75,000 outstanding mortgage balance, will be fully paid for by retirement, which will reduce her living expenses. Her other assets are being held for purposes unrelated to retirement. Other assumptions will be made later about the value of Social Security, private retirement plans, and personal resources available at retirement.

OBJECTIVES

Most people planning for retirement begin with a general goal, such as: "I (or we) wish to maintain the same standard of living enjoyed during working years." One challenge is to translate this statement to dollars. Certain expenses, such as for travel and health care, typically increase during retirement. Other expenses will decrease or be eliminated. Those eliminated include work-related expenses, Social Security taxes, and retirement plan contributions. Income taxes (federal, state, and local) are likely to diminish because of larger exemptions for persons age 65 or older; part of Social Security income will not be taxable[3]; part of income produced by the liquidation of previously taxed personal investments will not be taxed; and total taxable income from all sources is likely to be less than taxable income during working years.

Two primary methods help quantify retirement objectives. The first requires an itemized list of expenses for the first year of retirement. The total of this "pro-forma budget" becomes the amount of uninflated income needed annually in retirement. Persons who do not maintain a detailed record of family expenses will have difficulty constructing a detailed budget for retirement years. The second method is simpler. It begins with an **income replacement ratio,** recognizing that some expenses will stop upon retirement and others may change. Studies show that desired replacement ratios range between approximately 70 percent and 85 percent of total income just before retirement.[4]

Lori Dowd's objective is to have her retirement income from all sources equal 75 percent of her earnings in the year before retirement. Further, she wants to retire at age 62.

ALTERNATIVE SOLUTIONS/EXPOSURE EVALUATION

With the objective established, the next step in the financial planning process requires estimating:

1. The amount of money needed at retirement to meet the objective.
2. The portions of this sum that will be met by Social Security and employer plans.
3. What shortfall (i.e., necessary personal resources), if any, exists.
4. The amount of annual contributions needed to overcome the shortfall.
5. Alternatives available to close the gap.

Assumptions

Assumptions must be made to estimate needs over many years. Lori Dowd makes the following assumptions:

1. Inflation in consumer prices will average 4 percent per year (i.e., the approximate average rate since 1950).
2. She will remain with her current employer until retirement. This employer will continue to offer a defined benefit retirement plan with no change in the current provisions.

---

3. This assumption may change in the future.
4. See, for example, Bruce A. Palmer, "Tax Reform and Retirement Income Replacement Ratios," *Journal of Risk and Insurance,* vol. LVI, no. 4 (1989): pp. 702–725.

3. Her nominal income will increase at 5 percent per year through age 50 and at the rate of inflation (4 percent) between then and retirement at age 62.

4. Anticipating the government's need to reduce overall Social Security benefits in the future, Lori's benefits are projected at 85 percent of current levels. In addition, a 30 percent reduction, from age 67 benefits, is taken for early retirement at age 62. Benefits are expected to increase with inflation between now and the end of Lori's retirement period.

5. Her current $15,000 401(k) plan balance is assumed to earn 8 percent per year. In retirement years, this fund will remain invested at 8 percent and be liquidated in equal payments.

6. No future contributions to her 401(k) plan are recognized, since we are determining how much she needs to invest in the future.

7. Retirement income objectives can be expressed adequately in before-tax dollars. Assuming continuation of current income tax laws and achievement of Lori's desired level of retirement income, 85 percent of her Social Security benefits, all of her defined benefit pension, and all of her 401(k) income will be taxed (after exemptions and deductions).

8. Recognizing the trend in life expectancy, Lori's retirement period is projected to span her ages 62 through 89.

Analysis

We recommend using an electronic spreadsheet to make calculations. For this case, inputs at the beginning of the retirement period were calculated manually. The manual calculations are simple, provided you have a financial calculator or annuity tables. Otherwise, you may want to include pre-retirement years in the spreadsheet. A calculation of the shortfall for Lori's retirement years is shown in table 23–1.

Lori's salary in the year before retirement at age 62 is expected to be $160,021.[5] Her retirement income objective in the first year of retirement is 75 percent of this salary, increased by the 4 percent rate of inflation. Inflation results in nominal dollar income needs of $170,820 at age 70 and $359,891 at age 89.[6]

Three sources of retirement income are recognized in table 23–1. Only Social Security increases with inflation. The defined benefit plan is what retirees call "fixed income."[7] While the 401(k) payments are shown as level

---

5. Salary at age 50 = (current salary) $(1 + i)^n$, where i = 5 percent and n = 15; $103,946.41 = 50,000 (2.078928), and salary at age 61 = (Age 50 salary) $(1 + i)^n$, where i = 4 percent and n = 11; $160,021 = 103,946.41 (1.539457). The calculations reflect inflation at 4 percent for the entire period and 1 percent annual productivity gains in the first fifteen years.

6. A 3 percent inflation rate during retirement years, ignoring any change in salary prior to retirement, would result in assumed retirement income needs of $158,114 at age 70 and $277,255 at age 89. A case can be made for assuming that retirees do not bear the full impact of inflation. Housing costs and property taxes for those owning homes, for example, may not fully reflect inflation.

7. Some employers make ad hoc, discretionary increases in defined benefit pension payments from time to time. None are assumed in this spreadsheet.

amounts, the 8 percent earnings assumption implicitly recognizes inflation.[8]

The next step in the spreadsheet calculation is to add the three sources of retirement income. Then annually subtract "total sources of retirement income" from the "retirement income objective." The result is the "shortfall" found in table 23–1. If retirement income objectives are to be met, funding for the shortfall needs to be accumulated by the beginning of the

TABLE 23–1

Retirement Income Needs for Lori Dowd*

	1995	2021	2022	2023 ...	2026 ...	2029 ...	2032 ...	2035 ...	2038 ...	2041 ...	2044 ...	2047 ...
AGE	35	61	62	63	66	69	72	75	78	81	84	87
Gross Income	50,000	160,021										
Retirement Income Objective (.75)			124,816	129,809	146,017	164,250	184,758	207,828	233,778	262,969	295,804	332,739
Sources of Retirement Income:												
Social Security			20,184	20,991	23,612	26,561	29,877	33,608	37,804	42,525	47,834	53,807
Employer's Defined Benefit Plan			47,475	47,475	47,475	47,475	47,475	47,475	47,475	47,475	47,475	47,475
401k (from 1995 balance)			10,957	10,957	10,957	10,957	10,957	10,957	10,957	10,957	10,957	10,957
Total Sources of Retirement Income			78,616	79,423	82,044	84,993	88,309	92,040	96,236	100,957	106,266	112,239
Shortfall			46,200	50,385	63,973	79,257	96,449	115,788	137,542	162,012	189,538	220,500
Present Value of Shortfall at Age 62:												
at 6 percent (beg. of period)			1,379,205									
at 8 percent (beg. of period)			1,060,838									

*The retirement income objective and Social Security benefits keep pace with cost of living changes, assumed to be 4 percent per year. Retirement income from the defined benefit plan remains constant in nominal dollars. Income from the 401(k) plan reflects an 8 percent return on the unused principal balance as it is amortized by level payments.

8. While the 401(k) payment is calculated as a level amount, its 8 percent return in pre- and post-retirement years can be viewed as covering expected inflation of 4 percent plus a 4 percent risk premium.

Calculation of the annual income from the 401(k) plan was done manually. First, the future value at retirement age of the $15,000 age-35 account balance was determined. That is, future value = $15,000 $(1 + i)^n$, where i = 8 percent and n = 27; $119,821 = 15,000 (7.98806). The annual payment was calculated with the formula for the periodic rent of an annuity: $R = A_n \left(\frac{1}{a_{\overline{n}|i}} \right)$, where R is the periodic annuity rent (payment) throughout retirement. A_n is the present value at the beginning of the retirement period, and $a_{\overline{n}|i}$ is the present value of an annuity of 1 per period. From the future value calculation made above, we know that A_n = $119,821. The value of $\frac{1}{a_{\overline{n}|i}}$ can be calculated $\frac{1}{a_{\overline{n}|i}} = \frac{i}{1 - (1 + i)^{-n}}$ or obtained from a table, $10,957 = 119,821 (0.091448). (Note: the formula assumes end-of-year payments which are sufficient for estimates over many years.)

retirement period. Notice the shortfall begins at $46,200 when Lori's age is 62. The shortfall is $84,765 at age 70 and $243,261 in the last year of the analysis.

The present value of the projected shortfalls, as of the beginning of the retirement period, constitutes the total personal resources needed when retirement begins. We have instructed our spreadsheet program to calculate the present value using two alternative interest rates. Assuming 6 percent interest during retirement years, Lori needs to accumulate $1,379,205 by age 62. If she is willing to trade off more investment risk for a higher expected return of 8 percent, the necessary accumulation is reduced by 23 percent to $1,060,838.

Is it reasonable for Lori to accumulate sums of this magnitude during the remaining 27 years of her employment? In search of an answer, we first calculate the level contribution required if the investment medium earns 8 percent tax deferred.[9] The result of $11,239, 22.5 percent of Lori's current annual salary, exceeds what seems reasonable as savings.[10] Alternatively, we can calculate an amount of annual contribution that will increase each year to match her increasing preretirement salary. This amount in the first year is $4,756.[11] Continuing to contribute 9.5 percent of her salary with 8 percent investment returns would accumulate the necessary sum of $1,060,838 by age 62.

From examining Lori's current cash flow statement (table 22–2), we realize that she is currently contributing 4 percent of gross salary to her employer's 401(k) plan on a tax-deferred basis; her employer is contributing an additional 2 percent; and she is saving an additional 1 percent of salary for nonretirement purposes, such as college funding for her children. When a person considers the amount to be invested for retirement as too large, two major adjustments deserve thought. First, consider increasing the assumed rate of return on investments by taking more investment risk.[12] Assuming a 9 percent rate of return in Lori's pre- and post-retirement years reduces the percentage of future salary to be saved for retirement to 6.6 percent. Second, Lori could lower her retirement income objective. If Lori assumes a 9 percent return on investments *and*

----

9. $1,060,838 / \left[\sum_{n=1}^{27} (1.08)^n \right] = 1,060,838/94.38829 = \$11,239$

Note: Contributions are assumed to be made at the beginning of the year. Financial calculators and annuity tables may assume contributions at the end of the year. If you make similar calculations with either of these, use the annuity due mode, or add interest for the final year to your initial future value.

10. See Lori's current cash flow statement in table 22–2.

11. $1,060,838 / \left[\sum_{n=1}^{27} (1.08)^n (1.045556)^n \right]$

$= \$1,060,383 / \sum_{n=1}^{27} (1.129200)^n$

$= \$1,060,838/223.05931 = \$4,756$

Note: The salary growth rate of 4.5556 percent is a weighted average of 5 percent for fifteen years and 4 percent for twelve years.

12. See the Consumer Applications for this chapter.

lowers her replacement ratio to 70 percent (from 75 percent), the percentage she needs to invest for retirement becomes 5.7 percent.

DECIDE ON INVESTMENT PLAN

After deciding how much to set aside for retirement, the next step in retirement planning is to decide on an **investment plan.** Decide the agency through which you will invest and the investment medium (or media) that best fit your risk profile. When you have adequate sources of liquidity (e.g., savings, insurance, and credit cards), tax-deferred plans should be preferred. They offer two definite advantages:

1. Deferral of income taxes on contributions during preretirement years.
2. Deferral of income taxes on investment returns in pre- and post-retirement years. Tax-deferred contributions result in earning investment returns on money normally paid in taxes.

In addition, some plans (such as Lori's employer's 401(k) plan) provide for employer matching of employee contributions, subject to a maximum. Lori, for example, could contribute all but 0.5 percent (6 percent from Lori and 3 percent from her employer) of her 9.5 percent total need to a 401(k) plan.[13]

Non-tax-deferred plans, often called "non-qualified plans," that allow individual investors to defer income taxes on investment earnings but not on contributions include:

1. Annuities, with no limit on the amount of maximum annual contribution.[14]
2. IRAs, with a $2,000 per income earner maximum annual contribution.[15]

Often, participants in tax-deferred plans are given choices of investment funds ranging from low-risk bank money market accounts to common stock funds. Non-qualified investment media available to individuals include the entire array of investment opportunities: bank savings instruments, annuities, mutual funds, individual bonds and stocks, and real estate.

Key advice on individual preretirement planning consists of four points:

1. Begin at an early age to allow sufficient time for numerous contributions and the magic of compound returns (for example, $1,000 per year earning 8 percent over ten years grows to $15,650; the same annual investment at 8 percent for forty years grows to $279,780).
2. Contribute new funds at regular intervals.

....

13. Other tax-deferred plans, not available to Lori in her current employment, include IRC Section 403(b) plans, IRC Section 457 plans, Individual Retirement Accounts or Annuities (IRA), Keogh plans, and Simplified Employee Plans. For discussion, see chapter 20.
14. Annuities are discussed later in this chapter.
15. Municipal bond returns are tax-exempt. Their returns, however, are lower than those of taxable bonds with similar risk, discounting in advance for their favored tax status.

3. Take as much investment risk as your personal risk tolerance will allow in order to have higher expected returns.

4. Diversify your portfolio.

In addition to using the 401(k) plan, Lori's 8 percent return reflects a willingness to take modest risks. Perhaps she decides to place half of her 401(k) contributions in a corporate bond fund and the other half in a high-grade common stock fund.

The primary decisions made at the beginning of the postretirement period are:

1. If employer-sponsored plans allow **lump-sum distributions** (i.e., one cash payment equal to the expected value of lifetime benefits from a defined benefit plan or the account balance of a defined contribution plan) as an alternative form of distribution, should a lump sum, partial lump sum, or no lump sum be selected?

2. What are the tax effects of taking a lump sum distribution, and how will you invest this distribution?

3. If lifetime income options (for example, income for as long as either you or your spouse lives) are available in an employer-sponsored plan or through an individually purchased annuity, which option will you elect?

4. Will you purchase an annuity to hedge the risk of outliving the principal of individual investments or lump-sum distributions?[16]

IMPLEMENTATION

Above all else, successful retirement planning requires a commitment to making the necessary periodic contributions. Then you enroll in available employer-sponsored plans, select financial intermediaries (e.g., an investment-mutual fund company or insurer), do the paperwork for an IRA or other account, and decide on an investment strategy. Unless you are a retirement planning specialist, you may want the assistance of an agent or planner with a CFP, CLU, or ChFC designation. One reasonable strategy is to take more investment risk at early stages of life and become more conservative as retirement approaches.

PERIODIC REVIEW

Especially when planning is done at an early age, the assumptions are unlikely to mirror future reality. Thus, estimates of necessary contributions will be approximations needing periodic adjustment. The assumptions that Lori Dowd, for example, will remain with her current employer and that the employer will make no changes in its retirement benefits over the remainder of her work life are speculative. All assumptions must be reevaluated periodically.

....

16. Other financial decisions that may be made at this stage of life (if not made earlier) involve purchasing of Medigap coverage (see chapter 21) and of long-term care insurance (see chapter 22), and handling estate planning matters (see chapter 22).

Annuities

Annuities are the primary insurance company product that helps individuals accumulate funds for retirement. During preretirement years, annuities are primarily investment vehicles. During retirement years, the product provides a periodic payment that continues throughout a fixed period and/or for the duration of a life or lives. Although annuities are frequently used to save for retirement, their unique function is the *scientific liquidation* of a principal sum, usually during retirement years. During this period, they protect against the risk of outliving the financial resources invested earlier in the annuity. If the duration depends upon the expected length of a life or lives, the contract is known as a **life annuity.**

As the United States population has aged, an increasing portion of life insurer income has come from annuities. In 1953, annuities accounted for 9.1 percent of insurer income. By 1973 this percentage was 10.46 percent, and in 1993 annuities made up 33.55 percent of total insurer income. Between 1985 and 1994, total individual annuity sales more than tripled to $99.3 billion.

PARTIES TO AN ANNUITY

The person or entity that purchases an annuity is the **owner.** The person on whose life expectancy payments are based is known as the **annuitant.** For annuities sold directly to individuals, the owner and annuitant are usually the same person. The **beneficiary** is the person or entity who receives any death benefits due at the death of the annuitant.

MECHANICS OF ANNUITIES

Premium Payments

Annuities may be bought either on the **installment plan** or with a **single premium.** Most people use the installment plan. Usually, the owner chooses a flexible plan where premiums may vary in amount and frequency. In the event the annuitant dies before benefit payments begin, deferred annuities sold to individuals promise to return the accumulation value at the time of death.

When you buy a deferred annuity on the installment plan, you are engaging in a savings program during the accumulation period. There is no protection (insurance) element involved, any more than would be the case if you made monthly deposits in your savings account at the bank. Both will guarantee the return of your account value.

Accumulation versus Liquidation

The time during which premiums are being paid and benefits have not begun is called the **accumulation period.** The value of the contract during this period consists of premiums plus investment earnings minus expenses and is called the **accumulation value.** The time during which the accumulation value and future investment returns are being liquidated by benefit payments is called the **liquidation period.**

ETHICAL *Dilemma*

Suitability and Annuities

Edwin Able is employed by a commercial bank. He is licensed to sell both fixed dollar and variable annuities. One of his duties is to sell annuities on which the bank receives commissions from the life insurer. He also promotes bank savings instruments such as certificates of deposit.

Assume that at the present time the interest return for the fixed dollar, single premium annuity is 7 percent guaranteed for the next three years. The high-quality common stock separate account that supports the variable annuity product has averaged a 10 percent investment return since its inception in 1970. Last year, its return was a minus 11.4 percent, indicating the investment risk in the variable annuity. Edwin, age 24, is a risk taker and likes to sell people on the higher expected long-run returns for the variable annuity, always pointing out the tax-deferred nature of annuity investment returns. Both annuity products have expense charges of 1 percent per year; they both have surrender charges that begin at 5 percent for the first year and decrease 1 percent per year. The current return on a certificate of deposit with a three-year maturity is 5 percent. If a certificate is surrendered before its maturity date, interest is lost for three months.

Mrs. Maria Gonzales, age 50, is conferring with Edwin. She is financially unsophisticated, believes Edwin is trustworthy, and intends to follow his investment advice. Her $20,000, 6.5 percent, three-year certificate of deposit is maturing today for $24,159. The interest income on the certificate is taxable yearly at Mrs. Gonzales' 15 percent marginal rate. Mrs. Gonzales earns enough income to support the modest lifestyles of herself and her 15-year-old daughter, for whom she provides the sole support. Her only other significant assets consist of a small house and an automobile. The investment's primary purpose is to finance the daughter's college education, beginning in three years. Security of principal is of utmost concern.

When Edwin finds that Mrs. Gonzales is disillusioned upon learning of the 5 percent return if she renews her certificate of deposit with the bank, Edwin reminds her that the certificate is guaranteed by the Federal Deposit Insurance Corporation, an agency of the federal government. She is still disappointed and says she wants to convert the maturing certificate into cash and consult a Merrill Lynch broker for advice. At this point, Edwin cheerfully informs her that he can put her money in an annuity. He proceeds to tell her about the 10 percent historical return on the variable annuity.

Should Edwin try to sell Mrs. Gonzales a single premium deferred annuity? If so, should he recommend the fixed dollar annuity or the variable annuity? Will your decision be influenced by expense and surrender charges? What about the 10 percent penalty tax on certain withdrawals?

Commencement of Benefits

Annuities may be classified as either immediate or deferred, reflecting when benefit payments begin. An **immediate annuity** begins payments at the next payment interval (for example, month, quarter, or year) after purchase. They require a single premium. **Deferred annuities** begin payments sometime in the future as elected by the owner, such as at age 65. Deferred annuities may be funded by a single premium, equal installments, or, more commonly, by flexible premiums.

Denomination of Benefits

During the accumulation period and the liquidation period, your annuity is classified as either a **fixed dollar annuity** or a **variable annuity.** Fixed dollar annuities earn investment returns at rates guaranteed by your insurer, subject to periodic changes in the guaranteed rate for the next period. A set amount of benefit per dollar of accumulation (varying also by life expectancy when benefits begin) is paid during the liquidation period. Variable annuity returns vary with the investment performance of special investment accounts. The amount of benefit payment may vary from month to month or at another interval.

SETTLEMENT OPTIONS

Generally, an annuity owner does not set a precise retirement income goal in advance. Instead, the retirement benefit becomes the amount that can be provided by the savings accumulated by retirement time. Further, the amount accumulated is a function of the amount of your contributions, their timing, and the rates of investment return credited to your account over time. This concept is illustrated in figure 23–1. If you die before you begin annuity payments, the accumulation value is returned to your beneficiary. When the annuitant lives until the liquidation period and selects an income option based on the life expectancy of the annuitant alone, it is considered a **single life annuity.**

FIGURE 23–1

Hypothetical Values for the Flexible Premium, Deferred Annuity Concept

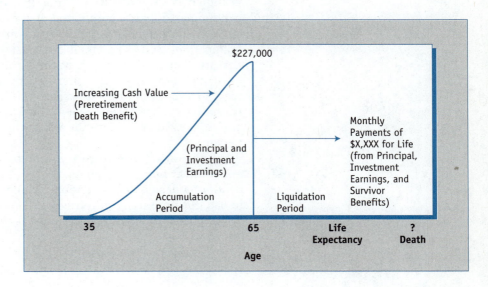

Your originally specified beginning liquidation (retirement) date can be moved forward or backward, if you want a change. Upon retirement, you have several options:

- lump sum cash payment
- fixed period payment
- fixed amount payment
- life annuity
- refund annuity
- temporary life annuity
- period certain life annuity
- a joint life annuity
- a joint and survivor annuity

The typical options include taking cash in a lump sum equal to the accumulation value of the contract. A **fixed period annuity** makes payments for a specified period, such as twenty years, and then ceases. A **fixed amount annuity** pays benefits of a set amount per period until the accumulation value at the time benefits begin plus investment earning during the liquidation period are exhausted. The amount paid under these three options is not influenced by anyone's life expectancy.

When the owner selects an option based on the life expectancy of the annuitant, minimum lifetime amounts of payouts per dollar accumulated apply and are based on guarantees made by the insurer at the beginning of the contract. The guarantees reflect a minimum guaranteed interest rate and assumed rates of mortality. These guarantees throughout the life of the contract constitute the major way in which annuities during the accumulation period differ from mutual funds. The owner pays for the guarantee through a mortality charge (for example, a 0.25 percent annual charge) levied on the accumulation fund.

An annuity in which benefit payments are guaranteed for life, but cease and the premium considered fully earned upon the death of the annuitant, is known as a **life annuity.** While this annuity pays the maximum periodic benefit per dollar accumulated at the time benefits begin (or per immediate single premium), far more common is the selection of a payment option that, under specified circumstances, provides benefits to another person following the death of the annuitant. Most people do not like the idea that they might die shortly after beginning to receive benefit payments from an annuity in which they have made a large investment. Insurers have, therefore, made available refund annuities, period-certain life annuities, and annuities that reflect the life expectancies of more than one person.

A **temporary life annuity** is a combination of a fixed period annuity and a life annuity. Payments stop at the end of a specified period or at the death of a designated individual, whichever comes first. You might choose to use this option if you retire early (e.g., at age 55) and want income from the annuity until other retirement benefits such as Social Security begin at age 62.

A **period-certain option** guarantees a minimum number of annuity payments whether you live or die. Thus, you can purchase a life annuity with five years certain, ten years certain, or some other period certain. If the annuitant dies before the end of the specified period, payments continue to a beneficiary for at least the period specified. A cash payment may be available to the beneficiary equal to the present value of the remaining payments. If the annuitant lives through the period certain, payments continue until the death of this person.

A **refund annuity** is one which guarantees that the annuitant and/or beneficiary will receive minimum payments, during the liquidation period, equal to the single premium in an immediate annuity or the accumulation value in a deferred annuity. For example, assume an accumulation value of $250,000 at the time of annuitization and that the annuitant receives $100,000 before death. The beneficiary would receive a lump sum payment of $150,000. The annuitant is also promised lifetime benefits. Consequently, benefits can far exceed the accumulation value at the time of annuitization, plus future investment earnings on this amount. The annuitant pays for the refund feature by taking a reduced amount of periodic benefit compared to that for a life annuity.

With a **joint annuity,** two people are named and payments stop when the first joint annuitant dies. In contrast to the joint annuity, a **joint-and-survivor annuity** continues payments as long as two specified people live, plus the remainder of the life of the last to die (i.e., the survivor). A husband and wife are the typical users of the joint-and-survivor option. The annuitant can decide at the time of annuitization for the amount available to the survivor to be the same as that received when both parties were living. Alternatively, the decision can be made at the time of annuitization for the amount available to the survivor to be reduced (e.g., to 50 percent or 66.66 percent of the original amount).

Some annuitants want the full refund guaranteed by the refund option, while others are satisfied with a period certain guaranteed. Others select a joint or joint-and-survivor option because of concern for another person, possibly over their lifetime. The effect of such guarantees is to reduce the monthly installments that can be purchased with any given sum of money. The option selected depends upon one's situation and viewpoint. Figure 23–2 presents a classification of annuities and their features.

TYPES OF CONTRACTS

Annuities commonly used to help fund retirement include:

- the flexible premium annuity
- the single premium deferred annuity
- the single premium immediate annuity

All three are available with fixed-dollar guarantees or as a variable annuity.

The **flexible premium deferred annuity** allows you to change the amount of contributions, stop contributions, and resume them at will. For example, you may use a payroll deduction plan in which you authorize your employer to transfer $100 per pay period to the insurer. For a period of time you may want to discontinue these contributions and later resume them at $200 per pay period.[17] Without payroll deductions you might pre-

....

17. Most payroll deduction annuities are part of a tax-deferred program. Tax-deferred programs for individuals will be discussed later in this chapter.

FIGURE 23–2

Classification of Annuities

1. Method of Premium Payment
   A. Single premium
   B. Installment premiums
2. Commencement of Benefits
   A. Immediate
   B. Deferred
3. Denomination of Accumulation Values and Benefits
   A. Fixed dollar
   B. Variable dollar
4. Settlement Options
   A. Without life contingencies
      1. Lump sum payment
      2. Fixed period payments
      3. Fixed amount payments
   B. With single life contingencies
      1. Life annuity—no refund
      2. Temporary life annuity
      3. Period-certain life annuity
      4. Refund life annuity
   C. With joint life contingencies
      1. Joint life annuity
      2. Joint-and-survivor life annuity

fer to submit premiums on a monthly, quarterly, annual, or some other basis. Earlier in the chapter, we referred to this as the installment plan.

For fixed dollar annuities, the insurer guarantees a minimum rate of interest. Initially, a current rate of return (for example, 8 percent) will be promised on funds in your account for a certain time (for example, two years) during the accumulation period. As returns vary over time on your insurer's investments that support fixed dollar annuities, the guarantee for future periods is likely to change. The degree of change may reflect partly the need for your insurer to remain competitive with annuity returns offered by other insurers, bank certificates of deposit, and other competing investment vehicles. Often, two or more interest guarantees are made by the insurer. One set of guarantees applies to funds contributed to your account in past periods. The other rate applies to funds you contribute during a future period. For example, at the time this material was written, the Teachers Insurance and Annuity Association had announced the rates reflected in table 23–2.

During the liquidation period (typically, retirement years), a fixed dollar periodic annuity payment is based on a guarantee of your principal and an investment return between 3 and 4 percent. Additional investment earnings are shared with you through dividends. Annuitants who die before life expectancy forfeit some principal and/or interest that creates a "survivor benefit" to continue payments to those who live beyond life expectancy.

The **single premium deferred annuity** differs from a flexible premium deferred annuity primarily in the manner of premium payments. As the name implies, only one premium is paid. The motivation for purchase usually is driven more by the tax deferral of interest on earnings than by the promise of lifetime income during retirement. Another difference between the single premium deferred annuity and its flexible premium cousin is the longer period to which the current rate of interest is

TABLE 23-2
....
Fixed Dollar Annuity Interest Guarantees

FOR AMOUNTS CONTRIBUTED	EFFECTIVE ANNUAL INTEREST RATE
Future Period of:	
1/1/95–6/30/95	7.50%
Past Period of:	
10/1/94–12/31/94	7.25%
7/1/94–9/30/94	6.75
1/1/93–6/30/94	6.50
1/1/91–12/31/93	7.15
Prior to 1991	7.15

SOURCE: "TIAA Traditional Annuity New Rates," Teachers Insurance and Annuity Association, New York, December 1994.

guaranteed (above the absolute minimum of 3 to 4 percent that applies during the lifetime of the contract). With the single premium annuity, the initial current rate may be promised for three or more years. At the end of this period, you may renew the annuity at a new current interest rate that applies for one or more years.

Mortality expense charges were described earlier. Other expense loads will be explicit or implicit both for fixed dollar and variable contracts. Many insurers have either no sales load or a low sales load. This feature is often accompanied by a *surrender charge* (a percentage attached to withdrawals) that applies during the first five or more years. For example, 7 percent of the amount withdrawn can be retained by the insurer if your contract is surrendered for its cash value in the first year. The penalty decreases 1 percent per year, disappearing at the end of the seventh year. The surrender charge has two purposes. First, it discourages withdrawals. Second, it allows the insurer to recover some of its costs if the contract is terminated early.

The agent or broker may receive a normal level of sales commission on no-load and low-load annuities, but the commission is not deducted directly from your contributions. Instead, the insurer must pay the difference between the commission and any sales charge deducted directly from you, from its "profits." For example, the insurer may be earning 8 percent on investments and crediting 7.5 percent to fixed dollar annuity accounts. The spread of 0.5 percent will not produce a profit for the insurer for this product line until all expenses associated with the product have been recovered. A surrender charge helps provide funds to cover the commission and other expenses when the contract has not stayed in force long enough to produce enough profit to cover the commission.

Annual expense charges levied on all assets are usually around 2 percent. Part of this charge is used to pay marketing expenses. Recently, several organizations (including discount investment brokerage firms, mutual funds, and life insurers) have begun issuing no-load variable annuities that are sold without surrender charges.[18] (Fixed dollar annuities with the same insurers maintain surrender charges. This discourages surrenders of contracts where the insurer guarantees the value of principal and might be forced to liquidate investments while financial markets are depressed.) In addition, their annual expense charges are about half of the usual 2 percent

....
18. Variable annuities are described more thoroughly later in this chapter.

average. Some of the no-load (really "low-load") products are designed for distribution by fee-only financial planners; others are sold directly over the phone, in banks, or by mail.

The **single premium immediate annuity** is best understood by emphasizing the word "immediate." Benefit payments to the annuitant begin on the next payment date following the premium payment, usually a large sum. The primary purchase motive would typically be interest in lifetime income. A primary source of funds for these annuities is lump sum distributions from corporate retirement plans (see chapter 20). Other sources of funds include various forms of personal investment and life insurance death benefits.

Another use of annuities arises out of legal liability judgments. As explained in chapter 7, personal injuries often result in a liability insurer making a lump sum payment to cover some combination of general, specific, and punitive damages. Liability insurers are increasingly interested in making periodic payments to the plaintiff, to lower the total cost of the liability. A **structured settlement annuity** is a special type of single premium immediate annuity that achieves the goal. Issued by a life insurer, its terms are negotiated by the plaintiff, the defendant, their attorneys, and a structured settlement specialist. The market for structured settlement annuities is highly competitive. Consequently, the successful insurer in this market is likely to have a high rating for financial soundness (see chapter 25), a competitive assumed rate of investment return, and a mortality assumption that reflects the plaintiff's life expectancy. Life expectancy for the plaintiff may be shorter than average as a result of his or her injury.

Variable Annuities

Variable annuities are more complicated than fixed-dollar annuities. Their nature is clarified by a discussion of objective and mechanics.

Objective: Stable Purchasing Power When people think of future income needs, they usually think in terms of today's dollars. What they will really need is a constant purchasing power, regardless of future price levels. The objective of a variable annuity is to provide this purchasing power stability. The contract is expressed in terms of units rather than dollars. The theory underlying the variable annuity is the same as that underlying variable life insurance (see chapter 14). That is, certain investments, primarily equities, are expected to keep pace with inflation over the long run.

Mechanics In the variable annuity, two types of units are employed: accumulation units and annuity units. Some accounts invest primarily in variable-dollar assets such as common stocks and real estate. Investments are made in separate accounts like those that fund variable life insurance. The value of each unit varies with the current market value of the underlying investments in the portfolio.

When you pay the periodic premium in dollars, you are credited with a number of **accumulation units,** the number to be determined by (1) the amount of your premium and (2) the current market value of an accumulation unit. For example, if the monthly premium after expenses is $50 and the current value of a unit is $10, you are credited with five units. If the current value of a unit has changed to $9.52 when you pay your next $50 premium after expenses, you are credited with 5.25 units. If, the value of a unit is $10.42 when you pay the premium, you are credited with 4.80 units. As you pay the premium month after month and year after year, you accumulate units of investment (accumulation units) rather than dollars, as would be the case with a conventional annuity. Your *surrender value, or maximum withdrawal,* at a specific point in the accumulation period is:

(Total number of units × Current market value per unit) −
Surrender charge, if any = Surrender value

This same calculation determines the death benefit received by your beneficiary if you die during the accumulation period.

When you reach the liquidation period, **annuity units** are exchanged for accumulation units. The determinants of your dollar income are: (1) the number of units to which you are entitled considering your age, sex, and settlement option, (2) the current market value of each unit, and (3) an assumed investment return, such as 4 percent. If the market price of the investments purchased by the annuity company for its separate account rises above the assumed investment return, your income will rise. If the investment return declines below the assumed return, your income will decline, hence the name "variable annuity." This contrasts with a fixed dollar annuity payout that will remain at the exact same dollar amount (e.g., $1,079.68 per month) for the remainder of the annuitant's life (assuming a life annuity option). However, excess interest payments or dividends may be made.

Many variable annuities offer a choice of investment media. The choices are similar to those for a family of mutual funds. In fact, some variable annuities are funded by a family of mutual funds rather than by separate accounts maintained by the insurer. For example, your variable annuity might offer the following separate accounts:

1. Money market.
2. Long-term commercial bond fund.
3. High-grade common stocks.
4. Balanced fund with bonds and stocks.
5. Growth stocks.

You could divide your funds among two or more accounts in a manner that reflects your personal risk propensity. Then you could pursue a long-run investment strategy by maintaining this mix (e.g., 40 percent long-term bonds, 40 percent high-grade common stocks, and 20 percent growth stocks) until your risk propensity shifts.

Alternatively, you could place all your funds in one account and then periodically transfer funds to another account, subject to contractual limitations. Limitations control the number of transfers between accounts and/or the amount that may be transferred during a contract year. If you wanted to try to increase returns by predicting interest rates, you might keep funds in the short-term money market account when you believe long-term bond rates are low. Then, when you think long-term bond rates are high, you could switch to this account. You could later switch to common stocks, perhaps when you think interest rates have fallen near a new low and a bull market for growth stocks is beginning. As you near retirement, you might prefer a mix of 40 percent bonds and 60 percent high-grade common stocks. These are just a few examples of how a managed annuity lets you develop a personal investment strategy. It does not assure that you will earn higher returns than might be realized with a regular fixed dollar or another variable annuity for which the insurer's investment department chooses the mix of assets. But many individuals think they can forecast money and capital markets and thus time the markets. Annuities offering a choice of investments are designed for these people.

A Word of Caution   It is clear that fixed dollar annuities are unsatisfactory during periods when the dollar is depreciating rapidly in value, but there are legitimate risks associated with the variable annuity as well. After experiencing success during the stock market boom of the 1950s and 1960s, variable annuity owners faced a lackluster performance by common stocks in the 1970s. During the 1980s, up until this chapter was written in the mid-1990s, performance again became very attractive because of rapidly rising common stock prices.

Figure 23–3 confirms the effect of investment market performance on the unit values for the oldest variable annuity in the United States, the College Retirement Equities Fund. End-of-year accumulation unit values are plotted for the twenty-five years from 1970 through 1994. This annuity began with an accumulation value of $1.00 per unit in 1952. By 1970 the unit value was $6.17, ending at $69.86 in 1994. End-of-year values were lower than those for the previous year in five of the twenty-five years. The accompanying annuity unit values (not shown) for retirees reflected greater variability and less overall growth than accumulation unit values because the calculation of the number of annuity units to which one is entitled assumes that investment returns will be at a specified percentage. The mid-1970s brought significant decreases in annuity payments for retirees holding this variable annuity. The values did not reach the 1972–1973 level again until 1981–1982. Since then, experience has been pleasing. Such is the nature of variable insurance products. The entire investment risk is borne by the owner, negative and positive. There are no minimum guaranteed rates of return, as there are for fixed dollar annuities.

Taxation of Annuities

Now we examine how funds in annuities are affected both by income taxes and estate taxes. The discussion of income tax is divided into the accumulation period and the liquidation period.

INCOME TAXATION DURING THE ACCUMULATION PERIOD

The first major tax question is: Can individuals deduct annuity contributions (premiums) from adjusted gross income each year? Generally, premiums are not deductible. A "yes" answer to the question requires that you qualify for one of several tax-deferred programs. Tax-deferred programs for persons who are "employees" include Individual Retirement Annuities (IRAs); employer-sponsored Internal Revenue Code (IRC) Section 401(k) savings/profit sharing plans; IRC Section 403(b) plans for employ-

FIGURE 23–3

Accumulation Unit Values for the College Retirement Equities Fund: 1969–1994

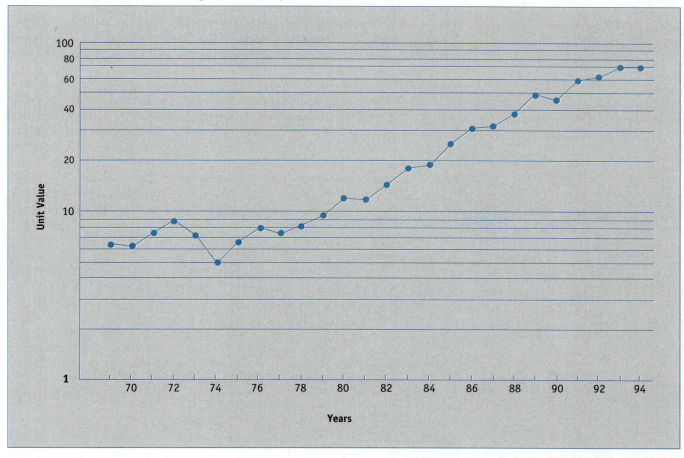

SOURCE: "Charting TIAA and the CREF Accounts" (New York: Teachers Insurance and Annuity Association College Retirement Equities Fund, 1993) and TIAA-CREF Quarterly Summary, 1993 and 1994.

ees of educational and certain other tax-exempt organizations; and IRC Section 457 plans for state and local government employees.

If you are self-employed you are eligible for tax-deferred contributions if you establish a Keogh plan or a Simplified Employee Plan. Without establishment of one of these two plans, as a self-employed person you are eligible to make tax-deferred IRA contributions. Except for IRAs, these plans were described in chapter 20 because of their frequent ties to employment.

The interest of individuals in deferred annuities increased significantly after 1974 when **IRAs** were first authorized by Congress. The Tax Reform Act of 1986 reduced their attractiveness among higher-income people, but left the program essentially unchanged for others.[19]

19. At the time this material was written, Congress was considering three proposals to modify IRA restrictions. All three would allow early withdrawals for college expenses, first-time home buying, major medical expenses, and long-term unemployment. Two of the three propose qualifying more people to make contributions.

Who is eligible to make tax-deferred IRA contributions? *If you are not a participant in an employer-sponsored retirement plan in a particular year,* you can make contributions up to $2,000 per year (or 100 percent of your earned income if you make less than $2,000). *If you participate in an employer-sponsored retirement plan* (that is, an employer makes contributions or provides credits on your behalf), the maximum amount of tax-deferred IRA contribution depends on income earned from work, but not from investments, Social Security, and other nonemployment sources. The relationship is shown in table 23–3. Single people earning less than $25,000 and married couples filing a joint income tax return with less than $40,000 are eligible not to pay current income taxes on contributions up to $2,000 per year. Above these income levels, tax-deferred contributions are phased out. Single people earning more than $35,000 and married couples earning in excess of $50,000 have zero tax-deferred contribution limits. If you are married and make an IRA contribution, you may also contribute up to $250 into a spousal IRA for a spouse with no earned income. The spousal account must be separate from your IRA or be a subpart of your account. The accounts cannot be joint.

People who are not eligible to make tax-deferred IRA contributions and those who were allowed to contribute less than $2,000 (because they were single with earnings between $25,000 and $35,000 or married joint-filers with earnings between $40,000 and $50,000) may still make nondeductible IRA contributions. If you are ineligible to make tax-deferred contributions, you can contribute up to $2,000 per year on a nondeductible basis. If, instead, your income level allowed you to make a tax-deferred contribution of less than $2,000, you may make a nondeductible contribution up to the difference between $2,000 and your tax-deferred contribution for the year. For example, if you are single and earn $30,000, you are eligible to contribute:

1. *Tax-deferred.*
   $[(\$30,000 - \$25,000) \div 10,000] \times \$2,000 = \$1,000$

2. *Nondeductible.*
   $\$2,000 - \$1,000 = \$1,000$

The advantage of making tax-deferred contributions to any of the several tax-deferred, "qualified" programs is the deferral of income taxes until you withdraw the funds from the annuity (or other tax-deferred plan such as a mutual fund). Ideally, withdrawal takes place in retirement, many years in the future. If you had not made the qualified contributions, a

TABLE 23–3

Maximum Tax-Deferred IRA Contributions for Retirement Plan Participants

INCOME LEVEL	CONTRIBUTION LIMIT
1. Individual earning less than $25,000	$2.000
2. Married couple filing jointly with earnings less than $40,000	$2.000 per wage earner; $2,250, including a spousal IRA when the spouse has no earned income
3. Single person with earnings greater than $25,000	$2.000 minus [(Adjusted Gross Income − $25,000) ÷ 10,000] times $2,000 = Maximum Contribution*
4. Married person filing jointly with earnings greater than $40,000	$2.000 minus [(Adjusted Gross Income − $40,000) ÷ 10,000] times $2,000 = Maximum Contribution*

*Subject to minimum contribution of $200 when the result is more than zero.

significant portion (e.g., 28 percent marginal federal tax plus 7 percent marginal state tax) would have gone to government treasuries in the years they were earned. When contributions are made to qualified plans, the money that would otherwise have gone to pay income taxes earns investment returns, along with the remainder of your contributions.

Income taxes are also deferred on annuity investment earnings. This is the rule whether or not an individual qualifies for tax deferral of contributions.

During the accumulation period, there are no income taxes due *unless* you make premature withdrawals or surrenders. Such events, however, subject you to income taxes and potential tax penalties. All dollars withdrawn from tax-deferred annuities are subject to income taxation. The first dollars withdrawn from post-1982 non-tax-deferred annuities are taxable up to the point that they equal the sum of your investment earnings (i.e., the "interest first" rule). After this point, withdrawals create a nontaxable return of your cost basis (usually the sum of premiums paid).[20]

Further, a 10 percent federal penalty tax applies to premature withdrawals (i.e., those prior to age 59 1/2). The penalty does not apply to:

1. Withdrawals due to death.
2. Withdrawals due to disability.
3. Payments taken in essentially equal installments over your life expectancy (or the joint life expectancy of you and your spouse).
4. Withdrawals allocable to contributions made before August 14, 1982.
5. Withdrawals from a structured settlement contract.

The penalty taxes have the purpose of encouraging savings for retirement. The use of annuities as short-term, tax-deferred investments is discouraged.

In summary, certain contributions and all investment earnings for annuities, fixed dollar and variable, escape income taxes during the accumulation period. The exception is premature withdrawals.

INCOME TAXATION DURING THE LIQUIDATION PERIOD

All payments from a tax-deferred annuity are subject to ordinary income taxes during the liquidation period. Remember that neither contributions nor investment earnings have been taxed. Liquidation must begin by April 1 of the year after you reach age 70 1/2 to avoid penalties. Lump-sum payouts are subject to five-year tax averaging. This usually produces more taxes than payments over an extended period such as your remaining lifetime.

For non-tax-deferred annuities, you need to pay ordinary income taxes on the return of previously untaxed investment earnings. The amount of each payment representing previously taxed contributions is not taxable. Each payment is divided between taxable and nontaxable amounts at the beginning of the payout period by calculating an **exclusion ratio.** The ratio is then multiplied by each periodic payment to determine the amount of each annuity payment that is excluded from gross income. The exclusion ratio is:

$$\frac{\text{Investment in Contract}}{\text{Expected Return}}$$

20. For annuities purchased before August 14, 1982, withdrawals are subject to the cost recovery rule. This rule allows full recovery of the cost basis first; then subsequent withdrawals are taxable.

Your investment is the sum of nonqualified contributions minus any dividends you have either received in cash or used to reduce required premiums. The expected return is the product of a fixed payout period or your life expectancy (in years based on a government table) multiplied by each year's expected payout.[21] For example, assume $100,000 has been contributed. This amount becomes the numerator of the ratio. For the denominator, assume an annual payment of $9,600 (i.e., $800 per month) and a life expectancy of 26.04 years. Thus, the "expected return" is $249,984, and dividing this amount into $100,000 tells us that 40 percent of each payment will be excluded from income. If you die before life expectancy, your estate qualifies for a tax adjustment. If you began the liquidation period after 1986 and you live beyond the life expectancy used in the calculation, all payments thereafter are fully taxable because your full investment in the contract was previously received.[22]

ESTATE TAX TREATMENT

IRC Section 2039 governs the federal estate taxation of annuities. If you die during the accumulation period for your annuity, the entire cash value becomes part of your gross estate. Marital and other deductions are unaffected by the annuity.[23]

Death during the liquidation period creates no increase in the value of your gross estate if the annuity payments stop at your death. For example, a life annuity option or a period-certain life annuity option where the annuitant lived beyond the period certain would discontinue payments at the death of the annuitant. However, if payments are to continue to the estate or another person following the death of the annuitant, the present value of those payments are includable in the gross estate. The present value calculation discounts for both interest and the probability of the beneficiary's death. Refund options and the joint-and-survivor option often result in benefits for survivors. If the survivor is the spouse of the owner, the payments should qualify for the marital deduction. If the deceased annuitant had paid only a part of the contract's purchase price (e.g., a spouse had made 60 percent of the contributions), only this proportionate share of survivor benefits is included in the gross estate. The same rule limits the amount included when death occurs during the accumulation period.

This chapter has been divided into two major segments: one covering how to plan for retirement and the other describing the fundamental nature of annuities. The need for individual retirement planning is important because income from Social Security and employer-provided retirement plans is often less than an individual's desired level of retirement income. We have demonstrated the usefulness of spreadsheets in determining how much to contribute to retirement savings. Annuities have the unique feature of providing options guaranteeing lifetime income. They often play a major role in individual retirement planning.

21. Adjustments must be made for the value of the contingent beneficiary's interest created by a period certain or other refund feature.
22. Any excess interest payments or dividends are fully taxable in the year they are paid.
23. Proceeds received from life insurance settlement options (see chapter 15) are taxed with the same exclusion ratio as described for nonqualified annuities. See chapter 22 for the method of determining federal estate taxes.

Consumer Applications

Understanding Historical Rates of Return for Different Investment Instruments

Historical investment returns help us form expectations about the future performance of certain types of investments. A positive relationship between investment risks and long-run expected returns is a well-accepted concept in investment management. That is, individuals can expect to earn more in the long run (defined, perhaps, as more than ten years) by investing in higher-risk instruments. This strategy helps achieve retirement objectives; however, a random survey of United States residents over age 25 shows substantial distaste for financial risk. Those willing to take different levels of risk were: 44 percent only minimal risk, 33 percent average risk for average gain, 17 percent above-average risks, and 5 percent substantial risk for substantial gain. Males, younger respondents, those with at least some college education, and those with annual household incomes of $25,000 or more were more likely to express willingness to take average or higher financial risk.[24]

HISTORICAL RETURNS[25]

Historical returns are presented for several major types of securities in table 23–4. The period covers 68 years, including the stock market boom of the late 1920s, the 1929 stock market crash, World War II, the historically high bond interest rates in the 1979–1982 period, the historically high depreciation in bond prices during 1994, and other abnormal periods. Inflation between 1926 and 1994 averaged 3.1 percent, with a standard deviation of 4.6 percent.

Market performance since 1945 excludes the Great Depression of the 1930s and World War II. Is this a better period on which to base forecasts? During this later period, geometric, compound, mean returns by broad category were: treasury bills, 4.7 percent; intermediate-term government bonds, 5.6 percent; long-term government bonds, 5.0 percent; long-term corporate bonds, 5.3 percent; large company common stocks, 11.9 percent; small company common stocks, 14.4 percent. After adjustment for inflation (an average of 4.4 percent) since 1945, inflation-adjusted average returns (and risk) for the two periods would be quite similar. Undoubtedly, short-run future returns will differ widely from long-run averages. Who knows if future long-run averages will approach historical ones? This is one major risk inherent in seeking higher returns.

TABLE 23–4

Geometric Mean Total Returns and Standard Deviations for Major Categories of Securities: 1926–1994*

CATEGORY	GEOMETRIC AVERAGE	STANDARD DEVIATION**
U.S. Treasury Bills	3.7%	3.3%
Intermediate-Term Government (U.S.) Bonds	5.1	5.7
Long-Term Government (U.S.) Bonds	4.8	8.8
Long-Term Corporate Bonds	5.4	8.4
Large Company Stocks***	10.2	20.3
Small Company Stocks	12.2	34.6

*Total returns consist of income return, capital appreciation, and reinvestment of dividends and interest.

**The standard deviation in returns is a common measure of financial risk, reflecting variability in returns. The higher the standard deviation, the higher the risk.

***Large company stocks are defined as those in the Standard & Poor's 500 Stocks index.

SOURCE: *Stocks, Bonds, Bills, and Inflation,* 1995, p. 118.

24. *Retirement Confidence in America: Getting Ready for Tomorrow* (Washington: Employee Benefit Research Institute, Special Report SR-27, Issue Brief Number 156, December 1994): p. 11.

25. The long-run returns presented in this section cover the period of 1926 through 1994. They were obtained from *Stocks, Bonds, Bills, and Inflation 1995 Yearbook* (Chicago: Ibbotson Associates, 1995).

personal resources
income replacement ratio
retirement income objective
investment plan
lump-sum distributions
life annuity
owner
annuitant
beneficiary
installment plan
single premium
accumulation period
accumulation value
liquidation period
immediate annuity
deferred annuity
fixed dollar annuity
variable annuity

single life annuity
fixed period annuity
fixed amount annuity
life annuity
temporary life annuity
period-certain option
refund annuity
joint annuity
joint-and-survivor annuity
flexible premium deferred annuity
single premium deferred annuity
single premium immediate annuity
structured settlement annuity
accumulation units
annuity units
IRAs
exclusion ratio

Discussion Questions

1. What are the three major sources of retirement income in the United States? What uncertainties exist for a relatively young person in projecting these sources into retirement years?

2. What constitutes "personal resources" in the individual retirement planning process?

3. Describe two methods of quantifying a person's (or couple's) retirement planning objectives.

4. Describe the assumptions that must be made in the typical retirement planning calculation. What data would one normally gather at the beginning stage of this planning process?

5. Name the tax-deferred retirement programs that may be available to help fund the personal resources segment of a person's retirement plan.

6. Under what circumstances might a risk-averse person decide to take a life annuity income option?

7. Under what circumstances might a joint life annuity be suitable?

8. Why do you suppose the flexible premium annuity is the most popular form of deferred annuity?

9. Who assumes the investment risk in variable annuities? Does the same party assume mortality and operating expense risk?

10. What is the primary way in which a single premium deferred annuity differs from a flexible premium deferred annuity? How might the typical motivations for purchase differ for investors in these two types of annuities?

Cases

23.1 Like most people, Dr. Richard Beneventano, a sole-practitioner psychiatrist, has waited until his 40s to become serious about retirement planning. He will reach age 45 next month; his net earnings are $95,000 per year, he wants to retire at age 65, and he desires to maintain the same standard of living during retirement years as he enjoys now. Assume Dr. Beneventano anticipates 4 percent annual growth in his income between now and age 65.

1. Project his income to the year before retirement for the purpose of determining his potential standard of living at that time.

2. Since he has decided on a 75 percent replacement ratio, how much will his retirement income objective be at age 65?

23.2 Use a spreadsheet to calculate the percentage of future income Dr. Beneventano should plan to invest between ages 45 and the beginning of age 65 if he is to attain his retirement income objective (see Case 23.1). Assume the following:

a. He is eligible for a Keogh tax-deferred retirement plan.

b. His Keogh plan, established ten years ago, is of the defined contribution type (see chapter 20) and has a current account balance of $100,000.

c. He plans to continue allocating Keogh contributions partly to a government bond fund and partly to a variable annuity separate account invested in high-grade common stocks. The average expected combined, after-expense return is 9 percent both in the accumulation and liquidation periods.

d. The same retirement funding vehicles and the same investment return assumptions apply to postretirement years.

e. Retirement income is expected to keep pace with a 3.5 percent inflation assumption.

f. Social Security benefits for Dr. Beneventano and his homemaker spouse, at his age 65, are expected to equal 16 percent of age 64 income.

g. Social Security benefits are expected to increase annually at a 3.5 percent inflation rate.

h. There are no additional vested retirement benefits.

i. By retirement time, his home mortgage and children's college expenses are expected to be fully paid.

j. Recognizing that most of the risk of "living too long" will be hedged through the use of a variable annuity, assume the postretirement period terminates at the end of his age 84.

1. Based on the assumptions shown above, determine the annual shortfalls (gaps) between Dr. Beneventano's retirement income objective and sources of income (from Social Security and the current Keogh balance). Calculate the present value of these shortfalls as of age 65.

2. Determine the annual contribution between ages 45 and 65 that is required to fund his retirement objective, expressed as a percentage of his increasing stream of future income.

23.3 Mrs. Abigail Dozier, age 66, is asking your advice about how to use a lump-sum distribution of $500,000 she expects in three months from her employer's money purchase retirement plan. She is single, has no close relatives, lives in a rented condominium, and has nonretirement certificates of deposit valued at $75,000. She wants to leave, at her death, the balance of her nonretirement fund assets to Bard College, her alma mater. She hopes the balance will be substantially more than the current $75,000 value. In addition to Social Security benefits, her lifestyle, including travel and treatment of a chronic (non-life-threatening) health problem, will require liquidation of approximately 90 percent of the $500,000 lump-sum distribution over her twenty-year life expectancy.

1. What financial instrument is designed to keep Mrs. Dozier (and others) from being without income due to having lived beyond the time a principal sum is liquidated by periodic withdrawals that include principal?

2. Help Mrs. Dozier decide between fixed dollar and variable annuities, or a combination of the two.

3. Assume Mrs. Dozier uses 90 percent of her lump-sum ($450,000) to purchase a variable annuity that offers a family of separate accounts. How would you recommend that she divide her funds between (1) a money market account, (2) a corporate bond account, (3) a high-grade, large-companies common stock account, and (4) a small-companies common stock account? Further assume she needs an expected long-run return of 8 percent. (Hint: You may want to read this chapter's Consumer Applications before answering this question.)

P
A
R
T

IV

Insurance Markets and Regulation

The Insurance Institution

Introduction   As a risk manager for a family or organization, you will make better decisions when you know about different types of insurers and the work performed by their employees. Knowledge of insurers will help you select among the approximately 5,700 U.S. insurers and lead you to an appropriate insurer for your particular needs. In a search for glass insurance or a homeowner's policy, you do not want to waste time contacting a life-health insurer. For personal automobile insurance, you might want to know about reciprocals.

As an educated person, you will want a historical perspective on how the insurance industry has evolved to its current configuration. Thus, we begin with a short history of insurance.

At the end of the chapter, you will have considered:
1. How the social device called insurance developed.
2. The types of private organizations that provide insurance.
3. The types of government organizations that provide insurance.
4. The career opportunities in insurance.

Development of Insurance

Because of a lack of reliable records, there are differences of opinion concerning the origin of insurance. Something similar to modern insurance may be discerned, however, in certain historical developments.

ANCIENT PRACTICES

Perhaps the earliest forerunner of property insurance was a scheme used by merchants in Babylonia several thousand years ago. They engaged sales representatives to sell goods in faraway places. To assure the return of the representatives with the merchants' shares of the profits, the representatives were required to pledge their own property as a guarantee. In the beginning, a sales representative who was robbed while away from home sacrificed the pledged property, just as in the case of dishonesty. This arrangement, however, created too heavy a burden for the sales representatives and led to a new system in which the pledge was not forfeited if a loss was caused by robbery, provided it was not the fault of the representative. Thus, the risk was shifted from the sales representative to the merchant. This system soon spread to all kinds of shipping in Phoenicia and other parts of the ancient world.

A similar shifting of risk originated in ancient Greece. When a Greek moneylender financed a voyage for a shipowner, the ship or its cargo was pledged as collateral for the loan. When the ship was pledged as collateral, the contract was called a **bottomry** contract; cargo as collateral created a **respondentia** contract. With either, the lender agreed that the loan would be canceled if the ship or cargo failed to return. In effect, the lender insured the ship or its cargo for the amount of the loan. The incentive for the moneylender was an interest charge that was larger than the percentage charged on loans for less risky ventures. The charge covered both a normal rate of interest and a charge for risk. The charge for risk was called a **premium,** the term that is still used to describe the financial consideration in insurance transactions.

The forerunners of modern life and health insurance are found in ancient Greece and Rome. In Greece, religious groups collected funds from their members for funeral services, providing what was probably the first form of burial insurance. The Romans adopted similar arrangements for life insurance. Their schemes, however, were open to the general public. In some cases, rather broad forms of coverage for death, disability, and pensions were developed for particular groups, such as soldiers.

MIDDLE AGES

During the Middle Ages, trade associations (or guilds) contributed to the development of insurance by establishing insurance schemes financed by *regular payments* from their members. Guilds paid benefits for a wide variety of losses, such as those caused by fire, shipwreck, theft, and flood. The guild system also offered health benefits similar to those currently available through health insurance companies. Loss of sight, serious illness, and old-age dependency were compensable by insurance.

There is no general agreement concerning just when marine insurance (or transportation) contracts came into existence. It appears, however, that contractual marine insurance may have been written as early as the middle of the fourteenth century. By the middle of the fifteenth century, rules governing the conduct of the business had been adopted by several Mediterranean port cities.

MODERN DEVELOPMENT

In 1574, the English Parliament created a Chamber of Insurance to sell marine insurance. Later, instead of roaming the streets looking for business, risk-bearers adopted the practice of meeting in coffeehouses to transact business. One coffeehouse proprietor, Edward Lloyd, attracted risk-takers to his establishment by gathering risk-related shipping news, which he published as *Lloyd's News*. The popularity of his coffeehouse among insurers ultimately led to the establishment of Lloyd's of London in 1769. We discuss modern aspects of Lloyd's later in this chapter.

During this period, a marine insurance company was also formed in Paris to compete with individual underwriters. Later, British law enabled King George to grant charters to two marine insurance companies, that were subsequently empowered to write fire and life insurance also. The risk-bearers became known as *underwriters* because of their practice of signing their names under the contracts on which they were willing to assume part of the insurable risks.

Even though London had disastrous fires in every century from the eighth to the thirteenth, fire insurance developed slowly. After four centuries without a conflagration, the Great Fire of London in 1666 caused such huge losses of property and life that attention was called to the problem of inadequate fire insurance. Dr. Nicholas Barbon responded by building houses to replace those which had been destroyed and offering fire insurance to the purchasers. In 1667, he established the world's first fire insurance company, known as the Fire Office.

One of the first life insurance policies to be offered by professional insurers was a term policy written by a group of marine underwriters in London on the life of William Gibbons, early in the sixteenth century. The first life insurance organization, as measured by modern standards, was the Society of Assurance for Widows and Orphans. It was established in London in 1699 for the purpose of paying a stipulated amount at the death of a member. It collected premiums weekly and selected insureds on the basis of health and age. The oldest life insurance company in existence today is the Society for the Equitable Assurance of Lives and Survivorship, usually called "Old Equitable." Established in England in 1756, it originated such practices as a *grace period* for premium payment and the payment of *dividends* to the policyowner.

DEVELOPMENT IN THE UNITED STATES

The major development of insurance in the United States began after the colonies became independent. Prior to that time, most insurance was written by foreign insurers. Although some small United States marine insurers did a thriving business, most insurers were hampered by a lack of capital. In 1792, however, the Insurance Company of North America was established. Its success encouraged the formation of other marine companies; by 1800, more than thirty had been created. Marine insurance grew as the United States merchant fleet grew.

Fire Insurance

Fire insurance in the United States developed as a result of the formation of fire-fighting companies. Benjamin Franklin helped establish the Union Fire Company in Philadelphia in 1730, and the movement spread to other cities. One of the first United States fire insurance companies was The Friendly Society in Charleston, South Carolina. Founded in 1735, it went out of business after a major fire swept the city in 1740. The Philadelphia Contributionship for the Insurance of Houses from Loss by Fire was formed in 1752. It issued perpetual policies financed by earnings from the large deposits made by insureds. Establishment of other fire insurance companies soon followed. The Insurance Company of North America added fire insurance to its marine business in 1794, and by the end of the century fourteen fire insurers had been formed.

In the nineteenth century, fire insurance companies evolved to their present status. Early in the century, fire insurers were small and operated in relatively small areas. The disastrous fire of 1835 in New York City showed the necessity for spreading such risks. From that time on, fire insurance companies built their businesses on a much broader geographical base. As a result, they were able to survive disasters such as the Chicago fire of 1871 and the San Francisco earthquake and fire of 1906. Over time, fire insurance evolved into "property" insurance, with protection for numerous other perils in addition to fire.

Life Insurance

Early life insurance policies in the United States were issued by individual underwriters for short terms at high premium rates. The first permanent life insurance organization in the United States was the Presbyterian Ministers' Fund, established in 1759. In 1794, the Insurance Company of North America became the first United States commercial company to write life insurance. The oldest incorporated insurance company still writing life insurance is the Mutual Life Insurance Company of New York (1842). In 1988, the number of life insurers reached an all-time high of 2,343, declining to 1,840 companies at the end of 1993. The decrease reflects many mergers and consolidations motivated by the need to lower operating expenses in smaller companies that did not benefit from economies of scale.

From Specialization to Affiliated Groups

Other forms of insurance, such as inland marine and liability insurance, developed during the nineteenth century. At that time, insurers were licensed only for specified types, or "lines," of insurance. A company, for example, could write fire insurance but not life insurance, life insurance but not marine insurance. To fill the need for more than one kind of insurance, multiple insurers were created. This led to the formation of fleets, or groups, of companies that could offer several different types of insurance under one management. Eventually, a movement to abandon insurance compartmentalization was successful in getting changes in legislation.

Today, all states permit **multiple-line underwriting,** which enables a single insurer to write all types of insurance (other than life-health insurance) in one policy. Many multiple-line property-liability insurers also have an affiliate or subsidiary writing life-health insurance. For example, in 1982 the Insurance Company of North America (primarily a multiple-line property-liability insurer) merged with the Connecticut General Life Insurance Company (a large life-health insurer) to form the CIGNA Corporation. CIGNA offers insurance products and related services to handle all exposures faced by the typical family and the typical business (including global exposures) or governmental organization. Other large insurers offering both life-health and property-liability contracts include Aetna, ITT-Hartford, Allstate, Nationwide, and State Farm.

Other large insurers, such as Equitable Life (of New York), New York Life, and Northwestern Mutual have chosen to remain concentrated in the life, annuity, and disability income areas of insurance. Northwestern Mutual has also specialized in the needs of individuals and small businesses, as opposed to larger organizations. The Hartford Steam Boiler Group is an example of a property-liability insurer that specializes in boiler and machinery insurance and open perils property insurance for commercial facilities, both domestically and globally.

Property-liability business is conducted by approximately 3,900 U.S. companies. However, 900 companies conduct virtually all the business; the ten largest companies issue over 40 percent of all U.S. property-liability policies. The largest company services 12 percent of the market. Concentration is even greater in the personal market, where the largest insurer, State Farm, in 1993 covered 23 percent of the homeowner's market and 19 percent of the personal automobile market. Total property-liability premiums are split fairly evenly between commercial and personal lines. Private automobile insurance alone accounts for almost 40 percent of total property-liability premiums.[1]

Financial Services

A recent development affecting insurers in the United States is the movement toward organizations that offer a full line of financial services, insurance being only one. A financial services firm offers investments, money market funds, tax assistance, insurance, and other services needed by individuals and families in the management of their personal finances. These services are often marketed through the financial planning technique.

The financial services movement created new competition for insurers and their agents. Securities firms like Merrill Lynch are now offering banking and insurance services. Commercial banks such as Citibank and Nations Bank are expanding their role in offering insurance and investment services. Regulation still provides barriers between banking, securities, and insurance; however, these barriers are gradually being broken.

DEVELOPMENT INTERNATIONALLY

Insurance has three multinational dimensions:

1. U. S. domestic insurers (that is, those organized in the United States) often buy or sell reinsurance from or to insurers in other countries.

---

1. *The Fact Book 1995: Property/Casualty Insurance Facts* (New York: Insurance Information Institute, 1995): pp. 7–9.

2. U. S. domestic insurers often follow clients with multinational operations to provide them complete service.

3. Insurers open operations in other countries to expand their markets and diversify risks, thus becoming multinational in scope.

International insurance in the form of reinsurance has existed for centuries. The worldwide growth of "jumbo" exposures, such as fleets of wide-bodied jets, super tankers, and off-shore drilling platforms, creates the potential for hundreds of millions of dollars in losses from one event. No single insurer wants this kind of loss to its income statement and balance sheet. One mechanism for spreading these mammoth risks among insurers is the international reinsurance market. Approximately 15 percent of the world's property-liability insurance premium volume is written as reinsurance. Nearly three-fourths of this business is conducted outside the United States.

In 1992, the world spent approximately $1.5 trillion on insurance premiums. The U. S. leads the world in total insurance premiums (35.6 percent of total 1992 expenditures) and is the major consumer of property-liability premiums (50.9 percent). Japan leads the world in the consumption of life-health insurance, with 34.6 percent of expenditures in this category. Other leading consumers of insurance include Germany, United Kingdom, France, South Korea, Canada, Italy, The Netherlands, and Spain. Switzerland led the world in 1992 per capita insurance premiums ($2,923), followed by Japan ($2,576), the U. S. ($2,068), Luxembourg ($1,935), and the United Kingdom ($1,769). Direct international comparisons, however, have less significance than you might think because the need for private insurance varies greatly with degrees of socialism and with different rules (laws) for deciding when one party is liable for injury to another.

Whereas the largest insurance markets are in the developed economies, the fastest growing markets are in developing economies. Premiums in the Latin American region were growing annually at 13.2 percent, 8.5 times as fast as the U.S. market during the same period. However, insurance markets in most Latin American countries are relatively underdeveloped because of the instability that has characterized these economies.[2]

Private Insuring Organizations

Private insuring organizations are owned and controlled by private citizens, rather than by the government. They engage in risk-bearing for a fee. In some cases, the objective is to make a profit. In other cases, it is to provide insurance at cost.

Insurance is offered by several types of insurers:

1. Stock.

2. Mutual.

3. Reciprocal.

4. Lloyd's of London.

2. *The Fact Book 1995: Property/Casualty Insurance Facts,* pp. 11–12.

5. Lloyds Associations.

6. Savings bank.

7. Health care plans.

The first five types are sometimes referred to as **commercial insurers.**[3] Insurance is a sideline for savings banks, and they are not considered commercial insurers; nor are health care plans, which originated primarily as prepayment plans rather than risk-bearers.[4] The various types of private insurers have more common characteristics than differences, but each has distinguishing features.

STOCK INSURERS

Stock insurers are organized in the same way as other privately owned corporations created for the purpose of making a profit. Individuals provide the operating capital for the company by purchasing its stock. As stockholders, they own the firm and elect its board of directors. The stockholders are induced to invest their funds in the firm by the prospect that it will earn a profit. If the firm operates successfully, the value of their investment will increase as the firm grows. Thus, they may benefit by both income from stockholder dividends and appreciation in the market price of the stock. Stockholders may or may not be policyowners of the stock insurer. In either event, they have the option of disposing of their ownership interest by selling their stock.[5]

Much of the insurance issued by stock insurers has fixed premiums without policyowner dividends or other refunds. Thus, they are "nonparticipating." Stock insurers in fact cannot issue assessable policies. Assessable policies contain provisions allowing the insurer to demand, before a policy expires, an increase in the premium quoted when the contract began. Stock insurers can, however, issue participating insurance contracts containing provisions that allow insurers to return a portion of the premiums to policyowners. Some contracts, such as universal life policies, have participating features even though they technically are nonparticipating.

Participating insurance differs from nonparticipating insurance by having a refund, or dividend, feature. **Dividends** are paid to policyowners at the end of each policy year. The funds to pay dividends typically come from two sources. The first is an extra charge in the initial participating premium. For example, a participating life insurance premium may be set at 110 percent of what the nonparticipating premium (e.g., a universal life target premium) would be for the same insurance. Over time, all of this

---

3. Commercial insurers (i.e., private as opposed to governmental) sell both personal and commercial lines. Types of insurance are discussed in chapter 3.

4. Health care plans such as Blue Cross and Blue Shield, dental service plans, health maintenance organizations, and preferred provider organizations were discussed in chapter 19. Our discussion in this chapter is confined to the other types of insurers.

5. A unique type of stock company is the so-called "captive insurer." Such an insurance company is owned solely by the organization for which it provides insurance. This may be one firm or a group such as a trade association. The captive is likely to provide insurance to others also. Tax incentives encourage the generation of at least half of the captive's income from sources other than the parent firm.

extra charge is expected to be refunded as dividends. Extra (redundant) premium charges are uncommon among property-liability insurers. The second source of funds to pay policyowner dividends is a share of the insurer's *profit*. To be competitive with mutuals and self-insurance schemes, stock insurers frequently use refund features in certain insurance plans (for example, group health and workers' compensation) that are sold to employers.

To attract prospective insureds, stock companies emphasize the services they render and the capital and surplus of the company, as well as the reserves, that help to guarantee payment of claims. The insurer bears the risk as an entity separate and apart from the insureds. Stock companies predominate in property-liability insurance and are especially strong in commercial lines of property-liability. In addition, they had issued 59.5 percent of all life insurance in force at the end of 1993.[6]

MUTUAL INSURERS

Mutual insurers are owned and controlled, in theory if not in practice, by their policyowners. They have no stockholders and issue no capital stock. People become owners through policyowner dividends of the company by purchasing an insurance policy from it. Profits are shared with owners. Officers who run the company are appointed by a board of directors that is, at least theoretically, elected by policyowners. The stated purpose of the organization is to provide low-cost insurance, rather than to make a profit for stockholders. Insurance is only a low-cost bargain when managers employ specific techniques to (1) keep operating expenses low, (2) avoid the payment of invalid claims, and (3) maximize investment portfolio returns.

Recent research shows that mutual and stock insurers are highly competitive in the sense that neither seems to outperform the other. There are high-quality, low-cost insurers of both types. A wise consumer will want to analyze both before buying insurance.[7]

Many *mutuals* in both the life-health and property-liability fields are of great size and operate over large areas of the country. This is particularly true in life insurance, where the largest insurers are mutuals. Until a mutual reaches the financial requirements (e.g., size of capital and surplus) for a stock company of the same type, it must issue assessable policies. At this point, nonassessable premiums are charged.

These large mutuals do a general business in the life-health and property-liability insurance fields, rather than confining their efforts to a small geographic area or a particular type of insured. In 1950, they had about two-thirds of the life insurance in effect in the United States. Now, 110 mutuals have a little over 40 percent of the business and manage approximately 39 percent of assets held by the life-health sector of the insurance industry.[8]

6. *Life Insurance Fact Book, 1994* (Washington: American Council of Life Insurance), p. 19.
7. Mayers, D. and Smith, C., 1986, "Ownership Structure and Control: The Mutualization of Stock Life Insurance Companies," *Journal of Financial Economics,* 16, pp. 73–98 and McNamara, M. and Rhee, G., 1992, "Ownership Structure and Performance: The Demutualization of Life Insurance," *Journal of Risk and Insurance,* 59, pp. 221–38.
8. *Life Insurance Fact Book, 1994* (Washington: American Council of Life Insurance), pp. 108–109.

Mutuals in the property-liability sector are overshadowed by stock companies, which have over two-thirds of the business. The property-liability mutuals, however, have grown more rapidly than stock companies in recent decades by offering very competitive rates in the rapidly growing personal automobile and homeowners insurance markets.

There are several types of mutual insurers other than the general mutuals discussed above. They include county or farm, class or specialty, factory, perpetual, and fraternal companies. The key features of each type are described in the appendix to this chapter.

RECIPROCAL INSURERS

Reciprocals are similar to mutuals in that both are formed to provide insurance at cost, rather than to make a profit for a third party. Each policyholder in a pure reciprocal, however, insures part of the risk of each of the other policyholders. If there were 100 insureds in the group, for example, and each had the same value at risk, each would, in effect, say to the other, "I will pay 1 percent of your losses if you will pay 1 percent of mine." The reciprocal itself is not liable to policyholders; instead, they are liable to each other. In a mutual, on the other hand, assets belong to the insurer, which is liable to policyholders. The reciprocal holds assets contributed by the policyholders as premiums, but the assets are pooled and each policyholder beneficially owns a proportionate share of that pool.

Whereas a mutual is incorporated, a reciprocal is unincorporated. Whereas a mutual is controlled by a board of directors, reciprocals are managed by an attorney-in-fact, whose powers are enumerated in a power of attorney granted by the policyholders. Part of the premium is paid to the attorney-in-fact for his or her services in soliciting business and managing the operations of the reciprocal, and the balance is credited to separate accounts maintained for each insured. When losses are paid, each insured's account is charged with his or her proportionate share of the loss. At the end of the year, funds remaining in each account may be left in the reciprocal or paid back to each insured as a dividend.

Reciprocals in their pure form are a minor, declining type of insurer. They are still strong in the western U.S., especially as writers of personal automobile insurance. The Farmers Insurance Exchange of California held a 5.6 percent national market share of automobile insurance in 1993; only State Farm (18.9 percent market share) and Allstate (10.6 percent market share) have more automobile business. The bulk of reciprocal business is now written by **interinsurance associations,** which are more like mutuals than the pure reciprocals described in this section. They do not keep separate accounts for each member, and losses and expenses are not prorated among insureds. Furthermore, insureds do not have a claim to any portion of surplus funds. The United States Automobile Association is of this type. In 1993, it sold 2.8 percent of all U.S. automobile insurance and 3.1 percent of homeowners insurance.[9]

....
9. *The Fact Book, 1995: Property/Casualty Insurance Facts* (New York: Insurance Information Institute, 1995), pp. 8–9.

LLOYD'S OF LONDON: A GLOBAL INSURANCE EXCHANGE

Lloyd's of London, the oldest insurance organization in existence, conducts a worldwide business primarily from England; it is also licensed in Illinois and Kentucky. It maintains a trust fund in the U.S. for the protection of insureds in this country. Approximately 40 percent of its total business is on U.S. exposures, 10 percent is on European exposures, and the remainder is from the rest of the world.

In states where Lloyd's is not licensed, it is considered a "nonadmitted" insurer. States primarily allow such nonadmitted insurers to sell only coverage that is unavailable from their licensed (admitted) insurers. This generally unavailable coverage is called **surplus lines insurance,** and it is Lloyd's primary U.S. business.[10]

Lloyd's does not assume risks in the manner of other insurers. Instead, individual people called "Names" do. Names, who are members of Lloyd's, accept insurance risks by providing capital to an underwriting syndicate. Each syndicate is made up of many Names and accepts risks through one or more brokers. Surplus lines agents in the United States direct business to brokers at one or more syndicates. Syndicates, rather than Names, make the underwriting decisions of which risks to accept. Various activities of Lloyd's are supervised by two governing committees—one for market management and another for regulation of financial matters.

The arrangement is similar to that of an organized stock exchange in which physical facilities are owned by the exchange but business is transacted by the members. The personal liability of individual Names is unlimited; they are legally liable for their underwriting losses under Lloyd's policies to the full extent of their personal and business assets. This point is sometimes emphasized by telling new male members that they are liable "down to their cufflinks," and for female members "down to their earrings."

In addition to Names being required to make deposits of capital with the governing committee for financial matters, each Name is required to put premiums into a trust fund that makes them exclusively encumbered to the Name's underwriting liabilities until the obligations under the policies for which the premiums were paid have been fulfilled. Underwriting accounts are audited annually to assure that assets and liabilities are correctly valued and that assets are sufficient to meet underwriting liabilities. Normally, profits are distributed annually. Following losses, Names may be asked to make additional contributions. A trust fund covers the losses of bankrupt Names. A supervisory committee has authority to suspend or expel members.

Seldom does one syndicate assume all of one large exposure; it assumes part. Thus, an individual Name typically becomes liable for a small fraction of 1 percent of the total liability assumed in one policy. Historically, syndicates also reinsured with each other to provide more risk sharing.

The practice of sharing risk through reinsurance within the Lloyd's organization magnified the impact of heavy losses incurred by Lloyd's members for 1988 through 1992. Losses for these five years reached the

----

10. In addition to large organizations like Lloyd's, nonadmitted insurers include many offshore captives and other entities that sometimes have little, if any, capitalization (see chapter 26 for more on nonadmitted insurers).

unprecedented level of $14.2 billion. Reinsurance losses on U.S. business were a major contributor to these losses: long-tail liability claims due to asbestos and pollution, Hurricanes Hugo and Andrew, the 1989 San Francisco earthquake, the Exxon Valdez oil spill, and product liabilities.

The massive losses wiped out the fortunes of many Names. In 1953 Lloyd's consisted of 3,400 Names, most of which were wealthy citizens of the British Commonwealth. By 1989, many less wealthy, upper-middle-class people had been enticed to become Names with unlimited liability, pushing the total number of Names to an all-time-high of 34,000 in 400 syndicates. By mid-1994, only about 17,500 Names and 178 underwriting syndicates (with only 96 accepting new business) remained. As a result of the mammoth total losses (and bankruptcy or rehabilitation for many individual members), Lloyd's had reduced underwriting capacity and was experiencing difficulty in attracting new capital. What started in a coffeehouse was getting close to the inside of the percolator.

Among Lloyd's reforms was the acceptance of corporate capital. By mid-1994, 15 percent of its capital was from 25 corporations that, unlike Names, have their liability limited to the amount of invested capital. Another reform consisted of a new system of compulsory stop loss insurance designed to help members reduce exposure to large losses. Reinsurance among syndicates has ceased.

Lloyd's, an organization that reports its underwriting results with a three-year lag, was expected to be profitable in 1993 and subsequent years. Its capacity is very important in both surplus lines and reinsurance markets. Thus, its return to profitability is important around the world.[11]

LLOYDS ASSOCIATIONS OF THE UNITED STATES

There is no connection between Lloyds Associations of the United States and Lloyd's of London. **Lloyds Associations**—sometimes called "American Lloyds"—are corporations, partnerships, or associations made up of individuals who join together to offer insurance. Each individual assumes a specified portion of the liability under each policy and specifies a maximum amount of liability. The liability of each individual is limited. Rather than operating through syndicates like Lloyd's of London, Lloyds Associations are managed by an attorney-in-fact. Several have failed over the years.

INSURANCE EXCHANGES

Organizations similar in design to Lloyd's of London began business in Florida, Illinois, and New York during the early 1980s. The primary purpose of these **insurance exchanges** was to increase the financial ability of the United States insurance industry to handle reinsurance needs and

11. Parts of this discussion have been based on "Lloyd's Chairman to Address Annual Conference," *Coverage,* Vol. 2, No. 2 (February 1993): pp. 1–2; "David Rowland: Lloyd's of London One Year Later," *Coverage,* Vol. 3, No. 5 (July 1994): p. 5; "Lloyd's Lost £2.048 Billion in 1991," *National Underwriter,* Property & Casualty/Risk Management ed., No. 21 (May 23, 1994): pp. 1 and 42; "The Deficit Millionaires," *The New Yorker* (Sept. 1994): pp. 74–93; and "Lloyd's Lost £ Billion in 1992," *National Underwriter,* Property & Casualty/Risk and Benefits Management (February 6, 1995): p. 2.

ETHICAL *Dilemma*

Management Practices at Lloyd's of London

Undoubtedly, numerous factors contributed to the recent worst losses in the history of Lloyd's of London. Other insurers overcame the lower operating expense advantage that had been held by Lloyd's, resulting in greater price competition by the 1980s, and multiple natural disasters were the most devastating in history. Yet, what role was played by questionable management practices? Instead of several layers of reinsurance each being held by a separate insurer (or syndicate at Lloyd's) in the 1980s, Lloyd's placed several layers in the same syndicate as well as among syndicates. Each time a layer of reinsurance was placed, a syndicate underwriter received a share of the premium and a broker received a commission, yet all risk still remained with Names. When one syndicate accepted several layers of risk on the same exposure, several commissions were paid to brokers but the same Names held the risks.

Could the motivating force behind reinsurance practices at Lloyd's in the 1980s have been greed for excessive brokerage commissions, resulting in less premium remaining to pay losses borne by Names? Likewise, where any line of insurance in the U. S. is compulsory (e.g., workers compensation insurance), should agent/broker commissions (including Lloyd's business) be less than on voluntary business to reflect less marketing effort? (Of course, competition for market share would remain intense among insurers.) To what extent did Lloyd's have a moral responsibility to see that investors (Names) meet a "risk suitability" test, especially considering the unlimited personal liability they assumed? Does this responsibility extend beyond disclosure of basic facts?

insure unusual exposures without relying heavily on Lloyd's of London. Because of large losses, the Florida and New York exchanges closed in 1987. The Illinois exchange is still in operation, concentrating on large property-liability exposures.

BANKS AND INSURANCE

For decades, savings banks in Massachusetts, New York, and Connecticut have sold life insurance in one of two ways: by establishing life insurance departments or by acting as agents for other savings banks with insurance departments. Savings banks sell the usual types of individual life insurance policies and annuities, as well as group life insurance. Business is transacted on an over-the-counter basis or by mail. No agents are employed to sell the insurance; however, advertising is used extensively for marketing. Insurance is provided at a relatively low cost.

In recent years, many savings and loan associations have been selling personal property-liability insurance (and some life insurance) through nonbanking subsidiaries. Commercial banks have lobbied hard for permission to both underwrite (i.e., issue contracts and accept risks as an insurer) and sell all types of insurance. Approximately two thirds of the states have granted state-chartered banks this permission. At this time, national banks have not been granted such power.[12] Perhaps the two main arguments for allowing banks to enter the insurance business are:

1. To allow them to develop into full-service financial institutions.
2. To reduce insurance marketing costs.

Critics claim that insurance marketing costs (particularly commissions to agents) are excessive. If banks could make more sales per marketing person by spending less time locating clients, the costs of marketing insurance might fall, especially in the area of personal life-health insurance that (for all except a few companies) pays high commissions in the first year of a sale. Insurance agents have lobbied to keep banks out of the insurance business, claiming that a bank might coerce borrowers to place their insurance with the bank. Bankers deny that they would put any pressure on borrowers.

The U.S. Supreme Court recently approved (with a 9–0 vote) the sale of fixed-dollar and variable annuities by national banks, reasoning that annuities are investments rather than insurance. In 1995, banks sold about 20 percent of all annuities.[13] Consequently, this Supreme Court decision did not answer the question of whether banks will gain unlimited powers to underwrite and/or sell all types of insurance. Banks can be expected to continue to pursue this goal through Congress and the courts.

Government Insuring Organizations

Federal and state government agencies account for nearly half of the insurance activity in the United States. Primarily, they fill a gap where private insurers have not provided coverage (in most cases, because the exposure does not adequately meet the ideal requisites for private insurance). However, some governmental programs (e.g., the Maryland automobile fund, state workers' compensation, insurance plans, crop insurance, and a Wisconsin life plan) exist for political reasons. Government insurers created for political goals usually compete with private firms. This section summarizes state and federal government insurance activities. Most of the programs were discussed in detail in earlier chapters.

STATE INSURING ORGANIZATIONS

1. All states administer unemployment compensation insurance programs.
2. All states also have **guaranty funds** to assure that the burden of insurance company failure will not be borne solely by certain poli-

12. Except that national commercial banks in communities of less than 5,000 have for many years had the right to sell insurance.
13. John R. Wilke and Leslie Scism, "Under the Gun: Insurance Agents Fight an Intrusion by Banks, but Other Perils Loom," *The Wall Street Journal,* Vol. CCXXVI, No. 26 (August 8, 1995): p. 1.

cyowners. Covered lines of insurance and maximum liability per policyowner vary by state. Financing is provided on a post-loss assessment basis (except for pre-loss assessments in New York) by involuntary contributions from all insurance companies licensed in the state. An insurer's contributions to a particular state are proportionate to its volume of business in the state. No benefits are paid to stockholders of defunct insurers. The funds are responsible for obligations of insolvent companies to their policyowners.

3. Eighteen states have funds to insure workers' compensation benefits; some are monopolistic, while others compete with private insurers.

4. Several states provide temporary nonoccupational disability insurance, title insurance, or medical malpractice insurance. Many states provide medical malpractice insurance through **joint underwriting associations** (JUA). JUAs are created by state legislation which gives them the power to assess all insurers writing liability insurance in the state if the JUA experiences losses in excess of its expectations. However, rates are supposed to be set at a level adequate to avoid such assessments. Some states have also created JUAs for lawyers and other groups that have experienced insurance availability problems in the private market.

5. Seven states along the Atlantic and Gulf coasts assure the availability of property insurance, and indirect loss insurance in some states, to property owners of coastal areas exposed to hurricanes and other windstorms. Insurance is written through **beach and windstorm insurance plans.** Compliance with building codes is encouraged for loss reduction.

6. The state of Maryland operates a fund to provide automobile liability insurance to Maryland motorists unable to buy it in the private market.

7. The Wisconsin State Life Fund sells life insurance to residents of Wisconsin on an individual basis similar to that of private life insurers.

8. In recent years, several states have created health insurance pools to give uninsurable individuals access to health insurance. Coverage may be limited and expensive.

FEDERAL INSURING ORGANIZATIONS

1. The Social Security Administration, which operates the Social Security program, collects more premiums (i.e., taxes) and pays more claims than any other insurance organization in the U.S.

2. The Federal Deposit Insurance Corporation insures depositors against loss caused by the failure of a bank. Credit union accounts are protected by the National Credit Union Administration. The Securities Investor Protection Corporation covers securities held by investment brokers and dealers.

3. The Federal Crop Insurance Corporation provides open-perils insurance for farm crops. Policies are sold and serviced by the private

market. The federal government provides subsidies and reinsurance.

4. The Federal Crime Insurance Program covers losses due to burglary and robbery in both personal and commercial markets. In 1995 the coverage was available in eleven states and the Virgin Islands, where availability problems exist in the private market.

5. Fair Access to Insurance Requirements (FAIR) plans have been established in a number of states under federal legislation. They are operated by private insurers as a pool to make property insurance available to applicants who cannot buy it in the regular market. Federal government reinsurance pays for excessive losses caused by riots and civil disorder.

6. The National Flood Insurance Program provides flood insurance through private agents in communities that have met federal requirements designed to reduce flood losses. Most of the 2.8 million flood policies have been written through the Write Your Own (WYO) program, in which private insurers sell and service their own flood policies. The federal government accepts all underwriting risks (i.e., all losses and expenses that exceed income from the program).

7. The Veterans Administration provides several programs for veterans.

8. Several agencies insure mortgage loans made by private lenders against losses due to borrowers failing to make payments.

9. The Pension Benefit Guaranty Corporation protects certain retirement plan benefits in the event the plan sponsor fails to fulfill its promises to participants.

10. The Overseas Private Investment Corporation protects against losses suffered by U.S. citizens through political risks in underdeveloped countries.

Careers in Insurance

The purpose of this section is to provide enough information about careers in the insurance business so you can decide whether or not you should investigate the opportunities. The discussion also will give you a better understanding of functions performed by insurers.

INSURANCE EMPLOYMENT

The insurance business in the United States employs over two million people. About 30 percent are engaged in marketing and related services; the rest perform other functions. Insurance agents are the "visible minority" in the insurance business. For every agent you see, there are two or more other people working directly for insurers in less visible but equally important jobs. About 60 percent of those employed in the industry work for life-health companies, 40 percent for property-liability insurers.

To call attention to the variety of jobs in insurance, one company refers in a recruiting advertisement to "our 2,400 different job descriptions." Table 24–1 provides some examples. Some of the jobs listed are common to

TABLE 24-1

A Sample of Insurance-Related Jobs

FINANCE AND INVESTMENTS	
Actuary	Investment manager
Director of Finance	Securities analyst

MARKETING	
Agent	Broker representative
Advanced underwriting consultant	Employee benefit representative
Bonding representative	General agent
Branch manager	Pension consultant
Broker	Special agent

UNDERWRITING	
Medical director	Underwriter

ADMINISTRATION	
Accountant	Personnel manager
Customer service representative	Premium auditor
	Risk manager

COMPUTER SYSTEMS	
Systems analyst	Programmer

LOSS CONTROL	
Loss control engineer	

LEGAL	
Government relations	Legal counsel

CLAIMS	
Claims adjuster	Claims processor
	Private investigator

INDUSTRY-RELATED POSITIONS	
Employee benefit consultant	Regulator
Financial planner	Risk management consultant
Public adjuster	

all types of business organizations. Others, such as the actuary, the claims adjuster, the risk management consultant, and the underwriter, are closely associated with insurance. Positions such as those in employee benefits and risk management may also be held in noninsurance organizations.

You can gain some understanding of careers in insurance by observing the flow of an insurer's operations. We will describe briefly careers in each of the following functional areas of an insurance operation, as well as some insurance-related careers:

1. Management.
2. Actuarial.

3. Marketing.

4. Underwriting.

5. Administration.

6. Investments.

7. Legal.

8. Claims.

Management

As in other organizations, an insurer needs competent managers to plan, organize, direct, control, and lead. The insurance *management* team functions best when it knows the nature of insurance and the environment in which insurers conduct business. Although some top management people are hired without backgrounds in the insurance business, the typical top management team for an insurer consists of people who learned about the business by working in one or more functional areas of insurance. If you choose an insurance career, you will probably begin in one of the functional areas discussed below.

Actuarial

What is an **actuary?** An actuary is a highly specialized mathematician who deals with the *financial* and *risk* aspects of insurance. This individual determines proper rates and reserves, certifies financial statements, participates in product development, and assists in overall management planning.

Many large companies hire college graduates, primarily with majors in actuarial science, mathematics, or statistics, for entry-level actuarial positions. These trainees are expected to demonstrate technical expertise by passing the examinations required for admission into either the Society of Actuaries, for life-health actuaries, or the Casualty Actuarial Society, for property-liability actuaries. Passing the examinations requires a high level of mathematical knowledge and skill. Actuarial department employees are frequently given incentives such as time off for study during working hours and reimbursement for books and tuition. Passing all ten examinations required for a designation is expected to take several years. Many actuaries work for insurance companies, while others are employed by government or private consulting firms.[14]

Marketing

Most marketing positions involve direct sales. However, product development, advertising, market research, direct mail sales promotions, and other activities that support the sale of an insurer's contracts are conducted by salaried specialists in the home office. Most insurance is sold by **agents** (that is, sales representatives) who make face-to-face contacts with buyers. A number of agency arrangements have evolved for marketing insurance

---

14. For futher information about actuarial careers, write to: Society of Actuaries, P.O. Box 95668, Chicago, IL 60694, or Casualty Actuarial Society, 1100 N. Glebe Road, Suite 60, Arlington, VA 22201.

in the United States. In some respects these agencies are similar, but they also exhibit significant differences, particularly when the system used in life-health insurance is compared with that in property-liability insurance.[15] Although some insurers have been successful selling without a sales force, most rely entirely on local sales agents. The apparent assumption underlying the heavy reliance on agents is that most of us do not like to think that losses will happen to us. We like to believe that losses only hit others. Thus, we do not face our own need for insurance without an agent selling (motivating) us. Effective salespeople can earn large incomes in the insurance industry. In the process, they help people and organizations with an important part of their financial planning and risk management programs.

Salaried experts are available to help agents with complicated sales. For example, an **advanced underwriting consultant** is a problem solver and source of information for a life insurance company's sales force in the technical aspects of business insurance and estate planning. This job involves both researching technical material and working with agents on a one-to-one basis. A law degree helps the consultant understand the application of tax and other laws to advanced insurance planning.

An **employee benefit representative** helps agents and brokers sell life, health, retirement, and other insurance for employee benefit plans, installs the plans after they are sold, and provides continuing service to employers. This job requires both technical knowledge of the employee benefits field and the ability to work with agents, employers, and employees.

A **bonding representative** works with agents and their clients on financial and technical matters concerned with qualifying for contract bonds. After an intensive company training program, the bonding representative is considered an expert who frequently deals with contractors, engineers, attorneys, and top management in virtually all types of businesses. The representative's recommendation plays an important part in the bonding company's decision to write contract bonds involving large sums of money.

Underwriting

An **underwriter** decides whether or not to insure exposures on which applications for insurance are submitted. When the underwriter decides that insurance can be issued, his or her next decision is the proper premium rate. Premium rates are determined for classes of insureds by the actuarial department. An underwriter's role is to decide which class is appropriate for each insured.

Underwriters must exercise sound judgment. For example, if an applicant has a history of arson, an underwriter would not issue insurance even on "fireproof" property. Underwriters work closely with insurance agents; insurance majors often choose this career.

A **loss control engineer** surveys the facilities of a company that applies for insurance and provides crucial information for the underwriting department. After insurance has been provided, recommendations designed to reduce losses are made following regular safety inspections. This service

15. The different types of marketing systems are explained in chapter 25.

helps keep the insurer informed about the risks it has assumed and helps reduce premium levels for the insured.

Administration

After insurance is sold, records must be established, premiums collected, customer inquiries answered, and many other administrative jobs performed. Administration is defined broadly here to include accounting, information systems, office administration, customer service, and personnel management.

Investments

Investment income is a significant part of total income in most insurance companies. Liability accounts in the form of reserves are maintained on balance sheets to cover future claims and other obligations. Assets must be maintained to cover the reserves and still leave the insurer with an adequate net worth. Assets consist of bonds, mortgages, stocks, and other investments. Security analysts and investment managers are employed to attain the highest possible investment income, subject to the constraints imposed by state insurance laws and prudent management principles. Investment department employees, are typically expected to have majored in finance. Many insurers require an MBA degree with a specialization in finance.

Legal

Law pervades insurance industry operations. *Lawyers* help draft insurance contracts, interpret contract provisions when claims are presented, defend the insurer in lawsuits, communicate with legislators and regulators, and help with various other aspects of operating an insurance business.

Claims

The **claims adjuster** is the person who represents the insurer when the policyholder presents a claim for payment. Relatively small property losses, up to $500 or so, may be adjusted by the sales agent. Larger claims will be handled by either a *company adjuster* (an employee of the insurer) or an *independent adjuster*. The independent adjuster is an employee of an adjusting firm that works for several different insurers and receives a fee for each claim handled.

As a claims adjuster your job would include (1) investigating the circumstances surrounding a loss, (2) deciding whether the loss is covered (or excluded) under the terms of the contract, (3) deciding how much should be paid if the loss is covered, (4) paying valid claims promptly, and (5) resisting invalid claims. The varying situations give the claims adjuster opportunities to use knowledge of insurance contracts, investigative abilities, knowledge of law, skills of negotiation, and tactful communication. Most of the adjuster's work is done outside the office or at a drive-in automobile claims facility. Satisfactory settlement of claims is the ultimate test of an insurance company's value to its insureds and to society. Like underwriting, claims adjusting requires substantial knowledge of insurance.

Insurance-Related Careers

Many insurance specialists are employed by noninsurance organizations as consultants, risk managers, regulators, and so on. Financial planners and consultants offer advice for a fee. Some large financial planning firms include an insurance specialist, an investments expert, a tax specialist, and so on. Risk managers perform the risk management function as it was described in chapter 2. The position requires substantial knowledge of insurance as well as other risk-financing methods. The interest of organizations in protecting assets and employees and also managing the liability exposure makes risk management a challenging and rewarding career. Insurance regulators work for state governments and perform the regulatory functions discussed in the last chapter of this book.

SATISFYING CAREERS

The jobs we have discussed are only a small sample of the career opportunities in insurance. Most have the same two requirements in common. First, employers prefer college graduates, although an insurance major is not usually required. What insurers and agencies are looking for is a person with excellent communication skills, strong drive, and the ability to learn. If you want to become an actuary, however, you must have a mathematics background. If you want to become legal counsel for an insurance company, you must have a law degree.

Second, there is a strong emphasis on continuing education and training. Many students who enter the insurance business are surprised to learn that graduation from college does not mean the end of studying. Promotions and personal development are enhanced by pursuing education and training programs, some in-house and others external. These are part of a satisfying career.

Pursuing a Career in Insurance

Whatever your interest may be, there is an insurance job for you. Some require specialized knowledge and skills, but many are similar to other kinds of business. Specific information can be obtained from (1) insurance company publications, (2) insurance company offices where you live, (3) local insurance agents, (4) your college placement office, and (5) various associations of insurance specialists.

It may be a good idea to find out how an insurance career could satisfy your interests so you can compare it with other alternatives. How do you find out about insurance careers?

IF YOU HAVE ANOTHER YEAR OF COLLEGE

If you are a typical full-time student, you probably have time to get some job experience and learn about the insurance business firsthand. The available options include (1) a part-time job during the school year, (2) a full-time job during summer vacation, (3) an internship, and (4) volunteer work with an insurance organization.

How do you find a summer or part-time job in the insurance field? First, contact your college placement or cooperative education office. Second, contact insurance company offices in your area. There may be some home offices or branch offices; look in the Yellow Pages. Third, contact insurance agency offices in your area (also in the Yellow Pages). They may have a job for you. In any event, they will be eager to help young people who express an interest in an insurance job. Fourth, you, your parents, or someone else you know may have bought insurance from someone. Contact that "someone" and tell them you are looking for a job in insurance. Fifth, association managers and staff know what's going on in the business and hear about jobs from time to time.

The associations include:

- Certified Employee Benefits Specialists
- Independent Insurance Agents
- National Association of Independent Brokers
- Professional Insurance Agents
- Risk and Insurance Managers Society
- Society of Chartered Life Underwriters and Chartered Financial Consultants
- Society of Chartered Property and Casualty Underwriters

What is an internship and how do you get one? An internship is a temporary, part-time employment arrangement between a student, an employer, and a college or university. Its purpose is to give the student a sample of the business through on-the-job experience. Generally, you are paid by the employer and granted academic credit by your college or university. Figure 24–1 is an excerpt from an internship report for a University of South Carolina student who interned with a life insurance company one semester. It shows some of the special assignments for which she was responsible. Your faculty adviser can help you get this experience.

IF YOU ARE GRADUATING THIS YEAR

1. Decide whether you prefer direct sales or an entry-level position in another insurance company function.
2. Register with your college placement service.
3. Study insurance company recruiting brochures.
4. Interview every insurance recruiter who visits your campus.
5. Write to several insurance organizations you would like to work for, including a resume (addresses can be found in *Best's Reports*).
6. Tell your insurance agent you want an insurance job.
7. Tell your faculty adviser you want an insurance job.

FIGURE 24–1

Internship Project

Project: Policy Filings—State of Indiana. Our company filed all policy forms in Indiana upon approval for admission. Several policy forms were disapproved and had to be adjusted by endorsement or addition of further policyowner information on the policy face. Kathy coordinated refiles of these forms and circulated an interoffice memo to update all areas of the entire set of filings.

Project: Article for Quarterly Newsletter. Kathy prepared an article on selling life insurance to dual-income families for use in our quarterly field publication.

Project: Field Manual Revision. To provide our field people with current home office operations information, Kathy revised the company field manual. This project took her into virtually every area of the home office.

bottomry

respondentia

premium

multiple-line underwriting

commercial insurers

stock insurers

participating insurance

dividends

mutual insurers

reciprocals

interinsurance associations

Lloyd's of London

surplus lines insurance

Lloyds Associations

insurance exchanges

guaranty funds

joint underwriting associations

beach and windstorm insurance
    plans

actuary

agent

advanced underwriting consultant

employee benefit representative

bonding representative

underwriter

loss control engineer

claims adjuster

factory mutuals

perpetual policies

Discussion Questions

1. Why do you suppose The Friendly Society in Charleston, South Carolina, went out of the insurance business after a major fire swept the city in 1740?

2. How do stock insurers differ from mutuals with respect to their ownership?

3. Do you think all states (and federal authorities) should permit commercial banks to engage in the life insurance business? Why, or why not?

4. Name several of the leading countries in insurance consumption. What are some of the ways they differ from lesser users of private insurance?

5. As a consumer, should you buy from a stock insurer chosen randomly or a mutual chosen randomly? Why, or why not?

6. A person buying insurance from a pure reciprocal transfers risk to the group but also assumes a risk. Does this seem rational to you? Please explain how this differs from buying from a mutual insurer.

7. How much of the business conducted by Lloyd's of London is associated with United States exposures? What kinds of U.S. exposures contributed significantly to massive losses at Lloyd's in the late 1980s and early 1990s?

8. Name three international dimensions of insurance. Why has the growth of "jumbo" exposures influenced the use of reinsurance?

9. Describe the kinds of decisions made by insurance company underwriters on applications for insurance.

10. What functions are included in the job of claims adjuster, and what knowledge/skills are required for the successful adjudication of claims?

....

24.1 Your aunt Celeste Salane (age 54) knows you are taking an insurance course. While you are visiting, Aunt Celeste receives an annual report on a life insurance policy that her father purchased for her when she was twelve years old. The annual report lists, but does not explain, the following facts:

- Annual premium of $450 due on November 12.
- Annual dividend of $1,000 being used to purchase paid-up additional insurance.
- Increase of $722 in cash value during the last policy year.
- Total death benefit available is $72,000

Aunt Celeste has heard that life insurance dividends are simply a return of an initial overcharge in premium. When she looks at the relationship between the premium and dividend on this policy for the latest year she is delighted but confused. Annual dividends have exceeded the annual premium for quite a few years.

1. Does this appear to be a nonparticipating or a participating contract? On what do you base your opinion?

2. Explain to Aunt Celeste whether you believe a premium overcharge is the sole explanation for the level of dividends for this policy.

24.2 Some life-health insurers have moved into the property-liability insurance marketplace. They formed new companies at a time when profits in the property-liability business were more volatile than those in the life-health part of the industry. Between 1987 and 1992, the rates of return on end-of-the-year net worth, based on generally accepted accounting principles, were 15.9 percent, 13.2 percent, 10.0 percent, 8.5 percent, 8.8 percent, and 4.4 percent for the property-liability industry. During the same years, returns for the life-health industry probably varied above or below 12 percent by less than 2 percent. Why might a life-health insurer have made such a move when it would have to spend a great deal of money to enter the property-liability marketplace, and when the profit outlook for this new business would be less predictable than for its existing lines of business?

24.3 Teri Tunell is a sophomore in college. She has a major in English and a minor in mathematics. She has enjoyed working part time as a salesperson in a local clothing store for the past two academic years. Last summer, she was a counselor in a summer camp for teenagers in Colorado. She told you recently that she is beginning to wonder about a career after graduation but really doesn't know what she wants to do. She knows you are taking an insurance course, so she asks you about job opportunities in that field. She tells you, "I enjoy sales work, but I don't want to go around knocking on doors like some magazine subscription salesperson. Also, I have made A's in all my math courses and am thinking of changing my major to mathematics."

1. Should you tell Teri about insurance opportunities, or should you tell her how to find out for herself?

2. If you decide on the latter approach, what would you tell her?

3. How can she find out what kind of job she may be qualified for? Might learning about the actuarial profession influence her choice of major?

Other Mutuals

County or Farm Mutuals

County or farm mutuals are local or statewide insurance operations that offer property-liability insurance primarily on farm property and its owners. Some of them insure only property in small towns. Most of them, including some that are fairly large, operate on an *assessment basis,* rather than collecting a premium in advance. In a pure assessment mutual, the manager adds up the losses for a specified period, such as a month; divides the total losses for the period by the amount of insurance; and assesses each insured. Most assessment insurers, however, charge an annual assessment in advance which provides funds to make prompt loss payments. These insurers also retain the right to levy additional assessments if losses exceed expectations. The customer is obligated to pay the additional premium. Some farm mutuals limit additional payments by insureds to one assessment, while others have unlimited assessments.

Considerable publicity has been given to a few instances in which mutual members have suffered severe losses because of the assessment feature. Be sure to read the policy and understand any obligations imposed by the contract. Otherwise, you may assume a risk you have neither identified nor evaluated. In general, assessment features should be avoided.

Several county mutuals collect premiums on a nonassessment basis and are reasonably large organizations. The New London County Mutual and the Barnstable County Mutual, both operating in the New England area, are each more than 150 years old. They primarily sell property insurance to preferred (low-risk) customers at rates well below standard (normal) rates for similar coverage.[16]

In Texas, county mutuals have come to fill a unique market niche. Organized many years ago to sell fire insurance in small areas, the Texas county mutuals now are major statewide writers of high-risk physical damage automobile insurance. That is, they sell property (but not liability)

16. San Antonio CPCU Chapter, "Texas County Mutuals," *CPCU Journal,* vol. 40, no. 1 (1987): p. 21.

insurance to automobile owners who must pay high rates because of bad driving records, among other reasons. The rates are nonassessable. Unlike other Texas automobile insurers, the county mutuals can change premium rates up or down quickly as their losses and market conditions change. Other insurers in Texas must appeal annually to a State Board of Insurance, a cumbersome procedure that produces rates that, from the insurers' financial perspective, are adequate for average but not high-risk drivers. In servicing this high-risk market, the Texas mutuals have moved away from their original purpose of providing fire insurance for farmers.[17]

Class or Specialty Mutuals

Class or specialty mutuals specialize in insuring particular kinds of businesses or offering specific types of insurance. For example, some specialize in insuring hardware stores or lumber firms, others concentrate on automobile insurance, boiler and machinery insurance, glass insurance, and so on. Many general mutuals started as specialty insurers. One company specialized initially in insuring glass but has now grown into a general mutual writing all lines of insurance. Nearly all the class mutuals are now in the general insurance business, although many of them continue to do a substantial amount of business in their original specialty class.

Factory Mutuals

Factory mutuals came into existence because a New England manufacturer thought insurance rates were too high for businesses that practiced careful loss prevention and control. This manufacturer persuaded others to join in organizing a mutual that would specialize in insuring factories that met high standards of construction and emphasized the prevention/control of losses. Insurance on superior properties continues to be the focus of factory mutuals. Four **factory mutuals** joined forces to create the Factory Mutual System.[18] These companies share risks through a reinsurance agreement and maintain an engineering division for *frequent inspections* and service to policyholders.

Insurance provided by factory mutuals is limited to the larger and better exposures to loss because of high underwriting standards and the cost of inspections. The factory mutuals have a practice of charging high premiums and then returning over half of the initial premium as dividends. They also own a stock insurance company that issues participating policies to organizations failing to meet the high safety standards for factory mutual insurance.

Perpetual Mutuals

A few mutuals provide property insurance on brick and stone dwellings through the use of **perpetual policies.** One of the first companies to offer perpetual insurance was the Philadelphia Contributionship, established in

17. San Antonio CPCU Chapter, pp. 20–29.
18. A group of large stock insurers later jointly formed the Industrial Risk Insurers to compete with the factory mutuals. This group also confines its coverage to large businesses that use sprinklers and other loss prevention/control programs.

1752 under the leadership of Benjamin Franklin. The initial premium, or deposit, in a perpetual is large enough so that investment earnings are the equivalent of an annual premium.

From the perspective of a consumer, this system of paying premiums is similar to paying insurance premiums from personal investment earnings. Since the investment earnings are not taxable to consumers, these insureds are actually paying premiums with income that is not subject to income tax. This is the main consumer appeal of these contracts. When losses and expenses are less than investment earnings, a dividend may be paid to policyowners. Perpetual insurance has no expiration date, but can be canceled by either the insured or the insurer. When a policy is cancelled, the deposit is refunded. The drawbacks of perpetual mutuals are that they do not operate in most locations and they require large initial deposits.

Fraternals

Fraternal societies are social organizations. Many of them, however, offer life and health insurance to members on a mutual basis. When fraternals first began to experiment with insurance, their efforts were more social than scientific, and many insurance schemes ended in failure because premiums were not adequate to pay claims. In more recent decades, their insurance operations have been subjected to greater regulation, which has tended to strengthen them financially. In the past, fraternals relied heavily on their ability to increase premium rates when more funds were needed, but today they emphasize adequate rates calculated in the same manner as for other insurers. Whether or not a fraternal offers financial security at a low cost depends upon the quality of its management. Fraternals are usually exempt from taxes because of their charitable nature. The major fraternal companies include Aid Association for Lutherans, International Order of Foresters, and Woodmen of the World.

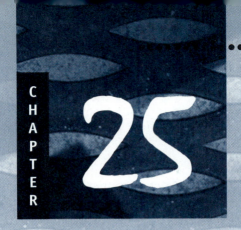

Risk Management
Implementation: Insurance

Introduction   When the decision to buy insurance has been made, you, as risk manager, must make important decisions. If you are in the personal or small-business insurance markets, an agent or broker probably will assist you. Will you select this advisor carefully, or just buy from whoever calls you? When losses occur, will you be equipped to negotiate with the insurer's claims adjuster?

This chapter aims to help you become a better insurance consumer, using premium dollars to the greatest advantage. We cover:

1. Insurance buying principles.
2. The insurance market.
3. How to select an insurance agent.
4. How to select an insurer or insurers.
5. How to select insurance coverages and compare costs.
6. How to settle losses.

Insurance Buying Principles

Many people spend enough for insurance to provide an adequate program of protection, but fail to achieve this objective because their premium dollars are improperly allocated. They spend too much for some parts of their insurance program, too little for others. You can make the best use of premium dollars by adhering to the following two fundamental buying principles:

1. The large-loss principle.
2. Avoidance of first-dollar coverage principle.

LARGE-LOSS PRINCIPLE

The **large-loss principle** tells us that the possible size of loss is a better measure of the significance of a loss exposure than the probabilities associated with various size losses. The fact that there is a low probability of death this year may be comforting, but it has little significance when you make plans. Either you will die this year or you will not. The significant factor for planning purposes is that dependents may suffer a *large loss* if you do. The liability risk is similar. Most people have a low probability of being held liable, except through the use of an automobile. But there is a possibility of becoming liable for thousands or even millions of dollars as a result of negligent behavior.

A possible large loss with a low probability is ideally suited for insurance.[1] The possibility of being held liable for a large loss to another person that results from activities around your home is an example of such an exposure. A large loss is one which you cannot bear and for which you cannot prepare other than through the use of insurance. Your first priority in deciding what kinds and amounts of insurance to buy should be determined by the size of your potential losses.

AVOIDANCE OF FIRST-DOLLAR COVERAGE PRINCIPLE

The avoidance of first-dollar coverage principle means that insurance dollars should not be used to protect against the part of a possible loss that can be borne financially. When the maximum possible loss is bearable, the risk should be handled entirely by retention. When the maximum possible loss is unbearable, deductibles permit retention for the first (bearable) dollars of loss.[2] For example, you can pay for minor damages to your automobile, but probably need insurance for losses greater than $200, $500, or some larger amount. A deductible allows you to retain the first dollars of loss and still have insurance for situations in which the large-loss principle calls for insurance.

The more probable small losses are, the easier it is for you to handle them without resorting to insurance. If they are small, you can stand the strain on your budget. If they are burdensome, perhaps the frequency can be reduced by loss prevention or the severity can be reduced by loss reduction. In any event, these losses may be predictable and budgetable.

1. The ideal requisites for insurance are discussed in chapter 3.
2. See chapter 2 for additional discussion.

Small losses cost the insurer far more than the amount of claim payment, due to adjustment and overhead costs. For many small claims, the amount you receive is less than the cost of processing and adjusting the claim. Insurers must charge premiums high enough to cover all costs of doing business; therefore, first-dollar coverage is the most expensive.

Table 25–1 illustrates this point. Note that for comprehensive coverage, which pays for damage to an automobile other than that caused by collision or upset, full coverage costs 19 percent more than coverage with a $200 deductible for an under-age-25 male driver of a Honda Accord garaged in Columbia, South Carolina. Full coverage (that is, with no deductible) comprehensive insurance requires the insurer to pay *all* the costs of damage caused by vandalism and other perils except collision and upset. Thus, every time such damage occurs, no matter how slight, the insurer has to pay for the repairs and the insured pays nothing. This insured would save an additional $19 of premium by increasing the deductible from $200 to $500.

For the same kind of automobile in the same location, $50 deductible collision insurance costs 22 percent more per year than $200 deductible. A $200 deductible exposes the insured to the risk of paying $150 more of a collision loss than with a $50 deductible, but reduces the annual cost of insurance by $104. If you cannot bear such a loss, you may be better off paying the extra premium for a $50 deductible. But if the loss is bearable, you should buy the coverage with a $200 deductible because paying $104 per year to protect yourself against one or more $150 losses in a year is expensive protection. By assuming the first $500 of each collision loss, you could save an additional $153. Does it seem reasonable to pay $153 per year for $300 ($500 deductible—$200 deductible) of collision insurance per accident? The answer is "yes" only if you are a much worse driver than your zero points in the last three years indicate.

It seems easy to conclude on the basis of looking at premium savings per $100 of insurance protection that minimum deductibles of $200 for comprehensive coverage and $200 for collision coverage would be desirable. It is more difficult to decide whether it is wise to increase deductibles beyond these levels without information on the expected frequency and severity of claims for this specific driver. For all insured passenger cars in the U.S. for 1993, the claim frequency per 100 insured vehicle years was 8.3. The average loss severity per insured vehicle year was $193. The insurer knows more about these factors than the typical consumer, and it is

TABLE 25–1

Annual Property Insurance Premiums for a New Honda Accord*

	COMPREHENSIVE	COLLISION
Full Coverage	$184	—
$50 Deductible	—	$568
$100 Deductible	$165	$494
$200 Deductible	$154	$464
$500 Deductible	$135	$311
$1000 Deductible	$113	$200

*Unmarried male, under age 25, driver training, no points, auto garaged in Columbia, SC, and driven to and from work less than 10 miles each way.

probably reasonable to conclude that when a possible loss is bearable, it does not pay to buy insurance to cover the risk.

The same principle is found in the rating of other types of insurance policies. In long-term disability income insurance, for example, the maximum duration of benefits can be markedly increased for the same premium if you will accept a policy with a longer waiting period.[3]

The Insurance Market

Before you start using the buying principles just discussed, you need to know something about the insurance market. Insurance may be bought through agents, brokers, or, in some cases, directly from the insurer. An agent legally represents the company, whereas a broker represents the buyer; both are compensated by the insurer.

It is important that you as an insurance consumer understand how insurance is sold because agents are likely to contact you before you draw up a plan for approaching the market. The point is that often *insurance is sold* rather than bought. This is particularly characteristic of life and health insurance products that are not compulsory. You are more likely to initiate the contact with a property-liability agent than with other types of agents because your automobile insurance may be compulsory as a result of state law, and, in addition, the lender on your automobile or home loan requires evidence of property insurance on its collateral. In any event, your main contacts with the insurance industry will be with agents or brokers. Thus, it is valuable to know how they differ.

Because life-health insurance and property-liability insurance developed separately in the United States, somewhat different marketing systems evolved. We will therefore discuss these systems separately.

LIFE-HEALTH INSURANCE MARKETING

Most life-health insurance is sold through agents who are compensated by commissions. The remainder is sold by salaried representatives and by mail or television. In the latter arrangements, the buyer may deal directly with the insurer or with an intermediary who promotes the insurer's products by telephone. Fee-only financial planners often recommend **no-load life insurance** to clients. The term "no-load" means that the product is not priced to include the agent's sales commission. However, the financial planner charges a fee for his or her advice, and this fee in effect pays for the counseling aspects of the marketing mechanism. You then buy directly from the no-load insurer. Total marketing costs are not necessarily lower if you need the counsel of a financial planner, yet you may reduce the incentives for being advised to buy a high-commission product.

Some companies insist that their agents represent them exclusively, or at least that agents not submit applications to another insurer unless they themselves have refused to issue insurance at standard premium rates. Others permit their agents to sell for other companies; these agents usually have a primary affiliation with one company and devote most of their efforts to selling its policies.

3. For discussion, see chapter 21.

Some insurers sell through brokers who often serve as agents for one or more other insurers. For example, some small- and medium-sized life insurers sell only through independent agents who mainly sell property-liability insurance.

The two dominant types of life-health marketing systems are the general agency and managerial (branch office) systems. Both systems are commonly called career agency systems because money is invested by both general agents and insurers to hire and train new agents. In return, general agents and insurers hope that many of these people will make careers with their companies.

General Agency System

A **general agent** is an independent businessperson, rather than an employee of the company. The general agent's contract with the insurer authorizes him or her to sell insurance in a specified territory. Another major responsibility is the recruitment and training of subagents. Subagents usually are given the title of "agent" or "special agent." Typically, subagents are agents of the insurer rather than the general agent. The insurer pays commissions (a percentage of premiums) to the agents on both new and renewal business. The general agent receives an override commission (i.e., a percentage of agents commissions) on all business generated or serviced by the agency, pays most of it to the subagents, and keeps the balance for expenses and profit. Agent compensation agreements are normally determined by the insurer.

In most cases, the general agent has an exclusive franchise for his or her territory. The primary responsibilities of the general agent are to select, train, and supervise subagents. In addition, general agents provide office space and have administrative responsibilities for some customer service activities.

In recent decades, general agents have lost some of their independence with many life insurers. Some insurers have agreed, for example, to absorb certain types of expenses for the general agent. The general agent compensates the insurer by accepting a lower override commission and by giving the insurer more control over agency activities. For example, it is not uncommon for an insurer to have veto power in the selection of new subagents.

A large number of life-health insurers use **personal producing general agents.** Such agents seldom hire other agents; instead, they sell for one or more insurers, often with a higher-than-normal agent's commission. The extra commission helps cover office expenses.

The trend is toward an agent representing several different insurers. This is desirable for consumers because no one insurer has the best products for all needs. For example, although your agent's primary insurer may have the best life insurance product to meet your needs, the best disability income policy for you may be offered by another insurer. In this example, to meet your insurance needs more completely, your agent needs to have the flexibility to serve as a broker or a personal producing general agent for the insurer with the desirable disability policy.

Managerial (Branch Office) System

A branch office is an extension of the home office headed by a **branch manager.** The manager is a company *employee* who is compensated by a combination of salary, bonus, and commissions related to the productivity of the office to which he or she is assigned. As an employee, the manager is subject to control by the company and may be transferred from one branch office to another.

The branch manager employs and trains agents for the company, but each agent's contract is between the company and the agent. The manager cannot employ an agent without the consent of the company, and it is from the company, rather than the manager, that the agent derives his or her authority. Compensation plans for agents are determined by the company.[4] All expenses of maintaining the office are paid by the company, which has complete control over the details of its operation.

Except for the degree of control by the insurer, a general agent and a manager perform essentially the same work from day to day. In many instances, only minor differences exist in the amount of control exercised over general agents and managers. It matters little to either agents or consumers whether a life insurer uses a general agency or a managerial marketing system. As a result of several insurers having recently been held legally liable for large damage awards to consumers claiming misrepresentations by agents, insurers are taking a new interest in controlling the market conduct of agents.[5]

Group and Supplemental Insurance

Group life, health, and retirement plans are sold to employers by agents in one of the systems described above, or by brokers. An agent may be assisted in this specialized field by a group sales representative. Large volumes of group business are also placed through direct negotiations between employers and insurers. A brokerage firm or an employee benefits consulting firm may be hired on a fee-only basis by the employer who wishes to negotiate directly with insurers, avoiding commissions to the agent/broker. In these direct negotiations, the insurer typically is represented by a salaried group sales representative.

Supplemental insurance plans that provide life, health, and other benefits to employees through employer sponsorship and payroll deduction have become common. These plans are marketed by agents, brokers, and exclusive agents. The latter usually work on commissions; some receive salaries plus bonuses.

PROPERTY-LIABILITY INSURANCE MARKETING

Like life-health insurance, most property-liability insurance is sold through agents or brokers who are compensated on a commission basis, but some is sold by salaried representatives or by direct methods. The independent agency system and the exclusive agency system account for the bulk of insurance sales.

---

4. You may notice that this is essentially the same arrangement as described above for general agents who have lost some of their independence.
5. Larry M. Greenberg, "Crown Life Loses a $50 Million Ruling Involving Vanishing—Premium Policies," *The Wall Street Journal*, Sept. 14, 1995, p. C18.

Independent (American) Agency System

The distinguishing characteristics of this system are the independence of the agent, the agent's bargaining position with the insurers he or she represents, and the fact that those who purchase insurance through the agent are considered by both insurers and agents to be the agent's customers rather than those of the insurer. The **independent agent** usually represents several companies, pays all agency expenses, is compensated on a commission plus bonus basis, and makes all decisions concerning how the agency operates. Using insurer forms, the agent binds an insurer, sends underwriting information to the insurer, and later delivers a policy to the insured. He or she may or may not have responsibility to collect premiums.

Because there is competition among insurers for the services of talented agents, such an agent has a strong bargaining position with the companies he or she represents. In a sense, the agent sells business to the insurer. Legally, these agents represent the insurer, but as a practical matter they also represent you, the customer.

An independent agency has the valuable right to contact you when your contract is due for renewal. This ownership right can be sold to another agent, and, when the independent agent decides to retire or leave the agency, the right to contact large numbers of customers creates a substantial market value for the agency. The insurer cannot interfere with this right of contact.

This marketing system is also known as the American Agency System. But it is best recognized for the "Big I" advertisements sponsored by the Independent Insurance Agents of America. These advertisements usually emphasize the independent agent's ability to choose the best policy and insurer for you. However, the portion of all property-liability insurance sold by independent agents, as opposed to direct writers, declined from 61 percent in 1984 to 55 percent in 1993. Meanwhile, the portion sold by direct writers increased from 39 percent to 45 percent.[6] This trend, especially strong in the personal lines of insurance, was well pronounced prior to 1984.

Direct Writers

Several companies, called **direct writers,**[7] market insurance through **exclusive agents** who are permitted to represent only their company or a company in their group.[8] This system is used by such companies as Allstate, Nationwide, and State Farm. These insurers compensate the agent through commissions that are lower than those paid to independent agents, partly because the insurer absorbs some expenses that are borne directly by independent agents. The customer is considered to be the insurer's rather than the agent's, and the agent does not have as much independence as do those who operate under the independent agency

---

6. *The Fact Book 1995: Property/Casualty Insurance Facts.* (New York: Insurance Information Institute, 1995), p. 6.

7. The term "direct writer" is frequently used to refer to all property insurers that do not use the Independent Agency System of distribution, but some observers think there are differences among such companies. Two types are discussed in this and the next section.

8. A group is a number of separate companies operating under common ownership and management.

system. Average operating expenses and premiums for personal lines of insurance tend to be lower than those in the independent agency system. Some independent agency automobile and homeowners products, however, have very competitive prices and should be considered in any insurance purchase decision.

Some direct writers place business through **salaried representatives,** who are employees of the company. Compensation for such employees may be a salary and/or a commission plus bonus related to the amount and quality of business they secure. Regardless of the compensation arrangement, they are employees rather than agents. Such representatives pay none of the expenses connected with securing or servicing business. In many cases, they are specialists providing engineering and inspection services to commercial insurance customers and devoting only part of their time to soliciting new business. Factory mutuals, for example, often use salaried representatives.

Brokers

A considerable amount of insurance and reinsurance is placed through brokers. A **broker** solicits business from the insured as does an agent, but the broker acts as the insured's legal agent when the business is placed with an insurer. Unlike independent agents, most property-liability brokers do not have ongoing contracts with insurers—their sole obligation is to you. When it appears desirable, a broker may draft a specially worded policy for a client and then place the policy with an insurer. Some property-liability brokers merely place insurance with an insurer and then rely on this company to provide whatever engineering and loss-prevention services are needed. Others have a staff of engineers to perform such services for clients. Modern brokerage firms provide a variety of related services, such as risk management surveys, information systems services related to risk management, complete administrative and claim services to self-insurers, and captive insurer management.

Many life insurance agents broker business with insurers other than the one with which they are primarily identified. Career agents with insurers that insist on exclusive representation primarily broker business that is not acceptable to their own company. Such business is known as "substandard," and there are brokers who specialize in placing it for agents. These brokerage agencies, unlike the typical property-liability broker, maintain ongoing contracts with several insurers.

Brokers are a more significant part of the marketing mechanism in commercial property, liability, employee benefits, and marine insurance than in personal lines of insurance. Brokers are most active in metropolitan areas and among large insureds, where a broker's knowledge of specialized coverages and the market for them is important. Some brokerage firms operate on a local or regional basis, whereas others are national or international in their operations.

MASS MERCHANDISING

An increasing amount of insurance is sold on a **mass merchandising basis** by mail, telephone, or television. Marketing through electronic mail systems such as Internet are also underway. At one time, most insurance sold by mail was health insurance, but a number of insurers are now selling life insurance and, to a lesser extent, automobile and home insurance by this method. Mass merchandising sales are created through advertising in newspapers, magazines, television, and radio, as well as by direct mail (or direct response). Such sales account for 7 percent of the personal insurance market.[9] Some mass merchandising insurers are licensed in only one or two states; insureds who live in other states may be at a serious disadvantage in the event of a dispute with the insurer.[10]

Mass merchandising often involves a sponsoring organization such as an employer, trade association, university, or creditor; however, you are likely to be asked to respond directly to the insurer. Some mass merchandising mixes agents and direct response; an agent handles the initial mailing and subsequently contacts the responding members of the sponsoring organization.

In some cases, you can save money buying insurance by mass merchandising methods. Direct response insurers, however, cannot provide the counseling you may receive from a good agent or financial planner. Whether counseling is crucial depends upon how much you know about risk, insurance, and the market. If you need counseling, you should buy through an agent or broker and be sure this person takes a reasonable amount of time in helping you. Few agents are willing to help you with your entire risk management program unless you buy enough insurance through them to compensate adequately for such service. The insurance distribution system is summarized in figure 25–1.

FINANCIAL PLANNER

A **financial planner** facilitates some insurance sales by serving as a consultant on financial matters, primarily to high-income clients. An analysis of risk exposures and recommendations on appropriate risk management techniques, including insurance, are major parts of the financial planning process. A fee-only financial planner, knowledgeable in insurance, may direct you to good-quality, no-load insurance products when they are priced lower than comparable products sold through agents. You are already paying a fee for advice from the financial planner. Why also pay a commission to an insurance agent or broker?

In many instances, it is appropriate for the financial planner to send you to an insurance agent. Products available through agents may be superior from a price and quality standpoint to the still limited supply of no-load products. Also, your financial planner is likely to be a generalist with respect to insurance, and you may need advice from a knowledgeable

---

9. John Wilke and Leslie Scism, "Under the Gun: Insurance Agents Fight an Intrusion by Banks, but Other Perils Loom," *The Wall Street Journal,* Vol. CCXXVI, No. 26 (August 8, 1995): p. 1.

10. You can call the state insurance department and ask if a company is licensed in your state, or call the reference desk of your city or state library. Appendix G provides information on insurance commissioners.

FIGURE 25–1

Insurance Distribution System

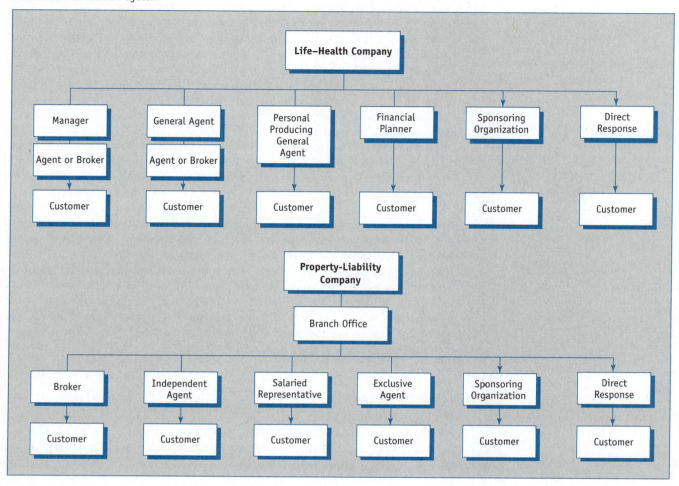

agent. In any event, financial planners are now part of the insurance distribution system.[11]

Selecting an Agent

Many agents merely sell insurance. Others render valuable service in addition to selling; they act as advisers as well as motivators. The quality of

11. Some state insurance laws prohibit an agent from promoting himself or herself as a financial planner. Other states do not have this prohibition. The result is some poorly qualified insurance agents and stockbrokers calling themselves financial planners. Some persons who sell products on a commission basis probably experience a conflict of interest between leading you to their line of products and to others on which they might not earn a commission. This conflict would not apply to some "product-based" financial planners, but it probably pays to be somewhat cautious of commissioned agents who call themselves financial planners. The potential conflict is reduced somewhat among fee-based planners who offset commissions earned on sales against the fee they charge for initial advice. You should also be cautious of financial planners who claim to be risk management and insurance experts, because a financial planning generalist, or one who specializes in investments or taxes, may know far less about insurance than a knowledgeable insurance agent.

insurance agents ranges from awful to mediocre to excellent. Since the premium for insurance includes the agent's compensation, it costs no more to buy through a superior agent than through a poor one. In this case, it is true that "the best costs no more." In fact, it may cost less; a superior agent can help you devise your risk management program and implement it by getting the most for your insurance dollar.

A superior agent is familiar with the risks confronting you, the proper insurance coverage to seek, and the market in which coverage is available at the right price. His or her interest goes beyond the sales commission. The superior agent has a genuine interest in your welfare and is always ethical.

Even ethical, professional agents and brokers must spend their time with prospective clients who offer them enough potential commissions and/or fees to compensate for the time they spend in counseling and selling. You will be more appealing to an agent or broker, therefore, if you concentrate your personal insurance purchases with one individual. Alternatively, try to work with one life-health specialist and one property-liability specialist. This concentration will also help the agent or broker keep track of what insurance you have and what you need. The same principle applies to the purchase of commercial insurance.

Superior agents will help you identify and evaluate your risks and will recommend the proper coverage. They will also explain what the policy covers and what it does not cover, as well as what it costs. They will attempt to reduce costs and keep the coverage up to date by regularly reviewing both the policy and the insured exposures. Superior agents have good working relationships with their companies, enabling them to get the best deal for you, both in placing the insurance and in settling claims. This does not mean that they will cheat the company for your benefit, but rather that they will take a responsible attitude toward the best interests of both you and the insurer. An agent who will cheat an insurer may do the same to you, according to the universal character theory.

Ideally, an agent has several years of experience before giving advice on complicated insurance matters. You will be interested in the agent's experience and educational qualifications, which should cover an extensive study of insurance, finance, and related subjects. A major route for life-health agents to gain this background is by meeting all requirements for the Chartered Life Underwriter (CLU) designation or the Chartered Financial Consultant (ChFC) designation. Property-liability agents gain a good background by earning the Chartered Property and Casualty Underwriter (CPCU) designation.[12]

The **CLU** designation is granted by the American College, Bryn Mawr, Pennsylvania, to those agents who meet experience, character, and educational requirements. They must pass a series of ten comprehensive ex-

---

12. In selecting a financial planner, you should look either for a person who holds the ChFC designation or one with the Certified Financial Planner (CFP) designation. The CFP program, administered by the College for Financial Planning in Denver, Colorado, has only two introductory-level insurance courses. Thus, persons with a CFP designation may have been exposed to only an elementary study of insurance. An alternative to the prestigious CPCU designation is the Certified Insurance Counselor (CIC) designation. The CIC designation is earned by attending a series of seminars and then successfully passing examinations administered at the conclusion of each seminar.

aminations on life-health insurance and related subjects. The examinations are similar in difficulty to those for junior– or senior-level college courses. The **ChFC** designation, also offered by the American College, is broader in scope than the CLU program. The ChFC program includes more study of the financial planning process, investments, and taxation, yet it still has a significant insurance content. The **CPCU** designation is granted by the American Institute for Property and Liability Underwriters, Malvern, Pennsylvania, to those who meet similar requirements and pass ten comprehensive examinations in property-liability insurance and related subjects.

Superior agents will represent one or more good insurers; if they represent poor ones, they are not superior. For the most part, once you have chosen the agent with whom you wish to do business, you will have selected your insurer(s). Thus, your agent must know something about evaluating an insurer. The superior agent possesses knowledge of risk and insurance, concern for you, ethics, experience, and contracts with good insurers. (Finding a good agent is one of the subjects for the Consumer Applications section of this chapter.)

Selecting an Insurer

It is not necessary to leave the matter of insurer selection entirely in the agent's hands. You should participate. To make an informed choice, answers are needed to the questions listed in figure 25–2.

STATE LICENSE

If you do business with an insurer licensed in your state, the state insurance commissioner's office may be able to help you in the event of difficulties. If the insurer is not licensed in your state, the regulatory authorities are in a weak position to help you. Hundreds of insurers are licensed in every state, so avoiding an unlicensed one does not greatly restrict your choice.

As is frequently the case, there are exceptions to this advice. Occasionally, especially in the case of large commercial buyers, the agent may need to place property-liability insurance in the surplus lines market.[13]

FIGURE 25–2

Insurer Checklist

1. Is the insurer licensed in my state?
2. Is it financially strong?
3. Does it charge reasonable prices?
4. Are the types and amounts of coverage I want included in the contract?
5. Are its claims practices fair?
6. What is its cancellation policy?
7. Does it have adequate underwriting capacity?
8. What services does it provide?
9. How does its complaint ratio (maintained by your insurance commissioner) compare with that of other insurers?
10. Does it have a reputation for integrity in all aspects of its operations?

13. The surplus lines market is defined in chapter 24.

FINANCIAL STRENGTH

When you buy insurance, you are buying a promise to be kept in the future. Will the insurer be able to keep its promises? Clearly, **financial strength** and stability are of prime importance to an insurance consumer. **Due diligence** is the process of determining the degree of financial strength that characterizes a financial services firm. Advisors such as agents, brokers, and financial planners perform due diligence examinations for three purposes. First, such knowledge is a prerequisite to rendering reliable advice to clients. Second, through doing their homework, agents maintain professional credibility with clients. Third, they reduce the possibility of being sued by a client for having provided incompetent advice.

The risk manager for a large organization may conduct the same due diligence as an advisor. What is prudent for the family or small-business risk manager? Perhaps the answer is to obtain the advice of a trusted advisor *and* check the ratings given by two or more rating organizations. When you use direct marketing, the rating services may be your only source of reasonably reliable financial information, assuming you are not an expert in insurance finance.

Historically, the Alfred M. Best Company was the primary source of financial ratings for insurers. Now there are five rating organizations (see table 25–2). You need a guide such as that in table 25–2 to interpret just how near the top a rating is. For example, Duff & Phelps, Moody's, and Standard & Poor's each have seven ratings with the letter "A," which the general public tends to associate with excellence. Weiss is the only service that uses grades like those typically found in schools. A distribution of grades for insurers rated by a particular rating organization is enlightening. For example, *Best Reports* gives their distributions in the preface. Separate reports are given for life-health and property-liability insurers. Best's 1994 distribution for the property-liability insurers it rates is given in table 25–3.

TABLE 25–2

A Variety of Financial Grades

BEST'S	DUFF & PHELPS	MOODY'S	STANDARD & POOR	WEISS
A+ +	AAA	Aaa	AAA	A+
A+	AA+	Aa1	AA+	A
A	AA	Aa2	AA	A–
A–	AA–	Aa3	AA–	B+
B+ +	A+	A1	A+	B
B+	A	A2	A	B–
B	A–	A3	A–	C+
B–	BBB+	Baa1	BBB+	C
C+ +	BBB	Baa2	BBB	C–
C+	BBB–	Baa3	BBB–	D+
C	BB+	Ba1	BB+	D
C–	BB	Ba2	BB	D–
D	BB–	Ba3	BB–	E+
E	B+	B1	B+	E
F	B	B2	B	E–
	B–	B3	B–	F
	CCC	Caa	CCC	
		Ca		

TABLE 25–3

Distribution of Financial Ratings
Assigned to Property-Liability
Insurers by the A. M. Best Co., 1994*

SECURE		VULNERABLE	
A++	125	B	54
A+	394	B−	22
A	488	C++	6
A−	426	C+	6
B++	116	C	8
B+	108	C−	3
		D	8
		E	26
		F	25

*The rating of FPR (i.e., "financial performance rating") with accompanying numbers ranging from 1 = "Not Assigned" to 8 and 9 = "Strong" are assigned to small or new companies. The FPR ratings (209 in 1994) are listed in a manner implying how they compare to the other, latter ratings. For example, an "FPR = 4" is listed between the B− and C++ ratings.

A significant portion of insurers are assigned ratings of "NA" (i.e., "not assigned"), accompanied by a number that suggests why no assignment was made. For example, NA-6 relates to insurers with a significant volume of reinsurance ceded with an unrated reinsurer. In 1994, Best gave NA ratings to 378 property-liability companies.

SOURCE: *Best's Insurance Reports: Property-Casualty* (Oldwick, N.J.: A. M. Best's Company, 1994): p. xii.

Professor Joseph M. Belth recommends that a conservative buyer select an insurer with a very high rating from at least two of the rating organizations other than Best. He defines a "very high rating" as:

Duff & Phelps:	AAA and AA+
Moody's:	Aaa, Aa1, Aa2, and Aa3
Standard & Poor's:	AAA, AA+, and AA
Weiss:	A+, A, A-B+, B, and B-

In the authors' opinion, Best's A++ and A+ may also be considered very high ratings. Belth also recommends that you read the reports provided by the rating organizations.[14] Any downward trend in financial ratings is a danger signal requiring exploration. As you explore further, watch for the hierarchy of adjectives used by some rating services. When you read the analysis of a particular life insurer in *Best's,* for example, you may think a "low" expense ratio sounds quite desirable. But after consulting the preface you will see that *Best's* uses "remarkably low" to describe the most favorable range of ratios. The adjective "low" classifies an insurer's expenses in the third category, which is really faint praise in comparison.

Your state insurance department has risk-based capital (RBC) ratios and Insurance Regulatory Information System (IRIS) ratios that are calculated annually (more often for troubled companies) by the National Association of Insurance Commissioners (NAIC). They are developed for regulatory purposes, and regulations prohibit their dissemination by insurers and agents. You can obtain the numbers that comprise the numerator and denominator of RBC ratios by requesting them from the insurance commissioner of a state where the insurer of interest is licensed. Certain IRIS

14. Joseph M. Belth, "Financial Strength Ratings of 1,600 Life-Health Insurance Companies," *Insurance Forum,* Vol. 22, Nos. 3 and 4 (1995): pp. 146–47.

ratios are available by request from the NAIC in Kansas City, Missouri. The nature of IRIS and RBC ratios is described in chapter 26.

Financial ratings are evaluations of financial solvency, liquidity, and profitability. *Financial solvency* exists when assets exceed liabilities. All insurers that are currently in business meet this requirement, assuming their balance sheets are correct. The question is: how much financial cushion (or degree of solvency) exists? The most common measure of the degree of solvency is the ratio of net worth (capital plus surplus) to assets (or to liabilities). Relating net worth to assets produces a measure that considers an insurer's size. Giant Company A may have five times as much net worth as Small Insurer B, yet B's ratio of net worth/assets may be twice as large as A's. Contrary to the impression created by a comparison of the absolute amounts of net worth, Small Insurer B may be financially stronger than A. Size alone does not make an insurer strong.

Ratios must be carefully interpreted. They are subject to manipulation. One management team, for example, may make lower estimates of reserves (liabilities) than another for similar future claims; the result would be a higher accounting-based net worth. Another interpretive problem is that mutual life-health insurers typically have much lower net worth/asset ratios than comparable stock insurers. This is misleading because the typical mutual charges higher premiums on some products; in the event of financial adversity, it could use the excess premiums to cover operating losses and simply reduce current policyowner dividends. An even greater problem for a very small proportion of companies is that managerial fraud could be distorting financial statements and rendering ratios unreliable.

Financial liquidity concerns the ability of an insurer to pay current debts, including claims. An insurer could be financially solvent and still have a negative cash flow. The degree of liquidity is measured by a comparison of current assets and current liabilities. Any comparison is hindered, however, by the difficulty of identifying all the insurer's current assets and liabilities. Some investments (for example, common stocks) may be more liquid at a given point in time than you might conclude from their categorization on a balance sheet. Likewise, it is difficult to identify all current needs for cash; for example, commitments to make investments in the future will not appear on the balance sheet and may be overlooked. Perhaps a reasonable indication of management's concern about liquidity is an insurer's past claim practices. An insurer's reputation for fair and prompt claim payments is a clear sign of management emphasis on liquidity as well as fairness.

Profitability refers to the extent to which an insurer's income exceeds its expenses. In addition to the absolute amount of profit (or loss), you will want to relate the amount of profit to a measure of company size. For example, calculate a return on book equity ratio by dividing the amount of profit for a year by the average of net worth at the beginning and end of the year. Also consider the trend in profitability over the last five years or so. Being reasonably profitable improves both financial solvency and liquidity.

Policy Transfers

In recent years, insurers have developed the practice of selling entire blocks of policies to other insurers. When buying new insurance, deter-

ETHICAL *Dilemma*

Enforcement of Financial and Marketing Integrity

In the first half of the 1990s, life insurers faced two assaults on their integrity. First, their financial soundness was questioned. The high interest rate environment of the 1980s and deregulation of financial service markets led to intense inter-industry and intra-industry product competition. The competition to illustrate higher returns on the investment elements of individual life insurance, annuities, and guaranteed investment contracts caused many insurers to take more investment risk than normal in an effort to produce higher investment returns. Some insurers, Executive Life being the prime example, invested too heavily in low-investment grade (junk) bonds. The value of these bonds fell substantially around 1990, leaving several insurers technically insolvent and without the liquidity to meet policyholder demand for funds. Heavy investment commitments in real estate also proved disastrous. Values in the real estate market fell drastically, due partly to overbuilding in the 1980s, followed by less-favorable tax laws and an economic recession. Insurers, including the large, respected Mutual Benefit Life, had promised high returns on guaranteed investment contracts (GICs), backed by heavy real estate investments. Contract owners such as pension plans surrendered large blocks of GICs; with an illiquid investment portfolio, Mutual Benefit had to seek protection from the New Jersey Insurance Department. After a history of meaningless financial solvency requirements, the NAIC hurried to develop their RBC requirements for both life-health and property-liability companies.

Later, deceptive marketing practices of agents in the two largest life companies (i.e., Prudential and Metropolitan) were exposed. Top management officials for both insurers admitted that agents in certain field offices had misrepresented the nature of cash value life insurance products. In some instances, sales materials had been approved by insurer marketing executives. Consumers (e.g., large numbers of nurses) had been convinced by Metropolitan agents that whole life policies were ideal for achieving certain retirement investment objectives. The agents involved were disciplined. Company and industry credibility had been damaged.

Who is responsible for policing honesty, uprightness, and decency among agents and insurers? Is integrity just the concern of regulators or is it within the purview of management? Does the typical consumer care whether or not his or her insurer has a reputation for financial and marketing integrity? (What about underwriting, pricing, administration, and claims integrity?) Should enforcement of ethical standards be left to lower levels of management (e.g., branch sales managers)? Does being very large in organization size mean that top management of large insurers should strictly delegate enforcement of marketing standards to lower levels of management? What is the proper level of investment risk and expected investment return? Are marketing gimmicks necessary?

mine if the contract gives the insurer the unilateral right to transfer the policy without the owner's consent. If your insurer notifies you that your contract is being transferred to another insurer, investigate the new company. If it is not as financially sound as your original insurer, you may want to enforce any right you have to reject the transfer.

PRICES

Price is another major consideration. Other things being equal, why buy insurance from a company whose prices are higher than those of its competitors? The notion that "you get what you pay for" has long since fallen into disrepute.

When comparing insurance prices, you must make sure that nonprice factors are the same for each alternative. Nonprice factors include those listed in figure 25-2 p. 622, such as financial strength and service. In addition, the types and amounts of insurance coverage must be the same for the alternatives you are comparing. Otherwise, you would be comparing the prices of apples and oranges. Small organizations often ask several insurers to submit bids on a particular type of insurance, without being specific about such matters as the perils to be covered and the maximum amount of insurance needed. The result is proposals that are not comparable.

You can better compare price of coverage by furnishing your **insurance specifications** to each insurer, agent, or broker. Specifications describe the types and amounts of coverage you want, minimum qualifications that insurers and agents must meet, service requirements, and other characteristics of your insurance needs. Bids that fail to meet your specifications may be discarded. For the remaining alternatives, you are ready to compare prices as well as various nonprice factors. (Methods of determining life insurance prices were discussed in chapter 16.)

CONTRACT PROVISIONS

Insurance contracts are not all the same. Like automobiles, insurance contracts of a specific type have certain basic features, but also significant differences. All automobiles have motors, transmissions, and other basic parts. Yet these basics vary (for example, an automatic versus a manual transmission) and some cars have more options (such as stereo tape players, electric door locks, and so forth). All insurance contracts of a given type, such as homeowners policies, have common provisions. All cover fire, lightning, explosion, and certain other important perils. But not all types cover falling objects, freezing, and several other perils. Earthquake requires a special rider in almost all policies. Flood coverage requires a separate policy. Amounts of coverage need to be tailored to your specific circumstances.

For these reasons, it is important to be sure the insurance contract you buy meets your needs. This requires an ability to analyze contracts, either by you or your agent/broker/financial planner. You can help your representative to adequately perform this analysis by asking some probing questions, such as the ones in figure 25-3.

FIGURE 25–3

Contract Analysis Questions

1. What perils are covered?
2. What is the limit of liability?
3. What property or kind of liability is insured? or, Whose life or health is insured?
4. What is the duration of coverage (for example, six months, a year, or continuous until canceled) under the contract?
5. What is the method of indemnification at the time of loss?
6. Will there be a deduction for physical depreciation?
7. What losses are excluded by the contract?
8. Does the contract cover only direct losses, only indirect losses, or both?
9. What hazards or limitations exclude or suspend coverage?
10. Would endorsements improve the contract's ability to meet your needs?
11. What deductibles and copayments apply?

CLAIM PRACTICES

It is unreasonable to expect an insurer to be overly generous in paying claims or to honor claims that should not be paid at all, but you should avoid a company that makes a practice of resisting reasonable claims. Even when claims are paid promptly and fairly, a loss is unpleasant and inconvenient. When the company balks and you have to fight for your rights, the whole process is frustrating and time consuming, and you may wind up accepting less than you are entitled in order to get a settlement. Unfortunately, no reference book grades insurer claims practices.

You do, however, have several sources of information. First, you can ask your state insurance department's complaint section if any of the insurers you are considering have generated an excessive number of complaints. Not all complaints are justified, but an insurer that generates more than the average for the amount of business it does should be avoided. Second, you can be on the alert for articles in the press concerning insurer claims practices. Third, you can ask the agent what experience other insureds have had. A top-quality agent will not represent an insurer with bad claims practices, but not all agents are experienced, knowledgeable, and ethical. Finally, you can ask your friends and business associates how their insurers treat them. This provides a small sample, it is true, but additional information may be helpful. By making these inquiries, you decrease the probability of doing business with the companies that contest or otherwise delay payment of just claims.

CANCELLATION POLICY

The insurer's cancellation philosophy is important. Will the insurer cancel or refuse to renew your policy the first time you have a loss? Most companies do not do this, but some do. You can get some information from the state insurance department's complaint section and from people who have had insurance with the company about the existence of any undesirable practices. You may also be able to depend upon what insurance agents say about the insurer; a superior agent will not represent an insurer that cancels too readily. Many insurers now limit their cancellation right by policy provision, especially in automobile and health insurance. Also, some states have legislation that restricts the right to cancel. You should evaluate the extent to which such extra protection is provided when you select a company. Ask the agent to explain the policy's cancellation provision, as well as applicable state law.

UNDERWRITING CAPACITY

In many cases, the amount of protection needed exceeds an insurer's **underwriting capacity.** Underwriting capacity concerns an insurer's financial ability to provide new insurance. For property-liability insurers, it relates the insurer's volume of premiums written for recent years to its net worth. As a generalization, the ratio should not be higher than three to one. As discussed earlier, reinsurance facilities are used to enable an insurer to issue a policy with higher limits than it is able or willing to retain. Reinsurance, however, does not make it possible for every insurer to offer the same amount of coverage. Insurers differ not only in size but also in the amount of reinsurance they can obtain. Thus, there is considerable variation in underwriting capacity. Underwriting capacity and reinsurance arrangements are important considerations for the business risk manager who wants to avoid having several insurance policies issued by different insurers to cover one risk. When buying large amounts of insurance, include questions in your specifications about the insurer's retention limit. Also obtain the names of the company's reinsurers and financial ratings for all reinsurers. This will help you judge overall financial soundness.

SERVICE

Insurance is a business in which the quality of the product depends on all the factors previously discussed, but only financial strength could be considered more important than **service.** An agent's or broker's advice and an insurer's claim practices are the primary services that the typical individual or family needs. In addition, however, you will want prompt, courteous responses to inquiries concerning changes in your policy, the availability of other types of insurance, changes of address, and other routine matters. You will also want a premium payment method that fits your budget. For example, it is cheaper to pay premiums annually, but your budget may demand monthly or quarterly payments.

Another service that some insurers offer, primarily to commercial clients, is *engineering and loss control.* Over a decade or so, through premium adjustments, a medium or large organization will pay for its own insured losses, plus its share of the cost of operating the insurers with which it does business. In addition, it will bear the cost of direct and indirect losses that are not insured. The *prevention* and *reduction* of loss whenever the efforts required are economically feasible are, therefore, of major significance. Much of the engineering and loss control activity may be carried on by the insurer or under its direction. The facilities the insurer has to devote to such efforts and the degree to which such efforts are successful is an important element to consider in selecting an insurer. Part of the risk manager's success depends upon this element. Engineering and loss control services are particularly applicable to workers' compensation and boiler and machinery exposures. With respect to the health insurance part of an employee benefits program, loss control is called cost containment and may be achieved primarily through managed care techniques.

Selecting Coverages and Comparing Costs

You can select appropriate coverages if you know exactly what you want and follow the buying principles discussed in this chapter. Knowing exactly what you want involves, first, knowing which loss exposures and perils you want to transfer to an insurer, and second, which insurance policy or policies will cover them. In earlier chapters, we discussed the risks to which you are exposed and how to select the insurance most appropriate for you. Because there are significant differences in prices charged by various insurers for similar policies, we also discussed how to compare costs.

Settling Losses

If you buy insurance through an agent, you usually notify him or her when you have a loss. If you do not buy through an agent, or if you are away from home when a loss occurs, you may notify the insurer directly. In either case, it is worthwhile to know something about how losses are settled, both in property-liability and in life-health insurance.

PROPERTY-LIABILITY INSURANCE

In property-liability insurance, the process of paying claims for losses is known as **loss adjustment.** In most cases, the person representing the insurer is called a **claims adjuster.** Insurers use several different types of adjusters: agents, company adjusters, and independent adjusters.

Some *agents* have the authority to pay the insured directly for small property losses and make recommendations concerning payment for larger losses. **Company adjusters** are employees who work out of the home office, branch office, or drive-in claim facility of the insurer and devote their full time to loss settlement. **Independent adjusters,** on the other hand, work on a contract basis for several insurers. In contrast with these, a **public adjuster** represents the insured rather than the insurer. He or she generally charges a percentage of the amount received from the insurer as a fee for services.

When you notify the insurer that you have had a loss, the function of the company or independent adjuster is to determine if the loss is covered by your policy and, if so, the amount of the loss. Determining the amount of a loss and whether or not it is covered can be simple in some cases and complicated in others. As a claimant, you will not want to pay for the services of a public adjuster unless you think the insurer is unjustly handling your claim or unless your claim is especially complicated.

LIFE-HEALTH INSURANCE

Benefits payable under life and health insurance contracts are seldom negotiated; they are either paid or denied. The process is simpler than in property-liability insurance because there are no partial losses; a claim is almost always paid in full or not at all. When proof of the death of the insured is received by the insurer's claims (or benefits) department, records are checked to determine that the policy was in force at the time of death and that the person who is requesting payment is the one entitled to receive payment. Situations in which complications may develop were pointed out in chapter 15 when we discussed policy provisions. When complications exist, life-health insurers use their own claim representatives or local attorneys to make investigations and recommendations. Typical investigations address questions such as those in figure 25–4.

FIGURE 25–4

Claim Investigation Questions

1. Was fraud and/or misrepresentation involved?
2. Was death from normal causes, suicide, or an accident?
3. Was the insured's age or sex misstated?
4. Can a disappeared insured be located?
5. Is the party claiming benefits the beneficiary named by the insured?
6. Is the claimant truly disabled in accordance with the policy's definition of disability?
7. Has the physician submitted an excessive bill?
8. On exactly what date did disability begin (or end)?
9. Is it reasonable to encourage a disabled insured to pursue a program of rehabilitation?
10. Is an otherwise covered health claim the result of an excluded preexisting condition?

Consumer Applications

Finding a Superior Agent and Settling a Claim

A superior agent can help you, but how do you locate one? We discussed how losses are settled, but what if you have a problem? These practical questions confront every insurance consumer, so let's discuss them.

FINDING A SUPERIOR AGENT

Insurance agents are not hard to find. Just look in the Yellow Pages, or, wait until one finds you. But how do you identify a superior agent? There is no sure-fire method, any more than there is for identifying a superior attorney or physician. The questions listed in figure 25–5 may, however, help you identify those most likely to meet your needs.

Except for surplus lines insurance, it is illegal to sell insurance without a license from the state in which it is sold. Avoid buying insurance from unlicensed people. Agents who have CLU, ChFC, CPCU, or CIC designations have demonstrated that they were well-informed in the field of insurance at the time their designations were earned. A life-health agent who is not a CLU or a ChFC, or a property-liability agent who is not a CPCU or CIC, may be just as well-informed and have just as much ability, but he or she has not demonstrated these characteristics in a way that can be easily identified.

An agent's *freedom* refers to his or her ability to shop the market. Some agents represent only one insurer or group of companies and cannot place business with others. There is nothing wrong with this arrangement and it may fully meet your needs, but you should be aware of it so you will know what to expect. An exclusive agent will offer you only

the insurance provided by his or her companies. To find out how much freedom an agent has, ask the person with how many companies he or she is affiliated.

Ask how long the agent has been in the insurance business. At least five years is preferable. There is no substitute for experience. Why do business with a beginner when your family's financial well-being is at stake?

For the same reason, a *full-time* agent is preferable to a part-time agent. Even full-time agents find it difficult to keep abreast of developments in insurance; it is impossible for most part-time agents to do so. You can find out if an agent works full time by asking him or her and then verifying the answer with the agency.

Does the agent *keep up in the insurance field?* How can your agent help you if he or she is out of date? Ask your agent what he or she does to keep up. Be specific: What do you read? What insurance seminars have you attended during the last two years? Figure 25–6 shows some good answers.

Does the agent *render service?* Ask the agent for the names and telephone numbers of several people who buy

FIGURE 25–6
What the Superior Agent Might Do to Stay Current

READ:	ATTEND:
Benefits Quarterly	Agent's association seminars or
Best's Review	meetings
Business Insurance	CLU, ChFC seminars, meetings, or
CFP Journal	classes
CLU, ChFC Journal	CPCU or CIC seminars or classes
CPCU Journal	Estate planning seminars or
Employee Benefits Journal	meetings
Financial Planning	Industry-sponsored seminars
The Insurance Forum	Risk management seminars
Journal of Commerce	State bar or CPA association seminars on insurance and legal issues
National Underwriter	University management center
Risk Management	seminars
Rough Notes	Insurer training schools
Wall Street Journal	Million Dollar Round Table meetings
Weekly Underwriter	

FIGURE 25–5
Superior Agent Checklist

1. Is the agent licensed in your state?
2. Is the agent a CLU, ChFC, CPCU, or CIC?
3. Does the agent have sufficient freedom to place your business?
4. How long has the agent been in the insurance business?
5. Is the agent a full-time agent?
6. Does the agent keep current in the field?
7. What services does the agent render to clients?
8. Does the agent seem truly interested in your needs?
9. Does the agent seem ethical?
10. Do people knowledgeable about insurance recommend the agent?

insurance from him or her. Ask those people the questions listed in figure 25-7.

The superior agent is a professional in the sense that his or her primary interest is your insurance needs, considering all the circumstances surrounding your situation. Other agents may be primarily interested in making a sale simply to collect a commission. You will need to judge the agent's professionalism by observing the degree of the agent's interest in your special situation. See if the agent takes time to answer your questions, or if the objective seems to be to quickly sign you up and run to the next prospective sale. In the process, try to separate the agent's legitimate interest in an efficient use of time and a lack of concern about your needs.

Try to develop a feel for the agent's ethics. As an ultimate test, ask whether he or she thinks you should report a modest amount of earnings received in cash on your income tax return. The agent who would advise cheating the government might also cheat you.

While formation of your own judgment is important, the recommendation of another person with well-above-average knowledge about insurance is useful and comforting. If you know a superior property-liability insurance agent, he or she may recommend a superior life-health agent, and vice versa.

HANDLING YOUR CLAIM PROBLEM

If you have a problem settling a claim, ask your agent for help. If a superior agent cannot get you what you want, he or she can explain why. It is time-consuming and emotionally draining for you to fight with the adjuster, who is (usually) well-informed and experienced. It is particularly distressing to do battle and then learn that the adjuster was right. So be sure of the facts. Your conviction that the insurer is wrong should be based on careful consideration of all relevant information. What does your contract say? How does the contract language fit the facts surrounding your claim? Once that is established, you are ready to proceed. Figure 25-8 suggests questions to ask yourself.

FIGURE 25-7
....

Agent Service

1. What has the agent done for you lately?
2. What did the agent do when you had a loss?
3. When was the last time you called the agent?
4. When was the last time the agent communicated with you by telephone, mail, or in person?
5. Has the agent suggested changes from time to time to keep the coverage current?
6. Are you reluctant to ask the agent for service? If so, why?

FIGURE 25-8
....

Checklist for Handling a Claim

1. Am I a named insured or beneficiary under the policy?
2. Have I fulfilled all the conditions of the policy?
3. Have I done all the policy requires of me?
4. What does the policy cover?
5. Does the claim fit a policy exclusion?
6. What values are involved?
7. Is the amount of money worth fighting about, or is this a matter of principle?
8. What is the problem from the insurer's point of view?

What to Do

Take photographs, including the scene of any accident, bruises, property damage, and other relevant physical evidence. Talk with witnesses. Once you are sure of the facts regarding your claim and policy, you are ready to begin negotiating with the claims adjuster. Claim negotiations are usually conducted orally, but you should put them in writing as soon as possible after each conversation to provide some record of what was said. If a situation arises in which you may have to fight for your rights, you would be wise to communicate in writing and request that the adjuster do the same. Written statements tend to be conservative; they are created with more care than oral statements. An unreasonable position may not be as obvious when expressed orally as it is when written—and this applies equally to both sides of any controversy.

Resist the temptation to be in a hurry about settling. Insurance company management does not like to have resisted claims on the books for an extended period. Disputed claims usually cost more than those settled promptly. Moreover, insurance regulators become concerned about an insurer with an excessive number of claims pending.

If a disputed claim involves both bodily injury and other losses, you may be able to apply a little leverage by delaying settlement until you are confident about the future effects of the injuries. For example, suppose the negligence of an insured driver causes physical damage to your automobile and the insurer is attempting to pay less than you believe is reasonable on the repairs and on the rental of a substitute vehicle. Letting the adjuster know about potential long-term health problems or disability will place property damage in proper perspective. We are not advocating false claims, but we do subscribe to the view that sometimes it is necessary to level the playing field with an experienced adjuster. Assuming you have suffered some bodily injury or pain, tell the police something like, "My arm hurts but not badly enough to need medical attention at this time." Under these circumstances, don't say, "I'm okay; I'm not hurt."

Also avoid admitting negligence or liability following an accident. The facts will determine this later.

Sources of Help

It may be worthwhile to write to the state insurance department for help with a claim payment problem.[15] Insurance commissioners do not want to become claims adjusters, but they can use moral suasion if they think an insured is being treated unfairly. It is insurance company policy to "get along" with commissioners.

Another approach is to write a courteous letter to the insurance company president and explain the problem.[16] Most top executives are concerned about their company's image and alert to the consumer's problems. In many cases, they are not familiar with the treatment given their insureds and appreciate hearing from them. Keep a copy of your letters and those from the insurer. You may need them as evidence later.

A request for arbitration may lead to an efficient solution. Some policies provide an arbitration or appraisal pro-

15. See Appendix G for addresses and telephone numbers of state insurance departments.
16. You can get his or her name and address from your agent, the state insurance department, *Best's Insurance Reports: Property-Liability United States*, or *Best's Insurance Reports: Life-Health United States*.

FIGURE 25–9

Claim Negotiation Checklist

1. Read your insurance policy for coverage, conditions, and exclusions.
2. Perform all your obligations required by the contract.
3. Keep a written record of conversations.
4. Communicate in writing; keep copies.
5. Take your time.
6. Use leverage.
7. Write the company president.
8. Contact the state insurance department.
9. Use arbitration.
10. Get a public adjuster or lawyer.

vision. Arbitration is much cheaper than litigation. Finally, if all else fails, get a public adjuster or a lawyer. He or she will tell you if you are right or wrong and if it is worthwhile to engage his or her services. In many cases, a company that has ignored your pleading for decent treatment will bend upon receiving a letter from an attorney or public adjuster. If such is not the case, you may need to take legal action. It is better to negotiate than to fight, but negotiation is most effective when it is based on strength perceived by the insurer. Consult the claim negotiation checklist in figure 25–9.

Key Terms

large-loss principle
avoidance of first-dollar coverage
    principle
no-load life insurance
general agent
personal producing general agents
branch manager
independent agent
direct writers
exclusive agents
salaried representatives
broker
mass merchandising basis
financial planner

CLU
ChFC
CPCU
financial strength
due diligence
insurance specifications
underwriting capacity
service
loss adjustment
claims adjuster
company adjusters
independent adjusters
public adjuster

Discussion Questions

1. Are small deductibles preferable in most instances?

2. Your friend says, "I don't bother insuring against losses that probably won't happen. If the insurance company can be guided by probability, why can't I?" How would you respond to this statement?

3. Many people say, "I don't have to be concerned about the financial strength of my insurance company because we have a guaranty fund. Furthermore, a weak company could not get a license in this state." Do you agree? Why, or why not?

4. It is sometimes asserted that you should avoid small insurers and always buy from the largest one you can find. Bigger companies are more financially secure! Do you agree with this advice? Why, or why not?

5. Some insurers that do business by mail or by television advertising state prominently, "No agent will call on you." Is this really an advantage to you, or is it their way of making a virtue out of a shortcoming? Please explain.

6. How do agents and brokers differ?

7. Advertising by the Independent Insurance Agents of America extols the unique features of the American Agency System and the Independent Agent whose logo is the "Big I." Does this advertising influence your choice of an agent? Do you prefer one type of agent to others? If so, why?

8. Upon hearing the advice that, "It is usually best to buy life insurance from a person who has been in the business at least five years," a life insurance company general agent became upset and said rather vehemently, "How do you think we could recruit an agency force if everybody took your advice?" How would you have answered that question?

9. Under what circumstances would you advise an insured who has suffered a loss to hire a public adjuster?

10. List several approaches to negotiating with an insurer that does not seem to be settling your claim properly.

Cases

25.1 Your acquaintance, Nancy Barns, recently commented to you that she and her husband wanted to reevaluate their homeowners insurance. Nancy said that it seemed the only time they ever had any contact with their present insurance agency was when a premium was due. Nancy asked if you knew of a good agency. She also asked what the term CPCU meant.

1. Help Nancy set up standards to evaluate and choose a "good" agent.
2. Review with her the standards of education and experience required of an agent with the CPCU designation.

25.2 Fred A. Juster recently wrote to you indicating that his company would consider settling your insurance claim for approximately one-half of what you believe you should receive. This was Mr. Juster's final offer, according to his letter. Bill, your neighbor, suggested you discuss this matter with the insurance commissioner. Jack, your other neighbor, said as far as he knew, the state insurance commissioner's office didn't settle claim disputes.

1. In a case of this type, what position does your state's office of insurance take?
2. What other alternatives could you pursue to seek a fair claim settlement?

25.3 Ms. Judy Maxwell, a 22-year-old single woman beginning her career in real estate sales, recently asked you to help with a perplexing decision. Judy said she must soon purchase some health coverage for herself. Her budget will not allow her to buy both "first-dollar" coverage and major medical. She likes the idea of health insurance that pays part of the bills common to everyday types of ailments. What she doesn't like is that this coverage is rather expensive and pays up to a rather low maximum amount, then pays no more. Judy realizes that major medical appears to be just the opposite. For the type of major medical Judy would choose, she would have to pay the first $250 and then the policy would pay 80 percent of the bills up to the point where she had to pay $1,000 (above the deductible) in a calendar year. Then it would pay 100 percent of covered charges up to maximum payments of $1 million. She has $200 of savings and expects to earn $25,000 per year beyond her business expenses. She admits she finds this decision hard to make. It is confusing.

1. Make a recommendation for Judy.
2. What buying principle applies in a case such as this?

25.4 You are reading the Sunday newspaper when you notice a health insurance advertisement. Upon reading the ad, you note that you can get the first month's coverage for one dollar, and that the insurance seems to be a real bargain.

Are there any problems you should be aware of when buying insurance through the mail? List them, and explain how you could cope with them if you did purchase coverage in this manner.

CHAPTER 26

Regulation[1]

Introduction To regulate or not to regulate? And if we regulate, should we do so at the state or federal level? These questions have appeared often before the U.S. public and legislators. Throughout the history of the United States, we have oscillated between extensive and minimal overt regulation of most industries, and have vacillated between federal and state authority. Insurance, because of some specific product and industry characteristics, has long been actively regulated. Most of it has been at the state level, although repeated discussions of federal involvement leave the issue open for consideration. A full understanding of insurance requires some knowledge of how it is regulated. In this chapter, we will discuss:

1. The rationale for insurance regulation.
2. The historical development of insurance regulation.
3. How insurance is regulated and by whom.
4. Questions currently being debated regarding insurance regulation.

1. We are grateful for the insightful and thorough review of this chapter provided by Joseph M. Belth.

Rationale for Insurance Regulation

As suggested, the decision of whether or not and to what degree to regulate business is not obvious. Experts tend to provide compelling arguments in favor and against regulation for any given situation. Generally, however, we can categorize the reasons for regulation into three areas:

1. Industry members have monopoly, oligopoly, or other excessive power over consumers.
2. Information is imperfect.
3. Public policy calls for regulation.

These reasons imply that competition might not exist in some situations and/or might not succeed in producing satisfactory performance for consumers. Perfectly competitive markets are considered to exist when the industry involves (1) a large number of buyers and sellers, (2) free entry and exit for firms, (3) perfect product knowledge among buyers and sellers, (4) homogenous prices for homogeneous products, and (5) no collusion among firms. If one of these elements is missing, excess power may exist and government regulation may be appropriate. Recently, however, economic theorists have come to recognize that perfect competition might be too stringent a requirement. Instead, they have proposed the concept of "contestable markets" as the standard against which to measure the need for government intervention. Contestable markets exist when entry and exit are free, and the product or service can be produced at competitive costs by relatively small companies. These three reasons for regulation apply as well in a contestable markets framework as in a competitive markets framework.

What about the insurance industry? How does it measure up against the three reasons generally offered to regulate an industry? In the United States, thousands of companies sell insurance. Further, while there may be some disagreement, most research indicates that no single firm enjoys excessive power.[2] An interesting point is that the law of large numbers favors having insurers share information about losses and expenses. Regulation against collusive behavior, therefore, differs for the insurance industry. This concept is discussed more fully in the section on the historical development of insurance regulation.

Information, however, may be considered imperfect in the insurance industry. Before taking this class, had you ever read an insurance policy? Did you feel knowledgeable in purchasing insurance coverage? Most consumers feel unable to negotiate with insurers or even to comprehend the product offered, and most probably are unable to negotiate. Often the complexity derives from insurer efforts to provide the exact coverage they intend to sell. The complexity is an unfortunate by-product. Differences among insurers, furthermore, are unclear. Aggravating these conditions is the fact that the consumer cannot sample the product or take it out for a test run to determine how it works. If the product works differently than desired, we cannot return the policy for a new one until it is too late—until a loss has occurred. Furthermore, long time periods may exist be-

---

2. Cummins and Weiss ("Regulation and the Automobile Insurance Crisis," *Regulation,* Spring 1992) note, however, that even a market involving more than 1,000 firms nationally may portray high concentration in certain high-risk categories.

tween policy purchase and occurrence of a loss. As a result, maintaining insurer solvency is critical and is uncertain at the start. Imperfect product knowledge is one reason to regulate the insurance industry. Some regulations implemented to meet this need include financial disclosures, approval of policy provisions, and pricing restrictions.

Insurance is considered "vested in the public interest," meaning that society is enhanced by the proper functioning of an insurance industry. Public policy, therefore, calls for the regulation of insurance. In chapter 9, for example, we discussed programs to assure the availability of automobile liability insurance. These programs are designed to protect the financial interest of both drivers and automobile accident victims. In chapter fifteen we discussed the suicide clause and incontestability provision of life insurance, both required policy provisions to protect beneficiaries. In chapter 20 we talked about various efforts throughout the United States to make health insurance available and affordable for everyone.

History of Insurance Regulation

For most of U.S. history, insurance has been regulated primarily at the state level. Understanding why this is and what the limitations are of state regulation may help explain the entire insurance regulatory scheme. The constant tug between state and federal control also should be noted.

PAUL v. VIRGINIA AND THE NAIC

For its first one hundred years, the United States developed primarily as a set of very independent entities (the states). Federalism was not given great strength, and perhaps to some extent was feared. Physical barriers to communication enhanced the separateness. The advent of the Civil War, however, forced the states to unite, first on sides and then finally as a whole.

Undoubtedly, the historical development of the country affected the development of all regulation, including that of insurance. Initial regulation of insurance involved company charters. A charter broadly defines the organization and establishes a state of domicile. Early in our history, most states required very little else of an insurer.

Yet insurance needs to be geographically spread to minimize the likelihood of insurer insolvency. Licensing requirements that permitted insurers chartered in one state to sell insurance in another state developed as a result. States later began to monitor insurer financial performance, license companies and agents, monitor business practices, and tax insurers. In 1841, New Hampshire organized a special state department to regulate insurance. All the other states soon followed suit. Most of these state organizations have been called **insurance departments,** whose director is called the **Commissioner (or Superintendant) of Insurance.**

As a result of this development, insurance became subject to relatively independent state regulations. As the country became more unified and insurance became more readily available across state borders, the insurance industry sought a uniform regulatory body that would allow insurers to operate in many states without facing differing and sometimes conflicting state laws and regulations. Their efforts to unify regulation culminated in the 1869 case heard before the U.S. Supreme Court, *Paul v. Virginia.*[3]

The plaintiff in this case, Samuel Paul, was an agent for a New York insurer working in Virginia. He argued that the state's (Virginia's) imposition of a licensing fee was unconstitutional, because he was in the business of interstate commerce. U.S. laws hold that interstate commerce is regulated by the federal government unless otherwise specified by the U.S. Congress; therefore, Virginia would be able to license intrastate commerce, not interstate commerce. The Supreme Court found against Paul, holding that insurance is not commerce, could not be interstate commerce, and therefore would not be regulated by the federal government.

Thus, the High Court had set down a firm rule for insurance to be state regulated. Still believing that some uniformity of regulation and sharing of information were desired, the state commissioners of insurance organized themselves and in 1871 formed the National Convention of Insurance Commissioners, later changed to the **National Association of Insurance Commissioners (NAIC).** The organization developed with the purposes of (1) developing the uniform statement blank; (2) sharing information (thereby saving the effort of each commissioner to deal with the same or similar problem); (3) promoting consistency across states through the use of "model laws," which are prototypes of regulatory legislation preferred by NAIC members who then work to have the laws passed by their individual states; and (4) organizing some political clout by working together.

U.S. v. SOUTHEAST UNDERWRITERS ASSOCIATION

Over the years, state regulation expanded in breadth and depth. Insurers and their regulators came to know what to expect from one another. Simultaneously, commerce (including insurance) became increasingly interstate, requiring increased federal regulation. Some of the more significant federal laws involve antitrust regulations, which forbid collusion, sharing of information, and similar abuse of industry power. Insurers were believed not to be subject to these federal antitrust laws because of *Paul v. Virginia* and a number of subsequent cases that followed the *Paul* reasoning. Insurers, therefore, shared information about premiums, losses, and expenses through organizations called **"rating bureaus."** The rating bureaus were able to apply the principles of the law of large numbers (discussed in chapter 1) to calculate relatively accurate prices for coverage. Some states even required adherence to bureau rates unless given specific permission to deviate. The bureaus also developed standard policy language.

In 1944, the federal government brought suit against one of these bureaus (the Southeast Underwriters Association, SEUA) for violation of federal antitrust laws.[4] The Supreme Court agreed with the federal government that SEUA inappropriately violated federal antitrust laws (the Sherman Act, specifically). *Paul v. Virginia* was distinguished, in that *Paul* involved the state's power to tax and license insurers operating in the state

3. 75 U.S. (8 Wall.) 168, 19 L.Ed. 357 (1869).
4. United States v. Southeast Underwriters Association, 322 U.S. 533, 64 S.Ct. 1162, 88 L.Ed. 1440 (1944).

while *SEUA* involved the federal government's right to regulate the interstate nature of insurance activities, including regulation against collusive sharing of information, as SEUA had been charged with.

THE McCARRAN-FERGUSON ACT

As might be expected, the states and insurers found themselves in some turmoil over the SEUA decision. Authority for insurance regulation was unclear, and the ability to use rating bureaus (considered critical by some) was placed in jeopardy.

Rapid and extensive lobbying of the U.S. Congress followed, and **Public Law 15 (The McCarran-Ferguson Act)** was quickly passed in 1945. This law provides for state regulation of the insurance industry to the extent that such regulation is adequate (leaving room for federal intervention). Further, federal antitrust laws are specifically held not to apply to the insurance industry, *except* for instances of boycott, coercion, or intimidation.

While we write these pages, insurance remains primarily state-regulated; however, there is movement in the U.S. Congress toward greater federal involvement. Current federal involvement includes security regulations related to variable life insurance and similar products, and indirect regulation through the Employee Retirement Income Security Act (ERISA), federal flood insurance, and other related activities. Discussions of extended federal regulation of insurance currently center on insolvency concerns. The question of antitrust laws also is in doubt, as several states recently sued members of the insurance industry and a rating organization for harm caused by collusion. These issues are discussed later in the chapter.

Nature of State Regulation

State legislatures pass insurance laws that form the basis for insurance regulation. Common forms of insurance regulatory laws are listed in table 26–1. Insurance laws are concerned with licensing requirements for insurers, agents, brokers, and claim adjusters; and with the circumstances under which such licenses may be denied or revoked. They also provide standards of financial solvency, including methods of establishing reserves[5] and the types of investments permitted. Provision is made for the

TABLE 26–1

Common Types of Insurance Regulatory Laws

- licensing requirements
- solvency standards
- liquidation/rehabilitation provisions
- rating (pricing) restrictions
- trade practice requirements
- subsidy programs
- taxation

5. Reserves are described later in this chapter.

liquidation or rehabilitation of any insurance company in severe financial difficulty. Solvency is affected by product pricing (setting rates), and rate regulation represents a very public and time-consuming part of the commissioner's job. Trade practices, including marketing and claims adjustment, are also under the purview of the commissioner's office. Legislation further creates schemes to make certain types of insurance readily available at affordable (i.e., subsidized) prices. The taxation of insurers, at the state level, is also spelled out in the insurance code for each state. Several of these items are discussed here.

Every state has an insurance department to administer insurance laws. In some states, the commissioner of insurance is also another official of the state government, such as state treasurer, state auditor, or director of banking. In most states, however, acting as commissioner of insurance is the person's sole responsibility. In some states, the commissioner is appointed, in others she or he is elected. Most insurance departments have relatively few staff employees, but several are large. The small departments are generally ill-equipped to provide anything approaching effective regulation of such a powerful industry.

COMMISSIONER OF INSURANCE

The commissioner of insurance is a far more powerful official than most people outside the insurance industry realize. Perhaps no other official has as much influence over a major industry.

The insurance code requires the commissioner to enforce its provisions and carry out the duties it imposes. It confers certain powers upon him or her specifically; others may be implied from the provisions of the code. The commissioner is empowered to:

1. Grant, deny, or suspend licenses of both insurer and insurance agents.
2. Require an annual report from insurers.
3. Examine insurers' business operations.
4. Act as a liquidator or rehabilitator of insolvent insurers.
5. Investigate complaints.
6. Originate investigations.
7. Decide whether to grant all, part, or none of an insurer's request for higher rates.
8. Propose new legislation to the legislature.
9. Approve or reject an insurer's proposed new or amended insurance contract.
10. Promulgate regulations that interpret insurance laws.

Most insurance departments handle complaints from consumers, and some of them do a good job. Some departments provide ready access for consumers by making toll-free telephone lines available and publicizing their interest in the consumer. A number of departments have published consumer guides to buying insurance, some of which are well done and can be helpful.

LICENSING REQUIREMENTS

An insurer must have a license from each state in which it conducts business. This requirement is for the purpose of exercising control. Companies organized (i.e., chartered) in a state are known as **domestic insurers.** **Foreign insurers** are those formed in another state; **alien insurers** are those organized in another country. The commissioner has more control over domestic companies than over foreign and alien ones. He or she has generally less control over insurers not licensed in the state.

An insurer obtains licenses in its state of domicile and each additional state where it plans to conduct insurance business. Holding a license implies that the insurer meets specified regulatory requirements designed to protect the consumer. It also implies that the insurer has greater business opportunities than do nonlicensed insurers. A foreign insurer can conduct business by direct mail in your state without a license from your state. In addition, nonadmitted or nonlicensed insurers are used for the placement of surplus lines or excess insurance unavailable from licensed insurers. That is, nonlicensed insurers are permitted to sell insurance only if no licensed company is willing to provide the coverage. You have access to nonadmitted insurers through persons who hold special "licenses" as **surplus lines agents** or brokers.

Financial Requirements

In order to qualify for a license, an insurer must fulfill certain financial requirements. Stock insurers must have a specified amount of capital and surplus (that is, net worth), and mutual insurers must have a minimum amount of surplus (remember that mutual companies have no stock and therefore do not show "capital" on their balance sheets). The amount depends upon the line of insurance and the state law. Typically, a multiple-line insurer must have more capital (and/or surplus) than a company offering only one line of insurance.[6]

Insurers must also maintain certain levels of capital and surplus to hold their license. Historically, these requirements have been set in simple dollar values. More recently, requirements for **"risk-based capital"** are being implemented in many jurisdictions. Remember that capital reflects the excess value a firm holds in assets over liabilities. It represents a financial cushion against hard times. Some assets, such as common stocks, may have values that vary widely over time; that is, they involve more risk than do certain other assets. To account for variations in risks among different assets, commissioners of insurance, through their state legislators, have begun requiring firms to hold assets sufficient to produce a level of acceptable capital on a risk-adjusted basis. The extent to which such requirements will be implemented is uncertain at the time of this writing, but many states appear interested in moving toward risk-based regulations.

....
6. The theory of this requirement is that a company offering all lines of insurance may have greater variations of experience than a company engaged in only one or a few lines and, therefore, should have a greater cushion of protection for policyholders. It seems reasonable to believe, however, that the opposite may be the case; bad experience in one line may be offset by good experience in another line.

Other Qualifications

Even when financial requirements are met, a license may be denied under certain circumstances. If the management is incompetent or unethical, or lacking in managerial skill, the insurance commissioner is prohibited from issuing a license. Because unscrupulous financiers have found insurers fruitful prospects for the milking of assets and stock manipulation, some state laws prohibit the licensing of any company that has been in any way associated with a person whose business activities the insurance commissioner believes are characterized by bad faith. The Equity Funding case, in which millions of dollars in fictitious life insurance were created and sold to reinsurers, for example, shows how an insurer can be a vehicle for fraud on a gigantic scale.[7] Some commissioners may believe that executives involved with fraud should not be allowed to form other insurance companies in the future.

SOLVENCY REGULATIONS

Investment Requirements

The solvency of an insurer depends partly on the amount and quality of its assets. Because poor investment policy caused the failure of many companies in the past, investments are carefully regulated. The insurance code spells out in considerable detail which investments are permitted and which are prohibited. Life insurers have more stringent investment regulations than property-liability insurers, because some of the contracts made by life insurers cover a longer period of time, even a lifetime or more.

Reserve Requirements

The investment requirements discussed above concern the nature and quality of insurer assets. The value of assets an insurer must hold is influenced by capital and surplus requirements and the regulation of reserves. **Reserves** are insurer liabilities that represent future financial obligations. The total amount of reserves (plus other liabilities) determines the minimum amount of assets necessary to meet any given capital and surplus requirement (capital and surplus is what remains after liabilities are subtracted from assets). A company required to have $1 million capital and surplus, for example, must have $10 million in assets if its liabilities are $9 million. Reserves constitute the bulk of insurance company liabilities, so in effect the calculation of reserves determines the assets required. An insurer short of assets could conceal its financial situation by underestimating its reserve liabilities. If management integrity or regulation prevents such concealment, the insurer is forced by reserve liabilities to accumulate assets needed to meet future obligations. Because integrity and good judgment are not always present, *reserve requirements* are an important aspect of insurance regulation. Insurance regulation influences the size of an insurer's minimum reserve by specifying the method and assumptions to be used in their calculation. Compliance is verified during company examination.

....
7. See Raymond L. Dirks and Leonard Gross, *The Great Wall Street Scandal* (New York: McGraw-Hill Book Company, 1974).

Life insurance policy reserves are the main liabilities for an insurer that concentrates on the sale of cash-value (e.g., whole life or universal life) insurance. These reserves are conservative estimates of the extent to which the *present value of future claims by policyholders* exceed the *present value of future net premiums*. As each year goes by for a specific group of insureds, the present value of future claims increases on a per policy basis; those insureds remaining in the original group are older, the probability of death is higher, and less time remains for investment earnings to accumulate before claims are paid. At the same time, the present value of future premiums decreases, because fewer premiums remain to be paid and they have a shorter time to earn investment income. The present value of premiums is calculated without including the portion of the premium originally intended to cover the insurer's operating expenses. This is why the reference is to "net premiums."

Because the present value of the promises made by the insurer rises each year while the present value of future net premiums declines, the difference between the two—the reserve—rises over time. These reserves are estimates of the extent to which future payments will exceed inflows of money and are, therefore, liability items in your life insurer's balance sheet. Reserves indicate the need for the accumulation of assets to help meet future obligations to the extent that such obligations exceed premium income.

An annual valuation of reserves is required by the law of every state. As mentioned above, the law also prescribes the basis upon which minimum reserves are calculated, but an insurer is permitted to use any other basis that produces reserves equal to or greater than those produced by the statutory method. The basis prescribed by law for life insurance states the mortality table to be used, the maximum rate of interest to be assumed, and the formula to be used. Some insurers may estimate reserves on a more conservative basis than that required by law.

Property-liability insurers are required to establish unearned premium reserves and loss reserves. The **unearned premium reserve** is essentially a debt to policyholders for protection not yet delivered; the full premium does not belong to the insurer until the policy term has elapsed. If the premium charged for one year's protection is $1,200, for example, the insurer earns $100 each month. After twelve months, the whole premium is earned. At any point during the policy period, the amount earned is the product of the portion of the term that has elapsed and the total premium for the period. The balance is unearned, and a reserve must be set up for the unearned portion. This reserve calls attention to the fact that part of the money taken in has not yet been earned. In the event of cancellation of the policy by either the insurer or insured, the unearned premium would have to be returned to the policyholder. For example, if the insurer cancelled after six months, it would be required to return to the policyholder one-half of the original premium, or $600 in this example.[8]

Loss reserves must also be set up to indicate the obligation to policyholders for losses reported but not yet paid and those that have occurred

---

8. When the insured cancels, something less than the pro rata portion (called a "short rate") is returned, under the theory that the insured incurred expenses that the insured should pay for if the insured chooses to cancel.

but are as yet unreported. The expenses of adjusting losses are included as part of loss reserves.

For both unearned premium reserves and loss reserves, the method of calculation (or estimation) is prescribed by law. The purpose of this requirement is to see that future obligations are not underestimated. Yet for losses associated with asbestos, hazardous waste, and some other substances insurers have had grossly inadequate reserves. Some insolvencies do occur (future obligations are insufficiently reserved). As a result, we see that the system does not always work.

Guaranty Associations

In spite of the best efforts of insurance executives and regulators, some insurers fail. When an insurer becomes insolvent, it may be placed either in rehabilitation or liquidation. In either case, policyholders who have claims against the company for losses covered by their policies or for a refund of unearned premiums may have to wait a long time while the wheels of legal processes turn. Even after a long wait, insurer assets may cover only a fraction of the amount owed to policyowners. In the aggregate, this problem is not large; only about 1 percent of insurers become insolvent each year. Fortunately, most of these insurers have historically been small. If you are affected, however, such losses may be catastrophic for you.

Until the 1960s, policyholders were lucky to receive a sympathy card from the insurer or the insurance commissioner when such a disaster occurred. Now, however, all states have **state guaranty associations** for both property-liability and life-health insurance to assure that you do not bear the entire burden of such losses. Instead, unpaid claims and return premiums owed to insureds or claimants of a defunct company are paid through a guaranty fund that requires involuntary contributions from solvent insurers doing business in the state. Most guaranty associations limit the maximum they will reimburse any single insured, and most also provide coverage only to residents of the state.

The guaranty association in your state assesses each company on the basis of the percentage of its premium volume to cover the obligations to policyholders. A solvent company that writes 10 percent of the automobile insurance in a state, for example, is required to pay for 10 percent of a defunct automobile insurer's obligations to insureds and their beneficiaries. No assessment for "riskiness" is charged. The same procedure applies under a separate fund for life-health losses. New York is the only state with any advance funding of its guaranty association. Other associations make assessments only after losses are incurred. Thus, the insolvent insurer never contributes to payment of its own losses. In addition, many states' guaranty assessments can be offset against state premium tax obligations. This in effect transfers the impact of insurer insolvencies to the taxpayers of the state.

Guaranty associations operate only for the protection of you and your beneficiary. They are not designed to pay for losses suffered by stockholders of an insolvent insurer. Some argue that the insolvency of a giant-sized insurer would severely strain the capacity of the system of state-by-state guaranty associations; they recommend federal guaranty programs.[9] Furthermore, most states place caps on the amount an insurer can be assessed for the insolvency of others, which may limit the ability to reimburse affected policyholders for their covered losses. Proponents of federal guaranty programs also argue that the insolvency of one insurer should not affect policyholders differently simply because the policyholders reside in different states.

POLICY FORM APPROVAL

Insurance contracts prepared by insurers must be filed with and approved by the commissioner, prior to use in each state. Forms with inconsistent, ambiguous, or misleading clauses are likely to be disapproved. Some laws even indicate how the form should be printed.

Some lines of insurance (for example, workers' compensation) have the entire form standardized. In other lines, such as life insurance, specific provisions must be included and others are prohibited.

PRICING REGULATIONS

Rate Control

One of the more visible functions of a state insurance department is the regulation of rates (i.e., the charge per unit of insurance) for certain types of insurance. Recognize that the regulation of rates is inherently related to the regulation of insolvency. Rating is given separate attention, however, because solvency is not its only objective.

All approaches to rate control have the objective to produce rates that meet three tests or criteria:

1. Adequacy.
2. Reasonableness (not excessive).
3. No unfair discrimination.

Adequate rates are high enough (considering actuarial estimates of losses, expenses, and investment income) to maintain the insurer's solvency. *Reasonable rates* are not *too* adequate! That is, they do not produce unreasonably high profits for the insurer. The requirement of *no unfair discrimination* means that differences in rates must be based on differences in loss distributions; insureds with similar loss distributions must be charged similar rates. This protects the small insured who has little bargaining strength in lines of insurance (for example, liability coverage for daycare centers) where a seller's market tends to exist. Strong disagree-

....
9. For discussion see Kenneth H. Nails, "Guaranty Funds: The Growing Burden," *Best's Review* (Property/Casualty Ed.), July 1987: pp. 26–28, 81–82. Also see: Arthur O. Dummer, "Lessons of Baldwin-United," *Best's Review* (Life/Health Ed.), vol. 87, no. 4 (1986): pp. 12–16, 102–4. An ISO study estimated that an Aetna bankruptcy would require 97.9 percent of the nationwide total capacity of all state guaranty funds; an Allstate insolvency, 86.8 percent; and a Hartford insolvency, 67.8 percent (from Kenneth S. Abraham, *Insurance Law and Regulation* (Westbury, N.Y.: The Foundation Press, 1990): p. 97).

ment exists over what are fairly discriminating rates.[10] We discuss some of the relevant issues regarding rate discrimination at the end of this chapter.

Most states consider property-liability rates not adequately regulated by market forces. Minimum rates for individual life insurance and annuity contracts are regulated indirectly through limits imposed on assumptions used in establishing reserves. Competitive forces are the only determinants of maximum rates for individual life, individual annuity, and group life-health insurance. Rates on individual health insurance are regulated in some states. Individual disability and accident rates are controlled in some states by refusing to approve policy forms in which at least a target level (for example, 60 percent) of premiums is not expected to be returned to the policyholder as benefits. Expenses are ignored in the indirect regulation of life-health rates where reserves are based on "net premiums." Net premiums only reflect assumptions about losses and investment income.

The dominant type of property-liability rate regulation is the **prior approval** approach. In states that use this method, an insurer or its rating bureau must file its new rates and have them approved by the commissioner before using them. Another approach called **file-and-use** allows an insurer to begin using a new rate as soon as it is filed with the commissioner. The commissioner can disapprove the new rate if it is determined to be undesirable within a specified period, such as thirty days. A few states have adopted **open competition** rating laws. This approach requires no rate filings by an insurer. The underlying assumption is that market competition is a sufficient regulator of rates. Although results are mixed, studies of the effects of different types of rate regulation generally find no significant differences in the prices paid by consumers under different systems for the same service.

Expenses

Expenses of property-liability insurers are not regulated directly, but they are affected by rate regulation. If expenses are too high, they may cause rates to be too high for approval. To demonstrate further, if a rate of $1 is approved, income is increased to $1.10 by investment earnings, and loss payments require 80 cents, only 30 cents is left for expenses and profit. Assuming a given level of losses, rate limitations indirectly put a ceiling on expenses for the insurer who will at least break even financially.

The New York expense limitation insurance law places separate restrictions on how much can be spent to attract new life insurance business and on total operating expenses. These restrictions apply to all life insurance companies licensed to sell insurance there. This is significant because companies licensed in New York account for a major portion of the life insurance written in the United States. If they are licensed in New York,

---

10. The NAIC as far back as 1978 recognized the limitations of using only statistical factors in determining proper rating categories. ". . .[P]ublic policy considerations require more adequate justification for rating factors than simple statistical correlation with loss; in this regard the task force recommends consideration of criteria such as causality, reliability, social acceptability and incentive value in judging the reasonableness of a classification scheme." National Association of Insurance Commissioners, *Report of the Rates and Rating Procedure Task Force of the Automobile Insurance (D3) Subcommittee,* November 1978, pp. 5–6.

ETHICAL *Dilemma*

What Are Acceptable Pricing Factors?

The business of insurance inherently involves discrimination; otherwise, adverse selection would make insurance unavailable. Recall from chapter 3 that adverse selection may occur when pricing categories are so broad that both good and poor "risks" are lumped together to pay the same price. Under these conditions, low-risk individuals or organizations will choose not to participate, because they realize they are getting a bad deal. With only poor risks participating, insurance becomes prohibitively expensive. To prevent this market failure, insurers must charge low-risk insureds lower rates than high-risk insureds; i.e., they must price discriminate.

The dilemma arises in considering which factors are acceptable to use in pricing and underwriting decisions. Are all factors acceptable? Think about the use of race as a life insurance rating element. Statistically, African Americans have shorter life spans than do other Americans. Remember that you are being asked to consider a hypothetical situation: race has not been used as an underwriting factor for several decades, because its use is considered socially unacceptable. We could use different categorization schemes, such as state of residency, gender, rural versus urban, or a host of other factors. Ellis provided a strong opinion: "The fact of the matter is that all actuarial groupings are either entirely arbitrary, or based upon social value judgments, or, in the worst case, are merely reflections of social stereotypes and prejudice."[11] Which of these factors, then, are acceptable?

Some people believe that any characteristic over which we have no control, such as gender, age (although in life and annuity contracts, age seems to be accepted), or race ought to be excluded from insurance underwriting and rating practices. Their argument is that if insurance is intended in part to encourage safety, then its operation ought to be based on behavior, not on qualities with which we are born. Others argue that some of these factors are the best predictors of losses and expenses, and without them, insurance will function only extremely inefficiently. Additionally, some argument could be made that virtually no factor is truly voluntary or controllable. Is a poor resident of Chicago, for instance, able to move out of the inner city?

What is the answer? Could and should insurers be forced to find less socially significant factors for pricing and underwriting? Do insurers have an ethical responsibility to minimize race, gender, age, and other discrimination, even if actuarially appropriate? Does society benefit by limitation on insurer practices? Or is society negatively affected by higher insurance costs overall? Where one group is aided, another may be made less well off by experiencing higher insurance costs. Is this "fair" discrimination? These are extremely difficult issues to address, especially in an era of AIDS, wealth imbalances, and rapid technological changes. Creative input from people like you is needed.

11. Statement on behalf of the American Civil Liberties Union by Deborah A. Ellis before the Elimination of Discriminatory Insurance Practices Study Committee, Des Moines, Iowa, November 17, 1988, p. 2, taken from Donald W. Hardigree and Robert J. Carney, "Gender-Neutral Insurance Rating issues," *CPCU Journal* (September 1990).

the expense limitations (and some other aspects of the New York insurance law) apply to their operations in all other jurisdictions as well. The New York insurance department has the reputation of being a tougher regulator of insurance than that of any other state. Most other states are not as well equipped in terms of personnel, strong laws, and budgets. As a consumer, you can have more confidence in the quality of an insurer when it is licensed in New York. The expense limitation law is one example of this strength. Illinois has some minor life insurer expense regulation. Other states rely solely on competition to be an adequate force to control expenses.

The New York expense limitation law was implemented soon after the Armstrong investigation of 1906. The investigation discovered numerous extravagances and abuses of executive power, particularly in the operation of large mutual life insurers. Insurers lured agents from each other by offering higher and higher commissions. This competition for agents raised expenses and reduced dividends to policyholders. New York's expense limitation law is based on the premise that at least in some companies, no one is looking out for the interests of participating policyholders. In the absence of expense regulation, it is reasoned that some insurers will pay more than necessary to agents and company executives. The ultimate concern addressed in passing the law likely is insurer solvency, which may give New York justification for extending its effect to business activities outside the state.

REGULATION OF TRADE PRACTICES

Control of Agents

The qualifications and activities of persons engaged in selling insurance are controlled through licensing requirements and prohibition of certain practices. Agents and brokers in all states are required by law to be licensed prior to, or soon after, engaging in the insurance business. Some states also require adjusters and fee-only insurance counselors to be licensed. There is considerable variation in the licensing requirements. Some states have pre-exam educational and training requirements; others only require passing a written examination prior to licensing. Most states require only an elementary understanding of insurance, although continuing education requirements are increasing. In states with continuing education requirements, applicants must attent eight or more hours each year at commission-approved seminars, classes, and other organized educational experiences. Additional examinations are not usually required.

Insurance laws also prohibit certain activities on the part of agents and brokers, such as: (1) twisting, (2) rebating, (3) fraudulent practices, and (4) misappropriation of funds belonging to insurers or insureds. **Twisting** (also called churning) is inducing you to cancel one contract and buy another by misrepresenting the facts or providing incomplete policy comparisons. An unfair or misleading comparison of two contracts can be a disservice if it causes you to drop a policy you had for some time in order to buy another that is no better, or perhaps not as good. On the other hand, sometimes changing policies is in the best interest of the policyholder, and justified replacements are legal. Twisting regulations, therefore, may include the requirement that the resulting policy change be detrimental to the policyholder.

Rebating is providing (substantial) value as an inducement to purchase insurance. This is the same as price-cutting on cars and other products. Rebating, when for example the agent or broker shares his or her commission with you, is prohibited because:

1. It is considered unfair competition among agents.

2. Some knowledgeable consumers would buy a new policy each year if first year commissions are larger than renewal commissions; higher lapse rates increase long-run cost.

3. More sophisticated consumers could negotiate larger rebates than the less informed, and this would be unfair.[12]

4. Agents may be encouraged to engage in unethical behavior by selling new policies over renewal policies, due to the larger first-year commissions.

Some insurers adjust to rebating laws by offering their agents and brokers two or more series of contracts with the same provisions but with rates that reflect different levels of commissions. A particular insurer's "personal series," for example, may include a normal level of commissions. Its "executive series," however, may pay the agent or broker a lower commission and offer a lower rate to you. In competitive situations, the agent or broker is likely to propose the "executive series" in order to gain a price advantage. A few life insurers market individual life insurance contracts through fee-only financial planners, without paying any commissions. Commissions also are not built into premiums for products sold through the mail and other direct marketing channels. Group life-health insurance and commercial property-liability insurance often are sold on a bid basis, where specifications call for no (or low) agent or broker commissions. Thus, commissions are negotiable when the policyholder is an organization.

Given the evolution of different commission levels in individual insurance products and negotiated commissions on commercial/group products, questions exist concerning the need for continuing antirebating laws. The Florida Supreme Court decided in 1986 that the antirebate law was unconstitutional. This decision had the potential to increase pressure on other states to reconsider the practice, but very little activity on the subject has occurred since then. California's Proposition 103 (passed in 1988), however, includes a provision to abandon the state's antirebate laws. The ultimate effect of California's vote remains unclear.[13]

Unfair practices is a catch-all that can be applied to many undesirable activities of agents, claim adjusters, and insurers (including misleading advertisements). Unfair practices may lead to fines, removal of licenses, and, in extreme cases, to punitive damage awards by the courts. *Misappropriation* refers to situations in which the agent keeps funds (primarily premiums) belonging to the company, you, or a beneficiary. For example,

12. John S. Moyse, "Legalized Rebating—A Marketing View," *Journal of the American Society of CLU,* vol. 40, no. 5 (1986): p. 57.

13. See Tracy A. Bateman, "Insurance Anti-Rebate Statutes: Validity and Construction," *American Law Reports* 90, 4th ed., 1991: pp. 213–252.

an insured was killed by accident; his $1,000 life insurance policy had a double indemnity rider. In order to impress the beneficiary with the value of this rider, the insurer mailed two checks in the amount of $1,000 each to the agent for delivery. The agent gave one check to the beneficiary and then induced the beneficiary to endorse the second check to the agent, on the grounds that its issuance was in error and so it had to be cashed and the money returned to the insurer. The insurance department recovered the $1,000, paid it to the beneficiary, and revoked the agent's license.

Control of Claims Adjusting

Every insured has contact with an insurer's marketing system, most often through an agent. Regulation of agents, therefore, has significant impact on most insureds. Only those who make claims on their policies, however, have contact with claims adjusters. This is the time when an insured may be vulnerable and in need of regulatory attention.

Insurance commissioners control claims adjusting practices primarily through policyholder complaints. Any insured who believes that the insurer improperly handled or denied a claim should contact the insurance commissioner's office with details of the transaction. The commissioner's office will investigate the complaint. Unfortunately for the insured, the commissioner's office cannot require an insurer to pay a claim, although a letter from the commissioner's office that the insured is "in the right" may be persuasive. The most common form of "punishment" for wrongdoing is either a reprimand or fine against the insurer. Some commissioner's offices keep track of the number of complaints lodged against insurers operating in the state and publish this information on a standardized basis (e.g., per $100,000 of premium volume). The vast majority of complaints involve the insured's misunderstanding of coverage. Still, an insurer receiving many complaints probably is operating in some fashion that is undesirable from the consumer's standpoint, even if it is just to cause misunderstanding.

Control of Underwriting Practices

We have discussed the ways in which insurer pricing practices are regulated. Closely tied to ratemaking is an insurer's underwriting function. Over the years, insurers have used a variety of factors in their underwriting decisions. A number of these have become taboo from a public policy standpoint. Their use may be considered unfair discrimination.

In automobile insurance, for instance, factors such as marital status and living arrangements have played a significant underwriting role, with divorced insurance applicants considered "less stable" than never-married applicants. In property insurance, concern over redlining receives public attention periodically. Redlining occurs when an insurer designates a geographical area in which it chooses not to provide insurance, or only to provide it at substantially higher prices. These decisions are made without individually considering insurance applicants. Most often the redlined areas are in poor urban locations, which tends to place low-income inner-city dwellers at an even greater disadvantage than when insurance is available. Discussing a recent redlining case, Deepak Bhargava, the legislative director for the Association of Community Organizations for Reform

Now, said, "Insurance availability is a real economic development and poverty question. It is one of the few products poor people have to protect themselves."[14]

Over the years, the factors considered appropriate for underwriting have changed. We consider the issue more fully in the next section on regulatory debates. For now, realize that the insurance commissioner's office has some authority to regulate against inappropriate underwriting practices.

Regulatory Debates	### *AVAILABILITY AND AFFORDABILITY*

Making various types of property-liability insurance available at affordable prices has been a major regulatory concern in recent years. Most individuals and organizations want access to all the insurance they believe they need. At first blush, from an insurer's perspective, this seems like a desirable situation of high product demand. Elementary economics tells us that the high demand would increase prices and profits—an ideal situation from the insurer's perspective. Up to the point where prices become unacceptably high to consumer budgets, the private insurance system works well. Consumers have access to the insurance they need, and insurers make a satisfactory profit. But the high frequency and severity of claims for some forms of insurance produce such high supply-determined (actuarially fair) prices that the insurance is unaffordable for many. In some cases it is unavailable at any price, because adverse selection is too great.

The sometimes joint and sometimes mutually exclusive problems of availability and affordability are fueled by the following factors:

1. High frequency and severity of claims for certain types of insurance, sometimes only for particular insured groups.

2. Societal belief that insurers ought to provide universal access to all types of insurance at affordable prices.

3. Industry and regulatory practices that promote cost-based pricing.

The existence of highly frequent and severe claims leads to unaffordable and often unavailable (due to adverse selection) insurance, which is in direct conflict with society's belief that affordable insurance should be made available as a right. This societal belief is an excellent example of the ways in which insurance is "vested in the public interest." In 1994, debate over national health insurance provides an example of this phenomenon. Voter revolts (e.g., Proposition 103, approved by California voters in 1988) over automobile insurance pricing and marketing practices represent further examples.

Even when insurance is available, the public may consider pricing practices inappropriate because some segments of society cannot pay the price. Actuarially fair prices require insurers to set rates according to the insured's expected costs (the actual price will also account for insurer operating expenses, risk, and profit). Economic theory holds that prices ought to reflect expected costs, otherwise market decisions will be inefficient. Un-

14. Jennifer Sereno and Andy Hall, "Insurer Less Likely to Cover Blacks," *Wisconsin State Journal*, June 1993: p. 141.

derpricing, for instance, leads to excess demand for certain goods. In insurance, inadequate rates may lead to unsafe practices (e.g., inadequate loss prevention and reduction on the part of insureds), actually raising costs above what would be market-determined expenses.

In response, regulators and legislators have devised various mechanisms intended to meet social objectives. These include **automobile insurance plans** and **reinsurance facilities,** discussed in chapter 9. **Joint underwriting associations** in automobile liability and medical malpractice insurance markets also exist. Some states have similar programs for workers' compensation and health insurance, and other programs exist for property damage to beachfront property or damage caused by riots.

Each of these programs requires insurers to subsidize, in some form, the underpricing of insurance to high-risk insureds. The result is overpricing of coverage to the rest of the population and a divergence from cost-based ratemaking. Such a situation violates the requisite of "reasonable premiums" discussed in chapter 3. Many economists believe the result is a less efficient insurance industry, which ultimately is a hindrance to society. Other commentators believe such subsidizing is the best social policy available for these particular issues.

IS STATE REGULATION ADEQUATE?

This is another way of asking if state regulation is preferable to federal regulation. Proponents of state regulation claim that much insurance is local, and the state can regulate it in accordance with local needs and conditions. They say that the states are doing a fine job. Critics argue that state regulation is expensive, because it involves duplication for multistate insurers. At the same time, lack of uniformity among the states complicates compliance for these insurers. These critics say federal regulation would be more uniform and effective.

A report by the Subcommittee on Oversight and Investigations of the Committee on Energy and Commerce of the U.S. House of Representatives (John D. Dingell, Chair)[15] caused serious concern over current regulation of insurance, and has been a catalyst for various proposals to impose some federal regulatory control. In the report, six areas were highlighted as "the key weaknesses in the present system of solvency regulation." These were: (1) delegated management authority; (2) ownership structures involving holding companies and affiliates, leading to overleverage of insurance companies; (3) nonregulation of reinsurance, either in the market or by state commissioners; (4) use of unreliable information for assessing solvency; (5) insufficient regulation, due to inadequate resources, lack of coordination, infrequent regulatory examinations, poor information and communications, and uneven implementation; and (6) inadequate enforcement of illegal and/or negligent management of insurance companies.

Since publication of this report, Representative Dingell (among others) has worked to pass legislation designed to include federal involvement in insurance regulation.[16] The most widely discussed federal activities are the

---

15. "Failed Promises: Insurance Company Insolvencies" (U.S. Government Printing Office, February 1990).
16. Insurance regulators have responded by developing risk-based capital requirements and accreditation standards.

implementation of a national guaranty fund and the development of federal financial standards. Given that the Dingell report focuses on solvency, it is not surprising that proposals for federal regulation also focus on this issue. One concern with dual state-federal regulation of this sort is that it splits pricing regulation (apparently still under the state regulator's authority) from solvency regulation. Under such a strategy, state regulators may have little incentive to worry over the adequacy of rates, focusing more on the consumer's concerns about price fairness (which may incorporate societal issues or proper rating factors) and affordability.

Other federal proposals attack the McCarran-Ferguson Act. Some call for the complete repeal of McCarran-Ferguson. Others focus on the antitrust exemption. Most commercial purchasers of insurance, as well as most insurers, prefer to maintain the legality of information sharing. Their economic rationale is that information sharing mostly aids smaller insurers who are less able to predict losses than are large insurers. Oddly enough, therefore, imposition of federal antitrust regulations on the insurance industry may diminish competition, because only larger insurers would be able to function competitively.

SHOULD UNDERWRITING FACTORS BE LIMITED?

In the discussion of control of underwriting practices, we mentioned the public debate over acceptable underwriting and pricing factors. Race and gender are two factors that historically have caused negative public reaction. Most recently, any factor not within the control of the insured appears open for debate.

In 1988, the issue received extensive media attention with the passage of Proposition 103 in California. Prop. 103 affected insurance regulation in a number of significant ways, including the imposition of a rate rollback, limitations of acceptable profitability measures, and elections for state insurance commissioner (as opposed to governor appointment). The initial media attention on Prop. 103, however, seemed to concentrate on limitations on rating and underwriting factors for automobile insurance.

Under Prop. 103 rules, the three primary rating factors for automobile insurance must be (1) the insured's driving record; (2) the annual miles driven by the insured; and (3) the insured's number of years of driving experience. What is missing? The big item eliminated is territory. Voters within the city limits of Los Angeles overwhelmingly voted in favor of Proposition 103, primarily to eliminate the large difference in rates between urban and rural drivers. Also missing from the listed factors are gender, age, and marital status. Other factors may be used by the insurer, but only in a lesser proportion to the influence of the three primary factors.

The dialogue between proponents and opponents of Prop. 103 has been voluminous and heated. Only with the passage of time will we be able to assess the validity of either side's arguments. What may be most significant today is the question about the value and legality of limiting underwriting criteria generally. Should insurers be told which criteria are acceptable? Some experts believe that underwriting restrictions will raise prices for the entire population. Others believe it will force insurers to be more creative and efficient in their business practices.

Regulations That Restrict Global Insurance Activities[17]

Multinational insurers face a variety of restrictions on trade; just as there are barriers to international trade in other industries, there are restrictions on *the free flow of insurance* across national borders. A variety of categorization schemes could be used to describe trade restrictions. Skipper[18] classifies protective measures regarding insurance services as one of three: those related to (1) establishment within the host country; (2) access to the domestic market; and (3) insurer operations. He further categorizes rationales for protection in the provision of international insurance services into three sets: (1) consumer protection justifications; (2) economic justifications; and (3) sociopolitical justifications. Tables 26–2 and 26–3 list the sub-elements associated with types of trade restrictions and the reasons for such restrictions.

The most direct restriction on import insurance trade takes the form of a government prohibiting both individual and corporate residents from placing insurance or reinsurance with alien insurers, and imposing penalties on anyone who does so. Another somewhat less severe form of restriction is to require that all forms of compulsory insurance, such as workers' compensation or automobile insurance, be purchased from a state-operated insurer. These restrictions become particularly burdensome to industries that cannot find adequate coverage from state-operated insurers, either for reasons of capacity or the types of coverages available.

Another method of direct restriction is through the use of *exchange controls.* This method effectively prohibits purchases from alien insurers by preventing individuals and companies from obtaining the necessary for-

TABLE 26–2

Common Forms of Protective Measures Used in Provision of International Insurance Services*

Measures Related to Establishment in Host Country
  Monopolist markets
  Licensing requirements
  Differential deposit/capital requirements
  Domestication
  Localization of ownership/insurance
  Local placement of transportation insurance

Measures Related to Market Access
  Nationalization
  Government procurement
  License and product limitations

Measures Related to Insurer Operations
  Employment of nationals
  Reinsurance placement
  Localization of reserves/assets
  Exchange controls
  Differential tax treatment
  Trade association membership

*Harold D. Skipper, Jr., "Protectionism in the Provision of International Insurance Services," *Journal of Risk and Insurance* (March 1987).

17. Much of this material was written by Frederick W. Schroath for the fifth edition of this book.
18. Harold D. Skipper, Jr., "Protectionism in the Provision of International Insurance Services," *Journal of Risk and Insurance* (March 1987): p. 56.

TABLE 26–3

Consumer Protection Justifications
    Availability of insurance
    Quality of insurance
    Reliability of insurance
Economic Justifications
    Development of local insurance industry
        Increase business written
        Increase retention capacity
        Protect local markets
    Balance of payments concern
    Enhancement of local capital market
    Avoidance of destructive competition
    The "status quo" factor
Sociopolitical Justifications
    Government philosophy
    National security/sovereignty concerns
    Religious and cultural beliefs
    Vested business interests

**Harold D. Skipper, Jr., "Protectionism in the Provision of International Insurance Services," *Journal of Risk and Insurance* (March 1987).

eign exchange; only domestic currency is available and, unless it is accepted outside of the home country, only domestic purchases can be made.

Although reinsurers are generally not subject to the same degree of restriction as primary insurers, some countries limit their freedom in several ways. In some countries, primary insurers are required to place all reinsurance with a state-owned reinsurance company. Even in countries where freedom is given to direct insurers to choose their reinsurer, alien reinsurers may operate with handicaps. Many less–developed countries have enacted restrictions on the export of both primary insurance and reinsurance premiums. Developed countries have formed regional economic trading groups that act as barriers to trade.

Various indirect barriers are frequently applied to alien insurers and reinsurers. Perhaps the most prevalent of these is some form of discriminatory tax treatment. This usually takes one of two forms. Since the foreign insurer sometimes is not subject to local corporate income and property taxes, local authorities may tend to over-compensate with substantial premium taxes. This results in the greatest discouragement to the alien insurer when keen price competition produces lower-than-expected profit margins. Another form of differential tax treatment is imposed by not allowing domestic policyholders to take tax deductions for premiums paid to alien insurers.

Other kinds of indirect barriers take the form of additional capital costs. In most insurance markets, newly formed insurers (or the branches or subsidiaries of alien insurers) are required to meet minimum deposit or capital and surplus requirements. Often these requirements are set higher for alien insurers, despite the financial strength of the parent corporation. More stringent solvency requirements in a number of markets impose higher capital costs on alien insurers.

Regulators and the Consumer

The underlying purpose of all insurance regulatory action should be the protection of consumers, both individuals and organizations. Most insurance regulations have impact directly or indirectly on consumers. For example, the emphasis on insurer solvency, including the provision of guaranty associations, increases your probability of collecting claims above what they might be in the absence of regulation. An occasional disciplinary action and the threat of punishment, through potential fines and the removal of licenses, probably make many agents, brokers, consultants, and insurers more honest than they might be otherwise. The list of indirect ways that insurance regulation benefits you as a consumer could be extended, but that is not the main purpose of this consumer application. We want to discuss the kinds of help you may be able to obtain from your state insurance department.

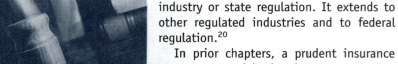

INSURANCE PURCHASES

Let's assume that you want help in making an insurance purchase decision. The insurance department might seem a reasonable place to seek basic information. After all, the department receives extensive information through annual statements, with all types of financial data, periodic (usually triennial) examinations of insurers, receipt of complaints from consumers, occasional contact with insurer executives, and other sources. In addition, the department is technically a watchdog/police agency charged with protecting the public interest in insurance.

The critic, of course, is aware that half of all commissioners come from executive positions with insurers, and half will return to the insurance industry. NAIC advisory committees[19] that drafted most of the model legislative proposals were dominated by insurance industry lobbyists, government relations officers, and other insurer personnel. State legislatures, like Congress, are also frequented by insurance industry lobbyists. A critic would have to wonder to what extent insurance regulation in most states is a clear example of the "fox guarding the henhouse." This situation is not confined, however, to regulation of the insurance industry or state regulation. It extends to other regulated industries and to federal regulation.[20]

In prior chapters, a prudent insurance manager was advised to know:

1. How to select an insurance agent, broker, or financial planner.
2. How to select a company or companies.
3. How to select insurance coverages and compare costs.
4. How to settle losses.

The issue addressed here is: What help can be obtained from your state insurance department in answering these questions?

Selecting an Agent

Insurance departments have two functions with respect to agents/brokers/financial planners. First, they license agents and brokers. (Fee-only financial planners may or may not need an insurance license in a given state.) Thus, your department sets a hurdle of knowledge for those who sell insurance. Unfortunately, most states hold the hurdle low. The typical high school graduate who has spent forty to sixty hours studying for the insurance licensing exam will pass the tests given by most states. A few states require more rigorous preparation, such as attendance at ninety class hours of insurance instruction. Separate examinations are required for life-health sales and property-liability sales. Some states also require annual attendance at insurance seminars/meetings for eight or more hours before renewing a license.

Second, your insurance department will discipline agents who have engaged in unfair trade practices. Usually this discipline does not take place unless a consumer like you files and pursues a formal complaint against an agent or broker.

If you call your department for information about an agent's qualifications, you are unlikely to learn anything

19. Advisory committees were dissolved in 1993. What will be used instead is not yet clear.

20. Monica Langley, "Friendly Terms: Thrifts' Trade Group and their Regulators Get Along Just Fine," *The Wall Street Journal* (Eastern edition), July 16, 1986: pp. 1, 15.

beyond whether he or she is currently licensed. Thus, the department weeds out persons who cannot pass a rather simple test, one that probably does not require as much knowledge as you will have to demonstrate to pass this course. In addition, the department's disciplinary procedures will take the license from those who are caught engaging in unethical insurance conduct. It is rare to find an unlicensed person posing as an insurance agent, but it does happen. For example, in the early 1990s, it was discovered that many stockbrokers without insurance licenses had sold annuity contracts. Even though licensing requirements are stringent in most states, your odds of getting good advice are better with a licensed agent or broker than from someone who is unlicensed. You are likely to find your insurance department of no help in furnishing information about an agent's educational credentials, number of companies he or she represented, experience, full-time or part-time status, quality of service, or other important factors. Your department can tell you, however, whether someone is licensed to sell the type of insurance you are considering.

Selecting an Insurer

Previously we indicated that hundreds of companies are licensed in every state, so avoiding one that is not licensed does not greatly restrict your choice of insurance. This is good advice for the majority of consumers, except commercial buyers who need to shop with Lloyd's of London and other surplus lines insurers. The functions of your state insurance department with respect to insurers are to license, monitor financial and market conduct performance, and discipline if necessary. As with the licensing of agents, some states have more stringent requirements for insurers than others. Arizona, for example, has very low capital and surplus requirements, whereas New York has much higher requirements. It means more to be licensed in New York than in Arizona. This problem may be alleviated somewhat when risk-based capital requirements become effective in all states.

All states have access to the results of a computerized analysis of financial statement data. This insurance regulatory information system (IRIS) compares eleven ratios for property-liability insurers and twelve for life-health insurers to standards for each ratio. Deviations of actual ratios from the standard ratios are like warning flags that help regulators identify potential financial insolvencies. The early detection of financial problems should allow regulators to intervene and prevent some insolvencies. Ratios, unfortunately, can also mask financial problems. For example, a life insurer with an acceptable net worth-to-liabilities ratio and other reasonable IRIS ratios at the end of 1984 might have to be rehabilitated in 1985 with some losses of foregone

interest on annuities. One would have to look deeper to see that this insurer had a large volume of questionable investments, primarily in overvalued securities of affiliated companies, and was placing reinsurance with financially weak affiliated companies.

Learning whether or not an insurer is licensed is about all you can learn by calling your insurance department. For example, you cannot learn that an insurer has several abnormal IRIS ratios or that a recent insurance department examination found a significant volume of questionable investments. Regulators typically guard adverse financial information, up to the point at which an insurer must be liquidated or rehabilitated. They follow the philosophy that the disclosure of adverse financial information might cause a run on an already weak insurer. Thus, about all you can conclude from learning that an insurer is currently licensed by your state is that it is not technically insolvent at the current time. This may help some existing policyholders and stockholders, but it will not help you as a prospective buyer. You must rely on the various rating agencies, including Best's, Moody's, Standard and Poors, Duff and Phelps, and Weiss.[21] You might also consider using the analysis of a top-quality agent, broker, or financial planner and your own analysis to weed out all but the financially worst insurers. Reliance on the rating agencies, however, is still your best bet.

Appraising Contract Provisions

Your state insurance department employs contract specialists who compare all proposed new policies with the requirements of your state's insurance code before they are sold in your state. Some proposed policies must be amended to exclude prohibited provisions, include requested ones, remove misleading clauses, and so forth; a small percentage never qualify. The point is that meeting state requirements only guarantees a minimum level of acceptability. As with cars and emission standards, Cavaliers and Cadillacs are both General Motors cars that meet the standards. But your needs may call for more than emissions tests. You may not need a Cadillac policy to meet your insurance needs, but if your needs are at all complex, you may need more than a Cavalier contract. Thus, calling your insurance department and learning that an insurer's contract provisions meet legal standards is insufficient. Rely on the analysis of a good agent/broker/financial planner, along with some probing questions of your own. Insurance departments almost never assume an advisory role.

---

21. See *The Insurance Forum*, September/October, 1993, for a discussion of these agencies.

Judging Price

A few insurance departments, beginning with Pennsylvania's in the late 1960s, have viewed the provision of "shopping guides" as within their public interest function. The philosophy is to fill gaps in consumer knowledge and enable you to make better-informed choices. Shopping guides usually include price information on personal lines of insurance. Your department may be able to provide you with price information for the larger insurers writing automobile, homeowners, and life insurance in your state. Early in your search for personal lines of insurance, request a guide that includes price information. It may lead you to a low-cost insurer. Because insurers are low-cost for some products and rating classes but not for others, you will still need to analyze the particular proposal presented to you.

Judging Claim Practices and Helping Settle Claims

The first step in deciding whether your prospective insurers have admirable records for paying just claims promptly and equitably is to check with the complaint division of your insurance department. Consumer-oriented departments will relate the number of complaints it receives on each licensed insurer to its volume of business for your state, although some states choose not to provide such information because of the belief that it may be misleading. A complaint does not necessarily reflect insurer wrongdoing. You do not want to do business with an insurer that does not deliver its product in a relatively complaint-free manner. The insurance department can perform a useful consumer function if an insurer delays or refuses to pay your claim. Insurers do respond quickly and thoughtfully to insurance department questions about specific claims. Aid also is available when you are unable to recover the unexpired premium on a canceled contract.

SUMMARY

Your state insurance department may, or may not, be consumer oriented. But your purchase decisions can be improved in any state by contacting your state insurance department about the licenses of agents and insurers. In addition, your department may be able to provide helpful information on prices and on the absence or existence of a high ratio of complaints to volume of business, as well as consumer guides that explain types of coverage and provide shopping tips. The department is most helpful in intervening in the settlement of claim disputes and in getting premium refunds on canceled policies. The regulator cannot require an insurer to pay your claim, but the threat exists that the regulator can cancel an insurer's license to conduct business in your state.

Key Terms

insurance departments
commissioner (or superintendant) of insurance
National Association of Insurance Commissioners (NAIC)
rating bureaus
Public Law 15
The McCarran-Ferguson Act
domestic insurers
foreign insurers
alien insurers
surplus lines agents
risk-based capital reserves

life insurance policy reserves
unearned premium reserves
loss reserves
state guaranty associations
prior approval
file-and-use
open competition
twisting
rebating
redlining
automobile insurance plans
reinsurance facilities
joint underwriting associations

1. Describe the requirements of a competitive market, and how well they are met by the insurance industry.

2. What criteria are applied to the regulation of premium rates? Are these reasonable criteria?

3. What are life insurance policy reserves, and why must they increase over the years for a given group of insureds? How would reserves be affected if the state insurance department lowered the maximum rate of interest assumed in reserve calculations?

4. During a certain period, St. Petersburg Insurance Company has a gross income of $9 million. However, in the same period, total benefits (claim payments and changes in reserves) and expenses are $10.2 million. How does the company make up the difference without becoming insolvent?

5. How can a legal limitation on life insurer expenses, such as that specified in the New York expense limitation law, be justified? What effect do you think market competition has on insurer expenses?

6. What are risk-based capital requirements, and what is their purpose?

7. How are you, as a policyholder, protected if an insurer fails? Are stockholders protected? Do you think the method of financing such protection is fair?

8. What factors have contributed to making availability and affordability regulatory issues?

9. Discuss the implications of insurance regulation at the federal level. What would happen if the industry were not regulated at all?

10. How does a state insurance department help you as an insurance consumer? Suggest ways by which such services could be extended.

Cases

26.1 The Happy Life Insurance Company is a stock insurer licensed in a large western state. Its loss reserves are estimated at $9.5 million and its unearned premium reserves at $1.7 million. Other liabilities are valued at $1.3 million. It is a mono-line insurer that has been operating in the state for over twenty years.

1. What concern might the commissioner have if most of Happy's assets are stocks? How might regulation address this concern?

2. If a minimum of $4 million in capital and surplus is required by state insurance law for this type of company, what minimum asset value must Happy hold to meet these requirements?

3. If Happy fails to meet minimum capital and surplus requirements, what options are available to the commissioner of insurance? How would Happy's policyholders be affected? How would the policyholders of other life insurers in the state be affected?

26.2 Two months ago, Peter Kimson bought a new car and at the same time purchased automobile insurance (at a cost of $420 for six months). Peter's employer just filed Chapter 11 bankruptcy, and so Peter is expecting to lose his job. As a precaution, he is considering the sale of his auto. He is unsure about his auto insurance coverage, for which he has already paid.

1. How would a return of premium be calculated for Peter?

2. What type of reserve is this, and how is the insurer's financial statement affected?

3. What variations exist if the insurer cancels, and why?

26.3 Roger Randall has had whole life insurance coverage with Moon Life Insurance Company for several years. He was recently contacted by an agent for Star Life, who, after looking over Roger's present policy, told him he had been deceived about his coverage and offered to refund 20 percent of the premium if Roger switched to a Star Life policy. Roger does not really understand either policy and cannot evaluate the agent's claims.

1. What would the state insurance commissioner think of the agent's refund offer?

2. Who would gain from a premium rebate? To whose advantage is the prohibition of such "unfair competition"?

26.4 Meri Randall is president and CEO of International Monumental All Lines Insurance Company. It has been in business for forty-seven years and is licensed in all states except New York. It has offices in fifty other countries, primarily in Europe and South America. One trade association it belongs to is publicly in favor of federal regulation of insurance, to the virtual exclusion of the states. Another has taken a firm stand against federal regulation and is very much in favor of continued state regulation.

Meri is well known and highly respected in the insurance business, as well as in banking and related fields. She is recognized as a proponent of big business, but is a political moderate. Friends in the insurance business who favor federal control are urging her to come out in favor of it, whereas those who favor state regulation want her to make a public statement supporting their position.

1. What would be potential arguments Meri could make both for and against federal regulation?

2. Who would benefit by replacing state regulation with federal regulation?

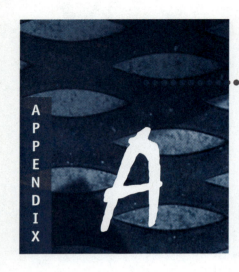

Homeowners 3
Special Form

HOMEOWNERS 3
SPECIAL FORM

AGREEMENT

We will provide the insurance described in this policy in return for the premium and compliance with all applicable provisions of this policy.

DEFINITIONS

In this policy, "you" and "your" refer to the "named insured" shown in the Declarations and the spouse if a resident of the same household. "We," "us" and "our" refer to the Company providing this insurance. In addition, certain words and phrases are defined as follows:

1. "Bodily injury" means bodily harm, sickness or disease, including required care, loss of services and death that results.

2. "Business" includes trade, profession or occupation.

3. "Insured" means you and residents of your household who are:

   a. Your relatives; or

   b. Other persons under the age of 21 and in the care of any person named above.

   Under Section II, "insured" also means:

   c. With respect to animals or watercraft to which this policy applies, any person or organization legally responsible for these animals or watercraft which are owned by you or any person included in **3.a.** or **3.b.** above. A person or organization using or having custody of these animals or watercraft in the course of any "business" or without consent of the owner is not an "insured";

   d. With respect to any vehicle to which this policy applies:

      (1) Persons while engaged in your employ or that of any person included in **3.a.** or **3.b.** above; or

      (2) Other persons using the vehicle on an "insured location" with your consent.

4. "Insured location" means:

   a. The "residence premises";

   b. The part of other premises, other structures and grounds used by you as a residence and:

      (1) Which is shown in the Declarations; or

      (2) Which is acquired by you during the policy period for your use as a residence;

   c. Any premises used by you in connection with a premises in **4.a.** and **4.b.** above;

   d. Any part of a premises:

      (1) Not owned by an "insured"; and

      (2) Where an "insured" is temporarily residing;

   e. Vacant land, other than farm land, owned by or rented to an "insured";

   f. Land owned by or rented to an "insured" on which a one or two family dwelling is being built as a residence for an "insured";

   g. Individual or family cemetery plots or burial vaults of an "insured"; or

   h. Any part of a premises occasionally rented to an "insured" for other than "business" use.

5. "Occurrence" means an accident, including continuous or repeated exposure to substantially the same general harmful conditions, which results, during the policy period, in:

   a. "Bodily injury"; or

   b. "Property damage."

6. "Property damage" means physical injury to, destruction of, or loss of use of tangible property.

7. "Residence employee" means:

   a. An employee of an "insured" whose duties are related to the maintenance or use of the "residence premises," including household or domestic services; or

   b. One who performs similar duties elsewhere not related to the "business" of an "insured."

8. "Residence premises" means:

   a. The one family dwelling, other structures, and grounds; or

   b. That part of any other building;

   where you reside and which is shown as the "residence premises" in the Declarations.

   "Residence premises" also means a two family dwelling where you reside in at least one of the family units and which is shown as the "residence premises" in the Declarations.

SECTION I - PROPERTY COVERAGES

COVERAGE A - Dwelling

We cover:

1. The dwelling on the "residence premises" shown in the Declarations, including structures attached to the dwelling; and

2. Materials and supplies located on or next to the "residence premises" used to construct, alter or repair the dwelling or other structures on the "residence premises."

This coverage does not apply to land, including land on which the dwelling is located.

COVERAGE B - Other Structures

We cover other structures on the "residence premises" set apart from the dwelling by clear space. This includes structures connected to the dwelling by only a fence, utility line, or similar connection.

This coverage does not apply to land, including land on which the other structures are located.

We do not cover other structures:

1. Used in whole or in part for "business"; or

2. Rented or held for rental to any person not a tenant of the dwelling, unless used solely as a private garage.

The limit of liability for this coverage will not be more than 10% of the limit of liability that applies to Coverage A. Use of this coverage does not reduce the Coverage A limit of liability.

COVERAGE C - Personal Property

We cover personal property owned or used by an "insured" while it is anywhere in the world. At your request, we will cover personal property owned by:

1. Others while the property is on the part of the "residence premises" occupied by an "insured";

2. A guest or a "residence employee," while the property is in any residence occupied by an "insured."

Our limit of liability for personal property usually located at an "insured's" residence, other than the "residence premises," is 10% of the limit of liability for Coverage C, or $1000, whichever is greater. Personal property in a newly acquired principal residence is not subject to this limitation for the 30 days from the time you begin to move the property there.

Special Limits of Liability. These limits do not increase the Coverage C limit of liability. The special limit for each numbered category below is the total limit for each loss for all property in that category.

1. $200 on money, bank notes, bullion, gold other than goldware, silver other than silverware, platinum, coins and medals.

2. $1000 on securities, accounts, deeds, evidences of debt, letters of credit, notes other than bank notes, manuscripts, personal records, passports, tickets and stamps. This dollar limit applies to these categories regardless of the medium (such as paper or computer software) on which the material exists.

   This limit includes the cost to research, replace or restore the information from the lost or damaged material.

3. $1000 on watercraft, including their trailers, furnishings, equipment and outboard engines or motors.

4. $1000 on trailers not used with watercraft.

5. $1000 for loss by theft of jewelry, watches, furs, precious and semi-precious stones.

6. $2000 for loss by theft of firearms.

7. $2500 for loss by theft of silverware, silver-plated ware, goldware, gold-plated ware and pewterware. This includes flatware, hollowware, tea sets, trays and trophies made of or including silver, gold or pewter.

8. $2500 on property, on the "residence premises," used at any time or in any manner for any "business" purpose.

9. $250 on property, away from the "residence premises," used at any time or in any manner for any "business" purpose. However, this limit does not apply to loss to adaptable electronic apparatus as described in Special Limits 10. and 11. below.

10. $1000 for loss to electronic apparatus, while in or upon a motor vehicle or other motorized land conveyance, if the electronic apparatus is equipped to be operated by power from the electrical system of the vehicle or conveyance while retaining its capability of being operated by other sources of power. Electronic apparatus includes:

    a. Accessories or antennas; or

    b. Tapes, wires, records, discs or other media;

    for use with any electronic apparatus.

11. $1000 for loss to electronic apparatus, while not in or upon a motor vehicle or other motorized land conveyance, if the electronic apparatus:

a. Is equipped to be operated by power from the electrical system of the vehicle or conveyance while retaining its capability of being operated by other sources of power;

b. Is away from the "residence premises"; and

c. Is used at any time or in any manner for any "business" purpose.

Electronic apparatus includes:

a. Accessories and antennas; or

b. Tapes, wires, records, discs or other media;

for use with any electronic apparatus.

Property Not Covered. We do not cover:

1. Articles separately described and specifically insured in this or other insurance;

2. Animals, birds or fish;

3. Motor vehicles or all other motorized land conveyances. This includes:

a. Their equipment and accessories; or

b. Electronic apparatus that is designed to be operated solely by use of the power from the electrical system of motor vehicles or all other motorized land conveyances. Electronic apparatus includes:

(1) Accessories or antennas; or

(2) Tapes, wires, records, discs or other media;

for use with any electronic apparatus.

The exclusion of property described in **3.a** and **3.b.** above applies only while the property is in or upon the vehicle or conveyance.

We do cover vehicles or conveyances not subject to motor vehicle registration which are:

a. Used to service an "insured's" residence; or

b. Designed for assisting the handicapped;

4. Aircraft and parts. Aircraft means any contrivance used or designed for flight, except model or hobby aircraft not used or designed to carry people or cargo;

5. Property of roomers, boarders and other tenants, except property of roomers and boarders related to an "insured";

6. Property in an apartment regularly rented or held for rental to others by an "insured," except as provided in Additional Coverages **10.**;

7. Property rented or held for rental to others off the "residence premises";

8. "Business" data, including such data stored in:

a. Books of account, drawings or other paper records; or

b. Electronic data processing tapes, wires, records, discs or other software media;

However, we do cover the cost of blank recording or storage media, and of pre-recorded computer programs available on the retail market; or

9. Credit cards or fund transfer cards except as provided in Additional Coverages **6.**

COVERAGE D - Loss Of Use

The limit of liability for Coverage D is the total limit for all the coverages that follow.

1. If a loss covered under this Section makes that part of the "residence premises" where you reside not fit to live in, we cover, at your choice, either of the following. However, if the "residence premises" is not your principal place of residence, we will not provide the option under paragraph **b.** below.

a. Additional Living Expense, meaning any necessary increase in living expenses incurred by you so that your household can maintain its normal standard of living; or

b. Fair Rental Value, meaning the fair rental value of that part of the "residence premises" where you reside less any expenses that do not continue while the premises is not fit to live in.

Payment under **a.** or **b.** will be for the shortest time required to repair or replace the damage or, if you permanently relocate, the shortest time required for your household to settle elsewhere.

2. If a loss covered under this Section makes that part of the "residence premises" rented to others or held for rental by you not fit to live in, we cover the:

Fair Rental Value, meaning the fair rental value of that part of the "residence premises" rented to others or held for rental by you less any expenses that do not continue while the premises is not fit to live in.

Payment will be for the shortest time required to repair or replace that part of the premises rented or held for rental.

3. If a civil authority prohibits you from use of the "residence premises" as a result of direct damage to neighboring premises by a Peril Insured Against in this policy, we cover the Additional Living Expense and Fair Rental Value loss as provided under **1.** and **2.** above for no more than two weeks.

The periods of time under **1.**, **2.** and **3.** above are not limited by expiration of this policy.

We do not cover loss or expense due to cancellation of a lease or agreement.

ADDITIONAL COVERAGES

1. **Debris Removal.** We will pay your reasonable expense for the removal of:

   a. Debris of covered property if a Peril Insured Against that applies to the damaged property causes the loss; or

   b. Ash, dust or particles from a volcanic eruption that has caused direct loss to a building or property contained in a building.

   This expense is included in the limit of liability that applies to the damaged property. If the amount to be paid for the actual damage to the property plus the debris removal expense is more than the limit of liability for the damaged property, an additional 5% of that limit of liability is available for debris removal expense.

   We will also pay your reasonable expense, up to $500, for the removal from the "residence premises" of:

   a. Your tree(s) felled by the peril of Windstorm or Hail;

   b. Your tree(s) felled by the peril of Weight of Ice, Snow or Sleet; or

   c. A neighbor's tree(s) felled by a Peril Insured Against under Coverage C;

   provided the tree(s) damages a covered structure. The $500 limit is the most we will pay in any one loss regardless of the number of fallen trees.

2. **Reasonable Repairs.** In the event that covered property is damaged by an applicable Peril Insured Against, we will pay the reasonable cost incurred by you for necessary measures taken solely to protect against further damage. If the measures taken involve repair to other damaged property, we will pay for those measures only if that property is covered under this policy and the damage to that property is caused by an applicable Peril Insured Against.

   This coverage:

   a. Does not increase the limit of liability that applies to the covered property;

   b. Does not relieve you of your duties, in case of a loss to covered property, as set forth in SECTION I – CONDITION **2.d.**

3. **Trees, Shrubs and Other Plants.** We cover trees, shrubs, plants or lawns, on the "residence premises," for loss caused by the following Perils Insured Against: Fire or lightning, Explosion, Riot or civil commotion, Aircraft, Vehicles not owned or operated by a resident of the "residence premises," Vandalism or malicious mischief or Theft.

   We will pay up to 5% of the limit of liability that applies to the dwelling for all trees, shrubs, plants or lawns. No more than $500 of this limit will be available for any one tree, shrub or plant. We do not cover property grown for "business" purposes.

   This coverage is additional insurance.

4. **Fire Department Service Charge.** We will pay up to $500 for your liability assumed by contract or agreement for fire department charges incurred when the fire department is called to save or protect covered property from a Peril Insured Against. We do not cover fire department service charges if the property is located within the limits of the city, municipality or protection district furnishing the fire department response.

   This coverage is additional insurance. No deductible applies to this coverage.

5. **Property Removed.** We insure covered property against direct loss from any cause while being removed from a premises endangered by a Peril Insured Against and for no more than 30 days while removed. This coverage does not change the limit of liability that applies to the property being removed.

6. **Credit Card, Fund Transfer Card, Forgery and Counterfeit Money.**

   We will pay up to $500 for:

   a. The legal obligation of an "insured" to pay because of the theft or unauthorized use of credit cards issued to or registered in an "insured's" name;

   b. Loss resulting from theft or unauthorized use of a fund transfer card used for deposit, withdrawal or transfer of funds, issued to or registered in an "insured's" name;

   c. Loss to an "insured" caused by forgery or alteration of any check or negotiable instrument; and

   d. Loss to an "insured" through acceptance in good faith of counterfeit United States or Canadian paper currency.

We do not cover use of a credit card or fund transfer card:

a. By a resident of your household;

b. By a person who has been entrusted with either type of card; or

c. If an "insured" has not complied with all terms and conditions under which the cards are issued.

All loss resulting from a series of acts committed by any one person or in which any one person is concerned or implicated is considered to be one loss.

We do not cover loss arising out of "business" use or dishonesty of an "insured."

This coverage is additional insurance. No deductible applies to this coverage.

Defense:

a. We may investigate and settle any claim or suit that we decide is appropriate. Our duty to defend a claim or suit ends when the amount we pay for the loss equals our limit of liability.

b. If a suit is brought against an "insured" for liability under the Credit Card or Fund Transfer Card coverage, we will provide a defense at our expense by counsel of our choice.

c. We have the option to defend at our expense an "insured" or an "insured's" bank against any suit for the enforcement of payment under the Forgery coverage.

7. **Loss Assessment.** We will pay up to $1000 for your share of loss assessment charged during the policy period against you by a corporation or association of property owners, when the assessment is made as a result of direct loss to the property, owned by all members collectively, caused by a Peril Insured Against under COVERAGE A – DWELLING, other than earthquake or land shock waves or tremors before, during or after a volcanic eruption.

This coverage applies only to loss assessments charged against you as owner or tenant of the "residence premises."

We do not cover loss assessments charged against you or a corporation or association of property owners by any governmental body.

The limit of $1000 is the most we will pay with respect to any one loss, regardless of the number of assessments.

Condition 1. Policy Period, under SECTIONS I AND II CONDITIONS, does not apply to this coverage.

8. **Collapse.** We insure for direct physical loss to covered property involving collapse of a building or any part of a building caused only by one or more of the following:

a. Perils Insured Against in COVERAGE C – PERSONAL PROPERTY. These perils apply to covered buildings and personal property for loss insured by this additional coverage;

b. Hidden decay;

c. Hidden insect or vermin damage;

d. Weight of contents, equipment, animals or people;

e. Weight of rain which collects on a roof; or

f. Use of defective material or methods in construction, remodeling or renovation if the collapse occurs during the course of the construction, remodeling or renovation.

Loss to an awning, fence, patio, pavement, swimming pool, underground pipe, flue, drain, cesspool, septic tank, foundation, retaining wall, bulkhead, pier, wharf or dock is not included under items **b., c., d., e.,** and **f.** unless the loss is a direct result of the collapse of a building.

Collapse does not include settling, cracking, shrinking, bulging or expansion.

This coverage does not increase the limit of liability applying to the damaged covered property.

9. **Glass or Safety Glazing Material.**

We cover:

a. The breakage of glass or safety glazing material which is part of a covered building, storm door or storm window; and

b. Damage to covered property by glass or safety glazing material which is part of a building, storm door or storm window.

This coverage does not include loss on the "residence premises" if the dwelling has been vacant for more than 30 consecutive days immediately before the loss. A dwelling being constructed is not considered vacant.

Loss for damage to glass will be settled on the basis of replacement with safety glazing materials when required by ordinance or law.

This coverage does not increase the limit of liability that applies to the damaged property.

10. **Landlord's Furnishings.** We will pay up to $2500 for your appliances, carpeting and other household furnishings, in an apartment on the "residence premises" regularly rented or held for rental to others by an "insured," for loss caused only by the following Perils Insured Against:

a. **Fire or lightning.**

b. **Windstorm or hail.**

This peril does not include loss to the property contained in a building caused by rain, snow, sleet, sand or dust unless the direct force of wind or hail damages the building causing an opening in a roof or wall and the rain, snow, sleet, sand or dust enters through this opening.

This peril includes loss to watercraft and their trailers, furnishings, equipment, and outboard engines or motors, only while inside a fully enclosed building.

c. **Explosion.**

d. **Riot or civil commotion.**

e. **Aircraft,** including self-propelled missiles and spacecraft.

f. **Vehicles.**

g. **Smoke,** meaning sudden and accidental damage from smoke.

This peril does not include loss caused by smoke from agricultural smudging or industrial operations.

h. **Vandalism or malicious mischief.**

i. **Falling objects.**

This peril does not include loss to property contained in a building unless the roof or an outside wall of the building is first damaged by a falling object. Damage to the falling object itself is not included.

j. **Weight of ice, snow or sleet** which causes damage to property contained in a building.

k. **Accidental discharge or overflow of water or steam** from within a plumbing, heating, air conditioning or automatic fire protective sprinkler system or from within a household appliance.

This peril does not include loss:

(1) To the system or appliance from which the water or steam escaped;

(2) Caused by or resulting from freezing except as provided in the peril of freezing below; or

(3) On the "residence premises" caused by accidental discharge or overflow which occurs off the "residence premises."

In this peril, a plumbing system does not include a sump, sump pump or related equipment.

l. **Sudden and accidental tearing apart, cracking, burning or bulging** of a steam or hot water heating system, an air conditioning or automatic fire protective sprinkler system, or an appliance for heating water.

We do not cover loss caused by or resulting from freezing under this peril.

m. **Freezing** of a plumbing, heating, air conditioning or automatic fire protective sprinkler system or of a household appliance.

This peril does not include loss on the "residence premises" while the dwelling is unoccupied, unless you have used reasonable care to:

(1) Maintain heat in the building; or

(2) Shut off the water supply and drain the system and appliances of water.

n. **Sudden and accidental damage from artificially generated electrical current.**

This peril does not include loss to a tube, transistor or similar electronic component.

o. **Volcanic eruption** other than loss caused by earthquake, land shock waves or tremors.

The $2500 limit is the most we will pay in any one loss regardless of the number of appliances, carpeting or other household furnishings involved in the loss.

SECTION I - PERILS INSURED AGAINST

COVERAGE A - DWELLING and COVERAGE B - OTHER STRUCTURES

We insure against risk of direct loss to property described in Coverages A and B only if that loss is a physical loss to property. We do not insure, however, for loss:

1. Involving collapse, other than as provided in Additional Coverage 8.;

2. Caused by:

Copyright, Insurance Services Office, Inc., 1990

a. Freezing of a plumbing, heating, air conditioning or automatic fire protective sprinkler system or of a household appliance, or by discharge, leakage or overflow from within the system or appliance caused by freezing. This exclusion applies only while the dwelling is vacant, unoccupied or being constructed, unless you have used reasonable care to:

(1) Maintain heat in the building; or

(2) Shut off the water supply and drain the system and appliances of water;

b. Freezing, thawing, pressure or weight of water or ice, whether driven by wind or not, to a:

(1) Fence, pavement, patio or swimming pool;

(2) Foundation, retaining wall, or bulkhead; or

(3) Pier, wharf or dock;

c. Theft in or to a dwelling under construction, or of materials and supplies for use in the construction until the dwelling is finished and occupied;

d. Vandalism and malicious mischief if the dwelling has been vacant for more than 30 consecutive days immediately before the loss. A dwelling being constructed is not considered vacant;

e. Any of the following:

(1) Wear and tear, marring, deterioration;

(2) Inherent vice, latent defect, mechanical breakdown;

(3) Smog, rust or other corrosion, mold, wet or dry rot;

(4) Smoke from agricultural smudging or industrial operations;

(5) Discharge, dispersal, seepage, migration, release or escape of pollutants unless the discharge, dispersal, seepage, migration, release or escape is itself caused by a Peril Insured Against under Coverage C of this policy.

Pollutants means any solid, liquid, gaseous or thermal irritant or contaminant, including smoke, vapor, soot, fumes, acids, alkalis, chemicals and waste. Waste includes materials to be recycled, reconditioned or reclaimed;

(6) Settling, shrinking, bulging or expansion, including resultant cracking, of pavements, patios, foundations, walls, floors, roofs or ceilings;

(7) Birds, vermin, rodents, or insects; or

(8) Animals owned or kept by an "insured."

If any of these cause water damage not otherwise excluded, from a plumbing, heating, air conditioning or automatic fire protective sprinkler system or household appliance, we cover loss caused by the water including the cost of tearing out and replacing any part of a building necessary to repair the system or appliance. We do not cover loss to the system or appliance from which this water escaped.

3. Excluded under Section I – Exclusions.

Under items 1. and 2., any ensuing loss to property described in Coverages A and B not excluded or excepted in this policy is covered.

COVERAGE C - PERSONAL PROPERTY

We insure for direct physical loss to the property described in Coverage C caused by a peril listed below unless the loss is excluded in SECTION I – EXCLUSIONS.

1. **Fire or lightning.**

2. **Windstorm or hail.**

This peril does not include loss to the property contained in a building caused by rain, snow, sleet, sand or dust unless the direct force of wind or hail damages the building causing an opening in a roof or wall and the rain, snow, sleet, sand or dust enters through this opening.

This peril includes loss to watercraft and their trailers, furnishings, equipment, and outboard engines or motors, only while inside a fully enclosed building.

3. **Explosion.**

4. **Riot or civil commotion.**

5. **Aircraft,** including self-propelled missiles and spacecraft.

6. **Vehicles.**

7. **Smoke,** meaning sudden and accidental damage from smoke.

This peril does not include loss caused by smoke from agricultural smudging or industrial operations.

8. **Vandalism or malicious mischief.**

9. **Theft,** including attempted theft and loss of property from a known place when it is likely that the property has been stolen.

This peril does not include loss caused by theft:

a. Committed by an "insured";

b. In or to a dwelling under construction, or of materials and supplies for use in the construction until the dwelling is finished and occupied; or

c. From that part of a "residence premises" rented by an "insured" to other than an "insured."

This peril does not include loss caused by theft that occurs off the "residence premises" of:

a. Property while at any other residence owned by, rented to, or occupied by an "insured," except while an "insured" is temporarily living there. Property of a student who is an "insured" is covered while at a residence away from home if the student has been there at any time during the 45 days immediately before the loss;

b. Watercraft, and their furnishings, equipment and outboard engines or motors; or

c. Trailers and campers.

10. **Falling objects.**

This peril does not include loss to property contained in a building unless the roof or an outside wall of the building is first damaged by a falling object. Damage to the falling object itself is not included.

11. **Weight of ice, snow or sleet** which causes damage to property contained in a building.

12. **Accidental discharge or overflow of water or steam** from within a plumbing, heating, air conditioning or automatic fire protective sprinkler system or from within a household appliance.

This peril does not include loss:

a. To the system or appliance from which the water or steam escaped;

b. Caused by or resulting from freezing except as provided in the peril of freezing below; or

c. On the "residence premises" caused by accidental discharge or overflow which occurs off the "residence premises."

In this peril, a plumbing system does not include a sump, sump pump or related equipment.

13. **Sudden and accidental tearing apart, cracking, burning or bulging** of a steam or hot water heating system, an air conditioning or automatic fire protective sprinkler system, or an appliance for heating water.

We do not cover loss caused by or resulting from freezing under this peril.

14. **Freezing** of a plumbing, heating, air conditioning or automatic fire protective sprinkler system or of a household appliance.

This peril does not include loss on the "residence premises" while the dwelling is unoccupied, unless you have used reasonable care to:

a. Maintain heat in the building; or

b. Shut off the water supply and drain the system and appliances of water.

15. **Sudden and accidental damage from artificially generated electrical current.**

This peril does not include loss to a tube, transistor or similar electronic component.

16. **Volcanic eruption** other than loss caused by earthquake, land shock waves or tremors.

SECTION I - EXCLUSIONS

1. We do not insure for loss caused directly or indirectly by any of the following. Such loss is excluded regardless of any other cause or event contributing concurrently or in any sequence to the loss.

   a. **Ordinance or Law,** meaning enforcement of any ordinance or law regulating the construction, repair, or demolition of a building or other structure, unless specifically provided under this policy.

   b. **Earth Movement,** meaning earthquake including land shock waves or tremors before, during or after a volcanic eruption; landslide; mine subsidence; mudflow; earth sinking, rising or shifting; unless direct loss by:

   (1) Fire;

   (2) Explosion; or

   (3) Breakage of glass or safety glazing material which is part of a building, storm door or storm window;

   ensues and then we will pay only for the ensuing loss.

   This exclusion does not apply to loss by theft.

   c. **Water Damage,** meaning:

   (1) Flood, surface water, waves, tidal water, overflow of a body of water, or spray from any of these, whether or not driven by wind;

   (2) Water which backs up through sewers or drains or which overflows from a sump; or

(3) Water below the surface of the ground, including water which exerts pressure on or seeps or leaks through a building, sidewalk, driveway, foundation, swimming pool or other structure.

Direct loss by fire, explosion or theft resulting from water damage is covered.

d. **Power Failure,** meaning the failure of power or other utility service if the failure takes place off the "residence premises." But, if a Peril Insured Against ensues on the "residence premises," we will pay only for that ensuing loss.

e. **Neglect,** meaning neglect of the "insured" to use all reasonable means to save and preserve property at and after the time of a loss.

f. **War,** including the following and any consequence of any of the following:

(1) Undeclared war, civil war, insurrection, rebellion or revolution;

(2) Warlike act by a military force or military personnel; or

(3) Destruction, seizure or use for a military purpose.

Discharge of a nuclear weapon will be deemed a warlike act even if accidental.

g. **Nuclear Hazard,** to the extent set forth in the Nuclear Hazard Clause of SECTION I – CONDITIONS.

h. **Intentional Loss,** meaning any loss arising out of any act committed:

(1) By or at the direction of an "insured"; and

(2) With the intent to cause a loss.

2. We do not insure for loss to property described in Coverages A and B caused by any of the following. However, any ensuing loss to property described in Coverages A and B not excluded or excepted in this policy is covered.

a. **Weather conditions.** However, this exclusion only applies if weather conditions contribute in any way with a cause or event excluded in paragraph 1. above to produce the loss;

b. **Acts or decisions,** including the failure to act or decide, of any person, group, organization or governmental body;

c. **Faulty, inadequate or defective:**

(1) Planning, zoning, development, surveying, siting;

(2) Design, specifications, workmanship, repair, construction, renovation, remodeling, grading, compaction;

(3) Materials used in repair, construction, renovation or remodeling; or

(4) Maintenance;

of part or all of any property whether on or off the "residence premises."

SECTION I - CONDITIONS

1. **Insurable Interest and Limit of Liability.** Even if more than one person has an insurable interest in the property covered, we will not be liable in any one loss:

a. To the "insured" for more than the amount of the "insured's" interest at the time of loss; or

b. For more than the applicable limit of liability.

2. **Your Duties After Loss.** In case of a loss to covered property, you must see that the following are done:

a. Give prompt notice to us or our agent;

b. Notify the police in case of loss by theft;

c. Notify the credit card or fund transfer card company in case of loss under Credit Card or Fund Transfer Card coverage;

d. Protect the property from further damage. If repairs to the property are required, you must:

(1) Make reasonable and necessary repairs to protect the property; and

(2) Keep an accurate record of repair expenses;

e. Prepare an inventory of damaged personal property showing the quantity, description, actual cash value and amount of loss. Attach all bills, receipts and related documents that justify the figures in the inventory;

f. As often as we reasonably require:

(1) Show the damaged property;

(2) Provide us with records and documents we request and permit us to make copies; and

(3) Submit to examination under oath, while not in the presence of any other "insured," and sign the same;

g. Send to us, within 60 days after our request, your signed, sworn proof of loss which sets forth, to the best of your knowledge and belief:

(1) The time and cause of loss;

(2) The interest of the "insured" and all others in the property involved and all liens on the property;

(3) Other insurance which may cover the loss;

(4) Changes in title or occupancy of the property during the term of the policy;

(5) Specifications of damaged buildings and detailed repair estimates;

(6) The inventory of damaged personal property described in **2.e.** above;

(7) Receipts for additional living expenses incurred and records that support the fair rental value loss; and

(8) Evidence or affidavit that supports a claim under the Credit Card, Fund Transfer Card, Forgery and Counterfeit Money coverage, stating the amount and cause of loss.

3. **Loss Settlement**. Covered property losses are settled as follows:

a. Property of the following types:

(1) Personal property;

(2) Awnings, carpeting, household appliances, outdoor antennas and outdoor equipment, whether or not attached to buildings; and

(3) Structures that are not buildings;

at actual cash value at the time of loss but not more than the amount required to repair or replace.

b. Buildings under Coverage A or B at replacement cost without deduction for depreciation, subject to the following:

(1) If, at the time of loss, the amount of insurance in this policy on the damaged building is 80% or more of the full replacement cost of the building immediately before the loss, we will pay the cost to repair or replace, after application of deductible and without deduction for depreciation, but not more than the least of the following amounts:

(a) The limit of liability under this policy that applies to the building;

(b) The replacement cost of that part of the building damaged for like construction and use on the same premises; or

(c) The necessary amount actually spent to repair or replace the damaged building.

(2) If, at the time of loss, the amount of insurance in this policy on the damaged building is less than 80% of the full replacement cost of the building immediately before the loss, we will pay the greater of the following amounts, but not more than the limit of liability under this policy that applies to the building:

(a) The actual cash value of that part of the building damaged; or

(b) That proportion of the cost to repair or replace, after application of deductible and without deduction for depreciation, that part of the building damaged, which the total amount of insurance in this policy on the damaged building bears to 80% of the replacement cost of the building.

(3) To determine the amount of insurance required to equal 80% of the full replacement cost of the building immediately before the loss, do not include the value of:

(a) Excavations, foundations, piers or any supports which are below the undersurface of the lowest basement floor;

(b) Those supports in **(a)** above which are below the surface of the ground inside the foundation walls, if there is no basement; and

(c) Underground flues, pipes, wiring and drains.

(4) We will pay no more than the actual cash value of the damage until actual repair or replacement is complete. Once actual repair or replacement is complete, we will settle the loss according to the provisions of **b.(1)** and **b.(2)** above.

However, if the cost to repair or replace the damage is both:

(a) Less than 5% of the amount of insurance in this policy on the building; and

(b) Less than $2500;

we will settle the loss according to the provisions of **b.(1)** and **b.(2)** above whether or not actual repair or replacement is complete.

(5) You may disregard the replacement cost loss settlement provisions and make claim under this policy for loss or damage to buildings on an actual cash value basis. You may then make claim within 180 days after loss for any additional liability according to the provisions of this Condition 3. Loss Settlement.

4. **Loss to a Pair or Set.** In case of loss to a pair or set we may elect to:

   a. Repair or replace any part to restore the pair or set to its value before the loss; or

   b. Pay the difference between actual cash value of the property before and after the loss.

5. **Glass Replacement.** Loss for damage to glass caused by a Peril Insured Against will be settled on the basis of replacement with safety glazing materials when required by ordinance or law.

6. **Appraisal.** If you and we fail to agree on the amount of loss, either may demand an appraisal of the loss. In this event, each party will choose a competent appraiser within 20 days after receiving a written request from the other. The two appraisers will choose an umpire. If they cannot agree upon an umpire within 15 days, you or we may request that the choice be made by a judge of a court of record in the state where the "residence premises" is located. The appraisers will separately set the amount of loss. If the appraisers submit a written report of an agreement to us, the amount agreed upon will be the amount of loss. If they fail to agree, they will submit their differences to the umpire. A decision agreed to by any two will set the amount of loss.

   Each party will:

   a. Pay its own appraiser; and

   b. Bear the other expenses of the appraisal and umpire equally.

7. **Other Insurance.** If a loss covered by this policy is also covered by other insurance, we will pay only the proportion of the loss that the limit of liability that applies under this policy bears to the total amount of insurance covering the loss.

8. **Suit Against Us.** No action can be brought unless the policy provisions have been complied with and the action is started within one year after the date of loss.

9. **Our Option.** If we give you written notice within 30 days after we receive your signed, sworn proof of loss, we may repair or replace any part of the damaged property with like property.

10. **Loss Payment.** We will adjust all losses with you. We will pay you unless some other person is named in the policy or is legally entitled to receive payment. Loss will be payable 60 days after we receive your proof of loss and:

    a. Reach an agreement with you;

    b. There is an entry of a final judgment; or

    c. There is a filing of an appraisal award with us.

11. **Abandonment of Property.** We need not accept any property abandoned by an "insured."

12. **Mortgage Clause.**

    The word "mortgagee" includes trustee.

    If a mortgagee is named in this policy, any loss payable under Coverage A or B will be paid to the mortgagee and you, as interests appear. If more than one mortgagee is named, the order of payment will be the same as the order of precedence of the mortgages.

    If we deny your claim, that denial will not apply to a valid claim of the mortgagee, if the mortgagee:

    a. Notifies us of any change in ownership, occupancy or substantial change in risk of which the mortgagee is aware;

    b. Pays any premium due under this policy on demand if you have neglected to pay the premium; and

    c. Submits a signed, sworn statement of loss within 60 days after receiving notice from us of your failure to do so. Policy conditions relating to Appraisal, Suit Against Us and Loss Payment apply to the mortgagee.

    If we decide to cancel or not to renew this policy, the mortgagee will be notified at least 10 days before the date cancellation or nonrenewal takes effect.

    If we pay the mortgagee for any loss and deny payment to you:

    a. We are subrogated to all the rights of the mortgagee granted under the mortgage on the property; or

    b. At our option, we may pay to the mortgagee the whole principal on the mortgage plus any accrued interest. In this event, we will receive a full assignment and transfer of the mortgage and all securities held as collateral to the mortgage debt.

    Subrogation will not impair the right of the mortgagee to recover the full amount of the mortgagee's claim.

13. **No Benefit to Bailee.** We will not recognize any assignment or grant any coverage that benefits a person or organization holding, storing or moving property for a fee regardless of any other provision of this policy.

14. **Nuclear Hazard Clause.**

   a. "Nuclear Hazard" means any nuclear reaction, radiation, or radioactive contamination, all whether controlled or uncontrolled or however caused, or any consequence of any of these.

   b. Loss caused by the nuclear hazard will not be considered loss caused by fire, explosion, or smoke, whether these perils are specifically named in or otherwise included within the Perils Insured Against in Section I.

   c. This policy does not apply under Section I to loss caused directly or indirectly by nuclear hazard, except that direct loss by fire resulting from the nuclear hazard is covered.

15. **Recovered Property.** If you or we recover any property for which we have made payment under this policy, you or we will notify the other of the recovery. At your option, the property will be returned to or retained by you or it will become our property. If the recovered property is returned to or retained by you, the loss payment will be adjusted based on the amount you received for the recovered property.

16. **Volcanic Eruption Period.** One or more volcanic eruptions that occur within a 72-hour period will be considered as one volcanic eruption.

SECTION II - LIABILITY COVERAGES

COVERAGE E - Personal Liability

If a claim is made or a suit is brought against an "insured" for damages because of "bodily injury" or "property damage" caused by an "occurrence" to which this coverage applies, we will:

1. Pay up to our limit of liability for the damages for which the "insured" is legally liable. Damages include prejudgment interest awarded against the "insured"; and

2. Provide a defense at our expense by counsel of our choice, even if the suit is groundless, false or fraudulent. We may investigate and settle any claim or suit that we decide is appropriate. Our duty to settle or defend ends when the amount we pay for damages resulting from the "occurrence" equals our limit of liability.

COVERAGE F - Medical Payments To Others

We will pay the necessary medical expenses that are incurred or medically ascertained within three years from the date of an accident causing "bodily injury." Medical expenses means reasonable charges for medical, surgical, x-ray, dental, ambulance, hospital, professional nursing, prosthetic devices and funeral services. This coverage does not apply to you or regular residents of your household except "residence employees." As to others, this coverage applies only:

1. To a person on the "insured location" with the permission of an "insured"; or

2. To a person off the "insured location," if the "bodily injury":

   a. Arises out of a condition on the "insured location" or the ways immediately adjoining;

   b. Is caused by the activities of an "insured";

   c. Is caused by a "residence employee" in the course of the "residence employee's" employment by an "insured"; or

   d. Is caused by an animal owned by or in the care of an "insured."

SECTION II - EXCLUSIONS

---

1. **Coverage E - Personal Liability** and **Coverage F - Medical Payments to Others** do not apply to "bodily injury" or "property damage":

   a. Which is expected or intended by the "insured";

   b. Arising out of or in connection with a "business" engaged in by an "insured." This exclusion applies but is not limited to an act or omission, regardless of its nature or circumstance, involving a service or duty rendered, promised, owed, or implied to be provided because of the nature of the "business";

---

c. Arising out of the rental or holding for rental of any part of any premises by an "insured." This exclusion does not apply to the rental or holding for rental of an "insured location":

(1) On an occasional basis if used only as a residence;

(2) In part for use only as a residence, unless a single family unit is intended for use by the occupying family to lodge more than two roomers or boarders; or

(3) In part, as an office, school, studio or private garage;

d. Arising out of the rendering of or failure to render professional services;

e. Arising out of a premises:

(1) Owned by an "insured";

(2) Rented to an "insured"; or

(3) Rented to others by an "insured";

that is not an "insured location";

f. Arising out of:

(1) The ownership, maintenance, use, loading or unloading of motor vehicles or all other motorized land conveyances, including trailers, owned or operated by or rented or loaned to an "insured";

(2) The entrustment by an "insured" of a motor vehicle or any other motorized land conveyance to any person; or

(3) Vicarious liability, whether or not statutorily imposed, for the actions of a child or minor using a conveyance excluded in paragraph (1) or (2) above.

This exclusion does not apply to:

(1) A trailer not towed by or carried on a motorized land conveyance.

(2) A motorized land conveyance designed for recreational use off public roads, not subject to motor vehicle registration and:

(a) Not owned by an "insured"; or

(b) Owned by an "insured" and on an "insured location";

(3) A motorized golf cart when used to play golf on a golf course;

(4) A vehicle or conveyance not subject to motor vehicle registration which is:

(a) Used to service an "insured's" residence;

(b) Designed for assisting the handicapped; or

(c) In dead storage on an "insured location";

g. Arising out of:

(1) The ownership, maintenance, use, loading or unloading of an excluded watercraft described below;

(2) The entrustment by an "insured" of an excluded watercraft described below to any person; or

(3) Vicarious liability, whether or not statutorily imposed, for the actions of a child or minor using an excluded watercraft described below.

Excluded watercraft are those that are principally designed to be propelled by engine power or electric motor, or are sailing vessels, whether owned by or rented to an "insured." This exclusion does not apply to watercraft:

(1) That are not sailing vessels and are powered by:

(a) Inboard or inboard-outdrive engine or motor power of 50 horsepower or less not owned by an "insured";

(b) Inboard or inboard-outdrive engine or motor power of more than 50 horsepower not owned by or rented to an "insured";

(c) One or more outboard engines or motors with 25 total horsepower or less;

(d) One or more outboard engines or motors with more than 25 total horsepower if the outboard engine or motor is not owned by an "insured";

(e) Outboard engines or motors of more than 25 total horsepower owned by an "insured" if:

(i) You acquire them prior to the policy period; and

(a) You declare them at policy inception; or

(b) Your intention to insure is reported to us in writing within 45 days after you acquire the outboard engines or motors.

(ii) You acquire them during the policy period.

This coverage applies for the policy period.

(2) That are sailing vessels, with or without auxiliary power:

(a) Less than 26 feet in overall length;

(b) 26 feet or more in overall length, not owned by or rented to an "insured."

(3) That are stored;

h. Arising out of:

(1) The ownership, maintenance, use, loading or unloading of an aircraft;

(2) The entrustment by an "insured" of an aircraft to any person; or

(3) Vicarious liability, whether or not statutorily imposed, for the actions of a child or minor using an aircraft.

An aircraft means any contrivance used or designed for flight, except model or hobby aircraft not used or designed to carry people or cargo;

i. Caused directly or indirectly by war, including the following and any consequence of any of the following:

(1) Undeclared war, civil war, insurrection, rebellion or revolution;

(2) Warlike act by a military force or military personnel; or

(3) Destruction, seizure or use for a military purpose.

Discharge of a nuclear weapon will be deemed a warlike act even if accidental;

j. Which arises out of the transmission of a communicable disease by an "insured";

k. Arising out of sexual molestation, corporal punishment or physical or mental abuse; or

l. Arising out of the use, sale, manufacture, delivery, transfer or possession by any person of a Controlled Substance(s) as defined by the Federal Food and Drug Law at 21 U.S.C.A. Sections 811 and 812. Controlled Substances include but are not limited to cocaine, LSD, marijuana and all narcotic drugs. However, this exclusion does not apply to the legitimate use of prescription drugs by a person following the orders of a licensed physician.

Exclusions e., f., g., and h. do not apply to "bodily injury" to a "residence employee" arising out of and in the course of the "residence employee's" employment by an "insured."

2. **Coverage E - Personal Liability,** does not apply to:

a. Liability:

(1) For any loss assessment charged against you as a member of an association, corporation or community of property owners;

(2) Under any contract or agreement. However, this exclusion does not apply to written contracts:

(a) That directly relate to the ownership, maintenance or use of an "insured location"; or

(b) Where the liability of others is assumed by the "insured" prior to an "occurrence";

unless excluded in (1) above or elsewhere in this policy;

b. "Property damage" to property owned by the "insured";

c. "Property damage" to property rented to, occupied or used by or in the care of the "insured." This exclusion does not apply to "property damage" caused by fire, smoke or explosion;

d. "Bodily injury" to any person eligible to receive any benefits:

(1) Voluntarily provided; or

(2) Required to be provided;

by the "insured" under any:

(1) Workers' compensation law;

(2) Non-occupational disability law; or

(3) Occupational disease law;

e. "Bodily injury" or "property damage" for which an "insured" under this policy:

(1) Is also an insured under a nuclear energy liability policy; or

(2) Would be an insured under that policy but for the exhaustion of its limit of liability.

A nuclear energy liability policy is one issued by:

(1) American Nuclear Insurers;

(2) Mutual Atomic Energy Liability Underwriters;

(3) Nuclear Insurance Association of Canada;

or any of their successors; or

f. "Bodily injury" to you or an "insured" within the meaning of part a. or b. of "insured" as defined.

3. **Coverage F - Medical Payments to Others,** does not apply to "bodily injury":

a. To a "residence employee" if the "bodily injury":

(1) Occurs off the "insured location"; and

(2) Does not arise out of or in the course of the "residence employee's" employment by an "insured";

 HO 00 03 04 91

b. To any person eligible to receive benefits:
   (1) Voluntarily provided; or
   (2) Required to be provided;
   under any:
   (1) Workers' compensation law;
   (2) Non-occupational disability law; or
   (3) Occupational disease law;
c. From any:
   (1) Nuclear reaction;

(2) Nuclear radiation; or
(3) Radioactive contamination;
all whether controlled or uncontrolled or however caused; or
(4) Any consequence of any of these; or
d. To any person, other than a "residence employee" of an "insured," regularly residing on any part of the "insured location."

SECTION II - ADDITIONAL COVERAGES

We cover the following in addition to the limits of liability:

1. **Claim Expenses.** We pay:
   a. Expenses we incur and costs taxed against an "insured" in any suit we defend;
   b. Premiums on bonds required in a suit we defend, but not for bond amounts more than the limit of liability for Coverage E. We need not apply for or furnish any bond;
   c. Reasonable expenses incurred by an "insured" at our request, including actual loss of earnings (but not loss of other income) up to $50 per day, for assisting us in the investigation or defense of a claim or suit; and
   d. Interest on the entire judgment which accrues after entry of the judgment and before we pay or tender, or deposit in court that part of the judgment which does not exceed the limit of liability that applies.

2. **First Aid Expenses.** We will pay expenses for first aid to others incurred by an "insured" for "bodily injury" covered under this policy. We will not pay for first aid to you or any other "insured."

3. **Damage to Property of Others.** We will pay, at replacement cost, up to $500 per "occurrence" for "property damage" to property of others caused by an "insured."

   We will not pay for "property damage":
   a. To the extent of any amount recoverable under Section I of this policy;
   b. Caused intentionally by an "insured" who is 13 years of age or older;
   c. To property owned by an "insured";
   d. To property owned by or rented to a tenant of an "insured" or a resident in your household; or

   e. Arising out of:
      (1) A "business" engaged in by an "insured";
      (2) Any act or omission in connection with a premises owned, rented or controlled by an "insured," other than the "insured location"; or
      (3) The ownership, maintenance, or use of aircraft, watercraft or motor vehicles or all other motorized land conveyances.

      This exclusion does not apply to a motorized land conveyance designed for recreational use off public roads, not subject to motor vehicle registration and not owned by an "insured."

4. **Loss Assessment.** We will pay up to $1000 for your share of loss assessment charged during the policy period against you by a corporation or association of property owners, when the assessment is made as a result of:
   a. "Bodily injury" or "property damage" not excluded under Section II of this policy; or
   b. Liability for an act of a director, officer or trustee in the capacity as a director, officer or trustee, provided:
      (1) The director, officer or trustee is elected by the members of a corporation or association of property owners; and
      (2) The director, officer or trustee serves without deriving any income from the exercise of duties which are solely on behalf of a corporation or association of property owners.

   This coverage applies only to loss assessments charged against you as owner or tenant of the "residence premises."

We do not cover loss assessments charged against you or a corporation or association of property owners by any governmental body.

Regardless of the number of assessments, the limit of $1000 is the most we will pay for loss arising out of:

a. One accident, including continuous or repeated exposure to substantially the same general harmful condition; or

b. A covered act of a director, officer or trustee. An act involving more than one director, officer or trustee is considered to be a single act.

The following do not apply to this coverage:

1. Section II – Coverage E – Personal Liability Exclusion 2.a.(1);

2. Condition 1. Policy Period, under SECTIONS I AND II – CONDITIONS.

SECTION II - CONDITIONS

---

1. **Limit of Liability.** Our total liability under Coverage E for all damages resulting from any one "occurrence" will not be more than the limit of liability for Coverage E as shown in the Declarations. This limit is the same regardless of the number of "insureds," claims made or persons injured. All "bodily injury" and "property damage" resulting from any one accident or from continuous or repeated exposure to substantially the same general harmful conditions shall be considered to be the result of one "occurrence."

   Our total liability under Coverage F for all medical expense payable for "bodily injury" to one person as the result of one accident will not be more than the limit of liability for Coverage F as shown in the Declarations.

2. **Severability of Insurance.** This insurance applies separately to each "insured." This condition will not increase our limit of liability for any one "occurrence."

3. **Duties After Loss.** In case of an accident or "occurrence," the "insured" will perform the following duties that apply. You will help us by seeing that these duties are performed:

   a. Give written notice to us or our agent as soon as is practical, which sets forth:

   (1) The identity of the policy and "insured";

   (2) Reasonably available information on the time, place and circumstances of the accident or "occurrence"; and

   (3) Names and addresses of any claimants and witnesses;

   b. Promptly forward to us every notice, demand, summons or other process relating to the accident or "occurrence";

   c. At our request, help us:

   (1) To make settlement;

   (2) To enforce any right of contribution or indemnity against any person or organization who may be liable to an "insured";

   (3) With the conduct of suits and attend hearings and trials; and

   (4) To secure and give evidence and obtain the attendance of witnesses;

   d. Under the coverage – Damage to Property of Others – submit to us within 60 days after the loss, a sworn statement of loss and show the damaged property, if in the "insured's" control;

   e. The "insured" will not, except at the "insured's" own cost, voluntarily make payment, assume obligation or incur expense other than for first aid to others at the time of the "bodily injury."

4. **Duties of an Injured Person - Coverage F - Medical Payments to Others.**

   The injured person or someone acting for the injured person will:

   a. Give us written proof of claim, under oath if required, as soon as is practical; and

   b. Authorize us to obtain copies of medical reports and records.

   The injured person will submit to a physical exam by a doctor of our choice when and as often as we reasonably require.

5. **Payment of Claim - Coverage F - Medical Payments to Others.** Payment under this coverage is not an admission of liability by an "insured" or us.

6. **Suit Against Us.** No action can be brought against us unless there has been compliance with the policy provisions.

No one will have the right to join us as a party to any action against an "insured." Also, no action with respect to Coverage E can be brought against us until the obligation of the "insured" has been determined by final judgment or agreement signed by us.

7. **Bankruptcy of an Insured.** Bankruptcy or insolvency of an "insured" will not relieve us of our obligations under this policy.

8. **Other Insurance - Coverage E - Personal Liability.** This insurance is excess over other valid and collectible insurance except insurance written specifically to cover as excess over the limits of liability that apply in this policy.

SECTIONS I AND II - CONDITIONS

1. **Policy Period.** This policy applies only to loss in Section I or "bodily injury" or "property damage" in Section II, which occurs during the policy period.

2. **Concealment or Fraud.** The entire policy will be void if, whether before or after a loss, an "insured" has:

   a. Intentionally concealed or misrepresented any material fact or circumstance;

   b. Engaged in fraudulent conduct; or

   c. Made false statements;

   relating to this insurance.

3. **Liberalization Clause.** If we make a change which broadens coverage under this edition of our policy without additional premium charge, that change will automatically apply to your insurance as of the date we implement the change in your state, provided that this implementation date falls within 60 days prior to or during the policy period stated in the Declarations.

   This Liberalization Clause does not apply to changes implemented through introduction of a subsequent edition of our policy.

4. **Waiver or Change of Policy Provisions.**

   A waiver or change of a provision of this policy must be in writing by us to be valid. Our request for an appraisal or examination will not waive any of our rights.

5. **Cancellation.**

   a. You may cancel this policy at any time by returning it to us or by letting us know in writing of the date cancellation is to take effect.

   b. We may cancel this policy only for the reasons stated below by letting you know in writing of the date cancellation takes effect. This cancellation notice may be delivered to you, or mailed to you at your mailing address shown in the Declarations.

      Proof of mailing will be sufficient proof of notice.

   (1) When you have not paid the premium, we may cancel at any time by letting you know at least 10 days before the date cancellation takes effect.

   (2) When this policy has been in effect for less than 60 days and is not a renewal with us, we may cancel for any reason by letting you know at least 10 days before the date cancellation takes effect.

   (3) When this policy has been in effect for 60 days or more, or at any time if it is a renewal with us, we may cancel:

      (a) If there has been a material misrepresentation of fact which if known to us would have caused us not to issue the policy; or

      (b) If the risk has changed substantially since the policy was issued.

      This can be done by letting you know at least 30 days before the date cancellation takes effect.

   (4) When this policy is written for a period of more than one year, we may cancel for any reason at anniversary by letting you know at least 30 days before the date cancellation takes effect.

   c. When this policy is cancelled, the premium for the period from the date of cancellation to the expiration date will be refunded pro rata.

   d. If the return premium is not refunded with the notice of cancellation or when this policy is returned to us, we will refund it within a reasonable time after the date cancellation takes effect.

6. **Nonrenewal.** We may elect not to renew this policy. We may do so by delivering to you, or mailing to you at your mailing address shown in the Declarations, written notice at least 30 days before the expiration date of this policy. Proof of mailing will be sufficient proof of notice.

7. **Assignment.** Assignment of this policy will not be valid unless we give our written consent.

---

8. **Subrogation.** An "insured" may waive in writing before a loss all rights of recovery against any person. If not waived, we may require an assignment of rights of recovery for a loss to the extent that payment is made by us.

   If an assignment is sought, an "insured" must sign and deliver all related papers and co-operate with us.

   Subrogation does not apply under Section II to Medical Payments to Others or Damage to Property of Others.

9. **Death.** If any person named in the Declarations or the spouse, if a resident of the same household, dies:

   a. We insure the legal representative of the deceased but only with respect to the premises and property of the deceased covered under the policy at the time of death;

   b. "Insured" includes:

      (1) Any member of your household who is an "insured" at the time of your death, but only while a resident of the "residence premises"; and

      (2) With respect to your property, the person having proper temporary custody of the property until appointment and qualification of a legal representative.

         HO 00 03 04 91

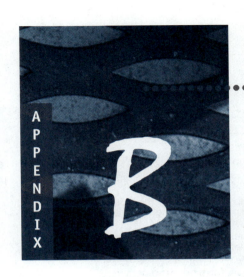

APPENDIX B

Personal Auto Policy

PERSONAL AUTO POLICY

AGREEMENT

In return for payment of the premium and subject to all the terms of this policy, we agree with you as follows:

DEFINITIONS

A. Throughout this policy, "you" and "your" refer to:

1. The "named insured" shown in the Declarations; and

2. The spouse if a resident of the same household.

B. "We", "us" and "our" refer to the Company providing this insurance.

C. For purposes of this policy, a private passenger type auto shall be deemed to be owned by a person if leased:

1. Under a written agreement to that person; and

2. For a continuous period of at least 6 months.

Other words and phrases are defined. They are in quotation marks when used.

D. "Bodily injury" means bodily harm, sickness or disease, including death that results.

E. "Business" includes trade, profession or occupation.

F. "Family member" means a person related to you by blood, marriage or adoption who is a resident of your household. This includes a ward or foster child.

G. "Occupying" means in, upon, getting in, on, out or off.

H. "Property damage" means physical injury to, destruction of or loss of use of tangible property.

I. "Trailer" means a vehicle designed to be pulled by a:

1. Private passenger auto; or

2. Pickup or van.

It also means a farm wagon or farm implement while towed by a vehicle listed in 1. or 2. above.

J. "Your covered auto" means:

1. Any vehicle shown in the Declarations.

2. Any of the following types of vehicles on the date you become the owner:

   a. A private passenger auto; or

b. A pickup or van that:

(1) Has a Gross Vehicle Weight of less than 10,000 lbs.; and

(2) Is not used for the delivery or transportation of goods and materials unless such use is:

(a) Incidental to your "business" of installing, maintaining or repairing furnishings or equipment; or

(b) For farming or ranching.

This provision (J.2.) applies only if:

a. You acquire the vehicle during the policy period;

b. You ask us to insure it within 30 days after you become the owner; and

c. With respect to a pickup or van, no other insurance policy provides coverage for that vehicle.

If the vehicle you acquire replaces one shown in the Declarations, it will have the same coverage as the vehicle it replaced. You must ask us to insure a replacement vehicle within 30 days only if you wish to add or continue Coverage for Damage to Your Auto.

If the vehicle you acquire is in addition to any shown in the Declarations, it will have the broadest coverage we now provide for any vehicle shown in the Declarations.

3. Any "trailer" you own.

4. Any auto or "trailer" you do not own while used as a temporary substitute for any other vehicle described in this definition which is out of normal use because of its:

   a. Breakdown;
   b. Repair;
   c. Servicing;
   d. Loss; or
   e. Destruction.

This provision (J.4.) does not apply to Coverage for Damage to Your Auto.

INSURING AGREEMENT

A. We will pay damages for "bodily injury" or "property damage" for which any "insured" becomes legally responsible because of an auto accident. Damages include prejudgment interest awarded against the "insured". We will settle or defend, as we consider appropriate, any claim or suit asking for these damages. In addition to our limit of liability, we will pay all defense costs we incur. Our duty to settle or defend ends when our limit of liability for this coverage has been exhausted. We have no duty to defend any suit or settle any claim for "bodily injury" or "property damage" not covered under this policy.

B. "Insured" as used in this Part means:

1. You or any "family member" for the ownership, maintenance or use of any auto or "trailer".

2. Any person using "your covered auto".

3. For "your covered auto", any person or organization but only with respect to legal responsibility for acts or omissions of a person for whom coverage is afforded under this Part.

4. For any auto or "trailer", other than "your covered auto", any other person or organization but only with respect to legal responsibility for acts or omissions of you or any "family member" for whom coverage is afforded under this Part. This provision (**B.4.**) applies only if the person or organization does not own or hire the auto or "trailer".

SUPPLEMENTARY PAYMENTS

In addition to our limit of liability, we will pay on behalf of an "insured":

1. Up to $250 for the cost of bail bonds required because of an accident, including related traffic law violations. The accident must result in "bodily injury" or "property damage" covered under this policy.

2. Premiums on appeal bonds and bonds to release attachments in any suit we defend.

3. Interest accruing after a judgment is entered in any suit we defend. Our duty to pay interest ends when we offer to pay that part of the judgment which does not exceed our limit of liability for this coverage.

4. Up to $50 a day for loss of earnings, but not other income, because of attendance at hearings or trials at our request.

5. Other reasonable expenses incurred at our request.

EXCLUSIONS

A. We do not provide Liability Coverage for any "insured":

1. Who intentionally causes "bodily injury" or "property damage".

2. For "property damage" to property owned or being transported by that "insured".

3. For "property damage" to property:

   a. Rented to;

   b. Used by; or

   c. In the care of;

   that "insured".

   This exclusion (**A.3.**) does not apply to "property damage" to a residence or private garage.

4. For "bodily injury" to an employee of that "insured" during the course of employment. This exclusion (**A.4.**) does not apply to "bodily injury" to a domestic employee unless workers' compensation benefits are required or available for that domestic employee.

5. For that "insured's" liability arising out of the ownership or operation of a vehicle while it is being used as a public or livery conveyance. This exclusion (**A.5.**) does not apply to a share-the-expense car pool.

6. While employed or otherwise engaged in the "business" of:

   a. Selling;   d. Storing; or
   b. Repairing;   e. Parking;
   c. Servicing;

   vehicles designed for use mainly on public highways. This includes road testing and delivery. This exclusion (**A.6.**) does not apply to the ownership, maintenance or use of "your covered auto" by:

   a. You;

   b. Any "family member"; or

   c. Any partner, agent or employee of you or any "family member".

7. Maintaining or using any vehicle while that "insured" is employed or otherwise engaged in any "business" (other than farming or ranching) not described in exclusion **A.6.**

   This exclusion (**A.7.**) does not apply to the maintenance or use of a:

   a. Private passenger auto;

   b. Pickup or van that:

      (1) You own; or

      (2) You do not own while used as a temporary substitute for "your covered auto" which is out of normal use because of its:

      (a) Breakdown; **(d)** Loss; or
      (b) Repair; **(e)** Destruction; or
      (c) Servicing;

   c. "Trailer" used with a vehicle described in **a.** or **b.** above.

8. Using a vehicle without a reasonable belief that that "insured" is entitled to do so.

9. For "bodily injury" or "property damage" for which that "insured":

   a. Is an insured under a nuclear energy liability policy; or

   b. Would be an insured under a nuclear energy liability policy but for its termination upon exhaustion of its limit of liability.

   A nuclear energy liability policy is a policy issued by any of the following or their successors:

   a. American Nuclear Insurers;

   b. Mutual Atomic Energy Liability Underwriters; or

   c. Nuclear Insurance Association of Canada.

B. We do not provide Liability Coverage for the ownership, maintenance or use of:

1. Any vehicle which:

   a. Has fewer than four wheels; or

   b. Is designed mainly for use off public roads.

   This exclusion (**B.1.**) does not apply:

   a. While such vehicle is being used by an "insured" in a medical emergency; or

   b. To any "trailer".

2. Any vehicle, other than "your covered auto", which is:

   a. Owned by you; or

   b. Furnished or available for your regular use.

3. Any vehicle, other than "your covered auto", which is:

   a. Owned by any "family member"; or

   b. Furnished or available for the regular use of any "family member".

   However, this exclusion (**B.3.**) does not apply to you while you are maintaining or "occupying" any vehicle which is:

   a. Owned by a "family member"; or

   b. Furnished or available for the regular use of a "family member".

4. Any vehicle, located inside a facility designed for racing, for the purpose of:

   a. Competing in; or

   b. Practicing or preparing for;

   any prearranged or organized racing or speed contest.

LIMIT OF LIABILITY

A. The limit of liability shown in the Declarations for this coverage is our maximum limit of liability for all damages resulting from any one auto accident. This is the most we will pay regardless of the number of:

1. "Insureds";

2. Claims made;

3. Vehicles or premiums shown in the Declarations; or

4. Vehicles involved in the auto accident.

B. We will apply the limit of liability to provide any separate limits required by law for bodily injury and property damage liability. However, this provision (**B.**) will not change our total limit of liability.

C. No one will be entitled to receive duplicate payments for the same elements of loss under this coverage and:

1. Part **B** or Part **C** of this policy; or

2. Any Underinsured Motorists Coverage provided by this policy.

OUT OF STATE COVERAGE

If an auto accident to which this policy applies occurs in any state or province other than the one in which "your covered auto" is principally garaged, we will interpret your policy for that accident as follows:

A. If the state or province has:

1. A financial responsibility or similar law specifying limits of liability for "bodily injury" or "property damage" higher than the limit shown in the Declarations, your policy will provide the higher specified limit.

2. A compulsory insurance or similar law requiring a nonresident to maintain insurance whenever the nonresident uses a vehicle in that state or province, your policy will provide at least the required minimum amounts and types of coverage.

B. No one will be entitled to duplicate payments for the same elements of loss.

FINANCIAL RESPONSIBILITY

When this policy is certified as future proof of financial responsibility, this policy shall comply with the law to the extent required.

OTHER INSURANCE

If there is other applicable liability insurance we will pay only our share of the loss. Our share is the proportion that our limit of liability bears to the total of all applicable limits. However, any insurance we provide for a vehicle you do not own shall be excess over any other collectible insurance.

PART B - MEDICAL PAYMENTS COVERAGE

INSURING AGREEMENT

A. We will pay reasonable expenses incurred for necessary medical and funeral services because of "bodily injury":

1. Caused by accident; and

2. Sustained by an "insured".

We will pay only those expenses incurred for services rendered within 3 years from the date of the accident.

B. "Insured" as used in this Part means:

1. You or any "family member":

   a. While "occupying"; or

   b. As a pedestrian when struck by;

   a motor vehicle designed for use mainly on public roads or a trailer of any type.

2. Any other person while "occupying" "your covered auto".

EXCLUSIONS

We do not provide Medical Payments Coverage for any "insured" for "bodily injury":

1. Sustained while "occupying" any motorized vehicle having fewer than four wheels.

2. Sustained while "occupying" "your covered auto" when it is being used as a public or livery conveyance. This exclusion (2.) does not apply to a share-the-expense car pool.

3. Sustained while "occupying" any vehicle located for use as a residence or premises.

4. Occurring during the course of employment if workers' compensation benefits are required or available for the "bodily injury".

5. Sustained while "occupying", or when struck by, any vehicle (other than "your covered auto") which is:

   a. Owned by you; or

   b. Furnished or available for your regular use.

6. Sustained while "occupying", or when struck by, any vehicle (other than "your covered auto") which is:

   a. Owned by any "family member"; or

   b. Furnished or available for the regular use of any "family member".

   However, this exclusion (6.) does not apply to you.

7. Sustained while "occupying" a vehicle without a reasonable belief that that "insured" is entitled to do so.

8. Sustained while "occupying" a vehicle when it is being used in the "business" of an "insured". This exclusion (8.) does not apply to "bodily injury" sustained while "occupying" a:

   a. Private passenger auto;

   b. Pickup or van that you own; or

   c. "Trailer" used with a vehicle described in a. or b. above.

9. Caused by or as a consequence of:

   a. Discharge of a nuclear weapon (even if accidental);

   b. War (declared or undeclared);

   c. Civil war;

   d. Insurrection; or

   e. Rebellion or revolution.

10. From or as a consequence of the following, whether controlled or uncontrolled or however caused:

    a. Nuclear reaction;

    b. Radiation; or

    c. Radioactive contamination.

PP 00 01 06 94

11. Sustained while "occupying" any vehicle located inside a facility designed for racing, for the purpose of:

    a. Competing in; or

    b. Practicing or preparing for;

    any prearranged or organized racing or speed contest.

LIMIT OF LIABILITY

A. The limit of liability shown in the Declarations for this coverage is our maximum limit of liability for each person injured in any one accident. This is the most we will pay regardless of the number of:

    1. "Insureds";

    2. Claims made;

    3. Vehicles or premiums shown in the Declarations; or

    4. Vehicles involved in the accident.

B. No one will be entitled to receive duplicate payments for the same elements of loss under this coverage and:

    1. Part A or Part C of this policy; or

    2. Any Underinsured Motorists Coverage provided by this policy.

OTHER INSURANCE

If there is other applicable auto medical payments insurance we will pay only our share of the loss. Our share is the proportion that our limit of liability bears to the total of all applicable limits. However, any insurance we provide with respect to a vehicle you do not own shall be excess over any other collectible auto insurance providing payments for medical or funeral expenses.

PART C - UNINSURED MOTORISTS COVERAGE

INSURING AGREEMENT

A. We will pay compensatory damages which an "insured" is legally entitled to recover from the owner or operator of an "uninsured motor vehicle" because of "bodily injury":

    1. Sustained by an "insured"; and

    2. Caused by an accident.

The owner's or operator's liability for these damages must arise out of the ownership, maintenance or use of the "uninsured motor vehicle".

Any judgment for damages arising out of a suit brought without our written consent is not binding on us.

B. "Insured" as used in this Part means:

    1. You or any "family member".

    2. Any other person "occupying" "your covered auto".

    3. Any person for damages that person is entitled to recover because of "bodily injury" to which this coverage applies sustained by a person described in 1. or 2. above.

C. "Uninsured motor vehicle" means a land motor vehicle or trailer of any type:

    1. To which no bodily injury liability bond or policy applies at the time of the accident.

    2. To which a bodily injury liability bond or policy applies at the time of the accident. In this case its limit for bodily injury liability must be less than the minimum limit for bodily injury liability specified by the financial responsibility law of the state in which "your covered auto" is principally garaged.

    3. Which is a hit-and-run vehicle whose operator or owner cannot be identified and which hits:

        a. You or any "family member";

        b. A vehicle which you or any "family member" are "occupying"; or

        c. "Your covered auto".

    4. To which a bodily injury liability bond or policy applies at the time of the accident but the bonding or insuring company.

        a. Denies coverage; or

        b. Is or becomes insolvent.

However, "uninsured motor vehicle" does not include any vehicle or equipment:

    1. Owned by or furnished or available for the regular use of you or any "family member".

    2. Owned or operated by a self-insurer under any applicable motor vehicle law, except a self-insurer which is or becomes insolvent.

    3. Owned by any governmental unit or agency.

    4. Operated on rails or crawler treads.

    5. Designed mainly for use off public roads while not on public roads.

    6. While located for use as a residence or premises.

EXCLUSIONS

A. We do not provide Uninsured Motorists Coverage for "bodily injury" sustained:

    1. By an "insured" while "occupying", or when struck by, any motor vehicle owned by that "insured" which is not insured for this coverage under this policy. This includes a trailer of any type used with that vehicle.

2. By any "family member" while "occupying", or when struck by, any motor vehicle you own which is insured for this coverage on a primary basis under any other policy.

B. We do not provide Uninsured Motorists Coverage for "bodily injury" sustained by any "insured":

1. If that "insured" or the legal representative settles the "bodily injury" claim without our consent.

2. While "occupying" "your covered auto" when it is being used as a public or livery conveyance. This exclusion (B.2.) does not apply to a share-the-expense car pool.

3. Using a vehicle without a reasonable belief that that "insured" is entitled to do so.

C. This coverage shall not apply directly or indirectly to benefit any insurer or self-insurer under any of the following or similar law:

1. Workers' compensation law; or

2. Disability benefits law.

D. We do not provide Uninsured Motorists Coverage for punitive or exemplary damages.

LIMIT OF LIABILITY

A. The limit of liability shown in the Declarations for this coverage is our maximum limit of liability for all damages resulting from any one accident. This is the most we will pay regardless of the number of:

1. "Insureds";

2. Claims made;

3. Vehicles or premiums shown in the Declarations; or

4. Vehicles involved in the accident.

B. No one will be entitled to receive duplicate payments for the same elements of loss under this coverage and:

1. Part A or Part B of this policy; or

2. Any Underinsured Motorists Coverage provided by this policy.

C. We will not make a duplicate payment under this coverage for any element of loss for which payment has been made by or on behalf of persons or organizations who may be legally responsible.

D. We will not pay for any element of loss if a person is entitled to receive payment for the same element of loss under any of the following or similar law:

1. Workers' compensation law; or

2. Disability benefits law.

OTHER INSURANCE

If there is other applicable insurance available under one or more policies or provisions of coverage:

1. Any recovery for damages under all such policies or provisions of coverage may equal but not exceed the highest applicable limit for any one vehicle under any insurance providing coverage on either a primary or excess basis.

2. Any insurance we provide with respect to a vehicle you do not own shall be excess over any collectible insurance providing coverage on a primary basis.

3. If the coverage under this policy is provided:

a. On a primary basis, we will pay only our share of the loss that must be paid under insurance providing coverage on a primary basis. Our share is the proportion that our limit of liability bears to the total of all applicable limits of liability for coverage provided on a primary basis.

b. On an excess basis, we will pay only our share of the loss that must be paid under insurance providing coverage on an excess basis. Our share is the proportion that our limit of liability bears to the total of all applicable limits of liability for coverage provided on an excess basis.

ARBITRATION

A. If we and an "insured" do not agree:

1. Whether that "insured" is legally entitled to recover damages; or

2. As to the amount of damages which are recoverable by that "insured";

from the owner or operator of an "uninsured motor vehicle", then the matter may be arbitrated. However, disputes concerning coverage under this Part may not be arbitrated.

Both parties must agree to arbitration. If so agreed, each party will select an arbitrator. The two arbitrators will select a third. If they cannot agree within 30 days, either may request that selection be made by a judge of a court having jurisdiction.

B. Each party will:

1. Pay the expenses it incurs; and

2. Bear the expenses of the third arbitrator equally.

C. Unless both parties agree otherwise, arbitration will take place in the county in which the "insured" lives. Local rules of law as to procedure and evidence will apply. A decision agreed to by two of the arbitrators will be binding as to:

1. Whether the "insured" is legally entitled to recover damages; and

2. The amount of damages. This applies only if the amount does not exceed the minimum limit for bodily injury liability specified by the financial responsibility law of the state in which "your covered auto" is principally garaged. If the amount exceeds that limit, either party may demand the right to a trial. This demand must be made within 60 days of the arbitrators' decision. If this demand is not made, the amount of damages agreed to by the arbitrators will be binding.

PP 00 01 06 94

INSURING AGREEMENT

A. We will pay for direct and accidental loss to "your covered auto" or any "non-owned auto", including their equipment, minus any applicable deductible shown in the Declarations. If loss to more than one "your covered auto" or "non-owned auto" results from the same "collision", only the highest applicable deductible will apply. We will pay for loss to "your covered auto" caused by:

1. Other than "collision" only if the Declarations indicate that Other Than Collision Coverage is provided for that auto.

2. "Collision" only if the Declarations indicate that Collision Coverage is provided for that auto.

If there is a loss to a "non-owned auto", we will provide the broadest coverage applicable to any "your covered auto" shown in the Declarations.

B. "Collision" means the upset of "your covered auto" or a "non-owned auto" or their impact with another vehicle or object.

Loss caused by the following is considered other than "collision":

1. Missiles or falling objects;
2. Fire;
3. Theft or larceny;
4. Explosion or earthquake;
5. Windstorm;
6. Hail, water or flood;
7. Malicious mischief or vandalism;
8. Riot or civil commotion;
9. Contact with bird or animal; or
10. Breakage of glass

If breakage of glass is caused by a "collision", you may elect to have it considered a loss caused by "collision".

C. "Non-owned auto" means:

1. Any private passenger auto, pickup, van or "trailer" not owned by or furnished or available for the regular use of you or any "family member" while in the custody of or being operated by you or any "family member"; or

2. Any auto or "trailer" you do not own while used as a temporary substitute for "your covered auto" which is out of normal use because of its:

   a. Breakdown;
   b. Repair;
   c. Servicing;
   d. Loss; or
   e. Destruction.

TRANSPORTATION EXPENSES

In addition, we will pay, without application of a deductible, up to $15 per day, to a maximum of $450, for:

1. Temporary transportation expenses incurred by you in the event of a loss to "your covered auto". We will pay for such expenses if the loss is caused by:

   a. Other than "collision" only if the Declarations indicate that Other Than Collision Coverage is provided for that auto.

   b. "Collision" only if the Declarations indicate that Collision Coverage is provided for that auto.

2. Loss of use expenses for which you become legally responsible in the event of loss to a "non-owned auto". We will pay for loss of use expenses if the loss is caused by:

   a. Other than "collision" only if the Delcarations indicate that Other Than Collision Coverage is provided for any "your covered auto".

   b. "Collision" only if the Declarations indicate that Collision Coverage is provided for any "your covered auto".

If the loss is caused by a total theft of "your covered auto" or a "non-owned auto", we will pay only expenses incurred during the period:

1. Beginning 48 hours after the theft; and

2. Ending when "your covered auto" or the "non-owned auto" is returned to use or we pay for its loss.

If the loss is caused by other than theft of a "your covered auto" or a "non-owned auto", we will pay only expenses beginning when the auto is withdrawn from use for more than 24 hours.

Our payment will be limited to that period of time reasonably required to repair or replace the "your covered auto" or the "non-owned auto".

EXCLUSIONS

We will not pay for:

1. Loss to "your covered auto" or any "non-owned auto" which occurs while it is being used as a public or livery conveyance. This exclusion (1.) does not apply to a share-the-expense car pool.

2. Damage due and confined to:

   a. Wear and tear;
   b. Freezing;
   c. Mechanical or electrical breakdown or failure; or
   d. Road damage to tires.

   This exclusion (2.) does not apply if the damage results from the total theft of "your covered auto" or any "non-owned auto".

3. Loss due to or as a consequence of:

   a. Radioactive contamination;
   b. Discharge of any nuclear weapon (even if accidental);
   c. War (declared or undeclared);
   d. Civil war;

e. Insurrection; or

f. Rebellion or revolution.

4. Loss to:

a. Any electronic equipment designed for the reproduction of sound, including, but not limited to:

(1) Radios and stereos;

(2) Tape decks; or

(3) Compact disc players;

b. Any other electronic equipment that receives or transmits audio, visual or data signals, including, but not limited to:

(1) Citizens band radios;

(2) Telephones;

(3) Two-way mobile radios;

(4) Scanning monitor receivers;

(5) Television monitor receivers;

(6) Video cassette recorders;

(7) Audio cassette recorders; or

(8) Personal computers;

c. Tapes, records, discs, or other media used with equipment described in a. or b.; or

d. Any other accessories used with equipment described in a. or b.

This exclusion (4.) does not apply to:

a. Equipment designed solely for the reproduction of sound and accessories used with such equipment, provided:

(1) The equipment is permanently installed in "your covered auto" or any "non-owned auto"; or

(2) The equipment is:

(a) Removable from a housing unit which is permanently installed in the auto;

(b) Designed to be solely operated by use of the power from the auto's electrical system; and

(c) In or upon "your covered auto" or any "non-owned auto";

at the time of the loss.

b. Any other electronic equipment that is:

(1) Necessary for the normal operation of the auto or the monitoring of the auto's operating systems; or

(2) An integral part of the same unit housing any sound reproducing equipment described in a. and permanently installed in the opening of the dash or console of "your covered auto" or any "non-owned auto" normally used by the manufacturer for installation of a radio.

5. A total loss to "your covered auto" or any "non-owned auto" due to destruction or confiscation by governmental or civil authorities.

This exclusion (5.) does not apply to the interests of Loss Payees in "your covered auto".

6. Loss to a camper body or "trailer" you own which is not shown in the Declarations. This exclusion (6.) does not apply to a camper body or "trailer" you:

a. Acquire during the policy period; and

b. Ask us to insure within 30 days after you become the owner.

7. Loss to any "non-owned auto" when used by you or any "family member" without a reasonable belief that you or that "family member" are entitled to do so.

8. Loss to:

a. Awnings or cabanas; or

b. Equipment designed to create additional living facilities.

9. Loss to equipment designed or used for the detection or location of radar or laser.

10. Loss to any custom furnishings or equipment in or upon any pickup or van. Custom furnishings or equipment include but are not limited to:

a. Special carpeting and insulation, furniture or bars;

b. Facilities for cooking and sleeping;

c. Height-extending roofs; or

d. Custom murals, paintings or other decals or graphics.

11. Loss to any "non-owned auto" being maintained or used by any person while employed or otherwise engaged in the "business" of:

a. Selling;   d. Storing; or
b. Repairing;   e. Parking;
c. Servicing;

vehicles designed for use on public highways. This includes road testing and delivery.

12. Loss to any "non-owned auto" being maintained or used by any person while employed or otherwise engaged in any "business" not described in exclusion 11. This exclusion (12.) does not apply to the maintenance or use by you or any "family member" of a "non-owned auto" which is a private passenger auto or "trailer".

13. Loss to "your covered auto" or any "non-owned auto", located inside a facility designed for racing, for the purpose of:

a. Competing in; or

b. Practicing or preparing for;

any prearranged or organized racing or speed contest.

 PP 00 01 06 94

14. Loss to, or loss of use of, a "non-owned auto" rented by:

    a. You; or

    b. Any "family member";

    if a rental vehicle company is precluded from recovering such loss or loss of use, from you or that "family member", pursuant to the provisions of any applicable rental agreement or state law.

LIMIT OF LIABILITY

A. Our limit of liability for loss will be the lesser of the:

    1. Actual cash value of the stolen or damaged property;

    2. Amount necessary to repair or replace the property with other property of like kind and quality.

    However, the most we will pay for loss to any "non-owned auto" which is a trailer is $500.

B. An adjustment for depreciation and physical condition will be made in determining actual cash value in the event of a total loss.

C. If a repair or replacement results in better than like kind or quality, we will not pay for the amount of the betterment.

PAYMENT OF LOSS

We may pay for loss in money or repair or replace the damaged or stolen property. We may, at our expense, return any stolen property to:

    1. You; or

    2. The address shown in this policy.

If we return stolen property we will pay for any damage resulting from the theft. We may keep all or part of the property at an agreed or appraised value.

If we pay for loss in money, our payment will include the applicable sales tax for the damaged or stolen property.

NO BENEFIT TO BAILEE

This insurance shall not directly or indirectly benefit any carrier or other bailee for hire.

OTHER SOURCES OF RECOVERY

If other sources of recovery also cover the loss, we will pay only our share of the loss. Our share is the proportion that our limit of liability bears to the total of all applicable limits. However, any insurance we provide with respect to a "non-owned auto" shall be excess over any other collectible source of recovery including, but not limited to:

1. Any coverage provided by the owner of the "non-owned auto";

2. Any other applicable physical damage insurance;

3. Any other source of recovery applicable to the loss.

APPRAISAL

A. If we and you do not agree on the amount of loss, either may demand an appraisal of the loss. In this event, each party will select a competent appraiser. The two appraisers will select an umpire. The appraisers will state separately the actual cash value and the amount of loss. If they fail to agree, they will submit their differences to the umpire. A decision agreed to by any two will be binding. Each party will:

    1. Pay its chosen appraiser; and

    2. Bear the expenses of the appraisal and umpire equally.

B. We do not waive any of our rights under this policy by agreeing to an appraisal.

PART E - DUTIES AFTER AN ACCIDENT OR LOSS

We have no duty to provide coverage under this policy unless there has been full compliance with the following duties:

A. We must be notified promptly of how, when and where the accident or loss happened. Notice should also include the names and addresses of any injured persons and of any witnesses.

B. A person seeking any coverage must:

    1. Cooperate with us in the investigation, settlement or defense of any claim or suit.

    2. Promptly send us copies of any notices or legal papers received in connection with the accident or loss.

    3. Submit, as often as we reasonably require:

        a. To physical exams by physicians we select. We will pay for these exams.

        b. To examination under oath and subscribe the same.

    4. Authorize us to obtain:

        a. Medical reports; and

        b. Other pertinent records.

    5. Submit a proof of loss when required by us.

C. A person seeking Uninsured Motorists Coverage must also:

    1. Promptly notify the police if a hit-and-run driver is involved.

    2. Promptly send us copies of the legal papers if a suit is brought.

D. A person seeking Coverage for Damage to Your Auto must also:

    1. Take reasonable steps after loss to protect "your covered auto" or any "non-owned auto" and their equipment from further loss. We will pay reasonable expenses incurred to do this.

    2. Promptly notify the police if "your covered auto" or any "non-owned auto" is stolen.

    3. Permit us to inspect and appraise the damaged property before its repair or disposal.

BANKRUPTCY

Bankruptcy or insolvency of the "insured" shall not relieve us of any obligations under this policy.

CHANGES

A. This policy contains all the agreements between you and us. Its terms may not be changed or waived except by endorsement issued by us.

B. If there is a change to the information used to develop the policy premium, we may adjust your premium. Changes during the policy term that may result in a premium increase or decrease include, but are not limited to, changes in:

1. The number, type or use classification of insured vehicles;
2. Operators using insured vehicles;
3. The place of principal garaging of insured vehicles;
4. Coverage, deductible or limits.

If a change resulting from **A.** or **B.** requires a premium adjustment, we will make the premium adjustment in accordance with our manual rules.

C. If we make a change which broadens coverage under this edition of your policy without additional premium charge, that change will automatically apply to your policy as of the date we implement the change in your state. This paragraph (**C.**) does not apply to changes implemented with a general program revision that includes both broadenings and restrictions in coverage, whether that general program revision is implemented through introduction of:

1. A subsequent edition of your policy; or
2. An Amendatory Endorsement.

FRAUD

We do not provide coverage for any "insured" who has made fraudulent statements or engaged in fraudulent conduct in connection with any accident or loss for which coverage is sought under this policy.

LEGAL ACTION AGAINST US

A. No legal action may be brought against us until there has been full compliance with all the terms of this policy. In addition, under Part A, no legal action may be brought against us until:

1. We agree in writing that the "insured" has an obligation to pay; or
2. The amount of that obligation has been finally determined by judgment after trial.

B. No person or organization has any right under this policy to bring us into any action to determine the liability of an "insured".

OUR RIGHT TO RECOVER PAYMENT

A. If we make a payment under this policy and the person to or for whom payment was made has a right to recover damages from another we shall be subrogated to that right. That person shall do:

1. Whatever is necessary to enable us to exercise our rights; and
2. Nothing after loss to prejudice them.

However, our rights in this paragraph (**A.**) do not apply under Part D, against any person using "your covered auto" with a reasonable belief that that person is entitled to do so.

B. If we make a payment under this policy and the person to or for whom payment is made recovers damages from another, that person shall:

1. Hold in trust for us the proceeds of the recovery; and
2. Reimburse us to the extent of our payment.

POLICY PERIOD AND TERRITORY

A. This policy applies only to accidents and losses which occur:

1. During the policy period as shown in the Declarations; and
2. Within the policy territory.

B. The policy territory is:

1. The United States of America, its territories or possessions;
2. Puerto Rico; or
3. Canada.

This policy also applies to loss to, or accidents involving, "your covered auto" while being transported between their ports.

TERMINATION

A. Cancellation. This policy may be cancelled during the policy period as follows:

1. The named insured shown in the Declarations may cancel by:
   a. Returning this policy to us; or
   b. Giving us advance written notice of the date cancellation is to take effect.
2. We may cancel by mailing to the named insured shown in the Declarations at the address shown in this policy:
   a. At least 10 days notice:
      (1) If cancellation is for nonpayment of premium; or
      (2) If notice is mailed during the first 60 days this policy is in effect and this is not a renewal or continuation policy; or
   b. At least 20 days notice in all other cases.

3. After this policy is in effect for 60 days, or if this is a renewal or continuation policy, we will cancel only:

  a. For nonpayment of premium; or

  b. If your driver's license or that of:

    (1) Any driver who lives with you; or

    (2) Any driver who customarily uses "your covered auto";

  has been suspended or revoked. This must have occurred:

    (1) During the policy period; or

    (2) Since the last anniversary of the original effective date if the policy period is other than 1 year; or

  c. If the policy was obtained through material misrepresentation.

B. **Nonrenewal.** If we decide not to renew or continue this policy, we will mail notice to the named insured shown in the Declarations at the address shown in this policy. Notice will be mailed at least 20 days before the end of the policy period. If the policy period is:

1. Less than 6 months, we will have the right not to renew or continue this policy every 6 months, beginning 6 months after its original effective date.

2. 1 year or longer, we will have the right not to renew or continue this policy at each anniversary of its original effective date.

C. **Automatic Termination.** If we offer to renew or continue and you or your representative do not accept, this policy will automatically terminate at the end of the current policy period. Failure to pay the required renewal or continuation premium when due shall mean that you have not accepted our offer.

If you obtain other insurance on "your covered auto", any similar insurance provided by this policy will terminate as to that auto on the effective date of the other insurance.

D. **Other Termination Provisions.**

1. We may deliver any notice instead of mailing it. Proof of mailing of any notice shall be sufficient proof of notice.

2. If this policy is cancelled, you may be entitled to a premium refund. If so, we will send you the refund. The premium refund, if any, will be computed according to our manuals. However, making or offering to make the refund is not a condition of cancellation.

3. The effective date of cancellation stated in the notice shall become the end of the policy period.

TRANSFER OF YOUR INTEREST IN THIS POLICY

A. Your rights and duties under this policy may not be assigned without our written consent. However, if a named insured shown in the Declarations dies, coverage will be provided for:

1. The surviving spouse if resident in the same household at the time of death. Coverage applies to the spouse as if a named insured shown in the Declarations; and

2. The legal representative of the deceased person as if a named insured shown in the Declarations. This applies only with respect to the representative's legal responsibility to maintain or use "your covered auto".

B. Coverage will only be provided until the end of the policy period.

TWO OR MORE AUTO POLICIES

If this policy and any other auto insurance policy issued to you by us apply to the same accident, the maximum limit of our liability under all the policies shall not exceed the highest applicable limit of liability under any one policy.

C

Building and Personal Property Coverage Form

BUILDING AND PERSONAL PROPERTY COVERAGE FORM

Various provisions in this policy restrict coverage. Read the entire policy carefully to determine rights, duties and what is and is not covered.

Throughout this policy the words "you" and "your" refer to the Named Insured shown in the Declarations. The words "we," "us" and "our" refer to the Company providing this insurance.

Other words and phrases that appear in quotation marks have special meaning. Refer to SECTION H – DEFINITIONS.

A. COVERAGE

We will pay for direct physical loss of or damage to Covered Property at the premises described in the Declarations caused by or resulting from any Covered Cause of Loss.

1. Covered Property

Covered Property, as used in this Coverage Part, means the following types of property for which a Limit of Insurance is shown in the Declarations:

a. Building, meaning the building or structure described in the Declarations, including:

(1) Completed additions;

(2) Permanently installed:

  (a) Fixtures;

  (b) Machinery; and

  (c) Equipment;

(3) Outdoor fixtures;

(4) Personal property owned by you that is used to maintain or service the building or structure or its premises, including:

  (a) Fire extinguishing equipment;

  (b) Outdoor furniture;

  (c) Floor coverings; and

  (d) Appliances used for refrigerating, ventilating, cooking, dishwashing or laundering;

(5) If not covered by other insurance:

  (a) Additions under construction, alterations and repairs to the building or structure;

  (b) Materials, equipment, supplies and temporary structures, on or within 100 feet of the described premises, used for making additions, alterations or repairs to the building or structure.

b. Your Business Personal Property located in or on the building described in the Declarations or in the open (or in a vehicle) within 100 feet of the described premises, consisting of the following unless otherwise specified in the Declarations or on the Your Business Personal Property – Separation of Coverage form:

(1) Furniture and fixtures;

(2) Machinery and equipment;

(3) "Stock";

(4) All other personal property owned by you and used in your business;

(5) Labor, materials or services furnished or arranged by you on personal property of others;

(6) Your use interest as tenant in improvements and betterments. Improvements and betterments are fixtures, alterations, installations or additions:

  (a) Made a part of the building or structure you occupy but do not own; and

  (b) You acquired or made at your expense but cannot legally remove;

(7) Leased personal property for which you have a contractual responsibility to insure, unless otherwise provided for under Personal Property of Others.

CP 00 10 10 91   Copyright, ISO Commercial Risk Services, Inc., 1990, 1991   Page 1 of 10 ☐

c. Personal Property of Others that is:

   (1) In your care, custody or control; and

   (2) Located in or on the building described in the Declarations or in the open (or in a vehicle) within 100 feet of the described premises.

However, our payment for loss of or damage to personal property of others will only be for the account of the owner of the property.

2. Property Not Covered

Covered Property does not include:

a. Accounts, bills, currency, deeds, food stamps or other evidences of debt, money, notes or securities. Lottery tickets held for sale are not securities;

b. Animals, unless owned by others and boarded by you, or if owned by you, only as "stock" while inside of buildings;

c. Automobiles held for sale;

d. Bridges, roadways, walks, patios or other paved surfaces;

e. Contraband, or property in the course of illegal transportation or trade;

f. The cost of excavations, grading, backfilling or filling;

g. Foundations of buildings, structures, machinery or boilers if their foundations are below:

   (1) The lowest basement floor; or

   (2) The surface of the ground, if there is no basement;

h. Land (including land on which the property is located), water, growing crops or lawns;

i. Personal property while airborne or waterborne;

j. Pilings, piers, wharves or docks;

k. Property that is covered under another coverage form of this or any other policy in which it is more specifically described, except for the excess of the amount due (whether you can collect on it or not) from that other insurance;

l. Retaining walls that are not part of the building described in the Declarations;

m. Underground pipes, flues or drains;

n. The cost to research, replace or restore the information on valuable papers and records, including those which exist on electronic or magnetic media, except as provided in the Coverage Extensions;

o. Vehicles or self-propelled machines (including aircraft or watercraft) that:

   (1) Are licensed for use on public roads; or

   (2) Are operated principally away from the described premises.

This paragraph does not apply to:

   (a) Vehicles or self-propelled machines or autos you manufacture, process or warehouse;

   (b) Vehicles or self-propelled machines, other than autos, you hold for sale; or

   (c) Rowboats or canoes out of water at the described premises;

p. The following property while outside of buildings:

   (1) Grain, hay, straw or other crops;

   (2) Fences, radio or television antennas, including their lead-in wiring, masts or towers, signs (other than signs attached to buildings), trees, shrubs or plants (other than "stock" of trees, shrubs or plants), all except as provided in the Coverage Extensions.

3. Covered Causes Of Loss

See applicable Causes of Loss Form as shown in the Declarations.

4. Additional Coverages

a. Debris Removal

   (1) We will pay your expense to remove debris of Covered Property caused by or resulting from a Covered Cause of Loss that occurs during the policy period. The expenses will be paid only if they are reported to us in writing within 180 days of the date of direct physical loss or damage.

   (2) The most we will pay under this Additional Coverage is 25% of:

     (a) The amount we pay for the direct physical loss of or damage to Covered Property; plus

(b) The deductible in this policy applicable to that loss or damage.

But this limitation does not apply to any additional debris removal limit provided in the Limits of Insurance section.

(3) This Additional Coverage does not apply to costs to:

(a) Extract "pollutants" from land or water; or

(b) Remove, restore or replace polluted land or water.

b. Preservation of Property

If it is necessary to move Covered Property from the described premises to preserve it from loss or damage by a Covered Cause of Loss, we will pay for any direct physical loss or damage to that property:

(1) While it is being moved or while temporarily stored at another location; and

(2) Only if the loss or damage occurs within 10 days after the property is first moved.

c. Fire Department Service Charge

When the fire department is called to save or protect Covered Property from a Covered Cause of Loss, we will pay up to $1,000 for your liability for fire department service charges:

(1) Assumed by contract or agreement prior to loss; or

(2) Required by local ordinance.

No Deductible applies to this Additional Coverage.

d. Pollutant Clean Up and Removal

We will pay your expense to extract "pollutants" from land or water at the described premises if the discharge, dispersal, seepage, migration, release or escape of the "pollutants" is caused by or results from a Covered Cause of Loss that occurs during the policy period. The expenses will be paid only if they are reported to us in writing within 180 days of the date on which the Covered Cause of Loss occurs.

This Additional Coverage does not apply to costs to test for, monitor or assess the existence, concentration or effects of "pollutants." But we will pay for testing which is performed in the course of extracting the "pollutants" from the land or water.

The most we will pay under this Additional Coverage for each described premises is $10,000 for the sum of all covered expenses arising out of Covered Causes of Loss occurring during each separate 12 month period of this policy.

5. Coverage Extensions

Except as otherwise provided, the following Extensions apply to property located in or on the building described in the Declarations or in the open (or in a vehicle) within 100 feet of the described premises.

If a Coinsurance percentage of 80% or more or, a Value Reporting period symbol, is shown in the Declarations, you may extend the insurance provided by this Coverage Part as follows:

a. Newly Acquired or Constructed Property

(1) You may extend the insurance that applies to Building to apply to:

(a) Your new buildings while being built on the described premises; and

(b) Buildings you acquire at locations, other than the described premises, intended for:

(i) Similar use as the building described in the Declarations; or

(ii) Use as a warehouse.

The most we will pay for loss or damage under this Extension is 25% of the Limit of Insurance for Building shown in the Declarations, but not more than $250,000 at each building.

(2) You may extend the insurance that applies to Your Business Personal Property to apply to that property at any location you acquire other than at fairs or exhibitions.

CP 00 10 10 91   Copyright, ISO Commercial Risk Services, Inc., 1990, 1991   Page 3 of 10   □

The most we will pay for loss or damage under this Extension is 10% of the Limit of Insurance for Your Business Personal Property shown in the Declarations, but not more than $100,000 at each building.

(3) Insurance under this Extension for each newly acquired or constructed property will end when any of the following first occurs:

(a) This policy expires.

(b) 30 days expire after you acquire or begin to construct the property; or

(c) You report values to us.

We will charge you additional premium for values reported from the date construction begins or you acquire the property.

b. Personal Effects and Property of Others

You may extend the insurance that applies to Your Business Personal Property to apply to:

(1) Personal effects owned by you, your officers, your partners or your employees. This extension does not apply to loss or damage by theft.

(2) Personal property of others in your care, custody or control.

The most we will pay for loss or damage under this Extension is $2,500 at each described premises. Our payment for loss of or damage to personal property of others will only be for the account of the owner of the property.

c. Valuable Papers and Records - Cost of Research

You may extend the insurance that applies to Your Business Personal Property to apply to your costs to research, replace or restore the lost information on lost or damaged valuable papers and records, including those which exist on electronic or magnetic media, for which duplicates do not exist. The most we will pay under this Extension is $1,000 at each described premises.

d. Property Off-Premises

You may extend the insurance provided by this Coverage Form to apply to your Covered Property, other than "stock," that is temporarily at a location you do not own, lease or operate. This Extension does not apply to Covered Property:

(1) In or on a vehicle;

(2) In the care, custody or control of your salespersons; or

(3) At any fair or exhibition.

The most we will pay for loss or damage under this Extension is $5,000.

e. Outdoor Property

You may extend the insurance provided by this Coverage Form to apply to your outdoor fences, radio and television antennas, signs (other than signs attached to buildings), trees, shrubs and plants (other than "stock" of trees, shrubs or plants), including debris removal expense, caused by or resulting from any of the following causes of loss if they are Covered Causes of Loss:

(1) Fire;

(2) Lightning;

(3) Explosion;

(4) Riot or Civil Commotion; or

(5) Aircraft.

The most we will pay for loss or damage under this Extension is $1,000, but not more than $250 for any one tree, shrub or plant.

Each of these Extensions is additional insurance. The Additional Condition, Coinsurance, does not apply to these Extensions.

B. EXCLUSIONS

See applicable Causes of Loss Form as shown in the Declarations.

CP 00 10 10 91

C. LIMITS OF INSURANCE

The most we will pay for loss or damage in any one occurrence is the applicable Limit of Insurance shown in the Declarations.

The most we will pay for loss or damage to outdoor signs attached to buildings is $1,000 per sign in any one occurrence.

The limits applicable to the Coverage Extensions and the Fire Department Service Charge and Pollutant Clean Up and Removal Additional Coverages are in addition to the Limits of Insurance.

Payments under the following Additional Coverages will not increase the applicable Limit of Insurance:

1. Preservation of Property; or

2. Debris Removal; but if:

   a. The sum of direct physical loss or damage and debris removal expense exceeds the Limit of Insurance; or

   b. The debris removal expense exceeds the amount payable under the 25% limitation in the Debris Removal Additional Coverage;

   we will pay up to an additional $5,000 for each location in any one occurrence under the Debris Removal Additional Coverage.

D. DEDUCTIBLE

We will not pay for loss or damage in any one occurrence until the amount of loss or damage exceeds the Deductible shown in the Declarations. We will then pay the amount of loss or damage in excess of the Deductible, up to the applicable Limit of Insurance, after any deduction required by the Coinsurance condition or the Agreed Value Optional Coverage.

E. LOSS CONDITIONS

The following conditions apply in addition to the Common Policy Conditions and the Commercial Property Conditions.

1. Abandonment

There can be no abandonment of any property to us.

2. Appraisal

If we and you disagree on the value of the property or the amount of loss, either may make written demand for an appraisal of the loss. In this event, each party will select a competent and impartial appraiser. The two appraisers will select an umpire. If they cannot agree, either may request that selection be made by a judge of a court having jurisdiction. The appraisers will state separately the value of the property and amount of loss. If they fail to agree, they will submit their differences to the umpire. A decision agreed to by any two will be binding. Each party will:

a. Pay its chosen appraiser; and

b. Bear the other expenses of the appraisal and umpire equally.

If there is an appraisal, we will still retain our right to deny the claim.

3. Duties In The Event Of Loss Or Damage

a. You must see that the following are done in the event of loss or damage to Covered Property:

(1) Notify the police if a law may have been broken.

(2) Give us prompt notice of the loss or damage. Include a description of the property involved.

(3) As soon as possible, give us a description of how, when and where the loss or damage occurred.

(4) Take all reasonable steps to protect the Covered Property from further damage by a Covered Cause of Loss. If feasible, set the damaged property aside and in the best possible order for examination. Also keep a record of your expenses for emergency and temporary repairs, for consideration in the settlement of the claim. This will not increase the Limit of Insurance.

(5) At our request, give us complete inventories of the damaged and undamaged property. Include quantities, costs, values and amount of loss claimed.

(6) As often as may be reasonably required, permit us to inspect the property proving the loss or damage and examine your books and records.

Also permit us to take samples of damaged and undamaged property for inspection, testing and analysis, and permit us to make copies from your books and records.

(7) Send us a signed, sworn proof of loss containing the information we request to investigate the claim. You must do this within 60 days after our request. We will supply you with the necessary forms.

(8) Cooperate with us in the investigation or settlement of the claim.

b. We may examine any insured under oath, while not in the presence of any other insured and at such times as may be reasonably required, about any matter relating to this insurance or the claim, including an insured's books and records. In the event of an examination, an insured's answers must be signed.

4. **Loss Payment**

a. In the event of loss or damage covered by this Coverage Form, at our option, we will either:

(1) Pay the value of lost or damaged property;

(2) Pay the cost of repairing or replacing the lost or damaged property;

(3) Take all or any part of the property at an agreed or appraised value; or

(4) Repair, rebuild or replace the property with other property of like kind and quality.

b. We will give notice of our intentions within 30 days after we receive the sworn proof of loss.

c. We will not pay you more than your financial interest in the Covered Property.

d. We may adjust losses with the owners of lost or damaged property if other than you. If we pay the owners, such payments will satisfy your claims against us for the owners' property. We will not pay the owners more than their financial interest in the Covered Property.

e. We may elect to defend you against suits arising from claims of owners of property. We will do this at our expense.

f. We will pay for covered loss or damage within 30 days after we receive the sworn proof of loss, if:

(1) You have complied with all of the terms of this Coverage Part; and

(2)(a) We have reached agreement with you on the amount of loss; or

(b) An appraisal award has been made.

5. **Recovered Property**

If either you or we recover any property after loss settlement, that party must give the other prompt notice. At your option, the property will be returned to you. You must then return to us the amount we paid to you for the property. We will pay recovery expenses and the expenses to repair the recovered property, subject to the Limit of Insurance.

6. **Vacancy**

If the building where loss or damage occurs has been vacant for more than 60 consecutive days before that loss or damage, we will:

a. Not pay for any loss or damage caused by any of the following even if they are Covered Causes of Loss:

(1) Vandalism;

(2) Sprinkler leakage, unless you have protected the system against freezing;

(3) Building glass breakage;

(4) Water damage;

(5) Theft; or

(6) Attempted theft.

b. Reduce the amount we would otherwise pay for the loss or damage by 15%.

Copyright, ISO Commercial Risk Services, Inc., 1990, 1991 CP 00 10 10 91   □

Building and Personal Property Coverage Form

A building is vacant when it does not contain enough business personal property to conduct customary operations.

Buildings under construction are not considered vacant.

7. **Valuation**

We will determine the value of Covered Property in the event of loss or damage as follows:

a. At actual cash value as of the time of loss or damage, except as provided in **b., c., d., e.** and **f.** below.

b. If the Limit of Insurance for Building satisfies the Additional Condition, Coinsurance, and the cost to repair or replace the damaged building property is $2,500 or less, we will pay the cost of building repairs or replacement.

This provision does not apply to the following even when attached to the building:

(1) Awnings or floor coverings;

(2) Appliances for refrigerating, ventilating, cooking, dishwashing or laundering; or

(3) Outdoor equipment or furniture.

c. "Stock" you have sold but not delivered at the selling price less discounts and expenses you otherwise would have had.

d. Glass at the cost of replacement with safety glazing material if required by law.

e. Tenant's Improvements and Betterments at:

(1) Actual cash value of the lost or damaged property if you make repairs promptly.

(2) A proportion of your original cost if you do not make repairs promptly. We will determine the proportionate value as follows:

(a) Multiply the original cost by the number of days from the loss or damage to the expiration of the lease; and

(b) Divide the amount determined in (a) above by the number of days from the installation of improvements to the expiration of the lease.

If your lease contains a renewal option, the expiration of the renewal option period will replace the expiration of the lease in this procedure.

(3) Nothing if others pay for repairs or replacement.

f. Valuable Papers and Records, including those which exist on electronic or magnetic media (other than prepackaged software programs), at the cost of:

(1) Blank materials for reproducing the records; and

(2) Labor to transcribe or copy the records when there is a duplicate.

F. ADDITIONAL CONDITIONS

The following conditions apply in addition to the Common Policy Conditions and the Commercial Property Conditions.

1. **Coinsurance**

If a Coinsurance percentage is shown in the Declarations, the following condition applies.

a. We will not pay the full amount of any loss if the value of Covered Property at the time of loss times the Coinsurance percentage shown for it in the Declarations is greater than the Limit of Insurance for the property.

Instead, we will determine the most we will pay using the following steps:

(1) Multiply the value of Covered Property at the time of loss by the Coinsurance percentage;

(2) Divide the Limit of Insurance of the property by the figure determined in step (1);

(3) Multiply the total amount of loss, before the application of any deductible, by the figure determined in step (2); and

(4) Subtract the deductible from the figure determined in step (3).

We will pay the amount determined in step (4) or the limit of insurance, whichever is less. For the remainder, you will either have to rely on other insurance or absorb the loss yourself.

Example No. 1 (Underinsurance):

When:

The value of the property is	$250,000
The Coinsurance percentage for it is	80%
The Limit of Insurance for it is	$100,000
The Deductible is	$250
The amount of loss is	$ 40,000

Step (1): $250,000 x 80% = $200,000 (the minimum amount of insurance to meet your Coinsurance requirements)

Step (2): $100,000 ÷ $200,000 = .50

Step (3): $ 40,000 x .50 = $20,000

Step (4): $ 20,000 − $250 = $19,750

We will pay no more than $19,750. The remaining $20,250 is not covered.

Example No. 2 (Adequate Insurance):

When:

The value of the property is	$250,000
The Coinsurance percentage for it is	80%
The Limit of Insurance for it is	$200,000
The Deductible is	$250
The amount of loss is	$ 40,000

Step (1): $250,000 x 80% = $200,000 (the minimum amount of insurance to meet your Coinsurance requirements)

Step (2): $200,000 ÷ $200,000 = 1.00

Step (3): $ 40,000 x 1.00 = $ 40,000

Step (4): $ 40,000 − $250 = $ 39,750

We will cover the $39,750 loss in excess of the Deductible. No penalty applies.

b. If one Limit of Insurance applies to two or more separate items, this condition will apply to the total of all property to which the limit applies.

Example No. 3:

When:

The value of property is:	
Bldg. at Location No. 1	$75,000
Bldg. at Location No. 2	$100,000
Personal Property at Location No. 2	$75,000
	$250,000
The Coinsurance percentage for it is	90%
The Limit of Insurance for Buildings and Personal Property at Location Nos. 1 and 2 is	$180,000
The Deductible is	$1,000
The amount of loss is	
Bldg. at Location No. 2	$30,000
Personal Property at Location No. 2.	$20,000
	$50,000

Step (1): $250,000 x 90% = $225,000 (the minimum amount of insurance to meet your Coinsurance requirements and to avoid the penalty shown below)

Step (2): $180,000 ÷ $225,000 = .80

Step (3): $ 50,000 x .80 = $40,000.

Step (4): $ 40,000 − $1,000 = $39,000.

We will pay no more than $39,000. The remaining $11,000 is not covered.

2. Mortgage Holders

a. The term "mortgage holder" includes trustee.

b. We will pay for covered loss of or damage to buildings or structures to each mortgage holder shown in the Declarations in their order of precedence, as interests may appear.

c. The mortgage holder has the right to receive loss payment even if the mortgage holder has started foreclosure or similar action on the building or structure.

d. If we deny your claim because of your acts or because you have failed to comply with the terms of this Coverage Part, the mortgage holder will still have the right to receive loss payment if the mortgage holder:

(1) Pays any premium due under this Coverage Part at our request if you have failed to do so;

(2) Submits a signed, sworn statement of loss within 60 days after receiving notice from us of your failure to do so; and

(3) Has notified us of any change in ownership, occupancy or substantial change in risk known to the mortgage holder.

All of the terms of this Coverage Part will then apply directly to the mortgage holder.

e. If we pay the mortgage holder for any loss or damage and deny payment to you because of your acts or because you have failed to comply with the terms of this Coverage Part:

(1) The mortgage holder's rights under the mortgage will be transferred to us to the extent of the amount we pay; and

(2) The mortgage holder's right to recover the full amount of the mortgage holder's claim will not be impaired.

At our option, we may pay to the mortgage holder the whole principal on the mortgage plus any accrued interest. In this event, your mortgage and note will be transferred to us and you will pay your remaining mortgage debt to us.

f. If we cancel this policy, we will give written notice to the mortgage holder at least:

(1) 10 days before the effective date of cancellation if we cancel for your nonpayment of premium; or

(2) 30 days before the effective date of cancellation if we cancel for any other reason.

g. If we elect not to renew this policy, we will give written notice to the mortgage holder at least 10 days before the expiration date of this policy.

G. OPTIONAL COVERAGES

If shown in the Declarations, the following Optional Coverages apply separately to each item.

1. **Agreed Value**

a. The Additional Condition, Coinsurance, does not apply to Covered Property to which this Optional Coverage applies. We will pay no more for loss of or damage to that property than the proportion that the Limit of Insurance under this Coverage Part for the property bears to the Agreed Value shown for it in the Declarations.

b. If the expiration date for this Optional Coverage shown in the Declarations is not extended, the Additional Condition, Coinsurance, is reinstated and this Optional Coverage expires.

c. The terms of this Optional Coverage apply only to loss or damage that occurs:

(1) On or after the effective date of this Optional Coverage; and

(2) Before the Agreed Value expiration date shown in the Declarations or the policy expiration date, whichever occurs first.

2. **Inflation Guard**

a. The Limit of Insurance for property to which this Optional Coverage applied will automatically increase by the annual percentage shown in the Declarations.

b. The amount of increase will be:

(1) The Limit of Insurance that applied on the most recent of the policy inception date, the policy anniversary date, or any other policy change amending the Limit of Insurance, times

(2) The percentage of annual increase shown in the Declarations, expressed as a decimal (example: 8% is .08), times

(3) The number of days since the beginning of the current policy year or the effective date of the most recent policy change amending the Limit of Insurance, divided by 365.

CP 00 10 10 91   Copyright, ISO Commercial Risk Services, Inc., 1990, 1991   Page 9 of 10   □

Example:
If:

The applicable Limit of Insurance is	$100,000
The annual percentage increase is	8%
The number of days since the beginning of the policy year (or last policy change) is	146

The amount of increase is
$100,000 x .08 x 146 ÷ 365 =$3,200

3. Replacement Cost

a. Replacement Cost (without deduction for depreciation) replaces Actual Cash Value in the Loss Condition, Valuation, of this Coverage Form.

b. This Optional Coverage does not apply to:

(1) Property of others;

(2) Contents of a residence;

(3) Manuscripts;

(4) Works of art, antiques or rare articles, including etchings, pictures, statuary, marbles, bronzes, porcelains and bric-a-brac; or

(5) "Stock," unless the Including "Stock" option is shown in the Declarations.

c. You may make a claim for loss or damage covered by this insurance on an actual cash value basis instead of on a replacement cost basis. In the event you elect to have loss or damage settled on an actual cash value basis, you may still make a claim for the additional coverage this Optional Coverage provides if you notify us of your intent to do so within 180 days after the loss or damage.

d. We will not pay on a replacement cost basis for any loss or damage:

(1) Until the lost or damaged property is actually repaired or replaced; and

(2) Unless the repairs or replacement are made as soon as reasonably possible after the loss or damage.

e. We will not pay more for loss or damage on a replacement cost basis than the least of:

(1) The Limit of Insurance applicable to the lost or damaged property;

(2) The cost to replace, on the same premises, the lost or damaged property with other property:

(a) Of comparable material and quality; and

(b) Used for the same purpose; or

(3) The amount you actually spend that is necessary to repair or replace the lost or damaged property.

H. DEFINITIONS

1. "Pollutants" means any solid, liquid, gaseous or thermal irritant or contaminant, including smoke, vapor, soot, fumes, acids, alkalis, chemicals and waste. Waste includes materials to be recycled, reconditioned or reclaimed.

2. "Stock" means merchandise held in storage or for sale, raw materials and in-process or finished goods, including supplies used in their packing or shipping.

BUSINESS INCOME COVERAGE FORM

AND EXTRA EXPENSE

Various provisions in this policy restrict coverage. Read the entire policy carefully to determine rights, duties and what is and is not covered.

Throughout this policy the words "you" and "your" refer to the Named Insured shown in the Declarations. The words "we," "us" and "our" refer to the Company providing this insurance.

Other words and phrases that appear in quotation marks have special meaning. Refer to SECTION G – DEFINITIONS.

A. COVERAGE

Coverage is provided as described below for one or more of the following options for which a Limit of Insurance is shown in the Declarations:

(i) Business Income including "Rental Value."

(ii) Business Income other than "Rental Value."

(iii) "Rental Value."

If option (i) above is selected, the term Business Income will include "Rental Value." If option (iii) above is selected, the term Business Income will mean "Rental Value" only.

If Limits of Insurance are shown under more than one of the above options, the provisions of this Coverage Part apply separately to each.

We will pay for the actual loss of Business Income you sustain due to the necessary suspension of your "operations" during the "period of restoration." The suspension must be caused by direct physical loss of or damage to property at the premises described in the Declarations, including personal property in the open (or in a vehicle) within 100 feet, caused by or resulting from any Covered Cause of Loss.

1. Business Income

Business Income means the:

a. Net Income (Net Profit or Loss before income taxes) that would have been earned or incurred; and

b. Continuing normal operating expenses incurred, including payroll.

2. Covered Causes Of Loss

See applicable Causes of Loss Form as shown in the Declarations.

3. Additional Coverages

a. Extra Expense.

Extra Expense means necessary expenses you incur during the "period of restoration" that you would not have incurred if there had been no direct physical loss or damage to property caused by or resulting from a Covered Cause of Loss.

(1) We will pay any Extra Expense to avoid or minimize the suspension of business and to continue "operations":

(a) At the described premises; or

(b) At replacement premises or at temporary locations, including:

(i) Relocation expenses; and

(ii) Costs to equip and operate the replacement or temporary locations.

(2) We will pay any Extra Expense to minimize the suspension of business if you cannot continue "operations."

(3) We will pay any Extra Expense to:

(a) Repair or replace any property; or

(b) Research, replace or restore the lost information on damaged valuable papers and records;

to the extent it reduces the amount of loss that otherwise would have been payable under this Coverage Form.

b. Civil Authority. We will pay for the actual loss of Business Income you sustain and necessary Extra Expense caused by action of civil authority that prohibits access to the described premises due to direct physical loss of or damage to property, other than at the described premises, caused by or resulting from any Covered Cause of Loss. This coverage will apply for a period of up to two consecutive weeks from the date of that action.

c. Alterations and New Buildings. We will pay for the actual loss of Business Income you sustain due to direct physical loss or damage at the described premises caused by or resulting from any Covered Cause of Loss to:

(1) New buildings or structures, whether complete or under construction;

(2) Alterations or additions to existing buildings or structures; and

(3) Machinery, equipment, supplies or building materials located on or within 100 feet of the described premises and:

(a) Used in the construction, alterations or additions; or

(b) Incidental to the occupancy of new buildings.

If such direct physical loss or damage delays the start of "operations," the "period of restoration" will begin on the date "operations" would have begun if the direct physical loss or damage had not occurred.

d. Extended Business Income. We will pay for the actual loss of Business Income you incur during the period that:

(1) Begins on the date property (except "finished stock") is actually repaired, rebuilt or replaced and "operations" are resumed; and

(2) Ends on the earlier of:

(a) The date you could restore your "operations" with reasonable speed, to the condition that would have existed if no direct physical loss or damage occurred; or

(b) 30 consecutive days after the date determined in (1) above.

Loss of Business Income must be caused by direct physical loss or damage at the described premises caused by or resulting from any Covered Cause of Loss.

4. Coverage Extension

If a Coinsurance percentage of 50% or more is shown in the Declarations, you may extend the insurance provided by this Coverage Part as follows:

Newly Acquired Locations

a. You may extend your Business Income Coverage to apply to property at any location you acquire other than fairs or exhibitions.

b. The most we will pay for loss under this Extension is 10% of the Limit of Insurance for Business Income shown in the Declarations, but not more than $100,000 at each location.

c. Insurance under this Extension for each newly acquired location will end when any of the following first occurs:

(1) This policy expires;

(2) 30 days expire after you acquire or begin to construct the property; or

(3) You report values to us.

We will charge you additional premium for values reported from the date you acquire the property.

This Extension is additional insurance. The Additional Condition, Coinsurance, does not apply to this Extension.

B. EXCLUSIONS

See applicable Causes of Loss Form as shown in the Declarations.

C. LIMITS OF INSURANCE

The most we will pay for loss in any one occurrence is the applicable Limit of Insurance shown in the Declarations.

The limit applicable to the Coverage Extension is in addition to the Limit of Insurance.

Payments under the following Additional Coverages will not increase the applicable Limit of Insurance:

1. Alterations and New Buildings;
2. Civil Authority;
3. Extra Expense; or
4. Extended Business Income.

CP 00 30 10 91 ☐

D. LOSS CONDITIONS

The following conditions apply in addition to the Common Policy Conditions and the Commercial Property Conditions.

1. Appraisal

If we and you disagree on the amount of Net Income and operating expense or the amount of loss, either may make written demand for an appraisal of the loss. In this event, each party will select a competent and impartial appraiser.

The two appraisers will select an umpire. If they cannot agree, either may request that selection be made by a judge of a court having jurisdiction. The appraisers will state separately the amount of Net Income and operating expense or amount of loss. If they fail to agree, they will submit their differences to the umpire. A decision agreed to by any two will be binding. Each party will:

a. Pay its chosen appraiser; and

b. Bear the other expenses of the appraisal and umpire equally.

If there is an appraisal, we will still retain our right to deny the claim.

2. Duties In The Event Of Loss

a. You must see that the following are done in the event of loss:

(1) Notify the police if a law may have been broken.

(2) Give us prompt notice of the direct physical loss or damage. Include a description of the property involved.

(3) As soon as possible, give us a description of how, when, and where the direct physical loss or damage occurred.

(4) Take all reasonable steps to protect the Covered Property from further damage by a Covered Cause of Loss. If feasible, set the damaged property aside and in the best possible order for examination. Also keep a record of your expenses for emergency and temporary repairs, for consideration in the settlement of the claim. This will not increase the Limit of Insurance.

(5) As often as may be reasonably required, permit us to inspect the property proving the loss or damage and examine your books and records.

Also permit us to take samples of damaged and undamaged property for inspection, testing and analysis, and permit us to make copies from your books and records.

(6) Send us a signed, sworn proof of loss containing the information we request to investigate the claim. You must do this within 60 days after our request. We will supply you with the necessary forms.

(7) Cooperate with us in the investigation or settlement of the claim.

(8) If you intend to continue your business, you must resume all or part of your "operations" as quickly as possible.

b. We may examine any insured under oath, while not in the presence of any other insured and at such times as may be reasonably required, about any matter relating to this insurance or the claim, including an insured's books and records. In the event of an examination, an insured's answers must be signed.

3. Limitation - Electronic Media And Records

We will not pay for any loss of Business Income caused by direct physical loss of or damage to Electronic Media and Records after the longer of:

a. 60 consecutive days from the date of direct physical loss or damage; or

b. The period, beginning with the date of direct physical loss or damage, necessary to repair, rebuild or replace, with reasonable speed and similar quality, other property at the described premises due to loss or damage caused by the same occurrence.

Electronic Media and Records are:

(1) Electronic data processing, recording or storage media such as films, tapes, discs, drums or cells;

(2) Data stored on such media; or

(3) Programming records used for electronic data processing or electronically controlled equipment.

This limitation does not apply to Extra Expense.

Example No. 1:

A Covered Cause of Loss damages a computer on June 1. It takes until September 1 to replace the computer, and until October 1 to restore the data that was lost when the damage occurred. We will only pay for the Business Income loss sustained during the period June 1 – September 1. Loss during the period September 2 – October 1 is not covered.

Example No. 2:

A Covered Cause of Loss results in the loss of data processing programming records on August 1. The records are replaced on October 15. We will only pay for the Business Income loss sustained during the period August 1 – September 29 (60 consecutive days). Loss during the period September 30 – October 15 is not covered.

4. **Loss Determination**

   a. The amount of Business Income loss will be determined based on:

      (1) The Net Income of the business before the direct physical loss or damage occurred;

      (2) The likely Net Income of the business if no loss or damage occurred;

      (3) The operating expenses, including payroll expenses, necessary to resume "operations" with the same quality of service that existed just before the direct physical loss or damage; and

      (4) Other relevant sources of information, including:

         (a) Your financial records and accounting procedures;

         (b) Bills, invoices and other vouchers; and

         (c) Deeds, liens or contracts.

   b. The amount of Extra Expense will be determined based on:

      (1) All expenses that exceed the normal operating expenses that would have been incurred by "operations" during the "period of restoration" if no direct physical loss or damage had occurred. We will deduct from the total of such expenses:

         (a) The salvage value that remains of any property bought for temporary use during the "period of restoration," once "operations" are resumed; and

         (b) Any Extra Expense that is paid for by other insurance, except for insurance that is written subject to the same plan, terms, conditions and provisions as this insurance; and

      (2) All necessary expenses that reduce the Business Income loss that otherwise would have been incurred.

   c. **Resumption Of Operations**

      We will reduce the amount of your:

      (1) Business Income loss, other than Extra Expense, to the extent you can resume your "operations," in whole or in part, by using damaged or undamaged property (including merchandise or stock) at the described premises or elsewhere.

      (2) Extra Expense loss to the extent you can return "operations" to normal and discontinue such Extra Expense.

   d. If you do not resume "operations," or do not resume "operations" as quickly as possible, we will pay based on the length of time it would have taken to resume "operations" as quickly as possible.

5. **Loss Payment**

   We will pay for covered loss within 30 days after we receive the sworn proof of loss, if:

   a. You have complied with all of the terms of this Coverage Part; and

   b. (1) We have reached agreement with you on the amount of loss; or

      (2) An appraisal award has been made.

E. **ADDITIONAL CONDITION**

Coinsurance

If a Coinsurance percentage is shown in the Declarations, the following condition applies in addition to the Common Policy Conditions and the Commercial Property Conditions.

We will not pay the full amount of any loss if the Limit of Insurance for Business Income is less than:

a. The Coinsurance percentage shown for Business Income in the Declarations; times

b. The sum of:

   (1) The Net Income (Net Profit or Loss before income taxes), and

   (2) All operating expenses, including payroll expenses,

   that would have been earned (had no loss occurred) by your "operations" at the described premises for the 12 months following the inception, or last previous anniversary date, of this policy (whichever is later).

Instead, we will determine the most we will pay using the following steps:

1. Multiply the Net Income and operating expense for the 12 months following the inception, or last previous anniversary date, of this policy by the Coinsurance percentage;

2. Divide the Limit of Insurance for the described premises by the figure determined in step 1; and

3. Multiply the total amount of loss by the figure determined in Step 2.

We will pay the amount determined in step 3. or the limit of insurance, whichever is less. For the remainder, you will either have to rely on other insurance or absorb the loss yourself.

Example No. 1 (Underinsurance):

When: The Net Income and operating expenses for the 12 months following the inception, or last previous anniversary date, of this policy at the described premises would have been $400,000
The Coinsurance percentage is 50%
The Limit of Insurance is $150,000
The amount of loss is $ 80,000

Step 1: $400,000 x 50% = $200,000 (the minimum amount of insurance to meet your Coinsurance requirements)

Step 2: $150,000 ÷ $200,000 = .75

Step 3: $ 80,000 x .75 = $60,000

We will pay no more than $60,000. The remaining $20,000 is not covered.

Example No. 2 (Adequate Insurance):

When: The Net Income and operating expenses for the 12 months following the inception, or last previous anniversary date, of this policy at the described premises would have been $400,000
The Coinsurance percentage is 50%
The Limit of Insurance is $200,000
The amount of loss is $ 80,000

Step 1: $400,000 x 50% = $200,000 (the minimum amount of insurance to meet your Coinsurance requirements)

Step 2: $200,000 ÷ $200,000 = 1.00

Step 3: $ 80,000 x 1.00 = $80,000

We will cover the $80,000 loss. No penalty applies.

This condition does not apply to the Extra Expense Additional Coverage.

F. OPTIONAL COVERAGES

If shown in the Declarations, the following Optional Coverages apply separately to each item.

1. **Maximum Period Of Indemnity**

   a. The Additional Condition, Coinsurance, does not apply to this Coverage Form at the described premises to which this Optional Coverage applies.

   b. The most we will pay for loss of Business Income is the lesser of:

      (1) The amount of loss sustained during the 120 days immediately following the direct physical loss or damage; or

      (2) The Limit of Insurance shown in the Declarations.

2. Monthly Limit Of Indemnity

a. The Additional Condition, Coinsurance, does not apply to this Coverage Form at the described premises to which this Optional Coverage applies.

b. The most we will pay for loss of Business Income in each period of 30 consecutive days after the direct physical loss or damage is:

(1) The Limit of Insurance, multiplied by

(2) The fraction shown in the Declarations for this Optional Coverage.

Example:

When: The Limit of Insurance
is $120,000

The fraction shown in the Declarations for this Optional Coverage is   1/4

The most we will pay for loss in each period of 30 consecutive days is:

$120,000 x 1/4 = $30,000

If, in this example, the actual amount of loss is:

Days   1–30 $40,000
Days 31–60   20,000
Days 61–90   30,000
             $90,000

We will pay:

Days   1–30 $30,000
Days 31–60   20,000
Days 61–90   30,000
             $80,000

The remaining $10,000 is not covered.

3. Agreed Value

a. To activate this Optional Coverage:

(1) A Business Income Report/Work Sheet must be made a part of this policy and must show financial data for your "operations":

(a) During the 12 months prior to the date of the Work Sheet; and

(b) Estimated for the 12 months immediately following the inception of this Optional Coverage.

(2) An Agreed Value must be shown in the Declarations or on the Work Sheet. The Agreed Value should be at least equal to:

(a) The Coinsurance percentage shown in the Declarations; multiplied by

(b) The amount of Net Income and Operating Expenses for the following 12 months you report on the Work Sheet.

b. The Additional Condition, Coinsurance, is suspended until:

(1) 12 months after the effective date of this Optional Coverage; or

(2) The expiration date of this policy;

whichever occurs first.

c. We will reinstate the Additional Condition, Coinsurance, automatically if you do not submit a new Work Sheet and Agreed Value:

(1) Within 12 months of the effective date of this Optional Coverage; or

(2) When you request a change in your Business Income Limit of Insurance.

d. If the Business Income Limit of Insurance is less than the Agreed Value, we will not pay more of any loss than the amount of loss multiplied by:

(1) The Business Income Limit of Insurance; divided by

(2) The Agreed Value.

Example:

When: The Limit of Insurance
is $100,000
The Agreed Value is $200,000
The amount of loss is $ 80,000

Step (a): $100,000 ÷ $200,000 = .50

Step (b): .50 × $80,000 = $40,000

We will pay $40,000. The remaining $40,000 is not covered.

4. Extended Period Of Indemnity

Under paragraph **A.3.d.**, Extended Business Income, the number "30" in subparagraph **(2)(b)** is replaced by the number shown in the Declarations for this Optional Coverage.

G. DEFINITIONS

1. "Finished Stock" means stock you have manufactured.

"Finished stock" also includes whiskey and alcoholic products being aged, unless there is a Coinsurance percentage shown for Business Income in the Declarations.

"Finished stock" does not include stock you have manufactured that is held for sale on the premises of any retail outlet insured under this Coverage Part.

2. "Operations" means:

a. Your business activities occurring at the described premises; and

b. The tenantability of the described premises, if coverage for Business Income including "Rental Value" or "Rental Value" applies.

3. "Period of Restoration" means the period of time that:

a. Begins with the date of direct physical loss or damage caused by or resulting from any Covered Cause of Loss at the described premises; and

b. Ends on the date when the property at the described premises should be repaired, rebuilt or replaced with reasonable speed and similar quality.

"Period of restoration" does not include any increased period required due to the enforcement of any ordinance or law that:

(1) Regulates the construction, use or repair, or requires the tearing down of any property; or

(2) Requires any insured or others to test for, monitor, clean up, remove, contain, treat, detoxify or neutralize, or in any way respond to, or assess the effects of "pollutants."

The expiration date of this policy will not cut short the "period of restoration."

4. "Pollutants" means any solid, liquid, gaseous or thermal irritant or contaminant, including smoke, vapor, soot, fumes, acids, alkalis, chemicals and waste. Waste includes materials to be recycled, reconditioned or reclaimed.

5. "Rental Value" means the:

a. Total anticipated rental income from tenant occupancy of the premises described in the Declarations as furnished and equipped by you, and

b. Amount of all charges which are the legal obligation of the tenant(s) and which would otherwise be your obligations, and

c. Fair rental value of any portion of the described premises which is occupied by you.

CP 00 30 10 91   Copyright, ISO Commercial Risk Services, Inc., 1990, 1991   Page 7 of 7   □

CAUSES OF LOSS – BROAD FORM

A. COVERED CAUSES OF LOSS

When Broad is shown in the Declarations, Covered Causes of Loss means the following:

1. **Fire.**

2. **Lightning.**

3. **Explosion,** including the explosion of gases or fuel within the furnace of any fired vessel or within the flues or passages through which the gases of combustion pass. This cause of loss does not include loss or damage by:

   a. Rupture, bursting or operation of pressure relief devices; or

   b. Rupture or bursting due to expansion or swelling of the contents of any building or structure, caused by or resulting from water.

4. **Windstorm or Hail,** but not including:

   a. Frost or cold weather;

   b. Ice (other than hail), snow or sleet, whether driven by wind or not; or

   c. Loss or damage to the interior of any building or structure, or the property inside the building or structure, caused by rain, snow, sand or dust, whether driven by wind or not, unless the building or structure first sustains wind or hail damage to its roof or walls through which the rain, snow, sand or dust enters.

5. **Smoke** causing sudden and accidental loss or damage. This cause of loss does not include smoke from agricultural smudging or industrial operations.

6. **Aircraft or Vehicles,** meaning only physical contact of an aircraft, a spacecraft, a self-propelled missile, a vehicle or an object thrown up by a vehicle with the described property or with the building or structure containing the described property. This cause of loss includes loss or damage by objects falling from aircraft.

   We will not pay for loss or damage caused by or resulting from vehicles you own or which are operated in the course of your business.

7. **Riot or Civil Commotion,** including:

   a. Acts of striking employees while occupying the described premises; and

   b. Looting occurring at the time and place of a riot or civil commotion.

8. **Vandalism,** meaning willful and malicious damage to, or destruction of, the described property.

   We will not pay for loss or damage:

   a. To glass (other than glass building blocks) that is part of a building, structure, or an outside sign; but we will pay for loss or damage to other property caused by or resulting from breakage of glass by vandals.

   b. Caused by or resulting from theft, except for building damage caused by the breaking in or exiting of burglars.

9. **Sprinkler Leakage,** meaning leakage or discharge of any substance from an Automatic Sprinkler System, including collapse of a tank that is part of the system.

   If the building or structure containing the Automatic Sprinkler System is Covered Property, we will also pay the cost to:

   a. Repair or replace damaged parts of the Automatic Sprinkler System if the damage:

      (1) Results in sprinkler leakage; or

      (2) Is directly caused by freezing.

   b. Tear out and replace any part of the building or structure to repair damage to the Automatic Sprinkler System that has resulted in sprinkler leakage.

   Automatic Sprinkler System means:

      (1) Any automatic fire protective or extinguishing system, including connected:

         (a) Sprinklers and discharge nozzles;

         (b) Ducts, pipes, valves and fittings;

         (c) Tanks, their component parts and supports; and

         (d) Pumps and private fire protection mains.

(2) When supplied from an automatic fire protective system:

   (a) Non-automatic fire protective systems; and

   (b) Hydrants, standpipes and outlets.

10. **Sinkhole Collapse,** meaning loss or damage caused by the sudden sinking or collapse of land into underground empty spaces created by the action of water on limestone or dolomite. This cause of loss does not include:

   a. The cost of filling sinkholes; or

   b. Sinking or collapse of land into man-made underground cavities.

11. **Volcanic Action,** meaning direct loss or damage resulting from the eruption of a volcano when the loss or damage is caused by:

   a. Airborne volcanic blast or airborne shock waves;

   b. Ash, dust or particulate matter; or

   c. Lava flow.

All volcanic eruptions that occur within any 168-hour period will constitute a single occurrence.

This cause of loss does not include the cost to remove ash, dust or particulate matter that does not cause direct physical loss or damage to the described property.

12. **Breakage of Glass** that is a part of a building or structure. This cause of loss does not include breakage of neon tubing attached to the building or structure.

We will not pay more than:

   a. $100 for each plate, pane, multiple plate insulating unit, radiant or solar heating panel, jalousie, louver or shutter; or

   b. $500 in any one occurrence.

13. **Falling Objects.**

But we will not pay for loss or damage to:

   a. Personal property in the open; or

   b. The interior of a building or structure, or property inside a building or structure, unless the roof or an outside wall of the building or structure is first damaged by a falling object.

14. **Weight of Snow, Ice or Sleet.**

But we will not pay for loss or damage to:

   a. Gutters and downspouts; or

   b. Personal property outside of buildings or structures.

15. **Water Damage,** meaning accidental discharge or leakage of water or steam as the direct result of the breaking or cracking of any part of a system or appliance containing water or steam, other than an Automatic Sprinkler System. If the building or structure containing the system or appliance is Covered Property, we will also pay the cost to tear out and replace any part of the building or structure to repair damage to the system or appliance from which the water or steam escapes.

We will not pay:

   a. The cost to repair any defect that caused the loss or damage;

   b. For loss or damage caused by or resulting from continuous or repeated seepage or leakage that occurs over a period of 14 days or more; or

   c. For loss or damage caused by or resulting from freezing, unless:

      (1) You do your best to maintain heat in the building or structure; or

      (2) You drain the equipment and shut off the water supply if the heat is not maintained.

B. EXCLUSIONS

1. We will not pay for loss or damage caused directly or indirectly by any of the following. Such loss or damage is excluded regardless of any other cause or event that contributes concurrently or in any sequence to the loss.

   a. **Ordinance or Law**

   The enforcement of any ordinance or law:

      (1) Regulating the construction, use or repair of any property; or

      (2) Requiring the tearing down of any property including the cost of removing its debris.

   b. **Earth Movement**

      (1) Any earth movement (other than sinkhole collapse), such as an earthquake, landslide, mine subsidence or earth sinking, rising or shifting. But if loss or damage by fire or explosion results, we will pay for that resulting loss or damage.

Copyright, ISO Commercial Risk Services, Inc., 1990, 1991 CP 10 20 10 91   □

(2) Volcanic eruption, explosion or effusion. But if loss or damage by fire, breakage of glass or volcanic action results, we will pay for that resulting loss or damage.

c. Governmental Action

Seizure or destruction of property by order of governmental authority.

But we will pay for acts of destruction ordered by governmental authority and taken at the time of a fire to prevent its spread, if the fire would be covered under this Coverage Part.

d. Nuclear Hazard

Nuclear reaction or radiation, or radioactive contamination, however caused.

But if loss or damage by fire results, we will pay for that resulting loss or damage.

e. Off-Premises Services

The failure of power or other utility service supplied to the described premises, however caused, if the failure occurs away from the described premises.

But if loss or damage by a Covered Cause of Loss results, we will pay for that resulting loss or damage.

f. War and Military Action

(1) War, including undeclared or civil war;

(2) Warlike action by a military force, including action in hindering or defending against an actual or expected attack, by any government, sovereign or other authority using military personnel or other agents; or

(3) Insurrection, rebellion, revolution, usurped power, or action taken by governmental authority in hindering or defending against any of these.

g. Water

(1) Flood, surface water, waves, tides, tidal waves, overflow of any body of water, or their spray, all whether driven by wind or not;

(2) Mudslide or mudflow;

(3) Water that backs up from a sewer or drain; or

(4) Water under the ground surface pressing on, or flowing or seeping through:

(a) Foundations, walls, floors or paved surfaces;

(b) Basements, whether paved or not; or

(c) Doors, windows or other openings.

But if loss or damage by fire, explosion or sprinkler leakage results, we will pay for that resulting loss or damage.

2. We will not pay for loss or damage caused by or resulting from:

a. Artificially generated electrical current, including electric arcing, that disturbs electrical devices, appliances or wires. But if loss or damage by fire results, we will pay for that resulting loss or damage.

b. Explosion of steam boilers, steam pipes, steam engines or steam turbines owned or leased by you, or operated under your control.

But if loss or damage by fire or combustion explosion results, we will pay for that resulting loss or damage.

c. Mechanical breakdown, including rupture or bursting caused by centrifugal force.

But if loss or damage by a Covered Cause of Loss results, we will pay for that resulting loss or damage.

3. Special Exclusions

The following provisions apply only to the specified Coverage Forms.

a. Business Income (And Extra Expense) Coverage Form, Business Income (Without Extra Expense) Coverage Form, or Extra Expense Coverage Form

We will not pay for:

(1) Any loss caused by or resulting from:

(a) Damage or destruction of "finished stock"; or

(b) The time required to reproduce "finished stock."

This exclusion does not apply to Extra Expense.

(2) Any loss caused by or resulting from direct physical loss or damage to radio or television antennas, including their lead-in wiring, masts or towers.

(3) Any increase of loss caused by or resulting from:

(a) Delay in rebuilding, repairing or replacing the property or re-suming "operations," due to interference at the location of the rebuilding, repair or replacement by strikers or other persons; or

(b) Suspension, lapse or cancellation of any license, lease or contract. But if the suspension, lapse or cancellation is directly caused by the suspension of "operations," we will cover such loss that affects your Business Income during the "period of restoration."

(4) Any Extra Expense caused by or resulting from suspension, lapse or cancellation of any license, lease or contract beyond the "period of restoration."

(5) Any other consequential loss.

b. Leasehold Interest Coverage Form

(1) Paragraph **B.1.a.,** Ordinance or Law, does not apply to insurance under this Coverage Form.

(2) We will not pay for any loss caused by:

(a) Your cancelling the lease;

(b) The suspension, lapse or cancellation of any license; or

(c) Any other consequential loss.

c. Legal Liability Coverage Form

(1) The following Exclusions do not apply to insurance under this Coverage Form:

(a) Paragraph **B.1.a.,** Ordinance or Law;

(b) Paragraph **B.1.c.,** Governmental Action;

(c) Paragraph **B.1.d.,** Nuclear Hazard;

(d) Paragraph **B.1.e.,** Power Failure; and

(e) Paragraph **B.1.f.,** War and Military Action.

(2) Contractual Liability

We will not defend any claim or "suit," or pay damages that you are legally liable to pay, solely by reason of your assumption of liability in a contract or agreement.

(3) Nuclear Hazard

We will not defend any claim or "suit," or pay any damages, loss, expense or obligation, resulting from nuclear reaction or radiation, or radioactive contamination, however caused.

C. ADDITIONAL COVERAGE - COLLAPSE

We will pay for loss or damage caused by or resulting from risks of direct physical loss involving collapse of a building or any part of a building caused only by one or more of the following:

1. Fire; lightning; explosion; windstorm or hail; smoke; aircraft or vehicles; riot or civil commotion; vandalism; leakage from fire extinguishing equipment; sinkhole collapse; volcanic action; breakage of building glass; falling objects; weight of snow, ice or sleet; water damage; all only as insured against in this Coverage Part;

2. Hidden decay;

3. Hidden insect or vermin damage;

4. Weight of people or personal property;

5. Weight of rain that collects on a roof;

6. Use of defective material or methods in construction, remodeling or renovation if the collapse occurs during the course of the construction, remodeling or renovation.

We will not pay for loss or damage to the following types of property, if otherwise covered in this Coverage Part, under items **2., 3., 4., 5.** and **6.** unless the loss or damage is a direct result of the collapse of a building:

outdoor radio or television antennas, including their lead-in wiring, masts or towers; awnings; gutters and downspouts; yard fixtures; outdoor swimming pools; fences; piers, wharves and docks; beach or diving platforms or appurtenances; retaining walls; walks, roadways and other paved surfaces.

Collapse does not include settling, cracking, shrinkage, bulging or expansion.

This Additional Coverage will not increase the Limits of Insurance provided in this Coverage Part.

D. LIMITATION

We will pay for loss of animals only if they are killed or their destruction is made necessary.

COMMERCIAL PROPERTY CONDITIONS

This Coverage Part is subject to the following conditions, the Common Policy Conditions and applicable Loss Conditions and Additional Conditions in Commercial Property Coverage Forms.

A. CONCEALMENT, MISREPRESENTATION OR FRAUD

This Coverage Part is void in any case of fraud by you as it relates to this Coverage Part at any time. It is also void if you or any other insured, at any time, intentionally conceal or misrepresent a material fact concerning:

1. This Coverage Part;

2. The Covered Property;

3. Your interest in the Covered Property; or

4. A claim under this Coverage Part.

B. CONTROL OF PROPERTY

Any act or neglect of any person other than you beyond your direction or control will not affect this insurance.

The breach of any condition of this Coverage Part at any one or more locations will not affect coverage at any location where, at the time of loss or damage, the breach of condition does not exist.

C. INSURANCE UNDER TWO OR MORE COVERAGES

If two or more of this policy's coverages apply to the same loss or damage, we will not pay more than the actual amount of the loss or damage.

D. LEGAL ACTION AGAINST US

No one may bring a legal action against us under this Coverage Part unless:

1. There has been full compliance with all of the terms of this Coverage Part; and

2. The action is brought within 2 years after the date on which the direct physical loss or damage occurred.

E. LIBERALIZATION

If we adopt any revision that would broaden the coverage under this Coverage Part without additional premium within 45 days prior to or during the policy period, the broadened coverage will immediately apply to this Coverage Part.

F. NO BENEFIT TO BAILEE

No person or organization, other than you, having custody of Covered Property will benefit from this insurance.

G. OTHER INSURANCE

1. You may have other insurance subject to the same plan, terms, conditions and provisions as the insurance under this Coverage Part. If you do, we will pay our share of the covered loss or damage. Our share is the proportion that the applicable Limit of Insurance under this Coverage Part bears to the Limits of Insurance of all insurance covering on the same basis.

2. If there is other insurance covering the same loss or damage, other than that described in 1. above, we will pay only for the amount of covered loss or damage in excess of the amount due from that other insurance, whether you can collect on it or not. But we will not pay more than the applicable Limit of Insurance.

H. POLICY PERIOD, COVERAGE TERRITORY

Under this Coverage Part:

1. We cover loss or damage commencing:

   a. During the policy period shown in the Declarations; and

   b. Within the coverage territory.

2. The coverage territory is:

   a. The United States of America (including its territories and possessions);

   b. Puerto Rico; and

   c. Canada.

I. TRANSFER OF RIGHTS OF RECOVERY AGAINST OTHERS TO US

If any person or organization to or for whom we make payment under this Coverage Part has rights to recover damages from another, those rights are transferred to us to the extent of our payment. That person or organization must do everything necessary to secure our rights and must do nothing after loss to impair them. But you may waive your rights against another party in writing:

1. Prior to a loss to your Covered Property or Covered Income.

2. After a loss to your Covered Property or Covered Income only if, at time of loss, that party is one of the following:

   a. Someone insured by this insurance;

   b. A business firm:

      (1) Owned or controlled by you; or

      (2) That owns or controls you; or

   c. Your tenant.

This will not restrict your insurance.

D

Commercial General Liability Coverage Form

COMMERCIAL GENERAL LIABILITY COVERAGE FORM

Various provisions in this policy restrict coverage. Read the entire policy carefully to determine rights, duties and what is and is not covered.

Throughout this policy the words "you" and "your" refer to the Named Insured shown in the Declarations, and any other person or organization qualifying as a Named Insured under this policy. The words "we", "us" and "our" refer to the company providing this insurance.

The word "insured" means any person or organization qualifying as such under WHO IS AN INSURED (SECTION II).

Other words and phrases that appear in quotation marks have special meaning. Refer to DEFINITIONS (SECTION V).

SECTION I - COVERAGES

COVERAGE A. BODILY INJURY AND PROPERTY DAMAGE LIABILITY

1. Insuring Agreement.

a. We will pay those sums that the insured becomes legally obligated to pay as damages because of "bodily injury" or "property damage" to which this insurance applies. We will have the right and duty to defend any "suit" seeking those damages. We may at our discretion investigate any "occurrence" and settle any claim or "suit" that may result. But:

(1) The amount we will pay for damages is limited as described in LIMITS OF INSURANCE (SECTION III); and

(2) Our right and duty to defend end when we have used up the applicable limit of insurance in the payment of judgments or settlements under Coverages A or B or medical expenses under Coverage C.

No other obligation or liability to pay sums or perform acts or services is covered unless explicitly provided for under SUPPLEMENTARY PAYMENTS – COVERAGES A AND B.

b. This insurance applies to "bodily injury" and "property damage" only if:

(1) The "bodily injury" or "property damage" is caused by an "occurrence" that takes place in the "coverage territory"; and

(2) The "bodily injury" or "property damage" occurs during the policy period.

c. Damages because of "bodily injury" include damages claimed by any person or organization for care, loss of services or death resulting at any time from the "bodily injury".

2. Exclusions.

This insurance does not apply to:

a. **Expected or Intended Injury**

"Bodily injury" or "property damage" expected or intended from the standpoint of the insured. This exclusion does not apply to "bodily injury" resulting from the use of reasonable force to protect persons or property.

b. **Contractual Liability**

"Bodily injury" or "property damage" for which the insured is obligated to pay damages by reason of the assumption of liability in a contract or agreement. This exclusion does not apply to liability for damages:

(1) Assumed in a contract or agreement that is an "insured contract", provided the "bodily injury" or "property damage" occurs subsequent to the execution of the contract or agreement; or

(2) That the insured would have in the absence of the contract or agreement.

c. **Liquor Liability**

"Bodily injury" or "property damage" for which any insured may be held liable by reason of:

(1) Causing or contributing to the intoxication of any person;

(2) The furnishing of alcoholic beverages to a person under the legal drinking age or under the influence of alcohol; or

(3) Any statute, ordinance or regulation relating to the sale, gift, distribution or use of alcoholic beverages.

This exclusion applies only if you are in the business of manufacturing, distributing, selling, serving or furnishing alcoholic beverages.

d. Workers Compensation and Similar Laws

Any obligation of the insured under a workers compensation, disability benefits or unemployment compensation law or any similar law.

e. Employer's Liability

"Bodily injury" to:

(1) An "employee" of the insured arising out of and in the course of:

    (a) Employment by the insured; or

    (b) Performing duties related to the conduct of the insured's business; or

(2) The spouse, child, parent, brother or sister of that "employee" as a consequence of paragraph (1) above.

This exclusion applies:

(1) Whether the insured may be liable as an employer or in any other capacity; and

(2) To any obligation to share damages with or repay someone else who must pay damages because of the injury.

This exclusion does not apply to liability assumed by the insured under an "insured contract".

f. Pollution

(1) "Bodily injury" or "property damage" arising out of the actual, alleged or threatened discharge, dispersal, seepage, migration, release or escape of pollutants:

    (a) At or from any premises, site or location which is or was at any time owned or occupied by, or rented or loaned to, any insured;

    (b) At or from any premises, site or location which is or was at any time used by or for any insured or others for the handling, storage, disposal, processing or treatment of waste;

    (c) Which are or were at any time transported, handled, stored, treated, disposed of, or processed as waste by or for any insured or any person or organization for whom you may be legally responsible; or

    (d) At or from any premises, site or location on which any insured or any contractors or subcontractors working directly or indirectly on any insured's behalf are performing operations:

        (i) If the pollutants are brought on or to the premises, site or location in connection with such operations by such insured, contractor or subcontractor; or

        (ii) If the operations are to test for, monitor, clean up, remove, contain, treat, detoxify or neutralize, or in any way respond to, or assess the effects of pollutants.

Subparagraphs (a) and (d)(i) do not apply to "bodily injury" or "property damage" arising out of heat, smoke or fumes from a hostile fire.

As used in this exclusion, a hostile fire means one which becomes uncontrollable or breaks out from where it was intended to be.

(2) Any loss, cost or expense arising out of any:

    (a) Request, demand or order that any insured or others test for, monitor, clean up, remove, contain, treat, detoxify or neutralize, or in any way respond to, or assess the effects of pollutants; or

    (b) Claim or suit by or on behalf of a governmental authority for damages because of testing for, monitoring, cleaning up, removing, containing, treating, detoxifying or neutralizing, or in any way responding to, or assessing the effects of pollutants.

Pollutants means any solid, liquid, gaseous or thermal irritant or contaminant, including smoke, vapor, soot, fumes, acids, alkalis, chemicals and waste. Waste includes materials to be recycled, reconditioned or reclaimed.

g. Aircraft, Auto or Watercraft

"Bodily injury" or "property damage" arising out of the ownership, maintenance, use or entrustment to others of any aircraft, "auto" or watercraft owned or operated by or rented or loaned to any insured. Use includes operation and "loading or unloading".

CG 00 01 10 93 □

This exclusion does not apply to:

(1) A watercraft while ashore on premises you own or rent;

(2) A watercraft you do not own that is:

(a) Less than 26 feet long; and

(b) Not being used to carry persons or property for a charge;

(3) Parking an "auto" on, or on the ways next to, premises you own or rent, provided the "auto" is not owned by or rented or loaned to you or the insured;

(4) Liability assumed under any "insured contract" for the ownership, maintenance or use of aircraft or watercraft; or

(5) "Bodily injury" or "property damage" arising out of the operation of any of the equipment listed in paragraph **f.(2)** or **f.(3)** of the definition of "mobile equipment".

h. Mobile Equipment

"Bodily injury" or "property damage" arising out of:

(1) The transportation of "mobile equipment" by an "auto" owned or operated by or rented or loaned to any insured; or

(2) The use of "mobile equipment" in, or while in practice for, or while being prepared for, any prearranged racing, speed, demolition, or stunting activity.

i. War

"Bodily injury" or "property damage" due to war, whether or not declared, or any act or condition incident to war. War includes civil war, insurrection, rebellion or revolution. This exclusion applies only to liability assumed under a contract or agreement.

j. Damage to Property

"Property damage" to:

(1) Property you own, rent, or occupy;

(2) Premises you sell, give away or abandon, if the "property damage" arises out of any part of those premises;

(3) Property loaned to you;

(4) Personal property in the care, custody or control of the insured;

(5) That particular part of real property on which you or any contractors or subcontractors working directly or indirectly on your behalf are performing operations, if the "property damage" arises out of those operations; or

(6) That particular part of any property that must be restored, repaired or replaced because "your work" was incorrectly performed on it.

Paragraph **(2)** of this exclusion does not apply if the premises are "your work" and were never occupied, rented or held for rental by you.

Paragraphs **(3)**, **(4)**, **(5)** and **(6)** of this exclusion do not apply to liability assumed under a sidetrack agreement.

Paragraph **(6)** of this exclusion does not apply to "property damage" included in the "products-completed operations hazard".

k. Damage to Your Product

"Property damage" to "your product" arising out of it or any part of it.

l. Damage to Your Work

"Property damage" to "your work" arising out of it or any part of it and included in the "products-completed operations hazard".

This exclusion does not apply if the damaged work or the work out of which the damage arises was performed on your behalf by a subcontractor.

m. Damage to Impaired Property or Property Not Physically Injured

"Property damage" to "impaired property" or property that has not been physically injured, arising out of:

(1) A defect, deficiency, inadequacy or dangerous condition in "your product" or "your work"; or

(2) A delay or failure by you or anyone acting on your behalf to perform a contract or agreement in accordance with its terms.

This exclusion does not apply to the loss of use of other property arising out of sudden and accidental physical injury to "your product" or "your work" after it has been put to its intended use.

n. Recall of Products, Work or Impaired Property

Damages claimed for any loss, cost or expense incurred by you or others for the loss of use, withdrawal, recall, inspection, repair, replacement, adjustment, removal or disposal of:

(1) "Your product";

(2) "Your work"; or

(3) "Impaired property";

if such product, work, or property is withdrawn or recalled from the market or from use by any person or organization because of a known or suspected defect, deficiency, inadequacy or dangerous condition in it.

Exclusions **c.** through **n.** do not apply to damage by fire to premises while rented to you or temporarily occupied by you with permission of the owner. A separate limit of insurance applies to this coverage as described in LIMITS OF INSURANCE (Section III).

COVERAGE B. PERSONAL AND ADVERTISING INJURY LIABILITY

1. Insuring Agreement.

a. We will pay those sums that the insured becomes legally obligated to pay as damages because of "personal injury" or "advertising injury" to which this insurance applies. We will have the right and duty to defend any "suit" seeking those damages. We may at our discretion investigate any "occurrence" or offense and settle any claim or "suit" that may result. But:

(1) The amount we will pay for damages is limited as described in LIMITS OF INSURANCE (SECTION III); and

(2) Our right and duty to defend end when we have used up the applicable limit of insurance in the payment of judgments or settlements under Coverage A or B or medical expenses under Coverage C.

No other obligation or liability to pay sums or perform acts or services is covered unless explicitly provided for under SUPPLEMENTARY PAYMENTS – COVERAGES A AND B.

b. This insurance applies to:

(1) "Personal injury" caused by an offense arising out of your business, excluding advertising, publishing, broadcasting or telecasting done by or for you;

(2) "Advertising injury" caused by an offense committed in the course of advertising your goods, products or services;

but only if the offense was committed in the "coverage territory" during the policy period.

2. Exclusions.

This insurance does not apply to:

a. "Personal injury" or "advertising injury":

(1) Arising out of oral or written publication of material, if done by or at the direction of the insured with knowledge of its falsity;

(2) Arising out of oral or written publication of material whose first publication took place before the beginning of the policy period;

(3) Arising out of the willful violation of a penal statute or ordinance committed by or with the consent of the insured; or

(4) For which the insured has assumed liability in a contract or agreement. This exclusion does not apply to liability for damages that the insured would have in the absence of the contract or agreement.

b. "Advertising injury" arising out of:

(1) Breach of contract, other than misappropriation of advertising ideas under an implied contract;

(2) The failure of goods, products or services to conform with advertised quality or performance;

(3) The wrong description of the price of goods, products or services; or

(4) An offense committed by an insured whose business is advertising, broadcasting, publishing or telecasting.

COVERAGE C. MEDICAL PAYMENTS

1. Insuring Agreement.

a. We will pay medical expenses as described below for "bodily injury" caused by an accident:

(1) On premises you own or rent;

(2) On ways next to premises you own or rent; or

(3) Because of your operations;

provided that:

(1) The accident takes place in the "coverage territory" and during the policy period;

(2) The expenses are incurred and reported to us within one year of the date of the accident; and

(3) The injured person submits to examination, at our expense, by physicians of our choice as often as we reasonably require.

b. We will make these payments regardless of fault. These payments will not exceed the applicable limit of insurance. We will pay reasonable expenses for:

(1) First aid administered at the time of an accident;

(2) Necessary medical, surgical, x-ray and dental services, including prosthetic devices; and

(3) Necessary ambulance, hospital, professional nursing and funeral services.

2. Exclusions.

We will not pay expenses for "bodily injury":

a. To any insured.

b. To a person hired to do work for or on behalf of any insured or a tenant of any insured.

c. To a person injured on that part of premises you own or rent that the person normally occupies.

d. To a person, whether or not an "employee" of any insured, if benefits for the "bodily injury" are payable or must be provided under a workers compensation or disability benefits law or a similar law.

e. To a person injured while taking part in athletics.

f. Included within the "products-completed operations hazard".

g. Excluded under Coverage A.

h. Due to war, whether or not declared, or any act or condition incident to war. War includes civil war, insurrection, rebellion or revolution.

SUPPLEMENTARY PAYMENTS - COVERAGES A AND B

We will pay, with respect to any claim or "suit" we defend:

1. All expenses we incur.

2. Up to $250 for cost of bail bonds required because of accidents or traffic law violations arising out of the use of any vehicle to which the Bodily Injury Liability Coverage applies. We do not have to furnish these bonds.

3. The cost of bonds to release attachments, but only for bond amounts within the applicable limit of insurance. We do not have to furnish these bonds.

4. All reasonable expenses incurred by the insured at our request to assist us in the investigation or defense of the claim or "suit", including actual loss of earnings up to $100 a day because of time off from work.

5. All costs taxed against the insured in the "suit".

6. Prejudgment interest awarded against the insured on that part of the judgment we pay. If we make an offer to pay the applicable limit of insurance, we will not pay any prejudgment interest based on that period of time after the offer.

7. All interest on the full amount of any judgment that accrues after entry of the judgment and before we have paid, offered to pay, or deposited in court the part of the judgment that is within the applicable limit of insurance.

These payments will not reduce the limits of insurance.

SECTION II - WHO IS AN INSURED

1. If you are designated in the Declarations as:

a. An individual, you and your spouse are insureds, but only with respect to the conduct of a business of which you are the sole owner.

b. A partnership or joint venture, you are an insured. Your members, your partners, and their spouses are also insureds, but only with respect to the conduct of your business.

c. An organization other than a partnership or joint venture, you are an insured. Your "executive officers" and directors are insureds, but only with respect to their duties as your officers or directors. Your stockholders are also insureds, but only with respect to their liability as stockholders.

2. Each of the following is also an insured:

a. Your "employees", other than your "executive officers", but only for acts within the scope of their employment by you or while performing duties related to the conduct of your business. However, no "employee" is an insured for:

(1) "Bodily injury" or "personal injury":

(a) To you, to your partners or members (if you are a partnership or joint venture), or to a co-"employee" while in the course of his or her employment or while performing duties related to the conduct of your business;

(b) To the spouse, child, parent, brother or sister of that co-"employee" as a consequence of paragraph **(1)(a)** above;

(c) For which there is any obligation to share damages with or repay someone else who must pay damages because of the injury described in paragraphs **(1)(a)** or **(b)** above; or

(d) Arising out of his or her providing or failing to provide professional health care services.

(2) "Property damage" to property:

(a) Owned, occupied or used by,

(b) Rented to, in the care, custody or control of, or over which physical control is being exercised for any purpose by

you, any of your "employees" or, if you are a partnership or joint venture, by any partner or member.

b. Any person (other than your "employee"), or any organization while acting as your real estate manager.

c. Any person or organization having proper temporary custody of your property if you die, but only:

(1) With respect to liability arising out of the maintenance or use of that property; and

(2) Until your legal representative has been appointed.

d. Your legal representative if you die, but only with respect to duties as such. That representative will have all your rights and duties under this Coverage Part.

3. With respect to "mobile equipment" registered in your name under any motor vehicle registration law, any person is an insured while driving such equipment along a public highway with your permission. Any other person or organization responsible for the conduct of such person is also an insured, but only with respect to liability arising out of the operation of the equipment, and only if no other insurance of any kind is available to that person or organization for this liability. However, no person or organization is an insured with respect to:

a. "Bodily injury" to a co-"employee" of the person driving the equipment; or

b. "Property damage" to property owned by, rented to, in the charge of or occupied by you or the employer of any person who is an insured under this provision.

4. Any organization you newly acquire or form, other than a partnership or joint venture, and over which you maintain ownership or majority interest, will qualify as a Named Insured if there is no other similar insurance available to that organization. However:

a. Coverage under this provision is afforded only until the 90th day after you acquire or form the organization or the end of the policy period, whichever is earlier;

     CG 00 01 10 93   □

b. Coverage A does not apply to "bodily injury" or "property damage" that occurred before you acquired or formed the organization; and

c. Coverage B does not apply to "personal injury" or "advertising injury" arising out of an offense committed before you acquired or formed the organization.

No person or organization is an insured with respect to the conduct of any current or past partnership or joint venture that is not shown as a Named Insured in the Declarations.

SECTION III - LIMITS OF INSURANCE

1. The Limits of Insurance shown in the Declarations and the rules below fix the most we will pay regardless of the number of:

   a. Insureds;

   b. Claims made or "suits" brought; or

   c. Persons or organizations making claims or bringing "suits".

2. The General Aggregate Limit is the most we will pay for the sum of:

   a. Medical expenses under Coverage C;

   b. Damages under Coverage A, except damages because of "bodily injury" or "property damage" included in the "products-completed operations hazard"; and

   c. Damages under Coverage B.

3. The Products-Completed Operations Aggregate Limit is the most we will pay under Coverage A for damages because of "bodily injury" and "property damage" included in the "products-completed operations hazard".

4. Subject to **2.** above, the Personal and Advertising Injury Limit is the most we will pay under Coverage B for the sum of all damages because of all "personal injury" and all "advertising injury" sustained by any one person or organization.

5. Subject to **2.** or **3.** above, whichever applies, the Each Occurrence Limit is the most we will pay for the sum of:

   a. Damages under Coverage A; and

   b. Medical expenses under Coverage C

   because of all "bodily injury" and "property damage" arising out of any one "occurrence".

6. Subject to **5.** above, the Fire Damage Limit is the most we will pay under Coverage A for damages because of "property damage" to premises, while rented to you or temporarily occupied by you with permission of the owner, arising out of any one fire.

7. Subject to **5.** above, the Medical Expense Limit is the most we will pay under Coverage C for all medical expenses because of "bodily injury" sustained by any one person.

The Limits of Insurance of this Coverage Part apply separately to each consecutive annual period and to any remaining period of less than 12 months, starting with the beginning of the policy period shown in the Declarations, unless the policy period is extended after issuance for an additional period of less than 12 months. In that case, the additional period will be deemed part of the last preceding period for purposes of determining the Limits of Insurance.

SECTION IV - COMMERCIAL GENERAL LIABILITY CONDITIONS

1. **Bankruptcy.**

   Bankruptcy or insolvency of the insured or of the insured's estate will not relieve us of our obligations under this Coverage Part.

2. **Duties In The Event Of Occurrence, Offense, Claim Or Suit.**

   a. You must see to it that we are notified as soon as practicable of an "occurrence" or an offense which may result in a claim. To the extent possible, notice should include:

   (1) How, when and where the "occurrence" or offense took place;

   (2) The names and addresses of any injured persons and witnesses; and

   (3) The nature and location of any injury or damage arising out of the "occurrence" or offense.

   b. If a claim is made or "suit" is brought against any insured, you must:

   (1) Immediately record the specifics of the claim or "suit" and the date received; and

   (2) Notify us as soon as practicable.

   You must see to it that we receive written notice of the claim or "suit" as soon as practicable.

c. You and any other involved insured must:

(1) Immediately send us copies of any demands, notices, summonses or legal papers received in connection with the claim or "suit";

(2) Authorize us to obtain records and other information;

(3) Cooperate with us in the investigation, settlement or defense of the claim or "suit"; and

(4) Assist us, upon our request, in the enforcement of any right against any person or organization which may be liable to the insured because of injury or damage to which this insurance may also apply.

d. No insureds will, except at their own cost, voluntarily make a payment, assume any obligation, or incur any expense, other than for first aid, without our consent.

3. Legal Action Against Us.

No person or organization has a right under this Coverage Part:

a. To join us as a party or otherwise bring us into a "suit" asking for damages from an insured; or

b. To sue us on this Coverage Part unless all of its terms have been fully complied with.

A person or organization may sue us to recover on an agreed settlement or on a final judgment against an insured obtained after an actual trial; but we will not be liable for damages that are not payable under the terms of this Coverage Part or that are in excess of the applicable limit of insurance. An agreed settlement means a settlement and release of liability signed by us, the insured and the claimant or the claimant's legal representative.

4. Other Insurance.

If other valid and collectible insurance is available to the insured for a loss we cover under Coverages A or B of this Coverage Part, our obligations are limited as follows:

a. **Primary Insurance**

This insurance is primary except when **b.** below applies. If this insurance is primary, our obligations are not affected unless any of the other insurance is also primary. Then, we will share with all that other insurance by the method described in **c.** below.

b. **Excess Insurance**

This insurance is excess over any of the other insurance, whether primary, excess, contingent or on any other basis:

(1) That is Fire, Extended Coverage, Builder's Risk, Installation Risk or similar coverage for "your work";

(2) That is Fire insurance for premises rented to you; or

(3) If the loss arises out of the maintenance or use of aircraft, "autos" or watercraft to the extent not subject to Exclusion **g.** of Coverage A (Section I).

When this insurance is excess, we will have no duty under Coverage A or B to defend any claim or "suit" that any other insurer has a duty to defend. If no other insurer defends, we will undertake to do so, but we will be entitled to the insured's rights against all those other insurers.

When this insurance is excess over other insurance, we will pay only our share of the amount of the loss, if any, that exceeds the sum of:

(1) The total amount that all such other insurance would pay for the loss in the absence of this insurance; and

(2) The total of all deductible and self-insured amounts under all that other insurance.

We will share the remaining loss, if any, with any other insurance that is not described in this Excess Insurance provision and was not bought specifically to apply in excess of the Limits of Insurance shown in the Declarations of this Coverage Part.

c. **Method of Sharing**

If all of the other insurance permits contribution by equal shares, we will follow this method also. Under this approach each insurer contributes equal amounts until it has paid its applicable limit of insurance or none of the loss remains, whichever comes first.

Copyright, Insurance Services Office, Inc., 1992   CG 00 01 10 93   □

If any of the other insurance does not permit contribution by equal shares, we will contribute by limits. Under this method, each insurer's share is based on the ratio of its applicable limit of insurance to the total applicable limits of insurance of all insurers.

5. **Premium Audit.**

   a. We will compute all premiums for this Coverage Part in accordance with our rules and rates.

   b. Premium shown in this Coverage Part as advance premium is a deposit premium only. At the close of each audit period we will compute the earned premium for that period. Audit premiums are due and payable on notice to the first Named Insured. If the sum of the advance and audit premiums paid for the policy period is greater than the earned premium, we will return the excess to the first Named Insured.

   c. The first Named Insured must keep records of the information we need for premium computation, and send us copies at such times as we may request.

6. **Representations.**

   By accepting this policy, you agree:

   a. The statements in the Declarations are accurate and complete;

   b. Those statements are based upon representations you made to us; and

   c. We have issued this policy in reliance upon your representations.

7. **Separation Of Insureds.**

   Except with respect to the Limits of Insurance, and any rights or duties specifically assigned in this Coverage Part to the first Named Insured, this insurance applies:

   a. As if each Named Insured were the only Named Insured; and

   b. Separately to each insured against whom claim is made or "suit" is brought.

8. **Transfer Of Rights Of Recovery Against Others To Us.**

   If the insured has rights to recover all or part of any payment we have made under this Coverage Part, those rights are transferred to us. The insured must do nothing after loss to impair them. At our request, the insured will bring "suit" or transfer those rights to us and help us enforce them.

9. **When We Do Not Renew.**

   If we decide not to renew this Coverage Part, we will mail or deliver to the first Named Insured shown in the Declarations written notice of the nonrenewal not less than 30 days before the expiration date.

   If notice is mailed, proof of mailing will be sufficient proof of notice.

SECTION V - DEFINITIONS

1. "Advertising injury" means injury arising out of one or more of the following offenses:

   a. Oral or written publication of material that slanders or libels a person or organization or disparages a person's or organization's goods, products or services;

   b. Oral or written publication of material that violates a person's right of privacy;

   c. Misappropriation of advertising ideas or style of doing business; or

   d. Infringement of copyright, title or slogan.

2. "Auto" means a land motor vehicle, trailer or semitrailer designed for travel on public roads, including any attached machinery or equipment. But "auto" does not include "mobile equipment".

3. "Bodily injury" means bodily injury, sickness or disease sustained by a person, including death resulting from any of these at any time.

4. "Coverage territory" means:

   a. The United States of America (including its territories and possessions), Puerto Rico and Canada;

   b. International waters or airspace, provided the injury or damage does not occur in the course of travel or transportation to or from any place not included in **a.** above; or

   c. All parts of the world if:

      (1) The injury or damage arises out of:

         (a) Goods or products made or sold by you in the territory described in **a.** above; or

(b) The activities of a person whose home is in the territory described in **a.** above, but is away for a short time on your business; and

(2) The insured's responsibility to pay damages is determined in a "suit" on the merits, in the territory described in **a.** above or in a settlement we agree to.

5. "Employee" includes a "leased worker". "Employee" does not include a "temporary worker".

6. "Executive officer" means a person holding any of the officer positions created by your charter, constitution, by-laws or any other similar governing document.

7. "Impaired property" means tangible property, other than "your product" or "your work", that cannot be used or is less useful because:

   a. It incorporates "your product" or "your work" that is known or thought to be defective, deficient, inadequate or dangerous; or

   b. You have failed to fulfill the terms of a contract or agreement;

   if such property can be restored to use by:

   a. The repair, replacement, adjustment or removal of "your product" or "your work"; or

   b. Your fulfilling the terms of the contract or agreement.

8. "Insured contract" means:

   a. A contract for a lease of premises. However, that portion of the contract for a lease of premises that indemnifies any person or organization for damage by fire to premises while rented to you or temporarily occupied by you with permission of the owner is not an "insured contract";

   b. A sidetrack agreement;

   c. Any easement or license agreement, except in connection with construction or demolition operations on or within 50 feet of a railroad;

   d. An obligation, as required by ordinance, to indemnify a municipality, except in connection with work for a municipality;

   e. An elevator maintenance agreement;

   f. That part of any other contract or agreement pertaining to your business (including an indemnification of a municipality in connection with work performed for a municipality) under which you assume the tort liability of another party to pay for "bodily injury" or "property damage" to a third person or organization. Tort liability means a liability that would be imposed by law in the absence of any contract or agreement.

   Paragraph **f.** does not include that part of any contract or agreement

   (1) That indemnifies a railroad for "bodily injury" or "property damage" arising out of construction or demolition operations, within 50 feet of any railroad property and affecting any railroad bridge or trestle, tracks, road-beds, tunnel, underpass or crossing;

   (2) That indemnifies an architect, engineer or surveyor for injury or damage arising out of:

   (a) Preparing, approving or failing to prepare or approve maps, drawings, opinions, reports, surveys, change orders, designs or specifications; or

   (b) Giving directions or instructions, or failing to give them, if that is the primary cause of the injury or damage; or

   (3) Under which the insured, if an architect, engineer or surveyor, assumes liability for an injury or damage arising out of the insured's rendering or failure to render professional services, including those listed in **(2)** above and supervisory, inspection or engineering services.

9. "Leased worker" means a person leased to you by a labor leasing firm under an agreement between you and the labor leasing firm, to perform duties related to the conduct of your business. "Leased worker" does not include a "temporary worker".

10. "Loading or unloading" means the handling of property:

    a. After it is moved from the place where it is accepted for movement into or onto an aircraft, watercraft or "auto";

Copyright, Insurance Services Office, Inc., 1992   CG 00 01 10 93   □

b. While it is in or on an aircraft, watercraft or "auto"; or

c. While it is being moved from an aircraft, watercraft or "auto" to the place where it is finally delivered;

but "loading or unloading" does not include the movement of property by means of a mechanical device, other than a hand truck, that is not attached to the aircraft, watercraft or "auto".

11. "Mobile equipment" means any of the following types of land vehicles, including any attached machinery or equipment:

a. Bulldozers, farm machinery, forklifts and other vehicles designed for use principally off public roads;

b. Vehicles maintained for use solely on or next to premises you own or rent;

c. Vehicles that travel on crawler treads;

d. Vehicles, whether self-propelled or not, maintained primarily to provide mobility to permanently mounted:

(1) Power cranes, shovels, loaders, diggers or drills; or

(2) Road construction or resurfacing equipment such as graders, scrapers or rollers;

e. Vehicles not described in a., b., c. or d. above that are not self-propelled and are maintained primarily to provide mobility to permanently attached equipment of the following types:

(1) Air compressors, pumps and generators, including spraying, welding, building cleaning, geophysical exploration, lighting and well servicing equipment; or

(2) Cherry pickers and similar devices used to raise or lower workers;

f. Vehicles not described in a., b., c. or d. above maintained primarily for purposes other than the transportation of persons or cargo.

However, self-propelled vehicles with the following types of permanently attached equipment are not "mobile equipment" but will be considered "autos":

(1) Equipment designed primarily for:

(a) Snow removal;

(b) Road maintenance, but not construction or resurfacing; or

(c) Street cleaning;

(2) Cherry pickers and similar devices mounted on automobile or truck chassis and used to raise or lower workers; and

(3) Air compressors, pumps and generators, including spraying, welding, building cleaning, geophysical exploration, lighting and well servicing equipment.

12. "Occurrence" means an accident, including continuous or repeated exposure to substantially the same general harmful conditions.

13. "Personal injury" means injury, other than "bodily injury", arising out of one or more of the following offenses:

a. False arrest, detention or imprisonment;

b. Malicious prosecution;

c. The wrongful eviction from, wrongful entry into, or invasion of the right of private occupancy of a room, dwelling or premises that a person occupies by or on behalf of its owner, landlord or lessor;

d. Oral or written publication of material that slanders or libels a person or organization or disparages a person's or organization's goods, products or services; or

e. Oral or written publication of material that violates a person's right of privacy.

14. a. "Products-completed operations hazard" includes all "bodily injury" and "property damage" occurring away from premises you own or rent and arising out of "your product" or "your work" except:

(1) Products that are still in your physical possession; or

(2) Work that has not yet been completed or abandoned.

b. "Your work" will be deemed completed at the earliest of the following times:

(1) When all of the work called for in your contract has been completed.

(2) When all of the work to be done at the site has been completed if your contract calls for work at more than one site.

(3) When that part of the work done at a job site has been put to its intended use by any person or organization other than another contractor or subcontractor working on the same project.

Work that may need service, maintenance, correction, repair or replacement, but which is otherwise complete, will be treated as completed.

c. This hazard does not include "bodily injury" or "property damage" arising out of:

   (1) The transportation of property, unless the injury or damage arises out of a condition in or on a vehicle created by the "loading or unloading" of it;

   (2) The existence of tools, uninstalled equipment or abandoned or unused materials; or

   (3) Products or operations for which the classification in this Coverage Part or in our manual of rules includes products or completed operations.

15. "Property damage" means:

   a. Physical injury to tangible property, including all resulting loss of use of that property. All such loss of use shall be deemed to occur at the time of the physical injury that caused it; or

   b. Loss of use of tangible property that is not physically injured. All such loss of use shall be deemed to occur at the time of the "occurrence" that caused it.

16. "Suit" means a civil proceeding in which damages because of "bodily injury", "property damage", "personal injury" or "advertising injury" to which this insurance applies are alleged. "Suit" includes:

   a. An arbitration proceeding in which such damages are claimed and to which you must submit or do submit with our consent; or

   b. Any other alternative dispute resolution proceeding in which such damages are claimed and to which you submit with our consent.

17. "Your product" means:

   a. Any goods or products, other than real property, manufactured, sold, handled, distributed or disposed of by:

      (1) You;

      (2) Others trading under your name; or

      (3) A person or organization whose business or assets you have acquired; and

   b. Containers (other than vehicles), materials, parts or equipment furnished in connection with such goods or products.

   "Your product" includes:

   a. Warranties or representations made at any time with respect to the fitness, quality, durability, performance or use of "your product"; and

   b. The providing of or failure to provide warnings or instructions.

   "Your product" does not include vending machines or other property rented to or located for the use of others but not sold.

18. "Temporary worker" means a person who is furnished to you to substitute for a permanent "employee" on leave or to meet seasonal or short-term workload conditions.

19. "Your work" means:

   a. Work or operations performed by you or on your behalf; and

   b. Materials, parts or equipment furnished in connection with such work or operations.

   "Your work" includes:

   a. Warranties or representations made at any time with respect to the fitness, quality, durability, performance or use of "your work"; and

   b. The providing of or failure to provide warnings or instructions.

CG 00 01 10 93   □

Whole Life Policy

The Northwestern Mutual Life Insurance Company agrees to pay the benefits provided in this policy, subject to its terms and conditions. Signed at Milwaukee, Wisconsin on the Date of Issue.

James A. Ericson
PRESIDENT AND C.E.O.

John M. Bremer
SECRETARY

WHOLE LIFE POLICY

Eligible For Annual Dividends.

Insurance payable on death of Insured.
Premiums payable for period shown on page 3.

Right To Return Policy -- Please read this policy carefully. The policy may be returned by the Owner for any reason within ten days after it was received. The policy may be returned to your agent or to the Home Office of the Company at 720 East Wisconsin Avenue, Milwaukee, WI 53202. If returned, the policy will be considered void from the beginning. Any premium paid will be refunded.

NN 1

Northwestern Mutual Life®

INSURED	JOHN DOE	AGE AND SEX	35 MALE
POLICY DATE	AUGUST 1, 1995	POLICY NUMBER	11 111 111
PLAN	WHOLE LIFE PAID UP AT 90	AMOUNT	$ 100,000

NN 1

**This policy is a legal contract between the Owner and The Northwestern Mutual Life Insurance Company.
Read your policy carefully.**

GUIDE TO POLICY PROVISIONS

BENEFITS AND PREMIUMS

SECTION 1. THE CONTRACT

Life Insurance Benefit payable on death of Insured. Incontestability.
Suicide. Definition of dates.

SECTION 2. OWNERSHIP

Rights of the Owner. Assignment as collateral.

SECTION 3. PREMIUMS AND REINSTATEMENT

Payment of premiums. Grace period of 31 days to pay premium.
Refund of unused premium at death. How to reinstate the policy.

SECTION 4. DIVIDENDS

Annual dividends. Paid-up additions and other uses of dividends. Dividend at death.

SECTION 5. CASH VALUES, EXTENDED TERM INSURANCE AND PAID-UP INSURANCE

Cash surrender value. What happens if premium is not paid. Basis of values.

SECTION 6. LOANS

Policy loans. Premium loans. Effect of policy debt. Interest on loans.

SECTION 7. CHANGE OF POLICY

SECTION 8. BENEFICIARIES

Naming and change of beneficiaries. Marital deduction provision for spouse of Insured.
Succession in interest of beneficiaries.

SECTION 9. PAYMENT OF POLICY BENEFITS

Payment of surrender or death proceeds. Payment plans for policy proceeds.
Right to increase income under payment plans. Guaranteed payment tables.

ADDITIONAL BENEFITS (if any)

APPLICATION

NN 1,4

BENEFITS AND PREMIUMS
DATE OF ISSUE - AUGUST 1, 1995

PLAN AND ADDITIONAL BENEFITS	AMOUNT	ANNUAL PREMIUM	PAYABLE FOR
WHOLE LIFE PAID UP AT 90	$ 100,000	$ 1,533.00	55 YEARS

A PREMIUM IS PAYABLE ON AUGUST 1, 1995 AND EVERY AUGUST 1 AFTER THAT.

THE FIRST PREMIUM IS $1,533.00.

THE OWNER MAY ELECT THE SPECIFIED RATE OR THE VARIABLE RATE LOAN INTEREST OPTION. SEE SECTIONS 6.4 THROUGH 6.6 OF THE POLICY. THE SPECIFIED RATE LOAN INTEREST OPTION WAS ELECTED ON THE APPLICATION.

THIS POLICY IS ISSUED IN A SELECT PREMIUM CLASS.

DIRECT BENEFICIARY   JANE DOE, SPOUSE OF THE INSURED

OWNER   JOHN DOE, THE INSURED

INSURED	JOHN DOE	AGE AND SEX	35 MALE
POLICY DATE	AUGUST 1, 1995	POLICY NUMBER	11 111 111
PLAN	WHOLE LIFE PAID UP AT 90	AMOUNT	$ 100,000

NN 1   PAGE 3   090

TABLE OF GUARANTEED VALUES

END OF POLICY YEAR	AUGUST 1,	CASH VALUE	PAID-UP INSURANCE	$100,000 EXTENDED TERM INSURANCE TO
1	1996	$ 0	$ 0	--
2	1997	1,078	5,000	JAN 14, 2001
3	1998	2,201	9,800	NOV 28, 2004
4	1999	3,371	14,400	APR 15, 2008
5	2000	4,588	18,700	APR 27, 2011
6	2001	5,852	22,900	JAN 11, 2014
7	2002	7,165	26,800	SEP 8, 2016
8	2003	8,528	30,500	MAY 13, 2019
9	2004	9,942	34,100	SEP 16, 2021
10	2005	11,411	37,400	OCT 13, 2023
11	2006	12,933	40,600	AUG 15, 2025
12	2007	14,515	43,700	APR 9, 2027
13	2008	16,156	46,600	OCT 11, 2028
14	2009	17,860	49,300	MAR 3, 2030
15	2010	19,629	51,900	JUN 19, 2031
16	2011	21,466	54,400	SEP 2, 2032
17	2012	23,370	56,800	OCT 18, 2033
18	2013	25,341	59,000	NOV 6, 2034
19	2014	27,380	61,100	NOV 2, 2035
20	2015	29,486	63,100	OCT 11, 2036
AGE 60	2020	38,328	71,800	MAY 31, 2040
AGE 65	2025	47,545	78,800	SEP 7, 2043
AGE 70	2030	56,741	84,400	SEP 19, 2046

VALUES ARE INCREASED BY PAID UP ADDITIONS AND DIVIDEND ACCUMULATIONS AND DECREASED BY POLICY DEBT. VALUES SHOWN AT END OF POLICY YEAR DO NOT REFLECT ANY PREMIUM DUE ON THAT POLICY ANNIVERSARY.

INSURED	JOHN DOE	AGE AND SEX	35 MALE
POLICY DATE	AUGUST 1, 1995	POLICY NUMBER	11 111 111
PLAN	WHOLE LIFE PAID UP AT 90	AMOUNT	$ 100,000

NN 1   PAGE 4

STATEMENT OF POLICY COST AND BENEFIT INFORMATION

FOR INFORMATION CONTACT YOUR AGENT   OR THE HOME OFFICE

ROBERT S HOUSER   THE NORTHWESTERN MUTUAL LIFE INS. CO.
4330 GOLF TERR, STE 209   720 E. WISCONSIN AVENUE
EAU CLAIRE WI 54701   MILWAUKEE, WI 53202

PLAN AND ADDITIONAL BENEFITS	AMOUNT	PREMIUM IF PAID ANNUALLY	YEARS PAYABLE
WHOLE LIFE PAID UP AT 90	$100,000	$1,533.00	FIRST 55

		- DIVIDENDS USED TO REDUCE PREMIUMS -		- DIVIDENDS TO ADDITIONS* -	
POLICY YEAR	DEATH BENEFIT	GUARANTEED CASH VALUE END OF YEAR	CASH DIVIDEND PAYABLE AT END OF YEAR*	TOTAL DEATH BENEFIT END OF YEAR	TOTAL CASH VALUE END OF YEAR
1	100,000	0	0	100,000	0
2	100,000	1,078	62	100,290	1,139
3	100,000	2,201	142	100,936	2,410
4	100,000	3,371	224	101,928	3,821
5	100,000	4,588	309	103,260	5,384
10	100,000	11,411	753	114,686	15,880
15	100,000	19,629	1,169	133,161	32,151
20	100,000	29,486	1,511	156,492	55,870
AGE 60	100,000	38,328	2,441	196,603	89,879
AGE 65	100,000	47,545	3,035	250,991	138,594

	BASIC POLICY	
	10 YEARS	20 YEARS
SURRENDER COST INDEX*	3.58	.69
NET PAYMENT COST INDEX*	12.22	9.18
EQUIVALENT DIVIDEND INDEX*	3.11	6.15

NOTE-This statement is recommended by the National Association of Insurance
     Commissioners. It may not necessarily reflect all the benefits contained
     in the policy. An explanation of the intended use of the cost indexes
     and the equivalent level annual dividend is included in the Life
     Insurance Buyers Guide, available from your agent.

 *Dividends assume no loans; loans will reduce dividends. Dividends are refunds
  of premium and are determined annually. They reflect mortality and expense
  savings and investment gains. Not an estimate or guarantee of future results.

8% LOAN RATE-APPLIED AT END OF LOAN YEAR   PREPARED AUGUST 9, 1995

THIS POLICY IS ISSUED IN A SELECT PREMIUM CLASS.

INSURED   JOHN DOE   AGE AND SEX   35   MALE

POLICY DATE   AUGUST 1, 1995   POLICY NUMBER   11 111 111

PS-NN 1   WI 99999 090

SECTION 1. THE CONTRACT

1.1 LIFE INSURANCE BENEFIT

The Northwestern Mutual Life Insurance Company will pay a benefit on the death of the Insured. Subject to the terms and conditions of the policy:

- payment of the death proceeds will be made after proof of the death of the Insured is received at the Home Office; and
- payment will be made to the beneficiary or other payee under Sections 8 and 9.

The amount of the death proceeds when all premiums due have been paid will be:

- the plan Amount shown on page 3; plus
- the amount of any paid-up additions then in force (Section 4.2); plus
- the amount of any dividend accumulations (Section 4.2); plus
- the amount of any premium refund (Section 3.1) and any dividend at death (Section 4.4); less
- the amount of any policy debt (Section 6.3).

These amounts will be determined as of the date of death.

The amount of the death proceeds when the Insured dies during the grace period following the due date of any unpaid premium will be:

- the amount determined above assuming the overdue premium has been paid; less
- the amount of the unpaid premium.

The amount of the death proceeds when the Insured dies while the policy is in force as extended term or paid-up insurance will be determined under Sections 5.2 or 5.3.

1.2 ENTIRE CONTRACT; CHANGES

This policy with the attached application is the entire contract. Statements in the application are representations and not warranties. A change in the policy is valid only if it is approved by an officer of the Company. The Company may require that the policy be sent to it for endorsement to show a change. No agent has the authority to change the policy or to waive any of its terms.

1.3 INCONTESTABILITY

The Company will not contest this policy after it has been in force during the lifetime of the Insured for two years from the Date of Issue. In issuing the policy, the Company has relied on the application. While the policy is contestable, the Company, on the basis of a misstatement in the application, may rescind the policy or deny a claim.

1.4 SUICIDE

If the Insured dies by suicide within one year from the Date of Issue, the amount payable by the Company will be limited to the premiums paid, less the amount of any policy debt.

1.5 DATES

The contestable and suicide periods begin with the Date of Issue. Policy months, years and anniversaries are computed from the Policy Date. Both dates are shown on page 3.

1.6 MISSTATEMENT OF AGE OR SEX

If the age or sex of the Insured has been misstated, the amount payable will be the amount which the premiums paid would have purchased at the correct age and sex.

1.7 PAYMENTS BY THE COMPANY

All payments by the Company under this policy are payable at its Home Office.

SECTION 2. OWNERSHIP

2.1 THE OWNER

The Owner is named on page 3. The Owner, his successor or his transferee may exercise policy rights without the consent of any beneficiary. After the death of the Insured, policy rights may be exercised only as provided in Sections 8 and 9.

2.2 TRANSFER OF OWNERSHIP

The Owner may transfer the ownership of this policy. Written proof of transfer satisfactory to the Company must be received at its Home Office. The transfer will then take effect as of the date that it was signed. The Company may require that the policy be sent to it for endorsement to show the transfer.

2.3 COLLATERAL ASSIGNMENT

The Owner may assign this policy as collateral security. The Company is not responsible for the validity or effect of a collateral assignment. The Company will not be responsible to an assignee for any payment or other action taken by the Company before receipt of the assignment in writing at its Home Office.

The interest of any beneficiary will be subject to any collateral assignment made either before or after the beneficiary is named.

A collateral assignee is not an Owner. A collateral assignment is not a transfer of ownership. Ownership can be transferred only by complying with Section 2.2.

NN 1,4

5

SECTION 3. PREMIUMS AND REINSTATEMENT

3.1 PREMIUM PAYMENT

Payment. All premiums after the first are payable at the Home Office or to an authorized agent. A receipt signed by an officer of the Company will be furnished on request. A premium must be paid on or before its due date. The date when each premium is due and the number of years for which premiums are payable are described on page 3.

Frequency. Premiums may be paid every 3, 6 or 12 months at the published rates of the Company. A change in premium frequency will take effect when the Company accepts a premium on a new frequency. Premiums may be paid on any other frequency approved by the Company.

Grace Period. A grace period of 31 days will be allowed to pay a premium that is not paid on its due date. The policy will be in full force during this period. If the Insured dies during the grace period, any overdue premium will be paid from the proceeds of the policy.

If the premium is not paid within the grace period, the policy will terminate as of the due date unless it continues as extended term or paid-up insurance under Section 5.2 or 5.3.

Premium Refund At Death. The Company will refund a portion of a premium paid for the period beyond the date of the Insured's death. The refund will be part of the policy proceeds.

3.2 REINSTATEMENT

The policy may be reinstated within five years after the due date of the overdue premium. All unpaid premiums (and interest as required below) must be received by the Company while the Insured is alive. The policy may not be reinstated if the policy was surrendered for its cash surrender value. Any policy debt on the due date of the overdue premium, with interest from that date, must be repaid or reinstated.

In addition, for the policy to be reinstated more than 31 days after the end of the grace period:

- evidence of insurability must be given that is satisfactory to the Company; and
- all unpaid premiums must be paid with interest from the due date of each premium. Interest is at an annual effective rate of 6%.

SECTION 4. DIVIDENDS

4.1 ANNUAL DIVIDENDS

This policy will share in the divisible surplus of the Company. This surplus is determined each year. This policy's share will be credited as a dividend on the policy anniversary. The dividend will reflect the mortality, expense and investment experience of the Company and will be affected by any policy debt during the policy year.

4.2 USE OF DIVIDENDS

Annual dividends may be paid in cash or used for one of the following:

- **Paid-up Additions.** Dividends will purchase paid-up additional insurance. Paid-up additions share in the divisible surplus.
- **Dividend Accumulations.** Dividends will accumulate at interest. Interest is credited at an annual effective rate of 3 1/2%. The Company may set a higher rate.
- **Premium Payment.** Dividends will be used to reduce premiums. If the balance of a premium is

not paid, or if this policy is in force as paid-up insurance, the dividend will purchase paid-up additions.

Other uses of dividends may be made available by the Company.

If no direction is given for the use of dividends, they will purchase paid-up additions.

4.3 ADDITIONS AND ACCUMULATIONS

Paid-up additions and dividend accumulations increase the policy's cash value. They are payable as part of the policy proceeds. Additions may be surrendered and accumulations may be withdrawn unless they are used for a loan, for extended term insurance or for paid-up insurance.

4.4 DIVIDEND AT DEATH

A dividend for the period from the beginning of the policy year to the date of the Insured's death will be payable as part of the policy proceeds.

SECTION 5. CASH VALUES, EXTENDED TERM INSURANCE
AND PAID-UP INSURANCE

5.1 CASH VALUE

The cash value for this policy, when all premiums due have been paid, will be the sum of:

- the cash value from the Table of Guaranteed Values;
- the cash value of any paid-up additions; and
- the amount of any dividend accumulations.

The cash value within three months after the due date of any unpaid premium will be the cash value on that due date reduced by any later surrender of paid-up additions and by any later withdrawal of dividend accumulations. After that, the cash value will be the cash value of the insurance then in force, including any paid-up additions and any dividend accumulations.

The cash value of any extended term insurance, paid-up insurance or paid-up additions will be the net single premium for that insurance at the attained age of the Insured.

5.2 EXTENDED TERM INSURANCE

If any premium is unpaid at the end of the grace period, this policy will be in force as extended term insurance. The amount of the death proceeds under this term insurance will be:

- the plan Amount shown on page 3; plus
- the amount of any paid-up additions in force (Section 4.2); plus
- the amount of any dividend accumulations (Section 4.2); less
- the amount of any policy debt (Section 6.3).

These amounts will be determined as of the due date of the unpaid premium. The term insurance will start as of the due date of the unpaid premium. The period of term insurance will be determined by using the cash surrender value as a net single premium at the attained age of the Insured. If the term insurance would extend to or beyond age 100, paid-up insurance will be provided instead. Extended term insurance does not share in divisible surplus.

If the extended term insurance is surrendered within 31 days after a policy anniversary, the cash value will not be less than the cash value on that anniversary.

5.3 PAID-UP INSURANCE

Paid-up insurance may be selected in place of extended term insurance. A written request must be received at the Home Office no later than three months after the due date of an unpaid premium. The amount of insurance will be determined by using the cash value as a net single premium at the attained age of the Insured. Any policy debt will continue. Paid-up insurance will share in divisible surplus.

The amount of the death proceeds when this policy is in force as paid-up insurance will be:

- the amount of paid-up insurance determined above; plus

- the amount of any in force paid-up additions purchased by dividends after the policy has become paid-up insurance (Section 4.2); plus
- the amount of any existing dividend accumulations (Section 4.2); plus
- the amount of any dividend at death (Section 4.4); less
- the amount of any policy debt (Section 6.3).

These amounts will be determined as of the date of death.

If paid-up insurance is surrendered within 31 days after a policy anniversary, the cash value will not be less than the cash value on that anniversary reduced by any later surrender of paid-up additions and by any later withdrawal of dividend accumulations.

5.4 CASH SURRENDER

The Owner may surrender this policy for its cash surrender value. The cash surrender value is the cash value less any policy debt. A written surrender of all claims, satisfactory to the Company, will be required. The date of surrender will be the date of receipt at the Home Office of the written surrender. The policy will terminate and the cash surrender value will be determined as of the date of surrender. The Company may require that the policy be sent to it.

5.5 TABLE OF GUARANTEED VALUES

Cash values, paid-up insurance and extended term insurance are shown on page 4 for the end of the policy years indicated. These values assume that all premiums due have been paid for the number of years stated. They do not reflect paid-up additions, dividend accumulations or policy debt. Values during a policy year will reflect any portion of the year's premium paid and the time elapsed in that year.

Values for policy years not shown are calculated on the same basis as those on page 4. A list of these values will be furnished on request. A detailed statement of the method of calculation of all values has been filed with the insurance supervisory official of the state in which this policy is delivered. The Company will furnish this statement at the request of the Owner. All values are at least as great as those required by that state.

5.6 BASIS OF VALUES

The cash value for each policy year not shown on page 4 equals the reserve for that year calculated on the Commissioners Reserve Valuation Method. Net single premiums are based on the Commissioners 1980 Standard Ordinary Mortality Table for the sex of the Insured; except that for extended term insurance, the Commissioners 1980 Extended Term Insurance Table for the sex of the Insured is used for the first 20 policy years. Interest is based on an annual effective rate of 5 1/2% for the first 20 policy years and 4% after that. Calculations assume the continuous payment of premiums and the immediate payment of claims.

SECTION 6. LOANS

6.1 POLICY AND PREMIUM LOANS

The Owner may obtain a loan from the Company in an amount that is not more than the loan value.

Policy Loan. The loan may be obtained on written request. No loan will be made if the policy is in force as extended term insurance. The Company may defer making the loan for up to six months unless the loan is to be used to pay premiums due the Company.

Premium Loan. If the premium loan provision is in effect on this policy, a loan will be made to pay an overdue premium. If the loan value is not large enough to pay the overdue premium, a premium will be paid for any other frequency permitted by this policy for which the loan value is large enough. The Owner may elect or revoke the premium loan provision by written request received at the Home Office.

6.2 LOAN VALUE

The loan value is the smaller of a. or b., less any policy debt and any premium then due or billed; a. and b. are defined as:

a. the cash value one year after the date of the loan, assuming all premiums due within that year are paid, less interest to one year from the date of the loan.

b. the cash value on the due date of the first premium not yet billed that is due after the date of the loan, less interest from the date of the loan to that premium due date.

6.3 POLICY DEBT

Policy debt consists of all outstanding loans and accrued interest. It may be paid to the Company at any time. Policy debt affects dividends under Section 4.1. Any policy debt will be deducted from the policy proceeds.

If the policy debt equals or exceeds the cash value, this policy will terminate. Termination occurs 31 days after a notice has been mailed to the Owner and to any assignee on record at the Home Office.

6.4 LOAN INTEREST

Interest accrues and is payable on a daily basis from the date of the loan on policy loans and from the premium due date on premium loans. Unpaid interest is added to the loan.

The Specified Rate loan interest option or the Variable Rate loan interest option is elected on the application.

Change To Variable Rate Loan Interest Option. The Owner may request a change to the Variable Rate loan interest option at any time, with the change to take effect on the January 1st following receipt of a written request at the Company's Home Office.

Change To Specified Rate Loan Interest Option. The Owner may request a change to the Specified Rate loan interest option if the interest rate set by the Company under Section 6.6 for the year beginning on the next January 1st is less than 8%. The written request to change must be received at the Home Office between November 15th and the last business day of the calendar year; the change will take effect on the January 1st following receipt of the request at the Home Office.

6.5 SPECIFIED RATE LOAN INTEREST OPTION

Interest is payable at an annual effective rate of 8%.

6.6 VARIABLE RATE LOAN INTEREST OPTION

Interest is payable at an annual effective rate that is set by the Company annually and applied to new or outstanding policy debt during the year beginning each January 1st. The highest loan interest rate that may be set by the Company is the greater of (i) 6 1/2% for the first 20 policy years and 5% after that or (ii) a rate based on the Moody's Corporate Bond Yield Averages-Monthly Average Corporates for the immediately preceding October. This Average is published by Moody's Investor's Service, Inc. If it is no longer published, the highest loan rate will be based on some other similar average established by the insurance supervisory official of the state in which this policy is delivered.

The loan interest rate set by the Company will not exceed the maximum rate permitted by the laws of the state in which this policy is delivered. The loan interest rate may be increased only if the increase in the annual effective rate is at least 1/2%. The loan interest rate will be decreased if the decrease in the annual effective rate is at least 1/2%.

The Company will give notice:
- of the initial loan interest rate in effect at the time a policy or premium loan is made.
- of an increase in loan interest rate on outstanding policy debt no later than 30 days before the January 1st on which the increase takes effect.

This policy will not terminate during a policy year as the sole result of an increase in the loan interest rate during that policy year.

SECTION 7. CHANGE OF POLICY

7.1 CHANGE OF PLAN

The Owner may change this policy to any permanent life insurance plan agreed to by the Owner and the Company by:

- paying the required costs; and

- meeting any other conditions set by the Company.

7.2 CHANGE OF INSURED

Change. The Owner may change the insured under this policy by:

- paying the required costs; and

- meeting any other conditions set by the Company, including the following:

  a. on the date of change, the new insured's age may not be more than 75;

  b. the new insured must have been born on or before the Policy Date of this policy;

c. the new insured must be insurable; and

d. the Owner must have an insurable interest in the life of the new insured.

Date Of Change. The date of change will be the later of:

- the date of the request to change; or

- the date of the medical examination (or the non-medical application).

Terms Of Policy After Change. The policy will cover the new insured starting on the date of change. When coverage on the new insured starts, coverage on the prior insured will terminate.

The contestable and suicide periods for the new insured start on the date of change.

The amount of insurance on the new insured will be set so that there will be no change in the cash value of the policy at the time of change. If the policy has no cash value, the amount will be set so that premiums do not change.

Any policy debt or assignment will continue after the change.

SECTION 8. BENEFICIARIES

8.1 DEFINITION OF BENEFICIARIES

The term "beneficiaries" as used in this policy includes direct beneficiaries, contingent beneficiaries and further payees.

8.2 NAMING AND CHANGE OF BENEFICIARIES

By Owner. The Owner may name and change the beneficiaries of death proceeds:

- while the Insured is living.
- during the first 60 days after the date of death of the Insured, if the Insured just before his death was not the Owner. No one may change this naming of a direct beneficiary during this 60 days.

By Direct Beneficiary. A direct beneficiary may name and change the contingent beneficiaries and further payees of his share of the proceeds:

- if the direct beneficiary is the Owner;
- if, at any time after the death of the Insured, no contingent beneficiary or further payee of that share is living; or
- if, after the death of the Insured, the direct beneficiary elects a payment plan. The interest of any other beneficiary in the share of that direct beneficiary will end.

These direct beneficiary rights are subject to the Owner's rights during the 60 days after the date of death of the Insured.

By Spouse (Marital Deduction Provision).

- **Power To Appoint.** The spouse of the Insured will have the power alone and in all events to appoint all amounts payable to the spouse under the policy if:
  - a. the Insured just before his death was the Owner; and
  - b. the spouse is a direct beneficiary; and
  - c. the spouse survives the Insured.
- **To Whom Spouse Can Appoint.** Under this power, the spouse can appoint:
  - a. to the estate of the spouse; or
  - b. to any other persons as contingent beneficiaries and further payees.
- **Effect Of Exercise.** As to the amounts appointed, the exercise of this power will:
  - a. revoke any other designation of beneficiaries;
  - b. revoke any election of payment plan as it applies to them; and
  - c. cause any provision to the contrary in Section 8 or 9 of this policy to be of no effect.

Effective Date. A naming or change of a beneficiary will be made on receipt at the Home Office of a written request that is acceptable to the Company. The request will then take effect as of the date that it was signed. The Company is not responsible for any payment or other action that is taken by it before the receipt of the request. The Company may require that the policy be sent to it to be endorsed to show the naming or change.

8.3 SUCCESSION IN INTEREST OF BENEFICIARIES

Direct Beneficiaries. The proceeds of this policy will be payable in equal shares to the direct beneficiaries who survive and receive payment. If a direct beneficiary dies before he receives all or part of his full share, the unpaid part of his share will be payable in equal shares to the other direct beneficiaries who survive and receive payment.

Contingent Beneficiaries. At the death of all of the direct beneficiaries, the proceeds, or the present value of any unpaid payments under a payment plan, will be payable in equal shares to the contingent beneficiaries who survive and receive payment. If a contingent beneficiary dies before he receives all or part of his full share, the unpaid part of his share will be payable in equal shares to the other contingent beneficiaries who survive and receive payment.

Further Payees. At the death of all of the direct and contingent beneficiaries, the proceeds, or the present value of any unpaid payments under a payment plan, will be paid in one sum:

- in equal shares to the further payees who survive and receive payment; or
- if no further payees survive and receive payment, to the estate of the last to die of all of the direct and contingent beneficiaries.

Owner Or His Estate. If no beneficiaries are alive when the Insured dies, the proceeds will be paid to the Owner or to his estate.

8.4 GENERAL

Transfer Of Ownership. A transfer of ownership of itself will not change the interest of a beneficiary.

Claims Of Creditors. So far as allowed by law, no amount payable under this policy will be subject to the claims of creditors of a beneficiary.

Succession Under Payment Plans. A direct or contingent beneficiary who succeeds to an interest in a payment plan will continue under the terms of the plan.

SECTION 9. PAYMENT OF POLICY BENEFITS

9.1 PAYMENT OF PROCEEDS

Death proceeds will be paid under the payment plan that takes effect on the date of death of the Insured. The Interest Income Plan (Option A) will be in effect if no payment plan has been elected. Interest will accumulate from the date of death until a payment plan is elected or the proceeds are withdrawn in cash.

Surrender proceeds will be the cash surrender value as of the date of surrender. These proceeds will be paid in cash or under a payment plan that is elected. The Company may defer paying the surrender proceeds for up to six months from the date of surrender. If payment is deferred for 30 days or more, interest will be paid on the surrender proceeds from the date of surrender to the date of payment. Interest will be at an annual effective rate of 5 1/2% during the first 20 policy years and 4% after that.

9.2 PAYMENT PLANS

Interest Income Plan (Option A). The proceeds will earn interest which may be received each month or accumulated. The first payment is due one month after the date on which the plan takes effect. Interest that has accumulated may be withdrawn at any time. Part or all of the proceeds may be withdrawn at any time.

Installment Income Plans. Payments will be made each month on the terms of the plan that is elected. The first payment is due on the date that the plan takes effect.

- **Specified Period (Option B).** The proceeds with interest will be paid over a period of from one to 30 years. The present value of any unpaid installments may be withdrawn at any time.

- **Specified Amount (Option D).** Payments of not less than $10.00 per $1,000 of proceeds will be made until all of the proceeds with interest have been paid. The balance may be withdrawn at any time.

Life Income Plans. Payments will be made each month on the terms of the plan that is elected. The first payment is due on the date that the plan takes effect. Proof of the date of birth, acceptable to the Company, must be furnished for each person on whose life the payments are based.

- **Single Life Income (Option C).** Payments will be made for a chosen period and, after that, for the life of the person on whose life the payments are based. The choices for the period are:

  a. zero years;

  b. 10 years;

  c. 20 years; or

  d. a refund period which continues until the sum of the payments that have been made is equal to the proceeds that were placed under the plan.

- **Joint And Survivor Life Income (Option E).** Payments are based on the lives of two persons. Level payments will be made for a period of 10 years and, after that, for as long as one or both of the persons are living.

- **Other Selections.** The Company may offer other selections under the Life Income Plans.

- **Withdrawal.** The present value of any unpaid payments that are to be made for the chosen period (Option C) or the 10 year period (Option E) may be withdrawn only after the death of all of the persons on whose lives the payments are based.

- **Limitations.** A direct or contingent beneficiary who is a natural person may be paid under a Life Income Plan only if the payments depend on his life. A corporation may be paid under a Life Income Plan only if the payments depend on the life of the Insured or, after the death of the Insured, on the life of his spouse or his dependent.

Payment Frequency. On request, payments will be made once every 3, 6 or 12 months instead of each month.

Transfer Between Payment Plans. A beneficiary who is receiving payment under a plan which includes the right to withdraw may transfer the amount withdrawable to any other plan that is available.

Minimum Payment. The Company may limit the election of a payment plan to one that results in payments of at least $50.

If payments under a payment plan are or become less than $50, the Company may change the frequency of payments. If the payments are being made once every 12 months and are less than $50, the Company may pay the present value or the balance of the payment plan.

9.3 PAYMENT PLAN RATES

Interest Income And Installment Income Plans. Proceeds will earn interest at rates declared each year by the Company. None of these rates will be less than an annual effective rate of 2%. Interest of more than 2% will increase the amount of the payments or, for the Specified Amount Plan (Option D), increase the number of payments. The present value of any unpaid installments will be based on the 2% rate of interest.

The Company may offer guaranteed rates of interest higher than 2% with conditions on withdrawal.

Life Income Plans. Payments will be based on rates declared by the Company. These rates will provide at least as much income as would the Company's rates, on the date that the payment plan takes effect, for a single premium immediate annuity contract, with no charge for issue expenses. Payments under these rates will not be less than the amounts that are described in Minimum Payment Rates.

Minimum Payment Rates. The minimum payment rates for the Installment Income Plans (Options B and D) and the Life Income Plans (Options C and E) are shown in the Minimum Payment Rate Tables.

The Life Income Plan payment rates in those tables depend on the sex and the adjusted age of each person on whose life the payments are based. The adjusted age is:

- the age on the birthday that is nearest to the date on which the payment plan takes effect; plus
- the age adjustment shown below for the number of policy years that have elapsed from the Policy Date to the date that the payment plan takes effect. A part of a policy year is counted as a full year.

POLICY YEARS ELAPSED	AGE ADJUSTMENT	POLICY YEARS ELAPSED	AGE ADJUSTMENT
1 to 8	0	33 to 40	-4
9 to 16	-1	41 to 48	-5
17 to 24	-2	49 or more	-6
25 to 32	-3		

9.4 EFFECTIVE DATE FOR PAYMENT PLAN

A payment plan that is elected will take effect on the date of death of the Insured if:

- the plan is elected by the Owner; and
- the election is received at the Home Office while the Insured is living.

In all other cases, a payment plan that is elected will take effect:

- on the date the election is received at the Home Office; or
- on a later date, if requested.

9.5 PAYMENT PLAN ELECTIONS

For Death Proceeds By Owner. The Owner may elect payment plans for death proceeds:

- while the Insured is living.
- during the first 60 days after the date of death of the Insured, if the Insured just before his death was not the Owner. No one may change this election made during those 60 days.

For Death Proceeds By Direct Or Contingent Beneficiary. A direct or contingent beneficiary may elect payment plans for death proceeds payable to him if no payment plan that has been elected is in effect. This right is subject to the Owner's rights during the 60 days after the date of death of the Insured.

For Surrender Proceeds. The Owner may elect payment plans for surrender proceeds. The Owner will be the direct beneficiary.

9.6 INCREASE OF MONTHLY INCOME

A direct beneficiary who is to receive proceeds under a payment plan may increase the amount of the monthly payments. This is done by the payment of an annuity premium to the Company at the time the payment plan elected under Section 9.5 takes effect. The amount that will be applied under the payment plan will be the net premium. The net premium is the annuity premium less a charge of not more than 2% and less any premium tax. The net premium will be applied under the same payment plan and at the same rates as the proceeds. The Company may limit this net premium to an amount that is equal to the direct beneficiary's share of the proceeds payable under this policy.

MINIMUM PAYMENT RATE TABLES
Minimum Monthly Income Payments Per $1,000 Proceeds

INSTALLMENT INCOME PLANS (OPTIONS B AND D)

PERIOD (YEARS)	MONTHLY PAYMENT	PERIOD (YEARS)	MONTHLY PAYMENT	PERIOD (YEARS)	MONTHLY PAYMENT
1	$ 84.09	11	$ 8.42	21	$ 4.85
2	42.46	12	7.80	22	4.67
3	28.59	13	7.26	23	4.51
4	21.65	14	6.81	24	4.36
5	17.49	15	6.42	25	4.22
6	14.72	16	6.07	26	4.10
7	12.74	17	5.77	27	3.98
8	11.25	18	5.50	28	3.87
9	10.10	19	5.26	29	3.77
10	9.18	20	5.04	30	3.68

MINIMUM PAYMENT RATE TABLES

Minimum Monthly Income Payments Per $1,000 Proceeds

LIFE INCOME PLAN (OPTION C)

SINGLE LIFE MONTHLY PAYMENTS								
MALE ADJUSTED AGE*	CHOSEN PERIOD (YEARS)				FEMALE ADJUSTED AGE*	CHOSEN PERIOD (YEARS)		
	ZERO	10	20	REFUND		ZERO	10	20	REFUND
55	$ 4.48	$ 4.43	$ 4.28	$ 4.29	55	$ 4.09	$ 4.07	$ 4.00	$ 3.99
56	4.56	4.50	4.34	4.36	56	4.15	4.13	4.05	4.05
57	4.65	4.59	4.40	4.43	57	4.22	4.20	4.11	4.11
58	4.75	4.68	4.46	4.50	58	4.30	4.27	4.17	4.17
59	4.85	4.77	4.52	4.58	59	4.38	4.34	4.23	4.24
60	4.96	4.87	4.59	4.66	60	4.46	4.42	4.29	4.30
61	5.07	4.97	4.66	4.75	61	4.55	4.50	4.36	4.38
62	5.20	5.08	4.72	4.84	62	4.65	4.59	4.43	4.46
63	5.33	5.19	4.79	4.94	63	4.75	4.69	4.50	4.54
64	5.48	5.32	4.86	5.04	64	4.86	4.79	4.57	4.62
65	5.63	5.44	4.92	5.15	65	4.97	4.89	4.64	4.71
66	5.80	5.58	4.99	5.26	66	5.10	5.01	4.71	4.81
67	5.97	5.72	5.05	5.38	67	5.23	5.12	4.79	4.91
68	6.16	5.86	5.12	5.51	68	5.38	5.25	4.86	5.02
69	6.36	6.01	5.18	5.64	69	5.53	5.39	4.93	5.14
70	6.58	6.17	5.23	5.78	70	5.70	5.53	5.01	5.26
71	6.81	6.33	5.29	5.93	71	5.88	5.68	5.08	5.39
72	7.05	6.49	5.34	6.08	72	6.08	5.83	5.15	5.53
73	7.31	6.66	5.38	6.25	73	6.29	6.00	5.21	5.67
74	7.59	6.83	5.43	6.42	74	6.52	6.17	5.27	5.83
75	7.89	7.01	5.46	6.60	75	6.77	6.35	5.33	5.99
76	8.21	7.19	5.50	6.79	76	7.04	6.54	5.38	6.17
77	8.56	7.37	5.53	6.99	77	7.33	6.73	5.43	6.35
78	8.93	7.55	5.56	7.20	78	7.65	6.93	5.47	6.55
79	9.32	7.72	5.58	7.42	79	7.99	7.13	5.51	6.76
80	9.75	7.90	5.60	7.66	80	8.36	7.34	5.54	6.98
81	10.20	8.07	5.62	7.90	81	8.76	7.54	5.57	7.21
82	10.69	8.23	5.63	8.16	82	9.20	7.74	5.59	7.46
83	11.21	8.39	5.64	8.43	83	9.67	7.93	5.61	7.72
84	11.76	8.54	5.65	8.71	84	10.18	8.12	5.63	7.99
85 and over	12.35	8.68	5.66	9.01	85 and over	10.74	8.30	5.64	8.28

LIFE INCOME PLAN (OPTION E)

MALE ADJUSTED AGE*	JOINT AND SURVIVOR MONTHLY PAYMENTS						
	FEMALE ADJUSTED AGE*						
	55	60	65	70	75	80	85 and over
55	$ 3.79	$ 3.93	$ 4.07	$ 4.19	$ 4.29	$ 4.35	$ 4.39
60	3.87	4.07	4.27	4.46	4.61	4.73	4.80
65	3.94	4.18	4.45	4.73	4.98	5.19	5.32
70	3.99	4.27	4.61	4.99	5.37	5.70	5.94
75	4.02	4.34	4.73	5.20	5.72	6.21	6.60
80	4.05	4.38	4.81	5.35	6.00	6.67	7.24
85 and over	4.06	4.40	4.86	5.45	6.18	7.00	7.75

*See Section 9.3.

NN.LIFE.(0194)

It is recommended that you ...

read your policy.

notify your Northwestern Mutual agent or the Company at 720 E. Wisconsin Avenue, Milwaukee, Wis. 53202, of an address change.

call your Northwestern Mutual agent for information -- particularly on a suggestion to terminate or exchange this policy for another policy or plan.

Election Of Trustees

The members of The Northwestern Mutual Life Insurance Company are its policyholders of insurance policies and deferred annuity contracts. The members exercise control through a Board of Trustees. Elections to the Board are held each year at the annual meeting of members. Members are entitled to vote in person or by proxy.

WHOLE LIFE POLICY

Eligible For Annual Dividends.

Insurance payable on death of Insured.
Premiums payable for period shown on page 3.

NN 1

Northwestern Mutual Life®

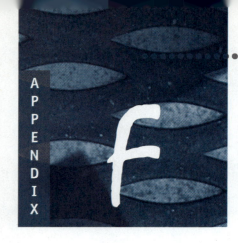

CSO Table

Commissioners 1980 Standard Ordinary Mortality Table

	MALE		FEMALE			MALE		FEMALE	
Age	Deaths Per 1,000	Expectation of Life (Years)	Deaths Per 1,000	Expectation of Life (Years)	Age	Deaths Per 1,000	Expectation of Life (Years)	Deaths Per 1,000	Expectation of Life (Years)
0	4.18	70.83	2.89	75.83	50	6.71	25.36	4.96	29.53
1	1.07	70.13	.87	75.04	51	7.30	24.52	5.31	28.67
2	.99	69.20	.81	74.11	52	7.96	23.70	5.70	27.82
3	.98	68.27	.79	73.17	53	8.71	22.89	6.15	26.98
4	.95	67.34	.77	72.23	54	9.56	22.08	6.61	26.14
5	.90	66.40	.76	71.28	55	10.47	21.29	7.09	25.31
6	.86	65.46	.73	70.34	56	11.46	20.51	7.57	24.49
7	.80	64.52	.72	69.39	57	12.49	19.74	8.03	23.67
8	.76	63.57	.70	68.44	58	13.59	18.99	8.47	22.86
9	.74	62.62	.69	67.48	59	14.77	18.24	8.94	22.05
10	.73	61.66	.68	66.53	60	16.08	17.51	9.47	21.25
11	.77	60.71	.69	65.58	61	17.54	16.79	10.13	20.44
12	.85	59.75	.72	64.62	62	19.19	16.08	10.96	19.65
13	.99	58.80	.75	63.67	63	21.06	15.38	12.02	18.86
14	1.15	57.86	.80	62.71	64	23.14	14.70	13.25	18.08
15	1.33	56.93	.85	61.76	65	25.42	14.04	14.59	17.32
16	1.51	56.00	.90	60.82	66	27.85	13.39	16.00	16.57
17	1.67	55.09	.95	59.87	67	30.44	12.76	17.43	15.83
18	1.78	54.18	.98	58.93	68	33.19	12.14	18.84	15.10
19	1.86	53.27	1.02	57.98	69	36.17	11.54	20.36	14.38
20	1.90	52.37	1.05	57.04	70	39.51	10.96	22.11	13.67
21	1.91	51.47	1.07	56.10	71	43.30	10.39	24.23	12.97
22	1.89	50.57	1.09	55.16	72	47.65	9.84	26.87	12.28
23	1.86	49.66	1.11	54.22	73	52.64	9.30	30.11	11.60
24	1.82	48.75	1.14	53.28	74	58.19	8.79	33.93	10.95
25	1.77	47.84	1.16	52.34	75	64.19	8.31	38.24	10.32
26	1.73	46.93	1.19	51.40	76	70.53	7.84	42.97	9.71
27	1.71	46.01	1.22	50.46	77	77.12	7.40	48.04	9.12
28	1.70	45.09	1.26	49.52	78	83.90	6.97	53.45	8.55
29	1.71	44.16	1.30	48.59	79	91.05	6.57	59.35	8.01
30	1.73	43.24	1.35	47.65	80	98.84	6.18	65.99	7.48
31	1.78	42.31	1.40	46.71	81	107.48	5.80	73.60	6.98
32	1.83	41.38	1.45	45.78	82	117.25	5.44	82.40	6.49
33	1.91	40.46	1.50	44.84	83	128.26	5.09	92.53	6.03
34	2.00	39.54	1.58	43.91	84	140.25	4.77	103.81	5.59
35	2.11	38.61	1.65	42.98	85	152.95	4.46	116.10	5.18
36	2.24	37.69	1.76	42.05	86	166.09	4.18	129.29	4.80
37	2.40	36.78	1.89	41.12	87	179.55	3.91	143.32	4.43
38	2.58	35.87	2.04	40.20	88	193.27	3.66	158.18	4.09
39	2.79	34.96	2.22	39.28	89	207.29	3.41	173.94	3.77
40	3.02	34.05	2.42	38.36	90	221.77	3.18	190.75	3.45
41	3.29	33.16	2.64	37.46	91	236.98	2.94	208.87	3.15
42	3.56	32.26	2.87	36.55	92	253.45	2.70	228.81	2.85
43	3.87	31.38	3.09	35.66	93	272.11	2.44	251.51	2.55
44	4.19	30.50	3.32	34.77	94	295.90	2.17	279.31	2.24
45	4.55	29.62	3.56	33.88	95	329.96	1.87	317.32	1.91
46	4.92	28.76	3.80	33.00	96	384.55	1.54	375.74	1.56
47	5.32	27.90	4.05	32.12	97	480.20	1.20	474.97	1.21
48	5.74	27.04	4.33	31.25	98	657.98	.84	655.85	.84
49	6.21	26.20	4.63	30.39	99	1,000.00	.50	1,000.00	.50

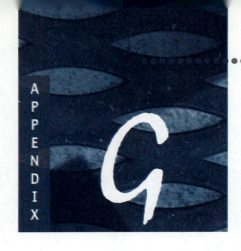

State Insurance Commissioners

STATE	NAME AND TITLE	ADDRESS	TELEPHONE/FAX
Alabama	James H. Dill Commissioner of Insurance	135 South Union St. Room 200 Montgomery, AL 36130	205-269-3550 T 205-240-3194 F
Alaska	David Walsh Director of Insurance	P.O. Box 110805 Juneau, AK 99801	907-465-2515 T 907-465-3422 F
American Samoa	Moetulu'i T. Iuvale Insurance Commissioner	Office of the Governor Pago Pago, AS 96779	011-684-633-4116 T 011-684-633-2269 F
Arizona	Chris Herstam Director of Insurance	2910 North 44th St., Suite 210 Phoenix, AZ 85018-7256	602-912-8400 T 602-912-8452 F
Arkansas	Lee Douglass Insurance Commissioner	1123 South University Ave. Suite 400, Univ. Tower Bldg. Little Rock, AR 72204-1699	501-686-2900 T 501-686-2913 F
California	John Garamendi Commissioner of Insurance	One City Centre Building Suite 1120, 770 L Street Sacramento, CA 95814	916-445-5544 T 916-445-5280 F
Colorado	Jack Ehnes Commissioner of Insurance	1560 Broadway, Suite 850 Denver, CO 80202	303-894-7499 T 303-894-7455 F
Connecticut	William J. Gilligan Acting Commissioner of Insurance	P.O. Box 816 Hartford, CT 06142-0816	203-297-3802 T 203-566-7410 F
Delaware	Donna Lee Williams Insurance Commissioner	The Rodney Building 841 Silver Lake Blvd. Dover, DE 19901	302-739-4251 T 302-739-5280 F
District of Columbia	Robert M. Willis Commissioner of Insurance	441 4th St., NW, 8th Floor N Washington, DC 20001	202-727-8000, x3007 T 202-727-8055 F
Florida	Tom Gallagher Insurance Commissioner	State Capitol Plaza Level 11 Tallahassee, FL 32399-0300	904-922-3101 T 904-488-3334 F
Georgia	Tim Ryles Insurance Commissioner	2 Martin L. King, Jr. Dr. Floyd Memorial Building 704 West Tower Atlanta, GA 30334	404-656-2056 T 404-657-7493 F
Guam	Joaquin G. Blaz Insurance Commissioner	378 Chalan San Antonio Tamuning, GU 96911	011-671-477-5106 T 011-671-472-2643 F
Hawaii	Lawrence Reifurth Insurance Commissioner	250 S. King Street, 5th Floor Honolulu, HI 96813	808-586-2790 T 808-586-2806 F
Idaho	James M. Alcorn Acting Director of Insurance	500 South 10th Street Boise, ID 83720	208-334-4250 T 208-334-4398 F
Illinois	James W. Schacht Acting Commissioner of Insurance	320 W. Washington St., 4th Floor Springfield, IL 62767	217-782-4515 T 217-782-5020 F
Indiana	Donna Bennett Commissioner of Insurance	311 W. Washington St., Suite 300 Indianapolis, IN 46204-2787	317-232-2385 T 317-232-5251 F
Iowa	Terri Vaughan Commissioner of Insurance	Lucas State Office Bldg., 6th Fl. Des Moines, IA 50319	515-281-5705 T 515-281-3059 F
Kansas	Ron Todd Commissioner of Insurance	420 South West Ninth Street Topeka, KS 66612-1678	913-296-7801 T 913-296-2283 F
Kentucky	Don W. Stephens Insurance Commissioner	215 West Main Street Frankfort, KY 40602	502-564-6027 T 502-564-6090 F

STATE	NAME AND TITLE	ADDRESS	TELEPHONE/FAX
Louisiana	James H. Brown Commissioner of Insurance	P.O. Box 94214 Baton Rouge, LA 70801-9214	504-342-5423 T 504-342-8622 F
Maine	Brian Atchinson Superintendent of Insurance	State Office Building State House, Station 34 Augusta, ME 04333	207-582-8707 T 207-582-8716 F
Maryland	Dwight K. Bartlett, III Insurance Commissioner	501 St. Paul Pl., Stanbalt Building 7th Floor-South Baltimore, MD 21202-2272	410-333-2521 T 410-333-6650 F
Massachusetts	Linda Ruthardt Commissioner of Insurance	470 Atlantic Avenue, Sixth Floor Boston, MA 02210-2223	617-521-7794 T 617-526-7770 F
Michigan	David Dykhouse Commissioner of Insurance	611 W. Ottawa St., 2nd Floor North Lansing, MI 48933	517-373-9273 T 517-335-4978 F
Minnesota	James E. Ulland Commissioner of Commerce	133 E. 7th Street St. Paul, MN 55101	612-296-6848 T 612-296-4328 F
Mississippi	George Dale Commissioner of Insurance	1804 Walter Sillers Building Jackson, MS 39205	601-359-3569 T 601-359-2474 F
Missouri	Jay Angoff Director of Insurance	301 W. High Street 6 North Jefferson City, MO 65102-0690	314-751-4126 T 314-751-1165 F
Montana	Mark O'Keefe Commissioner of Insurance	126 North Sanders Helena, MT 59620	406-444-2040 T 406-444-3497 F
Nebraska	Robert Lange Acting Director of Insurance	Terminal Bldg., 941 O St., Suite 400 Lincoln, NE 68508	402-471-2201 T 402-471-4610 F
Nevada	Teresa Rankin Commissioner of Insurance	1665 Hot Springs Road, Suite 152 Carson City, NV 89710	702-687-4270 T 702-687-3937 F
New Hampshire	Sylvio L. Dupuis Insurance Commissioner	169 Manchester Street Concord, NH 03301	603-271-2261 T 603-271-1406 F
New Jersey	Drew Karpinski Commissioner of Insurance	20 West State St., CN325 Trenton, NJ 08625	609-292-5363 T 609-984-5273 F
New Mexico	Fabian Chavez Superintendent of Insurance	P.O. Drawer 1269 Sante Fe, NM 87504-1269	505-827-4601 T 505-827-4734 F
New York	Salvatore R. Curiale Superintendent of Insurance	160 W. Broadway New York, NY 10013	212-602-0429 T 212-602-0437 F
North Carolina	James E. Long Commissioner of Insurance	Dobbs Building, 430 N Salisbury St. Suite 4140 Raleigh, NC 27603	919-733-7349 T 919-733-6495 F
North Dakota	Glenn Pomeroy Commissioner of Insurance	600 East Blvd. Bismarck, ND 58505-0320	701-224-2440 T 701-224-4880 F
Ohio	Harold T. Duryee Director of Insurance	2100 Stella Court Columbus, OH 43266-0566	614-644-2658 T 614-644-3743 F
Oklahoma	Cathy Weatherford Insurance Commissioner	1901 North Walnut Oklahoma City, OK 73105	405-521-2686 T 405-521-6635 F
Oregon	Kerry Barnett Commissioner of the Oregon Department of Consumer & Business Services	440 Labor and Industries Building Salem, OR 97310	503-378-4271 T 503-378-4351 F
Pennsylvania	Cynthia Maleski Insurance Commissioner	1326 Strawberry Square, 13th Floor Harrisburg, PA 17120	717-783-0442 T 717-783-1059 F

STATE	NAME AND TITLE	ADDRESS	TELEPHONE/FAX
Puerto Rico	Juan Antonio Garcia Commissioner of Insurance	Fernandez Juncos Station 1607 Ponce de Leon Avenue Santurce, PR 00910	809-722-8686 T 809-722-4400 T
Rhode Island	Alfonso E. Mastrostefano Insurance Commissioner	233 Richmond Street, Suite 233 Providence, RI 02903-4233	401-277-2223 T 401-751-4887 F
South Carolina	Lee P. Jedziniak Insurance Commissioner	1612 Marion Street Columbia, SC 29202	803-737-6160 T 803-737-6205 F
South Dakota	Darla L. Lyon Director of Insurance	500 E. Capitol Pierre, SD 57501-3940	605-773-3563 T 605-773-5369 F
Tennessee	Allan S. Curtis Commissioner of Insurance	Volunteer Plaza 500 James Robertson Pkwy. Nashville, TN 37243-0565	615-741-2241 T 615-741-4000 F
Texas	J. Robert Hunter Commissioner of Insurance	P.O. Box 149104 Austin, TX 78714-9104	512-463-6464 T 512-475-2005 T
Utah	Robert E. Wilcox Commissioner of Insurance	3110 State Office Building Salt Lake City, UT 84114-1201	801-538-3800 T 801-538-3829 F
Vermont	Elizabeth R. Costle Commissioner of Insurance	89 Main Street, Drawer 20 Montpelier, VT 05620-3101	902-828-3301 T 802-828-3306 F
Virgin Islands	Larry Diehl Director of Insurance	Kongen's Garden #18 St. Thomas, VI 00802	809-774-2991 T 809-774-6953 F
Virginia	Steven T. Foster Commissioner of Insurance	1300 East Main Street Tyler Building Richmond, VA 23219	804-371-9694 T 804-371-9873 F
Washington	Deborah Senn Insurance Commissioner	Insurance Building P.O. Box 40255 Olympia, WA 98504-0255	206-753-7310 T 206-586-3535 F
West Virginia	Hanley C. Clark Insurance Commissioner	P.O. Box 50540 Charleston, WV 25305-0540	304-558-3354 T 304-558-0412 F
Wisconsin	Josephine Musser Commissioner of Insurance	121 E. Wilson Street Madison, WI 53702	608-266-0102 T 608-266-9935 F
Wyoming	John McBride Insurance Commissioner	Herschler Building 122 W. 25th Street, 3rd Floor East Cheyenne, WY 82002-0440	307-777-7401 T 307-777-5895 F

Glossary

Accident   An event or occurrence which is unforeseen and unintended.

Accident and health insurance   Provides hospital, medical, surgical, and income benefits in the event of sickness, accidental injury, or accidental death.

Accidental bodily injury   Injury to the body of the insured as a result of an accident.

Accidental death benefit   Provides additional benefit in case of death by accidental means.

Accidental means   The unexpected and unforeseen cause of an accident. The cause of the mishap must be accidental in order to claim benefits under the policy.

Accumulation period   The time during which premiums are being paid and/or investment returns are being accumulated on an annuity contract, before benefit payments begin.

Accumulation value   The difference between *income,* consisting of net premiums paid, interest guaranteed, and excess interest, and *outgo,* consisting of mortality charges, management and marketing expenses, and withdrawals or loans in an interest-sensitive life insurance policy.

Acquisition cost   The immediate cost of issuing a new policy, including cost of clerical work, agent's commission, and medical inspection fees.

Actively at work   A condition that you must be at work on the day your group insurance coverage would normally become effective. Otherwise your insurance will not become effective until you return to work.

Actual cash value   The cost of repairing or replacing damaged property with other of like kind and quality in the same physical condition. Commonly defined as replacement cost less depreciation.

Actual dividends   Policy dividends paid during a past period. See Projected Dividends.

Actuarial cost methods   Systems for determining contributions to be made under a defined benefit retirement plan. In addition to forecasts of mortality, interest, and expenses, some methods involve estimates of future labor turnover, salary scales, and retirement rates.

Actuary   A mathematician trained in the insurance field. The person who determines premium rates, reserves, and dividends along with the conduct of various statistical studies.

Administrative services only   An arrangement under which an insurer or another third-party administrator contracts to provide specific recordkeeping and claim payment functions to a self-funded group insurance plan.

Administrator   A person appointed by the court to serve the function of executor. The duties include assembling of assets, paying all debts and taxes, and making proper distribution of remaining property in an estate.

Admitted company   An insurance company licensed in your state.

Advanced funded plan   A retirement plan that accumulates funds during the time employees are actively working.

Adverse selection   Tendency of people who have a greater perceived probability or severity of loss than the average person to seek insurance.

Age limits   Stipulated minimum and maximum ages below and above which the insurer will not accept applications or may not renew policies.

Agent   The independent agent is an independent businessperson who represents two or more insurance companies under contract in a sales and service capacity and who is paid on a commission basis. The exclusive agent represents only one company, or a group of companies, usually on a commission basis. The direct writer is the salaried or commissioned employee of a single company or a group of companies.

Aggregate limit   The maximum dollar amount which may be collected for a single occurrence or during the policy period or during the insured's lifetime, as specified in the policy.

Agreed amount endorsement   An endorsement which establishes the value of property or gross earnings. It prevents a coinsurance penalty for inadequate amounts of insurance. Instead, the insurer agrees to a valuation of property or earnings.

Aleatory   Performance of insurance contract conditions is based upon an event which may or may not happen.

Allied lines   A term for forms of insurance allied with property insurance, covering such perils as sprinkler leakage, water damage, and earthquake.

Allocated benefits   Benefits for which the maximum amount payable for specific services is itemized in the contract.

Annuitant   The person on whose life expectancy annuity payments are based.

Annuity   A contract that provides an income for a period of time, such as a specified number of years or for life. Annuity payments are usually made monthly but can be quarterly, semi-annually, or annually.

Application   A signed statement of facts requested by an insurer for the purpose of deciding whether or not to issue a policy.

Arson   The willful and malicious burning of, or attempt to burn, any structure or other property, often with criminal or fraudulent intent.

Assessable   A policy which gives the insurer the right to require policyowners to pay additional premium during a policy period.

Assignment   Transfer of the ownership or benefits of a policy.

Assumption of risk   A defense against liability, such that if the plaintiff (injured person) knew of the dangers involved in the act that resulted in injury, but chose to act in that fashion nonetheless, the defendant may not be held liable.

Attorney-in-fact   One appointed to act for another; e.g., I give you power-of-attorney to sell my car and sign the required documents on my behalf.

Automatic premium loan provision   Provides that if a life insurance premium is not paid, a policy loan in the amount of the premium due will automatically be made at the end of the grace period, provided there is enough unborrowed cash value to cover the loan and its interest for one year.

Automobile insurance plan   A program under which automobile insurance is made available to persons who are unable to obtain such insurance in the voluntary market.

Automobile liability insurance   Protection for the insured against loss arising out of his or her legal liability arising out of the use, operation, or maintenance of his or her automobile.

Automobile physical damage insurance   Coverage for damages or loss to an automobile resulting from collision, fire, theft, and other perils.

Aviation trip insurance   A policy protecting individuals as passengers of a scheduled aircraft. It is generally obtained at airports.

Avoidance   A risk management technique that often is not feasible because it keeps one from engaging in a desired activity.

Bailment   The transfer of risk associated with property by placing it in the hands of another for safekeeping, servicing, and so on.

Basic health care policies   Provide coverage for hospital, surgical, and physicians' visit expenses, as well as a limited number of other medical services named in the policy. Basic policies usually require little or no cost-sharing by the insured and provide relatively low limits of coverage.

Beneficiary   A person designated by the policyowner to receive a specified payment upon the insured's death.

Benefit duration   The maximum period during which disability income benefits are payable.

Binder   A temporary insurance contract made by an agent of the insurer.

Binding receipt   A receipt given for a premium payment accompanying the application for life insurance. This binds the company, even if the applicant is not insurable, while the application is being processed. If the proposed insured dies while the application is being processed, a claim for the death benefit will be paid.

Blue Cross   An independent, not-for-profit membership corporation providing protection against the costs of hospital care.

Blue Shield   An independent, not-for-profit membership corporation providing protection against the costs of surgery, physician charges, and other items of medical care.

Boiler and machinery insurance   Coverage for loss arising out of the operation of pressure, mechanical, and electrical equipment. It may cover loss to the boiler and machinery itself, damaage to other property, and business interruption losses.

Bond   Written contract in which one party (the surety) guarantees performance of an agreement between a second party (the principal) and a third party (the obligee). The surety makes the guarantee to the obligee on behalf of the principal.

Bottomry   An agreement made in ancient Greece whereby a loan made on a ship was canceled if the ship was lost. A similar agreement in which the cargo was collateral was called "respondentia." Both these arrangements combined lending with insurance.

Branch manager   An insurance company marketing manager who selects, trains, and supervises sales agents. He or she is a company employee.

Broker   Represents buyers of insurance. Deals with either agents or insurers in arranging for insurance required by the customer.

Burglary   Act of stealing property that involves forcible entry into or exit out of the premises burglarized.

Business coalition   A group that has made statistical analyses and other efforts to control health care costs through business alliances in a city or region to enhance medical care purchasing power and identify low-cost providers.

Business interruption insurance   Coverage for loss of earnings in case the policyowner's business is shut down by fire, windstorm, explosion, or other insured peril.

Buy and sell agreement   An agreement made between the owner, while living, of a business and a potential purchaser of that business. In the event the owner becomes totally or permanently disabled and/or dies, the agreement goes into effect. This allows the owner to protect himself or herself against loss due to the inability to sell the firm for its full value.

Capital sum The maximum amount payable in one sum in the event of accidental dismemberment. When a contract provides benefits for kinds of dismemberment, each benefit is an amount equal to, or a fraction of, the capital sum.

Captive A form of risk retention by which a subsidiary corporation provides insurance coverage to its parent and other affiliated organizations.

Captive agent An uncomplimentary synonym for exclusive agent.

Cash accumulation method A procedure used to compare the costs of two or more life insurance policies, concentrating on differences in investment elements.

Cash value The investment amount or surrender value of a life insurance policy.

Catastrophic loss A loss (or related losses) that is unbearable in the sense that it causes severe financial consequences such as bankruptcy to a family, organization, or insurer.

Ceding company An insurance company that shifts part or all of a risk it has assumed to another insurance company. The latter is the reinsurer.

Certified employee benefit specialist A professional designation offered by the International Foundation of Employee Benefit Plans and the Wharton School of the University of Pennsylvania to persons who: (1) pass a series of ten exams on subjects related to benefits, and (2) subscribe to a code of ethics.

Certified financial planner A professional designation offered by the Institute for Financial Planning to persons who: (1) pass a series of six examinations on subjects related to insurance, investments, taxes, and their integration through the financial planning process, (2) are currently employed in financial planning or an affiliated field, and (3) subscribe to a code of ethics.

Chartered financial consultant A professional designation offered by the American College to persons who: (1) pass a series of ten examinations on subjects related to insurance, investments, taxes, and their integration through the financial planning process, (2) have at least three years of experience in one of the subject areas, and (3) subscribe to a code of ethics.

Chartered life underwriter A professional designation offered by the American College to persons who: (1) pass a series of ten professional examinations on subjects related to life-health insurance, (2) have at least three years of life-health insurance experience, and (3) subscribe to a code of ethics.

Chartered property and casualty underwriter A professional designation offered by The American Institute for Property and Liability Underwriters to persons who: (1) pass a series of ten professional examinations on subjects related to property-liability insurance, (2) have at least three years of property-liability insurance experience, and (3) subscribe to a code of ethics.

Claim A demand to the insurer by the insured person for the payment of benefits under a policy.

Claims Adjuster A person who settles insurance claims for an insurer.

Class rating A system of premium rate determination in which all risks with similar characteristics are charged the same rate; e.g., all females the same age and in good health are charged the same rate per $1,000 of life insurance by a particular insurer.

COBRA See Consolidated Omnibus Budget Reconciliation Act of 1985.

Coinsurance A property insurance policy provision that requires the insured to carry insurance equal to a specified percentage of the property's value or receive less than full reimbursement for any loss. Also, a health insurance policy provision that requires the insured to pay a percentage (for example, 20 percent) of each covered charge.

Collision The upset (turning over) of the covered auto or collision with another object.

Commercial insurance Contracts sold to businesses or other organizations. The term is usually confined to descriptions of property-liability insurance contracts. Life-health insurance for organizations is usually called group insurance.

Commercial insurer A company that issues property-liability insurance to businesses and other organizations.

Common law Body of law based on custom and court decisions.

Comparative negligence A defense by which the court compares the relative negligence of the parties and apportions recovery on that basis.

Comprehensive medical insurance Provides benefits generally equivalent to those provided by both a basic and a major medical health insurance policy. It is characterized by a low deductible amount, a coinsurance (participation) clause, and high maximum benefits.

Concealment Intentional omission of a material fact by the insured.

Conditional receipt A receipt given for a premium payment accompanying the application for life insurance. This binds the company, if the applicant is insurable, to make the policy effective from the date of the receipt. If the proposed insured dies while the application is being processed, a claim for the death benefit will be paid only if the applicant would have been judged to be insurable.

Consequential loss Loss which results from (is a consequence of) a direct loss; e.g., a loss caused by fire causes loss of earnings while the damaged premises are being repaired. (Also known as indirect loss.)

Consideration One of the elements of a binding contract. Consideration is what each party to a contract gives up to induce the other party to make the agreement.

Consolidated Omnibus Budget Reconciliation Act of 1985 (COBRA) Law which requires employers to allow employees to continue group health coverage at the employee's expense for up to 36 months following certain events that would otherwise lead to termination of coverage.

Constructive total loss A partial loss so large that repairs would cost more than the insured property would be worth after being repaired. For example, it may cost more to repair an old car damaged by collision than to buy a replacement from a used car dealer.

Contingent beneficiary In the event that the primary beneficiary does not survive the life insurance policyowner, the contingent beneficiary is entitled to the proceeds of the life insurance policy when the policyowner dies.

Contract bond A type of surety bond that guarantees the performance of a contract. It is used frequently in building construction.

Contributory benefit plan One that requires employees to pay part or all of the costs (e.g., part of the premium) for group benefits.

Contributory negligence A defense against liability that disallows any recovery by the plaintiff if the plaintiff is shown to be negligent to any degree in not avoiding the relevant harm.

Conversion privilege The right given to an insured person to change insurance without evidence of insurability.

Convertibility option The right to convert a term policy to a whole life or other type of life insurance, before a specified time, without proving insurability.

Coordination of benefits (COB) A method of integrating benefits payable under more than one health insurance plan so that the insured's benefits from all sources do not exceed 100 percent of allowable medical expenses.

Copayment The fixed amount paid by the insured for a physician office visit, an inpatient hospital stay, a drug prescription, or other specified service. For example, a copayment of $10 per doctor office visit may be required in a medical expense insurance contract. See Costsharing.

Corpus The property of a trust.

Cost containment Effective methods to control the growing cost of health insurance.

Cost of living adjustment A retirement plan provision that increases benefits during retirement years in accordance with a cost-of-living or wage index, perhaps subject to a maximum increase of 4 or 5 percent per year. A similar provision may increase amounts of life insurance.

Costsharing The amount paid by the insured for medical insurance deductibles, coinsurance, copayments, or premiums.

Credit insurance A guarantee to manufacturers, wholesalers, and service organizations that they will be paid for goods shipped or services rendered. It is a guarantee of that part of their working capital represented by accounts receivable.

Credit life A type of life insurance that provides benefits to a creditor in the event of a debtor's death.

Credit risk Involves the insolvency of the purchaser of U.S. exports.

Crop-hail insurance Protection against damage to growing crops as a result of hail or certain other named perils.

Cumulative probabilities The sum of probabilities.

Current assumption whole life insurance A whole life insurance policy requiring a fixed premium, and clearly separating its expense, protection, and savings elements. Investment returns similar to those currently being earned by the issuing insurer are credited to the savings element.

Declarations Statements made by the insured that identify the person(s) or organizations covered by the contract, give information about the loss exposure, and provide the basis upon which the contract is issued and the premium determined.

Deductible A provision that requires the policyowner to contribute up to a specified sum per claim or per accident toward the total amount of the insured loss. Insurance is written on this basis at reduced rates.

Deferred annuity An annuity under which payment will begin at some future date, such as in a specified number of years, at a specified age, or upon request.

Defined benefit plan A pension plan which promises to provide a clearly specified amount of retirement benefit that will be available at each participant's normal retirement age.

Defined contribution plan A pension plan which provides benefits based solely on the clearly specified amount contributed for each participant, plus investment earnings and forfeitures, minus expenses.

Dependence Exposure units are dependent if loss to one increases the probability of loss to another.

Deposit administration contract Requires a retirement plan sponsor to make regular contributions to an insurer on behalf of employees. Principal and interest are guaranteed, but the adequacy to fund all benefits is not guaranteed. Annuities are purchased as employees retire. A separate account is a special type of deposit administration contract that does not make guarantees. See separate account.

Deviated rates   A rate other than the rate that gained approval of the appropriate regulators upon application by a rating organization. This rate is filed by an insurer independent of the rating organization, and is based on the insurer's own loss and expense data.

Diagnostic related groups (DRG).   A classification system for medical or surgical conditions that recognizes age, sex, and other determinants of hospital treatment costs. A predetermined fixed payment is made for a patient's care based on the patient's DRG classification.

Difference in conditions policy   For domestic exposures, the DIC policy is written as a separate contract to supplement underlying insurance. It is an all-risk contract that typically includes a broad array of perils including flood, earthquake, and building collapse, while excluding perils covered by the underlying insurance. For international exposures, the DIC fills in the gap between the coverage on U.S. exposures and coverage purchased locally for international exposures.

Direct loss   A loss that causes actual physical destruction (or taking) of property.

Direct writers   Companies in the property-liability field that market insurance through agents that represent only their company or companies in their group.

Disability   Inability to perform one or more duties of one's occupation because of injury or illness. After a period such as two years, the definition may switch to any occupation for which the person is reasonably suited by education, training, or experience.

Disability income insurance   A form of health insurance that provides periodic payments to replace income when the insured is unable to work as a result of illness, injury, or disease.

Disappearing deductible   Deductible which decreases as the amount of loss increases, eventually reaching zero.

Dismemberment   The loss of a limb or sight.

Dividend   A policyowner's share in the insurer's divisible surplus funds apportioned for distribution, which may take the form of a refund of part of the premium on a participating policy.

Dividend addition   Paid-up life insurance purchased with a policy dividend and added to the face amount of the policy.

Doctrine of Stare Decisis   Once a court decision is made in a case with a given set of facts, the courts tend to adhere to the principle thus established and apply it to future cases involving similar facts.

Double indemnity   A life insurance rider that doubles the death benefit when death is caused by accident.

Dramshop laws   Laws that impose special liability on anyone engaged in the distribution of alcohol.

Dread disease insurance   Insurance providing a benefit, subject to a maximum amount, for expenses incurred in connection with the treatment of specified diseases, such as cancer, poliomyelitis, encephalitis, and spinal meningitis.

Dynamic life insurance planning   A computer approach with the flexibility to produce amounts of net death need as it changes over time due to changes in income, number of children, and other factors.

Early retirement   A benefit which permits retirement of a participant prior to the normal retirement date, usually with a reduced amount of annuity. Early retirement is generally allowed at any time during a period of 5 to 10 years preceding the normal retirement date.

Earned premium   That portion of a policy's premium payment for which the protection of the policy has already been given. For example, an insurance company is considered to have earned 75% of an annual premium after a period of 9 months has elapsed.

Eligibility period   The period of time during which you may sign up for a group insurance plan without giving evidence of insurability.

Eligibility requirements   This term refers to conditions which an employee must satisfy to participate in an employee benefit plan, or conditions which an employee must satisfy to obtain certain employee benefits.

Employee benefits   Employer-sponsored programs to increase the economic security of employees. Insurance and noninsurance benefits are included.

Employee Retirement Income Security Act (ERISA)   Retirement plan legislation passed by Congress in 1974 which provides minimum standards to protect employees in most retirement and welfare (nonretirement employee benefit) plans.

Employee stock ownership plan   A retirement plan in which all employer contributions are not a function of profits and all contributions are in the form of the employer's common stock.

Employer's liability   A section of a workers' compensation policy that protects against potential liabilities not within the scope of the workers' compensation law, yet arising out of employee injuries.

Endorsement   A document which modifies the protection of a policy, either expanding or decreasing its benefits, or adding or excluding certain conditions from the policy. Same as a rider.

Endowment   A life insurance contract that pays the face amount either if the insured dies during the premium-paying period or at the end of this period. It is primarily an insured savings plan.

Equities   Investments in the form of ownership of property, usually common stocks, as distinguished from fixed income bearing securities, such as bonds or mortgages.

Equivalent level annual dividend   The average of annual life insurance policy dividends paid (or projected) during a specified period, adjusted for interest at a specified rate.

ERISA   See Employee Retirement Income Security Act.

Estate planning   The process of arranging for the conservation and transfer of property (the estate) to heirs upon death.

Evidence of insurability   Any statement of proof of a person's state of health and/or other factual information affecting his or her acceptance for insurance.

Exchange rate risk   The potential loss arising out of transactions in two or more currencies.

Exclusions   Specific perils, property, locations, or losses listed in the policy for which the policy will not provide benefit payments.

Expected loss   The sum determined by adding the products formed by multiplying the severity of each possible loss outcome by its probability of occurrence. The expected total dollar loss is the average annual loss an organization with a large number of exposure units can anticipate during a year.

Expense ratio   Ratio of insurer expenses to premiums received.

Experience rating   Variation of the group premium rate based on the organization's own past loss and expense record.

Exposure   The property or person facing a condition in which loss or losses are possible.

Exposure analysis questionnaire   A checklist that itemizes various losses to which an organization is exposed. Used in exposure identification.

Extended coverage insurance   Protection for the insured against loss or damage to his or her property caused by windstorm, hail, smoke, explosion, riot, riot attending a strike, civil commotion, vehicle, or aircraft. This is provided in conjunction with a property insurance policy.

Face amount   The amount stated in a life insurance policy to be paid upon death of the insured or upon the maturity of an endowment policy.

Factory mutual   Four mutual insurers that emphasize high underwriting standards and loss prevention for commercial property.

Fair plan   A facility, operating under a government-insurance industry cooperative program, to make property insurance available to those who cannot buy it through the regular market.

Family dependency period   In planning for death, this is the period during which children (and usually a surviving spouse) will be provided for financially.

Family purpose doctrine   Makes the owner of the family car responsible for whatever damage it does regardless of which member of the family may be operating the car at the time of the accident.

Federal crime insurance   Insurance against burglary, larceny, and robbery losses offered by the Federal Insurance Administration, an agency of the federal government.

Fellow-servant rule   This old workers' compensation defense prevented an employee who was injured as a result of a fellow worker's conduct from recovering damages from the employer.

Fidelity bond   A contract which idemnifies an employer for losses caused by dishonest or fraudulent acts of employees.

Fiduciary   Any person or organization who manages the property of another acts as a fiduciary. In this text, fiduciary refers to one who exercises discretionary authority or control over management of a retirement plan or disposition of its assets; renders investment advice for a fee with respect to moneys or property of a plan or has authority or responsibility to do so; or has discretionary authority or responsibility in the administration of a plan.

Final, average formula   A retirement plan benefit formula that bases the defined benefit on compensation during a number of recent years. This keeps the initial retirement benefit up with inflation and productivity to the extent that a retiree's earnings have kept pace.

Final expenses   In planning for death, this is one of the major categories of total death needs. Final expenses include funeral costs, debt repayments, and payment to a person representative who settles the estate.

Financial planner   An individual who serves as a consultant on personal financial matters to integrate insurance, investment, and tax matters into a sound financial plan that has the purpose of achieving a person's financial goals.

Financial responsibility law   A law under which a person involved in an automobile accident may be required to furnish evidence of financial responsibility, usually by auto liability insurance.

First-dollar insurance   Contracts that start paying losses without any retention, perhaps in the form of a deductible, by the insured.

Fixed-dollar annuities   An annuity under which investment returns, subject to a minimum guarantee, are specified periodically by the insurer and the amount of each annuity payment is a fixed number of dollars.

Fleet   A group, as of automobiles. Or, a group of insurance companies operating under one management.

Flexible benefit program   Allows each employee to choose among types and amounts of employee benefits. The plan sponsor may require minimum amounts of certain benefits such as health insurance to meet its social responsibility goals.

Flexible premium annuity An annuity that allows the contract owner to change the amount of contribution, stop contributions, and resume them at will. It is the required type of annuity for funding an IRA, Keogh, or other tax-deferred plan because contributions may vary over time as earnings change.

Floater policy A property insurance policy in which the protection follows the property wherever it may be located.

Flood insurance Coverage against loss caused by the flood peril.

Fortuitous losses Losses that occur as a matter of chance. Losses are not controlled or influenced by the insured.

Franchise deductible Retention by the insured up to the deductible amount. For losses in excess of the deductible amount, the entire loss is paid in full.

Franchise insurance A form of insurance in which individual policies are issued to the employees of a common employer or the members of an association and the employer or association agrees to collect the premiums for the insurer.

Fraternal insurance A cooperative type of insurance provided by social organizations for their members.

Future service benefits Benefits accruing for service after the effective date of coverage under a pension plan.

General agent An independent business person whose contract with an insurer allows him or her to sell insurance in a specified territory, and to appoint and supervise sub-agents. It is a major method of life insurance distribution.

Gift tax rule The rule allows that the first $10,000 given each year per donee may be excluded from federal estate and gift taxation. When a spouse agrees to the gift, the exclusion increases to $20,000 per donee.

Grace period A period after a life or health insurance premium payment is due, in which the policyowner may make such payment, and during which the policy remains in force.

Group annuity contract A pension plan providing annuities at retirement to a group of persons covered by a single master contract, with individual certificates stating the coverage issued to members of the group.

Group insurance Any insurance plan under which a number of persons and their dependents are insured under a single policy, issued to their employer or to an association with which they are affiliated, with individual certificates given to each insured person.

Group underwriting Provision of insurance to a group. Instead of selecting individual insureds, the insurance company decides whether to issue a group policy based on characteristics of the organization.

Guaranteed insurability option Allows the periodic purchase of additional amounts of life insurance without proof of insurability.

Guaranteed renewable A policy provision that gives the insured the right to continue a policy by the timely payment of premiums to a specified age during which period the insurer has no right to make any change in any provision of the contract while it is in force, other than a change in the premium rate for classes of insureds. The term, "guaranteed continuable," is synonymous with the term "guaranteed renewable."

Guaranty associations Associations created by state insurance law to protect the policyowners of defunct insurers. Their financing comes from solvent insurers doing business in the state.

Hazard A condition that increases the probability or severity of loss.

Health insurance A generic term applying to all types of insurance indemnifying or reimbursing for costs of hospital and medical care or lost income arising from an illness or injury. Sometimes it is called Accident and Health Insurance, or Disability Insurance.

Health maintenance organization (HMO) An organization that provides for a wide range of comprehensive health care services for a fixed periodic payment. The HMO can be sponsored by a variety of entities, including, government, medical schools, hospitals, employers, labor unions, consumer groups and insurers.

Hold-harmless clause A contractual provision that transfers risk from one party such as a property owner to another party such as a tenant.

Hospital imdemnity A form of health insurance which provides a stipulated daily, weekly, or monthly benefit up to a specified amount during hospital confinement. The payment is not based on the actual expense of hospital confinement.

Immediate annuity Payments begin at the next payment interval.

Income replacement ratio The portion of pre-retirement income that one wants during retirement.

Incontestable provision A contract provision that provides that the insurer may not contest the validity of a life insurance contract after it has been in force for a specified period, such as two years.

Indemnity A principle that says an insured should not collect more from insurance than the amount of loss. A health insurance policy with indemnity benefits pays actual charges up to a specified amount per day, per hospital confinement, or per procedure.

Independent adjuster A person who represents an insurer in settling loss claims but is not an employee of the insurer.

Independent agent An agent who sells insurance for several companies as an independent contractor rather than an employee.

Index linked policy The face amount of life insurance, and the premium, increases with the Consumer Price Index, subject to a maximum increase such as 5 percent per year.

Individual policy pension trust A trust created to buy individual life insurance or annuity contracts to provide benefits under a pension plan.

Individual retirement accounts IRAs allow a person not participating in any other type of qualified retirement plan or having earned income below a specified limit, to contribute up to $2,000 annually to a retirement fund and defer federal income taxes on the contributions and the fund's earnings. Persons not meeting these participation requirements may contribute up to $2,000 per year to an IRA and have the fund's earnings alone qualify for deferral or federal income taxes.

Inland marine insurance A broad type of insurance, generally covering articles that may be transported from one place to another as well as bridges, tunnels, and other instrumentalities of transportation. It includes in transit (generally excepting trans-ocean) as well as numerous "floater" policies such as personal effects, personal property, jewelry, furs, fine arts, and others.

Insurable interest If the occurrence of a loss, such as destruction of a house by fire, will affect you adversely, you have an insurable interest.

Insurance A social device in which a group of individuals transfers risk in order to combine experience, which permits mathematical prediction of losses, and provides for payment of losses from funds contributed by all members who transferred risk. Those who transfer risk are called insureds. Those who assume risk are called insurers.

Insurance Commissioner In every state, the head of the insurance department in charge of administering insurance laws. In some states, he/she may also hold another office (for example, State Treasurer) or have a different title such as Superintendent of Insurance. The Insurance Commissioner is a very powerful official.

Insurance exchanges Organizations similar to Lloyd's of London. They began a business of handling reinsurance and property-liability insurance on unusual exposures through exchanges in Miami, Florida; Chicago, Illinois; and New York City, during the 1980s. Only the Illinois exchange remains operational.

Insured In life-health insurance, the person on whose life or health a policy is issued; the subject of the insurance. In property and liability insurance, the person to whom, or on whose behalf, benefits are payable.

Insuring clause The clause which sets forth the type of loss being covered by the policy and the parties to the insurance contract. (Also known as the insuring agreement.)

Integrated retirement plan One that dovetails Social Security benefits (or contributions) into the private plan's benefit (or contribution) formula.

Interest-adjusted net payment cost index A measure of the cost of protection, including the time value of money, for a life insurance policy if it is kept in force until an assumed date or death.

Interest-adjusted surrender cost A measure of the cost of protection, including the time value of money, of a life insurance policy if it is kept in force for a specified period and then surrendered for the cash surrender value.

Intestate To die without a will.

Irrevocable beneficiary The beneficiary of a life insurance policy may only be changed with the consent of that beneficiary (for example, a divorced spouse may be given an interest in life insurance on a former spouse as part of a divorce settlement).

Joint-and-survivor annuity A contract that provides income periodically, payable during the longer lifetime of two persons. The amount payable may decrease at the death of one or the other or either person included in the contract.

Joint life policy A special contract that insures two lives (such as a husband and wife) and pays only upon the first death.

Joint underwriting association An association created by a state insurance law for the purpose of issuing one or more types of insurance that have become difficult to obtain or afford from insurers in the free market.

Keogh Plan A retirement plan with tax advantages for people who earn self-employment income.

Key employee One whose contribution to an employer is crucial to its success.

Key-person insurance Life or health insurance to protect the firm from loss caused by the death or disability of an employee who makes a significant contribution to the firm.

Lapse Termination of a policy caused by the policyowner's failure to pay the premium within the time required.

Large-loss principle The consumer principle that the possible size of a loss is a better measure of its significance than the probabilities of various sized losses.

Last clear chance A legal doctrine by which a plaintiff who assumed the risk or contributed to an accident through negligence is not barred from recovery if the defendant had the opportunity to avoid the accident but failed to do so.

Law of large numbers An important statistical theorem that, in essence, says as a sample becomes larger, the outcome for the sample becomes closer to the true prediction of probability. The theorem is very important to the prediction of losses by insurance company actuaries and risk managers.

Leasehold interest An interest that exists when a lease stipulates a rental that is greater or less than the prevailing market price for similar facilities.

Level premium A premium which remains unchanged throughout the life of a policy.

Liability insurance Provides protection against loss arising out of legal liability resulting from injuries to other persons or damage to their property.

Liability limits The stipulated sum or sums in a liability insurance policy beyond which an insurance company is not liable to protect the insured.

Liability Risk Retention Act A 1986 amendment to the Product Liability Risk Retention Act of 1981 which permits the formation of retention groups (pseudo-captives) with fewer restrictions than existed before the Act was passed.

Life annuity A series of payments that continue throughout the life of the annuitant but not beyond.

Life expectancy The average number of years of life remaining for a group of persons of a given age according to a particular mortality table.

Life insurance Provides for payment of a specified amount at the insured's death, or at a specified date.

Limited policies Contracts which cover only certain specified diseases or accidents.

Linton Yield Method A method that ascribes a value to the protection element of a life insurance policy for each year based on renewable term premium rates and then calculates an implicit rate of return for the policy's savings element.

Liquidation period The time during which the annuity makes payments.

Living/inter vivos trust A trust established during the lifetime of a creator; used to provide outside management and reduce the cost of probating an estate.

Living will A legal instrument that gives a designated person(s) authority to have life-sustaining efforts discontinued under specified circumstances.

Lloyd's of London The oldest insurance organization in existence. Lloyd's does not assume risks. However, underwriters who are members of Lloyd's engage in the insurance business at that London location under the supervision of a governing committee.

Long-term disability income insurance Pays benefits to a disabled person for an extended period, to retirement age, or for life.

Loss A disappearance or reduction in economic value.

Loss control Activities that reduce the frequency or severity of a loss that has occurred.

Loss frequency A measure of how often a loss has occurred in the past or is expected to occur in the future.

Loss prevention An effort that reduces the probability of loss.

Loss ratio Ratio of losses to earned premiums.

Loss reduction An effort that reduces the severity of loss.

Loss severity A measure of the amount of loss.

Loss transfer A technique (such as insuring potential losses) to shift the financial consequences of loss to another party.

Lump-sum distribution One cash payment equal to the expected value of lifetime benefits from a defined benefit retirement plan or the account balance of a defined contribution plan.

Major medical expense insurance Pays for the expense of major illness and injuries. Provides large or unlimited benefit maximums. The insurance, above a large deductible, pays the major part of all charges for hospital, doctor, private nurses, medical appliances, and prescribed out-of-hospital treatment, drugs, and medicines. The insured person pays the remainder.

Malpractice insurance Liability insurance for professionals, such as physicians and surgeons, to protect them against the risk of claims for damages in connection with professional services.

Managed health care A cost containment method where insurers and health care providers cooperate on a case-by-case basis in selecting methods of medical treatment that will be effective and minimize costs.

Management Information Systems Computer packages designed to assist the risk manager in making decisions by organizing and analyzing data available to the risk manager.

Marital deduction Allows that all property left outright to a surviving spouse becomes a deduction in federal estate tax calculations.

Mass merchandising A method of selling insurance by direct mail or on a payroll deduction basis through a sponsoring organization such as an employer.

Master policy The contract between an insurer and an employer or other sponsor of group insurance benefits. Employees are issued certificates or booklets as evidence of their participation in the plan.

Maximum probable yearly aggregate loss The dollar amount of aggregate losses in a year, with a probability of less than X percent.

Medicaid State medical programs of public assistance to persons qualifying on the basis of low income.

Medicare Hospital and medical insurance provided by Social Security.

Medigap insurance Policies that pay for all, or part of, health care expense not covered by Medicare.

Morbidity table Shows the average number of illnesses or injuries for a large group of persons. It indicates the incidence of sickness and accident the way a mortality table shows the incidence of death.

Mortality rate The percentage of people expected to die at a specified age.

Mortality table Shows the number of persons living or dying, at a certain age. It is used to calculate the probability of dying in, or surviving through, any period.

Mortgage protection A term life insurance contract in which the amount of insurance decreases at the same pace as the principle on a mortgage loan. Proceeds usually are paid to a mortgagee.

Multiple line underwriter An insurer that writes all or several types of property-liability insurance.

Multiple peril insurance Policies that combine many perils previously covered by individual property and liability policies.

Multiple protection policy A combination of level term and ordinary life insurance that pays a multiple (e.g., four times) of the face amount if you die within a specified period or the basic face amount if you die after this period.

Mutual insurers An insurer that has no stockholders.

Named-perils Type of policy which covers only losses caused by perils listed in the policy.

Negligence The failure to use such care as a reasonably prudent and careful person would use under similar circumstances.

New money rate An approach that credits an investment account with the return an insurer earns on its latest investments.

No-fault automobile insurance A form of insurance by which a person's financial losses resulting from an automobile accident, such as medical and hospital expenses and loss of income, are paid by his or her own insurance company without concern for who was at fault.

Nonadmitted company An insurer not licensed to write business in a state or in a foreign country.

Noncancellable, or noncancellable and guaranteed renewable, policy A policy which the insured has the right to continue in force to a specified age, such as to age 65, by the timely payment of premiums. During the specified period the insurer has no right to make any unilateral change in any provision of the policy while it is in force.

Noncurrency Two policies issued on the same interest that do not agree in their terms.

Nonconfining sickness An illness which prevents the insured person from working but which does not confine him or her to a hospital or home.

Noncontributory benefit plan One in which the employer pays all costs. Employees do not contribute.

Nondisabling injury One which may require medical care, but does not result in loss of working time or income.

Nonforfeiture options Alternatives available to a life insurance policyowner who stops paying premiums before the end of the normal premium payment period. The options include: (1) the cash surrender value, (2) a reduced amount of paid-up life insurance, and (3) extended term insurance for the policy's original face amount.

Nonoccupational policy A contract which insures a person against off-the-job accident or sickness.

Nonparticipating policy A policy on which no dividends are paid to the policyowner.

Normal costs The actuarial cost estimate for defined benefit retirement credits earned during the latest year.

Normal retirement age The normal age at which private retirement plan benefits are designed to begin. Most plans specify age 65. Some also provide for early or late retirement. See early retirement.

Objective probability An estimate of loss frequency based on observing what has happened in the past and assuming the same will happen in the future. Insurers prefer to have objective probability estimates rather than subjective ones.

Occupational Disease An injury arising out of employment and due to causes and characteristics of, and peculiar to, the particular trade, occupation, process or employment, and excluding all ordinary diseases to which the general public is exposed.

Open perils Type of policy which covers loss by all perils except those excluded. (Also known as all risk.)

Optionally renewable A contract of health insurance in which the insurer reserves the right to terminate the coverage at any anniversary or, in some cases, at any premium-due date, but does not have the right to terminate coverage between such dates.

Ordinary business All types of life insurance and annuities sold to individuals, other than industrial and credit life.

Ordinary life policy Whose life insurance on which premiums are paid for life. Also called straight life.

Other insurance clause States the way a loss will be shared when more than one property or liability policy covers the exposure.

Other states insurance A section of a workers' compensation policy that states that an employee injured while working out of state may be covered by that state's compensation law.

Over insurance An amount of insurance larger than the loss that could befall the insured.

Overseas private investment corporation A federal agency that sells political risk insurance to United States citizens who invest in certain underdeveloped countries.

Package policy A single insurance policy that includes several types of insurance, such as the Homeowners Policy.

Paid-up policy A policy that will remain in force without further premium payments.

Partial disability An illness or injury which prevents an insured person from performing one or more of the functions of his or her regular job.

Participating insurance Insurance that allows insureds to share in the profits of the insurance operation. Profits are shared in the form of dividends which may also include the refund of part or all of an initial increase or overcharge in premium.

Past service benefits Benefits for service before the effective date of coverage under a retirement plan, or prior to a date on which a plan is amended to improve benefits.

Peril The cause of loss, such as fire, flood and theft.

Period certain life annuity An annuity that provides periodic payments throughout the life of an annuitant, but for not less than a specified period such as ten years to a contingent beneficiary.

Permanent total disability A situation in which the injured person is not expected to be able to work again.

Permanent life insurance All forms of life insurance other than term. Actually a misnomer.

Personal insurance A category of insurance that protects against premature death, injury and sickness, unemployment, and dependent old age.

Personal producing general agent An agent for a life-health insurer who holds a general agent's license but sells directly to consumers rather than hiring subagents.

Pension benefit guaranty corporation (PBGC) A federal agency that protects vested retirement benefits up to specified monthly amounts in the event the sponsor of a private defined benefit plan fails to meet its promises.

Policyowners' surplus The net worth of an insurer, adjusted for overstatement of liabilities.

Policy loan A loan made by the insurer to the owner of a life insurance policy, using its surrender value as collateral.

Policy term The period for which an insurance policy provides coverage.

Political risk Unanticipated political events that disrupt the earning or profit-making ability of an enterprise. Nationalization and expropriation are examples.

Portability The transfer of pension rights and credits when a worker changes jobs.

Portfolio rate An approach that reflects the average return on a portfolio of debt investments with various purchase and maturity dates.

Pre-existing condition A physical and/or mental condition of an insured person which existed prior to the initial date of coverage.

Preferred provider organization Group of hospitals, physicians, and other health care providers that contract with insurers, third party administrators, or directly with employers to provide medical care to members of the contracting group(s) at discounted prices per unit of service.

Premium The payment made for an insurance policy.

Prepaid group practice plan A plan under which specified health services are rendered by participating physicians to a group of persons, with fixed periodic payment in advance made by or on behalf of each person or family.

Principal sum The amount payable in one sum in event of accidental death and, in some cases, accidental dismemberment.

Probability distribution of losses A figure or table that shows the probabilities associated with various sized losses. The losses can be of a specific type such as losses caused by fire or for total losses of all types for a given period of time.

Probate The process of settling an estate either in accordance with a will or if no will exists in accordance with state law.

Probationary period A specified number of days after the date of the issuance of the policy during which there is no coverage for sickness. The purpose is to reduce adverse selection. In group insurance, the probationary period is the period during which a new employee is ineligible to participate in the plan.

Profit-sharing plan A type of defined contribution plan in which a firm puts a share of its profits in trust for the benefit of employees. Contributions are a function of profits.

Projected dividend A portrayal of future policy dividends based on certain actuarial assumptions. Dividends cannot be guaranteed. See Actual Dividends.

Prolonged life risk The possibility that at some time a person may be kept alive through the use of life support systems for a long period at great expense and suffering.

Pro rata liability clause If a loss covered by this policy is also covered by other insurance, the insurer will pay only the proportion of the loss that the limit of liability that applies under this policy bears to the total amount of insurance covering the loss.

Prospectus A document that must be given to a potential purchaser of variable life insurance or a variable annuity prior to signing the application. It states the risks to be borne by the purchaser and how death benefits and cash values would perform if future investments result in various rates of return (for example, 0, 4, and 8 percent).

Proximate cause The cause actually responsible for the loss; the one that set in motion the events that led to a loss; e.g., a fire that led to water damage while putting out the fire.

Public adjuster An adjuster who represents the insured in settling a claim for loss covered by an insurance policy.

Punitive damages Damages awarded separately and in addition to compensatory damages as punishment for the wrongdoer.

Qualified plan An employee benefit plan which the Internal Revenue Service approves as meeting the requirements of ERISA and results in certain tax advantages.

Quid Pro Quo "This for that." Used in workers' compensation to describe the rights and responsibilities exchanged between employers and employees.

Rating organizations Industry-sponsored organizations that accumulate loss data for large numbers of property-liability insurers and file requests for rate changes with state insurance departments.

Rebating The practice of an agent refunding part of an insurance premium paid at the time of sale in order to entice people to buy insurance.

Reciprocal An insurance organization in which each insured assumes a share of the risk brought to the organization by other insureds. They are managed by an attorney-in-fact on a not-for-profit basis.

Recurring clause A provision in some health insurance policies which specifies a period of time during which the recurrence of a condition is considered a continuation of a prior period of disability or hospital confinement.

Reentry term A provision which allows the insured to redemonstrate insurability periodically and qualify for a new select table of rates applicable to term life insurance.

Reinstatement The resumption of coverage under a policy which had lapsed.

Reinsurance Assumption by one insurance company of all or part of a risk undertaken by another insurance company.

Reinsurer An insurer that accepts part of the contingent liability under insurance initially issued by another insurer.

Renewability option The right to renew a term life insurance policy for a specified number of additional periods, without proving insurability.

Renewal Continuation of coverage under a policy beyond its original term by the acceptance of a premium for a new policy term.

Replacement Cost Basis Compensation of property losses based on replacement cost with no deduction for depreciation.

Reporting form A method of updating, monthly or quarterly, the amount of inventory to be insured under a commercial property insurance contract.

Representations Statements of the insured to the insurer concerning exposures to be insured.

Reserve A liability entry on an insurer's balance sheet that recognizes a financial obligation.

Residual market Market for people who cannot buy auto insurance through the usual channels.

Res Ipsa Loquitur Legal tactic made by plaintiff to shift the burden of proof to the defendant. It may be used when the defendant had total control over the event that caused loss and loss would not have occurred had negligence not existed.

Respondentia An agreement made in ancient Greece whereby a loan made on cargo was cancelled if the ship was lost. This combined insurance with lending.

Retention The opposite of transferring a risk to another party. You engage in an activity or own property without buying insurance or using other contracts to transfer loss.

Retired lives reserve A method of funding, during the employees' working years, yearly renewable group term life insurance for retired workers.

Revocable beneficiary The person to whom the proceeds of a life insurance policy will be paid either upon death or upon reaching the end of an endowment period. The designation may be changed at will by the policyowner alone.

Rider A document that modifies the protection of a policy, either expanding or decreasing its benefits or adding or excluding certain conditions from the policy. Same as an endorsement.

Risk A state of the world in which losses are possible.

Risk evaluation The process of deciding how important is an exposure to loss. Measure of severity, frequency, and variability are involved.

Risk management An organized, formal approach to dealing with pure risks.

Robbery The taking of property by violence or threat of violence.

Savings bank life insurance Life insurance sold over the counter by mutual savings banks in Massachusetts, New York, and Connecticut.

Second injury fund A state-administered fund, generated by contributions required of insurers, intended to compensate employees for the combined effect of two work-related disabling injuries.

Second surgical opinion A cost containment method where greater payment of surgical costs is made by the insurer when a second opinion is sought prior to undergoing elective surgery.

Second-to-die life insurance A policy that pays upon the last death of two people. Usually purchased to pay estate settlement expenses.

Section 401(k) plan Allows the flexibility for employees to defer certain income on a tax-deferred basis or take the income in cash. It may or may not involve employer contributions. It must meet strict nondiscrimination requirements.

Self-administered plan A pension or profit-sharing plan funded through a fiduciary, generally a bank, but sometimes a group of individuals, which invests the funds accumulated instead of using the services of an insurance company.

Self funding A risk retention scheme that funds losses but typically does not include loss reserve funds nor use of the law of large numbers.

Self insurance A scheme that handles risk like it is handled by insurance, except that the risk is not transferred to an insurer. It is a retention program that involves the law of large numbers and loss reserve funds. The scheme meets the ideal requisites of insurance reasonably well.

Separate account A life insurer fund that is separate and apart from the insurer's general assets and is generally used for investment of retirement and variable product premiums. The majority of separate account money is invested in common stocks.

Service benefit An insurance benefit in the form of hospital or medical care services rather than money.

Short rate table A schedule of less than pro rata premiums that will be refunded if an insured cancels a contract before the end of its term. The less than pro rata refund is justified by the fact that most of the insurer's expenses of selling insurance are incurred at the beginning of a policy period.

Short-term disability income insurance A policy that pays benefits to a disabled person for a specified period not exceeding two years, and usually not more than six months.

Simplified employee plans Employer-sponsored IRAs. A form of defined contribution retirement plan that is relatively simple to administer.

Single limit Auto liability coverage in which the insurer will pay on the insured's behalf all losses up to a stated limit, for any single accident, whether property-related or injury-related.

Single premium life insurance A whole life insurance policy with one premium equal to the present value of future benefits, discounted for investment earnings and mortality.

Social insurance substitute A provision of a long-term disability income policy under which Social Security disability benefits are replaced if the insured does not qualify under this program's strict definition of disability.

Social Security option An option under which employees may elect higher annuity payments before a specified age (62 or 65) and lower payments thereafter to produce level annuity payments, including Social Security benefits when they start.

Specifications A description sent to potential bidders (in-surers), describing the types and amounts of desired insurance, minimum qualifications for bidding agents and insurers, service requirements, and other characteristics of one's insurance needs.

Split funding An arrangement whereby a portion of the contributions to a retirement plan are paid to a life insurance company and the remainder invested through a corporate trustee, primarily in equities.

Split limit Auto liability coverage that defines the maximum payable by the insurer in amounts specified for particular types of losses (as opposed to a single limit).

Spouse's dependency period This is the period for which the person planning death needs may want to provide income for a spouse who is not caring for children.

Staff adjuster An insurance company employee who settles claims for losses on its behalf.

Static life insurance planning A technique that considers only the worst possible scenario of death now and does not recognize various changes that may occur in the future.

Standard fire policy Part of a property insurance policy, containing an insuring agreement and general policy provisions. It standardizes basic parts of a contract and is completed by the attachment of a form to tailor insurance to a specific type of exposure.

Statutory law Body of written law created by legislatures.

Stock insurer An insurer created to make a profit for stockholders.

Stop limit provision A provision that eliminates the co-insurance feature after an insured's out-of-pocket expense reaches a specified amount.

Stop loss insurance A form of excess insurance. For example, in a group health plan, the stop loss coverage may begin benefits when self-funded claims exceed 125 percent of the claims an insurer would have expected under a fully insured contract.

Straight deductible Requires insured to pay for all losses less than a specified dollar amount and that specified amount of all other losses.

Straight life policy Whole life insurance on which premiums are paid for life, also called ordinary life.

Strict liability Liability without regard to fault.

Structured settlement annuity A special type of single premium immediate annuity that achieves the goal of providing certain levels of income to the plaintiff in a lawsuit.

Subjective probability An estimate of loss frequency based on logical reasoning and personal judgment.

Subrogation Gives the insurer whatever right against third parties you may have as a result of the loss for which the insurer paid you.

Substandard risk A risk with higher than average probability of loss, such as a person with a physical impairment who applies for health insurance or a person with a bad driving record who applies for auto insurance.

Suicide provision A provision that precludes the payment of life insurance death benefits and potential adverse selection, for a specified period of one or two years, after which suicide is treated the same as death from natural causes.

Supplemental costs The actuarial cost estimate of the amount necessary to amortize any past service liability in a retirement plan over a period that may vary from ten to thirty years.

Surety bond An agreement providing for monetary compensation, should there be a failure to perform specified acts within a stated period. The surety company, for example, becomes responsible for fulfillment of a contract if the contractor defaults.

Surgical expense insurance Health insurance policies which provide benefits toward the doctor's operating fees. Benefits usually consist of scheduled amounts for each surgical procedure.

Surgical schedule A list of cash allowances which are payable for various types of surgery with the maximum amounts based upon the severity of the operations.

Surplus line Insurance not available in the regular market from admitted companies. May be placed in the surplus lines market with a nonadmitted company under special provisions of state law.

Survivor income benefit A form of group death benefit that provides monthly benefits to an unmarried spouse and children under a specified age, upon the death of an employee.

Target premium A premium payment for an interest-sensitive life policy that is expected to keep the policy in force for an entire lifetime under a given set of mortality and interest assumptions.

Temporary life annuity An annuity payable while the annuitant lives but not beyond a specified period, such as five years.

Temporary partial disability A condition qualifying a worker for payments that are most likely to be made following a period of temporary total disability.

Temporary total disability A situation in which an injured employee will be able to return to work at some future time.

Term life insurance A type of life insurance that pays if the insured dies during a specified time such as a year. Term insurance usually has an increasing pattern of premiums over time and is pure protection (no savings).

Testator The person who signs a will setting forth instructions to be carried out upon death.

Theft Any act of stealing.

Tort A wrongful act or omission arising in the course of social relationships other than contracts, which violates a person's legally protected right, and for which the law provides a remedy in the form of action for damage.

Tortfeasor Person who commits a tort.

Total disability A disability that prevents a person from continuously performing every duty pertaining to his or her occupation or from engaging in any other type of work for remuneration. (This wording varies among insurers.) See disability.

Traditional net cost A measure of the surrender cost of a life insurance policy which ignores the time value of money.

Transfer A technique such as insurance or a hold-harmless agreement whereby financial aspects of a potential loss are shifted to another party.

Travel accident policy A contract that covers loss caused by an accident that occurs while an insured person is traveling.

Trust A legal arrangement by which money or property is entrusted by party A to party C. Party C is to invest the money/property and give the proceeds to party B.

Trust beneficiary The party who receives income and other disbursements from a trust.

Trustee A person or institution legally responsible for the management of money (property) in the interest of a third party according to the terms of a trust agreement.

Trust grantor The creator of a trust. It is this person who establishes a trust and contributes money/property to fund it.

Trust plan A noninsurance mechanism to accumulate funds and (usually) disburse benefits from a retirement plan. The typical trust plan is administered by the trust department of a bank. Neither principal nor investment earnings are guaranteed.

Umbrella liability policy A form of insurance protection against losses in excess of amounts covered by other liability insurance policies; also protects the insured in many situations not covered by the usual liability policies, subject to a deductible.

Unallocated benefit A policy provision providing reimbursement up to a maximum amount for the costs of all extra miscellaneous hospital services, but which does not specify how much will be paid for each type of service.

Uncertainty The state of mind one experiences when he or she becomes aware of risk. It is unmeasurable and subjective.

Underinsured motorist coverage Fills in the coverage gap that arises when the negligent party meets the financial responsibility law of the state, but the auto accident victim has losses in excess of the negligent driver's liability limit.

Underwriters Companies that are willing to assume risks for some promised payment. Also, persons who make underwriting decisions for insurers.

Underwriting The process by which the insurer decides whether or not and on what basis it will issue a policy.

Underwriting capacity The financial ability of an insurer to underwrite new insurance. It is generally measured by the relationship of premiums written to surplus (net worth) and is modified by access to reliable reinsurance.

Unemployment compensation A state-administered program which pays weekly income benefits to workers who are involuntarily unemployed.

Uninsured motorist protection Indemnifies an insured who is injured by a hit-and-run motorist or a driver who is at fault but has no liability insurance.

Unisex mortality factors A weighted average of male and female mortality rates. Required for employer-sponsored employee benefit plans, after August 1, 1983.

Universal life insurance A flexible life insurance contract that clearly separates its insurance, investment, and expense elements.

Unsatisifed judgement fund Funds found in several states which respond to the problem of an injured motorist who obtains a judgement against the party at fault, but cannot collect because the party has neither insurance nor resources.

Utilization review A review by a group of physicians, surgeons, and nurses offering peer judgments on (1) whether hospital admission is necessary, (2) whether the length of stay is appropriate, and (3) whether the quality of care is commensurate with the patient's needs.

Utmost Good Faith   (uberrimae fidei) A high standard of candor and honesty is expected of the parties involved in insurance contracts.

Valued policy One in which the value of the property insured is agreed upon and specified in the policy. Life insurance is also a valued policy.

Valued policy law Statute that requires payment of the face amount of the policy in the event of a total loss, regardless of the actual value of the property.

Variable annuity An annuity under which the amount of periodic payments vary according to the investment experience of the insurer's separate account.

Variable life insurance An ordinary life policy in which the fact amount of insurance changes in relation to the performance of its investment element, subject to a guaranteed minimum face amount. The investment element is held in a separate account. The objective is a face amount with stable purchasing power.

Variable universal life A policy which combines the premium and death benefit flexibility of a universal policy design with the investment choices of variable life.

Vesting A provision concerning the right of pension and profit-sharing plan participants to contributions made by the employer.

Waiting period Time between the beginning of an insured's disability and the beginning of benefit payments. Also called an elimination period.

Waiver Intentional relinquishment of a known right.

Waiver of premium A provision which exempts the policyowner from paying premiums while totally disabled.

War clause Controls adverse selection by those who buy life insurance during wartime. The clause prevents collection of death benefits following either death from all causes during war or death caused by war, depending on the wording of the contract. The clause is usually cancelled at the end of hostilities.

Warranty A statement made by the applicant for insurance which, if false, provides the basis for voidance of the policy.

Whole life policy A life insurance policy which remains in force throughout the life of the insured.

Written premiums Premiums on policies issued during a specified period, as opposed to earned premiums.

Yearly rate of return A formula that determines the rate of return on a cash value life insurance policy during a particular year.

Index

definitions, 272–73
identifying insured, 271
limits of insurance, 271–72
policy format, 266–67
Commercial insurance, 65, 589
Commercial package policy (CPP), 126
Commissioner of insurance, 641, 644
Commission on Social Security Reform, 417
Common disaster provision in life insurance contract, 375–76
Common law, 142
defenses, 284
Company adjusters, 630
Comparative negligence, 145–46
Competent parties in contract, 81
Complete comparative negligence rule, 145–46
Completed operations, 158
Comprehensive Environmental Response, Compensation, and Liability Act (CERCLA), 154
Comprehensive medical insurance, 456, 503
Compulsory auto liability insurance law, 210
Concealment, 84
Conditional binder, 78
Conditional receipt, 103
Conditions, 110–13
Confiscation, 124
Connecticut General Life Insurance Company, 587
Consequential losses, 11, 107
property, 122
Consideration in contract, 80
Consolidated Omnibus Budget Reconciliation Act (COBRA) (1985), 459–60, 515
Construction and physical hazards, 13
Consumers and regulators, 660–62
Contingency fee, 161
Contingent beneficiaries, 375
Contingent business interruption, 123
Contingent liability, 158–59
Continuance provisions
in health insurance policy, 510–12
for medical insurance, 459–60
Contracts. *See also* Insurance contracts
of adhesion, 84–85
appraising provisions, 661
bottomry, 584
competent parties in, 81
consideration in, 80
legal form in, 81
legal purpose in, 81
offer and acceptance in, 80
respondentia, 584
of suretyship, 18
Contractual arrangements and transfer of risks, 17–18
Contractual liability, 143

Contribution by equal shares, 136
Contributory negligence, 145–46, 284
Contributory plans, 431, 432
Control of claims adjusting, 654
Control of underwriting practices, 654–55
Conversion factor, 391
Conversion privilege, 435
Convertibility option for term insurance, 324
Coordination of benefits for medical insurance, 457–59
Corporations
close, 544
and transfer of risk, 17
Corpus, 540
Cost containment initiatives for traditional fee-for-service policies, 460–61
administrative and funding techniques, 461–62
plan design techniques, 461
utilization monitoring techniques, 462–64
Cost-of-living adjustment (COLA) clause, 486
in health insurance, 513
in life insurance, 345, 359–60
in workers' compensation, 291
Costs
of defense, 150
normal, 488
provisions for sharing, 455
psychological, 26
shifting of, in health care system, 458
supplemental, 488
Coverage
selecting, 630
suspension of, 111
voidance of, 111
in workers' compensation, 293–94, 301–2
Covered losses, 129
Covered perils, 129–30
Covered property, 129
Creator of trust, 540
Credit life insurance, 325, 336
Credit shelter trust, 548
Criminal law, 143
Currency inconvertibility, 124
Current assumption whole life insurance, 326, 350–51
Current investment return and universal life insurance, 349
Current mortality rate and universal life insurance, 348
Custodial care, 508

D

Damages
economic, 142
general, 142
to property of others, 191

punitive, 142
special, 142
Data sources, 9
Death
and income continuation needs, 525–26, 527–33
probability of, and life insurance, 314–16
Death benefits
accelerated, 381
options for universal life insurance, 344–46
pattern and term insurance, 324–25
and variable life insurance, 351–52
Debris removal, 178, 244–45
Decision maker, risk manager as, 27–28
Declarations, 104
Declarations page, 173
Deductible, 130–32
disappearing, 132
straight, 131
Defendant, 142
Defense
in automobile insurance coverage, 215
cost of, 150, 268
against negligence, 145–46
Defensive medicine, 160
Deferred annuities, 565
Defined benefit pension plans, 484–87
cost factors, 487–88
Defined-benefit pension plans, 556
Defined contribution plans, 488–89
Definite losses, 63
Dental care, and income continuation needs, 527, 535–38
Dental insurance, 503–4
Dental service plans, 589n
Dependent exposure units, 62
Determinable probability distribution, 63–64
Diagnostic related groups (DRGs), 464
Difference in conditions policy (DIC), 257–58
Direct loss, 107
Direct recognition, 374
Direct writers, 617–18
Disability
definition of, 378–79, 437
freeze, 422
and income continuation needs, 527, 533–35
insured status, 407
partial, 289, 505
permanent partial, 289
permanent total, 289
temporary total, 289
total, 289, 505
Disability benefits, 409
Disability income, 379, 447
Disability income insurance, 504–5
Disability income insurance contracts, 504–5